DAYBREAK ON THE LAND

DAYBREAK ON THE LAND

The National Library of Poetry

Chris Tyler, Editor

Daybreak on the Land

Library of Congress
Cataloging in Publication Data

ISBN 1-57553-162-3

Manufactured in The United States of America by
Watermark Press
One Poetry Plaza
Owings Mills, MD 21117

EDITOR'S NOTE

Our lives are filled with beginnings and endings. Many beginnings are cause for celebration: the birth of a child is anticipated by family and friends, the dawn of a new day brings the possibility of a fresh start. Conversely, endings tend to bring disappointment, sadness, or fear. Finishing a good book is disappointing, broken relationships may bring sadness, those uncertain about death fear the conclusion of their lives. As endings leave little room for hope, it is not surprising that they often weigh heavily on our souls and demand expression. Various poems within *Daybreak on the Land* explore this concept of having to let go.

Eileen Casey's "Fade Out" (p. 135) expertly portrays an aging woman's painful loss of youth. Much of her present is unused as ". . . she lives / time ticking by, drowsing away her once / needed vigour." Defining life by her vanished youth means her life is essentially over: "Life has become a waiting room / suspended somewhere between / bingo halls and terraced suburbia." Since her youth will not return, words like "waiting room" and "suspended" describe a life perpetually on hold.

The persona is enlivened only by memories of her past beauty. A peek into her bedroom serves as a study of her thoughts, where the past is associated with vivid colors:

> *when swan songs in dusty covers breathe again*
> *on the radio,*
> *she longs to dye her hair the colour of brandied*
> *peaches*
> *make scarlet slashes on her dry lips . . . .*

As comforting as such memories are, they are romanticized. Floods of memories come to her "when her bedroom is lit pinkly / like a Spanish sunset . . . ." Literally, the persona may have a pink shade on her lamp. Yet this rosy glow also emphasizes the tendency to view the past with rose-colored glasses, recasting it as wonderful and exciting -- "like a Spanish sunset."

A wish to "be marilynned on a street corner, / warm air billowing her skirts above dimpled knees" stresses the dead-end direction of the persona's glamorous dreams. Marilyn Monroe's early death meant the star is recalled as a sensuous younger woman. While not necessarily wishing for death, the character also wants to be remembered only as what she once was. Therefore, her dreams remain locked in the past and she drifts unhappily toward her life's end:

> *. . . she remains framed*
> *like a photograph*
> *slowly fading*
> *slowly fading.*

i

The form of Casey's poem further emphasizes the path of the character's life. The first stanza, which discusses middle-age as an in-between status, is middle-sized. The second stanza, however, swells as the woman's memories of youth and beauty unfold. The final stanza is diminutive in comparison; it trickles to the poem's end like the persona's fading life.

While the pain discussed in "Fade Out" comes from a gradual loss, David Fowler's "The White Fence" (p. 479) addresses a more tangible end: a loved one's death. The characters in this piece are literally repainting a fence, and their discussion of the death mirrors this automated action:

> *We talked about the mechanics of it all;*
> *the family in attendance, the ending ceremony,*
> *and the facts; brain and lung tumors, that she had smoked*
> *or hadn't, that she loved herself or not.*

The central image of painting the fence white is packed with meaning. Aspiring to a house with a white picket fence is a symbol for the American Dream, or the perfect life. In addition, the fence is a barricade like the wall used to halt the flow of emotions, and the characters are whitewashing this object as well as their pain.

The speaker realizes, however, that such emotions are too strong to remain hidden. He says, "We avoided the other stuff / that creeps among us in light or darkness / lurking behind a familiar smell, word, or song." Despite the best efforts, one emotional trigger results in "pushing aside those carefully erected barriers . . . ." Mechanized behavior aside, these stifled feelings charge the poem's atmosphere and the reader easily perceives the hidden anguish:

> *It is this we avoid in our wordplay talking about the end*
> *always fearful of losing it all*
> *right here,*
> *painting a white fence.*

Jason M. Miller's poem, "[The Uncollected Poet]" (p. 330), demonstrates that people may exit our lives in ways other than, but equally as devastating as, death. The speaker is a poet seeking artistic greatness. Ironically, his ambitions are dashed by his partner's leaving to fulfill her own aspirations. She leaves him as their child's caretaker, so he must write to make money, not art:

> *-- the mother in England, seeking*
> *a mildewed dream, the father writing*
> *poems for bedding, passing invisible*
> *in an age he meant to shape . . . .*

This departure ruins the persona by simultaneously signaling rejection and preventing his identity-defining writing. Thus, he is not only missing a loved one but also mourning the end of his dream. In turn, their child becomes the burden of the man's unfulfilled dreams.

This poem's literal setting supports the emotional landscape described. The scene is a basement, a stagnant atmosphere in which the persona writes -- and where he feels trapped:

> *In the basement warm papers couch*
> *the glass-eyed newborn staring*
> *at the ceiling the darkness textured*
> *by a shattered window, six feet high . . . .*

The "shattered window, six feet high" could be referring to the devastated man, as six feet is a common male height.

The window image is also applied to the love he and his partner once shared:

> *-- dream of love like an open window,*
> *and with wings let us collide;*
> *knowing a child now exists*
> *where we dreamt in colour.*

The atmosphere portrayed above was fertile in more than one way; it led to the couple's expression of love through a child as well as a place where creativity could flourish ("where we dreamt in colour"). Such description succeeds in communicating feelings without being overly sentimental, allowing the reader to grasp the tragic situation described. The reader can understand the speaker's barely being able to hold himself together, a difficult task which is mirrored by Miller's construction of the poem's title -- the words, most notably "uncollected," are held within brackets.

In "Palm Sunday Fugue" (p. 127), by Robert L. Ferrante, the father is the absent parent. Ferrante skillfully uses contrasts to construct a complex atmosphere. Palm Sunday precedes Easter Sunday and carries connotations of triumph; the palm reeds given out in churches on that day are a reminder of this joy. Hence the poem starts with an air of celebration, furthered by the young speaker's excitement. He can hardly wait to show the reeds to his loving grandmother: "I clutch my trove of yellow reeds on that holy day / eager to transpose them into Grandma's coos and wet kisses."

Yet the dismal state of his immediate family is drawn through a clash between the persona's innocence and harsh reality. The character says:

> *Sharp talk on the way home*
> *breaks the rhythm of new shoes on the concrete sidewalk.*
> *They're fighting again,*
> *but I listen to . . .*
> *. . . the snap-flaps of the sailor boy suit collar*
> *that the wind syncopates against the back of my head.*

Ultimately, palm reeds, innocence, and a grandmother's love cannot overcome the family's disintegration. That message is expressed by the palm reed's final appearance in the poem: "For days after my father left / it lay at rest on the dresser in my room . . . ."

Evelina Zarkh's "Commencement" (p. 1) also expertly uses contrasts to illustrate the confusion associated with a major life event: graduation. The poem's title alone wonderfully captures the emotional turmoil at hand. "Commencement" literally means "beginning." Although this term is meaningful applied to school graduations, students and even their parents often see commencement as a sad conclusion.

Initially, the speaker is determined to view commencement as an exciting start rather than a dismal ending. Full of knowledge and plans, she is ready to take on the world. This atmosphere is established by her thoughts on a common source of wonder, the night sky: ". . . under the presence of some miracle celestial orb, / comet, I think, . . . really nothing more than a strange stain on the sky. / In fact, it is the only thing that's indistinct . . . ." She categorizes this celestial sighting in terms of her concrete plans. The sight is not awesome or beautiful; rather, its significance rests in it being one thing she does not fully grasp.

Her apparent certainty is continued into the second stanza. Contrary to her father, who dwells on his past, the speaker resolves to live in the present. Zarkh effectively uses allusions to T. S. Eliot's "The Love Song of J. Alfred Prufrock" to illustrate the disparity:

> *My father dreams of white trousers, like Prufrock,*
> *on the streets of Rio de Janeiro during the Carnival,*
> . . . .
> *I think perhaps my sweetest days will be spent eating peaches,*
> *and not dreaming of peaches past.*

Peaches, being sweet and juicy, aptly symbolize pleasure. Eliot's Prufrock is a man who fears risk-taking and, thus, contemplates whether or not he should eat a peach.

This contrast works on an even deeper level when considered with the poem's third stanza. The difference between the speaker and her father is solid and easily understood, unlike her internal conflicts. Alluding to the complicated Eliot poem demonstrates the graduate's sense of increased intellect. Therefore, she tries to rely on knowledge and to shun wistful recollecting. Yet her confidence in intellect falters by the final stanza. While she describes the tearful graduating class as "so many miracle weeping

Madonnas," she is surprised to find herself weeping: "And God! Here I am crying rivers down to my boots / so caked with the earth of some seven states . . . ." The reference to "the earth of some seven states" suggests that her family moved often and she once believed she did not become easily attached; her tears prove otherwise.

By the poem's conclusion, the speaker has learned something more than textbook knowledge, that emotion has a place next to intellect. While her mind chases lofty pursuits, she cannot relate to the feelings of those like her father. Sentiment, on the other hand, connects her to others. It is when she is "crying rivers down to . . . [her] boots" that she declares, "I can feel the ground in my soles." The wordplay in that concluding line shows that emotion is the force that grounds her soul.

Zarkh's powerful images successfully portray the bewildered graduate, stuck between childhood and adulthood, torn by intellectual goals versus feelings. This imagery, in turn, adds considerable depth to her poem's message. Evelina Zarkh's accomplishment resulted in her being awarded the Grand Prize for "Commencement."

Other noteworthy poems to read include: "Oma's Arms" (p. 11) by Ulli Elia, "Zooponics" (p. 228) by Christopher J. Nohl, "The Morning Meeting: 9:00 AM" (p. 191) by M. J. Canuel, "Belly Buttons" (p. 27) by Janet Williams, "Villanelle" (p. 381) by Daniel J. Welty, and "Sunday" (p. 306) by Deborah A. Paggi. Please do not end your reading here, however; there are many other fine poems to consider on the following pages.

The production of *Daybreak on the Land* was made possible by the contributions of many individuals. Thank you to the editors, assistant editors, and office personnel who helped with the creation of this anthology.

Chris Tyler, Editor

Cover Art: Tracy Hetzel

Winners of the North American Open Poetry Contest

Grand Prize Winner

Evelina Zarkh / Island Park, NY

Second Prize Winners

M. J. Canuel / Lorraine, PQ, Canada
Eileen Casey / Dublin, Ireland
Ulli Elia / Cote St Luc, PQ, Canada
Robert L. Ferrante / Fairfield, CT
David Fowler / Santa Fe, NM

Jason M. Miller / Kenosha, WI
Christopher J. Nohl / Mequon, WI
Deborah A. Paggi / Sebastopol, CA
Daniel J. Welty / Waco, TX
Janet Williams / Jenison, MI

Third Prize Winners

Charlotte Alexander / Schofield, WI
Elizabeth Arthur / Powys, United Kingdom
Rotimi Opeyemi Babatunde / Ondo State, Nigeria
Sharon Bells / Aurora, ON, Canada
Dina Bogecho / Montreal, PQ, Canada
Don E. Bottorff / APO, AE
Atila Breti / Vancouver, BC, Canada
Karen Bruggemann / Albuquerque, NM
Bernadette Carroll / Las Vegas, NV
Denice M. Casteel / Ocala, FL
Cynthia / Freehold, NJ
Tracy Derynck / Calgary, AB, Canada
Ken Dudgeon / High River, AB, Canada
Dana Dumas / Inglis, FL
Glenn Fogle / Atlanta, GA
Claude R. Foster Jr. / West Chester, PA
R.S. Fotheringham / Portland, OR
Len Fraser / Brooklyn, NY
A.W. Gillidette / Queensland, Australia
Donna L. Gober / Lumberton, TX
Julie Haroutunian / North York, ON, Canada
Kathleen M. Hill / North Vancouver, BC, Canada
David Hyde / Harlingen, TX
Vance S. Jennings / Tampa, FL
Shannon M. Keesaw / Danville, CA
Susan King / Tuxedo, NC
John King-Farlow / Edmonton, AB, Canada
Margaret D. Kirkland / Owensboro, KY
Stanley Koehler / Amherst, MA
Betty Krantz / Long Beach, NY

Erika Kulnys-Brain / Halifax, NS, Canada
Karen E. Lippold / Los Angeles, CA
Margaret A. Lort / Highlands Ranch, CO
John McKinley / Bloomington, IN
Doramae Norr Michael / Saint George, UT
Jason P. Moore / Albuquerque, NM
Monik Nordine / Montreal, PQ, Canada
Rayford Norman / Raleigh, NC
Florence Olszewski / Jersey City, NJ
William C. Papke / Rockford, IL
Robin Parker / Mount Sterling, KY
Danyelle Pearson / Somerville, MA
Justin Pope / Denville, NJ
Olga Postnikoff / Edmonton, AB, Canada
Alex Prijic-Smith / Westmount, PQ, Canada
Caroline Sag / Queensland, Australia
Tim Scannell / Port Angeles, WA
Nancy Y. Schafer / Poulsbo, WA
Joy J. Smith / Ruby, MI
L.H. Soldanels / Kansas City, MO
Heather Thayer / Moscow, ID
Bonnie Trusler / Port Coquitlam, BC, Canada
Daphne Tsang / Vancouver, BC, Canada
Navin K. Varma / Ann Arbor, MI
Carolyn Weatherly / Mission Viejo, CA
Michele Wegman / Encinitas, CA
John A. Wehner / Langley AFB, VA
Marjorie Powers White / New York, NY
Helen B. Yarborough / Mullins, SC

Congratulations also to all semi-finalists.

Grand Prize Winner

Commencement

And so it goes: Walking up that aisle is just like hearing my boots
scrape gravel against asphalt in the dark crisp night, hearing nothing but the street,
the street responding, echoing under the presence of some miracle celestial orb,
comet, I think, but really nothing more than a strange stain on the sky.
In fact, it is the only thing that's indistinct,
unamplified, and somehow a blur:
all else is examined under a high powered microscope,
or so it would appear.

My father dreams of white trousers, like Prufrock,
on the streets of Rio de Janeiro during the Carnival,
and while I look at my classmate's wisps of hair, like melodrama,
I think perhaps my sweetest days will be spent eating peaches,
and not dreaming of peaches past.

Still, the tassels on our caps would be streams of tears
so we look like so many miracle weeping Madonnas
walking down the aisles.
And God! Here I am crying rivers down to my boots
so caked with the earth of some seven states
and the gravel of the other night and cracked practically in half
I can feel the ground in my soles.
Evelina Zarkh

Here's To You

There's naught etched on her face,
But grace,
Years of sacrificed duty created more beauty,
Time passes by, she stays fresh as a flower,
With resources of power.

There's naught flows from her lips, but sweet grips
Sounds of melody drift from her breath,
Are met by ears of reception,
Without an exception.

There's naught shines from her inner countenance,
But moral sustenance;
Didn't she conquer all foes and resolve her woes,
Yet rear a dainty family tree, with dexterity?

There's naught wrought to mankind,
So divine, as her tending folks — youth,
Attesting the truth to their minds,
To her own, most, full-grown,
For all that, Here's A Tribute

Rev. Willie F. Stanley

Untitled

The breath, eternal life;
a wisdom all her own. There comes a time
when the ageless heirs of forgotten days
surface underground, and as the seeker of dreams
we follow hidden treasures in the sand.
But at the end of every rainbow
a puppet plays a clown
and we become the circus...
From the real to the image
we create a sight unseen,
and in the structure that once was
there lives the unknown.
So with a wandering soul and an aching heart
a struggle to survive
becomes not only ones destiny
but their will to live...

Andreja Kovacevic

Cabin In The Pines

I never dream of castles that will crumble down in time,
just a little 'ole log cabin nestled deep within the pines.

All surrounding areas, I'd add beauty with my touch,
just to make you happy, the man I love so much.

The atmosphere that I would weave, like spiders do their web,
would encircle you, my darling, with nary thought nor dread.

I'd smother you with kisses and hugs, not just a few,
just to see you happy, would be my daily due.

The kitchen in my cabin, with savory smells subdue,
all the tantalizing ardor for my hungry man, just you.

In the parlor near the fireplace, gold red embers steal the night,
I could cuddle oh-so-closely, within your arms that hold me tight.

Then we'd wander off to dreamland after all our needs were met,
dreaming of a great tomorrow, some new challenges we've set.

I can smell the scented roses, see the honeysuckle twine
all around an open window of my cabin in the pines.

Sometimes I think that I'm not dreaming and your dreams are just
like mine, always sharing, always caring, in our cabin the pines.

Emma Noon Reed

She

She was lovely and gentle
Thoughtful and kind
She had keen perception
Had a wonderful mind
When trouble came haunting
She understood
No matter what evil, She
    always did good!
Her strength and her courage
    a real inspiration
Her understanding heart
    needed no compensation
It near broke my heart
    the day She was stricken
Why should one such as She
    have this pain and this aching?
No earthly being, could help my poor mother
She was destined to be in the hands of another
As a shining example she'll always remain
'Til together we are, in a Heavenly domain

Kathryn Titus

Sunrise On A Spring Morning

A glimmer of light across the hill,
The shadows flee, as if by will.
They mount above the treetops high,
that scan the margin of the sky.

All 'glory' breaks with the rise of the sun,
As tho' it were pleased that day has begun.
A glimmer of light across the hill;
How breathless it is, when all is so still!

I, too, feel lifted above the earth;
My heart is merry - so full of mirth!
Life seems so glorious, so promising still;
When a glimmer of light comes over the hill.

Bessie Sawatsky

Silent Tears

A scared, solitary tree sways in a field
Wind caresses her leaves and bark.
Lonely thoughts that refuse to yield
Leaving her completely in the dark.

The wind dies down, the sun shines below
The metal monsters slowly disappear
As she surveys the wooden tombstones
Of her fallen compatriots so near.

Her memories go back to a time
Now lost, once fertile, once green
Destruction of forest — a crime,
Their cries echoing against the fiends.

Lorelei Reeder

"I Am"

I am the sweet taste of cold lemonade on a hot summer's day
I am the lab animal who will never see another sunset
I am the only cat in a world of dogs
I am the doormat everyone steps on
I am the first flower that blooms in spring
I am the security blanket a scared child runs too
I am the busy bee that people shoo away
I am the twinkle in a mother's eye
I am the rainbow people see after the rain
I am the first one to be forgotten but the last to forget.

Malgorzata Grzelak

"Together Again"

I know this is something that few people think about or know for sure,
But this is something I think about and pray
in my heart it's true and a cure
for the way we feel when we lose loved ones again and again,
I can't believe in my heart that God would put
us upon this earth to love and have family and friends,
And then take them away from us to never know
or see then again,
There has to be a reason for all of us being
here knowing one another and caring,
There has to be a more wonderful place where
we'll all meet again and be sharing,
In a better place for all of us to make up
for the pain and sorrow we have here upon this earth,
We'll go to a heavenly kingdom that's full of
beauty and love with all our loved ones and
there will be a rebirth.
So believe that we'll all be together and see
one another again.
And where we're going there will never be an end. Amen, amen

Barbara C. Rackesperger

Gramps In My Pocket

Gramps in my pocket and I hold destiny
Even though it's just a picture
That I can always see.

Looking at all my pictures
Thinking of good memories
Oh! Pictures are what I love to see!
I keep them in my photo album and I just let them be
And when memories can do nothing for me
Oh! Pictures are what I love to see!

I wish I could visit yesterday
From this present I want to get away.
Yeah, Gramps is right here next to me
I know yesterday holds nothing real
I just wish I could be with Gramps
And that Gramps could be with me.

Oh! That's who I want to be with, that's just how I feel.
I pray everyday that Gramps is ok
Oh! I wish I could live in my world and never leave
I wish I could live in yesterday, yesterday, yesterday,
Just Gramps and me.

Omar David Castro

Memories

Memories fade of yesterday
among the adventures past.
How does one reclaim the time
when life was moving fast.
You sit, you think, you ponder,
you shake your head in wonder.
Oh, but it is the laughter and the smiles
that lead you through the endless miles.
The joy, the sorrow, the tears, the fear,
all seem so distant and far from here.
And yet, life seems like such a mystery
when one relives his days in history.
So, dream and remember the days ago
for tomorrow maybe the final you know.

Donna Bradigan

Headed Home

Between flight tedium is dull!
Everything looks limp and tired;
Some folks are tense; some full of bull.
Things seem drab, uninspired.

The lady in slick, brown attire
Lumpy, frumpy, wrinkled and in slump,
dozed, head bobbing, no fire...
Brown beads and bag... dump... dump.

Three men in beards, chubby,
Poorly trimmed, frowning,
Glowering; lonely hubbies
Anxious to be home, loving.

The big, fat guy looking like sleaze,
Waddled, puffing, bags lumping,
Plopped with a squash and a squeeze,
The chair bent, groaning, sunk-in.

Heading home... many miles still to pass.
Only an hour yet... to be there,
To see Claire, happy at last,
To be with her, touch her hair.

Richard Knowles

The Lament Of An Embryonic Novelist

I sat, a-thinking, deep in thought;
Searching, planning a story to be.
I tried in vain to grasp a plot
From the storehouse of my memory.
It's very easy to decide,
Before you've penned your story, rare,
That you'll succeed before you've tried —
Only to end in deep despair
Of ever accomplishing that aim
Whereat you guided uncertain feet.
After all, life is still a game
Of hoping, striving, failure to meet
That goal of everlasting fame,
Does not let you think defeat.

While in despair, I can resist
The urge to be a novelist.
So, I conclude my dreaming time,
By writing lines of words in rhyme.

L. H. Soldanels

True Love

What is true love? It is but pure love, real love
The admiration of another, the sharing of feelings
To be compassionate
As your hearts beat as one
Just the two in a world of their own
It is unconditional love, endless love
As to share your future, a lifetime together
To feel the love from within
To be in love for every reason
Unconditionally
Accepting differences, sharing likeness
To dream as one
To be true as one
When a glance means so much
Only a smile, yet a connection
Eyes linked forever to the same Eternity...
Only you and me
That is true love.

Trisha Yee

"What's The Point Of Life?"

What's the point of life and why do we cry?
Is there a point to living if we're all gonna die
why do we have parents and a family
if we're all gonna leave at different times
and why do we have money
like nickels and dimes
is there a real meaning
because we are all just grieving
why is there death and everyone has to die
this pathetic life just makes me want to cry.
Seasons, colors, warm and hot what's the
difference it should all be the same in one spot
different people, places and things and then people
die and we have to bounce back like a bunch of springs.
Why do we feel, hurt, and have minds
its all gonna be forgotten when we die
why are we here
and why are people so far and near
this will never go away we'll have to find
out soon like why do we have the sun and moon.

Marissa Hughes

Reflections

We are one in God,
    but apart from each other.
If we are to love Him as ourselves
    then shall we not love ourselves first?
How are we to love if there are not
    examples as to see what the Lord is?
Reflections of you through my reflections
    might best show a window to Him.
Seeking many reflections as we go gives a
    brighter light to melt shadows
        that needlessly cling to the ends of man.
Whereas His light shines around me,
    then I shall shine around you.
In turn, you will shine love to others
    who search and shall capture their barren souls.
Suddenly, dots of light encompass dark lands
    and hope plants seeds in the center.
Come! Let's search!

Fay Giaimo

Our Home

There's a place to rest on weary days
A window where you sit and gaze
Where a pretty picture hangs on the wall
And a friendly voice I heard just call
There's a pot to tea to wet your lips
A faulty tap starts to drip
The radio plays my favourite tune
The roses waft their sweet perfume
A book lies open to be read
There's hungry people to be fed
The dog lies down, the fire is lit
The night draws in, it's time to sit
The curtains are closed, it's cosy inside
An armchair's waiting for our pride
A clock ticks gently, the kettle boils
A bed to ease the hard day's toils
It's a place to feel safe and warm
Where children feel they're secure
A place of bustle or all alone
This is what we call our home

Pauline Hodson

Cat And I

Oh cat and I live by the sea,
in a cabin we found not long ago.

Some call it a shack,
but we have a garden out back,
and a table with a pot of tea.

Cat likes fish and so do I,
but friends we could never be.

Because fish we are a threesome,
and cat and I, are a twosome,
and buddies cat and I, will always be.

For cats eyes shine bright
and he waits with delight.

And I shall wait and see, in the pale moonlight, and if the wind
is just right, a fishing we could be.

Hey, if you're out our way, I hope you will stay and
have a cup of tea.

When the sun goes down and the moon comes around, we shall
find another quay.

And the three of us shall fish, when the sun goes down
and the moon comes around, on Semiahmoo Bay.

Dale Davidson

You

As the wings of life carry me forward
I look into your eyes and see a life I long to live
The door of reality holds me back
The tradition of the past gives me hope to give
Chains of pain, bring on guilt
Yet, I dream on for the days of old
Forever trapped in the nature within me
Holding on to the dream dripping with ice so cold
Somehow the light still burns
Reaching out into the darkness looking for the source
Like the cycle of life, I too take my turn
Waiting for your soft touch I've yet to feel
The burden of the beast knocks at my door
Faced with reality the pain is so real
As I open the door I see the emptiness
The path to your reality is so clear
The dogs of doubt bite at my soul
Yet the road is bloody with haste and fear
Perched up like and angel I wait at your door
Fear fills me, I can fight no more

Troy E. Lavallee

"Tribute To A Black Woman"

Beautiful black woman - Mother of Nations
Your blackness reveals a perfect creation
Four centuries of pain imposed on our race
And yet you endured without losing faith
He brutally raped you but only to find
He stole your black body but not your black mind!

Beautiful black woman - Lady of Color
You're my black sister and I'm your black brother
But if destiny chooses to join both our hands
You'll be my black woman - I'll be your black man
But I'll always give credit where credit is due
And believe me, black woman, we're all proud of you

So, lovely black woman, just hold your head tall
For you are respected and loved by us all
For too long, black woman, we took you for granted
You gave us black warriors from seeds that we planted
With your undying love and your strong guiding hand
You're the proud Mother of today's changing Black Man!!

Theo Harris

Peace

O' Peace you're a pretty messenger dove,
Flying over Asia, Europe and Black Cove,
Transcending north and south, and east and west,
Bring with you a magnificent friendship best.

O' Peace you're a messenger dove pretty,
Sharing freedom, harmony among brothers.
There would be no national boundary,
With tribe equality, dealing with each other.

O' Peace, you're a pretty messenger dove,
Cherish a wonderful great ladylove,
Construct a strong bridge for culture knowledge
And break through the vastness of the earth's edge.

O' Peace, you're a pretty messenger bird,
Sing us a poetic verse with sweet rhymes,
Inspire us to have sympathy aft'ward,
Ring in the big bell of the bounty chimes.

O' Peace, you're a cute messenger pigeon,
Reconcile fighting, dispute and difference,
Soothe strife, overbearing, and violence,
Get to the future new-era region.

All's fused into oneness, into oneness.

Happiness's indeed, indeed happiness.

Hor-Ming Lee

Graceless Lady

Graceless lady—
it is dark and I
am not used to the smell
Throw your gaze over here
Tell me   what is this
Why is my spleen twisted around
and my mind only a symptom of my body
I am floundering and touching all the wrong places

Tell me lady
Give me your wing
and let us fly artlessly through birth and ruin
Teach me Arabic and Pig Latin
Will that help that undeniable feeling
of dark of heartburn of dis-control
Am I bipolar bisexual or both
What is this crack and why am I crying
Do you know lady   Can you tell me
Can you sing in excelsis deo and grant me my three wishes
Graceless lady—
I am here

Jennifer Lee

Pain And Fear

Pain hurts.
And nightmares get you scared.
In the world without pain or nightmares,
Many people would like that world better
You imagine a world just like that;
No pain, no nightmares.
You can't feel the pain, and you won't get scared.
You forget the feel of all pain,
You forget how it is to be scared.
There may not be much meaning to life for you.
For you do not accept to feel all you should feel,
Or experience what you should.
Pain and Fear
We must all learn to bear.
It is part of our lives.

Karen Chang

"My Love"

We tried to love each other once,
and found it failed.
We went our separate ways, and
suddenly you reappeared.
Now all those feelings I once
thought were gone, have now returned.
What can I do, when my heart won't
stop loving you but, now I find, you're
only here for a short time.
What will happen when we say
good-bye?
Will you ever come back for me?
Will my heart ever be the same?
All these questions fill my mind, but
one thing will stay the same, I will always
love you.

Lori Henson

All Over My Cake

I saw you today.
Well, I didn't really see you but....
I saw you today.

You were the icing on my birthday cake.
At first I didn't recognize you but...Eva said,
"Look at your cake!"
And there you were, all over my cake.

You were an icy cream, brand name "Supreme"
Supporting my candles, very delicately handled.
But better yet, is when I get
to eat my cake with you.

No one will know and we won't show
just how much we're enjoying
the icing...all over my cake.

Zaida Torres-German

Shadowland

Dark but light, the indeterminate state
A cave of hopes, dreams, still to be fulfilled
We await release, but yearn to return
The knowing is the comfort.

In space, perhaps, it would not matter
Each would be separate, thus, affirmed
But here, on Earth, we are together.

No eraser voids the lines that part us
For they are the bane, and our being, yet.

To emerge from the shadows and grasp a hand
Is not a certainty to escaping light.

Despair envelopes the moment
Darkness swiftly descends.
Isolation.

Blackness is complete, now.

Ramanie Hemamala Kumara

P

P is for present with big fluffy bows that children try to see
standing on their tip-toes.
From the time that presents get under the tree, the children are
wondering what is in the present they see.
They shake and they look trying to guess what they are.
A doll or a truck, or maybe a game?
Nobody can guess what the presents contain.
Then on Christmas morning the children hope they got what they want.
The presents are opened and the guessing has stopped!!!

Lindsey Fosse

To My Own

Do you think of me as often as I think of you?
constantly I'm wondering about who you are.
Do I already know you? Or will I meet you later?
Every day, even without knowing, I think of you;
so much that it seems as if I might go crazy not knowing
and having to wait for what seems like an eternity.
I can't wait to meet you, to know you, to love you!
for you are the person that I have waited my whole life for.

Even though at times I can't stand it, I know that when I find
you the wait will have been worth it.
Even in the times of despair, thinking it will never be
I think of you and it comforts me.
Because you are the person I have waited my whole life for.
You are the person that God has hand picked for me,
and you are the person I will spend the rest of my life with.
Until then, I'll be satisfied, just wondering.
        Molly Goen

The Year Of The Rat

The rusty house,
Rotting leaves on the
    Slanting porch,
East winds,
Crisp, discordant sounds, whispers,
    All fly away

When once we knew and awakened,
When the waves roiled and spilled on the
    rolling sands,
We climbed, sweat on the cheek,
White cliffs, holding on,
    Why is it now empty?
The rusty house.
        Harry Fishtown

Animal Rights

Animals are loving creatures
Who have many unexplained human-like features.

Animals have rights
For which I fight.

I'm asking you to fight for animal rights
Because we need to rescue animals from disastrous plights.

Please look to the animals side
For which your "Best Friend" may reside!

I ask you to take in the consideration
For all the animals under experimentation.

I hope I have changed your point of view;
For I hope you realize the animals need you!
        Dana Grygo

On Spiritual Intent To Invest Yours

For sooth, the day is cloudy and cold.
Green leaves tipped too slain drizzle-drip . . .?
Why werest that mood's lipped-might meant a body's emotional fit so morbidly told,
Its words' worth wouldst maim the Verily Earth a liarous-quit.
But Sweet Spring's Vital Vision willst add'eth Her steep, ALWAYS, into the say:
Of its Quiet Breathfull Sense (a biased aim either'd sane)
Relegates an Inner Most Insightful Recollective Depth, too such a weigh,
Everything of its Owned Natural Permanent Accord, doth hold possessed, Its Own Tenuous Gain:
For look'eth there now! what be the wealth of all the flowered flare — shared sunneth air:
Beheld pungent, a wet-blossomy-rainbow, quietethly bodacious;
And note'eth also, howeth the robin, the beak willethed the Worketh Wear
Doth mold any mood's slouch into a moment engaged vigorous and interested loquacious.
Ahhh, Ruffled Season! filleth mine eye with all the endureth wonderment of God's breasted grace;
And withstandeth thy delicate blue-schell to form as strength in everything . . . some child's face.
        Melvin J. Kramer

Dante's Inferno

The day was mellow, the day was gold.
It's days like these when you don't feel old.
Dante's Inferno is where we be,
from sun-up to noon down drinking with glee.
The boys were ecstatic, fly rods in hand,
catching the big ones, wouldn't fit in the pan.
My lover, my wife sat on the shore,
romancing the scenery, need I say more?
She'd caught her limit and oh, such a sport,
released all the small ones, when I rowed her to port.
We climbed up the mountain and caressed all the rocks,
the volcanics and igneous, man what a walk.
Out on the rangeland looking down,
feeling the freedom that nature abounds.
My day was pleasant, my day was Great.
        Duncan Gillespie

Wasted Away

We love because we must
    were bitter because we cannot trust
We lie because we're ashamed,
    there's so many problems in which we get blamed
We wear the clothes and play the part
    not realizing the strain put on the heart.
We walk through life with a smile
    letting no one know of the triumphs on the trials
We're swallowed by humanity
    then give up claiming insanity
Joking and laughing and wondering why
    staring in the mirror and starting to cry.
Realizing we've wasted it all away
    wishing to do it all over, praying for one more day.
It seems we've committed suicide
    by never getting off the crazy life ride.
We've done it the same as everyone before,
    never taking a new path, or opening a new door.
Now life has passed us by,
    and we look back and forever wonder why.
        Abby Manatt

One True Fairy

Fairies are my favorite things,
I especially love it when one sings,
And I love how they play
All throughout the whole long day.

I wish I could join them in
Their daily routine of taking a spin
Through the deep blue sky;
But I can't because I can't fly.

I am hoping to go with them when they play,
If they're in the woods, or by the bay,
I don't even care if they are in a tree;
Because I only wish and hope to see
One true fairy.
        Erin Kathleen Sutton

A Final Prayer

Now I lay me down to sleep
Pray the Lord my soul to keep,
Cherish those I love so much
Keep them precious in your touch.

Goodbye my child; I love you so
But I guess how much; you'll never know.
Please dear, don't be sad
I'm here now, and I am glad.

For no more pain I'll have to face
Here in heaven, it's all erased.
So please hold my memory in your heart
And I promise we will never be apart.

Live you life, as I lived mine
Because no one knows of our time
For today, I did not awake
And my soul, the Lord did take.

Candace M. J. Grant

Dad

The first time I saw you I knew you were my dad
Someone who would love me even if I were bad
You were busy farming, so mom mostly took care of me
But you are my dad, something she can never be
Time has passed by and now I understand
You must spend time to farm our land
You could almost call that garage your home
There all day you work and roam
After school I come to see if you need my help
When I leave, you whine and you yelp
Dad, I hope this is only beginning of the good times we'll share
Because growing up without you I would not be able to bear

Brandice Scraba

Keeper Of The Dreams

There are dreams that are of happiness,
dreams of far off places,
dreams of what was,
and what is,
dreams of what may of been,
there are dreams of what will be
But the keeper of the dreams decides what you see
so beware!

Crystal Bassett

Life's Repairs

Someone once broke my heart
I told them not to worry I've
got glue to make it new.
Someone broke my heart again, and
Again like a stupid never learning fool
told them don't worry I got the stuff to make it new!
Again someone broke my heart but,
this time I couldn't tell them I've
got the glue, to make it new!
How can I go without repairs to my heart to
make it trusting and brand new?
Oh, God help me find the glue
to make my heart brand new!
Soon someone will
come along and break my heart again.
But, this time I have a
deep, dark feeling I won't
make it through the awful,
horrible pain to get
the glue to make my heart brand new!

Muriel Zimmerman

Beyond The Darkness

Life at times seems like an endless journey
In a vast wilderness of darkness.
Yet, beyond life's struggles and sadness.
There is a nourishing garden of eternal bliss.
And all who achieve admittance to that garden
Reflect its radiant beauty.

For that is the garden of God's purest light.
How do I know? I have glimpsed into that garden
And was enchanted by its light.
Thus, I will not rest until I am completely out of
This bleak, miserable place of emptiness.

I know that as long as I keep moving
In the direction of God's pure light,
I will eventually come upon its source.
Then! My soul will absorb its magnificent rays.

So that all who are near me, and are approaching
The garden of bliss, will see a reflection of
Its pure light shinning through me.

Magdalene Patricia Balloy

Never Too Late The Lesson?

One day long past they stood here
in loud, long lines of blue and gray,
the stench of powder in their nostrils,
eyeing each other across their cold steel
the vacant, lost stare of death and hate
written indelibly on their sad faces,
mostly too young, yet old unto death.
Now on this place now stands a tree
spreading its quiet green canopy
softly over the still, warm earth
bedecked with the delicacy of life,
whispering soundlessly to all to listen,
pleading with us to search in our hearts,
begging us silently to understand
that theirs was not the answer,
that the question should not again be asked.

Richard M. J. Thurston

Untitled

I stumble as I walk thru the woods by the lake,
So confused, weeping, weeping, weeping
Will I ever come out of this valley of tears and grief

There is no anger
Only why why - all alone - you're gone, really gone
I want to go with you
I don't want to live without you

Will I ever be with you again?
My darling, my darling Spirit, please stay here with me
Please, don't leave me here all alone

I must have hope that I shall see you again
But I know, I must wait, here,
till, at last
I shall see your beloved face again
I will feel your strong arms about me
ever enfolding, OH, my dear,

We shall be together again
forever throughout eternity
Only Forever

Sally Hartley

Dolores

I sit alone in a comfortable chair
Half expecting someone who will never again be there
A song is playing on the radio
Tears run freely from my eyes, I can't stop the flow
You are the wind beneath my wings
Every word of that song reminds me of all of the things
I should have said to you then
Now you will never hear any of my words again
I'm sorry Dolores that I didn't do more for you
When I had the chance
The rest of my life I will spend in a half trance
Part of me goes on with everyday chores
and part of me is forever lost because
When you left me I prayed I could follow
It was not to be and so I swallow
My tears and carry on
Looking forward to the day, when it's my time
and I will find the way, back to you.
My beautiful Dolores.

Joseph A. Buhler

The Web

The spider, toiling, struggling to exist,
Weaves out a web, as pliant as a reed,
Adhesive, powerful. He has no need
For heavy bonds; few insects can resist
The soft, deceptive strands, decked with the mist.
His web is strongly spun. A creature's speed
And strife are useless; rarely is it freed.
The spider is a clever strategist.

He catches in his web, high-thrown, far-spun,
The means to make his simple life complete.
So man throws out a web that none
Can conquer: supple strands of love that greet
And catch all things that come — an aged one,
A girl, a child, a lawman on his beat.

Based on the following quotation from Leo Tolstoy:
"Yes, the means to gain true happiness in life is, without any rules, to throw out from oneself in all directions, like a spider, an adhesive web of love, and to catch in it all that comes: an old man, a child, a girl, or a policeman."

Eleanor W. Serio

My Bible

My Bible; so full of adventure and strife
With so many lessons to teach me, of how to live my life.
My Bible; is something I read everyday
And if I have a problem, it tells me how to pray.
My Bible; the heroes inside are many, but one that really stands out
He turns his back on no one, he loves us without a doubt.
My Bible; has a man named Jesus, who gave his life on a cross
To cleanse us of our sins, and help redeem the lost.
My Bible; the story begins with Genesis - of how we all began
It tells of all creation, and the wonderful creation "man"
My Bible; the story ends with Revelation, the scary end of time
It tells us of trials and tribulations, and the ones to be left behind.
My Bible; if you have a problem, I guarantee you'll find
The answer inside the pages, of this wonderful Book of mine.
My Bible; is not prejudiced, against color, race, or creed
You can see all of this yourself, just open the pages and read.
It's hard to end this poem, about this Bible of mine
There's so much that needs to be told, so many souls to find.
So I'll end it with a message - Be true to God and your faith
To love and help one another, and all go to Heaven one day.

Cristy Knobloch

Flame

On evenings cold, within my hearth she'll dance
to rhythms ever changing, never heard.
With spirits bright, for all and none she'll prance;
quite unaware of ev'ry heart she's stirred
to draw to near, but then recede in pain
before her essence ever finds a grasp to tight.
How'er, a loose embrace will find her fain
to share her warmth throughout a lonely night.
For thus I love this splinter of the sun
enough to offer forth my tinder care
to stoke her passions higher once begun
to burn upon the brand which e'er I bear.
Oh beauty, delicate and fair, whence came
my inspiration pure, thy name is Flame.

Burton Morron

Waiting Room

Sadness and loneliness creeps insidiously
Between the cliffs and clouds
In chant and motion, enchanted motion
Capable of adapting thru primal screams...
Is this a daydream?
Schizoid society in a classic moral sense
Decisions... unthought... untouched
A Jewel in a dream, as the fire still smolders
I'm engulfed; as the emission of light slowly
Creeps to a lost eternity and sight
Dangers awaits...I'm at the point of self-destruction
New graffiti, old revolutions, a show of exaggerated emotion and energy
Who's waiting?
Innocence in a sense! As the arms of destiny keep you from me
I'm in the waiting room of...Tomorrow.

Perry Wilson

Floodlight

Fearing the night while watching its darkness fall
wondering at the sun that flees to the horizon in
her timely fashion, off to deliver on promises made
to other places worthy of her bright spectacle.
See you tomorrow! I shout after her with my eyes.
My words fall soundlessly on a deafened sea, but
somehow I know she heard me. I return my attention to
nights cold embrace (even darkness has its time, I guess)
Now fear subsides to pity as a sudden feeling of loneliness
is felt from the ashen murk around me. It does have a time
but it has no place, and time is growing short.
When day breaks you can see the source suspended in plain
view, means to an end, tangible. But darkness has no source.
You could travel its expanse eternity tenfold and all
you will find is more darkness. Suddenly the mood grows
darker as loneliness and pity turn to elements of anger
and spite. But for these I have neither time nor a place.
It will be time for bed soon, and I have an early morning
destiny at the edge of the horizon, where I will anxiously
await the arrival of my brightest friend once again.

Todd Robertson

Negatively Constructive

I destroy what is good with my sporadic web
Entangled in boxes of my wrecking
Spilled happiness forced into the hunted melancholy
My mirror standing beside me
Compressing feelings in unreflected wounds of a
messed conception
Causing me to scratch apart my joy
Murdering my ability to be
All alone inside my head
Eating my happiness.

Venessa Capo

Coward

The wind lacks courage.
Untamed he mocks, he ridicules, he jeers at all those things
cursed beneath his heal.
At his disposal is the power to consume
within himself
not only that which is on the earth, but that also which is above it.
At his howling command
structures of nature and inventions of man
bow at his feet.

And through it all, he has the audacity
Not even to show his face.

Tamie Harkins

Past Paths

Rolling thunder soars through the skies
The words pour down like rain
yet the lightening passes by

The wind blows down all my starting blocks
It's alright, I've already chosen more

If all you have is hatred and past wrongs
All you have is pain
I must walk in the footsteps of the Wise One

Until I learn life begins with each new day
I will never own friendship and love

The wind is the one that blows my blocks down
Only for me to start again
For if your blocks have fallen

It only means you have chosen the wrong path to follow
Choices are many, the decision is mine

If I envelop myself in a cocoon of the past
I'll never emerge safely
So reach out for your dream

Rachel Ann Brenart

It's Raining!

As the sun rises to reveal a new day
Life reaches out to drink of happiness
To quench the dryness of everlasting searches

Life is sometimes hard and full of dryness
Overcoming obstacles of the world

Some are fortunate and find an abundance of happiness
Others find it hard to come by

Some find it in books
Others in Friends
Some find it in spirit
Others in mind

As for me I can say that I am drenched
For I have found someone special
As for my life
It's raining!!

William D. McCullough Jr.

To Mom

For all the things you did without,
And all the times you watched us pout,
You gave your love most everyday,
And showed it in your special way,
We took so much and gave so little,
And never did you ever quibble,
As now we see the sacrifice,
You gave your love, your time, your life,
We wish we would have thought to say,
We love you with each passing day.

Tracy Foden

Teens In 1996

He says he loves you,
And you believe every word is true,
But after he gets a piece of you,
Your relationship is through.

You see him every day in the hall, and wait at
Home hoping he'll call.

3 1/2 months go by,
And you're pregnant (no word of a lie)

You're nervous, and not sure of what to do,
So you tell your ex-boyfriend "I'm having a set of two.

You don't like needles, and pins,
But what do you expect, you're pregnant and having twins.

Teen pregnancy is usually never planned,
And next to you only a real man will stand.

Katie Ingalls

He's Only Sleeping

Shattering the silence in the still of night,
The dreaded call rang out,
Gripping our hearts with fright.

While clutching to hope for his recovery yet
To the hospital we raced.
Our pounding hearts nearly choking us,
Then the terrible news, he's gone, we faced.

Disbelief, numbness, and shock overwhelmed us with grief.
So swiftly, death stole him from us!
Ripped savagely from our earthly lives!
Our broken hearts can't comprehend,
His life here so brief!
Finality leaving horrid emptiness thus.

His gentle heart is still
But free now of pain.
His beautiful eyes are closed.
But he's not alone, he's with God,
Held, safe in his arms,
Till we'll all be together forever, in eternity, again.

Patricia J. Reister

The Little Lad

Please O Lord, don't think I'm a pain,
Seems I'm asking for things again;
Just make me a proper Dad,
When I hold the hand of the little lad.

The road he goes is long and rough
Make sure he's made of proper stuff;
Stand him firm straight and tall and true,
Tell him what he must and mustn't do.

Keep his eyes on goals on high,
Before he wins he first must try;
Be not afraid to fly or fall,
And love of all creatures great and small,

Help me halt the headlong rush,
And when to say and when to hush;
And find a moment the tears to dry,
When troubles find the little guy.

And would it Lord be too much,
If he would sort of stay in touch;
Maybe someday make him a little glad;
That he held the hand of dear old Dad.

Bernard Hann

Oma's Arms

On the underside, velvety, silken
I'd like a blanket as soft
On the outside, wrinkled as wet, brown paper
Extensions to rough, skin-taut hands

Arms fleshy from homemade soups
Twitching as she tugged at threads of unsuitable seams
Wobbling as she kneaded with pride
   the dough of a strudel none of her daughters would make

Enveloping grocery bags she carried upstairs
Outstretched with the annual washing of windows
Anchoring the paperback that lulled her to sleep
Rarely cold on winter nights
   Never needing the bed jacket I bought for her birthday

Arms swinging by her side like a brave soldier
Folded under her breast
  Crossed like a barrier
   Armed for battle

And still
My fading hand print evidence of our embrace
     Ulli Elia

Magic

No one can ever know
How your wisdom, your love, your magic
Helped me grow.

Sitting on the arm of your chair
Sharing pain, sharing stories, sharing life
You were always there.

You loved me so much and nurtured me
Through the rebellion, the anger, the doubts
The adolescent lunacy.

The frantic calls from far away
"Use flour, cook it slower, don't get upset,"
You'd calmly say.

Now I'm where I want to be
And you're gone, and I miss you, but I know
Your magic is inside of me.
    G. D. Mason McLemore

"With No Lies, Looking Into His Eyes!"

When I looked at him in his eyes,
I knew at that moment he spoke no lies.
His eyes were breezy; like windy, skies.
They were different; not like the other guys.
As the girl who sits down behind me sighs,
Wishing she were in my place; looking into his eyes,
Held close to him in his arms;
They wrapped around me like knotted bow ties,
Together we are wise!
Happy I'm his only prize,
But as the tears fall heavily from his eyes,
I know he can no longer tell me any lies.
As I lie in his arms my heart cries;
"Please, tell me the truth, no more lies!"
Since he has, I want him to know,
as this relationship dies,
That for once, I did something wise!!!
    Bobbye L. Turnbough

Storm No More

Rhythmically, at first, slow, drops sprinkle the dust
soon steady, ready to swallow the crumbling crust
   Drink deeply my friend
   rejoice in my mirth

Clouds deepen and darken, mumbling their madness
rush swiftly like faces from sweetest smiles to sadness

   But not I or you follow
   joy overflowing the earth

Wind whips gently then stops, start faster and faster
sing low, reach high, she is lost without the master

   Which guides you to me
   and us to our birth

Then thunder and pour, resonate and soar
becomes one under, overpower, strengthen and roar

   I love you and love you
   the storm is no more
    Karen Tompsett

Upon Returning Home...

The wheels kick up the gravel;
The car door slams and jars a silent night.
Hurried steps...
A hand reaches, quivers.
So slowly the key turns and
A door creaks open.
Echoes in the foyer...
   Then the old familiar scents
   embrace me as the luggage drops to the floor.
Destination unknown...
   The armchair beckons.
I am absorbed by the surroundings.
Now, the echoes diminished by
  Memories...
   warm, loud and clear.
    The house is not empty.
Physical absence only...
   my heart never left.
    Justin Pope

On The Path At Last

Waiting so long for my path to appear,
Finally it's here!
For years waiting at the bottom step
I now climb eagerly toward the top
Enjoying the process of my journey,
Climbing the time-worn celestial stairs
Many others have traversed before me,
Pausing on some steps
As difficult lessons are learned,
Then bolting upward to higher levels,
Knowing I may not reach the top in this lifetime
Perhaps not for many, many lifetimes to come
But listening to my Higher Self
Pulling me ever upward,
My Spirit taking flight
And my heart opening to the world.
May I shine as a beacon for others to follow
As others shine for me.
Together, linking hearts and hands,
Enlightenment for all becomes a reality!
    Marilyn J. Dowle

Springtime In May

I love the Springtime that comes in May
When all the little children come out to play.
Their voices are ringing, the birds are singing.
'Tis such a happy day when Springtime comes around in May.

When the little flowers peep up
   through the earth,
'Tis a glorious sign of nature's new birth,
Their color all glowing to give such a ray:
'Tis the sign of Springtime as it comes in May.

The trees all dress up in their finest glory,
They too, can tell of such a wonderful story,
Their beauty is here for a while to stay
As they too, welcome the Springtime when it comes in May.

Could you too, not look about you and see
All the beauty that God hath given to thee?
A child, a bird, a flower, or a tree,
   by such He dresser the earth to see;
And then waits for the day, when the beautiful
   Springtime — comes once again in May.

Virginia W. Cameron

These Things I Remember Of A Past I Can't Forget

I remember Big Ben ticking, and the sound of my grandfather snoring nearby.
I remember the sound of the train going through the valley, and a cow bellowing from the barn yard door.

I remember going fishing and catching lots of bullheads.
I remember the sound of crows flying through the air, and at night, you could hear the bullfrogs saying good night.

I remember the cats that would parade around at my grandfather's feet. I remember the sound of him playing the fiddle, going to square dances, and milking the cows, with once actually falling into the drop.
I remember picnics in the yard and the chicken my grandmother always bought. I remember eating onion sandwiches, watching soap operas, and the candy bars we would share just between us.
I remember my grandmother's smile and the funny faces my grandfather made.
I remember the unforgettable love and security I felt with them, and most importantly the acceptance I felt because I knew no matter what, I was loved unconditionally.

I remember the 'I love you grandpa' pin he wore to his grave.
I remember the strawberry daiquiris my grandmother and I shared just before her death. But the one thing, the best thing, to remember is that they are together once again having the time of their lives.

Jeanne M. Brunelli

Nostalgia

Tonight I took a journey to the year of '53,
I wandered through the pages of a book that used to be.
I walked back down the hallway of Mobile's Murphy High,
And seeing once more those happy faces,
   remembering brought tears to my eyes.
It seemed as if I stepped across that bridge, infinity, and caught,
again, a moment of a life that used to be.

No doubt, as many years have gone, some faces are no more,
I wonder, as I think of it, just who has gone before?
Could it be Mary, Sue or John, perhaps it's Joyce or Bea.
Or could it be that impish face now smiling back at me.
I stumble o'er the threshold, my eyes are full of tears,
My steps no longer light and gay; they've slowed down
through the years.

I turn and look behind me, I see where I have been,
And then I look across the veil to a life that might have been.
My two sons and little daughter, pleasant dreams race through
their heads.
If I had lived life differently, there might now be three empty beds.

Margaret Kasey

Reverie

I am the wind
that gently urges lost clouds into destiny,
I am a drop of water
in an endless sea called humanity.
I am a spark of Life
twitching in a fury of emotions.
I am the soil of friendship
where a prosperous seed is sowed.
I am the desire, everyone has to be loved
I am a page, upon which Life is written.
I am a dream
stirring within a restless mind.
I am the essence of Love
awaiting a form of expression.
I am the song of joy
lonely hearts never hear.
I am universal, yet divinely unique.
I am limitless, bound only by my possibilities.

I am your imagination, let me grow with you.

Nancy Maria Bonnier

Sorrow Of War

The most important thing about war is pain mixed with sorrow,
Because our soldiers are dying with pride,
When bloody battles of pain rise.
Taste the death with your eyes,

Sickening fear is in mind.
Tears of destruction, our soldiers cry,
Winds of gun shots, make their way by.

Families worry of their men fighting through explosions,
Death by each side, men in dozens.
Sleepless nights or awakening to God,
No one will know the way you've gone.

Whether it was with defeat or with failure,
All they know, is that you were a millionth soldier.
They may go through your bags to find a black secret,
But they only find letters of love and engagement.

Don't make any friendly soul,
Because later on, will be his time to go.
Why wait until tomorrow?

   -Because-

The most important thing about war is pain mixed with sorrow.

Michelle R. Husser

The Gray House

The gray house was the old house.
The shutters fell off of it,
From hinges weather-beaten and rusted.
A little girl, Mildred,
had many a dreams in,
And went to school from.
The gray house was not to do all things in;
A house to do good and a mother with morals.

From the gray house was wed,
From the gray house a poet was born.
Gray was the name of the poet,
wrote 'Memories Of Childhood'
About Ray, and Ruth and Margaretta.
But Mildred now has moved to a new house,
Way up on the hill,
and the little Gray house is needed no more.

Mildred Pearl Griffiths

Caring, Courage, Professionalism:
Army Nursing In Vietnam

The history books will say little of us, and we received no accolades.
Yet every soldier who served in Vietnam knew us and remembers
- we were there. Army Nurses.
In Quang Tri...
   We were there looking into the wide, glazed eyes of a shocky
   19-year-old infantryman from small-town Georgia who lost both
   legs to a Vietcong mine a half-hour earlier.
   We cried with him and we cared - we were there...
In Pleiku...
   We were there as Huey's roared in and out of the compound, whipping
   an eerie veil of dust and dirt about, leaving their stretches of
   still and moaning warriors, as rockets whistled in the black night.
   We prayed for courage, guidance, and for another day.
   Amidst the turmoil, we continued to triage-we were there..
In Binh Thuy...
   We were there in the sweltering heat of the Delta dispensing
   ointment and toothbrushes to the elders and kids on Medcaps;
   assisting the young corpsmen with the care of a badly burned
   Vietnamese mother; and we were there carrying on the finest
   traditions of the Army Nurse Corps.
Today, on the wall, in Washington, D.C., the etched names of 10 of
   our fellow nurses gleam into eternity. Others of us were wounded,
   injured, or have vivid remembrances of our long year in that small,
   far away Asian country.
But, we were professionals, and proud to serve our country.
We were Army Nurses in Vietnam...
And the soldiers still remember.
   Timothy A. Jacobs

Song For Autumn

Kind summer's gone and burnished amber leaves
Are floating down upon the frosted air.
And we who smiled and found warm summer fair
Are sad to see the wheat bound up in sheaves,
For summer's green we cannot ever hold,
Nor stop it when it turns to Autumn's gold.
North winds will shake the black and barren trees
And they will sing their bleak and stormy song,
While snow is falling softly all day long,
A blanket for the faded golden leaves.
And you will say, "Once bloomed a red rose here"
As if it 'twere in some long forgotten year.
Then silence like a pall' will smother sound
When snowflakes deepen, deepen on the ground.
   Elizabeth Dudley Baker

The Promise Of Old

And over the cloud HE set his bow:
The signet of his promise to men,
a glorious bridge, the Arch of Hope
that clads the earth in robes of gold.

The promise of the Things to Come,
Of Beauty, Joy and Grace,
Of Peace on Earth, Goodwill to Men,
A world united in Truth and Faith.

HE set His bow right o'er the cloud,
The Bridge into Eternity;
And mankind, seeing the holiness,
Looks up, newborn in purity.

My heart leaps up when I behold
  The Promise of the Lord —
The clouds are dark, the clouds are near:

  Y o u, Youth of today,
   are this 'Promise of Old'!
   Rose Lesser

Gift Givers

Delight the eye, wild flowers do.
In time they grow in fine-tuned space.
With hues (not few) and gifts on cue...
Alluring scents - herbs - foods to taste.

The Vitamin C of Rose hips gay
Keep colds afar - thus we are free
To scatter smiles along life's way
And cheer those cast on stormy sea.

Untouched by mud, they quietly float
With enchanting fragrance - gift so rare!
Those lilies white, the "perfect boat"
for animals. Buds roots they bear.

Those gifts of God are ours for aye.
Their seeds and roots are harvests cast.
Of love and cheer may others say:
"Their roots and seeds also - will last."
   Marguerite L. Taylor

A Tribute To Rabin

A tragic event in the Middle East
Where a fierce man of war but a strong man of peace
Was struck down by the Devil's hand
As he fought for peace in that troubled land
Firmly schooled in strategic ways
He won a war in only six days
With a mighty hand he vanquished the foe
Yet planted the seeds in which peace could grow
Like a magician waving his wand
He dared to shake his enemy's hand
A commanding general so noble and wise
He went on to win the Nobel Pace Prize
And though a monster shot him dead
Many will follow the path that he led
Who mourn his passing but shall still strive
To honor his memory and keep peace alive
Like Lincoln, Sadat and so many sages
He leaves us inspired as he departs for the ages
   Israel Siev

The Essence Of My Dad's Soul

You watched as I waved from
  the horse on the carousel,

Sheltering me from life's pains,
  Uncertainties and fears-I could tell.

Your childhood was poor-and
  Times, they proved hard.

While your strength as a man shown bright,
  Still the pain in your voice, I could tell had been marred.

The shoes that you shared as a child on the farm.
I'll never forget, as you spoke of your past,
  The night that you wept, so close in my arms.

You loved as a husband, you guided as a father-
No man in my eyes, will I love and respect as deeply,
  For there could be no other.

It was undying love, compassion, and wisdom
  That created the essence of my dad's soul.
For the sacrifices, the support, and the values which he emanated-
  Never once took their toll.

Your death leaves me empty; for who can I turn to,
This hollowed gut feeling inside me is all too new.
   Carol Hignite

Untitled

It seems that when I am with you,
You take up all my time,
And when we take some time to think,
You only mistake my words,
One minute we are together,
And the next I am out of the picture,
The only thing keeping me going,
Is that everything I have reminds me of you,
And when I look into the mirror,
I see terror and shades of sadness,
But only a few weeks ago,
Was I looking and they weren't there,
And everything keeps falling apart,
Nothing ever fixes itself,
You tell me it won't work, but can't we even try?
And you never seem to understand,
What I am really talking about,
I get the feeling that I am just a memory,
And what am I supposed to do about this mess, leave it and just wait?
I'd rather pick it up and start all over again.

Heather George

The New Puppy

I celebrate exuberance!
I had forgotten it in my advancing years.
Though joy still peeps around
The door way of my life when least expected
In the written word
In music heard
I am conversant with content,

But exuberance!
Four gangling legs jumping for the butterfly
Only to folk akimbo.
The coltish leaps
The wild abandonment of motion
For love of motion
For love of life
The velvet eyes shining with good health
The kisses for no reason
These are the joys I had forgotten.

Joan G. Day

To My Husband On Our 47th Anniversary

I see the tree you planted years ago,
But we were younger then; I could not know
The passing years would in the future bring
This glorious spring.
They told us we could never have
A child,
But then our baby daughter came
And smiled.
They said we should enjoy
This only one,
Till we were over joyed;
A baby son
Came to add stature to our years
And joy and tears.
You have inspired our flourishing.
The tree is taller, and the days
And nights inspire
Only praise.
And through it all, I always knew
That there was you.

Virginia Nedrow

Something Beautiful

This is the moment I believe in:
Another moment and this feeling will depart.
But this is the instant of attainment,
No other ever never will perceive.
We are alone, so like each other;
   no one can see how much we share,
We are so sad in isolation
   knowing this no antidote to fear.
When touching souls we feel transcendence,
   so slipping fast no time to grasp,
And left alone, we bemoan shadows
Veiling the sense of one in all.
So walk the streets without companion,
   the touch of death - black feather's fall;
And all is lost in time of touching...
And all the same - nothing at all...

Douglas Baird

The First Snowfall

Its scent had filled the air for days
And fences, doorways, walls all creak,
Far in the distance
The eyes can see
A change fallen o'er the mountain peaks.
Cobblestones convert to gems,
Shining smooth beneath one's feet;
Glistening silver lights up the night
A mirror reflection from the streets.
A town in waiting,
Silent, anticipation
Awaiting the return of a long forgotten friend,
His pattern, his destination.
Then, ever so softly
In the still of the night,
A spellbound arrival
The valley, now white!

Angelika Loewen

The Tao Of Rose

How can I find my inner peace?
   By closing the door on my ancient war.
How can I heal a hurting heart?
   By touching the heart of my hurting soul.
How can I be the truest friend?
   By being a friend to my truest self.
How can I tap my greatest joy?
   By embracing and blessing my greatest pain.
Where can I see the brightest light?
   In the heart of the dark of my darkest night.
Where can my courage arise and take form?
   In the depths of my fear, in the eye of the storm.
Where can I hear the sweetest song?
   In the promise of dawn when the night has been long.
Where does my dying lead... to the earth?
   The seed is but sleeping, in dying there's birth.

Rose Kramer

Untitled

For all the things you've done and thanks never received
For giving me the strength to go on when I had the need
You were always giving always took the time
Gave me special memories that will always be mine
Even if I travel abroad or near
In my heart I'll always hold you so dear
For all the miles I've traveled all the places I've been
You've always given smiles, been there as my friend
I should have long ago took the time to say
I love you more with each passing day

Perry Keaton

Alone In The Dark

Sitting.
Blankly staring into nothingness,
looking around for signs of others,
but nothing shows.
Darkness surrounds,
no shimmering brightness to comfort us.
Alone,
forever alone in the darkness.
The night of a jungle.
Nothing in the eyes of a panther
searching for his food.
Preying on others in the darkness of a city,
all alone,
No one to hunt with.
He sits alone, alone in the dark.
People could learn from him,
learn to live without others,
learn to live with themselves,
learn to live alone.

Alone in the dark.

Leslie Crockett

Fear

I gnaw at every man's brain,
I'm like a parasite that won't go away.

Every man tries to hide me,
but eventually I show through.

No man lives without me,
though some like to believe they do.

Psychiatrists specialize in getting rid of me,
movies are made that star me.

I come out full force at night,
I am what nightmares are made of.

Children believe I live in their closets,
when in truth I only live in their souls.

I am every man's worst fear,
I am fear itself.

Laura A. Francis

"The Visit"

My grandmother came to me one night.
Looking especially lovely in God's glowing light.
She said "hush" don't be afraid, it's me your grama.
Listen to what I've to say.
Life on earth was truly good to me.
But I came sick so God set me free.
Heaven is a wonderful place.
Where all around you can feel God's grace.
It's peaceful here there is no pain.
No more heartaches no more strains.
All my friend's are her with me.
To laugh about what use to be.
So tell your Mother that I'm alright.
And in her mind my memories are held tight.
Tell her often that she is loved.
Even from her Mother who watches above.
I'm her guardian angel she cannot see.
But by her side I'll always be.
So take care of her for there is no other.
That can take the place of your dear sweet Mother.

Wendy Brisseau

Choices

Sometimes I wonder - where has it gone - this life,
this youth of mine?
The years that once had lie ahead now gone in
instant and never ceasing time.
The dreams, the hopes that I had planned -
seems like not so long ago - I held them in my hands.
But when we love, and love I have, we open up our hands,
then dreams slip through as if they were
mere grains of sand.
I guess if I had stood more firm and turned my
hands to fists - I could have held on to those dreams
but oh - what I would have missed -
I think I cannot give half myself - part to this
and some to that - I must give all myself,
choose one thing or another -
So right or wrong - choose I did -
I chose to be a Mother.

Bettie Lee Moore

Untitled

Women I have known and been are too numerous to count.
Spiked heels to make me taller,
just so we can sleep our way to the top,
and keep us from running.
Laws taped to my flesh about a baby I've never seen,
just so we can feel our duty;
that we are all potential mothers.
Women I have known and been are too numerous to count.
Silicone implants to make me bigger,
so we all resemble Barbie.
But you can't rape the willing
even though we all screamed "no,"
and they'll never know how that feels.
Women I have known and been are too numerous to count:
We were taught to keep quiet
We were groomed to be beautiful
We were marketed as toys
We were supposed to be dumb
We were trapped into devotion
Women I have known and been are too numerous to count.

Laura Petrella

Why

Why is it that parents are the last to know?
In fact most parents are never told.
What is a child supposed to do?
Hide and cry and pretend it ain't true.
Live like a rat afraid of the cat.
Scared to come out in the light of the day,
Afraid of the night, the sounds and the dark.
Seeing the shadows move with the moan of the wind;
Somebody is coming to visit again.
There's no one to tell, nobody cares,
We stay in silence, no breathing, not a tear.
In hopes that the visitor,
Will no longer return.
And that one day someone will care.

Corina S. H. Benoit

"Her"

She's more than words can describe,
The memory of her, enough to keep a man alive
The sweet smell of roses brings her countenance to mind,
She's a heavenly creature, truly one of a kind,
There's a spot reserved for her in every man's heart
Neither time nor destiny shall keep us apart.

Peter Brown

Broken Heart

I'm looking for something,
I know I once had,
But when it broke, I lost it,
Now I'm feeling real bad.

It was something that was,
From deep down inside,
I know I can live without it,
But I don't want to pass it by.

It was shattered into many little pieces,
After being hurt so many times,
So after a while, I denied.
That it was even mine.

Well this little thing,
That I once had.
Well it's been left in your hands...

So if promise to love it,
And treat it with care,
When you open your hands,
It will always be there.

Lisa Kelley

One More Day (A Poem About Anorexia)

One more day to dream and laugh
But now I cannot change the past
I have just one more day to last
Then it's over, just like that

I stooped so low to get out fast
But now I cannot change the past
Who knew I'd end up this way
All I need is one more day

I'm past the mission that I once sought
To be the thinnest girl, I thought
But now I'm fighting to stay alive
And no one's here on my side

It started as a simple diet
Now there's no way to deny it
My life is over, it's taken control
I'm not the same old normal girl

It has taken all of this
For me to learn just what pain is
Here I lay in my hospital bed
Knowing one more day and I'll be dead

Elizabeth Frazier

Help Me God

Sometimes I wonder,
Sometimes I doubt,
What this faith is all about.
I've heard you parted the deep blue sea,
Healed the sick, made blind people see.
You wore a crown of thorns on your head,
Left on a cross hanging, until you were dead.
The tears you wept, I'm told were for me.
So what is this faith I can not see?
I wish that I could understand, why I can not feel your hand.
If your with me night and day, why don't you answer when I pray?
Have you closed your doors, turned me away?
So tell me God, what must I do?
To fill a part of me with you.
I need to know your by my side
So I no longer run and hide,
Help me see you're really there
Let me know you truly care,
Give me a sign from up above,
Tell me God, it's me you love...

Carla Grewatz

Lucy's Charm

Little Miss Lucy just stared at her charm.
It dangled from the bracelet attached to her arm.
Upon it there was a sight to behold,
a unicorn with wings standing rigid and bold.
The longer she stared, she saw a twinkle in his eye.
The next thing she knew he began to fly.
He flew across her room and onto her bed.
Her bracelet was now dangling from the horn on his head.
When she went to retrieve it, she brushed past his hair.
He disappeared when she touched him,
but she knew her friend was still there.

Timothy L. Miller

I Love Today

I love to hear the songbirds sing,
　About their nest of twigs and string.
I love to see the blooms of spring,
　So many colors and smells they bring.
I love to feel a gentle breeze,
　A western Zephyr, if you please.
I love to watch a butterfly, fly.
　It seems to float as it flutters by.
I love to see the setting sun,
　A quiet notice, the day is done
I love to see the moon come up,
　An catch moonbeams in my cup.
　Today I heard birds sing.
　Today I saw blooms of spring.
　Today I felt a western breeze.
　Today I saw a flutter-by.
　Today I saw the setting sun
　Today I saw the moon come up.
　Today I totally filled my cup
　I love today.

V. F. Gontero

Untitled

I can imagine moonlight over the depthless ocean,
shimmering upon the waves with serene emotion.
I can see you walking upon soft summer sand,
beneath a velvet sky in a far away land.

I'd die a thousand times to be with you tonight,
to be in you arms under the stars so bright,
to be by your side as we endlessly roam
along the beach and snow white foam.

I can feel you lips brush against my face,
and your arms around me in an eternal embrace.
Your heartbeat echoes my trembling kiss
as I lose myself within passion's bliss.

I believe in love, in all our dreams.
I believe in Destiny, in starry schemes.
If we hold true and love each other,
nothing can keep us from being together.

Albert Nguyen

Love On A Card

You came to me on a card today
Scented with heart of you so gay.
I instantly took it, and stepped inside
Your home so fresh where you abide.
And there we had a frolicsome time
Telling events so very sublime.
Just a breath of refreshment, a taste of joys
Being with you and all the boys.
Oh, it was good that you came to me
On a card so filled with joyous glee!

Mada S. Scott

"When Dreams Bless"

When dreams bless the entity
  or the present existence at last,
   all our hopelessness and despair
   will soon be a thing of the past
And should the blushing of one's flesh
  set flames to a party pastence,
   the tranquility of this blessing
   will be its own strongest defence
For hearts that have been slaughtered
  on loves battlefield before,
   tread longer no merciless memories
   or pains anguish ever more
Because how many tears in the oceans
  or the storms they eventually arise,
   can deviate our peace on earth
   and then devour our heavenly skies
So standfast my dearest darling
  and take this factual heed to breast,
   always trust in love, hope and faith
   and the Lord's Prayer will do the rest!

    Walter Lussow

The Pansy

I planted a seed in the warm brown earth,
And watched every day for three weeks, till its birth.
Two tiny green leaves popped up through the ground,
I watched, and I watered, and fussed, till I found
that the speed of its growth, was amazing to see.
How quickly it flourished, and all 'cause of me!
One day I ran out, my plant to behold...
And there was a flower, its face trimmed with gold!
The inside was purple and black as the night
with tiny gold stamens all furry and bright,
Its velvety texture to touch, oh so soft,
And its scent through the air, it gently did waft.
This sweet little flower, this pansy so small...
Its beauty, true beauty, I shall always recall.

    Liz Humphreys

Spirit

Our life is like a candle,
For when we're very young,
We're full of strength and passion,
Like a flame we stand up strong.

We challenge life with many goals
And strive to reach great heights,
But heartaches caused by love and grief,
Can shade and dim our light.

Emotions take their toll on us
Like a candle in a draught.
For as we age with passing years
Our lives are quickly halved.

We know life's not all happiness
As hardships play their part,
Appearing as grey shadows
Causing nightmares in our dark.

Just as the candlelight will fade,
We'll see our dreams diminish.
And like the vision of a ghost,
Our spirit too, will vanish.

    Valerie Taber

Special Angel

God opened up the heavens
And said come home my son
Your life here on earth
Is over and is done.
Your parents they will miss you
Your sister, brother-in-law and nephew too
Some day you'll be together
Now there's something "I need you to do"
Right now I need a "Special Angel"
to brighten heavens place
you can do it best of all
with your sweet and smiling face
I lent you to your family
for 25 years and more
Some day you'll be there
Waiting to welcome them
In at "Heaven's Door."

    Ellen M. Woods

For You

Night comes,
  with sounds of silence.

Night comes, with dark beauty,
   quiet magic, mysticism, with mystery.

Night comes,
  with silent lights, bright stars and dreams.
   Dreams of you.

Night comes,
  with thoughts of you, sounds of you,
   feelings of you. The presence of you.

Night comes,
  bringing your spirit, your presence,
   your soul. Love.

Night is you, magic and mystical,
  silent and brooding,
  beautiful and embracing.

Night is you,
  bright and shining.

You are the moonlight and it's magic.

You are the stars and
  their shine in a midnight sky. I love you.

    Samuel C. Miles

Untitled

I have given all that is humanly possible
There is the vastness of empty eternity inside of me
First there was anger, followed by tears, now pain
Now a nonexistence of warmth has escaped from my body
A dry death begins to creep from within
There is always more pain when death has ignited from an
inward spark
If only my soul could rain and drown the spark
But in the end even my soul has been given to unknown forms
If only there was one moment to grasp, one emotion to remember,
  but absolutely nothing comes to me
Momentarily all good and evil will combine and a slow breeze will
  add air to the fire
As all storms begin and end so does another mere existence

    Jennye S. Miller

Behold As I Look Into Your Eyes

Behold, as I look into your eyes
nothing can be comparable, to the sparkle that I see.
Your beauty delights my senses
to the point that my body beckons you.
For now as I look upon your picture
I must be content within your smile
the smile that resembles its beauty like the sun.
Unmistakably it's you whom have unsettled this
moment that lay dormant within me.
I have only but one wish to forsee,
I have only one dream to see clear,
to enter unboundedly to your domain and extend
myself to you fully and completely.
Comprehend my words and make yourself compatible to me.
You and I are unique, universal, and opulent with
feelings that must somehow find their way.
Read their words and open your heart
for they are mine until the end of time.

Anthony Hope

Lord, You Become My Hope

Lord, will You walk with me and go where I go?
Lord, will You touch me, so Your presence I may know?
Lord, will You teach me and show me the right way?
Lord, will You answer, when I remember to pray?
Lord, will You help me, when I can't help myself?
Lord, will You give me food, when there's no money to stock the shelf?
Lord, will You give me clothes, when there's no money to buy?
Lord, will You dry my tears, when all I can do is cry?
Lord, will You show me, what is Your perfect will?
Lord, will You give me peace about it, so my heart can be still?
Lord, You have done all this and ever so much more;
Lord, You died for me, and Your love was at the core.
Lord, You gave me something that is a help to cope,
Lord, when things look darkest, then You become my hope.

Penelope Buzzutto

Moments Forever

When by death the strife between thy flesh and spirit ceased,
The gate of the dead to pass to the glories beyond;
Pain beyond compare, drop! Drop! Falls upon the heart
Until in my despair, there comes comfort by providence.
　But if only the assembly of the overcoming Saints to join
　　Immortal to stand in his likeness forever;
　　If only the throng of the triumphant church to join
　　Never never more to die again,
　　Better therefore it is to die than to live.
Blessed thou art, the golden way to have found,
The connect gracious of the great divide;
Thy end was therefore better than thy beginning
For to thee the feet of the master was granted thy race to end.
　Oh mother! Thy gain falls to my loss indeed
　If a thousand choices I be granted this Mother's Day,
　Thy loving child I still shall chose to be;
　To enshrine the fragrance of thy memory in sundry hearts.
Is never more to die! Only loving and beloved forever!

Obiora Ohia Mbrey

Why Me?

Lifelong coddled by love, care and guidance
Protected by angels of merciful power
To keep my walk straight
My sight high, in heaven.
My pride down, in ashes
In brokenness joyful,
In solitude, thankful,
And I ask: "Why me, My Lord,
　Why me?

Elena R. Jimenez

Journey

For some the door opens early
for some a journey ends with rain

From a lonely cave voices ring
call out names; in a faraway den
lions roar in conversation
for some, silence pretends death

A pious miser scatters the pack
saves minor blessings
a tired benefactor grumbles in sleep
on dusty caravans the journey smells of sand

For some, the road prolongs mourning
for some a journey ends with rain

Kunal Basu

The Homebody

"Why?" You may ask, "Are you walking around,
With your head in the clouds while your lips make the sound,
Of a warble of wrens on a seed covered mound
While your feet stand a foot off the floor?"

I could tell you, my friend, of a girl that I know,
Or a tale of just how I once got her to show
That no matter how bright shone my loving hearts glow,
It always was dim next to hers.

But, no, I'll just say that I love this dear girl,
That I'll work my life through just to give her the pearl
That I'm told can't be bought with the gold of this world,
And, that, I am willing to do.

Now don't think that any can touch on my love
For I swear by the heavens and God up above
That no power or beauty nor soft wing of dove
Could ever come 'tween me and her.

So humor me now and don't think it too strange
With a smile on my face in the heat of the day
For it's homeward I'm bound and I'll never seek change.
For me, where there's fam'ly there's life.

Jim Mackey

On The Beach

Ah, joyful hours of lassitude
And idle hands display,
With naught to do but lie and brood
Long summer hours away.

As languid fingers sift the sand
And thoughts are far transported,
Then peace filtrates one's very soul and
Problems are neatly sorted.

In and out my mental trend
I catch a lapping of the waves,
As they wash around the bend
And fill the rocky caves.

The gulls that scream in wild defiance
As they swoop low to the sea,
Proudly sharing an alliance
From which they never can be free.

And, oh, it is such a blessing
As I lie in this peaceful repose
To feel the warm breezes caressing
As gently the summer wind blows.

Phyllis D. Murphy

Fantasy On "Summer Starlight"

Maestro, liken me to your instrument,
Provoke softly from my strings the melody of secret longings.
Whisper to me not with words, but with fingers,
With dexterous hands.
With impassioned grace touch my keys and play the Sweet-Sigh
Symphony which only we may hear,
(Other's ears would find discord).
Let your wrists move fluidly as I tremble beneath your virtuous
    Fingertips.
Caress each phrase, let it swell and recede, (Oh Blessed rubato!)
Let our bodies resound in unison, both of your hands moving
Solidly upon me, as we approach the final note of our Masterpiece.
But as starlit sky brightens, my keys are still, and I am covered again,
With my shroud of silence;
And she who dances to your music in the sunshine will never know
That upon my strings remain the midnight sighs,
And upon the fingers of (my) her maestro is a quiet memory of a
Secret song that can never be played again.

Kristin Leigh Chabot

Sisters

Here I sit, upon the floor, wishing I were someplace more. I feel in
love with my sister in Moncton, I really think that that is something.

I felt my sister with tears of sorrow. I'd be there tomorrow. Out
the car window the cities went by, but I only sat, stared and cried.

On the radio "Susan" sang, "Suffer in Silence" was the name. I sit
here thinking, writing and crying, but inside I feel like dying.

I wish my sister were here with me, we're such a terrific family. I feel in
love with my sister in Moncton, I really think that that is something.

I thought I knew you all I could, but there's more to life than
childhood. We both grew up without each other, I just thank
God we have our mother.

I learned a lot while I was there, now I know you really care. My
sister is the tops for me, she's the tallest branch on my family tree

I cannot write another letter, until I make myself better.
Now you know how I feel for you, I hope you feel the same way too.

This poems poured through without much thought, from heart,
to paper to mailbox. I hope you read this from the start, and
know it comes from deep in my heart.

I feel in love with my sister in Moncton, I really think that that is
something. From within my heart I love you so, but now I really
have to go. Our letter writing now begins, without the sadness
from within. I'll watch for letters, from my sister far away.

Lisa Burden

Sanctuary

Entering your home, filled with people looking for forgiveness,
I discover I am not alone.

I know I will see you again as I am seeing you now;
Yet, your power is overwhelming, I have no right to stare - I bow.

My parents have taught me the meaning of caring, sharing and love;
Having a mind of my own, I rely on judgment felt from above.

My insides start turning and my heartbeat races;
Lowering my head to shadow my tears, ashamed of my lack of graces.

Realizing I've taken the wrong path, I retreat;
My destination, your home, so sweet.

I cry because I know what you want of me, and I know what I'm capable of;
I see what I'm making of myself and am aware I have to forgive,
    plus offer more love.

One day you will call on me and I will be tremblin';
Please look deep inside me when judging for Heaven.

Having faith my wishes for goodness shall not falter,
I raise my eyes to your celestial altar.

Renee A. Collins

Baseball Is A Game Of Life

Baseball is a sport, but much more than a game,
Like living life day by day, the feeling is the same.
Sometimes you get a hit, or score the winning run,
At other times you strike out, as if you are coming undone.
Often you're at bat, you swing, and think the ball is out of sight,
Then, in the distant left field you see the Green Monster
    standing high.
Much like when your life is happy, and you're living burden free,
Then all of sudden one thing goes wrong and complications are
    all you see.
If only you were playing at Wrigley it would be over the ivy fence.
But unfortunately you're playing on a bigger field,
Where there are no batting hints.
Much like when you childhood education changes into a career,
There are no maps or guidelines to tell you what's far and
    what's near.
Baseball is no longer a sport or a game, but more of a business
    or a job.
Whatever happened to Joe Dimaggio or the great Ty Cobb?
Much like baseball, life's meaning is sometimes lost.
And at times, like "Shoeless" Joe, we have to pay the cost.
Be the best at what you do, by practicing as they say.
Remember that everyone strikes out,
But tomorrow is a new day.

Traci Clark

The Rose In My Garden

There's a rose that grows in my garden,
It's a blossom of rarest of hue;
And the rose that grows in my garden
I planted, my darling, for you.

And I bring you the blossom at evening
To tell you, my dear, of my love;
But the glory that glowed on the vine, dear,
Seems to fade like the sunlight above.

In your presence the rose has no beauty,
Its scent fades away like the dew,
For as rare as the beauty it owns, love,
I can't begin to compare it with you.

Judith B. Ethridge

War Of Races

Wild horses run across the white sands,
Of the breathless ocean.
One by one, fading to sand,
As the air becomes a blinding mist.

To which way freedom runs,
We shall never know,
Until all of the people can join together
To follow the trace of wild horses.

This world is too prejudice,
For anyone to care about each other,
And in each separate world, everyone sleeps.

The custom today goes unnoticed by some,
But it does not pass by me,
I am aware of the war of the races,
Running through some peoples minds.

Why were we portrayed as unequal,
Each colour, has something to give to another,
If only the skin could be looked passed,
And the inside could shadow the outer layer,
And racists would go blind.

Kim Davies

A Star So Bright

Do you have a star shining in the heavens tonight?
Let me tell you of one of my stars that shines ever so bright.
It was on an early Thanksgiving eve,
When a loving, gray-haired man, crashed into an ugly tree,
from caring for a neighbor who had a need.
On that cold and early Thanksgiving Eve.
I will always wonder why he was on the wrong street,
that caused his confusion and hit that ugly, naked tree.
This loving, gray-haired man, was my father you see.
And his death that night, put one of those stars that
shines ever so bright, in my heavens each night.
I feel no sorrow...for every night I can see
my father's love shining back at me!

Gloria McBrayer

Papa Dillon

As I lay in bed last night unable to sleep
All at once I thought of my father-in-law and I began to weep

I thought of what a kind and gentle man he was to me
You had to know and love him for these things to see

At the age of thirty two I still didn't know how to drive
Who but this wonderful person was there by my side

He never complained about the mistakes I made
Until I could do them right there he stayed

He was so proud when I showed him that I had passed
Then he knew he had finally finished his task

No greater grandfather could my children ever find
He helped us to teach them to be honest, loving and kind

The day he died I thought my heart would break
But I had to hold myself together for the children's sake

I felt I had lost one of the greatest friends of my life
No longer would I have this wonderful man to help me with life's strifes

I know all our family has been blessed by knowing this fine man
I am sure he has a beautiful home in God's heavenly land

I'll always remember him as long as I live
Because he had so much love for everyone to give

Mildred Dillon

The Sun God

Everyone hail to the sun God, the eliminator of pain.
Who frees us from misery, of a white frozen rain.
Bathing us with the warmth that nourishes our soul,
the golden sun is the peak of our eternal hunger,
as we are showered by its residue.

The skeleton trees are recovering from defeat,
they too will soon be flowing with nurturing kindness.
Mother earth is once again fertile and full,
soon it will receive our tobacco of gratitude.

It is a pleasure to once again see the rebirth of a land,
that I have almost forgotten.
Sitting on the grass and feeling its earth surroundings,
reveals the scars of war.

Children, run to where you desire.
Only a pointless chase will reward you with your goals.
Awake, my fellow people and repurify your faces!
For your shelter is no longer needed.
For it is thanks to our sun God who has liberated us,
from a frozen seed of pain.

Daniel Natanblut

Mobility

Our global sphere is laced
With countless roadways, spaced
To bear the traffic of a mobile world.
From the country lanes to super highway chains
Are travel styles and scopes and modes unfurled.

And perhaps unseen but still part of the scene
Are air paths in the sky above the ground.
And on the ocean blue ships and boats sail too,
And railway tracks supporting freight is found.

Intricate indeed the travel routes, agreed.
Though perfect if all moves in faultless form.
But harmful if by chance
An error - path nuance -
Pivots accidents and injuries aswarm.

So too our lives are made,
Chance's mashed cascade
Can smooth our paths or pull our lives apart.
How much depends on luck,
Good judgment, skill or pluck,
Our lives' result, serene or counterpart?

Marguerite Moser

An Idea

A decision must be made; an idea must be thought.
A goal must be reached; a lesson must be taught.
A wish must be made; a dream must be caught.
A want must be desired; a battle must be fought.

No one should give up; no heart should be tamed.
No names should be called; nobody should be blamed.
No hate should be felt; no love should be shamed.
No confusion should be known; no names should be named.

What is so wonderful about kids getting high?
What is so wonderful about saying goodbye?
What is so wonderful about learning to die?
What is so wonderful about wondering why?

Everyone needs to stop and take a look around.
Everyone needs to keep their feet firmly on the ground.
Everyone needs to strive for what can't be found.
Everyone needs to think about where they are bound.

We all need to stick together and go hand-in-hand.
We all need to love one another and take a stand.
We all need to love our neighbors so that hate can be banned.
We all need to once again make America the promised land.

Pam Walls

Any More

Lord I'm down here where people come and
go everyday. Just thinking of themselves, oh, it
seem like, there is no love in their hearts, any
more, any more. Lord, it seem like, there
is no love, in their hearts any more,
any more. Lord it seem like, there is no love,
in their hearts anymore, anymore.
I'm down here and I can't hear and
I can't see your beauty any more, any more.
I'm down here and I don't feel at home
any more, any more.
I'm down here and I can't get no peace,
no rest, no joy, no joy, any more, any more.

Lord I'm down here where people come and go everyday.
Just thinking of themselves, oh, it seem like, there is no love
in their hearts, any more, any more. Lord, it seem like,
there is no love, in their hearts any more,
any more Lord, it seem like there is no
love in their hearts, any more, any more.

Mary Marva Blue

Change

The familiar faces of parents and places,
I always love to recall,
The smiles and love,
the old rocking horse,
I rode when I was small.

I thought it was to cool to move away,
spread my wings and live in the city,
I found it cold,
a transient place.
Few friends, no love, no pity.

Even kids in the street, with pockets all full,
From selling illegal brown sugar
No respect for themselves,
Let alone their folks
In a few years, they'll just be a number.

I wonder if they know, in villages small,
How lucky they really are,
Having age-old friends
Where time stands still,
The only change, the clock on the wall.

Margaret C. Acton-Wood

I Am Like A Wave

I am a surfer, I am like a wave
It is as if I never close out, always barreling perfectly
I barrel like the perfect wave every surfer dreams of
I am a surfer, I am like a wave
It is as if the face of my wave is a mirror
You look into the face of the wave and see nothing but yourself as
You would a mirror
Out of all bits darkness you look ahead and see a light like your
Looking out of a deep dark cave
I am a surfer, I am like a wave
As you fall back in the tube, as if you and the board froze in time
But the wave kept breaking you here the roar of the white water all
Around you as if it were thunder
Fear grips you, so you take a half a step forward and speed up like
A cheetah chasing its prey I am a surfer, I am like a wave
The light gets bigger as if it were a train coming straight toward
You finally you come out, you're as happy as when you caught your
First wave your stomach feels like there is a million butterflies in
It I am a surfer, I am like a wave
You swerve down into the through as a cheetah's prey would make a
Sharp turn now closer to the shoulder you turn up the face of wave,
Then off the lip and catch some air as a motor-cross racer would
Stunned from all that happened in that wave, looking like a statue
You paddle out to the line up I am a surfer

Collin Briley

Mother Oh! Mother

You were there when I had my first cold,
You taught me not to be shy, but to be bold.
You taught me to be strong and never to cry,
You told me to always keep my head up high.
Mother oh! Mother, you are my heavenly gift from above,
Because you are to me as rear as a dove.
Very unique not often seen,
You are all of these things to me.
When I become a mother my child will be blessed
Because just like you love me, I won't love her any less.
You were there for me when I was born as you child,
And your love will be with me all the while.

Carlene Riley

Willow

Sometimes there are frosty stains
on broken glass,
And lilac scented roses can tremble
and reflect their arrogance amongst the
cruel cracks within the window.

The infernal night cannot hide
the softness of lazy petals from vain eyes;

I wish I could paint waltzes
with their delicate footwork,
and slim, frilly Victorian skirts circling
upon polished floors. Tempered
tiptoes; two fingers politely
clicking to the beat upon a pale, idle hand.

Or I could sketch the wind, or
cut out shapes of respect from fragile cardboard...
The insolence of intangible entities,
and their delight in slipping through our fingers-
or through broken glass:

Chipped icicles of ice can't know whose integrity to pierce,
nor how to battle the sunlight.

Dina Bogecho

Kite

Rise highward Kite
Ascend in gustful certainty to freedom which is sky
Climb the wind stretch out to sun's light
(What string and hand and arm can reach
At tip-toes on the hill)

Last night I dreamt a huger Kite
That raised me breathless from the earth
And matched my wish with her delight
To marvel soaring skywide

But you are not that kind of Kite
You'd rather leave me emptied here
To sail more distant from my sight
And simply vanish like the dream
You strain against my hold

Yesterday I though to give you flight
Closed-eyed I counted down from ten to one
And held my breath for longer than it takes to lose a Kite
Yet clutched you tight, afraid

Brent Haas

White Trash Lament

She left Sioux city back in 93,
gave me a book about Nom Chomsky.
I didn't read it.
I didn't care.
I knew I'd follow her anywhere.

I lost my job back in 95.
She left me the next day by 9.
So much for collectivity.
My sister knew she'd be the death of me.

The library's open and waiting for me.
You can learn what you want and it's always free.

I go to the library almost every night,
read up on Gramsci and some other guy
The library lady don't know what to think about that.
She gave me a book about a Siamese cat.

The library's open and waiting for me.
You can learn what you want and it's always free.

Bill Blood

Let Me Know

Why must we fight like cats and dogs so much,
when there's love in every touch.
Every time the road starts to bend,
we know we can turn to our friends.
They say you're such a bad friend,
but I don't want this relationship to end.
Everyone sees how much we fight,
let's just tell them to fly a kite.
When you proposed that we get married,
all our problems we tried to bury.
Each day I love you more,
but it seems you love me less.
So please let me know,
if you really love me so.

Nicole Smith

A Baby's Blanket

Now I lay me down to sleep.
With this blanket, warm I'll keep.
Cover me over up to my chin.
Just check my blanket now and then.
Now I'm at my very best, Mommy take this time to rest.
While the sugarplums dance in my head,
My blanket will comfort me in my bed.
Put your feet up in a chair,
For in your mind I know I'm there.
But, when I awake and open my eyes,
You better come when I cry.

Evelyn Sue Oswalt

Sunny

Once upon a Christmas time
a pet store caught my eye,
And drew me to its storefront
window as I was passing by.
'Midst yips and yaps and puppies'
paws against the windowpane,
A tiny ball of coal black fur
kept coming back again.
She wriggled and waggled her little
tail and struggled, her freedom to gain,
I paid the man and took her home,
and Sunny is her name.
Nurturing her through puppyhood,
her antics warmed my heart.
Watching her grow, just happy
to know that I had been a part.
She's all grown now, such a
beautiful dog, but to me she will remain
That puppy in the pet store window,
and Sunny is her name.

Wanda G. Weaver

Gone

The easiest part of loving you is falling,
falling like a rock dropped from a cliff,
wanting is hard waiting for hours for that which never comes,
then you forget that I exist,
I fade to extinction until your love is gone.
Yet mine still burns strong,
yet I know it is wrong, that I love you so long,
thinking for hours of the love we once had.
Wishing for months that it was not gone.
But like your love,
not but a scar of the love that is gone.
Then quickly like yours it is all gone
not even the scar is still among us.

Tawnya Casey

For Anne

Sometimes, it's like I'm standing frozen.
In a field.
Suspended by the silence and the vastness.
There's no difference, inside nor out.

Your coming
is like a wild rose,
whispering in my ear, giving substance and dimension
to the frightening stillness.

Rollicking the stillness
serene is so full of whispers, is it a she shell?
simply such a spirit
sounds I can't here
around (warmth) and around (warmth) and around
standing with soft flannel
standing in sunlight
this be me, every little thing.

Gillian Ferrabee

Predestined

From the beginning of time
God has had me on his mind
Before there was Adam and Eve
God had already planted my seed
Before there was Cain and Abel
God had a place for me at this table
Before Moses raised his staff
God had already laid my path
Before Joseph took Mary to be his wife
God had laid out a diary, a book of my life
Before there was even a disciple
God had me on every page of the Bible
Before Jesus cried when he heard Lazarus was dead
God had already anointed my head
Before the woman had an issue of blood
God had already given me his Love
Before Jesus died on the cross at Calvary
God had already sacrificed his son for me
All these people had to come and had to go
Because this was God's plan to save my soul

Doris A. Reed

Ahwahnee

The blue, cool lake
protective trees
singing chants in the gentle breeze

Children's voices
laughing, calling
"Watch me!"

The small local cafe
smells of flavored coffee
folk singers from our past singing
voice of my beloved friend
speaking of cosmic things
or
mundane things becoming cosmic

Children growing
goats kidding
vegetables sprouting
up to touch the sun

This is the universe.

This is God touching our world.

Patricia Bruketta

Untitled

Sometimes there are those days
When all seems so bright
Sun shining upon us and your eyes so blue
Then sometimes there are those days
When nothing goes quite right
Do you understand why you do what you do
The other woman is the forbidden juice
Hiding in your green bottle
If it is nothing I have done
You can know I am here for you
So you may share your fears and thoughts
In doing so this will give us a better understanding
Give us strength to stand by one another
I would rather leave
Than watch you destroy yourself
To such a forbidden disease
Which has such a powerful destruction to oneself
So please allow me to be your only woman
Share with me so I may share with you
And we may grow together

Carol McKinnon

Reflections

How can I express what you mean to me?
You've let me become what I've wanted to be!
The love that I've known for so many years,
Has helped me through sorrow and dried many tears.
You give to me willingly, asking nothing in return,
Took time to teach me when I had so much to learn.
You've offered opinions but always listened to mine,
Treated me like a queen when I scored my first nine!
You taught me to love and showed me to care,
In good times and bad you've always been there.
Would I feel such confidence, when time came to leave home?
Of course, you taught me to stand on my own.
The examples I live by and the excellence I pursue,
Come deep from within me; reflections of you.
With many thanks and my love forever.

Larissa Lowing

Life

The cry of a child.
The voice of a scream.
These things hurt me,
I wander what they mean.

Life is so wrong.
Why should we go on?
Take the time to look at life today,
Then you will see why I say death is the best way.

I need someone to hold me,
to let me know he cares,
to whisper in my ear he will always be there.

If I had these things I believe I could make it,
But the way I feel right now, I just can't take it!

Kandi Oxner

The Night

The night it engulfs me, suffocates me.
With the night the pain starts, the loneliness.
Blackness, nothingness all around.
The ticking of the clock is deafening.
Pounding out each second of the night.
The streets below are empty the darkness has taken them to.
Then out in the distance I see the golden hues of morning.
The darkness is afraid it runs and hides, taking my pain with it.

Susan Best

Welcome Baby Larkin Rose

Baby cries; Dixie is barking.
Dixie alert to a new girl said, "Woof."
Amelia amazed at the beauty of Larkin Rose,
Cries out with joy, "Welcome Larkin Rose."
Caitlin no longer our little girl, happily
Turns her title to Larkin Rose.
Shouts "We love you Larkin Rose."
Daddy, face all a glow, smiles and kisses
TeriLee and Baby Larkin Rose,
Mother Teri, after many long days,
Gives birth on Friday, 12 August 1994,
To eight pound, thirteen ounces,
Gorgeous Baby Larkin Rose.
Welcome Baby Larkin Rose.

James P. Crowley

He

Coming at me, like a solidified dream
Puddles of liquid cerulean
    hold my stare, through the cliche haze
Gnawing at my soul
    like a maddening dog
and sleep will not comfort me.
And flying dreams with butterfly wings
    try to penetrate my mind
        but are crushed to fairy dust
with fists of exaltation.
    Crush my bones
your touch would send shivers
    down my broken spine
    Deny me oxygen
the sight of you would leave
    my choking body breathless
You look so good from the corner
    of my eye
        ugly head-on
Lust became a cannibal.

Alex Prijic-Smith

"Little Lambs"

Behold the man, the king, the lamb!
He was a friend to all, even down
to the littlest lamb, He is the shepherd
we are his lambs.
He's there when you need him, he won't
let you down. He'll be with you through
it all, the good times and the bad,
He cares about you when you're sad
He's joyful when you're glad.
He hears your cries in the midnight
hour - our shepherd our dearest friend.
He loves us as no other, he's closer than
a brother. Thank you Jesus, for being there
for your little lambs.
Amen

Melrose L. Hurst

Simply Written, Simply Told

Tales of the young, and tales of the old.
Beginnings are fast, endings are slow
Much in between as onward you go
Stay firm, stay fit, stay positive in mind
Take sorrow, worry, fatigue, and leave it behind
A new morrow arises
bringing forth many surprises
Breath in the sunshine, breath out the sunset
Make ready for the world of internet.

Genevieve A. Brett

It Is April And Life Is Springing Forth

It is April and the earth has warmed beneath the now friendly sun and air,
The earth is quaking and splitting as the life beneath awakes.

I smell the lilacs now in bloom and remember childhood days when
Mother's lilac filled the house with their sweet scent,
Who can smell the lilacs and not release a sigh of joy?

The trilliums now spread their threesome leaves and above or
below their dainty blooms nod in the breeze.

Our dogwood looks like a field of snow when viewed from my bedroom
window in the morning, it is an old tree but proud of the years it
has held my eyes and it envies not the young pinks out front.

The weeping cherry won't weep this year. Winter's late grasp
has seen to that but new leaves are emerging and next year will
provide another chance. As I pass it by I tell it, "Don't be sad, I
love you even in your frock of green."

Oh, April, I am so in love with you. Carry me in to the ages left
to me and show me that you care. Each winter as the cold and
dark descends let me remember you and all the loveliness you
bring and as I look out on the snow and cold a smile shall break
upon my lips as I remember you.

Robert P. O'Brien

The Admiration

Unconquered spirit of a dove
Freedom of an eagle's flight
Vulture's focus of its prey
Cat's eagerness of exploration

Awesome strength of a sturdy oak tree
Slow but steady growth of a flower blooming
Crystal clarity of a sparkling blue ocean
Unrestrained power of a mighty river

Energy of a fiery light
Mysterious nature of a complexity
Deepness of a bottomless pit
Grace of a peaceful night

Happiness of a winning fighter
Intelligence of a humble academic
Hunger of a competitive athlete
Vision of an imaginative child

The qualities that make you who you are
The qualities that impress and inspire

Raymond Anthony Pary

Who Is This Come Up From The Fires

Who is this come up from the Fires
And black with the heat of Love?
O Thou Nubian! Thou Ethiope!
With Lips of ebony
And Breasts like the wind-carved mountains!
O Locks of fluted jet!
Thighs of blocks of obsidian
And fire-blackened steel!
O Legs of bronze
On Feet of beaten gold!
Thy Feet like the sun in incredible noon!
Black Arms, black Limbs inlaid with gold
And set with diamonds,
With precious gems,
With emeralds and with uncut stones!
With agate and black pearls!
Thine Eyes are a gathering of suns!
Thy Tongue richer than the makings of the bees!
Thou movest like a barge hurled against the sea!
And all my bowels are moved!

Jean Trinité

My Precious Black Child

My precious black child I wish that you could see,
You being my child, means a lot to me,
(My Precious Black Child) and as your parent in every way,
It's my duty to protect you everyday, (My precious black child.)

My precious black child sometimes things can get a bit perplexing,
But I beg you, my child (To never give up!)
Stay optimistic, I know it's easy for me to say,
Trust me my Black child,
I've been down that pathway, (My Precious Black Child.)

My Precious Black Child, My heart cries out, like rainy day,
Because I as a parent know,
That my black child is in a lot of agony and pain,
And me being a female, makes it harder for you to confide.
My Precious Black Child. (It's O.K.)
Give your burdens to me, so that I can help work them out,
My precious black child

My precious black child, my precious black child,
Hold your head up; put on put best smile,
Let the world know that you are happy to be,
My Precious Black Child.

Janis Gattu

Oh Black Man, Where Are You?

I've looked everywhere, yet can't seem to find
That strong black man who will be all mine
This tiresome journey is becoming an endless game
Open up to me black man, reveal thyself, tell me thy name
I can't give up on thee, my nubian king
Because I need thee by my side
To catch me when I fall and to hear my cries
Oh yes! I've been hurt by thee a thousand times before
Yet still, I seek thee to fill me and I come back for more
Why can't thee understand; where ever thou are black man
I need for thee to share with me thy knowledge, not just to
Hold my hand
Stop the violence, the lies, and all of the deceit
Because thy strong black queen is getting weak
This is a cry out for help, love, and affection
Can't thou understand?
Where are you black man?
Oh black man, where are you?

Donna L. Dukes

The Looking Glass

Gazing into the looking glass, so very thoroughly...
Gazing back as far as the mind will see
Quite often deleting thoughts, not willing to see...
Questioning past happenings, could it really be
Snowflakes fall and soon melt away.. unlike life's problems day to day.

From little girl to grownup wife...like a box of surprises, isn't that life.
Teach our children A, B, and C...but more important how to see. Cry
and laugh and learn to love...know the gentleness of a dove.

Obtain a little confidence along with some pride...
The 10 Commandments to abide. Do what you can, what will it cost...
Allow them to learn the nailing upon the cross

For emotions are real, he well aware
Seek not to hide them, they'll always be there

Like a wound unattended it festers and grows...
Accept this as knowledge, thus you will know

The key to success and complete harmony... allow eyes to open, most
important to see, understand your own person, hesitate, do not run...
understand others in this way then you will have won. For life's
path is long and falls we will take, the happiness is real, it's all
what you make!

Vickie Di Vergilio

America

America was discovered in 1492.
I just can't wait until 2002.
America, I call it my home.
It has lots of space to roam.

America gives you the right to vote and freedom of speech.
The moon and stars are always in your reach.
The population is on a deadly rise.
Our problem is the polluted skies.

In America we have prosperity, poverty, and slums.
Also cherries, apples, peaches, and plums.
The huge farms produce lots of grain.
While the cattle and sheep graze on the plain.

The colors red, white, and blue form our flag.
In America, industry shows no lag.
The historic places and beautiful cities to see.
These are all a benefit to me.

Go north, go south, or go in between, you are still in America the Great.
Where freedom is sought by every state.
Fifty states we chose to raise.
America you deserve lots of praise!

Amanda McDannell

Loneliness

Here I sit frightened and very much alone,
Emotionally drained, and cold.
I hear no voices on the phone,
I contemplate the horrors of growing old.

I am alone.

What do I do to dispel this feeling,
Of grief within a void; of gloom.
I count the lines upon the ceiling,
I know that now my life will never bloom.

I am alone.

I constantly ponder that if I took my life,
If I would help the world become a more beautiful place.
I need to put an end to this unbearable strife,
And save humanity from the horrors of my mangled heart and face.

Andrea Boothby

A Valentine Greeting

When we pause a moment through the day
To ask God's love to guide our way
To thank our Father in heaven above,
for making this world in His wisdom and love,
For his greatness in making all things here below,
The sunshine, the moonlight and the colored rainbow,
For making the mountains and oceans so great,
For making the creatures-each one to his mate
For placing the soft puffy clouds in the air-
The blue starlit sky and the birds which fly there,
Each tiny one knowing that it has a worth-
A gift of nature to us here on earth-
God wants us to know that he loves each one-
For this reason He sent His own son.
He shows his majestic being in the greatness of trees,
He shows his beauty and his love in the ants and bumble bees,
The seasons too He changes and life and death arranges-
No one else has the power over these,
He made the snowflakes, and the raindrops and sweet morning dew,
But most of all I thank Him, for making both of you.

Norma C. Brander

Pure Darkness

The darkness takes over the light
For as many days there is, there is also that many nights,
As the blackness swallows the sun it also devours your vision
Because you're frightened you cannot see darkness unlock the prison
Some see it as a handicap but it's an advantage to be blind
Unhindered by sight you can look into one's soul, heart, and mind,
Looks no longer matter such as weight, height, or the colour of one hair
Rather love comes from the ability on how much each person can care,
As years pass people age, but in the darkness no one grows older.
For youth is a state of mind and beauty is in the eye of the beholder,
Listening to what is said rather then staring at one's face
No more hate of fear for in the darkness everyone is the same race,
Looking back through history at monsters of the past
If you take away their deformities would they still be outcasts?
The elephant man would not be in a circus, rather thrive to be a teacher
The hunchback could have been a saint, he could have been a preacher,
For beauty would be seen on the inside not the scars of the out
Beauty contests don't exist for inner beauty is what it's about,
But they were seen as ugly, men looked with hate women with fright
The reason stopping them from being a hero, is the impurity of the light.

Mark Mason

Puppets And Pawns

Bitter stars among already lit dreams
of mother's, of father's timeless scenes
who preach, who pray, who want to live
the lives of those aren't willing to give.

Every door is locked in this endless maze
every door but the one wished to be closed
reading a script already written
standing on a pedestal perfectly posed.

We follow the book of unwritten rules
the sons and daughters of powerful fools
who need, who try, who want to live
the lives of the soul's God unselfishly gives.

We wish to climb the castle walls
we hope to cut the umbilical strings
from the binds that tie us to who we are
master's puppets and pawns of kings and queens.

Tracy Burns

Memories

Whose head is this that lies upon my pillow,
　With shrouded lids that cover eyes of blue,
　With softened lines etched from life's hardships,
　With faint traces of a smile that lifts my heart?
'Tis you, my belovéd, 'tis you.

Whose body is this that lies upon my bed,
　With limbs entwined around me,
　With strong heart beating against mine,
　With manlihood nestled in its womb?
'Tis you, my love, 'tis you.

Whose lips are these that brush my brow,
　That chase my sorrows away,
　That whisper tender words of comfort,
　That makes my heart beat with happiness?
'Tis you, my dearest, 'tis only you.

And when your head no longer graces my pillow,
　When the spark of life no longer shines in your eyes,
　When your cold lips no longer speak my name,
　Who will fill my thoughts as old age creeps upon me?
'Tis you, my darling, 'tis always you.

Debbie Thompson

Speckle Eyes

I saw you sitting there, just a small twinkle
glistened from your tiny eyes.
Such a story behind all the lines on your face.
Such a world behind the so-neatly styled puff of gray hair.
Oh... you seem so tiny, so frail, to withhold it all
Something about you marveled me, something so
appealing that I caught the little glisten
from your tiny eyes.
Could it be you're asking for love; or perhaps
you're just trying to find a reason to hold on to life.
To someone you were once quite a gal.
To someone you are quite a memory.
Now you are to me so marvelous, so dainty...
For you are little speckle eyes.
I will not forget, for you captured a part of me,
You made me smile, something that's very hard to do.
You will always be a memory to me, so old, yet so wise;
How could I ever forget those tiny "Speckled Eyes"!

Jacqueline D. Keys

Broken Heart Within A Dream

My dream finally came true,
I had her in my arms,
for a minute or two.

It came and gone to quick for me
I'm hurting so bad,
this, I hope she doesn't see.

My heart is aching,
I'm missing her, more and more,
with every breath I'm taking.

I'm trying not to be down, I'm trying not to pout,
but, when I look at her picture,
the tears just trickle out.

It hurts so much inside
my true feelings, I'm trying to hide

I try to go out and have a good time with my friends,
I miss her so much, when will all this heartache end?

I can't get her off my mind, happiness,
I don't think I'll ever find

Unless, she comes back to me, but deep down in my heart,
I know, this will never be.

Jake Knight

The Homeless

They live on the streets
They live on their own
And have no place to call home
They beg for money every day
But are ignored by the people who pass
them on the way

They sleep in boxes
And wear rugged clothes
And eat from the garbage
And where else only God knows
They are the homeless

I pray to God every night
That they will be O.K. and alright
I know that one day they will go to a better place
Where they will be appreciated
By God because of his love and wonderful grace

Fitzann Reid

Dying Soul

Seek the world, find yourself,
Stop if you need help.
The pool of blood, reminds me of mud
Body, black and blue
Eyes wide, hands to her side.
Is she dead?

She sat there in the bathroom,
Stared at the way she gloomed.
She picked up the blade,
That seemed to make her day.

She placed it on her wrist,
Because, she knew she wouldn't be missed.
She pressed, yuck, she made a mess.

I hear her screams,
Or, was it all just a dream?

Now she lays on the floor, her life was much of a blur.
No one cried, no one lied,
They hated her, but then she died.

Jennifer Ashby

A Dream

The breeze felt so cool against her face
Grass tickled her toes 'neath the tree
The sky was so clear, not a cloud in sight
A spirit so happy, so free.

'Twas too good to be true. A dream perhaps
Enjoy it before you awake from it
Once shattered to pieces, you can't put it back
Like a match that burns out too fast once lit.

You're enjoying each moment. You feel it won't end
You'll live in this dream forever or more
Then suddenly — blackness. A shrill is heard
"Oh mommy! Oh mommy!" from outside the door.

Reality hits you — no longer alone
On some island so far, far away
Perhaps when you've dealt with disasters at hand
This dream will start over some other day.

So few, few moments these days can be found
To be all alone with your dreams
So enjoy them the fullest then lock them away
On dark, lonely days they're your sunbeams.

Helen Symkowycz

I Hired On Full-Time

Nine months of anticipation;
Nine months of waiting;
A new beginning with no ending;
A lifetime of being a Mother.

I thought I knew what being a Mother would mean;
Bathing the baby, feeding the baby, watching it grow...but now I know.

Night comes and I welcome the rest and the quiet,
But with the quiet I keep listening for sound.

Sound of my baby's crying;
A softer sound of my baby stirring;
The whisper soft sound of my baby's breath.
I wait...there is no sound.
We (my baby and me) hold our breath till the next one comes.

Now my babies are grown and I welcome the nights,
I welcome the rest and the quiet.
But with the quiet I keep listening for sound;
A car driving up, the opening of a door or the ringing of the phone.
I cannot rest until I hear the soft sound of my baby's breath
For I hired on full-time.

Diane Thompson

Overcome

Trials, tribulations, troubles and pain
   Why you may ask and what do I gain
No one can really tell you for sure
   Until you have overcome and endured
It's not easy to deal with some things in this life
   And you wonder if you can handle the strife
But always remember in the darkest of night
   That day will return and with it the light
You'll endure through the clouds and the rain it will go
   The sun will come out and you'll bathe in the glow
Then looking back on where you have been
   You'll see all the times you were able to bend
Without being broken by the winds of the storm
   Coming through all the troubles and into the morn
Much stronger and wiser with some bruises it's true
   But knowing you've done the best you can do
So when you feel you're at the end of your rope
   Just look to the light and remember the hope
Of a better tomorrow with a bluer sky
   When your dreams and your spirit take wing and fly high.

    Michelle Covington

Snow Blossoms

Swiftly thru the night
While all the town was still
Snow fell silent, soft and white
To awaken the sleeping town with a thrill.

Thru my kitchen window
I looked with delight
The dogwood tree had blossomed
With snow cones - pure and white!

Each cluster of twigs in the shape of a cone
Was like a dainty cup
Catching snow flakes one by one
Until they filled it up.

The clusters of red berries
Scattered all among the tree
Together with the white snow
Blossoms, was a lovely sight to see.

    Creola Starnes

Belly Buttons

A twirling mass of sweaty fingers,
Climbing inside his crooked hand.
Its spindle twigs hold my melting palm,
As it drips buttercups onto the patchwork ground.

Crunching leaves with hungry feet,
We mimic fireflies and dig for worms.
Colored kites thrust us through sculpture clouds,
Then spit us out into tall iced teas.

Sipping melons in a box of chatter,
Till the moon burps the secrets out.
Our ears uncurl to tickling reflections,
Of belly buttons and their connection.

    Janet Williams

Perhaps

Perhaps if I'd been there more, listened more, talked more.
Perhaps if I had not hid behind this mask.
Perhaps if I had opened up and showed you what I felt.
Maybe you would know me, love me.
Perhaps if I had laughed more, pretended less, said what was on my mind.
Maybe you could have taught me, shown me.
Perhaps.

    Kathryn Leigh Brackley

Untitled

I close my eyes and see yours,
You, sitting there looking at me.
Your eyes how they shined
I will never forget.
To see them like that,
See what you feel,
I never want it to fade.
Every so often, I look into your eyes,
And there I see and know,
That it's still there, that your still feel,
Because of what they say.
I can't describe the way they looked
But it was wonderful to see,
And every so often they will shine
Reminding me what's there
And also what can't be.
The feelings there that must wait,
Or be kept locked up,
But never to die, because they can't,
Only to be kept inside.

    Natasha Sweet

The True Colors Of Life

The true color of youth is bright red, a fiery orange with which
to prove its stead. To right the wrongs of generations past,
to free the world and make peace last.

The true color of adults is sky blue, fluffy clouds in a
springtime hue. The soft caress of love that turns lime green
and will forever remain to be seen.

The true color of parenthood is a beloved pink standing in
awe of its lifetime link. Proud mother and father they shall be,
creating the joy of infancy.

The true color of again being alone is a satisfying grey of
such pleasant tone. When the grandchildren hint that
they'll come to stay, not so, if the grandparents have their way.

The true color of old age is snowy white, no color at all,
just a struggle to live with all of their might. From honey and
darling, Mom and Dad, then Grandma and Grandpa,
it all seems rather sad.

The true color of life is a shimmering rainbow above, of hate
and of forgiveness, strife and of love. The pastel shades that
fade with age will forever burn brightly on one's memory stage.
For these are all the true colors of life.

    Roger Bottman

Two Things

The yellowed paper,
The out-dated styles,
The now-unpopular melodies,
The crackling cassette.

Two things improve with time.
Two things can still make goose bumps run through us like lightning.
Two things can bring back the moment when we had everything.
Two things are sometimes all we need to survive.

Photographs and songs recall people now absent from us.
Photographs and songs make us remember what we had.
Photographs and songs find our lost loves.
Photographs and songs are the only time machines we have.

The beautiful bronze-tinted paper,
The creative styles,
The timeless melodies,
The cassette with character,
The physical proof of memories.

    Jessica McNamara

"I Am Somebody's Child"

I was born, I love life, I am somebody's child.
I know that I have not always been good,
And sometimes misunderstood.
But, I am somebody's child.

I might have spoken out of turn;
I might have looked at you very stern;
I walked down the street;
My mind was clear; or it might have
Been perplex, never realizing the end
Was near, I had no fear.
I am somebody's child.

You looked at me with anger and strife;
We spoke no words, you took my life;
What did I do to provoke you;
You too are somebody's child.

You got away on that dreadful day;
The people who were there will not say;
Don't they know someone must pay;
I was born, I loved life, I was somebody's child.

Clarissa Craig

Northern Lights

I often wondered what the Northern Lights represent. Are they just mere flashes of light shining and shimmering in the dark recesses of space or more? I wonder if they may be shimmering heavenly souls of the departed of this earth, dancing in the heavens, bathed in the glorious light of the Almighty, dancing carefree and happy, showing their earthly loved ones that they are joyous in their afterworld, making us believe in jubilation, love and life after death.

Or are they souls that are forever searching, flickering in and beyond the heavens, waiting, hoping for the light that may never come, to bathe them in the glory and splendor of the Almighty.

I have sat and watched these mysterious lights, forever dancing their own breathless and spectacular rhythm. I wonder and pray that they are the joyful souls that have been granted the heavenly radiance of God. The Northern Lights are in the darkened sky of night to show people of the earthly world that there is still hope, peace, and beauty after death of the human body. The soul may join the heavenly Northern Lights and know peace and contentment. I pray that this is what the Northern Lights may represent.

Dale Henton

The Price

I thought possessiveness was caring,
and jealousy was love.

I was the object of his desire,
and as such, I was scrutinized.

I lived in shame and fear,
and learned to believe this was normal.

I paid for his insecurities
with my flesh and blood.

I paid for his love
with my emotional scars.

When I freed myself from this bondage
that some called marriage,
I believed I was truly free.

But who can afford to love again,
when you have already taken such a chance
and paid the price?

Who can love again
when there is nothing left to give?

Tonya Arrington

Life Is What You Make It!

L is for the little things that challenge you each day.
I is for the inspiration that helps you on the way.
F is for faith the provides insight.
E is for effort that helps you win the fight.

I is for the image that shows you a plan.
S is for strength which tells that you can.

W is for the wish that points to a star.
H is for your horoscope that tells who you are.
A is for ambition to help you reach the top.
T is for the task that inspires you not to stop.

Y is for the yen to be the very best.
O is for the opportunity to stand the test.
U is for the unity of mind and body for a peaceful rest.

M is for the magnificent control of life's demands.
A is for the assertiveness to keep your head out of the sands.
K is for the keen responsibility to get the job done.
E is for the ease with which the victory is won.

I is for the initiative to find the best way.
T is for the tenacity to succeed from day to day!

Joan E. Pate

Designs

There's a drop upon the window
There's a way it decides to go
Why this direction? Not that, and because
Of this is meets another, from over there.

The sun illuminates, designs
Etching out the dust, leaving marks
Until a cloud blots out the ray.
Not till the next day will it
Appear as part of something bigger.
And then again,
There's a drop upon the window...

Henry Stonnington

Spirit Of Nature Anew

Do not grieve for me when I am gone,
But listen to the sweetness of a bird's song.
Look unto mother nature's wonderful things,
Of woodland creatures, flowers, trees and birds on the wings...
Snow-capped mountains, running brooks and shady nooks...
There God's wonder to behold.
For this was my world,
To love, to cherish and to fulfill my soul.

Mary Jewel Ramey

First Snowstorm

Little snowflakes in the air,
  Little snowflakes all so fair;
    Dancing jumping swirling by
      Flying quickly from the sky.

Here they come with much delight,
  Could it be a party tonight?
    Little snowflakes why the hurry
      Here come more in a flurry
        Dancing jumping swirling down
          Each in a pretty tinseled gown.
        Little snowflakes in their play
          Rushing past my window today
            Could they be angels from the heavens
              Coming quickly in sixes and sevens?
                Look! Here's the queen in finest array,
                  I'll ask her what's the rush today
                  I'll ask if it's a party tonight,
                    Or just a little flight
                      Of snowflakes all in white.

Helen-Gene Erickson

Untitled

My God listen to my plea, I know you hear me,
why do you not answer me. I know you know what's
best for me as I can't tell what's best for me.
My life is in your hands I know, and I do trust
you so. But why O Lord have you not heard my
plea, for I can sense you close to me. My heart
is aching so, but I have such faith in you. Even
thou I don't understand, I am sure you will let
me understand. For no one knows the power of
prayer, as it does not go unheard.

Rita DeLurey

Gossip

Words passed by people, from lip to lip,
Intentionally mentioned, never by slip.
Tugging and tearing until they rip,
Never giving a thought to the morale they strip.

People who indulge in this 'sport',
Are of the most destructive sort.

Gossiping is the illegitimate right to claim
The taking of someone's good name.
Whether the words are serious, or making 'fun and game,'
The soul which becomes undressed, will never be the same.

Debevon Lee

A Letter From Grandpa

When you were just a little boy a letter was wrote from me,
It was written by your grandpa as you sat upon his knee
There's something I'd like to tell you but your much too young today
By the time you read this letter I'll have probably passed away
You are to young to know why and would not understand
That's why I left this letter, till you become a man
The day that you were born a star fell from the sky
That's where you got that smile and that twinkle in your eye
Your grandma was so happy and I was full of joy,
Your parents were delighted that they had a baby boy
Now what I want to tell you as you grow up in this world
Take care of Mom and Grandma cause there just to fragile girls
And now about your sisters listen to what they say
Because they are a little older and they already tried that way
Now when you get a whole lot older and have a grandson on your knee
Remember this old letter that was left to you from me
Just tell him to show respect and to love mankind and kin
and it will make a better world for their family to live in
So now that you read this letter I hope that you agree
And enjoy your life as I did you when you were on my knee

Ray J. Schulze

My Daughter My Friend

It's hard to be a grown up when inside you want to be
Cradled like a baby and rocked so lovingly

We all need to feel the love surround us like a cloud
We have to know we're safe with our loved ones all around

I'm glad I am your mother, but I feel more like your friend
You're a truly beautiful person on whom I do depend

We have done some things together I never will forget
You are the sunshine of my life I'm so glad that we have met

I know that you are frightened now, I assure you, you're OK,
You have a beautiful bright tomorrow and right now you have today

They say we choose our parents before we are conceived
I feel so very honoured, and lucky, you chose me

Willene Price

The Spirit Truth

Opening himself up,
And venturing into the unknown past.
He saw the fate that had been hidden.
His unconscious self saw
What people of the old days would never believe.
Their beautiful paradise broken, battered, and shattered.
Their future skewed
In the wrong direction.
After the fires fell from the sky,
Burning and destroying,
Chasing away the inhabitants of the place of the Gods.
The survivors fled to the forest,
Abandoning their sacred cities,
So their future may never be repeated.

J. P. Merz

So Sad, Too Bad, That's Just The Way It Is

We can never be the same you and I.
Try as we might the chasm runs between.
The great, shifting shell of the earth,
Rent, torn, twisted,
leaves no neutral ground.

All the woes that have gone before:
Digging... digging deeply into the flesh,
Into the tunnels and creases of my veins.
That sharp, pointed blade cutting...killing:
Leaving a bloody trail of need.

We can never be the same you and I.
Through countless encounters no healing occurs.
Fragile bridges crumble! cables cut! loosely hanging.
Only the frozen plains of need, of want
Connect us.
And warm tears only widen the gap.

Fern Gordon

The Storm

Black overhead are the storm clouds that gather
Off in the distance the thunder's deep roll
The wind that a moment ago was so restless
Stands quietly by and breathes not at all.

I stand and I watch as the sharp lightening flashes.
Like neon lights, lighting the heavens aglow
Casting a weird, eerie light o'er the landscape
Of rivers and valleys and hills here below.

Weary the clouds with the burden they carry
Open their arms and send forth the rain
Drenching the earth with the tears of their sorrow
Hoping to ease their dark, ugly pain.

Then back of the clouds the sun is seen peeping
Chasing away the thunder and rain
And over the mountain God's archway of color
The beautiful rainbow of promise again.

Pauline F. Bell

Trains

Do trains get tired of running on tracks?
Do they ever get tired of signing contracts?
Do they ever get tired of people standing on them all day?
Do they ever wish they could go another way?

Matthew John Phillips

"Ode To A Cowboy"

We would like to be————
a better cowboy than anyone could see—
We have one down the road——
He travels by horse, that's his mode.
Working from morning to night——
He always travels light.
A roper with magic in his hands—
We all think that's pretty grand.
Horse-breaking is his trade——
Finer cowboy's haven't been made!
But——Life to him is all grit!!!
An older man now—
He still knows anybody's cow.
He'll help you if you get down and out—
and try to teach you what life is all about.
A neighbor and a friend——
Always ——to the end.

Joella J. Palmer

Pain

As she walked through all the rows of beautiful flowers;
  she stopped to think for hours and hours.

She told herself everything was going to be okay;
  but there was no place for her, no where to stay.

Life was hard, life was rough;
  she always knew she had to be tough.

She had no home, food or family;
  her life was nothing but a big tragedy.

What did she do? What's so wrong;
  she's talented, unique and really very strong.

Why was life so cruel to her?
  she can't think straight, her mind in a blur.

Nowhere to run, nowhere to hide;
  she just sat down ready to die.

She was crying, trembling and some what dirty;
  she wished her life was more sturdy.

I think about that girl sleeping under a tree;
  I think a little harder and that girl is me!

Kasandra Passmore

The Long Day

The Long day is at an end.
The golden sun has gone down beyond the horizon.
The shadows are becoming longer as if beckoning
  in the night.
The red, yellow and green hues light up night skies.
It is now time to reflect on the passing day.

What have I done with it?
Did I make the best use of it?
Do I wish I could have it back and live it all over again?
Did I say a kind word, or do a kind deed?
Did I brighten someone else's day with a smile?
Can I say yes! This is a day well spent?

Can I joyfully look forward to tomorrow now that the
Long Day is at an end?
The day I worried about yesterday,
Did I have cause to worry? Not if I did my best.

Karietha Marks

The Millionaire

We window shop, but seldom buy,
I wake each morning wanting to cry.

Sometimes I think our labor is in vain,
But, I receive a blessing and feel ashamed.

I wish for more than what I have;
Not so much for me, but for those of whom I care.

I remember the scripture, "God provides for our needs"
He never said, "He would supply for our greed."

I took an audit of my life, to justify my worry
I could hardly read the pages, my tear filled eyes become so blurry.

How selfish can one be?
I realized God has been so good to me.

Our children are healthy, there's food on the table
They have clothes to wear, tho not stitched with designer labels.

As I sat reading, my assets grew
I knew what I had to do.

Drying my eyes, I realized
"I have so much to share."

I lowered my head in silent prayer
Thank you God for making me a millionaire.

Jerri Smith

Lonely Child

Huddled in an archway, alone and afraid
A waif of a child, scantily dressed and cold
Shivering a little as clouds shroud the sun
And the sky grows threatening and dark.

Raindrops splash down, slowly then faster
She gets drenched and still the sky pours
Rivers of rain and tears stream down her face
As merciless torrents beat down upon her.

She whimpers at the lightning and thunder
Thinking and hoping for the sun
Until soon the drenching rain slackens and stops
The air stills and solitude surrounds her.

The clouds slowly begin to move away
And the little one hopes and prays for the sun
When a ray of heavenly light shines down
She locks on that ray with tears in her eyes.

Wishing for warmth and escape from the cold
She watches the clouds part to blue sky
Like a heaven sent hand from above
The sun gently surrounds her and the little one smiles.

Lin Clutter

Stay Awhile

  I miss your touch, your warm smile
The way you hold me, please stay awhile
  You always loved me, regardless of how,
Always thought of me, I know that now.
  Your warm caress, how much I long for
Your tender caring is all I live for.
  Yet now I know as time has passed,
Our future forever, it could not last.
  Your lost time has shortened the days
You need your space to help find your way
  Oh, how I want to be by your side
To guide you, to support you, through life's rough ride
  I love you, I miss you... your hug, your touch
I want to search with you, for I need you so much...
  To be my friend, my lover, for life's many miles
Please, for me, for you... stay awhile.

Charles T. Nason

Burneast

Mother's day is a special kind of day,
When children honor their mother in some large or small way.
A time to say thanks for loving, caring, and sharing,
A time to embrace, reflect, and look ahead.

Need money for airfare, sick and need much care,
Simply shopping for an outfit to wear,
Or if your burdens get too hard to bear,
Call on me, and I'll be there.

Although we live within a few miles,
I seldom get a chance to see your smile.
I'd love to hear you sing those old familiar hymns,
That bring back memories every now and then.
We live in a world where people are distant,
But I am always here to talk or listen.

So in honor of this special Mother's Day,
I say, "thank you" as I send my undying love your way,
Mixed with compassion, sprinkled with forgiveness,
Cultivated with understanding, overlaid with affection,
And wrapped with God's amazing grace!

Kathleen W. McGriggs

Casey's Prayer

Thank you, God for this great day
And all the things that came my way.

And with tomorrow's coming light
Help me to always do what's right.

Please help me walk in happy shoes
And learn from every path I choose.

The lessons that are there for me
to be the best me I can be.

So as I lay me down to rest,
We'll know I've done my very best.

And Lord, my strength, my friend, my guide,
Thank you for walking by my side.

For helping when the road is rough,
For laughter when the times are tough,

For tears that was away the pain,
Thank you, Lord, for everything.

R. Michael Smith

Why Do You Care

Why do you care
How I dress or how I do my hair
I have problems just like you
I'll try to forgive them out, that's what I'll do
I don't care
Go ahead and stare
I had braces why I don't know
I can't sell my teeth or put them on show
I have green eyes and short brown hair I'm 5 feet tall
But them why do you care
I don't want to be different
Here is were I was sent
There are many things I do not know
Like how to live or how to sew
We all breath the same air
I'll ask one last time, so why do you care?

Chelsea Pinkel

Trueblue

Working class working man,
strong to the finish, does the best he can.

Up in the morning, to bed at night,
works all day, makes it all right.

Makes your factory, makes your home,
makes your car, makes your astrodome.

Salesmen sell it, managers manage it,
scientists think it, engineers design it.

Working man makes it, working man maintains it,
working man modifies it, working man uses it.

Look at your ceiling, look at your floor
look through your windows, look out your door.

Working man does it, he does it all and more,
working man does it does for rich and poor.

Mama calls, baby calls, sister calls, brother calls,
working man comes, he comes to all.

He's a carpenter he's a working man,
He's Lord of all Jesus Christ King, carpenter, God and man.

When you're feeling blue and not so true,
remember Lord Jesus, he's a working man and true blue too.

Bill Bowen

Talk With Nature

I see you in the trees, I see you in the skies,
I see you everywhere, in ants and butterflies.
You talk to me so gently with fallen rustling leaves
I love you mother Nature, you're one who all forgives.
But people disregard you and underestimate
Still you're the only witness, you can predict our fate
Oh, Nature you are gorgeous and still you can avenge
By sending droughts and flooding, you show us your revenge
You're owner of the talents and you divide them all
Among the every person who use them in part small
You're right, she said with whisper some people do deny
That they have any talent when talent's standing by
I'm giving everybody his own unique skill
But it's not every person who can develop still, his own talent!
And now all my beauty yet vanishing by now
My Mother Earth is bleeding but you can save us.
How?
If you still love your Mother and want it to survive
Do give example others and I will start revive!

Yulia Rud

That Night

When I think of that night
I long for the next time we shall be together.
We were as one,
Breathed as one,
Two hearts beating as one.
Time seemed to stand still
And all our petty problems magically disappeared.
A whisper here, a gentle touch there,
What was happening outside of that room?
We didn't care.
The climax unfolded,
Our hearts raced, though still beating as one.
Then suddenly, it was over.
You cried tears of happiness and tears of pain.
That was great; Let's watch that movie again.

Jason Scott Gentry

My Surroundings

I live in a place where I am free,
With blowing wind and a swaying tree,
With tiny little ponds full of frogs and toads,
I sink into my thoughts

The birds, the grass, the sun, a bee,
It's hard to believe this revolves around me.
With night falling quickly and clouds in the sky
I sit on my porch steps as cars go by.
Then everything's still, I sit and wait,
Until...

The morning comes quickly,
Gentle birds are flying free,
I say, fly away birdy, fly free for me.

Paige Pronovost

Freedom Fantasy

Had I wings today, I would be far, far away.
Like you my feathered friend, I would be free — free to be me!

No caged existence, no unopened doors,
No staged performance, just free — free to be me.

In timeless eternity, across pastures green,
High above crystal blue waters, I would spread my wings.

Through virgin forests, not yet known by man,
To the mountain peaks, I would extend my plan.

Ever onward and upward, what a breathtaking sight!
And a perfect escape to a world that is right.

Beyond misunderstandings and worn-out years,
To peace everlasting where there live no fears.

Where love is a blessing and allowed to grow free,
And I have no boundaries — just free to be me!

So, soar where you want to, perch where you may,
Go where God leads you, for today — today you are me!

Addine Ramsey

Caution To Camelot

King Arthur's edicts proclaim
"In serving each other we become free for
we are the land of justice and the hope of mankind.
Sit at the round table.
Surrender your sword within the Circle of Brothers
who vow to be yours in life and death."

Lancelot forewarns
"Watch the empty seat, my Lord.
Remember beyond Camelot live the lesser people
those who follow the Master of Nothingness.
If you go to the land of forgetting
where King Tyranny rules
everlastingly, guard our principles.
Protect Merlin.
Don't make choices in the dark.
Hold your lance tightly
and always put armor over your heart."

Penny Lee Reasinger

"Time"

As time goes by, we wonder. Just when
we think we have it all, we end up with
less than we started with. They always
say life is what you make it, but that
is not always so. Life is what it wants
you to be, not what you have achieved.

Sarah Travagline

Merlin's Tower

Brooding within my castle borders
stone walls pulled about my shoulders like a cloak
black bird phantom echoes my spirit
healer, heal thyself.
The chess game of life is
stalemate, checkmate, wizard, bishop, king, rook,
moat dragons, copper scales flashing
brilliance on granite tower.
Shadows drip like blood from mortal wounds
with a flash of wing, death.
Verdant fields stretch open
on my burial knoll giants play
Obliviously they too must cross the causeway.
Castle walls my fortress, my prison, my madness.

A. M. Kat

Golden Anniversary

Life is a game of give and take,
   Love makes it all worthwhile.
There are problems and heartaches most every day,
   But Fran meets it all with a smile.

So we've walked together these 50 years,
   Sometimes the wind rose to a gale.
But Fran stood tall with his head held high,
   As a shield for Ruth to walk through.

Then came the day life's price must be paid,
   Fran's body lies still and cold.
Strength comes from God as Ruth walks alone.
   The golden years are done.

Once more love shines through the gloom of life tasks,
   Memories become very real.
Heaven is dearer than earth ever could be,
   Fran is at Home, and the latchstring is out.

Ruth E. Hillick

Her Love

She has money to lend, money to spend
A diamond ring and ev'rything
A mansion so fine, she calls it divine
But somehow her love isn't mine

She loves bracelets and things, golden earrings
And fancy clothes, labels she chose
My money's her toy, her pride and her joy
But somehow her love isn't mine

Yes, my wealth is her love
And it's all she dreams of
I wish she had time to spend with me
But her love's not worth a dime if it's not free

Maybe someday she'll be lonely and see
Love's a thing money can't bring
That her love and mine is something divine
And that's when her love will be mine

Louis J. Pourciau

Anne

   Red hair brushed with sun
Face with summer's fading blush, liberally sprinkled with freckles
   A mustache of breakfast orange juice
A stain of raspberry cool-aid decorates her once blue jumper
   Knees streaked with grass green
   Feet a fudge brown as she runs through the mud
      Here comes my Anne

Carolyn A. Lewis

I Thanked The Lord For You Today

Today I needed to feel loved and I found you loving me.
Today I felt so alone until I felt your hand around mine.
Today I started building walls until your safety tore them down.
Today I was in so much pain until I felt your healing touch.
Today I felt so worthless until your eyes told me I meant everything.
Today I tried to hold back the tears until you gave me your
    shoulder to cry on.
Today I couldn't find my smile until you made me laugh.

Yesterday I was looking for your tender eyes.
Yesterday I was missing your beautiful smile.
Yesterday I was yearning for your strong arms around me.
Yesterday I almost stopped believing in you.
Today, just in time, the Lord brought you to me.

So I thanked the Lord for you today.

Stephanie Lynn Cummings

Footprints

Walking through the warm sand
Watching waves of water land on the shore
Looking up at the sun resting above the horizon
Feeling the cool wind blow
Listening to songs of birds echo through the sky
Storing at cracked sea shells
Wondering why I'm here and no where else
Thoughts about life swim through my mind
Searching for reasons but not many to find
For why I'm here to live and then die
Footprints in the sand are what we look back of
And stones we wish not to have thrown

Mervat Khader

I'm Thinking Of You

The way I think of you
Night and day, until I'm through.
I look to see if you're there
But when I turn around it's only a chair.

My heart calms down,
My eyes look around.
Can I say hi to you once more
Or should I sit and adore?

My mind focus on your attention,
My eyes light with vengeance.
When I see the girl of your past,
I wonder, will her beauty last?

The sunshine in my heart is for you.
Will it be like that once I'm through with you?
Sincerely, I'll look again for someone else,
But I realize I can't; you're the only someone else.

Amanda Quaye

For I Am Not

Some are born to compete
others are not, for I am not.
Some are born to be athletes
others are not, for I am not.
Some are born to care for others
others are not, for I am not.
Some are born for academics
others are not, for I am not.
Some are born to be leaders
others are not, for I am not.
Some are born to explore
others are not, for I am not.
But I don't let this get me down,
Because this is what makes me an individual.

Buck Breazeale

I Wish I Could Remember

I cling to fading shadows of your memory, Daddy,
wishing I could remember
the first time you held me,
or your laughter at my baby smiles.
I wish I had paid more attention
Which way was your hair parted?
What was your favorite color?
Which song on the jukebox made your heart beat faster?

How beautiful you must be now;
You are every color, every note,
Every shade of light around me.

A year has passed, and all I have left
are pictures of you,
Along with the guilt of never telling you my deepest
secrets, my greatest dreams,
or the fact that I like purple best.

Roberta C. Hiner

Fairy Tale Dream

Mr. Right where are you?
Did you find my glass shoe?
Beauty and the beast were quite a pair.
Where are you? This isn't fair.
Snow White found the Prince Charming,
but I'm still out there farming.
Rapunzel was locked away from sight,
yet she still found her Magical Knight.
Sleeping Beauty was to sleep for life,
but that didn't stop her from becoming a wife.
I'd tell you more,
but I have to run to the store.
But alas, I see him on the way.
Stop! Don't let him get away.
As I acknowledge the full moon...
Oh Mother, did you have to wake me so soon!

Theresa B. Kozakwicz

Thoughts On Statistics

Oh, why am I so masochistic, as to take the course, "Statistics"
the sums of which I cannot comprehend.

The data is continuous, if measuring feet or inches,
while books and cars can only be discreet.

The mode and median can be mean...at times I think it quite
obscene, that standards can become so deviate?

Combinations and permutations only lead to more frustrations,
to which degree there is some variance.

I think that I shall never see a simple probability,
distributed within a normal range.

One factorial! Two factorial! I hope they'll build a bell memorial,
for those of us who vainly tried...and died.

Oh, why am I so masochistic as to take the course, "Statistics"
the pain persists, but soon the task will end.

And even though there's strength in suffering, from this text
I can't help running....trying to find a random sample, or some
brain cells which are ample....
Only God can help these wounds to mend!

Jacquelyn A. Hassett

Lost Love

I remember the picnics in the park,
And the sweet smell of roses so divine.
Those days I was as happy as a lark,
And it was not because of the red wine.
That evening in front of the fireplace,
Reflecting the dancing flames in your eyes.
A look of serenity on your face,
As you knelt and proposed, to my surprise.
My only wish had been granted to me.
I thanked my lucky stars that it was true.
Why could not technology let us see,
That fateful cancer that left our days few.
    You would not be suffering, as in Hell,
    If only I were still alive and well.

Dorcas E. Webster

Floating Fame

The night is surrounded by eerie stillness
The full moon floats within silent stars
The water creeps upon the shoreline
A shadow lurks behind the rocks

Her eyes stare longingly at the horizon
Wondering what lies beyond its reach
She steps up to the foamy sand
Then wades in past her slender knees

Dawn arrives in wondrous splendor
Children splashing at the seashore
Sounds of laughter twist to horror
The shadow has returned she's blue

Headlines splash across the papers
As they read Jane Doe is found
Lifeless on our sandy waters
Identification is unknown

Fame that had forever alluded her
Has now so boldly appeared in print
Not necessarily the way she dreamed of
The unknown lady is well known now

Conni Kroeger

The Essence Of Love

The very essence of being in love
Is the joy that fills your heart;
True love never diminishes,
Whether you're together or apart.

True love changes everything,
So long as it is true;
The birds sing happier melodies,
The sky shines forever blue.

While in love you walk through life,
Always bearing a smile;
That smile shows the world,
That loves makes life worthwhile.

So if you ever fall in love,
You must never let it go;
And the enchanting joy that lovers feel,
You will also come to know.

Deborah Sprague

Ghost In Your Heart

I am the voice you hear
    outside your bedroom window
I am the chill that tickles your spine
    when you crawl into your bed
I am your evil succubus
    visiting you in your dreams
    turning them into nightmares
I am the demon who laughs at you
    when you wake up alone; spent and shivering
        because you can still hear my seductive whispers
        amidst the silence
        echoing in the stillness of the night
I am the ghost - like face
    you think you see behind you
    when you look into the mirror
        that face being indelibly stained
        upon your memory forever
I am the ghost in your heart
    hauntingly persistent, forever insistent
        that you always remember me and never without remorse

Jill Reese

The Limit Of Your Vision

Are you seeing me as me, or just another night surprise?
Is the limit of your vision the seduction in my eyes?
If it is I don't want beauty or its comforting disguise.
Or its camouflage distorting of what underneath it lies.
I have always wanted everything, everything the world could give,
I have wanted for true love, and accompanying feeling felt within.
I am yearning always for the truth. Which is the moral way to live?
What a question for this yearning soul, an answer only you can give.
All the heartaches we have battled to make it through another day.
To have finally arrived in such a state of disarray.
Yet to find more paths to follow with not a clue as to the way,
Surely questioning the future. Shall I go or shall I stay?
So to end mistakes before they are, you have to make a choice.
Are you comforted within me, or do you find comfort in my voice?
As we age we'll surely wrinkle, And as you that's what I'll be.
But if you truly love me, all you'll see is that I'm me.

Jean M. North

The Peaceful Sky

The peaceful blue sky rises from the song
The beauteous peoples underneath the broad sun
Cool, calm, and free broods over this land
The holy time is quietly everlasting
For the love, the lasting love, not cease

It has footprints under the sky
Full of my struggle, my tear, my breath
And also my youthful smile
The endless hope in the future appears in my eyes
In the peaceful blue sky in Canada

Like the scenery of an oil painting
Variety of colors from deferent worlds
Blissful and warm in the gentleness of heaven
No anger, no envy, no hate, no fear
In the solemn thought of this big land

The country is prosperous and at peace
The people live in happiness
God bless this big land lucky forever
The blue sky stays eternally
Long in time, Canada! Long in time.

Blake Hsieh

Wind and Rain

Wind is better than the rain - most of the time;
(I hope I can write an interesting rhyme!)
The wind can move the leaves, people, papers, and a rabbit hutch -
drifting, cooling, hurling, "crispy," heavy and swirling so much;
My hair is tossed about and it sticks up and out - it is appalling,
It looks like it's "snowing" outside when the new tree blossoms are falling,
from the wind, winding and whistling and constant - all month long,
and when it is hot at noon, I enjoy the wind, so strong;
The rain is needed for the flowers to grow,
I'm happy that it too has replaced the snow;
Rainy days really used to make me feel extra anxious and very sad;
but, there's nothing to fear any longer - and with an umbrella, I'm glad.
Also, the water gets very choppy on a windy day;
so, you require sturdy fishing poles at Raritan Bay.
You need a light, peaceful wind to fly a kite,
and real friends to make our lives good and all right.

Linda Zabala

A Ballad

The dark night fell upon me
It caught me unaware
The moonlight smiled upon me
As it glimmered off your hair

With movements lithe in the star-filled sky
And eyes set bright aglow
You smile a tender smile at me
Love from your smile doth flow

So waltz with me in the nighttime
Come run through the fields of day
But never forget, for long years yet
Where love shown through our play

My robes flow now with whispering folds
You dance with simple grace
I take your hand, on one knee stand
To gaze upon your face

James T. Descheneaux

He Answered

Many years ago, I began a battle I could not comprehend....

I ask, "Oh Lord, how could you leave me here
With not even a friend?"

He answered.... little one, fear not for I am with
you always.... even till the end.

The hours turned to days, weeks,
months, and then into years.

I ask, "Oh Lord, please, please will you come near."

He answered, "my precious child,
Look....I am right here."

I wanted to be faithful but it seemed
I failed him time and time gain.

I ask, "Oh Lord, can you forgive me for all my sin?"

He answered, "Oh, child of God
Your life is only about to begin."

I wanted to serve him, never to let him down.
Only to be worthy

I ask, "Oh Lord, how could you want to love me?"

He answered, "Dear one, please remember,
It was I who chose to die on Calvary.

Dottie Scarbro

November

Wind-swept clouds streaked
the azure sky,
Chasing geese southward
Escaping winter's whipping winds to come.

A single hawk circled lazily
beneath the afternoon sun,
ascended and cascaded,
played in season's last thermal weather.

Wild yellow weeds, patch worked
on arid red clay,
bowed in graceful grandeur.
A farewell gesture to harvest's end.

I closed my eyes
and laid among the weeds
while clouds drifted overhead
the hawk glided
in autumn's last breath.

Thomas Reese

Yea! Christopher

I look at you in awe, not quite believing the beautiful person you
are... inside and out.
Your happy face and engaging smile brightens every place you
go, for a moment, or for hours.

How little it takes to make you happy.
The look of pure joy on your little face when anyone claps and says
"Yea, Christopher!" for whatever it is you've accomplished -
no matter how insignificant.
The recognition alone delights you.

The sparkle in those remarkable eyes,
The mischievous look when you're teasing someone.
The body language when letting people know what you want or need.
If we listen to you... really listen with our hearts and minds...
we understand.

You cannot talk, but you do communicate, and make yourself understood.
If we pay attention we could learn from you...
Important things, like smelling flowers, watching ants build a hill,
waiving hello to the clouds.

It does a heart good to see that little ray of sunshine in a six year
old boy who cannot talk, but does communicate.
Pay attention and you will learn, and in spite of yourself,
you'll be saying "Yea! Christopher".

Brenda L. LaPointe

A Tree In The Fall

In the yard I see a Tree,
the oldest and largest and shady tree.

You can hear a faint whistle winding through
the big and mighty limbs of the tree.
The leaves shake with fear,
for soon they will fall down and wither and die.

The sun dies down a little bit each day,
the tree dies down a little bit each day.
Soon the cold will give the tree frostbite
and it shall shed its leaves leaving it bare.

But one day the sun will live again,
one day the tree will live again,
The tree shall retrieve its scattered pieces
and people will stop in front of the yard
to sit under the tree,
the oldest and largest tree.

Teresa Racanelli

"Grace Abounding"

Amazing grace how sweet the sound
His love for us has no bounds.
He placed his life upon the cross
So the souls of man would not be lost.
Once our hearts were full of sin
But all is forgiven when we pray to him.
We once were blind but now we see
He shed his blood to set us free.
The wonderful grace of Jesus abounds
His love for us always surrounds.
    Thank You Jesus!
    Mary K. Pulley

River Of Life

The river flows as life itself
Curving, changing with different setting.
We grow and flow with life itself...
Not knowing where we're headed, or what we're getting.

All through life we seek the best,
sometimes discouraged too soon.
Try again and head straight forward
Keeping dreams high as the moon.

We must flow with life itself
and if not so good, must change it.
Although nature sets the river's course,
Time and care can rearrange it.

    Linda Pedley

M e

I know not where I'm going, only where I've been
Life for me full of rewards, where shall I begin.
My mate is gone, my family grown -
Will I find love again? That happiness I've once known.
Must life now mean simply to survive -
Warm, loving, gentle, I'm very much alive.
There must be someone waiting for me -
Where shall I seek her, who will she be.
Always getting hurt, I wonder why -
Laughing on the outside, while inside I cry.
They say time is a healer, it will fade away -
Thoughts that make me weep will all be gone someday.
I won't give up, though the pace is very slow -
I will succeed, with each and every blow.
Life is tough with its twists and turns -
As everyone, at sometime learns.
I must go in this promise land -
Find that special woman, then ask for her hand.
To be honest and faithful, and just be me -
What more could she ask for, I'll wait and see.

    Lonnie L. Hennings

Do You Know?

Indifference in men is the meaning of hate.
    It's apathy saying that love holds no weight.

Then hate is the chosen tool of a man
    Relentlessly battling his own Divine Plan.

Yet hate, when seen through the sages eyes,
    Is the veiling of Truth; Love's total disguise.

Then, what is wrong as compared to right,
    But another step as we journey toward Light.

And what's a mistake, whether big or small,
    But a road in the map of Divinity's all.

What is fear, but a call to the wise,
    To bring to awareness, love in its guise.

Love is the answer, as me and you.
    So choose, at this moment, False image or True!
    Veronica Grogan

Mass Murder In A Cathedral Town

Dunblane, a 13th century Cathedral town,
on the edge of the Scottish Highlands
Was ineradicably stained at the Ides of March, by the murder
most foul of 16 kindergarten bairn, mercilessly gunned down in
their school's gym, their teacher too, at the sanguine hands
Of an outraged, busted boy scout leader, rumored a pervert;
now a site needing a cairn.

Twelve other children, though injured, survive,
never able to blot out this horrid scene
Wrought by a loner, a psychopath dubbed "Mr. Creepers,"
not previously charged with any crimes
Hence, licensed by local police to own four semi-automatics --
this executioner most obscene
In a kingdom roundly lauded for stern gun laws,
strictly enforced, doomed way ahead of the times.

Her majesty paid a royal visit to lay a floral wreath just outside
the school's gate.
A stunned Great Britain observed a national silent minute to
honor the prematurely dead
Who though, so innocent met a mindless, violent end on this
ignominious date.
All cry out, "God, is there no sanctuary from such tragedy, such
loss, such dread?"
    Norman R. Nelsen

The Treehouse

This poem is bout my treehouse;
    Which is filled with elm tree leaves!
I like to sit here and read my book,
    And feel the cool summer's breeze.
I write on the walls if I want to;
    For there are no rules up here,
But if that squirrel steals my food again,
    I'll scream and rip out my hair!
I like to listen to the blue-birds,
    Why, they always have a song,
And I always hear the church bells ring...
    Ding-dong, ring-a-ding, ding-dong!
    Amber Lippick

Ellis Island

Babel of tongues,
heaps of rags, unloaded from old ships
and left on the windy shore
in the darkness of their uncertain future.

Emaciated bodies,
bright and frightened eyes,
sore from broken roots,
thirst for life and fear to fail.

So the immigrants,
thousands and thousands,
arrived at Ellis Island, America's door —
threshold of the great dream.

Today, throngs of pilgrims,
proud of their fathers' boldness,
come to honour the seeds
of their prosperity.

But sobbing and groaning
I hear within these walls,
and to the wretches driven back on the sea,
pity and love, I bestow.

    Caterina Parisi Mehr

The Wind

I am the wind...
The wind that floats quietly in and out of your life.
You know me when you feel me
but wonder if you really do when you don't.

I am the wind...
The wind that fuels embers into a raging angry flame
The strong driven wind that extinguishes the inferno of an
    uncontrolled forest fire

The wind that suddenly warms you on a crisp winters day
The cool breeze that dries the sweat of a hot humid night

I am the wind...
The wind that brings dark angry skies that scare you in the night.
The morning calm on which glide the white clouds of hope.

At dawn, I carry the singing birds afloat.
At dusk, I whisper to you gently through the trees and leaves.

I am the wind...
Don't ask me why, because I don't know
Remember me when the winds die, but don't despair.
Because what is still wind? But air!

I am the wind...and as long you breathe, I am there...

Gilbert M. Escontrias

Boredom

Not a thought, not a sound,
Silence spills upon the ground,

It lingers in this misty room,
Inside the soul of ignorance,
That carries on a scent of doom,
Upon her sullen deliverance.

She hears, nor sees, a single word,
On ivory wing doth fly the bird.

But in her heart floats the hate,
That sparkles and fades against the eye,
Against the night so often late,
Against the tears of repressed cries.

" So cry," the smut of boredom says,
" For I know what death and boredom is,

To those whom fear his awful sight,
Alone in his loneliness does he weep,
Shaded against the grace of light,
And in only his pain shall we hear him peep."

So boredom is alone at last,
With his heavy burden of no past.

Brady Frey

My World

Today I live in a world so complex I don't understand.
People don't have time for others to lend a helping hand.
Yesterday was simple, no locks upon my door.
That time is gone forever and there may never be anymore.
Tomorrow makes me shudder to think of the life I'll live.
What will become of the children, what heritage will I give?
Each day I stop to look at how nothing stays the same.
To live in this world one must learn to how to play the game.
A nation at peace is full of guns, drugs, and crime.
I'd rather to back to the years at war, a more simple time.
As I think of the children I long to have some day,
It makes me weep to know that for my cause they'll pay.
I live in a world of electronics, everything right in reach.
But religion, morals, and the value of life we do not teach.
I live in a world that everyday takes away from the youth.
The Lord is my shepherd, I want no more and that is the truth.

Jennifer R. Bass

Struggling With Christianity

Trapped in a web of deceit,
    bound with satan's hands and feet.
Mind of a child of fortune,
    bearing the pain of Jesus Torture.
Little care about tomorrow,
    welting in forbidden sorrow.
Again I shall never hear,
    the beautiful cries of Mother dear.
Darkness shall forever close,
    on a face as precious as gold.
Grace shall take me far away,
    relieve the pain I feel someday.
Deliver me to the Holy Land,
    into my Father's arms as he stand.
    Crossing over is no fear,
        to understand is so clear.
Walk the way of joyous cheers,
    praise his name throughout the years.
When you finally reach the rapture,
    he will fill your heart with laughter.

Margaret Garrett Hendrix

In Solitude

You called to me with a voice so filled with love,
I could hardly hear the roaring of the water.
The wind carried your whispers through the air,
And my body absorbed its precious melody...
So I closed my eyes to all the world and in my mind, saw only you.
As your voice grew softer and more silent still,
I ached for the sweet echo now barely heard in the breeze above —
Completely lost in my quest for love.
In solitude I shed a thousand tears,
And watched them as each one landed on the water,
Making circles on the glass which held my reflection
For a single moment in time...
In that moment there was quietness,
And I held my breath as if my heart would shatter if I should breathe.
And then the bittersweet stillness of the air filled with thunder,
And I was awakened from my sleepless sleep and dying dream...
The roaring of the water filled my ears and pierced my body
And somehow I listened for the wind, yet the wind could not be heard.
So I closed my eyes to all the world, and in my mind, saw only you.
As the water's anger lessened and grew more silent still,
I ached for that sweet echo once heard in the breeze above —
Completely lost in my quest for love, yet found instead, my death...

Jennifer Bryan

Soliloquy On Solitude

In the depths of despair I floundered,
when suddenly it occurred to me
only I have the strength and wisdom to set my own mind free.
In the beauty of the garden of solitude,
I cherished my happiest hours;
I reached for the blossoms of patience and searched
through the bowers of prayer.
I drank from the fountain of serenity, its pool a mirror of me...
as I opened the gate of reflection, remote as eternity.

An invincible spirit welcomed truth and rejected the facade...
the dual between me and them,
between me and me, between me and God.
I tasted the wine of the multitudes and refused this heady brew.
In the hours before dawn I discovered me;
to my own self be true.
This solemn message of peace revealed to me,
on the meandering path where each footstep rings...
a soul weary of winter, joyfully embraced the songs of spring.

Rebecca Odom

Transient Of The Theory Of Relativity

Moving moving bubbles of the distortion
   (reverberations, a trailing note)
Swaying swaying leaving of waving

Timing timing the holes of the sky
Cosmosing cosmosing inside of the things
Staring staring changing of the time
Moment in seasons momentarily like
Human minds and hearts with natural water

Midoro Saito

The Old Maple

Just a little twig was I yet so much time has passed
I've laughed, I've cried, I've lived life so- and I'm so glad
   you've asked me
At each spring thaw they craved the sap which flowed like honey sweet
And very soon a crown green with majesty I'd greet.

Young lovers ran to my feet to chat their affection
Curved deep witness of their love engraved as if protection
I cradled nesting families, provided shelter from the rain
And smiled as chirps of feathered friends got comfort from my mane.

The weather chills I still as nature blesses me
I stood so proud quiet beautiful as all did come to see
But one dark day so sorrowful is etched upon my heart
As one lone man took his dear life of which I was a part

As days go by and I grow old I'm losing my resistance
The rain burns now the sun is hot, my friends are at a distance
When time seems long, I close my eyes fond memories caress
I was a twig so long ago, thanks for your love....I'll rest.

Donna Ayotte

First Christmas

The sounds of the Christmas are in the air,
The music, the snow, a child so fair.
It is baby's first Christmas, although she doesn't know.
But it will be fun to watch her Christmas, as she grows
Christmas is for people to share.
Happiness and love should not be spared.
But alas, it does happen to a few,
I often wonder, "To Who?"
Spread the Joy and, Spread the Love!
Continue to pray to the one above.
This is His day when he was born.
The years have past,
but the message is never out worn.
Love never dies when it is pure and strong.
May Christmas win over the people who are wrong.
Love should shine forever and ever.
That way life could be like Christmas and BETTER!
Here's to the holiday season and birth.
We will always celebrate to show the "One's" worth!

Debbie Bludau

Inner Truth

I am inner truth. I may frighten you.
Only because I can make you see what you truly are.
I can't make you see what you will be.
I can change you and make you face your fears.
I can also make you face your true feelings.
I can also make you lose many things as well.
I am inner truth and I can make you lose your identity in a short time.
You look and see what you can.
But false identities are stripped clean away.
If you don't know who you are now. You will know after.
There is always a spark of hope with inner truth.
I hope that everyone can find their truths and their
personal best within themselves as well as around the.

Dawn Jones

Instincts

In my body all my instincts may return.
In the sun my eyes may burn.
In the stormy rain lightning shines.
Pain thrives from the inside.
Recovering, the voice is heard.
Make a choice, in control and unnerved.
Mud that once soaked my body leaves me as I rise.
Pain from the inside subsides.
Now I stand, alone but strong.
My fears once condensed...
now are gone.
I start to walk confident in stride.
Leaves crackle
trees sway
indications that I'm alive.
Tailwinds blow
my body yearns.
Instincts did not leave me...
they did return.

Derek Catanzaro

That My Child Will Walk Again

Dear God, she's such a little girl,
To try to understand.
Why other children run and play,
And she must hold my hand.

Her blue eyes fill with tears, oh God,
And her small voice asks me, Why?
And I feel my own heart breaking, God,
Until I want to die.

But I kneel down and hold her close,
And teach her how to pray.
And tell her if she's very good,
She too will run someday.

That soon she'll laugh and run and play,
With the joy of being young.
This is the prayer I make each night,
Whenever day is done.

I ask You God, in all Your love,
To touch the hearts of men.
And if it is Your Holy will,
My child will walk again.

Regina Scopelitis

Life Lives

Breathe in deeply and realize,
that you are a part of life.
Let your most intimate emotions arise,
and forget your most challenging strife.

Feel the strength life brings with love.
Feel the love that strengthens life.
Life gives you the right of wondrous creation,
for life is of astonishing emanation.

Discover within, the wall of pain
that you have constructed.
Disconnect yourself from your brain,
and you will see the mess it has instructed.

Destroy that wall and run free to the heart,
for that's where life truly lives --
and then you will forever be a part
of the everlasting life that lives...

Leilani C. Racoma-Lessnau

Details Of Ignorance

A blotch of colours splashed on a side
With systems of speech enabling a cry
Ask how many colours there are in all
See the motion of reflections crawl
Which reflection is yours you see?
Can you distinguish it from another cree?
Look at the millions of specks on that wall
If one disappears, would you notice at all?
Blink. And you've missed a tremendous change
Does anything seen a little big strange?
Listen to the cries from their systems of speech
Would you hear if one was out of your reach?
You see that wall others see as a spot
For you are now part of the wall that slowly rots
Back on the side, it is you that is heard
But it is you that can speak not a single word
Now that you are a speck on one wall
If you disappear, will I notice at all?
If you cry to me with your system of speech
Will it be within my hearing's reach?

Margaret Jou

Journey To Heaven

Some people say when we die we will take that journey alone, I don't think that happens because the bible says the Lord comes to take us home. I believe we have to die in order to gain, and I believe we will live forever with the Lord in His reign. The bible says that heaven is a beautiful sight to see. It says the streets are paved with gold and there is a mansion waiting on me, My name has been written in the book of life with God's own mighty hand. The bible says there will be no night, no need for candles nor fear. The Lord be our light and He will wipe away our tears. If we bear His cross as we walk through this old world we share His glory with Him. But we have to wait for this wonderful journey as all others have done. I heard as we stand in front of the great white throne that God is sitting on, Jesus will say to the Father these are my children welcome them home. When I think of all the beauty and the glory we will share, living forever with the ones we love and never having to care. I believe as we travel this journey we will never walk alone.

Renee Adams

"The Awakening Of Spring"

The crocus has arisen from her written bed,
To welcome the spring, so it is said.
The daffodil's adorning the meadow that's bare.
With glorious colors; luxuriant and rare.
From across the hills calls sweet Bob White,
With notes so shrill; what a delight!
The meadow lark is happily on the wing,
Singing the overture of spring,
The robin is nesting her eggs of blue,
The warmth of her love brings her tiny young through.
A caressing breeze embraces the trees,
The rhythm of summer rustling the leaves.
The air is fresh, the sun is warm,
Earth has awaken from winters storm.
Some slightly smile and think nature is add,
But way down deep, I know it is God.

Shirley Maiotti

Tired

Eyes need rest, head needs to lay down. Arms and fingers just need to stop moving. Chest, stomach, backbone all need eight hours of rest. Waist, hips and legs need no movement. Toes and feet need a hot soaking bath. Tired yes tired...whole frame tired. Eyes, head, arms, fingers, chest, stomach, backbone all tired. I must be named Derit. Turn it around, it spells Tired.

Gwendolyn N. Green

The Seasons Turn

They were late in coming
This year,
The season's first Redstart
and the Crane.
The Geese had left in March
and haven't come yet again.

But I saw the Redstart today,
confirming the nip in the air
is no freak turn of weather
But something that's coming to stay.
The Peacock's been moulting from his treetop lair.
The children have picked each feather.

I have come out to give the dog a little turn.
The cold wraps itself around my throat.
The smoke rises to lamps from leaves left to burn.
It will be time soon for muffler and coat.

Crane and Redstart, Redstart and Crane,
The scent of wood smoke from leaves left to burn.
When birds that were gone come back again,
That's how I know when the seasons turn.

Fateh Singh Jasol

Help

He relies on me for I am his youth
This white-haired old man in the bed
As ill as he is he gives me a smile
So trusting yet somehow misled

For days and days I have cried and despaired
While trying to get myself heard
"He is a person not just tired bones"
Yet they pass by without a word

Nurses and doctors are all overworked
With not enough time to show care
My dad needs a smile and a few kind words
But all he receives is a stare

Later! We're busy! Won't be a moment!
We owe our ill people much more
Let's put ourselves in their shoes for a day
To see what we will have in store

Stop in your tracks all you carers of man
And let love flow into your heart
So next time my father cries out for help
You treat the whole man not the part

Ruthie Segal

Untitled

When God blew out a candle;
Life was breathed into a small child.
When God set the fields aflame;
Warmth was given to a homeless son.
When God hung a picture;
Inspiration was given to a dying artist.
When God picked a flower;
Gardeners were blessed with large blooms.
When God went out to play;
An athlete was given victory.
When God smiled;
The world rejoiced.

Kelly Gruver

Hugs

Someone prescribed six hugs a day,
  he said I'd feel better in many a way.
A hug that would make me feel good inside,
  would always bring sunshine right by my side.
A hug that would make me feel secure,
  would keep me as cozy as a foxes fur.
A hug that would make me happy and gay,
  would bring good memories for many a day.
A hug that would bring me to a smile,
  would make me feel good for more then awhile.
A hug that would make my pain disappear,
  would also keep me away from my fears.
A hug that would make my loneliness expire,
  would make my heart forget the desire.
Six hugs a day, agree I do,
  some medicines aren't always taboo.
So thank-you my friend for passing this along,
  hugs from me to you all the day long.
    Regina Sherman

Precious Times

Even the most precious of times fade fast.
But all I ever wanted was for you to say "our love could last"
All I ever dreamt of was everything you are.
You're not just another guy I had meet in a bar

You were the light that made me shine.
I would have given you the world, if you would have taken the time.
I remember every moment we ever spent together.
I remember the love we shared and all the times
I wish we could have been together.

But you wouldn't give me the chance.
Even though I could see you wanted to with your every glance.
It could have been so right.
But you chose to turn out the light.

So I'm standing all alone with a heart full of hate.
Wondering how something so wrong could feel so right.
Wondering how you could put your arms around me and then
In a heartbeat fight me with all of your might.
    Jackie Pidgeon

Unsuspecting

Those brown eyes of yours was what first caught mine.
There was a certain twinkle to them that meant many things,
but it was difficult to tell what they held.
They had a hypnotic stare that would take my breath away
and make my heart beat ever so fast.
Those eyes were dangerous, for it caught not only me by surprise,
but also other women were intrigued by those deep, brown eyes.
Those eyes could break many hearts; for my heart was broken
by those very same eyes.
    Sheila Splichal

Threshold Of Forever

  Impatiently I wait; wanting that door to open,
The door beyond which all my loved ones wait;
knowing that soon I'll be there with them, all of
us together: and my beloved soul mate with whom
I've shared decades and moments; waiting for me
to be seated at that Splendid Table, Wait,
Listen, my Escort is here and I am eager to
pass thru.
    Velva Rosiere

A Highway Of Nature

An opening in a dark forest;
A road carved by nature's journey
From high in the hills.
Downward, winding, twisting, turning,
Cool, fresh, flowing water.
For how many years?
Ever since the glaciers passed—
Ever since a world was carved out.
A new world——carved by nature!
A world containing fish,
Amphibians, water fowl, rocks.

A world not planned for human-kind.
Yet we invade this world
And claim it as our own.
We cause the resident tenants to hide,
Making them fearful as we strut and swagger.
As we take over Nature's possession.
But the day will soon be upon us
When, along this water-course of Nature,
We will be turned into a tiny speck!
    Donald Burns

Rhapsody Of Nature

  The stars lean over the balcony of heaven, kissing fiery
fingers of dying embers from a lonely campfire... its sparks
leaping toward indigo skies.

  The Old Gentleman in the Moon, shakes himself from
slumber, blinks his sleepy little eyes, and peers from behind a
wispy bank of clouds...

  Far, far away, a lone wolf wails an eerie mating call
...a wily, sly fox slinks its way to his lair... an eagle in flight
makes a diving thrust, seeking an animal of prey... a gentle
breeze whispers an echo as it wends its way thru the canyons.

  The Rhapsody of Nature is in full revue
...the Old Gentleman in the Moon takes a bow

  To lowly earthlings, from his high, lofty throne
...and now

  Clasping his hands, he heaves a deep sigh
...radiating his mystical glow

  From the Great Milky Way, to Saturn and Mars
...touching emerald valleys below.
    Elga Haymon White

Eternal Fear

  Humans fear the unknown place that comes in contact with
their space. Spirits float, Angels fly, and the Demons from hell can
burn you alive. God and Devil fight back and forth for control
of an unknown force. Winged demons fly through the night,
carrying condemned souls to their rightful eternal fright. Angels
lead the hopeful souls, to the passionate light, that their peaceful
future holds. Lost souls are floating through the air. Drifting in a
realm called Sheol. In this place they must stay, and wait for the
light to come and carry them away. Humans fear the unknown
place that wraps itself through time and space. In this place,
they must learn, how to face the fear all alone.
    Jennifer L. Hambleton

Crack Kills, You And Your Family

I want to tell you about my brother's best friend,
He will take away your money until you have none left to spend.

He will make you do things you have never done before,
I'm talking about robbing people, houses and stores.

He will take away your confidence, sanity and responsibility,
As for now, you have no personality!

He will take you away from your friends and your family,
His stem is powerful, can't you see?

He will say, "Take one more hit, it's okay,
I'm going to kill you anyway"!

He will pull you towards him night or day,
You're hooked on him, he will always stay.

Someone has to stop him, he's too far gone,
He doesn't fit in, he doesn't belong!

His name is Crack, he's no damn good,
If my brother would have only understood!

I love you Brother, deep down inside,
Get help from crack and you will never have to hide!

Cathy L. Thornton

My Valentine

The loneliest day of the year, is just three days from here.
My calendar's marked, with a big red heart;
Cards with lace will be sent to cheer.

There'll be flowers and candy and chained lavaliers,
Velvet box with a ring, and a love song he'll sing,
A sweater of red in finest cashmere.

A book of treasured verse, a crimson satin purse,
They'll sit across a table, spend as much as he is able,
Sip the finest of wine, as the couples converse.

These are dreams of each sweetheart and as they meet Cupid's dart.
There'll be holding of hands and then they'll dance;
Going home as a last resort.

The one on my mind doesn't do valentines;
He'd bring raw fish, to fulfill my wish,
And I'd write him, hearts with rhymes.

We'd work in the yard and I'd make him a card.
"Let me love you", he'd say, "in my own way."
While eating fish, we discuss the Lord.

Now things have changed, it's been arranged;
As he passes by, he stops to say "Hi"
Visits her and leaves me pained.

Julia Dixon Collett

To Choose A Hero

I've heard all this talk about heroes
movie stars and athletes, and that's fine
Now if you will allow me, I'll tell you about mine

He came back from the World War two in 1945
Shot up in the war, was just glad to survive
Three years of healing before he could come home
Walking on a wooden leg, his real one was gone

He would ride a horse, or climb a windmill
Flank big calves, he had determination and will
I've seen him in awful pain
But he would keep on working, never complain

I've seen him dig post holes and build a corral
Rope and doctor a wild-eyed cow
I've worked right beside him as a boy and as a man
He taught me to love and appreciate this great land

This Great American is a hero to me
He's grown old now, and slowed a little with time
And if I were to choose a hero He Would Be Mine.

Leon Autrey

Sedona

Majestic wonders of beauty
surround the sacred lands
concealing the secret legends
of the ancient tribes

A hidden but mighty force
emanates from within the fiery towers
releasing profound wisdom,
provoking the strength of all human emotions.

Dignified and bold
this reflection of the past
teaches man to be aware,
to search for the true meaning of life.

Mindy Hoppe

Escape

While a thousand violins begin to play
    bits of colored glass
Become part of your embrace
    Blame it on love
Do it while you're still young
When the time is right take the first step.
Write with compassion about deceit
Without complaining
Pain is only another name for pleasure
    keep my secrets
    enjoy your games
For I have stopped caring about
the best route for escape.

D. Wolford

Fat Ladies Can't Jump!

Oh, to leap as a graceful gazelle,
    So high, you can touch the sky!
To frolic and romp, with your feet in the air,
    What a wonderful thing to try!

The more I watch a willow dance,
    The more I think "I" can be!
Forgetting the reality that weighs me down,
    It's impossible physically!

So, I try to leap in "any" style,
    But, too soon I come down hard!
I forgot, when I stepped off my "mind's trampoline"...
    And meeting the ground left me jarred!

Oh, to feel light and buoyed as the wind,
    A balloon...drifting away!
But my body is chained to the ground by pounds,
    And my heaviness stands in the weigh!

Melissa Ryane-Miller

What Is A River?

A little girl came up to me and asked, "What is a River?"
A river, I replied, is a messenger traveling foreign lands.
Or maybe a river is an artist, carving sculptures of rock.
Or perhaps a river is a snake that bends, and twists back
On itself, and winds through the desert sand.
Or maybe a river is a never-ending path on which many travelers journey.
Or perhaps a river is a voice, whispering and bubbling
And overflowing with laughter.

Amy Kangas

Sugar Sands

Though heat of night prevails,
there is coolness in the salty air.
Blue waters pound the shores
with timeless waves that roll,
smashing to their death,
their screaming roar to end.
Sands of sugar white,
like snow flakes in the dark
let patterns of moon light,
altered by wind and summer clouds,
dance against sea oats, that also
gently dance, as they succumb their bodies, to the wind and
sand.
The glow of eastern skies reveal,
rays of gold from breaking morn,
Ghostly shadows disappear
as waves calmed the breaking roar.
The wind as playful as a child has
formed new patterns on the land,
new summer hideaway, new life,
new sparkling hills of sugar sands.

Elisa F. Austin

Everlasting Love

Like the two lovers, Romeo and Juliet, they met one day,
Neither of them knowing that their paths would go the same way.
They learned to love and cherish each other,
And the bond between then grew stronger and stronger.

They thought their love would last forever,
But one day she decided it had to be over.
The man did not know what went wrong,
But he decided that he would be strong.

Days went by and his feelings did not die,
Because he knew that one day they would again pass each other by.
She never knew that he felt the same way,
And that his love for her was there to stay.

But as fate would have it,
Things never happened that way.
And he is still hoping and praying,
That she will come back one day.

Glen D'Souza

Old Man

At the beginning of time only pain and love were created
and time started at the moment of the first passion

I still hear the sound of crushing stars
I still feel the warmth of your look
I still touch the gentleness of your fingers
I still taste fire of your kisses
I still flow in the air of the passion and desire

I still experience the penetration of our souls:
it is embedded deeply in my existence

Only God alone knows
why true is best expressed by tears -
and infinite pain

On the grave of my youth high grass has grown
but I still live from penetration of our souls

At the beginning of the time only love and pain were created:
therefore true love is best expressed by tears
and infinite pain

I know it is infinite love

R. Baycar

I Can't Be Rich

I can't be rich.
I would worry his love is for my wealth.
But, why is he looking at me?
Already I question his motives.
We have not met.
I could introduce myself; start a conversation.
He could tell me about the food I'm wearing.
Am I afraid of rejection?
I'm already alone.
Duplicity?
I've certainly had enough of that.
Am I waiting for perfection?
Why not?
It's still morning.

Lisa R. Hall

The Thunderstorm

The thunder told me it was coming,
The lightning told me it was near,
And by the sounds all around me,
I knew the thunderstorm was here.

The storm creeping upon me,
The sky full of light,
The rain coming down,
Just like one big sheet of white.

The sounds of the thunderstorm,
Hearing it roar all around,
The crash of the rain,
Hissing as it reached the ground.

The wind loudly yelling,
As it reached around the wall,
As though listening to a question,
And then yelling back an answer against the rising squall.

And when all is silent,
And when the wind no longer yells,
And rain and lightning and thunder gone,
This scene, to all who wish, of this storm tells.

Molly E. Whitehurst

"Grateful Then Ourselves"

Truly there's a source of power most indeed.
Which causes a tree to grown out of a little seed.
Or how the sky can change its form from light to dark.
A horse looks like a dog, but only one can bark.
A cat runs after a mice with such tremendous speed.
A body when it is thirsty takes water for its needs.
The moon within the sky apart from all the stars.
Who gave them all a name from Jupiter to Mars?
And who shall keep the land from going under water?
The same who tells a seed to become a son or daughter.
And who can tell the wind what time it needs to blow?
The one who knows thee answer to which way it will go.
Then as the wind returns to the place where it is stored.
The heavens seem to open and, rain is truly poured.
But, in the forth season, the rain will turn to snow.
The flowers all will die but, again there soon to grow.
But, all these little things have somehow come to be.
Just like the best the beateth inside of you and me.
These things which been written in the book that's on the shelf.
For all these have come from powers, greater then ourselves.

Taniko Turner

Love

Love means you care for someone
You don't just like them as you would like anyone
It means you are kind to them
And you cherish them like you cherish your own life
You think about them all the time
And you'll never let them go as long as you shall live
Even if they are sick or gone you love them like they were your
own flesh and blood.
Love means that you find that special someone
And you love with all your soul until the day you die because
true love is as good as gold.
That's what love means.

Kimberly Sommerkamp

Seeking Peace

The search for peace begins with you
For to yourself you must be true

Exploring deep within your soul
There you will find peace and become whole

The center of your being is where peace doth lie
It's a feeling of elation; a natural high

You can ride on this feeling 'til the end of the Earth
For the feeling of peace gives a sense of rebirth

God gave us peace as a miracle token
Given this; we can hear His word that is spoken

For when God lives in the depth of your heart
You'll find you've had peace from the very start

Tammi S. Schuchard

The Lord Is My Shepherd

The Lord is my shepherd whom I shall always have.
He died on the cross to save me from the grave.

He will be coming back to the earth soon.
I don't know when, but it could be night or noon.

I hope you'll be ready when He decides to come,
so we can go together to our special home.

Shirley Tassler

Corruption

Evil is the thin-lipped smile on the greedy man's face
He smiles because he knows you don't have what it takes
Can't learn trickery fakery

You must burn with the will to grasp the crooked prize
with lip-smacking relish; and the snake-hooded eyes
that shield him from truth

He doesn't feel mother earth clean in new day's dew
His domain is a swamp-steamy marsh, drawing him into
the deceit of golden power

He's secretly lonely, howling insanely in fear and despair
Fear you'll reveal him; despair because he no longer cares
for his soul or yours

When he looks out and spies you hovering close to his lair
tempted to envy his piggily hoard, his urge is to lure
you down dirt-deep with him

He'll falsely promise whatever your heart desires — flatter
if you'll only enter his trashy heap. Say it doesn't matter
that dishonesty stinks

Evil exalts when innocence slippery-slides into the mire.
Only slightly less pleasing are those who resist hell-fire
and fall into despair anyway

Rowlanda Jones

Flash Dancer

Comet, comet, burning bright
Thru the darkest depths of night
Suffer all with eyes to see
Your great and grandeur mystery

Inspire me with your awesome light
As you travel thru the night
Reveal your pathway thru the stars
Tell me all you know of Mars

Comet, comet, streaking light
Newest star to brighten the night
Teach me the way that I should go
Show me what I want to know

A new generation will see your face
On your next journey thru time and space
But I'll always remember your milky way tail
And dream of the stars that dance on your trail

Comet, comet, burning bright
Take me with you on wondrous flight
As round and round the sun you go
To return in 15,000 years or so

Cheryl Phillips

Narrative Of A Secret Admirer
(A Young Woman's Point Of View)

A man I see, who never sees me, who will never know me,
Wandered into my life, unbeknownst to him,
I see in his eyes a beauty, tenderness within

I remain discreet, concealing my foolish love
Keeping blind faith we will meet
  'neath a twilight sky above

The way that he walks, his stride so sublime, puts me in awesome
Shock! Never fails, every time

His dark brown hair,
  unsuccessful in its battle to hide those fine eyes,
Gray as the sky are his eyes it seems, sparklin' like raindrops
  during a spring storm, never losin' that gleam,
  transcending anything I dreamed

This man I see, who will
Never meet me, who will
(Missing line)
Never love me, is my fondest daydream,
  though "It is not meant to be,"
Nothin's known for sure now, Nothin's carved in stone for
My fine man and me.

Eddie P. Alvarado

This River Of Life

Here we will go and will flow in this river of life,
Gently we're passing among the rocks we have strived,
There I can see all the trees that meet by the stream,
Trees that have drunk of the stream are a strong as can be.

As we are flowing in this river of life,
I want to be still water and rest in a pond,
There I will gather all thoughts and life unto me,
All peace that comes from the stream...tranquility.

There will be those who will take from this river of life,
Destroying those who has embrace and is of the pond,
Sweetness once dwelt in this still water pond,
Bitterness tries to take over put yet I must flee.

Others will come and will see how the pond has become,
Taking the time they will restore to me, innocence,
Keeping me others will gather by my side and sleep,
Waiting for peace and tranquility that comes from the stream,
But it is time to move on and look toward the sea.

Sandra L. G. Baez

Untitled

The hat flew off and tumbled,
tossed and turned,
funneled down the street.

The window washer shaves her legs,
cuts herself,
and smiles.
The post-man delivers mail,
caught up in worries for his child,
sick with leukemia and no insurance.
Countless bugs awaken each day,
soon to be smashed on windshields
or slapped by offended picnickers.
Glassy-eyed housewives push shopping carts
down yawning aisles of vacant shelves.
Awkward mousy girls enter schools each day
prepared to be shoved and belittled.
In Pakistan a boy gets killed
for questioning authority.

On TV the soap has ended,
and mother cries.

Erica M. Doyle

Rose Who Am I

To be but a tender flower
To which but a gentle Petal
Which sends its gentle fragrance.
To be but a gentle flower.
How worst but would I grow.

Tell me who should I be.
Shall I be a gentle seedling.
Blowing in the wind.
Or where should I lay myself to rest.

Even do when I rest.
I do not rest in sleep.
But set to do as I may.
But when should I do it.

As I find myself in my sister flower but a rest.
But should I say is it now.
I feel my self its so sweet and rosy.
I feel it ever so strange
For is it happening now.
Never again to blow in the wind.
I shall now be what I am to be.

J. P. Kenneally

My Day

It was raining that spring morning
My day looked gloomy and gray.
I was a little old lady with a walker
Headed straight for a closed door.
The door opened, a young man stood there,
He looked neither different nor dour.
As I crossed the threshold, I stumbled,
Righted myself and flirted,
"I am falling for you"
Right back he came as if on queue
"Lady, you have made my day."
I thanked him and went my way.
It was still raining outside
But my day was no longer gray.

Nancy Gay Hughes

Dear Patsy

Dear Patsy, although you and I are far apart,
Your lovely name remains in my lonely heart.
Though you may be a thousand miles away,
I could still see your smiles each day.

Your lovely hair and beautiful voice,
Are none to compare to one's only choice.
Your eyes are hazel and they may appear sad,
But with you, my heart is always feeling glad.

You who are so far across the wide blue sea,
Where I'm always longing and yearning to be.
No matter what the future may be for us,
Let us take it as if it were for thus.

I'm closing my letter to you this way,
And wishing you a lovely Christmas day.
So sending my love always a friend,
May our loving friendship never end.

Pearl W. S. Lambert

Black Or White?

Black is a Mysterious color
Like it's trying to hide something or
someone
Black is deceiving not knowing what's
going to happen
What's evil Black or White?
Many people would say black, but I would
say white, "cause white is blinding, not
being able to see past it or through it.

Sara Bassett

Direction

Twilight still and twilight broken,
As for me I go unspoken.
Hands shall pluck me to the heavens
And the eagles guide my flight.

Up from Earth the Wolves come hunting,
Exhausting beast so confronting.
Like the Vultures they pull me under,
Fastening my feet to Hell.

But the Harpies aren't so evil,
Pull me up for retrieval,
Then unwilling drop me on the wings of Heaven
And fly, I do, to safer ground.

Such a Lord in spacious Heaven,
Helps me choose the better path.
I shall stay with wing shaped sandals
And join the Gods of allopath.

Lisa Smith

Manchild

Can this be my child?
He who lies in slumber beside me,
His legs and arms askew,
His head resting on an open palm?

Can it be his voice I hear as his mind trips...
Lightly, on events I have no part of.
His dream world?

Can it be? Oh yes it is...
My name he calls when there is want, need, love
For I am his mother, lover, his mate..
His woman, his wife and he is all to me.
My man.

Wilhelmina Heyliger

Blue

Blue is the color of the Arctic winds blowing
Blue is the time of winter when it's snowing
  It's spring now, the bluebirds are calling,
    To let the world know that the snow has stopped falling
The river and streams are peacefully flowing

Blue is the color of the clouds in the sky
Blue is the rain that passes us by
  Come now, let us swim in the sea,
    Let us fly like the birds, happy and free
What a peaceful experience to be up so high

Blue is the color of the cool breeze blowing
Blue is the easy thought of knowing,
  The birds are flying happy and free,
    Looking down and smiling at the fish in the sea
They will be smiling until it starts snowing,

The birds will head southbound,
  Cheerful and knowing,
    That they will return when it has stopped snowing
    Troy Meyer

My Mother's Love

My mother is a sweet spirit. Shows her love for me
when she holds me in her arms, soft and tenderly.
When God chose my mother, I'm thankful I got you.
Your love flows unconditionally as he wants it to.
Words cannot express how special you make me feel.
Mom, hoping you know my love for you is real.
God knew exactly who I needed. Blessed me with his best.
Your beauty and sense of humor out-dazzle all the rest.
Always busy using talents God gave to you.
Still never too busy to give a hug or two.
Beautiful things you sew make home a cozy place.
A labor of love. I can see it in your face.
My mother's love is special. Nothing can compare.
Thank God for my mother's love. We feel it everywhere.
    Linda L. Jones

Mission Of Love

In your sorrow you have flown
  like an eagle to measureless heights.

There you rested above the storm
  in the burning aurora of His Presence.

In the silence of this encounter
  He kindled your soul in fires of His love.

So that in the morning's wakening
  your radiant luminous hope

Flashed far down the dew drenched valleys.
  His songs of love vanished all fears.

He reached out His strong Hands to you.
  His touch inflamed your spirit into high thoughts.

He bid you go forth and seek
  the inner glory of each soul.

Discover every separateness
  as though it was a spring.

Dig about it
  and make the living waters flow.
    Lucille Marie Nuncia Geise

The Stolen Love

Your movements and Your soul's full of grace,
forgotten waltzes returning to my ears.
I see clear eyes, I see Your lovely face,
I hear again Your inner, hidden tears.

You choked again from unexpected grief,
You were upset and could not rest and sleep;
when love is crushed by iceberg or by reef,
and drowned deeply like a cracking ship.

Since Love has stolen by Your close friend,
Your heart I'm keeping as a piece of gold.
I'm feeling guilty for the tragic end;
forgive me, darling, it was not my fault!

Your movements and Your soul's full of grace,
forgotten waltz's returning to my ears.
I see clear eyes, I see Your lovely face,
I hear again Your inner, hidden tears.
    Isaac Milgram

Comets

In ancient times comets were misunderstood.
Man did not know from whence they came.
Blight, plague, famine and other misfortunes no good.
They thought were caused by them and quick to blame
Were they who understood little astronomy.
They could not cast their gaze upon the stars
And see with telescopic clarity
Olympus Mons, tallest mountain on Mars
Or view the glowing gas and starlit dust
Of light years away faroff galaxies.
To early man a comet surely must
Have seemed an omen heralding tragedy.
Too bad they could not stellarly explore
And tell the superstitious dinosaur.
    Randolph M. Murphy

Open Your Eyes and See

Open your eyes and see the beauty of nature,
See the mountainous regions,
Their majestic landscape flows like running water in a river
  flowing with endless rapids,
See the hills run longer and longer until they just seem to fade away,
See the prairies that appear within the mountains,
Their tranquility spreads throughout the entire mountainside,
See the oranges and reds yearning to poke their heads out of
  the clouds to form a brilliant sunset,
See how peaceful and full of harmony the world looks from up here,
No roads, no wires, no houses, no lights,
This is the perfect world.
    Joseph K. Prior

The Way of Life

One spring morning God the Father
walked very quietly through the forest.
The tree branches whispered in wind.
It is nice to be alive. The birds are singing.
"Thank God the winter is over. Happy days
have returned." One lady bug, one bee,
and one fly flew on the hand of God and
thanked him, just for to being alive.
God said, "All my children in the world
must learn that all living things need love,
care and respect. This is the way of life.
If you learn this, my children, you will know
in your heart that love and life go hand in hand."
    Selma Schwarz

Martyr Of

I'm the martyr of your unconditional love,
Something I need very little of.
Pull the thoughts all from inside,
I wait while you ponder of where to hide.
My domain is limitless,
Unfortunately in it I uphold no bliss.
Time's refusal to say anything to me,
Makes me the martyr that here you see.

Elizabeth J. Bohler

What If...Poem

What if pain did not exist,
Would it be better or worse,
I think it would be a curse.

What if pain did not exist,
God gave us pain for a reason,
To know the limitation of every single person.

What if pain did not exist,
People would push themselves too far,
Until a mournful family prayed "au revoir."

What if pain did not exist,
Would it be better or worse,
I think it would be a curse.

Kyle Dennis

On Someone Else's Wedding Day

Funny, the things I remember
When I look back upon that day.
That day we drove to the wedding
Through that cozy town I've since forgotten the name of.
When the Sun was shining, we bought those crackers, in the blue box,
At the gas station where we stopped.
They were spicy, at first, I thought.
You said they were stale.
You had too much of a good thing, you had enough.
You could no longer stomach it,
You realized you no longer felt good.
I guess it goes way back, to when the communication stopped.
It might have happened
When we stopped sharing the fun times.
There's the possibility, perhaps,
The pay was stretched too thin.
It could have been the sheets, beige really was quite drab.
You said "It just got old, the spice was gone."
I no longer felt good and was left
With a bitter taste in my mouth.

Susan Schuett-Grote

To My Love

Cry when you cry! Hurt when you hurt!
Love as you love! This is how deeply, how strongly, my love,
how compassionate, how my love transcends all barriers and
cuts straight to the soul.
It lives in my loins, in my sweat and tears, in my every thought
and emotion, my love, visible and invisible, heavenly, devilish,
jazzy and soulful, my love, bitter and sweet, hot and cold,
moving and changing, with you and for you, with you and
without, always my love, my love!

Quinton Holloman

Shells

There are shells of many different colors
There are purples, reds, blacks, oranges, blues, peaches
and many other colors too.

Sometimes you could hear the ocean and
other times you could hear the animals in the ocean
Shells can be happy or they can be sad

Shells can be shiny like the ni'ihau or they
can be dull like the cowrie that is worn out.

Some can be round or they can be oval
Some can be big some can be small
Some can have living creatures in them and
some might not

All Shells Are Beautiful!!

Leialoha Hurwitz

The Top!

You stand at the top looking down,
You wonder what path to take.
The choices you see are infinite, yet you decide.
You decide your path and prepare to go.
Your palms sweat, your heart races, and your legs
Start to tingle.
You wonder were you will end up,
Even though you know were you are going.
Suddenly you are Off!
You concentrate not to stumble,
But you fall, then realize something.
You must keep on!
You are scared all the way through
Then finally reach the end.
You look back and think how electrifying
That it was,
And decide to go again!

Joseph Micek

Heartache

Dedicated with love to my little brother, Roger
He stands on a cliff, his face to the sky.
He's there, he's there, but why, oh why?.
He knows he is here, his love he has lost.
His heart, it is broken, it's cold as the frost.
Forget her, forget her, he tells to his mind.
To his soul, to his body, he begs thee, be kind.
The wind in his hair, the roar in his ears,
The blood in his veins, the salt of his tears.
As he thinks of her, he looks to the sky above.
I must die to join her, my woman, my love.
He walks to the edge and then he looks down.
He leaps to the cold water, where his heart will drown.

Jackie Robinson

Fear Of The Unknown

As I run wild with fear,
my thoughts and hopes are quite unclear.
The steady beating of my heart,
makes me want to fall apart.
Sweat is running down my face,
wishing I were in outer space.
Taking the blame for all to come,
I know there is so much I must overcome.
Wiping my tears with a trembling hand,
feeling alone and somewhat off hand,
now that I know that I can understand
maybe I can wake up from my horrible dreamland!

Sandra R. Kurup

Untitled

If you give an artist the eyes of a blind man, will he still be able to paint the colors of life? If you give a musician the ears of a deaf man, will he still be able to play the melodies that we love? And if you give a sculptor the hands of a machine, will he still be able to create the objects of desire? If the artist can see the colors as vividly as he can paint, then he needs not his eyes. If the musician can hear the music in his heart, then his ears are useless to him. And if the sculptor can create beauty with the love he feels within him, he needs not the hands he has. If you take the water from a rose, will it wilt and die, leaving its withered petals behind? If you take the riches from a man, will he crumble down, in shame and misery? And if you take the wings from a bird, will it still be able to fly, soaring high above the heavens? If the rose can survive on man's love for nature, then drought is no threat to it. If man can be content without materialistic possessions, then riches are no obstacles. And if the bird can float on a cloud of hope, then its wings were never needed. All of us have the artist, the musician, and the sculptor within us; We need not what we are given, but what we believe in. And all of us are the rose, the man, and the bird; The love within our souls surpass any of the streams that feed the rose, the riches that support the man, and the feathery wings that help the bird to fly.

Kanchan Sakhrani

Lynn

Sensitive, loving, caring, kind,
Mother of James.
Lover of plants, animals, and family.
Who finds happiness in cooking, talking on
  the phone and teaching.
Who needs her children, husband, and pets.
Who gives joy, freedom and money.
Who fears the dark, to be alone, and high places.
Who would like to see her mother again,
  Elvis, and grandchildren.
Who enjoys, sleeping, living and just being
  a mother.
Who likes to wear blue jeans, shorts, and
  dresses.

Mommy

James Misita

"Life"

I look at life in different ways
The many hours and the endless days
I see the good and I see the bad
Some happy people and some are sad
I see trees and flowers and a lot of joy
Little girls playing or a little boy
To hear the rain and see the snow
So much in life for us to know
Yet life can sometimes bring us pain
And still we have a lot to gain
To look at things in a different way
Our lives could change from day to day
To reach out and touch a life
A friend, a husband or a wife
I am glad I came to be
To see and hear and just be me.

Grace Ingenito

If Tomorrow Never Comes

If tomorrow never comes, would you hold onto my heart,
Forever loving me, if tomorrow never comes.

In the dawn of early light, resting throughout the night,
birds chirping
Hold onto all we loved, let comfort sing.

High noon, cool shadows crossing paths along the way
Ever present laughter, caress this passing day.

Evening dims to shades of purple, golden hues and
periwinkle, quiet fills the air;
And thoughts of you, no one to compare, thoughts of love
are everywhere.

If tomorrow never comes, I will hold onto your heart,
Forever loving you, if tomorrow never comes.

Elaine Shimskie

Jean-Louis Barrault

Trapped in two dimensions on a flat empty stage,
Defining his space by the span of his arms,
He called the third into being by tacit command
For air to solidify

Artistic medium: Motion on void,
Four dimensional figure;
Time: Heartbeat iambic;
Title: Mime.

Ivo Corday

A Day At The Beach

At the beach children play in the sand.
Building castles and burying people.
The ocean is blue like the sky and the
ocean has the saltiest water in the world.
The beach is open from sun up to sun down.
Different fish in the ocean from guppies to sharks.
On the beach you find treasures from sea shells
to hermit crabs. I look out my window and see the
sun rise over the ocean and see the people fill
the beach. Then it gets dark and I see the sun setting
over the ocean so beautifully.

Ashley Miles

Spirit

Into the evening shadows
The mounting darkness of night
From the deep recesses of ones mind
Dimming the illuminating light
Venture forth into the blackness
With faith and courage as your guide
Let he who is brave step forward
To lead us back into the dawn's warm light

Eric Tanaka

Poetry

Poetry is words that swirl into my mind and
fly down fast as if a slow bird.
They come down like rain but
leave with the sunshine
and all of a sudden there's a big bang
with words on my paper that
emerges into a poem.

Jeanna Marie Galasso

Rise

Above the hatred, the jealousy
Past the weak, the petty.
You rise, from the coming of dawn
to the slumber of the sun.
Around the bend, over the mountain
you rise, to a new me.
Forget the past, seek the day
In which life is lived and love is bred.
You rise, to quench the thirst,
And satisfy the hunger to live.
I do not suggest, I do not beg.
I command - Rise!

Matt Snow

A Road

Many aspects does love have, some we never see
But they're there, hidden and secret, growing between a friend and me
For I liked her, but she not me, at least not in that way.

I never ever really saw it, it came without me knowing it
Yet, through it all, I guess I knew, you really couldn't stop it
And then one day she came to me and she began to say:

I know you really like me, it shows in what you do
and you know well that I do not have feelings for you
But I think we both have been fooled by a feeling quite secret.

For since the day we met each other, our relationship has grown
And today we finally realize, our relationship is its own
And we can tell each other things we couldn't without it.

It doesn't tie us together, but provides a pal and friend
It knows no bounds, it's kind and sweet, it really doesn't end
And though we haven't seen it, it's probably always been.

And if I could've answered, I think I would've said:
Our friendship has been like a windy road which has led
You and me on a journey I would gladly take again.

Brian Guthrie

All Is Well

The sun fell down and the moon picked it up.
The streams went dry so the clouds began to cry.
The air was hot so the wind began to blow.
The sky was alone so a rainbow came to it.
The grass was green and the flowers were in bloom.
The deer was sad so the rabbit made it laugh.
The lion joined the fox in a game of hopscotch.
The bears began to play in a field of yellow hay.
Then the sun fell asleep as did all the other things.
And the moon stayed up just to see that all went well.

Kelly Carroll

The Phantom

The Phantom had no life.
He had no will.
He had no reason because he was set to kill.
He had feelings like everyone and fell in love.
She was the one he had been dreaming of.
She called him her Angel of Music,
the one her father had told her to marry.

She had a dream of him,
and saw the beauty within.
A hideous looking man who was hard to understand.
She couldn't understand why he was not acting like a regular man.
And all we know this very day.
She refused his proposal.
But she loved him in her own special way.
And up in heaven they will stay.

Jessica Harcrow

Untitled

As I lay,
my thoughts drift into a mindless confusion of past, present, and future.
The happenings of the past are now mere memories.
The present, secure and wise,
lingers not in front nor in back of you but within you.
The future holds nothing but mystery,
one can only guess at.
As I lay, my eyes close to open my imagination.
It is the one with the strongest, most vivid imagination who
becomes the wisest and happiest.
He is aware, yet dreaming,
cautious yet daring,
old yet young.
Because imagination is imagining,
it is anything and everything you can imagine.
As I lay, I grow weak.
A wide yawn uses the last ounce of strength out of my tired body.
I just lay there, my thoughts vanished,
and though my face wears no expression, I am content;
weak yet content.

Amelia Hileman

True Love

When to tell him how I feel
    the love I have for him is real.
My love is not built on lust,
    but, a new relationship built on trust.
Whenever he feels in disappear
    I'll give him a hug, and let him know I care.
True love is a hard thing to define.
    When you're in love with a certain someone he's
    always on your mind.
Your love can be near or a thousand miles away.
    When you find him you'll want him to always stay.
I can't wait to tell you
    if you only knew
It took me long to say it
    my true love is you.

Jill Stainthorpe

Do You See It?

He is so real to me.
I can hear Him in the thunder.
I hear His mighty power saying, "I'm here."
Do you hear it?

I see the beauty of Him in the flowers coming alive,
Saying, "See my beauty."
Do you see it?

I see Him in the rain as it cleans the earth
And brings forth the life in the Spring.
It feels so clean, the spring rain.
Do you see it?

The mighty power of His thunder brings forth the rain
That brings forth the beauty that He made.
I see **Jesus** everywhere!
Do you see it?

Sue Yates

Black

Black is the color of a witch's hat,
Black is the color of a witch's cat.
Black is the color of a starry night sky,
Black is the color of a very bad lie.
Black is the color of a lonely heart.

Katharine A. Michener — Age 9

Turmoil

The world is spinning around me,
In twists and turns like grease in water.
Ebony and ivory and gray.
Color explode in a violent hell.
Hey, could you slow down?
But no one understands.
Frustration and questions and things in between.
Are caught up in the massive snowball effect.
That tumbles and twists into the unknown.
I fall, I fall, down into the unknown abyss, I fall

Grayness befalls me, and I try to stay awake, but I'm slipping.
Drifting up and sideway, left to right, I can't stop
I drift, I drift, away into the unknown, I drift

Help, I cry out into the darkness,
No one understands.
A breeze blows as I go off track.
Loved one I once could see
Grow dim in the swirling abyss.
I try to reach them, but I can't.
I cry, I cry, all alone, I cry.

Josh Williams

Our Prayer

Heavenly father, savior divine,
Take these poor hearts of ours and make them thine,
This is the prayer we pray today.
Come into our hearts, come in to stay.

We are remiss, and we are poor
In help divine, but you stand at the door
And knock, hoping to be let in,
To help us to victory and save us from sin.

You stand and knock, we turn a deaf ear.
You say, "Let me in, I'll turn your fear
To a great triumph," we begin to pay heed,
Because we know we have a hungering need.

Oh Heavenly Father, do come in we pray,
We are ready now to let you stay,
We are tired of this sinful grind.
It is about to blow our mind.

Heavenly Father, Savior divine,
You have taken our hearts and made them thine,
We are glad we took time to pray
You have come in and you are in to stay.

Edgar P. Boslaugh

A Pressed Flower

Although your days have long since past,
In my mind you will forever last.
Like a yellow rose from a special time,
Pressed now between pages in a cherished book of mine.

You were the bloom with a scent so enticing,
Arousing hope and desire, a lure so enchanting.
To you I came and did submit,
Held captivated by the aroma which you did emit.

Your freshness as your petals did unfold,
Increased your beauty which time could not hold.
And now I keep you tucked away,
Within the pages of my heart, there to stay.

Patti Weber

Old Yeller

Wild
Long, dirty snout with a cut off ear
A dingy yellow covers him from head to toe
His dark brown eyes stare endlessly
He walked into their life as suddenly as an earthquake
He feels like a ping-pong ball, one minute he's getting kicked,
the next minute he's playing with Little Arliss in the drinking water spring
He finally gets accepted in and feels superb
In the eyes of Travis, his dingy yellow takes on a golden glow
Although he helps out, Travis wishes he'd do more work
But he's like a determined turtle trying to get to sea, he never gives up
Yelping young Yeller attacks his duties and never makes even a whimper
He would tree the squirrels, chase the 'coons, and even protect the family from dangerous wild animals
He may smell like a brown, rotten tomato, but they still love him
He's like a bomb ready to explode, a bomb of joy
They wouldn't get half the work done without him
What would we do without Old Yeller

Jordan Guidry

Old Yeller

Yellow face with one ear short and one long
Slick-haired yellow fur covers his body
His paws and teeth fight off enemies
As protective as a spy with secret information
He likes to have Arliss's companionship and love while running
    through fields, hunting wild animals, playing in the water, and having a lot of fun
Fearless when protecting the people he loves
Clothed by a dingy yellow coat
I wish all dogs were as protective as him
Though no dog could ever replace Belle, Travis loves Old Yeller
This smart stray stole food supplies from strangers
Without him hunting and protecting would be more difficult
Smelling an intruder who is far away is easy for him
As brave as a soldier, he wards off the enemy
But he never harms Travis or his family
Old Yeller was a very smart dog

Julie Roy

Thoughts Of You

The sunlight on wildflowers, still wet with dew,
early in the morn.
The fluttering little heartbeat, life's greatest miracle,
of a baby not yet born.
The wind ever blowing, softly through vales,
and roaring 'round high mountain peaks.
The warm summer moon, lightly resting on the water,
in soft, pale, ivory streaks.
The musical sound of water, tumbling over rocks,
of a waterfall hidden from view.
Always filling my mind, these things of beauty,
when I turn to thoughts of you.

Rodney S. Wilson

A Teddy Bear's Prayer

Dear Great Teddy, in the sky, I have one wish and I'll tell you why.
Here I am sitting on an empty shelf, being lonely all by myself.
I want someone to take me home, so I can have a friend to call my own.
Someone to teach me right from wrong, and I can teach them to be strong.
Someone to give me lots of care, and I'll be the Best Darn Teddy Bear.
Someone to tuck me in warm at night, and keep me safe, if that's all right.
Someone to give me lots of hugs, and who won't throw me on the rugs.
I'll be good, just you wait and see, there's a lot of LOVE stuffed in me.
Oh Great Teddy, my wish came true, I promise I'll behave for you.
I got a friend to go to now, NOW I have someone who will LOVE ME, WOW!

Nancy Forsyth

Senior Citizen Syndrome

Standing by the window on the second floor
Gazing at the scenes outside below.
Respectfully submitted to their lives alone,
Actors out of work without a show.

Sitting at the checkerboard or playing cards,
Or dominos rattling for the pile.
Doleful with their tragedies of growing old,
Crying for their freedom all the while.

Crowded little cubicles aline the halls;
A prison to the tenants of their kind.
Lonely hours waiting from their cruel neglect
Cater to the wasting of their minds.

Asking one some questions in the sitting room,
He wondered why a stranger came to call.
From his chair he paused as if in retrospect
Of the winters, springs, summers, and of falls.

He said, "We often sit and wonder
If life or death is really all it seems;
Mostly we just sit here tending idle hours
In our easy chairs, with our dreams."

Paul S. Wood

Kiss

Your kiss is, I believe, that of all and none and that tangy-sweet
wind of the breath of every forever ever...
and I think that your lips hold everything I need in the entirety
of existence and beyond...all I know is they...all I shall never kiss,
all I shall ever kiss is held deep within their two parting fractions...
One as lovely and sensuous as other and neither without beauty...
they are the two parts of my heaven full and warm and forever
the only and forever the one thing, yet two, that will remain in my
dried up memory after I shall no longer embrace their bodies with
these of my own...
when this incredible kiss is a memory and I with you for ever and
never I shall truly be in heaven...

Aaron Spradlin

A Talk With Mother Earth

Thick clouds of mist fall down from the sky
Seeming to fill the air with a haunting lullaby.
The trees seem ghostly in the pale moonlight,
And I see no stars in the sky tonight.

Hush, tired earth, for you may rest now.
Forget your children and their wickedness somehow.
Touching you and seeing you, I feel your love so near;
I wish we could talk and your words I could hear.

When, oh when, will you be a happy mother?
You ache from the hate that people have for each other.
Your pain is great, your sorrows grievous,
Your tears rain down and your sores are numerous.

We need to take care of you, bind your wounds and dry your tears.
We must change our bad habits and let go of our fears.
If people love each other, that will change how you feel,
For only through love will your wounds really heal.

Stephanie Billings

False Images

As through dense fog, jumbled words, recklessly mated,
reveal only false images, when peered through intently.

Neither a savant or Nobelist I, but a stater of fact that
unordered words, such as these, make a poet no more than
an unskilled brush makes an artist.

Paul Siemen

Who Are We

We ask ourselves who are we
We are the women with open minds,
     open arms, and open hearts.
We are United Nations Women's Guild
     standing together with joined hands,
     sincere hearts for the same cause
The children of the world.

We hear the cries from these children, we
     feel the pain and shed tears for them.

Who are we...We hope every day with all
     our efforts and strength we the United
     Nations Women's Guild will continue to
     hear and help the children of the world.

Joan Al-Salihi

The Logger

As he stood among the timber you could see the contented look
in his eyes. His tall, tan, muscular body bore scars from his
battles with the forest. He knew the dangers and the pleasures
of the forest and found each day a challenge.

He started up the skidder breaking the overwhelming silence.
The sun broke through the clouds making the morning dew sparkle
on the brilliant colors of green. You could hear the cracking
and falling of trees as he maneuvered the skidder with ease,
making a path through the dense forest.

The sweat drenched his clothes as he worked he saw among the
deck, stripping the limbs from the trees mighty trunks. He
never stopped working even when nature slapped the rain against
his body. The rain carved its ways through the dirt, making
its own way down the mountain.

The coolness felt good on his tired body as the day was fading.
The fallen trees over the mountainside looked like a battlefield.
Taking off his hard hat he began his journey back to
civilization, looking forward to tomorrow.

Sally Greenwalt

When We Are Broken

Some say... Love is healing
Others say... Positive thinking is the key
Still others say... Miracles are needed

But I have found...
God is Love
Positive thinking is faith in God's plan
And God sends Miracles to show us
"Rainbows through our tears"

Wanda Timmons

Magic In The Glass

What's that ugly thing hiding in the glass?
Under the leaves and bits of grass?
Are you dreaming of adventure and magical things:

A trip to the moon that shines like diamond rings
And traveling afar on the back of a star?
Good night; sleep tight.
Wake up in the gentle morning light.

What's that beautiful thing on top of the glass ring?
Did your dreams come true?
And away he flew.

Margaret Hoofe

No Tomorrow

This world may have no tomorrow,
For each day brings new sorrow for the lost souls of today,
whose dreams have shattered away,
Looking through the dirty window panes,
of their UN-foreseen future.

Can't turn around, will not dare to look back.
Drug-dealer in the door-way selling crack,
to a young mother of three,
scarf on her head, skirt above her knee.
With a baby on her hip,
Clenching that almighty pipe to her lip.

Tic-toc-Tic-Toc minutes passing, seconds lasting.
Everybody's rushing to something,
never realizing there may be no tomorrow.

Wake up world, end the sorrow,
rejuvenate all your tired energy.
Start now—so our youth can have a history.

Teach them—Guide them—Educate them to remain free,
From the negative, directly walking into the positive.

Or there will be no tomorrow!

Brenda Hardy

The Barn

I drove past a deserted farm
  and saw this old deserted barn.
Standing back among the trees
  with pigeons nesting in its eves.

Sunflowers blooming bright and tall
  grew along the outer wall.
An open door with a broken hinge,
  invite all outsiders in.

Inside, the loft was full of hay
  perhaps where children once would play.
Food for a cow, a goat, or sheep
  and a stable where the horses sleep.

A farmer with his plow in hand,
  once had owned and farmed this land.
He built a house for his family,
  then built this barn among the trees.

When I see this farm I feel so sad.
  What happened to that dream he had?
We'll never know where this family went
But the old barn stands as a monument.

Mitchell Langford

Evolve

What spirit grabs my heart in clutch
As talons of the eagle know
Can carry off a soulful much
With wistful looks below?
I've soared the heights of passion's mount
But failed with feeling's test
Been battered, floored and down for count
But know it's for the best
Can desperate life be so replete
With blissful moment's calls
Yet dwell in darker parts discreet
To cushion all its falls?
I've no answer to the truth
But beg to steer from wrong
Like pulling lever in the booth
Will outcome play my song?
We youth grow tooth; Absorb all blows
Til' heaven send a dove
And my weathered heart well beaten goes
To be kept aloft by love!

M. Chanatry

Awakened

There was a creak when the door opened.
And you entered like a soft breeze on
a still summer day.

I heard the sound first, but alone,
still convinced no one was there.

Then a rustling of spirit as the air
stirred around me.

No doubt, a portent of change.
Welcoming the breeze I inhaled deeply.

Then, surprised by the sound of a sigh.
Perhaps the door opening a bit more?

I really couldn't tell.
My eyes were closed.

Bruce Angeli

Loss

Hope wrenched from the grip of a clinging heart
Leaves the heart still shaped to what it has lost.
Shallow sensation at first, a peppery stinging
Until depth of knowing invades feeling
As a sponge drinking up sweet hot liquid.

And for a time the heart knows no purpose of what it can hold.
It begs for a skeleton of meaning
To mold itself to
Like a blanket agrees to the form that it covers

Then the heart is so open the wind whistles through
Both moaning and shrill it sings in dark emptiness
The name of what's gone.
The saddest of songs, with too many words.

A heart that held hope and purpose and meaning
Will call and demand to have something to love.
Renewal and freedom are the needs that it speaks of
Fluttering and squirming of a wild thing that's held.
Memory's edge curls and looses its moistness.
It is life a heart asks for,
For life is to be.

Dianne B. Camp

Cataracts

"My eyes are dim and cannot see"
Used to be a song to me
Sung by college gals and guys
With blurry, bleary, beery eyes.

They taught me there, now please don't smile,
That cataracts are in the Nile —
Imagine, then, my deep surprise
To find them growing in my eyes!

It seems that now I'm fifty-six,
My eyes are playing iffy tricks;
When navigating cataracts,
Dimming's how an eye reacts.

So, friends of mine, avoid surprise —
See the world with both your eyes,
And when they fade, why, sing with me,
"My eyes are dim and cannot see!"

Gerald B. Frank

Fire In The Sky

A fuse, a fizz. Silence. A bang. Smoke.
The smell of sulphur, an internal whistle.
A fuse, a fizz. Silence. A shower of color. Smoke
The smell of sulphur. Patriotism.

Mathew D'Angelo

In Search Of An Answer

My eyes watch what many do not see;
in pain, I watch as friends fade away.
They're lost in a bottle, their answers unknown,
drinking and searching, with questions unanswered.
They can't express what they feel deep inside,
so they open the bottle in search of an answer.
When will they realize,
the answer can be found
in Christ and Christ alone?
He's created and knows where our lives often lead.
Your life in His hands is the answer you seek.
Don't look in the bottle, the answers not there,
yet you still try and drink it away.
How can you overcome what you cannot express
for only in Christ is there true happiness.

Meredith J. Hoernemann

The Autumn Years

Time sweeps by on winged feet, more so as we age,
What we thought chic, just "yesterday," no longer is the rage.
Wrinkles etched upon our brows, gray sprinkled in our hair,
Aged marks upon our skin, that once was truly fair.

We've lived these many years, absorbing what life's dealt,
Our memories a treasure trove of experience and wealth.
The myriad things that we have seen,
The endless places that we have been.

The things that youth has yet to see,
Some they could learn from such as we.
But ears of deafness are turned to us,
And the youthful question, what's all the fuss.

You made your mistakes, let us take the reins,
While we pray not to see our mistakes again.
Take heed to the lessons we had to learn,
They are not trivial, not to be spurned.

Please draw on the wisdom we learned through pain,
And try not to repeat our mistakes again.

James G. Wilson

Forever In My Heart

We could be a thousand miles apart
And I could still be close to where you are.
No amount of distance,
Whether great or small
Can keep me from running to you
When you call;
And though I miss you
When we're apart,
You're always right here with me
Forever in my heart.

Becky Miles

Street Crossing

The sun gleams down from above,
reflecting the heat off the pavement,
sweat beads running down my face,
burning my impatient eyes.

The imprisonment of the crescent curb,
forbidding me to break loose,
from the invisible chains on my ankles,
enforced by my nervous mother.

The sound of their ever lasting laughter,
taunting me from the other side,
their broad smiles gleam in my direction
beckoning for my presence.

Why hasn't she come out yet?
She said five minutes.

Kelly Macdonald

I'll Love You Through God, Mom

I looked at some flowers and soon thought of you.
Enjoying the colors as you used to do.
And though you're no longer with us in this place,
I'll love you through God, Mom, through His holy grace.

Your friends sometimes stop by to share moments past.
Remembering the good times, which they thought would last.
But something then happened; some new work to do.
I'll love you through God, Mom, I know He's not through.

He's given us glory in order to share
That He is still working on each of us here.
And though He has called you ahead of us home,
I'll love you through God, Mom, I am not alone.

His presence is vivid as He reminds me
You're feeling much better, without agony.
And one day He'll let us approach toward His Throne;
We'll both love through God, Mom, when He calls us Home.

Cheryl B. Edgcomb

A Love Taken Away

Today is a day of grievance
All I hear is silence, go away, go away!
So that I may say
My sorrowing words that hurt me so.
I remember the day that we played
And laughed so joyously.
But now that day is done,
Yet I have not shunned
The evil deeds I have done.
So please forgive me. I am a lawful one.
God's lawful one.
The sheets that cover his cold, wretched, body are blood soaked
and soiled.
The one that killed him couldn't be spoiled.
He was a ruthless killer that killed my love,
And yet I feel no sorrow.
I just stare and wonder
  Why?

Meredith Stout

A Time So Calm

Searching for a reason to explain this most recent
and truly morbid turn of events,
we look back with longing and fear what is written
in prophecy that, to us, makes no sense.

One with a theory and each with another,
none reflected in the way that we live.
Sapped of our strength and too willing to accept,
we march on, unwilling to give.

What is suffered by us will be learned by our young.
Not learned in the sense that it ends.
No, our children will long for a time so calm
as what we are to weak to defend.

Jennifer Rast

Untitled

There is no way to escape the sadness
That will soon become my madness
A parasitical being that is feeding from my pain
Creating my nightmares and eroding my brain
Mind nor body can I control
Paranoia from the depths of my soul
Nothingness occupies my sight
For I am blinded by the fright
What I fear I cannot be sure
A foreboding shadow, a shapeless blur
That tightening grip encloses
And I know I am dying once again

Jacelyn Neufeld

Mother

A Mother is like a Rose.
She has pure relationship, and Oh how beautiful it is.
Her perfection is like the freshness of a spring morning,
As a Rose with drops of dew.

The love a Mother has runs like a spring of water
whose waters never stop.
Her compassion is like a watered garden
which brings forth a beautiful Rose of remembrance
as fresh as the morning's sunrise.

When a Mother prays, all Heaven stops to listen to the
Love, Joy and Compassion pouring from the heart
like rain from the sky into the River of Love.
The Grace of God flows through her words like a
stampede over the fence of a Rose garden.

Today is Her Special Day, and Just one Rose will do.
Mary McDonald

My Breath Of Life, My Precious Love

You walked into my life that day and caught me by surprise,
Never in my wildest dreams would I ever have surmised,
That deep within my lonely heart there dwelt a human being,
So full of joy and wondrous love, that I could all but sing.

The very precious time we shared though secret and far apart,
The passing moments that we had I cherish in my heart,
Entwined our love could never be nor openly shared a loud,
You gave so much of you to me and always I'll be proud.

But wasn't it beautiful this love we shared,
The bittersweet memories, oh how we dared
To try and change the hands of fate,
That had written our lives, but years too late.

I thank you for the gentle hands that touched my face with love,
Memories of our burning passion now lift me far above
All the lonely nights of fear and all the tears and pain,
You shared with me your gentle self and made me whole again.
J. R. Clift

Silent Murders

The sun disappears now the real day begins
They come from their homes, their branches, their caves
There is no sound except for the frantic breathing of the prey's lungs
And now there is not even that
No women scream no men faint and yet one little life is gone
And the killer is hungry for more silently it moves along the ground
hungry, searching
A young woman passes by - but she does not see no she is busy,
hurrying home to her man
She does not give the prey a thought- but the predator does
Oh yes the predator gives the new prey all of its thoughts it gives
its whole being to the hunt
To the death of its next target a gust of wind a hiss and one more
life has disappeared
No longer is it hungry are the silent murders over for tonight? It
looks like it but no what about the little ones?
For they are hungry too now another chase another death
A quickness of the wing a tiny squeak and another one is gone
Quickly back to the nest and they prey is given back, now easier
to eat and . . . The silent murders are done. For tonight.
Lauren Angel

A Broken Cross

Wearing a crown of thorns upon his head
His pain is measured in blood
Desperate cries from a broken heart
Fighting the fear of a damaged soul

The breakdown of a collapsing physical ability
A mental state faced with a meltdown
Covering up the damaged thoughts of his life
Thoughts with a melancholy theme

After the destruction of this immortal destiny
With his inner person twisted in knots
Bound together with hopeless turmoil

And now faced with an uncharted future
Distorted with confusion and doubt
Existing in a cesspool of infinite madness
Like 'A Broken Cross' on Halloween

Abandoned by the faith he came to know
Driven crazy by a psycho pinch
Is there any cure to insanity
Or is death his only door of hope...
Kris Hofmann

Aglori

When April showers touched hibiscus flowers
And moisture laden clouds, hung for hours and hours,
A stork came a flying
With a little girl that wouldn't stop crying.
She cried so often,
She cried so loud,
Yet what joy she gave
To parents so proud.
T'was such fun to hear, her cute baby chatter
To her, normal things just didn't matter.
She'd rather climb trees
Than play with toys,
Catch spiders and lizards
And dare little boys.
Junior A. Harris

I'm Thankful, How Are You?

When we meet, upon the street,
And pause to say 'How Do'
Let's share our heart, this thought impart
I'm thankful...How are you?

I'm thankful when the morning comes.
I waken, fresh and free.
The day is mine....my path to choose.,
In freedom's liberty.

Pretty soon it's off to work,
And singing, I will go.
For I'm a very lucky guy,
I want the world to know.

When my day of work is done
And I come home to rest
My family's there, my home is safe
I say to you, I'm blessed.

So let's all get together
We all, who here abide.
Let's show our thanks to one and all.
Let's show our thankful side.
Robert Swenson

My Savior

Jesus Christ is my Savior
Now my life has taken on a new flavor.
Jesus is my true and loving friend
Who loves me even when I sin.

Jesus has helped me give unconditional love
A love which comes from my Father above
To society's outcasts, downtrodden, and misfits,
Which encourages them to come out of their oppressed pits.

My Savior has opened my eyes to see
The ways he can use me in his earthly ministry.
Lord, "I am not worthy I say."
He replies, "Believe and I will make a way."

My soul now has a compassionate part
Since jesus has come into my heart.
My life is not free of care and woe
But Jesus is with me as through life I go.

So won't you accept Jesus as your Savior
So your life will take on a new flavor.
So you will have a true and loving friend
Who will love you even when you sin.

    Brenda Smith

Our Children Are Our Future

A hostage taking a prisoner of war
Guerillas will do anything to settle a score
Hijacking, murder, bombs going off
Do those guys really think they're tough

What is this world coming to besides disaster
When we no longer respect our Mother and Father
No longer good news on the television
No more love, just all sin

How can we stop this world from going up in smoke
All those fools addicted to coke
Causing trouble and making a mess
Robbing and killing for nothing less

All those children stuck in the middle
Don't they know that they're so little
Stuck on the street with no place for home
Out there hungry and all alone

Moms and Dads take them back in
All their anger comes from within
This world would be empty without them here
They're our future for each new year

    Nancy Amato

Now That You're Gone

No regrets, now that you're gone,
No thoughts of what was right or wrong.
Our yesterdays were full of dreams,
Some, vividly lived, some, unseen.
Our love was perfect, in that it was sound,
We had our spats, we did our rounds.
But, we loved, through all that came our way,
We respected each-other, and we each had our say.
We grew, and built, and even flourished together,
We never regretted us "being one", not ever.
We lived each day like a new verse to a song,
I held you, you held me, when things went wrong.
So, my love, I have no regrets, but one;
I am here, and you are gone.

    Maria Louisa Malandra

Untitled

In pain, I write this
I am so tired, my daughter
And you - who with your first cry
Are so very small

In joy, I write this
Holding you - touching your greedy hand,
Your hair, your curly feet.
You will have some happy days
My sweet
My daughter

In fear, I write this
For I know fear and anger
Sorrow and terror
Too

In love, I write this.
Let me be wise — for you
My daughter

    Margery M. L. Dudley

The Circus Life Of A Working Housewife

Twenty-two years of juggling, keeping all my plates spinning
    evenly, fairly, balancing on such a tenuous high wire.

No circus clown could make me smile.
Or distract and divert me from my extra mile.

Given daily, given freely, nothing required in return,
    as the hoops of fire grow higher and hotter,
    I leap through them with seeming ease.

And when the last trapeze flyer drops gently into their net,
I fall fatigued - the aches and pains of my needs never quite met.

    Molly R. Durante

Angels

Angels upon my shoulders, gazing up to the sky
Give me wings so I may fly
Let me soar above my life
Give me wings, give me flight
Let me gaze upon my children
Like stars give them hope
Angels so uplifting
Take me to that place
Set me free!

    Carrie Hansen

Love Nest

This isn't my idea of a love nest
but I'll follow docilely
Hope that it doesn't shatter my world.
Then die of pleasure
Her voice trailed off
Into a wall that swings open
What are my lines - now
It's more then that
My old love - new love
Exploring the body for the first time
smeary impression of a naked figure
Climbing - mission - danger - sublimity
Finally the summit
The door closed - softly
Another worlds dreams filled with fantasies
Love that we all need - can't have
From another worlds midnight visions
As realistic as we can get it
We'll take it

    Donald J. Woloski

Ever Fragrant

Marriage, is an honorable institution, respected and esteemed by all decree of divorce, nullifying the state is not higher licence to forgotten vows "Till death, do us part", is a promise a couple makes not as a frivolous jest some, for considerations other than love, put this vow to an early death.

Love is patient, love is kind, love is superlative, It never fails though its instruments, who profess to practice it, if marriage of love is falling apart, participants should commitments revisit, That garden of their lives where at first, had exchanged the best rose it could give.

Yet if failure is must, unremedied will remain and parting the only choice, The garden of life needs be tended with care for love's shorn shrub not to wither and die, Expecting no thankfulness in return if again, 'nother princely rose it can be yield.

A garden remains, a wasted wilderness if barred for entry or too far to reach where flowers grow and wilt hidden, unseen yet who really cares a whit? May blossoms only be, a life's fragrant offering and admiration left to picker's, Choice some will treasure it as priceless gift, others, just adorn tresses for a while...

Vinay Benjamin

Macabre Repose

In your shallow depths I lie, as a chill reverberates down my
   spine and through my whole being.
I am filled with your presence, which in itself, is an empty
   stillness that encloses everything.
This existence is cold and still.
It is a lifelessness that draws the moon closer, and spins
   translucent threads to bind me.
Your dreaming beckons me and catches me in a web of wonderment
   and illusions.
Where do your truths reside?
Are they a piece of this reflection; frozen and haunting?
This statuette in macabre repose speaks only of a quietude in heart
and mind that emphasizes the feeling of greatest desolation.
I know not the passing of time, only your placidity. My words are
   locked away behind clenched teeth.
They have fallen solely upon your unhearing ears.
In filling me you have left me bereft, with only a vast hollowness remaining.
Cold...
Still...
Lifeless...

I feel the warming kiss of death.

Cori Pradon

Masks

You used to smile when you spoke.
That aching grin, those dancing eyes.
You tried to hide it
Under a fancy facade.
I know you can't hide truth from one
Who knows you best, and
How can you smile when you know no one's waiting?

Have you ever thought that maybe
I felt a pain like yours?
An identical hurt, a like longing
For lost pleasures or unfound charm
In one you've loved so long, but
Can't seem to find.
How can you not love when you can't let memories go?

Is my smile like yours?
An actor's mask to hide the face
That pain has scribbled on?
I know "lonely" is written there, on mine and yours,
And we wear fleeting faces.

Tiffany Porter

Ocean Thoughts

This is a time of shifting
Shifting weight, shifting skin shifting purpose.

Like the sands shift on the shores with each tide
my body shifts with time to bring new form.

And like the sands of the shore are to the sea,
my body is to time.
Shifting, changing, appearing in various forms
Parts and eventually the whole worn down and
moved by gentle washes and violent crashes.

Time, untouched, stands witness to the shifts
as the shore relinquishes control to the power of the sea
and my body relinquishes control to the journey of my soul.

Caroline Johnston

Thoughts Of A Mother About Her Teen-Age Son

"I'll be late tonight, Mother, but please don't worry,
"I'm a big boy now, there's no need to hurry."
These words are both a sorrow and a joy,
To the one who's the mother of a teen-age boy.

"Don't worry about my driving, Mother, there's really nothing to it,
Just let ME have the keys, I'll show you how to do it."
To you he is still the baby with curls,
But he and his pals are beginning to date girls.

As you sit and watch him march right thru, precision movements
   with the band,
It seems like only yesterday that to steady his step, he needed
   your hand.
You know with an ache, that time really flies,
When you have to look UP, to look into his eyes.

The Cautiousness of Age bows to the Confidence of Youth,
They think we are old-fashioned, and that really is the truth.
We would not vainly sigh, for the "things that might have been,"
If we had Confidence at forty, that we had at seven and ten.

Rachel Baldwin

My Darling Sunshine

Another day my eyes have opened to the
beautiful treasures thee has placed upon me.

Not one moment has past without her shine
glistening in my visions.

From her glamorous rising to her
illustrious setting, She creates a joy of fulfillment.

Spreading her love through the 7 days
and all the deserving seasons.

None has appreciated her strengths and
flawless sphere, such as I.

For she is the inspiration of my yearning.

Without her power, nothing will prosper,
for she is that shine that reigns forever,

Whether the cloudiest of days, or the darkest
of nights... She enlightens my every forever.

For she is my guide; never changing...
The same every day.

She casts her rays upon me - which produce
My shadow that will never leave my side,
So long as I enjoy her everlasting glow.

She is my sunshine!!!

Sterlin'O'Keith Ruther Sr.

Beneath The Mask

Why was my grandfather taken away,
Upon silver-dusted angel wings?
"To dance with the stars and laugh with the moon."
She had a way of masking the grief that death brings.

Mother locked me up with the key in her pocket,
And thought my entire life could be controlled.
Not permitted to taste the bitterness of pain,
I never had a reason to be consoled.

Now that I've grown and I know how I cry,
I've been told of the suffering of his death.
The words of the story poisoned the air,
And choked me until I was gasping for breath.

I took joy for granted because I believed
That every day was a sparkling jewel.
I've been blindfolded from the tight grip of pain,
And grown up with only the thoughts of a fool.

When happiness gives you a kiss on the cheek,
Be sure to thank God for sparing the tear.
Though life has its scars, nightmares, and misfortunes,
Just be thankful for the rainbows of cheer.

Claudine Mead

Gateway To Heaven

The pastels of the dawn are now the earth tones of the evening
They span their rainbow of color across the canyon wall
Far reaching shadows cast a multitude of silhouettes
Against a fiery setting sun
The shifting colors accentuate the monastery cliffs
As the light quickly fades behind the deepest canyon wall
What beauty wanes at the close of day beyond the Sierra sun
Then as darkness creeps upon the forest awakening
Another drama unfolds before my eyes
The lunar of a thousand years exhibits her maiden visit
Over the majestic peaks her flame of light
Beams down on the stalwart pines and bowing bristle cone
Their branches arched heavenward as if in beseeching prayer
The restless pines give their scent
In each breath of nightly breeze that's spent
Among the gorge and rocky tor we find
Beauty for all to see and hear
My beloved Sierra so tenderly sleep

Marie Mahoney

The Old Woman

The old woman was a lonely woman. Her eyes were big bulging circles staring into your face. Her white hair was pulled back in a pretty bun. Her nose was like a little curled up ramp, and her legs were like a baby colt when it first learns to walk. Her eyes were little body's eyes when they are ready to cry. Her skin on her baby felt like silk. Her little feet were safely covered with cozy bunny slippers. When she stood up, she wiggled like a slippery pencil. Her wrinkles were like waves coming up on the shore. She was wearing a big blue sweater. Her fingers were long narrow twigs reaching out for something to hold. Her voice was like the whistle of a man playing a flute softly.

Cate Crain

Together

Once again I reach out
   to feel your breath, touch your lips, acknowledge your sigh
How I long for the day we finally embrace
   in passionate reality, we now can say hi

Together at last
   no longer apart
Until that day comes
   be still won't, my beating heart

Be still your beating heart
   the angels they will sing
For the heavens have brought you together now
   together you are blessed, worry not, anything

Go on forth, from this day
   fly with the doves, who will show you the way
We will seek the meaning of love, and I know we will find
   how a man and woman became one together,
   Body, soul, spirit, and mind.

Ralph Finizio

DEATH STRIKE

The attack comes swiftly, without warning.
   I jerk back my mind but it's too late —
      Its fangs sink deep —
      Its aim too true.

The venom rushes through my body,
   Paralyzing, bringing a terror too dark for words.
      Insidious, this slithering thought
      That coils around my mind
         Slowly crushing all hope for life from me.

Useless to struggle, I'm powerless to
   Fight against its strength, and the
      Last thing I hear before the poison destroys my sanity
      Is its hissing voice,
   "YOUR MOTHER'S DEAD."

Jann Muhlhauser

Be Contented

Be contented with what you have along this life that's yours;
   The Lord walks those beside you as long as time endures!
The bitter disappointments God will gently brush away,
   His loving arms will hold you forever and a day.

You need not ever worry that He will not understand,
   Or that He'll push you from Him with cold and careless hand.
He knows our deepest longings, and tears we try to hide,
   His hour is deep and lasting, with His arms open wide!

Be contented with what you have in this old world below,
   Follow Him whatever the cost, as Heavenward you go.
God's love for you does far surpass all human love you've known,
   In His heart forgiveness is treasures still unknown!

You must believe that you are very special in His sight,
   He understands and pardons, when you do all that's right!
And so by consistent living God's cause we will defend,
   By our honest influence, love to God extend!

And so now in my closing remarks I want you to know
   That all my prayers did reach God through hot tears which did flow,
There with the Lord and the angels, we'll know no pain nor tears,
   Only peace and happiness throughout the endless years!

Vera Mae Johnson

"On My Own"

My love, how I miss you.
The days are long,
The nights are longer
Without you, I despair!

You are gone,
Never to return.
I fill my days and nights as best I can,
But, oh how I miss you!

I wish you could hold me
To again keep me warm, safe and secure.
I know you are looking down from above,
But, oh, how I could use a hug!

My life is turning in another direction.
It is because of you and your everlasting love,
That I can go forward and seek
Someone else to admire, respect and hopefully love.

Thank you, my love,
God bless you, and keep you safe.
Good night, and all my love until we meet again!
Goodbye! Goodbye! Goodbye!

Kathleen S. Rusinak

Life Is A Present

Life is the present wrapped in pretty paper
    I run through the house to find
I spot a big, shiny box hidden in the attic
    Ah, the wonder it creates
Shaking the box, searching for clues
Finally, at last, the moment comes
I sit down on the couch
    Eyeing the big, shiny box in front of me
Undoing the bow, I can hardly wait
Ripping apart the pretty paper
    That binds my beloved box
Now, I'm ready to peer inside
A sense of happy anxiousness
    Enters my mind
I open the box to find
    An I.O.U note
    Taped inside

Michelle Marconi

"The Dog Beneath The Cross"

Many years ago I met an old man
    By the Sea of Galilee,
Who told a tale of the Crucifixion
    That has always stayed with me.

It seems that among the Romans there,
    Who threw dice for our Saviour's cloak,
Was a young soldier and his dog,
    Beneath the Cross of Oak.

This was the only dog present there
    And many question the breed of the hound,
But the old man had made a life long study
    And this is what he found.

Very few dogs have the mournful eyes
    Of today's Labrador Retriever,
So when he traced back that certain lineage
He himself became a true believer.

Today my own Lab's eyes still reveal
    This story of suffering and pain,
Passed on down by an early ancestor,
    From the day Our Lord was slain.

Tod McGinley

Untitled

The weatherman's forecast I follow each day,
    I dress for his latest prediction.
But time after time, to my utter dismay,
    His sunshine turns out to be fiction.

Economists' views of the future don't do
    Much better, though most scientific,
As forecast on forecast, like weathermen's too,
    Turns out to be less than terrific.

I have a solution — yes, here is the key —
    (And both would be free of their tether)
Have weathermen forecast the real G.D.P,
    While economists forecast the weather!

Robert G. Williams

A Poem For James

Secretly daydreaming of kisses
Seemingly intangible wishes
Absence of affection
For fear of rejection
Then suddenly brave at last
After fruitless time had passed
A request to have an engagement
Surprisingly led to embracement
Feelings unexpected
Caressed and protected
Hunger for love growing strong
Hoping it wouldn't be long
True passion for the first time is shared
Looking back there is nothing compared
With many others each
Neither could ever reach
What they now have together
An always and forever

Kimberly Anne Gack

"Will The Possum Fall"

I see the possum crawling
On top of the wall
At the mall
Will she make it, or will she fall
Or does it really matter to me at all
Crawl crawl possum crawl
On top of that wall at the mall
Will you fall?
I do not really know at all
But it seems to me
That the possum is not really worried at all
For the wall is truly the possum's hall way
To her home that lie's across the wall
And she know's this wall very well
For her children await her
Safe and well at the base of that wall at the mall
So now I truly see
For it is I who is play possum
For it does really matter to the possum after all

John G. Hernandez

Tiger

Red-striped, majestic, foe of man,
    Your hourglass is out of sand.
No longer will your roar strike fear,
    Into the hearts of all who hear.

Yet when you depart this earthly host.
    Man himself will lose the most.
He'll remember your glory in word and song,
    But forget his greed is why you're gone.

Joseph C. Greenfield Jr.

I Am

I know the one I am
tell them
I am that I am
Whatever you need me to be...
I am
The light that you see I am... your life force
I am
all you need me to be
I am
I give you the sunshine and the rain
I provide the substance for all
I am
the prime mover of all things
I am... mindful of the working of the universe
all things exist under my constant watchful eye
I am forever and ever
I am
capable of being ruler of all... because I am the maker of all I am
care and I care for all
I am that I am.

Dorothy Yarborough

Clever Youth

Under a collage of loose limbs
And over the fallen timber
Through a cripple creek
And into a meadow of wheat
Atop a rolling hill of green
Across a bunk of resting rocks
Down a cloven foot trail
And steelyard on iron rails
Jumping into mounds of hay
Swinging beneath an old oak
Straddling a half-cocked fence
While wielding each sinless sense
The sun regularly hounded our heels
So we raced harder and swifter against her
And even in our finest hours of clever youth
Did we ever imagine it to vanish so quickly

Cynthia

Mirror, Mirror On The Wall

You stare at your reflections in the mirror for a long time.
The image you see smiles at you, which seems normal until you
realize you're not smiling.
The reflection's smile wider and more demonic.
It realizes that you now know it has a mind of its own.

It begins to speak, though its lips don't move.
"For years I have been forced to shadow your every moment.
People don't comprehend the fact that I too am full of life.
Not a mere image of someone else, but my own person.
Now my fate will be yours."

The girls in the mirror seizes your wrist and drags you into her
prison of prisms.
You look out from your glassy cage with a saddened heart.
You understand that you will be held captive in the world of
reflections for eternity.
Not as a person, but a backwards shadow.

Courtney Collins

Spring

Spring has arrived, the grass is green
The birds singing sweetly, building nests in the tree
Trees are bursting with buds all around
Crocuses, daffodils and tulips burst up through the ground
Time to get the lawn mower out again
No time to sit and hold my chin
Rose bushes now are ready to trim
Lilacs in bloom, smelling so sweet
Children are riding their bikes in the street
The windows to clean and the house to paint
The fresh sweet smelling air after a new fallen rain
Watching the kids playing ball games
The girls riding their rollerblades, laughing aloud
Beautiful skies with white fluffy clouds
Winter has gone, spring is welcome here for a while.

Erma E. Pruett-Nielsen

Teaching Of Our People

They left behind symbols
to our people
words that run deep in our veins.
reflection of profound beliefs...
teaching that sheds light on our people.

Our sacred circle that
binds or wholeness
of creation... our journey...
to inner spiritual
growth. Our mysteries that will
guide us through our
visions...our quest.
To continue our
traditions as our elders did.

Lesia T. Bear

The Past

I lay awake in bed at night, before the time I can sleep.
Pictures fly by, through the soul in my eyes.
In my memory the past repeats!
The love that lasts
The faces I've seen.
Places to go, and the places I've been.
For all the wrongs, the points of the truth!
I, am at home, in the days of my youth.
The people I've met, and the few who have died!
Blood flows, my heart beats the sound.
New vision appear, in my mind crystal clear.
Feeling on still alive, content with myself!
At last, I, am a sleep, the future is here.
As I walk down dream street, I have to look back!
In a flash of light, I saw crystal clear!
The (past) that brought me here!
The soul of my life.

James D. Cronk

When Will The Hate End?

When will the hate end?
When will we realize our
country is sinking in quick-sand and
nothing can pull us up?
Will it take a bomb to kill
over 100 people and leave 400 injured?
It's been a year since the explosion.
The pain is still here, the tears
still fall.
But, we still ask ourselves,
"When will the hate end?"

Erin Coon

A Year Of Change

These past December nights have been star nights
with winter brilliant skies.
When I walk the roads at days end it seems
the entire universe accompanies me.
The stars sometimes lean so close if I stood
on tiptoes on the highest hill,
I might grasp one star in my tingling fingers.

Now as the year begins to sum up in its own inconclusive way,
the continuity of time makes any summary incomplete.
There has been sprouting, flowering and maturity,
there has been the falling leaves and harvest.

Now I rest in the quiet
attempting to consolidate the forces of change within me.
This is as near to summary and reflection as any years affords.

Life is never static and never will be - Life is change.
Tomorrow rises in the east;
all of the tomorrows.
I change with each new day,
but today - you are my star bright.
And I tingle when you're near me.

Philip M. Spears

Untitled

See not me for I see all, all who see shall be heard. Hear me,
dare me, and try and scare me, for I am God my begotten children.
You are mine and for that I shall watch all of you close, closer
than most. See me, for I am God. Well, it's fine day is it not?
My children, for today is the day which I shall glisten. For it's
everyday and every way I glisten. Listen to the Lord and listen
well, for I shall hear all. All above, all below, all in all I'm at your call.
Speak child for I listen, and listen well. You shall not hear my
thoughts for I don't think, I know. Do you ever question me?
I know. Now go with the wind and be free for I am your freedom.
Freedom is within the realm of the Lord, your God. Real goodness
is not, but I am forever or the feather shall wither. Fly today,
sing tomorrow, know not what I do but what I say. Say I, say why,
say cry, say no lie, say hi, say goodbye.

Todd L. Jean

Birdseed

Somewhere between the synapses, memories,
scattered like birdseed, give me reason to pause.
Winged creature, sparrow of conscience, claws
and pecks in crevices deep, once destiny.

Waiting for flight, black and white feathers freeze
in reminiscence of venomous love and draw
me further back, a dream where the jaws
of a villain grow wider by degrees.

Metamorphosed, I went north
as he traversed south. Degrade, defile,
you constrictor, as all the love you strangled
endlessly repelled and sent me forth
toward lumbering pines and sunflower smiles
where girls and snakes, like weeds, no longer tangle.

Nancy Y. Schafer

Night

Darkness is falling
The night looms long and quiet
Our thoughts run rampant in the dark
We toss and turn but sleep won't come
Too many visions abound
We wait and watch for dawn's golden light
With a quickening of breath, our heart feels light
Another dawn, another new day
A day filled with sunshine, laughter, and love
We thrill to the sight of oncoming light.

Rose M. Shaffer

Animals

What would it be like
to be an animal or any creature
to chase antelope at the speed of a cheetah
to soar like an eagle and snatch fish out of water
to strike with the venomous poison of a cobra
Oh just how would it be
to eat leaves from a tree with a tall neck of a giraffe
to hide in the shell of a turtle for protection
to hop around with the gracefulness of a rabbit
to protect your baby in the pouch of a kangaroo
Oh just how would it be
to jitter along with the legs of a crab
to squirm around in soil with the recklessness of a worm
to hang upside-down with slowness of a sloth
to swing around in trees with the playfulness of a chimpanzee
to talk with the voice of a parrot
to glow with the light of a lightning bug
and then to face the task that all creatures have to face
Survival
Just what would it all be like

Amit Raikar

Our Tea

A simple, innocuous bottle of tea,
That you placed in my hands after first meeting me.

It was mine to drink at a typical pace,
But I could not do so, in time or in space.

For so quickly it meant something deeper to me.
Something I'll now impart to thee.

Why couldn't my hands simply open the top?
Each time that I tried to, they managed to stop.

My logic and reason said, "Hey, it's your choice."
What was it that stopped me; your charm or your voice?

I had to depart from thoughts calculated.
As I did I then saw; it was magic related!

No way would I risk this move indiscreet.
For I did not know if again we would meet!

So I kept it to keep you close to my heart.
In case what we had thus far would depart.

Well, that did not happen. The antithesis held.
For our hearts and our souls have begun to meld.

And for all that we have with our chemistry.
It's so easy to see why we cherish our tea.

George Sellas

Alice

The link to which your very being belongs
the bonding that goes beyond
all biological ties.

The place the soul has travelled
bearing gifts of
guidance and strength.

Her infinite love
reflects light,
permitting comfort.

Knowing she's touched you
with her courage
dares to you breathe.

The epitome
of hope.
her name is Mother.

Susan Fridkin

Love

Your eyes are as blue as the sky
Your lips are as red a rose
Your hair is a brown as the bark on a tree
Your love for me is like the sea, peaceful and serene
I never knew you could be so beautiful

Dawn Benzie

Looking Forward

Life is a series of highs and lows,
The highs are an anticipation
As are waves softly rolling on the beach.
The lows sweep against you
As the rough waves break with the crash and hidden power
That can literally knock you off your feet.
Memory makes the highs stronger
So you may forget the lows.
Dreams and excitement ride on the high waves,
Doubt and worry lurk in the low waves.
We are blessed with the ability
Of time erasing the pain.
To ride the high waves of inner peace and tranquility.

Diane Meyers

"Caring"

The little girl sat on the front porch step,
Hoping someone would care.
Her clothes were ragged, her hair unkept,
Why was life so unfair?

The teenager sat by the side of the road,
On a suitcase, looking lost and forlorn.
She really had tried with all of her heart,
She wished she'd never been born.

The young woman sat at her desk at a school,
A caring teacher by her side.
Who encouraged, concerned, giving constant praise,
She now felt a feeling of pride.

Her parents weren't there to help her along,
In the trials life sometimes brings.
But someone cared enough to help.
And now, her whole body sings.

We each need someone who cares who we are,
Be it a parent, a teacher, a friend,
To give us support along life's way,
Right to the very end.

Muriel J. Unsworth

Thought I Was Dreaming

Milling about, renewed in abuse,
A coterie of angels did set me loose,
Ramose in their call, 'round me they spun,
I thought I was dreaming when I found but one,
A specious seraph with a tongue of gold,
Wertherian pride and a touch untold.
Healed by her amenity and cordial surprise,
I make ready my heart to get lost in her eyes;
Spoken in promise to come in and dwell,
Kissed by a dream into which I fell
Expressing afflatus in capricious display,
Disclosed in a heav'ly rapacious way;
Mellifluous assembly is the host of my lift,
Entrance denied to all else in gift.
And I thought I was dreaming when on her I'd reflect:
When all the while 'twas just her effect;
Absorbed and lost in adoration,
Yielding softly to mine new liberation.

Randy Markell

Sixth Street Kate

Oh where's the flame that burneth day and night
For the one I loveth with all my might
For whom many moons I've stayed awake,
My darling, my darling, Sixth Street Kate.

Cometh back to your Poppa, my little dove,
Returneth my Sugar, it's you only I love,
Don't leaveth me more nights to stay awake,
You cute little jitterbug, Sixth Street Kate.

Many moments will pass when I will pine
Just to dream of that gal of mine,
I'll hope and try to soon forsake
The memories I endear of Sixth Street Kate.

Alas, my thoughts are but in vain
To think that I could rid this pain
That lingers within me through and through,
Of the better times that I once knew.

Goodbye my darling, adios amour,
Seems we'll never meet once more,
Wherever I go, within me I'll take,
Sweetest memories of Sixth Street Kate

Lawrence Garifo

The Fuzz Ball

There was a fuzz ball on my bed
A fuzzy fuzz ball colored red
He had a sly grin on his face
He opened his jaws with skilled grace
His teeth were brightly shining in the light
He clamped to my finger with all his might
I tried to shake him but he wouldn't give in
I grabbed the neared object that was a pen
I popped him upside his scrawny little head
I hit him three times until he fell dead
Dead and helpless on the ground he lay
I got on my knees and blew him away

Cami Godwin

Old Yeller Faithful

He looks upon you with sweet eyes,
while his nose sticks out of his face.

His pale coat is a dusty shade of yellow.
When he's happy the bunt of his tail shows it.
His bark sounds like a child yelping in distress.

This dog proves to be incredibly brave and loyal
in situations threatening and involving his master.
He'll even fight the largest beast to save you.

He's the most faithful dog you'll ever see.
His coat is thick and furry to protect his soft hide.

Anyone would wish for a great pet like him.
Chasing coons and skunks,
happily he hunts with his master,
I'd describe him as loyal, brave, and kind-hearted,
he gives off the aroma of whatever he's
been rolling in, and holds that color too.

He's like a human member of the family.
His name is a result of his color and bark.
Old yeller proves that a dog is man's best friend.

Timothy Landry

The Heart

He shone on me like the light from the moon,
He left me yes, but I'll see him soon.
To say my goodbyes it hurt me much,
Soon again I'll feel his touch.
The face that left will be back I know,
For the time he's gone my love will be low.
I know I'll feel his hand with mine,
Eventually I will see his kind.
He walks to me as if to say,
"I'm leaving now but I'll be back next day."
Two days gone feels like years,
Even though I'll shed no tears.

Julia Tordjman

On The Beach

The wind settles around our enveloped bodies
quietly moving in rhythm with the thrashing surf.
The water foams and froths between our toes and legs
settling deep into our fervid thoughts.
Under the moon summer heat your skin slides and tenses
teasing my hard ambition causing me to grind my thoughts
longer...
Wrapping into a formless tide
the salts on our bodies meld and moan
mixing and emulating the peak of prurience
until settling aspired unto each others embrace.

Leo Sevigny

Untitled

I found some old pictures of cousin Jon-Jon,
He died a while back.
The last time I saw him, I was two,
So knowing him I lack.

There was a problem with his lungs,
He couldn't breathe too well.
Most surgeries didn't work,
He was suffering you could tell.

He was only a boy of eleven,
The sad day that he died.
Died of Cystic Fibrosis,
His family at his side.

And yet we know he's better now,
He's opened heaven's door.
Because we know he's with Jesus now,
And he's not suffering anymore.

Deanne Mallett

My Inner Being

My inner being reflects my present past and future
So I say unto my soul as my mind takes control
"The present may be good and I have done all I could
Or bad and it's the worse life I've had"
I do not know what the future may hold
When life will end or if I will grow old
I will erase unpleasant memories of the past that I harbor
Which hinder my progress for a brighter tomorrow
I must gird up my loins and bathe not in sorrow
And let joy saturate the chambers of my heart
To extract the negatives for a new start
I will laugh and be merry for it does good like a
medicine should
My faith will develop me so peace can envelop me
I must apply this formula every place with a smiling face
To strive master press forward and pray
Then my soul will rejoice for a brighter day

Esther E. Johnson

Lilacs

I often think how nice it would be,
To sit beneath a Purple Lilac Tree.
And listen to the 'Hum' of Bees,
Working in a warm June breeze.

I vision I see you in Times Square —
With blooms, of Lilacs, in your hair,
The fragrance of the Purple and Blue
Has the makings of the day for you.

Lilacs sparkle, with the morning dew.
They are of many colors, I'll name a few —
Purple, Pink, White and Blue.
They are not shy, they grow in view.

Lilacs, when in bloom, make a show —
In many places, 'Wild' they grow.
Around old foundations and hillsides —
Unsightly places, their beauty hides.

In Winter, when the skies are grey,
I vision, Purple Lilac blooms of June.
While in their branches, the Robins, nest.
And overhead, the swallows swoon.

William J. Lambert

The Day I Won The Lottery

I checked my ticket. I won! I won!
This was going to be so much fun!
I sat in my car with a heavy heart.
Please, oh please, will you not start?
I went to the bus stop to catch a ride.
But my wallet I left back inside.
I arrived at my door only to pout.
How will I get there? I locked myself out!
I climbed in a window, but that's where I failed.
The police picked me up, and then I was jailed.
I explained what had happened. They thought it was funny.
But they drove me down town to pick up my money.
I walked in the door to cash in my ticket.
Only to find that they closed down my wicket.
The next window over my winnings were counted.
I fell off the seat that on I was mounted.
The money I won! It just couldn't be!
Twelve thousand were winners of five sixty three.

Joy Oliver

Are You Proud Of Me Yet?

Daddy, I can sing my ABCs! "...."
Daddy, I can tie my shoelaces! "...."
Daddy, I got all As on my report card! "...."
Daddy, I can ride my bike all by myself! "...."
Daddy, I won at the HMTA piano contest! "...."
There were only three winners. "...."
Daddy, I won first place at the science fair. "...."
Daddy, I'm first chair flute in symphonic band now. "...."
Daddy, are you going to come to my dance recital? I'm doing my
    first ballet solo. "...."
Daddy, I got my first A in an honors class. "...."
Daddy, I have one of the biggest parts in the ballet we are doing. "...."
Daddy, oh never mind.
"You stupid girl, why did you have to embarrass me by taking your
    own life?!"

Joyce Chan

Every Good-Bye

A ventricle pump made of
stone - every good-bye is not
gone - helpless not hopeless
I do what I'm told - every
good-bye is not gone - a
perpendicular road leads
to discovery of who's left alone,
every good-bye is not gone -
It travelled like lightning into the future
It influenced a career and it influenced home -
all because every good-bye was not gone.
She knew, yet she didn't know,
because in her home - every goodbye was not gone.
The perpendicular road must now be horizontal or vertical,
it doesn't matter as long as it's straight
because in my home - good-bye
means gone.

Kara Golston

"Day By Day"

God, you know I'm getting tired
Please help me find the way
To have strength and courage
To live each passing day.

I hate when I get lonely
My nerves start wearing thin
They say, Life is what we make it
So were do I begin?

If life is, what you make it
Then I need some help from you
Please guide me through my troubled times
And tell me what to do.

As I get on my knees tonight
And fold my hands in prayer
I'll look beyond the clouds and stars
Because I know you're there.

I will pray to you for guidance
And help along the way
I need you "strength and courage"
To live, each day by day.

Dorothy Morrow

Missing You

On a cold, grey November day,
I suddenly felt lonely, my mind gone astray.
I wondered again why in all this time,
I've never had anyone whom I could call mine.

I longed for someone perfect for me,
Someone to carve my name on a tree.
The night we first met, I knew it was you,
For my heart was filled with love so true.

I approached you the first chance I got,
The sparks that were flying were burning so hot.
So hot, indeed, it burned all away,
Along with the car crash I see day after day.

You said you'd never leave me,
You said you'd always be there.
And now when my heart cries for you,
I can't find you anywhere.

I know you are with me, although out of sight,
And I wish I could hold you in my arms, so tight.
I know you're gone forever, it's true,
I just want you to know I'll always love you.

Zarina Khan

Dear Mother

Another love like a Mother's, no there is none.
   A mother will love you when all is said and done.

Many, many times our mother had to drink from a
   very bitter cup;
She would sigh and say, "I just want to live until
   my babies have grown up."
There were those times when we wouldn't listen
   and take our mother's advice;
And then we would end up paying a very high price.
   She would say "I tried to tell you because
I wanted you to know, even though I knew that
   there would be those times when you would have
to bump your heads in order to grow."

Oh Mother, Dear Mother, why did you have to leave
   us, why did you have to go?
We would give anything to hear your sweet voice
   whisper, softly, lovingly once again
"I told you so."

Carlene L. Ingram

Pure Soul

Deep within your secret self, lies your soul.
Sometimes it peeps out.
If you try to hide it, the attempt shows
Like a flashing light.
It makes a look come into your eyes,
A gleam of radar,
Stretching outwards,
Searching for the one, who skilled in the art,
Can read your soul.
You close your eyes and hope that when you open them
Nothing shows,
That no one can tell what was written in them.
It is futile.
Because every time your soul slips into your eyes,
It leaves a mark, eternal, indelible.
That is how, He, who is skilled in the art of soul searching,
Will find you, read your soul, and claim it for His own.

Hazel MacPhail

Old Immigrant

He was the strong one,
the demon of the valley,
the roar of the forest,
the muscular catapult
of a stream of life.
The trees tumbled
and the river silenced.
The torrential flame continued-restless.

The white hair moves in the wind
bringing a movement of life
in a dormant body.
The tempest ceased
in the soft, soft step of walking.
The tremulous hand has no rest
and the eyes no voice.
To live without a throbbing
and to die
under the frozen earth.

Carlo Millelire

The Roads Of Summer

Roads are like life. Twisting and turning they reveal hidden places that fill us with joy or sadness. As we tour our summer roads we realize the beauty of God's hand working all around us. His abundant generosity has wrapped the earth in an array of colors, shapes, and smells, which enhance our faith in Him and ourselves.

Have you ever wondered what our lives would be like without the never-ending green fields, life-giving air, puffy clouds, or skies that touch the blue lakes with a gentle kiss of friendship? Could we live without the majestic mountains that stand as mighty bridges to heaven? Or the stars that proclaim God's love for us again and again as they twinkle over the universe?

In this vast land of opportunity and plenty, God shows us His love is never-ending with the radiance of the sun and the glow of the moon.

Traveling God's country we are held spellbound and humbled because we know He is always with us—whether our roads are curved or straight, rising or falling, hidden or exposed.

Kathleen G. Vargo

How To Catch A Varmint

When I saw something move, that night in bed
It held my attention as my fears were fed.

Still mostly asleep, I wasn't seeing good yet
But I grabbed before thinking- like a trap was set.

Then I wondered, what'll I do next
Wishing I didn't have such a quick reflex.

Sitting there I began to realize - I was afraid
Reconsidering my options, since the move I'd made.

No one came to help, 'guess I didn't yell
But if I survived, I planned to tell.

Sitting there bent over, my back hurt with pain
So I squeezed even harder, ignoring the strain.

As drowsiness passed, I noticed other discomforts too
Thinking it would have felt better - had I worn my shoes.

It was strange, my right foot was getting numb
At this point I thought, this is dumb.

Here I was, squeezing my own foot hard
Thinking I'd caught a varmint from our backyard.

But I learned a lesson from dreams and tears
My worst enemy is me and my silly fears.

Richard Berry

The Revolutionary War

The war started in Lexington,
With hundreds of British and seventy minutemen.
With the tapping of the drum and the noise of the horn,
The fighting began one April morn'.

On June 16, 1775,
The militia took charge and started to strive
Against General Gage on Bunker Hill,
The only thought in mind was kill, kill, kill.

Crossing the Delaware on Christmas night,
Washington led his troops to fight with all their might.
To surprise the Hessians while they were asleep,
They snuck into camp without a peep.

There were also many fights on sea.
Without privateers, where would we be?
John Paul Jones won at Serapis,
For British commanders, that was a miss.

On October 17, 1781,
Cornwallis surrendered and the war was won.
In 1783, we were free,
Because Britain signed the peace treaty!

Nicholas Giacona

"When"

Imagine peace to all
  both friends and foes,
Imagine the sensation
  of sands between thy toes.

When your soul
  lies between destiny and fate,
When abnormalities
  rely on the decisions you make.

For this is when
  For when was then,
Vibrant color of illustrious hue
  For this is me; for this is you.

Utter forgiveness lives
  Although lonely at times,
As children worship songs
  and old nursery book rhymes.

If it's known, this when is to be;
For now that you know, is when you become me...

  "For Then and Only Then"
  "When"

  Britt Martin

Mother

White lace and pastels alive full of dreams
The colors of winter and summer and spring
Compassion and fashion and passionate whims
Like a clear morning sun that never grows dim
I'm a man now that's grown so proud and so strong
Still Mother's dear boy whenever I'm wrong
It seems when I'm cranky or nasty or bad
She rarely stops smiling even though she feels sad
There's still hope for this world because she can sing
With a heart filled with love and life full of dreams

  David D. Stuart

Letter Writing Romance "First Meeting"

With each day passing until our glorious joining,
My heart vigorously pounds while love is flowing.

To reach out our arms and warmly embrace,
A zealous dream fulfilled with heavens grace.

As I set here bored, lonely and shivering,
My mind and body is very nervously trembling.

I think to myself, are we compatible, will we click,
For all of life's dreams shall be fulfilled in a clocks tick.

To stand in wait with the desire to run,
Will we idolize each other with joy and fun.

She to be Queen Cleopatra with an eternal desire,
And he to be King Arthur with a heart of fire.

To feel cold, shaky and wet from anticipation,
While endeavoring to seek love and admiration.

For her, it's all about love, happiness and security,
For him, it's life's loving fulfillment of a happy family.

Loves judgment day is upon us today,
May we look upon each other in a delightful way.

As we stand hand in hand with eyes gleaming,
It is obvious destiny has been reached in our meeting.

  Thomas Edward Champ

My Home Town

The town isn't very big at all, and it
sure doesn't have much glitter,
It has lots of things most don't have,
Like the store where we could all ways
get the things that we needed, and the
church with the big tall steeple,
Every one there knew us, and called us
by our names,
Kids could stay out late and play, no one
would bother them, like they would now,
Everyone cared and gave so every one
could have a better day,
How I wish I could go back, and relive
the days of my past, and just enjoy the
peace and quiet, of the days in my hometown.

Rose Pate

Lost Love

Sad was my heart when I noticed!
Not the blooms were gone from the trees,
And a vision comes back to me clearly;
Most precious of all memories.

The stars and the moon in the Orchard!
Hung low over the blossoming trees;
And heaven was near with a fragrance;
That scented a lingering breeze.

The blooms made a white knell of wonder!
Enchanting for one to behold;
Sweet peace and contentment was present;
And it never can be fully told.
An angel was gnawing the orchard!
And she placed there a symbol of love;
That fled ever we knew it had been there;
And now you are gone, like the dove.
God took the blooms from the Orchard!
Just as he had taken from me;
The peace and the hope of was trusting;
As we stood neath the blossoming tree.

Orle Orlo

Just You And I

A walk under the shining light
holding you real tight.

Thinking how lucky I am
to have such a loving knight.

While walking under the light I say
please hold me tight, don't let me go
because I love you so.

As the night comes to an end he takes my
hand, holds me so close, and says,
"I never want to let you go."

RoseAnne Frazzetta

Tranquillity

Halo of clouds encircle like cascades
Tranquillity of bliss engulfs my presence
Tides seem to wash away the tedious tensions
Peace becomes my spirit in this sun drenched place
Take yield in the midst of the stream
With life flowing at each passing moment
The present forms within my midst
No longer to be held back with misconception
Take hold and go after life's pleasures
The form of fear has no name

Beth Dacus

History In Melody

Over 600 years ago, the melodies were slow;
The guitar music from the land of Morocco.
Mauritanians, Arabs and Berbers, sang of love,
So the Moors were peaceful 'neath stars above.

History in melody to remember,
Tenderly in May and December.
So old-fashioned jet teeners say,
Yet not so in history's way.

History in melody to remember,
Plaintive in April and September.
So thoughtful moderns decide,
When to the dictionary they confide.

Rings of gold to show in history,
Gems to display as in melody.
Darkened hands caressed a guitar,
Tribes of Barbary Coast came from afar.

James McMahon

What Is Love, What Is Life

Love is....
Love is,
   a rainbow bent on the rays of the sun
Love is,
   a cherry blossom silently spiralling to the earth
Love is,
   watching the lazy sun rising in the dark gray sky
     with someone dear
Love is,
   walking in the white covered park in a blizzard
     sharing the joy, sharing the pain
Love is,
   searching for the stars on a cloudy night
     sharing all moments together
Love is good times, love is bad
     sharing the times with each other is enough
Love is caring, dreaming, love is even hurting
   By living it together dreams become reality.
Life is.... life is....
     Having someone to love...

Peter Muratore

Three Killers

Twenty-five thousand die young, each year,
a victim of murder, which we all fear,
and fifty thousand go to an early grave
in that vehicle traffic we all must brave,
but, five hundred thousand and maybe more
die before their ten and three score.
And, how they die is certainly no joke,
they are victims of cigarette smoke.

James A. Hull

Life For The Moment

The sun set on the deep blue sea
visions of beautiful scenes and me.

Dreams and thoughts of times to come
wishing another day would be done.

I turned opportunities another way
and didn't live for the present day.

Time is passing and my mind is ahead.
"Life is to short," I often had said.

I found I'd be happier to live day by day
and trusted God would lead my way.

Jennifer Carlye Johnson

Space For Myself

Sitting here in the park is peaceful.
  Children's voices in the distance,
  The creek an endless comfort.
It goes on no matter what.
  Sparkly in the sunshine, cool on my face,
  Each trickle unique.
The cliff is jagged.
  It feels so very solid,
  My heart can feel the weight.
  It's too much - like the pressures of this world.
  Years erode away the surface;
    but deep down, the core doesn't change.
  Unless.... a miracle or enormous change takes place.
If it happens - will it be permanent?
Adjustment is difficult.
Why must we cope with change?
No more questions,
Find the answers around and within you.

  Patricia Bernard

Since You've Been Gone

Since you've been gone I've been very blue,
All I can do is have loving visions of you.
I miss you so much my words could never show it,
But now that you're here you can know it.
You've come back but only to visit,
So now I ask how's love? How is it?
Loneliness flocks around my heart and my soul,
I think it's determined and it's reached its goal.
Without you near I have no pride,
For I was told I would one day be your bride.
My dreams have been shattered though I know you don't care,
Because you just tell me I'll find more love somewhere.
So now I'll let go and be free from my burden,
But someday you'll be back I'm certain.

  Bambi D. Randall

Nature's Gift

The moonlight shines on the sea
Revealing a shimmering glow
As the trees are being decorated by snow
With clusters of sculptured forms
Making balls of twigs dance like horns

Suddenly the snow disappears
and the form of leaves appear
leaves weaving abstract nests
To hold the birds in rest
As the they fly from leaf to leaf
Nature is no place for grief

Nature's gift is to make us see that
spring is not the time for sadness
But for hope and gladness
To give strength to fight strife
To ease our pain and make us save to see
To be freed from avarice and greed
May she continue to use her
Magic wand for the autumn to be

  Helen Schott

Retired

They say these are the "Golden Years."
How come I do not know it?
For my old body to work must go it.
Now that I have retired I go to help the poor.
The ease I have envisioned has not entered my door.
Soon I will come to the end of my labor.
My loving saviour will take me home by his favor.

  Shirley Crowley

To My Woman

To my woman that's like onyx beautiful and
precious all honest that brings forth
life to her babies — she's harmless, loving,
powerful and a kind person.
She's a reflection of I symbolic to the moon
a beautiful bride to the groom.
She's a nuturer, a teacher,
my lover and heart healer
respect I treat her at
times a great leader...
she shouldn't be used
She shouldn't be abused
but be caressed and soothed
and taken upon a long cruise.
Watch as she enjoys this type of mood,
to my woman in my eyes you are appreciated
my love, my cup and everything is dedicated.
Behind every woman there's a man,
Behind every man there's a woman.

  O'Shannon McCants

Colleen

Who has hair like a bright sunny day
Who has eyes brighter than sunbeams
And who has a laugh like tinkling bells
None other than little Colleen.

Who makes a gray day turn into gold
And who makes the sad feel serene
Who tugs at your heart strings
With just a mere smile
It's our own darling Colleen.

She's a little bit feisty
And a little bit bold
Always wanting to help
Without being told.

She's as bright as the moon
On a cool harvest night
And as cute as a kitten
You'd like to hold tight.

A real living doll and
Perhaps a future queen
She's our own incomparable precious Colleen.

  Gladys Stark

Authentic

I asked myself how does he do that?
How does he make the moon sit in the
sky with no strings attached?
So full. So complete in its roundness.
Where does the light comes from shinning upon it?

Then I began to think how uniquely made I am
When my maker created me he made me unlike any other
Yes there are some who resemble but none like me

I'm artistically formed in shape and in color.
Like the satellite sitting upon the earth darkness.
No there is not one like me
And that light shinning upon the moon
Shines on me!

  Darlissa Steeples

Grains Of Sand

When first you met me
  I was a shell of a man
And like grains of sand by the sea
  A castle you began

You shaped with tender hands
  and a gentle smile
A mold of a man
  That was there all the while

The sea washed ashore
  Much like the crescendo from a band
And tried to erode with a roar
  This castle you began

But you stayed all the while
  With strength and belief in your hands
And would glare at the sea with a smile
  For in your hands were many grains of sand

Harry Carvalis

Your First Operational Jump

The green light's on, as you leave the plane
And throw yourself into space!
Many a thought's gone through your mind,
That may later show on your face.

It's too late now for turning back,
But you wouldn't if you could:
You're a man who wears the red beret,
And know for what it stood.

Your chute's abloom and you're floating down,
Wondering what's waiting there:
But you dropped with the best, your mind's at rest
Knowing nothing down there will compare.

Then you land in a foreign country
You may never have seen before;
If you're lucky enough to leave the place
You can tell 'em you've been in a war.

As the years go by and you're getting old,
Perhaps feel you're over the hump,
You can still stand tall and remember with pride
Your first operational jump.

William Nottage

Three Stages Of Love

To bring back love without the pain
To ease the wounds that still remain
To cross the bridge to the hurting one
To say you're sorry for things you've done
These thoughts run through your mind
If only you could turn back time.

When I was young I hurt so much
Then as time went by the most hurtful things
were put in the background of my mind
and didn't have the same intensity
Now that I'm growing older the hurt is
starting all over again.
Three stages.
Not wanting to believe the truth about someone if it hurts you.
Covering up the truth and letting other things take its place.
Finally, not being able to hide from the truth.

Diana L. Johnson

Within Me

Every time you turn around
I can not promise I will be there.
But inside of you I rest
And you inside of me.
Maybe not right on top
But somewhere inside of me you will always be.
When a tear trickles down my cheek,
Or a smile comes across my face..
Part of you will always be in it.
Like the moon in the sky,
You are a forever part of me.
You have touched my heart in so many ways
I can not remember all of them,
But I will always remember the friendship I
  share with you.
Words can not describe how very much you mean to me,
I hope you can paint that picture with all of the
  color you've added to my life.

Ashley K. Behrens

Garden By The Sea

The sea rolls in and greets with waves
Her strength is in command
Her whispered voice sings out to me
Your future's in my hands.

The peace you seek, you'll find it here
As you were gently led
Why me, why here, oh Lord I pray
The sands that I now tread.

Edna Dill

Beaches

The pure white sand goes on and on,
The breeze so clear
In the face of dawn.
The sea gulls spread their wings and cry,
As they appear into the clear blue sky.
But this is no ordinary beach,
It symbolizes eternity swept out of reach.
And as the milky sand sifts away,
It will come and live another day.

Karen Benrot

Wonders Of A Net Romance

Curious eyes, do like what you see, the images of letters on a screen,
Closing the gap between fantasy and reality,
Do you trust what's real, though it's heart nothing but words,
and soul, a group of sentences,
Fearful eyes, not need to be hostile,
For the joy from these will last for a long time,
Or is that when fearful eyes look upon tearful eyes,
Unbelieving to the truth, that behind the jargon,
there's possibly of this being reality,
Denying eyes, to well understood,
for you have seen the evil of the entity, when you were
surrounded by good,
But curious eyes can be gentle eyes,
Where gentle eyes excitedly express my need to be with curious eyes,
Beautiful eyes, loving eyes, yet they never get to see,
only curious eyes experiences the words and sentences,
that are withheld in thee,
So curious eyes, tell me to do you like what you see???
Do you see loving eyes, gentle eyes, beautiful eyes, or loving
eyes staring right back at thee....

James Dowling Jr.

Swiggie

If there be a doggie heaven
I know that Swiggie's there
Telling all her canine friends
Of the good food and loving care
She received while here on earth
She loved to walk and swim with me,
How sad! There is no water
In the sea of tranquility
A faithful friend and playmate was she,
Who guarded me from harm
Who welcomed my friends — not strangers
With her usual canine charm
Mr. Spaceman please throw a Frisbee
To her who waits so patiently
To see water flow so that she can swim
In the sea of tranquility.

Eloise Morris

Burst Of Spring

The trees shimmer in the wind
So light and airy in the Spring.
Leaves dance and shake
Bending high and low on slender branches.
Ever so often birds come to peck
For food beneath the tree bark.

High in the tree where people can't reach
The caterpillar moth get ready
To invade and ravage
All things green and succulent.

Life and death is the key
To our world - its existence harbors
A vestige of comic relief
Turning to tragedy like the comet
It flashes and disappears in the sky
Only to reappear another time.

Rain, snow, and sleet
Hit us like the bullets that kill
Yet we bring life back
With our hearts and a sigh and cry.

Grace Germann

The Ebbing

Time is but a fraction in life waiting to be put to rest.
When one has tears forming a mist in the eyes, as the dawn
burst thru the clouds of dreams. Like a void in an echoless
chamber, the heart beats a soft tune of memories.
In drifts the love that was forgotten in a timeless warp of life.
The feelings growing in a tight ring,
In an endless exodus as memories weave
a soft touch as the hands had met in a
grip of tenderness.
Fading slowly down thru time,
To be rekindled as love of long ago.
Fondly the memories float as if
on golden wings.
Carrying the dreams that tasted there
kiss with the passion in a moment of life.
For age is an enrichment in life that
brings life to life that lived and loved it all.

Bud Forrest

Quiet Flames

Have you seen a faun
in love with freedom and the beauty of nymphs?

He lives all the same
in green woods and
on airy islands

He stretches in abandon
and pleasure
an epitome of art

His body is made out of stone
the color of nude

His inside is made out of fire
the sound of air

His mind is champagne
His soul is boiling ardor
His touch is a river

His name is Passion
or is it Desire?

If ever you meet him
tell him he is
the gift of my life

Georgina G. Hewitt

Friends

No matter what you do
They always come through
They are always there
And always care
When you're sad
They chase away the bad
It's someone you trust
Someone who does not fuss
They can be someone like you
They can be very different too
They don't spread lies about you
They stick to your side too
They never drop you as a friend
They stick with you to the end
They don't whisper behind your back
And don't show lack of respect
They stick out their neck for you
They know who you are
And they say you're the best by far!!!!!

Sharon M. Skidmore

Talk To Me

Talk to me,
So I can listen to your life's long tale and
   hear your untold story of the world, and

Paint for me,
So I can see the canvas pigment splash
   the vibrant colours of your soul, and

Sing for me,
So I can let my spirit fly upon the wings
   of your sweet psalm and
   feel each tingling fibre touch
   the quiet softness of your song, and

Play for me,
So I can drift along your gentle melody and
   feel the deep dark rhythm's pulse
   drum down inside of you, and

Lay with me,
So I will feel so safe secure
   in your strong silent arms and
   share at last the secret
   rushing thunder of your heart.

Janet Modina

The Road Of Life

A country road.
One spot smooth;
Another spot like washboard.
A puddle of water is coming up,
The tire hits it with a splash
Then the front tire sinks.
The wheel spins but you cannot get free.
Thankfully, help arrives to give you a hand.
You realize you have a friend on your journey.
As you continue all is well.
A car is up ahead;
They wave and you wave back.
Another friend; you are not alone.
As you near the crossroad you see the stop sign,
It is time to stop and decide.
There are many different roads to choose.
You go straight through only to find
The exact same thing you just left behind.

Mary Hills

Daisy

I went for a walk today.
On the rocks by the lake I saw a flower.
Not a rose, just a daisy.
Standing straight,
Orange in the center,
White petals framing it.

I went for a walk yesterday.
In the wind and the rain the daisy was there.
Brave and innocent.
Strong against the rain.
Standing straight,
Oranges in the center,
White petals framing it.

The daisy is always there.
Growing where it can't, surviving when it shouldn't.
Not sophisticated, strong.
Not refined, beautiful.
Standing straight,
Orange in the center,
White petals framing it.

Onita Kovacs

1982

Today, I look into your eyes
    wishing you could stay.
Yet knowing that the dreams you have
    are steering us separate ways.
For years and years "friends" always were we
    but something's, maybe?...just aren't meant to be.
My love for you will grow each day
    and continue for...Lord knows when.
But my heart will always long for the moment
    until I get to see you again.
Someday maybe, we'll find one another
    and realize just what could have been.
But until that day, I hope...
    We'll always remain best of friends.
We'll reach for our dreams and our fantasies
    through the course of a hundred years.
But we'll say our goodbyes...through watery eyes...
    that will for years...
    drown a pillow...with tears.

Tammy Henderson Lampe

"Saving Inspiration"

Mere flash thought of just one noble near and dear
Pure, kind, gentle and indeed of rare breed
Rich in mind with the Midas touch of care and share
For me is inspiration infinite over and over to brood

Such for real, lights up my life, lightening its burden;
Lifts me ever so high to hope's those new horizons
That stood so far, by around and above me unseen;
Teaches me in content to give the best in me to near ones

But there exists not on earth many a happy face
That sheds around and above them such saving grace
Few though, if joined in hands to make others happy
Enough to mould after them this planet's whole face

Limited too we are to know and love such great faces
And often turn wrong to choose even those born for hearts
Confused too are those old reasons: of broken order,
Of fates unknown, of serpent's fakes, mixed with our own.

To save the known few at hand is a noble act of redemption
Paving the way for a far new creation, free of pretension

John Thanickal

Backsliding

Backsliding is a difficult art to master,
But I seem to have done it so well!
No new feelings of self-worth are showing faster,
Only in emotional pits do I dwell!

Where has all my energy for self gone?
Why am I still "other" focussed?
My head and the wind are calling, "come back home,"
Only my heart seems so obsessed.

God allows for U-turns,
Life creates backsliding;
Only in backsliding,
Watch out you don't get burns!

Nancy Ruth Allen

"My Dream"

In life we all have many dreams,
A dream is but a long deep thought.
And as I lay awake at night,
I ask myself but why, if all these things I dream about
could be real to us all...

I dream about the day, when the land will sing of peace,
For there will be no more fighting, only harmony will there be.
And there will be no more homeless, they will have a place to
call their own.
The land would also be free of disease, for too many people
have died, no more pain and suffering would there be, and
in "My Dream" life would be endless glory for me.
The hungry would be well fed, the bombings would never be
Our children would all be healthy, what a wonderful
things that would be.
Our streets would be free of drugs, it would be a thing of the past.
People would begin to love again, to trust in themselves and God.
My dream, is it just a dream, where did it all begin
Where does it all end?
This dream could be with everyone, reach out for it and make it yours.

Patricia Snock

My Prayer

Dear Father in Heaven, I know that you,
Can show me what you think I should do,
When I feel so blue and know not the way,
I can turn to you, and hear you say,
"Cheer up my dear, it's not all that bad
That you should sit and feel so sad,
Pour out your troubles now, to me,
So that together we can really see
Whatever it is, will work out in love,
So lift your eyes to the heavens above."

"Now count your blessings, one by one,
Then you will know what has to be done,"
So — I lift my eyes and look up to you
As I know you always have helped me through
The trying hours and the difficult days.
To my surprise!!! I am amazed!!!
Now how much better I really feel,
And all the wounds begin to heal.
I just feel like my old self again,
As I tear up the paper, and lay down the pen. "Thank You God."

Iona Boyse

Thoughts Of A Student Before Receiving Graded Test

Oh no, she's graded our tests
And is returning them to us!
I know I did bad on it,
I just know it!
Although I answered every question
I wasn't sure of the correct answer
On many of them!
She's coming closer.
How did I do?
How did I do?
I studied for hours for this test
And still I wasn't sure on many of them!
Like what year did the U.S. enter World War I?
Why were many opposed to the League of Nations?
What caused organized crime in the twenties?
Who was the prosecutor in the scopes Monkey Trial?
I just couldn't remember!
Why couldn't I remember?!
Well, there's the paper.
Just calm down and turn it over....

Paul Kuamoo

Abused Children

The battered child has a complicated life.
It is a life of much fear and abuse
The little children can't protect themselves
They are loved but somehow hated at the same time

The battered child is not just one who's beaten
For Mary's mother threw her down the stairs
And Jonnie was in the closet for a week
And Cindy's mom said she was dumb and ugly

One lonely day this boy was sent away
He's happy now with parents who care for him
No longer does he cry within a closet
But gaily plays outside with the other children.

Alice Wood

God's Winter Beauty

I looked out on the winter night,
    A storm was raging high.
The wind was blowing loud and strong,
    The snow across the sky.
The ground was covered in flurries of white,
    The trees were laden, but bare.
A bit of heaven opened wide,
    And I in a sense was there.
I stood in awe of the beauty there,
    As the wind grew calm and still.
A beautiful day was dawning now,
    As the sun crept over the hill.
There is nothing so rare as a winter night,
    As you sit by the fire and dream.
God has created a beautiful world,
    At a glance His beauty is seen.
Thank God for His wonderful world,
    And lift your prayers on high.
Thank Him for this winter night,
    For it's beauty you can't buy.

Pat Erickson

Untitled

Not in a folk faerie's land
Nor upon a golden grassed hill
It is knee-deep in reality I stand
Accompanied by my wit and will

Forefathers forsaken,
My life I've partaken,
To strive for the convictionless known

I stand on ground shakin'
In this life there's no fakin'
I'm givin', takin', holding my own

Rise up, rise up, out of the mist
Velvet glove on an iron fist
Perception deception is the solid real
What makes the difference is what you feel

Filth in the mouth, yet life without sin
To make it, you take it, again and again
Intravenously fed from the falsehood fount
What you ingest on your own, best make it count

Meg Holle

To My Daughter, Joy

Who would ever have thought
During all those years
That we quarreled and fought
Through laughter and tears
That there was a purpose to it all
Unknown to us then - the truth:
You can't walk before you crawl,
Adulthood only follows youth.
The Sun of all the yesterdays
Has granted us tomorrows,
The blacks and whites become the grays,
The "Joys" replace the sorrows.
From seedlings to brilliant flowers,
From cocoon to a butterfly.
So far above the rest you tower and, as I watch the time pass by,
I realize what was meant to be those years of climbing the mountain,
Of letting you go to be free to drink from life's Fountain.
Only now we both comprehend we had to scale the rough terrain
To have and be a friend; the Rainbow after the Rain.

Trudy Garman

If Not I

If not I whom shall gather the seeds of pine, harvest of the north
Secluded in hidden valleys of gold and red
Nestled beneath musty fragrance
Forgotten appendage, coveted by those who seek refuge
Lonely boughs who once gave life, castaway, forgotten
Solace only to those who seek warmth, damp, earthy, yielding bed

If not I then who shall travel with my lost love
That man who once more the insatiable badge of lover
With unequaled yearnings of all whom offered their hearts, dreams

Where once my lover nestled in the musty fragrance of I
Riding me, unpredictable winds of spring, soft breeze, stormy gales
The same winds that stir or bend those northern firs
Filling aching voids, velvet clothed in silk, soothing salve,
Warm milk to mons

If not I who shall it be
Whom shall become the philanderer who covets unknown trees

If not I who will it be nestled beneath musty fragrance
Like those forgotten, lonely boughs who once gave life long ago
Welcome bed to those who seek solace, damp, earthy, yielding bed
If not I who shall gather the seeds of northern pine.

Catherine Clydesdale-Henderson

The Pond

Surrounded by stately rugged oaks, fed by
Underground spring the blue-green pond
Provides habitat to varied life forms
Existing in symbiotic association.

A black drake with white duck waddle towards
The pond, leading four yellow and one black
Fluffy progeny, enter the water and begin
Bobbing down to gain sustenance from the algae.

Lounging in the shallows a base voiced frog
chants his symphonic melody.

Wiggling up from the lower depths a mosquito
larva breaks the waters calm then dives down.

Skimming over the pond's glassy surface a
water scorpion barely disturbs the smoothness.

Darting above the pond a red dragonfly stops!
Hovers! Landing on a pussy willow stem.

Though not eternal, this pond is destined to
serve as security, asylum, shelter, for aeons
yet to pass.

D. Rodger Long

The Eagle's Eyes

Flying high, up in the sky.
Looking down, through eagle's eyes.
Looking down and seeing trees,
Emerald fields, and living things.
A human here, a rabbit there,
A tiny mouse, beyond despair.
For the young ones, they will thrive.
Become like me, and then will die.
Too much pollution, not enough trees.
Bring them back, oh please, oh please.
We are diminishing, we go in pairs.
Hurry! Hurry! Any help out there?
Don't you see, what you've done.
You've killed us all, there's no more sun.
No more fields, or streams that run.
They're filled with sludge, and toxic gases.
A terrible sight, no grassy patches.
It's done, it's over,
You've killed all creatures,
But, there are many possible, different futures.

Matthew Russell Squires

Father's Idiosyncrasies

Lanky and frail with hints
of untapped muscular potential.
Receding hair, with remains
of a preceeding era.
Deep set eyes that are appropriately
magnified through less than spectacular spectacles.
A man with unbelievable patience
or extreme ambivalence.
The occasional stern feel could never conceal
the smirk, lurking behind the facade.
A mind so wise not to criticize,
only to stimulate and harmonize.
The combination of love, discipline and character
has been imprinted upon my entire existence.
All, because of father's idiosyncrasies.

Michael Douglas Miller

Author Of My Heart

My heart, like a book placed upon a shelf.
Every chapter containing its own storyline,
Some pages never being turned

Sometimes when the book is read again new meanings are found.
Some things often overlooked appear before your eyes.

The dust of time wearing heavy on the delicate pages
The pages, containing the mysteries and wonders of a knowledge
That not all dare to explore.

My heart like a novel; filled with romance, filled with suspense,
Every sentence like a vein with words flowing like blood.
Every chapter a new adventure to embark on.

I am the author of my heart

Yet never in total control of what my story may hold
For the one willing to open the hard leather cover.

Scuffed from mishandling, the pages sometimes torn,
Some possibly even missing.
Sitting on a shelf no purpose has my book
Except for someone to find it so intriguing they can't put it down.

Sunni Scheller

Melancholy

There is no time for petty excuses,
Nor time to think about the past.

The shadows emerge from the corners,
Engulfing my petrified soul.

The memories flood my mind,
Only adding to the pain,
And searching for a way out,
To leave me void of remembrances, torture.

It is exactly these experiences that
    call upon Death,
Guiding me to the other side.

Nobody understood my pain,
Or why I felt it.

Nobody bothered to understand,
Nobody bothered to care.

I only know that the separation my soul
    and body suffered was the only way to
    put an end to my afflictions...
The only way to lay my soul to rest.

Leticia Sanchez

"The Forest Through The Trees"

As the archer finds his mark,
You've found that spot in my heart,
As the arrow finds its game,
Our lives are to never be the same,
We found each other through the trees,
Every moment, meaning to please,
Learning, loving and laughing,
All the time being so happy,
Let us not make such a fuss,
Try and think 'bout the two of us,
I'll want you to have and to hold,
From now until I'm one hundred years old,
Tell me that you love me,
Tell me that you care,
Tell me you will never go away,
For you and I can be so happy one day,
You can see the forest through the trees,
Stop for a moment, see what you see,
A life together would never be bad,
I'd promise to make you happy, and never sad.

Bruce J. Marshall

Electric Death
(Or A Change Subtler Than The Electric Chair)

The neo-culture: Electric life!
A language of electric voices
Belonging to electric faces
   Tainted by electric smudges
And if you wish
   You can change your electric voice!
   Change your electric face!
Change is at your fingertips!

We are so fantastic, so sadly unbelievable
Dressed in electric lies
   Hiding farther behind electric lies

Touch my cold, metallic skin
Feel my electric pulse
Feel it shiver through your body
   Like sadness shivering through your body

Sleep in you electric bed
Rest your wired, electric head
Awaken refreshed— you're electric fed

Soon we'll all be
   Electric dead

James Patrick Surber

Family Tree

Where the warm winds blow

I liken it to a maple tree. It stands
alone in the field and it has been there for many years.
When you get close to it, you notice that it is not alone at all.
Many buds have spiraled down and met with the ground.
The new shoots vary in size and viability.

Sitting under the tree protects you. It gives you some comfort.
You feel awed by its size and renewed by its history.
You can always go to it - it can't abandon you.
You are thankful for this because this is where the warm winds blow.

They open your heart.

My family is near and dear to me. They provide a place to go,
to recede into when I need comfort. I depend on them.
I draw from them to rebuild my spirit.

When I am anxious, upset or just plain scared one of my family
is there to turn to. They say everything will be okay
and I believe this. Soon I find they were right.

Someday they will be gone, but so will I. We all will have been
better for having been together.
As just one we would have been less of a person.

Virginia E. Stewart

Untitled

Let's put history in its proper place:
It's just a record of the human race
Let's free ourselves from biased false belief
And turn once more to nature, for relief.
If we must worship things, let them be real
Things that we see, hear, taste, know, and feel
Worship the sun, the moon, the distant stars
Worship the many planets like Venus and Mars
Don't symbolize them as love or as war
But see them, in truth, no less and no more
As planets whirling, like our earth, in space.

Doreen Allred

Flashback Via Cinema

Tis' worse to fall in love with an overseas woman,
For all that is about her is intrigue;
Her phrases, expressions, life, country, past,
Lead to airmail in the extreme.

Hunger for information quickens,
Her little notes kindle the flames,
Dry TV shows, newspapers, magazines, books,
Feed a discovering, geographical affection.

Passion yearns over time and miles,
Days pass in a waking dream,
Till' at last transcontinental flight,
And contact with the beloved unseen.

Joy transforms to apprehension,
Knowledge to assumption, adventure to folly,
Mystery becomes irreconcilable difference,
Jet lag of the soul sets in.

I loved a woman I'd never met,
Till' one spring day I found,
A familiar face with stranger's eyes,
Who had read my deepest desires...

Ed P. Snead

The Last Tide

The saga of the mentally ill
that crave for something more than a pill
Stereotyped as crazed and wild
Forgetting conflicts built as a child

A single light shines from afar
Completely blocked by emotional scar
A lonely raindrop drops from the sky
Conditioned for years never to cry

Fantasies fill up the day
While reality leads us astray
Society says that we should hide
And drift away on the next tide

It's time to sleep so tomorrow will come
Although we know that we will be numb
The media takes away our dreams
So we may fall apart at the seams

The saga of the mentally ill
The system comes in for the kill
A human life that's pushed aside
Drifting away on the last tide

Frank Spiegel

Chameleon

My chameleon is very neat,
He has a long tongue and some good feet.
My chameleon as you know,
He sure likes to grow,
And sometimes to gunmen, he's a skeet.

Chameleons are so very weird,
And some people say that they have beards.
Chameleons hide a lot.
Some people like them, even tots.

So if you ever see a Chameleon,
Please don't think of him as a robot.
Kate Langenburg

Portraying Love

Love is sweet, like the spring day,
That moists bloomin' buds of May.
Like the song that's melting heart,
Whose note's touchin' his inner part.

True love, need not borrow bitterness.
Should not fade our happiness
But rise through life's petals bright,
As a star from the high angle, with her light.

Endurance of true love bears through morrows,
Many transient sorrows,
Yet tear's glare blends with kiss,
And turns love into Heavenly bliss.
Nevenka Simunic

Return Of Rome

Nothing rivals the possibility of love
when you're sitting on a gold mine
singing a melancholy ballad of chance,

Traveling the distant terrain of the mind,
searching for a phrase of affection
to capture the ear of the angel,
words more numerous than celestial bodies—
which feeds forth the brightest light?
which the greatest hope?
which could turn the head of Aphrodite, so grand in its perception?

When the bridges were built
I meant for them to be fortified, to last forever,
Instead they burnt down overnight—
that fire caused by the spark of false hope for another,

History teaches us time and time again, though,
that all great kingdoms come to an end,
and some, some return in even greater form,
if I was to catch your heart with precious words of passion,
do you think the greatest kingdom ever, the kingdom of love,
could return in even higher grandeur?
Benjamin Petre

The Happy Whale

The gigantic whale dives gracefully,
Smiling with his enormous teeth,
Singing in the moonlit ocean,
Eating hundreds of krills at a time.

A rusty old ship sails silently,
A harpoon races through the shining water,
Moving quickly the whale flees,
The harpoon hits loudly on the rocky ocean floor.
Jared Anthony Burton

Untitled

And it was the oddest thing:
    He took my skin
        folded it up
and put the hook through it, just below
    my head.
Hanging, dangling and submerged.
Blue and green around and within,
    And there he was.
His gaping mouth.
Geometric rows of infinite teeth revealed.
    Fins waving and the calming-hypnotizing
effect of barely perceptible gill arches. Like
    bellows.
He leaves me. The last I saw of him
    was the metallic flash of his tail.
As he swam off into the black.
And I was left to look around.
And hope that someone would find my pole
    left up on the bank.
Lori A. Dykeman

Mischievous Angel

Hands in the jam jar, then says, "No!"
    But the evidence tells you so.
Each one has their own sweet style,
    Mischievous Angel with a smile.

Tucked in bed with shut-tight eyes,
    dreams of candy clouds in the skies.
Wise little lady, who can beguile,
    Mischievous Angel with a smile.

Uses her milk to bathe the cat,
    Loses her mitts, and forgets her hat.
Dumps her clothes in a massive pile,
    Mischievous Angel with a smile.

Digs in the dirt, and buries her shoes,
    Lies in the flower bed for a snooze.
Dainty, daring, little elf 'chile,'
    Mischievous Angel with a smile.

Would not trade these years for anything,
    These happy times that only she can bring.
She'll be all grown up in just a while,
    My mischievous Angel, with a smile.
Margaret Robson Russell

Abortion

In my first month I'm as happy as can be.
You don't know yet; I can't wait until you see.

It's now my second month; I've got a while to go,
But I can't wait; mommy I love you so.

What's happening, why have I quit?
Abortion: Oh no! That must be it.

It would've been my forth, but I am no longer
If this happens again, I hope you'll be stronger.

On what would be my fifth, I kind of have a plead.
To be living, I have the need.

In this month, to go it would be three
I don't understand why my life couldn't be

In this month of seven, I think of what could've been
Being held by you, the thought may never end.

Even though I'm gone; I hope I'll still be loved.
And if you have a prayer, just send it up above.

Think about me every day and what may have been.
Just remember you might see me when into heaven you ascend.
Leigh Ann Lockhart

Rose Petals For My Mother's Grave

This is to release you and to let you go.
This is to sever the umbilical cord of energy that has connected us.
This is to release you and let to you go.

This is to give you back that old energy that has bound us and
held us and strangled us all these years.
This is to release you and to let you go.

This is to thank you for the good things. Your wise choices. Your
strength of character. Your generosity. Your endurance. Your intelligence.
This is to release you and to let you go.

This is to claim Me, Myself and I. My beauty. My choices. My likes.
My desires. My friends. My passion. My mission. My radiance.
This is to release me and to let me be.

This is to start in a new way to love you. One unique and beautiful
spirit to another unique and beautiful spirit. To love you as an equal.
This is to release us both and to let us both go and be.

Apart and together.
Together and apart.

Jeannie Mackay

A Tribute To The Nurse

No one knows the value of their work, until there's pain.
You cannot put a price upon their care, and what you gain
They change the face of agony and bring about a smile
From dawn to dusk, and though the night, their skill is there on trial

In gentleness their task portrayed, like angels on the wing.
No fear is shown within their deeds your care is everything
In sympathy there is no end, in them you put your trust
If gratitude must then be shown, to them we really must.

She is the life line between surgeon and patient of every ward.
And compliments she does not seek, she is grateful to see you cured.
For dedication in the nurse, is shown in all they do
And a purpose made within their lives is to tend and care for you.

There is no room for weakness of the mind at what they see
Their will is strong in tenderness, as ours could never be
This work is theirs and theirs alone it is built within their soul.
And they strive with care and thoughtfulness until they reach their goal.

Their presence makes life easier when in the hour of need.
They watch you rest subdued from pain, no matter what the breed.
And I for one, have known the care and love for life from them,
and yet, if gratitude must pay the bill, we will forever be in debt.

Bill Mander

Ambassadorial Inelegance And A Resignation

At an embassy reception there was a sad perception
    Of a diplomat in great shock.
He had discovered his fly was totally awry
    Wide open to the gaze of the flock.
When he discovered his error, he gazed down in terror
    In shocking and total dismay
For he turned his back on the snickering pack
    And proceeded to zip up his "disarray"!
But sad to say he met such delay
    For his zipper got caught in his tie,
But try as he would be never quite could
    Solve his problem on the diplomatic "front" that day!

R. Wallace Campbell

Angel With Wheels

Born of the love of two special people
Beloved daughter, wife, mother, grandmother
Family and home her world, mothering her worry and joy
Jean clad gardener, country music fan
Victim of the thief that stole movement and vision
Patient patient
Touching the hearts of all in her small place
Bed to wheelchair, wheelchair to bed
Eyes twinkling, muted voice chuckling
Hand and finger waving her "Whatever"
"making" her treat.
A light shining brightly, dancing, then flickering and gone too soon
Sorrowfully missed by those who love her
Comforted knowing she is free from suffering and pain
Now a loving spirit surrounded by Perfect Love
Watching over dear ones here
Remembered always

Barbara Vander Voort

Exquisite

Between the trees
Look up you'll see it with ease
The attraction
A twinkle within your eye
Delicious curves of thy lovely face
How can anybody else be so near
When my heart points the way clear

I see a vision
Blossoms of the lush velvet fields
Lips the perfection
Crimson red to black to a sharp edge of white
My fanciful delight
I press against you
I feel now that only love will pursue.

Did you know my white dove
I see our beautiful castle
You share with me your compassionate, caring love
Reach for me, my dove
Forever we will romance
But first you must take the chance

James Vipond

"Innocence Of A Child"

Each like a child when we kiss,
Full of innocence,
And when we hug there's innocent love,
Like God's blessing us with loving dove.
When we dance we step on each other's toes,
We do everything innocently which shows how much each of us knows.
Both of us enjoy the beach and building sand castles,
For us life hasn't any hustles.
Because everything to us in life is new,
As we grow older we'll learn, discover, experience, from what we do.
Excitement fills our hearts with the fall of snow,
Our faces light up with presents from Ho Ho!
Playing house and tea party's fun, dressing up,
Pretend becomes reality some, after drinking from the cup.
Life's path will show us new places and new faces,
Life's beauty and life's disgraces,
Yet young innocence can't be erased,
Since young innocence is as beautiful as bridal or baby's lace.

Pamela K. Walczak

My Dream

I saw her again last night.
In my vision, she sits before me as I wonder.
I feel her energy and know she is out there.
I see her face, so clearly as I rest.
Her hair, her eyes, her smile, my beautiful mate, the one I seek.
The one my destiny will find for me, but when I awake from
my unconscious thoughts she is gone.
I scramble in my mind to find the image, her image.
The details of her face, the mystery in her eyes.
I love her, but who is she?
She is waiting, I need to hurry, she can't wait forever.
Wishful thinking? Control of my heart?
I will know, I will feel her control over me.
Just like the dream, the dream of my future passing through my heart.
She will be the one, the one to hold me, the one that shall bear my name.
She will be proud of me, as I will be of her.
Please, my Destiny reach into my dream and bring her to me.
Then I can live free, free to know I have my dream.
Next time don't wake me up.

James R. Bradfield IV

My Love

I love you more than words can say.
I love you more each and every day.
I love you because you are my friend
and I hope that will never end.
I love because I am yours
and you are mine.
I love you for who I am,
for without you I never would have been.
We're been through some good
and been through some bad but I see now, we had;
to come to what we are today, for our love has grown more than
words can say.
I love you for who you are.
I love you more than I can express
for dear you are the best.
I love you more each and everyday,
my love

Michele Lee Adams

"What Is, Is What Is"

Bright sunlight, a sky of blue
More crime and violence, that's nothing new
A man dies and a baby is born
Some part of the world a war is going on
There's sadness, there's happiness
Some says life's a quiz
But to put it quite simply
What is, is what is
History seems to be repeating itself
Bosnia, Burundi, Rwanda need help
Murder, genocide and ethnic cleansing
People are dieing and no one is winning
Extinction of animals and toxic waste
World destruction, exploring in space
Then man says we've learned some lessons
I can't tell but let me make this expression
Lets forget about crime, hate and machines
Learn to love and make our world clean
Then we'll have love an happiness
And greatly acknowledge what is, is what is

Anthony Rhaney

Take My Hand (Ode To Martin Luther King)

Take my hand my work is done
  Lead me home my course is run
You my brother black or white
  Pray to God this very night
Ask Him now in strength anew
  To live and love for all that's true
That freedom's chimes will ever ring
  From mountain tops while valley's sing
America, America, both of you today
  Pray to God to light the way
That men may build and cease to slay.
  Oh kill not, my assassin fierce
Let love reign free and only pierce.
  His heart of hate, and woe
Put it down brother, take up that hoe.
  Cultivate your neighbor's heart
Shoot only freedom's power dart.

Dywane Momb

"A Loving Tribute To My Mom"

My dear Mother, I can't find the words to say how very special you are to me
  You are the "Rock of Strength" for me and everyone in our family.

I'll never forget how you taught me early in life about God's love
  And I could see how you lived your daily life, how you always
  prayed to Him above.

I know it is because of your daily walk with God, your witness and
  your Christian dedication that has made me who I am today, and,
  I'm so proud to say that "I'm a Christian."

You have always been there for me, if I need anything, I never have to ask
It seems you're there and know what to do, no matter what the task.

You never let anyone help you, but, you are always helping others
  And that's what makes you the very best of Mothers.

Your life hasn't been easy, you've had a lot of trials,
  hardships and pain, and you've always worked so hard
But, when this life is over and you get to heaven, you will receive
  your blessings from God and your crown full of rewards.

I know sometimes we seem to disagree, but I'm so thankful that God
  chose you as my Mother
I love you dearly, and I'm proud to be your daughter, if I could
  choose my Mother, I wouldn't choose another!

Happy Mother's Day!

Carolyn J. Allison

Imagination

In your imagination you can make your own convictions,
But all you see with your real eye,
are scenes of realistic non-fiction.
You can see anything you want to see,
a talking tree, a ghost, green flowers and
a blue and purple bee,
wizards, black flames, dragons and sword games,
a striped cow, a potted lamb, Pebbles and Bambam,
silver pennies, gold dimes, red bananas,
and purple limes.
A clipped winged bird that really flies, your friends,
Suzie, Molly and Kristin are really guys.
Everyday think of a new, weird, and wacky thing,
like you can hear a person without vocal cords sing.
In your imagination you can make your own convictions
but, all you see with your real eye
are scenes of realistic non-fiction.

Raya G. Ramsey

Two Hearts As One

God created two hearts to become as one
To share in laughter as well as the pain
To sing the songs of want and joy
While others are single and all alone
God created our hearts to become as one

Two hearts to live in peace and harmony
Together pressing, we are longing to be one
Yours and mine two hearts as one
Loving, caring, fulfilling every need
God created our hearts to become as one

With Love In Our Hearts
John W. Hairston

Nocturnal Dance

In a silver ray of moonshine she danced —
sparkling like a diamond
she twinkled
she pranced
with light leaps —
soundless, graceful

White and pure,
her eyes glowed like fire in the night —
on soft butterfly wings
she moved
she glided
with the wind —
slowly, carefully

Silent and meek,
she eventually became part of her surroundings —
faded away
to become
part of the sea —
a wave that had swept the shore.

Annette Hagberg

Are You There

My thoughts reach out to you.
But they go unanswered.

I can feel you in my heart
I need to know, are you there?
Do you feel the same?

A kiss,a touch, an embrace.
I need to know, are you there?
Do you feel the same-and be true to yourself,
Forget what's out there-facts, details.
How do you feel?
Go with your heart.

My thoughts are all about you,
When will we see each other next?
Will I see her smile? Hear her laugh?
I need to know, are you there?

I need you to say my name,
I need to hear your voice,
I need to see your eyes-so bright so alive!
You need nothing, perfection seldom does-
But I can see a place for me in your heart.

Adriano Paradiso

So There Was A Gal Who Mourned My Death

Fair Death you have brought me here
To tranquility in serene bed
To decay with nature who is so sincere
But I wish in life more ladies read

From heaven looking on the lamentation
My coffin being laid to sleep
Listening to my families anger and frustration
That hits my heart so deep

They should run in the fragrance of May
Not mourning over what cannot be
Moods should alter to ecstatic fun and play
Right now too hard to see

A young lady I've spent time with
Pours her heart on my grave
Great love she spoke, only heard in myth
Echoed like an endless cave

So there was a gal who mourned my death
Now haply here do lie
For when she weeps her dying breath
I'll catch her in the sky

Sean A. Stares

The Twilight Hour

The little pixy would come and sit under the pretty flowers.
Every evening at the twilight hour.
For he liked to see the fairies come out to play.
And watch as they flitter their wings and fly away.
Then he would laugh with glee,
As the little ones would come and sit upon his knee.
For their wings were ever so soft and fragile and small.
As they would sit and listen to the crickets call.
Then he would hear them chatter and chatter in their own little way.
And most times when they came he wished they could stay.
But that was not so.
For in evening they will have to go.
The he would watch as they flitter there wings to fly back home.
And he would sit there a moment with tears in his eyes for he
knew he would be left alone.

Esther Thompson

My Cloud

My cloud, my cloud
You look like an angel
You act like an angel
Oh no, there just was a big gust of wind
My angel is gone with the wind
If I turned to walk away, know what I hear
A tiny voice, it said, don't go now I just left to go get something
She shows me her necklace made of crystal cloud
I look at her amazed, she smiles and then she is gone
When I went to bed that night I dreamt of my angel
We are laughing and playing together
When I wake, know what I find
My angel's necklace left behind for me.

Lacy Orydzuk

The Harvest

Overcome by such kindness, you tearfully reminisced;
"I strayed from the way I was raised, but never dreamed I'd come to this.
I should have known that disdain for others would tag me one of these days;
I meet hard times and nailed up doors, no welcomes, or familiar layaways!"

Florrie J. Forbes

What I Need To Get By

When I am depressed, and I began to cry.
I remember God is all I need to get by.

I am trying to run this race.
So I can see Gods face.
That's why you see me trying to live by faith.
That's why I thank you God, I am save by grace.

If everybody believe the word of God is true.
There would be no reason to use me and you.

If you are a willing vessel to carry the truth,
We should ask God for power.
To do what he want's us to do.

That's carry the word into the world.
To try to save every boy and girl.

This is what God want us to do.
Yes me and you
and that's the truth,
yes that's the truth,

God is talking to me and you,
All about caring the truth,
not only me and you but others too.

Annie L. Moore

I Am Free, Independent, And Strong

I am woman, hear me roar
I am more than I thought of myself before
The ones who love and care for me help me see
What's deep, down inside of me
I am free, independent, and strong
If you think I'm weak, you're wrong
I earn my way to the top
So if you think I'm spoiled stop
My parents protect me from things in the world
That doesn't mean I'm their little girl
I don't steal, I receive what I earn
Watch me, and you'll learn
I'm not perfect, I make mistakes
I say what I think, and I'm not a fake
People hurt me, but I get over it
I stand tall and never quit
I know who I am and what I want
In the race of life, I'll be in the front
I am free, independent, and strong
If you think I'm weak, you're wrong

Nicole Walker

Silent Child

I was not blessed in my life,
  the secrets I did hold.
My mother, father, sister dear
  said they should not be told.
A crime did happen to a child,
  to this there's no excuse!
But all that came, of all that pain
  was a child who became a recluse.
My mother said, "I will not have it!"
  To your room you will not retreat!
But a shattered soul, of a child grown old
  I had no courage to meet
And as my tears fall down my cheek
  I whisper now to you,
Do you hear the cries of the silent child
  She's calling out to you!

Leighan Fales

My Love

As I sit by the water's edge alone
The morning's sun warmth soothing my face
I spend this time reflecting on our life
Looking back I can remember many moments
I remember the first time I saw you
The first time we met
The first time we touched
And the first time we loved
And I realize those memories are special
And I realize I still need to feel them now
For you are the one true love of my life
And with you by my side my circle is complete

Pam Kirchhoefer

What A Guy!

I've got a friend, who means the most.
He's always with me wherever I go.
He's been here for me through thick and thin;
Without Him, I don't know where I would have been.
I've had much suffering, heartache and pain
I know without that there is no gain.
He's helped me see the error of my ways,
And shown me a different path for my days.
What a guy! He's seen me through my troubled days,
And helped my pain go away.
He's there to help me celebrate a happy occurrence
And helps me see beauty in my everyday living.
I love the Lord who's there for me.
My friendship with Him helps me be more conscientious of others;
I can't describe how good He makes me feel.
What a guy!

Becky Thrush

Regrets

The time it passes quickly, although it seems to go by slow.
The things that I remember, I never seemed to know.
It seems it all is ending, although it's just begun
I hold tightly to the memories, of the things that we have done.
Gone but not forgotten, the memories always stay
I turn to say goodbye before I go my separate way.
I look to find your smile, though the tears I see your face.
The memories in my heart, I never will erase
our boats are pushed apart, by the forces of the tide.
Trying to forget, the feelings I must hide.
It's time to say goodbye, it's time to let me go,
it's time to move away, from everything I know.
Sometimes we must let go, although the feelings strong.
Sometimes we must hold on, although we know it's wrong.
But now it's time to part, with your face fred in my mind,
and the pictures of the places that we all must leave behind.
Some say no regrets, it all turned out ok.,
some wish it all were different, that they'd gone another way.
Be the memories good or bad, we never will forget,
as I look back in my past, there is nothing I regret.

Amy DeSantis

Early Morning Oneness

I am bursting with the softly blazing sunshine
  as I walk along the sandy stubble grass,
  making my way slowly to the seashore.
The fresh vanilla breezes toss the flowers,
the pale blue wildflowers growing by the roadside.

These gentle winds that take the dewey wetness
far away to places where no roads have gone,
that mix my breathing with the breath of stars,
make me ache to be at one with all that Is...

Gyatri Devi

Night Garden

What small phenomena occurs
in night's hidden garden?

We wear our day eyes blindly
and cannot see a shadow's birth
nor perceive a satyr's gelastic face.

Perhaps a daemon basks
in moon-drenched sorcery -
dancing an invisible minuet
before our night-veiled vision.

I would seek these things
from the haven of my lighted window -
but then...
they would flee
before its synthetic indelicacy.

So I chase will-of-the-wisps ceaselessly,
and only catch them...
...in sleep's little dramas.

Velma P. Brown

Life

Life is not great, now awful - it simply is;
We can make it great or awful by a simple
remark or gesture.

Life is endless, it goes on regardless of our
social, political or spiritual lives;
it does not end at death, or begin at
birth, it is as continuous as the suns rays.

Life is like a blank canvas, where your
ambitions, dreams and goals are on your
palette - you create your own picture.

Life is more powerful than all the worlds
nuclear weapons; more complex than
any of einstein's theories; and more
delicate than the smallest snow flake.

Life is dealt like a deck of cards, not
knowing what your hand will be, but
it is abused like an old second hand car,
thinking you can always get another one.

Trevor McAlmont

Mid-Night Sun

No sooner has the sun touched the horizon
Than she rises again
To glide over the southern sky,
Shedding her warm gentle light day and night,
Bringing life to animals and plants all alike!

At this time of the year,
All lives thrive and flourish here
In harmony and unspoiled at their own venture,
As nourished and cherished by Mother Nature!

Blessed shall be mankind
With the warm gentle light of the Arctic Summer Sun,
So gracious and kind,
That our lives shall be in harmony
And forever healthy and happy!

Yuk Wor Lee

Embraces

Embrace yesterday's modern world
today's fantasy spins
lye the devils grin
and famous smile that terror screams
they fall late at midnight
into the oldest yet most soft spoken woods
never to be found, leave no trail of evil
no evidence to trample upon
does bad things of nonsense happen
yet to another innocence? My soul,
never seen or heard of before
walk hand in hand with thy friends
until passing father's grave, friend's grave
or your grave
ask no more questions
for he the Lord has an answer for all.

Kimberly D. Stephenson

The Swimmer, Fisher and Fiddler

Warming as a hearth glowing,
orange, yellow, blue... a breeze gently blowing.
Swaying... tapestry dances from
boughs draping themselves upon a
flowing ground. Full; lazily
imperceptibly changing, pulling,
filling again and again and again.
Straw mats clinging stubbornly to a
temporary permanence of fluctuating duality.
Pulling stronger — a beckoning desire to roam
endlessly on an on... no destination, but a
destiny to wander back to no beginning.
Lazily pulling, filling again and again and again.
The swimmer cautious evading the fisher.
The fisher feigned no concern while the fiddler
fiddles his domain, his solicitous salute challenging.
The fisher stills himself; the swimmer approaches...
the swimmer is deep... the fisher moves on...
the fiddler retires.

Ray Thornton

Gaman Suru (To Endure)

From a distant land she came
Daughter of a farmer
Eighteen years young, picture bride to be
Of our father thrice her age, a stranger
With uncertain fear, she married
This stranger, our father
Toiled side by side by this man
In the sugar cane field
Bore him four children
Up at dawn, toiled till dusk
Nurtured us by her enduring love
Instilled in us, "Gaman Suru"
A mother's legacy of one's "Responsibility" and "Endurance"

Jane Tamae Carlson

Marriage

Marriage is like a cup of coffee:
The same old grind,
Usually a drip,
Never on sale,
Most likely goes stale.
But have no fear, marriage is always there
For people who really care.
Marriage is a true eye opener,
But I'd rather wear glasses.

Veronica Fernandez

The Loner In The Sky

When I go to bed at night,
there is only one light that shines bright.

I wonder how it feels,
all alone in the darkness.

But it does its job,
it gives the darkness a little light.

It changes from half to full,
and sometimes it isn't there at all.

What does this light do in the day,
all alone, with no one to play?

I will never know but,
I will always appreciate its bright light.

For it is the moon.

Mary Shemanski

The Raven And The Dove

The beckoning sounds sailed across
and embraced the scorn of the waves
Tamed and possessed, the furies at rest
now cringed with defeat in their caves

The challenge appeared in disguise
to the two that sang their song
A crushing tear was all they could hear
but they knew it wouldn't last long

Elevated above the perilous tides
the birds now mocked the doubting cry
Strength in their heart, alone or apart
the whispers of dissent were left to die

Time had trickled the amorous stream
that would unite the bird's desire
Deeply inflamed, the other's ashamed
and tossed their hopes in the fire

Dancing through tearless clouds of day
the harmony's voice again was heard
Conflicts were passed, failing to outlast
the Raven and Dove's final word.

Scot Lapierre

Terrifying News

The terrifying news strikes me
    from out of the blue
My stomach went weak
My chest turns uncomfortably tight
A wet salty tear runs down my pale face
She's gone

It hurt to hear the truth
About my cousin
My tears won't stop
My mind won't think
It hurt inside
To think she did not think we loved her soul
But we do!

After all the sobbing
Questions race my mind
My eyes are stinging painfully
I am still crying in my heart
I am very sorry

Jenna Tye

The Church Soup Kitchen

At Monroe Avenue and Oxford Street there's a church that's filled
    with love and hope
It clothes the poor and feeds the hungry, it's for us folk who cannot cope
The Soup Kitchen stairs are at the rear
And no one goes away hungry here
The pasta fusilli and the mulligan stew are always most agreeable
To the hungry and the lonely and to those of us who are less able
The hot rice is nice, and a warm pizza slice, always fill my belly
My carrot they dice and the meat pie they spice, and my sandwiches
    they make with jelly
"Welcome, everyone," "Welcome" is the reverend Father's sincere refrain
We say a prayer and then feed the hungry, it helps to ease the pain
The hall is filled with young and old, men and woman, and little kids
All need help or a guiding hand for they really are on the skids
Down in their luck their problems mount
If they had a buck, would it really count?
God Bless the folks and volunteers who give their time and serve the food
To do less than this, for this gracious brood, surely would be simply rude
Thanks to the stores and restaurants who give their surplus for our table
There's lots of deserts loaded with chocolate; my favorite is the sticky maple

George F. Shatzel

Dad, A Special Man

It takes courage to want to be a man;
knowing it will be expected you be responsible for the rest of your life.

It takes strength to stand up and be a man;
knowing you must be willing to fight nations to achieve your goals.

It takes discipline to decide to be a man;
knowing you will have to answer to many demands.

It takes skill to learn to be a man;
knowing you will need heart to conquer the fear in you.

But Dad it took a special man to be a father
and raise five daughters.

You were firm and sometimes hard,
which prepared us for the disappointments in life.

You were demanding,
but it taught us to be determinate and confident.

You were strict, and it made us posed and refined.

You were passionate, so we learned to be loving and understanding.
You were attentive, which led us to be bold and brave.
Most of all Dad, you were always proud of each one of us,
and that's why you will always be a special man to us,
and we'll always be your angels.

Nita Ford

The Dawning Of Spring

How quietly it always comes creeping,
Like the dawn of a brand new day.
Bringing with it the essence of life,
Which for a time had flown far away.

Gone are the bone chilling nights,
And blankets of soft fleecy snow,
Here are those beautiful sights,
Of the green lands beginning to grow.

And the daffodils poke their tips out,
To timidly test the air
While the robins up high in their tree tops,
Taunt "Come out, come out if you dare!"

All around floats a magical aura,
Like a faint, and joyous ring,
And one recognizes quite fondly,
That this is the dawning of Spring!

Stacey Bertsch

"Echoes Of A Whisper"

The very first words that are spoken by a child
A slow and soothing love song it makes the day worthwhile.
A sweet kiss from your first love creeps slowly through your mind
Echoes of these whispers will always seem so kind
The dripping of a faucet not turned completely off
The drizzle of a winter's rain the drops they sound so soft
Bless you is uttered caringly because someone has sneezed
Echoes of these whispers the ear at times do please
Free at last one day we'll be brave words from one so kind
One day we shall overcome became his frame of mind
By any means necessary these words another man's life
Echoes of these whispers reminds us of great strife
The sound of a pebble being thrown in a pond
Rustling of dry leaves under hooves of a fawn
Fluttering wings of butterflies basking in the sun
Can you remember whispers of Echoes that are long gone.

Rickey Gibson

Taylor Is Poem

Taylor is an eagle dancing in the wind.
Taylor is a shiney tear running down a sad cheek.
Taylor is a beautiful green grass blowing through the wind.
Taylor is a colorful butterfly fluttering through the breeze.
Taylor is a lacy white snowflake landing on a windshield.
Taylor is the cry of a new frightened baby.
Taylor is the crisp brown leaves falling from trees in the warm fall.
Taylor is a furry coyote howling to the beautiful lit moon.
Taylor is a furious tornado spinning round and round.
Taylor is the running hot fudge of a delicious ice cream sundae.
Taylor is the rays of the sun shining over the earth.
Taylor is the soft whisper of a small boy.
Taylor is helpful to her Mom and Dad.
Taylor is Taylor Robinson.

Taylor S. Robinson

Worship is Therapy

Worship is a therapy, that God requires of me.
Amazing things will happen, when I will use the key.
Praise unlocks the blessings that God has in store for me.
Yes, worship is a therapy, that God requires of me!

Worship is a therapy, that God expects of me;
To Praise And Glorify His Name, so I can be set free -
From all the poisonous darts that the Devil shoots at me.
Yes, worship is a therapy - I'm glad it's there for me!

Worship is a therapy, that God provides for me.
I will use it faithfully, so Christ is seen in me;
A refuge for the down - in - heart - it sets the captive free.
Yes, worship is a therapy, that God provides for me!

Worship is a therapy, a blessed joy divine.
God and I walk hand in hand, as I do upward climb.
He's always there to guide me, when I in prayer retreat
With worship as a therapy, there's miracles for me!

Marie Falck

Loving Arms

When I hold you in my embrace.
I feel above the human race.
I can always say sweet nothing in your ears.
Because in my arms you feel no fear.
Trust is a two way street.
But these loving arms make it sweet
When I am with you everything is all right.
Because I know, I will be with you tonight.

Gerald L. Murray

To Heathcliff (From "Wuthering Heights")

They think you are mad
but I know how much you love.
They think you are cruel
but I know your love is pure.
They think you don't feel
but Catherine is all you need.
She gave you life
and without her you feel you die.
She chose another man,
just because of her selfish pride.
You've gone, hoping
to come back and win her love,
but death and suffering is all you found...
The heights of clouds are coming
the light of God is shining...
no more silent cries
for the gypsy who is mad.
Go, go to her dear Heathcliff your time has come.
Probably it's there, in heaven,
where you both shall love.

Nanci R. Pensado

Let Me Be Free

Put me on a highway
with my pack against my back
take me where careless winds
blow tangles through my hair

Let me feel the soft earth on my naked feet
let me see the sunrise
when I need more light

Let my tender moments
be mottled by the sun
and my troubles washed away
by the summer rain

Let the trees be my shelter
stars above be my companions
nestled down with earth my comfort   let me find rest

On these quiet country hillsides
let me cry my childish cries
to my silent friends that listen
let me toss my cares let them ride
on the caravan of country winds
let me be   a carefree hitchhiker

Gwladys Koschinsky

Women Whispering

In the corner
within the darkness
there are women whispering

Behind desks and counters
and around the back
there are women, whispering

How more vulnerable could I be
as a man
having to watch women whispering

To only guess and never know
what's the subject
of those women, those women whispering

But I know
that if young girls weren't taught silence
there would be women shouting

David Lessinger

Sisters

Sisters are each other,
they are friends to one another.
Some sisters are too old to talk with together,
always telling you what to do, they seem like your mother.
Little sisters blabber everywhere,
if you get hurt, they don't give a care.
Other sisters are just about the right age,
but sometimes they do still put you in a rage.
Friends can be our sisters in a very special way,
of course, we could all be sisters if we took the time of day.
Each other's company sisters do enjoy,
unless between them comes a toy.
We live for our own flesh and blood,
thinking now, if we were not here would they be either?

Rachael Haedt

The Day The Clowns Cried

The rumors were ready to explode into violence
I didn't understand
Could it be Coincidence

The day the clowns cried
Is when I dreamt of peace.

Were the memories dangerous
I didn't know
They hurt me when they were gone, though.

Alison D. Kasun

"Never Alone"

When I am all alone
My thoughts become memories.
They are Sometime Happy or Sometime Sad.
I forget Then I remember.
Friends and Loved ones are within every thought.
I can not forget because I remember
The Past and the Present become one.
I am no Longer alone.

Patricia Schillace

Star Gazer

To me freedom is like a new joy,
But pain lies around like an old toy.
A shooting star races across the sky,
Holds great wonder for the human's eye.
The stars hold the answers to all eternal power,
But mankind can't find it, for they are all cowards.
All they see is a bright white light,
The power is just out of their sight.
This power I have seen, for I'm a dreamer of time,
And the taste of life is sweeter than wine.
In my world there is not time,
And pain is the only crime.
The power of this realm is the master of emotion,
Love runs through like a vast blue ocean.
Sometimes passion has so much force,
The only thing to do is let it run its course.
Sometimes there is pain,
And it carries forth a burden, like that of a heavy rain.
Eventually, it goes away,
Which starts a brand new day.

Nathan Eugene Hubbard

A Little Piece Of Heaven

Trees that stand tall and proud upon this land so green
A meadow full of wild flowers just waiting to be seen.

The sky so blue above, the suns warm touch upon my face
A peacefulness envelopes me from the beauty of this place.

Water so clean and clear; its surface just like glass
I've finally found a tranquil place; the perfect place at last.

So many emotions overwhelm me as I look around
The power of this piece of land, my God what have I found.

Perhaps its a little piece of heaven put here for everyone to see
Gods way of telling all the world, look what is yet to be.

Sula Saylor

We've All Been Down This Path Before

We've all been down this path before;
True, not well traveled, perhaps rocky and coarse.
You may find that a beautiful flower has died;
Or a bubbly brook once wet, now dried.
And all your thoughts will bring you sorrow this day
Of all the things that have gone away.
But remember, the rains will come and nourish the parched ground;
And a new and prettier flower will soon be found.
Just look ahead, you'll see where the path end lies;
Then you will have learned that the flower, the brook, and you
    survived.

A. L. Lelo

The Night Before Waking

'Twas the night before day
and all through my brain,
not a feeling was stirring,
not even a thought, astray.

I was frozen in my bed
while visions of nightmares
rumbled through my head.

The demons are waiting
in the corners of my mind,
in hopes I will soon lose my cool,
and give in to their ways, debating.

This is not Christmas,
no visions of sugar plumbs,
nor any sightings of St. Nicholas.

The time has come, the hour is upon me.
The time has come, to face the fear,
this nightmare we call living.
Beware the wicked, hidden, up a tree.

Robert Aaron Firth

Virtues

Friendship is too important to waste on people
with no self-respect.

Leadership is for the ones who cannot lead
themselves.

Compassion to the fellowman is wasted on the
lawless.

Shame is for the ones who have no pride

Integrity is for the ones who consider
life God's gift.

And Love; yes love is an emotion best kept
under control.

Rochelle Penelope Sorzano

Love Beyond Compare

The Lord is my divine Savior,
By His grace, I was saved and this has changed my life's composure.
Daily, my heart is filled with an unspeakable exhilaration,
That no one could deny me of my jubilation.
My faith rests upon evidence not demonstration,
But doubt leadeth to destruction.
While he ever bore Himself with divine dignity,
He denounced hypocrisy, unbelief and iniquity.
He died for our transgressions to suffer shame, insult and
humiliation, he loved us dearly, that he provided great propitiation.
The service of love is not a compliance but mere outward obedience,
And showing evidence of genuine repentance.
He is my light and fortress,
Always to my avail whenever I am in distress.
I need peace — Heaven's forgiveness and peace and love deep
in my soul. Money cannot buy it, intellect cannot procure it,
Wisdom cannot attain it; you can never hope, by your own
efforts, to secure it.
Salvation is free for all, without a price
He is my infinite sacrifice.
I call upon the Lord when I am in despair,
I am comforted with his unconditional love, it's beyond compare.

Denise Ramkhelawan

Look Inside

Where can I run to - where can I hide?
Who's going to listen - who'll take my side?
With all this pain, I just can't cope.
I've lost all my dreams and I've lost all my hope.

Everyone seems to forget about me.
I'm always neglect - why can't they see?
They never say what I want them to say.
They just turn their backs and they just walk away.

I asked God up in heaven to give me a sign.
I'm tired of hurting - I just want to shine.
I heard someone's voice say, "Look inside."
I went to the mirror and sat there and cried.

I realized for once that nobody's to blame.
Like the moth that flies to the deadly flame.
I must help myself - on me I must depend.
I must be my own, very best friend.

Thank God in the heavens above - He showed me that it's me I should love
It's me I should run to - my heart's where I can hide
It's me that should listen
Now I'll always "Look inside"

Merla-Lynne Pollitt

Left Me

You broke my heart, what can I do?
You said you'll love me, but that wasn't true.
You said you'll be there by my side,
now you left me here to cry...

How could you do this to our love?
How could you give your
heart and take it back away?
You said I was your one and
only, but that was a lie.
I gave you all the love I had, but
when you left all I had was
a broken heart. I told myself
you weren't worth it, but at
night I cry for your love.
You said you'll always be there
for me, but you left me here to cry...

Now you come running back for my love, but begging on
your knee won't change my mind,
because you left me here to cry.

Nelida Zavala

And God Was There

I saw a little church upon a hill today
With stained glass windows and steeples high -
It beckoned to me and I went within
To be with others who needed Him.

It was so peaceful with all heads bowed
And prayers rising to the skies -
We know He hears them "in the still"
In that little church upon the hill.

I felt a wonder in my secret heart
So very far beyond the telling -
For as the sun went down it cast a glow
Painting all the windows gold.

One and all are free to come
Blessings are bestowed if you just believe -
If you with your very heart to fill
Enter the little church upon the hill.
    He is there.

Evelyn Kimball Blake

Kitchens

Kitchens come and kitchens go
renters are never here to stay.
The landlord comes and tells you so,
and of course you always have to pay.
They lose their stay
and tell you they always have the right of way.

One day you get a letter in the mail,
it states the owners set a sail.
You find yourself without a home.
They come and take what they thought was theirs
we are left without a thing to cook on,
let alone something to put food on.,
For the kitchen was stripped
and the only thing I can say,
was we were ripped.

They think that we can bury the hatchet,
but in reality, they will pay for it in taxes.

Dawn Weaver

DYING TO MAKE A POINT

C arefully arranging the place and herself
O n a bed of clean linen in a completely swept house
N ot one, single, solitary
R egret, or positive remembrance
O verdose, a bottle full of pills
L et her finally hope in hopelessness

C ountless, endless, seem the days
A nd the pain, even at 19, of
N ever having been allowed to become or be herself

K indness demanded always of her she expects not to find
I s there any question why she didn't leave a note? What would
    be the point-they'd decide for themselves and tell her why
    even as a corpse. Gratefully she won't have to hear
    all their reasons that deny her hers
L ost Child swallowed up in
L oneliness, loss, abuse and all else caused and denied by an
    alcoholic family and addict society's all-consuming self

The moral of this story, tho simple is easy to miss, for those
"civilized" 'round d' Nial, the moral is this: **ASK, DON'T TELL**

Shauna Turner

Roll

We were young, we were free, now it's time to let it be
We were wild, we were mad, His time has come, it's much too sad
We were eight but now we're seven
One of us has gone to heaven
On the road, on the run, looking, searching just for fun
It is coming, it had came - who is the one to blame?
Time has passed, time gone by - trying so hard not to cry
Growing up, growing old - searching for that pot of gold
Moving here, Moving there. Leaving one to sit and stare
Thinking back, thinking when we were sitting in his den
Having laughs, having fun. But now the pain of what was done
We were young, we were free, but now it's time to let it be
We were eight but now we're one
All is said all is done...

Vaughn M. Rennols

Christina

You passed me by
You lived and died
I should have tried
But you turned aside

What happened to the dream?
A marvelous scheme
Like you and me
The dream was in my head

Did you feel it too?
Do you still think of me
In wistful remorse?
Why can't it be you?

When I looked into your eyes
I swam in pools of quiet fire
A serene place to live forever
And like fire, you appeared and now you are gone

Will I see you again?
I wanted more
You came ashore then
Washed away

Paul Festa

I Miss Him A Lot

I miss him a lot, for he was a
great man, and even though
I didn't know him, I'm sure
he would have been happy to lend me a hand.

He rode the bulls that no one could
and he tried the bulls that no one would.
He rode them good and he rode them
rough, for he was the toughest of the
tough. He rode the bulls straight to
his death, but everyone knows he was
the best. He's still my hero to this
day, but I sure wish he could have
stayed. He got me started
doing what I do, so here's to Lane,
this ones for you.

Jeffrey Johnston

When I Get To Heaven

The time has come for me to go
I'm not afraid cause I'm not alone
To live with Jesus has been my goal
And mostly all the people I know
For Christmas this is a special time
We'll all be reunited with family and friends
We are all forgiven even the sinners me are
To all live in peace and harmony again
As the pearls gates are opened up wide
I can see Grandparents are there waiting inside
Looking around I can see the people most dear to me
My mom, my sister, and my brother are happy as can be
I notice someone is missing from this joyous scene
One of the most important people in my family
The gates are closed for all the rest of eternity
I didn't get to tell him one last time
"I Love You Dad"!

Tiffani Cale

Alone...

Here I am
Alone in a crowd
A spirit suspended in loneliness
How can I free myself
How can I be free from fear
Like a bird, weightless, flying over a calm sea
I rise
I fall
I try
I fail
I hurt
I cry
I scream
My shrieks break the still air
They free me
I am not alone
I taste the sweet
And feel the pain
Here I am
Alone in a crowd?

Tehranique Miller

I Am . . .

In the midst of darkness, I am the Light,
For those who are blind, I am their Sight
In times of questions, I am the answers you seek,
For I am the strength, to those who are weak.

I am fierce a lion, but a meek as a lamb,
I am small as a puddle, but too large for a dam.
I am everything, yet nothing is what I choose,
For every time I win, I am destined to loose.

Try as you might, I will not break,
For my endless pride, you cannot take.
You cannot make me less than what I choose to be,
For I am Life Eternal, can't you see?

I am the yin and the yang, good and bad,
For I have given you everything you ever had.
For every pain, every hurt, every sadness, every sorrow,
Did I not give you, a promise of a better tomorrow?

Kelley M. Francis

Words of Love

My heart has a need to minister these words of love
so that it doesn't over flow with the joy I feel, that has
been kept in heart when were apart. I've walk thought
lonely dark nights carrying with me the thought of you
holding me, touching me, and loving you, and it weighs
heavy in heart and I haven't thy strength to lift this weight
in which has me bounded by your Love. A Love that is
unblemished and warm. That every time I'm alone I begin floating
on the notes of its mellow harmony. Running through
out the tunnels of my heart, echoing through out my body
leaving me to feel I've stolen moments of pleasure so much
pleasure that one would say it's only found in dreams. Yet am
I dreaming as well for when ever you have showered me with
love, it's like a gift of silver and gold sometimes it's almost
too much for my heart to bear whenever we love or touch, my
God I flourish the thought for thy heart skips beats and I
know without you there is no life and a life to live with out
you in it, is no life at all. Only you can keep me
alive in this paradise of perfect ecstasy.

Kenneth Saunders

The Race

The crowd roars like a killer tornado
As we stand upon the line like the last
Play at a scoreless super bowl with
Hard faces and the sweat pouring off
Of our faces from nervousness as we sit
Upon the line and wait for the gun.
"Ready" the man yells as stare down our path to glory.
"Set" our muscles tremble for we know this is it,
  "Bam" we explode off the line
  Like a pack of vicious, red eyed bulls
  We were all racing for fame and glory.
  I looked up at the finish line, it grew
  Gradually near like a small, timid spider.
  I glanced around, only one held my pace.
  As the race grew half over the man
  And I were neck and neck,
  I thought of how far I had come and
  How I had trained extra hard,
  But by the time I was done thinking
  The man had already won the race.

William H. Feaster

Ode to the Sea

O ocean great, O ocean deep,
O ocean proud with waves that leap.
The moon looks down upon your face.
The stars shine round with childlike grace.
If you could speak, or if you would;
If your roar could be understood
You would tell the tales of days of old
When greatest men set sail.
In simpler times when men were bold,
And women shy and frail.
You would tell of when you led the way
Across your treacherous sea,
Into a land so far away where everyone is free.
You know of everything that's passed
Across your waves; you knew the first you'll know the last
When we lie in our graves
And as I scan your ocean blue as far as my eyes can see.
I wonder, when life's trip is through, what will you tell of me?

Adam C. Brown

The Old Rocking Chair

I'm 80 today, were did they go those years
They bought me a rocking chair today.
Because now I'm in my golden years.
They tell me to sit and rock away

Help nan up the stairs
She may fall down and break her neck.
I'm to old to go up and down the stairs
There making me a nervous wreck.

Is this what they call the golden years.
Don't do this don't do that you may fall
They love you so much it brings tears
Don't get me wrong I love them all

It may be wrong and maybe not fair.
To sneak away to see my friends
Instead of rocking in my rocking chair
I may not find many out there, my friends

I'll take up the game of Bingo and pray
That all my friend who are left will be there
My golden years are not for rocking away.
I'm my old rocking chair.

Helen Miller

Saving Time

A sudden pressure on my chest,
A thrumming in my ears, and, half awake, I ask
"It's morning time so soon? Aren't you the early one?"
I stroke a silky head — and then, remembering,—the clocks!
Of course, the clocks.
"An hour to move ahead, — right now!
But, just a little minute here,...
How could a cat know that?"
"More of His light." she purrs, and smiles conspiringly.
"Alright, the first one's here, beside my bed."
And off we go.
We do the kitchen one, and by the piano bench,
The big one on the mantel-piece;
The radio has one;
And even in the car a clock, the last.
With pride we name ourselves, "Custodians of This Hour"
Of Sun Time
  Our Time
  His Time

John Langdon

The Willpower Of Man

How fascinating, interesting and looking so grand
What was that fruit that tempted the first created man?
As it hung on the tree without a blemish or spot
Holding on tight as the wind blew a lot.
The color of the skin is not the key
but what is important is the beauty you see.
So firm and solid as the hand reaches to touch
Now the temptation is great and the desires is much
Deep thoughts are pondered as the wish is to yield
Since the fruit seemed no different than others in the field.
While all alone and no one to look
The choice to taste was recorded in the Book.
Was it being deceitful or just committing a small crime?
History reveals this was the downfall of man at the beginning of time.
Throughout the years we have pondered in our mind
Why was this fruit so desired instead the picking of a different kind
We can't change the past but the decision we make today.
Will the fruit we choose be a burden of sin or Joy and Happiness in every way.

Mary Ann Adkins

"Spreading"

Here it comes in with the breeze
And nests itself up high
Upon the bodies upon the ones
Who doubt they'll ever be?

Infected with the gift of death
Eventually with year
As it rings its tolling bell
Who thought they'd ever be?

Drowned with Disease and Turmoil's Toys
With neck above the tide
Swimming for the final breath
Bobbing just to be.

A second chance is floating by
Waving as it spirals
In a whirlpool, in regret
With knowledge it will be

Spreading like the wings of birds
In and out new flesh
unbiased opinion upon destruction
To all of who have been.

David A. Valentin

Pre-Ordained Sacrifice

Because there always has been Pre-Ordained sacrifice,
The heart of earth imparts this timeless advice.

Do not mourn for me, or me, or me with funeral bells
So say the husks to the sprouting seeds.
We do not strain to go on.
We will remain as completed deeds; believe
Our death your gift of a freedom song
Which sings of a light such as these prison cells
Could never give nor now conceive.

The eternity of wisdom's power repeats each spring season
The WORD that God mixes into our plate both sacrifice and reason.

Frances E. DelaCuesta

Don't Want To Share

Cancer is something we don't want to share,
not even with our families that care.
We don't know their feelings unless we've been there.
The fear that all people with cancer must share.
It must be real hard to deal with each day.
Not knowing whether it's time for you to go or to stay.
So we really must show people we care
But cancer is something we don't want to share.

Maxine Roteliuk

Dream Keeper

You came to me in my dreams one night
The touch of your hand it felt so right
I felt shivers in my body when I thought of your face
I loved being with you no matter what time or place
You took me places that I've never seen
You kept me safe from all that's mean
You protected me from demons and lies
When something was bad you covered my eyes
And then suddenly I could finally see
And then I realized it was just me
I looked back on the things I had seen
And I realized then that you were just a dream

Jen Terrell

The Evil That Men Do Not

Skeleton key. Pass key to the soul.
  Imbibe of its Essence. Tune out that Darwinian
Nonsense. What's the difference between
  (Another, please)
Animal and human? Not important now.
  Oral fixation? No Freudian
Excuses. Not this time, Oedipus.

Personality? Sociological Convenience.
  No time for that! The ID now reigns supreme.
Irrevocable conduct. Who cares?
To do things one would normally
  (More!!)
Not, all in the name of the Animalistic is counter-Evolutionary.

Yet, it remains.
(Flourishes).

Garry Sled

Daydream

Dedicated to Ryan Mendoza

When the whispers sweet words into your ear,
When this is all you want to hear.
When you know love is in the air.
When he is there playing with your hair.
When he gives you things you've always wanted,
When life is full of love that's haunted.
You ask yourself, Is this dream?
Like a river of gold or even a stream,
Like golden swans on a silver lake,
Like cherries on a chocolate cake.
You wipe your eyes but you're still there.
You see horse with golden hair.
You wipe your eyes once again.
And there he is holding your hand!

Alexandra Anna Ashley Sokalska

Reflections

The sorrow in your heart is an emotion you must carry,
A burden that may be yours and yours alone.
The ache that you crave to repair is distant,
But it too will come.
A word is but word until it is verbally abused,
But the memory of a single violation can be forever.
Waste not your breath on an oration of anger,
Look deep and feel the emotions that are present.
Fell the fear, the anger, the soul rupturing confusion,
Let it ride thru your body, face each tragedy head on.
To yourself be honest amidst the turmoil,
Use words that instill no regret when faced with a mirror.
All that one encounters on the path of life,
Will someday be replayed.

Patricia Armstrong

Your Time Has Come

Your time has come
  To catch a dream,
  To fly with the eagles,
    To look past the sanctuary of today
    and face the challenge of tomorrow.

Your time has come
  To face your fears with a new courage,
  To feel the heartbeat of a legend,
    and be the voice of the legion.

Your time has come
  To be the one to take a step
  in an unknown direction.

Your time has come.
Your time is now.

Stephanie Goodrich

Guilty Vs. Innocence

Many people have negative thoughts in their head
Wishing and hoping for others to be dead
For the innocent they become very insecure
The guilty party knows not how much pain they endure
The innocent acts as if nothing is wrong
While actually on the inside they sing a sad song
The guilty party pecks away with a hateful phrase
The innocent feeling trapped inside a difficult maze
Never knowing how to find their way out
They become very frustrated and begin to pout
The innocent thinks the only way out is suicide
And the guilty party never understands why they died.

Adam D. Smith

Shattered Rainbows

When the rainbows turn to gray and the smiles leave your face
When the tears you cry and turned away
You hide
When your heart beats for someone true
When the road of love is just for you
When the special someone comes for you
You hide .
When a day of longing makes you sad and the night before has
    made you glad
When someone says you're all they have
You hide
When will the day come that you can say to just that one, that
    you can just love one and the tears of life will all be gone
When the rainbows turn to sun and life has just begun and you
    don'thide

Sarah Gajewski

I'll Come To Offer You My Heart!

When you find no one far or close
when you crave the smell of a red rose
when you need a hug, a kiss and a word
when you think it could not get any worse...
I'll come to offer you my heart!

There are times when all seems lost,
the good memories almost gone
and can't remember a happy song
when in solitude you need love the most...
I'll come to offer you my heart!

In your moments of deep pain
or in your nights of silent grief
when you feel yourself go insane
and your suffering is constant, and your peace is brief...
I'll come to offer you my heart!

We are two ends of the same rope
two souls in search for the same heaven.
When you feel you are loosing hope
remember that this unworthy man...
will come to offer you his heart!

Francisco R. Sulpizio

Secrets

Somewhere, deep inside, the guarded secrets lie
Inscribed in hearts, but not in stone
Of who we are, and where we're from
So deeply etched, so deeply honed
Forevermore, our seeds evolving, shall unrelent
Our history sets the precedent
Our right's and wrong's shall be our learning
Baptized by life, scarred, through enduring
The marked effects, suppressed from show
We build our secrets as we go.

David Whitby

Master Of Perfection

Overwhelming vastness of the Ocean;
Sacred ambience of the Sky;
Magnanimous Mountains;
Beauty of the starlit Night;
Green eye-coolers of the Earth;
Fragrance of the mud soaked in Rain;
Pearly dew on the lovely Blooms;
Creations of beings on Land;
Mysterious monolithic Cosmic;

The Power, sheer Glory, the Perfection;
Time and again, always in Motion;
Draws from me, an unexplainable Emotion!

Lord! It's beyond my Imagination;
If You, are the Creator, the Magician;
What or how could be You, the real You?

My mind, full of apprehension;
Dreads even to think of Your Form;
Could You be everything mould together?
Or could You be mould in everything forever
Though, You could be however; You are a Vision, a Dawn!

Rama Raman

Sonnet To Your Loveliness

I love the graceful way you hold your head,
Those tumbling curls that fall upon your brow;
Your slender hands that strike not, and instead
Caress - as though in offerance of a vow.
I love the stories that your two eyes tell,
The way each eyebrow quivers when it would;
They have the pow'r to show the thoughts that dwell
Inside you. Show you love me, if you should.
If wealth, indeed, were measured by one's smile,
And laughter were the rule by which we live,
With you a million-fold could dwell in style,
And each to each a new life you could give.

When God created Joy, He surely knew
And must have felt the love I feel for you.

Nord Arling Gardner

"Daily Devotional"

I thought of you today
In fact,
the day was you
I felt your loneliness, your fear
I saw your dreams
Hoped for what you hope for,
wishing your wishes to come true

But a heavy burden you carried,
my love
too heavy for just one

Oh how I wish I could carry them for you
I yearn to be your comfort
Two, carry the weight of this life together
Two, share in the journey of discovery
of themselves,
together
What makes them happy, their drive for one another
To serve God, as one

Eric Agee

I'll Take Care Of You

Rest my darling
while I sing you to sleep
let the breeze caress your hair
let the water touch your feet
and I while you sleep
a fairy tale will read.

All I need to rejoice
is to see you sleeping by my side
your body calmly relax
at the rhythm of my voice.

Make my song the weaver of your dreams,
the guardian of your soul
cause even while you sleep
serene and tranquil,
your dreams will always be.

Sleep, while I caress your body,
while the waves whisper in your ears
a song from the days when we were happy
when the moon witnessed the moment
that made your kiss last for all my years.

Estrella Martinez

"Transparent Questioning"

I know it's been a while, but I don't see the danger
   Of writing an old friend who has now become a stranger.

Have you ever stopped to think how good it used to be
   When forever wasn't long enough to contain our destiny?

When we were together we had the whole world by the tail.
   Now that we're apart I am scared that I might fail.

When people ask what happened, I say you stopped believing.
   That doesn't mean that I have. It was You who did the leaving.

I must admit I am curious, do you ever have any doubt
   That you did the right thing when you chose to shut me out?

Are there any dormant feelings? Is something missing in your soul?
   Or am I the only one who doesn't feel quite whole?

It's just kind of scary — I don't believe we're through.
   So until the day you marry, I still will wait for you.

Paul Schmiel

Wasted Life

As I glance through the window, I always see corruption,
I see a society that doesn't seem to function.
Everywhere I turn, someone's out to get me,
They threaten my life and try to see what I see.
I never ever knew how I messed up their lives,
But now they're out to get me and cut me down to size.

I didn't even know what drugs did to my mind,
But I made a mistake and now I'm one of their kind.
I have so many sins and I wanna' be forgiven,
But I can never change the way I've been livin'.
I see myself fade and I wanna' come back,
But every time I try, drugs always seem to attack.

People always said that I should get hooked,
But drugs messed up their lives and they hadn't even looked.
When it happened to me I didn't think it would turn out like this
But now that I'm dead, there are things I had to miss.

Don't ever try it, don't let it get through
'Cause the wall of life you build should always protect you.
What happened in that alley I do not know,
But my messed up life is all I have to show.

Daniel Bonventre

Animal Crackers In My Suit

One day I wished upon a star.
   I'd like to be there, but it's much too far.
It's hard to be so daring and bold.
   You see I'm only...five years old.
That very next day I built me a rocket.
   Out of ten bike parts and a wrench from Dad's pocket.
I packed my life support, lunch that is.
   I might be gone for years or be back in a wiz.
After I'd packed 'til my rocket was full,
   I buckled myself in and gave the lever a pull.
Whoosh! I was in space, lots of stars went by.
   I was the happiest person, I let out a cry.
I let out a squeal as loud as could be.
   When I hit the moon, I saw an astronaut jumping with glee.
I hopped off the rocket being very careful.
   One small step for me, a giant leap for all people.
It was like a trampoline, jumping around.
   It seemed like my feet never touched the ground.
The moon became dark which, I thought was always day.
   Then I heard a strange voice telling me to come home for the day.
I didn't want to leave, but as I turned to go,
   I noticed my animal cracker supply was low.
I got in my rocket and sped back to the house,
   then slipped in the back door as quiet as a mouse.
I told Mom about being in space.
   She smiled and said there was a permanent grin on my face!

Hilary Smith

Memories Of The Good-Old-Days

It's a pleasure to remember my life in West Virginia,
to take a trip back in time.
My repository of memories about the good old days,
placed for safekeeping in the storehouse of my mind.
My heart beats fast as I walked at last, where in childhood I played
in the clover grass. I turn my thoughts to the towering hills,
where at night comes the cry of the whippoorwills. At night we
filled the heating stove with wood, as much as it would hold.
In the morning, how we shivered, as we warm our hands and toes.
The aroma of coffee bubbling in the gray speckled granite pot, as
we curled our hair with the heating iron that seared and scorched
our locks. We rolled down the hill in a barrel, we climbed up high
and tall on our stilts. Carved a whistle from a willow, and made a
super-duper slingshot. To recall the view from the top of the
mountain, and the hush of the valley below...the carbine light my
Daddy wore to work, so many years ago. Times that stir a fond
emotion from a source so deep within. A time of love and
happiness, where my memory journey ends. And as I turn my
thoughts away, I weep for the child of yesterday.

Bonnie Hoover

Anniversary Thoughts

She sat and waited secretly,
For no one else had known,
From across the way she seen the flicker,
She smiled to herself..she could go.

The sign was his lit match,
In the darkness he was there,
Waiting for his one true love,
Not to meet they couldn't bear.

A family together they would share,
Laughter and triumph; sadness, despair,
Their power of loving, strong for life,
"Fifty years," they thought,
"Where went the time..."

Lisa Laliberte

One Of His Very Best

God sat upon His throne one day and looked upon the earth.
With wise ol' eyes and a little smile, He told of a special birth!
The angels sat and listened as the Dear Sweet Master spoke:
This extraordinary child is in need of special folks.

This babe's of my creation! Our Master did proclaim.
A boy so bright and lively his parents cannot tame.
Patience And Forbearance! The parents must possess,
If I'm to give to them one of my very best.

Patience and Forbearance! The master spoke out loud.
This child will grow into a man and make Me very proud.
So if you're the lucky parents of a bright and lively son,
Take comfort in the knowledge — you're also a chosen one.

Sally Fields Miller

A Land Forever Free

Neath that battle-darkened sky, grim but dauntless soldiers lie
Determined men with spirits high
Some with courage, some with prayer, some with just the will to dare
And brave the horrors of the field
Calm brave men who never yield.

Those with courage have no fear, those with prayer are conscience-clear
Hail those with just the will to dare
Strong and silent, cool and sure, not the perfect nor the pure
But they condemn a greater sin
And gaunt, determined, they shall win.

Nowhere is truth more grim nor bare, nor man's eternal faith in prayer
And trust in God so deep as there
His soul made pure, a man is sure his native land will long endure
And religious faith revives
The light of freedom in his eyes

Thus, these battle-weary men, endowed by Him with strength to win
Move forward, deafened by the din
Of roaring guns and bursting shells as Destiny its story tells
Of gallant fighting men who see
Ahead...a land forever free

Fred E. Fisher

What The Clouds Bring In

You never know what the clouds bring in,
the darkness of that hour, the coldness of the night,
or the speed of the wind that cuts through like a knife.

You never know what the clouds bring in,
rolling through our paths, seemingly deep and dark
with never ending power
to change that in which we feel is our hour,
hour of despair.

You never know what the clouds bring in,
thick, full clouds which seem to reach through the skies
to the heaven above.
With such kindness, beauty and an eternity of comfort
where the eye is its only boundary.

You never know what the clouds bring in.
I can't change what the clouds bring in.
The clouds, they will always come in,
bringing what they will always bring.
But my love, no matter what the clouds bring in,
they will always bring you my love.

Ernest J. Reilly

Untitled

When you look at my face you see darkness.
My skin is like onyx, my eyes are like coals.
Why did God choose to bring darkness upon me?
It's because he knew that my soul was created in darkness.
He knew that my life would be lived in darkness.
He knew that my thoughts would be consumed by darkness.
He saw me first and he knew it all.
So, I ask again, why did God bring this darkness upon me?
Why is there not a glimmer in my eye nor joy in my heart?
Now I smile, the darkness came first.
Yes I am the darkness but, after me there will be light.
The children will shine for me.

Bernice Love

On Taking Chances

I once saw a jay which liked to play
With a cat that prowled around.
He'd dive beeline, from the grand old pine,
Swooping slow and low to the ground.

With vicious claw Garf raised his paw,
But the jay rose swiftly away.
Still free, he perched on a distant birch,
Where he taunted Garf day after day.

From garden fence to bough up hence
Jay puffed out his breast and mocked.
With raucous call, while bouncing tall,
He laughed to see Garfield stalk.

But Garf, I declare, had a gourmet flair
For my sky-blue feathered friend.
Did he bide his time, this fat feline,
Could he plan the blue jay's end?

Would that day come? It had for some.
Say — Garf is nowhere around.
And no flash of blue — Ah, then I knew,
For jay feathers strewed the ground.

Phyllis Knoll

Glory

Have you ever stopped to marvel at the beauties of the world,
It's like a giant oyster, revealing its new pearl.

To stroll along a peaceful beach and listen to the breeze,
Is a special moment which one does enjoy to seize.

To espy a baby deer take its first few steps,
Or to have seen a forceful bear when it has gently slept.

To scale the rocky mountains and view the world below,
Or to watch the sun go down and revel in its gracious glow.

There are many different things in which we can behold,
Just sit and observe them quietly as the splendour does unfold.

Victoria Maystruk

"But I, Never Never"

You're always in my mind
You're so gentle, very kind
You may think that, love is blind, but I, never never!

When I look up, at the sky
I can see, the lovebirds fly
You may think, it's hard to try, but , never never!

Every new, may become old
Even those, as good as gold
You may say, that love is bold, but I, never never!

You know, when we two get mad
Our story, may become sad
You may forget, what we had, but I, never never!

Jeanne Amiri

Desert Dream

Clouds of spiky threads
billowy wads of cotton-
marshmallow pillows with whipping cream puffs
and a sheep's wool blanket
that shrouds the sky.
Icy cold to the left on mountainous treachery
while a desolate desert whispers to me at my right.
Dramatically out of place Lava rocks
pepper the land like spice
from a giant kitchen jar
broken and jagged in shapes
from beyond all reason
defying any sense of right or wrong.
And leading me for miles and more
this road insists on urging me further away from home.

    Perla C. Ortiz

The Standard

I get so tired of those who think they know me
They can never believe I did That
Not you, they'd say (as if they know me best)
I can't believe you'd do something like that
I hate the standards I must live up to
Some seem to have put me on a pedestal
If I step down to stretch my legs
They think I've taken a fall
Can't they see I'm far from perfect?
Perfect's not how I want to be
I can't live up to any more expectations
From now on, I think I'll just be me.

    Debra Rene Robinette

"Come Quickly Lord Jesus"

"Come quickly Lord Jesus," we hear the Bride say,
As she is made ready for her Wedding Day!

In spotless white garments made clean by the blood,
of Jesus her Bridegroom, the true Son of God.

In beauty she stands a Gentile, a Dove.
Watched over and cared for by the Master's sweet love.

Waiting and watching till the last lost sheep,
will enter the fold and make her complete.

The trumpet will sound a true Wedding March.
The Rapture will take place, just the right start.

Then to the Marriage Supper of the Lamb,
where our Bridegroom is waiting the end of the plan.

A new life beginning with Joy and real Peace.
A life full of worship, down on our knees.

Serving our Master, our Savior and Lord.
"Come quickly Lord Jesus "The Spoken Word!

    Kelly Batman

Untitled

I know not where my road will lead, but hope that I can leave a seed,
for the next who comes down this way, to find the seed and maybe say,
with this seed that I have found, I will sow it into the ground,
and watch it grow and mature, and build in grace and virtue,
to withstand all that comes along, that one day it may be among
the others who have studied hard, and never given in one yard,
to do anything but succeed, and follow the road that will lead
to where it's always wanted to be, and then be able to see
that I am proud of my deed, because I am that strong seed.
And when it comes my days do end, I do hope I am able to send
a seed to lay beside the road, that someone else may find and sow.

    Sandra Jordan

Mr Love Our Rabbit Filled Our Hearts With Joyous Moments

Mr Love was a beautiful little white rabbit who had the most remarkable pink eyes that glared like a diamond and sparkled like the stars in the sky.

This little rabbit was a very fascinating creature who brought joyous moments into our lives.
We loved Mr Love very much for he captivated our hearts.
He gave us peace of mind and happiness.

I can imagine sitting across my room seeing this tiny little white speck of life sitting in a corner with its eyes bright like the sun and his ears position up right like a t.v. antenna listening to every sound of life and taking every ounce of breath.

Mr Love lived the life of royalty such that of a king sitting high on his throne, he ruled for eight and a half years.

More than three years ago the angels came to take Mr Love to animal heaven one beautiful evening in February.
As Mr Love began to depart from us he heard our cries but gently went off to a heavenly sleep.
We felt tremendous pain and sorrow due to his departure from this earth.

    Beatrice Craft

Racing The Reaper

Living in a world of darkness, all alone
Looking for a life to call my own
Running from the reaper every single day
Waiting for the light to show me the way.
I turn the corner and see such a hideous sight
I see the reaper and I scream out in fright
He reaches out for me with bony white hands
My time is running like hourglass sands
Soon there's no sand left, not one grain
As I enter his clutches, I scream out in pain
I rip free from his grasp and pick up my pace
As I glance into his skeleton face
A shrieking laughter rings in both of my ears
And I have finally eluded the worst of my fears
The reaper screams loudly "I have failed indeed,"
"You escape me this day, someday I'll succeed!"

    Jason Beckham

What If?, What About?

What if, we didn't see men as color
And we saw every man
As our own brother?

What if when we
Decide to purchase a house
That because of our skin
Many problems, wouldn't arouse.

What about a job promotion?
Oh yes! We're qualified
But, come to find out
Our supervisor, just lied.

What about our children
Playing in the streets?
Every things alright
Until our parents meet

And if we took time out to consider
That color won't rub off, we wouldn't be so bitter

Do you want to know when all prejudice will end?
Allow Christ into your life
And let him wash away your sins.

    Terri R. Mays

Satan's Fire

Doors locked, windows barred,
Guard dogs prowling in the yard,
Won't protect you in your bed,
Nothing will from Satan's dread,
He'll tempt you with your secret desires,
To suffer eternity in a blaze of fire.

Even if God is on your side,
You can run but you can't hide.
Satan's near, you'd better fear,
Your life is over, don't shed a tear,
It's too late now to tell a lie,
Because Satan knows you're going to die!

Kevin Powell

Winter's Wake

Shimmering silhouettes standing silent,
Weathering the winter while waiting,
For the frigid frost to finally flee,
And, let the luscious leaves lift.
Children chatter in the chilling cold,
Bundled in their best bought booties,
Thinking tender thoughts of toasty times,
Pleasant patio parties and passionate play,
Sun sending showers of summer sounds,
Fancy flowers and foliage freely frolicking,
Waiting wondrously as the wind whispers,
Of times that thoughts turn to tall tales,
And, loving laughter lands lazily on the lawn.
Everyone enjoying endless easy evenings,
Swathed in the sultry sensuous summer sun.

Olga Postnikoff

Women So Special

Women so special, so special, so special
that brought enlightenment into my life.

Women so special, so special, so special
that show me that ways of a rose to be.

Women so special, so special, so special
that taught me the ways of the loving paths.

Women so special, so special, so special
That brought understanding with
experience to lead.

Women so special, so special, so special
that brought tears to my heart

Women so special
so special
So Special
that touch me
So Special,
I'll always feel special

Daniel Valentine

Ebony

Lips kiss floors of blackened tiles
Cold
   hard
      dusty
         cracked
Eyes dance in white-hot flames while
flocks of tangerine cinders spiral helplessly
   in the wind that chaps and stings
      gnarled fingers
Warm ribbons salted with memories
Drip down and over and stop —
forming tiny puddles of silent misery
   at my feet.

Denise Gretchen

For The Six Million

All through the night the world did turn
A deaf ear and blind eye
And now, though light morn' does burn
It still ignores our cry
To quell our plight the world did spurn
And we wish to know why.
Now we do learn that those with might
had reasons for delay
A chance to earn rather than fight
was the thought that held sway
So while we burned for foe's delight
they were collecting pay.
Our people bled, the gas and gun
Were friends to end the pain
When streets ran red for Nazi fun
The world did not complain
The dead are dead, what's done is done
But one thing does remain
Let it be said by everyone
"Never again." Amen.

Lee Loewinger

Death Of A Flower

Morning Glory stand so bright,
In the faint glow of moonlight,
Petals feel as soft as silk,
Flower's murderer has no guilt,
As the flower is ripped from the ground,
A sense of emergency begins to sound,
A weeping willow's cry is heard,
And the urgent rustling wings of a bird,
Morning Glory's time delays,
For no time to live the days,
Back beyond when days were sweet,
Never can these days repeat,
Morning Glory's time has come,
Every flower feels so glum,
Morning Glory about to die,
Has no chance to say good-bye.

Kristen Waddell

To A False Friend

Sing to me your siren song
Not too short, but not too long.
Make the mood a melody,
Which turns at length to rhapsody.

Hence your goal to let me sleep,
Whilst hand explores my pocket deep.
Misuse your time to crafty schemes,
Near-fool has awaked from lurid dreams.

My trinkets take - they're just a pittance,
The farce ends - and good riddance.
Stealth and avarice you ever conceal,
But, self-defeating, unwittingly reveal.

Angelo A. Vitanza

My Cat

My cat is fluffy,
She loves to eat treats,
When she has treats...
She goes a little bonkers.
My cat sleeps on my bed,
And snores herself to sleep.
Then she wakes up and comes and bites me.

Kaitlynn Osborn

Spring

What a wonderful spring
for the flowers to bloom
and to go to church
and see the bride and groom.

I opened up the windows
to smell the nice pine trees
and as I looked around
I saw the birds and the bees.

I hope we have spring
all year long
So we can see the birds stay
where they belong.

Britt Anakaer

Dream Of The Insomniac

Here I walk
Under a formless gray sky,
Frustrated.
Maybe I'll lie to rest,
Perhaps I could drift,
And sail the cold wind...
And my mind could send
A dream, the best
I've ever seen
Of a warm place where I've been.

Here I lie
On a bloody bed of nails,
Infuriated.
Was I not meant to sleep?
What I would do to only find
My simple wish for peace of mind.
None molest, deprive my need,
Oh, it would be best,
If only I could lie and rest...

Chris Eppler

Friend

Dear Jesus, you are my Friend
I need a Friend right now,
Sometimes I feel lonely, Friend.
Have you been there too?

My Friend, I know for sure
You understand my hurt
You left your Father, left family too.
Your friends left you.

Yes I believe you feel it too,
The emotions are real I can't deny
Though abandoned, never alone
When I cling to you.

Praise God, you never leave me
I never want to leave you
Maybe I can help the lonely too,
Teach them you are true.

Lois Short

The Storm

My mind has thunderstorms,
Dark and fierce.
Scurrying my mind,
Stifling my bliss.
Gaining control of my mind's gentle flow.
Losing my dreams,
No chance to grow.

Jeff Molson

A Dying Rose

In memory of beloved mother, Mrs.
Bertha Maxie Angulo
Mother, since you left this world
my life has not been the same
like a dying rose
that has not felt sun nor rain
My heart longs for healing
for sadness seems to be winning
Like a dying rose
happiness has become a stranger
to my soul
Like a dying rose
I wait to see
what the future holds
Mother, whether I survive or not
I will always love you a lot
Life is precious like a rose
facing life tomorrow
will be difficult I suppose
Mother, could my life be
like a dying rose?

Gerardo L. Angulo

Dove's Death

The wings of my soul
Have been twisted and wrenched
By this endless tempest of pain.

It buffets me to the ground
In a flurry of scattered feathers
Torn from my soul.

The freezing rain beats down on me;
A counterpoint of ice and mud.

And in a slowly filling puddle,
As I begin to drown,
I can hear the dogs.

Mitheldhae

Knowing

I always knew it was you for me,
Two souls come together, eyes meet...
Destiny.
It's more than a feeling
It's something you know
deep down inside.
No reasons to show.
It's in your heart
from the very start.
The moment your eyes meet.
Something has taken over.
It sleeps now, only to awaken
when the time is right.
I feel the stirring.
The journey has begun.
Can we face it?
Will we survive?
The answer is yes.
The knowledge is true.
Eternally it's me forever with you.

Wemi Ajigbotafe

...Of You

A reflection
touching
a sweet touch
a tear, heartfelt
to cry a tear
why am I here
and not you
this memory I have of you
there were flowers and you
and the reflection of you
in the water
we touched
a sweet touch
a sweet taste of you
lingers
on my lips
I smile at the thought
at the memory
of you
and I can go on

Laura A. Cline

The Pugilist

The sun is a slugger.
He stomps up the hill,
swinging those big
red gloves - a
boxer on a roll,
challenging all
contenders.
Reaching the top he
takes on a victor's
stance, his winning
smile warming
a chilly dawn.

Ina Fay Simonsen

An Island In The Sea

There is an ocean in my mind
A large expanse of sky and sea
And in its midst one can find
A piece of land that I call me.

There is storm within my soul
Upon this ocean deep and cold
The winter winds have lashed in fury
Quelled the song inside it buried.

On this island knoll of light
A sunken treasure in the night
Lies forsaken, lost, and deep
In the bleak and cruel sea.

There is something deep within
In a vision God has given
In my days both young and old
An incision in my soul
A well of wisdom and a song
A deep love both live and strong
All I can do is but feel
Let my heart release and yield.

Georges Duquette

Who's Song Is It?

Stillness enfolds my garden;
a new day has just begun.
Flower faces open up
with the rising of the sun.
Wait... I hear a song of praise,
even in this early hour.
I'm thinking: Is it my own heart,
or is it a cheerful flower?
Anyhow, it's a song of praise,
which every one may rehearse.
Yes, let's all make a joyful noise
in our Creator's Universe!

Aletta Van Oord

Untitled

I've written many journals
I've dreamt a million dreams
I've had the thoughts of mortals
And used paper by the reams

I've tried to sort my feelings
To put them into place
To have the right perspective
To wear a pleasant face

I've lived so many lifetimes
I've cried so many tears
I've looked into the future
That's clouded by my fears

I thought that life was over
That what was done was done
I saw the darkness looming
And nowhere left to run

Strangely though I wait to hear
What just one man can say
To know if there's the slightest chance
I'll live for one more day

Barbara Klusky

Dear Sister Dawn

You are my dear sister,
you are strong.
Believe me Dawn, You
did nothing wrong.

When your times are bad,
it upsets me to see you sad.
You can stand on your own,
Though, there are times,
you'll feel very alone.

Look at what you have,
hold it close to your heart.
It's never too late, for a fresh start.

Your children are your life,
you're doing what is right,
Protect them from fear,
Because, you hold them so dear.

When a marriage turns to one,
it is time it is done.

It's an up-hill climb,
You can do it, Dear sister of mine.

Linda Carpenter

My Little Seeds Of Life

Oh! How proud my heart does beat
For every little seed's discrete
Oh! How gracious I can stand
As I hold their little hand
Someday when they grow up
I hope that in their cup
Will be joy as great as mine
With seeds of their own kind

Anna Lewis Newman

Looking Down

Going to sleep, and waking
up in a place that's not
home. Not seeing family,
not a person you know.
Seeing kids you don't know
having fun. Not knowing
anyone, you must ask,
where you are. After you
find out you peer out of a
cloud, weeping. For your
family, for you are homesick
and never able to see your
family or friends again,
until they join you.

Danielle A. Lipman

Hurdles

There are those
Things in life
That stand
In your way.
Just another hurdle
One of those things
You must put far,
Far behind you.
Sometimes you
Get over them, and
Other times you
Get to the top
And everything,
Everything comes
Crashing, falling,
Tumbling down all on top of you.
You don't always
Get over those things, but you
Always, always put them behind you
And finish the race.

Amanda Lee Boyer

The Lost Child

A lost child is like a little squirrel,
Hopeless, helpless and lost.
Crying as if there's no hope
for her in the future.
Lost! No one to take care of her.
How Sad!

Walking along the streets,
Looking for someone to take her in.
Thinking, dreaming and hoping
to see and live in a home.
Waiting and waiting
to feel the gentle touch
of a loving mother,
And wishing that, one day
all that she had hoped and dreamed
will come true.

Cynthia Aung

Alone

They put me here,
in this little cage.
Full of fear,
full of rage.

I pass back and forth,
with a glow in my eye.
Breathing in cold air,
staring at the black sky.

I see no stars,
only the moon.
Which makes me think,
of all the lives I can ruin.

Just let me out,
just give me a chance.
To put you under,
my deep dark trance

Don't let anything stop you,
just open my cage.
And I will fill you with
fear and with rage

Holly Labuckas

My Tree

How did you know my tree?
Were you there with me as she
Twirled her chain round and round,
And I looked up
Into a whirl of rainbow leaves?

Did you hold on too,
As she eased her vine
To and fro, so little feet
Could land on tiptoe at the edge
Of the pit in my enchanted wood?

How did you know my tree?
My secrets, it keeps for me.
She took me in her arms,
Rocked me, sang a lullaby,
When I was ten and Grandma died.

Was she mixed, brown, gray,
Oak, Elm, maybe Bay?
Such clear pictures slip away
Into a place that is my tree,
Part then, part now, part tree, part me.

Ann S. Jenkins

Dad

Even though he's not here,
I sense him everywhere.
Even though he's not near
To hold me close
To still my fears,
His silence hurts.
Never responding,
Hardly there,
With care.
But with you
You hold me close
To still my fears,
Responding,
Always there
With care.
Lucky for me
You are my Dad.
Love your daughter

Lindsay Ellison

The Haunting Question

Who gives this bride away?
The question rings inside my ears
The question wouldn't haunt me so
If Daddy could be here

If he could take my trembling arm
And walk me down the aisle
He would look into my eyes
And answer with a smile

I give this bride away
And join the bridegroom's hand and mine
I can see this precious sight
So clearly in my mind

But who should walk me down the aisle
Now that he is gone
He will take my trembling arm
As I walk down the aisle alone

And what about the question
There'll be no one there to say
But we all will know the answer
Daddy gives this bride away

Rene B. Kennedy

A Mother

When I think of a mother
I think of my own;
And of how hard she works,
To tidy our home.

Kind words she bestows
On us everyday;
And loves us so much,
In her own special way.

I know in my heart
That a mother's love;
Can only come,
From God above.

So I thank my heavenly Father,
For giving her to me,
For I shall always love her,
Throughout eternity.

Stephanie Suzanne Guthrie

The Rain At Machu Picchu

A dream
A remote mountain
The rain
And the ancient walls
Of Machu Picchu.

But, was it rain?
Or, a cascade of tears
Tears,
From the old Inca Gods
Calling, to their daughters
And sons.

Silent tears
Washing the ancient walls
A long, kiss of tears
From the old Inca Gods
Remembering, the glory days
Of Machu Picchu.

And the rain, keeps falling down
On the lonely walls
Of Machu Picchu

Martha Guardado

Nature

Green trees, blue skies, strong
whispering winds,
The sound of nature all around,
Birds chirping, squirrels moving,
The life of nature everywhere,
Life is living everywhere,
To destroy it we don't care,
We don't know what we destroy,
Too hungry for land we are,
If we change the way we are today,
There will be the life and
sound of nature to hear and
feel for tomorrow.

Bridget Reid

The Snowman

A snowman stands in my backyard
    So cold, so straight so tall,
Imperial is his bearing,
    Majestic is his gall.

Though icy winds caress his frame
    He little cares not he,
He proudly stands and shivers not
    For Winter's King is he.

The children are his subjects
    And he regally sees their play,
And know as evening cloaks his realm
    They'll all be back next day.

But warmer days are coming soon
    With gentler breezes brewing,
And although he doesn't know it now,
    The sun is his undoing.

Ernest T. Todd

Michael In Three Acts

Just as the hunter aims
at plumes; seductive, bright
So too the suitor wins
his trophy of delight.

And as the hunter rapes
and strips what suits him best,
The husband eats his fill
and spits out all the rest.

The hunter leaves his mark;
a bloodied pelt, a shell,
A carcass on the path.
So too the Infidel.

Beverly Cole Earney

Why Poetry

Many may think my methods strange
    when poetry I conceive
To depict some treasured event of life
    in which I truly believe.

Perhaps it would be easier
    to write a book of prose
I would not then have to make it rhyme
    the essence of plot of expose.

But arranging thoughts poetically
    can give a lot of pleasure
To those who have but little time
    to fulfill their moment of leisure.

William Henry Jones

When It's Him I'm Thinking Of

I would have done so much for him!!!
But he didn't care
He meant the world to me
But was never there

I gave so much to make it work
But he didn't ever try
Now my world is falling apart
Since he said good-bye

He has his eyes
On someone new, he treats her very good
I can't help but wonder why
He didn't treat me like he should

Now I have a broken heart
That maybe time will heal
I wish I had another chance
To tell him how I feel

Now I sit here lonely
With no one to love
Not just anyone will do
When it's him I'm thinking of

Lynn Woods

Untitled

I sit here in a room full of warmth,
not from the heat of the fire,
nor the furnace,
but from the love of people
that fill it.

A ray of vibrance that strikes
my heart and over whelms me
like the color chart.

A vastness of life like a flying kite
so free and willing.

Like a newborn child unexplainable
but so beautiful it starts you crying.

To only make you feel like
one of gods children.

Steve Conley

Rain

Round, full drops
slide over a small
town washing away
yesterday.

Soon the rain slowly
disappears and the
yellow sun reappears
and tomorrow becomes
today.

Aleksandra Pavlovic

The Red Empire

Creation flows like a current,
In the room for only a second.
The starving caves
Built upon the foundation of naked steel,
Crave the martian
Who used to rule
The red empire,
Which now is only dust.
The sun is now earth.
This is the way of space.

Paul Smith

My Ode To Maw Maw

Lord God she is a cherished soul
Our memories of her are just like gold
Precious, gentle, kind and dear-
The ones you hold, oh so near.

So take her now to live with you
And give to her a life that's new
One of ease, no pain, no fear-
Not like it was when she was here.

Her loss to us is hard to bear
But knowing she is in your care
Makes it easier to let her go-
Oh Maw Maw, we loved you so.

Sherry Wright Clardy

Marriage

As you join hands together
and start a brand new life
May the love of God surround you
and bathe you in His light.

Your joy in one another
will have a healthy glow
If God is at the center
And you agree to grow

Let God into your marriage
And you will see your love
Grow beautiful and strengthen
with blessings from above.

He'll take care of your future
He'll bless the here and known
The past is but a shadow
when God is on the throne.

So do your best to please Him
and when the trials of life
attempt to overcome you
God's love will make it right.

Ruth Ness

To Fly

To fly
would be
my greatest dream come true.
Would be
the greatest thing
in all the land.
To fly
when the birds
swoop down
and
to be the queen
of flying.

Amanda Bryant

Secret Admirer

There you are across the room,
those eyes, that face, I can't
help but stare. My knees weaken
from the thought of your touch,
my heart jumps cause I love you
so much. But shyness has brought
me down so low, for who I am
you may never know.

Jess Wagner

"Ode To A Kite"

Soaring high in the autumn sky
  a little kite painted in blue -
Sailing in the dusky wind
  oh, so free and true.

Flying by and saying 'hi'
  to every little bird -
Going here and going there
  passing on God's word.

Speaking of how, what he knows now
  about the Lord above -
How God can change or rearrange
  what it is we think of.

How God alone can make a home
  a happy one or sad -
How God can make a mortal mistake
  turn someone back to glad.

And on this earth, since our birth
  God teaches us to pray -
So we can live, as He forgives,
  a happier life each day.

Terri Dillard

God Is Love

"I am who am!
So write for me."
So spoke to me, my mentor.
Loose now the bonds and set me free.
Go forth thou lone dissenter.
Tear down the walls that imprison me,
and let the poor souls enter.

Write and free me from this prison.
Free for me the inner vision.
Clarion bell ring loud and clear
so the inner ear can hear.

So the wound can really heal,
teach everyone to inner feel.

Some are blind and cannot see —
in awe of God's divinity;
blind to the truth that is sublime —
all of us are made divine!

Thru all of us flows the energy;
the impulse of Life that is Love.

Mercille I. Schmitt

Ruby Lee

She came into this world
with the name Ruby Lee.
But, she's always been
just Mama to me.

There were three kids before me
and two who came after.
Our house was always filled
with love and lots of laughter.

She taught us right from wrong
and good from bad.
To always work hard
and appreciate what we had.

Her hands are strong,
yet gentle and kind.
But, there were times when
they could sure sting my behind.

As I'm raising kids of my own
I'm praying I can be
as good a woman and Mother
as my dear Ruby Lee.

Lisha Boswell Aguilar

When I Saw Love

When I saw love,
I had joy and hope and trust.
And no other joy has been as ripe!
And no other hope has been as full!
And no other trust has been as strong!
As mine when I saw love.

When I saw love,
There was hurt and pain and tears.
Yet no other hurt has been as deep.
And no other pain has been as sharp.
And no other tears have been as sad,
As mine when I saw love.

When I saw love,
I had joy and hope and trust.
But no other joy has been as short,
And no other hope as been as crushed,
And no other trust has been as blind,
As mine when I saw love.

Mary Angela White

There Is No "WHY" In Heaven

As I look at all the souls
from Heaven
I understand why I am made
the way I am.
Some souls are angry with me
because of the body I occupy.
Some souls are angry with me
because of who my Father is.
But I have come to understand
the reason souls question
every situation.
The relationship.
A soul must have a relationship
with their Father before they can
know WHY God is Heaven
inside me.

Alien

"The Valley"

The valley, flushed with gold
Diamonds ripple on the stream
As the dark clouds unfold
The valley becomes a dream.

The valley, the forest's alive
Should you descend the trail
The swallows in their dive
The little deer so frail.

The valley, where shadows fall
The grass is wet with dew
The swaying pines so tall
The flowers that are new.

This valley, has no secrets now
That it held years ago
But it can show you how
Its beauty, as it grew.

This valley, lovers stroll
Amid the twilights glow
Hearing only the bells toll
They are alone you know.

Leslie R. Tidd

The Farewell

I weary this so battered world
My eyes, though dim, are more
As being here — yet trying to see
Beyond an opening door

My youth and its remembrances
Are forefront in my mind.
Remembered faces, so very clear.
More real than now, I find.

I wonder, if I look ahead,
That door would open wide
And oh! such happiness I'd find
Should I just slip inside

The way is clear. My heart is full!
The vision that I see,
with joy I step upon this path
And down eternity!

Jocelyn Martin Hurd

Remember, Look Up High!

When hasty words that you may say
Pour venom to a loving heart
Despite the pain and grief they cause
Instead of hurting in reply
The quiet spirit will just sigh
    Before you speak, my friend,
    Remember, look up High!

When in someone else's yard
Your eyes will dart in greed
Your fellow man, who's there for you
Will not suspect misdeed:
His faith in you will never die.
    Before you covet others' goods,
    Remember, look up High!

And when with suffering you shall meet
On life's meandering roads
Do not be blind to those in need
One day, you too may ask your "why."
    Before you take another step
    Remember, look up High!

Constantin Clisu

The Little Child (Of War)

The sun is shining brightly
On the valley far below
The little child is playing
As the gentle breezes blow

His heart is filled with laughter
All the world seems bright and gay
And only in the distance
Does the blue sky fade to gray

The little child grows older
In a place so far away
The air is filled with hellish noise
And all the sky is gray

An eerie silence hovers now
He hears no rifle crack
For the little child lies dying
As the gray sky fades to black

James F. Pettersen

Fantasy

You're a will-o-the wisp,
A beautiful phantom who teases me.
An enigma — an elusive delight
That just cannot be.
You're a jack-in-the-box,
A comical pattern of fantasy.
You're a puff of pink smoke,
A visual pun — inconsistency.
You're a thing of the past —
And a future to be
An Epiphany.

Lawrence Thailer

Bright Blue

It is true bright blue
To talk to those
Left behind in the treads.
Though a mark is left
Though is bereft
Memory of grand occasion
Not what the angel left on my shoulder.

Suddenly ignition spurs the mind.
Ear is willing to see
What others hope to bloom in kind.
My time
My wait
Our want
To find

Robert Foley

"Lost Light"

The belt snapped, the child cried,
And deep inside the joy has died.
The angry voice, a brutal sound,
Emotions driven underground.

Disconnected from the light
Darkness clouds my inner sight.
Fears invading, all alone
Searching for a safety zone.

Battered ego, damaged soul,
Abusive actions take their toll.
Hide the feelings, never share
Emotions buried deep down there.

Gini Sandler

My Love Forever

Since we have been together,
I've felt so complete inside.
You may have me for ever,
And I'll have nothing to hide.

You make me feel like sunrise -
After a moonless night.
I promise you no other light -
Will ever disrupt my sight.

You have made it to my heart,
You have made it to my dreams.
And every day without you,
Is harder than it seems.

I love you more than I express,
To you all the time.
And if you'd like me to confess,
I'm really glad you're mine.

Jacqueline Thibodeau

The Color Cry

There are many colors
Throughout this land.
In many places
On many of man.
But none quite like the color cry.
Why...
Through the eye of the color cry,
Everything is clear —
Like raindrops falling
From the sky...
With tears of joy
With tears of pain,
Our teardrops are the same
As we cry.
So let us cry
The color cry.
Then we can feel the rain
That is clear —
Through the eye
Of the color cry.

Bob Blakley

The Saturnine Sky

As I gazed upon the saturnine sky
I began to weep and cry
What makes people so ungrateful
Instead of satisfied

What makes them so discontented
With what they already have
Can't they see what God has done
And he's above them all
He can lift them up
Or gently let them fall

I hope our world won't always be
The type of world it is
With all of its ungrateful people
And Av-a-ri-cious-ness

But being optimistic as I am
I will always say
There is room in all our hearts
To work at making a change

Vivian Y. Stuart

My Prayer

Hear our prayer we ask of Thee
Fill our souls with ecstasy.
May we learn Thy truths divide
when we worship at Thy shrine.

Lord, our God, we praise Thy name
For our blessings, day by day,
For our earth so richly blest,
For the rains to quench its thirst.

When we leave this earth - so frail
Help us find the Holy Grail,
Heaven's gates swing open wide
Let us in Thine arms abide.

Stars of morning, shout for joy
When we reach the Heavenly shore
Angels sing with love divine
Welcome! Welcome! Child of Mine.

Patricia Marshall

"Success"

Varied are the goals
Of the wayward man,
Who vacillates in the wind
Scorned by those who excel
A dismal failure, they assert
But who defines success?
It's not that he lacks
The ambition to succeed
Nor the ability to surpass
But only that,
Triumph is construed
According to the standards
To which one clings.

Terrell L. Winkler

On Leaving

There is an art to leaving,
the way you show your back
hard and solid under
loose clothing-
the way you twist the doorknob
firmly
under your palm
and pull it towards you.

There is an art to walking out,
letting the cold air slap your face
better than any woman.

Lucinda Zimmerman

How Do I Feel?

My fear is gone.
I'm no longer lost.
It's you in my heart.
All else is tossed.

I need your love.
I'm ready to give
Anything you want.
I just want to live.

I have been scared
To show how I feel.
Now that I trust me
Everything seems real.

How do I feel?
I'm in love with you.
I wasn't aware
Until I lost you.

DJ Giesbrecht

Man

What is man?
 Let's turn our gaze in that direction.
Is he brain, blood, bones?
 No! He's reflection.
 Reflecting all
 that's good and pure,
Honest, upright, Godlike, sure.
Thinking rightly,
 Healthy, whole,
Governed by immortal Soul.

That's the man
 that I am seeing...
That's the man
 that I am being.

Helen Bayfield

"A Dawn Too Tough To Face"

What sort of disgrace
could bring this dawn
too tough to face?
Thought his friend.

A Captain's rank
he did obtain
on the good ship Hope
But who was to blame?

 A madman's cry
 they said to make;
 but he chose a lie,
 his life to take.

His wife took off
and left the man;
a divorce to stop
was the Captain's plan.

He was well respected
but cancer drove him mad;
insanity wasn't suspected
and his passing makes us sad.

 A madman's cry they said to make;
 but he chose a lie, his life to take.

Richard C. Jackson

The Road Of Life

I started on this road of life,
Before I really knew,
What it was to be,
A person on my own.

At the tender age of fifteen,
I traded in my childhood,
For the love of a husband,
And a home of my own.

Not knowing how hard life can be,
To those that chose to give,
More of themselves to others,
Than others give in return.

But one thing I learnt on this road,
That without the love and guidance,
Of the one who gave me life,
My road would not have been this long,

To all of those who think,
They hold the key to life,
Remember you don't travel well alone,
But the lord will guide you home.

Debbie Albury

Untitled

I'm dancing on a sunbeam
I'm wishing on a star
I'm living in a world
that's forever more than far.
I'm wishing on a four-leaf clover
I'm at the bank of a crystal stream
I'm living in a world
that's forever just a dream.
I'm dancing in a garden
where everyone is free
I'm living in a world
that's forever just a fantasy.
I'm swimming with the mermaids
in a place we'll never find
for I'm living in a world
that is only in my mind
 never stop dreaming.

Jennifer Gomes

Whalebacks

I weave my way among the whales
these great plains earthen pods
Covered in the grasses, short and brown
Migrate South with the snowbirds.
Archaic beasts,
they draw us with them
through the Dakotas and Nebraska.
Closer to the sun,
away from the snow and ice of Canada.
Their spouts are silenced,
but the awe they invoke
Make our hearts leap in joy.
We wait and we watch and continue along
in breathless anticipation.
But ere, not a sound or misty spray
appear on the horizon.
But eight white tailed mule deer
bounding effortlessly
across the Whalebacks.

Shannon Bond

Life

Who's said life would be easy?
 "Not I!" Said the Lord.
Who said there'd be no sorrow?
 "Not I!" Said the Lord

Who said life would be joyful
 so rewarding and kind?
Who said there would be sunshine
 and a great peace of mind?

Who said Life's what you make it,
 you give more than you take.
Life can be... oh so beautiful...
 but now let's take a break!

You don't get something for nothing,
 and you never, never will.
You get just what you work for...
 so work hard for that thrill.

Now continue to be thoughtful...
 charitable and kind,
Soon you'll know what the Lord meant,
 and true happiness find.

Rue Ann W. Craven

My Friend?

My friend, my best friend,
through good times
or bad
I thought.

Until the bad times
came,
you laughed at me
and didn't care.

Worry about
me you do
not,
I guess you
forgot.

Chelsea Pogorelac

Books

Funny mysterious title,
Heart touching animal book,
Calm steady beginning,
Climax begins to rise,
Exciting adventurous middle,
Enjoyable heart touching end!

Katie Chung

Loved And Lost

She cried out for
    Her lover, lost
To find him again
    Any cost
Round her heart wore
    Bonds of steel
Heart so hurt
    T'would never heal
She wept until
    She could weep no more
Then left her sorrows
    On Death's cold door -

Andrea Rybicki

Listen To Me

Listen to me breathe
when my ear is
to your heart and
I can hear all the words
you just can't say.
With every single beat
You laugh and cry
and scream like fire.
Listen to me
breathe as deep
and hold it in.

Melissa Dulski

Lost Son

I got divorced when you were ten,
Remarried another,
You left to go live with your Dad,
You said, "You're not my Mother."

Your Dad was not too helpful,
You hated me as one,
He turned your heart against me,
I lost you as a son.

So now you're getting married,
No invitation came,
I knew that this would happen,
It still hurts just the same.

Each day I pray a lot and hope,
A miracle to see,
I should be at your wedding,
But it's not meant to be.

I wish you'd look inside your heart,
You'd see your thoughts aren't sound,
A miracle would surely happen,
And then the lost is found.

Jan Zimmerman

Tomorrows

If only I could have known for us
there would be no more tomorrows
Not for you and me nothing
but burden and sorrow
For now you are a world away
and at peace as they say
So for you and me as life unfolded
Time spanned but few in years
Life's hand dealt many tears
And so for you and me
There will be no more tomorrows

Yolonda Oswalt

The Church

The Church is faithfully standing
So patiently, never demanding.

Imagine its warm smile
Saying, "Come in, stay awhile."

I invite you to my pew
Open up your hearts, feel brand new,

Have faith when you come in
Don't give up, you are bound to win.

It's lots of things to do,
Spiritual love and fellowship, too.

I will really lift you up,
Even fill your empty cup.

Spirit uplifting I will provide.
Open the Bible and abide.

Whatever problem you can't bear
Take it to the altar kneel in prayer.

I am happy as can be;
No longer lonely, can't you see.

Until the next time untold
Again my empty arms unfold.

Charlie Guyton

Reality

A flash of lightning
A spark from the fire
Seeing you, I was left with desire
Only a dream, that's what you were.
Couldn't open my eyes, afraid of fear.
Something inside said
You would not appear.
Yet my heart longed
for you to be near.
let me go to sleep,
and keep on dreaming
if I have to, then it's the way of being

Patti Ulaszonek

Life Is Love

Life ever unto love is thrust
Ever unto life bequests
Its own
Ever unto love is cast
Love alone is life bequests
Eternal hope
For all must know that
Life ever shall in One reside
This unity of love betides
That each from One arisen
Returns unto its own.

Paul Elwood Peckham

Lost Love

As I stare into the daylight hours
only to notice another long day
closes...to the night.
No reflections in the mirrors
edges, no images are seen..in
the darkest of the night.
I'm the only light you see, only
light..you don't see me!
Nothing is heard, only quiet you
see...no shadows, but you and me
pass through this motionless
stare. I close my eyes and
reach out my arms...only to feel
the empty cold night air...
It's quiet still, no movement,
can be seen, no images, no reflections,
no whispers of
laughter...as I notice once
to often... as this long day
comes to a close...into the night.

Mark A. Gregory

Untitled

The moon crept into the sky,
Silence broken by a muffled cry,
In the dark kneels a clown,
Tears enough for him to drown,
Pain has cut him so deep,
A broken heart is why he weeps,
I ask why he sobs alone,
Believing happiness is all he's known,
He turns so I see his face,
In his eyes is only empty space,
Just as I am about to flee,
He softly says to me,
I do not cry for me,
The tears are for what I see,
A lonely angel in love,
with the last known dove,
The things she'll never receive,
Because her heart will not believe,
A man lives with such feeling,
And cry's alone, kneeling.

Shane L. Halmi

Guide Dogs

I have worked alongside
my blind master for
many years.

My paws ache with
pain, while they rest
upon the hot cement.

But I don't mind.
My fondness has
changed to my master.

I work for him with
overwhelming pride
in my heart.

As I slowly walk down
the busy streets,

I think of my blind master,
my friend.

I will never leave him.
I am a loyal guide dog.

Katie O'Neil

Birthdays

Happy birthday
you turn one today
April 19 what a day in history
Oklahoma City bombing
and Jacob Ryan's
birthday
So many lost on
such a great day
for a family with a newborn
Maybe those that were
lost are somehow in you
I will always remember April 19, 1995
you turned up in the world
for the
first time.

Robyn Scott

The Night Of The Train

She passed through here,
outshining the moon.
Time measured by her whistle,
her lamp aimed at wondrous places.
Though heart of iron
and nerves of steel,
she knew our town,
she knew our men,
men of the shop.
The dandy dancers who cleared the way.
She was kin to the mill,
with its dancing sparks.
Prosperity in her wake,
a way of life,
life itself obligated to her.
Now she's gone,
lost in the night,
unable to find her way.
Tomorrow covered her tracks.

Bill Egan

First Impressions

When I first saw First Impressions
I was really not impressed
He was jumping to conclusions and
He always seemed obsessed

With the look of people's faces
And the colour of their hair
Native tongue in many cases
How they got from here to there

First Impressions judges people
When he knows them not so well
Brings their faults out in the open
Like some kind of "show and tell"

Yet we all use First Impressions
When we're meeting someone new
So be careful how you use him
Or they'll do the same to you

Cindra Finlay

My Mom

She loves us,
She cares for us,
She cheers us up when we are sad
She does many things for us,
So, she is really not
So bad.

Justin Aquino

Untitled

In the beginning
You were so far from
Knowledge
You could not see nor hear,
Your world was just a black
Silence.
You knew no light,
But then she came
The being who would bring
Your soul to life,
The one who would teach you,
Knowledge.

Jeremy Cahill

Heights

The endless rising up and up.
The dizziness.
Just sit down, close your eyes
Nowhere to sit.
Ready to get off the towering height,
But nowhere to get off.
It grabs me!
With his strong, rigid hands,
Round and round and round I go,
Where I stop nobody knows.
Push!
Down and down and down I go.
Everything is spinning.
Down I go off the mountainous top.
I won't stop, so I spin.
Helplessly I spin.

Christine Dauksewicz

Two Lives In One

Dying! Dying is what I'm afraid of.
Life! Life is what I want
I dream! Dream of ways to get there.

But "Where" is really there!

The sun becomes my enemy.
The moon becomes my Ally.
Blood becomes my feast.

But to feast upon the living,
Is to feast before their dead.
And as my master told me.

"No guilt within thy head or
Thy shell dye a painful death."

With the living!
Not the dead!.

Thy shell not take the living
Unless the living bleeds.
And if thy did, once long ago
Thy guilt will set you free.

Tracy Paul

"Old Mother Annie"

Old mother Annie
Was a very old granny
Who decided to learn to fly.
But when she got up in a plane
It started to rain,
And Old Mother Annie started to cry.

Christina DeMizio

A Child To Love

What can you say,
of time gone away.
When desire from the heart
can not start - a life.

You wanted a child.
Were you not ready?
Or, was your life so un-steady?
Remaining one - no 'little me.'

But, the love is still there.
Feelings to share;
To give of yourself;
To show you care.

There must be comfort
in reality.
Purpose - although you
can not see.

Perhaps in being the helping hand
will provide a special stand.
for love — to a child.

Michael Mary V. Pratte

For You

When time
Has cast aside
Her silvered mirror
And each season's
Beauty seen
Lovelier than ever,
Remember then
The warm starry night of June
With its blossoming world
And rounded moon
Encloses a haven
"My soul and love
Live for you."

Friedgard V. Van Eck

Neighborhood

Babies crying,
Little girls giggling,
Mothers scolding,
Loud music playing,
Fathers swearing,
Basketball bouncing,
Tires squealing,
Hammers knocking,
Lovers quarreling,
Drunk men squawking,
Dogs barking,
Sirens wailing,
Blue lights flashing.

Silence............
Sounds of my neighborhood.

Doug McAbee

You Didn't Know?

Be there.
Be cool.
They are.
Quiet. Listen.
Going where?
Listen. Feel it.
Be cool, dare.
Listen. Be it.
Jazz.

LaMont Johnson

The Little Boy

I can reach to tables,
I can fill up chairs and
I'm still growing,
When I grow all the way
up, my head will bump
the sky, I'll have clouds
for a bed, and a moon
for a pillow, and stars instead
of freckles on my nose.

Dustin A. Bielawski

Sounds

Oh how scary the thunder is
How mad the rain is
With its dripping.
How annoying my brother is
Making bad chicken scratches
On his journal.
It's so silent now.
That scares me.

Malcolm Parkinson

The Black Heart

A heart of stone
Through to the bone
It has no feeling
And is always shielding
The Black Heart never changes

It tries to hide
And cannot confide
On all the earth and sky above
There is nowhere it can feel love
The Black Heart never changes

The color of coal
The absence of soul
Free as a lark
But when you look, all you see is dark
The Black Heart never changes

It's scared to feel
Cause it's all so real
It doesn't know what things to do
So all it does is pay its dues
The Black Heart never changes

Phil Cravens

M e

Where to turn
Where to go
What to do
Who to know
uncertainly swims
confusion screams
flustered thoughts
disordered dreams
who could know
who can see
nobody understands
Nobody but me
I go on
brave the winds
fight for strength
and hope I'll win

Natalie Wright

Untitled

Twisting turning slowly burning
    lightening into flames
A spark ignites our fancied flights
    why is there anyone to blame?
        You took the steps
        Along the trail
        Saving your singing self
To what do you owe
    that lovely spill which
knocked you off that pitying shelf?

A day a night
Those passing hours
when dreams invaded heartache's hole
    You tossed and turned
    but yet it still burns,

That fire named your soul.

Adrianna T. Mack

Skinny Dipping

Primal night
Misty shadow-light
Intruding skin shed
Life and fluid wed
In velvet womb tingle
As the earth,
the sky,
the lake,
and I mingle.

Cara Reed

Cliché

Sitting on a bench
of ignorance
Nostalgic mirrors
cloud themselves
A symphony of
solitudes
Play transparent words
of love;
A duet of duos.

You are being lost
in oblivion
For no obvious
reasons
You search for reality
and only grasp fantasy
Like the others (like you)
you pay;
Renting life.

You almost became
the cliché.

Geneviève Lauzier

Apart

Apart from all the jokes
and bereavements you have made,

Apart from all the lies
for truth, I'd gladly trade.

Apart from all the anger
that deep inside I hold,

Apart from all the emptiness
all meaning I have sold.

Apart from all injustice
whose laws you do abide,

Apart from you who hurts me
there's truly life inside.

Doris Plitt

The Irish Princess

Her arms held out
Her smile so bright
When her grandpapa
Comes into sight
Her hair is red
Her eyes are blue
She's his Colleen
Through and through
Her name is Meghan Mary
Right from the Emerald Isle
And when St. Patty thinks of her
All the angels smile
So when grandpa talks about her
You can feel the love pour out
For she's his Irish Princess
And of that there is no doubt

John J. Hayes

Maybe Tomorrow

When hope seems shattered
and Love is threadbare,
or the things which one mattered
are no longer there.

Remember that each day
falls into tomorrow,
despite all that might
today bring you sorrow.

Has the sun ever failed to rise
when all darkness has passed?
Despite what we may now surmise
few things are meant to last.

For life is always changing
and the feelings in our souls
are also rearranging
to meet our present roles.

It is an eclipse of generations
both the old and the young
who's living educations
will determine what is done.

Ken March

"Killing Time"

I look at my watch
And it's three a.m.,
Nobody's awake
Except me and him.

I am playing solitaire,
And I'm losing;
He's playing Russian roulette,
But he's cheating.

Every-other-minute,
He changes his mind:
He's going to lose it
On a lucky wind.

And I'm looking for aces
Underneath the piles,...
Getting rid of the faces
With sarcastic smiles.

Yes, I'm playing solitaire
And cheating;
He's playing Russian roulette
And losing.

Sankey A. Brumley Jr.

Untitled

It's hard to be a child sometimes
   Especially at night
When you waken to a creaking sound
   An unfamiliar light.

Never be afraid to say
   Exactly what you fear
I'll be there to hold your hand
   To help you understand.

As you grow up
   And start along life's way
Though we're apart
   There'll be things to fear
But I'll be near to help you dear
   You're always in my heart.

Agnes Osborn-Flautt

My Love

As I close my eyes
and think of my love
calling out my name
my eyes open wide
to find him at my side
he grabs my hand
and holds me tight
then kisses me
all through the night.

Kari Reimer

Untitled

The wind passes across the sun
And leaves no shadow.
When my life on earth is done
May I leave no shadow.
Let me leave only brightness behind,
And if I come to mind,
Remember me with a happy thought.
Perhaps a little song I've taught
Back in your early years.
In memory the heart still hears
That which has gone before,
And never quite shuts tight the door.
So if some light comes shining through
'Twill be remembered love for you.

Elsie Louise Hamelin

Alone

   In some rare cases
you're all I need
   A sweet smelling sensation
my destiny.

   I think of you more and
more everyday.
   I wish you were here
so I could say
   All the things I have on
my mind.
   So I could see that daily
smile.

   But since you're not here
I'm all alone
   Wondering when you're
coming home

Tanisha Robinson

Pilgrimage

I, haunted Orphan
Of Cellophane winds
Crawl thing-like
On Granite Crags
Gaze wide
Through geometric spans
Of Morning Sky

Into the vapor vastness
Of Eye Temple's Dome

My homeless flesh
Compresses gleaming stone
While vision glides
Across the Waters
Wrinkled Skin

Shedding edge cells into the Sand

Suddenly two Moons appear
Then slowly melt
To Turquoise Crescents
I stare imprisoned
They are my eyes

Robert Lemme

Thoreau

The stream floats by
smiling to the sun
and he wonders what it would
be like to be the stream.

The trees sway
waving to the sun
and he wonders what it would
be like to be the trees.

The night comes
saying goodbye to the sun
and he wonders what it would
be like to be the night.

I watch him sit
thinking of the sun
and I wonder what it would
be like to be him.

Jenny Simpson

Marooned

Sitting by the ocean,
Waiting for your ship to come,
What happened to us?
Our hearts used to bleed as one,
But now I'm left stranded,
Marooned with the setting sun,
I don't think I'll make to sunrise,
The dark has nearly won,
If you don't reach me soon,
Then the life within is surely done,
Sitting by the ocean,
Waiting for your ship to come.

David Marr

Envision

Instead of suffering
Through winter days...
I shall use the darkness,
To dream of summer.

Lindy Atkinson-Matalone

"The Soldier"

He is of me, together we walk on
   undefeatedly
With my shield and sword, I fight
   only for the Lord
I seem to trip on the way
I get knocked around and start to
   sway
I know what it is, I stand tall and say
   no way, and turn towards the
   right way
The Lord says, "You'll learn as you
   get older, I know by your heart
   that you will always be my soldier."

Domonique Esquilin

Bay At Dawn

It sits silent, motionless
Its breathing is shallow
Like the hour of death
The heart is slow
The ears erect, listening
Listening intently for another heart

The head moves
The eyes of gold search
Peering over the ridge
It finds little
It finds the wet mist of morning

A star edges up
It strikes the land
And darkness falls
Where the gold cannot reach

Surviving on food
But living on friendship
It waits no longer
The great mouth opens
And bellows a note of loneliness

Lynn Duffy

Death Is Here

The black sky is shining
So many people dying
Gangs and crimes
Some people with little time
Schools with violence
Kids watch them in silence
Diseases spread
Like Communion bread
Innocent babies have died
So many criminals have been fried
Death is here
But Christians live in no fear

Crystal Van Deven

My Pet

I have a little pony
He really likes to play.
He is over in the meadow
I visit Him each day.
The meadow is full of flowers
He stop to smell each one.
He is over in the meadow
Having lots of fun.
Sometime he stop and play
With his pretty little friend.
They like to race each other
They both run like the wind.
So if you are sad and lonely today
Go over to the meadow and watch
them run and play.

Jacqueline Reid

Remember

They burned their books,
they burned their schools,
manic kooks?
No, paranoid fools.

Knowledge would hurt youth
they would be able to think,
to discern idiocy from truth,
to establish a logical link.

From history, no great lesson
taken or learned,
once again,
knowledge was spurned.

Only the witless
would repeat this mistake.
Ask those witness
to humanity's first break.

Edward Stevens

Daddy's Little Girl

One blessed day, so long ago,
A lovely child was born,
Into a world, so strange and new,
So helpless and alone.

As years went by, her heart yearned
For more than she had known;
She knew not why, yet deep inside,
The emptiness had grown.

She was reborn, when one fine day,
The truth, so long unknown,
Filled her eyes with tears of joy;
Her Daddy had come home.

Michael L. J. Martin

Looking Past The Reflection

I look in the mirror
and see the person I want to be
when people look my way, they see her
instead of me

In the mirror I'm happy
I don't have a care
I can handle whatever
problems are out there

But without the reflection
there is this hand
it's ugly and black and grips my heart
how much more can I stand

Why won't someone help me
Why can't they see
they're looking at her
instead of me

Jessie Ottolini

Release

When the shades were pulled down
   on my world
My worries ceased
And I could sleep.
All the tension was released
As my soul was now at peace
For I was in the hands of God.

Emma L. Bull

Testis

Through eons of distorted time
Under Sirius' perceptive vigilance
The halflings still distort the truth
Ethics and morality are in decline

False messengers give false hope
To a wounded and blighted terra
The dark ones are stirring ere now
The eternal womb cannot cope

The old beliefs are tossed aside
For electric wizard idolatry
Pain and doom merchants abound
The four horsemen are saddling to ride

Helpless are the leaders of the race
They search in vain for a medicament
The terrible wounds cannot be healed
In eternal shame luna veils her face

Patriarchal sun deities are no more
The golden age has vanished
The seeker of wisdom that cannot find
The path to yon elusive door

Rolf Fritz Lauterbach

Boys

All my friends can think of is BOYS,
For them they traded all their toys.
I think that they are icky,
But, feelings can be tricky,
I guess they're sometimes joys.

Erin Haney

The Prime Of My Life

Now that I've come to the
prime of my life

I find I'm not having
the time of my life

Arthritis has set in
and so has bursitis

And my husband complains
that the kids never write us

I struggled for years
just to get to this point

And now that I'm here
there's an ache in each joint

I don't mean to complain;
what I want you to see here

Is that all things considered
I'm just happy to be here.

Roxie Botelho

Waiting

Time gone is lost.
Yet it is not too late.
Time waits for no one.
But His love waits for all.

Where there is life, there is hope.
And life's hope is He.
For though time waits for no one,
He waits for me.

Peter Pastorelle

Today World

In this world of ours
There is so much troubled mind
If we go down the street
We have to look ahead
And wonder what next
Because what we see is
Not good for our troubled mind
Men, women, teens everywhere
Are trying to quit
The road is long for each one
In this world of our today
There are lots of things going wrong
So look ahead now
Before it's too late
Because what behind the wall
Will get you
If you don't quit now

Eleanor A. Lewis

Love Before It's To Late

There are times in a woman's life
When she must face this world alone
Everything has disappeared
Her family, friends and home.

Damn that doorbell
There it goes again
Can't they just leave me alone
"No you can't come in".

The phone rings continually
Just an echo in the hall
The light bulb is flickering
Like a ghost upon the wall.

It's been five years now
Since the laid you down to rest
Keeping myself together
Was life's hardest test

So when you find that special someone
I hope you never wait
To walk through life together
And love before it's too late

Judith Boyle

Meditation

When my thoughts go wandering
   from Thee, oh Lord,
To empty desert land,
The thorns take root within
   my heart,
I stand on sinking sand.

Thy light I can but faintly
   see,
When my thoughts go wandering
   from Thee.

Mamie Elizabeth May

Untitled

I feel at times
I need a passport to your heart
a key to your head

I don't want to break any locks
or come by forbidden entry
I need you to invite me in

I can't be a part of you today
and an alien tomorrow

Carol-Anne Moody

The Light

Through closed eyelids shines,
The light so bright.
Fear not, lone soul
All will be right.
Your mothers arms,
Await your arrival.
To guide you through life
And all its trials.

As the years of life pass by
You prepare yourself, for the
Promised land of high.
Fear not, lone soul,
The light so bright.
Your father's arms,
Await your arrival.
To guide your soul
To your eternal goal.

George J. Coe

My Cowboy

Tough man
Wyoming Cheyenne
Blue eyes
Brown hair
Hot body
Rodeo rebel
Shining star
Midnight hero
Stetson hat
Justin boots
Bull rider
Bronc buster
Dusty sweat
Muddy soles
Near death
Eight seconds
Whistle blew
75-points
Rodeo's through

Sara J. Tucker

Dry Roses

Roses dry,
Pale, stiff and
fragile. They crisp
and crumble as the memory
fades.

The smell still lingers,
The smell of death.

Dry roses,
Light and hollow,
the life sucked out.

Roses dry,
Withered and crumbled
by the hand of time into
sand piling in the hourglass.

The glass breaks
and the sand is free
on the wind of lost
and faded memory.

Ydaliza Burgos

Gratitude

The sun warms me
as I sit here
Sketch pad in hand
Inspiration in my heart

Autumn surrounds me
As the season sheds her tears
Sending them drifting down
To the Earth beneath my feet

A gentle rustling awakens me
with the breeze
Filling my senses with
October's sweet perfume

The sky burns blue above me
Letting the colors of Fall
Glisten and shine
In their last days of glory

Gratitude fills me
For sight, sound and touch
And for the artist of the Heavens
who allowed me to know these things

Lori A. Lawton

Catacombs

In the catacombs of my heart
you will find various passages,
beware of the one you choose
my friend for they all lead to
either your salvation or
destruction.

Amelia Masek

"Some People"

Some people are addicted to drugs.
    Some need money in their lives.
I'm addicted to you my love.
    I just need you to stay alive.

Some people don't believe in love.
    They've never been in love before,
Or maybe their true feelings
    they have just ignored.

Some people are filled with pain.
    Some just no longer care.
I would also feel the same,
    but I don't because you're there.

Some people no longer dream.
    They don't feel the way I do.
They would know what I mean,
    If they had someone like you.

Marina Rios

My Love

When I look in your
eyes I see the stars
twinkling in the night.
Your hair is like silk
against my skin when
we are close.
My heart starts to
race at your touch.
My mind fills with
ecstasy at the thought
of being with you.

Russell Ward

"Down Below The Bridge"

Imagine yourself walking along a
    never ending bridge.

So high but yet so very long.

Cars are passing, with every step you
    take chills travel up down
    your spine.

Imagine all the cracks as you look
    down trying to count them all.

Can you see yourself falling,
    falling down below.

Imagine the feeling and try to hold
    on to what ever is near.

If you fall below you'll never see the
    top again.

Keep your head up above the bridge
    and never look down, below is too
    far to go.

Patricia Mitchell

Today I Wake

Today I wake
a brand new day.
And on that note
then I should pray.

To tell the Lord
I love him true.
And without him
my life is thru.

To thank him for
each new day,
and all the toys
with which I'll play.

A wonderful day
I will make,
With hopes for tomorrow
I will wake.

Donna A. Kirkness

Sweet Terrain

He floats with the clouds
and wrestles with the wind-
His body becomes numb
with a sharp searing touch.

Plummeting into a deep abyss,
memories soar past his
outstretched fingers.

The memories, slapping his face,
with a cruel reality-
Death opens its doors,
beckoning, coaxing, pleading-
Come in.

Screeching to a dead halt,
he sees the beautiful
red light and weeps-
in horror!

Laurie Rupert

"To Be Or Not To Be"

Friends we've been forever,
Friends on every day.
Love considered never,
That was all okay.

We talk a lot together,
We flirted to much to say.
We've joked about each other,
Every different way.

Platonic been our motto,
Life in time has past.
Our friendship I believe,
Will live on until our last.

Now it's getting deeper,
Dusk has gone away.
Love is getting stronger,
stronger everyday.

Though this is surprising,
It still creates confusion.
Shall I dig deeper into your eyes,
Or fight of this long lost Cupid.

Doug Bellenger

"Coping"

Sometimes life seems too hard
   to handle,
When this happens sit down
   and light a candle.
Say a prayer and it will ease
   your mind,
Because you are not alone and
   are not one of a kind.
Knowing someone listens
   makes it easier to bear,
There is always someone there
   to take time to hear.

Maryann Hollenback

Rings

Rings are perfect circles
Without a beginning or an end
An unbroken form
Forged of gold

White is pure
A dress to beautiful to be worn
Made for the day
Stitched in Satin

Flowers are fragile
A profusion of colors
A wonderful bouquet
Made with silk

Bride and groom
The perfect couple
Everything ready for this day
Loves so strange

The Silk is in tatters
The satin stains
And the gold ring
Is all that remains

Angela D. Plummer

If Only

And what of this spin
   to oblivion?

Entrust it to the curators in
   the museum of hopeful memories

The wants and wishes
   of future passed

The dusty resonance of
   what could yet be

The near clairvoyance of
   what might yet be

Washed in the begins and
   brittle visions of naivete

A cosmic wrap and splash,
   disabled amongst the why

Noia and paranoia
   llel and parallel

Hedonist, mottled, clumsy
   a grasping with gloves on

Here in the mausoleum of the mere
   a disparate design

The slender promise of nothing.
   If only.

Darrel Hilman

Who Will Love You When You're Old?

Lines of silver, leaves of gold,
Frost writes on the marigold,
Writes with fingers, stiff and cold,
Who will love you when you're old?

Skies are deep, and stars are waiting,
Frost upon the gold is grating,
Life, her blooms evacuating,
Bows to earth, still contemplating.

Mom will love me, Daddy too,
My love, and just one more or two,
All in Heaven, they are who
Will love me when I'm old and blue.

Silent voices, sweet and mellow,
Haunt the heart of some true fellow,
Listening in the fields of yellow,
Waiting for a soft hello.

Russell Phillips

Born To Win

He and his dad
and next of kin
played only one way
and that was to win
they held and broke
but they were not vain
and they displayed
no stress of pain
thus, their task
was difficult and great
there was no doubt about that
they conquered all
with their power, arms, and legs
but played it fair
and committed no foul or sin
for they were destined
to be born to win!!

Larry L. Kuntz

Fragrance Of Love

It's hard to make a home into
a house "For Rent"
It's empty now and that particular
fragrance of you and home, cooking,
baking, love and concern are all
covered now by the odor of fresh paint.

"It smells so clean and fresh"
they say as they walk through
and look the house over.

"Yes" I say, but when they
leave I go to the one closet that
hasn't been emptied or painted. I
hug your special sweater to me —

"It smells like you, Mama."
I say, and I weep into the fragrance
of all that was but will
never be again.

Charlotte Alexander

Untitled

Dancing trees
and flying leaves,
Fairy tales that kids believe,
What becomes of all of these,
when trees fall
and take its leaves?

There'll be no more enchanted forest
with little girls and witches horror,
No tales to tell by camp site
No place to hide...
What bumped
in the night??

Lisa Ann Ohmer

The Golden Gates

The golden gates were opened wide
A gentle voice said come.
And angels from the other side
Welcomed our mother home.
A precious voice from us has gone-
A voice we loved is stilled,
A place is vacant in our home
Which never can be filled.
God in His wisdom has recalled
The gift His love had given
And though the body slumbers here
The soul is safe in heaven.

Dean McElrath

Journey

In a traffic jam
a squad car is also in
under the blue sky in May

A cool drink
with a slice of lemon

A wheel chair glides
into swinging heat haze

Summer grasses deeply root
in a red rock in Arizona

The trace of a snail
across a hot rock
journey to the Galaxy

Isao Sakano

Heaven's Sweetest Angel

Although she didn't have
Lots of this world's treasures.
She always was so happy
With life's simple pleasures.

Instead of spending money
Frivolously on herself,
It made her so much happier
Spending it on someone else.

She always had the time
For each and every one.
To make them feel so special
So they never felt alone.

Near the ending of her life
When she was oh, so ill.
She always had kind words for all
And through her pain, a sweet smile.

And now that God has called her Home
We miss her Very Much!!!!
But Heaven's so much richer now
Because of His Sweetest Angel's touch!

Susan Hill Casper

What Is Success To You?

All day I work . . .
It wouldn't be so bad
If only encouragement I had.
When success comes to me dear,
You won't be by my side
Because you always nagged.
What is Success to You?
Kind words I wanted, so
Why can't you change?
Then we would walk
The road of success.
Again I'll ask,
What is Success to You?
Helping the one you Love,
When you can.

Miss Delora DeArmon

The Last Cry

My pain and sorrow
 is no more
And with it I have taken
 away yours.

The tears no more shall fall
 from my eyes.
From yours, the crystals
 may drop

For now, but not for long.
Ice melts fast in the
 heat of the sun.

I am reaching my sun
 This is my last song of goodbye.

Leyla Adkins

Untitled

Hockey puck oh hockey puck,
hit me in the face
give me a bruise
in a nice, nice place,
and if you don't, I'll shoot you hard
and hit me, then you won't.

Gavin Lake

The Nowhere People

I look at the Nowhere People
As they roam down the street
They don't belong anywhere
So they keep on their feet.

Who are these Nowhere People
Who wander near and wide?
Living life in Nowhere
Can eat you up inside.

And to the Nowhere People
Life is full of daily pain
For the clouds never lift
They're always drenched in rain.

Yes, even these Nowhere People
Wish for a place to belong
Yet somehow they survive
And manage to stay strong.

For some of them have faith
No matter how far they roam
That the last road they take
Will lead them back to home.

Dena Leichnitz-Amos

The Utopians

Intruders to enclosed
worlds they march
singly trying
to change
inertia

Dressed in knightly
garb they are out
of step building
private castles
among the row
houses

A blind and deaf mass
wanders by
unaware
uninspired
seeking only
rest

Not

Solitary
musings

D. S. Austin

Our Prison Of Freedom

Who am I if I can't be free
am I the keeper or the one who is kept?
Is my time mine
or is it someone else's?
Are my thoughts only dreams in my sleep
are they made up for me
am I captured by you
or for you by some one to keep
Is our love natural
can we keep our respect alive
you're the victory in my heart
you're a bright summers day
you have changed my heart, forever
you molded me like clay
I love you free and easy
just the way you want it
you're like a soft gentle wind
you warm my life
and you take away my pain

Mr. Blair A. Smith

Never See It As O.K. But Totally Wrong, Or The Damage Goes On, And On

When you're an abused child
cry not, for what you have done, but
for what was done to you

Never seek revenge, yet
reach for the stars, and
shoot high

Never allow your false pride
to take you for a ride

Search and look deep in
your heart,
never forget where you came from

Never wait for the day
you grow up
so you can have your turn

Never see it as o.k. but
as totally wrong, or the damage
goes on, and on

Barbara A. Englund

Untitled

We live the cosmic moment
and every time we spiral,
begins a higher level
transcending time and space.
Whatever we are thinking,
we are precipitating.
Remembering our birthright
we are one, we are unity.
I am you and you are me.

Constance Spear

God Is My Strength!

Speak to me, oh Lord
 and I will listen.
Touch my heart and I will
 feel the warmth of your love.
Hold me close and I will
 feel the strength of your arms.
With your surrounding presence
 I am safe and secure.
How dare evil rear its
 angry head in the face of God.
God is my strength!

Jane L. Carte

Photos

Old Photographs are histories
With powers unsurpassed,
For bringing special joy
In looking at the past.

The photo book
For years was tucked away,
Until within the attic
It came to light one day.

In one you were laughing
In one you were sad,
But all in all, you loved it
Each day, each time you had..

Old photographs add unity
And nurture family ties,
By adding to the present day
A touch of days gone by.

Carol Baldwin Hoffman

Secret Of A Rose Garden

Down in the garden beneath the soil
Roots of roses begin to toil
All day and all through the night
Leaves, alive, look for light
Up and down the essence flows
Through some stems rose blood goes
And up atop in hidden splendor
Rose buds await, their wombs to render
Then the time will come to flower
Roses to brighten your darkest hour
All this work is done for two
A gift for me to give to you
And so the rose garden's secret you see
Is the love that grows for you in me

David Medley

Dreams

My feeling go so deep it hurts.
You make me feel so special
As if you really do care.
I have new hope.
New dreams
I now know I can do anything.
As frighten as I might be
Just to see your face
Makes me feel safe.
You give me joy and happiness,
I thought was gone for good.
You make me feel happy,
Just by being near.
I hope you are always here.

Cathleen Jefferson

A Hippo Song

When my child was born,
a hippo mother gave birth
at the Zoo
in the river.
The little one did not live,
for the water was dead,
the mighty stream across the plains
was dead.
A part of me died, too,
in that river,
when I nursed my baby
trembling.

Pirkko T. Parkkinen

Shooting Star

Oh shooting star, oh shooting star
How far in the sky you are
With your streak of light
Shining ever so bright
Knowing in a minute's time
That you will be out of sight
And not giving me a photo
Record of your frenzy star flight
With only a mental image to delight
To tell my grandchildren
That I had seen a shooting star
In the midnight sky

To write a poetic description
Of this strange sight
For not knowing of how many
More years will pass me by
Before my eye is quick enough
To catch the glimpse
Of another night shooting star

John J. Chironno

Chaos

There was once a man named Bob
Who loved to eat corn on the cob
He was in such a mad dash
He had a bad crash
And hit his head on the doorknob

Bob had a wife named Jane
Who had to walk with a cane
She forgot her name
No one said it again
And now she is insane

Bob had a son named Lee
Who was born in '83
He had to pee
But hurt his wee
And now he is a she

Lee had a friend named Pete
Who didn't have any feet
He fell down
And broke his crown
And never rode back into town

Sam Tucker

This Time

Wind blowing leaves through the yard,
the streetlights begin to shine.
The moon's impaled atop the trees,
I smile, this time is mine.

I hear the sounds upon the wind,
so distant, yet so keen.
I hear the laughter down the street
of children never seen.

The porch swing raps against the house
as I sit on the grass.
I cherish all these moments
because I know they'll pass.

When all is calm and tranquil,
and all is well and fine,
I think not of tomorrow,
I smile, this time is mine.

Brian Sullivan

I Love You

I love you
But do you love me
I love the way you talk,
The way you look and,
What you say
I love you
Do you love me
I know I could never have you
You wouldn't want me
I know I could never be good
enough for you.
I know you're too good
for me
I love you
I know you'll always be
in my heart.
But I know I'll never be yours
I love you

Lorraine Shaw

The Five Birds Of The World

I have five birds, one blue, one
black, one red, one white, and one
yellow. Red describes anger, power,
and heat. White describes goodness,
kindness, and nice, blue describes
the sky, the water, and a beautiful
blue jay, black describes darkness,
terror, and fear, though yellow
describes courage, strength, and cheer.

What do all of these birds have in
common? They all describe the world
around us. These are the birds of
the world.

Roy Anthony Burtchaell, III

I'm Praying

I'm praying today
And prayed yesterday;
I'll be praying tomorrow,
not for myself . . .
But for young generation,
and I ask;
    Where are they going?
    Don't they know that
    They're self destroying;
My soul searching, I despair,
young people I love you;
Don't give in to temptation,
You're destroying beautiful life —
    generation . . .
Pray, for blessed salvation.

Elizabeth Pavich

Do You Love Me?

Do you love me there,
    as you loved me here?
Do you love me now,
    as you loved me then?
Would you love me if I were anywhere,
    as you loved me when I was there?
I love you here,
    as I loved you there.
I love you now,
    as I loved you then.
I would love you if you were anywhere,
    as I loved you when you were here.
So please don't stop all the cares
    we used to share.

Nikki Lea Workman

I Won't Give In

"You only have six months to live."
That's what the doctor said.
"The cancer's gone too far to fight.
In six months you'll be dead."

He gave me this heart rending news
About three years ago.
Yet here I am still living,
It's just not time to go.

I'll not give in to cancer.
It will not conquer me.
I have so much I want to do,
And much I want to see.

Doctors aren't always right
When lives are on the line
Our human spirit brightly shines,
And glows with life divine.

Sheila B. Roark

Don

To my brother Don
Whom I deeply adore,
You are my only brother
And I love you more and more.

We grew up together
And much is the same,
Though we are quite different
We share the same name.

We're both much older
Though much I have missed,
You now have your life
Our childhoods dismissed.

Your life is in order
With a wonderful wife,
Your son is an honor
Who completes your life.

We'll always be together
And this is so true
You'll always be my brother
And for that, I love you.

Debbie Duncan

The Unhung Doors

The house on the hill
With flowers on the bank
Kids on the porch and
Two new doors waiting to be hung
Years passed by
The kids grew up
and left me alone
with the doors waiting to be hung
I don't need them now
For the rooms are so bare
I guess they'll stay there
til the house falls down
And no one will know
The doors were never hung.

Gail V. Geyer

Further Engagements

The child like spirit,
Within the depths of you.
The time may come,
When through your veins,
You will feel it too.
We have plans,
Of future unknown,
With thoughts that will abide.
Forever strong,
Forever young,
I'll be there at your side.
You take me to places,
I thought I'd never see.
My flesh in your palm.
And there I shall be...
Till the day you say no.
And push me aside.
Or the day you day yes,
And make me your bride.

Renae Demello

Letting Go

Nicole, my child, And yet not mine
for in your birth, you are a gift
So special. And,
In your tiny being, O Grace,
A sharing of The Essence.

You grew and cherished Life
I saw it in your laughter,
In your pain. As mother and daughter
We struggled, sometimes symbiotic
Sometimes needing to control
And sometimes,
Allowing a deeper, caring knowledge
Of the self and of the other

I reminisce, I contemplate
Did I present my needs
Or yours, through you?
Your Life

And now, my Precious
Where can we go?
You are God's Child

Valnere McLean

Arnemia

Follow down Euphrates
and here I am again
Cremate all my fantasies
a pale reflection of a man.
Pain is an indulgence
Constantinople falls
and a wolf will jump across your grave
shadows on the walls.
I'm outside the killing window
catch a shallow sigh of fright
clouds above, like running wolves
chase away the light.
So, set my soul on fire
oh sweet wind of the south
my darling Diabolitine,
let me taste your pale red mouth.
No angels beneath this wicked moon
of a land that never was
paint a picture in my mind
of Arnemia.

Michael S. Crouse

he Hummingbird

Is it too late for the hummingbird?
I asked the wind
and this is what I heard...

No, my child, no
open your hand
give the sweetness you sow

In one breath I'll blow
the seed to a far away land
for another child to grow

Will the hummingbird follow in the sky?
I asked the wind
and this was the reply...

Yes, my child, that is true
yet keep open your heart
the hummingbird will come back to you

Donna V. Minshull-Ford

To Men Who Gave Us Liberty

As I ride along and see
the bright blue sky
I think of all I've seen and heard
It almost makes me cry.

The Glory of this land of ours
Of men who set it free,
May we nev'r forget
You men of history.

God made this land of ours
A Nation proud and free
Brave men have fought
At what a cost, to give us Liberty.

I'm not very good at words.
I guess I'm getting old.
The many things I've seen today,
and many things untold.

The Patriots for Freedom fought,
On land and stormy sea
Their lives they lost, at so much cost
To set our nation free.

Charlotte Miller

My Dog

I have a dog
that's big and gray
I wash him every other day

He's so dirty
and smells so bad
I have to use a scratch pad

When I wash him all over
I wish to find a four-leaf clover
To give me luck throughout the day
and help my dog stay clean and gray.

Julia Braden

Hats

My love for hats
steadily seems to grow
when it first started
I really don't know.

But when I was young
I wore one to Mass
it just always seemed
to give me some class.

I've black ones, a pink one
a white one or two
a green one, a red one
just to mention a few.

When I wear a hat
I feel properly dressed
in slacks or a dress
I'm always impressed.

To church or to shop
just wherever I go
with a hat on my head
I'll be happy, I know.

Eileen Noll

Forsaken And Forlorn

Sorrow! Despair! Sadness!
I face everyday
Oh, mummy, where are you?
Why did you go away?

Parents I do not know
Why is it so?
No one to turn to in sorrow
Daddy also would not be there tomorrow

I have never seen loving faces
I have never known angelic ways
Why is it so?

A world of pain and sadness
Empty and void
No where to go
No one to care
Why? Why? Why is it so?

Lynda-Ann Ramlal

Forever Family

We recognized the whispering voice
That gently called her home,
And we, who would be left behind,
Felt only loss and gloom.

Yet now our eyes are opened wide
By constellations bright,
And we can see our sister's love
Reflected in his night.

We can see her star of hope,
Skipping through the sky.
We laugh with her and then applaud.
There is no need to cry.

She left her pain on this dark earth,
And traded it for wings.
She will always comfort us
When in the wind, she sings.

Someday her voice will call to us,
Dear sister and good friend,
Then safe in his protective arms,
We'll be a family again.

Marianna Rizzo

My Spirit Dances

The content of my character
Is not what you first see,
You see the canes or wheelchair
And that's not the real me.
Though my body may be broken
And I need help to get around,
Inside I'm the same persón
That I always used to be.
Being in a chair has given me
A new perspective on life,
I've had to look a way beyond
those things I took for granted.
I now can see the beauty
Of the simple things in life,
Like nature, love, and laughter
And the joy of each new day.
If you could look inside of me
To see what makes me who I am,
You'd see my spirit dances
And my soul yet soars and sings.

Rosemary E. Johnson

Risk

Senseless,
Tired,
Conflict rushing before my eyes.
Metamorphosis
Permitted? Denied?
Necessary.
Break free,
Unfold thy wings,
Take flight.
Soar.
Will there be other eagles?
Maybe,
trust and see;
or die
less than you were destined to be.

Kelly McClure

Gratefulness

You treated me with such kindness
You carried me through desperation
You made me realize I have dreams.
You gave me sweet dreams.
You are my destiny.

For the love you've given me
I am eternally grateful.
You make me feel so alive
with passion and love.
I cherish every moment we are together,
in one another arms,
now and forever.

Brooke M. Bailey

My Dream Knight

This poem is about a stranger
Who stands afar from me.
He's someone from a fairy tale
Who comes to rescue me.

He's like a knight in armor
Upon his horse he'll ride.
This man is forever handsome
And fully filled with pride

If this knight is in my dream again
And I know that he will be.
If he rides his horse my way
I know he'll rescue me.

Freda Burrel

Life's Patchwork Quilt

Like a Patchwork Quilt
The pieces of our lives.
Are stitched together
With understanding...
From lessons we have learnt.

The many colours reflect
Choices we have made.
Mistakes learned from
And interwoven
Through our lives in change

Threaded through Life's Patchwork Quilt
Searching for its home...
Is the 'child'
That lies within —
A restless, striving soul...

Teresa Seed

Epilogue

You thought you'd found the cynic,
the romantic, dead and gone.

Yet only for a healing time,
and now I prove you wrong.

The river still cascades for me
and moans of olden days.

Whispering tales of passion forgotten
it hints at loves true ways.

I sit so still, afraid to move,
for least I break the spell.

A magical enchantment all around,
unknown to heaven and to hell.

The river still flows into the ocean
and love will still go on.

So I revel in this mystic world,
as my Night becomes my Dawn.

Tanya Swindle-Fernandez

Ghetto Lullaby

When I was young and had my dreams
And all my thoughts were free,
My father turned the lights down low
And then he sang to me...

"Sleep my child
And don't awake
No matter how
The earth does shake.
And have your cake
And eat it, too
But remember,
You won't always be two.
For then will come three,
And then four, and then five,
And the trick then will be
Keeping the poetry alive."

V. Cordell Brown

Best Friends

I am a rose
You are my stem,
You hold my up,
You make me grow.

I am a bird,
You are my feathers,
You make me believe,
You make me free.

I am a rainbow,
You are my color,
You show me the way,
You make me understand.

I am a candle,
You are my fire,
You keep me alive,
You light me up.

I am one,
You are one,
Together we are best friends,
Forever!

Tina Watson

"Wind Blows"

The wind blows through the house,
it's quiet as mouse,
The wind blows through the trees
as it stirs up all the leaves.
The wind blows through the sky,
as the eagles fly high,
The wind blows through the night,
Even though its not in sight.
The wind blow through the
beginning,
But may turn up never having
an ending.

Yashica L. Tuttle

I'm A Snowflake

I'm a tiny snowflake
I really have no shape,
I'm rather lacy,
But also mighty.
I don't fall to hurt,
But to clean the earth.
My flake is harmless,
Except to the careless.
Please step on me lightly,
Because I am slippery.
This manna I am,
For the avid skiers,
For winter sports,
There is no better.
I'm a tiny snowflake,
Better give me a break,
For next year
I'll be back
As a bigger snowflake.

Alma Labrie St. Jean

Reality

Far, far away.
Lost inside this room.
Where dreams become reality,
Nothing goes too soon.
Anything you've ever wanted,
In a moment will be yours.
Mirrored walls portraying apathy
Sinking down into the floor.
Swirling colors of distortion
Begging you to see,
What they can become
If you would only set them free.
Strange thoughts out in the open
Echoing between stone walls
Will be there to catch you,
If you decide to fall.
Once you've had enough,
You can go back at any time.
Back into reality,
Where everything is denied.

Lisa Norton

Untitled

I've been given wings.
Free to soar above the rest,
Whose feet have been planted beneath.
Yet I am among the unfortunate,
I'm privileged to the joy and pain
So sweet...

Christina Taliento

"Explore"

There's a lesson to be learned
about life and its trials
and tribulations nothings
easy in this nation unless
you have an Education so
focus on your goals let
your imagination soar-new
horizons to explore so
much to be achieved if
you only believe within
yourself and in your dreams.

Lisa Marie Gentle

The Clock

How long I've stood on the shelf
How long it's hard to say,

My hands no longer cross my face
nor tell the time of day

There was a time, long gone by,
when I came from the store

'Twas then folks took pride in me,
But no more.

Blanchard H. Stell

Why Am I Alive?

The burning lamp burst
Into a rolling flame
Arguing inhabitants
Spread in fear
One running naked
Leaving his robe behind
One fleeing and screaming
Loudly - "Oh! My God!!"
Some broken thoughts
Came to my mind about
Death-in-life and
Life-in-death
People die in this world
By numerous means
In war, accidents, sabotage
Death by water and fire
This makes me think
Of the question sure
"Why am I alive?"
In this "little world!"

George Titus

When Angels Fly

When children die, Angels fly.
Fly, Angels fly.
We cry when children die; for
we don't understand why.
Fly, Angels fly.
Guide our children for we
will miss them. Embrace them in
your glorious wings as we have
embraced them in their
short time on earth.
Gods newest little
Angels fly in peace, for
we will soon meet
again.
All Angels fly.

Dawn Trehearne

Three Pictures

Three pictures
    hanging on the wall
Seen by some
    but not by all

A water lily, a 'mum'
    and a butterfly
That seems as if
    it wants to fly

Three pictures
    that I like
Three pictures
    not quite alike

Done by the
    same artist
I find no fault
    that, I insist

Three pictures
    hanging on the wall
Three pictures
    that will never fall

Tomas Marmolejo

Rick

Your presence creates romance
Your voice rich with allure
Making my heart dance
You are unique, and oh so sure

Fireworks in the skies
Stars and butterflies
Topsy turvy for awhile
Within this moonchild

Caution to your wind
Touch me once again
Surprise, surprise
My electric currents
Now stirring your insides

Your air, Mr. Incognito
Is inviting to me, you know
Withhold your kiss, it's ok by me
Control, well, next time let's see

Trish Tahfs

Tall City

Here houses rise so
Straight and tall
That I am not
Surprised at all
To see them simply
Walk away
Into the clouds this
Misty day

Nataly Dupiton

Untitled

Suddenly-spewed from the cloud-banks,
    Shining wings, and silver bodies,
    Flying diamonds, lines triangles,
    Rhythmic roaring rushing marvels
        Man made birds

Dipping, swerving, zooming, diving,
    And all in one perfect time.
    Scintillating in the sunlight,
Bird-like fine, deep-throated monsters,
        Airplanes.

Barbara Nowlin

Dragon Lord

A shadow looms across the sky
A great red shape arises
Over graves in which dead lie
Of life and death it doth surmises

Intelligence gleams within its eyes
Its scales shine as lava flows
On high with leathery wings it flies
Within the sun its body glows

Its hide is covered with thick scale
Stronger than the strongest mail
Its teeth are like a thousand swords
Guarding hidden treasure hoards

Of this beast great men do fear
A call to arms when it draws near
Armies gather at its sight
All is fallen with its might

Greed is shown in monstrous lust
Collecting treasure is a must
Hidden in vast treasure hoards
Lay the treasure of Dragon Lords

Jeffrey William Linda

Paths

There are many paths in life
That you can take,
Many choices in life
That you can make.

But one thing always
Remains the same,
A feeling for you
That I can not name.

Is it love? Or something
Entirely new.
A feeling, a heartbeat
That belongs to you.

Bernice E. Cater

Mary In The Autumn Of Time

In the autumn of time
The sweeping wind
Of the universe
Gathered its force
And at the height of love
Swept you up
Beyond the universe

To the arms
Of the waiting angels
Who with cherubic smiles
And heavenly music
Escorted you
To the paradise
Of everlasting love

John Sockol

Life

Life is just a stopwatch,
 letting time run down,
With memories and nightmares,
 and a few tick tocks,
 here and there.

But then, life starts to fade
And time slows.
Last but not least the clock stops,
and so do the memories of
 life itself

Carissa Savine

Diminishing Eyes

Scent, corruption and beauty
irresistible for an untamed prey,
dangled with the sweet bitter juice
to rest is where it will lay;

Its eyes open wide for hunger
with startling jaws of death,
saliva, sweet as fragrance
demise with a soft gentle breath;

Struggling for a last glimpse of life
as its eyes collapse with fear.
mangle and devour with hatred
a body laid without tears;

Fulfillment is once satisfy
motionless like an undying cloud,
the deadly smell spreads evilly
with the corrupted eye, it is proud.

Peter Truong

The Book Of Mormon

Your pages leaped time's
 Unhallowed chasm
  To ignite a sweet
  Familiar spirit
   God planted in my soul

Held near my heart
 They live, I felt them breathe
  The prophets spoke
   And loosed my heart in tears
    Your days hold hands with mine

One dawn in time
 When memories have done
  With teaching
   And wisdom turns
   From bud to bloom

When my Savior smiles
 Because I know you
  Then through our embrace
   Unbounded joy will grip my heart
    Because you were my friend

Doramae Norr Michael

Dreams

Oh how I dream of far-off lands
of places I have read about
From Paris to the wonders of the world
from Russia to the desert sands.

All I have is pictures in a book
and dreams of where I'd go
Lots of time to read and plan
to travel to each and every land.

Ruth Pelter

She's My Queen

The sunflower: Yellow, black and green
She's my Queen, tall and strong
The Queen of the garden
Watching over her kingdom of growing
vegetables and fruits.
The sunflower has strong roots.
Holding firm into the ground
She has the sun, shining down
The birds love her black face
The sunflower is full of grace.

Laurie Hogg

Introverted

People call her
introverted, involved
with the spirit world and such.
But, if you sit in the quiet
with her, allow her to lead
while you follow along paths
she chooses, you'll discover
knowledge by saturation,
cell by hungry cell.
You'll learn to catch
your breath, listen
deeply, look deeply,
feel deep as the
sea of life we
swim anyhow.

Sandy Fink

Holes

Is this but a daydream?
I've been like this for so long.
I like this haziness so much
—how could it be wrong?
It's so hard sometimes,
to live just another day.
So I inhale the cloud,
and my fear holes go away.
I feel like I'm alone,
yet when I look around,
the faces are as placid as mine,
their mouths make the same sound.
I realize I'm the same,
as all those wasted souls.
And I know that they, too,
are sick of all these holes.

Crystal Clark

She Raises Her Arms

She raises her arms
connects with the stars.
Power flows through
in calm detached clarity.
Aware of the unity of all spirit
irrelevant struggling slips away.

She focuses outside
her mind-dribble
Which ceases its celestial pull
on her heart and senses,
Aware of a fleeting peace
soft with awe and wonder.

Lowering her arms
she turns inside.
Voices awaken the ache and pain,
torturing her spirit within.
She crawls towards the light
and raises her arms.

Kimberly Slivka

Hermony

A rich man of Ughelli
Loved his wife most richly
He made his money her money
But alas, all his money
Brought them no hermony

Michael E. Aken'Ova

Crazy Teacher

I have a teacher who is crazy,
and is also very lazy.
She drinks Coke,
and that's no joke!

I have a crazy teacher,
who has crazy features.
She has blue hair,
and doesn't care!

I have a crazy teacher,
who likes to sit in bleachers.
She lays in the sun,
and does it just for fun!

Michelle Gagnon

Being Eternal

A primordial grain of sand
    explodes,
and builds a star.
The star so joyful of being,
    expands;
and a nebula is seen afar.
The nebula longs to be
    and soon
a galaxy is waxing fair.
To shine in the eyes of
    those who love —
a grain of sand is there.

Roy E. Tipton

Poetics

A poem, so seems, a work of art
Wells from springs within the heart
Sometimes in thoughts of deep despair
And some of better days, and fair

To catch the tune may take some time
Or then to rise to heights sublime
After a pause and meditations
Are timely hints for new relations

For loftier goals, one can aspire
To feel at peace and thus retire
So as the yeast to bread does leaven
The spirit soars as high as heaven

With a scope so varied and boundless
So much one may confess
Surely as the tide goes out to sea
Minds reach out to set spirits free

Virginia Ashby

Lonely

Lonely is a solemn word, one which
    stands alone.
And once you are forsaken by it,
    sinks into the bone.

You feel apart from all the world,
much different than the rest.
No matter how hard you try and try
you just can't pass the test.

Makes no difference about your friends
the feeling is always there,
the empty space inside of you
the one you just can't bare.

It doesn't matter where you are,
you still feel out of place
and it doesn't matter who is there,
it's the world you just can't face.

Debra L. Torres

A Child's Love

My mom is a person
    you could never replace
She's gorgeous, slim and tall
    with a beautiful face
She's been there for me
    through thick and thin
I've been in and out of hospitals
    so many times, her head would spin
She's so special and loving
    I thank God she's mine
I'd love to paint I Love You
    on a big billboard sign
I love her so dearly
    with all my heart
I love being with her
    and not when where apart
I could never thank her enough
    for all she's done
She deserves an award
    for being #1

Christine Gillis

TIMES OF...

These times of vacant passion
Habits void of reason
Reality checks are in the mail
Opinions exceeding demand
Skipping problems to emphasize symptoms
Travel agents dispensing guilt trips
Past impossible, present inevitable
Pruning our family trees
Memories we never had
Dogmas run over by Karmas
Denial as a hobby
Would you like fries with that?
The "FUN" stolen from dysFUNctional
Lock up on your way out

Timothy James Vernon

The Dressing Table

Lift that baby
From the bath,
So small, so wet....
So slippery!

Wrap your creation
In something soft,
And enjoy new
Serendipity!

That small wet face
Against your cheek,
While glowing warm
And moist....

Steam gently wafts,
As you breath in
Pure fragrance...
From your first!

John F. Donnell

The Smiling Face

A smiling face
can save the day,
as you go about your way.
The sun shines bright in the sky,
and allows your face to stay alive.

Deanna Lightbourne

Burning Wonders

A star that shines so bright and high.
A moon that glows in a midnight sky.
All the wonders of the earth
Burn upon the fiery hearth

A leave so green, a rock so gray
Lay upon the pile of hay.
All the wonders of the earth
Burn upon the fiery hearth

A bird chirping so loud and clear.
A wolf that's howling threw my ear.

All the wonders and sounds of earth
Burn upon my fiery hearth!

Alison Wells

My Poet

Each poem
Imprinted upon my heart
A part of who I am.
Written before my life
    in the heavens.
The beat of my heart
    reflected in the words.
The meaning, my soul.
If I expire my words live on.
Born a poet
A soul ever searching for the words.
When will the search end?
My eyes wonder as
my core aches.
Who understands my curse?

Nicky Blanchard

Black Hole

Stars shine high above,
as darkness
covers the earth.

As daylight surfaces,
the world awakens.

For some,
the darkness
embraces for eternity.

The agony,
has hollowed
a space within.

This space,
is filled with loneliness.

The loneliness,
has forever embraced
the hollow soul.

And the soul,
is forever seeking
to fill this space.

Jennifer McCarthy

Solitude

Such loneliness within her eyes
Staring up to starlit skies
Filled with clouds of grey and black
She smiles as she grabs her pack
And heads out on this dusty road
But in her mind a heavy load
That makes her weep
In dead of night
In which I cannot
Bear the sight.

Dave Hart

Dreams Of Love

Dreams are blowing
like the wind in the grass.

Thoughts are growing
like the flowers you just past.

Memories are like mountains
deep in your soul.

Words can destroy you,
if they are said in a bitter tone.

Hope can rebuild you
and give new light to your life.

Love can fulfill you
and restore your bleeding heart.

Ingegerd Bjorklund

Keeper Of The Night

The moon, a pale silent figure
Slipping through the dark folds
Of the deep night.
All of the people go in
To their warm comfortable homes
To sleep the night away,
Unaware of the twinkling sprites
And stardust fairies
Playing in the deep green forest
Underneath the wan moon glow.
The harsh brightness of the day
Has been overcome by the cool night.
The pale silent figure
Resides over the darkness
With her starflies keeping her company
Until the sun chases them away
With the dawn of a new day.

Jenifer Carlee

Contrasts

If we didn't know misery
How could we know bliss?
If we didn't know ugly
It's the beauty we'd miss.
Could we experience warmth
If we hadn't felt cold?
If we hadn't felt fear
Could we really be bold?
There can't be an up
If there isn't a down
There can't be a smile
Without somewhere a frown.
There can't be love
Without someone who hates.
There exists no one destiny
Without alternate fates.
So never judge life -
This is good, that is bad.
You'll never know happy
If you've never known sad.

Juliana Blawyn

Children

Adults work while children play,
children laugh and dance all day,
rarely kids would do some work,
but only if they get high pay.

Sarah Jordan

My Mother

She was always there when needed
To give a helping hand
He manner and her kindness
will always understand.

She was the heart of our home,
And we could count on her
To help us through our troubles
Without a bit of stir.

No matter what would happen
As days would come and go
She was always there to lend a hand
And soften any blow.

Mother are our angels
Who teach us what is right,
And she'll always be beside us
On any dark and fearful night.

Clara Oates

Hidden Motives

A sparrow chirps
And the heart knows this is so
With no hidden motives
A tiny sparrow grows.

People play games
Hidden motives run amuck
But the compassionate heart sees
Children stuck in a rut.

Life is so short
yet people run from who they are
Then one day someone finds
The only real thing
About the life that was led
Are the things that were
left behind.

Keith Brown

"My Wild Life Playmates"

In the far corner of my yard
stands 5 deer big as cows.
On the bank are 2 large turkeys
a mother and father with 14 babies
above them.
In front yard is a double wide
skunk with a wide white stripe
down back.
A quick glance, it looks like,
an all white skunk.
Thank you God for all the wild life
beauty in my front yard
I have named my front yard,
God's wild life play yard.

Helen L. Engle

Threshold

The somber winds of
Winter descend and
Scatter the fallen
Leaves
A vast emptiness
Invades my living
World
I wither and my ashes
Mingle with the morning
Dew
As I enter into oblivion
The twilight

Ann Edelmann

Dreams

An open expanse,
Of danger,
Of knowledge,
Flowing through ourselves,
Coming to us,
Scaring us,
Giving ourselves an existence.
Do you not realize,
That once you lose that special thing,
You lose your mind?
For without this thing you don't see,
The light of paradise,
That's always within.
This thing which makes men heroes,
Makes beggars, kings.
If you do not possess this thing,
You are the only lesser,
A slave to reality.

Jeremy K. Kessler

You

Every time I touch you,
I know this love is true
Whenever I am down,
Your love erases the frown
When I get to talk to you
And listen to your voice,
I know it in my heart,
I've made the right choice
When I see your picture,
I think of where we've been,
I think of the future,
My face begins to grin.
But the past is another story,
Filled with silent secrets,
Thinking of it may only
Bring out a few regrets.
For those who have hurt you
And filled your life with hate,
In the future death is coming,
All we have to do is wait.

Michael Kennedy

An Age Of Enlightenment

She is very old now,
ninety and three
Her eyes nearly blinded,
but clearly can she see
down the endless years to Eternity.

Her days slipped by
and left their trace,
Her cracked dry skin
on her wrinkled face,
Show a pain only death can erase.

She is awaiting His call,
her time is near
Hearing his voice say
she has nothing to fear,
Speaking to her of His love
Only now, she does hear.

Terry Astbury

X-Ray

I want the fall
to blow away the leaves
over your tree
so you only to carry
your skin
the color of my desire
which my eyes have drawn
over your body
each time my hands
have seen you around

Miguel A. Rangel

My Wish

There was a time when all I wished
was that you learn to talk,
And then my second wish came true
and you began to walk.

I wished for you to smile at me
you brightened every day,
And then I wished you healthy
so you could run and play.

I wished for you to always trust
and know I would not lie,
And when the plans have fallen through
I wished you knew I tried.

When I miss something special
I wish I could be there,
I wish sometimes that I knew how
to show how much I care.

But, you always must remember
no matter what you do,
Of all the wishes granted me
the best received was you.

Paula Rae Olson

Do Sing To Me

Please do - sing to me
A song I like to hear
One which will live in me
And destroy my fear

Please do - let me hear
The sounds of my music
A tiny bird chirping
A melody dear

Please do - don't whisper
You'll spoil the peace
'Cause I am with nature
Of which I'm a piece

Please do - listen with me
And see if you'll hear
This gentle, soft breeze
Which fills the air

Please do - come closer
Come and join with me
Come listen and enjoy
This melody!

Nadia Edwin

Moments of Grandeur

A gentle Breeze,
Caressed the mirrored Surface;
A ripple soon appears,
Extends in widening ring
Toward latent purpose;
Completes its timely task;
Then quickly disappears.
While on the shore,
Not eye nor ear discerning;
A grain of sand,
Lately of earth's firm grasp;
Like tortured Man,
His every fiber yearning;
The Lord gives praise,
In just a simple Splash.

Jose Herlindo Gregorio

"Sea Breeze"

I look beyond the
waves of the sea
Water. A different
vision every splash;
never a thought like the last.
All of the dreams washed
away; never forgotten,
but like old fruit they never rotten.
Along the waters, and
above the sky. Every
break of dawn an old dream dies.
If you listen to the breeze
of the ocean at night.
It's beyond any thing
you might think that seems right.
Just like a walk along
the sea shore, a look beyond
all the mist, and you'll never
be able to resist.

Alicia Smith

Untitled

My name is Pig.
I live in a sty.
That someone people question...
I think I know why.

"Tis safer, "I say,
"For no one comes near."
This makes them happy
And I have no fear.

My memories, my music...
They bring me no harm.
It's dear ones who wound me,
Who won't take my arm,

I lift myself up
As high as I can
And cling to a dream:
"I once was a man."

Hamilton I. Driggs

Jesus

Thank you, Dear Jesus
For the gift you've given me
Thank you, for walking by my side
you pick me up, Dear Jesus.
When I stumble and fall.
You carry me when I'm not strong.
You give me strength when I am weary.
You give me courage to go on
Thank you. Dear Jesus
Thank you.

Margaret Chant

Moments

Some moments last a lifetime.
A moment when you smiled at me
A special glance between us
A moment when you were
just so kind to me
A moment of silence
when we had to say goodbye
That moment I wish
we had never had
Some we cherish, others
we just endure
The moments of a lifetime
some are remembered
and some just pass away
The special moments
live in our hearts until
we live no more

Sheila K. Freeman

Sparks Of Insanity

Fish that thrive
in the
ocean depths
are not found in
shallow waters.

Voncille C. Smith

"Clouds"

Fluffy white
    Palest pink
        Glowing orange
        Silver lined
            Shining gold

Fluffy clouds
    Sailing by
        Changing shape
        Filled with water
            Growing cold

Heavy clouds
    Bursting open
    Rain is falling
        Crystals forming
            Snowing softly

Snowy clouds
    Soaring high
        Dropping snow
        Covering land
            Cold and white

Nadine E. Bush

Golden Opportunity

"Golden Opportunity,"
I say to morning sun.
Awakening to greet the day.
My life once more begun.
"Golden Opportunity",
Because, my heart desires
To know the wind
To know the stars
To set the world a fire.
A fire in so many ways.
By zeal - by zest - by bliss
Granted me by God above.
Complete contentment - this.

Viola H. Holeman

The Night Before Christmas

It was the night before Christmas,
And all the children to sleep,
Kids off to bed, not a worry or peep,
Sweet dreams and good night.
Or a gift for Mom and Dad,
But don't forget those wishes,
As I read a book about Santa,
As he's off to his toy land,
And he loves all you children

But you must go to sleep,
Or Santa won't leave you a gift.
A little doll or a doll house,
A trick or a two-wheel bike,
Or that plane set or train set.

You might be wishing for
A toy truck or a puck,
And maybe a CB of your own,
But whatever it may be,
The Merriest Christmas
For the whole family.
Monica Andrews

Procrastination

Today, and not tomorrow, please
Let it be today
If you have a special thing to do
Or a special thing to say
For procrastination is a word,
And a word just let it be
And get on with what you need to do
Say the things you need to say
You'll likely find it easy and
Find that you were wrong
In delaying what you had to do
And put off saying for so long.
For if you've hurt someone you love
Please make amends don't wait
Don't wait until tomorrow
For it then may be too late.
Rita Taylor

The Angel of Love

God made you mine, Jerry
    Jerry was like a taste of wine -
I was only to keep him for
    a short time.
God gave me the gift of love.
Love is like wine -
    So now he's not mine.
God needed Jerry in Heaven
    to teach his angels
    how to love.
Alma Fritz

"Embarkation"

Never will I forget that dreadful
day nor the boat that took my
darling away.
The smile on his face as he waved
to me, a smile as brave as a
soldier could be.
With a heart that was heavy
and eyes that were sore, I
watched till I could see no
more when a voice seemed
to whisper to me, he'll return;
Have faith and you'll see!
Wanda Crowe

The Way That I Love You

This is to the one I love;
Who's very dear to my heart.
I don't know what I'd do without him,
I don't ever want to be apart.

I miss your touch and your smiles.
The warmth of you being near;
When I'm alone, away from you;
I always want you here.

In my mind and my soul;
You are everything to me.
You are my husband, my friend, my life,
And you always will be.

I never knew that someone could love
The way that I love you;
It had to come from up above;
I guess that he just knew.

I'm glad you gave me
This change in life;
To make you happy,
As your wife.
Barbara I. Pate

Lost And Found

I wandered around
In my despair
Wondering why no one was there
I felt alone, searching for hope
As I cried myself to sleep
I remembered the Lord,
and that I'm His sheep
My day has brightened,
my hope has come
The Lord is with me
My despair's overcome
Deborah Goodall

Intimate Thoughts

Grasping time from my active day,
    To pen a poem for me.
With some of the things I do like
    And even thoughts of the sea.

Animals can be insane, but
    I adore them from the start;
Because they have magical ways
    Of stealing away my heart.

I savor the Christmas spirit
    Of happiness and good cheer,
I'm always yearning they abide
    Throughout the approaching year.

Children are for loving, always
    I fancy their sweet faces,
The help me know true happiness
    And fill my heart's blank spaces.

I also like to listen to
    The resplendent sea at night,
And watch the azure waves go swirl;
    By the moon's luminous light!
Charlotte Virginia Lippick

Spring In The City

On a day that drizzled
warm and mild,
I felt on my chin,
I felt on my cheek
not a beard
but the first grass sprouting.

— Of all places! I muttered
and tried to hide from passers-by.

As I was about to vanish underground,
someone gently took me by the arm:
"How foolish you are!
Where else should the grass sprout
When sprout it must —
on stone?"

I glanced at him:
on his cheek also
flourished young grass
and the first violets budded -

it was spring in the city.
Gunars Salins

The Greatest Gift

Love is caring and sharing
It is not wearing
Love is doing what we can
It's our best plan
Love cannot be bought or sold
It's ours to have and hold
Love is help and hope
It's how we cope
Love is from the heart
It's our best part
Love grows by the hour
It's our greatest power
Love is the only sure thing
That life can bring
Love, yes, love
Is from above
Love you see
Is in you and me
But, most of all
There is love for all
S. Joe Celesnik

Fire In My Heart

My heart was moderately
Intact when I met you.
Now my heart is feeling you presence.
There are flames of fire
Licking at my heart.
Waiting in anticipation
For me to surrender
To surrender my heart
To the fire that burns for you
I'm strong and I won't give up
I know if I do the fire will consume
My heart and burn all the more brighter,
Luring other unsuspecting hearts
To its calling flames.
Leaving behind burned and
Ashen hearts that are
Incapable of being repaired.
Laura Amador

My Need

The image of you is with me all day, there is no distinction, it lasts
through night and day. When we were together, the sun was our limit,
it laughed and glowed, we resembled it. Now it's winter and we're home, I miss it.

You are my sun, my night and day; you are an expression of me, the
other version of it. It's a shame we didn't connect sooner; I had so
much on my mind. I doubt we would have had much in common; we had two
different lives: you were sleeping with women, I just wanted to be a wife.

Now we are at the same point in life; it took so much to see, I've
finally discovered myself and the person I want to be. I have my
ex-husband to thank for much of this, through him I found the way; we
never shared our hearts, he only showed me a way. I had to be married
in order to be free; I know you understand this, you did the same thing.

Even though I've discovered this new existence, life hasn't been the
same. I know I'm in your heart, but I want you in my life. I want you
to be with me. This is the way love is supposed to be. I'm glad you
feel the same; when the time comes, I would like to have your name.

Susan Tipton

Citrus

He peeled me, layer by layer, segment by segment;
to my core, to my very essence, to karma far more exquisite and essential
than celibate imagination could ever have conceived.....

White satin, vanquished by his Will, released my hair
and wafted through the moonlight to abandon its purpose upon the bedstand,
beside where rested his tropic, his sunkist, his citrus metaphor,
succulent organ of his Sacred Intention,
visceral vehicle of his Determined, Undeniably-Olympic Deliciousness.....

Propelled by the melodic mysticism
of his ever-so refined-and-rhythmic-persuasion,
my earrings disappeared, dropped without defense,
into his pulsating palm piercing to ooze through his invisible membrane,
to explode within his equatorial euphoria like seeds,
spontaneously surrendered to undulating earth from over-ripe flesh-exposed.....

His South Sea pearls from my compliant throat,
seduced through the choirs of his Archangelic Whispers,
slip away into vanishment within the miracle,
rooting ravenously in barren thirst for the Ocean of His Garden's Lush,
Impressionist Landscape, where fascination succumbs
in the silence between the notes to the finale of fulfillment,
when Choice swallow Chance exhaling the naked canvass of newborn Covenant.....

The fragrant, fecund blend of Nature's lavish bloom,
pervades, permeates in dripping watercolors of asphyxiating nectar,
sweltering delirious droplets, moistening-to-fluid his facile fingers
to part my lips, fold open my soul, suspend my breath,
expand my breadth to receive his overflow,
the ethereal offering of his ceremony, His Elegant Delicacy....

The nights and days consumed
in the hallucinogenic ritual of his Primeval Delight,
are all that I never know, to Wonder,
of Mystery, of Truth....

Nancy Hammill Wheeler

Tomorrow's My Brother's Last Birthday

Tomorrow's my brother's last birthday - How do I tell him goodbye,
My stomach spills out of my mouth, the tears - they well up in my eyes.

Tomorrow's my brother's last birthday - how will I cope when it's past,
To know he won't have another - because he's going now - way too fast.

Tomorrow's my brother's last birthday - My heart feels broken, and sad,
For tomorrow's my brother's last birthday - he's the only true friend that I've had.

Tomorrow's my brother's last birthday - he made it to see thirty-five,
When the AIDS virus hit him 10 years ago - I wondered how long he'd survive.

Tomorrow's my brother's last birthday - he put up one hell of a fight -
I've prayed for my brother nightly - but I know now the end is in sight.

Tomorrow's my brother's last birthday - I feel my life falling apart,
Even though it's my brother's last birthday - he will always live on in my heart.

Beth Pawson

Collections From My Past

Baby dolls and paper dolls,
my table with two chairs.
Story books and color books,
lead soldiers lined in pairs.

A play house with a tea set
just right for "let's pretend."
Board games and card games
to share with my best friend.

Dodge ball and volley ball,
and a length of jumping rope.
Roller skates and hop scotch,
and a jar of bubble soap.

Remembering them, I cherish them,
these treasures from my past
and I find myself collecting them
to make the memories last.

Ruth Barnwell

Thank You!

The storms rage on,
Without control.
Without regret,
Without sorrow.
Taking away life,
Not giving a care.
People want it to stop,
But no one dares to try.
We run and hide from the beasts
That have been sent to us by God.

Becky Walle

My Friend Forever

When the twilight softly gathers
Making way for shades of night,
I rest upon my pillow
And sleep until it's light

He walks along beside me,
In sunshine and in rain
In illness and in sorrow,
He takes away the pain.

He's the dearest friend to me
In good times and in bad
His wonderful love for me,
Is the best I ever had.

His is a divine love,
So hard to comprehend,
Vast and wide and wonderful
And never does it end.

Oh, yes! I count my blessings,
At every long days end.
For He's my dearest treasure,
My master and my friend.

Luana F. Cottrell

Innocence

My own drowsy child
Tucked in angelic repose
Wrapped in innocence

Deloris A. White

The Curse Of Thor

Lightning streaks across the sky,
an angry message from on high.
Creatures tremble, birds take flight
as thunder roars - portrays Thor's might.
Dark clouds gather, black and gray,
blotting out the light of day.
Thrashing rain - a drumming sound,
a viking's ire vent on the ground.
Wind whistles through the trees,
blowing on their sodden leaves.
Flowers bow their pretty heads
as Asgard's rain upon them treads.
Once again the lightning flashes,
the vicious wind whips and lashes.
Crack! Thor's hammer makes more thunder
and in his rage, he silence plunders.
Suddenly the clouds disperse
as Woden's son withdraws his curse.
The wind and rain do soon subside
and in their place, the sun resides.

Caroline J. Weedon

Memories

As I look into my past I see a picture image,
    it's just a memory.
I was happy and smiling and you were there,
    we were so close it's just not fair.
You have gone to heaven it's so far away,
    but life goes on, so they say.

I love you, I miss you, I can only say,
    I'll keep your memory with me each and everyday.
My heart is broken it doesn't feel the same,
    but time can only see my pain.

You gave me life full of pleasure,
    those memories of you I will always treasure.
These are my last words my darling my love,
    thank you for my life full of love.

Tracey Ruddy

In Memoriam Of My Nephew

At the beginning was sunshine,
the storm approached
and the calm came forth.

In many instances he was a bird in a cage,
but now he is free, the gates have opened
to redeem his inculpable soul
from human flesh onto infinity.

His very compassionate heart, always had hope.
He was like Pagliacci, laughing and jesting
but weeping and suffocating inside.

He was affectionate, lovable and sincere,
and with a very special and unique personality.
Everyone who knew him well, loved Gregory very much.

As a child, he shone as a morning risen sun;
when he reached adolescence,
an uncontrollable rain storm came into his life.
It was as devastating as a tornado.

Now in his midlife, the calm came after the storm
and nothing was left, but his ashes
drifting on the surface of the sea.

Martha Kuppersmith

A Lost Love

Talked about so much . . .
  God . . .
    People . . .
      Things . . .
Opened up . . . Oh! so completely . . .
I could truly be myself.
  Walks were many . . .
    Places varied . . .
      Countries,
        Towns,
          Cities . . .
TOGETHERNESS prevailed . . .
  Nothing was concealed . . .
    Seasons were changing . . .
My Friend appeared steady.
Realization and Shock were encountered. . .
    As
      My
        Friend
              v
               a
                n
                 i
                  s
                   h
                    e
                     d . . .

Anne Mancini

I Reached For A Star

I reached for a star that was not there.
Yet, like a dream, it shone so clear.
I reached for a star amidst confusion then,
Alone, with hope, holding on 'til the end.

The days wind up; the weeks push on.
My star fades out...suddenly, it's gone!
I close the blinds, tighten the string
To keep the lights out from within.

The seasons change over; they find me anew.
The blinds slowly open to let in the view.
Again, I am startled by a dazzling glow.
The star is in place — hanging ever so low.

I reached for my star as the years roll by,
Knowing only the pain should I fall as I try.
Life completes its cycle, the children have grown up too.
Age now dims the rays of light; still I lay thinking of you.

Betty R. Neal

Fallen Leaves

I'm coming around full circle,
each day brings forth a new beginning.
As I awaken in the early morning hours
to the melody of birds singing outside my window,
I'm learning to take time out,
to look around and listen...
The fresh and cool morning air at dawn,
as this day begins anew, I watch.
At dawn I find serenity, solitude,
my peace on earth.
I have listened to the footsteps from Heaven
fall from the sky upon the rooftop above me and
watched the raindrops run across my window.
I watch the faces before me and look into the eyes,
the windows to the soul.
I have seen the limbs of trees become bare,
the leaves racing across the ground before me.
I have looked down at times and
found myself walking upon Fallen Leaves.

Robert Brian Shoots

Place Of Birth

The place of birth that gave life to me
Is always there for you to see.
It holds a dream that can come true
A dream for me, a dream for you.
If you can come and join me here
I know that I can ease your fear.
A star is here, that we call the sun,
It marks our place as third and one,
If you can see it from where you are,
Then maybe your journey is not too far,
So, if you decide to come someday,
I hope I'm here to show the way.
But if I'm not I hope you're shown,
This place, called Earth, where I was born.

Allison Davidson

Forbidden Love

Loving someone I dare not touch
Loving someone I yearn for so much
Waiting for that chance to be in your arms
Gazing in your eyes with their beauty and charm
You know that you have stolen my heart
I ache for your presence when we are apart
I want to hold you in my arms oh so bad
For now I can only be frustrated and sad
If by some chance we will be together someday
I will do all that it takes to make you want to stay
So please don't give up hope for it may come true
When by some fate my heart will no longer be blue

Panda

A Message From A Friend

Life is a long road
with its small and large rocks
And its freezing and burning roads.

Life goes up, life goes down
You might smile, you might laugh
Or maybe you'll cry; no one knows.

What is important and must be remembered is
You are not alone.

No matter what is the situation, I will be there
In happiness, in sadness
I will be with you as your friend.

So, don't you walk ahead of me,
Because you might leave me
Don't walk behind me,
Because I cannot lead you.

Walk with me
a friendship that will be forever
And ever...my friend.

Yoda Patta

Down At The Meadow

Bending in a gentle breeze green Grass
grows free in fields spreading wide
from across meadow sky larks glide
their sweet song echoes loud again
while the green fields wait for rain

Then every blade of Grass gathers
it fine as it falls on the land
Making the meadow green once more
filling every stream and lake galore
and bringing freshness to nature
gives the meadow life it's true
each time it rains on the plain
Fields seem to feel like new

Philip A. Burton

Untitled

My "self" sits as a boulder in a stream
Solid and serene.
She watches as events wash ever by,
Rapidly in some seasons
Calmly in others
Sometimes there is a crashing and a splashing
Shocking me from complacency,
Forcing an escape route,
Yet no change in "self."
She observes and waits,
Knowing the answers,
But not telling me

Barbara Titchenal

Animals Lament

Why do we bother to pollute the land, sea or air,
continue this till it's almost not there.
Why do we kill the vegetation,
till most of us die from starvation.
Why do we bother our fellow brothers,
because their shape is not the same.
Why do we shoot, kill or maim?
Why do we bother to stop the bird from its loud shrill,
when the echo of the question.
can be heard in the still.

Norm J. Shaver

Change

Drops fall from the sky,
Sometimes slow, sometimes fast,
Prompting us to forget the sun,
Until its inevitable, golden return.

The grey clouds cover the blue sky,
As bad times hide the good;
As the polluted rivers of the world,
Are hard to imagine clean and pure.

Yet, wet leaves waver in the breeze; trees dance.
Rain and wind combine to form a new scene.
Before the sun reappears,
Erasing it.

Farmers welcome the rain,
Which wipes out of existence
The dryness of the Prairies.
For a time.

Then the sun returns,
The clouds depart, and, after
A few days, many think:
"When was it ever different than it is now?"

Jan Thomson

The Sun And The Moon

Early in the morning before life restarts,
The sun, a warm burning ball,
Comes up to awaken us all.
Energy, light, heat, all sources from the sun,
Ready and waiting for us to use.
Yellow, orange, red, all colors in the bright burning sun,
Like a fire on a cold winter's night.
In the evening when the day is over,
Down goes the sun and up comes the moon.

After the sun goes down and darkness falls,
Up comes the crystal clear moon.
Have no fear, there is no time of total darkness,
After the sun is gone, the moon is already here.
The moon, clear, cool, clean like a frozen pond in the sky,
Dry and crater filled, it lies alone
In the darkness of the sleeping world.

Hanna Martinson

"Your Face"

The wind whistles,
The leaves scatter.
And the cold air blows against
the hard cement.
A feeling of anger, loneliness and
helplessness.
All the flowers are dead except
for one alone plastic rose.
Memories are flowing through my mind.
Only memories, no future plans
Everything is gone
No more laughter or drunken night binges.
All our plans shot down in a minute
No time for hello
No time for goodbye
What was once dirt is now grass.
Time keeps passing but I'll never
have what I want
To see your face again.

Christine O'Donnell

How I Lay Me Down To Trip

Dedicated to Shannon Lynn Armes

Now I lay me down to trip, I pray the Lord my head won't flip.
And if I die in the night, Lord you know I try to fight.
I've smoked, pushed and popped, after awhile I couldn't stop.
I got hooked when I was ten, now I get high on heroin.
I started crying for more and more, until I couldn't even see
  the floor.
I stumble and fall into bed, sometimes my parents think I'm dead.
Now I'm looking in the mirror, I see a woman in white.
She's saying I will die sometime tonight, I hear my mother
weeping
and crying
"My Lord she's dying!" I feel it's time for me to go
But Lord before I go, please let my little sister know
Don't take the drugs I took, it's too easy to get hooked...
Now the lights are going from dark to gloom, as they close me in
  this horrible room.
Now a white sheet is placed over my head, and they have just
  pronounced me dead.

Amber Ennis

Eternally Fifty

As I approached my sixtieth year,
  The Great Beyond seemed extremely near.
Just what did sixty mean to me?
  My thoughts delved on reality,
Since seventy five is the average age
  Of a woman's life at that stage.
Fifteen brief years were left for me,
  And more time was wanted as I could see.
So contemplating on that score,
  I dropped to fifty and gained ten more.
My option for birthdays is incredibly nifty,
  I just skip each one and I remain,
  "Eternally fifty"

Margaret Rehbein

Decisions

Please don't call me anymore,
You can't decide if I'm just a friend or maybe more.
You lead your life while I put mine on hold,
It shouldn't matter if we're young or old.
Make your decision or let it fly,
Like the wind in the trees and the clouds in the sky.
Make your decision and set me free,
Either go with him or stay with me.

Scott Rothwell

Untitled

Sometimes I feel like a bird,
That doesn't like to be heard.
But I don't let it get me down,
Because I can get up off the ground.
There is another thing I want to show,
It is the love for you... didn't you know?
You are the wings that help me up,
At times when I am down.
And you keep my feet on the ground,
I want to thank you my dear.
For letting me shed my tear,
Now that I can fly again.
I want you to come with me,
To repay you for what you done.
And to let you see...
Now it is my turn to let you fly,
Up up away and way up high.
I'm here for you at any time,
No strings no chains just you
Me and the sky.

Karen Scott

Blueberry Eyes

Coffee perfumes, polished leather,
Polo cologne, or Eternity,
eyes like light through blue stained-glass
windows, and velvet hands
come at me like flying colors
when he walks in.
His speech is music
of too many accents. They're all made-up,
affected, superficial... he tries. His art,
though he's not bad at painting,
is done in the kitchen.
Salmon in wine sauce,
spaghetti with crushed olives, garlic,
and mushrooms,
or Tabasco on crawfish,
all of them simmer in memory's stomach
long after my belly is full.
Yet desert comes
when he sets down his fork and stares.

Christina J. Hare

I Like

I like french fries
with molten cheese,
and the smell of pine
in the morning breeze.

I like to run on a sandy beach
with sea shells crunching under my feet
and the sun beating down
in the summer heat.

I like to sit under a tree and daydream
about astronauts, rockets and space
and reading comics at a fantastic pace.

Chris Papathanasiou

Friendship

To my friend this poem I give,
So our honesty will not end,
And our trust will forever live.
Now and throughout the rest of our lives,
We together will face a lot of hard times.
But our hearts have strived,
So our love can survive.

Tiffany Madrid

Introspection

Father thank you for leading me down the path of truth
A path I couldn't have trod in the days of my youth
You are opening my eyes to the things that really matter
It's not fame or fortune or silly prater
My spirit man is enlarged to perceive other's pain
Never let me go backwards — I appreciate the gain
When I look at situations, I see more than the outside
Maybe it's because You have helped me deal with my pride
Never let me look at a person's false smile
Because I will know better — and go the extra mile
Lord, give me words and deeds of comfort to lift up my brother
When he has been lifted to seek out another
Thank you for a heart of compassion softened by struggle and pain
Now it's clear why in my life there came rain
It's only when you have been hurt and learned to keep on living
That you seek to help others through sacrifice and giving

Barbara M. Jones

"I Am"

I am a shy boy who is friendly.
I wonder about the planets and stars.
I hear a child being born in Australia
I see all the nations in the world talking in harmony.
I want to be friends with everyone around me,
I am a shy boy who is friendly.
I pretend I am floating high in the sky.
I feel the sadness and fright of the world.
I touch the rays of the bright sunshine and the clouds
floating by in the sky.
I worry about the hatred of the world.
I cry at the poverty and crime
I am a shy boy who is friendly.

I understand why the universe is vast.
I say bring peace to the world.
I dream of one day becoming rich.
I try to make friends with other kids I know
are new because I know what they are going through.
I hope that everyone will love and trust and forget
about evil and hate.
I am a shy boy who is friendly.

Joel Anstett

Reunion

This woodland path I climb alone,
  Bare feet brushing cool damp grass.
Where once his steps beside me trod,
  This eve I walk alone.

Higher I climb to the naked peak,
  Closer to him I rise.
Where once we stood in wondrous awe,
  This eve I stand alone.

My life is done; how can this be?
  One soul where once were two?
A stark silhouette against blood-red sky,
  'Tis I who waits alone.

As the whippoorwill cries his evening song,
  And the sun's last kiss bestows,
My weathered hand his ashes strew,
  This vow I keep alone.

From this earthly realm I take one step,
  And feel him grasp my hand!
We go where two hearts beat as one,
  And no soul walks alone.

Robin Cox Marrin

Young Love

People say that were young and that we don't know what love is.
But what do they know?
How do they know how we feel?

Some say this is just a 'phase' that we're both going through.
But how long does a phase last?
Can it last forever?

They say there's no such thing as 'love at first sight.'
But if it wasn't love, than what was it?
Why did my heart skip a beat the minute I saw you?

I say that the feelings we share between us are very unique,
unlike any other I've ever experienced.
But do you feel for me the way I feel for you?
Can we overcome the distance between us and love one another like
we've never loved anyone before?

Jennifer Glenn

Missing Grandma

The cool lady you meet when you're a child.
She will always play with you when
the weather is mild.
From the first time you saw her you
knew she'd be the greatest.
If she ever, took you to school
you sure would be the latest.
With her you can watch movie tapes
and play crazy eights.
She will take you to JC Penny's but
after that you'll always go to Denny's.
When she doesn't want to play
you can see her start to fade away.
She knew in her heart, that nothing
could tear you two apart.

Kristen Holmes

Higher Powered

You believed in me when I was down
You brought a smile to my heart when my face wore a frown
You never gave up when I didn't care
You just showed me your faith when I needed you there.
I invite you in when I feel alone
I call on you when I need a home
I look for you when I feel you are far
I see your presence up in the stars
For all these things I feel you are close
Because you've always been there when I've needed you the most
I believe in you as you do in me
Because you've helped these covered eyes to see
I am so grateful I know you and honored you're here
I will never mislead you, I will walk through my fears.
You take away what is too much for me
Without hesitation, you help set me free.
Thank you my God for just loving my soul
With you in my life I will never be cold.

Seija Davis

Christmas At Monte Bello

May this Blessed Holy Season bring
On you and yours from the Infinite King
Note only worldly precious gifts, but
Treasures in our hearts and souls that sing
Eternal happiness for which we cling.

Brotherhood, peace and joy we're giving
Each one of you for your well-being.
Let happiness and charity in our heart ring
Love of God, peace on earth in everything
On this Holy Season adoring our Heavenly King.

Ann G. DeAngelis

Bobby's Gift

Waiting in the early morn
In the quietness of winter's storm
The house is silent except for the clock
Tick tock, tick tock

The sound stirs feelings inside
I try carefully to hide
But my eyes fill with tears
As the hands tick by the years

For it's your face I see
In a flood of memories
As I think of you awhile
Reflections make me smile

Made with love for Mom
By her youngest son
The clock on the wall
Tells it all

   Brenda Lake

A Bigger Place

This world must be a bigger place
That spans way beyond outer space
It just can't be wrong or right
Black or white, rich or poor
There has got to be so much more
This world's a bigger place, I'm sure

What lies on the other side
No one knows, cause it's oh so wide
How can we erect boundaries
When throughout the centuries we find
The more we know, the further we go
The more we seem to be behind
This world's a bigger place, a bigger Mind

Are we awake or merely just asleep?
Questions taunt us, how wide, how tall, how deep?
When will it be tomorrow?
How comes there is sorrow
That makes the happy weep?
Are loved ones really gone, or are they just beyond
This world's a bigger place, a bigger Bond.

   Madge Tomlinson

You And Me

We reminisce in travelling life's broad oceans
and strange exotic seas our ship has sailed
we faced the shoals and reefs and rocks together
and through it all our love has never failed.

We brought our crew abroad in youthful ardor
we tried to share their many hurts and joys
we always hoped they'd learn from our example
fitted to the needs of our three boys.

Three stalwart sons have all now left our vessel
they off-shipped as they grew up, one by one
to sail their own uncharted, endless oceans
through storms and gales and calms as we have done.

And now we sail into uncertain waters
the seas are calmer than they were before
the sun is sinking low on the horizon
as hand in hand we face that strange new shore.

We cannot know what seas we'll sail tomorrow
no one knows the future, none can see
we only know we'll leave no space for sorrow
we'll face it all together, you and me.

   Carl F. Kelly

On Awakening

How quiet the morn as the sun slowly
  rises in the heavens.
My eyes are drawn to the quiescent
  leaves of a hibiscus tree.
Their stillness broken by the mournful
  cry of a dove, echoed by its mate
  some distance away.
The rhythmical wheels of a distant train, perhaps
  on its way to some exotic destination.
A truck can be heard afar rumbling toward
  the town.
The stillness again broken by a mother
  bird calling to her young, warning of
  the approach of a carnivorous crow.
Mine eyes are again drawn to the hibiscus
  leaves; now dropping down to earth on
  grassy banks and beds of roses or
  marigolds.
Now gently bestirring me to fall out of my
  cosy bed and face the coming day with joy.

   Margaret Rowe

In Memoriam Ytzhak Rabin 1922-2995

Hate is the ore of all barbarism.
Hate is aversion, disfavor, grudge, ill will, and murder.
Hate pops up in unexpected places and situations.
Hate is the major part of patriotism.
Hate is the stuff of wars.

Hate is like a flood. It brings chaos.
Hate leads to social pressure, riots, and death.
Hate is the heart of violence—gender, domestic,
  child, athletic, national, and racial.
Hate in religion has a half-life of eternity.
Hate kills the servants and the seers.
  Without them there is no future.

  Hate killed Ytzhak Rabin
  and all humanity suffers.

   W. F. Pete Powell

"Black Woman"

Black as the night
Since black the night must be
A tribal maiden emerges
Though deign to be
The dawn might rival, but must lack
The resplendence as such I see.

Black woman, mother, sister wife
All gracious goodness
The beginning, the author of my life
Dear superior mother
Through whom all virtues bring
A lullaby, a love song when you sing

Your trembling hands and tired feet are sore
From sunny clime to wintry northern shore
Patiently and steadfastly you strove
To nurture unselfishly with an eternal love

Cast down your vassal burden
Oppression by a rude awakening is slain
Well done American woman
The President is your son!!!

   Kenneth Mekonen

What A Daughter Will Miss

When a mother dies there are simple things that a daughter will miss.
...From her healing reassuring kiss
...To the beautiful glow of her eyes
...To the tender voice that spoke no lies
...A daughter misses the birthday cards that were so carefully chosen
   by her wise mother.
    A card with words written for no other.
...The laughter shared over Yahtzee and cards
...The work done together in that huge yard.
...Especially the holidays that had her special touch
   Are now just memories that mean so much.
...The house that always smelled so clean
...And even the times when I thought you were mean.
...A daughter misses the scent of your perfume
   As you walked through the room.
...The noise of those silly flip-flop shoes you used to wear
...And the style that you kept your hair.
...A daughter misses the mother who always forgave and always
   loved with all her heart.
...And who always held out her arms when I was falling apart.

...A daughter misses her best friend, her mother, but a daughter
   holds the memories of her mother forever.

    Pamela Jo Merillat

"Imprints Of Love"

Magical...like watching a falling star-and when you make your
wish it comes true at that second.
Like...seeing a rainbow under a waterfall
   or
    over
   a waterfall

Like feeling the cool rain on a hot summer night.
Like watching the sunrise and counting each and every color
along the horizon.
And capturing those moments within your everlasting memory.
To keep every second imprinted within your heart and soul.

    Rosemarie Porreca

First Love

Sometimes alone I still picture your face
Wind in your hair, squinting in the sun
Under fierce blue skies we used to race
Over scalding white sand we used to run
Our bare feet slapped on hot red tiles
Bursting from trees through thistled dunes
Tanned freckled cheeks, endless smiles
Etched on my mind like unforgettable tunes
Years later I asked if you still remembered
Hoping to dance on the clouds again
But words were stilted, by time encumbered
Blushing, I left for the world of men
Always dreaming, in midnight's ashen peace
Of sun in your eyes, hair's golden fleece.

    Laurence Cole

Untitled

People walking in a daze
No more laughing
No more joy
Crying people in the halls
He was my friend
He was yours
Sharing no more your triumphs, hopes, dreams
Always will we remember
Never will we forget
Many of us he left behind
With one word echoing in our minds
Why?

    Courtney Smith

Death In The Autumn Woodland

He stood at the edge of a thicket and listened, his ears held high,
His moist nose sniffed the morning breeze for scent of danger near by,
His brown eyes turned to the thicket where lay a doe and fawn,
Then satisfied that all was well he left mid gray of dawn.
Swift as an eagle on open wing he left the narrow glen,
Over meadow and rivulet while dew glistened bright on the fen.
Sudden a movement caught his eye that filled his heart with dread,
For watching and waiting with thunder-stick crouched a man clad in hunter's red.
Quickly he turned and darted, as swift as lightning he ran,
Each bound took him closer to safety as he strove to elude the man,
But just as he gained the shelter of towering tamarack
He heard the roar of thunder-stick and felt sharp pain in his back.
His heart beat in deafening terror, he stumbled but still raced on,
He must lure this man from the thicket that hid his doe and fawn.
Each breath felt as fire within him, his eyes were glassy from pain,
His body, weak and trembling, was covered with red blood stain.
In panic this innocent creature turned blindly and faced the man,
His velvet eyes gently pleaded but thunder-stick roared again.
His poor broken body was mangled, he uttered ne'er a sound
As he fall mid moss and bracken and spilled his life's blood on the ground.

    Colleen M. Noble-Nason

Winter

High upon the mountain's brow
There appeared a mantle of snow
When out of autumn's barren lip
There came the cold of winter's grip.

Trees so newly shed of their jade
Accepted the snowflakes, as they laid,
The mountains above, full of icy glow
Brought skiers up, from below.

The ski tracks, made from ski blades
Dulled the white, to darker shades,
Over the world, there fell a hush
When winter's sun turned the ice to slush.

The skies then opened to the rains
The rains clogged up the earth's drains,
Stormy winds arose, uprooting trees
And brought the earth to its knees.

Suddenly out of winter's cold grasp
Spring emitted in a perfumed gasp,
Crocuses sprouted from the earths face
As spring put winter, in its place.

    Carmel O'Brien

My Prayer For You

I've been sitting here wondering just what I could do
To lend a helping hand to you,
I've been trying to think of some word, thought or deed
To comfort you in your time of need.

Cheerful words seem so out of place,
But . . . I've thought of someone with "amazing grace"
Who has power to comfort as only He can,
To heal you with a touch of His hand.

You need only to whisper a prayer
And He will be with you in your time of despair —
To bring you up from the valley of pain
And place you on the top of the mountain again.

And my heartfelt prayer is true . . .
May the Good Lord bless and comfort you.
May He be with you in your time of pain —
Lift you up and make you whole again.

    Barbara Lusk

Coda

These are the masks we wear
They sometimes serve to take us there
In poison-colored fear it seeps through
And finds a way to encompass you

Some for pain, some for sorrow
Worn today, killed tomorrow
There never is a happy ending
Just pain and heartbreak and tearful tending

Revenge is good to seek the bad
And it drains the memories we had
We lost sight of what we wanted
And found ourselves broken and stunted

It always hurts to be so kind
You can see it forever in your mind
The angels weep for love with remorse
For there is nothing to feel from a pale horse

True memory is never remembered
Tainted thoughtfulness is how it was hindered
So let us leave this abysmal shore
And become ghost-dwellers forever more

James Woodrow Wilson

In The Wet Sand

The river has been flowing through my hands
distant memories are the only crumbs
of truth like the small river stones
I can close them in my hand
and hurl them back into the water

The memories flow through my hands
I feel your arm around my back your hands are calm
like the quiet meadow on the bank of a small river

The memories have been buried in the wet sand
we can dig them up with a stick to stop time,
which flows through our hands

Somewhere, at the river of memory
the clocks have been shattered
the troubled old man lost the rest of his senses
in the drifting tides of memories

Somewhere, at the river of memory
the old man pours time through the strainer
and he crams his dear memories
into the pockets of his old trousers

Yvonna Goldberg

Untitled

Going home.........,
   Going home........,
      Going home.

Is home where the heart is?
Is home where the hearth is?
Is home at the journey's end, or......
Is it where we begin?

Going home.........,
   Going home.......,
      Going home.

Is home a place where we love,
Is home a place where we pray,
Is home a place that we'll ever find?
If I go, what do I leave behind?
Going home.........,
   Going home........,
      Going home.

Is home a meeting of body, soul and mind?
If I go, exactly what will I find?
Going home.

Mary Rood

My Heroin

She came to me a sweet surprise
Helped me through my sacrifice
Fulfilled my soul an empty hole
Gave me life in a time of end
The sweet nectar runs through my vein, once again I feel no pain

My only love runs astray once again she will betray
My heroin, I need her love everyday, I fear the end
My daily fix I need again

I don't fear the end of life
Quickly I learned it's not worth the strife
With her help again I will find the end
Please come to me without my call
Alone I wait prepared to fall

A call in the night faraway once again night is day
In gush of blood my soul is one
Only she can heal my wounds she will save me from my doom

Without my love I would be lost
The cold would creep and the frost would fall
Again I wish to see her face all I asked was for a friend
Alone I stand at the end

Joe Fernandez

The Dying Seed Among Us

From the shallow sky nothing will live
nothing will die
everything is darkness
hidden from light
concealed from love,
happiness and everything that life is determined
to be
every day and night it sits there wondering,
pondering, marveling what it would be like
noticed by someone
anyone
all it would be is one person who
would make a difference
in its life
its only
life

Sam Levinson

Why?

Once upon a time on a sidewalk,
once upon a time all in haste,
I drew upon with crayon and with chalk.
Why is this writing a waste?

My acts can't hurt all that much
making a picture or a tale of fun.
Yet, if I do this as such
and seen, must I turn and run?

The rains will wash my pictures away.
My tales will fade in the sun.
All this graffiti which is here today
will be gone when day is done.

What if everyone marked on the walk?
Where would we be? We are not free
to do as we please, using chalk, and
faded messages are certainly no fun to read.

So take pen and ink, write letters
or make a card that is for giving
to someone to make them feel better.
Messages Worth Writing Are Worth Re-Living.

Gloria Adamson

A Lonely Summer Day

I hear the silence
Quietness that is so intense.
I hear the wind blowing this beautiful green tree.
As the world sets me free - I am in my own world and imagination.
As I start my trance, I dream of lovely soft summer blossoms.
They are so beautiful to see, to smell, making me feel as though
I've really touched them
The silky, soft petals caress my cheek.

I dream of summer beaches;
Deep blue oceans welcoming me to a place filled with warmth and tranquility.
A place where my memories flow by.
The strong fragrance filling me with an emotion;
An emotion making me feel as though the beach is beside me.
The beautiful palm trees swaying, the blue ocean sparkling, the
seabirds flying overhead, the fresh breeze all set me free to step
into a tropical paradise, seeming so pure and true.

As the birds keep chirping, I continue in my trance,
I see this summer in a new way, that makes it seem very special
from others; A summer with beauty and passion -
enough to take my breath away.

As my heart keeps beating rapidly, I hope to fulfill my dreams one day
Dreams I can make and hold on to and Oh yes, I say to myself
This is another one of those lonely summer days.

Sultana Razia Ahmed

No Monet - But Rich In A Life Filled With Love

Love is more precious than we'll ever know
love is more precious the reason is so...
it cannot be bought or borrowed or sold,
it always is new, it never grows old.
It has to be given received and cherished,
or very soon precious love will just perish

Love grows in the heart of a person you find,
for the seeds have been sown by mysterious signs,
A tender touch, a caring word have blossomed and have grown
And soon love fills your world its limits unknown

It comes from the heart to live deep inside
It touches your world and makes it alive
Everything's newer, more bright, much more fun
when you fall in Love
Two people make one.

A. Colvin

By way of explanation...

It used to really bother me when you'd slug me in the head,
I thought you must be crazy, but I wished that you were dead.

At first you claimed you loved me: you'd respect me all your life;
I trusted in your promise, and agreed to be your wife.

Life brought good, and life brought grief, and life brought us frustration;
We laughed, we fought, we loved — you swore: I was your salvation.

But now you say I'm useless: you slap me on the face,
And I wonder what it is I did to cause my fall from grace.

By the quiet of the morning, I have time to search my soul;
I look back at all my choices, and I see I've missed my goal:

I've tried too hard to love you, tried to be your friend,
Tried to understand your demons, tried to help you mend.

I know a good dog can go rabid and bite his master's hand —
For so it is with you, my love — now I must take a stand.

Real love's demands are painful when the anguish only grows,
And the master's forced to raise his gun to the best friend that he knows.

Yet the mad dog never hears the shot that ends his agony —
Nor, I pray, will you my love — for so it is with me.

Michaelynn Varzari Diller

"Unseen Whisper"

She walks like a whisper this lady we know,
Who gives us hopes and fears as we grow,
You cannot see her in our form,
But she is with us all around,
She touched my heart with powerful force,
Up in my land, myself the North,
I had been lost, for she was there;
But not in the way I knew she cared.
The bitter winds
The falling snow
The gray clouds that let you know,
She's not to far although unseen,
Mother nature is her name,
She comes with beauty and also change,
Take this time to enjoy the scene,
Four short seasons are all you'll see,
Love's been found in so many forms
That's why this place is called the North.

Sandra K. Matson

Mother

As I sit here on my bed
Memories of us go through my head
Times when I was just a kid
All the wonderful things we did

You were always there for me
Through all my bruises and my scratches
you were there
with heartwarming patches

You were my uplift when I was down
When I was sad you were my clown
You were my confidence when it was low
When I was afraid of the dark you were my glow

Now that I'm older
I look back on those days
How you were there for me
In so many ways

You were my dad, my sister, my brother
You were the best because you are my
Mother

Monique Ramirez

Mountain Laurel

In June you'll find the Mountain Laurel -
    dressed in full array.
Through out the forest and woodlands,
    all along the way.

Their tender little branches,
    bear lance-shaped leaves of green.
While clumps of small pink flowers -
    are blooming in between.

These tiny little flowers,
    shaped like little Tiffany lamps.
Decorate the lawns of many of our
    woodland hunting camps

When in full bloom the Laurel covers
    mountains as far as eye can see.
So is it any wonder that the Laurel -
    was aptly chosen to be.

The honorary state flower,
    of our beloved state -
Pennsylvania - God's gift of land -
    to both little and the great.

Geraldine Borger

Hope And Despair

In its reduced element;
elaborate midcourse through
composite terrain.
If I should smile, or attempt a joke — nothing.
Leaning on silence until
the words can regain their meaning.

Re-enacted thought:
Numerous takes throughout the day
with pained hands grasping the hilt.
More piercing in memory, drawn crimson,
expectations of promise lingering.
"Hope and despair do not co-exist,"
sacred speech, double edged;
yet I feel them all the same.

Our reflected injury is still fading
a gleaming ribbon, heated. Diminishes
along the blade.
Beads pulled down as by gravity.
No longer an immutable subject, I invite
though back to previous and mended motives.

Christian A. Morgan

Gulf War: 1991

Grey black suffused with pale dull white, faint shot
of gilded red. So morning shoots my eye
with horrors of the hours to come; my throat
coughs up the bitter phlegm of blanching day.
I clutch the warm surround and struggle, not
to be reborn in dawn's dark early light,
bringing the ghosts of yesterday that feed on fear.
Does the gypsy feel the terror, shut
in dim damp cotton wool, before it spits
out life in white-barred flight, lays the quick
round eating-eggs, loosens the insect scourge
To meet the branching day? Do wet wings shudder
as now my body shakes, hearing the thud
of bloody-minded newsprint on the drive?

Nancy Hughes Owen

The Flame Of My Spirit

The flame of my spirit once burned bright
Now it flickers slightly, on the verge of dying
As the harsh winds of life try to blow it out

My spirit bears the scars of many battles
Fought and won over the years
It has become fragile, it can't take much more pain
But it's all I have, I need it to survive

If the flame of my spirit were to burn out now
Then the smoke which is my soul
Would drift up to Heaven and I would be free
But I don't want to die
I don't want to lose myself
Somehow I must rekindle the flame
And let my spirit burn bright again
Because without it I am nothing

Jennifer Parsons

This Is Not Good-bye

Today a family lies their youngest to rest
From father, mother to brothers who tried their best.
Something we've never experienced. Is this trial or test?
Many tears of sorrow fill an empty void in our heart.
I think joyful memories of John's life should fill that part.
He is with Jesus saving a room for us in a mansion in the sky.
So rest assured family this is not a final goodbye.
Trust in Jesus there's only peace in Him........

Darrin R. Vara

Listen

Listen -
do you hear it?
He is telling us.
He is guiding us.
Listen -
it is His voice.
As quiet as the rustle of the leaves,
As melodious as a bird's song,
As gentle as the whisper of the breeze,
As intense as a crack of thunder,
or as startling as the crash of a falling tree.
Listen -
and you will hear.
The Word.
The Truth.

K. A. Infusino

"Bonnie Jeanne"

She is an American Astronaut,
    whose name is "Bonnie Jeanne,"
And she is one of the bravest women,
    this world has ever seen.

Her first flight in "Challenger,"
    was made in nineteen eighty-five,
Doing tests on crystals, plants, and liquids,
    hoping they would all survive.

She was in "Columbia," five years later,
    and to allay NASA's fears,
She went to recapture a falling satellite,
    that had been in space nearly six years.

In "Columbia," once again, in ninety-two,
    she went around the world for fourteen days,
Carrying out Biology experiments,
    an achievement worthy of great praise.

His fourth trip was in "Atlanta,"
    and the year was ninety-five,
when it linked up with Mir, the Russian space station,
    to keep the world space programme alive.

Jean Hendrie

"Dear Mommy"

I cannot wait to meet you and be cradled in your arms and listen to you sing all the lullaby songs. I can hear you voice, but I don't know what you say, though the sound of your heartbeat makes me feel you love me in every way.

Can you feel me turn for you and kick my legs around? Or feel my hiccups when I am turned upside down? I have been growing quite a bit and there is less room in here, I believe my arrival to be with you is near.

I think today is the day mommy, can you believe? My waiting is finally over, are you excited to meet me?

I feel like I am falling and the water is going away, it must mean my entry into your life is underway. But, OUCH! Something is hurting me mommy, around my head. As I was drifting away, I could understand the two words the Doctors said, "Clinically Dead."

Why did you keep me and let me grow, to make me believe I would be with you and that you loved me so? I only wished you had given me the chance to let you know at our first glance, that I had chosen you from above to be my mommy always to love. I want to thank you for the time we did share, well no words can compare. If you ever think of me along the way, just remember these words I longed to say, "I LOVE YOU."

Jennifer P. Wurzelbacher

Untitled

My dear Sweetheart, although you are far away
You can rest assured that you are in my thoughts
Every lonely night and every lonely day

You have gone to help people in a distant third world land
As the Peace Corps has beckoned you to share your love
And to give a helping hand

As the long days go by and you speak in another tongue
You have come to find and exclaim, what is the depth of love
when it takes the poorest family in the village
To help and show concern and to reciprocate
that special love in return

For learning, children need to be inspired
and made to feel at home
With the smile and encouragement that comes from your eyes
They will see also, that you are there at home

You once said that you were listening
to the soft music in your heart
Those little children you are teaching to read and write
That has taken you so far away
Are listening, and are surrounded by your symphony of love

Liane Iaukea

My World

As I sit on the edge of my window
I day dream of how the world should be
flowers, nice clean air,
and everyone in peace with each other
But I stop day dreaming and realize that,
that's my world,
And every one else is stuck living
in a miserable world of killing
and pollution
I get up from my window and lay on my bed crying
hoping that someday the world will reach peace
and be like mine;
My World

Alysia Lee Laws

Untitled

If death should visit me tonight
I know I have to make things right
I should have told you how I really felt
That you should believe in the cards you have been dealt.
For I am the Queen of Hearts
I don't want us to be torn apart
I am not the Joker in disguise
I can't live with all of these lies
You are the King I have been looking for
I can't possibly love you more
I wish I had told you this before now
But we will get through this somehow
So hold me now before I die
And let me look you straight in the eye
I wrote my words down because I am so weak
I can not bare to try to speak
So read my note and say good-bye
And promise me you will not cry.
"I love you my king, even if you never knew, my feelings for you
are very true. Good-bye my love, someday I'll see you above.

Love, Your Queen

Jamie Kuhar

My Son Grows Up

My hands were busy through the day,
I didn't have much time to play.
You'd bring teddy bear to share your fun.
I'd say, "a little later, son."
I'd tuck you in all safe at night
and hear your prayers, turn out the light.
Then tip-toe softly to the door...
I wish I'd stayed a minute more.
For life is short, the years rush past
A little boy grows up so fast.

No longer is he at your side,
his precious secrets to confide.
The teddy bears are put away...
There are no longer games to play.
No good night kiss, no prayers to hear.
That all belongs to yesteryear.
My hands, once busy, now are still.
The days are long, and hard to fill.
I wish I could go back and do
the little things you asked me to.

JoBeth Dowell

The Station

Chances are not for the
weak and faint of steam.

We must be daring to leap off the platform
of stability on to the moving train of uncertainty.

Dreams can only be caught on a
speeding locomotive of determination.

Dark tunnels can only be traveled
with positive light.

No matter how many wrong turns you
take you must follow the tracks till
you find your desired station in life.

Donna A. Heyen

Have You Taken Time

Have you taken time to talk to the Lord today
Asked His forgiveness when you knelt to pray.
Have you thanked Him for the blessings He's bestowed on you?
For the tender loving care He has given you.
Do you spread a little sunshine everywhere you go?
Sow deeds of kindness and watch them grow?
Do you visit the shut-ins and show them that you care
By giving them the love that you have to share.
Always save some special time for the Lord each day.
Follow in His footsteps each step of the way.
He will always be beside you to comfort and to guide you
If you keep Him in your heart always.

Mildred T. Long

Evening Prayer

Lord, you are my transformation,
My truth, my life, my motivation.
Lord, you are my being supreme;
Energy, love, peace... absolutely serene.
Lord, you are eternal presence, spirit and power;
I am your essence — your love... my honor.
My faith is absolute, my vitality perpetual.
Lord, you are my breath, my word, my action — my essential;
You are my mind, my heaven, my glow,
Lord... I love you so... forever I know!
I am Thee Trinity Creation — eternally so.

Gene Faith

Two Hearts In Three Quarter Time

The music throbs, the lights grow dim
As he tenderly holds me close to him
Cheek against cheek you glide as one
Two hearts beating in unison

But hat's not the way it works at all
When a gal as ridiculously small as I
steps out on a heavy date
With a guy built more like the Empire State

When the music throbs and the lights grow dim
I break my neck to keep up with him!
My arm gets twisted out of its socket
Any my face is jammed in his weskit pocket

I'm lost in a crush way down there
While he dances around in the stratosphere
It may be romantic waltzing about
But I make out better sitting them out!

Kay Gramer

"Friendship"

Friends are not just two people,
They go together like a church and a steeple.
Always happy, always fair,
Like two clouds in the air.
When they're together,
Never in fright,
When it's light in the day and dark in the night.
Sometimes when you can't count on life,
A friend is there to ease the strife.
So keep your friendships going strong,
And your life will be as happy as a song.

Corinne Essock

Time To Time

Nobody wants to say goodbye
But everyone does from time to time
Nobody wants to lose a friend
But for every beginning, there is an end
Nobody tries to do something wrong
But the street of mistakes is forever long
Nobody wishes for someone to die
But there is a death from time to time
You try to live life perfectly sane
But there's never a tiger that wants to be tame
Nobody wants to start to cry
But there is a tear behind every eye
Nobody wants to say goodbye
But everyone does from time to time

Heidi M. Ortolani

Waiting

I've been waiting so long for you to wake up,
but I am too tired to wait anymore.
You mean so much to me,
I often day dream of what could be.
That night all my dreams came true - almost.
But then the music stopped playing,
and the fire stopped burning within you.
I saw it, I really thought I saw the warmth and affection
in your eyes.
I saw it and I want it to come back.
But all there is now are cold ashes, a chilling wind
takes the place of that warm summer breeze that I felt.
The excitement is gone and the fun is over.
The thrill of pure and true love has melted away,
my hopes have faded, my dreams disappeared - all with you.
But I am still waiting,
holding onto what might be,
waiting, waiting, waiting for you.

Krista Ambrosetti

Time

If the tide of time was turned back,
If the present time stood still,
If future we knew, what would we do?
Would we work with a better will.

What if the tide of time turned back?
Would we be so vain as to say -
"No change would we make, nor correct our mistakes
But do the same things today?"

The present we know is happening now;
The past every breath that we breathe;
The future is ours and will only brings forth
The treasure that's sown by our seed.

If we knew what's in store
Would we do a lot more,
Would we help and befriend all man-kind?
In God would we trust, have faith and be just,
In people the good only find?

Nora O'Donoghue

Lost Friend

Today I lost a friend at Death's door,
He went through and said no more.
I was not able to bid him farewell,
The heaviness my heart felt.

His body will be placed in the earth,
To return to ashes and dust.
His spirit will be awarded a new birth
Embraced by the light, as we all must.

He will always be with me in heart and mind,
A memory of laughs and mirth,
He was my friend, one of a kind,
And I will see him in my spirit's rebirth.

"Don't be sad," I can hear him say,
"For He has promised us a new life,
And we will meet again someday,
Free from worry, free from strife."

Today I lost a friend at Death's door,
He walked through and said no more.
I was not able to bid him farewell
But we will meet again in the plush Dale.

Susan D. Simcox

A Cat's Dream

He lies sleeping, there in the sun,
Dreaming of jungles and game on the run.

Twitching with passion, his tail as he dreams.
He's quenching his thirst at cool dreamland streams.

The world and its troubles are forgotten to him.
The sun warms his body and he twitches his chin.

This cat is a monarch in his dreams of the past.
His dreams are so fragile, too fragile to last.

And, when he awakens, he'll stretch and he'll shake.
This cat is proud, asleep or awake.

Clara L. Buchanan

Black Roses

Life flourishes and blooms into beauty
but behold the dark side of reality
under the shadow of the moon
Death lingers, awaiting to unleash unhappiness into the world
Like a rose growing in the mist
it possess a symbol of hope and despair
For all things death will overwhelm
and wither in the struggle to survive
This rose begins to blacken, petals fall to the ground
Societies cruel injustice takes another life
however, the memory of what has been lives on

William F. Turner

Thus

The problem with people today is their fascination
with their own degradation: Which leads to
mesmerization of deep contemplation: Resulting in a
biased observation.
    Thus, in shifting their desire, to planes extremely
higher, each becomes a buyer: From their Lord and
Master Sire: Who burns them with his fire — for he's
always been a liar.
    Thus, like puppets on a string, they laugh and dance
and sing: While reaching for the ring of magic gold.
With thoughts no longer needed, the master's words are
heeded. To gain the world, they promptly lose their soul.
    Thus, in blinding revelation, they assess their
situation, and find with consternation: They are bound
for obliteration. For, without hesitation, they fell
for propagation.
    Thus, when their time is over, they lie beneath the
clover: Their bodies decomposed into the dust. Upon
their tombstone proper, inscribed there by a scoffer,
you find the words, "The Fool Left Us Thus!"

Don Tackett

To Love Again

Memories of the past they dazzle me,
When life was sweet — and good to me.

Romance and love and dreams came true
Heaven that I spent my life with you.

The clippings and memories are yellow and torn
Each picture I treasure — I smile as I mourn.

Now, "our" best friend walked into my life.
Remember when I was best friend of his wife?
Fifty years passed like sands of time
Fifty years passed in 3/4 rhyme.

No dreams, no tomorrows — but just for today
Fate was kind when he came my way.

Thought I could never love again
But he's so much like you
I grasp happy moments
That are all too few.

With loneliness now gone, I look for the dawn
My second love — oh so true —
I bless you my darling that you love me —
And I love you — dearly too!

Blanche Norwick

Welcome To Motherhood

(Dedicated to my two beautiful daughters, Kathi and Kristi)
You are each so special in your own unique way
I love you so much words could never say, I
Welcome you to motherhood with all the joys
And sorrows and know you both will be wonderful
Mothers who loves and cares regardless of tomorrow

You give them life, you rock them at night, you
Watch them grow and soothe their woes. You teach
them to love, to joy, and to cry and teach them
of God, for he is most high

You will have many crossroads in your life, but love
For your children will never break ties, for a mothers
Love never dies

You always keep them close at heart, becoming their
Best friend right from the start
For with love and patience as you watch them grow
Great love and respect they will always show

Carolyn Green

Into the Light: The Beauty of Life

A woman's smile that sends my heart to heaven
A rainbow that stretches across the open sky
A blood-red rose and a summer night sunset
The beauty of sight and little money in my pocket.

Church bells chiming on a still Sunday morning
Meadowlarks singing and a small child's laughter
Rock 'n Roll music and Beethoven's Fifth.
The beauty of sound and little money in my pocket.

Burning wood permeating the crisp autumn air
Hot-buttered popcorn inside a movie theater
Flowers in bloom and an apple pie baking in a piping-hot oven
The beauty of smell and little money in my pocket.

Ice cream cones, lemonade, and watermelon on a hot summer day
Cotton candy, a hot dog, and a Coke at the state fair
Barbecued chicken and potato salad on the 4th of July
The beauty of taste and little money in my pocket.

An electric blanket on a frigid winter night
Freshly-cut grass underneath my feet and mud between my toes
The sun upon my face and a cool breeze through my hair
The beauty of touch and little money in my pocket.

Camdyn J. Ripp

"Judgment"

Don't judge me by only what you see-
Can you judge a person by clothing,
race, age, weight, beauty, or possessions?

Don't judge me by only what you see-
If you only look to see these things than
look the other way, you won't see me.

Don't judge me by only what you see-
If you take the time to know me,
ask me questions, see what I believe.

Don't judge me by only what you see-
I am a person just like you.
I can be hurt easily, laugh at a good joke,
get depressed now and then, and ponder
the reason for my existence.
I am just like you.

Don't judge me by only what you see-
But you have to ask yourself,
why do you have to judge at all?

Traci D. Findley

"Pull Loose End"

It is tear-down slip-apart survival.
To bear your indifference I burn myself,
matching pain to pain. The tightness of rock,
pointed tip of steel sunlight, fast and enormous
slap-sting of fire all bleed off your skin
all push and pin me herding me into
a straight walled, hunger lidded
quarry of gray eyed stone where all the
allegiance I wish for from you sinks like jewels
as quickly as I bend down for them.
They are mined out by the pound by you,
who turned away from me
who spends up my spirit like
inherited money. I cannot
reach this loose end.

Kim Susedik

I Dream A Dream

Verily, I sit dream of all I want to be...
Of all the things I never was and all I hope to see...
Within myself, and in the world;
In My reality.

I want to be the one who asks and answers all the calls,
of problems from the people when it seems that all is lost.
To lift the spirits and mend the pride
of proud black men who have fought and died
a million deaths in their souls and minds
and just like dust, they rise, without tryin'...

...Their eyes possess a vision now blinded
by time and circumstance.

Will a chance save our lives?
By giving us the courage to survive
the attacks, while our backs are turned
against the rain, to shield the pain
from our helpless children who cry out in vain
for our God-given right to
Exist?

Jeanine A. Butler

Friendship What's It All About

It's about trust and respect for each other,
It's about expression of thoughts and open
communication,
It's about our emotions,

It's about occasionally not getting along
with each other, then making up and
continuing on as if it never happened,
It's about being ourselves,
It's about having fun,

It's about those times when we each need
our own space,
It's about sharing quiet moments of
reflections,
It's about an ever changing relationship
which has many avenues,
But most of all it's about you,
My Friend

Andrew D. Wilson

Over Time

Distance, travel time.
Across roads with snow, needing a place
to call it home.
Disparate, starving needing strength
feel like falling and never landing, sink.
Find the tracks, get on the path its
all or nothing and nothing I've had.
Clean off my dusty bones and mind,
clear the mind. Think, just think, can
this get easier with time?
Just wanting a sigh of relief. Tired
but starving for a change of thought.
Dream's lost, so just expand the
mind. Laugh it off and cry later on.
Time minutes are extremely important.
Waste not the minute fill each day
with positive thoughts. Don't miss it
move fast or it will be past.

Leanne Kyselka

The Eve Of The Morning

In the eve of the morning
When the dark breath of life descends upon the earth,
It brings horrors far greater than any cloaked by darkness,
And each of us witnesses their birth.

The burning of the bloated moon
On the skin of those who walk alone the long mile,
Without the pretense of survival,
That made the midnight journey seem worthwhile.

At the cricket's death
We open our eyes to the blinding light of our deeds,
And bleed them as a sacrifice
To the gods of ignorance, blasphemy and greed.

When the lone wolf and the owl sing,
"There is a different of a soul," they say,
"Between solitude in the quickened pulse of night,
And solitude in the desperate apathy of day."

Bonnie Trusler

For You

Softly the moon rises over the western sea,
Tilting its beams of silver through the sycamore tree,
Silently the evening lulls into its breathless wake,
Casting a mystic shadow over the languid lake.

'Tis then that my thoughts are turning,
'Tis then that my heart is yearning,
For you, for you.

Thickly the roses twine 'neath their shadowy arms,
Breathing their balmy fragrance, shedding their hue charms.
Mystic night is falling, twinkling stars are calling,
Tapering trees are lolling, and nature is sublime.

'Tis then that my thoughts are turning,
'Tis then that my heart is yearning,
For you, for you.

Charles Berkeley Fisher

Palm Sunday Fugue

Church bells (pianissimo)
through early-morning South Bronx streets
where grit and Sunday papers pirouette
as I clutch my trove of yellow reeds on that holy day
eager to transpose them into Grandma's coos and wet kisses.

Sharp talk on the way home
breaks the rhythm of new shoes on the concrete sidewalk.
They're fighting again,
but I listen to the brushed-drum sounds my shiny soles make
and the snap-flaps of the sailor boy suit collar
that the wind syncopates against the back of my head.

For days after my father left
it lay at rest on the dresser in my room,
a small piece of palm I had composed in the shape of a cross
with Grandma's knurled-fingered help —
that first cross that I learned to cut, for him,
the last I ever cut for anyone on that yellowing, muted holy day.

Robert L. Ferrante

The Snow-Shoe Hare

Swift, swift, swift see the lovely Snow-shoe hare run
trying to live, trying to survive, the deadly hunters gun

Puff, puff, puff see her frantic breath in the frigid air
as she races away, away from the men that kill without care

Thump, thump, thump beats her frightened little heart
the cruel hunters she must outsmart

Crunch, crunch, crunch she hears the approaching hunters feet
down into her burrow she vanishes, the hunters she has beat.

Amanda Dimitrov

Love (...By Any Other Name)

I do
A Romanian poet once said
that
we live in a language
not a country
and we do
and I live in silence
which is why
I feel so close to you.

Taking the Vows
A Romanian poet once said
that
we live in a language
not a country
and we do
and I live in silence
which is why
I feel so close to you.

Sandra Pralong

The Child

Today, I saw a child
Who was aching from the cold
Upon her was a cotton dress
Which was thin and badly soiled
Her face was covered with crusted dirt
And her eyes were laden with pain
She spoke to no one, not even to us her name
But her silence exposed a little girl's life
Filled with terror, darkness, and shame
Robbed of her childhood pleasures and joy
Alone in this world with no one to blame
Her only companion a battered doll in her arms
Tenderly she caresses its face
As she speaks in a language all her own
She cares for her baby with mother-like grace
Oblivious of the other children around
She sings a melancholy song
Helpless, I watch her nurture a statue
Wondering what the future beholds
For this angelic little child lost in this world of scorn

Treann Tubbs

In Truth

In truth there is no ethnicity, no race of any kind
these words made up from pettiness
a flaw of all man kind

In truth we are all just the same
I don't know why we hide it
I think that we should be ashamed, for trying to deny it

People may be different hues,
Shades of black, green, white and blue
it does not mean they are different,
inside is where it counts
it only means that they are special,
In truth, without a doubt

Kate Allison Halpern

Masque In The Mirror

I alone know myself, and I alone have forgotten, these transparent
masques have become opaque through time clouding the vision of
What I was, What I am.

When I see my reflection in the bathroom mirror, I don't see
Myself anymore, I see what I have made, a cold doppleganger of
What I used to be.

I lost my soul to society, I led my heart astray
I stole my own identity, and cast it all away

No one sees me as I used to be, only a hard carapace in its
Stead. Where did I throw my mind, and the memory of
Who I was.

The tread of existence wore away my distinct features, flushing
Me to the norm, a smooth faced mockery of who I was,
What I used to know.

I lost my conscience in captivity, I cast my history overboard
I crushed those who would break my misery, and feasted on
their bones

Alone in the cell created for myself, rotting from within
A sickness I created and wholly refused to cure
The pain of memory, the memory of life
Of how I used to be.

Bryan Reisinger

My Tribute To Our American Flag

You Represent in the altar of our country
the sacrifice of all of those that have fallen in the battlefield
and have made it impossible for you
to fall down from the glorious pedestal,
that our ancestors have placed you.

You Represent the tradition of the people that yearn for freedom
in a country such as ours:indivisible, united and all-powerful.
You Represent with your fifty stars in a blue frame
a celestial cloak that receives from God
the impulse to be able to break the chains
of so many oppressed nations, that still exist in the world today.

You Represent the purity of the ideals of this nation
when you protect the most valuable treasure of this people:
their liberty, justice and human dignity.
You Represent the devoted mother,
that receives all pilgrims in the world,
wishing to have the opportunity to live
with faith, hope, progress and happiness.

You Represent the beacon that guides the world
toward a safe harbour of liberty and takes them away
from the fog of oppression and injustice
You also, have the blessing of the Lord
and You have at your disposal:....jour lives!...
which we offer if necessary, to defend You, once again.

Carlos M. Barba

Tending Fire And Love

It's not enough to start a great fire and expect it to burn
indefinitely without care. So too, even the greatest of loves
need attention and renewal.

The hottest embers are at the bottom of a fire and they should be
turned for intensity. Turning and stoking memories will inflame love.

A fire needs breeze from a bellows. Love is fanned from a song in
the heart, romance, and the whispered reassurance of love.

Just as ashes must be removed before a fire extinguishes, troubles
should be identified and removed before love smothers.

A drenching rain will put out a fire. A prolonged rain of stress
and worry should not be managed but ended.

Lest the fire diminish, contaminated fuel should not enter, nor
should personal habits be allowed to diminish love.

For the brightest flames, the fire must be gathered to center.
Thoughtfulness and kindness will do the same for love.

Lastly, a fire must have logs, and this remembrance is a log to
fire our love.

Stephen George

A Place In My Heart

"Please Sir. Come in Sir."
"I would be honoured if you did Sir."
"Yes my Son. I love you Son. But why do you want me here Son?"
"You made me Sir. You cleaned me Sir. You bled, you came to
save me Sir."
"I am the Shepherd and you are my lamb Son. Yes I will come in Son.
Forever and to stay Son."
"Thank-you Sir. I love you Sir. I am forever a child of God now Sir."

Marla Lynn Huffman

The Butterfly

Last night . . .
    I dreamed of a butterfly which was of such great
beauty that the image of it was not allowed into
my waking imagination. (After all, I'm not an artist.)
    It landed in the palm of my hand; and, knowing
that I couldn't bear to watch it fly, I did the
only thing I could do . . . I woke up.
Today . . .
    I met you.

Constance Demyris Helton

As We Speak

As we speak,
in silence not sound.
Our eyes abound in each others view.
Sometimes a wink of the eye, sometimes a smile.
Maybe even a nod or a bow.
Engaged in deep conversation by the silence all around.
I agree with a smirk,
you disagree with a frown.
What a pleasurable time that we have had together.
Not even a word exchanged,
as we have reached the end of our quiet conversation.
Our eyes touch for one last time to meet.
As we say goodbye,
as we speak.

Toni Smitherman

The Gathering Storm

It started as a whisper; as gentle as a breeze
A soft and silky voice that only aims to please.
It stirs a peaceful memory; a faint image on the mind
And echoes down the passageways of things we left behind.

It grew to be a murmur; a sigh among the trees
A gentle nudge or urging that forced us to our knees.
From a memory to perception, a picture started to unwind
A life of perfect understanding, with loving ties that bind.

A wind blew out of Zion but didn't rustle any leaves
It came to rest upon a tree to swirl between two thieves.
A storm grew out of Zion and spreading out across the plains
Its power all contained in one man's dying pains.

A storm that's full of promise and gentle as a dove
Bursting forth upon the earth to shower us with love.
Its fury, a warning to be felt;
of judgement and forgiving to be dealt.

The storm upon arriving blew clear a path to see
A strong, yet gentle, hand that said, "Come follow me,"
It drew its strength from numbers; a bond to last all time
A home within our hearts, giving reason to the rhyme.

John H. Turek

Silver Jubilee

One fourth a century of years
has passed and still I sometimes think
that if I closed my eyes
then opened them again, I would be
once more in Edinburgh,
that the castle rock would hover over me
and the royal mile descend beneath me
to Hollyrood and the Canongate,
that I could touch St. Giles Cathedral
and see the tattered banners hanging there
from some far off war, now long forgot,
that the skyline of that spired enchantment
would be there once again in from of me,
instead of here — inside.

Some say only the present exists,
to which I say, nonsense;
Scotland is as solidly here with me now
as the first time I stepped out of the train
and saw her spread herself around me,
earthly magic.

Glen V. McIntyre

I'm There

Listen on your darkest night, when all your world is blue;
Listen with an open heart, you'll hear me calling you.
You'll feel my hand is grasping yours, although we're miles apart;
But,... you must remember, to listen with your heart.

Close your eyes and settle back, and you will find me near;
Pretend, just for a moment, that I'm sitting by your chair.
Remember, that where love is strong, distance hath no meaning;
And the miles will melt away, with naught but love between.

Listen as you say your prayers, and while you kneel in prayer;
Listen, listen, with your heart, you'll feel my presence there.
For I am never very far, for dear heart can't you see;
Nothing separates us, but miles, for you're a part of me.

So listen, listen, precious one, when you settle in for night;
And pull your nice warm covers up, and tuck them in real tight.
What you think is a breeze upon your face,
Is me kissing you "Good Night"

Joan A. Bazewicz

Pensées

The purple pansies turn their faces to the sun.
All summer they will dominate the bed.
The tulips, radiant, came and went.
The lilies-of-the-valley, too have fled
Until next year. Such beauty cannot last!

Why do those pansy faces stir my soul?
They've no exotic scent nor slender shape;
Just a round cyclopean face gazing outward
Watching. Ever watching.

Perhaps they're tokens of past loves,
Down paths I might have trod
Had we not met. So they remain
Wistful shadows of the might-have-been
Had things been otherwise.
The fates were kind to me when our paths merged.

P. Marianne Gardner

"WHAT HAS HAPPENED TO OUR LOVE?"

What has happened to our love,
Love that was so sweet and true;
When you were my turtle dove,
And the skies were always blue
You ran your fingers through my hair,
As you kissed and hugged me dear;
You said you would always care,
When you whispered in my ear;

What has happened to our love,
Has your love all died away;
For now as I gaze up above,
The sky keeps changing to gray;
When I get home you're not there;
 I don't know where you could be;
But my dear if you still care,
 You'd be waiting there for me;

Now you're gone and I'm so blue,
Have you found another love;
Why'd you break my heart in two,
What has happened to our love —; —?

Hugh Kenneth Thornton

Upon Leaving, A Carnival Thought

Riding on a stream of air
I gaze at the make believe world
Below, wondering, quietly,
About the illusion of peace, of serenity!
I gaze at fairy tale sights
That were dreams two decades ago
So much has happened,
The winds of time and the river of space
Blow one onward upon the waves
Of life!
As I ride the current of air
This make-believe mind within
Caresses sweet sweet memories
While a tearful eye looks
Upon haunted eyes, fantasie's delight
I am merely spacing
On a river of air
A highway of light!

Roger A. Lipe

Actor

Your tickets please and welcome to the greatest show that ever deceived you and I,
For you will see a smile upon my face and not the tears in my eyes

A good show is guaranteed, for I'm the greatest actor to be unknown,
For if the make-up is wiped away, my true self would be shown.

My true self hidden underneath a collage of colors shaped like a smiling face,
Disturbed by my life as a child, upset at the time that as an adult I waste.

A painted face of content and happiness wiped away and thrown upon the floor,
For I can only be myself when no one's around and there's no need for a show anymore.

Five minutes to show time sire...thank you, I reach for my face,
This time a little less make-up and a little more of me I will give to this place.

Someday life's stage will see the real me and I will meet the curtain call,
I will stand and give the show of my life and will leave the child of forever
     as the curtain falls.

James T. Mounts

A Contorted Mandate

Timothy McVeigh and Terry Nichols
are alive and well...served and protected
Though locked behind bars, they're allowed controls
within our laws...now, criminal tested

The rights of the one hundred sixty-eight
are being ignored within the courtroom
The latest defense, now up for debate
is a contorted mandate to assume;

McVeigh's lawyers deceitfully connived
plans to force the prosecution to prove
that he intended to kill those who died!
In that way they hope, his guilt we remove

But, what other expectation is there
when a building is blown-up at daytime?
Are we so naive, that he meant to scare...
to merely alarm...if so, where's the crime?

How absurd and sick, but, may I propose;
If McVeigh's found guilty...what should work best...
At a firing squad, assure so he knows
we'll just scare him with a hole in his chest.

Bob G. Martinez

Memories Left Behind

I have a friend who's on his way, to a better place they say
One where only joy exists, away from pain, away from "this"
He's going very quickly there, he's going and he doesn't care
Day after day, drink after drink, further down my friend does sink

I don't think he has a clue, as to why he feels so blue
I don't think he wants to die, but I wonder what will make him try
Make him try to find the peace or find a way the pain to cease
And come to terms with what he needs, there are so many ways to bleed

But bleed we do and always will, patch the wounds, clean the spill
Who am I to judge my friend, his wounds only he can mend
Our roads are short, of this I'm sure, alcohol's a nasty lure
It draws you in and won't let go, it's hard to stop, this I know

But stop you can, there is a way, the price isn't cheap, you've got to pay
It's worth the cost you must believe, oh the tangled web we weave
But weave we do and always will, patch the wounds, clean the spill
An earthly death won't stop the war, it just means that you're no more

So stop your path to early death
Take some time and catch your breath
You'll awake one day and find
You have better memories to leave behind!

Kevin S. Pendleton

Heartstrings

On Valentine's Day and way before
My heartstrings sing out a sad folk lore
They thrive each day to see you more and more
When they fail they break, they have before

The songs ring true on my fool heartstrings
Fool in the way that my whole heart sings
Singing when you hear of happy things
Singing when you're gone till my whole heart stings

A fire, if you will, that burns so bright
A passion for your love keeps my heartstrings tight
To keep you to myself is out of sight
To set you free I've made it right

Whilst I am without you, love
My heartstrings songs will rise above
Rise above on the wings of a dove
And fill your heart with all my love

Debbie S. Moore

Struggling And Living

I have worked so hard
Life is but a dream, don't make me a wimp
I am not dropping out of sight, till my stars shine
I am not getting discouraged, 'cause you want me to
Let me have a life, let me have a mind, let me have a soul
I am a human being like you
Let me think, let me make decisions
I am not a robot, nor do I want to be one
I am a sophisticated being like you, surviving against all adversities
Let me explore the wonders of nature and create wonders of science
Much better than you
You always want to kick me around, but I am always ready, always a
    fighter
When I began to see the injustices, you call me a trouble maker and
    a rebel
I am an intelligent being like you, struggling to maintain human
    dignity
Join me keep up the struggle, don't send me away
Give me an answer, don't refuse me, struggling and living
Living will I, achieving will I, till I leave a legacy

Samuel Rumala

Disenchanted Rose

Edges turning a soft purple-black
The red slips away with each day
The petals too soon shall fall away
And they will never be back
The smell of beauty is also gone
Replaced by a newer scent
The stem, now thornless, is bent
Taking her last bow before dawn
For then, the petals will finally fall
To table, waiting closely beneath
Spiraling to the floor, far underneath
Her life was fragile and so small
Yet, her beauty was one to think about
Velvet smooth to the touch of every hand
We never wondered where she would land
For her beauty always seemed to shout
Now I take you from your sad pose
Placing you back from whence you came
Knowing no flower will look the same
This is your eulogy, oh Disenchanted Rose...

Mark Shannon Driesbach

Beauty Within

As you lifted me I travelled to distant
    golden shores

There came the inner story, to know
    what your love has meant to me

In the midst of knowingness your
    wisdom has been

Everlasting, radiant, and gracious
    in expression

The beauty of your love has
    filled my heart

If all could see and know such bliss

How different life would be

The grandeur of your being is beyond
    the words to say

The feeling that comes is above
    human thought

To express your presence can only
    come in deeds

That would be reflection of your love

Can't you see, can't you see, can't you
    see what love can do?

Park Maloney

Hope

Up where they mix the ages of man
To us, where the path runs not smooth,
We strive, rush exhaust the gift that is held
For justice, a course, truth or love.

How fast they forget good deeds that are done,
No tribute nor lauds do you get.
But the heart mind an soul does grow
Within light - soft blue, white and yellow of gold.

The story is told through the ages it's passed,
Of the old ones who knew of our heart.
Echoes they left must now us suffice
To teach, guide and glow beacon bright.

Jane M. Sembera

Paws

Take my paw, I'll guide you my friend,
Through peaceful valleys, that never end......

As you slip those earthly bonds of life,
We'll journey to a land without struggle or strife,

Leaving the ones you cherish behind...
With memories shared, of joyful times.

A stalwart companion of loyalty and trust,
They'll miss you, friend, but leave... you must.

Green fields beckon, cool streams await....
With flowers and trees beyond this gate.

We'll romp and nap with others in play,
Friend take my paw, and I'll show you the way.

Lorayne Hanson

Far Away

Far away, I feel as though I am in another
galaxy, except I'm really in the same world.

Far away, I feel as though I'm drifting, but I'm
really standing still.

Far away, I feel like a lost island looking
for its sea.

Far away, I feel as though my spirit was taken
away from me.

Today all this is happening to me, but if I try to
make it better, I might finally find my sea.
Sundus Hadi

Broken Doll

Her porcelain head,
Was torn off,
Her head lies limp beside her material body,
Even though she is only a doll,
She knows who did this to her.

She knows who cruelly tore off her legs,
And left them there beside her body,
She will no longer bring joy to a lonely infant face,
Now, when the child is sad, she has no one to embrace.

That fragile doll had a secret,
A secret of torment and personal hell,
A secret she would never ever tell.

Her lips are painted shut,
They will be that way forever,
The doll was in so much pain,
But now she will no longer suffer,
Because he took her life,
He killed that angelic figure.

He knew she was the only one who knew the secret,
A secret is the way he had to keep it.
Natalie Martin

Home Sweet Home

I wish I'll be home
Laughter and joy
Sweet smiles
Like a flowers that blooms.

I missed all this things
Because here I am far away
From my home sweet home
A place where I'm belong

But sacrifices count most in life
Different trials come on my way
Yet I remain strong
Because of faith and hope

Suddenly blessings comes on my way
Though here I am longing
To see my family soon
To feel the love I've waiting for

Love that I'm longing for
I know one day I'll be home
For them, to joined the said
Happiness that create the brilliant light...
Jocelyn Marybeth C. Salazar

A Poem For Peace

Let's hold hands brothers and sisters
Around our Mother Earth
Love encircling this lone blue planet
This giving home of our birth

We all are brothers and sisters
Regardless of creed or race
Hold hands my brothers and my sisters
Make our world a peaceful place

Let's sing praise to our Father in the heavens
Let's rejoice in our global family
Open hearts with love and understanding
Sharing lives in peace and harmony

Let's hold hands my brothers and my sisters
Let's all pray for everlasting peace
May we respect and love one another
May all wars forever truly cease

Let's stand united as brothers and sisters
As we spin through space and time
Holding hands, praying together
Ensuring peace for all mankind
Linda L. Dowd

The Surprise!

It was late and cold that night as I left the bus.
    The crosstown pulled away.
"Treat yourself to a cab," I thought.
The strong, cold wind objected to my choice
    But I forced myself uptown...And Then It Happened!!!
A cab full of happy, beautiful people...
    They all got out — smiling, joyful!
The last man out, turning, smiled and said,
"We just brought this cab over here especially for you!
    "Here! Let me hold the door!"

A strange, warm feeling filled my heart—
    Suddenly I felt so happy! I couldn't explain it!
I was far away from the harshness and sometimes rudeness of the city.
    I felt respected, decent, worthy, safe—oh, so safe!
For just a moment, I was home again!
It was so precious, so wonderful, so special! What a surprise!!!
    A moment to cherish and cling to—a moment to feel...
Home again, home again, home again,
    Home!!!
Hold onto this moment forever and ever!!!
Betty A. Bayfield

Lament

Of things certain
there are few:
The incredible lament
of the viola
in a Rimsky-Korsakov sonata.

Of moments cherished
that you knew:
The lament that seems to
linger longer
than tracks in the sand.

The lament that comes back
into your head
when pictures, visions, tracks
have been erased
from the grasp of the hand.

The lament that seems to encompass
A lifetime of suffering (and so has it encased).

The lament that seems to say:
"Catch me if you can" (and wants to be chased),
And knows it will never be caught.
Charles Mann

Watching You

I came to watch you sleep last night, kissed your cheek and said
good night.
You quickly rolled over and gave a slight smile, I wondered if you
were faking but that's not your style.
I was standing so close, yet we're so far apart, I wanted to cry
but I was afraid to start.
Don't know how much more I can take, so afraid to make a mistake.
No one has ever loved me quite like you, I'm sorry for all I've
put you through.
I know we'll never be the same, for this I solely take the blame.
Yet sometimes I think it could be better, and wonder if we'll
somehow get back together.
Still haunted by ghosts in my past, unaware of how long it will last
I know it's wrong to ask you to stay, but I can't seem to let you
walk away.
So, until I figure out what's wrong or right, I'll settle for
watching you sleep at night.

Stormie M. Polhemus

"My Secret Wish"

I sometimes wish I were a star
Up in the heavens, twinkling from afar.
With nothing to do, but be shiny and bright
To add beauty to the sky, and light up the night.

There is so much beauty in the world to see,
A world wide traveler, I'd love to be.
I would go first to the sea shore,
I would soak up the beauty, till there was no more.

Then to the mountains, to breathe the fresh air,
It would be so peaceful not a worry, or a care.
Stopping now and then, to pick some wild flowers
And, enjoying a lovely soft, summer rain shower

Then on to the desert, with wide open spaces
The cactus in bloom, are found in no other places,
The nice warm desert sand,
Is a good resting place, for beast or man.

Although I'd roam far, far, from home,
Without my happy thoughts, I would be alone.
So with all my toil, and all my strife,
I give thanks to God, for my kind of life.

Ruby McKelvey

Tomorrow Never Comes

The rods and cones of a human eye;
Or the iron staff of a forgotten soldier;
Man can never find the answers;
Or create new lies to replace them.

Relieve the final days of a gloomy decade;
Racing against a melting clock;
On the first days of a promising decade;
Will the truth ever surface?

Now we see the answers to a lie;
Escaping a place we don't want to be;
Viciously attacking a pleasant hope;
Escaping a sight we don't want to see.

Relive the final days of a gloomy decade;
Can we fight to stay alive again;
Or create new lies to replace the old;
Men can never find the answers.

Eventually being laid to whither away;
Soon we will be forced to say;
Tomorrow never comes;
Tomorrow never comes...

David J. Purdy

Black Queens

Black queens as me.
Sweet as tea
Grow as a knowledge tree.
Never look back but remember
What our ancestors been through.
We are free finally free.
We may still fight to make things right.
Although things still turn out wrong.
We pick ourselves up. Start over again.
Be free as the eagle like a eagle
spreads his wings and flies high above
proud as ever.
Black queens as me we must see
That this world is for us to.
It's time for us to see
We have equal rights to.

Barbara Powell

Dreams

Do you believe in the power of dreams?
Do you ever wonder why? What is it in our dreams that makes
us wake up and cry?
I don't have the answers to the many things God does
I only know He created this big wide world with love
Our dreams are deep within us they cry out in our sleep
Deep in our sub conscious then into our sleep they creep
Have you ever had a dream that woke you up crying?
It seems so real you thought you were dying?
A jerk back into reality a scare for sure
You wipe your brow relieved and pray for cure
But when sleep overtakes you and the dream comes rushing back
How can you stop it? How do you react?
Cold sweats-shivering cold, or hot flashes from the nightmare
that's growing old
To wake up screaming and pray for a healing
Needing to shake this feeling and wondering, why is my mind reeling?

Edna D. Cappelli

She Walks Where Angels Fear To Tread

She walks where angels fear to tread
And she never hangs down her head
She'll wipe away your tears
And take away your fears
She'll hold you tight all through the night
And make everything all right
She has a heavenly smile and a unique style
She'll come right in and take your heart
She's never afraid to finish what you start
She truly is a God send
And she'll be with you now until the end
She's more than a true friend
She's always willing to lend a helping hand
She's in your heart and soul
When she is with you, you will know
Her presence makes you whole
Sometimes it may not be always show
But she walks where angels fear to tread

Corrina Lee Gates Schemeley

Life

From the beginning of time the golden word was born, life,
And we have risen to lead this unfulfilled task
From every star from every light.
To fulfill our dreams is to fulfill our lives.
Greed is what makes life suffer tho death is also to suffer,
Climbing the stairs of life step by step, hand in hand,
In the circle of life.

Elcid Martinez

The Observer

Through my window I can see the world.
I watch it like a child does an ant farm.
Like a monarch watches his domain.
I see so little of so much...
or maybe it is so much
of so little.
No one sees me as I sit here,
on my window seat,
dissecting the world.
I am the silent observer.
I watch,
and see,
and understand.
And still I do nothing.
What could I do?
I merely watch.
And I can see the world.

Anaïs Koivisto

Trapped

You could hear the rings of her laughter
    bouncing off the walls.

Rings of laughter that sometimes just pierced
    the inner soul.

Sometime it would just make you smile;
    with the glimpse of a memory,
    like the birth of a child.

Oh! What joy it would just bring to the soul
I wonder what happen with the rings
    they ring so low.
Rings of happiness, rings no more

There really once was happiness, now pain
    the glimpse of that memory I can't seen
    to catch anymore.

You see, he snatched happiness from her as their life begin
    it's been so hard to watch her fad within.
It just kept happening each time he walked in
The laughter once heard, just finally left the room
Laughter of happiness, absorbed deep therein,
    old faded walls, just trapped her within.

Shirley J. Mackey Brown

Lois

How can I describe the warmth that fills my being
By the sweetness of your presence?
Helplessly tongue-tied by the failure of my mind to
Voice a point of reference, I can only feel.

So splendid to my senses is the smile of your face,
Your laughter, sparkling eyes, and thoughtful touch.
The softness of your voice is like Spring's gentle rain,
Quietly kissing tender green leaves.

How beautiful you are, that precious house of your soul.
A magnificent house fashioned by God's grand design,
Each phase of the building with its own unique grandeur.
Radiantly you glow through each cycle of His created order.

I am blessed to walk with you in that phase where
You are surely more beautiful than at any time in the past.
How fortunate am I to know the whole of you,
The inner person, untouched by the limitations of time.

Ever passing to others the riches of God's grace received,
Gifts of love and compassion and patience.
Wonderfully humble, a conduit of goodness in word and deed.
Oh that I could tell my love for you.

Don Cates

Slave To The Flesh

I am slave to the passions the world has forgotten.
A slave to things that may never have been.
I am a slave to love in a whirlwind of fire, to dreams
encased in perfect fantasies.
A slave to the thought of an open mind, that never learned
boundaries, or chose to ignore them.
The true brilliance of a fool.
A prisoner of things that never were, that might have, Or
should have, but could not.
I am a slave to the unknown knowledge, the fire of a
passionate soul, to the craving of a body of flesh.
And the bliss of ignorance or is it the ignorance of bliss.
I am a slave to the beckoning of the known, and the thrill
of the unknown.
My desire is tireless and timeless as love and craving
themselves.
I am the words and so do I live to reach out forever,
always in search of the new master.

Jennifer Crabtree

The Passion

How many times have I loved?
Not in a question of who, but what?
A slave to passion, I have been dubbed,
Yet, not a slave to another.

A love for life,
Is it wrong?
Opposers, sift your strife,
A passion for life, is life.

I have thought of sadness,
I have thought of sorrow,
But I will not drive myself to madness,
For the good outweighs the wrong.

Life is good,
As the father of life is good,
By strength I have stood,
The darkest of night, the strongest of storm.

My passion for life may battle some,
For life has its hardships,
Into understanding we must come,
Live life now, live life now.

Matthew Hester

Two Is One

Kissed by the stars, we have been so blessed,
    Our souls united in a spiritual sense.
As planets delight, in their orbital dance,
    Stirring the potion which makes love chance.

Together we hold, our souls will not part
    We are of one, the earth and the sun.
The beauteous lies in the song of our heart
    A mystic rhythm, two as if one.

It is not by chance or some given right,
    The sea and the sky become one at night.
The earth and the moon, play as if fun
    Our souls are bound, two is one.

Eric Shabronsky

Mother Nature's Music

She blows softly through her soldiers standing on guard,
With tall brown trunks and brilliant green hair,
Her breath rustles the leaves of hair as it wisps by,
Her small children play in the branches of the soldiers,
Gliding from branch to branch they sing their family songs,
Her hard working honey makers buzz through and around the campsite
as they annoy the poor campers,
A snap, crackle, pop comes from the campsite that frightens the
busy honey makers away,
She cries down on the site of her poor soldiers cremation,
Tap, tap, tap comes from outside the campers cloth shelter,
As the light rises, Mother Nature makes her music again,
She blows softly through her soldiers rustling up their hair,
Her children glide from branch to branch as they sing their
songs,
Her honey makers buzz 'round and 'round,
engulfed in the rich air that surrounds them,
The snap, crackle, pop from the children of God's flame
rings through the forest,
The orchestra of tap, tap, tapping originates from high above
as she cries for her burning soldiers,
And far, far away, I fall sleep on a forest bed.

Tara Helfer

Dig

Dig deep you wallowing soul,
  dig until you grow old.
Look carefully and you will see,
  that you dig because of me.

If you fall or you feel to small,
  look at me, for I will make you tall.
Do not worry if the storm brings deadly strife,
  for I am the giver of light and life.

When you are done, your task completed,
  come to me and then be seated.
For your troubles, worries, and shame,
  I shall reward you with life, and a name.

Joseph M. Osorio

The Seedling

As the warmth of the loam surrounds me,
A life of darkness is my only home.
I feel a sudden urge to flee,
But I soon adjust to being all alone.

Some unknown force is my nurse;
It satiates my hunger pains;
It never fails to slake my thirst;
And its comfort keeps me sane.

The desire to elude again fills my head.
Such an incredible strength of power overcomes my soul.
I struggle out of the shelter, my loathed bed,
Into an atmosphere where my new entity becomes whole.

I celebrate the death of my strife
As I bathe in the rapture of my rebirth.
But I'll never forget my first life,
For my roots remain deep within the earth.

Nikia Singleton

"If Only"

If only I had more time...
we could have done more things together
we could have laughed longer and played harder
If only I had more time.

If only I had more time...
we could have done so much more
we could have taken long walks and had more long talks
If only I had more time.

"If only I had more time" I'd say when you asked
for me to stay
"I've got so much to do and I'm very busy -
maybe some other day."

And now you're gone to a better place
and I realize I've got that time.
I wish I could thank you for slowing me down -
because now, I've got the time.

Lori Schramm

A Wedding Prayer

Today on this, the day you wed,
Long after all the vows are said,
And all the guests have gone away,
Alone with God, for you, I pray.

Dear Lord, I lift my voice to you,
In praises for these precious two.

For them, dear Lord, I ask you give,
Your blessing for long as they live.

And knit, for them, with golden thread,
The road on which their feet shall tread.

And in this world of push and rush,
Enrich them with undying trust.

I ask for hope and joy and peace,
And caring that will never cease.

Shine down on them from up above,
And keep them warm with endless love.

Peggy Jean Tyler

The Power Of Love

With you, I have soared beyond the highest peaks
And descended into the depths of the darkest valleys;
Because of you, I have wept the widest ocean
And you carried me back on wings of devotion.

You alone, have given meaning to my life
And in moments of exquisite joy, set my very soul a-quiver.
In grief, unashamedly you laid yourself bare
And breathed warm words that whispered care.

Without you, this space in which we mortals move
Would be as Sheol, a bleak and barren place.
It matters not what cloth you wear,
Your mighty power lives everywhere.

  For you - are Love
    Audrey Timberlake

"Fly"

Fly raven, fly through the darkest night, fly till you find the day
of light. Even though her tears, soak your feathers and weigh you
down. Fly through the garden of eden without a frown. Jupiter is
on fire, neptune is dead, so fly until you find that reason left unsaid.
The Blackness of your feather's reflect the light of Day, Deny the
temptations of man, for you of all know you cannot stay. Do not be
forced by empty promises that make you want to delay. Just fly
raven fly till you find the light of day.

Matt Lyons

"Where There's A Will There's A Way"

"Where There's A Will There's A Way"
I've got the way but no will
So where an I going to go this day?
Where no man has gone before?
But I haven't the money to explore
The secrets of our endless world
So, perfect I sit, my hair nicely curled
With my future planned out for me,
Yet I have the choice to be
My own, on my own, or not
With not even myself have I fought
My future, my fate my destiny,
And I am told I should see
That what you say is good for me
But I'm not you, nor you I
What lies ahead is in the sky
or down below - do we all go
Out of our world as the mind
leaves your soul to find...

Kathleen S. Malisani

Together Again

I see you walking hand in hand in
that far and distant land.

Gone is your strife, gone is your pain,
for you have found your love again.

You walk through gates of memory to
greet old friends and family.

Fate deems one day we all must part
but I keep you both within my heart.

So I will grieve for you no more
for you're both at peace on that golden shore.

Shirley Wendorf

Fade Out

Middle-browed, middle-aged, she lives
time ticking by, drowsing away her once
needed vigour.
Life has become a waiting room
suspended somewhere between
bingo halls and terraced suburbia.

Yet, sometimes when her bedroom is lit pinkly
like a Spanish sunset,
when swan songs in dusty covers breathe again
on the radio,
she longs to dye her hair the colour of brandied
peaches
make scarlet slashes on her dry lips,
be marilynned on a street corner,
warm air billowing her skirts above dimpled knees.

Instead, she remains framed
like a photograph
slowly fading
slowly fading.

Eileen Casey

Moment

The love of two friends torn apart
By nonsense for one short moment
One loves the other more than just a friend
The other does not care for a moment about the others feelings
The one is torn apart by the two types of love
Love is just nonsense for a moment
For a moment's notice no one cares

Marquia Nielsen

Jonathan's Promise

A laughter, a smile
unique, and all his own
A hunger for adventure,
and the yearning to roam.

To find an answer
to some unknown game,
Being the person he was,
wasn't just in his name.

In the very short time,
that he shared with us here,
He taught us the meaning
of a friendship so dear.

We can all stand to learn
how to spend each day,
If we just go about it
in Jonathan's way.

Take each dawn as it was meant to be,
believe in yourself and you too, will see.
That true treasures lie in the gift from above,
and can only be given in the truest of love.

Annette Adamczak

Lines In A Rainstorm

As the rain falls and cuts off the world
And darkness comes
And leaves me to thoughts not worldly,
Loneliness crashes down with the
Thunder that rolls above and
I know how I love you, want you, need you.

Thoughts of you drift to me
Like the sweet refrain of a Viennese waltz,
And in my mental world of fancy
I once again know your sweet caress,
The exotic scent of your perfume,
Your angel face with its frame of dark curls,
Your lovely form — its hint of Heaven,
The ecstasy of your surrendered kiss.

Reality explodes like artillery — and leaves nothing
But a letter in my hand,
A picture on the table,
A lonely room in the darkness and an
Emptiness in my heart that
Only your presence can fill.

Vance S. Jennings

"He Promised, He Lied, He Came Back"

He promised he'd be back, he promised he'd
be back, a week has past he still ain't back, he lied
he lied, I miss him, but I never kissed him. He
lied, he was so sweet but he beat me, he never
touched me but he beat me. I watched him play
basketball and wondered, is this the last day I'll
see him? When he was sad I made him laugh when
I was sad he made me laugh. Without each other
we'll never be the same, we'll never be the
same. About a day ago he came back I was so
happy, but it wasn't him, it wasn't him, it wasn't
him. He promised he'd be back, a week has past he
still ain't back, he lied.

Melissa Fry

Knowing When

When the tides roll in and the rain falls down,
When the seeds from the flowers begin falling
  to the ground.
When the future turns to the past and there's nothing
  left to see,
When nothing is what your always left to be.
When the clouds of grey and white begin covering
  the sunlight,
When all of the happiness has died out during the night.
When the world is really known not round but flat,
When the people make you feel lower then a rat.
When your life was nothing but a long
  boring dream,
When you finally realize your different then
  you seem.
When people of the world no longer seem
  to care,
That's when you can turn to me
Because I'll always be there!

    Rachel Dava Winneshiek

Ode To Spring

The icy winds of winter is past
I am alive to face spring, I say,
Death I have faced with its icy blast
The struggle within is held at bay.
This is the day in which to live
The spirit within is kindling a flame,
Spring in the heart has so much to give,
Love and hope is the eternal game.
Hope springs anew within my breast
Birds chatter anew outside my pane,
Rivers of love flow out on a crest
I am alive and God knows best.

    Joy Sabados Jessie

My Parents

My parents mean the world to me
For them I'd climb a mountain or swim the sea
They cloth me: feed me: and put a roof over my head
They also let me sleep in a nice cozy bed
Sometime they yell and get mad
But it's usually because I'm being bad
I know they love me
For that's easy to see
They hold me through the good and bad
And comfort me when I'm feeling sad
To me they are like a sparkling gem
I don't know what I'd do without them

    Elizabeth Rogers

Boot Camp

My grandson, a fine Marine
It's good he joined, while still a teen
Boot camp was tough, and
sometimes downright rough
Yelling drill sergeants, obstacle
courses, and rifle range
Marching here and there, my what a change
Twelve long weeks of very hard work
At times he thought he would go berserk
But he came through it all just fine
And on graduation day, was on cloud nine
I'm so proud of him, he's one of a kind.

    Mary F. Albert

Riddle Of Life

In later years if often seems that life brings just small joys
We hope, we wish, we're praying hard - but really have no choice.
We learn to nourish our soul from times that have gone by
From childhood days, from sweet young love, when our heart was shy.
We dreamt from future happiness, fulfilled in love so gay
And were in innocence so sure good times and love and would stay.
There's nothing on this earth that we forever call our own
The might of life, called "destiny", sits high upon a throne.
So many people say their prayer - not asking God for wealth
They know that riches can destroy, they pray for peace and health.
And pray that life be good again, that there were no more sin
And no more wars, no fight nor hate, and decency should win.
In some old hearts the wishes died, the dreams came never true
Why life is so unjust and cruel - no human has a clue.
And fin'lly tired souls are still, there's no more question "why?"
They are content with what God gave, and glad when they get by.
Forgotten are comparisons, all short comings in life
Once old enough, there's not much sense to struggle and to strive.
Mankind is too dehumanized, kind hearts can barely cope
They trust in God real patiently and pray to him in hope.

    Liselotte Reich

Untitled

Make it flood Mr. Floodmaker
I want to know who will float in your boat
You can watch me drown,
I don't want to live with you anyway
If you can live with yourself
I saw her sparkle last night
Guess she's just a better grip than I,
But I'm always me
I know you can say that, but can she
So often you eat your cake too,
I guess her icing is richer than mine,
But when she sees me, she doesn't wish that she were her
I don't know why, when she's got candles too,
She's got you
Funny how brave you are,
funny how clever you know you can't be
Simple how you go on
Simple how life just goes on without me
Once I watched a year on a clock, through a glass;
Sorry, it's too much to watch again.

    Mandee Lynn McKelvey

Untitled

Together forever,
we thought we would always be.
With you my friend,
just you and me.

Together forever,
in this place we now see.
The land of our friendship,
that stands before me.

Together forever,
in our eyes only we can find,
our friendship, the memories
that never leave the comfort of my mind.

So as we make this pact,
I hold dear these words,
they will last as long as there's a you and me,
and so will the memories
of those times oh so free.

Always together,
just me and thee.

    Jennifer Komis

Untitled

The moon. The stars
The moonlight glaring off the ocean blue.

A picture perfect night.
Thinking of you, is all I can due.

You are my moon.
You are my star.
You are my ocean blue.

You are a picture perfect knight.
Without you, my world would not exist.

No moon.
No stars.
No moonlight or ocean blue.

No picture perfect nights.
Life with you has been magical.

As the earth needs the moon:
And the night needs the stars,
I need you!

From the moment I met you!
I knew this love was made up above —

Among the moon and the stars....

Danielle Rosso

Raggedy Man

I never felt a cement pillow
or the endless rays of the sun.
Just around the corner
from you, from me,
I saw a man slouching
in an uncomfortable position.
He asked me for a quarter,
I searched my pocket
to chime his cup
he held tightly in his hands.
Red knuckles, dirty nails.
And then he smiled at me shyly,
to which I replied the same.
My shoes were magnets to the ground —
I managed to walk away from him,
but not my guilt.
Stuffing my manicured fingers
in my pockets
and walked two miles home
while my bus fare filled his empty stomach.

Kari J. Hilsman

Stradivarius

When you listen to the tunes I've played
    What kind of impression have I made
If you think, I'm a bit off key,
    I've missed a note or two,
Cut them short or added a few
    Just call it a Rhapsody,
A rhapsody in A, E, I, O or U
    You may see my name
On the sign board in the post office saying
    Reward for information leading
To the arrest of W. H. E., born in 1903
    But you may never see my name
On the marque or Hall of Fame
    Or as a Grammy award winner
But who knows - They say
    What ever's to be will be
Some of these days you may see me
    Down on the street corner at Broadway and Main
With my strad and a tin cup and cane
    And a sign saying "Brother can you spare a dime?"

W. H. Enlow

A Little Boy

A little boy's hopes a little boy's dreams
A little boy's fears that lead to his screams
A little boy's adoration on a pedestal placed
A little boy's tears of a life yet to be faced
A little boy's world on whom it revolve
A little boy's loss as promise dissolve
A little boy's self one of promise - bold
A little boy's sorrow of cruelty un-told
A little boy's thought where fantasy lies
A little boy's truth in which he but cries
A little boy's triumph over all he meet
A little boy's weakness of final defeat
A little boy's wonder of a perfection sought
A little boy's pain when all comes to naught
A little boy's longing of warmth long past
A little boy's wish that this once it last
A little boy's heart with a hollowness old
A little boy's delight come out of the cold
A little boy's dread for what all this means
A little boy's hopes a little boy's dreams

Cornell H. Riggs

Change

Now that she is gone both our lives have changed:
There's no more whispering back and forth
After the lights are out,
No more riding horses together
Or going places that we both liked,
No more help with my homework,
No more good ideas.
She's gone for a whole year —
Spending nights with strange people,
Trying different foods,
Learning different languages
Singing songs, dancing dances
And meeting new friends.
This is change for her and me.
More for her, less for me
And when the time comes for me to leave,
I'll have learned how to smile
When change overwhelms me.

Katie Gray

A Poor Man's Dream

Panning for river gold is how the story was told,
Men sifted through river sand to find a pan of gold,
They panned for gold nuggets in the white water stream,
This rushing river was a poor man's dream.

Along the rushing river, men walked at night,
River water sparkling from bright moonlight,
Men listened as the river whispered its theme,
I'm the rushing river of a poor man's dream.

They sat on rocks watching the water flow away,
Wondering how many dreams had gone astray,
This river bottom had no gold, it washed down stream,
This rushing river was a poor man's dream.

Men, panned for gold nuggets along its winding bend,
This old river was panned by some of the greatest men,
Hearing stories of gold washed down stream,
This rushing river was a poor man's dream.

Darlene White

Sunshine

I know it was a very bright day at the time you were shining. I could hardly wait to see you at a moment of warm sunshine of joy, that shiniest in the sky at day; it's a happy time sunshine with bright hope. It's an uplifting time of loving, sunshine and great peace on this earth of fun for everyone that loves the great out-doors. What a wonderful work of the sunshine to brighten up the little one's faces, to bring cheer and laughter. There's singing of the birds on spring days to just fly from one place to another one. The sunshine is a happy time for us all to be happy and full of love for one another, like it's supposed to be for all life on this earth. Sunshine is great to hold for one who just to watches the day go by.

Gary Brooks

The Underground

I have travelled your tunnels and your lines
with wind and speed and sound. Long have I loved
the thrill of juxtaposing light and darkness,
stop and start, man and machine with faint dreams
of dragons spitting sparks from steel.

I have felt the bellowing of your mechanical
thunder and stood in wonder gazing at
kaleidoscoping masses, slick, shiny,
paper salesmen and the electrical
aroma of your breath.

How I have anticipated descending
in the mazes of your neon bowels,
journeying the multicolored paths of your purgatories
only to emerge, semi-dantesque
into the dim daylight of Blake's Jerusalem . . .

Glenn Fogle

Ode To Persephone

My Heart's Darling,
On the surface,...I too can be Gallant!...and Charming!
But, My Wit...is more provocative...(yes!...) sometimes alarming.
'though Rationality and Reason are 'oft...tools of my trade,
...I' the midst of 'Things' real, prove banal and...quite staid.

So, *"Please,"* you beg. *"...what Beast Black art thee...!*
... who would so!...deceive, and hide from me?"
Blithe mistress..., I *pliantly* submit...
I'm but a creature of tellurian appetite and lust;
...but cautious of the light,...I...do what needs must...

I'll conceal in verse, my Soul's intent,
To unlock your more...passionate bent.
An' challenge you only,...to live deliberately,
... an' not so much celebrally.

Because I know the veiled light of your eyes...
...burns no less bright than mine.
An' that your prudish pretense,...
...speaks but softly...of (aye!) your magnificence.

Alas! come an' Live with me, an' Be!...my Love;
For I *shall* win your Heart,...w'thout fair warning,
An' slay your deamons,...b'fore the morning...
...w'ile behind Night's curtain, the Earth will move.

Yet, before you think my Marrow...b'nighted,... I invitingly beseech...
Bid your *Politesse!*, *"...take leave!"*
An' roll-up your sleeve!...
...and *verily!*,...my Sunflower,...dare to Eat a Summer's Peach.

Gregory D'Neil Chapman

One Very Special Lady

One very special lady of no relation gave and gave love with no question.
One very special lady was there when our needs were so great, she embraced our hearts.
One very special lady understood our needs, fed our bodies, encourage our minds.
One very special lady touched my heart and turned the cold stone into a warm glow.
One very special lady spent a lot of time watching me grow.
One very special lady hugged and rocked me, listened and heard me, liked and loved me.
One very special lady taught us all one basic fact - love with no strings is a priceless gift.
One very special lady whom we never gave a present, said we gave her something - we gave her the gift of love.
One very special lady was loved so very much but we didn't know until we lost touch.
One very special lady- did I ever tell you I loved you? I think not.
One very special lady was in my life from the moment I was born until the moment she died.
I am so lucky I had loved of a special kind. I regret I had love but failed to recognize it.

Caroline Power

When I Think Of You, Mom

Mom,
When I think of you,
I see skies forever blue,
With a shimmering sunrise,
In which the sunlight never dies.
I think of you and see a baby bud on a tree,
Which will one day bloom just like me,
And I will know when that day comes,
Still I am in your heart,
And that our love will never fall apart,
I love you.

Candi Strudwick

The Grand Piano

A grand piano sits alone in a living room.
It has some damages, yet it is still so beautiful.
It is so strong, yet it is so weak.
Its walls are so mighty, yet neglect could destroy it.

You don't hear anything if no one is there to play it.
Yet when someone comes, he only plays the white keys,
It sounds so wrong and dull.
But when the right person comes, he plays all the keys,
Black and White, high and low,
And it sounds so beautiful.
Every key uniting itself with all the others, harmonizing, making
  beautiful melodies,
As if the world had finally realized you need everyone to make
  good music.

Shelby Chlopak

Our Love

A love I once had is now gone,
hoping to regain it I feel so alone.
Our love wilting away like a rose,
Wondering if my love for you shows?
Trying to let you know how much I care,
The pain of not being with you is to much to bare.
I am not sure who is to blame,
but our love use to put everyone else to shame.
Hoping we can make it in time,
hoping that one day you will again be mine.

Melissa Naylor

Where Did The Violets Go?

Remember where the violets grew,
with clumps of grass upon a knoll;
through the woods or in a field?
Oh what a sight to feed the soul!

We'd gather bunches while we may,
those velvet gems of different hue;
I yearn again for yesterday
to wander where the violets grew.

Now that's past for with regret
I watched those concrete buildings grow;
They say that's progress, don't look back,
but say, where did the violets go?

Maybe progress goes too far
to enter where the violets are;
Stone so cold cannot convey
The warmth and peace where violets lay.

Margaret Williams

"This Fairnight"

Fairnight and darkness surrounds us softly.
Hidden where none in the world may see.
Here we are alone
This night is our own
Fairnights that we share joyously

Come love, for love is the force that binds us
Short is the time that we call our own
though night must soon fly,
Love will never die
It lives in the cherished memory of this fairnight.

Richard Harrison

"Just Thinking"

What makes a person think he is better than you?
Is it the clothes he wears or the things he do?
Or did he come here in some special way?
Unlike the rest of us who celebrate Mother's Day
And why do some people cause you strife?
They even feel obligated to ruin your life
Then there's the leaders who mix a nasty brew
When they preach I am for him but not for you
Who shakes your hand and says he understands
Then rob the treasury and rapes the land
They amass great fortunes and live real hardy
And they call themselves a Political Party
So what makes a person think he is better than you
Well....it's our ignorance and the things we let them do

Robert Thomas Lee

The Perfect Rose

The face of an angel 'tis my mother to me
As I recall fond memories

Her love toward me blossomed with each passing day
The fun things we did, and the games we played

The good things in life did my mother teach
They are with me always in my heart for keeps

Fragrant kindness lingered within our home
Her wisdom Godly, sent down from his throne

A mother's love stays with you wherever you are
deep down inside like a bright and shining star

Who'll always be with you through thick and thin
The perfect Rose, My Mother, My Very Best Friend

Gail Beattie

Expressions

People have different ways of
expressing things.
　For "Thanks," it's a Hallmark,
for "I Love You," it's rings.
　For "I'm sorry," it's tears,
for "I trust you," it's the sharing of
your deepest, darkest fears.
　For "Marry me?!", it's kneeling,
and for "I'm nervous," it's climbing the walls
all the way up to the ceiling.
　For "Goodbye," it's a wave,
for "I win the bet," it's making the loser your slave.
　For "You're my hero!", it's a kiss,
and for "Being polite," it's calling a lady Miss.
　For "A reminder of love," it's a hug,
　For "A reminder of an enemy," it's
being called a slug.
　For "Forgive me," it's folding your
hands and praying.
　for "No," it's simply just saying (it).

Jenni Klotz

Overture Of The Betraying

Amidst the fires and rage of a war consumed world
a great shadow arose from the seas of the west, to plunder
and rape the known world, and to bring havoc by the hands
of an engine of death.
Selling Liberty only to those who can afford it,
and feeding of its own spawn, to dominate and usurp
the crown of the world.
The crown of the world is as a drunken trull, wenching
and selling to whatever price might conjure, and the gauntlet
of dawn of peace and order, lies lost in a pool of man's reflection.
Hidden from the righteous, the poor, and the worker, by the pale
notion of union.
And the angels have fallen upon this darken domain as one
bleeding heart they lay upon the alter of the world.
And fear is a sense both unfelt and unfelt in the states and
principalities to which we are enslaved, a dog and his keeper,
standing awkwardly in the wake of the era of peril, where leaders
mislead and a monarch of pestilence arises. One Nation amidst
many we are, one people rivaling an unseen enemy. We are
betrayed and yet we cannot speak of it. We are dying yet we
refuse to look upon ourselves accursed are we, the lepers of
dawn, we strain against perceiving our own horrible reflection.

Russell Rockefeller

Daddy

Daddy, dear Daddy, where did your dreams go?
They fade away faster with each year you grow.
You give up your time, for the family you love.
Praying for strength, from the heavens above.

Remember the child, with the world in his hands?
Is he buried alive, in a world of demands?
Money or love, which will it be? All of a sudden, the
daddy is me. " I'll give it my best," I say to myself,
and the feelings inside, I put on a shelf.

I suppose I could whine, but who's going to care?
They know in their hearts, that Daddy's still there.

Daniel P. Schell

Liquefy

Liquefy our assets, come before us high and dry,
devour the many pieces left in peace.
Multiply our numbers, just like knowing the reason why.
Waiting for the day when life will cease.

Staggering in numbers that will count the final few,
disregard the few who never join.
Deplore the cries of mercy and lament because you knew
Depends on the position of the coin.

Seek the final judgement by the Royal Sovereign King,
obtaining all the answers that you seek.
Behold the blinding catacombs of lies behind that ring.
The tidal wave has reached its highest peak.

Washing from existence into nothingness all round,
bringing to a stop and final sleep.
Stay where feeling comfort in the stable you have found,
but remember more of nothing is to keep.

Beaconing the angels to the place where angels lay,
recalling the beginning of the world,
Hope to see a difference before the troubles gone away,
depending on the way the rings are curled.

Tom Granger

Angel

Today I saw an angel
and it almost made me cry.
For I've never seen an angel
with such sadness in his eye.

It was a sunny morning,
then the clouds rolled in.
I wished I could take away in sorrow
and put his happiness back in.

He's a wonderful little angel,
the best to ever be.
And certainly the best miracle
to ever happen to me.

It makes me sad
to see him his way,
but I've promised him
everything's going to be okay...someday.

Today I saw an angel
and it almost made me cry.
For I've never seen an angel
with such sadness in his eye.

NaHshonee Stillman

Memories

My memories forever haunt me
How well I remember by past life.
Now time passes slowly
Loneliness, filled with strife.

Please tell me, dear Lord, why is it
You've placed me upon this shelf?
Why me? Why me?
I must even ask myself.

"Stay strong," he gently whispers.
"This battle never ending, you have won.
Courage keeps you centred
And love makes you that special
   Innocent someone."

So I gaze out of my window
And watch life pass me by
Never giving up hope
No longer wondering why.

Patricia Dahl-Audziss

Support For My Husband

My husband, overweight, gained thirty pounds in five years,
Suffered with diabetes and hypertension, insomnia and stress.

Taking high doses of insulin, with attacks of low blood sugars,
Went to see a doctor for his medical problems, in November 1995.

The doctor told him to lose weight and ordered some lab test,
All test result were abnormal, and went to see a dietitian,

My husband started on machine home exercises thirty minutes daily,
Ate a very low fat diet, lost weight - about ten pounds in ten weeks.

Exercise duration was increase to sixty minutes on weekends,
Finally he got cured, lost weight, in hundred days with no pain.

Now he believes in exercise, low fat, low calorie diet for all,
To regain better health, he wants to share this secret with you.

My husband is ready to do Yoga and Meditation for insomnia daily,
He bends, twists, pushups, sit-ups, work on all body muscles.

Sits still and Meditates in front of a burning sandalwood sticks,
I videoed the actions, and showed it on local TV for others to see.

More to come on this in the form of poems and prose later,
I won't be surprised, a paperback book published in color by him soon.

What? When? Where? How? There he goes, day and night,
Keep watching the doctor, with smile, MY HUSBAND.

Chaya G. Raju

"Things To Come"

I wonder what it would be like to go out
with her. I wonder what it would
be like to feel her hand
in mine, as our lips touch for
the first time. What would it be
like to share the kind of love two people
share? Like a king's castle on top of a
hill, there are always peasants lined
up competing for her hand. She
doesn't look for thoughts in a guy,
she looks for looks and for popularity.
She needs to look deep within, and
she will find the person who
is true to her. In the end she
will know it was the right choice.

Jason Johnson

Country House

It stands alone in the field
Surrounded by weeds and memories.
Its weather-beaten boards breathe
But reveal no secrets of its life.
The men are no longer called from its fields
To enter into its warmth and love.
There it stands
A stark sentinel to days long past.

Helen M. Armstrong

My Thanks

You bless me today, and bring me tomorrow
When I am lost, you take my hand and
   lead the way
When I awake, you bring happiness as each
   day awaits
Jesus, thank you for showing me your way
You take the ache, when my heart breaks
The pain I no longer feel, is on your
   shoulders now
My thanks for God's will

Patty J. Sublett

"Parents"

As I reflect back over my life, it's strange
to remember such a small soul with eyes wandering
at the strangeness of it all, but at the same time
to feel a protective warmth never consciously
felt before nor will it be recaptured again. For
this cocoon of warmth is due to two souls named
Parents. As I start to grow physically and
spiritually and take a second look at this place
called Earth, gaining courage, knowing that at any
time I can retreat back into my cocoon of warmth,
but at the same time this giving of selfless love
by souls strengthening me for the path that I must
take.....As the years go by I will falter between
right and wrong, but with God's Spirit I will choose
the right path. Knowing again that the invisible
silver cord is there, not holding me back, but
allowing me to grow. To say...I Love You Both
is what I feel inside, was taught to me such a
long time ago.....In the beginning by two selfless
souls giving of their entire being Love!

Brenda A. Kadlik

Hope

Alone, I sat amongst a garden of weeds
wrapped in a blanket of fog
Tendrils of mist wound round my head like a crown
Feeling nothing but misery, I began to drown
A lady came to me in my need and pressed her cool lips to my brow
opened my eyes to a radiant light
Enveloped in warmth and blinded by the sight
She melted away with a fairy's grace
her healing touch removed.
strained my eyes
Yet, hard as I tried
could never see her face

Gretchen Boals

Dream Spell

Here
in Dreamtime's hushed cleansing,
the purity of this thought,
    this emotion,
shall reach for you
and become
    a magnet for your touch
    a beacon for your sight
    a flowering to scent each indrawn breath
    a savory flavor on your tongue
    a musical whisper as you exhale
and finally,
    a stroke of soul across your heart.

Marie Hinchy

Footsteps"

afety is leaving your footsteps behind
ootsteps are the lead to survival
f you follow the footsteps, they will lead you home.
You can leave footsteps on the sand,
then the ocean water will wash the footsteps away.
very footstep is a pace ahead of the last one
ootsteps are individual symbols of recognition.
ach footstep measures a personality
nd every footstep belongs to a person.

ootstep after footstep becomes a path to a persons life
lonely walk into the reality of life leaves a path of footsteps behind.
he longest journey may seem a lifetime of footsteps.
very footstep marks that one moment of existence.

Patty Fagiani

The Sea

Oh the sea,
    the unpredictable sea of love.
Where the wild breezes blow
    and the rain pours down softly...
        from above.

And as a swarming body of water
    rushes toward the sandy beach,
You see a gorgeous ball of fire,
    slipping...sinking...into the waters of
    the unknown deep.

And in the dusk you hear the gulls shrill cry.
    They are trying to find shelter,
        from the chill, of the night.

Then you stop, and realize,
    that the glorious drama you have just beheld,
        was never to be seen again.
For it was the
    Unpredictable Sea of love.

Keli Mayville

A Soldier's Prayer

Dear Lord, I ask one thing of thee
    If I must die for liberty.
My blood I'll shed, my life I'll give
So that justice for all will forever live

My loved ones are left full of pain and fear
Dreading each phone call of what they might hear.
Please give them strength, but most of all,
Give them courage if I should fall.

Into your arms, Dear Lord I'll be
My Guardian angel please send to me.
For Lord if this is my destiny
Our Nation, Under God, Invincible, and with Liberty

Brenda Zakeri

The Unspoken Answer

A loved one weeps. Pain, sorrow, hopelessness, cover his countenance.
Looking for an answer, I shift in my chair, frantically searching for words.
Adrenaline rising. What should I do? Do I touch? What should I say?
I have no answers, no solution to this problem, no cure for this
ailment. Help me, please, God, give me an answer.
An elderly patient, weak, unable to speak, desperately struggles to
raise her hand to me. Others say, "Yes, Yes, we know what you need.
You're out of your mind, but we will help you."
But wait. She's crying out in silence. What does she feel? What
does she want? How can we know? Listen! Don't speak. Touch,
Care, Comfort her. I have no answer. I can't cure you but I'll stay here
with you. You're afraid. It'll be ok. I care about you.
Speak softly, my friend, if you must speak, but please listen to me at
my turn. You hear me, yes, but please listen to me.
Know what I mean by my words. Question me when you don't.
I need this short time to express myself. Please don't interrupt.
I know you have no answers. I don't want answers. I want your mind
and spirit. Be with me now as I speak. I need not an ear but a
mind and spirit. Ears only hear words. Please hear my meaning.

Betty Beshir

The Voice Within

The voice within mine own soul,
Is the voiced of love, I know;
Some folks may say, it's your conscience you hear,
That may be right for them I fear.

I'm never alone or afraid of sinking
My voice within is there night and day,
It always knows just what I'm thinking;
Even if my thoughts are good or bad that day;

The love I feel from my voice within,
Makes me feel tender and safe and warm,
I know my voice inside comes straight from Him:
It helps me to see light at the end of the storm.

My voice within speaks soft and gentle,
But sometimes it roars with rage
Some folks may say, I'm going mental;
But my sweet voice will keep me straight all of my days.

My voice within is called pure love,
It's a comfort to me when I'm alone,
It has come to me from heaven above,
Has been with me since the day I was born.

June Rolson

Child Of Seasons

Wisps, winds, winter blowing,
Stars swirling, seasons going.
Time travels before my eyes,
Oh, the miracles of nature that pass me by.

The sun turning the sky blue, pink, red,
Now Autumn to Winter is wed
And nature drifts to sleep.

As the pure blanket covers the ground,
Silence,
Then the smallest sound.

A child is born, her name is Spring,
Nature begins to awake
And the birds to sing.

Now in her youth,
Spring turns to Summer.
Carefree days, full of golden weather.

Oh, child of seasons, how I envy you,
You laugh and sparkle, love and die,
In the eternal circle.

Ruth Hammond

Missing In Life

A lot of people miss many things in life.
But only some people know it, some people not.
Some people lost all the best, period, of personal life.
Some people's youth day has not seen sun shining.
Some people have not even seen mother's tender care.
Some people's happiness is kidnapped by destiny.
Some people miss most needed education in the path.
Some people think bright day will come towards them.
Some people miss their eyesight, they do not know what it light.
To them it's the same, day and night.
Missed people can understand missing people's sorrow and
depth of the
life, so don't shackle one shelf for dead past and unborn future,
live for present. Proceed your walk on dark without fear.
Think things are out of control of peoples,
But everyone's got good, right to the tune of His glory.
If you miss your right, esteemed time will say sorry.

Kamalini P. Vadera

Changes

Changes are in the mist, changes are near, changes of feelings
run deep—changes so clear. Changes can be seen, changes
of fear, changes no longer still, changes known well,
changes all can tell, changes from those who fell!

Changes are coming near, changes—not fear, changes of life
afire, changes in lives so dear, changes with given share,
changes all can bear. Changes are being made,
changes in moods at play, changes to show the way.

Changes will appear, changes of nature's breed,
changes of life's natural feed, changes at heaven's speed—
changes of danger take heed. Changes for today,
changes from yesterday—changes from inner fear.

Changes—be aware, changes from absence,
changes with dreams, changes with acceptance,
changes in need. Changes to feel—changes made real.
Changes in changes from changes to change.

Changes are at hand! Changes found from taking a stand,
changes to roar throughout this land, changes within a
life span. Changes denied. Do you think you can?
Changes are promised. Changes—be honest.

Julien Bain

"The Bell"

People near and far could not tell,
  the chimes secrets of the bell.
The bell chimes a haunted tune,
  for no one knows what lies within the cocoon.
On certain nights you hear a cry,
  The beast hath risen, so be aware or die.
Run and hide for he will roam,
  On certain nights when he comes out of the catacomb.
He seeks blood as he stalks the night,
  and when he finds you, you will shake with fright.
Because no one ever lives to tell,
  the secret chimes of the bell.

Holly L. Draper

To A Wildflower

Little Wildflower blooming in the dell,
What secrets can you tell?

Are there Robins nesting near?
Do you know where Bees their Honey store?

Do you love the kiss of butterflies and ask for more,
As they gently brush your face,
  And flit from place to place?

Do baby rabbits scamper
  In the grass around your feet,
Playing hide-and-seek?

And when the twilight falls,
  Do fire-flies search you out
And with you their secrets share?

Though no human eye may ever see your face
  Or feel your softness against their check,
Or see you glisten with the dew,

Still, there you stand! Beautiful and full of grace,
Giving all you have.

Happy! Knowing you have found your place; a perfect place,
In all of GOD'S CREATION!

Virginia Rose Wallen

Keepsake

Feelings and Emotions,
Pools of memories that wash ashore the very edges
of the solid Earth.
As we experience the various roads of life,
we test all -
Friendships, relationships,
Family Values.
Wondering what should be - what is.
Changing our perceptions of the world,
we savor our memories
and grasp at our very dreams.
What is it that I mean?
Always live every moment for what it is worth
for as you live on
so do your memories.
Cherish your love of life
and allow your passion to portray you
as you truly are -
Mind and Soul.

Sonal Sheth

The Sounds Of Winter

Winter has come and has made his home here
If you listen closely, you will find that it's near.

The crackling of the fireplace as it brings warmth to those around
The murmurs of snowmobiles as they race over the ground.

The screams of excitement as children slide down the hills
The tea kettle whistles - hot chocolate is ready to chase away chills.

The sounds of cars trying their best,
but engines that just won't roll over
The weatherman says, "You haven't seen anything yet,
the temperatures are going to get colder."

The sniffles, the coughs, the throats that are sore
Winter in Minnesota, who could ask for more?

The popcorn popping as favorite games are being gathered to play
As we all cozy on to enjoy a cold winter's day.

Sharon Whitmore

A Father's Precious Love For His Daughter

Love is a feeling that we all share,
    It's not something given just anywhere.
It is an emotion that must be earned,
    It can't be taught, but it must always be learned.
Sometimes through much heart-ached, but mostly by joy,
    It's not to be thrown around like some fifty cent toy.
A father's precious love for his daughter is just like a yellow rose,
    It starts off small, but it steadily grows.
It blooms and it blossoms in the warm spring air,
    To all this beauty nothing else can ever compare.
My love for you Angel is like a fine piece of art,
    It will go on forever, till death do us part....

Charles E. Hall

A Baby's Prayer

Dear Lord watch oven me as I lie
here not knowing what is wrong.
Look out for mom and me, please help
us both to become strong. I just came
into this world a short time ago. I
have so much to learn, to see, so much
love to give out, like mom has given me.
She carried me inside her for nine long
months, she protected me from harm.
Please let me experience life with
her. Put me back into her arms.

Sandra Young

You Are Never Safe

The circle is an object of safety,
a serene vault of asylum,
a dangerously dark place of no pain,
a gateway; a link to the past.

Join hands in evil covet.
Join hands and call on the spirits.
Our virgin minds and souls together,
empty bodies for you to make your own.

Nothing of you but spirit alone.
Though you are here no pain to us,
'cause we're in the vault of asylum, right?!
Yet the circle can only protect so far.

For if we go too far to your world,
and our minds are too full of knowledge,
there is only a simple dream left,
a hope, a prayer, a chance of return.

Kirsten Martin

H.I.V.

I've looked in the morning on the deep blue
Sea, I found the one with H.I.V.
The cry's, the pain, the sickness, the death.
The one's I've cherished are fading from
Health, I have to stop this pain inside.
I have to help them be alive. For all I know I can not beer.
There are so many things that harm. And worry the ones that care.
You just can't look,
And see the harm it's brought to them, for all
You know they're as healthy as you and me.
For all that seem to be alright.
I just hope you don't get to see the night.
As long as it's still light. I would take into consideration the
trouble that all this causes. They go through shots. So painful
inside. To just look once would provably change your mind.
In cases like this they don't know what to do.
All they can do, is say I love you. If I were one.
There would be one thing in mind, that would be that all would stop
to speak their mind. AIDS is the beginning of truth, to find the cruet,
is still not within youth.

Shannon Greaney

Standing On The Auction Block

As I stand here on this auction block
Waiting to be sold,
My old worn out clothes
Didn't make me look like a sight to behold.

The people in the crowd
Were whispering very softly,
By the way they were looking
I could tell they were talking about me.

I feel as if I'm nothing
As if nobody loves me,
Why do I feel this way?
How can this be?

While a single tear rolls down my cheek
Someone bids one hundred dollars,
Can I have one-fifty,
The auctioneer hollers.

How did this all start?
Where did it begin?
Although it seems very hopeless
Someday, I know, we'll win.

Carrie Janiszewski

Mystifying

The sky bleeds a crimson curtain.
An erie glow radiates from an unseen star.
Desolate, encompassed in my own shadow,
Surrounded in a shroud of darkness.
The echoing of my breath confirms my solitude.
Quivering, my body cringes into a ball of fire.
The foundation of my sanity crumbling

My eyes wander the choking darkness
Trapped in my own world.
My thundering breath deafening —
My body shudders in time with my racing heart.
Tormented by the ever closing gas.

My essence erupts in a shrill shriek.
The darkness retreats.
Blossoming I stand alone.
Mystifying?
Or is it my imagination running wild.
Wild within the wasteland of my dream.

Nathalie Babayan

Tack Så Mycket, Dad

We honored my dad,
the other day.
Respect, dignity and love,
a Swedish-American dove.
A Sweden flag hung from the wall.
Underneath, a wreath was installed.
Vikings and other nations
viewed the blue carnations.
A ribbon with "Vila I Frid"
inscribed in yellow plead.
"Rest In Peace," it decreed!
Two, who came, maybe more,
owed their lives to this physician of war.
Fifty years and no lawsuits!
"Why?" the preacher questioned,
"was this Swede in such a position?"
A surgeon, getting help from God above,
was now in the arms of the one he loved.

James E. Carlson

Friends

'Twas almost 15 years ago when I needed a friend, cause once again
I was alone,
So I look around, found a puppy, I bought her and brought her home.
She was the color of candy and had big brown eyes.
And so I names her Taphi - she was sweet as pie.
I could tell her all my problems and sometimes even cry.
She would snuggle closer and never question why.
I Had Really Found A Friend!

Time seemed to fly and all too soon, our roles seemed to reverse.
Now it was Taphi who was sick and feeling all alone.
Scales on her eyes affected her sight and she could hardly hear.
She lost her teeth and could no longer eat - she wore a look of fear.

The vet said the large knots were probably cancer and she
looked at me as if to say, "What is the answer?"

And so I took to her to the vet and held her in my arms.
She didn't fear cause she knew I loved her and would never do her harm
The shot was quick and she went to sleep knowing how much I cared.
It hurt me deep and the tears fell fast, but from more hurt and
pain she is spared. Taphi Had Really Found A Friend!!!

Neva Everett

A Song Of Spring

Spring! Where are you, this fine day,
While I am sitting in this angry room
'Midst April snowflakes, in the frosty gloom.
And leaden skies all laden, without ray?
I am weak-willed to wait for your ally;
To sit inside and see the leafless bloom
All trembling from the touch of winter's wint'ry tomb
Where are you, spring, so I can out and play?
The robin chirps your near ascent,
And builds his nest from tiny twigs and strings;
I am impatient for your warmth and wing-
For your warm kiss must be spent.
I am restless as the season sing,
But hark...I hear the sigh of Spring!

Larry Becker

My Lost Love

Tonight I walked along the beach,
And heard the ocean's roar.
And looked up at the starry sky,
And felt my spirit soar.

The moon light shone upon the sand
The waves kissed the shore,
There was peace and beauty everywhere
And I was young once more.

Walking with a boy that I loved so
And was so glad I'd met
And though many years have come and gone
Tonight I can't forget.

For our love was not to grow
Because it was a one sided thing
But often I still think of him,
Especially in the Spring.

And so I walk the beach alone
Scuffling through the sand,
And see again a boy and girl
Walking hand and hand.

Madeline Brower

What Happened?

Whatever happened to the hours and the days we used
to enjoy long ago?
Did they shrink and get smaller or change their shape?
Where did all that time go?
I used to make our house a home, looked after our
children too.
Was Secretary-Treasurer of local Red Cross
went to bridge club with friends good and true.
Walked to the library, drove to the store,
Did something worthwhile every day.
Won prizes yearly at our great fall fair, charter member of PTA.
Now I'm bogged down, and so far behind,
Two assignments to do - not just one.
Still owe many letters, though I write and write
And my knitting just does not get done.
So I wonder now, as I think about this,
Sometimes with a little frown.
Did the hours really shrink?
Did my days really change?
Or did I just slow down?

Margaret M. Ritza

I Wait Patiently

I wait patiently just to hear from you.
I long to hear your voice, just a word or two.
I listen for the phone but it doesn't ring.
Might as well go to bed, see what tomorrow will bring.
In my dreams you are always here with me.
Holding you feels great, through only fantasy.
The morning is bright but the sun doesn't shine.
There is a shadow hanging over this heart of mine.
You're on my mind twenty four hours a day,
I need to know who will win this game that we play.
I believe that every one has a destiny.
You can't fight what is meant to be,
but if you choose the wrong road you leave fate behind.
Now traveling separately is your body, soul and mind.
My body is here, my mind is lost, my soul must be with you.
How can you bring it back if you don't have a clue?
It is wrong for me to feel this way inside
but it is also wrong to take my love and hide.
Are you out there some where feeling alright?
What are you thinking of on a night like tonight?

Christine Murphy

A Verse Or Two....

The pen and mind have been longing for the ink to flow and ebb
I feel it is time to break the silent web
It has been a while since I have written a verse
My writings have been blessed, they have been cursed
The wondering of each aimed at ones demeanor
A pen can be gentle, or all the meaner
In the future, better the foremost than the latter
I much prefer a pleasant subject matter
The pen is a tool all of its own will
It is complex, abstract, and simple as it provides a thrill.

Stephen Saporito

An Immigrant's Journey

Land gradually disappearing; erased by carpet of white,
Torn heart crying to return
Listless hours haunted by memories,
Threatening unknowns, tomorrow will be a stranger.

Mind restlessly considering; facing the passing of time,
Worn heart clutching the present
Quickened thoughts unsure expectations,
Awaiting arrival, tomorrow may be a helper.

Now breathlessly encountering; piercing the carpet of white,
Waked heart seizing the moment
Renewed soul courage and determined,
Welcoming the entrance, tomorrow has become today.

Michael Pilapil

Day To Day

The morning light was shining through the shade.
It was time to get up and start the day.
Streaks of sunlight across the room played,
Creating a picture that said it's time to pray.
Also a reminder the bed was not the place to stay.
Covering your head is not the way to start a day
Get up. Bend a knee, before you start to play.
Say those prayers you had failed to say.
Thank him for what life brings. No day the same,
Each one a picture to remain in your memory frame.
Days to play, to live, create, to enjoy and play.
To kneel to say "Thank you"; it's so little to pay,
A prayer for that good life you have each day.
Each one beautiful, days of love, work, or play.
Just say "thank you Lord" there is no more to say.

W. Drury Clark

Grandma's Story

"Jesu Madia! Jesu Madia!" Grandma would sigh
Hands to her cheeks as she uttered her cry.
"The nun would shake me, wake me at four a.m.
Come on Tillie, it's time to get up;
the abbey need be fired up."

"It's cold and dark; please don't make me go today."
Her face puckered in pain, whimpering as if eight again.
Rocking back and forth, clasped hands beat her breast.
"I was afraid, so afraid, so afraid; but sister would say,
God goes with you, just pray all the way."

"Into the icy darkness, slowly, slowly, on tippy toe I'd go.
First raising my lamp through each doorway, I'd take a peek.
Into each empty room I'd sneak, kindling a fire in the dirt.
Then I'd run like the dickens from the lurking shadows that
would suddenly grow out of the hearth."

"Half walking, half running up hallways and down,
I'd trip on my nightgown during every morning round.
Finally done, in the chapel, I'd meet the sun.
Many a time this story was told when Grandma
was near and more then eighty years old!

Diana Loveric

I Shall Not Hide

Beneath the satin softness of my skin
    That you so cherished, lay deceit within.
My mask of honor, faith and decency
    But poorly hid the fear that burned in me.

All unaware, you let your dreams unfold
    Into those depths of sweetness, yet untold
That you beheld within your precious bride.
    If only that's what I had seen inside.

That wondrous love which we had brought to birth
    Would Eden's garden made upon this earth.
But there 'neath angel's eyes was death reflected
    That I knew not, from my own soul projected.

And oh, so far we've traveled now since then
    I fear I shall not see Love's face again.
Yet hope bids me to cry into the night
    Just once more, to behold that precious sight.

The vision of love's eyes caressing mine.
    A chance to climb love's mountains one more time
And from those heights proclaim both far and wide
    "Love, seek me just once more... I shall not hide."

Sheila M. Sliter

The Letter

I went to the mailbox, one beautiful day.
And found your letter, from far away.
It made me so happy, I started to cry
And realized then, I could never say bye.
To what I was feeling deep inside.
Even though we weren't together.
As lovers should be, I kept on believing in you and me.
I searched my heart, inside and out
And soon realized without any doubt
I didn't know what to do.
I only knew, I was in love with you.
I tried and tried not to let is show,
But something told me that you would know.
So I kept praying to God above
That somehow I would win your love
Then I got that little sign,
Even though it took some time
I got an answer to my prayer
God showed me you really cared. Now were together, you and me,
Thanks to God above, we were meant to be.

Katrina L. McAninch

Life, Love And Children

White all around, beautiful and cold
Sitting in my old chair, I wonder
How many winters lay asunder
Will we still be together, love behold.

I long for summer and birds singing
Flowers blooming, the rain and the sun
Squirrels rummaging, people walking and jogging
Teenagers on roller blades, children having fun.

Youth long gone, golden years remain
What will happen to us, we can still dream
Of good times past, of joy and pain
But we must keep living as a team.

My darling, I still love you with all my heart,
Everyday, I thank God for finding you
I hope and pray, we always remain together sweetheart
You are my constant companion, I belong to you.

Life was grand, we were dealt a good deal
What about our children, living day by day
Life not so rosy for them, misery is real
The rest of our life, dedicated for their happiness today.

John McMurtie

"The Wonder Why There Is Trouble In The World"

We wonder why there is trouble in every part of this world,
we over look those we call our leaders that cause the trouble and more
Things are not going to get any better because we fail to do our job,
to get rid of those trouble making leaders and give thanks to God.

The people must work together in every country that we know,
to stop the hunger and killing the whole truth must be told.
With the unholy alliance the United States have supporting
Israel and its crimes. So much has been hidden from the people
of the World there is no mistake.

The raiding of the Social Security funds by the C.I.A. and
others, the lies being told to the people that Social Security is
broke, is much the same being told by the U.S. Government
about everything else. Why the American people believe
anything politicians say is enough to have a stroke.

When people refuse to hear the truth and listen to politicians' lies,
they get exactly what they ask for and their complaints fall on deaf
ears. Instead of asking themselves why there is so much crime, drugs
and killing, they should be working to get all crooked politicians
out and put honest ones in.

God helps those that help themselves in doing the right thing in
dealing with all. He gives us six senses to learn much and know
when we are right or wrong. And when we fail to act and stand
up for right and put wrong to shame. Then what befalls us is
our own fault and one day we will take that great fall.

Rudolph V. Freeman

"Me"

If I were somebody who would I be?
Who is this person inside of me?
This person without an identity?
I've looked at myself, from without and within.
I need some direction, but don't know where to begin.
My whole life, I have wanted just to belong.
I would deny myself to please others,
I know now I was wrong
I have played the game, as so many do.
I've come to realize that true friends are so few.
I've played wife and mother.
I've gone from one marriage to another.
I've made my mistakes, one right after the other.
I still find myself searching, looking into this empty space.
Trying to face this person, without a name, without a face.
If I were somebody, who would I be?
How will I find this person... this person.

Laura Bates

Yosemite

This sir, surely is the gateway to my heaven.
The valley of light, waterfalls, and hard granite walls,
second unto none other.
El Cap, the master. Half Dome, the mother.
I, her son, her mate, my master.
Higher Rock, my elder brother is.
Bold and strong, stand he tall.
Middle Rock, my sister is,
beauty incomparable has she,
facing north while setting sun slides gently towards the west.
Oh, to sit upon my younger brother's shoulder,
Lower Cathedral,
and see the first rays of morning light touch my master's brow.
To quote a friend is, "To be amazed."
Born to the rock and life on a vertical wall.
To death, this life I choose to live, and would have none other.

Loyd Price

What Is The Measure Of A Man?

Is a man measured by wealth and fame?
Or by a bank account or a haughty name?
Or is he measured by other things
Like shiny cars of diamond rings?

No, I submit that is not at all
What makes a man seem strong and tall.
It's things like faith and humility
That makes a man seem like a strong oak tree.

It's love of his wife and his family
That makes him seem real strong to me.
The one whom we honor here today
Is one who has measured up in every way.

Though he never achieved worldly acclaim
He left his mark here just the same.
You see... he measured up in every way
To what a man should be today.

S. Eric Kyles

"Love"

Love which is the most difficult mystery,
Asking from every young one answers,
And most from those most eager and most beautiful,
Love is a bird in a fist,
To hold it, — hides it,
To look at it, — let it go,
It will twist loose if you
Lift so much as a finger,
It will stay if you cover it —
Stay but unknown and invisible,
Either you keep it forever with fist closed,
Or let it fling,
Singing in fervor of sun and in song vanish,
There is no answer other to this mystery.

Rachel Smith

Abandoned

The lonely house sits upon the dead grass.
As the wind cries out and whispers to the
shutters: Free me from the sky.
A loud cry sounds out to the sky,
As the totem poles lean toward the house.
An old man comes walking along
And spots a photo of himself as a boy.
Then a tear lands on the ground.

Heather Thompson

Bee

Life to the flower is a simple task
yet our fulfillment's hope seems vague and masked.
In sweet submission to beckoning spring
lilies surge, bloom, then die unflattering
into the whispered hush of winter's peace,
complete and one with nature's fond increase.
Behold the blossom of their radiance —
a Joy's reflection, Wisdom's immanence —
Truth through Beauty resting for awhile
rejoicing in the hymn hummed by The Smile
whose chosen instrument, the willful bee,
could teach the alchemist true alchemy.
Seeking, we remember that our birth,
Creation's highest art, is formed from earth —
the same sustaining grip that holds the flower —
and soul — a gift from Breath's instilling Power!
Finding, we are one with Mercy's Grace
to simply Be and be simply the vase.

Thomas R. Flebotte

Our Savior

Christ the Lord was born this day,
All have come to kneel and pray.

God and man, all in one,
Christ Jesus, the newborn son.

Lying in a manger outside na inn.
He came down from the heaven to forgive our sin.

He healed his people throughout the land,
With a prayer to the father and a touch of his hand.

John Baptized him in the Jordan water,
He came to save every man, wife, son and daughter.

A dove came down from heaven above,
"This is my son sent to you in love."

He told about a heaven of peace and no tears,
A home for all without any fears.
They all wept and begged him to stay.

Jesus shed his blood for all mankind.
Now we who are born again have peace of mind.

Praise to you, my Lord above,
You come to us with love, love, love!

Bill L. Roloff

Dancing Daffodils

Please believe me, I see them dancing.
I see the Daffodils dancing here and there.
They are dancing in the fields, the gardens,
through the hills, the mountains and along the rivers.

Please believe me, I see them dancing.
I see the Daffodils dancing by the sidewalks,
in the parks, the front yards, the back yards,
at the seaside, and all along men's steps.

Please believe me, I see them dancing
I see the Daffodils dancing an unfamiliar music.
In fact, they are dancing the Eternal Symphony of Nature,
Which is as subtle and as captivating as Nature itself.

Please believe me, I see them dancing.
I see the Daffodils dancing a music that spreads peace and love,
bliss and harmony throughout the globe.
Indeed, human race will be forever changed.

Please believe me, I see them dancing.
I see the Daffodils dancing and some people imitating them.
Alas! No one can catch up with the rhythm of this music.
Please! Do not give in and you will climb the steepest mountain.

W. Jean-Noel

Steel-Toed Blues

Reach out and touch the world that be
Construct a new life for he
The gentleness is gone; worn out
No more blocks to move, not for me

Thirty years of rock and sand
Dusty and grit on skinless hand
His worst limb is the back that cracks
Incidents to look at but he stops not at that

Retirement moons away
He fell under by just one day
A slave to employment this way
Fallen on concrete malaise

Yes he is quite blue
Blue as the wound in his steel toe shoe

Serena Weekes

Different Stride

I'll take a stand today, and this is where I will stay. To keep my
head high walk and with my own stride. I know now that I am not
the same person yesterday as I am today. Letting no one get in my
way. Listening not to what other people around me have to say.
Because I don't dress a certain way, they have certain things to say.
But I will keep my head high and walk on by, looking to the future and
not the past. This journey of life begins, with many heartaches.
Love and emotions take over my heart to make my heart feel weak.
I shall not dwell in the past. I'll move forward knowing God is at
my side, holding my hand, and leading me though life, and removing
my shell that has protected me for so long. Now my protection is up
to me, leaving my life that used to be. The people in my life who
have caused my pain, I still love them today Even though it will
never be the same. I know that it had to be for me to keep my head
high, just to be proud for what I stand for. No one can take that
way from me, because I know in my heart I can keep my head up
and high and walk with my own stride, and taking pride in my
accomplishments today and my goals tomorrow.

Sylba M. Lathem

Three Little Tears

Three little tears today I shed, for the one who brings me day.
Three little tears today I shed, for I miss my little boy.
For my thoughts of him bring laughter, and my thoughts of him bring
cheer and my thoughts of him bring sadness, for I wish to have him near.

Three little tears for him I cry, yet I know he doesn't know
That I really, truly miss him and I truly love him so
For I wish to hold him in my arms, and I wish to hold him tight.
And I know if he was with me now, he would wipe my tears on sight.

For to me he's one in a million, and he's all I seem to have
He's the one who makes me smile, though inside I'm really sad.
For you see, today I'm lonely, and my heart is full of shame
And my pride is torn to pieces, because of the day I walked away.

Three little tears today I shed, in all sincerity
Three little tears for him I cry, because guilty is my plea
Football, baseball, basketball, and swings over the sand
I'm guilty of missing his growing years, and it truly makes me sad

My son today I cry for you, cause I really miss you so
My son this pain is killing me, for it hurts within my soul.
All I'm trying to say my son, is I wish to have you near

Roger James

If I Had A Slave...

If I Had A Slave - He could not keep my books
He could not man my kitchen and surely he couldn't cook

He would be a servant so never could he be my friend
He could raise my cattle but never my children

If I Had A Slave - What would I say to God
Could I tell God that I'm fruitless without my slave with heart

What about my mom and dad who passed their ways to me
Who made me their beneficiary to deprive those who aren't free

If I Had A Slave - I'd chain myself to him
to feel the woes of what he knows about who gave life to him

If I Had A Slave - How could I sleep at night with closed eyes
seeing dreams of days of justice right

How could I reach for happiness and allow not bits for some
How could I own all gifts of joy and share not one with none

If I Had A Slave - I'd be wise enough to know

That God would not forgive me
That God would not forgive me

If I Had A Slave
        Alton L. Littles Jr.

Untitled

It was a beginning
Innocence, Safety and Love
There was growth
Friendship, Learning and Fun
I found something Out about Myself
Differences, teasing and isolation
Then I found my own kind
Passion, Truth and Prejudice
I developed my Pride
Independence, Responsibility and Success
I told all
Confusion, Doubt and Acceptance
I was my own Person
Love, Sex and More
What I learned next changed my Life
Anger, denial, bargaining, depression, acceptance
It Ended In The Blood
        Stacy Donnelly

The Hole In The Grass By My Parking Space

It's there in the church yard getting bigger each year;
The hole in the grass where I park.

I've been noticing it now for several years,
And at the first, couldn't see how it started.

But as I watched and observed at the end of each service,
The reason became perfectly clear.

The kids had been gathering to talk with each other,
And they always gathered right there.

I had made some remarks to friends as we talked,
Of the dirt that appeared in my car.

"Lock the doors," they would say, "keep them away,
For you know how disrespectful they are."

But I couldn't agree, for what I could see
Were the friendships that were growing there.

If my car needed cleaning after each trip to worship,
Why should I need to care.

For by the car use of my car and the hospitality it showed,
The kids made a bond that would last.

And it's pleasing to me as I continue to see,
By my parking space a hole in the grass.
        Connie LaValle

When Love Finds You

You awakened my heart from its slumbering state.
When you walk into the room
It's as if the sun has by passed the moon.

Every inch of me comes alive once again I asked myself "Why?"
When I don't see your face I miss you and a part of me dies.

When you stare in my direction, those eyes are like a match
that ignites a fire within me.

As I walk close by, you begin to blush
For me to cause this, is better than any touch.

I can't control how I feel because this seems so real

There's nothing in the world I'd want to see
Than when you turn around and smile at me.

Heaven is when I'm held in your arms
Feeling safe and protected from harm.

To me, life seems so fair because you truly care.
My soul sings when you're near
I wonder if you hear but at the same time I'm in fear....

Will I lose this love of yours
While now my heart still soars.

It is a chance and risk we all endure and what for....
This desire has taken me away with no say
When love finds you there's not much you can do.
        Julie Lachman

A Pause

Fishing in a mountain stream, deep in the woods
    Where not too many men have trod - just God.
A stream tumbling down a mountain of rock,
    Bounding through space into a pool at the bottom.
This mortal looks around - small and insignificant.
    Tons of rocks rising high on one side,
A mountain of stately pines on the other,
    At my feet the falls have subsided to tranquility.

Is this life rushing by, then pausing to meditate,
    Perhaps to reflect, refresh and to refuel?
A tall mountain of rock - could be my worry of yesterday.
    I turn it over, around and let it revolve
As the water tumbles downward.
    Suddenly a solution pierces my mind
Like the peaceful bubbling creek at my feet, and
    All is right within this mortal.
        Lahoma M. Cook

I Never Thought!

I never thought my life would be a total mess, a catastrophe.
I never thought I'd ask my pastor to pray for me and my disaster.
I never thought I'd be alone, without my family, without my home.
I never thought that she would leave, or how my heart would
ache and grieve.

I never thought that we would fight, throughout the day,
throughout the night.
I never thought that love would die, or how I'd hurt, or how I'd cry.
I never thought that I'd hurt her with my frustrations and anger.
I never thought problems I brought home would destroy her
love and our home.

I never thought that I would see my kids crying, saying
goodbye to me.
I never thought I could feel so old, or a lover's heart could turn so cold.
I never thought I would hurt my wife, I know I'll love her all my life.
I never thought of the trouble I've bought, all because ....
I never thought!
        Robert L. Hansen

What Kind Of World Is This?

As I sit here,
and watch the waves,
crash against the shore, I wonder,
What kind of world do we live in?

Is it a world,
of peace and tranquility,
or a world,
of hate and crime?

The waves crash hard,
like hate and crime,
but roll gently,
like love and peace.

The forest fires,
are like war, destroying everything,
and the sea gulls,
are our children, flying free.

Is it a question, that can be answered?
Because I think, we live in both.
We live in two worlds,
So different, they are the same.

Kristen Harding

Unpure Love

I trusted you, you let me down.
You turned my smiles into frowns.
I gave you everything I ever had.
Little did I know you'd treat me bad.
I cry for you now all the time.
Even while I write this rhyme.
You left me now, I'm all alone.
Now all I do is cry and moan.
I sit at night by my bed.
The nights we shared still in my head
Will these feelings ever end?
Can my broken heart make amend?
I wish these feelings would leave for sure.
I know that now your love
was unpure.

Jeannie Townsend

Unexplainable Love

How can I tell you how much I love you so, when they haven't made the words to hear, how I love you so.

You know I'll be here, when we grow old, just by looking at the tear in the morning glow.

I've learned from life, from my grandma so dear, how important it is to fulfill each year.

When we walked down the aisle, and said "I do," we became one instead of two.

When the day breaks, and I know you are near, it gives me the strength for the year.

We made our mistakes, that cost us so dear, but now we know how to say "that's alright honey, I love you any way."

God forgives us and protects us for he knows, how much we love each other so.

Norma Settle

No Tears

As you lay alone longing for companionship, you fe
depressions and despair
Yet you shed no tears and you do not weep
There seems to be no worth to your life
Though you feel the emptiness of your lack of emotion
You wish upon the first star you can find that your sanity will let
you free but the star isn't listening
It lets you down in its moment of glory
You are alone in the darkness of your sadness
Beyond the reach of all people
You see no light at the end of the tunnel
No second chance
Your dreams and aspiration lay in ruins
Leaving you alone again
You stare blindly at the darkness
The only lights is coming from the glimmering ember of your heart
You can't understand how you can feel this way
You are naive in your innocence; although you have a knowing stare
And as the tears finally begin to fall a smile appears
You have conquered the emptiness you have won.

Mike Dempsey

The World Today

If you think the world today is a paradise,
You're living in dreams, not real life,
So think about guns, rape, violence and death,
I'm not done yet, so hold your breath.

What about violence in the media today,
It influences kids in a very bad way,
Think about alcohol and drugs in the world,
Actually, just thinking about it makes me hurl.

The future of our kids is at stake,
They will suffer because of our mistakes,
We are the ones who pollute the air,
And the animals suffer, it's just not fair.

We have to stop polluting and doing things we'll regret,
And maybe somewhere along the line,
Our happiness will be met,
And our world will still have a chance,
For joy, harmony and even romance.

Simonne Mendes

My Journey

I can't see where I am going
But I know I'm being led
And I know my hungry spirit
By my Lord is being fed...
When I pray to Him in silence
I can feel my heart grow still
All seems wall within my spirit
When I say "Lord, do They Will."
Tho' my life is but a vapor
To my finite mind its long
And I've learned some painful lessons
But I've also heard life's song...
Tho' you've chastened me, you've loved me
Tho' you molded me thru strife
Thank you, God, and thank you, Jesus
For my journey thru this life!

Ardell Sipple

Friendship

God has given many things
In this great big world I pleasure
But Friendship is His greatest gift
And one thing your should treasure.

For nobody gets it for you
It's a thing we all must learn
That boughten friendship is no good
It's something you must earn.

Your friendly smile, or cheery words
The nice things that you do
All play a part in showing us
What makes the inner you.

So don't lock them up inside you
Please share them like a brother
And you will see whenever you do
Your friendliness touches others.

So pick your friends for what they are
Not for what they're worth
And you'll taste the pleasure of sharing in
God's greatest gift on earth.—— Friendship.

Kay Lafrenie

Love Of Others

O listen to my voice, and let me tell you about others
That give me peace within, and a smile with-out,
For the love of others is pure as yellow gold.
If it be a smile, or to see a tear that falls
From a cheek that has been weather-worn, I see
O the love of others, and what it means to me.
If it be Janet, Peggy, or Marie, one or all three,
For the years have been so gracious to these,
To one or all three, for in their eighties they be.
For each day for their eyes to see,
As they greet the rising sun and a new days dawning.
When others come along, and join thee others three,
For Mable, Ruth and others, also are a joy to me,
As they join and come along with others three.
O the love of others, and how can this be,
To know that God has been so precious to me.
In having others, come along with all of these.
O the love of others, come and see
All of these, and others, that have shown love to me,
As God has really been a blessing, from all of these.

Doris M. Friese

Car Poem

I get into the car; I look into the mirror,
My mother yells out, 'Good luck to you, Dear!'

I pull out of park, and I turn off the brake,
Then I run over the fence, and over the rake!

I turn around the corner; I'm on the avenue,
Then I hit a black Mercedes, and a fire hydrant, too!

So I look to the left; I look to the right,
Thank you God! There's not a cop in sight!

I screech into the parking lot; I run over the curb,
I listen very carefully. Was that a siren that I heard?

So I run into the building, excited as can be,
I go to straight to a clerk who says, 'Welcome to the D.M.V!'

I take the Driver's test; my hands are getting sweaty,
The clerk hands me an envelope, to open when I'm ready.

I hop into the car, to make the journey home,
And I open up the envelope with my favorite comb.

I walk into the kitchen; I'm greeted with a high five.
For after seven tests, I'm finally licensed to drive!

Now I'm finished with my story; I hope you won't complain,
Because my care keys are handy and I can drive you insane!

Kristen Adams

Reconciled In Our Sleep

If ever there's a thistle between us
Meteors belch in an acid sea
My love only honks from her distance
Like a Canada Goose

But once I hold her asleep
A rose lamb in our bed of mint
She breathes up and down her kitten nostrils
She clutches the joint of a bear's thumb

All through the whites, yellows, reds of a daisy's night
Our conflicts and stitches dissolve in rest
Our stems ooze more jokes through their fibres -
Emotions turn to such garden colours
As the fingers of dawn still show

John King-Farlow

I

Told my son to stay at home
For earlier he fed me a lie.
Slid out the window at a quarter to three.
Rebelling, and making me cry.

Invited my daughter to feed the pigs.
She despised it, and so this I planned.
Though when she was called, she did as requested,
Fearing, since I am at hand.

Then came the day to reward all the worth,
Patience warrants the treasure.
My daughter received, but my son was left dry.
He traded the life for his pleasure.

Anger became him as envy brewed.
And fighting to win at the game,
He killed half my sheep, packed and left home.
Tragically, he'll burn in the flame.

Chad A. Marbut

A Sunday Carousel Ride

There are perhaps no more endearing thoughts
of childhood than ones first carousel ride.
There is a charm, a feeling, an awakening
of imagination that happens, and makes
a child feel good inside.
The detail of the horses, each one so unique.
The music of the pipe organ, adding to the mystique.
Mother and dad so correctly dressed,
and we feeling so proud in our Sunday best.
Like knights holding their swords high,
we cling to the bar of the carousel.
Round and round, up and down,
Spinning to caliopied sounds,
A wonderful place to revisit this time,
The carousel memory going round in my mind.

Jack DeYoung

Friend

One who is attached to another by affection
And by ones being of respect in ways of
Love, moral rules and thought of purity
In the way of life pertaining to a humanistic being
And discipline to the religion of the law
"Of our father God"
When one entwines the golden web together
In joining with another one
She or he can claim that a
"Beloved friend is found"

Geraldine Cutler

Wonder

I sing for you, I sing a song that tells of the troubles and the hardships of our time and our people. I play for you, I play a melody as sweet as ambrosia that only the gods may drink. I read to you, I read a poem that voices the feelings of our time and our generation. I act for you, I perform a play that through the motions of my body expresses the life and form of my soul and of yours. I cry for you, out of my eyes flow tears that hold the sorrow of you and all the world. I pray for you, I pray that the gods may look down on the wretched Earth that they created and have pity for their wayward subjects and that they may show mercy to us as well. I wonder. I learn for you, I learn the philosophies and secrets and beliefs of the ancients so that I can share them with you. I ask why for you, I ask why do we torture ourselves over meaningless things and constantly do wrong to our fellow man? I wonder. I wonder for you. I sing for you. I pray for you. I read to you. I act for you. I cry for you. I learn for you. I ask why for you. I live for your beauty and your grace and I will miss you when we part.

Stephen R. Maynard

Black Rain

The black rain started to pour down from the sky,
They hit the ground with a silent cry.
A dreadful scream pierced my ears,
As people ran with streaming tears.
Instead of waving a simple good-bye
the message spelled time to die,
Many died throughout the night as rain did
not end till morning light.

Years have passed since that rain fell but
the memories live on from those days of Hell.

Kimberley Rose

"The Seduction Of Spring"

Warmth and light. The sun is shining.
Flowers blooming; beautifully striving.
Cabalistic yellows, golds and vibrant greens,
bubbling brooks and gentle flowing streams.

A light breeze, a soft cascade,
The sounds of nature: A calming synchronized serenade,
A bright pure and fresh beginning.
Whispers of the wind, bashful birds singing.

Rebirth. The cleansing of the soul,
new hopes and dreams to cherish and hold.
The canvas of life: The beginning that never ends.
Spring is a mystical seduction - a welcomed friend.

Elizabeth Bonham

Star

Why can't I be a star in the midnight sky,
Looking down from miles up high?
Everything would seem uncomplicated.
I would not have to deal with the things that I hated.
I would not have to look in the mirror each day
And wonder if everything will be okay.
I would not have to worry about hurting anyone,
Or if I was possibly... maybe... liked by someone.
Liked, or even loved, for who I am, me,
And not who I appear to be.
If I were a star in the clear night sky,
Looking down from way up high,
Then someone might look up at me,
    with even the smallest glance,
And see that I can be beautiful
    if given half a chance.

Joylyn Harvey

Nana

Nana is a fat old woman
She eats her food straight from the pan
She eats all day
She eats all night
Then she will pray
Help me in this fat fight

Nana just sits all time
The most she does is make a rhyme
She doesn't like to travel
Her road is made of gravel

Nana's not happy much
Until I give her a love touch
I take care of Nana we eat peanut butter and banana

Nana wears a great big dress
I hear her always say God Bless
Nana wears no shoes
She counts her toes by twos

Nana never wears underwear
And very seldom combs her hair
Nana has a heart of Gold
And she loves me I am told

Kaylyn Chandler

These Are The Precious Days Of Our Lives...

How much longer will man on earth realize.
We are living closer to nature called mother nature.
But it's threatened by man changes the environment in his hands,
with pollution yes it's a critical fact, but the trees grow back
ruin the earth, with drugs that whack, imagine food and shelter
for those who's laid back this is a warning a wide
spread good morning no time to waste he also dumped garbage
and oil all over the place contaminated the water for whose son or
daughter so I think, precious day's to think about chemicals
that's set like a time bomb ready to go off.
This type of pollution, thousands will be lost.

Nelson Norman

Untitled

My room is my world
My little window is the door
To the other, out there
I sit and watch life pass by
My room, my world
Each is going somewhere, someplace,
To see someone
Yet I sit and watch from my little
Window
For I have no where to go, no one to see
My room is my world
And there is no one in it but me

John G. Murray

Rainbow's End

A tale was told by my Irish kin,
about a pot of gold at every rainbow's end.
So I followed a bow for miles and miles,
over mountains and valleys to the Sandwich Isles,
and there is where I found its end,
the pot of gold were the eyes of a friend!
Oh, please wait, you must hear the end!
Not all rainbows end with a friend!
Some with candy, and some with money,
but that's not as good, nor very funny.
So be careful where you go, and what you do,
because someone's rainbow might end with you!

S. C. Wood

An Enduring Hour

So let us, of this hour, understand thee as nigh restless sea,
unformed and abysmal in its depths, yet bespeaking movement,
and in its roundness inexhaustible, bestowing life upon dawning
soil as is most reverent, and therewithal, amenable to its benefaction.
And lo! Benefaction sweet and enduring—tell us who of all shall
ne'er comprehend Thee in the subtlety of this sea's movement;
for o'erlong has Man been wooed by the nature of the word,
solemnest of appellations, *God*, Thy name, as it styles an object.
Nay, but Thou art more unauthorable than that, assuredly,
and descried Man not Thy face until he knew Thee as occurrence,
as noun become now verb, for Thou dost not see, but Thou art
Seeing itself, dost not know, but art knowing itself, unascertained.
And alas! For he is o'erfilled with joy who seeks not absoluteness,
who yearns not for a Being, but rather *Be-ing*, beseeches not a thing,
but only that suspiring ineffably betwixt all things; just as the sea,
unformed and abysmal, bestows its life upon, nay, *as* dawning soil,
so dost Thou as perseverance bequeath his own being to Man,
thus both appearing and concealed - at once - in Thy temporality:
He, Man: wooed by the very language as gift which makes him so;
Thee: Therein entrusting all Being; for veritably Thou art Thyself *Time*.

M. W. Robidoux

Summer Storm

Blue sky reigns unchallenged by clouds
Oppressive heat is provided by the ruling one
Movement is slowed, vitality drained
Earth's kingdom begs for mercy from the sun

The sun displays his power
Mocking his subjects the weakness of their way
Brown grass yearns for its youth
Cursing the despotic ruler of the day

Rule is not eternal. Dark warriors invade
Engaging the light in a violent duel
The sun senses the power of surrounding darkness
Slowly it retreats, surrendering rule

Waves of ebon claim the sky
The gift of rain enlivens the land
Green returns from its banishment
Branches stretch upward a worshipping hand

The dark saviors do not cease
Tyrannical, they honor night, shackling the day
A cowering Earth cries for relent
And shards of welcome light pierce the grey

Ken Dudgeon

The Prophet

Such is the detail for all to see
What is to come, and what is to be.
Death to oppressors, the beasts set free.
Those left living, damnation for eternity.

Yet what could bring about such a fate?
For surely these questions, one must ask.
But the answers, I fear, have come too late.
The dark one has undertook his task.

He knows no boundaries of riches or age.
Be they young or poor, they're all the same.
As life is his symphony, death his stage,
All are mere parts to fulfil the game.

So, close to hearts and souls they hold,
Generations to recite as best they can.
For never has such a tale been told,
Then the triumph of death, and downfall of man.

Sarah Bauder

The Rift

Marshmallow hands with knuckle-less skin
A tiny round baby he was back then
I had not planned, I had not said
Let's have a son, it's okay — go ahead

That mattered little when his eyes met mine
When he smiled, the whole universe was fine
I laughed when he buried his hands to the wrist
In his first birthday cake — oh, what a mess

As a teen he wrenched my heart and it bled
Isolation and sadness were his best friends
I kept thinking that soon his spirits would lift
The only thing we saw clear was the rift

Where life's promises once laid unspent
Now was the rift all rotten and bent
Being a dad is not what I'd thought
For my son is right here yet he's really lost

Sure, we spoke the right words, but nothing came out
Sounds empty and useless, yet thrown about
For I did not bend, I had not said
I love you son, it's okay — go ahead.

Dallas Orr

Blue Emperor

Beautiful to behold
Delicate and free,
Fluttering as you fly
In all your majesty.

Exquisite in form,
Intricate in detail,
Like the finest tapestry.

Blue Emperor is it any wonder that you are revered?
You are much more than a decorate ornament
A frame captured by a photographer's lens.

Resting on a petal of a white orchid
You remain motionless, reflective, undisturbed.

Suddenly a cupped hand reaches out to embrace,
But you are too quick, too clever, and escape its grasp
Leaving your humble abode just as swiftly as you entered.

You are a symbol of freedom
A better tomorrow,
A promise of hope
A negation of sorrow.

Pauline Pitcher

Life I Pray

My innocent life so tender and frail;
I cannot yet cry, breathe, or tell.
The pain I'll endure if I'm torn away;
All I ask is life I pray.

Oh mother dear, tell me what did I do?
I surely didn't mean to hurt you.
I came to be without a say;
Is nine months that long of a wait?

Are you too young?
Is it your career?
Or is it giving life,
What you really fear?

If I am gone, there's no angelical face;
No child to take to the zoo or some neat place.
Not a cry to hear, nor a whisper of laughter;
If I'm not wanted, give me up at birth, thereafter.

The choice is yours, what more can I say;
All I ask is life — I pray.

Diane Marie Sobota

One Tree Hill

Only the true shall walk upon the grounds of
one tree hill bare foot.
Only the depressed shall seek warmth and comfort
upon the trees arms.
And there they shall die by the arms.
The untrue shall die at the foot of the hill.
The true shall be mourned by the winds of God.
And the untrue by the bugs.
There they shall lie for eternity for all us to see,
And show us what might happen at our one tree hill.
But I shall stand at the foot of the hill,
For I am untrue.
And glaze upon he true with eyes of sorrow
and a heart of desire.

Anita Robidoux

I Love Snow

God made earth and God made sky
    God made you and God made I
He made high and he made low
    He made cloud and he made snow.
When I was a little boy, tender, silky and glow
    I jumped in my mother's arm and wanted to touch the snow
My mother pat, me kissed me and never let me go
    As I grew big I touched the twig and
Made the bubble blow.
    Sometimes I jump, sometimes I thump and
Sometimes resting on silky snow
Life became busy, work hard to pull the cart
    Sometimes it's loud, sometimes it's slow and
Sometimes it became pause
    Then one day when Christmas came I became Santa Claus
I saw snow on my head snow on my face
    Snow on the roof and snow on the surface.

God gave me snow from high to low because
    (I love snow)

Saroj Kumari Sikka

Messenger Dove

I had a dream last night
As the stars flickered bright
And in the form of a dove that is pure and free
The clouds gathered together and whispered this to me

She loves you and she always will
So calm your soul and set your heart still
She was sent to you from heaven above
To be yours alone to cherish and love
Yours is a bond so good and strong
In each others arms is where you belong
So smile and sing the days away
And listen to me for what I say
These are words I bring you from above
From Someone Great who knows real love.

Rena M. Niles

To Glory For Our Boy King - Henry V

In days of yore the knights were nuts
The Earls and Dukes no better,
They warred for King and bled till dead,
They also weren't too clever.
Took sword in hand and felt so grand
To settle scores in funny lands.
They cherished King and were well bred,
But had nothing much inside their heads.

Lottie A. Garfield

Just For A Little While

When we arrive upon this earth, we know not,
how long it will be,
    We only know we are a child of God, for all
eternity.

    Each of us will play a part that touches so many,
perhaps as child, spouse, parent or friend.
    We are thankful we had you for a while, the part
you played will never end.

    We have so many memories, some joyful, some
sad.

    But we can take comfort in knowing, that you
gave us the very best that you had.

    We will miss you with our tears and grief, then
one day we will smile.

    We will say "Thank you Lord." He gave us you,
just for a little while.

Bonnie H. Ricketts

Forever Is Ending

Each time you express how much the love has grown
how far we've come
pain arouses and fills my shell
what is so cherished by one
can be tumult for the other
it crushes me to know our time
our precious time
is limited
and cannot by nature
last for the nostalgic forever of my dreams
the becoming of two
is inevitable
the wind
slowly erases the names
gingerly engraved in the sand
as they become dissipated images
and the sun
blinds the curious eye
that looks upon it
we cannot question the knowledge buried in the sand

Lisa Simpson

Child's Train

I once heard a train I hear no more.
a train of shared sentiments on turns bent inward,
But no more as before;
The train sang, leaped, disappeared amongst celloid-thin
Iron valley slopes, bringing an innocent child's
Happiness upon my face,
But no more,
It whistle-jumped silver-believe mountains with electric
Smoke joy, only to appear while reappearing on light gauge
Dream driven track between sugar coated
Entrails of tunnels yet to come.
This, the train once heard but
No more.
Inside the head of a 1940's boy;
inside the head of a boy once,
But no more.

William Robert Evans

Ferris Wheels

Ferris wheels spinning through a glittering sky
Crackers were cracking, it was the fourth of July

Three shots for two bits, shoot a bear through the heart
Pop a balloon with the fling of a dart

Take a chance on the wheel, win a doll for your dame
There's nothing to loose when life is a game

Candies of cotton, cakes from a funnel
Fly wild through the air or find love in a tunnel

Bottles of fantasy sold at an auction
Brewed spices and herbs and other concoctions

Stragglers, hagglers and medicine men
All become heroes when you're only ten

With my hand in his I walked wide-eyed along
Never questioning once where such things belong

It was thrill upon thrill, my senses exposed
Just a dare to the spirit to remain composed

Absorbing it all for the moment, not more
In a time, place and game where no one keeps score

And while ferris wheels spun through a glittering sky
I thought I knew but I didn't really know why

Dan Del Peschio

Sunlight

The sky is lit up bright
By natural sunlight
The clouds dance
In a sleepy trance
The earth is woke from its sleep.

Everyday very early in the morn
The earth is to a new day born
People yawn and stretch
As the rays of sunlight catch
In their sleepy eyes.

Light full of colors like a rainbow in the sky
Its brightness delightful to the eye
Yellow, green and blue
All pure and true
Sunlight fades into night.

Kathryn Wood

Spirits Live On

In my world she still exists
In a hopeful heart more than a wish
A dream which I know will come true
It was a battle she had to lose

There is no thought where she's not there
And yet her presence now is air
Her face I see among the clouds
Her spirit nowhere near death shrouds

A smile which can never die
A kindly soul which never lied
A glow which made the world complete
That made it a greater defeat

Her life can never end again
To me she was more than a friend
A confidence which made her fight
Strong throughout the day and night

An inspiration in my eyes
On wings of God I know she flies
A life of love she did well fill
I will speak of her iron will

Ruth Catherine

Mama Seal

One bright day a mama seal
relaxed on the ice,
thinking, isn't this nice.

A hunter sneaked up from behind,
clubbing her 'til she thought
she'd go blind.

With blank eyes,
mama seal did implore,
Please! Please! Don't hit me any more.

The hunter with a
heart of lead,
hit her one more blow
to the head.

Dragging the mama seal,
bleeding and dead,
he hefted her onto
his sled, thinking:

Isn't this nice,
I found her just lying
on the ice.

Mary Rocks

Death Is The Desert

Hot, dusty winds across the desert blow,
There is no garden green, just heat and sand.
The fruits of labour here have naught to show.

Lush vegetation's difficult to grow;
A drop of water is in high demand.
Hot, dusty winds across the desert blow.

In the distance a mirage seems to glow;
Horizons in each direction expand.
The fruits of labour here have naught to show.

The sun will cleanse your brain of all you know.
Buried by gusting sand squalls where you stand,
Hot dusty winds across the desert blow.

The dryness of the desert is your foe,
The water craved is never close at hand.
The fruits of labour here have naught to show.

Vultures fly in circles, their prey below;
As final remnants decorate the land.
Hot, dusty winds across the desert blow.
The fruits of labour here have naught to show.

Lynne Hayes

Untitled

Should I smile at you?
You look empty, as though you're searching for
something to make you whole
or is it someone?
I've caught your eye now, so I'll smile at you.
I hope you smile back, you have such a beautiful face.
Your eyes don't look empty now; they look hungry.
My smile is returned
Shall I speak to you?
Will you speak to me?
It's my dream, so we will talk.
We will laugh and be happy together
Until my alarm rings
and wakes me up.
Then we'll part.
Forever.

Jennifer Wright

Sunday

Mmmm. Sunday.
I awake later than usual.
I stretch, then press my body deep into
The warm mattress, luxuriating
In the comfort and knowledge
That I can stay in bed all day,
If I want.
You reach over and touch me,
Pulling me close in your warmth.
We kiss, and I say,
"Where's my coffee?"
You laugh, then bound from bed as the
Puppy barks that she's ready for breakfast.
Allowing me a few more minutes of
Idle reverie.
And then you plop the Sunday paper
On my lap, arousing my senses with that
Marvelous coffee you brew.
How I love Sundays at home with you.

Susan A. Daum

Jacob Judith Jacklin Jawn
Simply Would Not Mow The Lawn

Jacob Judith Jacklin Jawn,
Simply would not mow the lawn.

He washed his hair, and made his bed,
He brushed his teeth, and books were read.

And though his mom would go on and on,
He simply would not mow the lawn.

And so the grass grew so very high,
Then it dropped and started to die.
For it was no longer green but turning brown
and Jacob Jawn was beginning to frown.

At last the grass could grow no more,
For the grass was becoming a real eyesore.

So children remember Jacob Jawn,
And always, always mow the lawn.

Justin G. Pruitt

In Retrospect

Give your flowers to the living, not the dead!
Consider all the kindly things that could be said,
When ears could hear, and warm hearts could respond.
Too late for smiles, when eyes look up in glassy stare,
But life no more is there.
This world of man for kindness is half-starved.
Yet kindness is the life-blood of the soul,
How oft too late for sad regret or deep contrition,
So many souls have died from malnutrition.

Margaret G. Perkins

Between The Lights

Awake without remembering much,
again experiencing terrible illumination—
smoky moons, headlights, silhouettes—

I apologize, forgetting everything
is inexplicable, poetry unforgivably.
It's reckless busy-work, really,

enshrining an opossum even
as dirty snow. Dislocated,
December rocks an eyeball,
twilit colorfield anesthetized, uncomprehending

Stephen Massimilla

One Last Time

As the sunsets
I sit there staring at his grave
Asking myself.
Why did he have to die
He was so young
And had so much to live for.

I would give my soul,
To have him back to love
But I know that will never be
Because he's dead and never coming back.

I just wish I could of been there,
To say good-bye
For the last final time.
I wish you all the luck
In your on coming life.

Michelle Smith

Gods Before Us

Gone is the landscape of future's past.
Clear is the crispness of winter's cold breath.
The masses assemble elbow to shoulder,
Pushing and tugging to shove to the fore.

The eyes in the back look on with despair,
It's obvious to them that most do not care.
The grumblings and matterings are heard upon wing,
They look upon themselves and see everything.

Desire is not passion, it's wanton neglect,
Not for their staples, but human respect.
We muscle our way atop those who falter,
And bend on our knee at the atheist altar.

Money's our God, our divinity of sorts,
We worship it daily and spare no retorts.
We'll topple the temple of life's lusty seed,
Unknowingly, unwittingly with our omnipotent greed.

Lay still, don't move and quiet your heart,
Each man together; a beginning, a start.
Every man's a beggar and some still the fool,
So live out your life by God's Golden Rule.

Bruce C. Stephens

Untitled

Silence lies across the water.
Golden rays slowly appear on the horizon.
The faint sound of eight oars slice the stillness of the water as
    they emerge from the mist.
This human machine thinks as one, pulls as one, fights as one.
As every stroke taken makes dreams of being the best become reality.

A hawk hovers overhead.
Fresh morning air fills their lungs.
The water glistens and ripples as the shell surges forward.
All eights bodies are focusing together, breathing together and
    hurting together.
As the will to win becomes stronger with every stroke.

A man watches silently from shore.
Bright yellow light is now painting the clouds with colour.
The wind has started to gently blow and scents of spring fill the
    air around the eight crew members.
Everybody remembers the past season laughing together, working
together, and winning together.
Knowing that yesterday's lesson have made them stronger
    today and for many years to come.

Cheryl George

Don't Be Afraid Of Dark Clouds

As I look above my head
I notice a very dark cloud
I could not take my eyes off it
In a few second the dark cloud opened
In the middle there was Christ on the cross
Around him was the prettiest blue I have
ever seen, so were the silver stars
blinking so brightly at me.
Oh it felt so good as the star dust
sprinkled down upon me; it felt
so good from my head to my toes.
Oh how it felt so good,
I stared at the cross and in a very
soft voice told my father how I
felt him and how good it felt.
So don't be afraid of dark clouds
inside there lies a silver-lining.

Shirley Henry

Golden Wings

When kids start to grow up, they expand.
  Not only physically,
  but their minds extend to the sky!
Everything - Anything! - is possible.
  Adult need to teach
  children how to fly.
We can test our wings, but we don't.
  We think and ponder endlessly
  about who or when or why.
When we take off we soar above!
  We think, then fall
  and, thus, again we try.
Our wings are small but powerful,
  And when we fall,
  we cry.
Yet up and up and up we go,
  And when we spread our wings,
  we're so high!

Andrea Frumples

To My First and Forever

The very soul sings a new melody when love is found
A song that is pure and clean, a virgin sound
Love fire all senses - touch, skin so soft that its feel alone is an addiction
A narcotic so powerful that when all alone the skin remembers
shadows of silk the essence clinging like a silky web which
cannot be shaken loose
A feeling which has knotted itself around the heart and
whose very presence sends it racing
Sight, beauty so riveting that it hurts not to look
Eyes so deep and dark that if stars shone there
One would feel like they were looking into the soul of the universe
During the darkest most peaceful night imaginable
A sight that has knotted itself around the heart and whose very
presence sends it racing.
Smell, the scent of her being excites the atoms of the soul
A scent which has knotted itself around the heart
and whose very presence sends it racing
Taste which nourished the soul, a sweet tasting emotion that
lingers in the mind
A mixture of all that was, is, and will be fine and pure
A substance that has knotted itself around the heart and whose
very presence sends it racing.
Sound, her voice alone a melody which the mind craves
A simple melody of consonants and vowels, of syllables and accents
A song which has knotted itself around the heart and whose
very presence sends it racing.

Peter B. Lee

Our Garden

Our garden is a special place, where we can see and feel God's grace,
in every foxglove spike and pansy face.
Each blossom in our garden fair,
beckons us to come close there;
to come and see what treasures grow,
to smell the scents when we bend low.
We work, we sweat, we tend with care,
for every life that finds home there.
The hues of blue, and pink, and gold,
all blended in a palette bold;
one the artist's brush could n'er uphold.
Sometimes we lose a plant in season,
hard to say what is the reason,
but overall we reap success and revel in the beauty blessed.
I'm glad we tend our garden's birth,
for there's no other place on earth,
where time, and love, and gentle care,
can give delight so rich and rare.

Evamarie John

Testimony Of The Tree

The branches were filled with green,
when the first inkling of illness, came
to light. It came, so abruptly, and was quickly known.
Throughout the fall, when leaves did fall.
I reflected, in the beauty, of that tree, and
wondered, if I might have, seen it all?
The bleakness, when winter came, and
left bare, and naked branches.
Seemed this illness left my soul, stripped
and, bare as well.
When, Spring's budding did occur, and I
too, had outlasted Winter.
I took heart in the miracle of Spring, and
Life. But, I barely saw the flowers, my
time was cut so short, but the fruit of
life and living I did bear,

Sharon Grove Mack

You And I

You and I are fortunate to have met,
And that is something we will never regret.

You and I began to make plans,
Walking down the beach holding hands.

You and I have grown together,
And formed a love that will last forever.

You and I will pledge to one another,
That from this day forward
There will be no other.

You and I

Paul Santaera

Between Two Cliffs . . .

One chooses what one's heaven is to be . . .
A breakfast peach full-ripened on the tree,
A child's smile, an arm around the waist,
A glimpse of dawn, of home-made bread a taste . . .

A flight of geese, an autumn view,
Of Indian-summer days a few,
A place where God and one can be
Between two cliffs beside the sea.

Stanton R. Gaylord

A Daughter's Love

When I look at two red roses,
I think of you and me,
And how we began a journey together,
Not separately -

Throughout my life,
You were always there,
Guiding, directing me,
Showing how much you care.

Then I stepped from your path,
onto my own,
Creating a life for me,
but I was never alone.

When we moved to this state,
I found a bright star,
And called it by "Mom,"
So you are never very far.

We've had our ups and downs.
Now, look at that bright star
And think, even though we're miles apart.
I'm really not that far.

Crystal Ann Erbes

Yours And Mine

A masculine structure of authority
created to be the head of his home
purposely designed for physical strength
yet gentle and sensitive to his woman's needs
Recognize his existence
Admire him
Value him
Treasure his presence
The Man The Father Gods First Creation
respectfully yours

An intriguing display of beauty
delicately formed for companionship and love
assertive and bold she humbly stands
rich and knowledge, powerful in strength
the back bone of the family
Appreciate her
Cherish her
Hold her dear
The Woman, The Mother, Gods Choice For Man
respectfully yours

Elois L. McCollum

The Window

Thank you Lord for my easy chair,
  It rocks and swivels me to where
There's a large window for me to look out
  And see what your world is all about.

Puffy white clouds drifting slowly by,
  Their background a Heavenly, light blue sky.
Tall pines, massive oaks, the maple too,
  Gum trees and dogwood that speak of you,
Shading the camellias and azaleas below
  And whatever else under trees will grow.

Birds with all their color so bright,
  They are truly a beautiful sight!
Butterflies coloring for me and you,
  Fluttering to flowers of equal hue.

Squirrels?—oh yes indeed!
  Eating buds and much bird seed.
Rabbits also eating seed
  And whatever they find in a chosen weed.
Thank you Lord for your gifts to me,
  Everything through this window I see.

Marion E. Sottile

There Must Have Been An Angel

Alone I stood against the convincing wind
Chilling me to loneliness.

My heart was on a journey
And my thoughts were made of illusions.

I walked in front of my life many times
Turning corners in search of you.

I ached for your finding, my ultimate being
To love endlessly.

There must have been an angel when you ascended into my life.
There must be an excellence to have delivered such an angel to me.

Never before did I possess such a strength more powerful
Than the stamina that masters my feelings for you.

How can I explain the loving feelings
You have stolen from my heart.

How can I rescue all ounces of energy
You've installed with my soul.

Pull me closer for the feeling that I most desire
Is to be near you.

Hold me tightly for no strength more mighty
Do I aspire to feel.

Kelly S. C. Cuff

So Near To Christmas Eve

The twenty-third of December,
The house is quiet now,
A prelude to the joyful time
Of "Oooh" and "Ahhh" and "Wow"!
The big clock ticks the hours away,
And strikes them one by one,
The kitchen's warm with oven smells
Of cakes with cinnamon.
The gifts are wrapped and tied with bows
We saved from former years,
And stacked by tree, and chair, and hearth,
To wait the coming cheers.
The family pet naps as if to guard
The treasure trove, it seems,
A peaceful sight, and fleeting fast,
So near to Christmas Eve.

Jearldine Markel

To Our Daughter, With Love

Through the halls of time we trod
  a single blink or tiny nod
The years fly by first two then ten
  never to return again
The small sweet cherub that we held
  now stands in a gown and veil
A rosebud about to bloom
  the role of wife to assume
Soon a mother she will be
  in quick succession one, two, three
A broken heart she must mend
  soon she heals, love comes again
With all these things she takes in stride
  add college graduate full of pride
Tears of love and joy we shed
  as we proudly lift our heads
This miracle of love we see
  God's precious gift to you and me

Linda S. Pittman

Ode To 309

Yesterday, I saw the Wrens as if to play they flew,
In and out the little house, but work came first-
A twig - some straw - and then the nest.
The young would come in time and in the warmth of love
Be sheltered from the rain and fed to grow up strong.
They would try their wings for places far from home.
The nest was gone, Fall and Winter came but....
Even in the cold and snow, the barren little house knew,
Another Spring would come and it would shelter once again.
So it goes as time goes by, the young must fly away..
To build their nest another place.. another time.. another day.
Life goes on and in it all, I saw God's plan.
I'm glad I stopped to listen, I'm glad I heard their song...
Yesterday, I saw the wrens.

Lewis T. Jones

To The One I Love

I sit here and think how lucky I am to be in love,
to have a love so deep for you that in a silent room
you can hear my heart pound. I have found a new
and dearest friend. It's to you my dearest friend
I tell you my secrets, my deepest fears and hopes and
dreams, and it's you that provides me with love and hope
of a beautiful life that's in both of our dreams. I say to
you my dearest friend you will not find a love to be
more true than the love I have for you. Our love
spreads to our families and friends to our future
children, and one day to theirs. You are my mate for
life my soul mate and when I am old and gray I will
think how lucky I am, not only to be in love, but to
have been in love with my soul mate and my dearest friend.

Annette Rochlin

Leave Me Alone, Again

Fly to me, beautiful butterfly, flutter your wings upon my cheek
You replenish my tears, I admire your freedom, for you
    are something I could never be
Brilliant are you, with your techni-colored life, the
    mirror of innocence, in which I long to find my own reflection
Rest upon me, fairy of jewels, diminish my sorrow for
    only a while longer, I, in my world, only a captive
Gliding with such grace, leading yourself into the last
    hours of your flight
I don't expect you to stay, enjoy your short time
    consumed in the vastness of mysterious scents
Propelled into the darkening of the horizon, sleep deep,
    exquisiteness, now leave me alone, again

Christal Randall

If

If you are rain, then it pour,
If you are wings, then let me soar.

If you are grass, then I am the flowers
If you are time, then I'm the hours.

If you are life, then let me live,
If you are love, then let me give.

If you are winter, then let it snow
If you are sunshine, then let it glow.

If you are water, then I am clear,
If you are sadness, then I'm a tear.

If you are artwork, then I'm a masterpiece,
We'll spend our lives together until world tends to cease.

Amaris McNair

Love At First Sight

With a single glance of her glistening smile, my heart was instantly
    pierced by a shaft from the passionate Cherub's bow.
The beating muscle within my chest burst with desire for this wondrous
    form that could only have fallen from the heavens above.
I was inspired to learn more of this mystifying woman, who could cause
    an uncontrollable tremor to pass through my body with a single look
    from her beautiful brown eyes.
Her name is Lisa, but should have been Hope or Faith. She brought a
    light into my life, brighter than the fullest moon in a blackened,
    starless sky. Like a sun that bursts through an overcast sky on a
    dim spring morning and frees the dead earth from the remains of winter.
She is indeed and angel, because only an angel is capable of the love
    and care which she does indeed possess.
I know not why she walks among the mortal people of the earth,
    bringing joy and happiness to all that view her splendor or hear
a kind word pass through her soft, delicate lips.
My heart has belonged to her from the first day she came into my view.
My only wish is that if someday she must return to the heavens, she
    shall grant me passage to accompany her so that I can continue to
    experience the wondrous pleasures of heaven which she has provided
    for me here on Earth.

William J. Turgeon

Unforgotten Hero!

I watch him grow old, my hero, my dad
The sight of it weighs heavy in my heart
no longer has he strength in body or mind
Age has taken its toll.

Fragile, yet determined, he continues his fight
Teetering on the edge of a past he does not want to forget
and a future he cannot imagine
why make memories of today if tomorrow he won't be able to recall

He is hindered with thoughts of today, yesterday and years gone
by he cannot comprehend their meaning
He endures the torture of envisioning people and places he cannot
identify with for he does not know them, he cannot remember

In time he will be plunged and locked into the darkness of his own
mind he will live in the past, alone
I pray for the moments when he will remember who I am
just long enough, so we can reminisce and I can tell him one last time
I love him, and he remembers!

Nancy A. Kolenski

Mystical Sunlight

Like cascading, sparkling water
Caressing imaginary rocks.
Crystalline traces of silver and gold
Illuminate your eyes with your essence,
Showering warmly over my soul.

As I drift through your words
To the melody of your voice
And dance to your whispers.
My heart will rejoice.
Like a mystical sunlight
Or magical spell
Your radiant smile
Is more than I can tell.

Each morning I linger
Tangled in your arms
Breathing in unison
And sharing your charms.
Pressed together like the pages
Of an unopened book
I browse the words of your passion with one single look.

Christopher A. Fontana

River Of Emotions

She still seems to be that overflowing river to me
She talks so fast like if she doesn't get it expressed
Then the current of her thoughts will take all reasoning from her
And just when I think she has settled down to an even flow
A torrent of emotions will rush around her bend
Exceeding from the banks of her memory to swamp me
She has waited so long to confide in someone that now I think she
    fears I will drift from her
So she talks in a rush like she's trying to shoot for some rapids
An out pouring to get to that all important sentence
A flooding of released feelings that will settle the rocking of her
    life's boat
Then when she has made her point the stream of her voice will become
    calm until she remembers more
Then she will wade back into the water for another dip of sorrow
And I am pelted once again with her tears but I do not mind
For I too have been floating down that brook of despair, floundering
    by myself
Longing for someone to steady the tide of emotions that flooded my
    senses
For someone to listen to the gush of words that poured from my mouth
So if I can help steer the course of her life to a better ebb
Or bring a stillness to her troubled waters
Then I will be glad to listen and do what I can for her
And there in we will both find a route to drown our woes in one
    another

  Linda K. Sorrells

Hello Out There

Here I am, another day.
Do you want to know what I have to say?
I can't work anymore.
It makes me to sore.
I didn't finish college,
So I hope my word's won't bore.
Let's see what fun
I can make today.
Sometimes people do hear what I have to say.
I know I'll eat dinner at breakfast time
And breakfast food at lunch.
See if that will give more punch.
I must be doing something right,
I am still living healthy without a fight.
I know: I'll go shopping
And stand on line.
Talk to someone and make a pun,
Someone will smile and let's have some fun.
Here we go again, thank God for the sun,
Let's keep folks guessing and on the run.

  Carolyn M. Warner

Heartache

Dedicated with love to my little brother, Roger
He stands on a cliff, his face to the sky.
He's there, he's there, but why, oh why?.

He know's why he is here, his love he has lost.
His heart, it is broken, it's cold as the frost.

Forget her, forget her, he tells to his mind.
To his soul, to his body, he begs thee, be kind.

The wind in his hair, the roar in his ears,
The blood in his veins, the salt of his tears.

As he thinks of her, he looks to the sky above.
I must die to join her, my woman, my love.

He walks to the edge and then he looks down.
He leaps to the cold water, where his heart will drown.

  Jackie Robinson

Out On A Limb

I've made a fatal error: I have climbed out in a limb.
My chances of a safe return are looking rather slim.
I've gotten myself in too deep, now I can't get out.
I fear for my longevity, my future is in doubt.
I should have heeded warnings as they came from all around,
Instead of climbing way out here, this far above the ground.
My situation's shaky, my foundation's not secure.
I don't feel all that stable, and my footing is unsure.
Security and safety seem a million miles away.
Perhaps I should have looked before I leapt into the fray.
But it's too late to second-guess: There's no way to retract.
Regretful things we so and say; we just can't take them back.
I wish that I could turn back time, and live that time again
Knowing all the things I know, but didn't know back then.
I know that I would make much wiser choices if I could,
But standing here wishing doesn't do me any good.
I'll still be in this quandary, in spite on my lament.
Remorse would just be still now, it's pointless to repent.
We cannot change our actions, or the outcomes that ensue:
I've told you I love you, and there's nothing I can do.

  David Roddick

You

You show me a glass figure of maturity,
exposing the child inside. You hide your
unpredictability deep down, but it's really
like a crashing tide.
I watch you from behind a wall, ignoring
that your out of reach. You see the thickness
of my skin, I wish that you would look beneath.
You cross my mind every day, I'm
waiting for a sign. I wait for you to show
me a way, or tell me that you're mine.
My flaws are very plain to see, yours are
likely few. There's so much that I would like
to tell you, if you only had a clue.
I dream of what are life would be like
together, knowing I haven't a chance. I doubt
you give me a second thought, or even a
second glance.

  Mike Simon

A Crying Child

Once I heard a crying child a
child that cries cannot smile.
No one to turn to, to be in peace.
No one to watch them while they sleep.
A child that cries and cannot smile.
Always has a reason why.
A reason of pain or fear and
a feeling that no one cares.
So if you see a crying child
go to them and find out why
let them know that someone cares.
For only you can help stop their tears.
So they can live like God meant for it to be.
To live in a life full of joy and peace.
And for someone to love them
and watch them while they sleep.
The world has so many children
some of tears and joy.
And God ears just don't want to hear.
No more crying tear.

  Brenda Hartley

Who's At The Helm?

Our ship of state of the economy
have minds of their own, it's plain to see.
Leaders and statesmen on the marque.
Campaigners instead, they turn out to be.

Should the Nation face an emergency,
whom could we turn to, who would there be?
The polished "entertainers" in the political realm,
or to the quiet master alert at the helm?

Elections determine them, or is it applause?
The louder the volume the greater the cause?
The voice of the people might not be ignored
if ethics and leadership were restored.

Show do not tell is a well known line,
as important to poetry as is the rhyme.
Why can't the same reasoning now apply
to our nations leaders on whom we rely?

The nation cries out for our leaders to be
true to their principles and family.
Their self-serving goals should be reversed.
Our nation and its people must come first.

Cleve Anderson

Come Back To Me My Lamb

In the flesh she is gone, but her spirits lives on
For she is a lamb of God!
Her pain was intense, your grief was immense
For someone you look to blame
If to blame you must choose, you can never lose
By sharing your burden with me.

Where I dwell, love never dies
So the secret my friends is this
Bring the anger from your heart, to my house
I'll store it downstairs
In the darkness where no one can see.

As you leave my house, if you should stumble and fall
Over others who block your way
Do not be surprised for they live without light
My goodness they choose not to see
I sent my Son to provide the love that's inside
All of those who choose to believe.

With free will I gave, the privilege to save,
All of those who honor my name.

Douglas J. Burgoyne

Chocolate Decadence

He ate chocolate decadence,
but into me his teeth shall not clench.
He is tired of the smack,
which he no longer finds useful.
Death's whispers have scratched his arm.
His body no longer is controlled,
but it is the controlling factor.
He, himself is free?
No wonder he's emerged into a deep black whole,
soon they shall both die.
Yet, he, himself abides on decadence.
He knows not where he's going.
How it pains me inside.
He's no longer able to exist within my framework.
Is there something I should know?
I no longer want to just sit by...
He angers me so,
He angers me so,
He angers me so.

Alison M. Hall

A Place In The Sun

The sun greets us each and every day
We wonder what will it bring our way
Will it be joy or will it be sorrow
Will we even see tomorrow
Let's live our lives by God's laws abide
To earn our reward, a place by His side
At the end of the day the sun will set
Let's take this time and not forget
To give Him thanks and praise
Let's not make our lives an unholy maze
Think of the joy and peace and fun
When we finally reach our place in the sun.

Carole A. Malanot

Watching The World Go By

Two fat old spinsters sat on the porch
   Watching the world go by.
"I'd go to Hawaii," said one to the other,
   "If I didn't have this fear to fly!"

The other old maid stroked her fat, hairy chin,
   And thought long and hard with a strain,
Then turned to her friend with a smile on her face
   And said, "Dear, then just take a train!"

"Don't be silly!" the woman said to her friend,
   "I can't take a train to get there!
Those Am-Traks move much too fast for me...
   And besides dear, I don't have the fare!"

Joan Lewis

As I Sit And Watch

As I sit and watch the moon-lit sky
I think of you and start to cry

I wish we could hold end tight other each
In the still of the silent night

My love for you will never
Just as sure as it began

I wish you would come back to me
Then maybe you'd finally see
that our love was meant to be

I want you to know that
my love is true
And someday I hope to be with you

Just remember that my love never die
Just as sure as the stars light
up the midnight shies

Tracy Lemback

The Journey

Together we were soul mates...both you and I
Sharing a secret bond; always together side by side
The strength of our friendship growing from within
Built with the knowledge of the battles we must win.

You always seemed to know when I needed a lift
Your advice and encouragement were much needed gifts
When we were together there was no need to pretend
We could be open and honest and the closest of friends.

Our souls have now parted, you are well on your way
Taking the journey we spoke of on that one rainy day
My heart is aching which I fear will not fade
Though I will cherish the memories that you and I made.

I once was told you never lose a true friend
They are with you always until your road ends
So my friend, I will keep you near until I too am gone
But until my journey begins, tie a knot and hang on.

Sandy L. Rouleau

Something

It must be the way
You made this blind man see
Or the way you opened up
My heart with a key

Or could it be the way
You always cheer me up
And show me hope
When I've given up

Or maybe it's just the warmth
I feel when you hold me
Whatever it is
I feel the way that it molds me

But to be honest, it'd be no surprise
If it happened to be something in your eyes

Garrett Cornelius

Rich Girl

Young, rich girl
Young, rich girl.
Smooth, sweet rose petals,
Smooth, sweet rose petals.
Soft, plush carpet, pointed shoes, feather pillow.
Sweet juicy apples, gentle summer breeze, fresh sour lemons.
Dark, dancing shadows, late Sunday evening, wearing hard,
leather
        shoes.
One young, rich girl.

Jessica Marshall

Relating

The spider moved across the busy walk way of the mall
Sit and watch his progress and hope for his success.
It is only he and I who care.
The stroller with the sleeping child passes harmlessly over his head.
The old couple, out for senior special sales day
    shuffle by - but still he moves on.
A family - mother, father, small girl and two young boys are nearing...
    One boy, unknowingly flicks the spider on his toe - and sends him
    sailing into space.
        Disoriented our spider strolls the
Center of the way - a dangerous decision -
    One final pedestrian goes by -
Our spider find his equilibrium restored,
    moves on and reaches the safety of
    the wall, then the doorway and then
    out of sight. Safe for the moment.
    I wonder - what are his plans for the Day?!

Elizabeth Pierson Koontz

Remember Thy Name

As I arise in the morning,
To worship the golden sky,
The night fades away,
And awakens a new day.
For millions of years,
a girl has awaken,
To play, and to hike,
To sing, and to dance.
She is a girl, she will state.
Remember thy name.
Remember thy soul.
Remember they name to the day of thy fate.
Place my name on a golden spear.
Do not behold fear.
Girl I am.
Girl I state.
Girl I am to the day of thy fate.

Jennifer Cohen

To Have The Plates Is Best

When you were little, did you ever dream of printing cash?
Of filling up your wallet with some money in a flash?
Creating money accurately means To Have The Plates,
The stamping of some paper into notes best demonstrates;

Or stamping metal into coins; or blips computerized,
Into you bank account deposits, checks now authorized.
Now if you printed it to spend, the others would bewail,
They'd call it counterfeiting and send you off to jail.

But what if government would let you print it up to lend?
With only what you could collect in interest to spend?
If you could print and lend a thousand out at ten percent,
You'd make a hundred interest on printing that you lent.

If government stops using its own plates and comes to you,
A billion printed nets a hundred million revenue!!
To service debt in ninety four, Canada's request,
A hundred and eighty billion dollars paid in interest.

We're taxed over five hundred dollars each per month to pay
For interest to holders of our plates they gave away!!!
With everybody being taxed to pay them interest,
Of all the scams in history, To Have The Plates is Best!!!

John C. Turmel

Oh Love, Do You Remember My Name?

Oh love, do you remember my name?
And all of those times playing the Game
We played it so well and always together
Now you have gone, and left me the sole player.

Oh love, do you my remember my name?
That ever-changing rhythm, yet the song was the same
Unsure of the outcome, and so left it to chance
I held out my hand, and asked for this Dance.

Oh love, do you remember my name?
I looked at the picture in its beautiful frame
It showed memories of what was, and the promise to be
But now, I fear, you may have forsaken me.

Oh love, do you remember my name?
You picked up your bow, and with unwavering aim
Had searched out my heart, and then let the arrow sing
Oh love, you opened my eyes to what happiness could bring.

Oh love, do you remember my name?
You conquered my soul, and made my heart tame
I add this to my sorrow, for I know it to be true
Oh love ... I will always remember you.

Glenn Marcotte

Whisper

When you look at me
the light in your eyes warms
my heart and it flourishes
like the daisy bathing in the early morning sun.
You reach out and touch me
an your softness unveils desires
I didn't know existed within my mind and soul.
I drink in the light and softness as though
it is mine to relish a life time
when I know it is only for a moment.
A moment of light and warmth
a moment stolen when the dark cloud
isn't there to shadow and bring a coolness
to what I feel when you speak my name.
I take what I can even though
it must remain a whisper like the sound
of evening winds brushing against the
gentle petals of flowers resting in gardens.
For now, I am patient, as time will nourish change
and change is waiting for us, I see it when you look at me.

J. J. Driever

The Sea

As the waves crash over the sandy beach,
The sun menacingly challenges all who pass,
The ocean deep and cool holds tiny fish with bright colors,
The ocean tide brings in new shells to be investigated,
Along the coast magnificent sand castles large and small,
Shells are lined up everywhere showing off their lovely colors,
Sand crabs walk around the beach protecting their small underground
    homes,
Turtles come ashore to lay their eggs where nobody can find them,
The laughter of children fills the morning air,
The salty sea water plays happily with the sand castles until they
    collapse,
The now dark evening sky warns everyone that it's time to go home,
The mournful seals wail on the rocks as if someone is lost,
The sea continues to roll over the sandy beach,
The sounds of the sea rock you to sleep with their constant lullaby,
This is the ocean blue and it will never die.

Rachel Bock

Feelings Of Hopelessness

Why is it so hard to get to know someone?
Trying to break down the barriers until there are none.

It gets so depressing to be rejected,
but it seems so much worse when you are neglected.

I feel so let down by the people I've cared so much about before
The feeling is so shattering it hits me as if I were falling to the floor.

What ever happened to faith, hope, trust, and happiness?
Are they just words said or do they even exist?

A part of me is so full of life and full of need,
but the other half has no more beliefs.

What is the use of getting close to someone again?
When they'll only leave you and the pain will definitely never end.

I'd like to find someone out going and fun,
just someone I can depend on.

I'm tired of hurting and feeling so numb,
but from what I've heard it's only just begun.

Will the pain ever go away
or will it just haunt me till the end of my days.

I give so damn much, but in return I get nothing,
not even a simple touch.

Maybe one day, it'll come "My Happiness",
but as of now I only have
—— Feelings Of Hopelessness!!! ——

Jesseth Mae W. Garcia

An Image Of God

To touch the hand of God would soothe my heart.
To hear his voice would be the loveliest sound
That could possibly come to my ears.
To catch a glimpse of His awesome beauty
would surely leave me gasping for breath and
paralyzed with amazement.
But I have touched the tender hand of God;
And I have heard His ever so sweet voice;
And I have seen His indescribable beauty.
For I have held my children's delicate hands
and have held my babies to my bosom.
I have heard their precious little voices
inquiring answers of me and telling me, "Mommy, I love you."
And the pristine beauty they possess, not only
in their outer appearance but in their inner being,
is that which nothing can compare and has
often been the cause of my tearful eyes.
God can be touched. God can be heard. God can be seen.
The nearest thing to God is a child.

B. Montgomery

A Ruin (Duntulm Castle: The Isle Of Skye)

Where are they all we wonder on this lonely
northern headland. But for sheep there's nothing
doing, only us, windblown, intent on narrow paths,
as if a cruelty of nature or the heart kept off
all complicated kinder things, all life but what
is spare or helpless, huddled there.
    What else survives

is simple, bare as earth, the cobbles of
a nameless cairn. Ahead, the ruin lifts its shape,
still facing to the sea, no shore below
and no way off but to be bundled in a boat,
the body in its poor disguise defenseless
to the sea and sky: and stones as gray, piled up

or falling in, thresholds to silence, unsilled
doorway to the dark inside, uneven ground, no footing
for the dance, nor any dignity of stance,
no thought of sound, but sighs, or of day, but
in the doorway where you stand, unfeatured by
the light behind you as the rain ends and the thought
    of company returns.

Stanley Koehler

"Old Age"

The rocking is easy, Though my days may be short.
I rock like a child and told I am smart;
Little does anyone know about my mind,
    That I feel good and my mind is fine:
My body looks wrinkled, wrenched and poor;
I keep rocking upon the floor:
Sometimes getting up and pacing to the door,
Is someone there to see me once more?
Oh! My childhood days have come, once-gone;
My family no more! I am alone.
But look! I can see the reversing of me,
and my head is fine as I sing this song.

Ron Phillips

Watercolor Of Life

The brush tip gently touched the paper.
The color spreads unevenly without boundaries.
Slowly the pastel hues takes form. Color is added
layer upon layer for shading and contrast until it is
just what the artist pictures in his mind.
So like a watercolor painting is the life of a child.
He starts out knowing no boundaries as he explores
the world around him.
Slowly people and events influences his way of living.
Year after year, he changes, as he is molded into his
own type of person.
His very existence is the watercolor of life.
He is the artist of his soul.

Sheryl L. Palmer

Beauty Of The Path

Walk with oneness, and the beauty of the path becomes you.
Although only a few steps are in your view, be not blue.
As a leisurely breeze unseized by the past fallen trees,
Go easy and pleased through the glow of yellow autumn leaves.
Gaze with gratitude as the supple sun's rays light the maze.
Raise hymns of praise as eyes blaze from your amazing days.

William C. Benni

"Subways"

Hustles and bustles everywhere
It's really tempting to make you scared
People standing all around
It's surely enough to get you down.

In the morning is a trip
Much too crowded to even slip
People packed like sardines
Man, it's really a bad scene.

Some stand tall, others small
Pushing up against the walls.
Bursts of laughter, loudly talking
Much too crowded for even walking.

It's comfortable at 7 o'clock
By then the rush hour has stopped
Go home and relax for the day
For the next morning, the price you'll pay.

Partricia Ann Hicks

Sunset

How shall I paint a sunset's glorious fires,
When torn and fragmented clouds are like a sinking wreck?
Turn the heavens tumults into multi-styled spires
And paint the late day which we, tired now, forsake.
Is there a prophetical man or an ancient sayer
Who may reach far enough in such a glorious sight
To see the trembling hero and monster-slayer
In the last glowing glory of the heavens' sinking light?
I have praised the sunrise with the purest Roman wine
And with the swelling of a baker's morning yeast
I see now the sunset in her richest colors shine,
Her wealth reflecting on the next morn in the east.
From blue to lavender, from crimson to timid rose,
From amethyst to purple like creatures with teeth, tails and tusk
But now, with the sun in its last and flaming repose
We feel warm and yet shiver in this crepuscular dusk.
From the heavens where the Godhead calmly dwells
Among the far flung clouds, now in waves and dark swells.
And in all the faded colors, the day breathes its last shine
While we sleep, I'll know Today's sunset was God's and also mine.

W. R. Schubert

U.S. Veteran, American Boys And Girls

I'm a veteran, and I fought, for, my country.
America - (Vietnam war)
And for you boys and girls.
Not to be mean. But to be good.
Not to hate. But to love.
Not to make fun of each other.
But to help each other.

Not to play around in class.
But to pay attention to your teacher.

Not to talk back to your teacher.
But to listen and respect your teacher.

Not to fight and hurt each other.
But to live in peace as good citizens.

Not to drop out of schools.
But to stay in school.

Not to join gangs. But to stay away from gangs.

Not to end up in prison, or on drugs.
But to be someone your parents and America - can be proud of.
A lot of soldier died for your freedom - boys and girls.

Don't waste it. I am a veteran and I fought for you.

Arthur C. Lopez

Loneliness

Anonymous as a toll taker on the G. W. Bridge
walking streets no one even looks at me
   am I invisible?

I have this hollow feeling deep inside
like my soul's been sucked out -
   from where it used to reside

The pain that I feel brings tears to my eyes
   that no one notices is no surprise

Don't know why I feel this way - this emptiness -
   this heartache - is it self induced?

I could join the ranks of the dearly departed
   but every new day I feel my life's just getting started

Dysfunctional family - divorced with three kids - that
   may have something to do with the state that I'm in.

The shrinks couldn't say - no more - just
   prescribe Prozac, Zoloft and meds galore

I've tried it all and it helped a little
   but what I need most is God's acquittal.

A need - a longing - an ache for what?
   to be held - cherished and loved a lot.

John R. McLaughlin Jr.

Alone

Lonely she sits, the girl who inside
Thinks of committing suicide.
Her feelings hurt, her trust dismayed.
Because, with her, life's game has been played.
Her thoughts tampered with, her actions impaired.
And now it seems like no one cares.
Then she smiles because she'll soon be gone
But until then she'll just sit......
   Alone.....

Tamecia Glover

Vulnerable January

January is in, lock the door
Stark raving mad from yesterday's eyes
Emotions spiraling downward on the killing floor
Last years carcass is now attracting flies

So January is bold and new
Fresh as baby's blood
Up to no good
Ragged and tired wearing December's shoes

"So new year, what's your promise?"
January protests already tired and sore.
Nothing new your brother didn't miss
Only you'll be just as poor

January puzzled naked with a crown of thorns
Martyred already to humankind
Desperately wishing he was never born
Exposed, unready, sweating profusely in this newfound bind

January on the edge of tears
Desperate now for an end
February the future full with fear
Life's cycle repeated once again

Atila Breti

The Mannequin

As I stand here with my new suit, white shirt and tie,
Watching the people as they go passing by
Some have smiles, some have tears,
But most are in between
Afraid to show their feelings to anyone it seems
As I stand here watching as they go passing by
They're always in a hurry with something on their mind
Oh well, maybe because its Christmas time.

As I stand here watching as they go rushing by,
I know who I'd like to be
Yes, I'd like to be santa clause
For I'd like to put a smile on everyone's face,
Especially this time of year
When everyone should be full of happiness and cheer
But
As I see it now, I'll never be anything
But
A mannequin dressing up this window this year.

Eddie Hendrix

"Upon The Gardens Of Heaven"

Daddy it's raining again as you sleep face down in the
sidewalk gutter across the street from Joe's bar.
Broken bottles of whiskey are shattered all around you and
make me only wish that a wrong move would cut you blood cold.
You begin to stumble back to life as I fly back to heaven
with the warm morning sun upon my little wings.
I don't want to hear you cry today daddy; mommy says that's
the alcohol talking.
Mommy and I are doing well daddy with the other angels of
fatal deaths upon the gardens of heaven.
Long ago, as it is in eternal time, I still remember being four
of earth years like other little girls.
The bedroom was full of love and laughter as mommy and I
read a book when you walked in from work angry one night.
You grabbed mommy with your rattlesnake tattoo arm and like
a rattler you struck and beat her to death.
Then, daddy it was as if you felt you had sympathy for my
crying and screaming; you pulled a gun out from the hallway
closet and shot my heart of love out for you.
I can fly free daddy, but as you are starting to get old, the law
will catch you and lock you away until you die and dance in the
fires of hell.

Paul Beare

Spirit Walk

Tread softly, for the ground on which you walk is holy
Hold lightly to life, lest it escape you
Row gently, gently down the stream
Speak softly, with the voice of love.
Touch tenderly,
Look deeply, into the heart:
So joyously, for every moment is precious!
Rest quietly in My hands.
Be still, and know that I am God.

Flow gently, noiselessly through the days,
quiet as a whisper, disturbing not a cobweb.
Listening, listening for My voice in the stillness about you.
Weightlessly walking through the grass,
that not a blade is broken.
Feeling the strength, the lift of My Spirit carrying you,
the steady rhythm of My Life within, and without.
So shall you rise up with wings as eagles, as you wait upon me
Resist not, for it is not by your might nor power, but
by My Spirit that all is accomplished.
Say "Yes" to Me, to Life!

Bobbie Thompson

Darkness

Somewhere in the world tonight light cannot be found.
Neither star nor moon light will reveal the blackened ground.
Beneath the rocks of the barren desert, and below the cold, cold sea
darkness as black as the miser's heart brings solace to those in need.
The darkness I've felt inside my soul is enough to wake the dead.
A bitter man is plain to see; evil is in my head.

Somewhere in the world tonight shadows lie all around.
Creatures dwell throughout the darkness unseen without whaling
    a single sound.
Behind a dumpster in an abandoned alley, and on a blank television screen,
darkness as black as the miner's lungs brings solace to those in need.
Deep in the hollows of the earth I've mined for copper and lead
without seeing light for days; evil entered my head.

Somewhere in the world tonight the spiral of darkness is wound.
Life exists, though seemingly dead, beneath a hard clay mound.
People continue to hustle and bustle, though them he cannot see.
Darkness as black as the blind man's eyes brings solace to those in need.
I've never seen the setting sun; my eyes have long been dead.
What's the use in getting up? Evil is in my head.

Keith Haynes

A Mother's Love

A mother's love
    Is like no other.
She spans the massive gulf
    Between the cold callous world
        And her child's tender ambitions.
Her love is encouraging;
    Like a refreshing cool breeze
        On a suffocatingly humid day.
Her love is unconditional
    And like copper poured over wire structures
        her love envelops the entire family.
Her love brushes away
    The tears of painful frustration.
A mother's love boldly holds
    The torch of truth in one hand
        And the law of the household in the other.
Freedom reigns when one obeys,
    But a mother's love will always prevail.
Thanks Mom for being my Mother!

Sara Stoker

Sorrow's Hope

Time denied my love's farewell
To brush your cheek with one last kiss
To tell you how you thrilled my heart
With wonder, pride and gentle bliss.

In sudden darkness you slipped away,
Stolen by mysteries of tomorrow.
What cruel game was this in play?
(I've learned its depths of sorrow.)

I search to know the joys we shared
But soundless voids come back to me.
To touch, to see, to hear once more,
My soul is pierced with agony.

And, yet sheer hope does lead me on,
This lonely grief somewhat to ease.
In anticipation I wait for your smile...
Tears and heartache then to cease.

For God has promised life eternal
Offering sweet "Pleasures forevermore."
You were my joy and my pleasure
And we'll meet again at Heaven's Door.

Janana

"Eternity"

I was conceived for eternity.
Than why was I abandoned?
Not old enough to really survive,
But some how I am still alive.
The pain and suffering,
Has made me stronger.
Never believed I would live longer,
Than age sixteen.
All the things that I have seen
Which I cannot believe.
Now not able to conceive.
Now I have been scolded for eternity.
What did I do that was so wrong?
All I was doing was trying to be strong.
Now all I do is cry all night long.
Crying for an eternity.
Amy Michelle Welsh

Sailing

Soon I shall be sailing
In a white sailing boat
Under the flaming sun and the cool stars
Towards endless days without nights
And without mornings, in the middle of the day,
Always in the middle of the day.
Riding with the waves
That comes and go in the infinite sea
Green and far from all,
I shall go with them and the blazing sun,
And some day, perhaps, return.
Oscar A. Lopez

The Attic

Once upon a wealthy day
In a room that kids did play
The sound of laughter rung out loud
The polished boards were bright and proud

As time passed by, the goods to store
Were placed behind this heavy door
Upon the floor things left to lie
Forgotten as the years gone by

Boxes stacked against the wall
Some six feet, seven feet, eight feet tall
Children's toys, books, games and cases
Bed-spreads, quilts and antique laces

But, as the passage of time, has filled this space
And dust has settled in its place
Its lustre gone, a sadness there
Yet, all's not lost to those who care

For when the cobwebs are brushed away
Behold what treasures are on display
Not only a chest of gold you'll find
But a host of memories left behind
Suzanne D. Jarrold

Scared

I'm scared
Not like a lost kitten scared
Not in the dark scared
Not scared like a child alone
But ready to burst out into tears scared
Afraid of losing everything
Afraid of knowing the truth
Afraid of not being loved
Catherine Jones

Problems Left Behind

I am a girl with many problems
I wonder why I am like that.

I hear nothing; the sound has left my mind,
I see the earth as a world of problems and don't know why.

I want the world to know but not right now, you see
I will try to be the best I can at whatever I may do.

I pretend to be so quiet, lovely and sweet,
and gentle, yet, I feel like taking all I do and throwing myself away.

I Touch The World With All My Heart!

I worry about what will happen today and tomorrow.
I cry the tears of all the sorrow and pain left behind.
I Am Hurting Deep Inside.

I understand everyone has problems
I say nothing behind my wooden door.
I dream a dream that has no moral to pursue.
I try my best to top everything I've done before, I hope to see
A change real soon but change will come no more.

I Am, I Will, I Do, I Try To See The Other Way;
But Day After Day I Look The Other Way.
Tamarah Kalynn Jenkins

"Inside Field"

Sometimes I'm lonely,
Sometimes I'm mad
Sometimes I hurt
Sometimes I'm sad
But mostly I'm blue for my thoughts still remain of you;
A friendship which at once could seem true
Only to leave me lonely and confused with feelings that have been
    severely abused.
The process to let go still seems mighty slow.
I surrounded myself in a field with a shield, one of which a flame
    can not yield.
For too many times within my life I had to fight the burning flames,
only to live with these - remains
scars that will not heal of which I thought a friendship so real...
Though I feel pain, and still alone, yes sometimes mad yet always sad
Within my field I shall remain away from more flame of that
    constant pain.
Vickie J. Lauzon   7/94

Miami Beach

On careless strolls in years gone by
We'd smile at those who came to die
It's not so hard to nod and smile
If you're the one that's got a while

Hunched and old with rueful stares
On Collins Ave. on plastic chairs
In cheap hotels; the 30's pride
Left deco-dry by fashion tide

From Brooklyn, Bronx and Queens the old
Who're bitten hardest by the cold
Arrived to claim the empty rooms
Where lately frolicked brides and grooms

And though the tide's turned yet again
— what's in is out, what's out is in —
A few hotels still harbor those
Whose days are coming to a close

And so they sit, the frail, the stout
Plagued by shingles, pleurisy and gout
Not as easy now to meet their eye
For there shall soon sit I, sit I
Dale Walker

Once

One day old and new friends met,
Once on a friendly, dinner date.
Once they thought on going out,
But now she thinks, she's in doubt.

Once she thought he's a friend indeed,
Someone she could trust, love and keep.
Someone she could cry on when tears do roll,
Someone she could lean on when sorrows fall.

Once she thought he was sincere and true,
In a lively conversation when the night was blue.
They built their dreams in a lovely situations,
Never realizing they're only fascinations.

Now, the once upon a time left her a sign,
Never to rely on words just on a line.
Building future dreams from someone so new,
For they're only expressions, never will glow.
But now, still friendly, she did say,
"It's better to have met a friend and left in dismay,
Than never to have any friends at all."
Time comes rolling on this world so small.

Dolly M. Rivera

"I Love You"

Why must children go through what they do?
They deserve to at least hear someone tell them, "I love you."

The pain, fears, walls, and cold-hearted eyes
 are all I see in children
because their heart and soul dies.

Broken hearts are all I see.
Why can't adults just let them be?

They can't trust anyone
Since a small child all they've done is run.

I reach out my hand and my heart as they look at me and wonder,
 "Is there really a God? Could things be better?"

The loss in their eyes...
Their loss of love...
Their disbelief in the God above...

I wish they could see my smile and my heart,
 and know my prayers are with them
Because all my eyes can say is,
 "I love you" my children.

Charise Casiano

"Happy At Eighty-Seven"

One never knows until he tries
and even then may not realize,
What poetry can do to open one's eyes
as he writes line by line
He is showing his creative mind
It's his way, to really show
how our lives can come and go
sometime they are happy
sometime they are sad
But as of now, I'm really glad
I feel like I am in Heaven
being so happy at eighty seven
When you feel down and cant keep going
Give some thoughts, to writing a poem
It will pick you up, and you will feel fine
It will get the worry, off your mind
And something else I would like to say
I'm so happy to the born in the U.S.A.
That's another reason, I feel I'm in heaven
and so happy, at Eighty-Seven.

Neal Bishop Langston

Rainbow Dreams

Red, orange, blue and green.
The prettiest colors I have ever seen
are the only colors in rainbow dreams.
At day with the sun's gentle beams
at night with the moons silvery glow,
my rainbow dreams seem to grow and grow.
 And when I look into my soul,
then all the fears that I've known
will melt away by the light of day.
 Like a ship sailing into shore,
like the closing of my favorite store,
like when I can't have it, but I still want more,
my rainbow dreams begin my day and end my night.
 As I go and turn out the light
I say good-night.
My rainbow dreams,
my diamond dreams,
that's how it seems.

Shabnam Ranganathan

Everyone's Hole

Little by little, they're digging a hole.
Many help to construct the pit,
 while few stall the advance.
By now, it is large enough for me to be pushed,
 stomped,
 kicked,
 and beaten into,
 until I rise no more.
Then, I'm smothered by the ill-placed contempt and hatred
 of those who do not know me, but fear me for my differences
which so closely resemble their own.

Norm Boivin

Pain

Pain is a feeling
that is hard to explain.
It hurts, it's bad,
it makes you feel sad.

Everybody feels pain
one day in their lives.
And when you feel that pain,
you feel like you want to die.

The day it hits you it hits you hard.
You want to crawl in a hole
and hit yourself hard.

Thinking it's all a dream,
The pain isn't real, but you can feel it,
Oh that pain you feel.

It hurts so much believe me I know.
I've been through it before,
you just want to let go.

When the pain finally leaves
You feel like you're free,
You can run and run and holler I'm Free!

Mindy Pollender

Untitled

Drinking and driving do not mix
No matter what the cost
And because of that lethal combination
A little boy's life is forever lost

Cindy Jean Watters

"Life"

I am young and life is fun
as I play around all day
sharing pranks and laughter
with friends rolling in the hay.

Then I leave my home, my friends
and lovely native land
to seek my fortune overseas
in countries with golden sands.

Life is serious and work is tough
but I always do my best
despite what odds might arise
I keep ahead of the rest

With responsibilities and pressures mounting
I question what its all about
Especially coming unexpectedly
and hitting you like a clout.

Now I look back and ponder
while striving to keep ahead
yet knowing the final consequence
that I will end up flat on a bed.

John Perry

Flowers

Sorry I forgot,
To give these to you.
And forever I've kept them here,
For at least a thousand years.

And now they're brown,
And kinda dead and dried.
But I'm telling you that I've tried,
Tried to give them to you.
But I never could.

And the water in the vase has evaporated
From its place, old and withered,
Failing away, wishing for a summer day.

Sorry I forgot to give these last year.
And who knows how long I've had them here?

And once again, springtime has come.
Last season will fade away, and maybe tomorrow.
Or maybe today, I'll give these flowers to you
Like I've been waiting so long to do.

Mia Dyan McInturff

The Cycle

Once on a hill there grew a flower,
From seed, to stem, to growing pride
Behold its beauty people muttered,
Soon after that same young flower
Fell, withered, and died.
Once a babe was born, a male to be exact
He grew from youth, to man,
Then he reached his peak of span.
Once there was a village pitied,
Because of size so small,
It grew, and grew to reach a city,
Then a kingdom, did behold,
It reached its peak, but not yet withered, struggling to survive,
Will this kingdom fall and die like all the rest?
The answer lies in you. You're the people, you're the kingdom,
The world is just your tool, like the seed that grew to flower,
And the babe that grew to man, the world will grow with you to an
Everlasting span, but if you treat it badly and hurt
Its heart inside, the world will turn like man and flower,
And coldly sink and die.

Robert Sanford Berlin

The High Side Of The Universe

The high side is where I like to float.
You cannot get there by train or by boat.
The high side will take you, where you've
never been before.
The high side will have you begging, and
stealing for more.
The high side of the universe is where I want to be.
Just try it once and you'll see.
Take my advice, everyone who wants to watch
the clouds turn in to demons, and the
demons turn into clouds.
You'll see what I mean you see everything in green.
So try your hardest not to give in.
But don't be stupid it's not a sin.
This poem is done,
and now it's time for some fun.
I'll see you on the other side.

Brian Trayer

Jeffrey Lee Powers

One man
His world in his hands
On a stage
In front of his fans
Closes his eyes, is it all real?
After all these years, how does it feel to finally make it
Almost gave up, on his own special dreams
He opens his eyes, it's as real as it seems
The roar of the crowd fills up his ears
He's finally made it, after all these years
Somewhere in his heart, he knew that he would
But he had no idea, it would feel this good to finally make it
All the work, all the years, all the lost dreams, all the tears
Are all gone now, no where to be found
He takes a minute and looks around
The stage, the band, all the screaming fans
The music, the song, the beat moving along
We're actually here, he was really a hit
And at that moment he knew...
He made it!

Carrianne Craig

A Walk Through The Woods

As I walk through the woods, the leaves crunch beneath my feet.
The hues of fall surround me like a warm coat.
Menacing bugs of summer gone, too cold for them now.
I breathe deep the chilly air, its freshness clears my mind.
The trees now void of their green life,
Give a clear view of the field, barren of life as well.
Soon the snow will fall, covering the earth like a blanket,
Bleaching the world free of color until spring begins to paint its way.

Tina L. Lloyd

Wonders

As I lay here in the dark
and stare up at the sky,
I see right through the starry
heavens and still I wonder,
why?

Why do stars fill the night?
Why must the moon shine so bright?
To create a glorious, heavenly light.
Such a marvelous, wonderful, glamorous sight.

The answers to these wonders,
I will never know.
My wonders for these answers,
will forever grow and grow.

Heather Berney

Olivia Rachel Atwood's Funeral

Full gray clouds bury bright green hills
In clods of meat that hide from sight
Icy boughs full of winter's will.

A church clock's thick bellow lies still
In lost hollows wandering through night
And gray clouds that bury green hills.

Black cars push through mist till they fill
Shallow lots shimmering street light
Through icy boughs of winter's will.

Black clothes gather and sit until
Olive rises to heaven's height
Above clouds burying green hills.

I watch her mother's tears lie still
On her grave and I fill my sight
With icy boughs of winter's will.

Olivia loved winter's chill,
So I love it, with all my might;
The gray clouds that bury green hills,
And icy boughs of winter's will.

R. S. Fotheringham

Queen Of Hearts

Days: Short, frigid, bleak. Lengthening into months
Punctuated by rain and snow.
They approached the other. Curious, tentative, open;
To the possibility of warmth
And longer days.
She; Rolling the dice, with a whisper to Lady Luck;
Laid her wages down.
He; sensing the stakes,
Placed his own.
Together they played; arranging and accepting,
What the other offered.
Discarding remnants
Of previous games.
It continues still. Days longer, warmer, softer.
Reflecting
Glowing embers from fires within.
Fewer clubs and spades
Remain to be drawn.
Left to play are
Many Hearts and Diamonds.

Brice A. Goodwin

God's Mole

He was standing in front of the bathroom mirror,
shaving himself with a straight-edged razor,
which he sharpened, daily, on an old strop, a leather relic
brought from Mississippi to New Jersey fifteen years into this
new century, an artifact his father, a freed slave, had passed on
to his son, my grandfather, whose large, wrinkled hands now
moved across the weathered regions of his massive, hawk-like face
with smooth, assured strokes, as though recalling, all on their own,
his long ago youth. The white, sleeveless T-shirt he was
wearing looked like an ad for Clorox,
luminous cotton against sagging, sable skin.
I believed, as a boy, that God was a towering, black man,
who shaved himself in front of the bathroom mirror every morning.
The mole, God's mole, was still there,
near my grandfather's right shoulder blade,
a protruding piece of skin, a seemingly small, undeveloped digit
that fascinated me without end when I was grown up,
which I recognized, now that I was grown,
as being simply the outward and visible evidence
of an imperfect and very human deity.

Louis Bryan

Thinking Of My Brother On The Mid-Autumn Night

When will there be bright moonlight?
Let me with wine ask the blue sky.
I don't know in the celestial height
    what year is tonight.
I want to go by wind to the sky,
    but I fear it is too cold in the height.
Though in the moon there is song and dance,
    yet it is not as on the world so nice.
The moon peeped into the red pavilion, the haren damask,
    and into the room where I lay awake.
We should not complain and rebuke
    why the moon is not always round.
As people experience union and separation, joy and pain,
    so the moon tends to wax and wan.
From ancient times this is the way,
    I only wish you live long,
And let us a thousand miles away,
    share the moon so round and fair!

Zhang Bing-Xing

Destiny In Thought

Good thought is a true jewel
Nobody can steal or sell
Beyond the scope of man's thinking
Lies another world glittering,
For what is where today, changes tomorrow
Nothing stays, happiness or sorrow
Smile to bring back the cheer
Watch the dismay disappear
When mind brings in a negative thought
Erase it with positive onslaught
Feelings of despair must be fought
All great achievements, begin with a humble thought
Destiny lies to be sought
Hold yourself, don't lose heart
For, struggle is always at the start of Success

Sangeeta Punjabi

Painted Facade

You clown around with your happy face,
You are loved by all in every place.
But what lies behind your painted facade,
A man of sadness and of rage.
Known by all, but not by one.

As the mask is removed and the shoes are small,
You are away from your stage or shopping mall.
The tears run down your cheeks at night,
The friends for which you had to fight.
Known by all but not by one.

A life you lead making people laugh,
In others hearts you've made your mark.
Going to places and joking around,
You are always known as a happy clown.
Known by all but not by one.

Your unmasked life is of sadness and sorrow,
All night long you pray for tomorrow.
When you can repaint your mask and personality,
Where you can clown around and make them happy.
Loved by all, but not by one.

Dale-Leanne Stephenson

For Allan Tung

Your tongue is silent now, you who could speak so many
and sing in any key the language of the heart.

Your gathered the pain of the world into your blood.
The pain of fallen angels, of doomed cities and people;
of crucifixion and extinction of races and monuments of culture;
and of the earth —
the crying elephants and clubbed baby seals.

With a wave of your band and the bowl of a wolf
echoing and re-echoing all around
you sent forth banners like waves of light
flying colorful rays on silken wings
floating up this great dome
up and up to the one above
in ever widening circles of swirling streams
on a departing ship in a final farewell.

Sailing right up there —
into the heavenly lap of Love.

Peace be with you Allan,
Peace, be with us.

Tamir

Autumn Cradlesong

Hushhhhh, Hushhhhhh, weary elm
Rest your long, strong arms of brown
Rocking gently to my sway
Yield, as I whistle my chilly lullaby,
Your ponderous, enchanted crown
Once a noble emerald, brilliant and bold
The mark of your power, now fatigues into gold
With it I will play
Make it dance and frantically fly
Tremble, trip and tumble
Then upon a grassy pillow let it lie
Where under a heavy foot it will crumble
Sleep now, mighty king
Deposed monarch of a frost-conquered realm
And dream of coronation in the spring

Bernadette Carroll

I Am

I am a kind person who loves all kinds of animals
I wonder what I will look like when I'm older
I hear the dinosaur's feet stomping hard on the ground
I see a pot of gold at the end of a rainbow
I want to help the whales and dolphins survive
I am a kind person who loves all kinds of animals

I pretend to ride a dolphin when I go swimming
I feel happy and warm inside
I touch the dew on a rose petal
I worry about when loved ones will have to die
I cry about my dog who passed away
I am a kind person who loves all kinds of animals

I understand why we need to go to school
I say that I have a guardian angel
I dream of having a good career
I try to obey my parents more often
I am a kind person who loves all kinds of animals

Christie Michele Todd

Birth

When the seed of the earth is inseminated
by nature's dew,
Life's greatest gift will be bestowed on you.

Earl A. Foster

When I Was Alone

When I was alone, you were there.
You picked up my heart when no one cared.
You were my friend during the
darkest night.
You lay down your gun when I asked for a fight.
When I cried on your shoulder,
you promised life would go on.
I believed you were right by the break of dawn.
My heart was broken my soul was crushed,
I thank you again my dear best friend,
I love you so much

Nicole C. Hyde

Growing Pains

If I had only known then what I know now,
   My life would be so different; you ask how?

I would have had the stability and security to stand on my own,
   I wouldn't have settled for almost anyone because I was
      scared to be alone.

Yes, the world at times is a very lonely and scary place,
   But to be alone and scared is learning and your mistakes
      you learn to face.

Mistakes make you grow and to grow is to learn,
   There are no easy answers and solutions to life, for
      knowledge you must earn!

Lenora R. Drew

The Final Journey?

Mortality is a provision vital for the transmission of life.
Frees the soul from the shackles of the past
And the trammels of life.
You have come of age
Your life edges up, closer to its final stage.
You approach the release from the toils of the flesh.
There's nothing to fear in passing into another world so fresh.

The shadows of eternal night creeps upon your sight
And when all sights are gone and you see no light,
When all sounds are no longer heard
And you loose consciousness of the things you feared,
Like the drifting clouds in the sky
The spirit glides off without cry.
Hail to man's over self
Death is birth!
The ethereal double is dissolved
The wheel goes on
For the silver cord is severed
And the golden bowl is shattered.
Death is birth!!

Kelvin Asare-Williams

Conch

As many colors as a rainbow,
But you'll never see me in the sky.
As finely-crafted as a diamond,
When you find me you might sigh.

I'm as hard as the strongest granite,
But I'm as frail as a pane of glass.
I make as much noise as the ocean,
And yet from my mouth no sound does past.

I've got points just like a porcupine,
But I'm as smooth as the finest vase.
And if I should stay where I was made,
In a hundred years you'd find no trace.

What am I?

Rick Albrecht

Gondaloon Revisited

Ne'r pained this mortal little girl
so strained in concert, never build
this castle in our tepid sand
did blast the sea, the waves, this man.
Vicious vice, oh malady
to bluff your way past unperceived,
lie loose arched passion on my bed
scourged of reason in our heads.
Dance, my modicum of spirit high
cracked needle-ice slides down your spine
to lodge and scream our moods abase
Dragonesbane now blocks the gate.
There lightning sullen shudders by,
seldom betrayal so shocking thrives

And so, as acid rain in trees
this Gondaloon mourns pain for me
these moon-dark demons scythe hard your soul
Passion stricken savagely

Bradley Smith

Why My Father Had That Look In His Eye

The school I attended was very small,
Twenty-four feet square plus a porch and entry hall.
My father had donated an acre of ground,
And this is where the school was found.

The school board is where my Father did "sit,"
And he ruled it just as he saw fit.
Mrs. Anderson was the teacher he hired,
Nine years she taught until she retired.
She was a big woman that's the least I can say,
Three hundred pounds was the guess of the day.

One day a new game she would teach us to play,
At how not to get angry at what people might say.
When it came my turn for something to say,
I told her what my Father said one day.
A good windbreak for cattle Dad said you'd make,
And I knew at once I'd made a mistake.

Right then and there class was dismissed,
And I knew my Dad would hear of this.
It's really sad when a kid of six,
Can get his Dad in such a fix.

Fred L. Verner

Two Hearts

Today I read a line
Which he wrote to me.
One day I have to thank him,
he will be leaving soon.
'Ere long I will forget,
and be without regret.
Right now I am upset
Trying to recall a hint,
Some proof that his love exists.

Before the tide of life runs out
Even the mistakes will return.
An action which was never taken
To haunt me when I'm old.
And now I'll try to convey
Some proof of my silent regard.
Only you have jet black hair,
No one else in my full eyes.
Eye to eye and heart to heart, you leave.

Carrie McClain

My Prairie

Out on the prairie so vast and wide,
  are hidden secrets, deep inside.
One day it's sunshine, one day so crisp,
  air so rejuvenating gives one a lift.

Never thought I'd make my dreams come true
  here, on the prairie, all brand new.
I came from a place, okay in its right,
  but changes have come to darken the sight.

I can't live there it's so stressful at times,
  so I'm bound for the prairie, where I'll make it mine.
It's an unexplained, anticipated thrill
  to a home temporarily built on a hill.
Then on to my final home in a small town waiting still.

Everyone goes for coffee early in the morn
  We never did that where I was born.
People so friendly and pleasant while walking, you meet,
  out in the crisp sunshine, going down the street.

What pleasant times await in this quiet place,
  ...almost a step back in time to trace.

Donna Schuh

The Stars

How can I look - and yet not see?
Knowing the stars twinkle down on me.
Their vast array of sparkling light
Shines through the velvet dark of night
Without earthshine or cloud or haze
or low horizon to make them dim,
As high above on mountaintop
where naught seems between me and them,
I lift my hand and gently brush the stars
into a swirling rush of light - a glimmering sight -
The nighttime sky so full of stars
All constellations are lost - except the Bears
who point the way
And yet today, as home returned
That sight upon my spirit burned,
I look - the stars are dimmed and lost,
Except in the mind's eye, the heavenly host above me
in all their beauty
A transposing of my innerself to there,
Even though I may be here - To see the stars!

Julie B. Courtney

I Am

You are purple passionate, seductive, beautiful
I am black dark, mysterious, lonely
Black is night, and you are the stars
Black is rain, and you are the rainbow
I am the sun, and you are the rays
I am God, and you have the power
If there was no purple the rainbow,
Would not be completed
It would not be whole
Black would not be missed
It is the color of depression
And the color of death
Purple is happiness and life
Without purple the world is black
And what am I

Joy Nowak

"With Out Love"

Millions of miles away, in another world, my heart looks for compassion, understanding and kindness. I have come to realize that love is leaving this planet, through problems, excuses and selfishness, it has ended.

In my thoughts I ask, why has God forgiven us?, Why is it that everything is turning back?, and why have we lost the touch of human beings and become savage animals? We don't believe in good things anymore, there's no caring; the tales of yesterday are mysteries today and there's no place where we can hear your music.

The Little Red Ridinghood has been eaten by malicious thoughts and Snow White has been raped, the beautiful smile on Pinocchio's face has turned to tears and the friends of yesterday are today's greatest enemies.

Armies of ferocious people march on the streets and friendship is only used to buy consciences; man has become a deadly worm and the earth cries for help; unity between families doesn't exist anymore and every soul is fighting against its own.

Come back my Lord, come and bring with you the light once more, bring us the purity of your eternal love; listen to the cries and pain of your Saints; put a new smile on your face and let the earth be born again; help us comprehend the beauty around us and teach us to live in harmony sharing all we have.

Jhadran Agmeth Rojas

Without A Cause

Why fretest thou, ignoble son of man!
At thy not achieving thine own goals.
For who art thee but a wisp of straw
With no hand in thy birth, growth and decay.

Conspiracy of forces unseen and unknown
Has shaped thy image, having themselves no father,
Only inter-twined, intermingled and shaped out of buffeting.

And thinkest thou it is you,
Someone special, something extraordinaire
Made particularly by one who exists
Unseen, guides unseen, is master of all
And had a purpose for you.
So must you feel special?

Do not forget creatures like you
Millennia gone past thought the same way
And created out of imagination
A source of effect, a cause, for what
They saw could not happen without a cause.

But what caused that cause
They forgot to ask and created a cause.

B. P. Nigam

"I Am, But Am I"

I am, but still I may not be myself yet,
How strange to be, but not know who you are,
The way is long and I can see no landmarks
To guide me to the unknown ways, afar;

I may be underneath a rose or any flower,
It's going to take sometime for me to know,
If I am me or am I just my shadow,
You know how long it takes for them to grow,

It may not be completely as it is, or is it?
I maybe wand'ring on a foreign star,
And if you ask the why and ask the wherefore,
I am but searching for myself, I am not here.

Christine Lay Armstrong

A Day At The Beach

Me and my friend come down off a bridge and onto a beach
The waves are up in the sky trying to reach and reach.

The sun is very bright
like a knight on his sturdy steed.

I look into his eyes an to my surprise
He really starts to beam.

My friend starts to run out into the water
I should call out to him but I don't really bother

He splashes around chasing bubbles but yet he cannot catch them
I think he's having troubles.

My friends sees birds on the beach and then he starts to chase them
The birds fly high up in the sky and this adds to his frustration.

My friend gives out a little yell almost like a moan
Then he slowly starts to drop behind, alone.

Then his energy is back just like that and then he starts to run
if he could, I know he would run into the sun.

He just wants to run and run and then he jumps a log
And by now you probably know that my best friend is my dog.

Trevor Stagg

"In Dreams We Fly"

Heavenly dreams had been interrupted
    Because my sleep was broken by a fool
I scorned him then, for he corrupted
    Younger, more innocent than I, and more cruel.

Half above and half below this bed I lie
    And thru my top-soil slumber, I can see him crouch
Beneath that blade, and die
    In the cancerous corner of his tobacco pouch.

My dream is lost now, and in this daylight hour
    I remember visions of the scorned one,
Then revenge and death were in my Power
    But the devils plans by moonlight, look sickly in the sun.

Yet in this waking world they all complain
    There is but war and death, and grown men cry
My friend the fool, the man insane
    He should dream too, for in dreams we fly.

Kevin O'Grady

Beneath Thy Waters Black

The pond was still, and deep, and dark.
It made her tremble through the park.
"Oh," She thought, "to join with thee!"
To rival thunder, sky and sea.
"To leave my plagued and troubled mind."
"What peace and succor I should find."
"Beneath thy waters black."
"To slip beneath thy murky depths,
And hold thy stillness to my breast."
"To be as rock, and sand, and log,
To be as rainbows and misty fog."
"Not to hear the children's laugh,
"Might even prove a pleasant task."
"Oh, in thy darkness would I bask...
Beneath thy waters black."
To slip beneath thy waters deep,
And join in thy eternal sleep,
"Ahh, such secrets we should keep...
Beneath thy waters black."

Donita Mullins

Special Hands

These hands belong to someone special.
When I was a baby,
These hands helped me cross the street.
When I was a toddler,
These hands took care of me.
When I feel off my bike,
These hands gently soothed the hurt.
These hands took me lots of places.
These hands are special,
And belong to my mother.

Orchadia McLean

No, Last Night Wasn't A Dream

I am a stranger where you're concerned
You didn't want to speak of what you learned
Drowning in denial
With preaching of survival
Leaving our relationship
Awkward and futile

So I won't be the person you hoped I would be
I'm a firm believer that love should be free
Free to love anyone
Even the same one
Love should be cherished
Before we all perish

If you think I would choose this, you're wrong
Mind and body are tired of being so strong
I will always love you
No matter how cruel
I don't require acceptance
Just love me no less

Joan Owens

Elysian Voyager

Eternal traveller, what have you seen?
For millennia untold, your bright face
Has gazed upon our tiny global scene,
Floating silently in the sea of space.
Heavenly pilgrim, will you ever sate
Our desire for knowledge? Will you confide?
Do you laugh at man's struggle against fate?
Or cry at our pretentious, human pride?
Immortal muse, with your wisdom and trust
Unsurpassed by mortal men, you will see
A grand new world where all I know is dust.
Can you notice one small man's mortality?
   Celestial sage, before you fade from sight,
   I ask - are there stars in the endless night?

Raiffe Sculthorp

Teddy Bears

Loved, and torn to tattered rags.
Yet always forgiving.
Tear stained, and peanut
butter and jelly stained.
   Yet always there to comfort.
Dusty and old.
   Yet cherishes memories without bitterness.
   Forgotten and alone.
    Yet never regretful.
Teddy bears our private
counselors until we out grow them.

Amanda Craig

Four Seasons Of Northwest Mountains

Brief warm summers in the wildwood
Surrounded by mountain peaks —
Blue skies obscured by mammoth green pine trees —
Wildlife are the only natives.

Leafage to autumn shades.
Mountains are snow-crowned.
Winter-like flurried scatter demised leaves from dormant Aspen trees.
Famished deer set our on a quest for fresh, green vegetation
   at lower elevations.

Winter sunbeams illuminate ice crystals on the surface of the
   frosty terrain.
Nature's towering alps hibernate beneath a blanket of snow dust.
Snowdrifts conceal any sign of civilization.
Animals anxiously await the season to change while they are
   temporarily moved from their dwellings.

Toasty spring days follow frigid spring nights.
Melting snow creates a clear of ice-cool water.
Flowers burst bloom at the edge of the liquefying snow.
Snowshoe hare leave behind prints in the snow that signify the first
   presence of wildlife for the season.

Mike Nichols

Love Hurts

He has taken my heart,
Forever he hold it.
I know we'll never be apart,
For he has told me he'd love me always.
Until that awful day had come,
He shattered my heart into a million pieces.
And he walked out of my life,
So quickly like it was all just a dream.
I no longer have a heart,
Since he has broken it in fear,
I will never be able to look him in his eyes,
Without shedding a single tear.
I know he's not here to stay,
But I now realize
He's only here to take my life away.

Katie Kenyon

Passing By

He stands scratching his head
mumbling incoherently.
A concrete bench - his bed and home.
He is alone.
We are not so different Him and I.

He crouches in the corner
smoking someone else's butts.
A plastic, grocery store bag - clutched to his side.
He is running.
We are not so different Him and I.

He sits embracing his mother
darting wide eyes around.
A worn filthy blanket - to keep out the cold.
He is afraid.
We are not different Him and I.
We are not so different
Him and I.

Shanni Rhoades

Untitled

I called to the brilliant sun
as it lay shimmering before me,
"Wrap your comforting rays
around me and
melt my frozen heart" —
but the sun only moved
a little closer.
"Let your soothing light
come touch me and
caress my tender skin" —
but the sun only moved
a little closer.
"Dance with me,
and only me, until
the moon does rise" —
but when I reached to pull it closer,
the flaming sun turned to water in my hand.

Courtney Arlington

Quiet Words Whispered

I wrote a letter today of yesterday
a script composed of dreams
words of hope and nights of desire

Even though I yearn to write of trees, kites, and pigeons flying
Today, I can only write of you
your dark shiny hair
your enchanting eyes
and your delicate curves where my hands always seemed to wonder

It was yesterday that I realized February's calling
and the quiet words whispered in the shadows of night

But, even in these days, words are all we can hope to trust
making time the only things possible of uncovering the truth
leaving nothing, but the distant sound of falling rain

Now again, another year goes by
and the leaves begin to change to their own springtime splendor
making me understand that life is like the openness of the sky
it never seems to end
just like our hopes and our dreams
they lie eternally in the arms of a single
blissful, harmless, kiss.

Michael J. Miller

A Poem Definition

A poem is synonymous to life itself
    Difficult to apprehend, yet impacting on emotion.
It is a song from the heart,
    Interpreting reality at a far more abstract dimension.
    Poetry triggers your inner mind, your imagination,
    Leading it to a more critical perspective.
A poem is the outcome of various feelings and
Untouchable emotions that one may endure.
    While being the trailblazer of soaring imaginations,
It vitally allows your thoughts a chance
To become the vanguard of reality.
    Some poetry distinctly leads us to a higher plateau
Of the thinking ability,
While others leave us with unanswered questions,
Crippling our understanding of its unique language.
A poem's deep instincts on life are like a force
That demand us to ponder the meaning of reality a bit more.

Keisha Valentine

Undiscovered Days

Icy arrows of light
through white birch and dark pine
waves of silver-plated frost, frozen rivers of gold
dark fingers unclasp the land
a new day lies glittering before me
in that soft second before the birds begin to sing
I light a candle, talk to the sky
let the sun rise within me
Then, in a sparkle of new laid snow
on a orange red horizon
the child in me begins to laugh, happy just to be
calling back the cranes that are flying south
letting them land in her arms
with the promise that she will keep them warm
through the heart-rending crack of fissured ice
at the very first call of spring
The child knows they will be happy to stay
to hear the vast and silent planes awake and sing
shimmering with the promise
of one more undiscovered day

Anna Lia Bright

Change Of Seasons

Glancing out the window of my home,
Observing the progress of wheat that has been sown.
Witnessing the contrast of dark green wheat with pale
    yellow ripened corn,
Acknowledging the demise of the old crop, and the new crop being born.

Thankful the long, hot summer is over at last,
Reveling a year's hard labor is now in the past.
Watching Mother Nature prepare for the cold days ahead,
Breathing a sigh of relief, another crop has been put to bed.

Each year it gets harder to make ends meet,
The rains never come, and you can't beat the heat.
Giving it all up, weighs heavy on my mind,
This big, cruel world is relatively unkind.

Suddenly the bleak cold winter is gone, Spring arrives.
A new crop will be sown, to renew our lives.
The wonderful aroma of fresh tilled ground,
Enticing my senses, to keep me around.

Barbara Haley

Untitled

Dear someone, someone close, someone tender.
Anyone who loves me with care.
I am out here waiting patiently
I call but I cannot hear, my
head spins in a dream, a springtime dream.
A vision of green, a vision of trickling water
in my dream. I hear, hearing the sweet, melodious
song, only a song so sweet can only be
from a mockingbird.
As I dream, I bathe in the sunshine,
lie in the bed of mother earth. I see
blue before my eyes far and wide from
one end to another.
A marvelous sight, this not heaven but
something more, something someone
has placed just for little me, me so relentless
and sporadic.
What gratefulness, such power of mind and heart
to work together, understanding, to make a perfect
dream, for me.

Jason H. Lilienthal

Between The Two

My anchor is my dreams.
Tho' anxiety interlopes along the way,
Wonders prevail.

Ants' hard work piling dirt
Might help a lazy one start to work.

Lilacs' aroma
Makes me resist other perfume.

The hummingbird's whir
Is an organic jet.

The frail, purple blooming iris
Is Gigi.

The honey bee
Is a politician on the stump.

Field stones awash in a mountain stream
Mirror the spectrum.

Soft rain on my roof
"Pings" like a harp of a ball room.

The moose, ignoring all about them
Makes me considerate of others.
Dayton M. Spaulding

Maieru

Mountains and hills are clothed in green
A glittering river is flowing between
In the valley the people are waiting
Expecting eternal flowers to bloom
Rejoicing I take it all to my heart
Unwillingly I wave goodbye and depart
Annika L. Watrous

A Rose

A rose has many different meanings that you may or may not know.
A rose may say the things that you just cannot show.
A rose can say "I love you" and "How was your day?"
A rose can say "I'm sorry but I must go away."
A rose can put a sparkle back into the eye.
A rose can ask questions, such as "Why"?
A rose can say "I'm sorry to hear the bad news."
A rose can say "I need you" and "You're the one I choose."
A rose can say "Hello" to a baby sweet and new.
A rose can say "Good-bye" to an old friend too.
A rose can say many silent things, so in a way a rose has wings.
A rose can pick you up when you're down and out.
A rose is precious without a doubt!
Rexan A. Wilkes

The Silhouette

Entering in my life, passing through vaguely,
I can see that mysterious silhouette in the garden by the waterfall,
   like a beautiful swan swaying in the water.
I can even hear the sweet and gentle voice calling my name,
   as I get closer the voice so vivid asking me to come and share
      the melody playing.
Is it my imagination or is it a dream?
Am I to wake up and realize my beautiful silhouette was just a dream.
G. Sookhu

Prism

Like the prism in a window
   I catch the sun, making beautiful rainbows.

As the Son encounters my diamond surface
   I come alive for you — creating dazzling colors
      speaking of beautiful things.

Let me be for you, beautiful imagery
   revealing truth
      bringing healing, like the Christ.

If you touch me, you will set me dancing, spinning,
   twirling, making beautiful splashing rainbows.

If you hold me, you will cut off my light and my life
   and I will become nothing, useless, taking up space.

Let the Son touch you and make you be alive for me
   dazzling, dancing, spinning, twirling,
      splashing beautiful rainbows on my life.

Become for me, beautiful imagery
   revealing truth
      bringing healing, like the Christ.

Be for me, the light and life of Christ,
   like the prism in a window.
Ann Jeffries

Gray Day

I was like them, but then came was him
there is his light, light in the night
the sun can be black, but black is bright
I was like them, but now I met him
out of place, in societies race
but he showed me pace
after the change, the change that I felt
who am I? Now I know
who can tell me, but myself?
This is the day before my tears
this is the day I first revered
trying to hide my mind, behind
I was like them, but now I have him
I can't pretend, my morals won't lend
I was like no one, until he was like me
I was truly loved by no man, until he loved me
and as the skies turn gray
I have but one thing left to say
as I closed in your heart - warmed letter
I really do love you and most of all I have me
Jodi Creager

The Corner By The Customs House

No words are spoken.
None need be.
An unmistakable cry reverberates
from pale chapped unmoving lips
unheard
except by the black silent shepherd
and me.

"Help, please help,"
a sign sighs
accompanied by a quiet jingling,
a light clinking
of little metal
on little metal.

I stop for a moment, certainly no more than two,
before my lateness ushers me
from his sightless solitude.

Though glitter may be added
and the jingling seem more bold
his windows, they'll stay dark
and the spirit - cold.
Nathan Hale

Was It Love?

Like the wind that comes and goes,
Like the roses grow and doom;
Feeling lost and feeling blue,
As if all the dreams were gone;
The picture stays but the feeling goes,
The tears fall down but the sun dries them all,
Tormented and destroyed, hearing another love song.
So, was it love or was it hate? That got in the way.
You sit alone but you don't complain,
Thinking about yesterday,
Rolling back the memories,
To those happy days;
So, was it love or was it hate? That got in the way.
People notice the pain,
But they just go away,
Thinking you were playing a game.
The game of the broken heart;
So, was it love or was it hate? That got in the way.
There is no use for the rain,
As the rose will grow again.

Nadiah Zaki Al-Gasem

Agony In Oklahoma

As I sit and watch TV,
I can't help but wonder,
What if that were me?

As I see one mother's worried face,
I wish for a moment,
I could take her place.

I take it back just as fast,
I wouldn't want my child dying,
In such a tremendous blast.

I wish I could be there,
Tell people I hurt with them,
Tell them I really do care.

"Look towards tomorrow,
Don't dwell on today,"
When you haven't lost a loved one,
That's a very easy thing for you to say.

Oh God, make it all go away,
Bring peace and happiness,
To the people in Oklahoma City, somehow, some way.

Heather Amberger

The Addict

Hokus, pocus! Find the locus of unrequited love,
The love that was never and not
Now magically appears in livid technicolor
Dimensional, having height, length, depth
Eternal, unfathomable, even unforgettable -
Wildest dreams steaming with fulfillment.

Hokus, pocus! Find the locus of unrequitable love
In the middle of a merry go around
With prancing horses, dancing painted pigs and ostriches.
"This time I'll get the brass ring and then I'll ride for free!
I'll find the mythical magical person,
Carved like the horses, as painted as the pigs,
But speaking! Come! Your dilly dream awaits you!"

Hokus, pokus! Find the locus of unrequested love.
The heart says to the mind, "Seek!"
Obediently the mind whispers to the body, "you must search,
Or else desire shall be happily never after;
Dear earth-bound body you'll be completed, done, spent -
Bathed in utterly bogus light, the better to see yourself."

John Anderson

Abyss

I stand perched on the edge, no more steps can I take,
but I must continue my dark journey to meet head on my fate.

The abyss is dark and forbidding but I cannot turn away,
it's almost as if it's familiar in some sinister and scary way.

Its cold encircles me, engulfs me with its dread,
there's an uncontrollable fear growing stronger in my head.

As I gaze into the darkness it's finally clear what I see,
the essence of the abyss is harbored deep inside of me.

My soul is black with lies and guilt my conscious gone array,
I've caused so much pain in your life and now it's time to pay.

My sentence is a painful one, a tragedy so true
for I have perched someone new on the edge and that someone now is you.

Oliver Harrell

Song Of The Sea

Did you ever look upon the sea, the sea of blue and black,
Where the waves show white on the darkest night,
And the ships don't leave a track?
Did you ever see the bloody sun seemingly rise from the deep,
Where the biggest ship is but a speck,
And the waves rock you to sleep?
For it you have, I've nothing to tell;
For you've seen the same as I.
I've seen the ocean a watery hell.
And the waves rise toward the sky.
I've seen the ocean smooth and clean
Like a plate of polished glass;
And I've seen the sun turn the ocean red,
Like the cheeks of a blushing lass.
This ocean is so much like a girl,
That you come to love it true.
Till you find its waves have a fickle curl;
And there's death in their depths of blue.

John W. White

Why

I try going thru life doing the right things.
I try being fair and just to everyone and everything.
Sure I falter and make mistakes at times.
So God why do you send me thru such a hard grind?
Do you have something in store for me and how?
But I am only human and I desire some good stuff now.
With me being who I am.
I will continue to be the sacrificial lamb.
So for now I will do my best in your eyes.
Until from here I have to say goodbye.

William L. White

Friends

A friend is a treasure your whole life long.
Someone who is caring, trusting, loving and strong.

A friend is a gift that we give to ourselves.
As precious as an antique we keep on the shelf.

But a friend is someone who believes in your dreams
Never doubting or judging and is on the same team.

A friend is someone who believes in you.
Not just the person but all that you do.

Treasure the friendship right from the start
Treat it kind, love it deeply, hold it close to your heart.

Polly A. Fullerton

Reality Bites

Realizing life is so deep,
You almost need a shovel;
In hopes there's not a heap,
So as not to grovel.

Anytime you think you want to die
Look up, look down, look all around,
Then you understand your reason to try.

There comes a time,
When there's no denying;
Anyone could be in this bind,
Without allowed any crying.

Never think you're above and beyond,
It could always happen to you,
Left lying lifeless in the bottom of a pond.

Always remember that Golden Rule,
It definitely has power to help you through;
Especially when there's nothing left to do,
With the exception of believing in only you.

Mary L. Armour

Fading Memories Of Melody

A flash of what once was is all to see of her face.
Few pictures with which to reminisce, hoping the mind does not erase
That sweet, subtle smile - those glowing, green eyes.
Fading memories lead to final good-byes.

Some memories last a lifetime; others seem to disappear.
Reflecting on good times, paralyzed with fear,
Sometimes incredibly unsure
If accurate memories of her will endure.

With memories fading only dreaming remains.
Dreams foster no miracles - only pain.
In them hopes of the past spark anew,
But reality lingers near - awake and without you.

The path of pain pierces to the core,
Bypassing the waves, straight to the shore.
Fading memories and dreams gone awry
Breed hopelessness sketched in sunless sky.

Steve Bratton

Message Of Good Wishes

On wings of Poem, I travelled here;
I shall speak, lend me thy ear;
Crossing great oceans, I've reached;
Your great country, new knowledge to seek.

I carry message of love and good will;
Straight into your loving heart, to fill;
India's cultural heritage I've brought;
To share among many things, thy thoughts.

Martyrs of America for ever live;
In pages of thy history, during our love;
Their heroic deeds on time's fleet, sing;
Bringing to our hearts, blossoms of spring.

On shores of inventions, United State stands;
Giving in its wake, a life grand;
Science and Technology claim to seek;
To ascend great heights like Everest's peak.

Hand in hand India and US march;
Showering on universe, Democracy's torch;
Almighty from heaven will always guide;
To achieve this, by being on our side.

Asokan Balasubramanian

Untitled

As she walked through the front door the screaming hurt her ears.
Her parents were ranting again she thought through streaming tears.

She tried to hide in her room, but the door slammed open.
As soon as she looked up out went all her hoping.

She tried to close her eyes and block out all the pain.
Every once in a while this helped to keep her sane.

It didn't always help, but she always got by.
This time she didn't; this time she wanted to fly.

She tried to talk to friends, none of them understood.
None of them had her problems; none of them ever could.

She wanted to go to a better place, she wanted to get there by eleven.
She grabbed a knife and slit her wrist, and hoped that she would go to heaven.

Amanda Beal

Folly's Drama

Is this it? The constant betrayal of those who I dared open my love to?
   I'm a joke when I exit the stage where the games are played;
I'm a fool when the podium belongs to me, where I speak the truth
of my atrocities of being weak, an occasional liar, a shameless
exhibitionist of seeming no self respect.
   Why hide the truth of these endeavors which belong to us all?
   I trip as I leave the stage, looks of disapproval, distaste, and
repulsion reject my entire presence. The judges have found me
guilty... but, when night falls, they all come to me, at sometime
or another, wanting to share my bed;
Almost pleadingly. They'll say anything. I see them. I always have.
   In my bed we are all alone, no stage, no jury. We are alone,
face, they cannot hide from me. They know. They feel safe. They
tell me of their atrocities, of their guilt, almost as if seeking my
approval, or giving a confession. I have no judgments to lay on
them, only those that they read in my eyes. They look away, ashamed,
or stand defensive, ready to fight or deny what I might have to say.
My heart open, I say nothing. "Sshhh...it's okay, shhh...it's okay."
   I know as well as they do that when the jury and I'm not there I'm
once more a mocked fool, a hidden night time accessory.
   As I enter, silence. Heads turn to look at me, but in my eyes.
Silence. Always I am thinking, looking at their fear, thinking,
"The damage I could do!" Four words await on the side of the line
where I stand and they never cross, "Let the games begin!" My smile
twists, my eyes speak, "I dare you. One at a time, all of you!"
   Alone. Self Will. Afraid, and Ready.

Shawna Walker

A Fallen Angel

Once upon a dewspun day,
the most magnificent creation was made.
An angel from whose lips came beautiful song,
had a heart that reached forever long.

But once upon a tear filled night,
an angel came upon the Lord to fight.
Sadness overwhelmed his creator,
but the Lord knew he was a traitor.

So once upon a midnight dream,
and angel stood and screamed.
He cried out to God with hate,
for he knew his fate.

And once upon a scarlet sky,
an angel laughed as a savior said, "Good Bye!"
And although once, in a pearl-gated palace,
and angel felt a great call,
we all know vanity was his fall.

And so once upon a time,
the Lord said, "Vengeance is surely mine!"

Eve Campos

Untitled

End all light that shines through light
and hides the day from the night
End the scandals that peer through the walls
and portray themselves as saints to the unfortunate
The ones who don't see
are to be pitied for being deceived
and worse yet the perpetrators
for being blind of their deeds
This is not God but the devil slipping his fingers
   into his prey
Making things pretty, and beautiful, and easy to catch
but will decay upon touch, rot upon inquiry
and die upon conviction
Look the other way and what you will see is beauty
which you thought you saw before
but this is eternal given from the soul of the creator
Just breathe and it is there
but you have to find it
buried in the depths of darkness

   Philip Lippman

The Words Of A Song

I sing not only that I'm happy,
I sing that a lonely one may know a moment of belonging,
As the melody I send drifts into their hungry soul.

I sing too, for all the joy
That awaits the sacred should they hear
And leave their darkness for even a glimpse of light.

I sing to drown the sounds of war and violence
And hope their rhythm changes to mine.

I sing to all that are taking from the earth
More than they need for their comforts,
That it may feel no more abuse
And silence its trembling of quakes and floods.

I sing the softest to little children
That I may guide their steps,
To smell, not crush the flowers along life's way.

I sing so humbly for the gift the Creator gave to me
And that he should keep giving me words
So I can sing.

And one day that they may be words
That the whole world will sing with me.

   Hope McNabb

Heaven's Flower

Small sandalfooted boy of yesterday
Sunshine soaked spirit flashing in my memory.
I see your gift of treasured dandelion
Well and slowly chosen from a meadow's grandeur
Thrust upward to my vision.
That sun warmed flower clasped
In your dear dusty hand
Still catches and invokes a mother's wonder
And bespeaks our love.

Dear little one, now grown tall and far away
The wonder and the love continue on.
And that past heaven's flower of love
A tender dandelion, lives in my heart's eye
Golden, satin to the touch and
Reverently placed still in an honored place
Upon my memory's mantelpiece.

   Rhys Stevenson

Golden Angel

Dew drenched fields
Lilies vast and white
Happiness that butterfly wields
In reckless abandons flight
Blue eyes fill with salty tears
Envisioning the memories
Black hole filled with fears
Soul soliloquies

Fleeting thoughts of time gone by
Sun burns hot with guiding light
No time left to woefully cry
As day fades into empty night

Left a star in velvet sky
Stands alone and shines as one
Separated from the rest...can't be seen by naked eye
Spirited golden angel known to none.

   Diana L. Simmons

Romancing the Whales

Listen quietly and their tales
The haunting sound and sight of whales
Rising up majestically
Frolicking and migrating across the sea.

Wondrous, strong, swimming side by side
Brilliant sunlight glistens off their hide
Blue, Hump, Orca, Black and White
Silently propelling themselves, into night.

Strong, playful, amazing to behold
Retreating, advancing, acting so bold
Brazen monsters, sometimes so shy
Bulleting from sea depth, aiming for the sky.

We watch and love, what would they be?
Without protection from land to sea
Their beauty gives good cause to cry
Diving deep, tails gracefully wave goodbye!

Water spouts in playful spray
Riding the waves on a winter's day
As the many years go passing by
We hear the echoes of their woeful sighs.

   Deborah S. Xanthakis

The Homeless Man

A young man sits painfully on the ground;
His hand outstretched, not making a sound.
His empty hand, frozen from the wind;
His heart guilty, for he has sinned.

He knows not what, he has ever done wrong;
He tried his best, yet all is gone.
His home and what money he ever had;
Have faded away, like a dying fad.

Some people give change, others turn the other way;
Then there are some, who have words they want to say.
Hurtful thoughts and demeaning words.
Can no longer damage those sensitive nerves.

He feels so low, that no one can strike;
He's lost the to try and fight.
What is left, what can he say?
Even his spirit, was taken away.

As time moves on, he awaits the day,
When his life will end, ridding him of all his pain.

   Kirk DeMatas

Life

A generic term, at the time of packaging
No hint to the sperm, as to the quality of product hatching
Pretty baby, all our own — not yet human, not yet grown
Thrust into the world alone.
Mother, Father, family dear, are you close enough to hear?
With folded arms and faded ways you cling to cherished good ole' days,
   'spite pressured peer
And when at last the bond is severed, free will complicates the
   choices
Where to go and whom to go with, too many options, too many voices
Adulthood an amass of noise is.
And does it matter whom we fight?
Enemies are future friends, seen in an unflatt'ring light
Probably why war is so confusing at night.
Does serving others make a better man, or merely one with a retirement plan?
A time clock starts your day, and puts an end to your play
Your children, babes as you once were — do they venerate, or
   repudiate, the values you take pains to oraculate?
Bummer!
And as twilight closes in, fragile veil, paper thin
You lose your deposit if you break your lease
Rest in peace.

Brett Hart

Who I Am

I am a man
Who lives on the 28th floor.
Every morning I go through the lobby
And out the front door.

In the afternoon,
I walk back in.
I get on the elevator,
And a number I punch in.

When I reach the 14th floor.
I have to get off.
I find the staircase
And the rest of the way, I walk.
I could do this for several reasons.

But which one is it.
I may be overweight or need the exercise,
But reality, I'm a midget.
And I can't reach the 28th floor button.

Kevin Dunlap

To Give And Receive

Give me the love that I seek
and I'll give you the child you want.
Give me the home I need
and I'll give you the warmth inside.
Give me the security that protects me
and I'll give you the friendship that you desire.
Give me your hand...
And I'll be your wife.

I gave you the love that you sought
and you gave me my sons.
I gave you the home that you needed
and you gave me the warmth.
I gave you the security to protect you
and you gave me a loyal friend.
I gave you my hand...
And you became my life.

Cynthia Green

Untitled

Do you think time would stop for me
   Do you think the winds would blow my way
Do you think the sunset would talk and
   if so what would it say

Do you think the thunder would call for me
   Do you think the rains would cry
Do you think the lightening would reach out
   to gently wipe my eyes

Do you think the waters would stand still for me
   Do you think I would lie and chat with them or
Do you think my mind would float away
   with cherished thoughts of him

Do you think the world would slow down for me
   Do you think it would not turn at all
I only wish it would pause a bit
   for I am so dizzy I may fall.

Maggie Clay

Colour: Meaning Broad Spectrum Of Color

Sitting in a chair, then into the kitchen I take a look. I see my mother cooking and reading recipes from a book. At that moment, she stops and turns to me and says, "Honey you're so beautiful, your skin so fair." I look at her strange wondering did she really say that — why? All of a sudden, I remembered watching her one night, as she looked into the mirror and started to cry.

Then I knew of her pain, the pain that's within. That she felt that being colored was a sin. It was contradicting to me since she always said "stand tall and be proud." To never forget where I come from and to never let anyone keep me down. I guess she wanted to break the chain and teach me something other than what she had been taught, but deep down I knew that that's not the story that I had bought.

But whatever the meaning, I guess I'll do as she wants me to believe, to pretend I don't see the prejudice portrayed onto people who look like me. I hope to see the day that people are judged for who they are and the virtues that they are built on, and not because if their race, sex, class, age or even religion. But for now I guess I'll take it one day at a time and for myself remember that being colored is not a crime.

Veronica Telles

To All It May Concern

My name is Bill Clinton and as President,
I'll mostly sign bills but won't have to pay rent.
This is my family and this here's my cat.
Here also are budget plans pulled straight from my hat.
I'll send you to Bosnia with artillery,
While I stay home and take advice from Hillary.
What's the difference between a mule and an elephant?
To you that question might be irrelevant!
Would you rather have Bob Dole, or maybe Ross Perot?
That Whitewater thing? You don't need to know!
Would I lie to you or doom you to fail?
You already bought that I didn't inhale.
Whatever you do, don't ask Limbaugh or Newt!
I'm too good a scapegoat to give me the boot.
So what do you say!
How about four more years?
At least I'm not Carter, whose brother sold beers!
Well, I've got to go catch a 6:30 flight
To resolve a dilemma in the House they call "White."
Seems it's my turn again, to do dishes tonight!
Thank you America!

William K. Kroon

The Holistic Bermuda Triangle

My father Sun, my Mother
Earth, I, the baffled embryo moon,
questions life. Rotating on my axis, with a
weeping curse, of a necrophiliac within a complex
wall of mist, asks questions, only to live an
unanswered meaningful life, of sorrow,
hate, and perished love. Pounding memories,
rape my heart of blooming memories,
now frozen in time. A smile
witnessed as a day age, becomes
an eternal gift, only the chemicals
within, hold the key to
rewind its contents,
acknowledging
the punishable
gift of
life.

Ricardo P. Enriquez

Morning Espresso

"Espresso, please," she thought and rightly said.
"Wait in line!" the repetitive replies.
A bearded, dark chimera appeared instead.
Red coat, the color of crushed tomatoes belies
His stature like Odysseus, proud and tall,
Who is this dashing stranger with staring eyes?
Must be a physics Nobel after all.
"Espresso, please," she thought and cries.
A tea was brought, but coffee hissed.
Odysseus took a sip and then sat down.
Her heart did pound imagining such bliss.
"Lack of coffee," sniffed the therapist, Dr. Brown.
"Espresso, please," she thought and screams.
Her wedding band grew tight in lacking caffeine dreams.

Anne Faynberg

Resolution

We didn't chose each other. It seemed like whimsy.
A disappointment for you, confusion for me.
Evaluated at birth and forgotten;
To be lost in your clamor and the howling bravado
You used to buy off your fears.

Tastefully decadent;
Your counterfeited insouciance betrayed you
And then the laughter stopped tinkling;
The roaring reduced to a hack.
Strangers wearing Monday morning smiles,
Gave way to bustling activity.
A small girl, the center of it all, reaching for the familiarity of oblivion.

Looking back, I'd like to say that our time together had merit,
that despite the shards your memory leaves, I am better for it all.
But caprice overused becomes routine;
Reason thrown away finds its absence rising vicious in the morning light.
I wouldn't have chosen you. There is hope for me in that —
And resolve.

Terry Pierce

True Love

Have you ever had a true love?
Someone to call your own.
To hold you in their arms at night.
To calm your fears and take away your fright.
Someone you love with all your heart, for whom you think
you'll never part.
You love him and he loves you.
Together you make the perfect two.

Kari Ludwig

Childish

I wish I could be a kid again,
Carefree, always having someone to depend on
Running around in the field of life, full of possibilities
No decisions or problems
I would run around and play all day
The grass rubbing against my legs and the wind in my hair
I'll never be a kid again
So many things are changing
Now life is full of worries
Problems with my family, friends, life, death, and love
Trying to figure out who I am and what I want to be
The grass is now vines grasping me, pulling me down
It is suddenly cloudy, it rains, it pours
My life is thunder and lightning
I must be strong and get through this storm
Because I know the sun will shine some day
I'm just so sorry that I wasted my childhood away.

Lauren Fabrizio

Please Hear What I'm Not Able To Say

You picked this place, cause you thought it was safe;
It's tidy neat and clean.
But please see beyond that; is this place nurturing?

The way that I react, is the only way you'll know;
If I'm really happy, If it's safe for you to go.

When you drop me off, do I fight, and kick, and scream?
Perhaps I have a reason, perhaps this place isn't what it seems.

Fussing and screaming in the beginning, is natural when you go;
But this reaction should subside, within a week or so.

For if this place you leave me in, allows for me to grow,
There's no question about it, of course, I'll want to go.

My attitude, when you pick me up, is another way to hear;
For it can say what's really going on, my excitement will be loud and clear.

I know you have to leave me, and you pay for the best of care,
so use these signs, they are the words,
I trust in you to hear.

Kathryn Blair

My Father

My father — who, you ask, was he?
He was the best as can be.
He was one of a kind.
And he always spoke his mind.
Don't you dare say he was a wimp,
'Cause he would have left you walking away with a limp.
Do you want to make a bet?
Whatever my daddy wants, my daddy gets.
And when it comes time to say "goodbye,"
We will cry and cry.
Now it's time for me to see,
In no more pain and suffering he will be.
I will see him, when?
When it's time to be a family again.
And do you know what's really nice?
My dad has gone to paradise!

Bridget Russell

Souldancer

When does the line 'tween light and dark
Divide and conquer restless ways?
Where is the space not black or white
Separating night from day?

What wonders lie within that time,
That moment when our sleep draws near;
That span between both life and death
In which great visions can appear?

What lessons learned will juxtapose
Each on each within that time?
What dreams will play upon the field
That lies within this heart of mine?

There are still some remembrances
That carry on in waking light
Of where I danced within the glen
Of the soul I joined last night.

E. M. Flavin

Peace Poem

Lets all try to get together
In the arms of mother earth
Thoughtful understanding
Night prove everything its worth

Let us dry the teardrops
And seek the reason for their cause
Utter nothing hurtful without first a careful pause

Try to share some bounty
With those who hunger so who can tell beforehand
Who will feel the coming blow

Is the grass beyond your fence
Really greener than your own?
Why not ask your neighbour's method
While your grass is being sown

Each of us is human and vulnerable to pain
Hurting one another has nothing much to gain

Wear your neighbour's moccasins to see just how he feels
And show some real compassion when from tragedy he reels

Our world is just a circle, so we should easily hold hands
And rather live together 'stead of fighting for their lands.

Gertrude Cohen

Untitled

Listening to songs in French
I can mouth the words
But I don't know what they mean
Don't know what I mean
Though I must be saying the right things
I think I make sense to someone

Turn up the volume
Till any song doesn't make sense, to
Listen to music
Without the burden of words.

Write a poem
With just the impression
No words.

Tally Helfgott

The World's Greatest Treasures

The world's greatest treasures is not what you might think
It's not silver or gold, not metal at all
It's not diamonds or emeralds nor gems that are rare
The world's greatest treasures are
A hug, a smile and a kiss

When you feel sad and blue
Alone that nobody cares
When you are ill and feeling low
Gold, silver or gems may give you a momentary thrill
But a hug, and a smile, and a kiss will give you a very real lift

They show you are not alone
That someone else cares
That's why it's plain to see
The world's greatest treasures
are a Hug and a Smile and a Kiss

Imelda Graham

The Eagle's Quest

On silver tipped wings set ablaze by the sun's fiery haze
Ore white topped mountains and arctic blue seas,
Across far reaching plains of purple green forests and
Lush coloured valleys and bright golden leas.

My senses keen and sight pinpointed on the light that streaks
From marshmallow like clouds
To the distant earth like luminous shrouds
I descend to the crest of the mountain from whence I came
To my nest of young eagles bearing my game.

Tis from this vantage point I'm made strongly aware of life's
Cries for help and desperate despair,
For freedom is king here and heaven is near
And man is a thing only other men fear.

On silver tipped wings I have soared high and long
With the wind rushing to me to sing its sweet song
Tis the song of the lion, the elk and the bear and all of
The creatures that together will share
The endless glory of natures domain
Where I, the eagle, my quest be to reign.

Bertram Reid Turpin

Homesick

Take your valley with mountain walls.
Take your city with gala halls.
Take the lakes and the boats that you paddle
But give me the range and my boots and saddle.

I miss the song of the meadow lark
And the sound of the farm dog's friendly bark.
I miss the chimes of the milk cow's bell
As she comes at night to the old corral.

Perhaps a deer has grazed its fill
and stands tonight on a Cypress hill.
The moon looks down on its beauty rare
'Till turns again to the forest's care.

Away out there on the prairie wide,
My loved ones sleep on a green hillside.
I mourn them not for when teardrops start,
Their love shines through to my homesick heart.

Ina Gordon

The Birth Of America

Three hundred years to this day
I'm still troubled by those who have walked this way.

Their foot prints are trails in my mind,
and in earth's bosom they're kept for all time.

Like the precious metal hidden in Mother Earth's tomb
they were pulled from the depths of darkness,
Yanked from the depth of darkness,
snatched from their Mother land's wound.

Oh! What an awful feeling
the scars are felt to this day
the birth of "Good Old" America
What a price to pay

Like black precious gold they were all thought to be
brought to this land you're a profit you see.

Brought under contract to America's soil
Chain to this land, to serve and to toil

Three million strong have come and gone
who have left me behind to tell of this wrong.

Seeking a dream on America's shore
Seeking a dream that is here no more
Paul Gray

Drive-In Shows

Do you remember those drive in
shows? Holding hands, necking and
anything goes but, just when everything
is going your way, the lights come on
as bright as day. The loudspeakers
come alive, "We have king size drinks,
burgers and fries." So out of the car
without delay, to the snack bar you make
your way. Food is the last thing on
your mind, as you take your place in
that great long line. Finally you're
there, you reach for your change, the
attendant stares, like you're
disarranged. Back to the car you rush
with the food, hoping she hasn't
changed her mood. But after the
snack, it's well understood, that
one special moment is gone for good.
Robert L. Taylor

The Country Drunk

He drinks whiskey at home
and anywhere he may roam,
behind the tobacco barn,
or in the field of yellow corn.
He drinks it where I've seen a mouse
scurrying about in the smokehouse,
He's told me a fib
about drinking it in the corn crib.
He hid it for a rainy day
in the cowbarn which stores the hay.
The woodshed holds empty bottles
of that which he enjoyed when he was idle.
The henhouse was spared
because when he entered, their wings flared.
All the mules in the stables
know the stories are not fables.
Margaret Glidewell Poole

Autumn Moods: A Time To Reflect

Can I compare you to another or would I even try?
No words can explain the radiance within your eyes.

Sun! Stand still! Darkness move no more. Noon day
shadows cast forth, as the sun's ray's begin to soar.

You are life at its fullest moments in time. My friend
at best, my love forever. I cannot compare.

When leaves fall at autumn's approach. No rain. Only
dew upon the sparsely covered slopes. When days seem to shine
with its brilliant rays of light and a cool wind blows on a
clear autumn's night. I find myself thinking of you.

I wish upon a star, in the stillness of the night. I
wish upon a star as the moon shines bright.

Forever wishing that you were here. As the night
fades slowly, my eyes fill with tears. Can one price love?
I question myself daily as I watch the sun rise high above
the horizon.

Each dawn's rising brings ever present hope. Each dawn's
rising brings another day to cope. For something is missing
from this time of year. It's the warm touch of your hand and
holding you so near.
Patrick Williams

A Time To Remember

The Bethesda Deaconesses
have lead the way
and now it's time
for us to say,

thank you for your leadership

It may have been
you didn't know
when starting out
so long ago

the gifts you would leave behind

You've planted an image
of care and concern
for all you have given -
this much we have learned

to be gentle with those whose lives we touch

Your lives are a blessing
and we hope to reflect
the same compassionate service
that we have grown to respect

because you have taught us well
Lin Thomas

No More Wars

See all the bright harbor boats,
Come, watch as they dance over the waves,
Sailors are dressed in their navy pea coats,
While, here we stand as free Indian braves.
Ships are all decorated in their gala array —
Here they come to cheer from far off shores.
We salute our red, white, and blue of U.S.A.
Let's all thank God, and celebrate — No More Wars!!
Evelyn G. Goss

"Platonium"

Come with me on a journey of time.
To a place so wonderful in the center
of your mind.
Let's fly so high above the moon
and stars.
In vision all the splendor of heaven,
Look! We just past mars.
Isn't it great looking through this maze,
To behold the beauty of all the cosmic rays.
Doth yonder to behold; a planet,
I can hardly believe, doth mine eyes deceive.
Colors of the rainbow dance before my face,
Fragrances so sweet I cherish to embrace,
Peace and tranquility doth fill my heart
and soul.
Joy unspeakable, Oh! I feel so bold.
Does one dare to take a voyage
out to sea.
Then come inside your mind
to Platonium with me.

Charles G. Miller Sr.

Common Bond

A bird that did not make its flight from the north
An apple bud that blossomed on a dead end tree
A patch of grey snow on a bed of red roses
A prisoner on death row still yearning to be free
A senile old woman locked up on the fifth floor
A vagabond in a cardboard box he calls his home
A leftover spring from a burned out autumn
This is the burning life
This is the common bond

Nadine C. Hoyer

Shattered Tomorrows

Do you think that you are better than me?
Do you think that's fair?
Did we not open up our trusting hearts and
land for a better tomorrow?
I have walked on both sides.
And have seen pain, hunger and suffering equally.
Do I ridicule you and your ways?
No!
Do our hearts not beat the same?
Do our lungs not fill with the same air?
Do we not have same fragile emotions?
Yes!
Then why do you think you are better than me?!

Kim Adams

In Praise Of Dolphins And Their Relatives

In the depths where the Cetacean sings
Under the reach and swell of waves
That ride over the eye of our globe
Saline, restless gyres dimly perceived
In those depths where sings the Cetacean
There is some light
But of a quality quite different
Spectrally shifted with depth
Thus, the perception of the Dolphin
And his companions
Is much at variance
With our myopic vision
And his song
Quite strange
To our air-filled ears.

Tom Berman

Lonely Nights

In the loneliness of the night,
I find my will trying to fight.
Holding back the tears.
Of the love my heart fears.
Desiring to hold someone who's true,
Someone who's in need of me too.
But as the night grows cold,
I have no one to hold.
So many nights spent alone,
Feeling the cold in my bones.
The only thing I hold in my arms,
Is the air that's lost its warmth.
And in the darkness of the night sky.
Even the stars have another by their side.
Making my loneliness so much more,
Harming the heart that's already sore.
This growing loneliness in the night.
Is causing me to lose my fight.

Elvie Hall

A Storm A Comin'

Listen, can you hear the storm a comin'?
Hear the rumble of a people frustrated and angry!
Yes, a dark and ugly storm, be sho nough a brewin'.
Building up with so much destructive energy!

The storm will move across this hateful land and
so much blood, sweat and tears will be shed!
A people will be in the grip of Death's hand and
the land will be fertilized with the human dead!

Bias, prejudice and discrimination is the eye of the comin' storm!
Prime conditions for the formation of a most violent atmosphere.
When it strikes, no man, woman or child will go unharmed and
the land will be left covered in a cloud of fear!

Lying, denying nor hiding will keep this storm away.
God, nor the Flag, will be the sheltered havens for cowards!
Truth and people partnerships will be the shelter that saves
a people to see the light of the Lord, to stop a horror!

Force and fraud can no longer be a people's virtues!
There must be a reinstatement of Hope, Faith and Charity.
For a people's spirit and a link with God to be renewed.
No more irreverence to God: bury Hypocrisy!

Daniel Meadows Jr.

A Song For The Children

Look up, look up!
There is beauty to see, colors abound.
There is love to warm and comfort you.
There is knowledge waiting for your attention.

Look back, look back.
What do you see?
Is it warmth and love or vacant stares?
How can I be sure you've learned what I longed to teach.

Now look here into my eyes.
The love is there to sustain you
As you go into the world on your own.
Do not forsake it.

Now look ahead.
Watch your step, where you walk.
Precious objects depend on your care.
We know not the width or the depth of the path
That we travel.

Shirley M. Stein

To A Chestnut Sapling

Welcome little Chestnut Tree,
You've just popped up to say Hello to me!!
Soon, high up you will grow,
Leaving all else down below.
Strong and sturdy,
Proud in splendour,
Yet, to the wind you will bow.
With sprawling branches
You will create a splendid shade
From the noon day heat,
And the birds
Will knit their nests
Among your twigs.
The rain, the snow and the sunshine
Will rest upon your leaves,
And, the star sparkle
Will stream through your peep holes.
Chestnut tree,
Grow and live in this wide, wide,
Welcoming World with me.

Sarojini Bertha Peters

"The Journey Of Life And Death"

A new beginning starts when you first inhale.
You begin your journey on a distant trail.
You encounter the sun and meet the rain too.
Sometimes your sky gray, sometimes blue.
You'll meet people whom you can count on; whom you can trust,
But then some will just vanish with the midnight's dust.
Sometimes you'll laugh.
Sometimes you'll cry.
You might lose sight of where you are going and wonder why.
You run and face more obstacles...mountains on your track;
But you must continue to press forward and never turn back.
You'll race 'till you cross the finish line...until you have
completed your trail.
Then with a sigh of relief, you take a breath and exhale.

Kimberly Taybron

Fallen Angels

You see them everywhere,
    out on the freeways, down on the malls,
Flightless, chewing gum, showing their legs, hiding their wings.
    No longer singing, they don't recognize each other.
They drift into the arms of strangers, who promise Eden
    Offering more than invisible love,
        intangible comfort.
    Offering the taste, the pure erotic glory of darkness.
Fallen angels open wide their heart,
    knowing heaven is in the touch that connects us all.
So they hide in the dark, stealing kisses.
    Kisses blown from the clouds,
that melt the moment they land,
    leaving them thirsty, wanting only more.
Their sweet passion's just a fleeting sip
    of a much Higher Bliss.

Marilynn Huseby

Days

Some days my thoughts are just boxed up,
all crammed and jammed inside.
They hang from swelled up tentacles
in the emptiness of my mind;
And other days they flutter and fly -
such bold and beautiful things!
I find emotions, left by the complex thoughts
that drift around inside.

Alex Bennett

When I Was In Love

When I was in love I felt so good,
I felt like a dove, I stopped eating food.

But now we broke up I felt so sad,
I felt stuck, yet others are glad.

I lost my dreams I'm going nowhere,
It seems, soon I will go somewhere.

I almost forgot he cheated on me,
Yet I miss him a lot but no one can see.

I am depressed, it all went so fast.
I feel like a mess but it's all in the past.

I feel so much sorrow, yet I have to go on,
Still, there's always tomorrow, the pain will be gone.

He was my guiding light, I miss him now,
His bod was a sight, Oh Wow!

Madelaine Cacatian

Cry Of A Dolphin

Please
Oh, Dear God, just let me be.
All I want is to live in my sea!

Oh, Dear God, just let me play.
I never meant to get in their way!

When I swim, I feel so free.
Thank you, Lord, for this gift to me.

Oh, Dear God, I never hurt a one
Why do they kill me for having fun?

I just want to play in my sea.
Why can't these humans let me be?

I hurt. I bleed. I cry a lot.
Just let me live the life I've got!

I love you. I trust you. Please be my
friend, for I don't want my life to end!

Lisa A. Bergholtz

The Quiet Time

Found—again! the quiet time.
A time to think in solitude.
No sound, no sounds, not a whisper.
Soft thoughts make a gentle mood.

Found! the quiet time. Listen!
Birdsong, babbling brooks, gurgling streams.
Cool winds breezing in the trees,
Silent thoughts of broken dreams.

The quiet time. Muted sound.
Seabreezes, conch shell moans, sea foam.
Hear a long-legged, snowy, crane,
Slowly winging its way towards home.

The quiet time. Without a voice.
Silver stars winking in the night,
The moon glazing down in silence,
Night owls fluttering into flight.

Gloria Armstrong-Mosely

Lurable

With entrancing eyes that reel you in
She casts a spell of magic.
And her fire drives a man to sin
With an ending oh so tragic.

I try to resist, but her scent is strong
And pulls me in with ease.
Her lips sing out the saddest song
And her body longs to please.

Run! Hide! Abandon Her!
My conscience yells from above.
But no is the answer that echoes here,
My heart is lost in love.

Joshua Mahon

Untitled

Am I from another time
When poetry would oft times rhyme
And I without sophistic wit
If I can't bear the foggy writ
Of shallow thoughts-disguised with words
Composed by philosophic nerds

A privileged lot of folks are we
Who know just why - free verse is free
Who wants to read this verbose trash
Oh please come back dear Olden Gnash

A new art form now fills the air
Alas! The answers to my prayer???
A generation spouting rap
A curse! Of adolescent crap

Oh yes there's meter and yes there's rhyme
But spare me this emetic slime
It's time to stand and make a choice
You take the rap - I'll take free voice.

James R. Bruening

Down The Ages

The distance seemed a haggard mile
And they trudged along - a weary file
Afar, where the sky met the earth
They knew was hope, or maybe, death.

To stand, to speak, to fight no more
But bear the burden of ghastly gore
Insane warriors fighting a fire
And innocent lives lost in the mire

The children know not to sing or play
For them it's guns that sway
No mirthful blithe fill their lives
Broken, they live in their hollow hives

For reasons, unknown, they say the cause
What cause proffers, sorrow and remorse?
For ages and more we have seen it all
Bloodshed, pain - sinners them all!

History will hide her ugly head
For her load is certainly heavy as lead
She will be cursed, sworn and hurled
While humanity moves like an unheeded herd.

Kalyani Gopinath

"Where Dreamers Hang Their Hat"

Somewhere in the shadows, lying in the grass.
Against the moonlights beauty, where dreamers hang their hat.
Hidden by the willows. Out beside the pines.
Where starlight gazes down, and dries my teary eyes.

That's where I am waiting. That's where I reside.
I'm somewhere. Can you find me?
   I'm where dreamers go to hide.

Past the winding river, along the drifting hills.
Against the silent darkness, where lovers sleep so still.
Taken by the current. Breathlessly and shy.
Lost inside the beauty. Taken by the sky.
Adrift on the ocean; between the water and the shore,
with the sand between my toes, never asking for much more.
Sweeter than the candy that was given as a child,
where dreamers dream their dreams, with their heads up in the clouds.

That's where I am waiting. That's where I will stay.
For tomorrow or forever, or forever and a day.

I'm there. Can you see me? That's where I am at.
Lost inside the beauty.
   Where dreamers hang their hat.

Cathy Farrar

The Human Synthesis

Sun God, we began in a melt of eons,
as portions of water, air and sperm —
we, the squatters at ground level,
You, in the galactic tiers of Heaven,
where a potter turned clay into man.

We recast old longings into shadows,
and parodied the suggestion of being,
the intrinsic emotion of compassion,
into a sequence of harmony, right, law —
human ideals scouting the road ahead.

On Earth's brow, we seeded futures,
of swords, plowshares, and libido, the mix
activated in human expediency, to endure
the voice and dream of the God Aspiration —
flame flaring the God call in man hearts.

The Olympian Dream became one in man,
what we were, and what we came to be,
in the migrations of life between the stars,
as we searched the roadways of hope,
before the flaring of dawn rising as stars.

Manuel Gomez

Untitled

Your voice slowly fades out,
As I slide down,
Wondering what will become of me,
Thinking back on what has produced me.
All of the love expressed,
Remains in every smile.
All of the pain and anxiety,
In every glance down.

I glance down too often,
Not taking the time to smile.

I'm not so concerned with your basic studies,
They will not complete my picture of happiness.

Many times I don't understand,
What it is I'm looking for.
I recognize my real goals,
After they've been accomplished.

When you continue to ask about my expectations,
I glance down,
Feeling the weight of your frustrating question.

Kim Bottita

Prejudice Is Wrong

God created us all equal, although there's many whom disagree
the color of a persons skin, it means nothing to me.
There is so much anger and bitterness, it's everywhere I go
why can't people just forget prejudice? Together work an grow

In todays world, there are many problems to burden one down
The saddest of them all prejudice, yet it's all around
Throughout each day, in all walks of life
Prejudice slurs, and they cut deeper then any knife.

Judged by the color of their skin, and nothing more
When in reality, it's all races, and of this I'm sure.
There is both good and bad, in all races (it's so clear to see)
It is told on the news each night, it's written in history.

We all should be teaching love, love for one another
Not all this judging and criticizing, based only on color
This world I know, would be a much better place to live
if we all would just learn to pull together, just a smile give.

It is just as easy to teach love, as it is to teach hate
Please stop the prejudice, stop it now, before it's too late
There is not a one of us, not a one promised tomorrow
When our last breath is taken, it will be to late for sorrow.

Shirley D. Edwards

The Desert

While wandering on the desert,
I've seen such wondrous things.
The beauty of the sunset sky.
The color of butterfly wings.
I've heard the rustle in the trees,
As a silent wind creeps by.
Felt the magic of the night,
As the moon glides 'cross the sky.
I've felt the heat of campfire,
Make me feel as warm as toast.
I've watched my children smile,
As we have a weiner roast.
I've kissed the sticky marshmallow spot,
On a child's upturned face,
And watched the embers glow and fade,
With my husband in this place.

Vickie Hatton

Three Close Friends

Side by side, many years we had shared
Just best friends...people talked and stared.
We would fall in love, they all just knew
eventually we did, it simply passed thru.

My feelings for him, they had to be known
over length of time, a strong love had grown.
He wasn't at all the man, I had made him to be
For some time, disappointment hung over me.

I wasn't looking for love, just for fun.
That is how our relationship had begun.
No shining armor, he didn't come riding
instead my knight appeared, to me in hiding.

I had to let him go, before I could see
there was love there, if only I'd let it be.
I pushed him away, he seemed to fall so fast
Love so quickly, I didn't think it would last.

One offered excitement, we were quite a pair
but sincere love, I would never find it there.
One offered romance and love that seemed to grow
we were three close friends, that was some time ago.

Stacie Johansen

Voices

From out of the mist of a mind — the siren call,
seducing with false promises.
From out of the dark of terrors unknown,
fragile and unseen — it whispers.
Be mine it tempts,
Soar on the wings of purples and golds.
Come to me, trust only me — the command
From out of the mist of a mind — a sinister hiss,
You are mine, have no others before me.
From out of confusion and fear — you cannot escape,
A terror echo from a demon within,
Trust no mortal — no sanctuary, no place to flee.
From promise to lie,
From lover to foe,
You cannot resist it screams!
From out of the mist — naked horror,
A mind.

Susan Pollard

"Ode To Donella"

In my room four walls I do see -
   silent, lifeless barriers keeping you from me.
Not so my heart -
   a place of no limits or bars,
   where you and I may dance to Hootie
   beneath a million bright stars.
A breeze in a safe forest upon our faces,
   a lake of blue, a meadow of green -
   so many places...
   to learn about you, to know your heart,
   a lifetime ahead, now is a good start.
Patiently I wait for more glimpses of you -
   to hear your voice, to hold you anew.
Until that day in my heart you will be -
   swimming as beautifully as a dolphin
   in some bright, clear sea.

David W. King

Dance To A Mountain Sunflower

Dance to a mountain sunflower
a silent waterfall is a
caressing shower.
To the best refreshment sip the
running river.
The trees will keep me warm
as the warm wind blows the comfort hither
it's impossible to keep a quiver
in the rain so I can not shiver.
Listen to the background I like the sound
of my only step just before
I walked the ground.
I used to walk now I run to find
leaving what I've kept behind.
No need to see again for this I've seen and done.
Times a while
my feet feel sore walking mile to mile
at last now I drink from my own hands
seeing the response of gentle reflection
comforting these mountain lands.

Candace Noftsger

Attempting Peace

Soldier has orders, placed there in his hand,
Commander in Chief, giving the command,
Sending out the best that our country can,
Peace keeping mission, sent to help out other lands.

Some are just boys, while others are men,
The United States of America, trying to help keep peace again,
Men and women, this time will go in,
How soon we seem to forget, a place and time called, "Vietnam"!

Off they go, as loved ones wipe their faces,
There on their cheeks, are left tear traces,
Those in high places keep telling us, "It's for peace, not war"!
Too many returned, in body bags, history tells us the score.

Families notified to check the remains,
On their hearts, you can feel the stains,
Lesson unlearned: "War is hard to tame"!
Too late for peace, too late now to refrain.

Amanda O. Lin

Dear Dad

When I was young, we had good times and bad,
now that I'm grown, I'm so proud of you dad.

A lot of things you did seemed so mean to me,
now I know better, you were protecting your seed.

When I thought I was grown, and tried to be bold,
you never gave up or left me in the cold.

We fought, we yelled, and caused so much pain,
I realize now it was all for my gain.

You've put up with a lot, how could I have known?
I see it now, now that I have grown.

I know it's not late, I know you're proud,
you never hold it in, not even in a crowd.

I have kids of my own, it's plain to see,
your teachings and patience were your gift to me.

When my kids grown, and they seem sad, please talk to them,
like you did to me dad, and tell them how hard it is to raise them,
in a world full of crime, drugs and mayhem,
we've tried our best, G-d knows we did, but I know how hard it
is to be a kid and if G-d is to erase us from this earth,
your love and strength has been with them since birth.

Mary Stellatos

Goblet

One perfect goblet.
Dirty ... discarded;
Hidden amongst other saleables great and small.

Unwanted,
Unclaimed,
Unappreciated,
Waiting...

For just the right hand to reach for it.

Clean it ... shine it,
'Til its facets catch the glow of
Candlelight,
Allowing it to bask in the true, deserved, long overdue
Glory it rightfully should have always
Possessed.

Lauding over a simple, brick mantlepiece, the goblet's simplicity
Permitting the full splendor of its ego to be realized.

Empty, or full of the wine of love.

Cherished,
Treasured,
Shared.

Linda Jill Lustgarten

Said The Wise Man To The Child

As the young girl walked towards the steps of the wise man's home
She pictured him all glorious on his throne.
She timidly knocked on the door with her hand.

"Come in, Come in" called out the wise man.
They sat down and had some tea and cakes
And she thought she saw a trace of sadness cross his face.
"Why have you come to see me, my child?" he asked
For he could see the determination behind her polite smile.

"I have the same questions that everyone asks time after time:
Why are we here? What is life?
Their questions are the same as mine."

He considered it for a while and then said,
"Your whole life has not yet been led.
You must live a bit and you will find
that the answer will come within a lifetime."

As she walked out the door, she was pleased and confused
Because one day she would know what the wise man knew.

Patricia Carole Davis

The Candy Dish

Think very hard. Try to remember
When you were just a tot.
At Grandma's house, above the sink-
The thing you loved a lot!

Always, always out of reach
You had to ask for help.
To reach this thing you loved so much
High upon that shelf.

It stood there like a statue,
With secrets tucked inside.
You couldn't reach it anyway,
No matter how you tried.

But, Grandma knows your heart's desires
She knows you every wish.
She reaches out, removes the lid
And hands you the candy Dish!!

Wanda Anglin

Transcendence

Along this path I traverse over footsteps of those before me
The essentiality of my being realized among the splendour
I comprehend to no end, that which eludes superficiality
Knowing, the human condition to be so fragile and so tender.

As imagination conjures visions upon the mind
I understand not, our adherence to the current paradigm
The spirit must be set free, and not confined to ideology
Material possessions are of no substance, as that of individual creativity.

Tearful of our idle complacency, amidst the ruins born of
technological advancement
I become shrouded in the darkness of a civilization that portends
its own demise
To surrender one's serenity in exchange for a monetary increment
It is understood, harbor not the fallacies manifest in dormant minds.

What wonder can excite those who deviate not from their slumber
Yet awaken to a pale reflection born of society's dictum
A time of innocence, for it they could only remember
Would surely render misgivings to the lethargy of their life-giving serum.

Bryan F. Clark

Now I Know

In the springtide of life
Under the beautiful stars of innocence
They stuffed my head with canards
How I could not think for my age

Gave my youth on a bargain-basement
To mortal gods and tethering ghosts
Was made to fight wrong wars and battles lost
They laughed; I drank with yellowed leaves

Like smoke that cannot shield
Truth itself a-sudden stood naked
Eve returned from the grim reaper
Adam's primordial truss to sever

The gods fell from their lofty heights
Their fibs across their sculptured grimaces
And I, left alone in the cold wonder
The sounds of silence that speak yonder

But I see the pennant of heroes
Now I know I shall emerge victorious
I'll pitch and toss my own way
By dawn, I shall win! I shall win!

Sylvester Itoyah

My Dog Zero, Distemper,
The Lady Veterinary
And Carter's Mountain...

The doctor said, "Your dog shall die."
The lady vet began to cry,
"I did my all to make her right.
Your dog can't live throughout this night!"

I took my dog to Carter's place
For Zero's sickness to erase.
I said to life, "I make this vow:
Let me trade places with her now!"

A blinding cloud of brilliant light
Then cured forthwith my Zero's plight
And made me for a deeper bond
And made my arm a magic wand.
I put my hand by Zero's heart
And felt the pulsing with a start.

To all of life I hardly spoke,
But after that my dog awoke.
If Zero's life was barely slight,
Then what was that most brilliant light?

Eugene Hubbard

"Reflections"

A growling dog awaits, outside my bathroom door -
his teeth are barred, white and sharp,
I refuse to look, not beyond -
His star like eyes glow, with light
reflective of what's within, a panting
tongue hangs remorsefully, deep within, a hapless grin.
Paws so razor sharp, the floor is scratched
beneath, yet heard I nothing; when we walked
close to me, on maneuvering his quiet feet.
Startled, shook, somewhat put aside;
My own eyes in the darkness, grew afraid and wide,
That growling dog seemed closer; closer
within the lighted shadow outside this room,
I looked behind me, no window to my advantage be;
Deeper, heavier, that growl seemed to get,
In the mirror the reflection wavered, I dared not interject -
All cleansed and ready dare I exit,
The only door? One step forward and realizing; it was just a box,
absorbing a reflection;
outside the bathroom door.

Michael W. Rubin

One Life To Live

Unlike the cat
I only have one life to live.
There will be no rehearsal.
The time I am given will be my only chance,
I hope I'll make the most of it.
I'd like to be a golden sun
Radiating loving energy on everything around me.
I aim at myself being a channel of love.
I dream of peace on earth.
The time I was given is going by.
The time I was given is running out.
Something must have gone wrong somewhere
For everywhere I look there's sorrow.
Even though people are seeking the truth,
Every time they face the light
And open wide their arms to love,
Their shadow looks like a cross lying on the ground.

Danielle Beaudet

Love Takes Time

I can't explain the way I feel
Because it's so hard to realize that it's for real.
It was like all of a sudden you were there
To prove to me that you really cared.
You grew to be a special part of me
You gave me something I thought would never be.
We say this love will last forever
But time can't tell how long we'll be together.
So, let's just take one day at a time
And see how long you will be mine.
Hopefully, you and I will be together till the end
And you are whom I can always depend
With trust, honesty, and having you there for me
I want this to be more than just a memory
And if we are ever to come apart
Just remember that you will always have a special place in my heart.

Kelly Marie Regan

Unforgettable

The glow on his youthful complexion, the aura of sheer delight,
Trailed long behind his coach as he traveled across Canadian highways.
As if drawn by a magnet, mesmerized, on him my eyes were glued at first sight,
As I sat diagonally to his seat. His professional demeanor, young age, and ways
Soon in my mind, were carving a deep, lasting impression, a rare musical note.
Without any warning, as if manned by a ruthless mechanical device,
His psoriatic right hand traveled incessantly to his mouth and throat.
As he gnawed desperately at his joints for relief that never came, in a vise,
I relieved his frustration in my own veins, with the same depth and intensity.
For him, I felt the caring feelings I had for my sixteen year old daughter.
A rare, invisible, sincere, benevolent bond that withstands the years to eternity.
A cold sweat made me shiver, as at most a chewing gum I could offer,
A soft drink, a few words. As my soul ached for him, hopelessly,
I pondered in silence, "If I could only his hands for mine exchanged."
Vowing help from home, with a broken lead pencil his address I obtained
On a discarded chewing gum wrapper, placed across a juice container.
For some intangible reasons beyond his control and my logic, within a few hours
This young man had changed my life, forever.
And as if he were my son, I was missing him even before his coach had disappeared.

Pierrette Gendron

Real Life

Authority figures arrested in a scam,
a youth is killed in a hardcore slam
We live in a world filled with drugs and crime,
many different criminals serving their time
It's all about the money so people on the greed,
say it isn't everything but it is what we really need
There is no respect left from the young to the old,
people seem to turn their back in this world so cold
Been beat down and robbed now I fight for life,
everyone is packing from a gun to the knife
We make things harder then they really have to be,
throughout this life I have always paid my fee
Live paycheck to paycheck my boss's scam and lie,
lucky I am alive and just barely getting bye
In an illegal world filled with violence and hate,
unsure of what will become when I reach my final fate.

"RoB $o¢¢i"

Acceptance

If Love is a Rose, Lord,
Then let it smell Sweet.
If Pain is a Knife, Lord,
Then let it be Dulled.
If Hope is a Bird, Lord,
Then let it Fly Free.
If the Silence is a Vise, Lord,
Then Pry it open with Your Strength.

But if I am to Love, Lord,
Then let the Flower Grow.
And if I am to be in Pain, Lord,
I accept the Knife as Your Will.
If I am to Hope, Lord,
Let the little Bird Fill my Soul.
Please, Lord if the Silence is to be my Fate,
Let it be Pensive, and not Filled with hate.

Jennifer Portice

My Pal

Oh careless driver where 'ere you may be
I want you to know what you've done to me.

You've taken the best pal I've ever had
She was only a dog but she wasn't bad.

Wherever I went she followed me
She was always happy, it was plain to see.

You came along speeding, you hit my Pal
She's dead now, but you kept going pell mell.

It might have been a child that you hit instead
Left in the roadway cold and dead.

Please, Mr. Driver, won't you do your part?
Slow down, and don't break another one's heart.

Marge Hill

Our Love

Walks along the silvery shores
....quiet...serene...
Tender moments-no words spoken - so much said.
Moonbeams dancing through the trees
Flamboyant's fiery-bold
Lady of the night's exotic- sweet perfume
Mysteries unfurl...
A flicker turns to flame
A beacon in the night...
Our love!

Eugenie Golden Kelley

Thoughts The Mind Has Fought

Rockets and bombs bursting in air
The roar of thunder; lightning everywhere.
A train gets louder as it comes down the tracks
The screaming and cries of victims being attacked.

The racing of motors,
The screaming of engines,
The mind has heard sounds that are never ending.

The night is falling, the wind starts blowing,
The body grows tired, but the mind keeps going.
Shadows thru the windows the mind sees,
Trees are whistling, the falling of leaves.

The clock goes on ticking,
As the mind keeps reliving,

The world turns around, another day is beginning.

Fears of the mind can be a terrible thing,
But the arms of security is a wonderful thing.

Taraleen Panvelle

"Reflections At Twilight"

Why go on when your loved ones have left you?
Why go on when the enemy takes?
But you do go on for the ones who still love you.
You do go on for the children's sake.

Why go on when the body crumbles
And life seems nothing but grief and pain?
But you do go on, even tho' you may stumble;
You pick yourself up, and go on again.

Why go on when the storms overcome you,
And your soul yearns for the distant shore?
But you do go on, not knowing but trusting,
You reach for the hand that will lift you once more

Rita M. Alt

Howl

She'd make a tidy morsel
of their meek and monkish ways;
with nostrils flared and feral gleam she waits —
in barefoot disarray.
She mocks the bogus trumpery,
the haughty nincompoopery,
and eyes their bawdy plumage
filing past in slow parade;
then sends a howl of glacial rage
in a-capella serenade,
to fill the holes
their steps had made,
an echo
from the past.

Robin Parker

To The Belle Of Brisbane

You were music I had never heard,
a strain I had forgotten could be played
though even in its silence I had known it,
and in my heart the harmony you made
vibrated strings that never had been stirred.

It seemed that you combined sweet sounds
of things of which you never were aware —
of winds of April errant as your thought,
echoes shaking the still autumn air,
whisper of the snow on far-off grounds.

John Mahoney

The Whitestone Bridge

Against the checkerboard of night
garlands of stars unfurl and build
the mountains for our dreams to scale,
where only sun and moon shone yesterday.

A virgin's breasts thrust up
in sweet anticipation of a kiss
stream rainbows through dark molten glass
like hopes of promised lands.

Harsh echoes of our restless City
forged from hard piercing shafts of light
are pacified and lulled
by a seductive cadence of the sea.

And through a misty dream we now behold
Atlas asleep in Venus' arms
above the fragile mirrors of the dawn
its fringes ruffled by the wind.

Henry Halama

Mary B and Me

We became friends many years ago
I believe she was sent from above.
The years we shared as I look back now
Were filled with nothing but love.

She shared memories of her military life
A proud soldier she always would be
As we sat at her table, I'd choke back the tears
When she'd say "Please remember me."

Her love for her country and fellowman
All animals, especially the birds.
Is difficult at a time like this
To even put into words.

I'll miss you, my friend, our joy and laughter
All the good times we shared together
So save me a spot near you in heaven
Where we will remain friends forever.

Lisa Driver

I Love You Mom And Dad

For teaching me to dress and walk
For being there when I needed to talk,
For bandages on skinned up knees
For teaching me thank you and please.

For bed time stories and good night kisses
Even for making me do the dishes,
For being there to help and guide
For always being on my side.

For wiping up my many tears
For helping me overcome my fears,
For swimming lessons and skating too
For teaching me to tie my shoe.

For help with homework that was too hard
For playing with me in the yard,
For hugs you gave when I was down
For making me laugh when I wore a frown.

For promising to be my best friend
For all the birthday cards you send,
For things you cleaned and meals you cooked
For the many things I've overlooked.

Rhonda MacEachern

Listen

Children are supposed to be our greatest assets
But do we all treat them that way?
Do you ever tell your friends to wait a bit
Because your child has a problem and wants to express it.

So maybe when they want to change the colour of their hair
Or you disapproved of the clothes they wear,
Maybe they're afraid, let them know you get scarred too
That you have fears and frustration just like they do.

It's tough being a parent, it's tough to be a kid too
So be patient and helpful as they work it through
Be willing to give them support and guidance
But don't be afraid to set limits they have to abide with.

An issue that seems trivial and small to some
For others it may be very hard to overcome.
There's sex, drugs and AIDS and peer pressure so great.
Put your hand out to them so alone they don't carry all the weight.

Whether you're a parent or guardian, it's time you were told
Listen to your child the same way you respect the old.
This may be a small step to help end prejudice and violence
To building a world where never again a child remains silent.

Carol Pemberton

While You're Gone

We've been through so much in our lives, it's hard to let go,
getting rid of the pain goes so slow.
I can still see you laying in bed, sleeping so peaceful and free,
but honey, while you're gone, will you watch over me?
We lived young and grew old, our grandchildren will never forget
the stories you told. Our walks on the beach hand in hand, I
remember the day so clearly, slipping on our wedding band. The
meals I used to cook, the way I felt by you saying how great I look.
I close my eyes and you're all I see, but honey, while you're gone,
will you watch over me? I know you're in good hands up there in the
sky, I never really had my chance to say a goodbye. You got real
tired so I tucked you in bed, you said you loved me and I kissed
you on your head. I told you goodnight and shut off the light.
I woke up the next morning and you were still asleep. I tried to
wake you up but you didn't make a peep. I realized then that you
had died, I held your hand and prayed and cried. When I let go of
your hand it was as cold as can be, but honey, while you're gone,
will you watch over me? I know there's always a time to leave, mine
may come soon, but until then honey, while you're gone, watch over me.

Micah B. Dallas

Peace Poem

On the path of guiding light, the love for it is burning
bright.....I pray for it day and night.....If it
were real, oh what a sight!

It if could happen, it just might, make the world quite
alright.....But we can never win the fight, when
everyone is so uptight.....

If the bark is worse than the bite, why are we all still
living in fright?
Peace on earth should make it right, so we can live
one fearless night.....

But we can't progress to a new height, when our
hearts are full of spite.....Take a stand, go into
flight.....Fill us all with delight.....

The outcome may be slight, but it's enough to excite.....
your heart, like wind through candlelight.....
Maybe one day we all will unite, and change the
blackness of our souls into white.....

Jennifer Slichenmyer

Dances With The Secrets

Dances with the secrets, one's heart does hold.
Gliding ever so lightly over the questions, others do have.
Answering ever so politely.
To protect you so the world won't know,
you're cold. For once I wish the shoes were,
on the other feet. But would I really be,
leaving the pain behind.
Dances with the secrets, of a love not complete.
It does so amaze me how much a heart can take.
To step out in a blaze of glory.
Because your love's not fake.
Dances with the secrets of yet another one side affair.
Sidestepping the reality it must be a mistake.
Dances with the secrets, going through the notes,
in my memory in which to compare.
Dances with the secrets, I've left in prayer.
My secret desire, to have a true love that has,
time for me as well as others.
That kind of love I can share.

   Mary Christine Lucas

"Life Is Full Of Twists And Turns"

Life is full of twists and turns,
sometimes it stings and sometimes it burns.
But one thing that will always remain true
is the fact that I am always here for you.

Things don't always go the right way.
There are certain things that may dampen your day.
But remember one thing when times seem blue:
I will always be here, waiting for you.

I may not know exactly how you feel,
but I'm always around to help you heal.
I may not have the best overall view,
but I will always be here, to listen to you.

Sometimes I may not fully understand,
but I will always give a helping hand.
I'll say one more thing, although it is nothing new

I will always be here, just for you.

   Brian James Stremlau

A Toblerone Box In The Reunited Berlin Underground

In the country of cleanliness,
   Among un-Aryan litter
In the Friedrichstrasse station,
   Lies a cast off candy box.

In the glow of fluorescence and Glasnost,
   Boy meets girl in free air
Long encased in communist concrete,
   Like all their thoughts till now.

"A Pen!" They accost the Auslander.
   Opening the box to a new sweetness,
She writes against his breast,
   The address he could only dream before.

Now east is west and west is east,
   Finally the two have met.
Children and grandchildren,
   Issue of a candy wrapper.

Reams of paper at Versailles,
   Helsinki, Yalta, Potsdam, Munich
Mean less than the empty checkpoint,
   And a candy wrapper in the Friedrichstrasse.

   Sherman McCall

Friends

For friends are so few and far between
Even from here to there
And from where I'd came from,
So far away.

I've come to rest my heavy load in this small but cute church.
With my heavy heart and a heavy load.
For I stopped to hear this beautiful song about your loving Lord.
Sad and my heart was heavy as I felt the tears streaming
down my face.
No hanky in my pocket, as I tried to hold back the rushing tears
Fearing that someone would start to stare.

For where you came from was not so clear
Only that you were there and you cared.
For all it takes is a kind word, a friendly face and loving
arms to embrace.
Heavy hearts will melt away and you see I'll have a special
friends on this day
So thank heaven for friends and
Thank God for you Velda, my special friend.

   Sylvia Shepperd

For My Husband

My home is large as large as can be
I am not lonely for he bought it for me

He was my man only one of his kind
With whit, kindness, smart, and intelligent mind

Kindness for those he new, and O! So much for me he did do
Smart in so money away Silver fox was a name called his way

Intelligent he was for well read was he
He knew so much about you and me

Twenty years I spent with my man,
what he taught me now I understand

The years went by as the days did to
He became very ill there was nothing I could do

God took him away it time for him to go
for my dear husband had suffered so

My home is large as large as can be but never alone am I you see
His body is gone but that is all, his love, and spirit fill each wall

May we open our eyes and try to understand
God has his reasons he has his plan

Never to forget what God did for me
for twenty years with my husband he gave to me

   Mary Lee Nielsen

Broken Goblet

How clear, how fragile the crystal goblet,
An artisan's prize, a work of art.
Facets gleaming prismatic fire
From sunlights beam or candles glow.
That fragile stem so cool to touch,
The bowl a globe of clear cut ice.

Color changes as liquid flows,
Ruby, Amber or Crystal clear.
Fragrance of grape and berry rise
Dizzying senses, as the world recedes,
The goblet falls from fingers numb.

Amid shattered glass one only finds
Remains of broken dreams.

   Ruth Craig

The Morning Meeting: 9:00 AM

(Not even Hollow men with three dimensions
Just silhouettes
Obstructions for the recessed lights)
They sit around the conference table with memos and reports
Inseminated artificially with numbers and words.
Their words like a plastic surgeon's stitches
Hold my face in tact
While other-worldliness rots within me
And I hear my voice disembodied and eviscerated of spirit
And hope sing discordant lyrics, while
Ink-stained hands lay before me useless and impotent.
They scratch endless lines leading to the edges of paper
And off.
Chords in my throat strike notes in a melody
Foreign to me.
And their faces on me watching
Watching the phenomenon that was me.
There is a spot on the crown of my head that reflects the light
And I cast my own shadow.
Thin. Thinner. Thinnest.

M. J. Canuel

Longing For Aberdeen (Scotland)

I long for the hills of home, and for the seashore foam
To smell the new grass mown, and roses in their loam
To hear again the pipes, watching to see who wipes
To walk along the street, friendly people there to meet

I want to walk the country lanes, in sunny skies and rains
To smell the salty air, that collects on skin and hair
I hear the wind that blows, in my mind that flows
Way back to my youth, when people were not uncouth

To see the northern lights, oh! the beauty of that sights
Where twilight lasts all night, and mosquitos do not bite
To visit majestic castles, along narrow roads of hassles
The history that is steeped, in courageous men that weep

To visit the local pubs, for they are truly the hubs
Lives may come and go, the local pubs will know
Then go for fish and chips, that broadens mind and hips
And join the singing groups, walking streets like troupes

Oh! the hills I'd like to roam, the bonny hills of home
Renew spirits that are flagging, and feet now a dragging
To walk along the sands, see the ships from many lands
And watch the waves that crash, with fury and backlash

Maureen Kreissl

The Kiss of Death

The kiss of death blew softly in through my door,
My life had passed some time ago, I knew it,
And frankly my life is wasted, I know, I blew it,
I dreamed the dreams of being rich, it's lore,
I'd say with credence, stick with me, I'm sure,
That life will lay a sumptuous feast for me,
The gate I'd hoped would open, ne're seemed to be,
And here, I lie, a dejected porcine bore,
Oh, what a fool! 'Tis me, I search, an aperture,
Yet I see no hole here to hide my soul,
And death is closing in on me, I'm naked!
No lies to cover and shelter me, I conjecture,
My end is here, the coldness chills my role,
I wasted life and precious time; I faked it.

Lorelei Marie Johnson

Always In Lead

Where from my heart you dare not tear apart?
What of my mind you leave forgotten behind?
Where buried is my soul of essence you stole?
How by my life you continue to strive?

What of this body you've drained of all natural purities?
And of this empty shell now worthless even as a bell?
How can you make me live kept from all I believe?
Why then take my life by the blade of your knife?

I am not as I seem; nor am I dead.
You make bleed my existence of tears I shed.
That which you've taken from me—an illusion of fake,
Cannot be replaced—not even for your sake.

I am and I am not that which you speak.
I come and I go like all flakes of snow.
Be not as you are but what must be
And then you'll not need to be always in lead.

Julien Bain

The Town Of No Can Do

'Twas the age of Never Was and Never Will Come To Be.
In the town of No Can do they rode, quite a calvary.

Upon the backs of broken dreams they came to save the day.
Bringing joy and encouragement to all who were in their way.

The first to fall unto their spell was a boy named Billy Dean.
A sad little lad with n'aer a friend and very low self-esteem.

"Look into yourself," they taught "and searching deep you'll find,
A happiness just waiting there for a boy who is loving and kind."

Billy did just as they said and chanted "yes I can".
He looked deep inside a scared little boy to find the courage of a man.

Little miss Becky Jones was next as she sat alone and cried.
"I wish I was much prettier, like a princess," Becky sighed.

The team gave her a magic mirror, told her to hold it up and peer.
"Beauty lies inside you," they taught, "see the lovely girl that's there."

Becky did just as they said and held the mirror up high and tall.
A beautiful woman glanced back at her, why she was never ugly at all!

The team rode on throughout the town up to every neighbor's door.
Changing frowns to smiles, sighs to laughs, the people's spirits rose and soared.

Today the town of No Can Do is the city of Yes We Can.
Now hope resides in the hearts of every child, lady, and man.

Jennifer Lang

I Have A Friend...

I have a friend, a friend so dear.
I know that He is always near.
He lives in me.
Right in my heart, so you see we are never apart.
He has healed the sick.
He has saved the lost.
He has paid the greatest cost.
He gave His life so we could be free.
Free from sin and all its costs, free from death and all its loss.
My friend is Jesus and now you see Jesus died
For you and me.
He is waiting for you to let Him in.
So He can get rid of your sin.
So let Him in and you will see,
Just how great His love can be.

Jennifer B. Asbury

October 6, 1995

Coming from the north to survive in the south.
Learning about a whole new different world.
A world that's in a capsule, trying desperately to stand perfectly still,
Not move so they'll go unnoticed by the rest of the world,
"It's always been this way,"
"We Southerners don't celebrate Memorial Day."
Coming from the north,
Seeing the intolerance, indifference, the economic shackles and chains
That continue to divide and bind everyone's mind
I'm better than, I've more than, I can outdo you,
I don't associate with your kind,
You're not the right shade, color, shape, denomination, social affiliation.
Coming from the north to survive in a small southern town.
Everyone knows or wants to know intimate gossipy details about
Everyone's lives, but no one's willing to
Be openly trusting, unsuspicious, caring, loving, giving,
genuinely warm towards one another
Coming from the north
Surviving the south.

Luanda J. Wesley-Foster

My Mother

I was sad...(when I was ten)...
I felt ignored...
others needed you more

When I was fourteen, I was angry...
I could not understand...your hardships
to clothe and feed your loved ones
Leaving home on cold winter nights
Working, working to keep me warm
You filled your days and nights working, working...
Giving of yourself till nothing was left
Unappreciated, exhausted and empty
You came home, you always did...

I could not understand
Your struggle, your pain
Your hurt, your loneliness...

I am a mother now
and I want to give you, my mother
My deepest love, my kindest thoughts
Because, now, I understand...
I love you, I always will.

Martha M. Coetzee

Untitled

You're everything I think of
You're everything I dream of
Guess what, this might be love
Everything I do I think of you
Everywhere I go you're with me to
You're constantly in my head
You will be till the day I'm dead
I'm in love with you
I want you to share it
I'm in love with you
I want you to care
Life sucks, life's not fair!
I've loved many people in thirteen years
And lots of them made me shed many tears
They were all players and play the same game
But I'll never show love for them again.

Crystal Barrett

Valentine

In Loveland where the Bluebird sings,
Cupid folded his gossamer wings.
He sat him down in a flowery nook
And reached inside for his Mating Book.
His chubby fingers traced the pages
For names of lovers-to-be through the ages.
A star he drew on your dear name,
Reaching mine, he did the same.
With the stars a spell he wrought;
You'd seek me while you I sought!
On rosy toes with a joyous shiver, an arrow he pulled from his quiver.
Aim he took: Zing! the dart flew, piercing your heart, my heart, too!
He gathered up each shattered bit and plied and tried until it fit!
He danced around, 'twas so much fun, making two hearts into one.
So perfectly the pieces blended, none could see
Where my heart began or your heart ended.
With airy grace and happy laughter
He filled the heart with Love to last a lifetime and ever after.
Binding the heart with golden twine,
He gave to us a Forever Valentine.

Zoila Conan

Emptiness

Emptiness finds us all at one time or another,
Usually when it's our fears we discover.
But with all this emptiness it can be said,
That sometimes some people just wished they were dead.

Taken for granted are the things that we had,
We look back on them now and it makes us sad.
The future holds many promises of an untold treasure,
But, the pleasure of things to come we just can't measure.

I could go crazy very easily in this bunker if I try,
The walls seem to close in and at your head they pry.
It consumes you with a feeling one can't quite explain,
Something from the dark side touches your soul and remains.

I sit in my bunker with memories from the past,
In all this madness I wonder how long will they last?
If my memories escape me I'll be in an endless abyss,
and all I will have to comfort me is my Solitude and Emptiness.

Aaron Hughes

The Re-Uniting

He took a rose and placed it in her hand,
He bent low to kiss her cheek.
As her eyes closed for the last time,
He knew one day again they would meet.

His heart so broken and this eyes so red,
Yet he held back the tears.
He would cry alone in the darkness,
And remember all their years.

As the memories would pass before him,
He'd remember how pretty she was.
So long ago on their wedding day,
Their hearts so full of love.

He'll miss her more than life itself,
But he knows they'll meet again.
For one day the Lord will come for him,
And touch him too with his hand.

When he passes through the gates of heaven,
He'll see her waiting there.
Once again they'll be together,
Their love to forever share.

Yvonne B. Goss

No Time For War

Let us look with care so we can see
Deep in our souls what life may be.
From mystic fragments in early times
To a gasping planet and grasping minds.

All life does battle as its form takes shape
With its struggle to breathe and steps to take.
But a will to live is not harm to another
We are all for one and each for the other.

A brain must mature and the spirit be free
So the disease called age can no longer be.
Then the morning star that shines with dawn
Was a promise from God if we but overcome.

Thus the solar system will become a step
For growing life that uses self-help.
Then the Milky Way will surely be
A human home for an eternity.

Ples Mason Phillips

To My Dear Ocean...

Ocean, my love.
Strong, determined in your movements and thoughts
You're never calm. Looking for cliff to break in
or for a coast to take out.
Attracted by the sound of your voice
I want to jump into your waves
but cold splash of your passion awakes me.
I stay distant. The waves constantly
approach me with new power.
They attack me crashing into the cliff
breaking off pieces of me.
But your fight won't destroy the shore between us.
And serene azure won't make me forget
your coldness, darkness and illusion.
Your alluring fake love won't fool me anymore.
And though you try to smooth the rocks of our life together
I am aware of your dim hidden thoughts.

Katya Nalivaiko

A Poem of Comfort

Is there any heart discouraged as it journeys on its way, does
there seem to be more darkness than there is of sunny day? Oh,
it's hard to learn the lesson, as we pass beneath the rod, that the
sunshine and the shadow serve alike the will of God, but there
comes a word of promise, like in the bow, that however deep the
waters, they shall never overflow. When the flesh is worn and
weary, and the spirit is depressed, and temptations sweep upon
it like a storm on ocean's breast, there's a haven ever open for
the driven bird, there's a shelter for the tempted in the promise
of his word; for the standard of the spirit shall be raised against
the foe, and however deep the waters, they shall never overflow.
When a sorrow comes upon you that no other soul can share,
and the burden seems too heavy for the human heart to bear.
There's a burden-bearer ready if you'll trust him with your load;
for the precious promise reaches to the depths of human woe,
that however deep the waters, they shall never overflow. When
the sands of life are ebbing, and I near the golden shore, when I
see its waters rising, and I hear its billows roar. I will reach my
hand to Jesus, in his bosom I shall hide, and twill only be a
moment till I reach the other side, it is then the fullest meaning of
the promise I shall know, when thou passest through the
waters, they shall never overflow!

Draper Lockhart

Of Pride And Honor

It was not but a simple choice. Pit your pride against
  your honor and find who truly reigns within you
Discover that part that dwells in your heart and gives you
  the strength to continue
to keep from confusing yourself in your choosing of the paths
  you will wander or follow
It was not a test you would have embarked upon alone,
  for well you believe you know yourself, but,
I am not so sure, and so, admit my deliberate plot
  that put you in such shackles as to choose.
I am not so dismayed that your choice has betrayed
  your honor - indeed, it was quite well expected.
My distress lies instead in your mistrust, I was led
  to believe it had not been neglected. Surely you knew,
After all we've been through that your pride would reside
  well tended in me. How could you not know that in trade of
  ego would have been given back loyalty? Have you lost
  yourself - found yourself, are you even aware of this
  dimension of focus? For these are the questions that,
  if we care, should matter enough to provoke us...

M. S. VanAllen

Summer Shadows

The heavy carpet of fallen leaves cushions and calms
my thoughts, mid-afternoon when day's warmth greets
autumn eve's early coolness.

Shadow played games of hide and seek, shadows of
empty trees, shadows of people now gone, shadows of
a summer that loved and embraced me.

Oceans and beaches that sang so merrily the summer long,
their beautiful symphonies are over, but I remember the
words and melodies to each and every summer song.

Shadows reaching into my soul, emptying in cool twilight,
wood burning fires toasting the air, stars smile at
me but I do not care, I look for summer everywhere.

November's evening shadows draining my summer soul.

Winter will soon come, with silent nights, frozen lakes
and sleeping fields of snow, burying those summer
shadows that now seem a million years ago.

Summer souls flushed away by fall and winter, hopefully
soon to be filled up again.

Peace my summer shadows, goodwill towards every child,
woman and man. Amen

Edward M. Fontein

For Pity's Sake

What drives a man to murder
the mother of his children

Feelings feed this hate, this love:
More than enough for one;
Never enough for the other starveling.
Except a smile will do in the dark
What hate cannot in the light.

And sorrow, poor sorrow,
Tries to tell us of pity and hope.
Love cannot scream in rage
But hate can tie the knot
That bids a head be hanged.
Hate will kill the beast as a new beast is born;
Hate needs no help as from our hearts our love is torn.
Laugh lightly in the devil's face,
cling to your lover's last mad embrace.

"Twas pity stayed his hand" I read:
The tin dividing line, the edge of the abyss,
Become the smile of hope, the path to bliss.

Patrick Ellen

Sinner Man

Lord, have mercy upon the Sinner, who lives in the path of darkness.
Who cares not for the word of righteousness.
Who neither knows of the hand of Mercy.

He lives a life of Useless Thinking, Heartaches, Pain and Harmful
Drinking. Knowing not of the Great Jehovah, who can cleanse
your soul as white as snow, all over
Yet, he goes on in his same old ways, living his life from day to day.

Sinner Man, Sinner Man, change your ways.

The all mighty is going to call us some sweet day.
If you live a worldly life, your soul would burn in a lake of fire
Will you be willing to let your soul burn in Hell, for all the
worldly makings?

If you'd only choose Heaven as your aim
Things would be different, your life would completely change

I was a Sinner, that's why I can say, get down on your knees
and pray ask God to help you and forgive you for your sins

For when the roll is called up yonder and I hear the voice of the Holy Son
I hope and pray, he will say unto me, well done my servant well done

Sinner Man, Sinner Man, change your ways!!!

Rev. Olevia Howard

A Child's Cry

There are many things that change my inner being. Seeing a
painful change as in a slow deterioration like flowers during a
hot dry summer, wilting slowly, turning brown then into nothing.
As children look up with open minds, waiting to be filled with
joyful thoughts, wanting to learn about the wonders of life.
When it was the time of life you thought very thing was nice,
some how every night was turned into tears and fright, having
no one to hold you tight. Underneath the covers you lie
through the night not wanting to ever wake up in the night or to
sunlight. As the pain eats at your soul and brain. Can you ever
start to claim to feel like a real person again? Some how, some
way, there comes a day when you stop wilting away. You feel
no pain, you sit there and smile. You act as if everything is okay.
You wonder does anybody see this pain? Am I really alone or is
it just a game? You beg, you plead, you don't want to keep
making your heart bleed. You reach for a hand, doesn't any-
body understand? Why didn't anyone grab my hand. Now you
learned to defend yourself, promising that no one will put you
through this hell. Until one day you learn to put the past away.
You no longer live in that dwelling place. You learn to save face.
You now long to live, anticipating the sunlight; and the moon-
light to set upon your face. Now you smell the flowers everyday
and you awake to know that everything is and will be okay.
Now I say thank you God for the day you grab my hand and
pull me away. Thank you Lord for everyday.

Linda Leighton

A True Story (Halloween)

I once had an elderly neighbor.
To her, Trick or Treating was new.
So when the wee Goblins and Ghosts
came to call - she said,
"But what kind of a trick will you do
if I don't give any treats to you?
The wee ones surprised but non-plussed,
were prepared. They promptly, obligingly,
stood on their heads!
What a fine way to bridge the Gap
which we're told seems to exist
'twixt the Young and the Old.
She got her Trick - they got their Treat.
Then they trotted off gladly
to homes up the street!

Alberta W. Arrasmith

Dear Lord

You are so good to us,
Being like you we will never fuss,
Gentle, thoughtful, loving and kind,
Are the qualities one needs to find.

Your love to us you have shown;
Although to evil we are prone.
Give us strength, dear Lord to endure
The conflicts inherent in life's daily chores.

Our World needs to be a better place,
For us each day to face.
Selfishness, greed and crime
Must be banished during our time.

The miseries of power struggle and poverty
We feel each day as our only property;
Can only be resolved to our satisfaction
As we experience your true reflection.

So, Dear Lord, give us the zeal to fight
For all things that are right
In such a way that pleases thee;
And to mankind the benefits will always be.

Muriel P. Morris

J.C.

Thou shalt not die unavenged, sweet sir.
Revenger for every cell thou shed will swell
And cleanse this land; but not through harm or hate,
Those have now long since been the wombs of hell,
But just by peace and warmth to burst our gate.

Thou shalt not die unavenged, sweet sir.
Your words shall cry out loud through time's embrace:
To run and cross all ears of those who'll hear;
To plant your seed and make us words in place,
Those words which form the phrase of songs so dear.

Thou shalt not die unavenged, sweet sir.
Your voice shall not have lost in vein its calls.
Nor will it be a mere event for lies.
You'll cross the thickest skulls and greatest walls,
And springs of love will bravely bloom and rise.

Thou shalt not die unavenged, sweet sir.
Oh, not while living minds caress your land.
While beats of hearts still join the souls of men,
And hence wilst these your gifts of love still stand.
'Tis yours sweet Christ our every breath. Amen.

Luis Alfonso Dau Farah

The Light From Within

My eyes close shut and I step inside my soul.
There is darkness, then light shines upon me.
As I stand in the light, I see that I am not who I thought I was.
I see that life is not as I had imagined it to be.
Rays of hope reach out to me from this light to touch me.
They hold me.
They tell me that I have been wounded, they tell me that I have been naive,
They tell me that I have been selfish, they tell me that I have been lost.
They show me the significance of my flaws and mistakes,
As they caress my humanness.
These rays guide me in forward motion,
And I explore the limitless possibilities that these caresses of
    forgiveness show me.

I see the art of Life and I see my true colors.
Murals are painted before my eyes of a joyful and courageous soul
Murals that could only be painted by the brush of yesterday's hand.
Uncompleted paintings are displayed in this gallery of light,
Where I see masterpieces in the making, as change continues on....

Karen Davis King

Hope Negotiated

Militarism is the way of Nations
Why should they rust in peace?
Everyone abandon the Fourteen Christian Stations
Citizens, their lives are out on lease.

World Leaders looking for blood to shed,
Military Intelligence, as truthful and clear as hazy mist.
Nuclear warheads and slugs of lead
Are spent on corrupted generals' infinite abyss.

Bay doors open and launch codes set.
Gold plated grins and fourteen carat rings
Place their pocket change on this costly bet.
Today...the fat lady sings.

Paul Story

Mother

Spring, then Summer, then Fall and snow,
Christmas come, and Christmas go.
Memory takes us to the past,
Reflecting on all the Christmas that we've had.

The food, the gifts, the fellowship, too,
But most of all, I remember you.
The cooking, the cleaning, and all the fuss,
As children, didn't mean anything to us.

But looking back over the past,
I see the love it took, to make Christmas past.
I thank you, Mom, for all you've done,
And I'm so proud, to be your son.

Richard A. Keiser

Untitled

There are many people who have crossed my path
I thank God for each one
I wouldn't have known what life's about
If their confidence I hadn't won.

It's a good feeling to do your best
But it's also good to have someone
You can talk to and tell them all
And someone to be with who's fun.

Life is meant to go on
Cross over the bridge and live
Forget all and try real hard
To see what it is you can give.

There are many solutions to problems
Everyone knows what to do
But you must do what's in your heart
This is the best for you.

I only pray for guidance
It's easy for me to live
Hoping when I do my best
It's all that's expected me to give.

Dorothy A. Patterson

Spring

When the season crept through the shadowy days,
when sunshine peeked through gray clouds making dozens
of glistening golden rays,
when they snuck through the branches of my old willow tree,
forming shadows upon the grass all around me,
When blossom started to bloom on trees bushes and plants,
when they started to approach from their little places,
those small tiny ants,
when the birds started to chirp and sing,
I knew then it was the coming of spring.

Kalina Torino

Doing For Others

It isn't always the thing you do
    More often than not it's what you don't
That leaves you with a heart that hurts
    When daylight ends and sleep just won't come

Those tender words you never uttered
    The missile still clinging to the pen
The roses that you might have sent
    Still at the florist regardless of your intent

The burden you might have lifted
    To ease a poor brothers load
The council you might have offered
    As you traveled and shared that road

The gentle touch of a loving hand
    The sound of concern in your tone
Those things you had no time for
    With all the troubles of your own

The little acts of thoughtfulness
    Forgotten though oh so kind
So many chances to help one another
    If you will only seek and find

Charles A. De Land

It Was A Time

It was a time;
The time when the skies raved and it rained lead,
When, above, lightning glowed and many groaned,
Others ate fruits of cruelty from the fields of rage.
The time when hearts bled and it rained dread,
When, undeserved, cherries at heart were reaved,
For many a world came to an edge.
The time when fiends fumed and it rained feud,
When, irefully, blades sighed and many frowned,
Lots offered morsels to a ravenous glebe.
The time when strife howled and it rained scald,
When by the flaming flood many were drowned,
Numbers were charred and numbers ceased to be.
The time when spite roared and it rained discord,
When the era for roam reigned and many roved,
By time were bred widows and orphans.
The time when currents shivered and it rained riptide,
When troubled the mighty Zambezi growled,
Her bosom riven by whales of arms:
It was a time.

Pious Haachizo

Reflections

I awaken in morn to a bright and sunny day
Are we putting down our roots, and finally gonna stay?
Life is very pleasant here, the people make it so
I could start a garden, and maybe it would grow.

My garden is a sorry sight, with weeds of every kind,
The vegetables are really there, just difficult to find.
it gives me pleasure just the same, but friends joke with glee,
Gardens may be their pride and joy, but not my cup of tea.

The neighbors say it's berry time and who is gonna pick
The berries for the Berry Fest, it's coming mighty quick.
The jobs are finally meted out, the work is getting done
Everything so festive looking, by gosh this could be fun.

And fun it was that year ago when we had the Berry Fest
Will there be another one? I can only hope and guess.
And though I'm not active in all that happens here
The time I can spend helping is certainly most dear.

And I'll not forget it, because I think I've found
The nicest place to live in and I want to stay around.
Only time will tell if I'll be here to enjoy another spring
But then none of us really know that life and time will bring.

Frances Hillier

She Doesn't Know

A woman sits, silently:
looking around at this massive void,
she calls her life.
Observing...Watching....Waiting...
She looks around this massive shell.
cluttered, with memories.
But how could this be?
A woman sits, observing a man,
she thinks she loves...shattered dreams.
She recalls her past...melancholy,
Was she happy?
She doesn't know.
She watches a screen...played only in her mind.
She needs a new writer.
But how could this be?
She longs for the dream...A small child's dream.
Would she be happy?
She doesn't know.

Laura E. Reed

Forgetting

Gazing off at a distance cloud; a single
bird goes by;
A quiet voice speaks to my mind; if only
I could fly;

I would search out the mountains and head
towards their peak; and never once look down;
For then I would remember all of my sorrows;
are here, on the ground.

I would clear the tree tops and scan the
valleys below; I would spread the wings of my
mind to see how far I could go.

I often come to visit this place: It has such
a peaceful setting; I always leave with a smile
on my face: After visiting the world of forgetting.

Michael Garrett

For You

There are many different types of songs
that are in the world today.
    Songs of joy and laughter, sorrow too.
    But this song I wrote was made for only you.

Just tell me you love me and that will suffice.
For you I'd do anything...I'd sacrifice.

I'll love you forever and never let you go.
I'll be your companion and never your foe.

You've given me your wisdom throughout all my life,
Through good times and bad times, during my strife.

Your smile gave me confidence and warmed my heart.
Now all I hope is that I can do my part.

Forever I'll hold you close my whole lifetime through.
'Cause I could never leave you and this is the truth.

No more talk of darkness, I will be your light,
I'll guide you, protect you, keep you safe at night.

Baby it's times like these that I must confess.
Can't seem to find the words that even express
the happiness I've come to know, the dreams that have come true.
And most of all, the joy I've found in living life with you.

Anthony Magturo

Goodbye

Will you know me?
I know you from the past.
I have seen you on the mountain tops where the snow never melts
And where men fear to tread;
I have seen you for a moment in the mist which shrouds the forest
And heard your laughter somewhere in the breeze.

Will you remember me?
I recognize the footfalls of your feet as they walk beside me;
I have glimpsed you in my mother's face as she turns around to embrace me.

Will you think of me?
I have often thought of the morning star which fades
In the daylight but remains there for eternity
Fixed in its celestial orbit and yet,
I can reach out and touch it and make it seem as real as my existence
Or perhaps, just as unreal. I will also know you in the years to come
When this Earth is no more and the heavens are filled
With the glorious beauty of peace
And where my existence clearly entwines with yours,
And forever remains the hope of my love.

Afia Serena Nathaniel

Drifting Love

Darling, you and I are on the same drift!
Of the same general intention the motion cause,
and we are drifting away from real life;
because, we are like earth, grovel, rocks, and fine sand
Which is being carried away by rivers, in our time
moving along with little effort, as if forever.

Our lives are off course all piled in a heap!
This glacier must be stopped and deposited now,
yes, it must be slowed before it is too late;
and our life must be a pit that will hold water
by doing this, it will stable our thinking minds
we must go forth, for flooding gets us no where.
Our love must be true, that brings happiness!
Like the ocean current, that brings us back to shore;
and we must all swim up stream to be gain with;
if not, we will stand still an make no headway
so, let us follow our hearts an such the truth
and let our God, the judging of our souls.

Let us not drift away for each other again!
And being together in spirit, our souls will win.

Orlo Marlatt

Meandering Creek

Life is like a meandering creek.
Slowly trickling past little obstacles.
Squeezing through little gaps in the soil.
Rolling over pebbles and rocks covered with green moss.
Tumbling over the little falls to land in a still puddle.
I sit for a second in the quiet little puddle,
Then I move again, around a bend.
Always moving forward,
Never turning back.
Each turn, each rock, each fall,
Are just memories in my life.
My life is a meandering creek,
Not a raging river that flows too fast.
It is gradual, steady, never stopping,
Just living, breathing, drinking,
Absorbing everything that comes my way.
Rhythmically I flow through this maze.
I hear a constant beat residing in my chest.
It tells me where to go, and who to love.
My life is like a Meandering Creek.

Mike Acocella

Reflections

Oh what is this before me I see
A reflection,
A reflection of me?
And just what is it I see,
An image,
An image of what I should be?
To refuse to see the reflection I see
Is foolish and unwise to me
For first the reflection I must see
Before an understanding of what I should be,
Though I may not like what I see
To see the reflection and know it's me.
For when I truly see,
The image becomes more clear to me
The image of what I should be.

Belinda Webb

Forbidden Fruit

Others may not approve of our time together, but they do not
know what I know, they cannot feel as I feel,
they've never been where I've been.

Instead, they see only what they want to see, that which is
scandalous, they believe only what they want to believe, which
revolves around sensationalism,
they heart only what they want to hear, it prick their ears.

If they were to search my heart, they would see something else,
they would believe a different story,
they would hear a song, gently in the night,
one that is soft and light, sweet and true.

The time we've spent together has been both a blessing and a curse,
both comforting and painful,
both liberating and binding.

But I am thankful for your tender fingertips,
when I could feel only harshness;
I am thankful for your attentive ear, when I thought no one cared;
and I am thankful for your smiling blue eyes,
when I thought I had forgotten how to laugh.

Deborah L. Irwin

Let Me Hold Your Hand

Let me hold your gentle hand and feel your warmth;
Let the stream of life flow through each other.
Let me take you with me to where time never ends,
To where love is divine, where two souls are one.

Walk with me on the soft sand of a thousand years,
Where each grain is an instant, a bit of eternity;
Where the footprints we leave are erased behind
By the incessant ocean's wave, the wave of time.

Let's embrace until we feel to be not two but one;
Until our hearts beat in unison, a pulse of love;
Until in your eyes I see your soul, you in mine;
Until your mysterious glow and mine become one.

Let me hold your gentle hand, let me kiss it softly.
Let me whisper from my soul my love you.
Let our lips come together into a kiss endless....
Then, in the glow of the moon, let's lie and rest...

Until the wave will take us to the eternal glow.

Silvino R. Foglia

A Prisoner's Blues

My home is one of headache
A place of stone and steel
An iron cell, a home you call hell
And here you sit all alone.
For one crime, you pay with time
Where lights glare day and night
And though you rage and pace your cage
You still must stay and pay.
Your home in hell is one small cell
That no man wants to call home
Your body cramps from cold and damp
That chills you to the bone.
It somehow seems that all your dreams
Must wait for a new tomorrow,
Your days are filled with misery headaches,
Your nights are filled with sorrow.
But don't be sad, it's not so bad
Because I hide it well within
No trace outside, it's deep inside
What my trip through this hell has been.

Ronald Keirs

Sights (Perception)

If I could, just once, see through your eyes.
Lay to rest, I s'pose, the doubts I comprise.

...I saw you, you looked like a rose.
...I noticed, a mind that explodes.

If I could, one time, connect mind to mind.
I to learn, a lil' bit, the thoughts you comprise.

As if eye to I; our skies, are one sky.

sights...
of different colored lights;
sights...
the wind could blow away;
sights...
to long show us a path;
sights...
to help make out our past.

Not to miss, understand;
We see it, not the same.
Fingerprints define;
Love twists
The sunshine.

Timothy A. Gettig

Earthquake Hangover

Dizzy from getting up too fast,
Light-headed in a fog of wonder.
Nervous burst of energy,
Blurry-eyed staring in the dark.
Stumbling to the bathroom,
Fumbling with the flashlight,
Groping walls to stay familiar.
Queasy with anticipation,
Straining to listen.
Finally reassured of momentary safety,
I return to prone tossing and turning.
Propping up, rolling over, plumping pillows,
An uncomfortable, restless dance,
A 4 a.m. Achy Breaky.
It seems just as I drift off,
My alarm startles me,
Reminding me I have responsibilities.
It forces me to sluggishly respond,
To another day with an earthquake hangover.

Laurel Robinson

Writer's Block

The pen remains still
Timid ballerina
Longs to release her pain
In a dance of beauty and of truth
Stage fright grows tiresome
With the passing of long tedious days
Emotion threatens explosion
Aching for the twists and turns of padded feet
To the rhythm of life love and hate
Her performance could make the sun rise or fall
Hiding in the shadows
Her body shudders in anticipation
Her day has come
The spotlight of opinion threatens
The purity of her truth
Smooth stage of white stretches before her
Blue ink footprints reflect her pain

Pamela M. Davis

Escape

Standing at the edge of infinity,
I look down at the swirling vortex.
The cold world below looks almost inviting;
A way out —
A transformation from one place to another.
Voices from behind calling out words of warning:
"Don't do it... you're young..."
Yes, young.
What world will I grow old in?
I must escape.
The voices echo away end in gasps
Then stop.
I enter the world I so longed for,
but receive no release
From hard felt pain.
Instead I get only suffering.
I should have listened to those voices,
those words of warning.
Now I will die for eternity,
Never gaining escape.

Gilad Moll

Hidden Yet Visible

He is white like a dove
And brings a hush of peace to everything
Wherever we go he is all around
Like the cool spring breeze and blue sky

He can be yellow and bright like the sun
Shining his love down upon us
We can hear him in the gospels
In the stories of his life for us

Whenever he is talking we can hear
In a rumble of thunder
In the bright flash of golden lightening
When the clouds part and the sun shines again

Even thought we cannot always see
We must believe in him and what he stands for
God is with us and his son died for us
This great man is hidden from us

Yet we can see him through the Bible
We can see him through each other
The Father, Son, and Holy Spirit
Believe

Courtney Johnson

Untitled

Your hair like the golden threads of finely spun silk.
Your eyes like looking twin jewels reflecting the
    vast openness of the sea.
Your lips like sweet nectar wine longing to be enveloped.
Your face like the sweet innocence of an angel.
You skin like the softness of freshly fallen rose petals.
Your touch like the gentleness of a newborn child.
Your body like a vision from heaven on earth.
Your voice like the whisper of the wind through the forest.
All this and more are you............

Dorothy Katona

Perhaps...

Perhaps you are more frightened than me,
or maybe you think I'm crazy.

Perhaps I cannot deal
with what they think is real.

Perhaps you believe life is not for you.
I can only hope, my words leave a clue.

Perhaps I choose a life of quiet desperation,
or void of any great aspirations.

Perhaps you're running from your own emotions,
apprehensive of causing commotion.

Perhaps your love was never a gift,
but something causing me to shift.

Perhaps you live an altruistic life,
avoiding any kind of strife.

Perhaps I choose not to trust,
and know without it, there can be no lust.

Perhaps material things are all you can give.
Is that all you need to really live?

Perhaps I, will never know,
why I love to watch it snow.

Terrill Nowak

Mistress

The emotions I feel are complex,
though in his mind my thoughts are of just sex.
My eyes long to see his strong face,
my skin to sense his warm embrace.
Wishing to tell him dreams and with him I want to belong,
hoping he'd listen to why I'm happy or what may be wrong.
He'll wine and dine me even give me furs,
belong to me in public, but at home he'll be hers.
Torn apart and lonely many nights I wept,
waiting and wanting a man that never left.
Watching couples in love, I'd cry,
imagining that they were he and I.
Touching, holding, loving and kissing,
all this I have, but something is still missing.
We argue at times because I have to hide,
everything I want to express inside.
The whole world sees, but one does not know,
unless she doesn't care and has a lover of her own.
Til I have the answer my heart will never rest,
Does he think of me only as his mistress?

Madeline Deniellcia Brown

You

I wake up each morning with you in my mind
I go to sleep with you in my dreams
I see you in my thoughts throughout the day
I feel your warmness in my heart
I smell your body with each burst of wind
I smile when I think of you
My spirit is lifted when I think of us together
I wonder if our hearts can combine to form one
My soul is lifted to heaven at each word you speak
I wonder if you'll ever return these words I say to you.

Pam Skilj

Groceries Bane

Oh, the woe! The decisions to decide!
Which aisle to start, which side?
Which food to select
or reject.

Dairy products first, I guess
I'll have only the best
Next, all the meats
Dinners, Lunches, hoping prices to beat.

Vegetables, will consist
of corn, beans, rice, hominy from my list.
Cereals, tea, coffee, plus drinks and of course sug'ar
As my husband acts like a coug'ar.

Condiments and garnishes to go with the meals
While looking for any special deals.
Last but not least, our cats —
Sebastian and Sushi need to stay fat.

Varieties, colors, tastes with texture
Fruits, breads are one more venture.
Hard part's still to go.
Paying, hoping enough money to flow

Rose Mary Fountain

You And I

Let our hearts fly to the heavens with all their might
I want to feel your heartbeat with mine

Every breath I want to take it in with my own
Tell me you love me and take me down into a sleepless slumber
I want to feel your arms around me and every moment like my own

Let our moment last forever
grasping every ounce of strength, so we can be as one
If only for those precious moments that we share
Let us forget the outside world
We can only think of ourselves

For just a short time we forgot everything except each other
So now, we came back to life to look into each other's eyes
And all we can say is the love we both share, the magic we both made

But as we now part, we will remember the time we had together
The passion we both made
Till another day, till another night, till we meet again.

My love forever yours!

Donna Lea Highsmith

Old Villa Revisited

"Hearts and flowers" - a foolish tune...
Meant for no one, not for you.
The rusty bell outside her home
played a chime that once meant more.
And, locked behind the gilded gate
cobwebbed mem'ries never slept;
I heard them past the wind -
exchanging words... with the dust!
Such loving words; so full of trust...
Then, when the clock hand bid goodbye
to five o'clock...
You tipped your hat.

Michael Lucien McComb

Life Discovers Love...

A butterfly that blooms - you are
flourished in a field without grass,
when a flower gave you life
playing with the wind
while dancing found herself in a branch;
Reaching out, in the warm sun,
within the transparency of light
rising to joy, you defy time!
Eternity - your space!
Your essence - the sky!
Proof of the earth - a paradise?
The crystal light that goldens
the vibrant leaves, ethereal wings that become
- butterflies
The infinite sound of universal bells,
while softly embraces the trees - slight wind;
Multicolored transparencies - petals;
Delicate awe of - children just born,
Being told by a glance - all of you - I love...

Susanna Iris Folli

Chocolate

Chocolate makes a perfect gift,
for any time of year.
Chocolate goes extremely well,
with a bottle of Dad's root beer.
Butterfinger is a treat,
even though it is too sweet.
If your hunger goes too far,
take a bite of a Hershey bar.
When it comes to a glass of milk,
eat Cadbury's Caramilk.
If you want a chewy treat,
it's a Rolo you should eat.
If you want Mega crunch,
on a Kit Kat you should munch.
If you want a milky snack,
it's an Aero that you lack.
I know this poem will never end,
'cause there's more chocolate around the bend!

Erin Mitchell

Bird Brain

Birds are smart I have found.
They fly South when there's snow on the ground.
They fly North in the summer,
But people are dumber;
They stay in the cold all year round.

Michael A. Wickham

"Burial At Sea"

Shrouded alive in the rough canvas
Of the forgotten sail.
Canvas neither yielding or forgiving,
But always keeping me in darkness-
The darkness that binds to destroy.

The seemingly inescapable trap is dumped into the sea,
Intensifying the darkness now I can't perceive.
Writing, searching, not an inch in either way,
Enclosed in cold steel teeth- trapping my immobility.
The depths pass me up slowly at first, then faster.

Frantically searching, I look up seeing the
Dim coin of light. Faint, blurry to my surprise.
With my heart I pull myself with inner desire.
I'm faithful 'til end to that light- all the while growing
More than whole with strength from split Singleness.

Pulled up towards light my bond is broken.
Triumphant return and entrance to my vessel.
Sailing towards the sun with no reservations
Until the next face with death
always in the dark of day, lurking for my soul.

    Chris Rauh

Romance

Romance is mythic.
It starts in the soul, pierces through
the skin, resounds in the eyes and the ears, and captures the heart.
A sweet voice, an inviting look, the melodious wind, the soft touch
of the moonlight spurs it on. The man stands in front of a girl.
She wants to get a response from him, but he is immersed in himself
with no thoughts but only feelings. She gives a hint with the dart
of her eyes, but he only watches her breasts rolling like waves.
She gestures with her fingers in a movement, which says:
"come on," but he keeps looking at her body shaped like a
banyan tree, spreading its shade through her dark hair;
her beguiling hands floating like the branches of the tree;
her feet waving her whole body as if it is ready to fly
with saffron wings. "Why is he waiting there?"
"What does he want?" Perhaps he does not know what he wants.

He came on the wings of time,
he will stay there beckoning humanity to enjoy the escapades
of two lovers.

    Baidya N. Varma

In The Mind Of A Lonely Daughter

Whenever times are tough
They'll never be tough enough
To pull two people apart
Who are bounded at their heart.

As so much time passes by
You can't help but wonder why
You've been apart for so long
So many years that are now gone.

A daddy gives you his love
And more then ever dreamt of
A daughter sheds her tears
Because her dad has been gone for years.

A daughter has been left behind
A victim of those tough times
She can't accept his distant hand
But she tried her best to understand.

But for now she's got a mother
And the cutest little brother.
Someday her dad will realize her pain
And maybe he'll realize there's no one to blame.

    Brooke Renfrow

Looking Into Your Soul's Eyes

When we first met back in March, I started into your deep dark brownish black eyes, Trying to remember why my soul knows your eyes.

Why? Where you my brother My father, My sister or maybe my Lover. Only the soul knows the truth. We strive to rekindle the Burst of Cosmic energy we feel toward one another.

When I look into your eyes, I see conflict, I see fear, I see strength of many nations. I see lust and trust. The soul is the mirror to the real you. The soul is the part that goes back to God.

The Soul knows where to Go! Who you are, Who you were and where you're going. So when I figure out who you are I wont be shocked. I'll just

Welcome You Again.

    Kelly D. Scott

Foundling

The first night was the worst.
Sharp whimpering, soft puppy fur.
The need for someone who has known and loved her well.
Whimpering ceased, she played with sock and rubber bone.

We ran an ad. Somewhere in the time before her family came
and called the foundling by her proper name,
We became hers.

There is a silence now.
Almost as loud as whimpering, in its own way,
For sameness, that first hard night and the last day is this:

To these two things the heart is slow,
The getting, and the letting go.

    Donna J. Gallardo

Why...?

Why is there war,
When everyone wants peace?
Why is there famine,
When others are leaving plates half-full?
Why are loved ones dying,
When many have never even gotten the flu?
Why do innocent children get brutally beaten,
When some kids lead the pampered life?
Is there an answer?
Is there a reason?
Maybe it's just the path of life,
Or maybe there is no reason at all.

    Jillian Levy

Unknown

Unknown is this, the flare of desire
It burns within all, strong as a fire
We know not its purpose, nor reason of being
Whether good or bad, or deeply deceiving
It may devour our hate, the many battles we've fought
All this has an answer, though I do not know
Look deep inside, for its special glow
I have searched many places, many skies have I flown
But after all this searching, I know not the unknown

    Adam Anderson

Understand The Black Man

He's been there, done that,
Been put down like a dog.
Always blamed for things,
Never right, always wrong.

He tries hard to take a stand,
But yet they don't understand,
Why the black, black man
Stands and had never ran away
From his mother, father, sister, brother and children
And he knows how the world has been to him.
But yet the black man, black man, black black black man can win.

Danielle McKinney

Roots On The Variegated Bush

Crowded together, they were enjoying the hush:
The long leaves of the variegated bush.
A melancholy patient, the day almost spent,
Picked four of them for her enjoyment;
And along with them a not-too-young shoot.
She placed them all in a bottle to root.
And everyday they seemed to saunter —
She nourished them all with some fresh water.
In the bottle they stayed; the shoot bore a new leaf;
And after one week, much against one's belief,
There was to behold, and I wish one to know,
A sign that the shoot and the leaves would grow.
At the base of the shoot, there were splits in the bark;
The swollen leaf bases made her happy as a lark;
Because of a truth the leaves started to root.
So also did the not-too-young shoot.

Grace Henderson

"Lasting Thoughts"

Tonight when the lights are dim
and your lids are closed
Think of me.

With lips so moist like sweat on fruit
Until the sweetness is instilled in the corner of your mind
Dream of me.

For dreams can become reality
and in our minds reality can be forever.

Vanessa R. Allen

Hands Of Darkness

Hands dripping with the blood of many souls
a face you only see as darkness
hatred to be fooled into love
a world that is full of sadness

Dry tears that never stop
gripped tight as death touches me
caressing with a serpent's tongue
slithering in and out of me

A film of slime that doesn't wash away
a feeling of death that circles in the air
colorful eyes turned gray in the darkness
and a heart that has lost sight and care

Once there was a happy bright child
and then her soul slipped away in the night
to be reborn into the undead
far from reach with no hope to fight

The hands of darkness that cover the earth
War, Murder, Rape
the faces of death are out there
and there is no hope for escape.

Janet Hise

Done Gone Past My Mind

As a young man of cheery ilk
With a flip delivery, smooth as silk
Seldom concerned with matters of state
Hardly an item committed to memory
Had "Done gone past my mind".

As the years sped by and family size decreased
The flip delivery began to slowly cease
Followed by a slower, more mature canter
No one would longer call it banter
Until prior tales mostly had "Done gone past my mind".

As I approach the date of never ending slumber
With a start, at night, I awake and wonder
After I depart
Will everyone, once I knew, only say
He's "Done gone past my mind"?

James F. Russell

Living Epistles

Living Epistles are read, when the Bible are not,
The Christian life is "not trying to be good."
It's being a Christian in name, faith, work no matter what,
Without thinking, - living the way that you should,

Help me, Lord, that when others read my life each day,
They see smiling service prompted by love.
Don't let strife, or envy, or bitterness mar the way,
That keep some person from heaven above.

May others see Christ when looking at me,
May my life brighten the lives of those in need.
May I lead some soul to Christ, to be saved,
By my actions, my word and deed.

When at the judgement seat of Christ I stand,
May there be others near with this story-
"I'm here because you gave me a hand,
By living only for Christ and His glory."

Bonnie Lee Holman

This Day's Agenda

As I begin daily hygiene and select my attire
Today, a new door of life stands ajar.
Be this a day of work or one of leisure
Without seeking, may I truly find pleasure.

Now, separate chores, duty, and responsibility
Let's choose what's important, label necessity.
My schedule, though flexible, will remain clear
Be I taking lead or, simply, bringing up the rear.

I will remember trials and follies of the past
And attempt to create some change to last
May I manifest proper attitude and open-mind
Today, oh Lord, help me do my best to be kind.

Deliver me from, "Acting like I care"
Wondering what's right; doing out fair.
Instead, help me harmonize with fact
And honestly, "care enough to act."

Donna M. Baker

An Angel's Tears

The snow is falling silent and still
    Quiet as a baby's sleep
It looks like tears from an angel's eyes
    Because sometimes even angels weep

Jerald Reaves

The Angels Gift

You can see the angels hands praying freedom's
grace upon dawn's earliest morn'...piercing ill wind's
pains and wrongs, pouring praise's blessings, singing
goodness' song; and, whenever heaviest burdens bind,
take heart to know that the angels blessings sweetly
chime, resting upon you in judgement's test and times;
and all the evils around you are but the angels hands,
freeing you from the earth...separating dust from
bewitching's darkness'...and, in the mercy's prayer,
guiding to love's sunshine, the angels hands blessed
you in eternity's purest rhyme...and, in the peace of
morning's star, hugged in summer's truth, the angels hands
held sunshine's golden soul...blessing upon you the hearts
sunlight, - eternal life; and, freedom's tear wiped away
every darkness' fear, in eternity's sunshine flowers...
   -blessing upon you the light of the world
in peace's angelic rosebud...sent within the
angels gift, with everlasting love.
    Sheila Wainscott

I'm Going To The Sun Today

Sunny days, good winds and I'm heading your way;
Sailing to the sun, I am going to find a better day.
I am all by myself, but I am not alone;
Sailing to the sun, I am on my way home.
Forty-seven days and it has seemed unending;
So long is my wait just to see you again.
Rays escape the sun and fall onto my face;
I wake to see that you are in my space.

I have been so lonely lately;
Now I am making my way.
I will be home and this time I will stay;
I'm going to the sun today.

I can still make it by, loneliness does not disease my brain;
When my emotions rain, the sunny day will ease my pain.
When my mind wanders, it always finds you;
You do not hide from me, your light comes shining through.

Today I am coming back to you;
And I am finally making my way
I'm going to the sun today;
I'm going to the sun today.
    Andrew M. Stephens

Untitled

God pick me up and set me free this life I live, is running over me,
Walk beside me, on this rocky road, life gets better, I've been told,
I don't believe those foolish words,
But if you lead me, I'm willing to learn.

God talk to me and give me a sign,
Is dying the same as losing my mind?
Take my hand and care for me, it's not much to ask, you will see,
Lead me to the peaceful land, let me walk your footprints in the sand.

If you should let me live this life,
Try to pull me through all the strife,
If you don't, I may die inside,
Although no one will see how I cry,
Try and hold me up, don't let me fall,
Maybe someday we can tear down this wall.

I figured my life would change in a way,
And then everything so bad would be different someday
But God, what will happen to my soul?
What will happen with this life that's so cold?
Tell my mind the answers it demands,
Then maybe someday I'll understand.
    Jennifer Phares

Believing In The Lord

Something is right for I can feel, my life is healthy and almost healed,
I've made mistakes in the years I've went thru,
Things I've learned from and things not to do,
Once it's lived you can't go back, that's the way you lay the track,
Work on the day as it comes by,
It will all be recorded at the end of night,
Give unto others and think not only of yourself,
In the end you will be blessed with riches and great wealth.
Look forward to tomorrow it's a new day,
Follow God's word and he'll lead the way,
From pain and sorrow to happiness and joy,
God made a promise on the birth of a boy,
Jesus Christ is his name, from heaven above he has came,
But he was murdered by human man,
His last words "Forgive those upon this land,"
He asked for forgiveness, it wasn't a game,
He knew they'd remember, remember his name
Believe in him with your soul, body, mind and heart,
Follow the lighted path, don't be afraid of the dark,
Cause just when you think you're all alone,
You'll hear two voices saying "Welcome home".
    Jacalyn L. Splawn

The U.S.A. Speaks

I'm known to all as the U S A
And it seems that Doom is now my Fate
For there's dissension everywhere
Morality reduced to Satan's scale.

The land itself is slowly dying
While all society itself is crying
Bewailing morals of those in power
While sating themselves with liquid fire.

The Rivers, Lakes, Ponds and Streams
Are all polluted and killing the fish
The forests once so filled with trees
Are now destroyed by people's greed.

The birds and animals are endangered too
By hunters and trappers who are truly cruel
Then too, the earthquakes, storms and floods
Cause grief, destruction, much death and blood.

The people themselves are totally to blame
For my Destruction, Downfall and Shame
They're selfish and greedy, lax about sin
My Problems Are Great, There's No Way To Win.
    Mabel E. Lane

The Homeless

The Homeless are in the world, with
  no where to stay
  Lord! Give them a special love, to
  survive another day
The Homeless heart's, are as pure as gold
  They live in the street's, and even sale
  their souls
The Homeless will eat, anything they can find
Oh Lord! Bless them, with a peace of mind
The Homeless are human, just like you and me
  God gives us your sight, so we may see
The Homeless need people, who really will care
That's why we as Christmas, should always share
The Homeless can love, just like me and you
  God created us, and the Homeless too
    Ulysses Collier Jr.

Lost Life

Under the bridge the three of them lay, an empty brown bottle in each hand,
Weathered and dirty, unkempt and grey, all that's left now the shell of a man.

Lost love, lost job, lost home, lost life, each has his own story to tell,
Soul mates by day they brag and they skite, till the drink wears off and it's hell.

Salvation draws nigh as they take their fill, old memories and emotions grow dim,
Today is a haze, yesterday unfulfilled, tomorrow a dreamer's whim.

Beneath the stars, out under the sun, neither seeing nor heeding the same,
A life is lost and somewhere, someone, grieves for a man with a name.

Elaine Delaney

My Struggle In You

A cry within strains to reach beyond the barriers of
your fears. To approach the secrets of your true self,
the struggle must be done.
I seep above the darkness mist to see the person within. To
find a beauty that few have seen. Rare that it may be, it's
a strength that's as bright as a moon.
Your enemies are great, larger within you. Yet, the moon that
my truth has found are brighter that the fears.
The passage of time has left a mist of doubt. The moon has
a darkness that I struggle to remove. A deep need to see your
brightness has become a task which have longed to finish.
My struggle in you is the breathe of all the love that passes
between us. Only together can we beat the fear, the darkness
and the silence.

Jennifer Osborne

The Chase

Running from no one but myself, I stop and think
We run through our lives for one reason: we are afraid to slow down
Afraid to see who we are, more afraid to see who we're not
Afraid to see what little we have; always wanting what we haven't more and more
Thinking too much as we hurry along, never taking the time to stop and wonder
Never wondering why and what and how, always demanding
And because of this we get no answers, no explanations
And so we hurry along not noticing each other and not noticing ourselves
Running from everything, seeing nothing

Aaron Payne

Hope After The Storm

Battered like the mountains
Of a planet in outer space;
Burnt like the abyss of hell;
Forsaken like dry bones in a desert,
Then I saw hope, I saw a flower bloom.

Volcanoes erupted in my mind,
Earthquakes shook my body.
Rivers flowed from the cleft of my eyes
Thunder rolled in the hammer of my ears;
Then I saw hope, I saw a flower bloom.

Tell me that the sun will shine again,
That dust will be human once more,
Convince me that life is more than just a birthday
And that laughter will roll over the waves.

Softly, so softly I was touched
By a tender loving hand; straightened
Like a flagpole in the wind.
Patience calls me here to soothe my soul
And duty tells me I must arise,
Cause now I have hope, I've seen a flower bloom.

Patricia J. Adams

Awakening Of My Mornings

At the beginning of each day,
a ritual of love is shared.
Gentle tickling and soft caresses,
replace the harshness of an alarm clock.
As the mornings peep over the thick quilts,
smiles reflect the loving affection.
Their beautiful, large brown eyes,
reflective of their mother's.
Their dark smooth olive skin,
soft, tender and innocent.
The stretching reaching arms of awakening,
painfully remind me of their brief stay.
With each sunset I await in anticipation,
for the next awakening of my mornings.

Jerry L. Sparks

Unknown

Where's my life and wheres it goin'
    I'm falling through and I'm unknowing;
I need to know more; wake me at last
    Where's reality, not in the past,
    I've tried too long to make it last
So here I go down and unchosen road
    Lonely and weary from too heavy a load
Here I sit lonely and trying. But it's a hard
sell and no one is buying.
    Have I really made life's choice, or was
    It picked by someone else's voice?
For so eager an answer I'd like to know
    Where is my life and where should
    It go?

Brian K. Rick

Safe

THERE IS A PLACE THAT'S JUST FOR ME
WHERE RAINBOWS END BY THE CANDY TREE.
PIXIES WITH FLOWERS ROAM THE SKIES,
AND FAIRIES SING ME LULLABIES.
I AM SAFE THERE

but when i awake
the pain will return;
the hurt and the fear,
and the tears that burn.

But again I'll escape
In my mind I will hide
You can't find me there
You can't make me cry
You have no power there
You can't hurt me
I am safe.

Wendy Wellington

Growing Up In The 90's

He gazed into her insipid eyes
He damned her inviting thighs.

Her father had screamed with self-righteous Morality
Since he had jump-started her youthful fecundity.

His conscience and his ego underwent some strife
But he did the right thing and made her his wife
    With two rings of gold
    for his fresh planted soul
He ended his life.

Peter Brooks

Walls

The blisters in the cracked concrete wall swell with sweat and
secrets murmured.
Dirty and bloody socks line the parapet, and piles of live
people dance lying down in the bed of a rickety pick-up truck.
A casserole of human flesh, salted with desperation, melted with a
family portrait of despair, bakes and shakes in the psycho sun.

A cancer of hate and a disease of "I own this land and who the f***
do you think you are?" Await these accident persons on a pilgrimage
to the land of idols, where its alleged people need what they want and
make scapegoats of the desperate. Shadows of music and wisps of
opaque angel wings side along walls of sweatshops, move across winery
fences and swim quietly through strawberry fields forever.

A shout is heard and a coronet blasts a warning. Ants scurry.
Some later lie smashed and brain damaged from police batons.
Others make it to Compadre Juan's, to fuel an urban underclass fire that
heats a stew so polluted that Uncle Dick is already dead and doesn't know it.

Scrawls of handwriting pepper the otherwise perfect walls of the
white world, but no one knows how to interpret the nagging tagging of
emptiness. Mary and Joseph read the evening paper and sip chardonnay.
Pedro and Jesus pick grapes until seven, eat a bean sandwich, and
send their paychecks home to Madre.

Joe Corcoran

Where We Stand Out

Don't you remember back in the 'hood
That everything we owned and valued would be jacked.
It's hard to stop the gang bangin',
'Cause no one's got your back.
We're in the '90s, and kids are havin' sex.
Some think life is easy, but in reality, it's complex.
Gangs are killin' each other for what we wear in style.
My homeboy just shot someone, and now he's in juvenile.
Now I figga... we gotta be straight up with one anotha.
We can't keep goin' around callin' each otha a f**ka.
I hide a loaded gun in my jacket for protection.
Why go through all this sh**, 'cause of what we wear for fashion?
My homegirl got stabbed in the leg; needed 84 stitches,
But my girl, Streek, don't mix in with the rest of them b*t*hes.
I stood up for my homies. Got beat-up and shot someone.
I was put in jail; couldn't get bailed. Damn!!! I thought
my homies would come.

Anna Liza Aseoche

The Witch

Early morning, the sun stretched her arms
To radiate the sweltering heat of the day
Below, a lone woman beauty in every pore
Stood bound and tall to a wooden stake
An ivory shell with no cotton to cover
Raven hair long and limp
About her neck a wreath of dead roses
An angel fallen from grace
An enchantress with black magic to cast
Her time was now, fate was waiting
Mortals gathered as the stake was lit
A spectacular view she had become
Her eyes bled water as she paid for her sins
An agony filled scream tore through the valley
As shouts grew louder and pain ripped her apart
Burning flesh from her self she could smell
Skin melting like candle wax, bones cracking
Greedily the hot devil groped her, licked her , touched her
Finally pulling her in to join his hunger
Leaving death clinging to the air as the crowd departed
Alas far away a bang shuddered the sky
Hiding the sun, and bringing the dark
Sweet pellets of rain fell upon her ashes
An apology for the wrong, they never knew they did

Nichole Quiring

"The Priest"

I've stepped into an octopus garden
An uncircumcised hardon
Seduces by God
Loves by God
A beautiful garden
Alluring and inviting
Some edges frayed
Gone unnoticed
Wrapped arm in arms
Suction swarms
Concuss alarm
Who is crazy here?
Beauty disguises fear
Captivating, big and rare
Why the mistakes?
All at once depart this place
A heavy shadow still lurks
In the garden's secret curse
Love lies deep
For what it must keep
Buried with obsession
In this brutal lesson.

Tammy Allen Deloyht

"Go Ahead"

Turn the screw...The rue!
Wood is Tree, agree?
Root grown. Still! Free
earth life. Like D.D.T.
knot...For the turn.

Gay baby! Burn...
like fern. Primitive,
fire life...
Mick use the knife.

You-ow, Me0ow!
Bee, Tree, me, Thee, we
is life. Mate
rate, at the gate.
For goodness sake.

Clifford Rose

The Black Sisters

Dark lines eyes
and rouged up cheeks
and black, something black.
Whether it be tight tops or short skirts
we matched in harlot, jezebel ways.
Back then,
Brett Micheals, Axle Rose, and Sebastian Bach
were men of our shared fantasies
until real men came along,
we passed them back and forth too.
Remember one, he called us the black sisters,
quite the fitting name.
From the days of malls
and forbidden parties,
to cars and smoke-ridden apartments,
we passed it between us.
And when the sexual, psychedelic dreams
eventually became reality,
it consumed us both together
Black sister to Black Sister,
Best Friends Forever.

Veronica M. Villareal

The Once Series: The Second Bleeding

Once, when the heaving, hacking stomach of benevolence puked its pungent putridness onto my head to share its inner warmth with me, I decided to help a little old lady across the street by jamming six sticks of dynamite up her saggy butt and lighting the fuses, thus propelling her charred, scarred, and haggard form safely to the other side. Boy, she didn't even say, "Thank you."

Once, when the twirling, swirling drill of Commandments burrowed into my head to purée my thoughts, I decided to covet my neighbour's adulterer, steal the honour of my father and mother, vainly make graven images of God's name, be a false witness against the people I've killed, and bow down before the Once God. Boy, it's gonna be tough gettin' into Heaven.

Once, when the tiny, shiny shadow of sadism spotlighted my head with its darkness, I decided to pin my anatomy teacher to a dissecting tray and open her, brand 7 run-on sentences onto my english teacher's face and tongue, fold my algebra teacher into a right triangle and bisect him, wrap my spanish teacher into a piñata and beat the goodies out of her, and lastly, ghastly, I sundered my acting teacher's legs and arms and propped her torso up with them so she can act like a table. Boy, I guess I don't gotta go to school tomorrow.

Once, when the freeloading tenant of writer's block shacked up in my head to bum off my thoughts, I decided to...........Boy,...........

Jeremy Walter

Frog Green Grass And Skyscrapers

This is not my life
I live in the city
Where too tall buildings
Prick and scratch
The delicate flesh of sky
Innards oozing out
In dazzling colors and
Dripping down tall walls
Pulled hopelessly towards pavement and screaming cop cars
A victim of gravity

There — only stars crowd the sky
Elbowing each other with their brightness
I mean . . . they're so much clearer there
And Orion's penis is much more visible
It isn't covered up by tight Calvin Kleins
Or cloaked in thick syrupy smog
The kind that's so sticky
If you had a little butter
You could pour it on pancakes
And have breakfast

Sarah Jane Sculco

Puzzle #7

Incessant rain
Pulsating bladder
Ceaseless bass from a stereo
Streams of metal barring beams of moonlight
From reaching faceless figures
Inebriated donkeys stumbling on four legs,
While they nay and bite at each others raised tails
A wall grows bored of being erect for twenty years
And lies down on the nearest bed
A reflecting glass desires to know what he looks like
Instead of a young couple having sex
Shrill sirens slice through the chocolate coated ceiling,
While marshmallows dip humans into scalding mugs of coco
A chicken curses a half-clothed man nailed to a post,
Blaming him for lost dreams of being beautiful.
A manufactured fortune from a cookie is read aloud
And a voice inquires, "What does it mean?"
Who knows? Who the hell knows?

Nadine Nardilli

Love, Sex, And Rock-N-Roll

Love,
Never felt by me.
Never old enough to understand THEY say.
Breaks my heart Every time I try.
I guess I wasn't ready.

Sex,
Too much internal pressure,
Not sure.
Not understood.
Don't understand.
I guess I wasn't ready.

Rock-n-Roll,
The only escape
Loud
Pounding
Rhythm through your veins.
Unlike the other two,
I guess I'm always ready.

Tanis Kaiser

Unarmored Therianthropic

Unshelled nuts sprout forth
Their branch-like semen
Enamored by the light,
It's a geranium fixation
An eternal sun habit,
Junkies and their beer, valium or T.V.
Mall mice and their charge cards for Macy's.
Spiders spin their arachnid religion
Of delicate fiber hands
To catch the firefly's spark
Whom dying sheds Promethean life
Insectual survival's sacrifice,
Shrimp curl like fingers
Reaching deep into the sea
With foreshortened limbs
Their half-formed shadow of the fetus
Still small in the embryonic ocean
Unarmoured and delicate,
The sperm whale's mouth shovels their lives
Into the caverns of his belly for love of its own being.

Jeffrey Kalman

Dear Mother

You have the face of a bulldog
but instead of the slimy saliva
dripping from its mouth
you have a Marlboro cigarette
dangling from your painted pink lips
I hate when you talk with it
and the cherry
bounces   around
and only half your mouth moves   while the other half
is left hugging the filter

You bought me a prosthetic umbilical cord
I slept with it under my pillow every night
but the tooth fairy tried to
steal it away
white fog lingers out from her throat
and she speaks robotically
a lot like you when you sing me to sleep

Leanne Nemes

"O.J."

The waves of circumstance carry him like an angry moor
Contorted in a jealous rage: An instrument of death.
Learning of it we somehow join him in this journey —
And odd and momentary alignment, unsupported by will or capability.
Our senseless signs support a trusted and familiar face
That hunts our credibility and scores our inclination like a valued
hide. Of course we know this man; this unrelenting, shining smile:
But not his dark and weighted soul, deformed intent, or
Fractured sensibility. Twisted rage is all...
A silenced scream, a howling dog and horror traced
Between the courtyard tiles. An ornamental prison with
Little space in which to die or self defend.
The act defies our need to comprehend and stands complete.
There is no understanding; only his denial of the deed.
But what of grief? And what of pain?
The beast moves quickly unrestrained and inattentive to
Involuntary visions of the act. With subtlety of conscious care
He moves beyond the slaughtered truths and mangled facts
To recreate himself. There isn't time to question why
The world is stranger than before.

Sandra C. Kelley

United States Of America

Land of equal opportunities for the crazy, hazy and lazy folks alike
With cities flung and scattered across varied landscapes and
climatologies, and peopled by creatures of diverse background,
Yet with a common dream — freedom and equality for her peoples

In derision I laugh at this dream, for in my Dad's words "the very
big butt and boobs that attracted me to your Mom was to be
the cause of our separation." Alas! where is the equality?
In a land of Sacred cows and Sacrificial lambs USA,
your founding fathers are weeping in their graves,

Their hope of reaping Unity, greatness and strength from these
diversities turns into a mirage. Divisive tendencies rear their
ugly heads - race consciousness degenerates into racism
Alas! freedom is dead. My life no longer in my hands or in hands
of those to whom our powers were surrendered.

Because the limits and boundaries of our "freedom" we cannot fathom.
Yeah, in God We Trust while clinging tenaciously to pragmatism,
existentialism and psychic readers
USA, turn to that God to avert a gradual disintegration and anarchy.
Remember, He is more jealous than Jehovah — the God of the Jews.

Emmanuel U. Chukwueke

struggle, daughters of evE

the serpent can take Many shapes, let the white dove be our sign!
always inferior A "superior" gender,
struggling against prejudices since edeN
Can we not hear; with our eyes see?
should the soft answer evil wIth evil or stay the undeserved whore of mother earth?
the temPtor tempt to meetings.
All weAk perish, rejected by society
in pain you gave life, in pain you deparTed - thank you?
beauty - worshipped, ugliness - despised; venus Ideals born out of hairfoam.
the pOnd reflects utopia
the sweetness of victory for our sex to eNjoy

Eva-Marie Stegeby

1988-AIDS

Panic Sex, General Anxiety disappearance of body
Cultured Dyslexia Telematic Society

Cyberspace

Technification of bodily fluids
Hygienic Politics, Eugenic ideology
Breakdown of Immunization, social isolation

Panic, Power, biological discourse
Pleasure of Catastrophe
The media shrieks as the body leaks, Politics of urination

Hyperspaced

Gather the Christians
Time for crusade
Brand the Jews, Tattoos for AIDS

Hyper Modern Condition

Sex, Religion, Money and Politics
Violent and Hellusinagenic

Transgression, media seduction
Post Modern body: Simulacrum, Phendoleminuim

Cultural Suicide: Dyslexia and Schizophrenia
Pleasure Pain: Tearing away living one's fantasy

Christine Ellis

Moral Mishaps

Man in heat
rabid and uncertain.
Laying with women
of another world...
Breathing mad blazing sins
and fusing into the arms
of someone forbidden...
The danger appends passion
something far beyond moral law...
Impels a necromantic insanity
through my bones...
for once I feel truly alive...

Phil Campbell

The Unheard Victory Of Us All

The bright cadmium puddle slowly trickles
down the side of the carefully sculptured
metal frame of the sleeper's humble abode.

The putrid odor of death made the coroner's
guts wrench as he stumbled upon the horrific scene,
Not to mention the recognizable colors left behind
by the unaccustomed rookies.

Finding the gun on the floor, one wondered how long
the young man layed in his own blood
Which over time had stained his pure skin
Poor bastard must have been pretty lonely to
have been lifeless this long.

Under the lifeless hand of this obvious tortured soul
rested a crisp white sheet. Sadly the meaningful
words had been disguised with the life that had
run out of the young ones body.

I supposed as fate had its way with the boy
No one was to know the immaculate words
So carefully planned by the brilliant mind
Which read death makes angels of us all

Rhonda-Faye Walker

Late Night Blather

All jewelry off, all accessories away.
We are caught right now in the vortex of lost dreams
Only to be remembered in a fog of hidden knowledge,
Insight into the confusion realms
The way you wish you were half the time
Not so inhibited when you want to be free
Not of responsibility but towards it and yet
We continue to reign as our own worst enemy.
Why the drive, destination senseless?
Numb - to reality, numb - for eternity
Until tomorrow, when we must continue the ironic cycles.
When he exclaims lucid, specific, graphic, lovemaking, pornographic
Sex scenes by one of the world's finest word crafters, emotion capturers
Gets him horny and I hear it, makes me sick and hot all at once
Most people find the best way is to live in the mean
But for those of us who cannot compromise we fluctuate through the
    extremes of the spectrum, killing time with useless rhyme which
        helps us see the whole picture clearer.
Opened minds vomiting truth all at once unconsciously, symbolically
Through words which only hinder inexpressible emotion.
You held such possibility, what happened to you and me?

Benjamin Malkin

Anonymous Love Notes From A Wife To A Husband

I have watched you from afar,
and in my heart you are a star.
Admiration from a distance, for me is new.
Do I dare to think you love me too?

Another week has now gone by,
when I get a glimpse of my heart does sigh.
Under you clothes I watch your muscles ripple.
Perhaps someday soon, we'll do a triple?

I love your eyes and your soft lips,
and those great buns behind your hips.
The rest of you is also swell,
what I hope to see, I will not tell.

I dream of the time when I'm in your strong embrace,
And we swim through sheets of silk and lace.
The time has come my darling, my dear.
When we lose ourselves, with nothing to fear.

Now is the time to read my lips,
while placing your hands on my waiting hips,
just fly to the east, to the rising sun,
To our cozy love nest so we can have some fun.

Gisela Hansen

The Laureate

I am the laureate, for those who'd like to know
My writing is darker than Hemingway, but it's also lighter than Poe
Yes I am the laureate, writing many a verse
Do you think these shoes go with this purse
You can call me the laureate, you can call me Jim
You can also call me sweet cheeks, depends on what mood I'm in

Sure I am the laureate, that isn't hard to see
Will you please excuse me, I have to take a pee
Me I am the laureate, poet tried and true
And if you don't like my poetry, well then f*** you!
Oh I am the laureate, my weapon is my pen
Not really into bestiality, even though that's a nice looking hen

I am just a laureate, follow me if you can
I have an extraordinary talent, but I am just an ordinary man
Man I am the laureate, writing poems at will
I actually got laid last week, sure hopes she's on the pill
Damn I am the laureate, it's getting near the end
Gotta kill me a rooster, he's making moves on my hen

James Kane

Between the Lines

Between the lines, between the sheets,
Between the curves, between the seams.
It's always been true and
All of those who looked
At you the way I do
Understand it all and
The things you do.
You look at me the same,
Way I do but you still
Don't understand what I
Mean to you.
The same words, the same lines,
The same sh*t, the same cries,
It's always changing but
We're still the same we
Watch the world and look
Away unashamed of what
We've become or once
Were before we lost the
Last war.

Wade Klein

An Empty Prayer

Oh take me sweet Lord to my doom,
Hide me in a lonely tomb.
Rip my heart out of my chest,
So finally I'll be at rest.
Torture those who are mean to me,
Kick and bite them, I want to see.
You push and push and then you'll feel,
My hatred for you is truly real.
Rid me of my pain oh please,
Toss me dead upon the seas.
Crush my dreams and my sorrow,
Take away my sweet tomorrow.
Right now I'm burning up in hell,
Into the devil's arms I've fell.
Suck the last breath from me,
'Cause dead is what I want to be.

Cara Miscia

Pleasure and Pain

He sits
staring at the woman in his life
and thinks . . .

Of the wonderful time he had
Last night
Enveloped in the voluptuous thighs
Of that woman in the small room
Upstairs, above the bar
While at home his woman and child slept

Then he, at three in the morning,
Or was it half past four?
Crept into her bed
Smelling of stale beer, and stale semen
That made even the old man, lying
By the corner post oblivious of the world,
Wrinkle his nose in disgust
That made her turn away from him . . .

Crying out in agony and shame
Even as he reaches out for her touch

Valerie Forbes Ndekhedehe

A Feather

A feather drifted down one day
It started on high
And hovered for a long time
Ever so slowly
It started to fall
Swaying back and forth
Lightly, comfortably and lovingly
Floating through time and tenderness
Bringing along with it
Love, compassion and happiness
A feather drifted down one day
And landed on my heart to stay

Kelly Morin

Autumn Muse

Turquoise skies contrast
the gold ginkgo leaves clinging
to ancient branches, as they did
when druids hid behind their fans.

Appliqued quilts of leaves
warm chrysanthemums, bowed
by time and frost.
Green tomatoes hang.

A red bird and yellow leaves
float in silence
out and down.

Wind-chimes strike the knell
for harvest's end,
sounding the quiet of buried seeds
and hibernating roots,
to come forth
in the staggered timing of creation.

Margaret D. Kirkland

Oh Lord Please Let Me Go

Let me sing
Let me go free
Let me express my internal glee
Oh Lord please let me go

I want to cry
I want to shout
I want to let my pain all out
Oh Lord please let me go

Hear my joy
Hear my fright
Hear my soul throughout the night
Oh Lord please let me go

I can hear you
I can feel your breath
I can now lay down and rest
Oh Lord I'm now with you

Robert Stowe

Life

Enjoying night, enjoying day
Enjoying life in every way

The Good, the bad
The ups, the downs
The happy, the sad
The smiles, the frowns

Just relish in the love of being
And only then will you start seeing
All this good, God has given
This special gift, the gift of living

Jimmie E. Jones Jr.

Desert, Sand, and Sea

Dry bushes, hot sand, and a
  shining blue sea.
On occasion there is shade
  near a twisted smoke tree.
Seagulls are finding their way
  to the shore.
Looking for whatever sea gulls
  like to explore.
Continuous hills in the distance
  Oh what a great sight!
Their colors ever changing throughout
  the day into night
Creosote leaves, lacy in their
  silhouettes against the sky
So peaceful, so quiet with exception
  to a cotes cry
This desert is home and
  forever there'll be
Dry bushes, hot sand, and
  a shining blue sea.

Vivian F. Wilkeson

The Things I Love

I love the way you dance with me
  To music sweet and clear,
The way you hold me in your arms
  And whisper in my ear.

I love the way you talk to me
  When we are all alone,
The way you kiss my lips, my dear,
  And know they are your own.

I love the very thought of you
  That's with me everyday,
I even love the love the loneliness
  I feel when you're away.

The things I love are countless
  As are the stars above you,
But what I love the most, dear one,
  Is the way you say, "I Love You."

Evelyn Masek

Talk To Me Tonight

Talk to me tonight,
and soothe my empty soul,
come to me now,
and fill the barren hole,
let me hear your whispers,
and make them last 'till dawn,
it's what I need to hear,
from you, it can never be gone,
let me rest on your voice,
and take me to your heart,
and lay me down next to it,
so they will never part,
help me come alive again,
and live my life of love,
talk to me tonight,
and let me rise above.

Julie L. Harriss

Fond Memories

Each new day brings fond memories
  of you and days gone by,
A time when we were young
  and kites could fly.
Our hopes and dreams soared
  like birds in the sky,
A time when love, could keep us
  cosy, on the coldest night.

Your warm and loving smile,
  can never be replaced...
Nor precious memories,
  ever be erased.
Knowing that God has you,
  in his kind embrace...
Makes each new day,
  a little easier to face.

Alice Marie A. De Decker

Place In My Heart

I lie awake most often
And think of what we lost
Are there answers to my questions
How much would they cost

I pray deep inside me
It's for the best someway, somehow
Though I can't seem to find
The better in it now

I'll be your friend in waiting
If you should ever need
I know life has confused you
So I have set you free

My heart shall never hate you
This should come as no surprise
For I love a part of you each day
I stare in our child's eyes.

Nicole E. Robert

A Good Day For A Ride

Today is a beautiful day I thought
as I stepped out the back door
I've just got to saddle my pony
take a ride and explore
So I saddle my pony with his objection
says he doesn't want to explore
he's seen it all before
but I stay with him
and soon were on our way
I spy a red tailed hawk
When all of a sudden my pony balked
there's a ditch full of water ahead
he starts to prance
sometimes pony's do a dance
his front feet go high in the sky
this sight you can't compare
as we go flying through the air
experiences like these are not uncommon
nor are they taken for granted
they are very much welcome on my planet.

Roy A. Ragsdale

Oneness

When you view a sunrise
across earth's vast land
still your thoughts...
and join the oneness
of God... universe... man.

Hazel S. Milnor

You Never Knew

The whole night I sat
near the rose bush
waiting for you,
but you never knew.
Till it was dawn.
I had melted into tears
that lay scattered on every petal
The tiny drops of dew
on the rose I left
for you.
You never knew.

Anupa Chakravorty

Me and Him

God is my bow,
I am his arrow.
My direction in life
is controlled by him.

My target is your 'Heart',
His is your 'Soul'.
Together we will love you,
Forever

Warren Conder

Moms

Moms are always there for you
Helping in every way
They were there when you sneezed a-choo
You took her heart away
Making you clean
Dressing you nice
Never mean
Cooking us rice
Giving us love
Giving us care
Like a dove
And a bear
Good cook
All the time
Buying us books
Reading us a rhyme
That's about my mom I love
Who reminds me of a special dove

Nicole Hochberg

Graduation Day

One two three
There's no stopping me
I'm going for the goal
Not putting anything on hold

The future looks bright
I'm taking the goal to a new height
Across the stage I go
No more play dough

All grown up
Not a second to spare
I turn around for one
Last glare

Ebony D. Lynch

Distant Angel

I'm sitting here dreaming
That you're here on my lap;
And we're singing a song
For it's time for your nap.

Here's a kiss and a hug,
And a wee squeeze or two,
For a sweet little girl,
And that girl is you.

So I rock you and squeeze you,
You look up and smile;
And you snuggle up closer,
So I hold you awhile.

Oh my dear little angel
Though you're far, far away;
You live in my heart,
And you're there to stay.

Evelyn McWilliams

Untitled

Our spirits float through the wind
like birds on the breeze
Any amount of time with you
I will spend
Like raindrops on the window
you fell into my life
Knowing it was right from the start
hoping we will never part
Lightning crashes as we make love
thunder rolls in the skies above
Loving you is all I need
we'll make it work, at any speed
The key to my heart
is what holds you dear to me
unlock my heart
The love inside is yours to be.

Christina D. Bauer

A Sad Day...

A sad day...
is agony slowly cruising
through the soul
is...
the lack of hope
the weakened faith
the heaviest weight
on a pounding heart...

A sad day...
is the longest journey
man has to face
without the sunshine
is...
a dark, cold night
without a soul
to share

Nelida Rodriguez

Untitled

Turning the pages back in time
Through the chapters of my mind —
Life is too short to leave behind
Living in a fantasy
Suddenly taken by reality
Does anyone remember me
You once knew me
Flashes of my days
I knew I was here to stay
But no one stays the same

Jason McIvor

Wanted or Unwanted

Conceited, no,
yet the fact
remains,
males find
me fair.
Many tell me so,
some for gain
some for flattery
but all in vain, because,
whatever portion of
beauty and character is
given me by my great Maker
is given freely,
to you, my beloved,
lover and friend.
I am eternally yours,
and happy in the fact.
Time may change you, my love
But I will remain yours,
Wanted or unwanted.

Mary Field Garrett

Love

Darkness fills the room
A gloomy gray filth
Engulfs my eyes
The smell of roses
Scare and frighten me
I'm left speechless
And loneliness fills my heart

Light
It blinds my baby blue eyes
And I see my
Father one last time
And I realize it's not
Loneliness, it's love

Amber McCarty

Reaching Hand

Where are you?
I can fell you...
An empty room portrays my heart,
And with its white untouched walls,
I cleanse myself.

You are my guide...
Translucent are my thoughts.
My senses swept away by winds!
I overcome though...
And find escape in your abyss of light.

Razvan Mihailescu

Love

I love a man his name
was Steave, I would watch him
play well I would weave.

He would write me letters,
he would sing me songs.
He would visit me when ever the
church bell tongs.

He would howl like a coyote,
he ran like the wind.
Then all I heard was a letter he
would send.

Lauren Gray Meisenheimer

Blue And Broken Hearted

Through the years, through the tears,
I'm forever haunted,
Have to know, how to show
Just how much you're wanted.

Needed too, it was you
Who comforted and guided,
Even tho' there were times,
It may have seemed one-sided.

Courageous, strength and love,
You gave me constantly.
There were times that I thought
I ought to set you free!

Once more Dear, still my fear,
Help me be light-hearted.
Nevermore, will we be
Blue and broken-hearted.

Christine Wilson

Waiting

Your love descended upon me
    like a snowflake from the sky.
It softly fell and kissed the Earth
    who responded with a sigh.

The whispers of music from heav'n
    brought magic to moonlight beams.
The trusting gentle Earth lay down
    to sleep in a cloud of dreams.

In snow-enveloped arms of love
    the Earth contented lay,
Unwary that tomorrow's Sun
    would steal his love away.

The laughing Sun in triumph blazed
    all across the morning sky.
The melting snow became his tears
    as earth bid his love goodbye.

Now the great Earth sits in silence
    hopefully gazing above,
As I, too, sit this lonely day
    awaiting return of love.

Gayle Vowels Williams

"Obsession"

Looking for a way out
Of this place of mixed emotions.
The door is closed,
There's nowhere to hide
From this uncontrolled obsession,
Obsession that chips away at your heart
While lifting you high into the sky.
Euphoria leaves you breathless,
The plunge down leaves you restless
For the love you long to have,
For the touch you long to feel,
For the words you long to hear,
From the one you long to hold.
The ride isn't over,
The rushing wind leaves you cold.
Just a few more twist and turns,
Just a few more dives and bends.
Hopefully soon the heartache stops...
And the torture ends.

Naomi Tacuyan

The Web

"Come into parlor"
said spider to fly,
"Come into make out
    Give it a try"
Fly soon late
    Did regret it
He soon later
    Did forget it.
Spider fly
    Girl and guy
Tricks they try
Keep it neat
    No retreat
No net, not yet.

Anne M. Adamson

"To You That I Have Loved"

Visions of you beside me,
Line the side of my face.
I feel your presence near,
Then, suddenly, gone without a trace.
A new life,
A new name.
It's not all so new,
Just part of the game.
I wish you the best,
I really do,
Just please don't forget,
Me, your Monica Sue.
In part,
Yours I will always be,
So don't shut that door,
For outside, it is me.
I will be here,
No matter where you are,
Whether you are near,
Or whether you are far.

Monica Sue VanBrussel

A Parent's Prayer

Our son was brought to us
from God above.
He is our source of
inspiration and brings so
much love
and tenderness to our
hearts.
Please God lead him on
through the paths of
righteousness.   As his
parents, give us the
strength and guidance to
help him to grow
and become a man.

Karen Luchtenberg

Marine, A Poem For Ernie

To battle he goes,
Pride lives in his heart.
Dying is for his foes,
Combat to him is an art.
But, oh too soon,
His youth will be forsaken
His heart with wound,
His soul will be taken.
And when all is done and seen,
He will still be a marine!

Ignascio G. Camarena

Untitled

America
let's
Make It A Positive Day;
Our
Schools
need
Karaoke
To turn this world around;
We need to pull
Together
In hopes to build new ground.
Our
Children
need some
Happiness
Somewhere along the way.
Teach them
Karaoke
and
Make I A Positive Day.

Rebecca Jean James

What Is Christmas?

It's a fading paper angel
Made with care so long ago,
A stolen kiss one winter night,
Or a late December snow.

It's a fresh-picked sprig of holly
Or a desperate prayer for peace.
It's a cry for help from children
So that all the wars might cease.

It is snowy pines that shimmer,
And it's silver tinsel, too,
A grateful hug, much needed,
Or a gift from me to you.

It's candles' glow and shining stars,
Your deepest heart's desire.
It's lovely smiles from folks so dear
And dozing by the fire.

But most of all it's simply love
That a baby came to give.
How humbly did he grow, then die
So that all the world may live!

Barbara Fogel

A Moment

Cigarette smoke spiralled in the air
stirring circles of the imagination
in a starlit night
scented with a soft breeze
the waves swish swashed amorously
and mermaids emerged beckoned
together we plunged into the deep blue
soon the charioteer appeared
and in his splendor cynthia yielded
and as they melted in his light
day and night were one
time and place conquered
and eternity created
a moment of joy in life.

Afroditi Panaghis

Trees

I love trees
They are amazing
I like to lie in your shade
And listen to the birds
Sing on you
And listen to kinds
Of music

Jonathan Pieton

Untitled

Faithfulness — the dog
Life and death devotional
Reminder of God.

Charity Kraeszig

YOU ARE ME

Dreaming vividly of you
Tossing your perfectly "round"
Into my chest as we
Re-cap our exercise . . .

Your voice so soft and listless,
Your lips, so soft,
These are my visions of pleasure
Repeated again and again.

We often wonder whether our happiness
Is real or made-up "bull" . . .
Bull for those who hear . . .
We do not hear; we experience
A joy beyond any known tangible . . .

You are me with every conversation.
Long distance in miles, but
Right here in my heart, right now!
You are my reason for existing now.
Stay in my heart for life,
As we "tick on" to eternity.

George Guy

Nightdream

I am not thinking of a time
When I shall fall asleep beneath
my sheets somewhere else,
not here, where I fall asleep holding
my own hand, smoothing over
the half-moons in my
finger nails.

I am not thinking of red
candles on nightstands,
two shadows, a white wall.

Nor am I thinking of him,
a blue kitchen
somewhere,
stirring soup in a gingham apron,
tied loose about his waist.

I do not think
of untying it one night,
moving closely behind him.

Shannon M. Keesaw

Mr. Wonderful

What is it with his gorgeous
smile? What is it with the
way he smiles at me? What is
it with how his eyes look sad
and sexy all at the same
time? What is it with his body
that makes him look like a
god? What is it with the way
his name goes perfectly with
his attitude? What is it with
the way I melt at the sound
of his voice? What is it with
the way I love him, but he
could never love me back?

Eileen Walsh

Hope

Sun sifted through a motionless tree
A small bit of light fighting its
    way to a patch of ground.
In desperation my eyes try to pull
    the rays through the leaves
A little sun is better than none
    and a little hope grows into
    a stronger and greater hope
A little faith in God will find
    its way through the haze.

Mary Gordon

Mirrors

Look it's Mr. Beautiful
Looking at me
He's all face and body
No brains in that one.

Look at Mr. Beautiful
Admiring his perfection
He's all precise beauty
Cultured to perfection.

Look at Mr. Beautiful
Looking jealously at me
I'm the smarter one here
He's just a shape.

Look I'm Mr. Beautiful
Looking at my reflection
The doubled image of myself
And perfect in every way.

Jay Little

Zone

A flower grows...a flower grows,
    Out in the fields beyond,
A raindrop falls...a raindrop falls,
    On the petals of hurt and bond,
Wake up love...wake up life,
    Shine down on the one below,
Light me up...pass me on,
    It's there the moon will go,
Far away...lost in time,
    Curled like a ball,
Fade away...fade away,
    Trapped behind a wall,
Darkness falls...shadows cast,
    Cold is now the floor,
Shine again...shine again,
    Take me there once more.

Stefan Konstantopoulos

Shooting Star

Today I turned my heart
backwards and
saw a dark shadow in my form
darting and dodging
from under and between
clouds of painful memories
and raining daggers

Scars were glistening across
my back like shooting stars and
I turned forward again because I
did not want to see
what I had already felt
over
and over before

Now still my heart rests
in darkness
slowly slipping
into a silent slumber
not to be awakened ever
lest by the touch of your love accepted

Plea for Basherta
January 13, 1995
Mariella Götz

The Lonely Heart

Happiness of love...
Silent distance
Years of tears
Drown endearments
Kissed on ears
Phantom faces
Faded smiles
Trace a path of lonely miles.

Flames of memory
Torch the heart
Echoes kindle embers spark
Reminiscence...
Song of the lark
Happiness of love
Warm embrace
Caress the lonely heart
Lost in empty space.

Sarah Ballantyne

The Kiss

I wonder if a kiss means marriage
Or if it's just a date
Or if it means good-bye
Maybe it's over rate
I wouldn't just know why.

Jessica Dennis

A Mother's Day Poem

When it comes Mother's Day
you do things your mother's way,
do your chores
sweep the floors
wash the dishes
with good wishes
When it comes Mother's Day
remember her favorite words
Go Away

Steven Stanley

Let Go

If I had a wish in this vicious world,
I would wish for myself to die.
No one would understand how I feel,
Why I want to die.
I'm dead within myself,
My body just living in hell.
If I had to tell someone,
They'd just think I'm crazy.
My life is going down hill,
I'm falling more and more.
I'm down too deep
To climb back up,
So don't anybody give me a hand.
Just let me go,
Let me go to where I belong.

Joli Vang

Mirrors

Mothers and daughters,
Fathers and sons,
Can be the tensest of relations.

Why does this happen?
Perhaps you'll agree
We see in the other
That very thing
We cannot accept of ourself.

The other's a threat
For the nearer they get
The closer ourself we see.

It's nice to be perfect
All polished up clean,
Wheeling and dealing
our tongue.

But little we know
Of the heartache below,
In ourself and the other one.

Elaine M. Kershaw

Young Torment

Restless, tearing, uncertainty
Raging fire within.
No way out
Dreaming of freedom
To soar like a bird.
Release the pain
Send it far, far away.
A sense of calm
You long to know.
Those around you
Think all is right.
Just make a choice
They say.
Trying this, doing that
A world of happiness awaits.
Peaceful, soothing, sunshine
Someday you hope — somehow.

T. J. Starratt

A Poem For Mama Bear

You disciplined me when I was bad,
You helped me when I was sad,
You helped raise me since I was young,
You yelled at me when I sung.

Mathew Stanley

Untitled

Each day, a quest
Started off to the best
A push, a fight
Opens a new light
You see that what you've got
Is not something that can be bought
Sometimes you regret
That you can forget
How friendship is so precious

Shivani Chandra

The Night Sky

As the sun slowly falls,
the darkness overtakes,
bright stars glow like fireflies,
a flash of light, a shooting star,
a night owl hoots, as the trees
sing in the wind, the bright
moon shining as far as he can,
as a wolf howls to him, the
stillness of the void of the
night scares a mouse bound
for its house, the silence is
broken as a cat starts to meow
in the void of the night.

Tanya Pateman

Liberty In The Cross

I am your Father God to thee
with freedom's holy light;
I am the Author of liberty,
guarding the loyal with My might.

To a nation who used My roots
and multiplied My grant;
Bringing forth more fruits,
and is glorified in My covenant.

Blest be liberty for all mankind
when Jesus came He said;
"Blest be the nations that find Me,
and by My hand are led."

Blest be the cross that binds
Christian soldiers for liberty;
March on for it is a sign,
so all will know of Me.

Blest be the soldiers of the cross
marching for peace in liberty;
Give a hand to the lost,
take up your cross and follow Me.

Phyllis Conant

Answer

Answers the call of change
Both spiritual, physical.
Begin anew,
or die without living fully;
without a spiritual life that after.
Take stock of your life,
your ambitions.
Retrain, reform, rebuild, renew;
to change the sum total,
a combined effort is call for.
Answer the call and live.

B. Miles Jackson

Used To Be

You can't
Take this
Away from me.
Maybe it doesn't
Mean that much,
But it's everything
To me.
Fragments left,
After the fall.
I stand here
In the ruins
Of everything;
Nobody else can
Help me
Put it back
Together.
This used to be
A safe haven.

Susan Ehlah Johansen

A Walk In My Garden

She had felt his touch,
The gentleness of his soul.
He had stopped to feel her petals,
And the beauty of her heart.

His brief interlude with her,
Was etched in her memory.
The warmth of his words,
Comforting her aching soul.

The surrounding flowers bloomed,
Whilst her petals became soft.
Her emotions drained,
Her stem weak.

He had given her sunshine,
She had begun to grow.
Now only his prints remained,
His touch lingering...

Elizabeth Scruth

Easter - 1994

At Easter time in 1994
the skies were as grey
as Welsh slate;
dark with white clouds interlacing.
The rain came,
the snowflakes too,
and tiny cannon-balls
of hail bombarded the daisies.

There was some glimpse
of hope, when the sun
steered through;
and the clouds sped away
leaving patches of blue.
But the sky seemed sad,
and it reflected on me;
and I thought of the cross at calvary;
and I wondered - was God, angry?
For despite his great sacrifice,
his world is still not perfect.

And were the hail-stones his tears!

Freda Ball

Untitled

She will cry sometimes, but not for him
she will care for all;
and for him.
She will hold it all and hold on
will she realize he is one?
He walks tall and worries not
she, a step behind,
will for him and her together.
She will listen with attentiveness
He will take with awareness,
although he is doubtful
she is hearing only the relevant
will she assure or deny his speech
he will live on and so will she
with full alliance to each other.

Anne Henning

Little Images — Not Nice

A dream
and a mystery cabbage
amble inverted
along
illogical dimensions.

The Wizard and the Okie
did a U-turn on the trail
and cut a turbulent rose —

The swamp pets,
the worms,
and the fire globes
joke
beyond illusions.

By the lake
on a day
I read
letters of cold fire.
A silver mask
noticed
the fungi.

Clark Hardman Jr.

Untitled

Tell me, what is beauty
Unless the price is free?
An eternity of sacrifice
And a soul lost to unhappy.

A face is only features
Until lit up with a smile
A body only skin and bones
'Til with love it walks a mile.

The inner spirit breathes it song
To soft for human ear
Smothered by impurities
It will die at the hand of fear.

Within the eye of a raging storm
Every troubled heart lives
But when the tear drops cease,
The truest beauty begins.

Miranda Medema

No Religion

No religion can ever heal you
No thoughts nor pain
can ever release you
It's just a photograph
of ancient summer's breeze
Life's a mirage

No Marx nor Lenin can ever free you
No stocks nor bonds
can ever secure you
It's just a stream of tears
of young girl's virgin fears
Life's a mirage

No cause or might can ever assure you
No Tao no how
can ever teach you
It's just a dusty trail
of old man's broken dreams
Life's a mirage

Life's a mirage

Dae Soo Hahn

Finally

I felt it.
You can't tell me it's not
Real.
I felt it.
I didn't see a bright light
Or hear a thundering voice.
It felt it.
Inside.
Deep Inside.
I felt it.
I believe in it.
You can't make me change
my mind.

Heidi J. Keparutis

Fisherman And The Fish

Oh great salmon
Rise from the sea
And take the bait I give to thee.
Child of the great spirit
Brother of the Tyee
Ask Quinnat to come to me.
The sea is wild
The sea is wide
But Quinnat my brother cannot hide.
He feeds my people
He sustains my life
Without King Salmon
There would be no might.
Oh brother who has called me
I have spent my life at sea
My spawning time has begun
I must return to rivers deep
To spawn and then eternal sleep.
And the cycle begins again
Fish and fisherman till the end.

Donald G. Lott

Interruption

Like an interruption to my sleep
the morning came
And I dragged out of bed and
stumbled to turn on the light

That's the way it usually happens
We fumble for the truth
and it runs right into us

As dancers in the dark
we flow together
Trying to make sense
out of circumstances

That's the way it usually happens
We fumble for the truth
and it runs right into us

As choosers of choices
We make decisions for the day
And all the while it is our
periphery lightning the way

Yolanda Poston

Single Mother

You see me
as the mistreated
relative
or the abused and defeated
neighbour.
You see tear-stained cheeks
on my child,
hang your head for the victims
of society.
My shadow lurks in your backyard,
uninvited.
I am your dirty laundry,
overflowing.
I am the annoying sting
of all your paper cuts.
I am the recurring nightmare
lying in your bed.
Inevitably,
I will be
the mother in your daughter.

Kelly Sedore

Looking Through The Mirror

I looked away infinite
I looked over the universe
I looked in the world
I looked at nature
I looked into the life
I looked for the peace
I looked back and didn't see God
I looked down on death
I look after myself

John Fontenele Araujo

Scent In The Air

Stop and smell the blossoms
of blues and pinks and reds.
Pause, take in the splendor
of field after field of beds.
This moment soon will pass,
never to repeat.
So know it while you can,
for time cannot repeat.

Ngaio Hotte

Kingdom Of Heaven

I had an escape from reality
within my dreams one night
I entered the kingdom of heaven
Where the world was a beautiful sight

I could hear angels voices singing
and as they rose in sweet harmony
I whispered how happy
I am, at last
Dear Lord to be with thee

Up there in the kingdom
Where beauty and peace
reign supreme
I found comfort and solace
Surrounding me
In my magical, mythical
dream

Charlotte C. O'Dell

Jesus Is The Way

Jesus is the way.
He makes a way out of no way.
He's my shining light everyday.
Only Jesus' light can lead and guide
You on your way. Jesus is on the
Main-line — pick up your phone and
Call on him anytime. The sun is
Bright, the moon is a light, the stars
They shine at night — but no light is
As bright, as the bright light of the
World. The light of love — the light
Of peace — the light of joy — that no
One can destroy.

Lottie M. Harris

Nana Loves!

His sweet, young voice beckons me
I glance in his direction,
Dragging on the floor I see
The froggy game collection...
Nana play!

His favorite book is in my lap
He squirms on well-padded knees,
Stalling for time before his nap
His soft voice gently prompts me...
Nana read!

Excitedly he rushes past
The other children playing,
His little legs are climbing fast
And as he slides he's saying...
Nana watch!

He waves at me and says goodbye
With tears flowing in sorrow,
His mother tells him not to cry
You'll be with her tomorrow...
Nana waits!

Pam Warden

Untitled

Four's more than a-plenty
to tell it in twenty.
Insisting on ten,
crank-out six with a roarrrr
remembering Meis: Less is more.

R. B. Cutler

Justice

Justice is a vulture
who sits over the scene
of man's lack of remorse;
the judge and jury are
its eyes,
probing into the unwashed
victim's entrails;
It's knotted ugly claws ache
for the action of its wings
to encompass its prey
and move on.

Florence Olszewski

Pearls

Woman is a hole,
mysterious, and bottomless;
all the suffering and futility
of the world,
pouring into her.
Through her flesh, it is reborn;
sanctified... purified...
She bares this burden of truth,
of trust,
like a torch in an endless night;
but it fails to shed
its healing light
upon her own darkened life.
Woman patiently bathing
in wells of pain,
to cleanse the ills of the world;
never doubting her faith
in what is right...
one day, her tears will be pearls.

Sheila Simonson

Someone Special

Shall I watch
each day go by, each
season with its change
of tides. And each road
I travel on, one day find
someone there beyond. I
feel a warmth within me
growing. My heart is full
and my eyes are glowing.
Someone is there so close,
will I ever be knowing.

Gloria Johnson

Only Him

It matters not where I may travel
Nor whom I chance to see,
Jesus is the only One
Who means so much to me.

I look at all the worldly things,
I weigh them one by one;
He is still my sole companion
When all is said and done.

I cannot stray from His precious wing
When I know my Lord is near
Because He is my Guardian,
And because I love Him dear.

I would not take the world
And all the devilish things within
In place of what it means to me
To live my life for Him.

Barbara J. Munn

Inspiration

I hope,
I pray,
And I dream every day
That things will go my way.

Minutes pass,
Hours pass,
Then they become a day
But nothing goes my way.

Still I hope,
Still I pray,
I still dream everyday
I know things will go my way.

Vicki Wolf

Our Of Minds

lightwave
    blue
'cross the
    morning
        nightsky

intiMe
    swoosh t'all
infiknitted
    afghan

people
    in their supposedly
right minds
    have trouble
        swallowing my existence

but since you're
    hanging from the big dipper
i s'pose
    i can hope
        things'll be cherry

i love you

Philip Barry Rosen

Reptile House

Snake in the house!
Snake in the house!
Snake in the house!
I just saw a small
snake in the house,
I don't know
what kind of snake
I saw, all I know
there is a snake
in the house. Look!
There is the small snake!
Pretty snake.
Will the snake bite me,
if I hold it in my arms?
I hope not!
There is a snake
in the house,
just go to the zoo
and visit the small
snake in the house,
at the reptile house.

Joyce Davidowicz

A Daughter's Love Promise

I send to you a special gift,
You can neither feel nor see.
It will last for many years to come,
And it's from the heart of me.

I offer you my helping hands
Whenever they are needed.
And to you both, my listening ears
Though things may be repeated.

I promise to take care of you
Should health or hardship fall,
And I'll try to fill your every wish
Though it be great or small.

I give to you my friendship
To use as you see fit,
It will always be here waiting
Should you have the need of it.

And last, but certainly not least
I give you all my love,
And a constant prayer to God on high
To watch you from above.

Diane Hall

Lightning

Thunder claps, lightning strikes,
rain pounds on the window.
It's a storm.
What I like best about a
storm is lightning,
The way it zigzags through
the sky.
Lightning looks like a bright
light zigzagging through
the dark sky.
When it hits the ground
it smells like burnt toast.
Lightning may be dangerous
but it's my favorite part
of a storm.
What's yours?

Daphne Hovey

Distant

Distant horizon
On the blue sea
I see the silhouette
Of my FAIAL
Normal reaction
Or indiscreet vision
A poet's dream
The Island lover
I want to return
Make it real
Or it is an idea vain
Of a fantasy
That was tenderness
To become suffering
An incessant pain
Blind stubbornness
Insane agony
Constant affliction
The immigrant's cross
On a distant land

Eduardo De Lacerda

Take Up The Slack

If you want to be like anyone,
Take up the slack.
If you would like a pat on the back,
Take up the slack.
The slack will always hold you back,
Take up the slack.
When you have found you have won,
taking up the slack has just begun.
Keep the slack always in back,
And keep on and never look back,
There is no room for slack.

Hattie B. Birth

Blue Monday

Today is Monday, day of blues,
But really it is what you chose,
And just what makes a Monday blue,
Give it thought, it could be you.

Don't get uptight, not for awhile,
But did you start out with a smile?
I don't mean beaming like a clown,
Just start your day without a frown.

With that much done relax your face,
A smile will easily fall in place
It takes less effort say the books
And really can improve your looks.

A smile can only prove to you
That not all Mondays are so blue.
So spread a smile along the way,
You'll surely brighten someone's day.

Penny Milne

Untitled

Now I remember why I saw your face
all along the harvest. The gold that
glistened in rows - was you.
    Fields of fire on earth, only
    put out by the setting sun.
        Such melancholy hung around the
        moon, that night.

A nice voice, you have one - I said.
Modulated to the perfect pitch, it
makes me shiver down the street when I
hear it.

Running water down a dry throat.
Harvest dust swept from my throat.
Azrael has run his golden scythe
over my tongue.
    So I am dumb.

I touch my tongue to remember
what I might have said, to you.
Maybe I would have said that you
have a nice voice.

D. R. Hanni

Time Traveler

Like the wings of doves
through sunshine fly
    of forests bound
    and feelings high
touched by nature
with the secret of time
be a traveler so open
and shine, shine, shine!

Donna M. Kosena

A Mother's Gift

Withered, trembling fingers,
upon white sheets lay.
Hallow cheeks, golden white hair,
sunken eyes, mouth feebly mumbles,
with gentle restless smile.
Eyes close from earthly light,
finale sleep prevails.
Painful breaths emerge,
time slips quietly away.
Stillness is within,
my human spirit rests.
The soul is at peace,
yesterdays are gone,
as dust in winds.
All my tomorrows are eternal,
Children, your inheritance?
Gifts of love,
memories embedded deep within.
Light of wisdom taught.
My life achievements,
each one of you.

Karolyn Ivie

Love In Silence

In the silence of the night,
when all the world is asleep,
my thoughts about you taunt me,
and feelings about you I keep.
    But not even you know this,
even less the way I feel,
my heart remains in silence,
and willing to keep still.
    How much longer I ask,
will I be able to hold,
my love for you, that with each moment,
keeps growing forever strong.
    As the dawn breaks,
I will keep my silence once again,
my love for you will still flourish,
but only in my heart will it remain.

Dania A. Garcia

Cry For Help

White silver,
Incandescent moon,
I stand and stare, weep and swoon

Smiling rock,
She who gives light,
Help me forgive his sins tonight

I'm all alone
Bowing before you
Asking that your advice be true.

For all the hurt
And unbearable pain,
You can make things right again.

Glowing crescent,
Satellite,
Deliver me from this stage of fright

Beautiful moon,
My only friend,
This bitterness I have must end.

Jessy Napper

The Quest

Life is but a temporary thing
Why must we struggle so?
A continuous search that ends in vain
Why can't we rest and let it go?

Is it because, way down inside
We feel, somehow, somewhere
That tho our dreams have been denied
There is a purpose - it must be there!

Some never seek, yet have success
To them, it's rightly so
What inner strength do they possess
Of which I do not know?

Some have found it and held it tightly
They know where their destiny lies
Others have had it but held it lightly
And in that loss is where faith dies.

How long must we wait before we know
If our searching is worthwhile
Or will that all come after we go
Then will be know how to smile?

Jeanne L. Sims

Butterfly

When I was a butterfly,
You would tear off my wings.
Then I learned to fly
wingless,
or rather, on wings
not visible to you.

Now I float and flutter
wherever I please.
My butterfly soul
tastes nectar, feels sunlight
hears birds sing.

Free, I follow my path
from flower to flower.
Heedless of your hand.

Mildred Bell Kaliss

The Oak Tree

I was always here.
I watched your forefathers
Fish, hunt, farm.
I never bothered them.

They never caused me harm.
But now streets must be paved.
Buildings made.

My life's juices no longer flow.
For they have cut me down.
Why?
I'll never know.

Tracey Veldhuis

Barbie

In the isolation of my pain
I wonder, am I real?
My captive heart lies silent
You don't want me to feel

Dress me, I'm your Barbie doll
I'm only here for you
My hair, my smile, my body
Are all you see as true
Hold me, I'm your Barbie doll
It's nothing but a game
You defile me, I must break
No, don't feel any shame
Kill me, I'm your Barbie doll
I'm screaming in my mold
Sugar, spice and all that's nice
I'm different, far too bold

In the isolation of my pain
I find that I am real
I cry to break the silence
And I learn that I can feel

Heather Dineen-Porter

True Love In The West

The girl she loved her cowboy,
The cowboy loved his girl.
Even when he rode away with a,
Lock of her curl.
He promised to come back for her.
And when that day had come.
She took his name.
And they lived until they,
Were done.
The west was hard and wild,
That we all know.
But the girl she had her cowboy.
And the cowboy had his woman.

Amy B. Peterman

The Vision

Standing on a bridge so high
Looking up I saw no sky
The earth was black
And so very cold
I then looked at myself
And I was not old
The dragon I saw was giving birth
To a creature so gross
That was not of this earth
As I stood and watched this awful thing
The dragon then turned
And came after me
I started running with nowhere to go
Through flames of fire
I had wished were snow
I jumped from a canoe
Into another one and another
Not knowing that Christ
Was my shelter
My brother

Derrick Jones

Other At One

An infinite line,
A point in time,
Both touch each other.

An addition of one,
A subtraction of three,
Both can equal the other.

An eerie shadow,
A loving figure,
Both can be the other.

An empty soul,
A searching heart,
Both want each other.

Dan W. Stott

My Mother

Has there ever been a mother
as lovely as my own?

With dignity and pride, as
no one else has shown.

A smile so sweet and honest,
upon her shining face.

Admirable and loving,
heart so full of grace.

Hands that have the power to
give the gift of healing touch.

A heart that wants to give
the love a child needs so much.

A voice that says "I love you"
in such a soothing tone.

And so I have this mother
I'm proud to call my own.

Alexandra Brooke

Untitled

The mayo brothers made for me
A dietary snickersnee,
made up of fulminating broths
That cut you down to smaller cloths,
The gourmandizing trends of man
No longer need deterring hands,
For now the mayo brothers two,
Have come through for me and you.
Shout Hosannahs, ring the bells,
For now society is svelte,
Molded into perfect forms,
Esthetic blobs, caloric norms.
So, if you care to be your own
Master owing none to all,
Tell the mayo Brothers to
"Wield your wicked snickersnew
And use it on that bunch of snobs
That cast aspersions on us slobs."

John Longo

Gingerbread House

Winter wears very well
the woolen wrinkled merry winkles,
dimples under wrap,
thick icing roof tops over
stove tops gingerbread warm.
Icicles on eaves
twinkle clearly,
pink clad faces cheerily
exchange well worn secrets
of sugar plum stockings
winter wears very well.

Monik Nordine

The Gentle Spring

The calling birds, the opening buds,
the clear blue sky.
The forest green, the fragrant scents,
the fresh clean air.
The babbling brook, the new mown hay,
this cheery day!
The fluffy clouds, the pleasant walk;
the call "hello."
The squirrel runs, the deer appears;
the gentle look.
The thoughts of life, the love of God,
this precious day!
And once again - the gentle spring!

Paul A. Trouve

Atom

The shape and fragrance of a rose
The curve of every tiny nose
Remembered with the perfect prose
Of atoms

My thoughts so carefully defined
The brain encompassing my mind
That which I think is me I find
Is atoms

Creations memory is vast
From deep space cold to novas blast
All shapes and forms come down at last
To atoms

So when I leave this happy place
And friends no longer see my face
Remember me somewhere in space
With atoms

Neil H. Higginbotham

A Sea Of Faces

I walk in crowded spaces.
People all around me,
But no one is there.
A sea of faces.

It's always the same.
"But you dance there in vain!"
My mentor cries,
"Go, like the wind — away"
I cannot go. It is too late.

Virginia V. Fox

Wonders

The dainty little snow drop, pushing
      its green blades of leaves
      through the dark, frozen ground
      in January, blossoming from
      February to April.
Watching birdlets leaving the safety
      of their nests for the first time.
A big handsome hawk standing on
      my nearby lawn.
Braking for a wild turkey strutting
      across my road.
Two-way traffic grinding to a halt
      as 5 beautiful deer gracefully
      leap across the highway, all
      without harm!
The birth of a child.
God's great love for man!!!

Lois MacNary Steele

Premonitions

The distant sound
      of flags
whipping in the wind
      sounds like
the footsteps of an
      approaching army

Roberta M. Frechen

We Love You Lord

We love you Lord 'O' Thou most
High we love to sing your praise
We'll sing them to you all our days
Rejoice in Thee everywhere and inside
Rejoice, Rejoice, Rejoice All ye people

Bobbi Lakin

To Mary Ritter

There once was a lady named Ritter
Who worked as a pet sitting sitter.
One day by mistake,
She sat on a pet snake.
Now guess where the damn critter bit'er.

Glennon Zehrt

Moments

Beating
Recording the course of time
Our clocks (hearts)
It flows through our veins
Like blood
Past
Present
Future
Time
Not so enormous
Never begins
Never ends
Dwelling on the past
Capture the now
Capture the heart
And hold it there
Forever
Never release it
It's always yours

Jason Murphy

From Whence I Came

Far far away I see green fields
richer in colour than I stand on now,
yet no path leads from here to there
no sign directs to show me how.
I yearn to tread these greener fields
and walk amid its wealthy grass,
beneath my feet a firm ground feel
to stand content and let time pass.
Yet I pause before I take a step,
and looking back from whence I came
I see the fields I left behind,
I look ahead and see the same.
The grass lies pale beneath my feet
as were the fields behind,
are the fields ahead to be the same,
are all fields of one kind.

W. Wilkie

Nurse P's Blistery Day

It's going to be a blistery day
Nurse P was heard to say
As kids filled the chairs
And coughs filled the air
Of her office.

It's certainly a blistery day
Nurse P was heard to say
As she gave Ned some ice
And checked Tilly for lice
In her office.

It's certainly a blistery day
Nurse P was heard to say
As she caught puke in a bowl
And put a parent on "hold"
In her office.

It was a Most blistery day
Nurse P Muttered away
As she watched the night news
And kicked off her shoes
Away from her office.

Joan Luckhurst

Just Like Dad

Father my one great desire
      When I grow to be a man.
Is to be just like you
      If I possibly can.
The places you go
      The things you say and do
Dad wherever you may go,
      I'll follow after you.

I've often asked Mama
      She says she thinks I can,
Be a lot like Daddy
      When I've grown to be a man.
Now, I'm just a little child
      Sometimes good and sometimes bad,
But I'm sure when I've grown up,
      I'll be just like my Dad.

Marguerite Diel

The Timeless Heart

In this vast kingdom,
My priceless Crust of ageless wisdom,
In the waiting . . . let It be known,
My extravagant Jewel glazed on my own,
In radiance glowing,
With all the elegance of knowing,
No key . . . do not fear!
No secret . . . I've always been here.
Noble of never ending . . .
I lavish purity from the beginning.
This stunning Timeless Heart,
Forever a splendorous part,
Of all that Be . . . as me,
Keeping precious time,
A moment so sublime . . .
Chromed in crimson gold,
This authentic story is told.

Elaine Bartuch Hayes

A Prayer Of Faith Away

Born in this world of sin
There is no love at all within.
You lie, steal, kill, and hate
In all kinds of evil you participate.
You cannot be what you need to be
You cannot see what you need to see
You are blind, and you're also dead
Your life is a total mess
Because you need to be fed.
But there is a way out and in
A way out from your world of sin
A way that allows you to win.
God loves you just like you are
He's everywhere; He's never far
Only a prayer of faith away
Confess with your mouth the Lord Jesus
Believe in your heart
And be saved today.

DeLores Harding

You Unforgivable

Fireworks are fading
And I am amazing
He is standing small
How can I control.....

Empty eyes and flesh
Trying more or less
To hide what remain
Task that won't repair.....

Stop that faking show
Is common and low
Be more brave my dear
Weren't we so near.....

Now when all are gone
And I lost my own
Shocking heart I carry
To one whom I marry.....

Donna Koto

Wings

They have clipped the wings
to a white butterfly.
Never again the
hovering speckle will linger
above the silent villa to behold
flowered windowsills
with flashy carnations
and scenting gentianella.
Never again it will rest
upon the moist, velvety moss
that cleaves to shaded rocks
by a chattering brook.
Never again it will hear
the rustic, gleeful, songs
of the country lass
whose moist back glimmers
under the burning sun.
Two broken, useless, stumps
that somewhere vibrate and die away.
Like shattered dreams.

Tony Lattanzio

A Valentine Poem For Matthew

Deeper than the oceans,
Bluer than the skies,
Nothing is more special,
Than when I look into your eyes,
A truly loving boy you are,
Far beyond compare,
To the burning beauty of the sun,
or the country side so fair,
Like fresh dew upon the vine,
early one spring morn,
your face shines truly beautiful,
As was the day you're born,
So hold my love deep in your heart,
A cherished place to be,
Never will we be apart,
Throughout eternity....

Lisa Middough

Unrequited Love

Love lost
before ever being found

Love everlasting
yet eternally fleeting

Love ending
though without beginning

Love blinding
but what a sight to see
the reality
that love hurts

But pain
can be pleasure

And if that be true
my life is love!

Michael P. Spangler

I'll Miss You

You said you'd be leaving,
That you found another home.
In a way I understand,
Why you'd leave me alone.

But you won't see me crying,
Even though I wished you'd stay.
You were great but not the best,
Ain't life funny that way?

You know I'll miss you,
But I don't care.
The time we spent together,
Was great to share.

I know I'll think about you,
When there's a moment I can spare.
But don't get me wrong,
I'll miss you but I don't care.

Jennifer Charlebois

The Turkey's Revenge

Once upon Thanksgiving Day,
We sat beside the table.

The center piece, who's now deceased
and very much unable.

To run, to jump, to gobbly gook,
to whisk its feathery back.

Within two days of hanging round,
will be a sandwich snack.

So, among the savory foods placed
round this day's feast.

Was once a walking, talking, squawking
twenty two pound beast.

So lick your chops my hungry friends,
Eat hardy as you can.

'Cause some day the evolutionists say,
The turkey might revenge.

Arthur D. Freeman

The Telling

His face showed how he felt
when he stopped and knelt
queen to him
mythical sprite
God to him
everything then
everything now
living only for me
sights set
just on me
no competition
from other stars
earth and sky
nothing to fear
his face showed how he felt
when he stopped and knelt
and then bravely
loving powerfully said
let me love for both of us.

*Ljiljana Milice Zikic-
Karadjordjevic*

Tender Loving Care

A seed in the ground,
will someday grow.
Reaching maturity,
it will glow.

A baby born,
also grows.
And in time,
he, too, will glow.

Plants or life,
are of the same.
The right ingredients,
gives one fame.

Be it a plant,
a girl or boy.
In each case care,
a common alloy.

Tender loving care,
a gift from the heart.
Needed by everything,
right from the start.

Robert M. Rampani

Destiny

Greatness comes when least expected.
  Finding hope in deep despair
    brings fellowship.
A man's heart can be broken
  by the hands of fate,
Repair comes from wisdom and
    depth of understanding.
Understanding brings Greatness;
  which comes when least expected.

Janet Lynas Loper

Untitled

Can the end be near
Fast or slow will I go
My ends brings a mighty year-
Let it not be slow.
Prove that God is real
Or prove that God is a fake
Can I make him a deal-
Or is my soul last in a massive lake.

Carol Strahan

The Dandelion

Dandelion
I choose you
out of loneliness
out of fields of others like you
so devilish in your tantric ensemble
so predictable.
Sway this way, sway that
still I shudder as your petals
sweep manhandling my ears
whispering a hundred I love yous
I'll never answer back
dan
de lion...weed...

Daniel Schulman

She Is Near

Come following me,
is the shadow of death.
Lingered for many years,
she beckons for me to heed her call.

I have eluded her once again.
Nevertheless,
her constant, gentle coaxing,
falls heavily on my ears.

In a different form,
yet I recognize her presence.

As my body yields to her invitation,
her beauty attracts my soul.

Nicole Kopacz

Pristine Maiden

Oh, pristine maiden in the woods,
Upon the deer-trail so narrow,
Where are you going this night,
To the glade at the waterfall?

Oh, warrior of untrod trails,
I have come to find my love,
Are you the warrior I love,
Or is it another farther on?

Oh, pristine maiden in the woods,
I am not your warrior lover,
For I wait to tell you of him,
For your warrior is surely dead!

Oh, warrior of untrod trails,
Can this awful thing be true,
Has my warrior that I love,
Truly died and gone away?

Oh, pristine maiden in the woods,
He was my friend and brother,
And though you weep for him,
Will you be my lovely bride?

Janet R. Montle

When Angels Cry

Oh rain from the heavens,
Why do you so pour?
Are many your griefs,
For such a downpour?
The heavens responded,
With thunderous light.
Why do you not heed,
My little ones' plight?
My angels from heaven,
I send to be born.
They are then forsaken,
And treated with scorn.
From their mother's womb,
They return to me.
Butchered like the lamb,
Before they're to be.
I command creation,
All that is to be,
Eternal damnation,
Will fall upon thee.

Felipe Chacon Jr.

Beyond

When I look into the ripples
  of a rushing waterfall.
I see a faint reflection
  like a shadow on a wall.

When I look into the waves
  along a sandy beach.
I see a lonely face
  that only you can reach.

When I look into the still waters
  of a lonely little pond.
I see behind the face,
  behind and beyond.

Catherine Styers

Mirror

For have you joy?
Then joy is yours to share.
And have you love?
Make light your neighbor's care.
Have you found courage?
Teach your friend to dare!
What power you have
In loving word or deed,
Is yours to give
To meet another's need.

Emma E. Glynn

Wonderland

On my window, ice paints flowers
Tells me of an artist's powers
Who created the design
Of the world I now call mine.

I of course am quite impressed
His art and skill are manifest
But its meaning He has hidden
Behind an art, to me forbidden.

Exhibition of his art
On a global, worldly mart
Was a mystery for all
After Eve's and Adam's fall.

On my window, ice cold flowers
Tell of his creative powers
Silent is the frozen sight
Will not reveal His plan, His might.

I know that I am frozen here
In an earthbound atmosphere
Cannot tell you what I felt
When icy flowers never melt.

Karin Dovring

Maybe

Definitions of the word "Maybe,"
Are perhaps and possibly,
Of possibly as being perhaps,
Of perhaps perchance you see.

But a classic example of "Maybe"
I'm sure you will agree,
Though 'tis not in the dictionary,
Is the 'oft used phrase "We'll see."

'Tis used instead of "Maybe,"
And at times perhaps possibly
And perchance one day conceivably
Will replace them all "We'll see."

Frank Jackson Elkin

Maybe

Something in your heart
is tearing into my brain
I don't want to be torn apart
I just want to stay the same

Something in your touch
is trying me for size
I don't like your touch
It sends cold down my spine

Something in your thoughts
is pulling me apart
I don't like the sort
that try to break my heart

Something in your eyes
just wants me to give in
I don't want your lies
I won't ever live in sin

But something in your smile
washes my fears away
I'll be yours for awhile
maybe I'll always stay

Leigh-Chantelle Koch

Playing In The Summer Sun

I sit and watch my children pure,
    So sweet and innocent, safe and secure.
To watch them play in the summer
    sun,
To know their lives have just begun.
    To hold their dreams in the palm
of your hand,
    To give them the best of whatever
you can.
    Children are a treasure so
precious and rare.
    Like a bird on the wind not
having a care.
    To watch them play in the
summer sun,
    To know their lives have just
begun.
Michelle R. Kloppenburg

Untitled

We, in a puddle of solipsism;
    In which love is a prismatoid;
    Solace is harmony.
I speak of a kingdom inside your id,
    Where flowers flow freely,
    And soak in the sun;
Where water glows luminary,
    And dripplets are seeds.
We baith in soft petals,
We play in the air,
We plant dreams in gift sacks,
    And place them in prayers.
I speak of a palace a bextra our heart,
    Where insects bred freely,
    And bleed for a harp.
In a land of swelled beauty,
In a ramulose of Light,
We blinked too many times,
In toto, we spoiled the sight
David Grmm

I Saw The Dream Arising

I saw the dream arising
From the mirrors of the sea,
The shifting family images
Of all that used to be.

Although age forms a film
Of patina on our past,
I knew these forms were moving
To a music slow or fast;

Dancing down the beaches,
Heading for the dunes
In a rhythm of reunion
Under many suns and moons.

We lunched on more than wishes;
We slept on more than beds,
In a landscape of forever
And the seascape in our heads.

And then the dream, arisen
From the mirrors of the deep,
Sank faster than poor Jonah,
And I awoke from sleep.

Alvin Landy

Most Versatile of Colors

The sparkle of a baby's eyes
Like sapphires faceted so true,
Delphinium tipped soft with dew
A ribbon for the highest prize.

Background for stars of white together
Representing this our nation,
Tones of subtle variation
Blending in a peacock feather.

Placid seas reflecting show
The azure of the summer skies,
And trace a spectrum which belies
The contrast of the depths below.

From palest tint to vibrant hue
Most versatile of colors — blue.

I. Louise M. Esterhai

God's Creations

Oh Lord, my God, I stand in awe
    and look with admiration,
At all the glorious splendor of
    Your creations.
All nature Your perfection, my
    heart bursts with pride
To know that one of these, am I.

Though Your enemy has caused a
    flaw in me to be,
I see the love You still hold
    for me.
With strength renewed and will
    to please,
I will strive to be just what
    You planned for me.

Lois Puckett

Entrapment

Life's doors closing,
The web is spun.
Only the good,
May come undone.

Strands of life,
The web that stayed,
Holds to deceit;
Randall L. Williams

The Country

Violet-grey sky
A warm in summer breeze
honeysuckle climbs
the tall pine trees
the crickets sing
their sunset songs
summer wild flowers
grow in throngs
a sweetness is here
relaxing and free
this is the way
life should be
Hannah Link

Devils And Angels

Devils in the sky
On clouds they fly
Though their wings
Are filled with screams
Of souls that never die.

Angels in the air
On clouds they stare
And their wings
Seem to dance and sing
To release all life's despair

Devils and angels in the sky
On the clouds they flight and cry
Though their wings
Are filled with stings
Neither will ever die.
Brandon Dame

How? Where? Scared!

In my life I've already seen
too many people taken away from me.
First my father then my friend
when is it all just going to end?
I don't quite seem to understand
how things work on, the other land.
I am so scared — so very scared
when I die where will I be?
No one knows...Exactly.
I am so scared,
    so very scared.
Laura M. Fajdich

Campfire Sparks

Like shooting stars from fire rage,
As madmen sit in unwary gaze,
What a picturesque sight to see,
The bizarre cremation of a tree.
Sandy Beaches

The Constant Vigil

Does he know the Vigil she kept?
The sleep she lost,
The tears she wept?
Did he feel her faith so strong?
Her undying love
When things went wrong?
Would he know before he'd go
The pain and fear
She never showed?
A constant Vigil she kept,
She wouldn't eat
She never slept.
Her love so strong and good and true
And now she's turned him over to You.
Please let him know she was there,
Her love surrounding him everywhere.
Let him know the Vigil she kept,
The love she had
The tears she wept.

Marilyn Rice

Ruth

People say...

Ruth is evil and bewitched.
She can have a walnut pitched,
ten thousand miles across the land
and it will land
on a bank of sand.

Ruth is cross and very mean
she won't even eat one single bean.

Ruth is nutty and quite crazy,
(rumor says she's even lazy).

Ruth was named after candy bars.
People say she's from Mars.
But, I don't care what people say
I think to this very day.....

People are not evil or bad.
Everyone counts
For who they are inside.

Jaimie Lee Hughes

Cry For Love

The trees, they whisper
   In the wind
But no one pays them heed
For what they whisper in the cold
Is but the homeless' creed.

Out in the cold
   Not once, not twice
But every time it rains
They whisper out and cry for love
When all is but in vain.

Yes, on the streets
   And in the parks
They always are alone
No family, friends or loved ones near
No music in their souls.

Come summer, winter, spring or fall
   No difference does it make
A baby's cry
A young child's smile
I pray won't land up there someday.

Priya Alphonso

Mr. President?

Why?
Why must we hide, in fear from
The growing wrath
Of the dark side?

Leaders
Why don't you lead?
Cause each passing day
We fall farther from the creed.

Why?
Why must we shy away
From good that would
Make us happy?
Cause we're choking sir
In the barrel of a gun.
So please act now
Before the death of another one.

Please quiet the riots
That grow in your glen
And make this place
Safe for our children.

Joshua Jair Whitfield

Love With Larry Dale

Absolute or relative
Absolute in the air
Absolute in spirit
Absolute in longing

Absolute in staying power
Touching earth relative
Relative and real
Love will be there

Like the earth changing
Like water surging and sluicing
Like light's velocity constant
Constant and real - Reality

Love with Larry Dale
Positive and negative
Constant and real
Absolute and relative

Barbara Bailey

Don't Tell Me

Don't tell me life is easy.
Don't tell me life is hard.
Don't tell me what's already known.
Don't tell me of things absurd.
Don't tell me what I need not hear.
Don't tell me what I've heard before.
Don't tell me of the future.
Don't tell me to live and learn.
Don't tell me what's right or wrong.
Don't tell me to decide alone.
Don't tell me I waste my time.
Don't tell me there's so much to do.
Don't tell me I worry myself sick.
Don't tell me I have no cares.
Don't tell me, just let me learn.

Michelle Hastings

Alone

To be without you is the
worst thing because
I'm all alone and
Afraid that it will always be this way
   and I have a
Longing to be with you but
Only I am here to hear my lonely cries
No one else understands and
   I feel so
Empty inside
   An emptiness that can only be
   filled by
   you
   you and your caring touch,
      warm smiles, and tender kisses
   But I know this can never
   ever
   be.

Aiesha Joseph

Mute Cannon

Mute in peace the cannons rest.
The idle dogs of Mars.
A warrior's peace is work
To erase battle scars.

Mute and cold the cannons point
Over loud and heated talk.
That drowns the muffled tread,
Of the ghostly ranks that walk.

With vanquished and the victor
Mars must once again have his jest,
They prepare for war again
And only weapons rest.

Again — Around Mother Earth
   The dogs of Mars are howling.
   While the hopeless young and old
Hide from their savage prowling.

George A. Bailey

My Cat

My cat has orange stripes
Like those of a tiger.
When he looks at me
I can see the gladness in
His beautiful yellow eyes.
The yellow in his eyes is like
That of the sun.
He has an orange spot on his
Stomach that looks like a bib on
A little baby of one.
I am very happy that he is mine.

Fauve M. Beaudin

He Is Very Near

It soothes the heart within me-
To read The psalms
In the stillness of the night-
For the sense of God's presence-
Fills me with great delight!
I reach out to touch Him-
For it seems He's very near-
And gently — very gently-
He wipes away each tear-
For it's His comfort only
That soothes my aching heart-
For, I know-
That in all eternity-
We'll never be apart!

Verna L. Gray

Losin' You

Don't know what I got-ta do.
The times we meet are gettin' few
You don't tell me where I stand
And things ain't goin' like I planned.
I'm all tore up and wish I knew,
How can I get through to you?

I'm always knockin' at your door,
But then I ask myself what for.
You've just gone out or so they say
It hurts me so to turn away.
I swear I won't return no more,
But I come back just like before.

You know I ache; you know I'm blue
But it don't mean a thing to you.
Could be you've got some other guy;
Just tell me so; just please don't lie.
Don't know what I got-ta do;
Can't bear the thought of losin' you.

William H. Averell
(Willie the Shake)

Untitled

Alone in the night
With the whispering wind
Cars rushing by
On a road without end
A river runs by me
But I am alone
I know that you
Will never come home
You had my devotion
My body and soul
I was yours to command
Abuse and control
You hit me and used me
You lied and you left
Yet I never complained
You were all that I had
And now that you're gone
I am alone
Twisted and broken
By the side of the river road.

Kristin Moore

"You Love Him"

You love him
You remember time and time again
how much you wish to see him.
You love him with all your heart
but to remember that night tears
you apart.
Now all you have is memories of him
You go to bed and pray that God would
erase that day
You wonder how come it happened to me,
Or how could it possibly be?
Now all that you can say
is we love you Marc and we're
sad that you went away.

Erica Lynn Gisclair

Yesterday, Today And Tomorrow

It's funny how three words we say
With time we all can see
Though we use them different ways
One the other will be
Though yesterday precedes today
And is a short time past
Today it quickly comes to be
And even then won't last
Now as we look a day ahead
Tomorrow is what we say
So yesterday, today and tomorrow
Are similar all in a way
A part of what God gives to us
Time goes by and time stands still
Whether a moment, hour, day, or year
It's all in Our God's will
So as we look to Mighty God our Creator
We may learn to understand
Yesterday, Today, Tomorrow and Time
Are all in God's Own Plan

Renee Pemberton

"Memories"

You can have my heart,
But not my soul.

You can have my love,
But not my being.

You can be my lover.
But not my mate.

You can have tonight,
But not tomorrow.

You can have these memories of us.
Take it in your heart,
And keep it safe.

For these memories
Will always be,
Special of me and you.

Ermelinda Maria Noriega Moyers

Unicorn Pool

Moonlight on the pool so bright,
Shining in the dark of night.
By the side what does appear
Soft and gentle as a deer?

Quietly it does not trod,
On the ground so thick with sod.
As it moves, I catch a sight,
Of its coat, a bright, clean white.

The pool ripples, touched by gold
That the creature's one horn holds.
What could it be with such a horn?
Simple answer: Unicorn.

It bows its head to take a drink,
I make a little noise, I think.
It lifts its head and looks around,
At the bushes, at the ground.

It turns and runs so far away,
I hope to see it soon one day.
But if you see it be forewarned,
You'll not forget the unicorn.

Heather O'Hearn

The Palette

This palette bleeds with color.
The shades change day by day.
Bare sketchings scream with passion
    as if there's words to say.

This canvas blank yet lively.
The brush paints stroke by stroke.
Impressions in the corner
    with every phrase that's spoke.

This picture slowly forming.
The brain grows thought by thought.
This work of art is changing
    with every lesson taught.

...and now my role is over,
I've done all I can do.
The painting now is given
    to a palette fresh and new.

Chad J. Anderson

Love Comes

Marriages take place everyday.
Love comes but once in a lifetime;
Quietly knocking upon the heart's door,
Tiptoeing through chambers,
Leaning close
To whisper in the ear,
Caressing the lobe,
Tickling the senses.
Like an angel with snow-white wings
Dancing across the sky,
Or, a dust-covered cowboy
Galloping across the desert,
Love is unstoppable
As it begins with an attraction
Which gives way to a bond.
Love is special,
Lasting a lifetime,
Hopefully,
Forever.

James M. Englum

Kitty Leisure

Sheba climbed onto the roof
Oh, that cat is so aloof
She didn't say good morning,
nor give me any warning
of the mouse upon her plate
and the other, I guess his mate
which I found under the chair
Now, aren't they quite a pair.
Sheba's licking her paws
and sharpening her claws
What a life, it's so ideal
as she thinks of her next meal
Watching the birdies in the tree
and couldn't care less about me!

Dolly Larson

May

May's exquisite fragrance of
lilacs in my room,
Has brought me joy and pleasure,
And kept my heart in tune.

The lilies of the valley
strike up their notes of cheer,
For Mother's Day and
May Day come at this time of year.

Florence E. Weaver

Unlocking A Love

A secret garden deep in your soul
Where many try to go.
But you keep those gates unlocked
Your reasons no one knows,
But there is one key
That you do not possess
The one that has earned your love,
Is the one with the success,
They have traveled in your mind
To see what it is you see
So my one question to you is
Do you know who holds the key?

Heather Tanaka

"Oh Day"

Oh day oh rising day.
When the sun shows
high in the sky.
I look down and see
how far I have come,
but it is the end of
my day now.

Jodi Stumbris

One Chance

I am
Unfairly judged
Upon my mistakes from
the past. I was not forgiven.
One chance.

Rebecca Vallas

Teaseday Afternoon

Straw in glass
  Bowl of berries
    Kissing the neck
Rain against the window flurries.

Kiss on lips
  Tongue on cheek
    Roll off side
Turn off passion security to seek.

Clam shell closes
  Venus fly trap
    Prey been caught
Black Widow's mission a wrap.

Jeffrey Wayde Puckett

"A Sudden Realization"

Hark! Hear the silence.
The darkness, so bright.
Behold with thine heart
as dawn turns to night.

The crow sweetly singing.
Cat and dog, hand in hand.
I shall run 'neathe the water,
then drown in the sand.

Emily Herman

Angle Of Love

I love that angel,
That molded our love.
So perfect he made it,
And calm as a dove.

He took away rough spots,
That other loves have.
He finished it gently,
On a silver white cloud.

He worked with our love,
By the bright moonlight,
And picked stars from heaven,
To make it more bright.

He wrapped it in tenderness,
He sealed it with care,
And singing of love,
He sent it down here.

When I look in your eyes,
There's a message of love,
That came down from heaven
On the wings of a dove.

Eva Opal Copeland

As True As The Sky Is Blue

My dear sweet man, this song I sing,
My love for you is true;
As true as the rosebuds in the spring,
As true as the sky is blue.

Your smile, your laugh I can't erase
My mind is filled with thoughts
Of your loving hugs, and strong embrace
You often to me have brought.

I know I don't deserve you
And yet praise God you're here
Loving me so kind, so true;
Your love I hold so dear.

So know tonight and every night
My love for you is true;
As true as stars so shiny bright,
As true as the sky is blue!

Susan I. Lancaster

Loss Of Time

Because of deadlines
I have to be on time
I place a watch upon my wrist
So the time I will not miss
Whatever's on my mind
I can't lose track of time
If my clock ever stops
I'll be in one hell of a spot
As they bury me on a hill
My time will then stand still

Danny VanHoesen

Untitled

If I only knew how to act,
no one does and that's a fact.
When you think about what to say,
it's not always from the heart,
and that special one just walks away.

Amber Myers

Sense

Much of what we do makes sense
We're schooled to use our brains
We do just what's expected
And tally up our gains

Much of what we do we think
Important to mankind
We build the world around us
With usage of the mind

Much of what we do makes sense
At least within the head
What would happen if we look
Into the heart instead

Much of what we do would then
Reflect the inner dream
And life would flow as it should
With love the major theme

Much of why we love makes sense
It leads us to release
Our daily fears and worries
To find our own true peace

Jane Geary

Sally

My daughter is a friend of mine
and will be till the end of time.
She lends a shoulder when I cry
without a need to question, why.
If I'm down, she'll find a way
to cheer and lift the clouds away.
She makes each day worth living for
no one could love a daughter more
and when I have to leave her side
I pray the Lord God will provide
a daughter who's as good as she
to love her, just as she loves me.
One more thing I pray I may
hear my daughter one day say,

My daughter is a friend of mine...

Kate Clarke

Children! Children!

"Children! Children!"
  "Yes Mama!"
"Where have you been to?
  "Grand-papa!"
"What did he tell you?"
  "Hurricane a come,
    So he not going to send us
    To buy no more rum,
      'Cause he want to be sober
        When hurricane come!"

Mary Geo Quinn

mine?

speaking of a distance
i see a distance in your eye
not so much an innocence
as a glamourous disguise

breathing of a softness
i feel a softness in your soul
and it's that particular feeling
that makes me feel so whole

listening to your mindspeak
i know you can speak your mind
but even as i stand and stare
i'm not quite sure you're mine

grae

Snow

I awoke this morning
to a beautiful sight
    A blanket of snow
had fell through the night
    A white glowing cover
lay on the ground
    Peace and beauty could
be seen all around
    Some little birds played
near by
    A couple of bunnies then
caught my eye
    This beautiful world
in which I stand
    God spread his love across
this land
    So let us remember where
the snow came from
    The blanket of white
that is God's Son.

Brent E. May

"No Game I Can't Beat"

Desperately thinking
of rivers that flow,
my mind is a stream
where no girl shall go.

Rocks slow my stream
my stream will still flow,
but where my stream runs
no one shall know.

My mind is locked up
so there is not a key,
I live in that box,
so no one shall see.

The point you should get
or the point that I make,
my mind plays no games
so no hearts shall break.

Spencer J. Rhodes

The Solo

I hear a song,
sung by a huge choir
that I am a part of.
Some in green, or black,
or gray, or white, or brown.
Some are stationary,
Some move,
but all are known,
Charted and explored
completely.

Except one.

Clothed in all colors and none,
It sings a beautiful melody.
In tune with the rest,
But standing out.
This is the human soul,
and as I listen,
I forget to sing.

Anna-Binney McCague

Kronos To Kairos

Passed I from Kronos
    to Kairos time,

From human boundary to
    Divine horizon,

Repetitive act bore forth
    creative urge,

Night's shadows yielded to
    day's eternal light,

Moment's pause lasted a
    countless forever,

From barren desert bloomed
    a thousand voices.

And love's Alpha gently
    embraced its Omega,

Passed I from Kronos
    to Kairos time.

Paul Hughes

Toge (For Alyce)

Thorns have no barbs,
    save those sometimes
Imagined when dispiritedness
Has seemed to win the moment.
Prize them for their use in
Teaching virtue, but prise them out
    not too quickly: we might mistake
The blood of life for that of
Death. Trust in Love, of which
Compunction is a part, that we
Can grow to be more perfect than
    even we might dream.
Trust in loving friends who hold
The promise of your sacred destiny
Above their own, who also wear your
Thorns, who speak your
Name with every prayer.

Alexandre De La Creche

Alone

Sometimes I feel alone
Like no one understands
Just what it's like to be
With so many problems on my hands

I want someone to listen
to the things I have to say
I don't want to be alone
not tomorrow or today

And when I have one of those days
When everyone seems against me
I would like a shoulder to cry on
And someone who understands me

I don't want to be alone
I want someone to be there
Someone who will listen
And someone who really cares

Melissa LePage

Golden Haired Lad

My Golden haired lad
My ray of sunshine
When family illnesses were mine
to bear alone

His happy-go-lucky ways
would brighten my day
and my cares and worries
Just melted away.

Lines around his eyes
Slightly stooped shoulders
Tell me life's toils
Have touched him, yet I see
Smiling blue eyes!

We will endure life here
Our faith grows strong
God's mercy and grace
have never been wrong
Rejoice for today!

Dorothy Lancaster Braswell

Jazzole

I am soaked
in the sound of it.
The dismal yee-ha
of backwoods grace,
a disgrace
to my own name.

What I would and
could never be
assaults me
in a thumbing through
of fizzled texts.

Rushing
in the winter warm,
the magic does me.
Where is my avant-garde?
The horn that cools me?

Michael Cartright

Untitled

I hear your voice
    and the darkness disappears.

Once again, I feel warm inside.

I feel your touch and
    I'm alive again.

I touch your soul
    and you are mine again.

We cradle one another's hearts
    and we are one again.

Loneliness is gone again,

If only in the depths of my mind
    and the memories of my dreams.

Sheron Babb

I Can't Absolve My Self

I gathered too many weeds
In my life...
To find a remedy for...
I pulled up one flower.

Rita Stilli

Edgar Allen Poe

Oh! What has become of my existence.
Do not know who benefits
from the depth of my soul.
Paths beyond tracing out
unsearchable judgments.
Suffering of sorrow.
Bitterness of hate.
Countless memories.
Pain of despair.
Death tortures my tomb.
Punishing pierced
my unmerited favor love.
Condemned to a sentence.
Eternally lost.
Transform gratitude.
Sacrifice mercy.
Envy and rude.
Stumbling persecution.
My existence in time is
well known Poe.

Terry Lee Boblett

Everlasting Love

The sun sets,
The days fade,
  But,
You and I never will.

People come,
People go,
  But
You and I will always be.

No matter where we go,
No matter what happens,
We will always be together.
Together till the world ends.

We have a special thing that
People call love;
We call it everlasting.

Sarah Hinrichs

Angel Dreams

In dreams of night
Angels take flight
As I lay sleeping upon my bed
And they fly near
Then I can hear
The flutter of wings by my head
Take me up on gossamer wings
To fly in the heavens with you
For away from earthly things
The cares of this life
And troubles too
Show me things that are lovely
and beautiful
As only angels can do.

Deborah Meeker

Nurses

God, I thank ya for nurses.
They're doggone swell;
If weren't for them
many a sick feller'd jump —
Down some lonely, haunted well.

Solomon B. Margolin

Sunrise

Dawn opened her sea washed eyes
And lifted her golden head.
Darkness was overhead,
Making his nightly rounds.
Dawn slipped her aerial body
Into a ruddy robe.

She floated off her celestial bed
And glided towards Darkness.
Her rosy garment
Spread across the sky
Like spilt wine.

Dawn swiftly overtook Darkness
And beckoned him
To relent his lofty position.
Darkness subsided,
And made his way to his
High mountain home.

Sommer Harrison

Chicken Lips

I noticed it
long ago
the bottom lip
back and forth
against the top
pulling each way
just a little.
I learned
how it went.
She'd get a call
he wasn't coming
or had to go,
then the lip thing,
never a word.

Robert E. Hawks

The Ocean

To sit again beneath the sky
And listen to the sea gulls cry
And never have to say good-bye
To the wonders of the ocean

To wish upon a shooting star
Gaze at the milky way afar
And count how many stars there are
Reflecting on the ocean

To walk beside the ocean swells
Collecting semi-precious shells
Hearing secrets conches tell
Known only to the ocean

To see white caps upon each wave
Like markers on a sailor's grave
In life - in death I'll always crave
To go back to the ocean

Noreen A. Wadman

Freedom

Dormant   Power
Creating   Caring   Surviving
With a knowledge of truth
Awakening!

Victoria Anger

Misguided Jealousy

A young, unblemished artist
genius exported on whim
the Midas touch on canvas
how I envied him

A most skillful musician
facilely expelled a tune
the Midas touch on guitar
how my ire consumed

A literary marvel
baffling teachers with prose
the Midas touch on paper
how my hatred rose

No matter how I tried
I just could not compete
A mere tenth of his talent
and I would have been complete

Alone beneath the soft earth
young grass glistening with dew
the Midas touch with suicide
how I had no clue

Kathleen Kinney-Gordon

The Reasons I Left

Tonight my world is sinking...
It never sank before
The thoughts I was thinking...
They were there before

But now I'm in darkness...
Where is my light now?
This place seems so vicious...
I want to leave now

Why has she left me?
She never went before
The reasons that she gave me...
They were there before

The bells are ringing...
My time has come here
To life I was clinging...
No more will I stay here.

Khurram Farooquie

Of Woman

Environs duster
Ornamental bed cluster
Lumps of meat
With a heart of wit
Kitchen joy
And kid's toy
Endowed vain lust
In love lost
Live furniture
Wanted creature.

Adewale Akande

Unfamiliar

Unfamiliar voices
Unfamiliar faces
Unfamiliar footsteps in
Unfamiliar places
I look around and everything is
Unfamiliar
And I think to myself, am I too
Unfamiliar?

Natasha Johnstone

Running

I ran the road with a woman
I thought I knew her name
Words came easy on the road
Laughter came wherever she was

Her stride was sheer delight
and joy rode in her eyes
She shared her joy with me
and saved my life

I hit the wall of life
Held her for a moment
and found that I could go on
running as I never had before

I ran the road with a woman
I thought I knew her name
Her name was love
God help me
Her name was love

Dwight Hearty

The Victim

Buried in my soul
Is the woman I've become.
Trying to climb out
Slipping - deeper yet.
Afraid to face the light
And more frightened-to not-
To grab at the night.
To seek refuge in the dark
And whisper just for one
Who can pull the victim out.

The words have cut my spirit.
The silence rips my thoughts.
I've lost the voice of reason,
I stare at silent thoughts.
They grew into the sulcus
And they took from me my mind.
If she can find her way out
Will she cease to look behind?

Liz Wenger

Our Anniversary

I have chosen you as my partner
For our journey through this life
And I have no regrets
Since we became man and wife.

As we continue on through life
Still walking hand in hand
May we still find contentment
In this, our promised land.

Tho the years go on by
As surely they must do
Our love grows even stronger
Because our love is true.

It was many years ago
When first we said our vows
I loved you then sweetheart
But I love you more right now.

Tho we will grow old together
You'll still be young to me
And you will remain my sweetheart
For all eternity.

Matthew Scopelitis

Memories Of Christmas

A lonely green bow
under the tree, where pretty
presents used to be.
Brings back memories
of laughter and cheer.
Beautiful flocked tree
stands so alone, all loved
ones have gone home.
Tears falling down my
cheeks, recalling memories
and seeing that lonely
green bow under the tree.

Roberta V. Kuhens

Run Little Children

Run little children
Run from the night
Run little children
Into the daylight
Run little children
Run from the fear
Run little children
Darkness draws near

Paul T. Schoch

Counsel

Seek that which replenishes.
Be renewed by my laughter,
Empowered by your own.
Find the stream of your youth.
It is with you even now,
Water to refresh your spirit.
Return to the land of your ancestors,
The wisdom of the Earth.
There you will find your soul.
Complete the circle,
Find the center,
All power is yours.

Kathie L. Adams

Silence

In this agitated modern world,
Where wars are raged daily
And peace is just talked about,
Where maturity comes in death
And life is just a very short breath,
Where hate has become a religion
And love has been completely forgotten,
Where young ones are restless
And forever seeking new bridges,
Where leaders are sought after
Yet never being discovered,
I turn to myself in wonder
And uncover the fortune that is,
The presence of silence.

Robert Maxwell Lloyd

At The Cafe

I try to enjoy my coffee
concentrate on the newspaper
But I am too aware
of a fixed silhouette
behind me
immobile.

In my mind's eye
I see him staring at me
holding me with his gaze
rigidly.

Angered, I decide to face him
glare at him
on the pretense of getting
another coffee.

Haughtily
I stalk toward the coffee urn
As I defiantly pass him
my breath catches in my throat-
He is staring into space
sightless.

Leona Enns Hepburn

The Feeling Of True Love ... Lost

I feel your thoughts
Even though they are not spoken
I can see your face
Even though I cannot touch it

I feel your love
Even though it is not shown
I feel your heat
Even though it is not near me

I feel your pain
Even though the pain does not touch me
I feel your sadness
Even when I am not sad

When we made love
Our souls became one
And when we parted
Our souls did not.

Now there is no foundation
How do you love again...
I can feel no other
For all I feel is you...

Telina Perkins

David And Goliath

A black one, a red one, a pill to kill.
Gone and done is David.
An upper, a downer, a ticket to exit,
A door to no more for David.

Goliath won the battle.
Unlike the Bible plot.
David ate his pebbles,
And he never got a shot.

Mary Joan Wickham

Life

The Lord is always with me
His hand is on my heart.
I see Him in the trees.
I see Him in the park.

I cannot wander far
He is there with me.
I see Him in the dark.
I see Him constantly.

Birds, animals, flowers
All the living things
Show He is hand upon them
And all the joy He brings.

The Lord is always with me.
His hand is on my heart.
If he should ever lift it,
My soul would soon depart.

Kathryn Bonnardel

Lost

I looked around the other day,
And much to my surprise
A total stranger looked at me
Through the darkness of my eyes.

I wondered when it happened,
And how it came to be
That the person who was looking back
Was now no longer me.

I was there one day, but not the next.
Gone where I do not know.
The stranger who resides here now
Has nowhere else to go.

This drab and beaten stranger
Who's looking through my eyes,
Still wonders at the loss of me
As she sits alone and cries.

I hope that I am happy;
Forever roaming free.
And this stranger left behind can bear
The pain of being me.

Sandra J. Paul

"Grace"

There is a girl name Grace,
who has a beautiful face.
She is always good and kind
with a smile, and never an unkind
word will you find.
She is gentle and nice, full of warmth
and joy, and never ever like ice.
Yes, there is a girl name Grace
who has a beautiful face and always
with ribbon and lace.
She loves flowers and candy,
even walks and talks dandy.
There is a girl name Grace
and yes she is my best friend.
She will always be my best friend
until the end and around the bend.

Cynthia A. Ramos

The Caressing Wind

As the sky fills
with beautiful blues and purples
the wind softly caressed me...

As I remember the smile
which warmed by heart
faster than the summer sun
and eyes that shined brighter
than a freshly cut sapphire.

The arms I've longed to hold me
is like the wind caressing the branches
of a tall tree
for the distance between us
is a long winding road.

As I drift and dream
thoughts of you inhabit my mind
like shooting stars
in a never ending sky.

Cynthia Hernandez

Awakening

I have lingered in the ebbing
    tidal wave of night
    and waited fevered fancy
    for the ascending sun
    in eastern sky,
    casting brilliant rays
    as fingers of light
    etched the lofty mountain peaks
    in silhouette.

As nature speaks
    of a fresh tomorrow;
    man begins a new eternity
    that stretches out
    like a road
    across the endless desert.

The world awakens
    to another beginning
    fraught with endless dreams
    and promises.

F. Richard Dieterle

Spring

I feel
Expectation in the air
Green grass
Green leaves
Baby's breath
And let us not forget
The crocus

Ruth Elvebak

My Dear Friend

I've never really told you
    What your friendship means to me,
I've never wondered what you saw
    In someone 'just like me!'
I've never even told you
    How much I really care,
But, I am 'oh, so thankful!'
    That you were always there.

Grace V. Knight

Write Like The Wind

Write like the wind
    Of a warm summer breeze
Gently swaying
    The boughs of the trees.

Write like the wind
    When its fingers tickle
The chimes on the porch
    And make them giggle.

Write like the wind
    When it swells with pride
Flexing its muscles
    To bring in the tide.

Write like the wind
    When in brief repose
It lies in the meadow
    Consoling its woes.

Write like the wind
    When its wind-some call
Beckons to us,
    "Write one, write all."

Joy J. Smith

My Granddaddy

He laid in a hospital bed
For what seemed like forever.
He was a very sick man
But give up, he would never.

One Sunday morning
It all came to an end.
I lost my granddaddy
As well as a dear friend.

He put up a good fight
He fought hard and long.
But the Lord realized,
He was no longer strong.

He left this cruel world
With no suffering and pain.
For a new life in Heaven,
He was certain to gain.

I loved my granddaddy
He was the only one I had.
Whenever I miss him,
I just look at my dad.

Dana R. Mobley

God Gave Us Moms And Dads

God gave us moms and dads
because they gave a life to
live and we learn from
our moms and dads and they
gave us love and kindness
and we should give
some of that kindness
back with love. They
teach us the value of
love just as God teaches
us the value of faith so
we shall love our moms
and dads for a while until they die!
So thank you God for
Ward "O" Bretz,
Elizabeth G. Bretz,
    and
Clifford G. Olson.

Denise Pfannkuche

"Never Letting Go"

How could I let you go?!
The pain hurts me so,
I had trusted and loved
only to be hurt!
You turned me away with
words that killed!
You could never understand
the passion that was left unfulfilled
You can't run from me,
there's no where to hide,
I'll always be there,
till we reach that big
blue sky.

Cory Lynn Morgan

Love Affair

I gathered you into my arms
It's been close to fifty years
And the magic lingers.
The eyes not so blue
The face etched by time
The body tired yet willing.
Ours has been a love affair
That stretched and pulled
And laughter rang.
One smile, one hug
and there is magic in our moment.

Edna B. Dufresne

Zooponics

A new dawn breaks from every mourn
with breath that reeks of fertile decay
A new deal for the waiting unborn
that missed their chance at yesterday
As water imbues their eagerness
they meditate on glory
and pray avoid the meagerness
of a raped sky's frigid story
Precursors fell in green, clandestine,
wombs, some gelled on barren soil
but few survived the philistine
that breaks the earth with toil
a seed before its first day light
must choose its type and grade
but when there is but a moonlight
they choose Deadly Nightshade
because the light of smogless sky
has ventured to the Siren's song
and now the seeds who claim this sphere
will swell to right the wrong

Christopher J. Nohl

Beauty All Around

There is beauty all around,
In each sight and in each sound,
In each newly risen tree,
In each warbled melody,
In the air and on the ground.

Each person has beauty of his own
When he's young and when he's grown,
In his smiles and in his sighs,
In mourner's tears when he dies,
In memory when he is gone.

Rebecca L. Wickham

And In Return

So soft, so pure, so white
So beautiful day or night
Always moving, always changing
As if someone was re-arranging

I've seen faces and figures
And loved ones lost
But just for a moment
And then they were tossed
Like waves on oceans

I've seen pictures and paintings
In frames of blue
But as swiftly created
As swiftly they're through
Erased in smooth motions

I could look forever
In constant awe
But I will never
Find a flaw

I'd spend my life to make God proud
And in return? Make me a cloud

David J. Lamereaux

Now Gone Into The Night

Reddened eyes with no expression
Had once wondered with delight
In awaiting all of life's possessions
Now gone into the night

Shattered dreams and broken home
Please Dad and Mom
Don't fight
When I was young you spoke of love
Now gone into the night

Love that made this house a home
Has vanished from our lives
You taught me well
I walk alone
Now gone into the night

Bill Dungan

Flaming Love

A candle burns
Like the lining of my soul
Dripping away time
Melting away my hope
Smoke in the air
Like dreams in my mind
Strong burning flame
Like the love I hope to find
Lasting forever
Constant and true
Alone in the dark
Each flame flutter new
Hot and unsettled
Like I in my search
I'm ready to put up my guard
The candle prepared to scorch
Alone and patient candle
Waiting to be blown away
Just as I.....
.....Waiting day by day

Marisa Abrignani

My Dear Daughter

You are newborn, my daughter;
A rosebud recently cut.
You are so precious!
So tender and beautiful
With your blushing cheeks.

You are a branch from the trunk
Recently cut.
You will grow, and tomorrow will come.
And you will be a trunk and
you will have branches...
But always, you will be a branch
Of this trunk who loves you.

Zoraida Guzman

Our Innocence In Love

Our innocence in love,
The creation of a bond.
The passion when we're together,
The anticipation when we're apart.
As for our innocence in love...
Only my heart survived.

Randy Machalk

"Gone But Not Forgotten"

They say memories are golden,
Well maybe that is true,
We never wanted memories,
We only wanted you.

A million times we've needed you,
A million times we've cried,
If only love could have saved you,
You never would have died.

In life we loved you dearly,
In death we love you still,
You're very special in our hearts,
No one could ever fill.

If tears could be a staircase,
And heartaches make a lane,
We'd walk the path to heaven,
And bring you back again.

Our family chain is broken,
And nothing seems the same,
But as God calls us one by one,
The chain will link again.

Brenda St. Coeur

"An Evening on the Marsh"

A serene evening creates
a memory —
Conjures a life long ago.

Sleeping though awake —
I dream of walking upon
a green marsh.

Though in the midst of ice and snow —
I am sinking into the
lush succulence of my surroundings.

An illusion of immortality fills me —
as the gentle snow
wakes me from this vision.

I have unlocked a frozen memory —
a glacier that was slowly melting
is now lifted on the breeze —

Letting flow with its passage
a gift of peace.

Anne Braam

"Here On My Bench"

Peaceful silence
Cool breeze blowing
Warm sun shining
Sounds of nature
Invade my mind
Drawing out the noise
Of the cruel, harsh world.
Here on my bench
I sit and ponder
Thinking of places
Beyond imagination
Dreaming of destinations
Beyond my grasp
Here on my bench
I sit and write.

Jennifer McClelland

The Garden

In front of us some trees are spread
a pomegranate and a fig-tree
a lemon tree almost kneeled
lemon carrying in quantity.

Near the fence a poplar stranded
a climbing vine embraced her
the branches tighten each other
bunches of grapes separated them.

Down the ground unfinished running
thousands ants loads transport
sweet melody cicada singing
from time to time branches abandon.

Marvelous odor of garden dispersed
showed different from morning sense
by the evening you can't satiated
it is incomparable, excited.

The moonbeams falling are throwing
shades extended here and there
a scene of theater inside the night
a prey of nature, a miracle of life.

Panagiotis S. Kollias

For Love's Sake

For love's sake
I'll remember you
I'll keep precious time spent
Alive in my memory
I'll remember your voice
Like it sounded
When you spoke close to my ear
I'll remember your touch...
I'll hear your laughter
When I sit in silence
And if I listen hard enough
I'll hear you whisper, 'I love you'
When I close my eyes tight
I'll see you smiling
See your eyes looking into mine
See you as you are
And I'll feel your presence
For all that it's worth
For love's sake
I'll remember you.

Ann M. Gakere

Autumn's Farewell

I walked alone in the deep
quiet woods, a carpet of leaves
'neath my feet, here and there
a frisky, squirrel would stare,
then scamper to a safe retreat
A few last leaves clung with
tenacity to the trees, almost
as if unwilling to go with
the chilling autumn breeze,
a lonely hawk on his routine
stalk gave out a hungry cry,
As he circled high up above
in the blue October sky
With a tinge of sadness I
headed for home, another
autumn had come and gone,
the sun's last rays held my
steady gaze until I was
almost home

Alice Chaussée

Dads

Dads are special,
Dads are fun,
They are the sweetest
people under the sun.
When you're down,
dads are always there,
they always have time
to spare. So when you're
down, your dad is always
around. I know my dad
is fun, he is also the
sweetest person under the sun.

Amanda Knight

"Wildfire"

Brown eyes flashing,
Little feet trembling,
Tiny heart pounding,

A little fawn stands
At the edge of
A burning forest.

Wildly looking
For its mother.
Who lies dead within
The green inferno

Margaret Rabatin

Darkness

Darkness...
it haunts me,
encompassing my body
never to set me free.

I feel its presence
creeping up behind me,
preparing to pounce,
never to set me free.

Its fingers encircle my neck
threatening to choke me,
cold, rigid, tightening,
never to set me free.

Darkness...
it haunts me,
encompassing my body
never to set me free.

Jennifer Clements

"June Wedding"

I'm waiting for June.
I'll be a Bride.
It can't come too soon.
He will be there by my side.

I'll be dressed in white,
And I want a long train.
Everything has got to be right,
An air of calm, we must maintain.

My bridegroom is very handsome.
I waited a long time for him.
We'll have our own home.
He is so tall and trim.

He loves children.
I would love four.
We will have a huge den.
It's alright if we have more.

He will be smiling at me.
I'll be his Lady Fair.
My bridegroom, I can see.
I know, he will be there.

Victor S. Wallace

Untitled

When I was young and in my prime
I gave no thought to Father Time
Life was just one big thrill
And my father paid the bill
But life is not a bowl of cherries
After all it is the berries
We only go this way but once
So why did I act like a dunce
Now I marvel that I'm still alive
In two more months I'm 85
My friends have all gone on before
I'll see them all at Heaven's door
They'll smile at me from lofty heights
And say "Did you turn out the Lights?"

Mary E. Davis

There it Stands

There it stands
In the centre of the field
Flowers of the field
Cover it from top to bottom
The door stands open
As though waiting
For some long over due message
What secret does this box hold?
Why does it sit
In the middle of nowhere?
Perhaps it symbolizes a lonely heart,
That is waiting
waiting for its love to return
many seasons have passed
but the box still stands open
forever waiting
with endless patience
but why waste the time
waiting for something that will,
never arrive or return

Jonny Werner

I Knew I Was Loved

There was love in your
heart so long ago
but you had no choice
to let me go

I knew I was loved

You lived with a loss
and felt so forlorn
but you had no choice
I feel no scorn

I knew I was loved

Many years later the call
finally came
the love in your heart
was there again

I knew I was loved

Joined as a family
here we are
Our love will never
stray afar

I knew I was loved

Shelly Le Geyt

Goodbye To Summer

A few summer stragglers
still remain,
Yet the ocean knows
that the seasons must change.

The foggy mist swallows
the warmth of the sun...
That echoed with laughter
and days full of fun.

The footprints that dimpled
the sandy earth,
Have been smoothed like a pebble
by the roaring surf.

And the water itself
turns from blue to gray,
to convince us that winter
is not far away.

But do not regret
the changes you see,
For changes occur.....
infinitely.

Sandy Jacobson

Zen Precipitation

Each drop —
    a flicker-
pseudomotion in the grass,
ripples in the pond.

Each ripple —
    an expansion —
building upon the smaller motions,
becoming part of the bigger picture.

Until in reflection —
    silent contemplation —
we see the answers,
as a flicker changes the whole.

Dmitri Arbacauskas

Mary

The bench was cold,
the music stung my fingers.
I could see her figure behind me,
I could hear her voice.
The sweet smell of her was all around,
it was on me,
my body.
The home was very antique,
warm, beautiful.
We knew we loved each other
because our hearts were lustrous.
Outside,
a beautiful garden of flowers,
and a hill soaking up the spirit.
In the kitchen,
steam seeped from the kettle
whistling on the stove,
Those were the days...
and all that's left now
are memories...

Kylie Meyer

The Drummer

The drummer sits
Behind his tools,
Flailing
His wooden appendages

The crowd cheers,
The masses yell
For him to continue
Performing

He is
A true artist,
Splashing his canvas
With multicolored passion
And rhythm

The lights flash
Into his eyes
He is blinded,
He cannot see...

Yet...He persists
In painting his masterpiece...
In completing his life's work...

Collin Garrett Ryan

Baja Mar (A Chantey)

Sailors trav'ling from near and far,
Marvel in every case;
Explores called it Baja Mar;
Astronauts saluted from space.

Refrain: Sail with me to Baja Mar;
Seven hundred islands, reefs and cays -
Paradise is Baja Mar:
Islands in the shallow seas.

The climate is a natural balm:
The fabled 'fountain of youth'.
Trade winds bring a relaxing calm;
'Sun, sea, and sand' of repute.

Sail with me on these shallow seas;
View the sand banks below.
Scenic beauty: Exhuma Cays -
Fishes coloured like the rainbow.

The people are kind and friendly,
Like the Lucayans of old.
Bask in warm hospitality -
A refuge from wintry cold.

Cecil A. Dorsett

Bath Creek

The little town
defies discernment,
ends at the curve of Bath Creek
or starts there — some
essential substance shared,
uneasy at first, in a world
where things must struggle
to belong.
The beauty here is not
the spectacular variety
mirage in travel books,
but something rested around
the commonness of tree and sky,
hazed in the sun bleached air,
yet bright, cupped in the
still, quiet twilight,
keeping for a space apart
a place where loneliness
is not unkind.

Rayford Norman

"Two Special Gifts"

Dedicated to Candice and Desiree Tesoroni

I am not old in years,
nor am I wed.
But I have two special
gifts so precious and dear,
that if one of them left
my heart would tear.
These two special gifts
contain love, laughter,
and even good cheer.
They bring joy to my
heart in all they do.
They are two special
gifts just like me and you!

MaryAnn Bartleson

Cast Off

I am ready
to cast off

Cast off coats
cast off cold
cast off the mask
of the outcast.

I am ready
to cast off

Loose the line
rev the motor
slip into gear
and go.

Margaret Dubay Mikus

"That Is Who I Am"

I am your friend.
I am your enemy.
I am both.
I am neither.
Who am I?
That is who I am.

G. J. Guerra Jr.

Terry Fox: Marathon Of Hope

Running, running down the road
That stretches on and seems so endless,
With Death pursuing at his heels
Unshakable as his own shadow.

Clippety-clop, clippety-clop,
With a leg and a will of steel,
But a heart of flesh that whispers:
Look over your shoulder, Death quickens his pace.

One thousand miles, two thousand miles,
From youth to age, from coast to coast,
Each man alive runs down this road,
Though some don't ever reach the sea.

Another hill, another bend,
But as the sun attained midday,
A strong hand grabbed him from behind,
And a gun sounded to end the race.

John Hart

Bleeding Heart

Another day has come to an end
as I watch slip away my best friend.
Is this the part where I start to cry
or is it when I ask myself why.
Has it gotten so bad we can't even talk
I guess love isn't as wonderful as I thought.
Why must love be such a cruel thing to me
why can't it be perfect, the way I want it to be.
Could it be wishful thinking on my part
or just another slash in my bleeding heart.
It's been a day now, but it feels like forever
how long before I smile again, probably never.
Is there anyone out there who knows how I feel
how long before I realize this loss is real.
Is there anywhere I can go to empty the tears
can anyone explain it after this many years.
The answer is no, and forever alone
the answer is there but doesn't want to be known
the solution I'm told, is to be apart
so I never again have a bleeding heart.

Jennifer Trudeau

The Vision

Throw Roger Rabbit screaming into the night maze
Square garbage cans, ice-cold in the shadows
Hiding, panting in the trash can
Dark, jumbled, scared
Jumping off the cliff
Silver waves circle and shimmer in the heat
Fortune and money, green in my eyes
Bright flash from the press blinds me
The smell of the crowd like a cartoon jail
Fame in front of the camera, dank bars with drinks in paper
bags behind
A multitude of people running breathing heaving eating
My nose smells lunch
My arm is tossed out of a soft, dry bed
I have slept on my hat
Bad dream

Camelia Chanel Rabet

A Day In The Park

One day on a hunch, I packed a lunch
And went to the park for the day
I drove around, until I found, a place out of the way
I got out my flask, quite an easy task
And made myself a cup of tea
I enjoyed my food, as I watched the brood
Parade in front of me
Then two old dears, getting on in years
Slowly waddled by
Plump like their dog, evidence they liked to hog
With heaps and heaps of pie
Their clothes were all right, maybe a little tight,
Especially around the stern
Each stitch was strained, by the weight they had gained
H'mph, some women will never learn,
Then a car it stopped, some garbage the man dropped
As causal as could be
A few cans and a bottle, Man! I had the urge to throttle
BUT! The man was bigger than me

William J. Shand

The Telethon For Sick Children

This money is for "All" the children,
Who need your healing Lord.
Please grant this prayer, that they may be,
Free from sickness and healthy once more.
It hurts us Lord, to see them suffering.
We thank everyone, for helping and giving.
For without it they would be lost.
All we want to see, is the children set free.
Healthy again, and our world a better place.
We give thanks to the doctors, and nurses to,
Who toil each day, to find cures and reasons,
why these children are so sick.
There is a reason for everything.
Please Lord grant this prayer.
That once again these children will be well,
Free from suffering and pain
You said "Suffer little children to come unto me".
Thank you Lord.

Joan Côté

Why Teach

When I see a child come to my class door.
They ask, are you the teacher and some more?

You say yes, come in for awhile.
Then you see that great big smile.

They say thanks in their small way.
You just helped me make my day.

Now when I go home to get some rest.
It feels so good knowing you've done your best.

Darlene Small

The Vampire

I soars through the night sky, the dark clouds of thought
circle in my mind.
The song of the dying wind echoes in the shadows.
The moonlight dances around me.
The silent beating of my heart breaks the thunderous silence.
Fear me not child of darkness, for I am only a reflection
of your dying light.

Natasha Kocher

A Mood of a Dissatisfied Housewife

Empty hours with timeless tasks
Wearing costumes of futile masks
Looking for ventures and meaningful days
Lost but lurking in hidden rays
Self discipline is a rigorous cast
Self deception is an easier past
Determination is hard to find
Only when boredom has erased one's mind
Search and discover your hidden labour
Then life will offer lots to savour

Betty Klimitz

Patchwork

My mother was good at patchwork.
She painted the days of our lives
with the colours
of discarded fragments of cloth.
Prim and proper squares,
mystical triangles,
rambunctious hexagons,
cut, trimmed, matched,
and joined together by the common thread
of her pain and tears.
Her deft fingers weaved the harmony
of surrealistic magic
and unfurled in splashes of remembrance
a blanket to warm our nights.
Mother is gone now
but I still hear her speak
in the flowers, colours, patterns
of this extraordinary patchwork
which is love's tapestry spanning time.

Ng Kian Seng

Untitled

Waking
Is an act of abandon
The start of a mad race
Round and round
Circles over formica

You grope gingerly for the rag that gags your madness
Lint - hairs of grief
A symphony of pain
Singed slivers seethe
To foamed perfection
I can't help but be engulfed

There is no escape
From the plastic café
Of the plastic people.

Tracy Ng

Prairie Owl

Evening stars ignite the darkening air
    over winter's chosen shroud
    as sharp eyes cruelly proud
discern their snow scaped fare

Plowed furrows like lifeless veins exposed
    as nature's corridors of death
    reveal with suddenness the furtive breath
of life with equal swiftness soon deposed

Perpendicular descent with deadly grace
    ends for one nocturnal quest
    and brings for the other rest
in resurrection at the pinnacle of space

R. Garth Niven

Sonnet

When life and all its promises seem bleak
And clouds of gloomy thought my prospects mar
The sun, to my sad eyes, with pallor weak
Pursues its course above like some pale star
And yet I am no fool, for well I know
The sun will always shine, though clouds and rain
Oft shield its yellow rays from eyes below
Despite our human joys and human pain
To live, to love, to be betrayed, to weep
To suffer every ill that can transpire
Such things cannot, though troubling mortal sleep
Subdue that mighty lamp's celestial fire
Yet to my eyes, because of petty woe
The sun's bright rays no longer seem to glow.

Diana Brady

The Eagle Feather

She told the story of the Eagle's Feather
The eagle, God's emissary to the Native people.
As she spoke the room was enveloped in silence,
An aura appeared to surround her,
An aura fuelled by the spirituality of the feather she held.
Her eyes reflected everything that the feather represented
Total freedom, to go anywhere, do anything, to hunt freely,
The feather represents the epitome of what was the Native way of life,
Her eyes, they also showed the sadness of that great loss,
She stared at the feather and the realization of what has happened was clear,
Awestruck she fought for words and hold back tears,
A way of life has been destroyed, a way of life she still holds dear,
Yet this moment is mystical, her very essence is laid bare,
Her fingers delicately, lovingly caress the feather and she is
momentarily at one with God.
This fleeting glimpse said more than volumes.
It told the whole story of what it is to be a Native Indian in this
land of the free,
This land where the soaring eagle is no longer an eagle but a caged canary.

Nigel Richard Gates

A Still Frenzy

I have only dreamed of perusing the beauty's of the world,
daydreamed about the open fields and walking barefoot in the muddy earth,
I have wanted to kiss the shores of famous oceans and swim in lonely
ponds, roll down violently green hills and rest under tall redwoods
so still, but a breeze runs under the earth's surface and a current
electrifies the subtlety of my existence, all of sudden I crave a
wicked storm, of a clash of titans...or tides at least...
Where is the redwood split by the seduction of a lightning bolt, the
metamorphosis of a pond rising to be a river, or the shiver that
follows the rain drop chasing coldness down my back?
Where is the Adam to accompany the Eve in such an exciting frenzy,
he is taken on another form, a transformation, Storm Adam...
electrocuting my frailty and making my innocent wishes to roam
the earth alone evil.
Now I wish to be forever lying in the wet grass, under a dripping
wet tree...waiting for you to electrify me... cause you do it so
well yes...yes...I do love April showers.

Kelly Elaine Letros

Sunflowers

S is for its silent song, stretching for the bright, bright sun.
U is for its unique colors, fuzzy green, yellow, and brown.
N is for its need to see winter days and winter nights.
F is for the friends it has; swarming insects and pretty birds.
L is for the love it brings to everyone that comes its way.
O is for its originality, its peony, stem and personality.
W is for its watchful eye looking down from up so high.
E is for its acceptance of life, sitting there so happy and glad.
R is for its readiness to sing and play all day.
S is for its simple ways sitting there day after day.

Sunflower so silent so strong, sitting on its stem singing its song.

Lynn Hawkins

Dear Mom

Memories Of Mom

I treasure every moment, mom, of fun times spent with you;
Like singing songs and playing cards, or just a game or two.
Memories just fill my mind of playing jacks with rocks.
Or how you paid a penny for each matched up pair of socks.

And then there were four corners that we played in our back yard.
To keep an eye on all six kids, must have been real hard.
You always had so much to do, like making homemade bread.
You took this duty upon yourself and seen that we were fed.

God had a special plan for you, by making you our mother.
He knew no one else could fill this spot; He knew there was no other.
Of course we had our moments when we made you feel insane.
We had no way of knowing we had caused you so much pain.

But as I've grown and raise my own, it's very plain to see;
God must have had a sense of humor; He made my kids like me.
It's funny how the roles reverse; with things I say and do.
But nothing makes me prouder, mom. I've grown up just like you.

Cynthia Elsa Bagaglia-Wood

Something's Missing

Two friends sat talking, one night after work
About the days happenings and different quirks
You know I feel like there's something
missing one friend, said to the other
I know what you mean came the reply
But God didn't forget us, up there in the sky
He's just waiting for us to reply
So if you feel something's not right
And you don't know what it is
Take a minute to pray and forgive
Sit down and take a look and listen
You'll soon get your reply
The peace that you find will amaze you
And to think it came from the sky!

Connie Rose

The Will Of Tree And Me

Ablaze the sun crests a topaz sky
Day's glistening gifts the world are fanned.
A King stands atop the verdure high
Erect and bold with growing size
Whose will has thrust him above a proud land.

Bathed with brilliance blessed the sun
Soaked sweet with life which filled the drive
To struggle upward until hath won
By arms to climb the wind how done
When plush fingers mesh with heaven alive.

As I stand within him intertwined,
My soul would meet a spirit free.
Our aim the same, his resolve touched mine
And fills me with, as I do find
A soul at peace, the sky achieved.

Trey Morgan

Misspelled Cosmos

Fresh moon amidst a dusky sky —
singing to the rain and drowning the clouds
in a faint glow.
Stars huddle close
basked in a silver spiral of dust,
waltzing quietly with the sad comets.
Desperately clinging to their newly found bliss;
their pristine darkness.

Elena Gottreich

Untitled

Walking down a seemingly direct path, passing the cars, and gas stations, and palm trees that resemble dead grass, when suddenly I think that I must have seen this before.

All at once my eyes go from my hand to her hand. And I allow my mind appalling flights of fantasy.

that *you* will...
that together...

But as my eyes travel towards her eyes and meet, I remember that *we* had said goodbye.

Is this?

Passing the apartments and houses that could, would, and do exist anywhere. I consider, are *you* and her the same also?

And as we walk down any street, going by the dogs and the garbage and the graffiti that pronounces I love -, was I holding *your* hand, or her hand?

Then I recall hearing *your* voice, seeing her face,
"It's a ring road," *you* said.

Mark Elden Hiller

I Want To Be Free

I want to be free
Free to know God in his fullness
To see, to feel his awesome presence
And to know his thoughts.

I want to be free
Free to know that higher authority
To agree, to obey his rules
And to be able to live by them.

I want to be free
Free to sense his miraculous power
That heals, that teaches
One's mind to be sound.

I want to be free
Free to recognize his protection
That keeps, that holds me safe from any type of harm.

I want to be free, free to know the Comforter
Who leads, who guides me in all the right directions.

I want to be free, free to know God intimately
For us to be one, intertwined in every way.

I want to be free, free to live, free to know him.

Jeff Mobley

Why???

Why do I think the way I do?
Even though I know you feel it too.
Why do I always feel blue?
Every time I think of you.
Why do you act as if I'm not there?
This is something I just cannot bear.
Why does it bother you so much?
When all I need is your touch.
Why when I ask a question?
You don't even pay attention
Why do you have to hurt me?
When everyone knows we were meant to be
Why do I love you like I do?
Maybe it's because no one can replace you.
Why do I feel it deep inside?
This is just something I can not hide.
Why can't we work things out?
You know you're the only one I care about
Why don't we try one more time?
And then you will always be mine.

Jennifer Swedowski

Longing To Be Free

One summer day as my family and friends were sitting around this tree;
laughing, chatting and enjoying the scene as usually.

Suddenly we heard this hissing sound;
everyone immediately began staring at the ground.

Everything was silent, and the hissing sound stopped.
We all thought a snake had fallen from the tree top.

As we continued to laugh and joke around,
again there was this hissing sound.

We all began to move away from the tree.
A snake we knew we would surely see.

But as the boards was removed from the tree side;
there was this grasshopper trying to hide.

That was the joke of the day, you see.
Only a little grasshopper wanted to go free.

Judy Hagwood

A Mother's Cry

They say these men are gay - go ahead and let them die,
but somewhere in the distant night - I hear a mother's cry,

Although he's just a statistic - and he means nothing to you,
She gave birth to him in the hospital - and she dressed him up in blue.

She showed him to her husband - "Look honey, here's your boy,"
She's never forget her husband's look - it was one of utter joy!

She'd guide him as he grew - she watched him as he play,
her love for him grew stronger - each and every passing day.

But time was ticking off the clock - and how quickly it flew by,
She realized how fast he'd grown and her heart let out a sigh.

One day she heard the awful news - that would leave her broken-hearted,
her beloved son had a deadly disease - but his life was just getting started.

Who knew someday this virus - would make them say goodbye,
And somewhere in the distant night - I hear a mother's cry.

Carol Eaton

Longing

More deeply than the anatomy of my
soul your scent lingers, drifting up
and a long the walls of my mind.
Tear-laden cheeks born from the
longing, and yet living without your
touch creates deadly havoc at my
inner depths.
Thoughts of passion moving me more
profoundly than imaginable have
absorbed my dreams and distorted my
reality.
Your imprint, your innocent touch,
Your scent, your fond tone I drink through
osmosis, to merge our spirits and keep
you forever a part of me.
Your name, sweet as nectar is all that
I shall ever taste, as it passes
delicately from my lips with secretly
whispered, I love you's.

Velerie K. Jochum

A Dry Grey Season

Black horses surge to a halt near the edge
of a cliff. Snow covered fields so perfect,
so white, so clean, cover this ugly plateau.
I ride on a horse not black, but pale.
Pale in comparison to the other majestic steeds,
Pale in comparison, pale in comparing them.
Rush at the others, standing still at
the edge - the edge of a page, sharp as
the dagger in their backs.
We draw near to the others, dark horses and
their masters, heads held high,
looking forward with fear,
crying in the sunshine for the season to end.
I urge us forward, my steed goes speedily
past the black horses and shallow men, off that
cliff and into the end.
The end of fear and foolishness
the end of cares and ceremony,
the end of a dry grey season.

And into... the answer is in the sea gull.

Peter Graham

"Why Just A Season?"

"Why do we have just one season a year?"
For loving and caring and giving and cheer,
Why we could do it all year long,
And help others to belong,
To the Family of God,
"Where these desires could be strong!"
If God is patient, long suffering and kind,
We could be more like Him in our mind,
These attributes you see,
Will take us to heaven to live eternally.

People argue and fight all year long,
And then in one season, they manage to get along,
It seems to me we all could be
Loving and caring and giving eternally.

"Why just a season?"
For loving and giving and joy and cheer,
"Why just a season?"
When we could and should do it all year.

Jerrie L. Roy

Untitled

Throughout the years I've thought of you,
And of the memories that we share.
Ten years I've tried to keep in touch,
Just to let you know I care.

You asked me why I wept that day,
The last time our bodies touched,
Well, twenty-four years and I have yet to find,
Someone who means this much.

How could there be another?
For no one should rise above,
This torch that I still carry for you,
You are my one true love.

And I would wait a lifetime or more,
For this love that's meant to be,
Because all of my dreams will come true that day...
The day that you come back to me.

Monique C. Elser

I'm Always There For You

At times like these when everything seems to be going
Wrong, I long to be able to hold you close and help
Ease your pain. I know that comforting words really
Don't seem to be the answer now, but just remember,
   I'm always there for you.

It's easy for me to say that tomorrow is another day.
How can you possibly believe such words can take away
The ache of a broken heart, the loneliness of a crushed
Spirit, the fear of the future? But please remember,
   I'm always there for you.

I can't give you all the answers, I can't even give the
Questions, but trust in me and I can help you search
For solutions that are true and lasting. I want to
Ease your pain, see you safely through, so remember
   I'm always there for you.

And when the gloom is over, and the sun appears anew,
I'll be there to share your laughter as the sad
Memories fade, replaced by the good ones you cherish;
And then, my friend, you will know at last that
   I'm always there for you.

   Susanne Matthews

Ready To Jump

Elevens bells are heard
Patches of stars break free
From the rising rain that fills the mind
Brick stones hold up what otherwise would fall
Far, far down into the void
Nothing exists.
No thorns will crush the body
Unapproached problems will need no solving.
The car drives by, its headlights dimming in the distance.
Fog settles in
The exit is hidden.
Another stone breaks free and falls.
Oh, how free that rock is!
Longing to be free is finally emancipated.
Rain falls harder.
The wind shield can't stop the rain.
The fog is too thick for defrost.
Standing along on the rocks.
The world begins to spin. Dizzy. Round and round.
Which way was down? The twelfth bell strikes.

   Daniel F. Mayo

The Morning Star

The cool breath of the early dawn dispels
The velvety mysticism of the dark..
A faint tremor vacillates the pearly lights
Tired from blinking through the long night..
Myriad stars grow dim and disappear
All except one at the vertex,
The morning star.

The morning star presides for a brief, high moment
Over the end of the night and the rebirth of the day
Till the burning, rising sun
Overwhelms it with glowing golden light...

When sleepless and brooding
I gaze at the dawny sky
Sheer ecstasy embraces me and graces
The hope of a brighter day
And I rejoice and marvel
Drinking to my brimming fill
The scintillant, miraculous majesty
Of the jewel of the dawn
The morning star...and my heart begins to sing!

   William Hovnan

My Child's Life Is Destined To Be

When you were first born and placed in my arms,
Mommy felt, the Lord had sprinkled you with special charms.

I looked into those big beautiful eyes,
and realized they are as bright as the stars in the skies.

You attract those around you, like a magnet.
They who know you will not regret,
But will always remember and never forget.

Your time will come and your light will shine.
Thank God for those who support and love you.
They will be first and not last on your mind.

Time shall pass slowly at first,
Then you appear as a brilliant burst.

I see great things for my child so dear.
So never give up.
For your dreams are quite near.

There will be days when you stumble and fall,
But in the end, you shall achieve them all.

   Erline Dennis

Untitled

Life is full of ups and downs
in the city and in small towns.
Going through it day by day,
Struggling through it along the way.
If you are in a happy time,
It won't last long with all the crime.
If people wouldn't just keep to themselves,
And put their hate up on the shelf,
What a wonderful place this earth would be,
We'd leave it for our kids to see.
For there is only just one race,
That is of course, the human race.

   Wendy Ottosen

Loving You

  Loving you is heavenly, like mist
of morning dew, like rain
falling, while the sun is shining new.
  Loving you is easy, your tender
love I share, your kiss is like
a rose blooming in the air.
  Loving you, I always will, never to
go astray, I'll follow in you
footprints, I want be far away.
  Loving you I'll be complete not
wanting be free, I'll go where
you go, do what you do, your love
will comfort me.
  Loving you always has forever
been my dream, no more broken
heart only laughter as I sleep.
  Loving you my mind is resting with
thoughts of how it's going to be, a life
of joy and happiness surrounding you and me.

   Guinn West

What A Friend Is...

A friend is someone who cares about you.
They share their thoughts and dreams with you.
Dares to go the distance the whole way through.
Good times, bad times, maybe even sad.
All along they're going strong,
striving to do what is right - always there day and night.

   Beth Ann Boucher

Pleading Cry

Through the years, my pain has had no toll on its inflicters.
My cry has yet to be heard.
Lord won't you answer me.
Do you hear my plea?!

Since the nights in slavery and the days of suffered freedom,
my people have achieved but rarely received.
The merit we deserve is quietly passed by while our pleading
    cries never die.
Lord won't you answer me.
Do you hear my plea!

Many a night slaves have sung and prayed that their God would
unbound their chains and let their children free.
Lord won't you answer me.
Do you hear my plea!

A pleading cry of an African slave saunters boldly towards the heavens.
Lord this is not what you promised.
On the dry tundra in my homeland Free you said you would
always take care of me.
Lord won't you answer me.
Do you hear my plea!

Finally from a pain and suffering rooted 400 years deep.
I am acknowledged for the strength within me.
Lord you heard me! You answered my plea!

Aj Danre Brown

Happy Birthday Jesse

You arrived only a year ago
And in our hearts we love you so.
Each day that you grew
You amazed us with the things you could do.
You made it harder and harder to let you go.
For it was only your independence you wanted to show.
This day is special to us as it soon will be to you.
On this day only a year ago.
We love you Jesse.

Cassie Aguilar

The Sun

Over the ocean, behind the hill,
I saw once a shiny second sun,
then I heard a silent call, real,
like a fading roar of a drum.

I stood still at the foot of the hill,
not the move, I stood really still.

The roar rumbled and struck my heart
clouds slowly vanished in the dim,
and the frame of the scene broke apart,
was it true, or just a blurring dream?

I stood still under the second sun.
Not the move, just my heart ran and ran.

There was no sound under the hill,
nor any light of the second sun,
but it wasn't a dream, it was real,
blazing shine, and the roar of a drum.

Nash Djurkic

A Place Revisited

The long, long drive,
The highway widens,
Ribbons of gray stretching ahead.

Slowly my body unwinds,
My mind relaxes in the joy of nature's purity.

My senses rejuvenate as the sweet smell
Of pine permeates the air.

Curling smoke from the cabins
Reminds me that soon I will feel
The first shock of the lake,
Transcended by its beauty
As I plunge into clear chilling water.

Night descends like a dark cloak.
Loon's plaintive calls fill the air
and I creep further under the covers.

Sleep overtakes my lonely thoughts
Nothing changes...everything has changed!

Dorothy M. Clauss

"Hell"

A place within no wonders
No dreams ever dreamed
Never to feel the sting of love
Only feeling bitter sorrow
Tasting pity, grief, and failures
Which will last beyond tomorrow
Your soul no longer yours, belonging to him.
Dead for past the deepest blue.
He knows you.
All of you.
He hates you.
But you're his child, Kim.
He's your weakness, fears,
Your suffering and sorrow
He will last beyond tomorrow.
This life has no end
Your heart's like a small shell
This is the place I like to call, hell!

Kimberly Welcome

Time

There was once a time when I was all alone,
'Til you came along and filled my days.
Taught me how two people could become as one
Took me in your arms and showed me all the ways
Of making love.

Time went by and you became more dear to me.
I vowed that I would never leave your side.
You promised me the moon, the stars, the heavens.
You swore we'd be together 'til we died
But now you're gone.

Time goes by and still I wait for you my love.
My heart aches from loving you so much
My mind is filled with memories of long ago.
My days are filled with longing for your touch.
Come back to me.

One day I'll be looking out my window
Waiting for your knock upon the door.
Suddenly I'll see you in the distance
For so long, it's just what I've been praying for.
I love you so.

Jeanette Goddard

Sail Away

I always wish I could sail away,
Sail away . . .
To an island where everything prays;
To an island where love is the only way out;
To a place where doves like to shout.
And as I sail along sail along,
I come to a boat with the Love of His song.
Where joy doesn't cease;
To a place with the Love of His peace.
Come on, let's sail away;
Come on, let's sail along.

Caitlin Star Adams

Angels

God sent us angels from up above
To comfort, protect and guide
They wrap their wings around us and share their love
So someday we can walk by his side

They wear a halo atop their head
Made of pure gold
It stays in place even while sound asleep in bed
Because they are so warm inside their halo never gets cold

When you need someone to care
Around me where no one can see
Just remember God's Angels are there
My guardian and watches over me

Don't ever give up when it seems like it's too much
Just reach out for an angels touch

Brandee Foster

Friends

"I'm all alone," I've oft' heard that said,
And I've pondered the thought round, round in my head
For who is alone in this wild world bright -
In the light of day or the dark of night?

It must be a person unable to see
The beautiful things God created for thee.
Unable to hear a song fill the air
Unable to smell a rose that's so fair,
Unable to dream as twilight descends,
For who is alone when they're among friends?

Eileen Baker

The Discovery

There is a glorious cloud that captures us away
From the earth, as it may seem, to the truth we seek each day.

A dream becomes awakened as we look beyond the cloud
And know that there's a greater work out there amidst the crowd.

Discovery is a process; the detours must be made
Past the logic of the mind, to the heart where reason must fade.

Within the very depth of soul a mighty power waits,
Covered ever so lightly, while we decide its fate.

Yield to the force abiding; venture to look within.
Take time to scratch the surface; the stirring will begin.

Dig deeper and you will find a still small voice within;
At times a resounding thunder will say, "Begin again."

What is this force abiding so vibrant and so strong?
God's gift of faith discovered, makes way for the dreamer's song.

Marjorie Watson

The Woods

At night the woods are dark.
Darker than the normal black
An insane horrifying void.

As I walk through this vast darkness
Tripping over stumps where trees once stood, I stumble and fall.
It's been so long since I have been here.

Owls can be heard overhead
Creatures prowling the night.
In the darkness of the woods I can become free.

Running through the woods I feel my native ancestry
How it must have been to be free.
Truly free.

Feeling the feathers in my hair
The buck skin pants against my legs
Nature surrounding me.

It offers a freedom to all of its inhabitants.
Here I can be free.
Here I can be who I am and what I am
Proud to be Mohawk
Proud and not ashamed.

William Bailey

Sentimental Fortitude!

What beauty lies in the innocent expression of...
The saddest of thoughts! Which touch! Which move!
Which stirs your emotions! Your conscious! Your very soul!
Which makes you say "God! Load me with the world's sorrow,
pain, tears!...But...spare my co-existers! My brothers, my friends!

I'm immune! To the sorrow, to the pain, to the tears...
In this world where 'Love is Eclipsed'!!
So, why not take benefit of my incredible immunity
And...spare the innocent humanity?

I know, I realize, what happiness lies, what satisfaction lies!
In sharing, in bearing, in braving, the sorrow, the pain, the tears!
Of those you love, you care for, you live for....! And ...
Of all those having a 'Human Heart, which is' as tender when sad
for want of love and care as a withered flower for want of water!

God! Load me with the sorrow of my fellow-beings! My friends!
In return, I'll give them all the love they need! All the love I have!
For, I bet you! Your stock of sorrow, of pain, of tears...
Will be over - before!....
My stock of love, of affections of tender care is 'cut short'
brutally! By...the daredevil of destiny....the death!!

Ritu Mehta Pistritto

A Good Omen

In ancient Soto Temple,
giant cryptomeria trees, stand guard over
lonely weathered tombstones, names of ancestors;
illustrious family crest; three-oak-leaves in a circle;
boldly inscribed more than four-hundred years ago.

After a long and weary journey from Hawaii, known as
the Golden Isle where Father worked on a sugar plantation,
as timekeeper and interpreter, and finally rewarded with
gold pocket watch and chain, I gently laid his ashes to rest,
in beloved village surroundings of his childhood.

As I knelt and clasped my hands in fervent prayer,
a black snake suddenly appeared out of nowhere,
encircled the tombstone thrice, then slithered
through the withered grass and disappeared from sight.

I froze and stood in awe. I had never seen a snake before.
"Do not be afraid," said my village cousin, "The omen is good.
The ancestral spirits are happy you have come, finally...
to the land of your birth, to pay your respects to them."

Barbara Kawakami

To My Husband In The Service

(And A Postscript 50 Years Later)

<u>1945</u>: I never knew that loneliness could make me feel like this -
That I would treasure so each day since first I felt your kiss.
  I never knew that missing you could make me feel so sad,
  Nor did I really know 'til now 'twas you who kept me glad.
    I never knew that loving you was such a part of me
    This slow, dull ache would always be within the heart of me.

But though I never knew 'til now, and though you're far away,
I sometimes think, my dear, it's not too great a price to pay:
  The things we took for granted then we know are priceless now -
  Each meal we've had together since we took the marriage vow -
    The snow we shared in wintertime, our garden in the spring,
    And waiting in the summer for the harvest it would bring.

We've learned it was a privilege to do each daily task -
To share our sorrows and our joys - My darling, all I ask
  Is that God keep you safe from harm and bring you back to me -
  That He be with you always - in the air, on land or sea.
    I miss you so, my dearest one, but one thing is so true:
    My recompense is that I know that you are lonely, too!

<u>1995</u>: A Postscript: And now that God has taken you, those words still hold so true.
But I wonder now, my dearest one, if you are lonely, too!

Elizabeth Daws Sturns

Questioned / Unanswered

The echoing silence pounds in my ears
and brings to life all my greatest fears.

Am I worthy of you, and all
Your love has to give,
Or do I exist only to live?

You stand tall and proud,
a mask under which you hide,
but does your love expand
like the rushing tide?

Do you always dream a deep
lingering thought,
or is yours a soul which is easily bought?

Do I dare to dream of you and I,
or do I stand in the
shadows, and whisper a final good-bye?

Deanna Westrop

Night After Night

I lay in bed one night, dreaming
A happy dream
I awoke suddenly, fearing
Someone else was there

Before me I saw an angel, flying
With gossamer wings of light
The light touched me, warming
She then spoke to me

My heart ached, knowing
She told me of her love
Tears streamed down my face, hoping
I could love her back

I saw my angel, crying
She said she had to leave
I lay in bed that night, dying
And was told to live

I said goodbye as my angel took flight,
but she would be back, night after night.

Chris Lecnar

The Mantle

All eyes turn toward as angry voices
Unleash their crimson spleen across the land
Voices crying from old hurts, humiliation
Long-festering frustration
Voices that will not be stilled (they say) 'till
Justice has been done
Their cause won

All ears are tuned to his wise counsel
As in quiet tones he pleads for sanity
Since when are causes won if violence leads to anarchy?
Change takes time, it must evolve as such
Grievances come to light
And, within the framework of the law
The wrong made right.

Some, still able to think dispassionately
Head his word and pause
But others, so surfeited with hate
That reason itself has fled
Only wish him dead.

Loretta Francis

Watching Providence On The Edge Of Night And Winter

I am looking at the underneath of leaves
Bathed in the golden light behind the day,
Caught by the chill beneath the sun
Of twilight falling autumn's way.

I perch atop a season,
All suspended—hanging clear:
The climbing rose disengaged from picket post
Nor frigid blanket here
As yet, to drape about the dead,
And set a crystal stone
At robin's foot and violet's head.

Trees, stained with surging night
Uphold a canopy of blue gone dark,
I sit serene in scarfed state
Deserted in the park
By those who, food and fire driven,
Stumble back to dwellings warm,
Too early gird against the storm,
And unthinking, roof out summer.

Catherine Anna Jackson

Mystic Of Caring

A mystic of caring has a new reality,
  Giving new life to my heart's ability.
To what force does it belong?
  Or is it disguised for a song?
The voice that sings is divine
  And mystic of caring so inclined.
A new bond has been created,
As a new horizon for a summer day,
  And be no clouds to incur,
For the mystic of caring can endure.
  A wizards wand so endued.
Will my hearts enervate as it continues?
  For the awkwardness of this caring
Has its own sense of loneliness,
  Yet the feelings, created the bond with bliss
Will be there to share.
The strength and courage acquired
  Will be a remembrance, "someone cares"
Like a song, for a moment,
The mystic of caring will have a new reality...

Sharon Stroud

For You

I see.
I think.
I wonder.
I do.
Life would be meaningless without you.

I think I see. I wonder, I do.
Without meaning less, life would be you.

I without life? You wonder I see.
Do I think? Meaningless, would I be?

Do wonder. I think I would be
Without life! Meaning you see less I.

Peter Haynes

What Is A Man Of God?

A man of integrity,
With kindness in his heart;
One who is righteous, never broken apart;

They stand with dignity,
Never ashamed of the Word;
One who is respected,
In awe to be heard;

A man with fear,
Surrendering his life;
One who teaches,
Honored for he is wise;

They are gentleman,
With hearts that care;
One who is concerned,
Never too far to be near;

This man of God,
A man with great love;
One who gives praises,
Thee Almighty above.

Abigail Lewis

Rain

The rippling water thunders against the shadowy shore.
The birds are all chirping. They glide and they soar.
The leaves on the trees by the dew have been kissed.
Then along came the silence. And then came the mist.
The mist brought the thunder, the thunder the rain.
The rain brought the sorrow, remorse and disdain.
The rain filled the rivers, the oceans and lakes.
It's a delicate balance that makes no mistakes.
The rain pours down like tears from above.
It nurtures the forest. It shows us all love.
It helps feed the planet. It helps to bring life.
Accompanied by lightning, it cuts like a knife.
From out of the sky, the rain it does pour.
And when it stops raining, it's sunny once more.

Carrie Stephens

Sleeper

Sleeper
  under the stars
    the ocean of stars
      above

That great big beautiful
  placenta of stars
    smiling warmly on our skin
cosmos mother,
  milky sea for our ships to sail in

Sleep on gentle child-man traveler,
  sleep on in sparkling diamond darkness

Timothy David Lancaster

The Changing Faces Of Girls

The two girls sit side by side;
the sun slowly sets on their delicate faces.
Their smiles do not show any emotion,
they could be strangers.

The two girls hide their hands;
darkness sets in over their bodies.
Their eyes, like clear pools of water, see everything;
they could be friends.

The two girls squeeze together;
the moonlight dances around them.
Their love is seen through their tranquility;
they could be sisters.

The two girls stand;
the dawn blinds them.
They see each other for the first time;
they could be one.

Andrea Statton

Jesus And The Sparrow

Jesus made the little sparrow.
It's the dullest of them all.
Maybe it was the first bird made,
Before the colors came along.

Jesus made our coat very feathery,
In tones of brown, you can see.
It keeps us just as warm as others,
As he made it just for me.

Jesus taught sparrows how to build their homes,
In the trees and in the corners of the barns.
We are so free as we go our way,
As Jesus watches over us each day.

Jesus gives to sparrows as he does the others.
Let us fly through the air from tree to tree.
Jesus loves all the birds the same.
This is why Jesus cares for me.

My heart is filled with gladness,
When I think of Jesus, how we cares.
With his outstretched hands to us he calls,
Jesus knows when a little sparrow falls.

Treva Lapham

My Biggest Regret

To never have known you
is my biggest regret.
The times we will never share leave me
desperate, alone and scared.
For I wonder what it would have been like
to have known a mother such as you —
— o honest and true.
On this special day,
I visit with you, saying "Happy Mother's Day,"
the best a daughter can do.
The few times you held me is something
I was too young to recall,
but they are all the memories I have
so I cannot let myself forget
that you hugged and kissed me once
when I was very small.
A mother that was so caring and very special —
— is what I hear.
But to never have known you
is my biggest regret.

Susanna G. Fiorino

Living In Pain

From deep within me...
I feel pain... I hurt to the
   point whereas I no longer
realize the feeling of pain...
   For I have became pain itself.
Yet, some say there is no gain
   without pain... But what
do I have to gain, when I continue
   to Pain... Pain in my heart...
Pain in my talk... Pain in my
   walk... Pain in my sleep... Pain
when I eat... Pain has become my
   Life... For I feel only hurt
and pain... That's how life has became...
   Fortune from within... a suffering
sensation that has no end... Pain... Pain

Milton Trotter

The Journey

The search for understanding
is a never ending journey,
One that we must take with great passion.
Passion for similarity, passion for difference.
The road is long as the passage demanding,
embrace the now, live each day,
feel free.
Feel tree to nurture all pain
and free to welcome the healing.
The lessons of learning
may not always be clear.
Time allows us to reflect and absorb.
Reflect on what gives us joy,
absorb the induction of many agonies.
The search for understanding
must be one of building,
Building of character through experience.
Experience with character will help us understand
the journey.

Lorri Livermore

i Feel Both Sides

You say love is happy,
You say love is grand;
But to me it's just a word-
And i don't understand.

Joy is real to you
But pain is real to me;
You have wonderful memories
While torment's all i see.
You have no reasons to cry-
While all i want to do is die.

You say there's things to live for
And i used to think the same,
But now my life's a battlefield
And i'm sick of this stupid game.

We no longer agree
And we don't see eye to eye.
i'm longing for empathy-
Every time i cry;
But you're always happy and carefree-
Someday i hope that's where i'll be.

Rachel Galbraith

The River, The Valley And The Falcon

The river gently running, the water emerald green,
the grass rolling and waving, in the brilliant summer sheen.

The trees standing proud, so regal along the distant rim,
the buffalo grazing among the stems; green, tall and trim.

The falcon soaring high, below the clouds big and white,
the rain falling softly, just before the long cool night.

The cracking of the whip, cutting the oxen's bleeding backs,
as men run shouting crudely, along the piercing wheel tracks.

The herds of animals milling about, trampling all of the grass,
men cutting huge trees faster, than the river can carry them past.

The rifle shooting the falcon, wounded as it flew away,
hardly any fowl or small beast, could find a place to stay.

The hills standing naked, let the rain escape oh too fast,
the river flooding the valley, with mud, stumps and man's trash.

The wind blowing hard and hot, with dark a acidic smoke and grime,
rain killing the fish, as a long drought failed the summertime.

The people leaving the stripped valley, none staying to begin the renewal,
nonetheless creating a fresh start for the grass, trees, wild beasts, and fowl.

The green grass sprouting again, between the dark red clay and stones,
the rains keep washing, as falcons once again nest in their tree homes.

J. Tony Litherland

Lace Meadows

The earth cool and inviting, the lure of the winds faint voice
sifting delicately through the strands of a lacy meadow playing
them as chimes, filling the air with a tender song.

Shining rays dance as they weave majestically between the wisps
of clouds, casting with delight upon the span of mountains below
basking in warmth.

Golden horses graceful and free, absorbing the beauty surrounding
them, steal a kiss from a glassy brook, trickling gently against a
rocky edge, offering sweet treats.

A home tucked amidst the rolling hills, resting peacefully within
a bed of trees while smoke lightly saturates the air, encompassing
with a release of security, creating its own island.

The waters that originate from my very core are tapped, unleashed,
welling up from deep inside crying out....
begging for the desires of my heart.

Cathy Dawn Thomas

Palimpsests

Again we throw our wild surmises upon the sea of thought
which yields up its paltry catch, grown thin with want.
The search is on for the deepest of creatures known,
that plays with our patience and tasteless bait.
Yards of unravelled line turn in spiral downwards.
It has escaped us once more in those uncharted wastes.
Slowly, we mark each zone anew with sophisticated care
encasing our findings in electronic memory banks,
for we no longer trust brittle age old parchments,
ancestral foreheads wrinkled over their map of life,
as weary minds stumble at recent facts disclosed
but a brief moment in the heaving upsurge of the day.
Again we are immersed in floods of data bursting through
to sweep away a million links wrought in force, in depth
and in complexity, until the very central core explodes,
shattering the universe like a crystal ball in which the future
beholding itself cannot be contained. Back to the sap of being;
return beyond aqueous slitherings on the brink of existence,
the slate of knowledge be wiped cleaner than the shores of our birth.
Silent sea-spray of particles in the hour-glass of our metamorphosis.

Alina Poplawska

Sisters

Four little sisters, we didn't know
Why Mama was an angel watching us grow.
Four little sisters growing wild and free;
One went to Heaven, then there were three.
The tall one, the little one, and me.

We didn't stay the best of friends
While traveling all the turns and bends.
Three little sisters life's sea;
Floating and drifting and lost were we.
The tall one, the little one, and me.

Three little sisters to share the blame
As years ago we shared our name.
Although we will argue and disagree,
Sisters forever and ever we'll be.
The tall one, the little one, and me.

Clara Sitze

Roads

I wish I could live forever with my wife.
Life will not permit it though.
Life will bring me to a crossing
one day, a crossing where I will say
good-bye to my wife. One road will
take me back to yesterday, where memories
are my only companion. Travelling alone,
tomorrow is not a possibility for me.
Courage is not a virtue I would need
on this road. I would choose yesterday.
The other road will take me to a place
That's dark and always cold, but where
My soul is free. Free to travel, alone.
I will wait for her on this road.
Will she know me? Will I know her?
Will she be waiting for someone new?
I will need courage.
I would choose this road.

Charles Ashley

"Crying Of The Mind"

The strings of a cello moaning a sad melancholy sound
Calling me, beckoning me, deeper and deeper
And deeper still, until I, too,
Cry out in anguish for its pain and lonely sorrow
Yet still deeper I go - swirling movement

Is there no ending, and yet was there ever a beginning
Reality, my nemesis, you are so powerful
What you bring me you take with you.
As you pass me by like the wind
I try to capture you in my arms and embrace you
For all the time there is or ever was
Still you flow on uncaring as if to taunt me.
Reality, my enemy, I hate you and yet I love you
For the beauty that is all around me
Won't you touch me, hold me, even love me
Won't you stop for a moment as I stand here
Shrouded in a blanket of emotion
Waiting for you to carry me
Deeper and deeper still
Never ending, never ending, the sorrow of a suffering mind.

James W. Case

Senior Treasures

To think of time that drifts away so fast
A craft in time of storm has anchor hold
For now this wooden box protects my past

We share our dreams today, and will they cast,
A solid hand to hold when tide turns cold
To think of time that drifts away so fast

We all are done we cry, Oh Yes, at last
The wind may leave a message that is bold
For now a wooden box protects my past

A new day now begins, let's have a blast
With water rough I know, I'll never fold
To think of time that drifts away so fast

The places left to go just seem so vast
You are the Captain now, for I've been told
For now a wooden box protects my past

Accomplishments we've made can't be surpassed
So thank the ones who helped attain the gold
To think of time that drifts away so fast
For now a wooden box protects my past

Tracie Bertsch

My Journey

I have travelled through the paths of time
in fear of choking air
heavy earth trapped in darkness
wind whom knocked me in violence
clouds angry in grey, rain in heavy storms
sun rampant in fire
In solitude I have sought shelter
my leave singed and worn, my thorns sharp and cruel
my petals in stillness
Shedding my leaves
brushing my thorns aside, I take to stem
returning to the earth
I search for the beauty in nature
gentle earth, running wind
cool rain, warm sun
precious air
give to me gently, so as I may grow to bud
leaves in colour of green
stem strong and sturdy, petals of soft yellow
guide me gently

Lisa Buckland

The Vice Of Life

Inside each vise is common ground;
The empty void.
The Solemn soul.
The seldom satisfied search.

But if we stop and look around;
The beauty.
The love.
The energy from the earth.

The vice divides and weakens its bounds,
To free you and your soul,
To live life as a whole
Forever!

Sonny Abed

Man's Search

The sun rises from the east as the clouds turn orange and blue.
I gaze from the mountains ledge taking in the beautiful hues.
The shadows of nighttime slowly fade away,
as the waves begin to crash upon the rocks of the bay.
Sea gulls seek into the sand for their morning feast.
Walking along the beach in total peace.
Boats begin to raise their sails setting out for the open sea.
The flags on their mast waving goodbye to me.
So I stand and wonder as I walk down the steep mountain side.
Can man ever find peace like those birds who have nothing to hide?

Charles E. Bruegman

Gravestone

So many times I have sat talking to you,
Showering you with roses of the warmest red.
Many tears I have shed thinking of you,
Wishing to see you just one more time.
Remembering skin of porcelain and emerald eyes.
The very cradle of your arms rocking me to sleep,
I never felt cold with a smile of such warmth.
A gentle touch as that of a feather.
Many times I have kissed this cold granite stone,
The very stone you lay beneath still
No longer holding my hand or brushing my hair.
Oh, how many times I've said all this before,
Hopeful that my words are heard.
Often running home with something to share,
Still forgetting you're no longer here.

Stephanie L. Setter

Dawn

The grass is fresh cut, the color emerald green
The morning air is crisp, smelling sweet and clean
An orange globe breaks the horizon, at the coming of dawn
I sit here and watch it, from my seat on the lawn
Trees are budding, another spring in full bloom
Removing all trace, of the winters cold and gloom
Morning dew hangs, on the long green blades of grass
I watch the world changes, as the sunrise does pass
I can feel the touch of warmth, from the sun on my face
As it slowly rises heavenward, at a majestical pace
The birds are in song, as the sky lightens to blue
The warmth of the sunshine, gently evaporates the dew
This sight once beheld, is so glamorous and nice
Filling my soul with song, that has no cost or price
Such wondrous freedom, to see this glorious sight
That happens each new day, at the end of each night

Henry Jeffs

Softly We Touched

I walked the lonely shore in the starry moonlight night,
The breeze was blowing ever so lightly onto my lover's delights.
She brings me joy and happiness, sadness and melancholy moods,
She gives all of herself and takes so very little in return.

They say someday she will be gone withered and dead.
Oh if you look into her soul, her beauty will unfold
Her love will engulf you, and spellbound you shall be held.
The lover of my life, the gift of my God, the magnificent —
"North Of Superior"

William D. Souliere

Special Letter For Peace

When we are born, and come on this great wonderful world,
We only have a certain span of life to live.
One should live a good life, and make people happy, be
kind and understanding.
Why take young people, and kill them for the sake of a land,
Make them limbless and blind;
We must end all wars for the sake of mankind and humanity,
Etc. Etc. Etc.
There should be a trade agreement, with all democratic
countries, and improve relationship with one another.
I am sure the people of Canada, and all over the world,
would like an everlasting peace, especially in the,
Middle East — Vietnam — and Ireland.
With Gods help, I hope to achieve to objective.

Pearl Marcus

Reality

Is today the day they'll die?
You can see the fire in their eyes.
Grave men, near death, who see with blinding sight,
Raging against the dying of the light.

Devoting their lives to fighting wars,
Cold winds burn right through to the core.
Soldiers fighting with their souls.
Smells of stale blood chill their bones.

All beauty has come to rest in their eyes
Sights of gun powder fill the sky.
Bombs so close, to feel the shock,
Dead bodies slumped against a rock.

Sleepless nights, reliving the horror,
Crippled soldiers fight no more.
Decisions made to stop the combat,
To save our country against attack.

Assemblies held to show regard,
For those who fought, long and hard.
To save our country from future war,
So loved ones will cry no more.

Andrea Ackrill

Silence

I want to say it but I don't know how
I want to hold you but I don't know why
I want to explain it but I don't understand it myself
I just want to tell you that I love you

When we talk I try to make it clear
When we walk I want to be close to you
When we're together I don't want to leave
When I'm alone you're always on my mind

If I ever find the words to say
If I ever find a way
I'll tell you
That I love you

Until then read my face
Because it just might be the case
That I've found a way to say
I love you;
quietly, in the silence of my heart.

Heather Joy Bruischat

Logic Of The Heart

Take heart, o weary soul of yesterday
Replenish those laid-waste dreams
For all subtleties perchance
Reveal the sanguine expectation
Of a new hope, of a new loving.

Logical as the mind, love seeks its way -
Climbs up the highest mountains,
Crosses the vast seas and oceans...
Now comes its hard-earned denouement -
Not an illusion but a real thing.

Dreams in snippets; no longer in pieces,
Gelid soul's no longer cold,
The percolating tears cease,
Heartaches and pain become a living -
Living memento of a dying past.

Mario Torreon Lugod

The Warning

The old rook rasped from the sky-searching fir
In the days of slow-dropping sand
When the apples hung low on the young, tender boughs
Just awaiting the touch of a hand.
He called to the seekers to look where the log
Was dying, wet-rotted with mould;
To observe the cocoon lying couched in its wrinkles
The colours of darkness unfold.
We watched its escape, saw its wings gather strength,
Saw the breeze catch its joy, toss it high
For a few days to gladden the world with its light
But soon just to crumble and die.
So the bright moth returned to its dark haunts of mystery
Beauty extinguished. We live and are free.
The elixir we savoured, though stale, is still flavoured.
The rook cackles on in the conifer tree.

Elizabeth Arthur

The Approach Of Spring

The long, cold Winter is slowly passing,
Vernal Equinox is now approaching.
The daylight hours are becoming longer,
The Sun's bright rays are now getting stronger.
The planet Venus, at her brightest and best
Follows the setting Sun into the West.
On cold, frosty mornings when all is white,
Just watch as the Sun climbs to its full height,
The frost melts away and blue skies are clear,
Surely this tells us that Spring is quite near.
Now look at the trees, swelling leaf buds abound
And delicate snowdrops piercing the ground.
No more will we shiver and huddle indoors
And listen to wind which rages and roars.
We'll be in our gardens or trips to the coast
And that is the season that I love the most.

Jeanne Ison

Grandchild #3

Hey Diddle Diddle, Hey Diddle Dee;
We're just as happy as we can be
Waiting the arrival of Grandchild #3;
Only this time we're not guessing what the baby will be;
They've learned it's a boy, and they're naming him Jeffrey;

Yes, we've felt much Happiness and Joy from Grandchildren 1 and 2;
And, we'll cherish that Happiness and Joy, as we welcome all the new;
Because when talking grandchildren, after All is said and done;
To Grandparents, each and every grandchild is considered #1;

Now, we really must get ready, for in just a little while;
We'll be greeting Grandchild #3, who I'm sure will make us Smile.

Welcome Baby Jeffrey
Rita Deimling

Trophy Fish

As every great fisherman knows
there is a trophy fish out there waiting to be caught.
I've had all the battles I want with the little fish
and now it's time to pull that special one in.
Once I catch that trophy fish I will put her on my shelf.
I will love her,
and protect her, and keep her warm and dry.
There she will always be in my heart and my eye.
This trophy is like no other.
She is very special.
This trophy will be
my wife.

Sean P. Abernathy

This endowment for the arts on national conversation
is what of lines the along falls
done here on these pages.. Get people
what reassessing, talking, thinking
language is and how it is
manipulated and used.
To find hidden meanings or
Are words. meanings misconstrued
powerful. And we must rediscover
sometimes—intricate the rediscovering by power their
hateful and opposite, trivialized and watered down
language a—ours of language English
we so readily accept
reject ignorantly or
We must redefine—clarify
conversation and change through
about this entangled—ironic nation
and outdated, undefined, misunderstood of
ignorantly beautiful words.

Cassandra Leach

Untitled

The sky gleams, but the shadows grow dark.
The shadows tell me, that night is falling.
As the boat settles down,
so does the endless pool of water.
The water is gentle and bright.
It brings me happiness and joy.
Oh, what a beautiful site!
I bask in the glory of the sun
as it goes deeper into the horizon.

The scene is smooth and serene,
but it will not be still for long.
For there is a storm building, inside and out.
Release your fear and anxiety into the wind.
Let it get caught in the clouds.
Be still in this uncertain sequence of events
that is about to partake upon you.
Let the evil one slip from your body,
and let the golden child in you take over your mind.
Be angry no more.

Elisabeth Harvey

The Stranger

Love is like a stranger
Who slips into Her life
Faster than a whisper in the dark
And touches Her innocence in a way she least
expects.
With an extended arm she reaches out
Only to withdraw suddenly as if burned by
imaginary passion.
Because love is like a glimpse in the mirror,
As quickly as it came, if not caught,
Disappears into the silver sunset
And she'll curse the Stranger who hurt Her so.

Rosie Voon

Cupid's Quest

Words drip like honey
From the hive of lips
And the heart drinks the nectar
From the cup of love.

In the Eden
Of their garden
The Siamese Pair
Stretch forth gentle hands
Towards the forbidden fruit
As the serpent of desire
Breathes the heat of the fire
Into the nostrils of their burning hearts.

Flaming tongues
Lick furiously
At the cup
But taste
Only gall.

Michael Duff

Give Love To The Children

Give Love To The Children, children need love every day
Give Love To The Children, guide them on their way
Love's like a burning flame, consumes all that stands in its way
Love is the only power on earth to take the hatred away

Give Love To The Children, set the children free
To make their own decisions, then they will clearly see
Love is the sun the moon and the stars, love is a golden ring
Love is the one thing the whole world desires, be it beggar or king

Give Love To The Children, youth has not long to stay
Love is a long term investment, the best you will find any day
Love's like the rising sun, takes all the darkness away
Our children will tell their children and their children's children will say

Give Love To The Children, they are our crock of gold
And if perchance they ever stray, they will come back to the fold
Give Love To The Children, the children of today
Give Love To The Children and love will come to stay.

Elizabeth Quinn

My Mother Will Always Be My "Queen"

Long before you had water or gas heat,
There was always lots of love and laughter on Penny Street.

Many times I went to school with stings from the belt,
But now I know how tremendously it helped.

You always worked hard night and day.
Always thinking of your children, and a better way.

Food, clothing, and shoes you always provided the best,
But you helped me to realized they were only material things and
Never let them put my integrity to the test.
Many night, I heard you and Dad laugh way into the night
Even though times were hard, and things were very, very tight.

You taught me to always to be proud, and hold my head high,
And never look back on the past and sigh.

You were always there when I was in trouble,
Discipling if needed, but with love always on the double.

Love, honesty, loyalty, peace, and hard work are what you instilled in us.
And told us never forget the meaning of the word, "Trust."

So Mom, I love you for all your fine qualities whether silent or seen,
And these are the reasons why you will always be my "Queen."

Annie Ruth Berry

Antietam

Lost plans wrapped 'round three dropped cigars
Left the small place Antietam with lasting scars.
In that second year of that bloody war
Was the bloodiest day, but there would be more.
Lee's invasion was stopped at Antietam that day
But the creek was red from where the dead lay.

McClellan, Hooker, Jackson and Lee—
All of these would doubtless agree
That victory wasn't for either side,
Or the living or those who had died
For who can say, "The victory was mine,"
When people lie dead line upon line?

Julie Stallings

Search For Freedom

Isolated and secluded from reality,
My soul remains morbidly
hidden behind a wall of fraudulent
Smiles forced to surface to conceal
Years of dismal, treacherous mental beatings.
My fate comically decided by an inhuman being
hysterical diabolical manner.
I find myself sword fighting with destiny
And past traumas every waking moment
I am manipulated by these masters of the soul.
Where is the symphony playing for lost souls?
No music heard
Only thumps of my heart pounding
Against an embankment of tears.
I always thought there was life beyond birth
Patiently I await the pearly gate
And the comic who guards the abode for lost souls.
Are my spirit guides brightening the light in my tunnel yet?
Freedom I shall find. Not here.
Only there.

John Ferrari

Dear Mother

Dear mother I know I'm not always there for you,
in your times of need,
but I also say things I don't really mean.

Dear mother on this day your special day,
I think we should forget those times
and start over again.

For you and I know that love beats all odds,
so if you love me and I love you
then we can do just about anything,
that life throws our way.

Jenny Norris

Lonely And Blue

I turned to reach for you,
But you were gone, said you couldn't take it and so long.
I laughed at first, and now I cry at last...
Because I believed our love, would last, and last.
I looked at you with love,
I used to thank God above...
For you were just what I dreamed of,
and everything I had hoped for...
You were everything that was pure and beautiful,
You were the twinkles, in the stars,
I loved you, and then I lost you...
Now I am feeling really lonely,
Feeling really blue, and it's all because I lost you...
I really care, I mean,
I really love you...

Mary A. Dobyns

Promises Kept

What can I say that will put me in your mind
Need I only say words that are gentle and kind
Should I promise you things like a dance on a star
When I know that the distance between us is so far.

Or maybe a picnic on Saturn or Venus
You think that would stop, all that could come between us
A candle light dinner, on the dark side of the moon
A moment of time, that would end all too soon.

Or how about a ride, in the eye of a tornado
Would that impress you, I would like to know
Or maybe go surfing, in the sea of Tranquility
Quite a journey no doubt, but it'd be just you and me.

The man in the moon, I could tell you his name
But you'd probably guess, it was all just a game
A game I invented, called Promises Kept
It would end when I broke one, and learned that you wept.

These few things I would share, to make our love live
For you see, I really don't have much to give
If my promises fail, which most promises do
Above everything else, know this now, I need you.

Suupz

The Bond

To see those piercing eyes
To dream within;
To touch a face so soft
To hear a very delicate moan;
To place a hand upon a warm body
To give a soothing hug;
To fill the ear with tender words
In response, a gentle snug.

A ray of light in almost darkness
Delicate tenderness, infinite warmth.

When all around has grown cold
Someone to listen when all has been said.

Who hears your tears of sadness
Who sees your tears of joy.

Who knows your deepest thoughts
Who is willing to share what has always been fought.

May we live this ultimate moment
In intimate silence
So as not to break the bond.

Seajay

Torn

I sit in the quietness of night
thinking and pondering of days gone by.
Feeling the void enclosing me tight
and seeing the dark in how and why.
Cold and chill are swirling;
Turmoil foremost and flying.
Thoughts chaotically unfurling
with contentedness slowly dying.
Like the flower than can wilt,
so is the soul that withers.
Drowned in remorse and guilt;
No life, while slow death slithers.
Gone are the days of joys past.
Now black nights of dismay.
Life fades and will not last,
as clouds of drear forever stay.
Day no more sets on my eye, that looks inward with lost hope.
A smile is, upside down, a sigh,
alas, to struggle up a vertical slope.
How I long to return once more to family and friends gone before.

Tye Morancy

"Fear"

Many fears rage deep inside your mind;
one's forthcoming and one's left behind.

The fear of living eternal life can become disrupting,
without the knowledge on mind.

You have a spirit, a mind, and a soul, all of which cannot be told.

You are your own person, it's your choice; you can ignore the devil
or listen to the Lord's voice; some good and some of bad,
should either make you sad or glad.

The fear of choice on any part is something that needs to be
decided in your heart.

The fear is awful and is sometimes lawful; although your fears
are serious, they can always become greatly mysterious.

You can't fight your fears, by running from them for years; but
by sharing them with your peers.

Fears play a big part on your mind so don't let them get left behind.

Fears can sometimes mess with your brain, and can also sometimes
make you insane.

Never must you forget that fear is in every human being's heart
and that you must not let it tear you apart.

Cassandra Herrin

The Promise

I gave you my heart, I gave you my love
I thought you were God's gift from above
But time together, we both felt the strain,
Our lives were just traveling in opposite lanes.

I gave you a promise I struggled to keep
I was an addict and sinking in water
So deep you promised to stand by me and see me through
That promise you gave just wasn't true

Now we're apart and I'm feeling the pain
My drinking was what caused me to act so insane
Unlike your promise, mine wasn't a line
Patience is a virtue, you just didn't give me the time

But you won't be there when my promise I'll keep
You left me sinking in that water of deep
Watching me drowning, not lending a hand
Not seeing me rescued and laid on the sand.

I was gasping for air, begging to live
So I could prove to you my promise I've kept
Now I'm so alone, but in my heart you'll stay
Hoping again our paths will cross the same way.

I'll have proven to your my promise was kept
You could have helped, me but you chose to have left
All I will give you is a smile and a wave of the hand
Remembering you weren't there when I laid on the sand

Hildreth Woodberry

Tribute To The Black Woman

Strong heads held up high
Shades ranging from pale beige to the black of the evening sky
Never oppressed for long
And the last person you would ever want to wrong
Mother to all that lives and breathes
Nurturer of all the Earth's living beings
Protect her she is your life support
To none but Allah must she report
The Black Woman there is no other
Our friend, girlfriend, sister, wife and Mother

Tamla Sears

Finding Each Other

Trapped and confused I was
In a relationship going down
Then I met you and from far away
I knew something special had been found.

When we met it was natural
And also very able
I wonder now if it was planned
Another chance to lay my cards on the table.

You helped me see clearly
Also lead me on my way
Down a better road of life
Something I had only dreamed of everyday.

You make things seems so easy
Life is one big adventure
So, with you to guide me
I know I'm going to go.

Far up the ladder of success
And finally have happiness
My body, mind and soul
Actually may find some rest.

Rudi Cromwell

The Face

I do not know if I really know her
The face looks so familiar.
The silent long stare fathoms deep.
From the depth of oblivion
Surface the memories of my ancient world.

Pale grey sky was pouring monsoon rain..
Were those the fish couple
Dashing and darting with entangled fins
In the torrent of mighty stream?
No sun was there.
The grey sky extended and came down,
Melted with the white sand and silver water.
Eternal rain was washing the two bodies...

Oh! Did she see how my grasshopper on its moves
carry the lives of wives and little kids?
Did she see the white wings of cranes
Gliding on the flowing green fields of my heart?

How can I tell her that
Those little birds and the grasshopper
Died with me long, long ago.

A. F. M. Billah Khan

Untitled

I am squirrel stuck in a plastic tree.
High up on a hill, the plastic world I am forced to see.
Among the branches of teflon and polyester
I sit and I sit as my mind continues to spoil and fester
About the day that I am finally to be free.
But within the endless wait
My heart and my soul is mangled with so much hate.
My freedom is my aggression, my freedom forms my obsession.
From this hate comes my strongest desire, to over come this plastic tree.
I cast down upon the plastic world those polymer nuts that are
near to be found
I cast them down among those who venture around.
I cat them down to those who are far below upon the ground.
But yet in all my anguish and in all my pain
One simple fact aven will forever stain
No mater what I strike, it will always remain
In this plastic world aug will always be
A squirrel, stuck in a plastic tree

A. J. Martin

Lonely Man

All alone upon a hill
I am here; I sit quite still.
I sit and watch the world go by
Seeing nothing but the silent sky.

Now and then the church bells ring
As the choir softly sings.
I notice not; indeed, what do I care?
I am here and they are there.

The world around me slowly turns
For awhile it's cold but then it burns.
No one sees me; hear I am
No one knows when I see their shame.

They put me on this forsaken rock
Shackled me with chains and turned the lock.
Here I'm bound for eternity;
Sitting, waiting until someone notices lonely me.

Elena Wolf

Goodbye

Goodbye —
What does it mean?
A moments parting?
A fond farewell spoken lightly with
No thought that love would end?
Forever?
A single word that holds the power to
Quench all hope till only embers glow
Where once the flame of passion soared
And turned to beauty every act of love
We shared.
What then when Hope is gone?
What of the void that parting left?
An empty shell that housed our dreams —
Where shadows lurk to haunt my every hour
And echoes of your laughter stab my heart.
What then of love?
Goodbye.

Evan G. Nelson

Searching

As time goes by, I stop and reminisce,
All the impulsive decisions, the opportunities I miss.

Where will I lead my crazy life?
I'm too stubborn to settle and just be a wife.

Where will I decide to set my goal?
When will I feel satisfied, fulfilled and whole?

Where will my temptations drag me to lead?
The ambition to be famous, not just to succeed.

I feel the urge that something does wait,
How far will I follow it in the hands of fate?

I dreamed I'd be rich and a famous star,
But the closest I've come is a fantasy so far.

I just can't fulfill the desire in my empty heart,
I feel I'm lost, left stranded in the dark.

So, where is life's big hidden treasure?
I just can't settle for any simple pleasure.

So frustrated I feel, but I continue to dream,
That life will be perfect, or so it will seem.

Simone Saeger

I Want To Be Blind

How do you know what my eyes see, and
What do you make of my disinterest in the world?
If I do not see brilliance, should I see ugliness?
Perhaps at times my eyes see nothing
Sometimes there is nothing to see
My eyes can travel the universe, if I let them be.

But the cause of my disinterest in the world only my heart knows,
Your eyes cannot see that far.
Enough infirmity has allowed my eyes to shed tears
My ears have dried them away momentarily

The tears that fall down my cheek can be dried with deception
But the tears that the essence of my being shed need veracity to
be wiped away.
So, who are you to say what I should make of the things I see?

When you look at a stranger,
What do your eyes see?

Lea D'Antono

A Christmas Wish From A Guy To His Gal

I wish I could find you
Under my Christmas tree;
Just there, just there, for me.

If I could find you there for me,
You would be the nicest Christmas present
That I would ever see.

If I found you under my Christmas tree,
And as I have above said, just there for me,
I'd be the happiest guy in the whole world.
Don't you see?

If you found it in your heart
To put yourself under my Christmas tree,
For me,

I'd give you all the best things in life
That would be possible for me;
And I'd give you me.

Albert G. Richardson

The Pigeon Fanciers

Grey shapes silhouetted against the glass
Motionless, as tho carved from stone -
Eyes transfixed upon a swath of grass
Filled with those who bill and coo in monotone.

Their rotund forms mesmerize the watching eyes,
As each tender morsel passes too and fro,
But many years have made the winged-ones wise
To tricks of predators, with heads held low.

Serenely they saunter about their task,
Seeking the choicest morsels from within the grass
Heads tho always turned, eyes hooded in the mask
To slyly note each movement, behind the glass.

Scratching feet and bobbing beak,
Bright plumage reflecting colours in the sun,
They find enough of what they seek -
Each and every strutting one.

Enough - our watchers can no longer wait
For, anxious now to take a chance,
They burst forth with swift and flowing gait -
As the winged-ones soar high in glorious, teasing, swirling dance.

Joan H. Yates

Untitled

I'm sitting here all alone,
No one to talk to, no one to phone.
I'm looking at the decors, it's not very good.
If only, if only I could.

In days gone by, busy, busy all day long.
No time to stop. No time at all.
Days were not long enough.

Children, Laundry, Garden and all.
Painting this, Paint that.
Not quite right, the paper is hung.
If only I could, if only.

Now sitting here all alone.
My children now married and gone.
Paper needs banging.
If only, if only my old bones would.
Let me do the things I used to do.
Sitting here all alone, nobody to talk to. No one to phone.

Still it's nearly Sunday when my family all here
No need to phone and all to talk to,
This makes this place a home.

S. A. Gunton

How Much Do I Love You?

Lord, how much do I love you? You're so very dear to me.
I love you for the little things which in this world I see
The things which you have made to make this world a pleasant place
Like the cheering and the laughter when children run a race
The butterflies which flutter round with iridescent wings
The robin with his red breast who in the winter sings
The greenest grass, the autumn leaves and fields of golden corn
The snow and frost and icicles on a cold and frosty morn.
The daffodils and crocuses which herald in the Spring,
The summer flowers and roses which their perfumes to us bring
A newborn babe, a toddlers walk, a mischievous boy's quick grin
As he looks up for forgiveness when caught in some small sin.
The lightning and the thunder, the tides and stormy seas
When in our fear we cry to you and fall upon our knees.
You're always there, You never change, we call upon Your Name
In a world of changing values, You always stay the same.
This lovely world You made for us, to bring us love and joy
But often we neglect You and cling to our own alloy.
Forgive us Lord, help us to see You made it for our pleasure
That we might give all praise to You and love which knows no measure.

Brenda P. Scarborough

'Freedom'

You may take my heart, my love or my cares,
You may make me hate and cry bitter tears.
Maybe you'll lock me up in a cell
Or beat me so much, my identity they can't tell.
You can take my home, my life or my fun,
You can make me insecure or carry a gun,
Maybe you'll kill me straight out,
Or knock me out with the first punch of the bout.

But one thing that you cannot rule,
No you cannot control me at all.
There's one thing you can never take
One part no earthly thing can break
The freedom of my soul.

Lucy Stuttard

My Little Miracle

I think about you all of the time,
the sweet face I would've seen, the soft skin I would've felt,
I could've seen you laugh, smile, and cry you are my little miracle
I could've been there when you needed you the most, but I wasn't
I think about you all of the time,
I dream about seeing my love cradling and kissing you,
I know that my life would've been different
But I would've loved it all the same
Because a little miracle would brighten my days,
I think about you all of the time,
And I wonder if I did the right thing, if you forgive me?
I think about you all of the time my little miracle
Are you in a better place with angels such as you?
I want to know if your spirit knows that I loved you,
with all my heart, soul, and being
I had to do it even though it was tragic and it hurt my baby
I'm truly very sorry
You will always and forever be in my heart until I die.
And on that day I will see your sweet face and feel your soft skin.
I think about you all of the time.

Erica Lantzer

My Dreams

Do not ever try to take away from me
The priceless possession, I always enjoy
The vast expansion of vision,
The power of mind - my dreams.

These unconscious efforts of mind revealed so often
The secrets, my heart ached so much, to know.

They enabled me to reach such places
Where I have never dreamt to go
And gave me the privileges
That were impossible to know.

Like each outcome of unique combination of genes
This ever fresh imagination of an aged mind
Lets me do the things impossible,
Meet people, who are no more to find.

Sometimes I give myself away to these dreams
Thinking all my problems are over and my desires won.

How I wish for a small place for myself
In your dreamy thoughts.
Please excuse me,
But this is what I want because I love you - my dream.

Ramni Thapar

In Full Conscience

Nothing breaks like the morning.
The dull cry of the spirit of darkness
isolates the light from its glare.
A parched fragment of some unknown breast
somersaults through weary-eyed clouds,
vaguely intruding into the skies.
A few sighs escape
the shutters of the stirring air,
and rupture the womb of silence.
Somewhere, a child sacrifices its tears
For the sake of attention.

Nothing sleeps like the night.
A handful of dreams bury their motion
under a creaking chair.
Pools of hurried notions
trip themselves over the pavement stones.
A memory of some long-dead ritual
trickles into the drain.
Somewhere, a man hides his tears behind the dark,
To forget himself.

Vidya Ramamurty

My Four Mothers

As I sit here and think this day
I think of things that have gone astray.
I think of the four mothers that I have known
And how things have changes as I have grown

My own Mother, of course, is number one,
Yours truly was her first born son
She loved and taught me by day and night
All in hopes I would grow up right.

The mother of my children is number two
Our life together turned sad and blue
She had four kids and then we went astray.
But in many ways I love her still today.

Wife number two is number three
She took over and made our lives what they would be
But now she to has gone away
She went with God on her judgement day.

My own daughter is number four
She to has had her face slammed in life's door,
So right now she lives only for her children three.
So they grow up the best that they can be.

Fred R. Downs Sr.

"Friends"

Friends, friends, how great they are,
Even if they don't have a car.
Special in a variety of different ways,
Always your friend know matter what you say.

A person you can count on through thick or thin,
Even if you have had a few shots of gin.
Someone you can tell your problems too.
They listen even if they have the flu.

No need to worry about boring friday nights,
Because you and your friends can always go fly a kite.
With friends you will never be down,
Because they make you smile when they see a frown.

Money can't buy a great friend,
Only love will make you mend.
What would life be like without true friends?
I can't imagine it; so thank you God for making friends.

Cheryl Hawkins

Desert Eyes Of My Dad

On the desert between pale mountains
Our cries search for answers, through the valley we mourn.
Our eyes pierce the skies above,
Far away whispers we hear,
Your truth is so real, then
An angel through you is born.
Creeping by are the memories of time
Only I can be in this moment;
Alone, with only you.
Our isolation allows our choice to
Be determined; through your strength we are
Inspired with feelings that are new.
For hear me with your heart
And know, that there will never be
A day in my life, that you will never be a part of.
My sadness, my anger, my pain, and my hurt;
At one time lacked the knowledge; yet now
As your silence speaks to my soul...
There is comfort, I know to wipe away my inner fears,
I say... and you say, together... I am besides you now.

Ruthie Walter

Expression

Words are beautiful
scraped from the backs
of our minds;

we discover rainbows of colorful thought;

sweet is the rain,
on a summer morning

dripping from flowers in the sky.

I love the taste
of your warmth,

- caressing my calmness

my face turns to
the sun

never seen before

one hundred different ways,
to see

- without wonder

my head rests gently
on my new
found friend;

his name is faith.

Suzanne Weitzel

"What Lies Beneath Our Eyelids?"

What lies beneath our eyelids
when we send them off to bed...
first you close them softly
and darkness is around you
then you reach out timidly
to see what all surrounds you
your dreams creep up on you
while you are asleep
there is nothing you can do
yet in your dream, you weep
what lies beneath my eyelids
when I send them off to bed...
are my hopes and dreams and fears
and the only thing that comforts me
are my warm and salty tears
the eyelids through which no one can see
and my thoughts run through
a sweet place in my head
there is no more I can do
when the whites of my eyes are red.

Heidi Taynton Smurfertte

Broken Love

I reach out to you, but you are not there
I try to tell you, but you do not care
We were once the same, you and me
We were meant to be together —
Why can't you see?
What did I do, to make you go away
Was it something I did, that I meant not to say?
Now I'm alone, to dry my own tears
The days you've been gone, have seemed like years
Can I maybe wonder, if you could change your mind?
That special love again, we should surely find
Until I know I cannot ever be free
Please turn around...
    and come back to me.

Melissa Wendt

Untitled

Youth in spring interlude brief
Brings cause and effect to play,
Pervasive will does wake
And make live what could
As easily be left to sleep,
And in that wintery sleep die.
But no, in some grand scheme
Whose nature we do not understand,
Nature, our nature of the same,
Both we would do violence to,
In bitter arrogance show contempt.
We however, struggle on in witness
To that Beauty who struggles
In silken gauzes of her own disguise
And would be free.
What we once could see with younger eyes
From ourselves keep hidden in older age,
Yet will be revealed when tomorrow
We sleep and in our last winter die.

Robert Rudolph-Abernethy

Antagonist

Turn back now after coming this far?
What are you thinking, all knowing?

Raising a formidable wall in front,
You may turn back if you wish..

Look ahead and see yourself
How the old familiar highway
Turns chaotic treacherous...
Let the coolest wind whisper in your ear,
"Who knows for whom the bell tolls."

No one stops you sailing on forbidden waters.
And going farthest against the high tide.

Zeenat Afroze

The Mourner

My parents are dead and I'm all alone
Amongst the trees with their graves of stone
No-one to care if I live or die
No-one to kiss me if I fall and cry.
No-one to carry the burden I bear
No-one who notices I still care.
Somehow I shall live and survive
If no one listens, I'll still be alive
So take care of those cold grey stones
That somehow makes me so alone.

Janice Taylor

The Grass

I cut my grass again today
I think it was time, it looked like hay
But oh how futile it all seems to be
It grows right back to laugh at me
As if to say you fool of fools
Put away those silly grass cutting tools
You slow us down, that much we concede
But do you really think you make us bleed?
For all your efforts to keep us down
We pop right back for another round
And from our example, a lesson you could learn
To never give up, but wait your turn
For someday when you are down and out
Your climb back up won't be shut out
You'll be top dog in your hometown
With no machine to mow you down
And when reflecting on hard times you did pass
Just remember this lesson learned from us, the grass

Douglas Jarrell

My Lover's Eyes

My lover's eyes are like the stormy winter sea.
Cold and dangerous as his treacherous soul.
As the sun's warmth never truly penetrates but only hides the
danger beneath,
So the gray-green sparkle of my lover's eyes hide
The cold emptiness of the winter sea that is his heart,
On whose rocks I have crashed headlong.
My soul lies bleeding and in pain, lacking the will to go on.
Against the punishing string of the salt spray
The numbing cold that settles on my heart.
And in my despair I wonder
How can I go on? Why I must I go on?
My heart seems scarred forever, But the will to survive is still there.
Now desperate for another chance to live, to find warmth,
Perhaps love, and hope that the eyes of another will not lie.

Beverly Anya Chesanek

Ultimate Reality

A form composed of elusive electrons
Within atoms of astounding coalitions

Possessing visions of radiant array of colors
And perceiving parcels of prose

Periodically scenting over-zealous moisture
At times in taking odorous concoctions

Relishing salty and sour sweet assemblies
Bits and pieces with pangs of want

Welcoming fragments of subtle tones
And the angelic sound of silence

Having a vast range of sensitive settings
up lifting the crest of awareness

Aligning movements of consenting upheavals
Expressing the resilience of changes

Designing diverse images exploring the vastness of space
Also assimilating myriads of mosaic patterns

All consummated to create the ultimate reality
That's me and you

Andrew S. Wastak

Lean On Me

Lean on me the Master said, when your pain is hard to bear
Lean on me when your faith is sorely tried
In the darkness of your sorrow
You will find a new tomorrow
Child of God, I understand, lean on me.

Lean on me when you fear your heart is breaking
Lean on me if you think you cannot go on
I am your God, I love you, I see each falling tear
Child of God, I understand, lean on me.

I am your help in trouble
The Rock on which you stand
I am your strength, your comfort
I hold you in my hand.

Lean on me when you are lonely, and friends all disappear
Lean on me I will whisper in your ear
I have been where you are now
I bore the cross, you wear the Crown
Child of God, I understand, lean on me.

Marlene Hutchison

That Weekend

I want to scream, I want to shout,
just the chance to let it out;
built-up emotions run deep inside,
urging me to slip up and cry;
should I be scared or even afraid,
in this world to drive me insane?
who can I turn to that will help me see,
without burning bridges on either side of me;
screwed up, big mistake, just a quest-
for a few moments I conquered.
What are the intentions of my goals?
hurts more inside than what they are told.
"keep it a secret" I am threatened,
or you'll always regret it;
catching one last breath of hope,
finding myself a way to cope.

Julie M. Williams

Vexillary

Almost unnoticed the old Gods departed,
Taking with then the alter cloths, the chalice and the gold.
Strong and eternal they were not,
Suffering the fragility of friendship, the finite quality of love.
It was thought across our lone and level promontory
New Gods would come, bearing countenances of confidence
and trust.
And day after day we waited and nights we watched
(like dogs resting on elbows) for signal fires.
Cold and shivering and alone we waited, sand in our shoes.
But they never come, and the old ones stayed
Silent and forgotten on their own Olympus.

Walter M. Bastian

"Homeless"

As I walk, below the stars,
what I see is only cars.
And barrels lite up, newspapers
as covers, but plastic bags sometimes on others.
I see the people, coughing and being sick,
they hate to admit that they're dying quick.
From lawyers to bums,
from rich and poor, if just one another would open up their door.
To help people through out the day,
and give them a warm place to lay.
To see the children as sick as they are,
and watching the riches go into the bar.
The people drive by, like they don't care,
and to give them a ride,
oh they wouldn't dare!
To Asia to Africa, to Iran to Rome,
as the parents pray for their children to have a home.

Jenny Harman

Tribute To The Black Woman

Strong heads held up high
Shades ranging from pale beige to the black of the evening sky
Never oppressed for long
And the last person you would ever want to wrong
Mother to all that lives and breathes
Nurturer of all the Earth's living beings
Protect her she is your life support
To none but Allah must she report
The Black Woman there is no other
Our friend, girlfriend, sister, wife and Mother

Tamla Sears

This Time

I am in a long dark overcoat
It doesn't fit me
I'm uncomfortable
Are you listening? Is anybody listening?
I'm small. Tiny. Miniature.
Where has everyone gone? Is it time to start again?
Or will I go back?
You! (yes you) are looking at frustration, anger, fear,
loneliness, yearning.
You are looking at a small spring with a latch on it
Ready to explode into a thousand shattering pieces or
simply get stuck and deteriorate
You are looking at a cat
You are looking at a mouse
But all you see is a long dark overcoat.

Kim Frischmuth

"God, Please"

Many a cry is heard throughout the night,
Mommy, where is Daddy? Please hush my child.
The shooting has stopped and you need your sleep,
tomorrow I'll find you something to eat.
Here, have some water, I saved just for you
and one little sip for your Teddy too.
Mommy, how long must I sleep on the floor,
the stones are hard, don't you love me any more?
My darling, we use the cellar to hide
so we won't get hurt, when the soldiers fight.
When daylight comes, I must leave you alone,
promise you'll hide here, until I'm back home.
Oh God! I rob the dead of shoes and clothes,
but my child is alive, in need of both.
Oh God! What I am? I steal and I loot,
just to give to my child a little food.
Her daddy was shot, I alone must strive
to provide a future with peace in her life.

Elsbeth Richards

The Hidden Sun

Where is the sun?
Nobody knows.
All that is felt,
Is how the wind blows.
Moving the clouds all around.
In search of the sun,
That cannot be found.
Tears falling from the sky,
On this humid day...
The clouds cry.
A loud rumble is heard,
From the distance.
The sun peeps out,
For an instant...
Only to hide for the rest of the day.
All that is left,
Is the mist of gray.
How amusing to watch this display,
Of what we experience in some minute way.

Ruby Kanegae

February

The damp ice cube coldness will start to go away
and oatmeal spring isn't faraway.
The young kids wait patiently for warm spring to come.
But some wait for the crystal orange summer
and others say school is a bummer.
They can't wait for great free summer.
They watch the ocean line jump rope
and they say when spring gets here everything will be mighty fine.

Jeanette Sullivan

Wonder

Do you ever wonder
How it came to be
You thought you had everyone and everything
Well you did
All except me....

You wanted more between us
I wanted less
You said you cared about me
So I put you to the test....

I said I loved you,
You said it too
But for real this time
We are finally through....

You're the one who decided
By going to someone else,
I hate to tell you this
But you're not the only one....

We've had our fun,
So lets get it over with
The test is through and sadly to say so are we.

Amanda Lovell

Near The Bottom

The end is near
Hate is the destruction of the world

The final story is
One of no pride
Receiver of the blood

The bottom
Bottom of the end
End is near death
Near the edge
Running to escape
Getting nowhere but back down to the bottom

Climbing
Then slipping back down
Can't get out of the bottom
Can't go anywhere
But to the bottom

Amy Collins

What Did They Think Would Happen?

In the City of Angels with poor people lacking,
While some folk lay back at the opera just clapping,
Ignoring the sounds of skulls that are cracking...
What did they think would happen?

When years of despair and urban neglect,
Make the sum of your life the gold on your neck,
And you look at your own people without any pity...
Letting dope and corruption engulf your own city...
What did they think would happen?

While they sat in the hills in complete isolation...
As Black on Black crime erased generations,
And the rich folk would say that..."They're just so mental!"
"And besides...it's only South Central!"...
What did they think would happen?

If you give two brothers just one piece of bread...
But the mother and father eat lobster instead...
Then drift off to sleep from the full good life...
But...left out the lobster...and the knife...
What do you think would happen?

(May '92 — L.A. Riots)

Arthur A. Bembury

Let There Be Love

There are two souls which control the body
one is the mind and the other is the heart
logic never prevails in matters
that the heart deems is in its control
this is why love never makes sense
for we never listen to our minds
we listen to our hearts
and most of the time we get hurt
it is only when we listen to them both
and let them function together as one
will we ever find the truth
and when that truth is found
we will find the one person who
was the cause of this cooperation
and then and only then will there be
true love.

Joseph M. Kyle

A Day Above All

On this day the year we wed,
   the best time came to be.
Down the aisle your beauty came,
   with love you married me.

I was the happiest man alive,
   with eyes for only you.
My heart went traveling over years,
   beating strong with love so true.

Your beauty goes beyond compare,
   with silky soft smooth skin.
All around you is a gentle air,
   and a love that glows within.

No greater person I've ever known,
   though none will be as fine.
The kindness and love that you have shown,
   I'll treasure through all time.

   Happy Anniversary!
   Michael Baptiste

Cowie

My dog Cowie wasn't the best dog, but she was mine.
I thought we would always be best friends, for all time.
A long time turned out to be almost two years,
Almost two years, and a life time of my tears.

I never knew how lonely I was till she came.
Now that she's gone will I ever be the same?
Who will protect me, now that she's not here?
Who will be my friend, when no one else is near?

My dog Cowie used to love only me,
That's what they mean by a dog's loyalty.
She was always by my side, my best friend,
Those walks that went on forever, never wanting to end.

I never thought a dog could make a house a home.
The property was always hers to roam.
Who will help ease my pain?
Who will walk with me in the rain?

My dog Cowie is deeply missed by those who loved her best.
I hope wherever she is, she is at rest.
In my heart she will always be my best friend.
In my heart she will be till the end.

Sheila Shedrick

Untitled

Waking to the morning light, I shudder as the darkness seeps
through every inch of my soul, making its way to my heart.
The heart I have frozen and hidden from good and bad to no avail.
The darkness brings its own coldness,
the offal of resigned melancholy.
Allowing the sun to shine through for a little while,
the returning darkness seems overwhelming and devastating.
Will the grinding of my soul continue
until the occultation is absolute?
My transient heart beats relentlessly in my ears.
Look forward - see the truth of the future.
I try to cover my ears to stop the roar.
But all I hear is the roar of aloneness.
Who would have known of my great vexation,
the desolation of my soul at my own hand.
How do I hide the desperation of my soul?
Let the shroud of cheerfulness settle on me.
Pushing ever deeper the darkness of my soul
filling the void of despondency and loneliness.

D. H. Howell

Dreams

I dream of majestic mountains, their peaks covered with snow,
Of the beautiful elk, deer, and moose, as they peek out among trees.
Of the scraggly mountain sheep, as they leap down the steep slopes.
And the sound of the wolf's howl at night, which causes the blood to chill.
So much beauty abounds, as one slowly winds around each turn,
Making nerve-wracking passes so high with no guards,
Looking down it seems for miles into empty space.
Seeing water rushing and leaping over rocks, making rapids white with foam,
And snow-clad branches, and skiers on the slopes.
Watching ski-lifts carrying merry-makers, on their ride to begin their fun;
And the blue ice of the glaciers, proves another had a hand in this.
As this majesty is far beyond man's hand.
If only man could not altar, what God's hand made to be enjoyed,
And this Paradise was left alone, as it is a Heavenly sight.
But, the new modern highways push the animals back from view.
And what is ruined in this beauty cannot be replaced.
Smoking volcanos with the lava beds below,
Leaves a deep impression of how the One Above has power we
   never will control.
These sights remain, as their glory cannot be forgotten,
But, it causes a loneliness to return to Heaven on earth again!

Gwen McLean

I Hear You 'Ode To Walt Whitman'

Through history gone and shadows passing,
your "barbaric yawp" still singing its song,
of lovers dancing the midnight song,
of mother breathing her silent earth,
of birds waiting for a mates return,
and of the ocean electric connecting us all.
I too am walking the paths, of whom crowds
have passed, passing and will pass,
celebrating my foot steps with theirs,
knowing that you are one, I am another.
I have come to join you on that ferry,
to watch the tides race past my feet,
while asking a stranger at my side,
'are you waiting or are you here?'
I am not the poet of all men and women,
for that is you and I will only follow,
by giving you my soul, myself and my song.
Hoping you haven't been waiting so long,
I sing to you my only song,
'I am listening to you, I hear you.'

Paul Tangonan

To My Mom

For giving me happy childhood days,
For teaching respect and responsible ways... I Love You.

For showing me truth and honestly pays,
For loving me most on my very worst days... I Love You.

For loving me always, sad, sick or depressed,
For staying beside me without any rest... I Love You.

For listening and being my very best friend,
When my world was collapsing and seeming to end... I Love You.

For your kind and constant helping hand,
For doing your best and being so grand... I Love You.

For keeping me strong while you were dying,
For holding me tight while I was crying... I Love You.

Now you are gone and through we're apart,
You'll always be with me, deep in my heart... I Miss You!

Cathy Winegar Komes

The Tree Of Life

Seeping through the fertile lands of
green, the ghostly sight of poison
lurked throughout the lighted
enchantment, until it found what
it sought: The pure, the innocent.
Then continued to soak into the soul
of a proud, tall crisp evergreen, unjustly.
Only then the tree would sprout out
hate, fear, and prejudice into the air
and hearts of many. Now the leaves
that were once crisp and green, lay
brown and fallen, all over the darkened land.

Amy E. Murphy

The Artist

With a stroke of a brush, The Artist adds color to the canvas.
With gentleness and compassion, The Artist adds color to my life.

With fine detail and precision, The Artist begins to create a
masterpiece. With great joy and anticipation,
The Artist adds fine detail to my heart.

With His dreams, visions, and imagination, The Artist forms a image.
With strong feelings and emotions,
The Artist shares His vision for my life.

With talent and passion, The Artist has with exhilaration.
With love and appreciation, The Artist paints inspired me so!

With great hope and expatiation, The Artist reveals His creation.
Lord, please never stop being The Artist
of my life, of my dreams, or of my soul.

Tracy A. Lindsay

Capitol Reef

Canyoned cliffs stretch high beyond belief;
Afar, rust-red, extends the rampart line -
Planed blocks compressed in Earth's deep oven core,
Infused with ferrous stain and brick-baked for
Ten thousand thousand decades thus until
On some infernal order thrust and bent to
Lacerated folds of crumpled crust.
Raging glacial floods have scoured. Here I
Exist this cosmic instant, and look up....
Enduring massive walls - how long before a
Fracturing 'quake crushes your ancient magic?

Pete Matthews

Behold

Behold the Lamb as he is born.
Behold the Lamb as he grows.
Behold the Lamb as he is accepted of God.
Behold the Lamb as he teaches and heals the people.
Behold the Lamb as the priests come for him.
Behold the Lamb as he is judges of man.
Behold the Lamb as he is scourged.
Behold the Lamb as they mock him.
Behold the Lamb as they shove a crown of thorns on his head.
Behold the Lamb as the blood runs down into his eyes and down his back.
Behold the Lamb as he struggles to carry his cross to Golgotha.
Behold the Lamb as they nail him to the cross.
Behold the Lamb as the soldier spears his side.
Behold the Lamb as he endures the sin of man kind.
Behold the Lamb as he forgives as he dies.
Behold the Lamb as he is put into the tomb.
Behold the Lamb as he rises from the tomb with the keys of hell in his hand.
Behold the Lamb as he sits on the right hand of God.
Behold the Lamb as he speaks to God for you.
Behold the Lamb.....Behold

Eric Sutter

Little Bubble

Sail on a gentle spring breeze
    little bubble of mine.
With your wonderful colors
    swirling gently about you.
You bring a sense of peace
    to the eyes that beholds you.
I watch as you sail peacefully
    on without a care in the world.
As this sense of peace you gracefully
    bestowed upon me lingers, your colors
Slowly fade away and you drift
Peacefully into silence.

Joanne Rondeau

The Family Of Man

We all belong to the family of man,
with many different faces and creeds,
some believe, their Gods allowed them, to do awful deeds.
Some think themselves more superior then the rest.
Not looking out for the next person's needs.
They kneel down on their foe without remorse,
and change with their actions the worlds course.
This beautiful, fragile world has gotten so small.
when this continues, where will it all end?
I hope it is not too late for a wake up-call.

Karin Gaysek

The Lamp Of Phoebus

The lamp of Phoebus slowly rose,
Shyly her light so feebly glows;
Reluctant to release her rays
To herald the extending days
And conquer melting winter snows.

Her sister lamp at times bestows
Companionship and proudly goes
Across the sky and homage pays
To the lamp of Phoebus.

A glorious season of beauty follows,
Warmth and colour highlight our tomorrows;
Forgotten the gloom of yesterdays,
Even rain and mist cause no dismays,
As ever bright in the wake of rainbows
Is the lamp of Phoebus.

Joan E. Clark

Side By Side

My special friend on earth and God,
Are both silent in their ways.
They love me and from that love,
I find the strength to continue through the days.

I need both of you, to carry on in this life,
If one left, my heart would grow cold.
One holds me tender in his arms,
The other reaches out and touches my soul.

Whenever I need someone to lean on,
To help me if I drift apart.
One is there in the flesh,
But both are in my heart.

I feel like the middle thread in a braid,
Surrounded by two who love and strengthen me.
But if one thread breaks,
Incomplete I would be.

What more do I need or want in life,
Than my two best friends to hold me tight.
I am ready to face the challenges ahead,
Because you are the strength that binds my thread.

Lori Gervin

The Twentieth-Century Europe

In his mind the prefabricated answer,
the wise man raised the question what is history.

With all her brothers, sisters and all my
cousins my dearest and wisest mother
were killed in purest innocents.

Who or what had killed all of them,
it was always history
in it the killeds and the killers
inseparable unity, inseparable unity.

I had always liked poetry,
the poems of the greatest and modest
minds of history.

Had they ever dreamed the day
when by wise men or by fate
history will become not the
Killeds and the killers
inseparable unity, not their
inseparable unity.

Endre Rosta

Forgotten Warrior

It looked to me
like the eyes of age
had swallowed him up in a dead man's cage.

Worn-out hands
and salty hair
Boots of dust that had been everywhere.

Painted lines on a
pencil-drawn face;
looked like time had run the race.

On the back of this man
who knows no name
Eagles fly, too wild to tame.

In a dust bowl hell
in a place long gone
You can hear his voice; hear his song.

He walks through worlds
he cuts right through;
With the freedom of a walking tattoo.

Terry L. Salata

Water

Water, a universal substance
Takes any form,
Eternally in motion, Regaining strength by quantity and movement;

Water, crushing brick walls, but cleansing your child,
Using all means of travel,
land, air, sea,
Eternally in motion, purifying the earth;

Nourishing all creatures it is excreted,
Yet it rises again, moistening the crust,
Falling at night to the dew-points delight,
It takes any form,
Solid, liquid, gas,
It has no comparison, and cannot be destroyed, contaminated, Yes,
Yet living on forever, Trapped for earth to use;

Tidal wave washing over land, like a stampede of wild animals,
All made of water,
So gentle but yet so destructive,
The substance influenced by earth's metamorphosis,
Like the butterfly but different action,
Not willing but destroying with no choice.

Jason L. Stile

Dear John (Please Forgive Us)

Millions cried, and people died,
one man took your life, but we
all pulled the trigger, you laid
upon the ground, in a pool of blood,
We all have seen your face before—,
Dear John please forgive us,
Dear John say a prayer for us.
Because, millions cried and people died,
The day that John was taken away!
Just a boy from Liverpool, that changed the world
Just a boy from Liverpool, who's changed the world (he's gone)
And, father please forgive us, we know not what we do!
Dear John, please forgive us, and please say a prayer for me!!
Just a boy from Liverpool, that changed the world,
Just a boy from Liverpool, that changed our world! (goodbye)
Dear John please forgive us and please will you say a prayer for
    me and this world,
Because I can't stay here thinking that everybody's sinking,
so, please, please, please, don't let it, Don't let it be!!!. John.

Paul Kingsley Hone

Blind Sight

I guess I didn't want to see my mother getting old,
I wanted to keep in my mind her vision, glad and bold;
I refused to see the wrinkles 'round her blue, yet dimming eyes,
Or hear and recognize the sadness in those last few goodbyes:

I saw here stooping posture though, but excused it just the same,
And held close, in arms embrace, her smaller, fragile frame;
I didn't want to think of how age was taking its toll,
One never sees the ravages, but our loved one's saintly soul!

Neither did I notice the slow trembling of her gait,
As she shuffled across her lovingly polished floor,
I kept her in my mind's blind sight, seeing only her grace,
And that sweet, and loving smile, just as she was before:

The supple skin dried and mottling, lines of worry and of wear,
No spring in her step was present, nor glow of healthy hair;
But now, I've finally lost her, she's gone toward the light,
She heard the call of heaven and took that special flight!

There's a certain bright blue sparkle that's missing now, I fear,
Although I sense her spirit always soothing, loving, near;
In memories I conjure, all the wise words that she gave,
Loving deeds and encouragements, my life's pathway, to pave!

Elsie (Loke) Linholm

Evan, LOL

It's this desperation
I can feel you slipping away.

The hurried responses,
The uneasy replies,
All means leading to a dubious end.

Will you be there when I call,
How can I expect you to be?

Do I have the right to make demands on
Your limited, adult time,
When I'm barely willing to give my own?

The irony of situation
Surrounding us,
Smothers my once contented heart.

I can't wait to see you,
But know that we can never meet.

We're in that hang time,
Too involved to abort,
Not familiar enough to share.

I've lost the desire for common things,
And now only ache for you.
Kirsta M. Mosconi

Temple Of Life

Nightingale, with simmering sobs
Bleeding heart, with feelings throbs
Tears of dew, with autumn's fear
Buds in spring, are kept so dear
Thorns and flowers, to dust - but why?
From a caterpillar, sprouts a butterfly!
   Glorious masks of my own face.
   Wonders of my noble grace.

The earth, the sky, the day, the night
And particles of traveling light
Show my mind a magic gate
To my destiny and their fate

Network of my thoughts can nurture
Eras of new days and culture
Eternity, when I walk and find
Just a single leap of mind

I am yet a humble human who can laugh and weep.
I have made eternal promise - that I have to keep
Built inside the triangle of self and time and space
Earthen temple of my life is greatest holy place.
Syed Iftikhar Haider

A Little One

A little child so beautiful and fair
Is loved by many everywhere
Whether it is a gift or boy
To your life they bring much joy
Maybe you don't remember all those happy times
They come and then they go
Sometimes you may remember
And a smile comes on your face
As you recall those memories
Yes a little one brings joy to your heart
As they grow up
And have children of their own
You enjoy them even more
June Videon

Love

There's a time in your life when you have a certain feeling,
You'll know it when it hits, but seeing is believing.

When you meet that certain someone, that will take your breath away,
This is a chance of a lifetime, and it doesn't happen everyday.

When your eyes first meet, the emotions start to flow,
With the very first touch, your heart is all a glow.

You begin to become closer, and you're sad when you're apart,
With every minute you're away, you feel you have a broken heart.

But you'll know it when it hits you, it's more beautiful than a dove,
It's a very special thing, it's falling in love.
Angelia Mullins

God Can You Hear Me?

God can you hear me when I
speak your loving words, look
out into the sky and see the little birds?
God can you hear me when
I pray for the living and the dead,
or when I'm thinking and lying in my bed?
God can you hear me when
I ask for little things, like what will
be in my future and what tomorrow will bring?
God can you hear me when I'm feeling all alone,
when I feel I have no one to call my very own?
God can you hear me when I'm going through
my trying times, or when I need help
because I'm not in my right state of mind?
God can you hear me when I'm taking care of business,
or when my mind is in such a big mess?
Tell me God can you hear me?
Nicole A. Davis

"The Dream Is Past"

When I think of the scorched earth
and the wind blowing thru the sand,
I dream of another time when
Buffalo roam this land.

I see General Custer with his Army,
Billy the Kid, the holster on his side,
The bloodshed between the white men
and Indian over the Buffalo hide.

The Old West, the winds of silence,
Out laws and heroes in grassy, sandy,
graves lie still.
No markers separate those on Boot Hill

The time for dreams now is past
as the evening takes its course.
Somewhere lost in time,
the sound of Battle cry and the hoofbeats of a horse.
Elaine Rita West Davidson

The Spider's Web

Spider, a spinning creature of patience and perseverance
Weaves overnight a dextrous cobweb of par excellence.
In shapes ranging from a perfect pentagon to polygon
It prepares with sticky, silky threads a snare, well-spun.
The gossamer's slender superfine thread floats in the air,
From the fortified webs connecting shrubs in a weather fair;
The eight-legged arachnid calmly in centre lies in wait
To trap any winged insect or fly as its prey of delight.
A careless insect gets stuck unawares in thin gluey snare,
Thus entangling itself unknowing the doom that lies there;
In no flurry, the killer drags the ensnared to its stronghold
To be numb and see-saw the victim with legs manifold.
Nature provides food for spiders in their own bastion
Proving patience has its reward to many a million.
D. Sarangapani

Destiny

With breaking heart and heavy hand
I lift my pen.
Oh! will this devastating pain
Ever end - and when?
A pain, that's raking body and soul profoundly,
All effort to stop this destruction soundly
Seems hopelessly in vain.

Hard have I fought to stay on top of sorrow,
Dreaming and hoping for a better tomorrow.
This hope is vanishing swiftly day by day.
Little time is left me on this earth to stay.
Hope fading rapidly.

With broken body, grieving soul and spirit low,
Alone with treasured memories of long ago,
And no-one to share those precious memories of mine,
The hours tick away, unbroken by life's sunshine.
What hopeless destiny!

Edeltraut Scheffler Plath

One More Chance

It seems like centuries since
my mother and I have sat
at the old oak table,
centuries since we have laughed, cried,
or simply existed.
A lost family —
slipping stealthily away through the
worn down fingertips of time,
lost to the unknown and
quite possibly forever irretrievable.
So many precious memories like snapshots
misplaced or gone astray.
But perhaps somewhere there exists
an unused roll of film —
one more chance.

Erika Kulnys-Brain

Soul To Soul

I knew I loved you
    the first time you held my hand
When our fingers and souls interlocked in a pattern
unique to only us

Your eyes penetrated the very depths of my being
    and my eyes, yours

We understand the secrets hiding there
We uncovered a freedom to love
    so long ago buried
The fear was gone
A breath of life so fresh, Yet so familiar
Felt like home...
    Felt like other half of me...
You are my dreams
    you are my destiny

Alesia Jenkins

Whispering Bones

Because whispering bones
call to me from places unknown,
the thread of my ancestry remains a blur.
A shrouded misty secret haunts my blood.
Dead voices find their way to my dreams,
speaking to me in words
I cannot hear but only taste and see.
In the morning, I am left with the emptiness
of thoughts like clouds.

Tania L. Rowe

No How No Way Will I Stay!

16 children were killed today.
16 people in the gutter.
They never tasted bread and butter.
No how no way will I stay

A bullet shot thru the air.
Killing a motherless child who did not care.
Another person was shot dead.
An eternal box was his bed.
A new war everyday.
No how no way will I stay!

Many lives in the universe.
Most now need a medical nurse.
A person got hit with a dart.
Many say he had a good heart.
He was killed for acting a way.
No how no way will I stay.

A big shot sent a shutter.
All people did was stare and mutter.
My heart is not made out of clay.
But no how no way will I stay.

Adeel Khamisa

Our Lost Sister

Look at the moon, the sun, the stars
    from above.
They are there and shining, but where is
    a sister's love?
Is it hidden in the mud pies, created
    in the summer rain?
Where are you, are you hiding, please let us
    share your pain.
Is it hidden in the flowers, that are
    blooming in the spring?
Where are you, are you hiding, please let
    us hear you sing.
Is it hidden in the autumn leaves, that
    turn from green to gold?
Where are you, are you hiding, please let
    us warm your cold.
Is it hidden in the winter, among the
    sleet, the snow?
Where are you hiding, dear sister?
    Please hear us, let us know.

Betty M. Luper

My Mile (Or The System)

Come with me, walk my mile. Let's look through my eyes,
see my world. Then maybe, just maybe, you'll understand
me and my mile. See the system. They want you to become
one of them. To act, to deceive, to lie. Then, just when
it all comes down, there you are, left alone. They say
it's just the way the system works. A new place, new
piece of tin, just to find the system is also here.
A shot in the night, then just when it all comes down
there you are, left alone. A new place, a new piece of
tin, this time you find where each that carries this
piece of tin believes in this system, see the mother
as she sits in the pew. Watching the stranger smiling
and laughing. As she holds a picture of her four year
old son, who will never smile or cry or anything,
because his life was taken by this stranger.
See my mile, feel my hurt. Let's hope, not for me,
but, for this mother, that justice will be done.
Then, just when it all comes down, there this mother is,
left alone. The system is even here.

Rickey Paul Miller

What'll You Do When I Get Old

What'll you do when I get old:
will you love me still heart and soul?

Will your smile still beam like high noon,
and will your voice be as sweet as the flowers in bloom?

Will the passions of my kiss make you refrain?
Will that sparkle in your eye still remain?

When my memory's short and the hairline's gone,
will you love me then all the days long?

When we've withstood the test of times
and visions of youth are mellowed in our minds,
tell me "plum pudding" will you still be mine?

What'll you do when I get old:
will you love me still?
I hope you will!

Zakiyyah Azeem

"Without"

Without bones, without muscles
I am taller then the trees, I am bigger then the oceans
Without feet, without hand
I move mountains, I wreck ships
Without blood, without a soul
I break up friends, I end lives
Without love, without hate
I am alive, I am dead
Without happiness, without sadness
I have no pain, I have no emotions
Without feature, without structure
I am life, I am death
Without friends, without enemies
I am black, I am white
Without pain, without pleasure
I have no color, I have no life
Without parents, without guardians
I am terror, I am hell
Without heaven, without hell
I am life, I am me.

Lesa Gidden

"Dying"

She sits upstairs, alone, knowing, sensing.
Her youngest gone.
Dead, alone in the beyond.
She is told and her hand comes up.
Do not tell. She already knows.
Separated again, and only memories remain.
A child, playful and full of life.
A corpse, stagnant, full of nothing.
A breath of life, passed on.
Though: Did she have a soul? Do I?
Where is she now? Will I see her soon? No thought.
Time passes.
She finds no soul, but knows a voice.
"There is nothing here."
Awake?
I hear you. Where are you? Speak, tell me.
Again, nothing.
Here, as there, nothing.
Empty space, filled by empty being.
United again, she knows that she knows nothing.

Pablo Gosse

The Tree's Closing Argument

I am tall I am big I am green I am strong
will I be here for very long?
My contribution to this land is it now in the
tree cutter's hand?

My leaves the sway in gentle breeze
My bark is hard and sturdy,
As I exhale the world inhales
Clean, fresh air I am glad I'm worthy.

I filter noise the paper make
am home for man and animal,
My roots are firm I take a stand
I'm sure you must now understand.

Recycling is the thing to do that I may
continue to contribute to every one upon
this earth who love the tree and know
it's worth.

Michael Alexander Sands

A Note To My Love

All I really want to say
Is I love you more each day.
Each time we touch
Love grows so much,
And when our lips meet and kiss
Dear one I'm lost in timelessness.
Words like joy cannot convey
The feelings I get from the things you say.
When we're apart
My life's so dark,
But when you're near
It's all so clear.
Darling dear my love I send
And let me say it will never end.

Carina Sawyer

A New Day

I arise still sleeping
    Must walk this morning

Start out slowly warm up a little
    Walk faster

Catch the beauty of a spider web
    Dew sparkling in the morning sun

Take a deep breath
    Smell a new day

Pass through the school yard
    Imagine the sound of children laughing
     A bell rings time to study
Walk a little further today
    Hurry home, shower's running, coffee's perking

Take a deep breath
    Smell a new day

Sharon Kueter

Autumn's Maiden

The summer has gone onto hibernation,
Until the warm spring winds coax it out again.
As I walk down the leaf-trodden path
I can feel Summer's elegant lady fading,
And the festive maiden of Fall approaching slowly.
The almost weeping trees are surrendering their bloom
To the whims of Winter.

Jessica Lauren Byrd

Fall And Winter

Fall has come, there is gold everywhere.
We are carefree and think nothing of the world.
It cannot harm us. We are young and innocent
Running down the well-worn street laughing, so alive.

Suddenly, a woman is lying there.
A man is stumbling and shouting,
"Get up, tell them you walked in front of me!"
But she does not move.

I look at her and she stares back, frightened.
I see it in her eyes. I notice her age and am relieved that she is
    not young.
Yet she continues to stare at me and I at her.
She has a family, I can tell, and now I am frightened for her.

The man has dumped can upon can away,
And fury rises inside of me.
Again, I look at her,
Unable to release my gaze for long.

Now many people have forgotten her,
Even those who saw her that day.
But I am now apart from them.
I will never forget that look and how winter came too soon for her.

Adrienne Duplessis

The Grocery Line

Scanning the aisles, I try to find
the fastest moving line.
When I choose one, the rest speed up
and mine comes to a stop.
The cashier yells "Price check, please"
or "I have a ninety two."
The wad of coupons that she reads
is like a paperback.
That kid in the cart drops the ketchup —
"Cleanup at register five."
But then at last that sweet refrain:
"Paper or plastic, Ma'am?"
I watch my cans and bottles packed quickly
...on my strawberries and eclairs.
Then that magic moment I've been awaiting:
"Have a nice day!"

Elizabeth Stacy-Hurley

Heart To Heart

Oh Lindsay, life was hard for you
Right from the very start
You came into this world so new
With a very complex heart

I don't know how this happened
And I'm so sorry that it did
You never let on that it bothered you
And we would clown around and kid

You were such a happy baby
I kept you close and near
You learned to stick your tongue out
And then smile from ear to ear

Four months wasn't long enough
We had so much love to give
But your little heart couldn't carry on
To sustain and help you live

Now my poor heart is broken
And I know will never mend
You were a part of my soul, my existence
This will be our beginning, not the end.

Lilian S. Carmichael

Sleep Becomes Death

I hear your fears,
I see your last breath,
As my finger pulls the trigger,
As I hear your Blood Run Through your veins,
As I feel your pulse seep through my fingers through your veins,
For you did not scream nor cry,
For you did not beg nor deny,
For you fell asleep before the end of your time.

Tasha Larson

Youth...

Old enough to be on my own,
yet young enough to come back home.
Old enough to have responsibility,
yet young enough to feel no pressure.
Old enough to work,
yet young enough to deserve time away.
Old enough to quit school,
yet young enough to go back.
Old enough to settle down,
Yet young enough to be restless.
Old enough to develop patterns,
yet young enough to search for something new.
Old enough to know a lot of answers,
yet young enough to keep questioning.

Marilyn Zuidhof Loenen

Gift Of Wings

Why is it God when I feel a need to be connected to my soul, it's
your hand I need to hold? Why is it when I feel sorrow, it's your
heart I need to borrow? Why is it God when I lose my way, you
send me your light whenever I pray? Why is it when my heart
becomes cold, you touch me and make me whole? Why is it God
when I feel life is too much too to bear, I turn around and you are
always there? Why is it when I feel overwhelming stress, I get on
my knees and suddenly feel blessed. I don't know why God you do
all these things. But one day God I would like to be an angel and
wear your wings.

Dale Pollard

Night Worker

After he leaves, she rushes into her bathroom,
Turns on her shower,
And washes herself vigorously...
As if speed can clean her completely.
Skin reddened by her scrubbing she dons a ratty old robe,
Goes into her kitchen, and finds the money,
On her table as it always is...
She puts the money in her purse,
Then grimaces and washes her hands in her sink.
She sighs and goes into the room,
Seeing the bed a mess, she makes it...
Turning back the corner invitingly;
The nicer the room, the quicker the job.
She gathers the cheap clothes,
Removes her robe...
Prods the bruise on her thigh,
A purple welt tinged yellow discoloring her white flesh;
She stifles a sob and dresses.
Not even an hour after he has gone,
She goes out, again.

Avrielle Riddler

Not Mine Anymore

What had happened to this child of his,
Whose nose had always wrinkled in bliss?
Two, then three, he had gathered her near,
Now her heart torn, he had fate to fear.

She, his little girl, playing him chess,
Now would leave him, she had to confess.
Her hero, her life, her love to obey,
Dear God, is it, already that day?

Silence besot him, would she compare?
Don't let her, please, it wouldn't be fair.
His heart filled with an awful dread.
As she waltzed through the door, don't, he said.

There's so much I haven't told you yet,
I don't want you, ever, to forget!
Live your life, sing your own special song,
Do this, and you will always belong;

To me, to you, to the love you chose.
I'll let you go now, that's how it goes.
Come back to me dear, if he's a cad,
Love you forever, bye now, your dad....

Hazel Rooney

Lost Loves

The sun drowns down beneath the comfort of the white
Just as coldness outlines the heart of the overturned society
Both digging down deep inside me.
Living amid the turmoil and among the grieving grandmothers
as they bury their tomorrow . . . Today!
Then little fingers trickle on top of the falling sun
Waving at the passing parade of a tank brigade
Unknowing that Mom buried their dad today.
The child smiles at this peaceful pissed off warrior
Completely unaware that his world died today.
For sorrow's bitter end has not a sweeter taste
in a rosebud's cup at year's end
Nor a frozen leaf that blows into spring
Frolics around and wonders if it can sing
will bring back a lost love.

Don E. Bottorff

Untitled

To the moms still caring for their young children,
To the moms who care for children who will never grow up.
To the moms who have lost their children to war,
To the moms who await the arrival of a child not yet born.
To the moms who feel as though they have failed,
To the moms who wait for a simple, sweet phone call.
To the moms who cry themselves to sleep,
To the moms who raise their children alone.
To the moms whose child has quietly slipped away.
To the moms holding a crying child of any age,
To the moms who need strength for one more day.
God bless you and keep you close to him
And may he fill you with the tenderness you need to give.
And may he give you the comfort of knowing your own success.
That you have fulfilled a special calling in life.
That you have given the start of life the chance to live.
That this world would have been nothing without your
    perspective, your spirit and your care.

Thom Verwys

My Little Cottage By The Sea

My little cottage by the sea — I dream, I dream.
When I escape in my mind I'm at my little cottage by the sea.

Small, cozy, and just for me.
Chintz, floral sofa, and big window looking at the sea.

It's not in the Caribbean or Down South — it's on our East or
West coast — where, though, I don't know.

I see myself standing in golashes, jeans and a thick warm sweater,
standing on a cliff with the wind and salt breeze blowing in my face
oh so nice, so calm, so relaxed.

I see myself sipping tea on my chintz sofa with my fireplace roaring,
my feet tucked under me with a good book in hand.

Every once in a while I look up and glance at the sea.

I see myself painting or writing — my children's stories —
I'm content.

My little cozy cottage by the sea!

Loraine Johns

This Land

I love this land, it's called America
for all the beauty that I saw.
Its mountain ranges rugged looks,
the rivers running swift.
The lakes and parks a pleasure, the waterfalls a treasure.
Pacific Ocean waves were beating
on endless shores, and sand so white
covered the dunes, a national pride.
The summit of Mt. Lassen, the view a special treat,
I could not help but feel the beauty at my feet.
The haunting ruins of Mesa Verde,
covered in a shrouded mist,
only to emerge a short time later,
seeing Cliff Palace sun kissed.
I heard Old Faithful rumble, before it spewed its plume,
of water, vapor, steam and mist, a truly wonderful artist.
And in the Redwood Forest, I felt so small and weak,
in awe of so much splendor, I let my heart surrender,
and carry me away with love.

Ingeborg Von Finsterwalde

Silent Morn

Still, silent morn, no shining light,
Good Friday black, oh dreaded night.
Our heads bent low, in tearful thought,
We think, remember, lessons taught.

In sombre quiet, we kneel, we pray,
As memories surge on this black day,
Safe in our hearts, Christ love we keep,
Our soul does mourn, we hurt, we weep.

Our minds drift back two thousand year,
Where on the cross, fell bloody tears,
On place of skull they nailed Christ down,
There echoed hammers, dreaded sound.

"My God forsook me," was his thought,
Had Lord, his Father, him forgot?
Christ gave his spirit, no more he fought,
As soldier for his coat cast lots.

To us a lesson Christ has told,
How on this day, this story showed
Upon the cross, his life he gave
For us, our sins, our souls to save.

Mary A. Solinger

Pain Inside My Foolish Heart

As I lay in my bed, when we are apart,
I feel pain, from deep within my heart.

A pain that hurts, I have to hide
A very sharp pain, from deep inside.

A pain my girl gave me so many times before,
But that pain, I'll feel no more.

As cold as ice, you have treated me,
But your turn will come, just wait and see.

If you think love and pain go hand and hand,
I think you should stop, and think again.

If you know about my pain inside,
You would leave me alone, you'd run and hide.

If you only know what I'm trying to say,
You would pack your things, stay away!

I will not be hurt by you again,
We played love's games, next time I'll win.

Michael E. Souders

Untitled

Reaching toward the starlit sky
You grabbed a piece of my soul
Holding it in your hands as you sat
Cross-legged on the floor.
I could see you pondering the thought of love
Gasping, you devour the evidence,
Making me a part of you.
And then the night we danced in the
forest, arm in arm, twirling, flowing,
The trees were so dense, I could not see.
A bright light shining suddenly breaks the
Tree tops into tiny pieces
As they shatter, they fall of the ground
Slowly . . . Slowly . . . Slowly
The first flake lands on my head, and the
next, and the next until they are dancing like
snow creeping onto my nose.
I open my mouth and let them land on my tongue.
I slowly, carefully swallow each piece.
Now you are a part of me.

Shannon Green

Untitled

   Death, the enemy and inevitable conqueror of life!
It joins us at the moment of conception, a joint adventure that
we can do nothing about;
   And yet, most people manage somehow to avoid its sting,
some for perhaps only hours, days or weeks, but most for
many months, even years;
   We are not, however, able to avoid the many attempts made
by death, as it marks us throughout life in the guise of
sickness, disease and strife;
   Yes, it's true, we spend our day upon this earth in denial of
our constant companion called death, wanting to make believe
that we alone are exempt from its call, yes, in denial that at
some point, it will take the lead and we must follow;
thus, would it not be wise, and comfort to the soul of mankind
to learn of death and acknowledge its presence from the very start?

Richard W. Ross

"Winter Of A Soul"

Have I not survived the winter of my soul,
Seduced strangers while fires burned,
Seen the shadows of my own reflections
And known summers to be not perpetual.

Who fractured my soul, that the winds of change
Blew or my fields
Which being left unploughed, became
Pregnated by winter's rape
Leaving no hallmark to fame.

The key shall turn to skeleton when autumn's
Leaves are crushed 'neath suppered boot,
For we crumble as toppled tombstones
Weathering in grip of decaying holdings.

Do not pray or weep for me at my crucifixion,
For I bequeath the burden of all
Mysteries unto thee,
So let not my epitaph read of agony but ecstasy,
For I travel now,
To a more forgiving place.

Helena Star Keddle

The Eyes

I was watching the door - I saw him enter - watching and waiting
for I knew not what.
His eyes raked the hall then coolly met mine
an odd feeling shivered my spine.

He stood with thumbs hooked in his belt loops, feet spread,
rocking back and forth on his heels.
His eyes were narrowed he looked unfriendly. For a second I
thought I saw his mask slip - saw shyness and fear shadow his face.

People at tables were talking and laughing absorbed in themselves
having fun - but no one else noticed him standing alone?
I sat to one side - wished he'd sit near me and maybe
let two lonely worlds become one.

He glanced again - barely stepped forward, but
his eyes flashed away. His mask hid his face.
How could he know what I had been thinking? He
sauntered past me and sat down alone.

He left by himself before the dance ended - minutes passed -
A white-faced man stumbled in (I sensed I knew who the boy was),
he said "come help - it was dark - I just run over some kid!"

Roxanne Marie Davies

To Die...

To die in one's arms
Is to leave your soul in their hearts
Leaving your sorrow
Your happiness, love and depression
Which you went through in the past
Not knowing to give your life a second chance.
But you went on to be free from the
hardships of life so soon
You went away to the far off future
That awaits everyone
No matter if we are strong, weak
Big, or Small.
Because I know in our hearts our
souls shall not surpass
And our love for each other shall
never die...

Diane Jean

Untitled

I love to walk the nature trails,
At Highlands Hammock State Park,
And enjoy the beauty of God's creations,
To hear again the song of a Lark.

I remember the Cat Walk of bygone days,
Across an over flowing Billy Bow Legs Creek,
And the cypress swamp hold fascination, as I gaze,
Or as I walk through its splendor primeval.

The dawn light brings deer out to drink,
While constantly alert, they began to graze,
Or when very early, as quick as wink,
Other of God's creatures appear in this maze.

Joyfully, forgotten memories stir, not to erased,
Of youth, and dreams that would bring me bliss,
As I remember another time and slower pace,
And I stop to smile, reflect and reminisce.

Patricia P. Nealy

The Inner Truth

Dark, uncanny clouds loom over the vastness of the sea,
as night's obsession for death grows stronger and stronger.
Tidal waves terrorize the coast's crying shorelines,
and the moon's shine starts to fade
as night's dreadful weariness drags on longer.

Thunder strikes and echoes chill the spines of the unwanted,
while lighting sucks life out of those who are called upon.
Her ghostly chants and haunting mantras call forth the powers of nature,
as the forces of Earth, Air, Wind, and Fire are gradually drawn.

Her eyes a shadow of balance with nature's fury,
as the winds of emptiness envelope bier with a phantasmic hate.
The flames in her eyes grow scorchingly higher and hotter,
as she battles destiny and the faces of her own fate.

Nature hears her cries and unleashes painful truths,
as the sands of time are desperately running to stand still.
Rain starts to pour down on her soul's lost innocence,
and the wish to discover her inner truth has been fulfilled.

Giuseppe Gatto

The Little Boy

The poor child was lost,
Between his parents he was lost.
Misery and abuse everyday,
Affected him in every way.

He was scared of coming home,
Was scared to be at home.
A decent moment with his dad,
Is what he wished he'd had.

Every single hit that he received,
Made him think why he had been conceived.
For him no one seem to care,
He came home cause there was no else were.

Nobody to turn to,
And nobody to talk to.
No friends there to be caring,
To him life had no meaning.

Why couldn't he be like the boys at school,
He felt like he was a fool.
This child could be anybody,
A friend of yours it could be.

Annie Pinet

"The Storm"

Wind rustling through the trees,
Sounds like a train rushing down the track,
Gush, gush, push, push
Swish, swish on it rumbles,
Bringing leaves about my knees.

Billows of clouds scurry along in the grey sky,
Chimney smoke bends over backwards
Unable to withstand the strain,
Suddenly the grey turns to black,
Down comes the pouring rain.

Blankets of water envelop the ground,
Puddles with endless rotating circles swirl around,
Needles of rain pierce the dark circles
Like an acher aiming for the target.

With a flash of lightning sparkling silver
Crooked evil and threatening,
Followed by a mighty crash and thud
Of the menacing deafening thunder clap,
Moving onward with an army of sound marching.

Carole Elizabeth Lawrence

The Days That Used To Be

If I try really hard and think far, far back,
I'm sometimes able to peer through a small crack,
Deep into the memory of my youth.
I was little then, so long ago,
And I was contented, that I know,
Even that time Billy knocked out my tooth.

Remembering can bring pain,
Or remembering can bring joy,
But now nothing is the same,
I've given away my last toy.

I can't believe it has been ninety years,
Since the warm summer day on which I was born,
I have had my share of smiles and of tears
And please, sonny, speak right into my ear horn.

Right now you're young, and you think you'll never get old,
Well I'll give you some excellent advice,
Because someday, you will be just like me.
You can sell everything, but onto this hold,
It's the one thing you have that has no price
Memories of the days that used to be.

Lee Richards

Make Me Worthy

Make me worthy of the spikes that they drove into your hands
Make me worthy of the blood you shed for me
For you died upon the cross so that I would not be lost
You gave your love; you gave your life;
just for me.

Make me worthy of the thorns that they placed upon your head
Make me worthy of each stripe that you bore
For you suffered, bled and died as they pierced your precious side
You gave your love; you gave your life; just for me.

Make me worthy of the trip that you took up Calvary's hill
Make me worthy of the shame you bore for me
For you opened blinded eyes that I might see and realize
You gave your love; you gave your life; just for me.

You gave your life of Calvary so that I could go free
You took my place upon that cruel tree
You could have turned and walked away
but for me you chose to stay
you gave your love; your gave your life;
just for me.

Belinda Quesenberry

Our World, Gone

The world around us is writhing in pain
the people are dying, children are crying.
What of animals is forests and plains,
the loss of tranquility and peace...they're slain.

The trees in the mountains as timber they fall
birds lose their homes, squirrels their domain.
What of the rivers so clear, filled with fish
now dark and troubled, all lost for gain.

What is this creation, our homing place
destroy, destroy, our minds gasping ill taste.
How smart we are to fly to the moon
while here at home...approaching doom.

The mass of humanity, spilling over in time
monsters on wheels..smoking down concrete lines.
The clock is ticking to the dance of wolves
howling and hungry, a shot rings out..Kill!

Now all is quiet, the forests are gone
no birds to sing, no beavers to build.
The rivers all slush, the skies cold...gray
that's the way it was when life went away.

Thomas W. Graham

To The Sun

I thought I saw myself go to the sun
I longed by day
A self undone.
The well of hope, and honour dry
To want near sun
Beyond a sky.

From within no sheltered cave my longing bring
A mourning grief
On angels wing.
Glory not, to ache alone
A sin to wish
Behind atone.

John R. Lebarr

The Chimney

Walls long since fallen with time
secret memories that will never decline.

Fevered children held lovingly on mother's knee
a medical cure consisting of a special tea.

Bitter winds that moaned on a frigid night
only to be staved off by a warm fire light.
A fireplace constructed of stone and clay
bequeathed assurance of another day.

Awakened to the aroma of baking bread
cause for grace from every bowed head.

Spring will emerge as all signs of winter pass
bringing singing birds, wild flowers and grass.

The old house served its purpose well
a wealth of memories mortal man may never foretell.

Reverent silence cries out in an ominous hush
attesting the still voices of days gone by....
as they attempt to return in a majestic rush.

This old house was so valiant, timeless and grand
bearing witness in memory forevermore to stand.

Marie Whitehead

Standing The Test Of Time

On the scale of life, you've got two ways to choose,
There is no in-between, you either win or you lose.
You gather information so you can make a choice.
You listen with your heart and answer with your voice.
You pick and choose, make a choice, there is no room for guilt:
And in the end you take a look at the kind of life you've built.
Your foundation should be sturdy, worth more than solid gold;
for all the things that it supports are all of the things you hold.

It your life structure cannot stand the biggest test of all;
then all you have, all you have done, will crumble and will fall.
This test that I speak of today is the weary test of time.
It takes the cake, it makes the breaks, puts rhythm in the rhyme.
If your structure cannot stand this rock-hard, flawless test;
then it shall be taken down, forever laid to rest.
But the hardest thing about this test is when you think you're done
you stand back, take a look, only to find you've just begun.

When you're through you'll use your tools to wipe away your fears,
and these three tools that you will use are blood, sweat, and tears
And the answer to the final test is all so crystal clear:
What you do is what you get with blood and sweat and tears.

Nick Rhea

God Is Master Weaver

While weaving life's pattern
God does try to teach you and me
He really allows us lots of freedom
Go fast or go slow as you can be.

Work can be done carelessly
As mistakes we oft' times make
Tho God expects the best from us
For the threads of life are at stake

One must grow in understanding
Know the depth of pain and sorrow
Find expressions in joy and health
To have harmony in the morrow.

Face up to all your responsibilities
Then stop treating life so casually.
For all those threads of life
Are woven into a pattern of destiny.

Helen E. Bean

Sun?

The rain and hail has just passed by,
And I, stayed, warm and dry.
Still, there's an ache in my heart and a tear in my eye,
for a servant of God, that I just let go by.
I'd seen him before and only smiled, so as not to offend,
not quite knowing if an offer of food could amend.

That was in winter, it was snowing, I dare say,
as I'm writing this ode, on a most sunny, warm day.
I'd seen him a second time, on a bench, I think.
I pointed him, out to my family, but he was gone in a blink.
At that point I knew what to do.
A kind word and a morsel of food, too.

I'd seen him a third time, two days before the storm,
as I was rushing home, which was the norm.
He was walking most slowly, on his way to no where.
Again I passed by, like everyone else, we didn't care.

As I turned a corner and sat at a light,
I started thinking about this man's plight.
I turned to go back, but it was too late to see,
If may be, He, could comfort me...

Donna Lohman

"Momma's Christmas Dream"

Twas' the night before Christmas, and the house was a sight,
And Momma was working with all of her might.
With dishes piled in the kitchen sink, Dad yelling for food, the kids for a drink.
The smell of turkey was in the air, packages piled in every chair.
With the tree to trim and pies to bake, How in the world, would she stay awake!
Suddenly, out of the sky so blue, Came the light of a sleigh, of you-know-who!
Ol' Santa himself did appear , to help poor ol' Momma dear.
He trimmed the tree and baked the pies, When suddenly sleep came to Momma's eyes.
Now Momma's sleep was very troubled Because all of her chores seemed to be doubled.
She dreamed the mice that lived in the wall, Were dancing and playing down in the hall.
The fleas had jumped from the back of the cat, For a game of ball, "who's up to bat?"
"I am" said the one, with a wart on his nose, So on this command, the rest of them rose.
And what a game they played that night, But the umpire caused a terrible fight.
Now Mamma yawned and turned and tried to get up, And stepped in the middle of Dad's favorite pup.
He yipped and he yelled and went into a dance, Mom grabbed her robe, Dad grabbed his pants.
They checked him all over for a bruise or a cut, There was nothing wrong with that little mutt.
They looked at the house, it was neat as a pen, It was time for Christmas Day to begin.
Christmas is a lot work it may seem, But Momma was glad it was only a dream!

Connie Rone

Memory Of The Sea

At night I go there to escape from everything
I notice the reflection of the moon dancing on the waters and wind-blow it sings
And the stars give off an iridescence more beautiful then the nightbefore
The moment I step my bare foot on the shore
It takes me away to nothing I've ever experienced before
I walk for miles through the thousand grains of sand
Then I reach down and touch the never ending sea with my hand
The sound of the ocean clear my mind and I soon resemble the mind of a sailor lost at sea
I become engulfed in the waves crashing upon me-but there is no fear
The sea- it whispers wind chimes in my ear
As they echo throughout my brain I feel the atmosphere disappear
A ghostly solitaire that whispers faintly I am alone
I still feel the cool wisps of night air
It caresses my skin and catches locks of my hair
Sweeping them away from my face so that I feel the dew-kissed showers of ocean-spray
Booming crashes are heard across the surface of the ocean shore-forever in a day
These are the beautiful times of the sea
That linger in my memory
And once again I am swept away by it all
As they echo through

Jennifer Ludwig

Blind Date

Filled with intrigue and romance, thank you for taking the chance.
We may never share blissful happiness, or even a simple slow dance.
But it's nice to know you were interested, even the tiniest little bit,
To take the time to trust a bold desire to come here with me to sit.

Although it is true we may learn naught of love and any deep feeling
With one short visit. What if our hearts are hypnotized and sent reeling?
Would it not be worth the effort to see what fate holds for you and me?
I want not to add complications, but give me a chance if it is meant to be!

So, first impressions are out of the way. It happens in seconds, so they say.
The damage is done and romantic thoughts may already be starting to play.
Please let me see you once again, if not for romance then for being a friend.
Drink now to happiness and joy, a toast that our meeting has a happy end.

Let not these words make me responsible for poor Shakespeare or bad rhyme.
It is just that I wanted to find some different way to thank you for your time.
The roses are for your courage and curiosity to meet me blind on this day.
If it is meant to be then many will follow (I hear my romantic heart pray).

David A. Minnich

Perfect Love

God grant perfect love
    the greatest of all,
With perfect love
    we cannot fall...

Give us faith
    for all human race,
Faith we need
    for our hurried pace...

Hope for all people
    when discouraged or blue
When our burdens are heavy
    we must look to You...

God grant us hope and faith
    but most of all love,
Something this world
    has too little of...

All these things
    we ask of thee,
But most of all
    let love rein free.

Helen L. Matthews

"Life"

Tick-tock,
sounds the clock,
as life continues on.

By and by
I slowly die,
as time seems to creep on.
I scream and scream,
and though it seems
my life continues on;

My screaming stops.
So does the clock,
while darkness swallows all.

I bow my head,
for now I'm dead;
the life I know is gone.

As my soul takes flight,
I see the light,
and how heavenly it gleams.

My soul rests,
as a heavenly guest;
happy now in heaven.

Darryl VanOudenhove

Mother

Mother
You confuse me
With your funny
Way of loving
Mother
I love you
So love me back
'Cause...
Mother
You confuse me
With your funny
Way of loving.

Bianca Sultana

Card Houses

I've shared this dream called life with you,
We took too much, and now we're through.
I can see now, my armour never shone that bright.
Maybe, after all, it was a trick of the light.
I've watched you drink to my defeat,
And swallowed deep of my loss, and conceit.

We've seen heaven, we walked through hell,
And on the other side, alone, I feel.
The light of heaven still shines in your smile,
The darkness of the pit has enslaved me for a while.
Each time I see you, it's a blessing, a moment of bliss,
Then each second alone becomes one long death's kiss.

Pain and sorrow bring strength so they say,
So why haven't I the strength to stay away?
How can I hope to ever love someone new,
When I still can't say no to you?
And even if I tried, and succeeded too,
A moment, alone with you, and we'd be through.

Philip Duperron

Missing You

My mother's father, My friend.
Remember the times we spent together,
now I sit missing you.

My comfort in trouble, my shoulder to lean on.
You used to give me such good advice,
now I sit missing you.

A healthy man, yet diagnosed with cancer.
I sat up nights weeping in prayer for you,
now I sit missing you.

The telephone rang, the news was broken.
Tears stung my eyes like an uncontrollable fire,
I sit missing you.

A man too young to die, yet God called you home.
Feelings of pain and grief overcome me,
I sit missing you.

Years have gone by,
Memories of you, are still placed deep in my mind.
I cry no more cause I know I will see you in heaven,
but still, I sit missing you.

Nancy Schwendemann

"Why?"

Why must we be so curious?
Why must we be so brave?
To stand up to a ten foot
Monster in a giant creepy cave.

Why must we climb the biggest, tallest things?
Why must we be the best?
Why can we see that we're
No better than the rest?

Why must we be the rebels?
Why must we be so different?
Why is it that we cover at
The mention of "who did it?"

Why must we do such things?
Have we no sense at all?
Can we stop for just a minute
before we take the great fall?

I can't understand this
but simply ask you "why?"
Why must we ask these things?
"Why?"

Rochelle Chavis

Poppies

Bright spots of color in the corn, soft fringes round the edge,
Where there, among the dark hawthorn, they grow, and so the fields adorn
　　With garnets in the hedge.
Likes rubies set in purest gold, they glow with vibrant hue,
So bright, so bountiful, so bold, with silky petals there unfold
　　And beautify the view.

Bobbing and dancing with the breeze, softly and gently, they
Like sailing ships upon the seas that fill our eyes, our senses please
　　Will with the breezes sway.
And seas of poppies overtake whole meadows painted red
Like dye that stains with crimson lake, they color in the whole landscape,
　　Like gems before us spread.

The brightness of their Summer skirts which in the gold fields nod,
Their frills and flounces soon deserts, to Autumn's fruitfulness converts
　　And leaves a seeded pod.
And then in Winter's iron hold each seed lies dormant, dead,
To wait for Spring in depths of cold and jubilantly then unfold
　　Once more in fields of red.

Jenny Dukes

The Divine Light

Oh God, you are the Divine Light
The irradiance of which shines in my heart
The glow of which warms me
The effulgence of which transmutes me
The brilliance of which illuminates me.

The transillumination of your light fills my soul
Expanding, overflowing into the worlds, spheres and dimensions
I think of you now - so divine a presence in my heart
So near - so near; you breathe your sublime breath into me.

I feel you coming closer to me
The expansion of you filling my mind
The wisdom, reality, perception, truth and understanding
Are all contained in this moment.

This sacred beam of light permeates the gloom
And I on a quest in the subtle realms
Found this golden pool of radiance
And I stepped in it to be near to you.

My heart is warmed in this blazing flame
And I am so innately glad
That you have become my companion on this holy path.

Luciene Azique

The Paradox of Birthdays

Glowing lights flickering for one soul every year,
Eternally signifying and counting away the years
and the lives.
The question of what to wish for
and the memories of the last wishes
which failed to hold true
drift annually through the untouched mind.
As the lights grow in number
and increase their intensity
they blind the feelings that were once there,
Only to crash through the embodiment
and the ritualness of the birthday as an idea
and turn the tide for another year.
And what happens when there is no one left
to relight the candles?
Birthdays are celebrated tragedies.

Stephen Potts

Saint James' Church Cemetery

Soft snow flakes
Alight, gentle as a feather,
Upon hard granite
Rigid stone sentinels
For those who here make their bed.
Christmas wreaths temper
The stern, silent, gray mien
Of the markers
With colors of white, green and red.

Each wreath guards the secret
Of a relationship which used to be,
Caressing the brief biography
On its peculiar stone
With a yearning for immortality.

Against the winter sky,
The church spire persistently points heavenward
Allegory of that apostolic word
For all to see,
O death, where is thy sting?
O grave, where thy victory?

Claude R. Foster Jr.

Pictures And Dreams

She sits in the corner of a solitary room,
Dreaming of things that should last,
Her fantasies have faded in a broken heart,
And all her tomorrows have died in the past.

Her heart is so full of agonizing pain,
As she slides away in tears,
Thinking of all the sad times she's had,
That seem like a million years.

All her hopes have shattered like glass,
Her feelings are all in vain,
Life is an ever changing destiny,
As she cries emotional pain.

Yesterday has come and gone,
There's nothing new to look forward to,
Looking at pictures of old memories,
Of dreams, that won't come true.

Susan Erika Robinson

A Christmas Ride

We hitched up the horse, to take a ride in the new sleigh.
With dad, mom, and a good
friend, Freda Gaye.

We covered up with a
blanket, marked with red, green, and gold.
As we traveled down the road
there in the pasture was a horse and her new fowl.

The sleigh bells jingle out good cheer.
The sound rings out that christmas is here.
A quick glance at dad's face, on his cheek is a tear.
Because in his mind he'd remember how much of
God's love he saw through out the year.

As we travel along it's getting cold.
So we stop at a place where hot chocolate is sold.
We get back home and we had a good ride.
Horses are stopped and we get off on the right side.

So if you get a chance to take a sleigh ride
Go look at the lights on your Christmas ride.

Jerry Randall

Lonely Moon

After twilight sets, and the stars shine bright, a majestic king comes out in sight. This regal giant dominates the skies, with the help of his thousand dark eyes. He keeps a midnight vigil over his many subjects of the night, who move slowly and cautiously as if in fright. But even in the midst of all this power and might, this great king stands lonely in the night. Alone he ruled for a million years, never showing his internal tears. The stars and comets beckoned his every call, while he stood proud and tall, but he never felt pride at all, for it was love that he wanted. Never feeling or seeing the warm, bright sun upon his massive self, he stayed dark and cold, and acted as if bold toward his true wishes and longings, too proud to let them be known, or to let his true emotions be shown.

His golden aurora shines luminescently in the night, showing outwardly the purity of his wrath and might. But never will his sadness be shown or told by his own, even after he has grown countless of eons in age, and he no longer has his fury and rage.
Alone the king stands, glowing proudly in the night,
Alone one moon stands, lonely in the night.

Mark Kuhta

The Summer Stillness of a Meadow

Love has come and gone as quickly as a shameless gust, aloft invisible wings, through the summer stillness of a meadow.

Regret perched high above the calm, awaiting the answer -
Denying the truth, swallowed in the past, longing the future.

Hurried thoughts rambling aimlessly within a grassy haven,
Probing the domain of the unknown to offer reason to the heart.

Alas more powerful, the mind triumphs, damaging the scenery - felling regret;
A thunderous torment severed, sends thoughts scurrying.

Pleasant memories drift, fade - as succession blessed with time -
Silently replacing

The Summer Stillness of a Meadow.

Craig Hemmerich

A Longing Heart

So desperate I am to partake
of your beauty.
To a restless soul, you breathe life
into me truly
I am strong at my weakest moment.
Touching me to my heart's content.
Of thee I know of no other
heavenly scent.
When we arise together our
two eyes shall meet
A joyful smile, a heartfelt blossoming.
We need not speak, for what
words can express.
Of loving spirit we long have suppressed.
Upon my divided chest ye shall lay.
As we comfort each other, from day to day.
A quickening pulse, a rising
temperature and a heart founded swell.
You unleash more emotion in me than
I dare not tell.

William R. Winston

Under The Waters

In well o' soul 'neath bubblin' waters
o' thought and world left a muffled noise,
seek you there for yourself and others
in lovin' brace stayed in blissful poise.

For love none there e'er as fancy suits,
nor need broken hearts for healin' there;
for planted there deep are nature's roots
in one braided weave o' lovin' share.

In depth o' mind 'neath the frothin' cool
where faintest kiss the lake and shore seem,
there dive you deepest the quiet pool
for time where commence the worlds to stream.

Who were you then 'fore night turned to day,
the time where commence the worlds to stream?
Who were we then, 'fore the mind's first ray,
which clothes the night whole in splend'rous dream?

> *Eric J. Gray*

Man's Disgrace

I held a baby in my arms
And looked into her eyes
Of all god's wonders in this world
I just then realized
The miracles bestowed each day
Since the beginning of all time
We accept so lightly -question not
Oh yes, it is a crime.
This tiny life so perfect
Reflects each person born
How many times has hate and hurt
A happy life has torn
From those most helpless in their need
For mother's love and care
No matter color, race or creed
I wonder how they dare
But each day an angry man will strike
No thought, nor care, no sorrow
A mother's dead, a child will cry
The pain to never end, as there is no tomorrow.

> *M. Grace Lutz*

A Man's Sonnet

Like a ray of sunlight piercing my heart
Akin to a fiery spear
My cold and trembling spirit's heated
As your beauty draws ever near

Naked we lay together, loose of the
Cumbersome shackles of a fettering world
Focussing only upon our coupling
Through space and time we're hurled

I celebrate your body, warm and firm
Electrifying to the touch
I rejoice in your soft moist petals
A flower capable of expressing much

When I am with you, our souls mesh,
Allowing you to be with me
So that we may release the children
In our hearts and rejoice for we are free.

> *Daniel Jody Moon*

Linda

Linda, you is like a first fresh of spring
just before summer about to begin

As the flowers, awakes from winter, sleep.
Your air breeze the gardens (Special) fresh smell so sweet.
Eyes, of hopes can see blue heaven. Smiling pleasant to be.
You is the one that makes Pleasant Joyful Sense.
I can see Bright vision of love that Right,
like a new born Happiness Taking Flight.
Linda, you awakes the thoughts you get to the heart.
they don't have no mind (Linda) just Smarts.
Linda you are A Winner.
For me there will be no other love as (Linda)
Linda, Because you is the (Best) Yet.
Why, the (Difference you Tells from All the Rest

> *Linda Dejan*

The Reflection I See

When I look in the mirror I see
A friend that has come to me
A friend of love, of faith and of hope
One of stories, of friends, laughter and jokes

But of this friend you see
Not one regret, in the reflection I see
Only tears of love and some of pain
A lifetime of devotion, a faith in God
I shall forever praise

I see a passion for life
Not for money nor gain
A giving soul of the timeless age

Not a gift too small
Nor a thank you someday's
But always a kind word
And the tears shall fade

For in the reflection, I see
Is the gracious beauty
Of my mother in me

> *Nikki de'Layne Grandstaff*

"Anthropology"

The subject anthropology brings all human need to mind
And certain terminology highlights help that one can find.
Important is pathology in all illness and disease
And turning to neurology some can find their way to ease.
Men study criminology, ask why crime in life will start,
Seek answers through psychology, find the truth only in part.
From evil demonology people really need to turn
To discover Christology, as of Jesus' love they learn.
Through genuine apology can come God's forgiveness true,
Real cause for man's doxology, praising God for mercies new.

> *Donald J. Price*

Growing Old - Gracefully?

I always looked forward to growing old
Gracefully, or so I was told;
To command the respect
Old people have earned,
But the whole world has changed
As, sadly, I've learned!

You have to be slender, attractive and hip —
No matter how tired,
Appear full of pep!
Well, I'm from the "old world"
And plainly I see
In spite of the "moderns"
I'd Rather Be Me!

> *Lynn Jordan*

The Lord Also Snows

Thus says the Lord:

I come to you as snow,
Living water blowing where I will,
On the wings of the Spirit.

I come to you as snow
In the quiet of the night
For the beauty of the new morn.

My purity feeds your deepest springs,
And fills the wells from which you dip The source of life.

I cleanse away the sins of iniquity,
And cover your folly With a blanket of purity.

Who can face my brilliance in the light of day?
Who is not overwhelmed by my generous abundance?

But woe betide to the unprepared,
To those who do not know my way,
Who will not heed my prophets.

I come to you gently in my season, In beauty unsurpassed,
A beauty of consequent magnitude.

I hide not my coming from you,
Hide you not from my coming.

Phillip A. Ross

Do You Know Me?

"Do you know me?" I said.
I'm the little girl you loved and taught things to.
I'm the curious shadow who asked millions of questions you calmly
    answered.
I'm the one you sang to and bounced on your knee after work.
    Heavy boots beside the kitchen chair, still warm.
    Supper's aroma making our stomachs growl.
Stepping out of the old Ford truck, smiling ear to ear with a bag of
    candy and a huge hug just for me.
    Clothes smelling of freshly plowed earth.

"Where have you gone?" I said.
Blue eyes staring, puzzled.
Hair white as snow.
Withered hands that once carried buckets of feed to hungry cattle
    and lifted me onto the backs of fat ponies.
Bony arms once rock hard that held me tight, riding on noisy
    tractors through sweet hay scented fields.

"I'm still here Dad. I wish you could remember me," I said.
More childhood images flood my mind as I gaze helplessly at him.
Thin and pale.

Could this be the father that loved me so?

Alzheimers, I hate you.

Eve Dalton

Grandmother

Her name and dates are chiseled on the stone
    That stands beneath the shrub above her head,
We know she didn't cry - did not bemoan
    The hardness of her toil for daily bread.
Her children numbered ten, all born at home,
    The youngest one asleep at her still side,
Her days ticked on, timed by a metronome,
    The dreams she had of life ungratified.
If she'd but known the future yet to come,
    Would she have married him who brought her here?
A man as mean - a man as quarrelsome
    As grandfather - he had to domineer,
And yet, I can't lament the life she chose,
For from the shattered pieces, I arose.

Wilma H. Lewis

Wait For Me

Love of my life, you are now gone
so I am left alone once more.
The minutes, hours and days pass
in a mindless blur until I am sure

You are really no longer here,
and I must face the rest of my days
without your laughter, comfort and cheer
to guide me in life's endless maze.

I wonder where you have gone,
is it really a better place?
Do you still feel all the emotions
which drive the human race?

A place where there is no suffering,
no torment, no torture, no pain...
only music, unconditional love and surrender
to the Master force who has nothing to gain

From the constant turmoil and strife
we feel in everyday living,
wait for me my love, until our souls are
joined in a world that is all forgiving.

Jan Goodwin

Loving Memories

If God should grant that I grow old, oh what a blessing that would be,
For I shall set and rock away and dream of days that used to be.

I'll wonder back when as a child and live my life anew,
If I should make some changes Lord I know there be but few.

I know the ways of growing old with feet that stagger out,
the steady hands that use to hold will scatter thing about.

The eyes that used to read God's word they now no longer see,
The ears that used to hear each sound they now are deaf to be.

And when I have live my life anew awhile in my rocking chair,
help me not to be afraid to know you are always there.
And if my love one they forget, my rocking chair and I,
help me not to grumble Lord and neither let me cry.
For it's then I'll know from with in my heart that I a burden be.
Bend low dear God and take me home to be at rest with thee.

Helen Link

How Did He Know?

How did he know?
The setting sun over a green covered mountain
The song of the bird
Such a fragrance only flowers could bring
How did he know?
Salt air, crisp clean...Sweet
Water...let us dive and play
Green green grass to roll and get dirty
How did he know?
A pat on the dogs head
The stroke of the cats tail
A jump or two of the frog
How did he know?
After a hard days work a nap under a tree
The smell of Sundays dinner in the air
The call of mother to come home
How did he know?

James R. Kerr

Book Review

Reading is part of your life

Read a book
  I am giving you advice.
  Reading is very, very nice.
  I ordered a good book.
  Which someone already took.
I said, oh well, at least I got another book which is bright.

  Read a book or two,
  Which won't make a flue.
  Start with "The Rice."
  Then read about the mice.
  And it won't make you feel blue.

  Please go to the library
  Because there you can see books.
First go to ask.
  Then you won't have to look and look.

    Auret Esselen

Mommy's Gift

Such love and closeness the feelings of need,
To know it began just from the first seed.

Into someone special just from the start,
And to know no one can pull you two apart.

Having a baby is special you see,
Them growing up looking like daddy and me.

Teaching them what your Mama taught you,
To know you're a good Mom and there are very few.

And to know when they are hurt you're always there,
To share a bond none can compare.

To take care of them good times and all,
To know it all started before they learned to crawl.

A baby made out of love and caring
A special gift for two to be sharing.

To raise a life in your own special way,
And to know in your heart they'll grow up someday.

Enjoy and love what was given to you,
And to know one day they will also love you too.

    Linda Hernandez

Oh Little Baby

Oh little baby so innocent and sweet
Rooting so close to your mom trying to find
That familiar heartbeat
Needing a bond only a mother can give
Gotta adjust in this climate where you came to live

Oh little baby so innocent and sweet
Before your life gets started you must learn defeat
Even before your first breath
Your mother has given you death
She's has given you AIDS
You're just another mistake she's made
No matter if from sex or drugs
You'll soon just be a memory of kisses and hugs

Oh little baby so innocent
You could have made a life complete
So many lives you have touched
You've been loved so much
You never asked to be born
You never asked to be here
In your coming and going you make heaven seem so near

    Doris Hall

Untitled

  As darkness falls on this nite, the moon hides her
face from sight, not to see a terrible fright.
  Horror befalls one who did betray, now, he has
seen his last day. In his life he did play, fore knew
he not that he would pay.
  Walled up alive in a basement room, this will be
his final tomb. Too late he learned what danger
loom, that led him to this ghastly doom. Ten feet
wide and three fives thick, with its archway sealed
up with brick. And to escape hath he no trick.
  To defraud he did devise, this hast led to his demise.
Long ago he sowed bad seeds, and he now loathes those foul deeds.
As he yells his desperate pleas.
  To scam and scheme was his delight, now he
screams with all his might. Honest dealing did he
negate, now he hast learned much too late, that
this would be his final fate.
  His best friend's lover thought he so sweet,
he beguiled her with his deceit. Now his destruction is complete.

    Augustus Rolfe Garton III

This Land America

For this then the hour
Of peace and hopes of the many, the care
For the free whatever the undoings
Whatever the course of justice is a calling:
This grand canyon that never die of featureless actions
Where the weak will not die in vain
And the hopefuls shall have their simple stories told
Or smile a little longer;
This Niagara Falls in ceaseless flow of hopes
For the young and old, rich or poor.
For this land America,
The prudent and pride of Liberty will lives in History
Where the sweet rhyme of the bell will be told forever
In the hot summer days of New York
And Juliet is in the arms of her true beloved,.
And the pompous fairy tale paces of Hollywood
Is in every child's mind. The rock and roll
Embraces the sons in togetherness or, in uppermost
Quality, meritorious quality under the sun.

    A. L. Junid

One-Some

The wind blows fresh and the leaves all rustle,
The sun casts long shadows in the yard.
Night's coming on so I must hustle,
Mother Mocking Bird is there on guard.
The music is soft and good, as always,
Everything is normal, and yet
I feel no pleasure as on other days.
You're gone and I can't seem to forget.
I fidget, I bathe, I smoke,
I review the places I could spend the evening.
I remember how it was when I awoke
and it really took some believing —
That whatever I do today, it will be alone,
And tomorrow and the next day, and the next.
I guess from now on till I turn to stone
I'll miss you terribly, and that's the text,
This being apart is harder to take —
Not easier, as the years roll by.
So I'll read my book and fake
The illusion you'll soon be here. At least I'll try.

    George D. White

Repetition

...Of the hellish kind
shrinks time
stuck in closure
steals the mind.

Mired in the morass of life un-replenished
We are lost to abundance — love affluence.

Omnipotence of power is an illusive obsession
   and unwillingness to relinquish control
   to the wellsprings of benevolence.

This vicious cycle
carves fine vice furrows
deepening the grooves of insanity
   dissociation with reality
hampering the transformation of repetition
   for mind and soul expansive networkings.

Creativity is unleashed in all its glory
   if culled out of true source not infamy.

Mary Angela Nangini

Grandpa

It was his time
The body weakened by years of fulfilling life.
The eyes blurred by beautiful memories.
The ears numbed by words of love.
It was his time to go to a place where beauty far surpasses;
hunger, poverty, and hurt.
It was his turn to sit at the side of his God,
and absorb all the knowledge of his being.
The time will come when we will join
in harmony and love once again.
As for now we shall be content
knowing he is surrounded by Heaven.
Where the eagles fly on wings of gold.
The flowers bloom and never wilt away.
The compassion of others never sours,
and the love of those he left behind never leaves his heart.
It was his time, and though a void is left behind, our memories
linger and our love grows stronger.
For he is watching over us, just as we have watched over him.

Brooke Ann Bunten

They Pay Us To Be Poor

They pay us to be poor, categorize us in work,
to make us look at one another like dirt.
'Nough of us don't even know pant from skirt
but I know what I'm worth
I'm a human being, my heart is pure and clean.
Who tell them say to turn me off the seen.
True 'nough a them eat pork and beans,
that's why they be acting so mean.

True you're earning a dollar, I'm earning a quarter, that's
why you're acting like you're better
Soon or later the unseen turn the chapter, then you gonna remember
Not because you went to college, think you're intelligent more than me.
Not because you're driving a fancy car, think you're better than me.
Not because you're in a position, think you're secure more than me.
Who the hell are you, to come disrespect me!

Dave Sinclair

Alone In The Grass

Leave me alone in the grass,
Leave me be in silence, in the peace of loneliness.
The great inspiration of the "pseudo" nature has such
a powerful effect upon the young scops and thespians,
Such actors and players of words hold much brigand power.

Leave me be, in my rest on the grass,
I shall pretend to fly and glance down atop all
the wondrous spectacles of man; I will be nauseous
I will hurl my spirit down upon the cities of the brave
and I will flush from the forests all of his degradation.

Leave me be as I fall asleep in the grass,
for I have caused an acre of land to replow and replant.
If I take such a credit without first sharing my
Strength, which is weakness for this time, then I am a bard,
A master poet myself, with all the answers to all the questions no one has.

Leave me be as I become a seed in the grass.
I will fertilize the future forests with orchids and meadows.
I can only hope, as I lay here all wasted and decayed, that
I shall become a pawn, to be used with precision and care.
I thank thee, oh Lord above, for my burial plot here, in the grass.

Jason Matthew Hollingworth

I Am What I Am

Life cannot demand of me something I am not.
It can only ask of me what I am.
My destiny is not held in my own hands.
I must receive form life before I can give to life.
I cannot bring forth what I do not have.
I must try to understand my own soul.
I must not deceive myself but be honest with myself.
I must have courage.
   Courage does not come from a cowardly mind,
   Yet there is cowardice is every courage.
I must be faithful. Faith does not come from doubt,
   Yet there is unbelief in every faith.
I must have love. Love does not come from a cold heart,
   Yet there is hostility in every love.
I must be watchful. For there is weakness in all strength.
I cannot pretend that I am strong,
But must acknowledge and accept my weakness,
Making my weakness my strength,
In passion and despair I ask
To be only what I am

Jane Hollis

Spirits

In a forest dark and daunting
Is a house most hexed and haunting
Where spirits wrought from long ago have seeped into
   its walls and floors;
Deep within these specters loom
Amid the all-pervading gloom
And conjure morbid memories as shadows stir in corridors.

These apparitions lodge and dwell, their incantations cast a spell
Of unremitting permanence, defying any apocalypse;
While decades pass they staunchly brood
And magnify the somber mood
As phantoms gather in this den where afterlife shall not eclipse.

So mystical, this fleshless life,
So full of woe, yet free from strife,
These restless souls that wander forth, drifting on,
   shall never die;
So powerful, and yet so weak,
The solace that in vain they seek
Shall keep their deathless prowling strong while man ignores
   their baleful cry.

Nancy Solum

In The Doorway

My love stood in the doorway near our bed
where I lay watching. Today he'd swim alone.
The room behind him glowed with summer-red;
his back-lit image lingered when he'd gone.
Each time I closed my eyes his form would gleam
bright orange, red and crimson; but his stance
a silhouette, never changed though it would seem
to drift across my mind's eye in a dance.

Like a child's experiment in school — memorize
a brightened image, trick our sense to see
what was no longer there. Our shuttered eyes
revealing to ourselves alone, the imagery.

The sun-draped man is gone, the doorway bare
just memory's photo of him standing there.

Kathleen M. Hill

What Every Woman Knows

On a June night, the lady of the lake walks
with gathered flowers at her heart and
holds the keys to the world in her expectant
motherhood and ponders
the nature of physical reality and the
origins of what every woman knows
about pure wisdom and
natural history.
She critiques true reason and decides
to take action by night
and paints the history of the
world
in colors of the republic and pins
the origins of safety to
her life
and names it all
apple
pie.

Sharie Sauve

God

Is God real is He dead
is He roaming in my head?

Is He a figment of my imagination
is He a martyr, is He a maven?

Is He real, is He fake,
is He the baker that baked the cake?

Did He add carbon with a little sage
is it His fault that we have a fate?

Is He controlling us like puppets
or is He giving us free will, not like a Muppet?

Some are weak, some are strong,
some have envy — which is wrong.
God is all of what we'll be,
ruler of the universe, maker of the trees.

Ari Kronen

Dreaming

It is late, and I lay on my bed listening.
The song, "At the End of the Road" plays and I listen.
And I dream and wait patiently for him.
When will I know if he's the one?
How will I know that I'm looking deeply into his eyes?
And I still wonder and dream.
A dream that will one day come true.

Abigail Ann Taylor

Unconditional Love

I love you more than you can imagine,
And pray for you everyday;
You are so important and special to me
I never want you to "just go away."

I always feel comforted when I look to the sky,
And see you there twinkling
Makes my heart seem to fly.

I have an unconditional love for you,
That's deeper and stronger than ever,
And hope with all my heart and soul,
We'll be best friends forever.

I want you to know
That you are never very far,
For you are my special star.
Yes, you are; yes, you are.

Mary L. Erbes

Raphael Sapphire IV

In Genesis, we are admonished to eat not
Of the fruits offered by members of the tree
Of knowledge of Good and Evil.
Those ancient Gods and Devils of Olympus,
Those Fallen of Paradise, who would reign over man.

In Revelations we learn why, we must eat not.
The Seven Lamps, tools of the Gods and Devils,
Have alternately illuminated and enflamed the world
With their psychology of religious philosophy
And their expedience of political ideology.

However, the One with hair white as snow,
Will soon extinguish those seven lamps,
For ignoring the prime directive of Genesis.
In their blind ambition to rule, all have fallen short
Of the glory and creating a just society.

Knowing the Gods and Devils have failed so miserably,
That so many innocents stand in harm's way,
Is it too late, even in this eleventh hour,
To return to the beginning and the wisdom of the Mind
Which created and still governs the Alpha and Omega?

Edmund Ralph Wright

My Little Light

If it's anything I want to be,
It's a light to others that they may see.

With darkness shining all around,
there is light to be found.

A cheerful hello can light the way,
of some lost soul who's sad and gray.

A smile can give a young person hope;
It may keep them from drugs or dope.
My little light has got to shine.
On young and old of every kind.

If I cannot light the way,
What's my purpose here today?

I won't go through life and whine
I'll just let my little light shine

Willie Mae Crisp

Avoiding Reality

Don't wanna know who died or
how many.
Don't wanna hear who's president
of what country.
Don't wanna see what race is
seeking refuge.
Don't wanna weep to another
terrorist attack.
Don't wanna hear of a natural disaster,
or of Ebola and AIDS spreading much faster.
Don't wanna know who died or how many,
Just wanna lock up my door and go to bed.

Mary Hevi

The Cage

Why is it when you live a life of freedom
Those around you want to cage you back in?

Do they feel their own bars and think it's security?
Is there a part of themselves that want the same thing?

They want me to question the freedom I have.
How do I justify breaking their rules!

What was the purpose the laws were given?
Are they to protect us? From what, ourselves!

But if I am not my own but am God's alone
He is my protection, I'm free from the law.

Which is more glorifying to the Creator?
A life of bondage under the law
Or a life of freedom living through Him?

Elizabeth Winters-McNabb

"To Balance The Equation"

Where am I going?... or had I been?
Who's to know what's out and what's in?
The "Big bang": Explosion / implosion...how do you fare?
It must be both as were not yet there.
Gravity, electric-magnetic, strong and weak forces...and
    Just what is your query?
Is there really a "Unified field theory"?
As most we see is mass in relation.
Where does energy dwell on the other side of the equation?
And now I'm traveling near the speed of light.
My insides are out and my body's packed tight.
I keep moving faster as my mass increases.
Swallowed by a "black hole" and pulled to pieces.
Now you might say I'm all over the place.
Bonding the elements of time and space.
Thirty billion years have passed in less than a year.
And I'm wondering if I'll ever get out of here?
For up is down and in is out.
It's hard to explain what I'm talking about.
And now there is peace and goodwill among men but wait a minute
...then?

Daniel Rolland Bastian

Nuptial Hymn

Awake dear old heart and celebrate
Two young hearts now beat as one.
Blessed beneath a canopy
Of forest green ferns
And sweet blooms of white tropical orchids.

Gently dear heart let go.
For he has found someone
To love and cherish
Now,
And, for all Eternity.

Teresita E. Croft

You
Dedicated to my husband

You are the aroma of hash browns, crisping on a cozy morning's stove.
You are an honest book full of wonderful paragraphs,
    a thoughtful letter from an old dear friend.
With the last stroke of my brush, You are the painting complete.
You are the song that lifts my spirits, my inspiration,
    my passion, my most precious companion.
You are a waving field of yellow mustard and the breath of
    cool mountain air, fragranced with pine and spruce.
Like a fog embracing a lazy fishing village, thoughts of You blanket my soul.
When You leave my side, my heart aches,
    but upon return I feel a moment of mysterious joy.
You are a warm, soothing bath after a long distance run.
You are the sunset, which appreciates all the secrets of the day.
You are a comforting shoulder in the darkness, swaying back and forth,
    like a mother soothing her child, as water relieves a thirst.
You are a supportive bed with freshly pressed sheets,
    and passionate love on a stormy summer's eve.
When strangers pass I perceive your face,
    because You are the earliest thought
in my morning and my latest thought at night.

Sharon Bells

The Elephant

I learned one thing I never knew
while at the San Diego Zoo.
The great grey beasties whom we see
in zoo, in circus, on TV,
are females — each and every soul.
The male, it seems, resists control
and runs amok with fearsome noise
that terrifies both girls and boys.
The keeper said they have just one
out in the wild where he has fun
and does his level best to see
he leaves a line of progeny.
    This should have come as no surprise.
Men are the same in any guise.

Kathleen A. Jortberg

The World

The dawn comes up ere the moon has set —
To bring upon us another day, and yet,
The bitter picture of the one just flown — Pervades our memory,
and has not gone.
The dawn when men wake to find: Another day, and yet, they
are blind.
Blind to see that as they toil, — their lives around their necks do coil,
And squeeze the very blood of men to the earth upon which
their lives depend.
They kill and tear, and rob and ravage —
With cunning and brutality so cruel and savage —
It does my very spirit in.

With a slyness of lust brought to bear — we cannot resist them
as they tear
Our very souls from out our selves — as deep, deep within us
they delve, and soon,
Soon is left ne'er but a shell.
And ere the day is flown, the moon comes up to hide our scorn.

And once again to sleep we go — to hide our faces and
thoughts of woe.
As once again the clock turns round, and ere we wake we are
once more bound.

Jacob R. Raitt

Irises

When I dug up the fat bulbs, I knew
That I had a prize worth keeping;
And I dreamt of the violet and blue,
But lo, I had never been sleeping.

Then I took them and gave them some earth
In a place that was flattened and worn;
And I dreamt of the rain and rebirth,
But lo, I am already born.

If not for the welcoming land,
What more did I have to beseech?
And I dreamt of a tired, old hand,
But lo, she is far out of reach.

The irises never did grow
In that place they were helpless to be;
And I dreamt that they never would show,
But lo, they now grow inside me.

Joshua David Baimel

In My Thoughts

In my thoughts,
Are the people I love most;
People I cherish and remember.
In my thoughts,
Are all my wishes that will soon come true;
My hopes and dreams come alive.
In my thoughts,
Are puzzles that are starting to form pictures;
Will it be someone I remember?
In my thoughts,
Are childhood secrets that are yet to be discovered;
Secrets that still burn high that want to be remembered.
In my thoughts,
I think and dream about tomorrow or maybe today;
Things that are beautiful and magical.
In my thoughts,
Are prized memories;
That will always be...
in my thoughts

Marilu Flores

Love Is...

Love is something on the bough of a tree?
No - love is a feeling so close to me!
Love is a substance you can get when you please?
No - love is a mutual wave on the seas!
Love is something millions can buy?
No - love is a fantasy high in the sky!
Love is a whale who frolics in the sea?
No - love is a passion most desired by me!
Love is a relationship which never lasts?
No - love is a feeling the atmosphere casts!
Love is a picture upon a wall?
No - love is a disease that controls us all!

Crystal Niskasari

Our World

Spinning on its axis slowly round and round
In the beginning it was perfection
It was rare and quite unique
There for all of us to use what a treasure to be found

It gave to us the air we breathe, the water that we drink
The soil to grow so many crops for the food we eat each day
It cared for us through all seasons in a very special way

So why have we in our carelessness taken more than we should need
We have destroyed such beauty with our lustfulness and greed
We cared not for those to come in later years as we planted human seed

Oh mighty Creator I stand before you and say
Forgive us of our ignorance give us one more chance to mend our ways
Let us save our one and only world
For yet another day

Ruby Jenkins

Untitled

Hello, Mr. Snowman! Where did you get your hat?
My oh my! You sure look good in that!
In the house behind you,
With candles burning bright
I hear voices of children
Laughing with delight.
I see gaily wrapped packages
All around the tree.
I see mom in the kitchen
Busy as a bee.
I see a child come to the window.
"Here's daddy!" He cried.
So goodbye Mr. Snowman
It's time I go inside.
But wait! Mr. Snowman.
Please excuse me for staring.
But I want you to know,
That's my hat you're wearing!

Juanita Vaughn Burger

Eve's Children

Some day I shall walk proud and free,
I think it's called Eternity.
I'll walk without a crutch of wood,
No wheelchair ramp for me!
No guide dog treads beside my hand,
My ears, unstopped, are free.
Polio shall not me enthrall
I shall know green from blue,
Words shall not dance upon the page,
My head shall know things true.
There'll not be several minds in me,
My brain and body whole,
No C.P., M.D., C.F. shall ruin
My daily casual stroll.
No job denied because I'm lame,
Or deaf or cannot see,
Some day we'll all walk brave and proud...
This life? Or in eternity.

Woody MacAllison

"Night Walk"

When it's dark and late at night
and the moon is shining and still,
I look up and see the stars shining bright
and listen to the call of the whippoorwill.

I walk silently on the path in the woods
straining to hear any noises around me,
listening, and shivering as I pull down my hood,
the wind is whispering around peacefully.

I hear the owl call me far-away
and know it's time to go home.
Starting on my way,
I stop and remember I'm alone.

Up head I see the well-lit house,
I shout for joy and begin to run,
calling greetings to my cat, Mouse,
glad that my night walk is done.

As I lay snuggled in bed,
looking at the moon shining bright,
I pull the covers over my head
and whisper to the world, "good night."

Camille Mendez Williams

Childhood Tor

There upon a tor so high, where I'd always go and wander around,
To see the animals I loved, taking natures hand, every precious sound,
T'was a steep tor, took a while to reach the top,
Was strong, solid, gave me a secure feeling in my heart, as did my Pop,
While climbing, the sun shining over head, the cooling breezes blowing,
T'was like the warmth of his smile, which brought a good feeling growing,
The tor was high, standing straight and tall,
Like my dad, was full of life, then I'd hear his call,
Then running as fast as I could down that beautiful hill,
Till by his side, still panting, I'd be standing still,
I can see those huge rocks on that tor, loving them with all my heart,
When sitting upon them to rest before going along my way, of me
    they'll ere be a part,
As like those rocks my dad was strong, upon him I could lean,
His strength to help me through a problem where ere I was down,
Like the sun his love was warm, as those cooling breezes, was ere around,
All these precious thing will ere be the greatest part of me,
Forevermore those memories of yesterday, 'twill be,
When he came in the door, that look of love for me upon his face,
Like that beautiful tor, from my heart, mind, time will never erase.

LaVerne A. Kerkoski

A Day In The World

A day in the world shouldn't have to be
To make up to hunger and poverty
To wake up and hear on the morning news
Someone was shot, robbed or abused

You shouldn't have to hear a child died on drugs
because they met a street-like thug.
You shouldn't have to hear, someone died in a crash
because someone was stoned, or totally smashed

You shouldn't have to hear there was a fight
With a knife, with the end results someone
lost their life.

So...wouldn't it be wonderful to wake
Up today,
And hear the newsperson have nothing to say.

Linda L. Dallas

I

Teetering on the Charles Street subway rails
Between wide wooden slats and polished steel,

Stepping between broken glass, rusted nails
Holding gravity, I walk toe to heel.

Bearing the blue weight, a sky descending
Through straight white panes, and open bedroom blinds,

Faint shadows rise, lay like stripes ascending
To blanket you with the horizon line.

Led to rooftops piled high with winter's
Last speech, we overlook damp concrete streets

Left to dry as a new season lingers
For a time; like your complete body sleeps

In hues of blue and green assuming spring,
Eager with soft brown earth spread for morning.

Danyelle Pearson

Welcome Me

As I give you an expression, warmth, a
mind that cannot be copied nor imitated
Love me
As I give you the sights of delightful
surroundings, the softness of sound soothing
the mind - serenity
Forgive me
As I give you only a short while, for death
Is stronger than I and I only exist for
a limited time.
Please love me or let me love you

Sharon Lee Malas

Children

Children, let them be the sparkle in your eye.
Let them be the 'thing' that makes your heart beat
Watch them in their slumber. See their quiet
innocence as they dream of sweet memories. When
they awake, take them in your arms, hold them close
and feel the love in their little arms as they hug you
back. As they grow older, help them to live and
enjoy the many joys of each year. Let them know you
love them. Tell them "I love you." Such sweet words
to grow up with. Give them confidence to become
their own person. When they aren't children
anymore, still take them in your arms, tell them "I
love you." If you're blessed with grandchildren, let
them be the sparkle in your eye. Let them be the
'thing' that makes your heart beat. Tell them "I love you."

Lisa Bernier

David's Space

Grasped from our time in an instant,
Handpicked by God, like a blossom from his garden.
A bloom,
Whose petals would open and spread each day,
To greet the rays of sun or the drops of rain,
Like open arms,
Ready to embrace each minute ticking by,
Like it was his first minute,
Or his last.
Where is now, the sparkle of those eyes,
Eyes that spoke of zest and zeal.
Why now, is the laughter so silent,
That only our memories can stir and replay.
Memories stowed away in a special place,

Reserved and remembered,
as David's space.

B. L. Lumley

The Fossil

The beetle wandered wayward
Over the weary weathered stone.
The fossil figured faintly,
Is it looking for its own?
I've had one trapped for eons out,
But time's changed my furrowed brow.
Winds wash will and water runs by
Will the beetle find out how?My Dear Heart
On this day you were loaned the greatest of treasures.
Another little being gifted to you for awhile.
In this silver heart you can hold dear to yours her image,
to always remember how short time is and how grand the gift is!

Alice I. Arsenault

West Virginia, My Home

When I think about living other places and
let my mind wander and roam,
I'm reminded to count my blessings
of all the things I have here at home.

Here in West Virginia you can walk in the hills for hours and hours,
and gaze upon the beauty and smell all the different kinds of flowers,
the mountains, the valleys and all the beautiful sights we can view.
The early morning sunrise and the grass covered with dew.

I love to stroll in the parks and feel the wind's gentle breeze,
See the many kinds of birds and hear woodpeckers in the trees.
Why would anyone want to go any other place to fish?
Here in West Virginia you can catch about any kind you wish.

When I think about all the treasures that I can call my own,
I think about West Virginia and the place I call home.
And if God lets me live a long life, I hope he'll let it be,
Here in the hills of West Virginia where I know God walks with me.

Delores Snow

Whisper

The silence...
    in the end, it feels like a scream.
Some things can't be taken back,
    and some hurt most if left unsaid,
When they sit in silence, growing cold
    and lie in the darkness under your bed.

Some gifts are really a debt in disguise,
    when the one who gives only really knows how to take away.
A few truly don't know better
    but the rest have only ceased to care,
and all anyone wants is more than they really deserve
    (although they'd never admit it).

Was I foolish, to alter the order?
    was that my crime?
I can't sleep anymore
    because the cold hurts too much.
and I can't escape the whispering voice;
    "Your crime," it tells me, "was love."

Heath Allen Reynolds

The Great Battle

Bang! the cannon blared
the impact of the ball flared
Soldiers cocking their guns
fathers and sons
fighting together
through the horrid weather

"Charge!" Were the captains orders
As the men crossed their borders
which once their line was confined
No longer would they be shot from behind
Although the blue attacked from both sides
The men charged with revolting pride
Although this brave charge had been made
The only men left standing were the men who prayed
For what reason on that dark and cloudy day
did those men with their lives have to pay
we all feel the sorrow and pain
that will never wash away in the rain
Our fellow Americans died that day
and now the battle is over between the blue and the gray

Andrew Ward

Teen Suicide

Another teenage suicide....
What a tragedy!
To see such vibrant young potential
Just die.

If I could but have held them in my arms of care,
Brushed away the dark, dank clouds of hopelessness,
And moved them with some pure impassioned prayer:
O, dear one, I know you're hurting bad,
And prob'ly just need someone who will understand.

Life's wounds run deep,
But there below our surface waved emotions,
They contact inner strength, no more asleep,
And blending with the currents of compassion,
Will buoy you up to chart uncharted seas.

You may be different from the rest,
But that's what makes you special,
Your talents are unique and precious,
Enough to help you reach your crest.
Don't throw it all away!
We need you.

Craig D. Nicholson

"Autumn Onset"

Autumn breath comes
To sharp the dead night awake
With knurled fists
And twisted limbs.

So relentless is the goal
To quickly devour
What little pulsating beauty remains
That the feast eliminates a season.

To strike and conquer
This crisp invader
Remains a futile war in the shadows.
Victory is given to the biting Autumn wind.

Meredith A. Frame

The Little Tree

It stands alone, this little tree,
way up on a hill.
Every little breeze ruffles the leaves
that are left on it.
Their colors are so beautiful.
Brown and rust, orange and gold;
and the branches are beginning to change, too.
The little tree looks around and wonders why it is so alone.
There isn't another tree around
to even catch the same breeze.
It's so lonesome up here.
Then the little tree realizes that fall is coming,
and soon it will turn cold.
All of its leaves will have fallen.
So it stands tall, and lifts its branches
high up to the sky and waits for another season,
and knows it will still be a little tree,
way up there on the hill,
all alone.

Gloria Przyborski

The New Year

The pathway lies before us untouched by human steps
Yet, full of weary pilgrims, each trying to forget
His pain and loss and suffering the former year has left.
Who will arrest this traveller and mercifully lift
The burden of his misery and self inflicted pain?
Shall I?
Perhaps it would be wiser to pass on than stop to care.
But wait?
His face reflects my own when I his pain did bear.
I hear the words of Jesus then..."Blessed are the merciful for
they shall obtain....Mercy."
I bend and listen his weakened voice petitions..."Help".
I hear the cry, compassion fills my breast, I have no choice...
The way is clear...His pain and misery must be bound in love!
But whose? Mine?
No! It is the love of Christ in me that exercises mercy...free!
To all who in this year will step into the pathway next to me.

Rhelda M. Evans

A Future Untold

Have you ever met anyone that
Had such an effect on you,
That you would never forget them?
I have and when our roads separated,
He left my life forever.
Sometimes I wonder if God,
Sent him to prove a point to me.
You see I hurt very easy,
And I thought that's all guys wanted.
You know to play with us,
And then when it was not convenient,
They would just get up and leave.
He helped me see a different side.
A side that I want to always
Have in my life and in my relationships.
Although words said blinded his feelings,
I know that body language never lies.
So in memory of my friend Brent,
No matter where you go I wish you luck happiness
And hope I will find someone like you again.

Veronique Anderson

Grandma's Love

Her hands were wrinkled, soft and white,
Her face was solemn, her eyes so bright.
Her voice gentle in the quiet of the night,
This was my Grandma reading the bible by coal oil light.

She sat my brother and me on the bed,
Where we listened spellbound while she read.
The birth of our Savior, his life, his death,
It was all such a miracle, we held our breath.

We heard the lessons he taught of faith and love,
To forgive your neighbor, to store your treasures above.
How the blind was given sight and the lame to walk,
We learned to be pure in mind, soul and thought.

These were the lessons my grandma read,
To my brother and me on her feather bed.
Lessons to grow by, live by, and cherish,
Not to be forgotten for ideas more stylish.

The years have gone by for my brother and me.
Our Grandma's in heaven, no more lessons to read.
Tears still fall as I remember the nights,
My Grandma read the bible by coal oil light.

Melody L. Jones

Love

Power beyond mere attraction:
a force to be reckoned with.
Heartache - joy; pleasure - pain;
conflict and consolation; desire and hate.
An intoxication; like addiction,
one feels incomplete without it.
Risk; coming into another's space;
exploring new borders; surveying frontiers;
crossing virgin thresholds.
Resist - surrender; dream - despair.

Necessity, not to live without.
Like hunger; an appetite that must be satisfied;
passion's thirst quenched.
Air of fulfillment breathed;
as sleep rejuvenates the spirit.
It adorns us, radiating joy;
clothes us in a shroud of sorrow.
Giving quarter to our dreams,
it shelters from the cold of loneliness; shielding us from
disbelief.

Divine, but not always kind.

Robert Keller

Precious Violets

I love the little Violets
With their sweet and loving smell.
They're pretty as the twilight
    and loving as a shell.

When on our way home from school at night,
    their sweet perfume gives out.
As in our hands, we press them tight,
And our hearts with joy do shout.

Till at last, our arms are filled
With the precious little flowers
as our hearts are thrilled,
With their warm and loving power.

We take them home to Mother,
Our hearts are filled with pride,
Because we know she is a lover
of God's Flowers from the wayside.

Ida Mae Alice Esperschied

On Learning Poetry

Q. Must we decipher every poem
As tho it were a code
And analyse - like Intercept
Each sonnet and each ode?
Why must a poem be obscure?
Why can't they say it plain and pure?
I'm getting tired of this manure;
Quite weary of this load!

   Anonymous

A. Speak not, Anonymous, of fertilizer
Come, learn along with us and be some wiser.

As builders build, so doth the poemwright
Create the work with width and depth and height.

Each form: The word, just so, is for a reason
Which, mark, you may discover in good season
If you are taught - or teach yourself - the art
Of sensing how the whole employs each part.

What beauteous delights we find
When we're inspired to stretch the mind!

Howard D. Clayton

The Night

The night's soft breeze gently clings
As the moon looks on
Its hushed voice, almost inaudible
Echoes in the darkness
Overwhelming but not fearful
For it is something craved.

A sparrow takes flight into the ebony night
Floats amongst the clouds
The willows weep for they cannot fly
And the stars ache to feel the ground.
A silent scream, a fallen star
The blades of grass wait to catch it.

Black-coal sky
Suspended by the heavens
Mesmerizes, takes the world into its arms
Protects it like a child.

Night softens the harshness of day
With its heavy cloak
And filters out the mocking,
Unbearable light.

Teresa Regan

"Our Daddy"

He has sailed the seas, weathered the tides,
Home again, home again, full of pride.
Steadfast in his love and life, that is true.
Never wavering in his morale or values.
For his eyes only, have known what they have seen,
Experienced many places on land and sea.
Discipline and respect, always a demand.
No regrets, for he is a honorable man.
A teacher of life, to the depths of his soul,
Striving to help achieve a goal.
Giving strength and advice when in need,
A love of family and tradition are his destiny.
Daughters, a son, grandchildren in all,
Loving, unconditionally, large and small.
Sacrifice is second nature to this man,
Never relenting until one could proudly stand.
Who is this man, we love and fills us with pride,
He is our Daddy, still weathering the tides.

Deborah Myers Snead

Ocean

A folded mushroom cloud on the far horizon catches my eye.
Large and cumulous, it changes with each glance.
Blue, blue sky meets the grey-black horizon
Where the earth drops off.
Colored umbrellas dot the sand
Between clusters of people on the beach.
Girls in bright pink, hot greens, and blue—oh, so many shades of blue!
Families, singles, and couples scattered in clumps on the well-trod sand,
Joined by the over-riding sound of the waves.
The swish and roar mingled with voices, music, wind,
And the hum of airplanes overhead.
The calm and peace of the waves rolling up the sand
Lingers at the center of my soul long after I return
To the hustle-bustle world of my everyday,
Until, I am drawn to it again.

Mary Susan Stakem

Negotiations

Her pleading question: "just *one* jellybean?"
Two grown ups. One of them, at least, convinced
Of her concern for justice and fair play.
The other, knowing and reluctant, winced:
"Come now, how many have you had today?"

Above her fearful gaze, they traded quips
About the hour, appetite and teeth.
They quoted Spock, agreed that he was wise.
Philosophy dismissed the child beneath,
A shield against her supplicating eyes.

"But one is all I want, a *little* one...
A *green*! I haven't had a green one yet."
She sensed the silent tension in the air;
Then felt her fate had finally been set;
And green became the colour of despair.

But later on, when on of them had left,
Her promises of "just one green" renewed,
Gentle hands brought forth the emerald treasure.
A silent bond of faith and trust ensued,
Sealing their complicity and pleasure.

Stephen Day

Midnight Clouds

Forgotten, unspoken memories
Drift quietly by the old castle ruin
While the highlighted mystic clouds
Are advancing like an army on the moon.
Astral assent into our deep shallow sky,
A magical journey throughout the stars
with Godly powers to make the soul cry.

The darkened clouds, suspended in confusion-
Periodically cloak the moons beams
while the icy cool breeze within the night
Alights the passion of one's warm dreams.
Oh-to melt into the clouds that intrigue so much,
To be the inspiration of the arts —
To be free and to explode in Glory at dawn's touch.

Brian Pierce

Paths Chosen

We sit around, all of us alone
In the silence of the night, we cry
Man enough to kill, but not shed tears in crowds
The memories wound our minds
The tears keep falling
Even behind the mask, it's seen
The hurt shows through, like a light in the dark
The time will come to face reality
All must fall but not at once
We all think about home, we dream of going
We see our friends, and loved ones in our visions
The night stretches on
The night holds no prisoners
The feelings of our past comes back more and more
Finally, we cry ourselves to sleep
Ready to face the challenges of the next day, we awake
To find it's coming again
  The Time Alone.

Kenny Woods

The Time Of Death

Death enters my chambers with the silence of doom,
He stands there silently, in the center of the room.
The silence is eloquent, I know it is time
To go and meet this Master of mine.
He moves toward me, touches my bed,
All I see now is his faceless head.
I must go now to see my God,
He knows I'm ready, but I give a nod.
I take his hand, I turn my head;
...My spirit's live but my body's dead.
        Mary Colvin

Heaven Came to Samson

"Gran-ma must I die to go to heaven?"
Says this brave young man, age not yet seven.

"My younger brother's there and I feel so alone,
Can I go to heaven? And then - can I come home?

They say joy and happiness, that's where it's at,
But if I go, I must come back -

Cause Mommy misses David, and I know she'll miss me too,
But for a little while in heaven - Gran-ma, what can I do?"

Gran-ma says," God promises love - and his promises are true -
One need not die to go to heaven, sometimes it can come to you."

Then four years had come, and gone...
And for him, three more brother's were born...
Now happiness is everywhere! Image of David, each one bares.

Gran-ma sees this young man, (whose now eleven)
Play touch-football with siblings, sent from heaven
Silently she says "Yes, God promises love and his promises are true,
One need not die to go to heaven - sometimes it can come to you -"

Yes Samson - Heaven came to you -
        Marlene R. Pae

Hurts So Good

When we're together there's fire
Oh yes, but I must resist the flame
You're a heart-breaker, a stallion
Half a man, half a mane

and to say less, I Want You
Been wondering how I'd kiss you for years
I wouldn't object to finding out
But I don't think I could handle it.

I've felt your arms,
Heard your words,
Don't you know I want you
To kiss me till it hurts
I'd love to be pinned to your wall
All night I'd watch you sleep
And I'd die to be your covers
I'd warm you as you weep

But the worst thing is we want each other
We're attracted when nobody's near
It's all so discretely mutual
I'm alone..... Come here.
        Amanda Ziegler

The Wild Rose Beyond

A wild rose once grew where all could see,
sheltered amongst nature's garden forest,
And, as springs solstice dawned,
and moons passed swiftly by,
it healingly spread its branches,
and stood spiritually for all,
sacred, busy, thorny, and tall...

One day, a sacred beam of light shone through
a crevice, sprung and opened wide —
The wild rose bent gently toward nature's warmth
then passed beyond to the other side...

The wild sacred rose spread open wide,
sharing its scent for all,
It whispered during winter and fall,
for sacred spiritual call...

Now you all sense comfort in serenity,
I am amongst the nature's beauty,
Hear me, see me, talk to me, use me
Sense the unique cleansing for I am nature's rose,
May my spirit always be with you all.
        Muriel F. C. Roberts

Revenge

O, you cunning love!
Lurking upon its victims
Letting them taste the numbing drink from a goblet
But never have it finished to the bottom.
Forcing the heart racing, begging the mind for one more drop
But never to the bottom.
Letting the body curl up in a fetus position
Suffering from the disease of solitude, hopelessness,
Purposelessness, lack of touch and desire
One drop were enough!-
But never to the bottom.
If I ever finish you
I'll shatter the goblet to molecules
I'll swallow the last drop
even if it cauterizes my insides
And watch you becoming part of me till I die!
        Marie Franek

"Paradise"

A spring of gardens that over flows with the scent of a rose,
A well of fresh water where pollution isn't exposed.
A place where smoke, in the air won't pollute,
A place free of contaminated meat, where we eat choicest fruit.
A place that's covered with cinnamon sand,
We can enjoy life it self from violent man.
A place where the air smells like the finest perfumes,
A place of perfect vows, for the bride and groom.
A place of joyful lives, not depending on wealth,
Where God provides goodness and no one else.
A place that makes the low class equal to all kind,
A place where we won't die before it's our time.
A place that's filled with the goodness of life,
Don't we all want Paradise?
        Spencer Battle

"Tinconderoga #2"

The pencils are like soldiers - pointed,
chafing for a scrape across the page,
nudging timely truces - small erasures
yet row on row, earnest that the battle rage.

So, worn and nubbed (a moment's breather won)
some craggy height or foggy strait prevailed
onto a new, untested footing farther on;
into a deeper sea or darker, reedy swale.

A kind of nervous joy, much careful listening
disallowed a map of the Grand Strategy
yet given scope for tactic and quick healing
at each appalling choice of diction's mystery.

Tim Scannell

A Message From My Guardian Angel

While all the earth is still and at peace,
I watch over you all night as you sleep.
I touched your hair with my Angel wings.
Fill your head with Angelic Host Singing.

My love for you is unconditional and everlasting
I'll be with you always even after your passing.
I stand in guard over your presence today
And watch as you kneel to God to pray.

My time with you is never ending.

Carolyn A. O'Riley

"Lonely Heart"

Internally rotten from holding millions of tear drops within.
Wandering the lonely earth, feeling as though your life will end.
The heart diminishing from lack of love being received.
A love promised by lips you strongly believed.
Giving up completely on God so you no longer pray.
So after life is no more, your soul
wanders where the black hearts lay.
So use to the black emptiness in your heart
you clearly see past the dark pathways.
Knowing light symbolizes happiness so you
fear the brightness the sun brings to days.
Years of running away from a familiar resemblance.
Never stopping to find out but only taking a short glimpse.
Continuously running breathlessly and never coming to see.
This resemblance was the medicine of love to
conquer that virus of forever being lonely.

Veronica Moore

The World Today

Today, I sit in a favorite chair,
my T.V. window open to the outside world.
I see a world made mad with thunder -
as nations fight, pillage and plunder.

So many people, none of which I would have seen,
had they not marched across my T.V. screen
and shared their tragedy; thus,
entering my pensive life.

My heart bleeds and fingers tremble
as I try to pen my thoughts and thus assemble,
a morsel of ability to aid these innocent victims,
caught up in the adversities of life.

Would that I could reach these wretched masses,
and extend to them a permanent passage
into a quiet, temperate zone; thus,
write an exodus to this masochistic history -
so no man need cry alone.

Elva D'Antoni

Joy Unlimited

Some people think a "Christian Life"
Is dull, plain, and bored
But oh what a pleasure
When you know and love the Lord

There's nothing like the joy
That the Lord will give to you
Which no amount of wealth, and fame
Could ever rightly do

There's nothing like the feeling
That the God almighty gives
Knowing he's your Saviour
And in your heart he lives

And no thrill, or no sensation
Could quite match or equal up
To the happiness you'll at long last know
Once Christ has filled your cup!

Briant George

Listen, My Child

We learn from the happy times and the sad times too;
We store up the memories and replay them for you.

If our lives were always wonderful there would be little to say;
And who would care, Anyway?

Understanding and wisdom come from the experiences of life.
We give you our knowledge so you can avoid the strife.

Protection and guidance, we provide;
Love and support, so yours won't be a rocky ride.

Our aim is noble; but can it succeed?
We try and we hope that it will, indeed.

Pat Whaley Trentham

Friendship

Friendship is the soft shoulder when the teardrops have to fall.
Friendship is the phone number you sometimes have to call.
Friendship means everything.

Friendship is the inspiration and the sunshine,
when you try to get through the rain.
Friendship is that big hug that helps you get through the pain,
and it's okay if you're not sure.

Friendship is a candle when you need a breath of air.
Friendship is that sparkle in your eye,
when that someone's there to care
and sometimes a slow goodbye.

Friendship is that someone special
I'm glad you're here to today
You make a difference.

Daniel Seymour

Unrealized Love

As you sit and watch the sky move,
You feel alone, and cold.
But as you watch the birds fly over,
you long for the company of her love.
You crawl to the back of your mind,
and remember that summers day.
When you met her,
While watching the sky grow bright.
The sun rises, as you looked into her eyes,
but you don't realize the feelings,
the emotions that flood over you.
You could not see past her tight film of beauty.
You smile as you remember her face.
And a watery tear slowly falls down your cheek,
As you remember that you're still alone.
Because of unrealized love.

Jeremy S. Bell

It's Just A Wishful Thinking

I still have a lot of love to give
But how can we both learn to live
When our friendship is tossed a shore
Doesn't anybody say, "I love you" anymore?

We can't let this problem drift away
And pretend it's just another bad day
It's not something you can easily ignore
Doesn't anybody say, "I love you" anymore?

For everything that I've said is true
And if that's not loving you
Well, I really don't know what is
Unless there's something else I miss

All I've got to offer you is a true confession
By now we should have learned our lesson
No body wants an endless cold war
Doesn't anybody say, "I love you" anymore?

It's very difficult to express my emotion
Only you can cause such as commotion
Your love is still worth fighting for
Doesn't anybody say, "I love you" anymore?

Yandhi T. Cranddent

Lookie Yonner Johnny

Lookie yonner Johnny,
is that a bluebird that I see,
sitting up there in that peach tree?
The pain is awful,
am I gut shot Johnny, would you look and see?

This is a terrible battle
that we are a fighting here at Shiloh.
Am I gonna die Johnny, is this my time to go?

Why no, Freddie, you ain't a 'gonna die.
Rest now, Freddie, and be still as there you lie.

The medics are a-coming soon, Freddie
they are just a couple of yards away
from this here peach orchard,
and they will patch you up.
I gotta go now Freddie,
and with the rest of the company catch up.

As I left to do my duty, I looked into Freddie's eyes
and I knew he was going to die.
And as I ran to catch up with the rest,
whilest I was a-running, oh how the tears did flow from my eyes.

Michael D. Jones

Life Is Like A Puzzle

Life is like a puzzle
In so many different ways
Sometimes when you put a piece together —
It will take you several days.
Sometimes you find that special piece
That seems a perfect match.
Then everything gets jumbled
and nothing seems to fit.
You straighten and you shuffle
And you move this way and that
Hoping to find a solution
to that never ending task.
Puzzles interlock together
Just as paths in our lifetime do.
Sometimes it takes that special someone —
To make that piece work for you.
So when you seem to be struggling
Don't - worry or fret.
Because the next piece to your puzzle —
Is right within your grasp!

Janie L. Gish

Nurse

God started with a dew drop from a field of flowers
Making her personality refreshing as spring showers

From the magical clouds in the sky so blue
Came her spirit, kind, sincere and true

Chopping up his herbs and zesty chives
He seasoned a soul to touch people's lives

He lassoed a sun beam from way up above
Filling her with warmth and everlasting love

From an angel he pulled a single golden tooth
Giving her vitality and wondrous youth

He painted her with colors of the rainbow so fine
Granting her wisdom and patience divine

Reaching down he touched a rose, admiring every part
Holding it so tightly he formed her tender heart

Sprinkling on some star dust in the glow of his moonlight
He dried her with a fire fly to make her twinkle bright

When he finally finished a tear rolled down his face
Splashing on this masterpiece with goodness and grace

Linda McInnis

The Crabbed Waking Hours

Dark, empty city, threatening sky.
Clouds leading nowhere.
No friendship, no smiles,
Strange summer warmness of dreams in the hay.
Sleepless heartbeats waiting to break away.

At the edge of the bridge life was swaying.
The feeling was free.....
A strange place to be.
He stood there. No motion.
Brusque images went by.
His mind was left breathless, his soul on fire.
Tears on a highway at racing time.

With naked body he walked in the rain;
season of Heaven or season of pain?
His eyes reflections of void illusions,
looking for sunshine where there was not any.

Songs, messages drying away.
Cause, the hardest times are the waking hours.

Margarita Sotiropoulou

Ode To Chloe

Gazing in my direction,
my purring friend ventures,
investigates strewn papers, books,
a top the table.

My pencil,
warming paper with thoughts,
searching for words,
like an unskilled typist hunting letters.

She finds my pencil fascinating,
its movements entertaining.
Claws distended, the game begins,
Swat swat, swat swat, swat swat.

I welcome the interruption,
she tires quickly.
Marble-like eyes blinking, she sniffs,
papers, books, empty dishes.

Circling the clutter,
she finds the most comfortable spot,
my fiction.

Michele Wegman

Yesterday's Child

I want to be a little girl again,
And play with kitty-cats out in the yard,
And dance and twirl and swirl upon the wind,
And discipline my dolls — but never hard!

To fly upon my swing while singing
Songs of the day — my Sister taught me how,
I free floated in my Neptune world
Where sadness never dared to take a bow.

To taste again small pies of cinnamon
My mother made on afternoons for me,
And to rest awhile within my Daddy's arms
The safest place in all the world to be.

Oh God! But how I miss that childhood place,
As middle age stares boldly in my face!
Old Saturn trudges slowly on his way,
But leaves fast behind the child of yesterday.

Laura Irrgang

Crystal Ball: The Revelation

In a dark corner, it lurks, cries my name; the future of
life it reveals.
The Crystal Ball has an incandescent glow, the eeriness
of its light conceals
The days of happiness, the day of death, of what my life
shall be.

The dark clouds fade into light
I see myself happy and bright.
The menacing of the unknown
Madly, gladly to me is show.

Shock and horror from what I see
Lying on the ground, I see myself bleed.
A tragic death is my demise
I will no longer see the sun rise.

With a wild yell and an angered scream, I destroy the
Crystal Ball and its wicked gleam.
Shards of glass shatter to the ground; I fall to my
knees, tears spilling down.
It wasn't the future I has hoped to see, a tortured end
is what my life shall come to be.

Jennifer Fraley

Untitled

We quiet our children's indignant cries
with death to their children of rage,
and silence our turbulent seed with lies...
Sh....

We help our children spurn their past
and show them how a stone is cast,
at those who are our brothers, ourselves....
Ahh....

We teach our children ancient psalms
hide in cells from singing shells,
then lay them in the ground to sleep....
Ll....

We bury our children before the night
sit and rip and grip with pain,
days that have no light.
Ooh....

To avenge our children's lives on edge,
we reach for and hold the hand of dread.
And piece by piece our hurt and fear becomes a new tomorrow.
Mm....

Ayala M. Zion-Levy

Aubade

And when you open your eyes the gold flakes in your irises will
glow again.
And your eyebrows, so thick, will dance to our synchronized groans.
And the sheet, crinkling with each sigh, will slip down your chest.
And your hand will not lie calmly by your hip, but will restlessly
untangle my hair.
And you will roll over to greet me.
And I will rest my cheek against your sweaty shoulder,
breathing in used air.
And through the thickness of morning, all the smiles I have stored
for you
will rush out and stream
like sun through the crack in the shade
and splash across your face.
And we will decide to stay in bed, under the covers,
Sheltered from the rain I have called forth.

Alicia Shems

He Died Of AIDS

He was a dear, dear friend,
Thoughtful, considerate, compassionate and all.
We looked forward to his visits
When on occasions he made a call.
He was an educated man
A friend of schools.
He revelled in life
And dispensed joy and cheer.
No opportunity missed to extend to us
Illustrated books and expensive gifts,
Inclined not to favor fools.
We thought of him as a friend,
Dear to our hearts
A sense of humor and
A person you could love.
Extensive travels he had made
And then, suddenly,
He died of Aids.

Les Hutchison

Twisted World

Welcome to a twisted world,
A world twisted around love,
Twisted around hate,
Twisted around fear,
Twisted around war,
A world twisted so tight,
That no one can get in or out,
No matter how hard they might try.
If you don't fit in, you are confined to a small corner.
If you do fit in,
You are allowed to take over any area that you wish to.
People who are of the wrong color,
Of the wrong religion, of the wrong education,
Are forced to suffer surrounded by this poor example of
intelligent life
If we are so intelligent,
Then why can't we find the answer for world peace that is right
beneath our noses.
Why, because we are all too afraid that we might actually
discover
something that would make the world a better place,
Not just for them, but for everyone

Amber E. Lipsky

Spring

Spring, Spring!
Season of sea breeze and cool air
what took you so long to come around?
That time of burning sensation you left behind is mortal
and that season that burns my ear and nose causes me to
bundle
Oh! Spring, Spring why can't you be eternal?
Summer and Winter bring in misery
from which I want to run away.
Spring, Spring! Your beauty is a mystery
full with joie de vivre and loveliness
Oh! Spring, Spring come back
and rid me of the Summer and Winter madness.
Remy Dure

Beyond The Veil

Why weep thee mother, over death?
Thy child is free from strife,
The Lord will hold your child securely
For death is the leaven of life.

She'll wander round with past companions
In robes of spiritual worth,
She'll serve a faithful mission
Much greater than on earth.

So dry your eyes dear mother
The memories linger near,
Just think of the life she'll be leading
Beyond the veil so sheer.
Darlene Stahler

Weep Not My Love

Weep not my love for hearts afire,
Desire burning higher and higher.
I looked into your weeping eyes,
With a heart full of lonely lies.
Weep not my love.

Feel not the wrath,
For there is always another path.
Leave that lonely life behind,
There is a world that's gentle and kind.
Weep not my love.

You see others in control,
With their hearts and minds so full.
Dry those desolate tears,
And lay aside all your fears.
Weep not my love.
Terry Michalski

The Best Of Friends

After all this time that has gone by
I am still asking myself why?

I love you all with all my heart
and soon forever we will be apart

This is our last year together
and all we have are past memories to last us forever

We have come to far to through it all away
I wish there was a chance we could all stay.

Elementary school was when it all began,
to grow up this fast we did not plan.

We have been through so much inside and out
miss you all, I will without a doubt!

The time is now coming sooner when we will all part
but the best of friends, will always stay in my heart.
Leanne Simser

Hi Sweetheart

Your body lying in the warm sand,
The sun dancing checkerboard patterns on your skin,
Waves caressing you
As silk sliding down your back
And lips evoking chills from eternity.

You seek that elusive youth,
And feelings of ecstasy
Have awakened your senses.

Ants racing across you universe,
Screams from a volcano erupting...
This moment only!

May you live in hopes of again opening
The old suitcase in the attic of your dreams,
For I have just massaged your mind ... the highest touch.

In deep friendship,
Christine Demers

Memories Of You

Beautiful were you my sister dear,
I often sit wishing you here.
Loving, caring, always there,
When it came to my despair.
I followed your footsteps through the years
But never could I quite compare
I burdened you with my problems no doubt
You told me not to worry, it will work itself out
I loved you, looked up to you and hoping too
That I would grow to be like you
Willing to give without any care
You made my life easy with little to fear
We shared a lot of things together
Even though it didn't matter
Yes I miss you, missing you here
Because you were you, my sister dear
Clarissa George

Show Me Your Care For Me

The voices the voices
Why do they nag me so
I tell them to go away
I shout at them to leave me.
But people stare.
They are afraid of me,
They are afraid of me.
But don't you see.
I am telling the voices to go away
It's my way of controlling them.
Oh, God why must I suffer so
Only sleep merciful sleep
I awaken to the darkness
I am alone in my nightmare
Often shunned and homeless I am mentally ill
Please help me see the light again
To smile, love and laugh again
My illness you cannot see
Take your hand in mine and walk a while with me
Show me you care what happens to me.
Patricia Cassidy

Beauty of the Human Soul

Beauty within the soul never dies,
as the skin about us wilts.
For the beauty within us will always flourish
and deepen as the years go by.
Michael J. Dant

Next To Me

Flaming muscle in this torso
  Burns, burns, yearns,
Yens for you to be here, safe,
  Next to me
Electrics, somewhat pulsing in this skull
  Sends, lends, tends,
Gives messages to me, you see
  Says to me
How this entire being enjoys you here next to me
  Kissing, touching, holding, talking, walking
   Or frolicking about in a field
    Green, green, scene,
Open land to run and play, lay
  Next to me
  Tingly skin making me writhe
   Shiver, quiver, slither,
Wiggle about the ground, around
  On the ground
Wishing that you my dear, were here next to me
  Dancing, talking, hugging, hoping dropping.

Ronald Vernon Stephenson

Autumn Journey

Standing here on new plowed earth, looking out over stalks of sun
bleached corn a new Autumn day is born
Off in the east the sun rises, lighting this glorious day
High above in sky of cobalt blue, wave after wave of geese fly south
They are in quest of winter lodging
Off in the mist I can here a mallard drake calling for its mate
The dew that has settled on the trees over night, glistens and
flickers in the new morning light
This old dog at my side has made this journey with me many a fall day
before the crisp autumn air sends a shiver down my spine
My old dog quivers at every new scent
Across the road, standing at the end of a corn row, the reason for our journey
A lone Ring Neck Pheasant stands a solemn sentinel
Seemingly, he is waiting for his fate
He need not fear us I come without gun in hand
I still come to see the bird spring to flight and the pleasure of my
old dog as he chases a bird to wing
I hunt no more I take no pleasure in my quarries demise only do I come
for the glory of his being and the peace of these surroundings

Robert Dyer

Ah, But To Dream

To dream of such an experience would be absurd.
For your words would have spoken,
And your touch would have left no scar.

Ah, but to dream this, such a difference it would make.
Your lips would have remembered me,
And your sincerity would not have stung me.

To make the night up in a dream in my head
Would wake me with not a care in the world.
I would have dreamt of a night where decisions
Would not haunt me,
And your love would not have left me in the cold.

Carlye Barat

A Friend's Prayer

I thought of you and said a prayer today.
For strength and faith and sunshine and laughter for your day.
For joy and peace and love and wisdom and grace abundantly.
To see, to feel, to know, you're never alone.

Katherine J. Ison

A Baby

The most wonderful thing in the world is a Baby's birth
The first cry or really a wail
Its kicking and struggling in the doctors arms
And finally placed in the mothers
Such a tiny object you're scared to touch
But only because you love it so much
The pain and hearing to bring its birth
Is really the most wonderful thing on earth
A baby doesn't stay little for long
You have to help him get big and strong
Soon he will be off to school
Help him obey the certain rules
Maybe high school maybe college maybe more
Don't ever let him become a bore
Because before you know it
Off he will go, who knows where
You'll worry and worry he will act like he don't care
But it's just his way so don't get mad
Remember he once was the tiny bundle you had
A Baby

Betty Lastra

For Tonight I Realized...

I forgot to tell you what I've been meaning to say
  It rests in my mind but not words until today.
That throughout the years. I have come to see
  How important you are to the family and me.

Your love and affection are engraved in my mind.
  And an unhappy moment is quiet hard to find.
In an age of split marriages, families and friends
  Our families so warm that it need no amends.

   And I thank you because...

Our lives side by side, hopes and dreams wall to wall.
  Our world could resemble a domino fall.
Yet your love so strong, generosity so grand
  That our family won't fall, but instead we will stand.

And we will stand tall, and our love will not end
  With one single person or special friend.
We will love each other and everything that we do.
  You've taught us to love and for that I thank you.

And by setting this example by helping us to grow.
  You've spread this love for others to know.
To love life is to love others; you knew this was true.
  And our lives are all happier because of you two.

Ian Elliott

The Mud Puddle

I was walking home one day feeling hot and tired
Feeling hot and tired, yes feeling hot and tired
I was walking home one day feeling hot and tired
When I saw this great big puddle

So I took off my clothes, then I got a scary thought
I didn't really know if I should go in there or not
This wonderful puddle, well it looked so very nice
Sometimes a little kid has to make a sacrifice

Then I slipped to my left, I splashed to my right
I am a happy kid but not a pretty sight
I did a belly flop with a big loud thud
The water disappeared and there was only mud

So I sneaked into the house and there was mom and dad
They looked at me in shock and then began to laugh
They got the camera out and took a lot of shots
But oh my goodness I really need a bath

What a wonderful day this turned out to be
This turned out to be, oh this turned out to be
What a wonderful day this turned out to be
At this great big wonderful puddle.

Jeanette Gamble

Yearling Serenade

A spring.
A place.
A rapid change affecting time.
Furious race of time
It must be controlled some how.
Guide my way to a good path,
River of time...
I dream of a future for you and me,
Shall we live or shall we die.
A decision will be made by the great river of time

Philip Mattia

Nostalgia

If only I could go back to that yard,
Where I played from dawn till dusk
Just one more time;
If I could sit under that mango tree,
And play house with my childhood sweetheart.
Oh, how much I wish to see that river,
To throw small rocks at the calm surface,
Making splashes along.
I wish I could go back to those days;
When I sang with the nightingales,
And ran with the west wind.
These wishes may never come true
But I still wish to wish.

Asha Sreedharan

Of Time

The duration of a life cycle is very short
The age of a judge is only in court
The period of decadence is an hour
The season of spring is found in a shower.

The era of man soon comes to an end
The eons of time are not a friend
The epoch we now live in
Is the term of our sin.

The sequence of numbers we call days
The course of events go different ways
The succession of kings come and go
The date of death we do not know.

The span of life is a year
The stage of living is not yet near
The interval of loving is being born
The cycle of hate is at the morn.

The past is not altogether gone
The present helps us see a little beyond
The future will come soon enough
The time of love is always tough.

Brian Hansen

His Image

Nearly half a year has passed
Since I stared at you,
My eyes, like thumbs sliding over moist, red clay,
Softly shaping my heart
To wear your face,
Preserving you within my breast, that someday,
When your absence is too much to bear,
I might rip it out,
To gaze upon your countenance
In my final
Breath.

Laura Eleanor Holloway

Thinking

Reliving, rewriting, rerunning, redoing, remembering
The past, passing through
Layers, layering layered
Continuation, going on, running through, going past
Future, near future, far future, in between
Tingling, shivering, movement

Going through, thinking rewinding life
As old as new
Trying again

Behind tree, house, behind house, yard,
Behind yard, street, behind street,
Life, behind life, death

In books, pages, in pages, paragraphs,
In paragraphs, sentences,
In sentences, words, in words, letters, in letters,
Life

Emily Kalah Gade

Men Don't Cry

Moved by good the heart cries out,
And a spirit kindled urges for shout.
Joyous feelings seek sweet release,
But man's response denies any peace:

His choking throat chords taut in din,
Form a lumpy knot from deep within.
And tear ducts redly swelled with dew,
Strain to spill from eyes once blue.

For fear of notice... pride to blame,
Suppressed emotion seeks acclaim.
Then fighting hard for self-composure,
Quick stifled sobs forbid disclosure.

Ashamed of baring a meek caring soul,
He aborts sweet release of joy to extol.
Tender emotions then gone all askew,
The spirit denied now fades from view.

To free true feelings there is no shame,
Nor to share ones soul in sweet acclaim.
Yet men shun emotion with teary eye,
For after all... "Men Don't Cry."

Farrell K. Morris

Copper Is A Curious Word

Copper is a curious word!
It rhymes with Whopper and Topper and Stopper - and Pauper,
Like thunder that rides the monsoon on a July day
And comes a popper down our canyon, to blow us to kingdom come
And make the desert drink quickly of rain, e'er it drain
To the nearest wash, or sink 'neath thirsty soil.
It makes paupers, this copper, - and kings!
And loosens stays and chains of all who live nearby.
Paupers who keep fierce dignity and rejoice in frugality,
And glory in prodigality that leaches copper, green from the rocks,
And by nature's alchemy turns red to bless the world
With pots and electric sparks and roofs.
Copper is a desert creature
Of superstition and roadrunners and cholla and wind;
And dust that stops the throat, and sunsets to stop the heart,
And nights ne'er dreamed in Araby, nor in moonlit Coyoacan
As near guitars speak soft of life and love.
Copper is a curious word; and curiouser the life invoked
For those who turn away from gold and cold and mould
To be bold - as is proper with copper and paupers.

Paul Jesse Baird

Nature

Nature is a wonderful thing.
It's the way the trees grow and the way birds sing.
Nature is by lakes, rivers, and streams,
And even in the sunbeams.
Gazelle will romp and deer will play,
While the White River weaves its way.
Winter snowflakes fall from the sky
While winter days go passing by.
In fall leaves turn yellow and red
While sleepy bears crawl into bed.
Summer is a time for fun...
And little ones like to play in the sun.
In spring the animals awake
And do not know what Nature will make.

Evan Newman

Inside A Book

Inside a book, you can let your
imagination run wild.
Inside a book, you can find your
inner child.
Inside a book, you can travel to distant lands,
or walk on the great sands.
But if it gets too scary for you,
all you have to do, is close the book.

Lacy DeWall

A View Through My Window

A weak and watery morning light,
Barely separates day from night,
As a shawl of bleak despair,
Settles on the poisoned air,
The sheltering mounds of glass and stone,
Seem like concrete skull and bone,
And in them robotic mortals move around,
Lamenting, wailing without a sound,
And trees stand death like hands held high,
Searching for salvation in the sky,
And on the blackened path of fear,
Shadows of footsteps do appear,
And turn to children with ghost like face,
Silent and with morbid pace,
Their burdens held on skeletal backs,
Treasuring their lives in their sacks,
And as they turn are seen no more,
A devilish bird takes flight and soars,
And with a twist of angry pain,
The clouds collide and it begins to rain.

Jane Owen

Olympic Spirit

Sweet spirits of the world,
    bring us together again.
Work hard to win your place
    at the front of every line.
Stand up, and be proud!
    Let your nation's blood flow.
All blood is red blood,
    and forever it is so.
Now take a stand in your place
    for everyone will win.
We are all the children of the same God,
    and the Olympics bring our
        family together again.

Ava Sparks

Freedom Fly

Race away on the crests of tide, ferry me on a lifelong ride,
Let the skies be bright or grey, carry me somewhere else today,
Fill my lungs with air so free, float me on the deepest sea,
Show me sights I never knew, clear my eyes with a novel view.
Earthbound anchors hold no thrill, like an ugly dungeon grille,
Same old practice, single rut, causing open minds to shut.
Gritty taste of salt sea tang, let me savour white wave's fang,
Take me to some distant reach, tarry at some golden beach,
Flaunt my mind beyond this place, jet me inside outer space,
Show me where the future's best, challenge me to do the rest,
Fly me to a land of worth, distanced from my place of birth,
Magic power of nature stole, supreme in all from pole to pole.
Elegant isles of earth be bound, cameos set in sight and sound,
Open plains like quiet brides, grassy slopes on mountain sides,
Volcanoes venting earthen crust, hurricanes no man can trust,
Waterfalls, that hiss and roar, canyons depths oft held in awe.
Parry all the whims of fate, rise and let me elevate,
Hostile forces lose your power, sanction under God's own bower,
Silence ending all my screams, guide me to the isle of dreams,
Act to be my wise redeemer, take me where the grass is greener.

Stan Mason

Hockey...The Way It Used To Be

I want my boy to play hockey the way I used to do,
Go out for fun and exercise without hearing a single Boo.

My parents stayed at home and let Me play the game,
Not a yell nor a scream could be heard not even a dirty name!

We scrambled for the puck and played in our own style,
We fell, we hit, we bumped each other and had nothing but a smile.

Outside we changed and put on our skates the weather as cold as could be
And worked to clear the ice for play, not a complaint they heard from me.

But times have changed and the people too who come and watch the game,
From an outside rink to an indoor forum where the fans yell out in shame.

I want my boy to play hockey with a coach who treats him as one,
No yelling, no screaming, no carrying on, just out to have some fun.

It's important to learn and play the game from the bottom of your heart,
And enjoy the sport for what it's worth, new friends you'll never part!

Mike Driscoll

My Little Angel Courtney Marie

When I heard that you were on the way, I thought my life would end.
But little did I know that when you got here, my life would just begin.
You were so beautiful and you had such a great smile.
I came to realize that it made my life complete, to have my own grandchild.
Of all the cute words that I ever heard you say,
there was nothing sweeter than Pappa, and Nay Nay.
You taught us so much in such a short year,
you brought to our lives, so much happiness and cheer.
Suddenly your soul flew away, like a snow white dove,
But, you left behind your memories, and your love.
Sometimes as I reminisce, I ask the age old question "Why?"
Then it comes to me, the Lord saw you as a special angel in the sky.
Sometimes I can close my eyes, and I can almost see,
you smiling up at Jesus as you sit there on His knee.
He strokes your hair as He looks down tenderly,
and says welcome home, my little angel Courtney Marie.
You look up at Him and you seem to be so content,
you're not sad at all that your days on earth are spent,
Our vision is so very dim, but clearly you see,
We'll all be home one day with our Little Angel Courtney Marie.

Roger P. Jones

Disabilities?!

It gave GOD great pleasure to create me.
In his eyes I am a trophy of his beauty.
Delicately crafted from his own great hand,
every curve fine tuned, to his master plan.
He made my mold, I am now official,
a creature born to be very special.

I did no wrong, was no accident of birth.
I'm not cursed although I thought that too at first.
I felt ashamed and did not want to be me.
I'm a miracle, not some tragedy.
But the average humans, they do not know.
So they let their ignorance out to show.

Children are not taught fundamental respect.
So they mock differences, they refuse to accept.
Adults offer their misguided sympathy.
"Oh, you're incomplete, that's such a pity."
They can't see, they just don't understand.
I have all I need to be the perfect human.

Beauty is not hair, light eyes, flawless skin.
It's the goodness of your spirit that shines from within.
It's a fine tuned mind, that's always turned on.
Balancing your nature, helps you sing a sweeter song.
It's the kindness that flows, commanding respect.
It's meeting new challenge, out doing your best.

It's holding your head high and never losing step.
It's loving yourself, and moving correct.
It's regarding all life as a gift, not your toy.
It's planting good seeds, and sharing your joy.
Beauty is in the eyes of the beholder. That's true.
It's your eyes that matter. That beauty is you.

Mutiya Sahar Vision

Attention Good Members Of The A.B.W.A.

There's a word or two I'd like to say,
On behalf of our lovely President.
A girl whose life has been well spent.

Once a nurse who carried pills, rubbed your back
  and soothed you ills,
A beautician too, may I add.
She does so much, I can never tell,
But does it all, and all quit well.

If we give our support at length,
Boosted by our time and strength.
She will save us well the year around,
As an undertaker will be the last to
  let us down.

Gladys Haimes

A Poem

An innocent musing mated with celibate silence.
Birth pangs dawned in the wee time.
Travailing to oust the nuisance inside of me
I'm stuck in a poem
And I can't get free.

Circling, spiraling symbols and sounds
Tear through tangles of obscurity.
One fruitful image — that's what I need
'Cause I'm stuck in poem
And I can't get free.

What will it be, when it finally is?
Will it mirror a little of me?
Oh God, here it comes!
Thoughts surge like the sea

Ah, a wee little poem
and I'm free.

Cecile Jeannette Durand

Time

If time was a picture to paint on the wall.
What would I paint?
Would there be anything at all?

Would it be of a circle?
Going round without end.
Like all of the clocks on which we depend?

Or is time something deeper, bigger, or taller-
Is it substance, or like wind?
Or something much smaller.

How does time creep up and snatch away lives?
Is it evil? It's not human.
Who gives time its right?

On time we depend, and of time we fear.
Time can be given.
Yet it takes away years.

I could not paint time, for it is both enemy and friend
But I'll use it for God.
His time will never end.

Amanda Robinson

We Will Never Get Use To Death

I stand tall trying to accept death
My mother is going. I try to be strong
My heart is heating. the pain is deep
I wipe away tear. my pillow is soaked
My eye is red, pain is near. death is
Silent, you never get used to it, we have to
learn to be strong, it comes again and again
We will never get used to death, it returns
and takes my loved one that is so dear
Only God know how we feel because he died
On Calvary, we try to go on with our life
The lonely empty is there, silent pain is
Near, my heart is lonely, the pain returns
year after year where there is life, death
repeats itself over and over again, death
is something we will never get used to,
as time grows the pain gets old, it slips
away like the moon under the cloud, you
look up, there it is again so have
Death return again and again.

Carolyn Lewis

Wishing

I wish I could be somebody
Who knew the world at large.
Who knew the great and mighty
The ones who are in charge.

I wish I could give them a message
A plea to their hearts and minds.
A plea for hope and help
To have mercy on all mankind.

I wish I could speak to the many
To the high and exalted of every state.
To the ones who could help the poor and weak
And end the prejudice, violence and hate.

I wish I could influence the purveyors of death
The men who design and trade in destruction.
The men who train in the use of weapons
So that they will abandon their worldly disruption.

I wish I could bring love to all people
Give lasting peace, quiet and tranquility.
Give lasting happiness, joy and fulfillment
And all things in which the lofty lack ability.

Seymour Schott

Ode To A Tennis Buffeen

How do we love thee?? - In countless ways;
Your lobs; cross-court forehands; crispness of your serve;
Your battle for every point, even on the hottest days
That would try the zaniest players' nerve

A competitor? - Yes, this thou art;
Sucker for pusillanimous drop shots?
Yes - but cagey and smart
Enough to tie your opponents in knots

The game to you is like a holy war
A partner who stands like a saint
Quickly feels your wrath and gets the door
For it's not a sport for those with spirit faint

Life is so like a tennis set
One may be down at two to five
When suddenly you begin to storm the net
And your team gets into over drive

Five straight games and the set is won
That's what it's all about, for after all is said and done
Coming from behind makes one shout:

"Attaboy - Girl!!- Hail, All Hail, Agassinia!!"

Joseph M. Pisani

To A Small Child

Oh little one so fresh, so new,
I wish I could impart to you;
Memories tucked away with care,
So little time - so much to share.

I was once young and new like you,
Full of blissful wonderment too;
No care or worry to trouble me,
Just free to be who I could be.

To share those times with you, my treasure,
Would fill my heart with open pleasure;
So you could know me as a child,
Cheerful, carefree, a little wild.

That we could have that time to share,
So little time to take you there;
Those youthful days so precious few,
When I was a child so fresh, so new.

Barbara W. Schmedding

Sea Of Lost Dreams

The morning sun erupt into day
  The sea gives off a gentle spray
I'd love to leave, but I have to stay
  As all of my thoughts run astray
Like the stream to the sea

I think of places I could go
  I think of people I no longer know
I see how I have nothing to show
  And remember the people who told me so

Then night arrives with hate in her eyes
  And I'm amazed by her frightening size
Only she can see through my lies
  And only the night hears my cries

And morning comes again to the stream
  Beautiful mourning, as strange as it seems
I pick up an arm full of childish dreams
  And throw them into the stream
And bid them 'Bon Voyage' as they drift off to sea.

Neil Keifer

The Cross

Once there was a Cross of olive wood,
  on which was sacrificed the Lamb of God.
His Blood so dear was running down the tree,
  to pay our ransom and to set us free.
It soaked the ground and filled the earth divine
  until one day, beside the Cross, there grew a vine.
It loved the Cross, for Life sprang from Its source;
  it grew and twisted, even hugged the Cross so coarse.
The vine enjoyed its life in the shadow of the Tree;
  it grew strong, it bore fruit and it became free.
It decided it needed not the Cross' support in time —
  the Cross was forgotten, decayed — then a new vine.
This vine became different as it flourished in the sun;
  its growth quickly entangled and choked the former one.
It formed a crown of thorns around that vine of old -
  the end of its growth as its branches grew cold.
The vine of old remembered the Cross and the Crown.
  Just ask for forgiveness — please do not frown.

Willy Effinger

Messenger Of Wisdom And Truth

As I glanced out my bedroom window, I gasped!
My eyes were drawn to the near spruce tree
Where nestled within was a superbly beautiful, breathtaking,
Tawny-gold, feathery Great Horned Owl!
I could hardly believe my eyes, but there it perched
With such a marvelous and gracious presence
That permeated the entire yard
And flowed directly to me through its steady gaze
and its serene countenance —
Time seemed to stand still.
There was a knowingness between us.
Only a few feet apart, for several minutes, we were as one
As we stared into each other's eyes.
This was a supreme messenger of unending love, peace,
Wisdom and truth —
I knew this such that it moved me and shook me to my very core —
That such a majestic presence
Would grace my yard
To unmistakably urge
My own deep inner wisdom and truth.

Janice A. Bohdan

Flowers In The Mist

Fluttering
Lazily along
On the cool, evening spring
Wind, there's an
Eager butterfly
Repetitiously
Swooping down

Into the
Never-ending field of blooming wildflowers.

The spiteful moon swings
Higher in the midnight sky, slowly
Ending the mild spring day.

Mist begins to form on the tips of leaves,
In the moonlight it begins to
Sparkle, generously handing out new hope
To all the flowers in the mist.

Stephanie Jensen

The Composure of Jimmy Sedgewick

The stately St. George's maintains its lofty place:
It finds its greatest pleasure in the pattern of its grace.
Gentlemen and ladies still often come to call
As the statesmen lie in state in the yard around them all.

T'was Sunday morning in '24, when people came to hear
How the Gospel of the Saviour can dispel the glummest fear.
The neighbours and the locals, who kept the fires stoked,
Welcomed all who joined them from valleys quite remote.

All seemed to be as proper as St. George's aught to be,
Until they lost the silence to a small, but loud, "tee-hee".
It was over in the corner that the laughter eased on in.
Where Jimmy Sedgewick always sat, appeared a tiny grin.

Mrs. Grimshaw tried to hide behind her soft gloved hand,
But not before the Reverend saw the laughter land.
Choir heads began to turn as Betsy Phillmore's snickers
And Bernard Jones's great guffaws threatened all dry knickers.

And all the while, poor Jimmy clutched his mouth and thought to pass:
When he'd swallowed his communion wine, he'd emptied out the glass.
Though all this happened long ago, the story still is told,
How Jimmy Sedgewick swallowed, whole, the big fly and the mold.

M. A. McAfee

You

My dreams are filled with the longings of love
The safety of fidelity, the security of being understood
You rise in them and I cannot define my wanting to try
from my separate wildness
If I were to let you know, would it be another sorry wave
My old heart had risen to and then, like God's eternal soldier,
Walked on from, soothing my pain with a dangerous intellectualism?
Yet with all my eyes have seen, all the skills in living I have learned,
It seems so strange that all this love should not be
conveyed to a kind and loyal reciprocator
To one who sees beyond this lovely shell into the depths
of a golden place wherein lies our legacy.
So if I reach out in this inspired moment, it is not that
I will not survive without you
Just that something in your eyes has not left me, though
your presence is removed by the miles and your private pain
Will you ever try again?

Beth MacPherson

Compensation

For every solitary gain
There's an equal corresponding loss.
The coveted prize one can attain,
But who can guess how great the cost?
The gentle breeze that fills the sails
And the fearsome,raging, ship-wrecking gales
Are but aspects of Mother Nature's winds;
Both the welcome and the unwanted she sends.
Rain often induces subtle moods of gloom,
But later abound fragrant flowers in bloom.
For every victor, elated and proud,
There is the vanquished, shoulders drooping, head bowed.
Some rise and some fall;
Some win; some lose all;
The give and take are both parts of the picture.
But whatever the time
And whatever the clime,
You will know that there's always a balance in nature.

John B. Calhoun Jr.

"Tear Drops Are Prayers Too!"

As I awoke to God's beautiful sunrise,
A large tear drop fell from my eyes;
"Thank you, dear Jesus," it said, "for one more day,"
"Thank you for your blessings sent our way."

As the beauty of the sun's rays slowly danced by,
I looked to heaven, still more tears filled my eyes;
"Heavenly Father, my heart is heavy and I pray to thee."
"Come my child, bring those tears to me."

"This tear is for the lonely and homeless of our land,
This tear is for the fighting on every hand;
We sinned, Lord Jesus, and evil is all around,
Hear my tear drops Father, and lift us off the ground.
This tear drop is for innocent lives taken,
This tear drop for our many hearts that are aching;
Send your love and peace from on high,
Please Lord Jesus, wipe our weeping eyes."

As each tear fell, he caught each drop in his hand,
"Hush little one, I hear my children's cries upon the land;
I will not leave you, nor forsake those who love me,
For through each tear drop, you can see me."

Anquinetta Yevell Boyd

My Valentine

Sweetheart though I've often tried,
There is no way to express the feelings I have inside.
When I have something special to share,
It is you who is always there.
When I'm hurting and need a helping hand,
You seem to be the only person who understands.
The love I have for you is special and rare,
I'll always treasure all that we share.
You're the one I think of when I hear a certain love song,
You always help me tell things right from wrong.
On this special day, I hope you realize,
How much you mean to me, and that you're the one person...
I love to love!!

Amy J. Scofield

"In The Window"

In the window there is an object
scattered around suffering.
Suggest that it would be written down,
But there was an error.
The extra limit of a minute of the modern flavor.
A hundred men and women inspected it,
And was inspired,
In an instant they shoveled the dishonored sign,
and entomb there shepherd.
The language of the choir of swords gave knowledge,
That echoed forming the mixture of helplessness
through the air.

Rainah Palermo

Tina

My daughter, Tina, if you only knew,
The feelings in my heart pertaining to you,
Your kindness and warmth my cup of tea,
A special friend you'll always be,
Your natural innocence captures my soul,
And the love you give a story untold,
A schedule so hectic and full of strife,
But you always remember me as part of your life,
Thank you sweetheart for a love so real,
Cause life without you would have no zeal.

Suzanne Klug

A Thousand Years

I am the ancient,
body wracked with disease.
The hypocrites of today,
my mind serves to them a feast.

I am the elderly,
the souls on my shoes worn thin.
The scars of war left on my legs,
ebony shades along my skin.

I am the timid,
lurking behind the grass.
Hear the monotone voices of our society,
patiently waiting for them to pass.

I am the immortal,
faintly spreading the word.
Life rushes by with feeling,
This message, it shall be heard.

I am the gifted,
blessed upon at birth.
The magic of self-expression,
A lover, one with the earth.

Julie Haroutunian

Hands

You extend them to the person you meet
  With love, or just a friendly greet
Used to wave in saying goodbye
  Or to dry the tear from your eye.

While Mother gently caresses her babe with her hand
  Father's working for their livelihood among man
For makeup for ladies, men to shave their face
  To bathe or shower in the bathroom place.

Receiving the nourishment the body to feed
  Preparing for your future need
Turning the page of a book you read
  Steering the car while viewing the speed.

Above all the most precious hand
  From a mere babe He came to save the world
Freeing from sin whoever human of the land
  Cares to pick up their cross as through this life they whirl.

As the work is finished at close of day
  We bow our head, place hands together, begin to pray
Thanking Him for our daily blessings we reap
  Asking for His guidance through the night as we sleep.

Ethel I. Carlton

The Little Bee

"Buzz", said the little bee, "I beg your pardon,"
"Is there anything I can do to help in your garden?
I watch as you work, hour after hour,
On your knees, pulling weeds, and setting out flowers.
Small I may be but I'm willing at heart,
Just whisper your wishes and I'll do my part."

"I'll dance through your flowers not missing a beat,
In and out, all about, till the job's complete.
With my tiny pollen mop I'll scrub everyone,
I'll dust them and paint them and when I am done,
We'll both sit together and gaze at the view,
I'm so happy I could be of help to you."

"No pay will I ask, it's all quite my pleasure,
A beautiful garden is everyone's treasure."

Edna S. Hughes

An Unlived Life

  It's so sad, they want me to die,
I want to do more than just lay here and cry.
  It's so sad, I want a mom and dad,
I was really looking forward to the fun times we could've had.

  I could've grown to be big and smart,
But she wants to take a pill to stop my heart.
  I could've grown to be tall and strong,
Take a look at me is there something wrong?

  She's taken the pill and I'm almost gone,
What in this world have I done.
  She's taken the pill now it's my time,
Why don't people consider death to us little ones a crime?

  It's a mystery, the answer I'll never know,
We're still people but they just let us go.
  It's a mystery this terrible sin,
They use our dead flesh to beautify their skin.

I am in heaven now, this wonderful place,
I study God's love, His power and grace.
I am in heaven now, the beauties I do see,
Daddy really wanted me, but Mommy didn't agree.

Tawana Brock

Where Once I Had A Heart

The light was vanished
Swallowed by the night
The Omega has come
The Alfa will not return

I long for answers
To the questions that destroy
Taunting my mind draining my will

Won't somebody listen?
Won't somebody care? Where once I had a heart

I long for release
From the unseen shackles that bind
Constricting my soul tormenting my heart

I long for friendship someone who will be there
Who will never be leave and will walk beside me

Won't somebody listen?
Won't somebody care?

I long for the love
No one has ever shown me that can't be bought
It comes from the heart I long for something
To fill this enormous void which has developed the place

Where once I had a Heart

Erin E. Hening

The Infant Deserves Breast Milk

The breast is to the infant
what the placenta meant to it, in-utero.
Breast milk, like blood, is alive:
From it, infant derives immunity and safety shields

Human breast milk advantageously nurtures
the human genes optimally;
No wonder breast-fed children have
higher Intelligent Quotients and developmental milestones

Humans are the only homo sapiens denying
their newborns of their breast milk!
Human breast milk is
Custom-made for human offsprings

Will you let your child lose-out?
Your baby deserves the real thing

Stephany Udi Ighedosa, M.D.

My Angel

On the special day you were born,
the darkness of the dreary day was masked by the clouds parting
to let the sun stream through.

So beautiful! So bright!

What a miracle...
An angel from heaven had come to acknowledge your birth
and wish me well.

The beauty of it will remain,
as seen through my eyes and felt in my heart.

You are my angel,
my sunlight
my inspiration.

Audrey R. DeBlasis

My Family

I wonder what my family will be like,
Will all my family still be alive?
Will I have to visit more grave sites?
If so, who will be next to go?
But if I have my way, everyone will stay,
No matter what, I know they are safe;
With God and angels they will be.
Will life still be the same?
No way — it's full of change.
I also know, I will see them again,
In the kingdom of God at the end.

Suzanne Clinton

Abysmal Change

The tree will lose its leaves each fall.
Again, winter arrives; the wind sounds its call

The tree is barren, cold, and alone
No mercy has the winter shown.

Each season takes its turn.
Never to recur, the realist will learn.

"The tree has back its leaves," some will say.
As if, again, the same leaves sway.

A mistake all too often made,
for an indefinite farewell was bade.

Merry Piper Allison

Goodby Precious, Goodbye

Souring in the misty grey sky, through great heights
A bird was discovered
It flew towards me as the rainy clouds drifted
My soul awakened to its immaculate song
As we communicated through a language of our own
Fascinated by its grace and style
I admired it for a while
Slowly I extended my hands towards it and held it
Then I fed it from its hunger
Nurturing and giving it affection
It got use to my voice
Coming back for my attention
Loving its company, its charm
I caged it, in fear that I would loose it
But when I least expected it, the bird escaped
My precious creature had left me
For it never belonged to me.

Iliana Lopez

China Doll

There is a special china doll,
Teetering on the shelf's edge.
The voice inside her tries to call,
Seeking answers from the ledge.

Inside torment long sequestered,
Domain of anguish, so alone,
Outside realm, she portrays a jester,
Needs a haven for pain not shown!

Her external world takes no heed
To understand her plight.
God gives his strength. His way to lead,
This dragon she must fight.

The challenge soars with powerful might!
Behold, this gentle soul will not stumble.
She is determined to preserve what is right,
Despite the terrifying storm's fierce rumble!

Diana J. Weigel

Walk With Thee

Lord let me walk with thee
If I stumble along the way
I know you will be there to
Keep me through the day.

Don't let me be made ashamed;
Because I know you can
help me to win it's not a game;

Please dear Lord hold
my hand as I journey through the land

Because Jesus I need Thee
I need Thee I know you care for
You are always there I don't want to slide
Just be my guide if I fall by the way
You will be there all the day
Because you shed your innocent blood
for me to trust you the best I could;
Lord if my way seems dreary don't let me get weary
I know you will be there to protect me
Because you are my guide so let me not go and hide

Alma L. Bailey

Alone

It seems my life is like an empty sphere,
I lost so much of what I once possessed
My cries for help nobody seems to hear;
By lonely thoughts my mind is now obsessed.

The joys I had in life are in the past;
The love I want has somehow passed me by.
For me it seems that happiness can't last,
And now I sit alone and wonder why.

I place my need on people that I know
And hope that there is someone who will care.
Rejection makes me realize that it's so -
I turn for help and see that no one's there.

If somewhere there is one who cares for me,
I pray that he will somehow hear my plea.

Amy Hyncik

Earth Reaches Sky

I glance at the sky,
 Through the eyes of my mind
 To see the life that you breathe
 Through the eyes of your soul.

It's there,
 For I see the life that you lead
 Brings smiles from beneath
 The soul that I keep.

I glance at the sky,
 Through memories of my mind
 To a soul that is free.

My place is the sea,
 The earth and the grass.

Yours is the wind,
 The clouds in the sky.

From here I can see,
 That earth reaches sky
 And sky reaches earth.

And nothing's as wonderful as the life that I see.
For it's your life that I breathe.

Lisa Diane Miller

"What Am I?"

I am a single blade of grass growing stronger each day and
I am dawn shimmering on a serene mountain lake, as two swans
 float by...
In the morning I am slithery snake sidewinding my way to work,
But in the evening I am a relaxed wave lapping gently upon the
 seashore.
Sometimes I am a grizzly bear yearning to hibernate in my cave,
But most of the time I am an ear listening to ideas about to become
 reality.
On Saturdays I am a cloud unable to awake from a dream, while on
Sundays I am a rubberband pulled in opposite directions,
 all stretched out.
Then there's Friday and I am a milkshake about to be savored.
This is me...this is what I am.

Janeen E. Marcel

"Moments Of Clarity"

An artist stares blankly at a white canvas
deciding what forms should be born, thoughts flash
through his mind at excessive speeds, for the wheels
are turning and his emotions are burning. For the
delicate stroke of the brush, begins the Adrenalin rush.
It is when we dispel all disparities we can embrace a
moment of clarity.
 A poet chasing down an idea, as he is filled with unintelligible
words that when presented must be clear.
 The poet fixated on the unmarked page as he becomes
an actor without a stage. Thoughts into words a
process absurd, for a thoughts intention but words
fail to mention. But when words reach a parity
we realize a moment of clarity.
 It is these moments we are most astute.
It is at these moments our surroundings are mute.
As it is at this precise time when our
spirits become sublime.

Adam Serritella

Life's Riches

May your life be filled with these riches:
Loved ones to give you comfort,
A career that provides joy and wealth,
Enough happiness to make each day inviting,
Achievements to give life meaning,
Goals to make life a challenge, and
Just enough adversity to add
mettle to your character.

Morsie L. Edgerson

The Garden Of Eden

The holy grail
Lies upon the ground
Dry as my mouth.
The want of a fresh fruit of the garden
Has caused my excommunication
From paradise.
Sin, such a deadly thing
Now to this I attribute my loss
Of everything.
With slender scaled eyes of deceit
I was ensnared,
To be one who takes a death warrant dare.
Plagued by knowledge I do not want
Wanting innocence I can never regain,
The constrictions are now before me
And each has a vulnerable subscript immaculate.

Sean R. Whiting

"The Real Me"

Where did the real me go? I used to be
so happy, I used to be so free, I used to
be the smiling one - that used to be me.

I know I've had my problems. I know I'm
not quite the same. I know my feelings
aren't normal - what's causing me this pain?

I'm doing my best with everything around me.
I try so hard to please. I do things for others
that most would not do. I am there for
everyone when they beg and plead.

I don't understand why I feel so blue.
I know there's always going to be hard
times, but what is there that I can do?

I have few feelings left, doesn't anyone
understand? Can't they see that I am
no longer happy and most of all, that it's
not really me.

Sarah A. Parrack

"World Of Doubt"

Can you truly grasp a world of doubt;
And no reality is a part of you;
Time seems to push you out;
Of a world you thought you knew.

Oh yes, I can deeply understand;
The words of wisdom one might employ;
To shrewdly think I am a man;
Of substance and heart, and not a toy.

Let's try to overcome this fantasy;
Trying to live in a world of perfection;
To do so, you must really see;
Is just a part of your imagination.

To say I've tried would be suffice;
Having all the money and clout;
A life of reality would be nice;
If it wasn't for this world of doubt.

Ray Kelling

Menopause

I'm absolutely nuts, I'm steady as a rock
I want to scream my head off, I do not want to talk
I'm laughing at the dumbest things, I'm quiet as a mouse
I want my friends to come for lunch, I crave an empty house
I wake up hot and sticky - don't touch me you're a jerk!
I know it's only 4 a.m. get up and go to work!
I truly love my family, I can't stand anyone
I want to sit alone and cry, I want to go have fun
My best friend say this too shall pass, what do you know I say
You're ten years younger, you feel good, come here - no go away!
If I survive this awful thing it's likely we will see
That I'll be happy in ten years and she'll become like me.
Joanie Haynes

Untitled

I'm eighty, and time has flown, like a bird on wing,
and I still haven't accomplished everything!

There are so many things I wanted to do!
But, I'll not despair,
I'll go back in time, and remember
a life of blessings, joys and sorrow,
and live in the knowledge,
I have precious children and friends,
to help fill my tomorrows.
Adele Kverno

And The Rain Poured Down

It was a cold March night, During a cold March storm
The wind was howling; the rain was warm.
A girl was there, without her soul.
A boy was there, with eyes like coal.
And the rain poured down.

The thunder clapped with her every shout
She screamed out No and squirmed about.
"Shut up; Don't cry; Or I'll make you pay."
Then he finished the job, And simply walked away.
And the rain poured down.

She turned to watch him go, Tears stinging her eyes
Why hadn't anyone heard her piercing cries?
She was left all alone, in the empty lot
She felt puzzled, confused; Stomach in a knot.
And the rain poured down.

She sat on the curb and Thought of what to do
He'd stolen her innocence in the light of the moon.
The lightning flashed as she picked up a knife
Then stabbed her aching heart and ended her life.
And the rain poured down.
Kate Ryan O'Connor

My Prayer

From this world where might is right
Comes an army aimlessly to fight
Some say oppression, brutality they fought
To me it is bloodshed, tears for naught.
Yet, I am here to settle a score
That should have been settled years before
By men who are wiser than myself today
But lacked the wisdom yesterday.
I pray to God that light will come
And that I can overcome this vast emptiness that
brings blood and pain
Gives me living a cause not to fight in vain.
Samuel Lieberman

Observation

I saw a young man today, made instantly old
In one quick second, the years did unfold
A letter of sorrow, clutched in a withered hand
Told a story of broken love, that we all understand

His sunken cheeks, quickly running with tears
His anguished mind, confirming his fears
He stumbles, age showing on decrepit thighs
And gazes at the world through his dead eyes

My heart aches with empathetic pain
"Look!", I shout, "See the beauty of the rain"
"Or the magic of the leaves, falling away!"
"Why even the trees and I, share common DNA"

But he dismisses each, with an old shrug
Seeing only devastation, amid troubles tight hug
How does one comfort the heartbroken!
And heal that gaping wound with words merely spoken

He shuffles off, maybe looking for a cane
Oblivious to all, except his pain
I look away, mentally wishing him the best
And begin in turn examining the rest!
Norman E. Shaw IV

Lord

Who is this man who died for me?
Who gave himself at Calvary?
Who is this man that heals the sick and the blind,
This man of love, this man so kind?
He teaches me to pray and to give.
He bled and died that I might live.
He conquered death, he conquered sin.
He bled and died and lives again:
It's Him I praise and whom saints sing:
Lord of Salvation, Christ our King!
Sarah Schroeder

The Single Red Rose

I walked into the room
and there upon the pillow
lay a single red rose, to symbolize
the love we share.
A single tear rolled down
my cheek, a smile spread upon my face.
I knew the love we had
would always be there
and we would be together forever
all thanks to a single red rose.
Nicole Guay

To Crater Lake...Oregon

Oh priceless gem of azure hue,
Bless the Gods who fashioned you
in the rugged crater of Vulcan's eye.
You gaze eternally at the changing sky.
No mortal sight can pierce the depth
Where your fires were quenched when nature wept;
No pen nor brush can your beauty tell
For in all men's hearts you cast a spell.
Would that I were the wisest sage
To learn your secret, how through the age.
Your matchless beauty and sereneness air
Have made a perfect jewel for God to wear.
Clarence King

Walls Of The Unknown Prisoner

Shackled to my wrists are chains of reality
Of knowledge that can never be
To caress skin of soft sweetness, to kiss love's lips yearning but strange,
Will come not to me.
My four walls are adorned with murals of the specters of my mind
Sometimes so close to my heart
Mostly, far beyond lies my life's shrine
The reason, what is the reason?
Choices, they say, made in haste
Am I doomed to live this way?
Is my soul worth nothing; is it a soul to waste?
I strive and survive
By gathering crumbs of love and kindness
That are sparsely scattered upon my path
I will do my time serenely, and accept society's wrath
My day will come when I'll walk among the best
Either with my former keepers
Or with God in final rest
My day will come

Brenda Gilbert

Shadows

Shadows of what used to be
Were memories for me
All the time
Come and gone
What could have ever gone wrong
It may have been a mistake
But it feels much worse
Every things gone
Nothing to spare
Almost to much times gone to care
The flames come now they're gone
All they left me are shadows of what used to be.

Laura Gibbs

Mom

You always make the sun shine bright on my rainy days,
You love me unconditionally, even though you may not agree,
  with all my decision or ways.
Like the mighty oak, you keep our family strong.
You stand by me when I'm right, and always there to pick
  up the pieces when I do wrong.
I know sometimes I get busy and I might not
  always thank you for the things you do or say,
But just remember even though I'm not always around,
I'm thinking of you every step of the way.
  So right now, I want you to enjoy your special day,
Again, thank you for being you, and molding me into
  the woman, I've become today.

"Happy Mother's Day"
I Love You!

Staci Cirksena-Baumgartner

A New Leaf

Leaves as green as emeralds holding on so strong
One by one the leaves dance off to a distant song

One lone leaf falls and simply blows around
Coming ever so close but never touching the ground

Another leaf blows into a stream giving way to the flow
It drifts along in the murky water never wanting to go

And then there is a beautiful leaf turning red and gold
It wants to find a purpose before it gets too old

It flings itself into the hands of a man passing through
He takes the leaf and then decides to turn it over anew

Linda Diaz

Who Am I?

How can you dance, and never hear a tune?
How can you travel, and never leave the room?
How can the sun shine, in the dark of night?
Where is the darkness, when there is no light?

How can you have, and never possess?
How can you hold, but never caress?
How can you give up, but never give in?
How can you start, but never reach your end?

How can you see, with eyes closed tight?
How can you be blind, and still have sight?
How can you be bold, and remain discreet?
How can you build, but never complete?

How can you drink, but never quench your thirst?
How can being last, help you to be first?
How can you work, and never tire?
How can you need, without desire?

How can you read, and never turn a page?
How can you grow old, but never age?
Who am I? But before you decide,
Align your heart and mind, and let your conscience be your guide.

I. John Turrentine

Why Pretend You Don't Need Family

Family is considered by some unimportant.
But wasn't your sperm-and-egg start vital?

Surely you don't expect us humans to be like dogs.
How do we know whose child thrives with who?

Hey, who knows your name and history best?
Yes, no invention or arrangement beats parents.

Parents are natural and most protect their own.
Most children get their prep in nuclear families.

They don't trick or pretend, or favor in bonding.
Unnatural bonding by others is predatory.

Others will feed on the young and unprotected.
Mental bondage by unethical relationship stinks.

Seductions or coercions makes child a prey.
Natural parents don't have to steal their own.

What parent doesn't look forward to being grandparents.
Generation follows generation for continuity of love.

Love and not money keeps health and sanity well.
Through all the good and lean years love holds up.

Money has its cycles of ups and downs in change.
Family keeps constancy and seasons celebrated!

Nicholas L. Zouras

My Grandfather And I

As my Grandfather sat down today,
I knew it was not time for play,
He's telling us about his past.
Grandchildren gathered on his knees and lap,
Waiting for the terrific story,
Telling us about the wondrous glory.
As I sat there and thought,
About all the things he has taught,
He's my doorway to a different time,
Just as I am his.
We share a common light you see,
I am his bridge to future,
He is mine to past,
In that sense we live in immortality.

Hilary Stockbridge

Someone Who

My needs are small,
My wants are few.
All I need is someone who...

Can make me laugh when I want to cry.
Someone to care of I live or die.
Someone to tell my troubles to.
Someone to say "I love you, I do"
Someone to reach and touch my hand.
Someone to say "I understand."
Someone to lead me from darkness to light.
Someone to show me wrong from right.
Someone to keep me close to home,
And quell the urge when I want to roam.
Someone to guard me from the rain.
Someone to keep me from feeling pain.
Someone to love, honor, and trust.

These are the things that must be must.
All of these things I've found in you.
My wonderful someone,
My someone who

Erin Baum

She Is Created

She is created.
She swims in the womb of a glowing face.
She is born.
She lets out a startled cry of uncertainty.
She is taught.
She's always looking for a challenge.
She's in love.
She melts in his every embrace.
She weds.
She cries as she repeats the words of God.
She creates.
She knows only to give the child everything.
She grows older.
She watches the years build on the faces of loved ones
She is a grandmother.
She sees herself in the child's weeping eyes.
She withers.
She prays in thanks with family by her side. She's gone.

She is created.
She swims in the womb of a glowing face.

Jessica Raley

Gratitude?

I flung my door back open wide,
To let in freshness from outside.
And golden shafts of flickering light
The sun had filtered through the night
Broke through the leaves and in my door
Then spilled like nuggets on my floor.

A wild canary, green and yellow,
A pretty little frightened fellow,
He found the path the sun had taken
Too late he found he was mistaken.
He flew about the room and tried
To find his way again outside.

The blue sky and the trees looked through
What was a little bird to do?
Then from my hands uncupped he flew
To freedom and the world he knew.
He seemed a most ungrateful bird.
Maybe a "Thank you" never heard.

Till swinging on a limb his song
Brought gladness to me all day long.

Lillian Maylor Grubbs

We're Missing You

I'm blue and hurtin' a lot
But can't go against the Master's plot.

I stare at your chair
Thinking you'd maybe be there.

I hear your voice talking to me
But, really I know it cannot be.

You're with the Master, you're His own
For 72 years, He gave you as a loan.

It had to end, to release your pain
His promise to us - we'll meet again.

Your name shall be carried on
By two sons, and six grandsons.

One daughter, and one granddaughter.
None of our love will ever falter.

Don't go too far, keep close to us.
Especially on Easter, Thanksgiving and Christmas.

Your advice and "know-how" we miss
Remembering memories, we can't resist.

Rest in peace, Pal, with our Savior
We'll meet again, our love will never waver.

M. M. Hoffman

Shadowman, A Mother's Cry

He's my Shadowman.
He leaves footsteps from another world. His shadow world.
He's lean and long and brown and earthy.
He has hair on his legs; his beard keeps growing.
His eyes are dark with rings tossed by his shadow friends.
They've landed true. He belongs to them.
(But he's My Shadowman.)
His hair hangs lank and sometimes curls.
A blank, hazed look. Shadow look. Not there look.
All he wants is to be left alone.
Leave him to his shadow world. He is of no substance.
Don't reach out to him. You'll get a handful of nothing.
Tell his friends: He's My Shadowman,
And you can't have him.

Cal Wilkerson

Evolution

When speaking of men I think it's a sin,
To compare them to the occupants of a pig pen.
It is most unkind and I must draw the line,
Why insult and malign the noble swine?

What you ask is the contrast,
Between a man and a jacka**?
One is a beast of burden with class,
The other is simply an a**.

Do not compare men with the canine,
The difference is in their design.
Dogs have faithfully served mankind,
While men have done nothing but whine.

To speculate man derived from ape,
Is a theory I will not tolerate.
Every woman can easily see,
The difference between a man and a chimpanzee.

And just as an addendum,
What species did man evolve from?
I refuse to believe men were conceived.
From anything in the animal kingdom.

Debbie Palmer

Thankful For Human Growth And Learning

I am thankful for life,
With its strange processes of ovulation and fertilization,
And some who call it pollination,
Genotype and phenotype and hormones and chromosomes.

I am thankful for the theories of development,
That enable me to study and change the direction of my life,
From assimilation to accommodation,
And from unconscious motivation to sublimation.

I am thankful for peers,
And some who are known as overseers and,
Parents and grandparents classmates and soul mates, teachers and
preachers, and bullies we hope can later become self-actualized fully.

I am thankful for people who care and stand firm in times of despair,
People who create and motivate,
People who live and forgive and,
People who continue to grow physically, mentally, and psychosocially.

I'm sure my list of thanks would continue to ramble,
But I must scramble to complete this preamble,
That's dedicated to growing and knowing, giving and living,
And being thankful and grateful.

Gloria Dansby-Giles

Ode To A Golden Retriever

When I felt alone, you were always near
When I needed help, you were always there
I treasure your memory and ache in my heart
For love that's been lost...since we've been apart

It takes endless pain, it takes endless time
To surrender your memories...from my mind
I'd been a better man, I'd had a wiser plan
If I had only known I was losing you

There can never be another who could take your place
You brought me happiness, you taught me grace
May God always bless you, wherever you are
You were always my hero, you were always my star

When darkness is coming and no longer can I see
I'll call for your love and your closeness to me
To be my final guide... to the other side
Till we meet again...

F. T. Williams

At The Bottom

Life ties us all to a sinking anchor, seas roll with waves of fear
like thunder, what a price we pay for glory, yet still it makes me wonder.

Is this the bottom of my soul, the end of what's to be
if I ever make my peace, will I ever really be free

Where do I go from here, how do I rise above
to find a better life, what's this thing called love

At the bottom of this ocean, I'm drowning in my tears
for me it's been eternity, yet only 34 years

Swim against the currents, I know I have to try
pray I find my way back home, and live before I die

The bottom of it all is where you have to start
to make it to the surface, the answer's in your heart

It's an endless struggle, will it ever stop
just take it nice and steady, you'll make it to the top

The bottom of the ocean is a dark and lonely void
keep your head above the water, or you'll go paranoid

The day you surface from the sea is when you know you've won
that's when your anchor rises, to your raisin in the sun.

Sheryl Marcia Schwartz

Come Home With Me

I had a dream
about you last night.

So I decided to visit you
this morning when it was quiet,
when the light was such that
the sun was just beginning its day,
and the moon was ending its night.

Let me take you away from the
city and the noise,
and bring you into my world.

Here I will make you forever.
I'll bring you to another level,
a dimension that is higher than anyone who walks by
during these numbered days on this earth.

You will become color,
beautiful color.

You will become the essence of nature in the confines of
my world.
Here you will never die.

Elizabeth Heidi Pearson

Those

Those who care about themselves and no one else,
    live in sorrow and misery.

Those who would see the world at war always,
    have no idea of what freedom brings.

Those who think violence is a way of life,
    have never known kindness.

Those who think that enemies are all around them,
    have never tried to make a friend.

Those who think that hate is a way of life,
    will never be able to love another.

Those who would never help someone in need,
    are themselves in need of someone.

Those who go among life with these thoughts and destructive
    feelings, are lost lonely souls that are truly not living.

R. D. Stanley

Eden's Poem

Little Miss Eden no buttons nor bows
But bathed in love from your head to your toes

With parents who'll love you a little too much
And Grandma's and Grandpa's who'll melt with your touch.

Like the potter's clay you lie in wait
For the forces of life to determine your fate

Be not afraid of the future my dear
For Jesus our Lord will always be near.

Like all new babies you'll be wrinkled and pink
We're all quite sure that occasionally you'll stink.

If the Good Lord is willing and your mother is able
We'll expect you for dinner the last day of April.

But should you decide to be a bit late
We'll forgive you of course and save you a plate.

So until your arrival be a good girl
And prepare yourself to give life a whirl

A. Troy Richards

Pearl Of The Sea

Pearl of the sea,
You are so beautiful to me,
When I look in your eye at night,
I see the starlight, to comfort me.
With the sound of the sea, to capture me,
To set me free, with the ocean breeze.
Waiting for the sun,
To warm me, to the time to come.

Steven Lusk

Spring

Air gently warming, to greet another day
Fresh green shoots, pushing through warm earth
To give us spring again in its rebirth.
Birds joyously singing on warm bright mornings
Greeting us again on a new day dawning.
Virgin leaves burst forth on branches
Giving joy and color before our eyes
Making lattice work of clear blue skies.
A glorious medley of flower and bud
Is like the discovery of a new love
the miracle of life is ours to behold
As old as the hills our ancient gold
Give thanks for it all in fallow and field
For spring once more and all it will yield

Sonia Richardson

The Dusty Cerebellum

She looks into her own orbs
    mesmerized by the shade.
Touching the terrain of her face...
She glances at the porcelain throne
    Throwing her head back in rapture.

Wanting the painting to absorb her;
    to bathe in vibrant color
To eat emeralds and rubies; to lay down
    in the music and dream.
"Close your eyes, "she says.
    "Do you see it now?"
Breathing in the toasted scent of grief,
    she grabs the sunlight and puts it in
Her Pocket.

Peri A. Bever

The Abused Child

Oh wretched child!
Your fate unknown
Why Heaven for you
No sweet flowers grow?
Instead, your days and nights are shadowed.

Abused! Abused! Oh child in anguish
Parental love is never showered
Upon your heart to light your paths
Oh child abuse! Oh battered child!
Why seldom kissed? Why seldom praised?

Oh child abused!
So often cursed, so often bruised
No smile across your wilting face
Pitied by few and scorned by many
Abused you are, oh child of sorrow.

Oh Heaven! Forget not the abused
How could angels chime those bells above?
And know that the abused no sweet chant could hear
No rose; but thorns for the child abused
Scorched is your world by adult's fury.

Pansy Patterson

Broken Promise

As I walk through the land of broken promises
I see love and dreams that are now departed
Whenever I see a broken promise
What I see is the broken hearted
Their dreams are all torn apart
Just like feelings ripped from the heart
Everyone around me is hurt and sad
Thinking, remembering what they once had
Nothing ever has to be like this
It was all gone in an ungrateful bliss
Somehow, we the broken hearted will prevail
So strong, we can stand in a storm of hail
The road to recovery is long and narrow
We fly it under the wings of a sparrow
I again will stand and rejoice
If only anyone, will hear my voice
The Great Spiritual Power within
Will strengthen my heart again
These things are long overdue
It should happen, when I once Loved You

Larry Thompson

Ageless Vision

It's sad to see the winter's force...
The cold, bare world is hard to face...

Time has set its bitter course...
and compels me to follow in reluctant pace...

Yes, time's fierce hand directs me now...
the essence of life's spring has flown

Spring is gone, and yet somehow.
I see the blossoms of loves I've known

I can see them in visions so vivid and true...
those who wooed me; hear their loving sighs...

I feel the soft lips of passion anew
and recount soft murmurs and tender cries...

Spring's flame, sadly, has gone out...
Its warm breezes are like daydreams

Life's lush green leaves, I must do without
and life's breath is now what winter deems...

And yet the dream-like scenes remain..
in a colorful, silent parade

All through life's cold winter, and the pain...
My soul won't let those visions fade.

D. Catananzi Snyder

Trinity

Realm of sorrow
Divine evil speeds its wings upon tomorrow
Over flowing beauty of the beast...darkness is blinding
Caressing the neck of life...its tail winding
Shut out the light of love
Salvation in the dark and stormy skies above
"Come hither wallowing child of being"
Passionate claws grasping
Fly away...
Leave the creature of pity in today
The past is the future
The future has passed
Yet today is caught between the two realities and it
    will always last
The cries of death die as the dragon, overhead flies
And with it...all sound is gone, leaving the mind
    to compromise
Fools are silenced

Summer B. Franklin

Victims Of Pride

Two boys were singing in a church choir,
The both were so off-key.
Yet one himself was ever humble,
The other prideful as could be.

The prideful one thought, "This poor lad,
His notes, they make me require,
Because his singing is unusually bad,
Myself to sing a little bit higher."

The most sour of notes he began to blurt,
His pride was in full bloom.
Some visitors said that their ears hurt,
Yes, some even ran from the room.

Later, one said to the other,
"Your singing was strangely sour.
Even though you are my churchly brother,
You scared some people in the hour."

The humble one replied, "Friend, I will
Not your own notes chide.
But those who ran while you swelled
Were only victims of pride."

Kyle Brown

The Apple Tree

Somewhere there is an apple tree with
luscious fruit hanging from its limbs.
But it grows in a forest where no one will see it.
Some of its fruit will fall to the ground,
to rot or be eaten by animals.
Some of its fruit will have holes punched
in its beautiful red skin by hungry birds.
But just because its crop was not harvested
by human hands, doesn't mean that its
fruit had no worth.

John A. Lomax

One Day At The Beach

Throwing starfish back into the sea —
Trapping Coquinas, then setting them free.

Seeing a porpoise, hard at play —
Tapping two sea-shells, wishing he'd stay.

Building a castle from sand that we pour-
When this one's done, we will build some more.

Walking back through sea-grass and all —
Swimming over creepy things that crawl.

Back to the homestead, we two go —
"Can we do it again tomorrow?" "I don't know."

Sandra Osborne Bator

Haunting

I live in myself, dripping with desire.
The paper walls are floating with some ease.
The windows whisper always and conspire,
So I don't open them; fear of disease.
I lock myself away in my small room,
No one can get me and I can't get out.
The walls of stone enclosed, I'm in a tomb.
My strength is torn from me, I have no doubt.
No longer can I breathe, she cut my air.
A surge of power and a surge of pain.
Our love no more because she does not care.
My life ends simply and I do not gain.
I see her near and I look up and wave,
In a pass she drops flowers on my grave.

Robin Gunning

Rude Awakening

What is it that you see, that you want to share with me?
I put the pillow over my head to drown out the sounds.
What is it that you see, that you want to share with me?
As I wasn't quite ready to meet the early dawn.
They shrieked and peeped, shrilled and squealed
And banged against my windowsill.
What is it that you see, that you want to share with me?
For I'm not quite ready to meet the early morn.
The sky is red, the sky is red, one bird shrieked
the sky is red.
I uncovered my head and turned to peek
And there it was, a deep, deep red.
That was at its ultimate peak.
With dimension of depth, with streaks of purple and other reds
That bled then blended into that deep, deep, red.
The sky was red, really red, and at its ultimate peak
That early morn, the birds did shriek just before the dawn and shared
with me one early morn.

Heather Sidney Farmer

This Golden Flower

Impatience, Roses, Tulips, yes,
All of these one can address.
Yet, one flower still remains,
That one flower stands unnamed.
No flower but one,
Can dance in the flaming sun.
This one flower can move around,
And it can rest on my ground.
And the color of most flowers,
Have no hypnotizing powers.
That is, except for one,
The one who can get up and run.
This golden flower! This glowing flower!
Who doesn't need a rain shower!
This golden flower! The strangest flower!
Who can move around at any hour.
Oh! Such a mane of gold!
Oh! How soft to hold!
I'll plant your seeds and watch you sprout,
What a sight to see you move about!

Jenna Scorza

Trash Now Runs Through It

The river runs deep and steady
  carrying with it many things
Leaves, branches and rubbish
  floods from a heavy Spring.

The river I recall as a child
  was fun for us to swim
Picnics on river banks
  often unplanned - done on a whim.

As a kid I knew that river
  like the veins on back of my hand
And all those places for fishing
  where hundreds of small fish once swam.

'Tis not the same this river
  seemingly angry as it flows
Once peaceful and for us gentle
  always our fun place to go.

That seems almost eons ago
  our river when we were kids
Now polluted by those uncaring
  with warning signs posted "Swimming Forbid."

William Henry Jones

My Golden Flower

My golden flower was born in the year of seventy three.
She was full of life, such a blessing to me.
As years passed, she blossomed, to her golden form.
Her petals grew stronger thru life's many storms.
Tears formed on her petals, like the morning dew.
Which gave her courage, to make it thru
The winds blew, tossing and turning her way,
No time to worry, no time to play
One night my Golden Flower, was caught off guard
She fought for her life, so long and hard,
Her petals were bruised, withered, and torn.
Not fresh, like the day when she was born.
At the tender young age of twenty one.
Her work on this earth, was done.
No one know's who her assassin could be.
Only God hold's this answer, just for me.
Now my golden flower is shinning so bright.
In heaven with Jesus, in his glorious light.
When all of my work, on this earth is done.
I'll be forever with my flower, Diana, my beloved one.

Gwendolyn Gail Washburn

Double Trouble

There was a little old lady driving down the alley
Minding her own business and treating folks fairly,
When suddenly appeared going ninety to nothing
A reckless old driver with his pick up jolting,
Flying past her, his vehicle too close to her side.
He forced her car bumping, scraping the wall's hide.
She stopped and he didn't, but sped down the lane.
She thought to herself, man, you must be insane.
So now stuck with repairs to her car very new,
She was shaken, oh yes, but got not even a bruise.

Now this dear sweet lady had a job to do,
Contacting insurance, getting estimates too.
That done, she headed for the best repair shop
Only to encounter another sad stop.
A nice young fellow in his girlfriend's jeep
To get out of traffic attempted a leap,
But alas and alas he rammed her rear end
More damage to metal that's now crackled and bent.
Oh, this spunky little lady had what it takes
Just said to herself, guess I'm not due all the "brakes!"

Elizabeth F. Elkins

"Specialists"

There were once two little brothers named Karl and Peter
Who were normal kids, but unique that neither
had mundane thoughts or average ambitions
But far and beyond routines and conditions
They aspired to make their mark, if they could,
by helping and saving and doing much good.
They studied the sciences, biology and such
and cut up their share of frogs and much
more, cadavers and stitches and all sorts of stuff
That strengthened their ability to deal with the tough.

They went on to accomplish what they sent out to do
In an office together without much more ado.
In very short order, people came to their door
with health problems galore and were assisted and more.
From the time that they entered, a calmness prevailed
and assurance replaced fear of what was entailed.
The aura of skilled knowledge these doctors imparted
gave a boost to the spirits of the ill and downhearted.
Each of these boys reached up to obtain
a Hand from God for their accomplishments gained.

Nancy B. Ott

"I'm In Love With Someone I Can't Have"

I was sitting down at my work site doing security.
Her head was down, she looked up for a second I noticed her beauty.
I stood up quick but it was too late, for she went away.
I thought silently, if it's meant to be I'll see her another day.
One of those days I let my feelings win and I lose.
Tick tock, clicking, and flipping of the time.
A couple hours later I see the woman I thought I'll see another time,
If it was meant to be.
Now it's time to introduce myself to this beautiful lady.
As she nearly slips away I catches her as I speak.
I say to her, "Why so late a beautiful woman like yourself
walk the street?"
I guess it's not meant to be; she says she's mad at her fiance.
"He's cheating on me and from Atlanta to San Diego I traveled to be with him.
Found some obscene letters by women that slept with him.
Also he has been spending time with his baby's mamma.
I came all the way from Atlanta to go through this drama!
I'm through with him like the marriage I once had."
"I'm in love with someone I can't have."

Damon R. X. Colbert

Diamond In The Rough

The storm clouds gather overhead, the sky turns ebony black.
Winds whip up with gale force strength, nature springs an attack.
Slashes trees, sways the lines, and sets the windows rattling.
Rocks the house, scatters the seed, sets our wits to battling.

Where shall we run, where can we hide, from fury's mighty roar.
Slashing rain, melting hail, and lightening bolts that soar.
Across the heavens, to the ground, that rocks as thunder rolls.
Deafening, scary, dangerous, it penetrates our souls.

Then in a blink the sun appears, and fluffy clouds so white.
A multi colored rainbow, creates a splendid sight.
A smell of freshness fills the air, trees like diamonds gleam.
The world puts on a happy face, mother nature's washed it clean.

Esther M. Steed

Better Off Dead

Like an owl in the night
He prowls with no light

High in the sky
For he is not shy,
He spots his prey

He hears in his head,
It's all about control,
I must have control.

As he looks down
He sees her on the ground

And there she lay,
For she does not say he may

She looks up to see
Her good friend at her knees
He says don't scream,
But it is what it seems.

Now he is no longer her friend,
And her heart cannot mend.

And she is better off dead. Enough said.

Sharla Wall

What Came Out Of The Bag

First, the damp, rumpled bathing suit,
then the enormous sunhat,
the tiny grains of sand
like pepper in a salad, everywhere,
even in the pages of my journal

To remind me over and over the swims
before breakfast and the last
before the evening sky turned rose.

It's the colors I wish I might have packed;
aquamarine from the sea, red from the hibiscus
almost too intense to believe.

Today the pictures came back, six rolls,
the light brighter than anywhere else, with
the Harbour Island families on Easter Sunday,
the fishermen's ebony skin against their white boats,
a young horse rolling in the sand,
and the ocean in sparkling greens
crashing in tiny waves of cream
over the pink beach and all of it,
gems swirling, like the best of dreams.

Marjorie Powers White

"Reality Check"

Well, today's the day, you always knew would come
Just like the call of the crow, or the heat of the sun
But you see these rules of reality, are very different between
You're ears, because behind your face, there's a secret
Place, with hopes and dreams and fears. So here you are
In another debate, with those two little critics, that
You love to hate. They have many names, and they vary
In size, the one with the truth, and the one with
The lies, they live on your shoulders, just outside your
Brain, the angel and the devil try to stake their claim.
It's up in the air, it's out on the tiles. Your personal
Odometer, is rackin' up miles. Just cruzin' along,
Try to keep it straight. The sign in the harbor says:
"Leave no wake". But if you're looking for
Advice, you won't get it from me, just as sure
As I'm sure, a wild thing be free.

Allen Luiso

Fix That Broken Cup

I peaked, felt happy, partied and puked blood
I freaked, left home, started to shoulder shrug
I gained friends, lost weight, knew I was in a confused state
I was a sculptor of self abuse carving out my fate.
I led, sometimes followed, bled and almost always borrowed
I was caught up in the world of complaint and self sorrow
I soaked up, was weighed down with premeditated self pity
A broken cup, I stayed around shunning health wittily
I panted, suited moments, addressed demons and tied knots
I was enchanted, constantly tense, when the test ends I'll cry lots
I didn't like analysis, and loved mental paralysis
I found lost kingdoms and invented personal palaces
I massaged madness for a year and a minute
I never once confronted the foundations of what was in it
I came down, got up, fell apart and was torn to pieces
I recovered, rediscovered why I was born in this species
I showed a clean pair of heels to an often walled road
I started planting my own plans that no other dreamer sowed
I juggled with these memories and dropped a few hurts
I struggled with these memories and stopped a rebirth.

Rupert Sexton

Sing A New Song

Thank you Lord for all my abilities
especially those that allow me to sing to thee
Each new day brings a brand new melody
to worship you and to give me serenity
Sing out your song it doesn't have to rhyme
as long as you always have him on your mind
Praise him in your own simple way
it will bring joy to you throughout the day
Change the words as your heart desires
do it often so you'll never tire
Sing to Jesus so heaven's bells may ring
and the notes they sound will harmonize with the words you sing
We can sing about his holiness and his unending love
and the justice that he sends down from up above
Some of us may sing like an opera star
and have a voice that is full and can carry far
Others may be mute or can hardly speak
but their unsung words will not be weak
What a joyful way to praise Our King
as we create our own - singphony

William M. Giakas

The Little Bird In The Tree

The little bird high in the tree.
He sings a song each morning to me.
Dreaming of a beautiful summer day.
Little bird in the tree

He calls to his mate so far away.
Come my dear lets go an play.
For you are the one I'm waiting for.
Oh yes I'll wed you don't say no more.

The little bird high in the tree.
He is God's gift to you on me.
He sings every day with a tweet tweet tweet.
He sings every day little bird in the tree

Ethelda Sink

The Nightclub Scene... The Lost Scene

Each person yearns for understanding and acceptance
Clothed in finery, adorned with jewels and smiles
Striving to attract and hold worthwhile attention
The words are empty, the smiles are frozen...
void of real emotion

Bodies dancing, mingle with promise and desire - the need to be
embraced is strong, misinterpreted for lust
Each person having a real life but not sharing it with another
Disappointment, despondency, regret and loneliness are
constant companions
Lost people, waiting to be discovered, signals crossing to cause
confusion and doubt

If only each would drop the fabrication of happiness, speak honestly,
touch the other lost person, make a connection with each other...
discover reality uncovered from the fantasy of pretentiousness

Then, and only then, can they hope to gain insight into uniting
with each other and the touch of reality...
of hope... of love... of joining with each other in truth.

The nightclub scene... the lost scene.

Shirley Leonnig

Friends

Make time to be with friends
Make them smile
Make their purpose in life
All seem worthwhile.

Be friends with people who don't have many
Let them know that they can lean on you
I'm sure that if you were in their place
They'd be kind to you too.

If you're struggling with friends
Try to talk your problems out
For this is much better
Than to scream or shout.

Be proud of your friends
Give them much praise
Always be friendly to them
That way your friendship won't go in separate ways.

Never tell them to leave you alone
Let them know you're always there
Lend them a hand when they need it
Let them know that you'll always care.

Amber Swedberg

Spring Death

Still, smooth waters
Air heavy with mist
Around the bend they come
Mother, father, nine little ones
And the hangers on beyond,
Plumed with brown, black, grey, green and white.

Babies uncertain, fragile
Clustering by their parents.
Then, so quickly, black and from the sky
Swooping shadow, one is gone.

Still smooth waters.
Mother speaks and gathers eight
And the air is heavy with mist.

Life, death, life again.

Barbara Lou Cohen

Seduction Of Generation X

It's a monster ever looming like an invincible tank of doom.
The stench of smoking guns and the blood of vacuumed wombs.

Lollipops and razors, sex abuse at age of two.
Contract executions, bludgeoned bodies stain the dew.

Fraternize, sodomize, reverse maternity.
Life is but a lifetime - to hell with eternity.

Muscle, sinew, flesh and bone, neither male nor female sought.
Images of wanton figures, paper pleasures seen and bought.

Rolling chairs for rocking chairs, hail the youth explosion.
Aim to maim, cloak the cult, reverence all revulsion.

Mutilate, manipulate, swap playthings for a hammer.
Educate to masturbate, expressing Godless grammar.

Tuck a monster in a cradle, to baby croak an eerie tune
"Drop a head down in a bucket," is a game for afternoon.

Weave a child a plastic basket, float it down a concrete Nile.
Measure mom a dumpster coffin, while imps and demons watch and smile.

Like the wooden horse for Helen, designed to wipe out Troy.
Is the Diabolical scheme in motion, this generation to destroy.

Rosemary Shaw

The Algonquin Supper

Running Wind sat at supper
on his hands and knees,
eating all the food that's good,
eating all the food that's right.
Eating through the moon light night, until the break of dawn.
Corn, rabbit and buffalo stew ate it till his tummy blew.

Things weren't easy,
things were hard, working in the open yard.
Tools it took to build our lives,
bows, arrows, and Indian knives
helped us in our simple lives.

Miles traveled,
miles gained in the open plain.
Proud and fearless - Fame was gained.

Brian Seaman

The Man I've Never Seen

I fell in love with a man,
Whom I had never seen.
I heard about him through a friend
and I know, on him I can always lean
    I've been following him for many years
and he's never let me down
I'm growing more and more fonder of him
And I know he's always around.
You see this man is Jesus,
and I've never wanted him to go
away and leave me lonely,
for you see I love him so.
    He's with me in the midnight hours
When no one else in there
There's just no one else like this man,
To comfort me in all my fears and cares.
I know that one day I shall meet him
and it fills my heart with love,
for I'm going to live with him forever
Somewhere in heaven up above-

Louise K. Sharpe

The Saga Of Death

Death is tragic!
I pause to breathe but one last time,
While scattered memories race through my mind.

Or, is it magic?
I see the light and feel my soul,
Reach deep within me and take control.

Surely, its havoc.
Amidst the bliss of warm golden light,
The chaotic energy becomes clear and bright.

But, I'm a maverick.
I momentarily depart from the chosen way,
To reassure my dearly beloved I'll be okay.

And, I feel fantastic.
My spirit will live on in everlasting memory,
As my soul continues on its eternal journey.

Life beyond death is ecstatic!
For beyond the warmth of the celestial light,
Exists the rapture and bliss of the afterlife.

Richard A. Gaffney

Lady 1983-1996

It was a long time ago, that our family felt incomplete,
When we found our new beloved member roaming the streets.
It all started with a towel at the door,
But it eventually became more and more.
It started by the door, and then next to the fire,
Then into my room when I would retire.
There came the time when she needed a bath,
But we had to keep it a secret for fear of Dad's wrath.
She finally felt comfortable living in our home,
But she still felt the need, she wanted to roam.
The time came when she wanted to stay here,
That is when, our beloved Lady became so dear.
Lady loved us for so many years,
That is why there were so many tears.
She grew old and grey without our consent,
Lady had no Idea how much her love meant.
And so the time came for us to say good-bye,
As we let her go, we sat down to cry.
Lady doesn't want us to be sad, but think of her often.
For it was the love of our beloved Lady that made our hearts soften.

Jennifer Beerman

free your mind

i feel so all alone
i wonder what im doing
lost out here in this world
i can feel a storm is brewing

deep in my inner most me
a void that must be filled
what is this empty feeling
could someone my soul be stealing

and if i had to guess it
who could do something so wrong
the finger would point to me
and ive been stealing way too long

so standing front and center, no one else in the room
my mind wonders to sacred places, i see loving and peaceful faces

im too deep inside myself to stop me
i keep traveling the roads of my mind
and suddenly a jolt from within, could it be im set free from my sins

so much to lay down and release
time and faith have finally tamed the beast
and i walk out the room feeling free, i dare you to try to stop me

Sabrina Berry

My Mommy

My favorite place to be, when I was a little girl
Was sittin' on my mommy's lap and it made me feel in a whirl

For if at all I got tired and wanted a place to rest...
I'd just lay my head up against her chest

It was such fun hearing that very strange sound
My mommy's voice was a rumbling, like something underground.

It was a special game, I had my mommy near...
For up here on my mommy's lap, who could get me here?

We are both older now fascinating as can be...
But, oh, those special memories, "A sittin' on her knee".

We had our picture taken on a special day...
Where my mommy and me are smilin' somehow, it turned out O.K.

The Dear Lord has given us a memory bank, as precious as can be...
For I still remember that feelin' a sittin' on her knee...

Ellen Kaye Webb

The Man I Love

The man I love lays beside me, still and quiet is his body,
His eyes are closed and in this atmosphere of calmness,
His presence in our bed is looming.

The man I love is unaware of my stare,
My eyes slowly crawl across his body, drinking in his masculine form,
They gaze upon his handsome face, it's the same face that sparkles when I laugh,
Shows anguish when I cry, all life he offers, flows through this handsome face.

The man I love shares his life with me,
Every intriguing aspect of it,
In this relationship we give freely of ourselves, wanting only to be loved in return

The man I love has stirred, he gently speaks of his longing for me,
He offers a compassionate kiss, as words of love spill from his lips,
He loves me and only me.

The man I love is honest and loyal, time will never alter his commitments,
Only enhance their beauty.
He proclaims his undying love for me,
Repeating often, we are soul mates.

The man I love is sleeping now, just being with him fills my soul with passion,
Knowing as we share our dreams and secret desires,
We have found our path towards eternal happiness.

Ida-May I. Wegner

When A Man Loves A Woman

When a man loves a woman, he will some how find a Way
To gather his thoughts and finally Say,
"Roses are Red, and Violets are Blue,
Honey, you are so beautiful, and I truly love you."

He tells her, "I love you," in words as well as in Deeds.
He avoids abusing her with malice, discontent, and Greed.
He is kind, gentle, thoughtful, and Tender.
And if they disagree, he is the first to Surrender.

He watches his behavior, and does not fret at every Whim.
He is strong and courageous and she can depend on Him.
He always makes sure he has money in the Bank.
When she uses the car, there is always gas in the Tank.

When she acts strange and indifferent, He loves her Nonetheless
He treats her with Tenderness, and gives her love and Happiness.
He tells her, "I love you so much, I am full of aches and Pains.
You don't always treat me right, but I love you just the Same."

When he takes her out to dinner, he compliments her on how she looks.
When she prepares the meals he tells her he loved the food she cooked.
Every day he tells her "I love you more and More."
He always greets her with a hug and a kiss when she meets him at the door.

James J. Ware Jr.

Dinner

Hanging about the Lazy-Boy
  the lazy man shifts to his right,
changing the channels as well as
  his mind on what he'll consume tonight.
Let's start with a simple chicken
  breast cooked lightly and never fried
then throw in a couple sweet
  vegetables placed neatly on the side.
And for dessert the taste of fruit
  is the best thing to come to mind —
Ah, forget all that, it's too much work,
  order a pizza or two and recline.

Scott W. Watson

A Prayer For The Astronaut Carrying The Fist Vehicle On The Moon

In these moments we look at you so brave, so courageous.
We one anxious, tense, the idea of materialism vanished.
We just hope and pray, you make it safe
and may all sacrifice and privation
be worth well in comparison to your boldness.
Please! Oh astronaut return safe,
return safe to this planet!
Not only for the ones who love you,
your beloved one, your family,
but we, all people of this earth,
and many in the world
pray that you come down sound and safe.
We have one exclamation:
"God let them be safe!"
You are the light of today,
the hero of tomorrow's history!

Maria Dickenson

'Tis Fall

I'm sitting on the porch. It's night.
Guess I'm going to have to fight
To make myself go to bed.
It's so cool, so nice.

The summer's gone. Let that suffice
To bring the thought:
So are Chiggers, Skeeters And Biting Flies!
Now, Blank Them Out, or otherwise
In my mind they'll grow
And, don't you know
I'll be wishing, wishing, wishing
For the winter's snow!!!

Lillian M. Cavil

Won?

The vengeance sore,
and yet,
The release to settle the score,
and yet,
The battle is not won, it's just begun,
and yet,
For yet a struggling soul, the heat is felt,
and yet,
You've won a battle, you, but one, your select
army on your side,
and yet,
When your victory is won, no one to share,
but you alone,
Where is your army lined abreast to cheer
you on your victorious quest?
And yet,
They sit afar with silent tongue,
and yet,
You won?

Carolyn C. Jaynes

Olympic National Park

Silent trails wind through Olympic firs
Under gold and green-rich light that lures
God seekers forever up,
Forever higher.

Nancy J. McLaughlin

Things That I Need

Out of the east, there cometh the sun
out of a cloud, there falleth the rain
up from the ground, there groweth the seed
bringing to me the things that I need

If I am cold, the fire is warm
If I have thirst, the vine gives me wine
The fears of death, make my soul believe
Bringing to me the things that I need.

Robert H. Zander

Untitled

When I see you
I feel relieved
a sensation that cannot be believed
your eyes don't deceive
When I see you
I believe
you're the only one for me
and I am the only one for you
I believe we will be together and be lovers forever
I believe that we go together
no matter what people say
I believe that you will always stay till the last happy day
When I see you
I believe
that some days will be blue
but, I believe that we will stick together like glue
I believe that some people will approve of us being together
I believe that we are forever
When I see you
I believe

Basma F. Al-zaid

In Today Of Your Life...

Allow yourself to excitement of good fortune.
Seek only that which quenches the thirst of temptation, but let it
be with a fervent appeal, not ideal persuasion.
Remember the road from whence ye came but strive toward the
residence of your most secret passion.
Carry only that which yields energy for a weary travel.
Lead thyself to pasture three times but never refuse the appetite
of fellow man.
Release the victory trapped within others but savor your own in
solitude and thanksgiving.
Hold fast the power that pushes and pulls when you cannot;
pay daily respect and tribute to His hands.
Always confide in what you have observed but never lose sight
of what you cannot see.
Ponder that trials come and go but realize today draws a line
between the verdure of life and the travesty of a moment.

Ken Coopwood

Aesclipian Fate

Inspiring obstacles of up from antiqued welled walls.
Is the message gone?...Crumbled, and the answer?
Maybe the spiritess is awake...Hope.
Channeled visions through long winding corridors
    of ancient hospitals an answer to Confusion.
Drink the healing pure springs
Your vision opens, you need no guide.
You have pinnacled teeth of rocks
Mists to capture between a crag
Mountains too steep to climb.
A button or a key will press your relaxing escape into
Modern Time - a plane of history
    which solved itself
Into Being.
Resolution-
The answer for all our questions.

Stephanie Voorlas

Unity

One nation under God, we claim to be.
Our forefathers did it, with perfection in mind,
But our hatred for each other is plain to see,
Sectional, racial, even the religion kind.

We call ourselves ridiculous names,
African-American, Asian-American, and even worse.
But we shouldn't play those silly games.
To not be one people would be a curse.

Slavery is a subject that's mighty sore.
We had slaves, black, white, red, and yellow.
But don't try to blame us anymore.
The slavers are long dead and gone, young fellow.

Mutual respect is what we must have.
And pride in this country that we call home.
Happy that we live in the land of the brave,
Trusting that God's kingdom will surely come.

Call us American, with no nutty additions.
We live where the bald eagle soars,
Here in the greatest of all nations.
Let us all be friends forevermore.

John E. Jernigan

To Imagine

To dream is only to imagine with an open mind;
To never see the memories left so far behind.
To never look back at past loves that have gone bad;
But to look ahead to a future to never again be sad.
To hold onto everything you cherish so dear;
To gather more and more love and dreams each and every year.
To smile like a child, so innocent and sweet;
To have your eyes wide open as a child who's spotted a treat.
To savor the days the Lord has given you;
To realize he put you on this earth for you to be true.
Be true to yourself, though it will get you far;
The range is beyond comparison of that of a star.
Love each other with all your heart;
Never take for granted anything from the start.
Be happy, be love, be shining from above;
Know the Lord will love you wherever you are.

Rosemary Zicafoose

Why, Why, Why?

Her eyes twinkle in the sunlight,
But she doesn't notice me, it's like I'm out of sight,
She is more beautiful than the bright, blue, sky,
Why can't we be friends, why, why, why?
We have a battle back and forth,
She's going South while I'm going North,
If only we could be together, together as friends,
I have to do something before my chance ends,
If only she knew how I was after school,
She wouldn't think I'm dumb, a wacko, or a fool,
The only way I could see the light,
Is if we were to stop this battle, stop this fight,
She may not know right now why I act this way,
But she'll know sometime, someday,
I'll just have to wait however long it will be,
And hope and pray that, that day, she will like me,
When this day comes what shall I do?
Should I be myself or try something new?
I guess I'll never know until I try,
Boy, I hope this day comes before I die.

David Lee Huryta Jr.

Suzy And Ben

When Suzy was one, and Ben was eight,
He'd hold her tiny hand in his small one
And help her toddle around the yard.

With money he earned from mowing lawns
He bought her a long blue gown
On sale at Marshall Fields.

(She told us all quite seriously
that someday she would marry him.)

Serenely she would smile at him
As he ran off to baseball games,
Then turn attention to her dolls.

We thought her tender heart might break when she
Found that her childish dreams were an impossibility

She brought home boys for lemonade,
And he taught history at school.

A chance encounter at a friend's
Rekindled an old flame,
And Sue and Ben are wed

There in her mother's yard
Where once he helped her learn to walk.

Marcia Kesmar

Broken Hearted Savior

It's 4:00 a.m. eye's glued to the ceiling
Can't stop this tossing and turning
Can't persuade these feelings.

When I wake in the morning
And look in the mirror
Who will I see the devil or God my savior.

Why is it that the self inflicted wounds
Are the hardest to stop bleeding,
but once they are healed
We're anxious to have the blood flow again.

So yet another stone loosen its way from the road
With an unknown destination and no hand to hold.

It's easy to loose your way
When the hand you depend on is pulled away.

So distressed you stand like a solitary tree amidst in the field
With no friends to laugh with and not secrets to reveal.
Good-bye.

Robert M. Del Grosso

"Unconscious Ties"

When the truth becomes a lie.
Desperate to wake up from this nightmare.
Standing in front of a mirror, not able to recognize the face I see.
My soul being help prisoner for your entertainment.
Exploring my non-existent conscience.
Hearing the devils laughter as I tattoo my name on to his
thigh, realizing everything I ever did wrong.
Then forgetting the point.
Feeling my heartbeat inside my chest, then watching
you cut it out with a dull blade.
It's too bad things weren't different.
What's to become of my faded memory?
Denying my regrets and letting go of what once was mine.
As I take the devil's hand, devastated to see what his
world is really like.
Thinking unconsciously, as darkness smothers my only existence.
Saying my forever goodbyes to the one's that I love.
I was living the truth, only to find out, it was a lie.
"Who'd believe these unconscious ties?"

Gloria M. Cheadle

Come Back To Me

I don't believe I still love you
After what you put me through
At times I wish it was just a dream
And I'd wake up to see you by my side
But I know now that it's not a dream
And when you left a part of me has died
You told me that you cared and wouldn't hurt my heart
But that was a lie it's been torn apart
It's been torn into pieces and hasn't mended yet
I forgave you but I'll never forget
I miss you more than you could believe
And I still don't know why you had to leave
I miss the way we use to cuddle up late at night
I miss the way you made all the wrong things right
But now we're apart and I don't think you see
How much you seem to be hurting me
You're the one I go crazy over every time I hear your name
The only wish I have for thee is you'd do the same
So I'll sit and wait for you to come back my way
So my dreams will come true and I can be with you night and day

Amalia Knick

Show Him The Way

Dear God, tell me what to do.
I have a special friend, who is feeling sad and blue.

He feels like he lost at life, and with love.
So I ask for your help, from so far above.

See this special friend has so much to give.
But he lost his trust and hope, and is unsure if he wants to live.

I want him to know, he has other friends who love him dear.
And that he can count on us, to help him with his fear.

He holds a special gift, that's honest and true.
He would do anything for me, and even more for you.

So how can I tell him, his hurt will start to mend.
That life is full of ups and downs, but it doesn't have to end.

Please help him through this, show him the way.
Tell him it will be slow, and to take life day by day.

So help him Lord, to see what's best.
That his life can be changed, it's not one big mess.

Let him see the beauty, of what he has to give.
To see that life is really great, and challenging to live.

Donna R. Caskey

Never Forget

Let friendships live on, the closeness stays strong.
Let the fun never end and the memories never lost.
Spirits don't fade and loves never die.
Let the memories not be forgotten.
We'll never forget sweet times and sweet people,
the unforgettable few will stay with us forever.
Dreams may not come true and times may be hard,
but spirits don't fade and loves never die.
Our feelings stay strong though we may never know why.
Time is a circle around our hearts,
sometimes it's sealed and sometimes it leaks;
often it's strong, seldom it's weak.
The memories are the barrier between crying and laughter.

Beverly A. Cheezum

Me

If you look out and see;
    it is not hard to please me.
And I'm not hard to find; I'm just one of a kind.
I love everyone very much,
    I don't try to prove it by going to church.
    You cannot prove love much;
I don't try to prove it by going to church.
    And you cannot prove love everywhere;
Although people do not care.
    I try to go around for you to see;
That it is not hard to please me. Trouble is in the air;
You can look and see, that it is everywhere.
    When I was out in the world drinking;
I did not realize that my body was sinking.
    I did not stop to think about who, I was running around with,
did not care; that they could take me anywhere.
    Later on I got sick; it came very quick
My mother took me to the hospital
She a shed for the church members for prayer;
Now I know who really care.

Bessie Sullivan

For My Grandson

Oh, loving bundle of endless joy,
whose eyes perceive
a wonderful pantheon absent of strife.

Will you run after the butterfly,
and skip, and jump and smell the narcissus, frolic in snow,
and ponder your way through the realms of tomorrow?

And with your ephemeral youth,
will you inspire those around you, as did
Buddah, and Christ (even as a child), and the blessed
Muhammad?

Will you beat swords into plowshares,
or will you nurse at earth's bosom, mindless of how to use
the sweet nectar that you remove?

Oh, blessed newborn
how we pray, for your every day to fold up the night,
without starvation, discomfort or blight.

Luqman Abdel Magied

A Winter's Day

As I wake the wet streets gleam bright,
In the early morning light.
The gray clouds layer themselves,
And kiss the mountain tops.
The rusty cedars stand proud,
Against the ghost winds of the morning.
Hemlocks stand with weary heads bowed,
As if weighted down by endless days of rain.
The white mists raise from mountains shoulders,
As smoke from a thousand sacred fires.
The dull gray day lays quiet in the morning light,
And surrounds me with silent joy and peace.
As I wonder at the mellow mood that fills my soul,
And marvel at the beauty of the muted colours of the moment.

Ingrid Backman

"Last Night I Was Kissed By An Angel"

Last night I was kissed by an angel,
or so it would seem it promised, long
life of happiness and many other dreams.
I listen very carefully as each line
was unfold, then my spirit said quietly
that this is only fool's gold.

Vivian Sherman

Untitled

Dear Dad
I thank you for teaching me,
to be honest and kind,
for instilling in me values and morals,
it's better to give than receive,
to treat others as myself,
that a person is measured by who he is — not by what he has,
God first — others next — self last,
not to take any wooden nickels.
that life is not fair,
to be an example,
to be a leader — not a follower,
to stick by my beliefs,
that I make a difference,
to believe in myself,
that all good things come to those who wait
for being my father.
I love you dad and I will always be your little girl.

Betty Anderson

The Weathered Souls

Thin lines of understanding
etched upon their faces.
Scars of yesterday mark their places.
Today is yet forgotten.
Tomorrow we begin anew.
But yesterday tells all in the hearts of a few.
Buried beneath the anger, frustration and pain,
lies the souls who yearn to live again.
They have weathered the storm
and brought forth the knowledge of understanding.
Knowledge that has stood still
on patience and is forever unending.
They are the weathered souls,
weathered souls of man
speak to them, if you can.

Kim Boshears

Spirited Heart

Faith had risen into fire, awakened heart.
Thriving on solitude, opening shadows of spirits.

Spirits bond, unite in song, emotions of earth.
Mankind must come together as one.

The crying must stop, darkness must fall to pureness of oneself.
Rain echoes on, rainbows sparkle, water breathes.

Wind guides our hearts, pureness is refreshed.
Strength is power, power is spirited heart.

Let tears flow upon the skies treasures, for we will heal.
In suffering becomes a new beginning for love.

Spirited heart has called. Are you listening?
To a heart made of gold, truth of words.

Peace becomes our world, spirited heart must heal.
Compassion must feel, spirits bond unite in song.

Winds crash, thunder praises among lightning.
Darkness lifts into dawn, spirited heart beams rainbows.

Angels forgive our cry, saving us from darkness.
Spirited hearts flourish rainbows that is ourselves.

Marie Tymchuk

Eternal Dream

The silence rested upon her lips
Once pale and pink, had lost their pitch
Her hands once gentle, soft and smooth
Now are still and will not move.
The wind still blows, the sun still shines
The children laugh, an infant whines.
The silent death, just crept on by.
And lifted her soul and let it fly.
I shall not weep, nor shout or scream
For now she's in eternal dream.

Christa Ann Sweet

Waterfall

A place to ponder
A place to pray
The wind whistles through the trees
While water explodes into a thunderous roar
This place it seems so loud
But yet quiet
A place to ponder
A place to pray

Josh Townsley

Renewal

One minute happiness,
The other tragic,
Old memories...now historical,
Black.
Death.
The loved one whom has restored a place in your heart,
Gone.
Yet, as the tears flow down my face,
She disappears into a wonderful place.

Natalie C. Jones

"Journey On"

They all think I'm pretty witty
My thoughts churn...so what's the pity?

...Gloomy countenance I encounter
I try to brighten by a bit of laughter-

I will also lean on those
    but I hope I won't impose!

One must stand both straight and tall
But not dun the ones who fall into
    baths - walkers - and chairs!

There's much less and love and understanding
In this Valley of Tears....

Jean Mohns McCann

Divine Decree

This Love can nest Again
Warm flow from Soul to Soul
I took the Lost Empire Down
Divine Love is God's Real Gold...

And now that it's all Over
My Flock can "see" Again
Touch My Being to Remember
I'm your Mirror in Earth Heaven...

Come to Silence to Find Me
In no Compromise or Lies —
I've waited in Love to Hold You,
Your Dreams soothed the Earth School Cries...

And when you want a Drink from Me
The Lovelight will take you in "to be"
This Love can Forever Nest Again
The Renewed Life with Me must now begin...

Kathleen Wells

Wings

Perched on the Grandma side of my heart, you try your wings
then eagerly burrow back for love and a hug
when your legs buckle and your smile wilts.
Your sleep-heavy eye lids slip silently down
in mute surrender to Grandma's soft lullaby sounds.

Saddle-seated on Grandma's hip you point at your world...
sailing birds, pink roses and yellow daisies;
I teach you words and your copy-cat sounds
gurgle like water tumbling from your lips.
I lose myself in your yodel-coo sounds,
your "I Love You" smile and delicious belly laughs!
Soon your real-life words will take flight.

But you won't stay molded to me long
as your perpetual-motion body flings you into space,
propelling you into realms unknown.

As you grow and change,
Grandpa and Grandma's prayers will glide over you daily,
challenging you to soar toward life,
your wing tips brushing your dreams.

Margaret A. Lort

Paestum

Greek ruins lay upon Roman soil
At once was the edge of sea.
A buried culture still echoes on winds
Amid timeless icons of antiquity.

Ancient chambers rest in silence
Fading frescos strive to survive.
And ageless art tells their story
As crumbling walls come alive:

A voyage to distant shores
Where the stone temples now stand.
Scenes from the future appeared
Far below between the dunes in the shifting sands.

Into time, time beyond
Above across the sand they see
Distant silhouettes, breaking horizon
Where weathered land meets ageless sea.

And in crumbling walls and faded dye
Lies the mystery
Of a since past culture's
Sacred history.

Timothy A. Del Vescovo

You're Not Alone

Yesterday you were in love and all aglow.
Then you were dealt a hearty blow.
Your whole world crashed down around you
Making you feel hurt, angry and blue.
You made a vow from deep within,
"Never ever will I love again!"

Our wise Creator saw your pain from above
And sent you another person to love.
Engrossed in your pain, you couldn't see
God's provision or how happy you could be.
You go it alone with a pain that won't cease.
Only finding love again will make it ease.

If you find yourself alone and hurting any time, anywhere,
Remember God's provision and call me, for I'll always be there.

Alice Montanez

Now

*Dedicated to my beloved daughters Jean and Joanna
and my 7 Grandchildren*
Alas! The flesh has altered my silhouette
My flying power facing the throes of my decline - the darkness
seeking annulment of objects distorted - brilliance dimmed
by clouds of doubt - flapping no longer soar, seeking
changing seascapes, far horizon unfathomed depths of distanced hills.
Behold! I hear an inner stirring - slowly I flap my wings -
suddenly - from depths beyond a benevolent voice - not yet! not yet!
The heart remembering the brilliance of sun and sky, perhaps
there is contentment in the knowledge that the moment is now,
not yesterday nor tomorrow - now.
Saro, Saro, fedele - e preziosa la vita.

Susan Burstein

Big And Little Bangs

At the very first, I had structure
If you do not believe it, go to Einstein
or Planck
Do not forget, we have scientists to thank
For making structure's purpose plain to us
The best of convincing arguments
are not learned by chance
But must be weighed
Put in proper sequence —
It all comes from academic learning
then probed and studied
And placed in proper complement —
How else did we get a look at relativity
If there's a big bang
Are we not all little bangs
Else how did we come into being
We floated a nine month's time
Before this air breathing
And becoming another universal entity.

Katherine Young

Winter Snows And Summer Rainbows

Can a winter snow be compared to a summer rainbow?
A summer rainbow talking to a winter snow.
"Your life is very short, as mine is"
"Are you as delicate and how long do you live?"

The winter snow blowing out his ego
"I dance and sing until it's spring"
"Then I melt away to give you room
"And turn into rain, even on a summer day."

"What happens," were very closely related
Winter snow sand summer rainbows,
"It's just our timing, you know."

I'm for Thanksgiving, Christmas, and New Year's
Valentine's Day too, once in awhile St. Pat's I do,"
"You're the Fourth of July lazy summer days
Delightful showers, sun shining, birds singing
And rainbows too the sky clinging."

"We can't compare, were both needed
Snowflakes in winter and rainbows in summer."
Greeting each other in a far away stream
Where sunflowers blow in the wind and lazy daises dream

Dianne M. Young

Anastasia's Palace

Anastasia's palace
is made of gold and wine,
It weighs in corporate heaven
like parliament and time;

From elegance of exports,
for filibuster tramps
To caring for our brethren
in altruistic camps;

With Rockefeller's pennies
placed upon my eyes,
A profit tear, the flooding fear,
of avaricious lies

The taste of time's repugnance,
when called a token's peer,
It wades through greed's indignity
and draws the future near,

A second insight beckons
"It's hope that holds us steady"
we'll build a dream, and from it scream,
the meek are getting ready

Steven Van Austin

Sustaining Love

Sixty-eight years, some think that's long,
But to us who have lived it, it's merely a song.
A whisper, a moment, the blink of an eye.
How can we slow them — they're passing us by.

First we are children enjoying our toys.
Then "know it all" teen aged girls and boys.
Next comes the time we make plans for life —
Choose careers—become husband or wife.

The children arrive — family life becomes real.
We reach the height in emotions we feel.
It all goes too fast — slips through our fingers.
But the love we establish to life's end lingers.

Grandchildren come to the children we bore.
Making life count for even more.
Strife intermingles — makes it hard to cope.
And we reach out for something to bring us hope.

And to our relief, as life passes by,
There's the love of God on which we rely.
All else fades and crumbles — on that depend.
But God's love sustains to the very end.

Erma Bradford

Early Morning Votive

Striving against the night, the little flame, having been lit,
Encroached upon the darkness.
Its wick too short, its wax too heavy,
The air around it cold and damp,
The draft too strong,
Yet it struggled on.

And as the dawn arrived, the flame took wing,
As if it had become one with the first new light.
It grew brighter and more visionary;
Taking its cue from the rising sun,
It drove away the dark,
And together they dispelled the night.

This is creative life itself — an act of worship.
It is amazing how the Creator speaks
Amidst the simplest things,
To once more give the courage to go on,
To become,
To fulfill the word made flesh within.

Yvonne R. Blasy

Sunday

The smell of bleach hot steamy sterile clean
Socks underwear and t-shirts churn in the drum
Tumbling and falling playfully on top of one another

A bundle of booties and sleepers
On delicate slowly humming formula out
Warm and sucking infant fresh as a hatchling
Duck-down and fur topped
Lays gently cupped in my one hand
I drink in the doughy and delicious urge
Nestled together and sealed by that
Instinctive maternal touch
Mother and child rocking gently in the silent
Void of a midnight feeding

That urgent oneness fades into sounds of dailiness
The complaints of an adolescent knock down the door
Clearing the strong memory
The bleach penetrates the soaking fabric
The core of the texture filled to capacity in a passing glance
Like the tiny red sock I keep in my winter coat pocket
To feel the innocence when I most need reminding

Deborah A. Paggi

My Mother, Myself

I remind myself of my Mother, in the things I say and do;
As time goes by, the more I notice; it's her I'm growing into.

It comes as no surprise, all my life within her care;
With pure love and heartfelt devotion; without question she was there.

She taught me to tie my shoes, and all those things I had to know;
With courage, wisdom, and gentle guidance; she looked on and let me grow.

Under her watchful eyes I played, for hours upon end;
Today we sit and talk; she is my Mother and my friend.

I feel a closeness with her now, it grows stronger everyday;
Sharing laughter, love, and memories; a strong bond that's come a long way.

Always ready with encouraging words, to comfort and protect;
I hold for her the greatest love; honor and deep respect.

It's funny, now that I'm grown, how very plain it is to see;
Myself inside my Mother, and my Mother inside me.

Deborah L. Sanford

Strange

Strange.
Yeah, it's strange to watch the window paintings change,
To the new seasons.
Pretty portraits —
No more.
I hate these seasons.
Something I've known for too many years now,
As I grew up from all those different stages,
It's past my bedtime
Guess I'll just sleep.
Sleep through all the paintings,
And the strangeness they express.
Expressions.
Yeah, you can say that's strange,
Watching all passing motion
Express themselves through expressions.
It's strange.
Like you
Like me.

Laura MacLean

My Heart

This picture of you in my hand causes my eyes to tear
I cry for this second chance, not in fear

Captured within my heart is a love which will never falter
For this reason I want to take your hand with mine
Before God to the altar

I anxiously await your soft lips to be pressed against mine
Renee, this is what I want for all time

I wish only to hold you, making love to you under the light
Of a full moon
Merely awaiting the day we say, I do
For you my bride, and I your groom

Did I forget to say I love you
Let me say it within the words I write
My thoughts are of you all day long I dream of you every night

Renee, my angel with wings of gold
Fly into my arms for me to hold

These words I write are from my heart
May the Lord never keep us apart

I love you, Renee
Be mine!

John C. Hensley

Winter Romance

True Love is what I need. Adventure is
a part of me. Playing, caring, sharing
and trusting is everything you see.

You showed me you cared by being there.
We shared our thoughts and you knew I couldn't be bought.
I learned to trust only to find out it was just about lust.

It's not the carrots on the strings not even carats on a ring.
They will never get you anywhere.
Money isn't everything!

The best gifts of all you cannot buy,
for they come from the heart of only one special guy!

Exclusive girl friend is only one!
Smoke screens are not any fun.
My eyes are open so I can see.
And there will be no control over me!

Time to learn, time to grow. Times we spent in the snow.
The times we shared everywhere.
Are what's important to me you know.
Winter is over and now I must go.
You taught me a lesson I will never bestow!

Susanne Smith

The Abortion

I was a being, born to be free,
but somebody took that freedom away from me.
I was created, to be loved and adored,
but now I'm destroyed because of hatred and scorn.
I had a heart, it beat just like yours,
but somebody decided that wasn't important anymore.
Did they resent me that much? For I do not understand,
how could they look at me and not call me man?
If I had my choice I'd have chosen to live,
but since you destroyed me, I guess I'm better off dead.
Your fun had a price and you blamed it on me,
you ended my life so that you could be free.
I don't understand why you did what you did,
I promise I would have been a good little kid.
Murderer I scream. Innocent you plead?
Would you want done to you what you did to me?
Any regrets? No, not about killing me,
the only regret you have was creating me.

Erica N. Lytle

My River

My walk takes me along the river's banks,
Where I hear God's creatures, giving thanks
For all the food and shelter it provides,
With its shrubs and trees on either side.
Its their playground, their swimming pool,
Their summer haven, a place to cool.

As I sit by the river, on my favorite swing,
I quietly wait for the show to begin.
A pair of orioles are playing quite near,
Don't seem to realize, that I'm sitting here!
Cardinals are flitting from tree to tree,
Occasionally stopping, to sing for me.

My river is always an interesting, lively place,
Every day is different, like a changing face.
It can be so peaceful, gently flowing, so serene...
Or like a raging bull, out of control...very mean.
I love my river, for it comforts me.
Like God's other creatures, here, is where...
   I Want To Be!!

Helen B. Spittler

Lonely Voyage

When moon was high and air blew;
I was astonish with some ideas new.

It was like missing people some;
whom I deserted when we were young.

The cooler I got, the sadder I became;
All my cries and sighs were in vain.

I heard to my heart then, I talked to my ears;
I could not realized how I passed those years.

Everything is perishable and followed by moan;
For some it is dark, for the others it is dawn.

Who born rich and remain so;
One way or the other, they fall even though.

Starting from scratches, they reach their peaks;
Never become divers, who don't cross the creek.

Image is reflection of spirit and soul;
Lean forward if you intend to achieve your goal.

Lagging behind is the result of your mood;
Speak louder if you are to be heard in the crowd.

Patience is fruitful, some wisers say;
No one reaps without action, I deny it may.

Man is vaster then his design, and has his intimation;
The nature vouches for him, and proves his creation.

Most are scared, but few may dare;
Pressed by the society, survive rather rare.

Tariq H. Malik

To Jim

On you my heart has fallen; cracked,
But through your strength it is made anew.
Where once was pain, sorrow, and broken pieces,
Now stands strong, sturdy, resilient sinew.
And though it lacks of old that perfect rhythm,
Which seemed so precious for precision's sake,
Your courage has made it more than a time-piece,
For through the cracks my soul escaped.

And if, as mine, your heart should untimely fall,
I will be there to comfort and mend you.

And together we will walk the coming miles.

Mark Tries

A Swing In The Spring

Did you ever swing in an old rope swing
  Your toes stretching up toward the sky,
With the soft wind brushing your glowing cheek,
As the rest of the world glides by?

The rays of the sun peek down through leaves,
  Like green baby hands unfurled,
Touching your hair as you gently sway,
  Content and detached from the world.

Guns may bloom on a far away front,
  Intrigue and taxes increase,
But when you swing in a swing in the spring,
  In your heart for a while, there is peace.
    Dorothy E. Griffith

Or Is It Love?

Can love turn the eyes
  outward
    to see
dimpled spiders
freckle-legged grasshoppers
paisley-winged butterflies
smiling, winkling, blue-eyed cats
and rhythmically, blinking fireflies?
Can love turn the eyes
  inward
    to feel
relaxed spaces between thoughts
a dance of words spinning toward intuitions
a song of desire to be alive in spite of struggle
and gentle intangibilities
in a friend's expressions?
    Janet M. Garnett

A Schizophrenic's Love Song

As he steps outside, he closes the door
He's in a place he hasn't been before
He talks to himself as everyone stares
They feel sorry for him, but he is unaware

A lady talks to him, he has never met
But somehow it feels like he just forgets
Sometimes he finds himself far from home
He hears voices, but he's all alone

She calls him later, and asks where he's been
The confusion flickers on his face unseen
As he hangs up the phone, in comes the emptiness
He doesn't know, but he begins to regress

He leaves this world and enters fantasy
Existence is insanity
This is the way he deals with the pain
This world to him is so mundane

The hole grows bigger on the inside
She killed him with the love she lied
Now he finds he just can't concentrate
He doesn't know it, but he's found his escape
    Brandon Post

Heaven

Heaven is a road of gold,
Where you never, ever, ever get old.
Jesus will be sitting on the highest chair,
People from the past and present will be there.
I'll give Jesus a hug and squeeze him tight,
He'll warm me like the sun's own light.
I'll say "Hi" to the people all around,
And give them a smile without making a sound.
When I die this is how it's going to be,
My family, friends, Jesus and me.
    Kali Guillas

No Forever

There's no forever, is there?
There's no life for us to share.
It's just sunbeams and golden dreams
Dashed to cold nightmare.

There's no tomorrows, all to scared,
Yesterday's to much compared
Spilt the tears, built the fears,
To wise to be laired.

There's no 'til death do us part.
Only head, head against heart.
Will there be sorrow, if we let tomorrow
Carry us to a new start?

There's no forever. Is there!
There's no life for us to share.
It's just sunbeams and Golden dreams
Dashed to cold nightmare.
    Faith Felton

Precious Promise

Precious promise God has given
That as my Shepherd, He
By waters still, the way will lead
And from want I shall be free.

When times are tough, the going rough
Of rest I am assured,
As burdens bear, and troubles wear,
My soul shall be restored.

When death shall stalk, and its path I walk,
He will reassure my heart;
And I can say through all the way,
Thou my rod and comfort art.

When enemies encircle me,
I will have no fear.
God will protect and fight, you see,
For He is always near.

His love and mercy, have been so free,
Down through my life, you know,
So I should praise Him, you'll agree,
For soon to Him I'll go.
    Calvin M. Lake

Come

Come—
  With me—
    To where the sun warms the brown earth,
And soft haired, dark-eyed maidens,
  Stroll through the corn fields,
And children roll and play,
  And drop pebbles in the stream,
    To scare the fish.
Lying, watch an eagle lofting easy
  At the edge where the sky comes down,
  There is peace!
    Richard Wingate

Spring Time

  The sun is warming, everything is green.
Flowers bloom and the robins sing.
  No more coats hats and mittens,
It's time for fun, baby birds and kittens.
  The children romp and play in the sun.
We watch the ball players hit and run.
  Sunday drives and church bells ring.
Thank you God, it's finally spring.
    Lynn Snedeker

Love

Love is beautiful as it sounds is nothing but a long term suffering
and that is why it's so difficult to let oneself fall in love, or be in love.

Love as I was always told stands for "Trouble Free". That once true
love has found you - you only have to embrace it with open arms.

Well, as I grew older I realized that people confused the term being
in "Love" with something of an idealistic term, as something
mysterious. People are so tired of being in plain their lives
desperately searching for a solution then invented something
beyond their capacity to understand and that "thing" is love.

For love is nothing mysterious. It is life, yes live. It is these
obstacles that one encounters in every day life which enable him to
define the true meaning of "Love." Yet these obstacles are regarded
as something evil. The troubles of life alone cannot tell whether
or not someone is in love, or falling in love, but is rather the
product of those obstacles.

The joy, the courage and the strength that one gets from the suffering
is the beauty of life, thus the beauty of being in love. For if one
cannot relates to those upheavals, one cannot love.

Manouska Saint Gilles

What Happened To The Dinosaurs?

Dinosaurs, Dinosaurs!
What happened to the dinosaurs?
Did they go because of the snow?
Did they die because the sun made them fry?

Dinosaurs, Dinosaurs!
What happened to the dinosaurs?
Did they disappear because of their fear?
Have they vanished because they were banished?

Dinosaurs, Dinosaurs!
What happened to the dinosaurs?

THE QUESTION ANSWERED
Some may say it's just a suggestion;
But I believe it's the answer to the question:
What happened to the dinosaurs?
Though some may not like the sound,
By an expert scientist it has been found:
The dinosaurs disappeared in layers of mud
Left behind by a great, mighty flood.
That's what happened to the dinosaurs!

Dorothy Hughlett Ethridge

Is He Crying?

When I look out and watch, rain fall from the sky,
I think to myself, do we make Jesus cry?
As he looks down upon us, tell me what does he see?
Is he filled with disgust, or do you think he's quite pleased?
I can't help but feel, he's really quite sad.
It seems like the good, might weigh less than the bad.
From parents that kill, the children they bore
If not to love, then what were they for?
And children that have no respect for their parents,
do they get what they deserve?
Or is it one of life's bummer deals
where respect isn't really earned?
The drugs, the booze, dirty sex that's exposed
I can't help but feel, it's all I suppose.
Instead of waisting time on such things,
we should teach our children what loving can bring.
And maybe then the sun would come by
and I wouldn't wonder, when it rains, does he cry?

LeAnn Pisar

Winners

No matter the face, a smile, a tear,
An overloaded mind entangled by fear.
But not all is gone, all hope is near,
For it is faith that carries us here.

But when we doubt and don't understand why,
When laughing is nowhere but a scream and a cry,
When everything around seems only a lie,
And the walls are crumbling - take a deep sigh.

For it is then, to take a look around,
When you feel so completely down.
When the weight on your shoulders is much more than a pound,
That no matter what, help can always be found.

For this is when I step in,
Helping to take away the pain of that pin.
Not all is gold, some has to be tin,
But we can never lose - only win.

Pamela Sue England

As I Grow Up

When I was born it was hot July,
    The doctor saw me and said, "My, My, My!"
My dad came to see me in the maternity ward,
    The nurses in that little room were certainly not bored!

After awhile I grew up a little,
    My grandmother said, "Fiddle de diddle!"
I started school and used a pen,
    My grandfather said, "I remember when....."

Fourth grade math teaches a lot about fractions,
    English was hard so my aunt taught me contractions.
In science I learned why the earth rotates,
    In religion I learned about God and the Pearly Gates.

Now I'm in seventh grade and very mature,
    I love writing and have imagination galore.
And I hope this poem opens my career's door.
    I would like to keep going on, but I cannot write more.

Amylynn Terry

Sonnet

A summer and a winter now have flown,
and still, my idle thoughts recall that scene-
Of bricks and bars and walls that drown a dream
of Hope in Hate, 'till then to me unknown.

The tramping beat of feet upon the stone
that we were forced to scrape and scrub and clean-
'Till our frames became both limp and lean,
Like gaunt and ghastly ghosts, too weak to groan.

I knew then how the howling wolf must feel
when standing, trembling, all alone in snow,
with one foot caught and crushed by jaws of steel.
I felt the wounds within my heart would never heal-
As if Life's flame were but a dying glow.

Jack Jesmer

Thomas - The Other Brother

Uncle
liked white
forbidden flesh
dipped in apricot sauce
Cherry Blossoms
bursting bright on warm taught coated extractions
sometimes he dreamt of
colored lights
huddled in the lilac lilies
sweating white as satin sheets

Alejandro McCartney

The Day The Starling Fell

Sitting in the shade of my garage door, gloating over how my
vegetables grow,
When from the slopping eaves of the house,
Tumbled a baby starling the size of a mouse.

The anxious mother with food to spare,
Flew erratically through the air.

There I sat Miracle-Gro at my side,
Wrestling with tears I could not hide,
Watching this creature there on the ground,
Mouth agape for what its mother had found.

I wanted to stand, but what would I do?
For just like the starlings, I was helpless too!

Then from the shadow it leaped like a light,
A bold black cat to dine without a fight.

I lament even now and tears still swell,
Just as they did the day the starling fell.

David T. Lawrence

The Clouds Have Parted

There is a dark cloud of sorrow
that fills the air -
When a loved one is taken away.
All tears and wailing will not diminish-
the feeling of emptiness that is here.

Yet, let us revel in the joy -
that they are no longer in pain,
and that our loss in but their gain.
The clouds have parted for them-
for they are in a greater place.

Rays more glorious than the sun -
exist beyond the sky we know.
Our friend has embarked on a voyage-
too wondrous for us to know
where they are warmed in heavenly love.

They have fought the good fight,
and lived the good life-
What more wondrous reward could be earned.
Weep not for they who are no longer with us,
but rejoice in the life with us they shared.

Ilo Jean Redifer

The Cross

Rising bright with truth for lies
On gossamer wings, with amber eyes
This soaring flight of pure emotion
Gives throbbing birth to a divine devotion
For earth and sun, the moon and sky
And the Golden Promise of days gone by
When life began at Heaven's door
For as time lay trembling on virgin shores
Our Paradise was born
To be
Creation, love, eternity.

But, the breath of life has atrophied
Le cup of purity, putrefied
For evil's root has crucified
This sacred child of God...
This finite, fragile orb
This shimmering lyrical sphere
This mystical perfection
This, our Covenant, born of fire
This...Eden.

D. Anderson

Alienation

Of late, dear one, I've taken note
Of your troubled brow and lack of hope;
Of your cold embrace—as glacial as a polar clime;
That your eyes seldom, if ever, meet mine;
That we, as strangers, are oft apart—
Unlike married lovers in the dark.

The question begs to be asked by me:
Has some fascination found your heart's key,
Drunk nectar from your luscious lips,
Enkindled cogent passions for your hips—
Taking you to new heights of rapture—
Forever your paramour, your obsession, your captor?

Your sensual beauty—your ecstasy—were both my treasures;
My love for you, the bounds thereof, I could not measure—
But one loves well who loves enough to give one up
And shun the sweet and drink the bitters of the cup—
Thus setting free forever a captive, yearning heart
To the victor invincible who stole the light and left the dark!

And now your silent answer speaks so truthfully and so certain:
To this play, this act, this scene of love—ring down the curtain!

Mitchel Walters

Love Prayer

Teach me to love dear Lord I pray,
teach me to love every day.

For I need to have love in my heart all the time.

When you have love for your sisters and brothers,
you'll have love for yourself and for all others.

Teach us to love dear Lord I pray,
teach us to love every day.

The world needs love for all mankind.

People young and people old,
need to have love or their heart will grow cold.

Give us the desire dear Lord I pray,
to keep the love in our hearts every day.

The world needs love to survive.

If your have this love the Lord taught us to know,
your heart will bloom like a sweet smelling rose.

Help us to use the love you gave dear Lord I pray,
help us to use that love on some one today.

The world was built on love for all.

Janet S. Bennett

Eternity

Today I am to tell thee
of what I wish us to be,
for I only have but one dream
of which you are the only theme.
I wish us to be together,
to be in love forever,
to have each other by the hand,
to live my life as I've hoped and planned.
We would lay out in the night,
illuminated by the moons gleaming light,
Which glorifies a scene of mountains high,
which spreads across the open sky.
Near the base of the mountains
starts the beginning of an ocean
yet, as it extends to infinity
so does my love for thee
soon enough we will live my dream
though a while it may seem,
but, I swear to thee,
I'll love you throughout eternity.

Michael Mravetz

Only

I am the one to wait behind while others
dance more rigorously than I, toward a
common goal I'll linger aside to let you pass.

Foresight warns to detour my decrepit
path of which I stumble. Vanity has not
the progress to which I still stay behind.
Few to many are qualified to venture blindly
farther than I yet I do not follow bye and by.

To the path I've failed to follow along this
life disappoints my wish to guide you beside.
Please along with me wander yet without
remorse I may not sigh.

I am the he who stands alone without friend
or foe to follow me home. My dreams to settle have
I the wish no more an endless journey now becomes
my throne; shackled to and from the essence of
my name to be undone and not called upon rarely
more again. I rest now to be forgotten.

David W. Rice II

Human Bodies

Human bodies, legs entwined.
Lulled to sleep with songs and wine.
Made to suffer made to love
Ruled by the God's and heaven's above.

Make me weep, let me know.
Bask me in your unearthly glow.
Torture screams and joy laughs.
Show me my alternate half.

Sunken levels, rooms of hate
Unknown to others but in dreams of late.
Thoughts to ponder, voices to explain.
Nothing to ease the pain.

Showers of lust and desire
Quelled by the morning fires.
Hopes and dreams begone me not.
Life, its meaning, has been fought.

Human bodies naked but clothed.
Beautiful inside yet loathed.
Trained to obey, trained to mate.
Destruction will surely be our fate.

Renee Gabrielle Michaud

Ode To A Shoe

It started out in a factory
with shoemakers and workers galore,
I was taken out of the factory
and sent to a nice cozy store.

I was taken out by humans,
out of that wonderful store,
I knew these people would be my masters,
and I would see that store no more.

I spent my nights in a closet,
my days were spent hugging feet.
I was worn by a world class jogger
with my soles beating down on the street.

Then I got thrown into a closet
with all the other "used" shoes
I knew that I was useless.
and now I'm singing the blues.

Michael Dufford

Snow

The Lord created the four seasons,
And we know He has His reasons.
So, I will love each one, as they come, and as they go,
But the one I have always loved the most,
Is the winter when He lets it snow.

Snow is so beautiful, in any kind of light,
So it is hard for us to imagine anything ever matching this sight.
The winter cold puts such a freshness into the air that we breathe,
As the snow falls gently upon the ground,
And there is a wonderful, sweet silence, since falling snow makes no sound.

Now when the earth around us is all blanketed with snow,
We may think of Him who gave it, to His children down below.
And this seems to bring us a message, and so silently this is done,
Telling us that He knows what we think is beautiful,
And so someday He will show us what beauty really is,
If we will only show Him we love His Son...

©1996 *James Davis Sorrels Sr.*

The Rope Of Life

The rope of life I cling to from my mothers womb, soon I'll be free
If she choose's it to be
Nothing wrong I have done but for some ungodly reason they say I
must not be born
I long to be in two loving arms to be cuddled and to be warm
Not left on the door step or in a car
Not cast into a ditch or thrown into a lane
But give me to a stranger to love and set me free
Even the animals do that to the one they conceive
But surely you feel something after you have carried me
Even after a month or two or three
But give me a chance and you'll see you can surely love me
But if you put me to eternal sleep you'll never know how sweet I'll be
They say you'll forget me but down deep in your heart I'll always be
But when you are old and alone
You will surely know that you were wrong
And you'll miss me saying mom are you alright
So from this wrong make it right
So please do not take my life
But let me keep the rope of life

Ruth Willis

Mysterious Romance

As I was walking late one night in New Orleans
on Saint Charles Street, it was transformed into a dark park covered
with trees as the ground become thick white clouds and the light from
a full moon laid a path.
My feeling were over-taken by the passion that filled the air. That's
when I saw a beautiful and mysterious 'Genie' standing in silence
upon a cloud in the middle of the path. She reached out her hands and
a cold chill ran down my spine then a cloud carried me into her arms.
We began floating down the path cuddled closely together in silence;
but I somehow felt her communicating with my inner most feelings.
When the clouded path come to an end, she turned and waved her hand
across my face; I closed my eyes and she kissed me. Moments later, my
eyes opened and she had disappeared from in my arms and the park was gone.

Wendell Delaney

Blue Violet

I'm one blue violet in a field
and perhaps my fate is sadly sealed...

I may be meant to only be
like a drop of water in the sea...

But I long to stand out from the crowd,
not merely blend in — I'm too proud...

And not to be of a large mass,
but to be chosen by the young lass...

Each day she comes by our place
and pleasures us with her grace...

She's so gentle in her selection
and even kind in her rejection...

She steps not on us, but in-between —
she's the gentlest girl we've ever seen...

I'll raise my petals toward the sky
so she will no longer pass me by...

My feeling was right about today —
she's picked me for her small bouquet...

I now feel important as one of a few —
I'm no longer sad, although I'm still blue.

Bonnie Tirabassi

Futility

Turning o'er the landscape
    deliberate in its roll.
Imperceptible motion,
    methodical control.

A never ending harvest.
    Grist before the mill.
A silent grinding cycle,
    mortality doth instill.

Relentless tide on an endless sea,
    Spirits awash
        A futile plea.

Oh merciless treadmill cease thy bidding!
    Reverse.
        Reward, an end befitting.
            Reward our toils, we beg of thee.

And still the wheel turns unto me.

Richard Pawelka

"Thoughts"

Contemplating dreams at night,
I stay awake listening to the early morning sounds.
Thinking of away out of sight,
Contemplating on how to avoid the hounds.

I can't believe all those who fall for me,
why must I be the loved one?
I never stay long enough for love to see,
Contemplating the thought of leaving all but none.

Contemplating dreams keeps me awake,
If only there was away out for my own good!
Contemplating on not causing any pain for their sake,
If only I could get out before I'm taken by my 'hood!

I don't know why people trust me,
Contemplating dreams and I don't know why?
When I get close I leave them; the reason I can't see,
I don't know why I'm always contemplating new schemes!

J. D. Lawrence

When Friendship Dies

When friendship dies
There should be no lies

Secrets that we told as friends
Should never be revealed again

Best friends for life we said we'd be
But something came between you and me

A misunderstanding I thought it was
For best friends should never lose their love

Grudges that are held for a long time
Makes us wonder did we cross the line

When friendship dies, you're all alone
Set feelings aside pick up the telephone

Who cares who is right or who is wrong
We promised to be best friends for so long

Now seal that bond that made you friends
And make a promise never to fight again

For if you don't and time will pass
The grudge you held will always last

Kathleen Bruce Calvanese

Life Without Love

What is Life without love
Sometimes it can be tragic
Without love your life can be lonely
It can sometimes be depressing
It can be like Kool-Aid without sugar
Like a car without driver
If you don't have sugar Kool-Aid
It taste dull, like it doesn't have pizzazz
A car without driver just sits there
It cannot move without driver
If I threw you a curve ball could you catch it?
What is dope without addiction
Dope without addiction is love
Did you catch that curve ball?
Just like life without God
You don't know which way to go
You don't know to go up or down
What do you have in any of those things if you have
Life without love, if you don't have love in your life
What a sad case it can be

Willie Johnson

"A Light Beyond Hope"

The race of man is shortsighted.
We see nothing beyond our own problems,
Our petty rivalries of long dead ancestors.
Once in a great while there is someone with vision.
He'll gaze past our clouds of ignorance that surround us,
To a light beyond hope, beyond peace, a light beyond love.
He reaches to this light of freedom, yearning for a second of happiness.
He reaches for the light, rallying others about him.
And as his fingers brush the surface he falls back,
Colder than he never knew was possible.
He'll look into the faces of sneering people,
And in the second before the life leaves his eyes
He remembers and smiles,
The clouds part and he gazes upward,
A light beyond sheds golden tears on a smooth forehead.
For one second he knows freedom.
At night they tossed and turned, imagining they'd seen a light
    beyond hope.
They'll come awake with tears in their eyes,
The image fades until they brave sleep again,
A sleep riddled with golden tears for a dying planet.

David Brodsky

That Old Gentle Man

He had long since retired, that old gentle man
My life was beginning, I was just barely ten
He taught me to fish, and enjoy the outdoors
And shared his wisdom while I helped with the chores

It was a simple life he'd always lived
Never knowing wealth, and preferring to give
It would be many years, before I would know
Seeds of wisdom he'd planted, continued to grow

Ours was a friendship few rarely find
Giving without asking, and responding in kind
I heard many stories of his younger years
He spoke only of happiness, saying nothing of tears

He passed on one summer while I was away
But his friendship remains in my mind to this day
I'm a better person for having known this man
Who's kindness and guidance I now understand

As I find myself in my later years
Sharing my wisdom and quieting fears
Of those who are yet to face life's test
Taking the punches and giving their best

Theodore Disko

A Silent Rumble

Thunder awakens the snakes.
They roam amongst the clouds,
waiting to land upon some unknown destination.
They fill the air with their cries and all who hear cringe.
They sail upon the ground in violence,
creating destruction in their wake.
The lighted serpents cause the heat to rise,
ensuring that fog and darkness will cover their pathways.
They travel upon the ionic trail that connects them to our world.
We run, we hide, we stand at awe of their might.
But we know that the fire lizards will pass
when the lighted orb returns.
The authority of the darkness fades away at the hint of a small
beam of purity.
The image of the beast's flashing instantly, all around, singularly
in a second of time,
pales in comparison to the lighted sky of Day where its magnitude
cannot be fathomed.

Denos Myrmingos

Mother Earth

Earth is a big blue and green ball,
That everyone takes for granted.
Earth has oxygen and nitrogen.
Earth has the ability to make you live.
That is why we call her our mother.
She cares for you when she gives you light.
When you are cold, she gives oil to heat you.
But yet we treat her wrong!
Cutting trees
polluting air
wasting energy
and killing animals.
That is how we treat her and much, much worse,
After all that, she still gives us
water
love and
life!!!

April Aspen

Meandering

Brought from the land of the River Nile
Chained, abused and oppressed for a long while
Struggled and toiled from sun up to sun down
Slaving for a master without receiving home or crown.

Found a heavenly father to trust and pray to
Bringing frustrations and woes, asking what can I do?
Asking for deliverance, seeking mercy and grace
Hoping for relief from a hard master's face.

The burden's were lightened, hardships decreased
We praised the heavenly Father for shackle released
We praised the heavenly Father for all of our gains
Until we received a bounty of fortune and fame.

We soon forgot, the same way the children Moses led
From the old ark of safety, we fled
To a master of lust, whoremonging drugs and greed
Soon to find out it's destroying our seed.

Back to our heavenly Father return ye this day
Bow beneath the cross and humbly pray
Rise up! put your vices down
Lest you lose your soul, home and crown.

Mary Alice Warren

If You Only Knew

If you only knew how your smile touches my heart. How your
laugh heals my soul. How your touch makes my eyes sparkle.
If you only knew.
If you only knew how you walked into my life not a minute too soon.
How your words inspire me. How you spirit catches mine.
How your eyes talk to me.
If you only knew.
If you only knew how your courage gives me hope. How your tears
dance with mine. How your voice brings sun into my body.
If you only knew.
If you only knew how your body captures mine. How your
wisdom gives me strength. How your power enlightens me.
If you only knew.
If you only knew how your unspoken words speak love. How
your eyes follow mine. How your heart whispers "in time"
If you only knew.

Denise Ingram

The Other Side Of The Night

There are two times of night:
Night begins with the dying of the day,
But the light doesn't die so easily.
The young night is filled with music, laughter, and lights
The sweet taste of the wine
A lover's soft voice and caress.

For many, there is only this.
Night passes from youth to sleep.

Others are not so fortunate:
Those who are awake to see night in its maturity,
When the darkness overcomes the light and the music dies
away into silence.
This the time of night when the warmth of day and cheer is
finally gone, and the world turns cold,
Those who see the time when the world is vast and empty, silent and dark,
And feel all its weight on their shoulders.
All that these lost souls can do is reach out into the empty night,
Hope someone will take their hands,
And pray for the coming of the light.

Matt Keville

The River Trip

We're drift'n down the river, the waters
flat as glass.
Ducks are in the reeds and coots are
cruising past.
The sun is shining brightly, the water's
on the cool side.
Anticipations mellow, expecting just a
smooth ride.
The river rounds a bend, the waters moving now.
There's slap'n on the gunnels, risings in the bow.
Attentions needed now to guide the craft along,
There's walls and rocks and pools, the river sings a song.
Fear begins an icy trail as round a bend we go,
There's sleepers and sweepers and haystacks all in a row!
Fear has got a chockhold, nerves are nearly shot,
Inverted Vees and waterfalls, our unfortunate lot.
The worst of it is finally over, Oh No, it's not!
Our craft is in a whirlpool caught!
At last we're free and round a bend.
The scare is over, the rivers run, let's go back and do it all again!

Joelyn Porter

Hunting Season In Paradise

A piece of paradise lies, not far from my home.
Lush valley, green and ripe, fertile with inspiration for poets and artists.
The sun casts a spell on all it touches, while the breeze tickles
    the foliage at play.
Early in the morning the only sights of habitation:
Overhanging cables and signs showing which way.
The silence is broken by the gurgles of a miniature stream.
Hungry chicks.

I am lucky! A lone bird swoops in the skies searching for food.
Minding his business, gracing us with his elegance and poise.
Yet even this Eden has its serpent.
Crouching in hides, slithering on his belly.
Aiming... aiming... Bang
The tranquility shattered by leaded rain tattooing my car roof.
Icarus nose dives and spins out of control
To fall broken to earth's fatal embrace near hungry chicks.
The stream keeps on gurgling, while foliage cover multi sins.
Not much to show after the echoes of the big bang have faded,
Except for a barren sky.

Mariella Cassar

I Remember...

Days when the world was new
When mother was always right
Every when she was wrong
I remember the Nile, the roses
Red, yellow, maybe blue and green
The bright miles from beautiful Egyptian women
I remember the tropical sun
    The tropical heat
I remember things not so good
But I remember love
I remember snow when I first saw it
Buildings so tall they could touch the sky
I remember family
    Sun, rain
    Hurricane
When the world was my playground
When I could reach up and touch the sky
And paint it any color I wished.
    I remember...

Azziza Oluwakemi

Who Are You? I Am A Book!

Who are you? - I am a book
The greatest journalist,
The predictor of the events,
The presenter of the intellectuals and genius.

Who are you? - I am a book!
The friend of the readers,
The companion of the professors,
The comrade of the politicians.

Who are you? - I am a book!
The messenger of the authors,
The fan of the multitudes in the world,
The teacher of the learners.

Who are you? - I am a book!
The witness of the court,
The narrator of the past and present,
The silent counsellor of the counsellees.

Who are you? - I am a book!
The heir of the eternal heroes of faith,
The commandant of the advisors and orators,
The advertiser of the ideologist and psychologists.

Tsotetsi

No Length Of Tune

Beyond the sounds of city and shore,
beneath the call of living and war,
blind to the look, no preference
to either broken or perfect.
No favorite mood, no reason to rule,
no strength is stronger or true.

Beyond the vows of willing and worn,
beneath the dance of season and storm,
deaf of all ears, full courage
to lay back in quiet honor.
What roots are these? This breath we breathe,
reaped and sowed us from seed.
Our souls are woven around the wind, the alms of love,
older than feeling, there is no length of time in love.

Taja Sevelle

Bluebird

my father surprised me with his dream, his highest hope,
sung so often (by so many), yet rarely heard in our house
                    surprised!   my father dreamt!
surprised!   my father imagined   a place perfect   where bluebirds fly
                    surprised!
        my father imagined silence   in soaring   and peace!
                surprised!   my father imagined!

I saw a human form, yet no dreaming soul,
I saw an animal, with a masters mind . . .   dreamless
                                oh, to be a bluebird!   yeah . . .
        he wanted to be a bluebird   but I'll be a sparrow   any day

my father   the Papa sparrow   a bluebird inside   flying on sparrows' wings
                        body   too laden   to reach rainbows
                    my Daddy . . .
and tears fall with the wings   feather to sticky feather   dust and grease
                tyre to the hotted road of our degradation . . .

            dreams . . .   ha!   dreams

and I dream of flowers   beckoning the dance of flesh from flesh . . .

        I dream of flowers . . .   ha!

Jill Campbell

Sweet Sixteen

What is "Sixteen"? To some it's just a number,
A dog at sixteen would just lie and slumber;
Some say it's being carefree and young at heart,
But to me, "Sixteen" is my big start.

Oh, Yeah! I'm "Sixteen", I'm on top of the mountain,
When I speak, brilliance flows like a fountain;
I'm the sharpest pencil in the box,
If intelligence broke you out I'd have intelligence pox.

Oh, Yeah! I'm "Sixteen", I'm nobody's fool,
No more "Sister" driving me to school;
I can drive by myself, no "Dad" with me,
No "Mommy's Little Boy", Oh, Yeah! I'm free.

I can do what I want, go where I please,
Girls just swoon and sigh, I'm the "Big Cheese";
I can kick up my heels, stay out late at night,
Oh, Yeah! I'm "Sixteen", I'm a sight.

I'm fearless, I'm brave, in courage I'm way ahead,
No more alligators under my bed;
Oh, Yeah! I'm "Sixteen", I'm nobody's dummy,
Alligators? Under my bed? "I want my mummy!"

Janet E. Clendenin

That One

There is an old proverbial phrase people say.
"In life you only get one true friend."
I am happy that I don't need to wait another day.
My search for that one has come to an end.

Of course I mean you are that one.
Who else could even compare?
In my heart you are second to none.
Look any further, no, I wouldn't dare.

If you weren't there, what would I do?
You are always standing by my side.
I know I can place my trust in you.
So in you I will always confide.

What is the most important reason you are that one?
My feelings are shared and returned times two.

Karen Michelle Hilko

"My Precious Little Boy"

Two Paths had crossed, my heart remembers well
Memories to make me smile, through the tears that fell
Asking the Lord in prayer, when I was all alone
Please lend me a helping hand, for now I'm on my own
With each passing day, the life inside me grew
Until the moment came, when I was holding you.
My precious little boy, how will you ever know
The feeling I get inside, as I watch you grow
With each smile you give, and every step you take.
When you have bad dreams, I'll be there when you awake.
Fairy tales and magic wands, even trips to the zoo
Making our own memories, and sharing my dreams with you.
A love so overwhelming, bringing back a heart once lost
creating something so wonderful, by the two paths that crossed.
I'll cherish every moment, and my tears will be of joy,
I'm so proud to be your Mom, my precious little boy.

Michelle Palmer

A Question For A Brown Man

Would you shake my hand
If I put it out and called you my strong brother or man?
Or would you slap it away
Like they did to you back in the day?
If you had the chance
Would you make me your slave
Throw me in a cave
Then do a dance?
Would you tell me you are mighty and brown
Then kick when I'm down?
Would you spit in my face
And rule my race?
Would you put me in chains
Beat my brains
Sell my son
And never let us run?
Or would you be a man
And shake my hand
Then say
You too are my strong white brother?

Glen D. Rockwell

Mama, Will You Pray?

Will you pray for me, if I'm not able?
If my body's tired and my mind's not stable.
Will you fall to your knees and pray all night?
Will you plead my cause if I loose sight?

Will you pray to The Father if I'm full of disease,
to give me comfort, and put my body at ease?
Will you help to feed me and clothe me just right?
Will you read me The Word as I prepare for my flight?

Will you pray for my child if I have to go?
Will you teach him of Calvary and reaping what you sow?
Will you pray for my spouse, whom I love and adore,
Please tell him to meet me on The Heavenly Shore?

Will you pray for my brothers and sisters and such?
And for my precious daddy, whom I love very much.
Will you pray for my friends, and tell them not to fret,
Remind them of the laughter and the pain they'll forget.

When I have to go, I'll dare not look back,
I'll be headed for Glory, where nothing is lacked.
I'm ready for Heaven, with Jesus I'll stay,
I'm asking one more time, mama, will you pray?

Mary F. Lockamy

My Old Guitar

My heart is broken and I'll never see
  that old guitar they stole from me.

Went to the bank and then when I got home
  I found that I was all alone.

Was it revenge for something that I did?
  Oh no - they stole it for a kid.

I worked so hard - oh yes, to pay for it
  Just a memories now I can't forget.

The nice policeman, here's what he told me
  "Relax - don't worry - let it be
for someday soon it surly will return
  some day when you are unconcerned."

Oh, years have passed and still no word of it.
  I'm old; and shaking quiet a bit.

My heart's still broken and I'll never see
  That old guitar they stole from me.

Broken heart - stolen guitar
  Broken heart - stolen guitar.

Alice Perrault

Blend As One

The city is still,
The sky with dancing stars,
The People sleep,
The coolness of the air,
My heart feels the power of love,
I am loved.

I am alone, yet he is in my heart,
For now we are apart, soon we will be one.
I have given my love, my being, shared my thoughts,
Gone beyond the line of owning myself.
I step into his heart, fill him with love,
Share my most private wishes.

I am a complete woman,
Now I love beyond this world,
And He loves me beyond life in return.
We blend as the sky touches the horizon,
Solid, blend as should be. Blend as one.
Touch as man to woman, day after day, forever.

Pat Turner

Ocean

Your water so blue,
Your horizon so distant
It's hard to believe that you don't last forever.
Your shores are so rocky,
Your sand is so smooth.
The deep murky, blue of the waters far below
Are filled with adventure,
I'd like to explore......
The things that are sacred,
To the ocean,
And are hidden from everything else.
The prizes you carry down into the deep
The treasure of ships is that what you keep?
You keep it hidden in the cold dark water.
A place where no man or creature
Will ever find it.

Down in the depths of the Ocean

Clay Taylor

Doubt

Where is my life going?
seems to be an everyday occurrence,
constantly stemming forth
Moods of frustration,
Feelings of inadequacy and depression,
or thoughts consumed about the Future.

Just being happy is no longer tolerable,
as thoughts of career choices predominate,
leaving behind the times for social gathering,
so what am I going to do?

Not knowing worries me more than
Anything, because this insecure condition
has emanated to drastic proportions,
giving way to failure and loneliness.

Searching for a comfortable living,
needing some threshold of security,
Yet, no ideas are springing forth,
and I am left stranded with uncertainty.

Andrew A. Dinh

My Heart Yearns For The Countryside

My heart yearns for the countryside
With the peace and quite of the day.
A fishing pole at the water hole,
Where the trout and the catfish play.

I yearn to walk a nature path
That winds beneath the trees.
And through meadows green with a wildflower scene
Swaying in the breeze.

My heart is filled with loneliness
When I think of the hills of home.
Of all my friends and family
And the countryside I roamed.

But when age moves in, though the soul is young,
The body needs its rest.
And though the yearning's there to return once more
The legs won't stand the test.

So I sit and think of my yesterdays
And how it use to be.
And though I can't return to my place of youth
In my mind the hills I see.

Brenda Johnson

Untitled

As we grow older,
we realize how much our parents have done for us.
No longer taking for granted crying on their shoulder
and regretting what we did in those days when we were rebellious.
At the time we thought that they were so unfair
and that we knew all there was to know about life.
Now we know just how much they cared
and that they just wanted us to do right.
So remember before it is too late
to thank them for all they've done.
For another day do not wait:
tomorrow they may not rise with the sun.

Carol Payne

The Power Of Love

Love, the greatest hope of all,
Yet the biggest fear of any man.
Every man is so scared to fall in love,
but when he's there,
He wouldn't trade it for the world.

Love comes with so many benefits,
But the loss of a true love,
Can create misery and havoc,
And a realm of broken-heartedness,
That I would wish on no man.

If only there were a way to make love safe,
To eliminate all the heartache,
To make it a place where two people come together,
And join forces, hearts, and hands,
On a journey to everlasting joy.

But alas, there is no way,
Love will always be a dangerous path,
To be taken even by the weakest man,
Because the hope of one day finding that love,
Can make any man conquer even his darkest fears.

Brian Zwak

My Contribution

What is it that stirs my soul to probe the Creator's heart;
To make the world a better place is my desired path.
When I just stand and see the things that surround me,
I do know I have a role to play, an idea to perceive.

When I search for that elusive truth that lies beyond,
Let me not tire, let me not fail to find and track it down.
Give me the sight to see, what no one else has seen,
And the mind to understand the interpretation of my dream.

In the final assessment of my life, will I grieve or delight,
Will I have made a contribution of all my inspirations.
Will the world be a better place when I have gone,
For all my thoughts and creations that I have done.

George Fonseca

Discovery

Violin clutched tightly, I wait.
The bus roars up, clattering,
The broken dinosaur from a bad movie.

Climbing the steps makes mountains easy.
Paper wrappers flap on rubber treads.
The fare box grins like a Gothic gargoyle.

I rise, just as you taught me, Grandfather,
To give an old lady my seat. She has pain
Behind the brown in her eyes. She yells at me.

When I go to the back to sit
The way we used to, Grandfather,
They all yell at me.
The driver throws me off the bus.

I'm lost and have no fare.
Why didn't you tell me, Grandfather,
That people are different if their skin's
Like night, like coffee with cream, like topaz?

Everyone's the same underneath,
Aren't they, Grandfather?
Their blood is red.

A. W. Gillidette

Grandpa Great

Gracious as a host, he is the most!
Red is how he's known, most will boast.
Always there in heart and in mind
Never holds back a word that is kind
Delights everyone that he sees.
Patience to all is his decree.
Abundance of honesty and goodness are his key.

Grand in every way, that's his history!
Remarkable, religious, reasonable he'll always be!
Endless amounts of consideration and caring
Admirable talents that make him our king
Today, we want to thank him for everything!

Karen Sweeney

The Olympic Games

The Olympic games bring many, different countries and people
together
To share in athletic events.
The spirits are high,
The competition is keen,
For the competing medalist to attain
One worthy event of the games.
Each entrant complies with the rules of the team,
While he tries to play fair with the others
And gives of his best, to excel, to the end of the mighty game.

Thera B. Sass

The Dance Of Intimacy

Two hearts meet, reaching out to one another,
willingly accepting, all they have to offer,
exposing their innermost thoughts, innermost feelings,
creating a rare, unique bond,
a harmonious connection...
a dance of intimacy.

As these two hearts communicate, entrusting their most private
thoughts and emotions, everything from their hopes and
dreams, to their deepest, darkest secrets, their weaknesses,
fears, vulnerabilities, mistakes, insecurities...
completely trusting one another, without apprehension of being
ridiculed or judged, conveying all about themselves, with an assured
confidence, because of the genuine, sincere, appreciative acceptance,
for who they truly are.

As these two hearts grow closer, continually strengthening, an
overlapping bond, uniting their spirits,
entwining their desires, their passions, their energies,
they create a force, a power...

The dance of intimacy, is the very essence...
of making love.

Rey Cerezo

Only I Cry

Only I cried when we came to an end,
      the final words that made us friends,
my eyes watered and my mouth remained closed,
deep within no words of explanation arose,
      I felt the anger build inside, but as
I thought about it, only I cried.
Only I cried when people said it was
      because I fell in too deep, so this
is what I deserve this is why I weep, Yet how can one control
their emotions, how I feel about something is not a
game, it is a devotion, when I see you and smile
it is only a disguise, but when I'm alone and in thought only I cry.
Only I cried day after day after day,
      for I had lost my guide, therefore
I had lost my way, we did not end up at the
same point, same destination, too blind to
      see through the darkness of aggravation,
in the end you made the final choice, you spoke
out your strong firm voice all the turmoil and pain that I kept
to hide, all came forth when only I cried.

Desmond Anderson

Mick Jagger's Love Child

Best young debater in the nation
Had to play Hoops to get
Respect.
Pushed around on the court;
Just like the squad room.
A strained ankle for his
Strained friendship.

Three year of abuse:
Jokes about his lips
Jokes about his virginity
Jokes about his lineage—Monkey or Mick Jagger?
Laughter
The response to
His anger.

Like the Joker
The wide grin he wore
Was a lie.
Twisted;
Forced by the pain
With each step.

John Atkinson

And So I Ask

I'm not asking you for the moon or the sky
someone had already asked other females without minds
without love and dignity I'm not asking you for the stars
Leave for the night to light
I don't want a sadness night nor the sky that you can't offer.
Give and keep on giving me your love.
Which is pure through all the
dust that falls right through
I'm not asking, for too much
only your love in one single touch.
The way you can and the way you may offer.
And if you give I'll give you
my love and everything that you may wish for
I don't ask for some fake words.
Which it'll make me lose control.
I'm not asking for the moon that rises.
Leave it there for good luck.
All I'm asking is for your sweet passion.
So don't give up on giving
me your sweet and tender passion

Lucia Preda

Tomorrow's World

Children are the future, the life as it could be
Holding all our hopes and dreams
The fantasies we see

Children should be handled, with only love and care
For one day soon they will rule
The world that we all share

So when our children make mistakes
Be gentle as you scold beloving in your punishment
For one day you'll be old

Treat all children with respect
And you'll see in return
They will show it back to you, a lesson they will learn

If you treat a child with hurt
With only hate and pain
See how they will repay you
A lesson learned again

So if crave a perfect world
With adults fair and mild
Then start today it's not to late
Go ahead and hug a child

Lorelei G. Brown

Christmas Blessings

I have a special present for you,
It may come wrapped in a blanket of snow,
Or whisper to you as the voice of the wind,
It is Joy.

I have a special prayer for you,
May you find it within your heart and
encircling the sphere you call home,
It is called Peace.

I have a special message for you,
It is shared by seeds and dreams alike,
It is Hope.

I have a special wish for everyone,
May we be filled with the spirit of Joy, Peace
And Hope this Christmas,
And let us remember,
We have been given a precious gift,
That will allow us to travel a road whose
design is our own,
It is Life.

Sarah Alexandra Randall

First Grandchild

Jonathan Paul, Jonathan Paul, Oh so sweet and oh so small
The pride of your Mommy and Daddy, the love of your grampy and granny
I'm sure the angels who worked on you in heaven's assembly line
Picked you to be mom's special love, for all your days in time
For your lips they picked a rose, that in God's garden grew
It had to be, for when you smile, it's moist and sweet with dew
Your eyes, two stars a shining, that twinkle in the light
They set your face a glowing, all through the day and night
And for your heart, they picked a very special kind
It ticks with love and laughter, and never skips a chime
For your wispy hair, they dusted off the stars
To make each strand gleam and shine, like solid golden bars
As you slid along the Milky Way, to this cold earthly floor
I'm sure the angels must have cried, as you slipped through heaven's door

Jeanette O. Sweeney

Untitled

Here's to a fine fellow named Pat
Who is actually quite a cool cat
Through tough exams he's just sat
Now returned to his old habitat

Indiana was the school he chose
Where term papers he did compose
And nary a word did he transpose

He did his best, passed every test
Wore the cap and gown, but in now leaving town

Now he proudly puts his G.P.A.
On his up-to-date resumé
And then starts to pray
For a job with good pay!

So let's pop the cork
Before he's off to New York

We will miss him indeed
But we know he'll succeed

Pat's such a good sport
And he's probably pleased
That this verse is so short

Vivian Wartenberg

Where Do You Go And What Do You Do, What Are You To Me And Me To You?

Where are the sun, slip into the eye
Under horizons, we think and it's believe.
Where does the moon, hide its face
To disappear, when we're awake.
Where do you go and what do you do, what are you to me and me to you?

Where do the stars, so bright and clear
Begin and end, when we're not here,
Where does the wind, rest, when at peace
At the end of the world, we hope at least.
Where do you go and what do you do, what are you to me and me to you?

Where do the waves, of the ocean deep
Splash and spray, when we're asleep,
Where does the fog, so thick and grey
Lift and fall, while we're away.
Where do you go and what do you do, what are you to me and me to you?

Where does the dew, with its freshness clean
Touch the earth, while we're at dream.
What am I, in the changing scene
Part of the past, or the present team.
Where do you go and what do you do, what are you to me and me to you?

Carol Hunt

Pensive Is A Deep Shade Of Red

Don't turn half hesitatingly as the sun
in time-worn dance,
illuminates you mid-thought.
Don't stand so silent still,
that your ancient face
and young child's mouth,
become obscured by shadows
that flutter in the corners of my mind.

Run, my friend, lest the moss that moves so
imperceptibly, gaining territory,
rots the leather of your shoes
and reaches out towards your heart.

Pensive is a deep shade of red;
So rather hold your soul in bloodied
hands above your head
towards the sun;
Rather run
than let it ooze across your feet
and seep out between the bricks
of the sarcophagus, some call mind.

Melissa Anne de Vere-Loots

Where False Faces Lie

I look in the mirror, and what do I see?
Through a wavering reflection,
I see a smiling face;
I see a calm face;
I see a face streaked with tears.

All of them inter-changing,
twining deceptively into one another
until I cannot tell them apart.
But I know that all of them;
every single image in the mirror is a mask.

I am not real.
I was born playing a role.
Who is to say which one I am?
I can be anyone,
but I can never be someone...
I can never be me.

Tracy Comeau

Life

You filled my heart with joy,
    you lifted my sole.
You helped through the toughest times,
    you made my life whole.
You tore me from the ones I loved,
    you left and said, we weren't one.

My life is ruined,
    my life is gone.
All because I chose to please you,
    and not to comprehend what I did wrong.

You shoved me away,
    and left me to die.
Now I have a little girl,
    with no daddy in sight.

I thought you loved me,
    I thought you cared.
Now I know you lied,
    and now I'm totally scared.

Amanda Lynn Farnsworth

My Holy Spirit Plea

Rain down holy spirit - come upon me now
So I can receive you, while you may be found

Cleanse my Holy Spirit - of all my iniquities
Then mold and shape me into what you have me be

Use me holy spirit - to do your holy will
Knowing the strength I need, only you can give

Lead and guide me Holy Spirit - to places I need to go
Just to tell others that you live, and why I love you so

Feed me Holy Spirit - for I am hungry for thee
To fill and keep me, until your face I'm able to see

Teach me Holy Spirit - to understand your will and way
So I will forgive others each and everyday

Give me love Holy Spirit - to show to all mankind
That joy and peace is real; not just a state of mind

Renew me Holy Spirit - when trials and troubles comes
To give me strength to continue, this race I must run

Protect me Holy Spirit - from dangers seen and unseen
For I'm bought with a price and my soul has been redeemed

Receive me Holy Spirit - into your waiting arms
So when it's all over down here, this world can do me no more harm!

Addie Sue Pyles

Now Love Is Here

The breath of Spring comes to a garden spot,
It comes the way that all the breezes blow.
Its healing, soothing touch is everywhere;
So love will cause a waning life to grow.

The haunting fragrance of a Summer rose
Brings to the heart a peaceful happy glow.
Just how it came to be is mystery;
And love brings hope, a brighter way to show.

The birds fly south beneath an Autumn sky,
Leaving behind the hint of cold and snow.
Who charts their flight or marks where they arrive?
Thus it is so that love is here, I know.

The hush of Winter comes with falling snow,
Flakes seem the same, and yet it is not so.
Each falls to earth and all blend into one;
All loss is gain wherever love shall go.

I can't explain the course of happiness,
Or if we lose it, just where it would go.
As long as we're together, joy remains;
And it is so that love is here, I know.

Fern M. Cooper

Tempest

There is a calm peaceful feeling inside me
As if after a storm
The lightning has struck
    emotions
The thunder has boomed
    angry voices
The rain has beat down
    tears
The wind has bent the trees as if they were match sticks
    the acceptance of discord
The storm is over
The streets are swept clean of trash
Like my mind, clear of unwanted thoughts.

Margo A. Stambleck

I Belong

To the snow capped mountains of the frozen north where
the ice stretching to the horizon is dotted with shades
of blue. The loose snow blowing and glistening like
diamonds in the morning air.

Where the hills, ablaze with the colors of wild flowers,
slope gently to the edge of a babbling brook.

To the plains sown with wheat and oats that blow gently
in the breeze. The desert where cacti bloom and living
creatures hide from the sun's rays.

I belong on the sea where the waves gently rise, push
forward and crash. Where dolphins with their acrobatics
and the whales teasingly play. And where, when the fog
comes rolling in, the fog horns blare their long and
lonely warnings.

To all this I Belong
  Clara Jelso

Gifts Of The Soul

When life seems to have dumped upon us
Much more than our share
Remember that God places upon us
No more than what we can bear.

So when you think it's all too much for you
Reach deep into your soul
To find the strength that's always been there
Just lying around and growing mold.

Dust it off and bring it forth!
Let that God-given strength show
So bright it will be that all your troubles
Will melt away under its glow.

And you will find that with every step
You take, you'll have a brand new gait
And from your whole body, and from your face
The divine blessings of God will radiate.
  B. Keturah Phillips

Autumn Rain

By the afternoon window,
The curtain drawn back
To the fuzzed, frayed forgetfulness rain
Windlicking the trees...

Windstruck,
Beating out tracks on the stream's clay bank,
Washing the maple leaf's stain from the stone
To puddle
The wee-filled hollow beyond
The trembling willows below.

Walk,
Not alone,
Under the cool grey silver-dancing,
Misting forgetfulness rain
On the face
In tears...

Lip-moisten the hair,
Soften the warm flesh,
Remain.

Touch one another.
  Robert A. Campbell

Protect Children

The love seen within a child's eyes
Is sometimes the only truth behind a painful disguise.
Many are forced into silence,
While living with all forms of abuse and violence.
People have heard them cry and moan,
as they continue to suffer all alone.
Don't just read their stories and think, "What a shame,"
Or waste time finding who is to blame...
A nightmare for them is more than alarming,
When death becomes their Prince Charming!
Rescue children from this tragic fate
Be their hero and make death wait.
Their story may not become a fairy tale
But at least there is hope that love will prevail.
So help to make the world a better place
For the children who are the Future of the human race.
  Himala N. Singh

"My Soul Moves On"

When the houses already rest
When the rooms are still,
And when they cannot admire the song
Of feet passing by the gate
My soul moves on

Let them alone
Who! In the morning
Leave their houses, as who! As sunset
Hurry back to lock themselves in their room

What is a house - a place of rest
Only those who! Need rest
The dying and the weak
Why mush you, as they mush,
Forever keep returning

Move on, my soul, move on.
What if the motions, end not
In realization of desire?
Just move, move away
From rested houses, and rested souls
My soul moves on.
  Harvey Matthews

Untitled

Mr. President, I think you are a fine
man that still believe in this great land.
I think you are an American through and through,
so may God rest his hands on you.
I know your job won't be easy as you
run this race, but I bet you come in,
in first place.
I know the Republicans have tried everything
to dirty you and Hillary's name.
All great men stand the test of time,
and Bill Clinton, you're one of a kind.
The poor are weary, the middle class
too, give us something to hold on to.
The politicians should live on the street
and ask for a handout or something to eat.
I pray for America that's in hard times,
and may God give you wisdom,
and great strength to make this Nation
a better place.
  Evelyn Mick

Words

Sometimes unspoken
words
can mean more than
a thousand spoken
words
I didn't understand
your actions
until I
heard the slamming
of the door
missed your touch
when I finally
fell asleep
when I awoke I
couldn't help but
wonder why
you chose to
leave so many
things unsaid

Roxanne Taylor King

Bog

Ensnared by indecision,
Transfixed by pending pain,
Love Wallows,
Listing heavily

Why did the chill not penetrate
At this bog's beginning.
Only when this gritty mire
Met my trailing fingertips
Was I inspired to shudder

Mud tugs at my calves,
And unsuspected dread
Suffuses me.
I have always known
What this place is.

I can tell I have arrived.
The pain of this destination
Is familiar,
Now that I'm sinking

Laura Warren

Green Eyes To A Departed Friend

It was her twenty-fifth birthday
and a joyous occasion
Which I did attend
with little persuasion.

I drove her home and she taught
me to kiss
Then confided in me something
no one else knew.

She was sick inside and would soon
leave this earth
And she cried in my arms
.. Oh God how I hurt.

I held her and comforted her
but could not speak
But instead I to began
to weep.

Someone later asked what she looked
like this girl who cried
I could only say to them she
had the most beautiful green eyes.

David Verolin

Gentle September Ocean

Abandoned summer yacht,
Oblique on the ocean,
Mainsail tilted,
Across the setting sun,
Resilient enough,
To stay the season.

Sea gulls call,
Arriving on shore,
Breaking the still,
They gambol for scraps,
And fly to the rocks.

A gentle September ocean,
Swallows the orange sun,
The pleasure yacht bobs,
Playful and serene,
In the sky above,
A gibbous moon.

Matthew R. Dow

Untitled

Winds whisper secrets,
Puzzling calm before a storm
Sometimes nature fools.

Rain pelts the green earth,
Thunder shakes the high heavens.
Puddles quickly form.

The sun peers through clouds,
Warm rays gently kiss my skin.
Rainbows seal the peace.

Emily Loebelson

Untitled

Awake, oh nation fair
and take in hand
  your destiny
which lies beneath the axe
now poised to sever you.

The common soul that binds
us must burn brightly
  now
healing the pain,
uniting hearts and minds.
False prophets heed!
We shall together stand
  We are one land.

Barbara Zacour

On The Nature Of Love

Time was,
I thought that
love was
like a river;
Now,
it seems
more
like an endless series
of bridges,
each more fragile,
each over more perilous
chasms;
Until finally
we take
leaps of faith,
balancing on silvery,
dew-spangled cobwebs,
while the abyss spins
below.

Frances M. Harrison

Looking Back

The days went by so quickly;
As we look back on them now,
But the time we've spent together
Remains close to our hearts somehow.
Each memory of the happy times;
The laughter and the tears,
We will keep close to our hearts
Throughout each passing year.
We've been each other's crutch;
Their support in times of need.
We've been each other's enemy;
In attempting to succeed.
But through it all by chance or fate;
A wondrous thing took place.
We gave each other friendship;
A bond that no one can erase.
Now as we go our separate ways,
Please keep this thought in mind.
Our friendships and our memories;
Will stand the test of time!

Brandy L. Boshart

Memories Of Mother

When I lay in my mother's arms
Away from all there is that harms
Of dark days which me alarms
Had not yet gone beyond her charms

To her I would turn at night
When father had switched out the light
Tell her that one day I might
Climb a mountain of great height

I remember I was told
A soldier must be very bold
Or if in business life I sold
Truth was better than all gold

When romance finally struck
For my love I started to look
Who could like my mother cook
Stitch and sew with needle and hook

Then one day inside my head
I knew nothing from A to Z
For my mother she was dead
Now my heart felt full of lead

Terence James Quinn

Reflections

My heart is my conscience.
Without it I am nothing.
  It determines my reason
for living.
  It guides me through my
everyday trials and tribulations.
  Sometimes it slows down
a bit, but it never gets
out of the kitchen because
of the heat.
  Sometimes it is sad, and
suffers pain, but somehow
or other it never seems to
complain,
  I realize more and more
each day of my life, that I
can exist without my sensibilities,
but I cannot live without my heart.
  Yes, my heart is my conscience.

Joseph T. Rouzan Sr.

Good Morning Lord

Good morning Lord!
I'm beginning a new day
Please come along to guide me
And protect me, come what may

Talk to me Lord!
I want to hear your wisdom
Then it's mostly up to me
You have given me much freedom.

Walk with me Lord!
Pick me up, should I stumble
Just give me a little nudge
If I complain and grumble.

You're my friend Lord!
Whatever happens you're there
You love me for what I am
Always showing that you care

I need you Lord!
Take my hand and lead the way
Together, there's no limit
Let us both have a great day

Claire Doyle-Beland

Memories

Roses and memories
of warm summery nights
when I was but a girl,
young at heart
spirits light.

Roses and wafts of dew
kissed scent,
the petals fell and the flowers
went the way of
memories
and
by gone nights.
The memories I knew were heaven sent.

Rosalind D. Blue

"Checkpoint"

Betwixt those who carpe diem
And the countless others who do not
There lies the fears of all living men
With which their hollow souls be bought

Like a plague fear comes and goes
And solely those that feel it know
That when a different world they see
Only then can they be free

Justin Thomson

Expressions Of My Feelings

Watching my Mother die,
I feel helpless, despair.
I hold her hand, and ask why?
How can I say goodbye -

Watching my Mother die,
I feel her pain, in bed as she lay.
Dear God, please make it go away.
How can I say goodbye -

Knowing life is part of dying,
Lovingly, I look at her and cry.
Until we are together again,
Farewell my sweet Mother,
I Can Not Say Goodbye.

Toula Petropoulos Karides

Robbie's Poem

I woke up on shaky grounds at first,
Prayed to God, He quenched my thirst.
Could find no reason to go astray,
My Higher Power kept alcohol away.

Now that I found a reason to live,
To another human being of ourselves we
must give.
To fight this disease from within,
To turn to God instead of gin.

When we learn to help each other,
Our love will grow for our brother.
Then we finally felt relieved,
When we came to believe.

Robert E. Lutes Jr.

Untitled

When she enters the room
I notice her beauty
I notice her class
Why does she not notice me
When she speaks
I laugh at her jokes
I laugh at her wit
Why does she not laugh with me
When I sleep
I dream about her
Why does she not dream about me?

R. J. Wojtowicz

Lost

I am alone,
Lonely on a dusty beach.
No one knows where I am,
Nor does anyone care.

The waves pound the surf,
Ceasingly without hail,
That one lone person
Ails to see their depths.

The air is tangy with salt,
And sea gulls a memory.

I am so tired.
I wish I could lie down
And have the tide wash
Me away to the place
Where the mermaids live.

In my dense fog,
Someone calls my name.
I look back,
As if in a trance,
To see, someone does care.

Michelle Holt

Seasons!

One spring to fall,
Then they knew it all,
The summer had passed,
It was not a great mass,
The short but hot days,
The kind you spend at the bays,
Then came winter,
To fight the cold,
You had to be bold,
Soon came spring,
To start another ring!

Andrea Crombez

The Evening Prayer

The clock struck nine
The crescent conquered the sky
The muezzin calls

I would like to walk into a mosque.

So wash your feet
Cover your head
And disappear with me
Under the dark wings
Of this blessed shrine
Where shoulder in shoulder
We fall on our knees
To bow our foreheads to the ground

Oh Lord, do you hear our cries?

The lights seem dimmer
The bare feet whisper

Go now, peace be upon you!

The sound still follows you
Like a faithful companion

And if you look upon the sky
You will see the bright crescent

Magdalena Stanislawska

"In Between Time"

We need to find new things
Making our dreams come true.
We need to find new reason
That will benefit all we do.

To find a purpose, beyond the sea,
Or a feeling we have never had before.
Being brave and enter in ——
A different kind of door.

Looking for an answer
New and wise.
Holding on to yesterday
Threw new and loving eyes.

And when it's time for reality
We'll fill that empty space,
With love and honor
And a very "Secret Place!"

Elizabeth A. McQuade

The Squirrel's Highways

High mountain wires run thin,
in chill air of Winter time,
out to cabins dotted here and there,
with small movement in the wind.
For squirrel's quick and autumn fat,
who now chatter loud and bold,
to race looped highways of the sky,
and bob ways to shingled roofs.
The tinny whine of motor saws,
distant below their trees,
tell of others too,
who quickly now prepare.
Chimes that summer people bought,
to leave beneath their eaves,
brittle jingle something strange,
while Blue Jays mimic them.
Gray fleets of clouds slowly wander on,
a promise of ice and snow to fall,
and travel on the highways end.

Nicholas J. Gardiner

My Only Love

One day there was a great tragedy
My love died
I went to the hospital
I ran to the room
I looked at him
And cried
I put him in my arms
I whispered to him
Even though you are gone
Our love will be for eternity

So Everyday at night
I see the moon shine so bright
I would walk to the beach
And stand on the sand
And cry and cry
For my love
My only love

Gema Pineda

Ascension

Washable,
Wearable,
The soul can be cleansed each day.
Worn over mind and heart —
Often smudged by whom it hugged,
But brighter for having been touched.
Finally, torn and mended,
Washed out,
Dripped dry,
It fades from view,
    heavenward —
Leaving the clothesline forlorn.

Karen A. Franklin

Distinguished illusion
Aborted confusion
Diluted with acid,
Brought on from afar
A never forgotten - internal scar
Of freeness that can only
be dreamed of.
Held down by insecureness
and so vaguely felt love.
Dreary alertness from
the outside I feel,
Alone and forgetting
brought on like an unknown pill.
Deep within sorrow multipersonality
image
of joy then loneliness glances
turn vintage.
Salvation what's that?
But pollution wanted then destroyed.
Like a lung breathing in life.
A wound seeping out blood.

Michele Ortiz

Joy

Listen to the warming winds,
    softly as they blow.
Listen to the waving grass,
    swaying to and fro.
Listen to the happy sounds,
    of children as they play.
Listen to the swish of waves,
    washing sand away.
Listen with both eyes and ears,
    listen with all your mind.
Gather up the joyous sounds,
    tune out the other kind.

Heather Hughes

Why?

A tranquil day
Early fall
In the park
A birds shrill call

Kids at play
The sun beats down
A cool breeze
Peace abounds

Is it so hard
For this to be true
For billions of others
The world through

On the swings
A game of ball
A tranquil day
Early fall

Joachim Peter Maagdenberg

Many Thanks

You bless me every day,
With gifts straight from you,
To reassure me what the Bible says
Is most definitely true.

I'm granted such glorious bounty
From your magnificent hand,
Therefore, you can count on me
To worship you the best I can.

But those gifts I am not needing,
I'll love you just the same,
I'll still feel chills when singing
And always bless Thy name.

Long ago You saved me.
For us, Your only Son died then,
So that we could sit beside Thee
In the Kingdom of Heaven.

I give thanks for all I have received
And thanks for my spiritual hoard.
Just know that I'll always believe
And have faith in you, my Lord.

Douglas B. Shaffer

Love Awakens

In the morning hours
When your face is
Washed with dawn's
First tiny sliver,
My love awakens.

I watch your features
Resolve from shadowed
Pillow creases.
I pleasure in the quiet
Lust of this morning
Voyeurism, and,
My love awakens.

Gentle breathes and eyelashes
Flutter in dreaming.
A sigh, a moan, a turn
Tells me that soon
My love awakens.

Allan L. Jensen

Katherine's Rhyme

She has chubby cheeks
And a double chin
Roly-poly legs
Right down to the shin.

Beautiful blue eyes
That shine when she smiles
And a fuzzy little head
Growing hair all the while.

A perfect shaped mouth
And a cute button nose
Round little belly
And ten tiny toes.

You are our sweetheart
And we want you to know
Your Mommy and Daddy
Love you so.

Angela Blacklock

Getting Older

You know you're getting older when:
Things aren't the way they were,
Your 20/20 vision is,
Now nothing but a blur

You go to rent a movie and
Forget which one's you've seen,
The teeth you used to dental floss,
You now take out to clean.

You walk into a room and then,
Forget just why you're there
Instead of getting high lights done,
You now use loving care.

Your one night out to bingo is
The highlight of your week,
But you have to wear depends now
Just in case you spring a leak!

Wendy Holsey Goodman

"Friends Forever"

There were fads to follow
But we chose our own trends;
Sticking together always
Buddies 'til the end.

We had our rough times
But through those we came;
With smiles and a few hugs
No other friendship could be the same.

We offer each other advice
On the problems teens have,
Knowing that someday,
We'll look back and laugh.

Up late at night talking
About clothes, make-up and guys;
Sharing our first experiences,
How we were worried and wondering why.

Even though we're pals
We have arguments here and there;
But if there's one thing we're sure of
We'll be friends forever.

Jennifer L. Wethington

Katy

Inside your heart your soul is fading,
Your eyes fill with never ending tears,
My heart goes out to you my friend,
your soul is over flowing with fears.
Your heart is so unhappy,
I can see it in your eyes,
No matter what it is you say,
I see through all your lies.
You need to learn to live again
and let your soul rejoice,
but I can't do that for you
it's strictly your own choice.
Life will get better one day,
one day you will see
one day you will be you again,
and so happy you will be

Jesi McPeak

Homeless

My enemy is
   not the rain
   not the cold
Nor is it the
   lack of shelter
   or my
     empty stomach

My enemy is
   indifference
   the apathy
Of those who
   have not been on
   my journey
    through hell

Dana S. Wickes

Silly Girl

Silly girl
Promise me this
You will never stop

Silly girl
You truly make
The world go round

Angela G. Champness

True Love

It flows as
  a Rushing River
    ever in
     its Rhythm
Growing, growing
    increasing in strength
Until it empties
    into the Vast Ocean -
      continually
  of Eternal Life
    "Heaven" -
We are then
    Face to Face
    with God
     oh Joy!

    Hallelujah!

Sophia Rzadca

Spirit

Spirits in the nights
Hopes on the winds
Our souls soar to such heights
Despite our many sins

Such men are we
Mere specks of dust
With eyes that can never see
Unless we, but trust

Our souls so shallow
Dreams of touching our soul
Our minds so hollow
Dreams not our to hold

Signs on the wind
Hopes forever to despair
Are we of God's kin?
Lives in desperate need of repair

There is hope
But only from within
It is the only way we can cope
Listen to the voice within!

Greg Knight

Together

Round the fire we all sit
With love and care everywhere
Love is holding hands together
Outside is awful weather
Makes me shiver just to look
And then mom will start to cook
It is just good to be together
It doesn't matter about the weather

Sandra McKeown

Memories Of A Dying Earth

I have watched the eons go by,
Caught in the endless vacuum of time.
I have watched generations come
and generations go.
I have also witnessed the
coming of the industrial era,
Bringing with it my ultimate demise.

You would think that my children
cared about me.
Do something to help their
poor old mother back on her feet.

But they don't care.
They only want to see how
long I'll last.
Before they have to find a new
Mother Earth.

Jo-Anne Nina Sewlal

Endless Journey

Around the far bend in the road
  Beyond the furthest hill
Something calls me on and on
  Yes, something calls me still
My hands are shackled
  To their task
Many things I'll never see
  Yet, like an eagle in the sky
My heart soars wild and free
Around the far bend in the road
  Beyond the furthest hill
Something calls me and on and on
  And it always will.

Lucy F. Billman

Chasing Rainbows

While chasing down the rainbow's tail
In search of golden ore
Much to my amazement found
An even bigger score
Standing just in front of me
Hidden in the shamrock patch
A tiny little leprechaun
For sure an easy catch
A tiny Walkman on his hip
Playing Celtic tunes no doubt
Singing praise to Danny boy
As he danced about
Swifter than the eagle's flight
I dove in for my prize
A feisty little man was he
As he blackened both my eyes
I've since relieved my quest for gold
Still rainbows come and go
Though now I fish the scottish locks
More relaxing don't ya know

Scott "Spider" Ferguson

Purple Night

I have become purple night
loved by orange lights.
Snow, soft and cold,
melts on lips.

She stares at luminous white
sending out waves purple bright.
Her spirit is aroused
and she listens
to the snow.

She gazes at the sky:
She sees me look into her eyes.
She drinks the air
and fills her lungs
with purple.

Greg Duhaney

Two Years Ago

Remember back two years ago?
  I watched you from afar.
So innocent and beautiful,
  I found it very hard to keep
My inner thoughts from coming out
  and ruining the dream.
But time has tolled the mask you wear
  and beauty only seems to be
A foolish trap that held me while
  your actions made me weep.
You should have left a year ago
  while I was still asleep.

Roland Curit

To Passions Flame
  Two Hearts Desire
To Healing Hands
  Safe in the Night
To one night Stands
  To passion's bite
To Harley Moments
  Lace and Leather
Memories Haunting
  Always . . .
     Forever

Dedicated to the memory
of survivors everywhere

Connie Van Patten Leland

When The Seeker Understands

The search for truth is fruitful
For we are the God/Man
Seed and fruitage, all in one
When the seeker understands

Looking to the 'gurus'
To reveal the master-plan
Is to look without and not within
When the seeker understands

Sublimation, renunciation
Is so hard on your glands
But these fixations too, must bend
When the seeker understands

Craving no desire
Is like a fire fanned
No smoke appears in thought and deed
When the seeker understands

The true reward of action
Is in the act at hand
There is no need to search for more
When the seeker understands

Adam Perle

Why I Let Her?!

Why I let her
I'll never know
But as she drove she lost control
And as I looked straight ahead
I saw my life flash before my eyes
And when I awoke
In the hospital bed
with pain all over
I had to ask
Is my friend okay, or did she die?
Then I saw my mother
Look that certain way
I knew what happened right away.
The friend I loved with all my heart
Was laying with the Lord
Until this day I'll never know
To why I let her go that far
But here's a tip to keep in mind:
Please Don't Drink And Drive!!

Kimberly Flear

My Lord

The Lord gave his life,
He hung on a tree.
He washed away my sins,
He set me free.

He gave me a second chance,
A chance to serve his name.
Once he entered my heart
My life was never the same.

I love him today,
I'll love him tomorrow.
He eased all my pain,
He released me from my sorrow.

I don't know what I would do
Without the Lord in my life,
To erase all the misery,
To take away my strife.

As I said before
He means everything to me.
I'll love him and serve him
Until the end of eternity.

Brooke VanDegrift

My Dark Side

My heart sinketh
unto the pith of my soul
a place where I seldom go
I see you there
I know not how you
got here in my world
my dark world you have no
invitation I've sent none afar
it is my place for no one
knows who I am or where I will go

James Halderson

Death Comes Twice

For many years when I was young,
Dad took care of me,
But then one day the roles had changed,
That could no longer be.

His mind was such a vibrant thing,
So delicate, yet so strong,
But something went amiss one day,
Something very wrong.

I searched his eyes to look and find
The Dad that I once knew,
But only saw an empty shell,
With a mind that was askew.

The love was gone, he did not know,
His only little girl,
To him his life was simple now,
In a strange and different world.

Death had come to Dad that day,
But only claimed a slice,
For death had known that he'd be back,
For Dad death would come twice.

Christine Balon

Our Wedding

Today we give our lives to each other
Each expressing love
One for the other
Holding hands joined by love
We walk down the aisles
Our faces aglow with amorous smiles

As to each other we say "I do"
We're expressing a love
That's deep and true.
Deep down inside us
Love's seed has been planted
We've found in each other
Just what we wanted.

Devon McCarthy

Untitled

Overworked, Underpaid, tired...
Debt, bills, death, pain, anger
Smog, traffic...
...Walk away.
Trees swaying
Waves purring
Mountains thrusting upward
   into the clouds,
Sun warming the face
Birds soaring overhead
...a breeze
A deep cleansing breath
Gods world -
Revitalized...

A. Y. Lacquement

No Oil My Dear!!

What happened?
A nightmare.........

On earth
Might is right
Back to the stone age.
Bread and butter
Available to giants
And monkeys... the same way..
Same in everything.

No oil, my dear,
And all around you
fail to breathe, to see, to smell,
To touch, to hear,
And the underground
will suffocate
The last drops,
Can only serve,
A lucky ghost...
Who managed ahead to kill the cat,
And to throw the bones over the well.

Nicolas Nicolas Gebran

Living For The Day

He shoots a predatory glance
At the one he wishes to entrance
Hoping for a trespassing dance
Living for the day
He hears the beating of a heart
Knowing the skills to play the part
A wise fool trying so hard to start
His emotions not going away
Burning bridges
One way doorways
Racing rats
In a maze
Feeling his options are few
Not knowing what to do
He drives the anguish away
By living for the day

Shaun J. Russell

Anger

It's building up inside of me,
tearing me up from the inside out.
It's becoming harder to control.
I must push it down as far as I can,
I must contain it.
I must control it before it overcomes
me and consumes me.
Pain, agony, destruction.
I can't control it.
I must.
Pain, Anger.

Shawn P. McAndrew

"The Tear"

The tear in your eye
   is not for me dear,
The heart your heart
   Cries for is not mine,
Dreams I had of you are shattered
   By that tear in your eye,
So take the tear in your eye
   Dear, turn it into a dream,
Tell him you will love him
   Forever, and forever you
   Will be free,
The tear in your eye
   Is not for me dear.

Jimmy Kelly Best

Birthday 96

An invite for lunch,
A bit early we were.
Greetings all round,
As our table we found
For our feast
Vegetable soup,
Rice and ham,
Turkey pot pie,
Salad, dill pickles,
coffee, fruit Jello
With whipped cream piled high.

To raise funds,
A draw and win
A basket of wine,
Cheese, crackers,
And pickled red peppers.

Then home I went
And found this advertisement
Poetry contest!

Joyce M. Kinsey

Beauty

If pretty is as pretty does
why is face all we ever see?
the true beauty to us all
is inside every you and me.
it comes out only when we search
for that little piece of heart
we have to dig down deep inside
to reach that little part.
it comes out when we least expect it
it shows our own true self
but instead we look upon the face
and see a false mask of ourself.
but the beauty is within the heart
a place where love resides
a place where love can sit at ease
a place where love confides.
for beauty is in the eye
of the beholder who is you
and you're the only one to judge
if a person's beauty is all true.

Katherine Chin

Passing

I have forgotten your name
I don't remember who you are
It was such along time ago
It all seems so far away,

That life belongs to someone else
Who I no longer am
I'm not the same as I was
And I like who I am,

I'm just a reflection you see
As you pass the store window
It's just a dream
That was never meant to be,

So keep your name to yourself
I do not wish for us to meet

I have forgotten your name
I don't remember who you are
I'll just keep on my way
So please pass me by.

Annette Winship

Your Blood Left A Stain

You gave me your love,
right from the start.
I gave you mine,
until you broke my heart.

I said in the beginning,
our love was the best.
I never knew,
it would not pass the test.

I said we had the love,
others can only wish for.
I changed my mind,
when you slammed the door.

I said that you hurt me,
just by raising your voice.
You said you never meant to.
You said I left you no choice.

I said I will always love you,
but still I felt the pain.
I said you must go.
Your blood left a stain.

Robert Wayne Manley III

Leaving

I have to go I told a lie,
I have to leave, I have to die.
I said that I loved you,
Now what do I do?
If only you could see,
But I don't think you'd believe.
I'm leaving this world fast,
It's all because of my past.
You just don't understand,
Why I ran.
I shall miss you very much,
Right down to your soft touch.
I have to go now,
The note will tell you how.
After the bullet has entered my head,
I shall be dead.
No more crying or pain,
No more lying or trying to explain.

LaDonna Goff

A Cycle Of Time

A cold summer's night
A dark cold embrace
Sunlight turns to moonlight
As time seems to race

Like the wind, time flies by
And then suddenly it seems to die
The stars dimly glow
As time seems to slow

Speeding up the beat
The night faces defeat
Rising to victory is the sun
Standing still, time starts to run

Simone Clark

Listen!

Have you ever listened
To the quiet
When it snows

Have you ever listened
To leaves rustle
When it blows

Have you ever listened
To babe's breath
When he sleeps

Have you ever listened
To sun rise
When morning creeps

Have you ever listened
To soft music
Eyes closed

Have you ever listened
To op'ning petals
Of a rose

Listen...

Joan Conley

Autumn's Song

The sudden changing of the leaves
Reflects a season's gone
Chilling winds blow restlessly
Singing Autumn's song.

Cool and silent evenings
Gives one a refreshing feel
Of hidden strength within us
Any weakness seems to heal.

As day is done and sunny rays
Steam across the sky
The golden moon replaces it
Arising full and high.

The wonder of it all, it seems
That thanks should now be given
For allowing us to view these things
Is our dear Lord in heaven

Cassandra Bowen

Any Of These Days

Any of these days
I'll keep the sea in my pocket
and gather sand at any time,
breathe sips of air
and use the remaining instant
to build castles.

I'll wander among hills
and climb the wildest greens
and get to see beautiful images
and the widest landscapes.

I'll hear the of flying birds
among the branches and the leaves
of weeping willows;
I'll sing the river and dissolve
my song in the freedom of the water.

And I'll travel to remote horizons
so I can rescue the lost souls
of the ones that never returned.
And it will be one day of these;
any day of these it will be.

Marta Abello Saura

I Am

I am a flower
   waiting to bloom
I am a child
   locked in a room
I am a book
   that has never been read
I am an old lady
   better off dead
I am a toy
   tossed aside
I am a seeker
   whose request has been denied
I am a lover
   whose heart's been torn
I am a shirt
   all dirty and worn
I am the one
   who's always there
But if I were to leave,
Would anyone care?

Brooke Martens

The Torchmaster

The music blares in silence.
A half-finished poem on my lap.
Alone except for a fire nearby,
With scorching flames I despise.
Reminding me too much
Of the one within.
One that has burned far too long
And won't let me go.
I seal my tear-soaked lids,
Extinguishing my vision,
Cloaking memories with darkness.
Still the fire burns within.
Its seething tongues
Lashing accusations at my soul.
Branding them upon of guilt.
Past a fragrance floating
On the ashes of my conscience.
Leaving nothing,
But cinders of regret.

Debra Dupont

Five Old Oaks

What is all of this life for
I ask myself and guess
Is it me or just the world
That's nothing but a mess
I've always felt I'd live my life
Along the Golden Rule
But many days I think I find
It never is returned
A pentagon of old oak trees
Just looked at me and stared
They said, "The things that you believe
Are not the things that's shared."
The hidden sun behind their boughs
Has opened up my eyes
I think of things that could have been
And silently I cry.

Michael Marquardt

Would You Sing Me a Song...

Would you sing me a song
   to brighten the skies?
Could you tell me a story
   with no sad good-byes?
Would you write me a poem
   that has lines filled with love?
Could you make me a rainbow
   in the heavens above?
Should I tell you a secret
   made for only us two?
I'll whisper it softly,
The words
   "I love you"

Bridget Olson

Yesterday

Yesterday seems long ago
   Like friends of days gone by-
Of relatives we held so dear
   Recollections that make me cry.

I think of all the lean years
   They called the Great Depression-
The times don't change so much
   Now they call it deep recession.

As memories drift into my mind
   Not all of them are sad-
When I think of all the pleasure
   My life was not too bad.

Now happy days are here again
   I'm in the present day-
Life is surely worth living
   No matter what some folks say.

Joyce E. Shafer

Dreams Of Baseball

Batter up! The ball is pitched.
Went so fast I barely twitched.
Two are out, it's inning nine,
Victory is on the line.
Score is even, we must win,
Pitcher throws the ball again.
I swing the bat, ball passes through.
Umpire hollers, "It's strike two!"
With sweaty palms and nervous stance,
I contemplate our final chance.
Pitch is thrown, bat hits its mark.
Crack!!! The ball has left the park.
My home run wins the game today,
Baseball's kind of fun to play.

Daniel R. Buckles

Tree Freedom

Trees, flinging themselves at the sky,
Yet anchored so deeply
That only the earth worms
Attend at their endings.

Do they resent, while their twigs
Strain upwards, the
Umbilical trunk
Chaining them earthbound?

Do their roots struggle to
Loosen their chaining,
Knowing leaving is dying?
Do they think that it's worth it
For the moment of flying?

Jan Davis

Live The Life

Each of us, in this life,
Must know we have a choice.
To make a little difference,
To make heard, our voice.

Everywhere around us,
People telling us what to do.
To make the right decision,
You have to trust in you.

Live the life you've been given,
Learn to be yourself.
You cannot ever change things,
Sitting there on the shelf.

Go out, get involved,
Discover who you are.
If you just sit and watch,
You'll never reach that star.

Virginia Click

I'll Die Twice

I had a cold dream,
that was horrid and fast.
That scared me to death,
and I left in the past.

I heard a loud roar,
and saw one body fall.
Blood swamped the floor,
and that wasn't all.

I heard a voice scream,
as it rang through my ears.
I remembered that voice,
I've known it for years.

I stepped near a shadow,
and heard some low cries.
Held up the body,
and looked dead in his eyes.

He said, "You cannot help,
so just leave me be."
And I started to cry,
'cause that body was me.

Christopher Ronald Brennan

"Walk Of Life"

Foot prints are not only made
in the sand, they are embedded
deep beneath in the soul of man.

Some steps were soft.
Some were formed hard
others were made by
the life of God's card.

Your walk may be very differently
of course from mine. Could of been
bitter, sour/might of been kind.

Foot prints are not only
made in the sand.
Foot prints could be caused
by the hand of man.

Anita Rhue

Doorstep

I was once at a doorstep.
It was your doorstep.
And you told me.
Not to sell my soul there.
But I did.
And now I am free.
Free from you.
Not the pain.
You gave me.
Now my courage rise.
And I am here.
At your doorstep.
Not to love.
But to forget.
Forget the memory.
And the pain.
Now the end is near.
But not far away.
From your doorstep.

Wanda Ritchey

Untitled

I am not what you see
I know your ears do not hear me
Your eyes are blind
I need not justify
You have painted over me
A picture I don't recognize
Now you wonder where I have come from
Where is the woman you once knew
I was buried by your judgments
I was misconstrued.

Cynthia Lemaitre

Vacant Streets

The minds of children oh so sweet
Gently playing on the street
That mind to young to understand
What wicked men will do with hand
All around this hate campaign
Struggles on so much in vain
And at last man's work complete
No more children on the street
Young minds fed up with pain and death
Have packed their bags, got up and left.

Stephen Woods

Untitled

Melting, swallowing within itself;
creating a state-of-mind
only understood if experienced.
One that is created easily
but takes more than outer
beauty to live on.
Its innocence like a young child's:
Its infinity like one's heartbeat.

Jeannette Eileen Thomas

"Nature's Way"

The future of man,
    has never been plain,
every since Abel,
    got murdered by Cain!
Violence has always,
    been part of the plan,
in all nature's creatures,
    and that includes man!
Nothin' you do,
    or nothin' you say,
    is goin' to change,
    nature's way!
    Most of earth's creatures,
    take only,
    what they need,
    only man,
    is born with greed!

John Search

Nera Bella

It steadily moved upon
the day
There came a happy
dream to me
To dream of a black dog
in the mist.
I came to the mountains
to find the black dog.
I brought her home to
keep with me
We called her Bella.
My dream and my prayers
have been answered
They steadily move upon
each day.

Angelina Delmastro Smith

Scorpio

Last night I sat alone
listening to the sound of the ocean
breaking hot waves over my belly,
waiting for your footsteps,
a sound I can't recall.

You come in the morning,
spent,
a pigment of my imagination
faded back to gray.

Pack my memories
    airline stubs from P.R.,
    notes in your handwriting,
not wanting to go
or stay.

Carolyn Weatherly

The Giant's Plea

We roam around in a
    bamboo forest,
Most of us are not
    that big of a pest.
But why do humans take
    our food away?
Then we will disappear
    some day.

Jessica Presnell

Eyes In The Night

All day long
eyes in the night are wandering,
but she cannot see them,
so longing for something to eat.

The bushes rustle,
a wolf growls, the wind whistles.
Through the trees, you can hear
the owls as the coyote growls,
just across the street.
Where are you?

Nobody around,
not a quiet sound,
not even for a minute.
Not a tree, not a flower in sight.
Where are you?

She, in the darkness of night,
But even to her dark is not light.
Why is this?
How come she cannot see these things?
She is blind...

Christina Paixao

Freedom

These eyes look out the
apartment window.
Freedom is but three hundred
yards away.
The Berlin Wall, then Freedom

Each day I watch the bus stop.
The people, the life on the
other side.
I wish to see my family united
How many years must go by?
To many I fear, will I ever
be united before I die?

A whisper of freedom reaches
my ear. A walk to the
other side. The smiling face,
the welcome hand shake.

The sun is shining on this
cold winter day.
I feel only freedom.

Joan Frame

I Love You More

I love you more than life —
When passion at its height —
Pulses through my veins —
When sight and sound and
    touch and taste —
Are more exquisite, than
    words can say.
I will love you more than
    death —
When I've grown old and
    weary —
And too weak to find a
    single joy in life —
When my every appetite
    has been appeased —
And the soul of me longs
    to be gone,
From which was once
    beautiful, and is no more.

Dawn Moiras

Our Love

Our love is like a circle;
It's continued,
Though we've been apart.
It's like a small oak tree,
Growing daily,
Becoming strong and mature.
Our love is everlasting,
Staying true till we were reunited.
It's like a ship's sail,
Holding fast,
Weathering the roughest storms.
Yet our love is new and fresh,
Like the air
When the rain has passed.
It's to be enjoyed in full,
Cherished always
For whatever time we have.
And too, our love is precious
Like a rare jewel,
For it's been blessed by God.

Jolene Moses

Untitled

Life, what about life
nothing everyday; something

Untrue, uncool. To afraid
so laid back crashed
half tanked.

Never nothing new
always something old
always lazy and always
crazy not surprising or
alarming. It's so real
and so true never
red always blue.

Lillian Machado

Authentic

Artificial Rose
perfect no flaws, pestilence
hasn't touched you
Your order is formed by man,
My rose won't grow old or die,
Nor fragrance has a gift for me,
lives beauty fades away.
But a real rose holds my
heart forever

Lois Yates

Winter Perils

The ice 'N' sleet 'N' snow 'N' rain,
Have caused us all a lot of pain.

When mother calls me out of bed,
My ears 'N' feet 'N' nose are red.

My teeth all chatter while I dress,
Oh this weather is such a mess!

Then off to school I must go,
In all this ice 'N' sleet 'N' snow.

I fall down and bump my head,
And think for a moment I'm surely dead.

It's like Antarctica more or less,
Oh this weather is such a mess!

Nannie Mae Yeager Stevens

Untitled

A midnight meditation
Waxes in my mind, disabling sleep.
I am aroused by the
Silence of the wind as it churns
The summer air over the screen.

All's quiet, at last, the children
Asleep in dream states of school
Friends and lollipops, flowers,
Fanciful dresses, and dressed up dolls.
Cherubs sleep, daytime devils forget.

My spouse browses dark chambers
Of memories unspoken and well kept.
Light moans, swoons in mystical
Embraces of torturous temptations.
Lances of lightning shimmer outside.

Dark rains echo from my heart as
Lifted burdens leave my soul.
No goal, no target, no task,
The day is over, the deeds are done,
Time stops for the wind, I am at rest.

Navin K. Varma

Cold/Lonely

Snowy mountains slumber
under this blanket of white.
A lone pine tree awaits
spring blossoms.
Hibernating like a bear,
dragging days go by,
solely, I await you.
Vibrant colours of life,
sweet smells of honey;
mischievous little creatures
scurry about.
Showers then sunshine,
a rainbow brightens
the horizon.
   Awakened,
     by the scent of
       your cologne.

Linda Bailey

An Analyzation...

Has it come to your attention
if not, then I will mention
that today is an occasion
that calls for celebration

For today I tell the nation
of our deep infatuation
the wonderful sensation
which comes from your affection

Your never-ending devotion
evokes in me emotion
my hearts in constant motion
pounding with a great commotion

After constant analyzation
I have come to this conclusion
my final realization
We're a perfect combination

Kathleen Kleiver

Your Touch

Somewhere beyond the blue
My thoughts are turned to you.
I feel your caring touch.
Caress me, Oh please!
I miss your presence so very much
And long to be in your embrace
somewhere in outer space.

Mary E. Rarey

Mystery Trauma

It takes you on a journey
You thought never possible.

It lures you into the
deepest darkness.

It plays mind games as well
as a physical experience.

Yet if you're in good hands
you feel less pain.

It sees your weakest spots and
brings you down by taking over them.

It knows all, it sees all,
it hears all, it is all.

It creeps and creeps until
It's the evermost powerful.

It takes over until you've given in.
And when you've given in it ends.
And you're finally at peace

Erica Alex Huzar

"Lilt Of Birdsong"

Lilt of birdsong,
Perfume of flowers
   How precious earthly things
Time lasts not long
Our earthly hours
Truly do have wings.

Good-bye blue sky
Good-bye green sod
My time draws nigh
For rendezvous with God!

Dr. John M. Fewkes VI
(1868-1939)

The Dreamer

I've skipped along the stars
I've read a book on Mars
I listened to the Moon
About the dream she had last night
She dreamt of life and triumph
Neptune running to the light
Heard the silent cry of Pluto
Who sits there on the edge
The darkness that surrounds us all
As we're placed there on the ledge
I've sung a song on Saturn's rings
Inside my head I scream of riots
And what time has to bring.

Jessica Gibbs

Let Me Look At Me, Lord

Lord,
Instead of findings other faults,
May I look at mine,
Instead of putting down my brother...
Let me lift him up each time.
Help me extend a helping hand,
When I see him tired and worn
And not speak out those evil words,
Of hatred, strife and scorn...

Help me relearn the lesson, Lord.
That others I can not change..
But I can work upon myself,
And call upon your name...
For life down here is very short,
We won't be here for much longer
So please prepare myself to be
Not weaker Lord...but stronger.

Gail Jennings West

My Little Band

Come one come all to the Concert Hall,
And hear my little band play.
We rock "n" roll,
So don't be a troll.
Bring your friends,
Cuz the fun never ends.
If you don't come,
It'll be a bum.
Don't go away,
I hope you stay.
The refreshments are yum,
So don't be numb.
Come and hear my little band play.
Today!

Jill London

Imagine (Thx J. L.)

Journeying thru the mind,
I see a time and place.
Dreams become reality,
Nightmares are not borne.
Eden is.
All peoples are equal,
Everyone is rich,
Beyond their wildest dreams.
Anything can (And Will) happen.
Life goes on forever.
So does love.
Tempers do not flare.
Sadness is not accepted.
Truth is the norm.
Lies are not even gestured.
And goodwill among men (And Women).
Peace all around.
Imagine. (Thx J.L.)

Frank S. Jasutis

Ocean

Dances under the sky
Color of sapphire,
Waves never die.
Boating, swimming, surfing,
Birds, seashells, sand,
Flying, hiding, sifting,
Oh, what a mysterious land.

Martin Perez

The Winner

I'd love to be the trash man's boy
  And get dirty as I can,
And sit on beds and springs and things
  Atop his great big van.

I'd never wash my hands and face
  Except on Sundays fair,
And all the folks in church would say,
  "There's goes a millionaire!"

And, oh, how they would envy me
  Because I'd look so smart
It tacks and ties and summer pants
  I'd find in that old cart!

Sally Robinson

[The Uncollected Poet]

In the basement warm papers couch
the glass-eyed newborn staring
at the ceiling the darkness textured
by a shattered window, six feet high
— the mother in England, seeking
a mildewed dream, the father writing
poems for bedding, passing invisible
in an age he meant to shape —
Subtle cries fall flat against cement,
where heaviness devours hope,
where once there was dancing
— dream of love like an open window,
and with wings let us collide;
knowing a child now exists
where we dreamt in colour.

Jason M. Miller

The Cookie Jar

I'm going for the cookie jar
How come they are so very far?

My toys are in a pile
They reach up half a mile.

Mommy will you get me some?
I don't always like chewing gum.

Alecia M. Grider

Untitled

It's a deep and dark and lonely place
That no one else can know
It's a secret, sad and awful place
Where I alone can go.

With no warming the mood descends
Like the darkness falls at night
It's a horrid, cold and gloomy place
From which there shines no light.

There's an invisible and menacing wind
It storms right through my heart
It's a hostile, damp and bitter gale
That rips my world apart.

I'd take you there and show you
but it's a place you'd not adore
An unwilling hostage of my thoughts
I don't want to go there any more!

Karen Ferguson

The Dreamless Night

Wilted rose before me droops,
petals heavy with decay
like dead blood within my veins,
blighted; all blooms rot away.
Hooded hollows of my eyes
trap old candle's poisoned flame;
Brighter light would rape my mind,
and destroy my spectral name.
Paper moths are watching me,
clinging to the rusted wire...
Little eyes reflect my sins,
and my shattered soul's desire.
Rasp of wind between the stars
draws cruel barbs across my skin;
at torment's caress I sigh...
Ecstasy awakes within.

Locked inside my cell of flesh,
smothering in pallid webs...
Blackest pulse, so moist and deep,
soothes me as my spirit ebbs.

Tracy Derynck

The Bride

She stood there in beauty
As the sun beams
Danced upon her hair.
Today is the day, she is to marry
And there are smiles everywhere.
She is dressed in white lace,
From her head to the ground,
With little white hearts
Landscaped throughout her gown.
She turned her head
And blushed with pleasure,
It was the moment she had waited for.
Then in a twinkle
They kissed, and all time
Seemed to stand still.
A tear fell from my eye
As she walked pass,
But the smile on my face told her,
It was for her dreams that I knew -
Would forever last.

Mark James Bourgeau

Let Me Be Gentle...

As I walk my daily path,
Trying, Lord, to know Thy will,
Oft I whisper this small prayer,
'Make me gentle, gentler still'

Lord, my praise to you I sing,
Though I know my will is weak;
Still this tiny plea I bring,
'Make my gentle, when I speak.'

Let me live as you would wish,
Mold me, Lord as to your will;
As I strive to be your child,
Make my nature gentler still.

Many blessings you have given
Many prayers you've answered too;
Let my life reflect the love
That tells me I belong to you.

While I live upon this earth,
Let me grow in grace until
I'm a better child of God....
Father, make me gentler still.

Laura M. Yates

Granite Cove 39

Cracked glass,
    Poised on edge,
Glistens, shatters, falls.

Shards in foaming
    Disarray,
Fragmented splendor,
    On display.
Roiling thought around
    My brain,
Glass on stone till
    Sand remains.

Sand to glass,
    On sun and stone,
Shimmers, spreads,
    Retreats alone.

Sea glass,
    Gleam wholly entrapped,
Blunted, salty, green.

Gerri Fusco

To Rob From Mother 1966

Eyes of blue and hair of yellow
Cheeks of rosy red
These things make my little fellow
Sleeping there in bed.

Not a care as he dreams onward
Into night so dark and long
Seeing armies marching forward
Hearing mothers loving song.

In the morning he arises
Fresh as dew upon the grass
Full of mischief and surprises
Playing as the day goes past.

All to soon he's grown from boyhood
Into manhood standing tall
Then you say my sons a man now
No more troubles big or small.

Then you say a prayer of gladness
Thanking God from up above
For the boy that you did cherish
And the man that you now love.

Linda B. Sartori

My Jim

I stand upon the lake shore
    'Neath the sunset sky aglow.
I am thinking of you, dear
    My Jim of long ago.

For it was here in the moonlight
    You asked me to be your wife.
But I was young and eager
    And wanted a different life.

So I travelled to a distant land
    To seek fortune and fame.
And the road was long and lonely
    Before the world would know my name.

Now in the autumn of my years
    I know what I have missed.
I hope that life's been kind to you,
    And you found great happiness.

Here on the lake shore
    'Neath the sunsets after glow.
All I have are memories of
    My Jim of long ago.

Jeanne Kennedy

"Gift Of Life"

We cannot perform the miracles
that Jesus did here on earth,
But I'm sure that he would say
you surely gave your worth.

If you gave your heart to a mother
so she could watch her children grown,
or perhaps, give your kidneys
to a neighbor down the road.

Eyes to someone who cannot see
or tell the day from night,
Oh! What it would be like
to give them back their sight.

When all is taken from the body
and there isn't no more to be saved,
Through research they may find a cure
for diseases such as Cancer and Aids.

After you have read or heard this poem
please think about it twice
If you decide to be a donor
You will give the "Gift of Life."

Joyce E. Gillespie

What Does A Smile Say?

A smile says — "Good morning,"
It says — "I'm glad to see you,"
It says — "I feel good,"
It says — "everything is alright,"
It says — "I'm here if you need me,"
It says — "Thank you,"
It says — "Yes,"
It says — "I love you,"
A smile is a universal language,
It says — "Hello friend."

Alberta Johnson

"My Love"

My love is like a flower,
That opens up in spring,
My love is like a bird,
When it start to sing.

My love is like an ocean tide,
Rushing to the shore.
My love is smiles and tear;
And so much more.

My love is like the laughter,
Like children when they play
My love can be like children
When they kneel down to pray

My love is like the loud roar
Of a rushing ocean tole
My love can be exciting,
Like a roller coaster ride

My love is brighter than the
Brightest star above,
My love was made for you
And forever will you be my love.

Cynthia Banyas

Gérard

An old man
leads a lobster
by a blue leash
down the street

I ask him
why he
doesn't
have a dog

He tells me
it doesn't bark
and knows the
secrets of the sea

Dylan John Jaconi

Summer Of The Morn

The daffodils woke in the early morn
amidst the stars of life and storm
and strode the bridge of no repair
footed the paths that so one dare.

The bubbling spring amongst the
shaded sycamore trees
Bubbled in the rocked creek
Stood to sigh, stood to cry.
What is life? What is joy?

When eagles never lover thought
for sight to ground
But ever bough then wedges paths
Where daffodils no tears can wink.

Estonlena Riddles

Lord, Do You Hear?

Where are You, Lord, when I need You?
I'm told that You're here inside.
If so, why can't I find You?
How and where do You hide?

Is there an icon to click on?
A window where You will appear?
This life is very confusing.
I'm calling, Lord, do You hear?

Should I be looking for E-mail?
Are You out cruising the Net?
(Wonder if You've found a Home Page
Where Justice and Peace have met?)

This isn't meant to sound pushy,
But without You, Lord, I am lost.
I'm willing to pay to follow Your Way.
I know that Your cross is the cost.

Where are You, Lord, now I need You?
The end of my life's drawing near.
I said I will pay to follow Your Way.
I'm calling, Lord, do You hear?

Janet M. McNabb

Here, Now

Sun for all seasons
From the East
This wintry dawn
Distils its reasons:

Ali-Baba rounds the cave
To furnish it
Aladdin rubs the lamp
To burnish it.

David Aivaz

The Playground

Smiling faces of endless days,
Laughter and noise, abandon play.
Running, hiding, climbing trees,
Dirt, sweat, and bloodied knees.

Huddled groups of serious intent,
Dispersed masses of energy spent.
Loners, leaders, and political friends,
Race and color with ethnicity blend.

Two worlds of exceptional play,
Joined by commonality of way.
Power and favor, an inborn bond,
With innocence subject to the strong.

Adrian C. Vroegindewey

My Hope

I often take the long way round
When I am traveling into town,
Then I can pass the ole' home place
Tho' little tears run down my face.

For I imagine I can see
My daddy's chair beneath that tree,
Where he and mom would sit and wait
And worry if I showed up late.

We're really glad you came today
I remember, mom would say,
And by their faces, I could see
I was as welcome as could be.

We're mighty glad to have you
Is what daddy always said,
And we'd bow our heads together
When dear mother broke the bread.

Someday, I hope the Savior
Will call them both by name,
And midst great joy, He'll tell them
We're mighty glad you came.

Nita S. Balma

Life's Journey

Life is a journey
embarked on at birth.
Choices we make
determine the route
we traverse.
Steep mountains
dangerous valleys,
challenges around each bend.
Eternal joy or sorrow
at journey's end.

Shirley May Davis

Insanity

The day lay before him in golden beauty
All was well, and peaceful.
And then
It came, it collided
The thoughts shattered
There was no proportion.
It came at its height in fullness
Then subsided and died.
And it took him when it left.

Lorna Hoyles

Inside

Bitter times cloud the mind
It's hard to live to find
Desperation becomes the game
It's hard to feel the same.

Aloneness is tranquility
Memories, images of infidelity
As needful as the sun
Memories, potent as a gun.

Black thoughts linger
Empty thoughts point the finger
Chaos and hate ever near
Empty thoughts disappear.

Judgement is a progression
Love, hate and depression
Inside is screaming flower
Love, emotion changing every hour.

Shon Laffin

My Barren Moors

All I see is a placid sky.
All except these barren moors.
I cannot run, although I try
I'm trapped between two silent floors.

Between two silent floors in which,
No other life form will ever be.
No trees, no grass, yet soil rich,
Presents a trace of oddity.

And when the sun replaces moon,
The beginning of another day.
I, myself, a hopeless swoon,
Will have sadly died away.

No one there to mourn the loss,
As did I when father passed away.
I lived a life as my own boss,
But never lived to see the day.

When on these barren rocks I'd lie,
A ray of sun would end my fear.
Feeling the warmth of God's loving eye,
Gazing down upon me here.

Kristin Roberts

An Eagle

It would be so nice
To be like an eagle
Soaring through the air
So free all the time

Spread your wings
And just fly in the sky
Rain or shine

An eagle is so special
An eagle is freedom
Not just to me, but to so many

An eagle is so beautiful
To watch flying so high
It would be nice
To be there with him

Fly over the world
Everywhere because
You're free like an eagle

So spread your wings
Go with the eagle
Fly and be free

Virginia Jones

If I Could fly

Oh God, if I could fly...
I'd paint you rainbows
Across the sky
I'd spread my wings
And climb the wind
Up to the stars —
And back again
I'd cry an ocean
For an hour
To wash the dessert
For a flower
And raise the mountains
Spring the trees
And drop the rain
Upon the sea
I'd stop the earth
And halt all time
To hold my place
Within the sky—
Perhaps, my love... When I can fly.

K. A. Maddock

Angel In The Sky

Jessica, she had a dream,
To fly among the clouds.
Her mama and her papa,
She sure did make them proud.
She realized her dream,
But died making it come true.
Now she's living with the angels,
And flying in the blue.

She soared up to the sky,
At the tender age of seven.
Why did she have to die?
At least she's now in heaven.

She loved to fly and ride her horse,
Among many other things.
Now she's up in heaven,
And flying on golden wings.

Yes, Jessie's now an angel,
And living with our Lord.
This precious little girl,
Has gone to her reward!

Kathi Wilson

My Son, Beware

I've known this trail before
My feet have touched
these stones of moss.

I've known these arms before
My lips have touched the petals
of your skin
somewhere

I've known this joy before
with the wind softly
pushing me away

I've felt this love before
When as a child
you romped about my legs

I've known this pain before
    these tears before
The waterfall over my cheekbones
washes away my age

My son,
I meant to tell you
Of life, Beware!

Ronda Savoy

Why Me?

Downsized!
Not me - cannot be!
Loyalty - hard work
Useless?
Confused - why me?
Paralyzed mind - darkness
The clouds of gloom hover.
So much sadness,
So much fear,
Chaos - failure
A wasted life!
What will become of me?
Who cares?
I'm useless - downsized!

Guy Renaud

The Adventurer

In the mind of a boy
Thought is like a toy
To that is so well deploy
In the realm of joy
  Upon the wave of dream
  Upon the wind of hot stream
  Upon the loud scream
  Upon the help of a team
The eyes are skimming
Into the wild upcoming
As hope and fantasy are beaming
At the future wealth becoming
  On the wing of vision
  It soars on prevision
  In a land of provision
  In a life of submission.
Oh Canada! I acclaim
To this country I aim
The land of my I claim
That no one will it maim,

Marcel Amprino

Together

Wipe away the tear,
Feel my breath so near,
Waking from dreams so real,
Embraced in love together we heal.

Washed in waves of life,
Passion entwined in earthly strife,
Touching the moon when we laugh,
Our journeys together on our path.

Thoughtful moments as we reflect,
knowing our hearts always connect,
so my love wipe away the tears,
For my breath at your side is near.

Amber MacDonald

Time Will Tell

Let the clouds gather.
Let the rain fall.
For like each and every one of us
It is destined for recall...
To disappear again!

But unlike the spring green plants
Left dripping
In the rain.
Only time will tell
If we have left this world
Better than when we came.

Mark Matthews

The Dream Of A Lonely Woman

The sun warms the morning sky
It warms the land of days gone by,
The grass so green
The flowers so serene
The love of a man in my heart
We can never grow apart,
Together we can conquer the world
Its mystery to us unfurled.

As the wind blows across the land
It sways the trees and moves the sand,
The ocean roars a mighty song
So sweet for so long,
Open your heart for the world to see
A magical place for you and me,
Believe in your heart and your soul
In order to achieve your goal.

Shirley Makowski

Spring

Spring, the most exciting
first part of the year
Mother Nature
unfolds for you
all her treasures fresh
for you to view
Snowdrops, Crocus,
and Daffodils too
her call to the trees
never fails to produce
her emerald greens
a finery true
take heed when you see
her magnificent views
because it is all for you,
just for you.

L. N. Whitelegg

Love

Love is something none can see,
a feeling in the heart.
It makes you feel so sad the day,
when one you love must part.

It's there when you are holding hands,
and when you walk together.
And when you kiss the one you love,
it's something you can treasure.

There's also something more to love,
it's something strong and real.
When I am with that special friend,
I know it's love I feel.

What I hope for most of all,
for my true love and me,
is peace, true love, and happiness
perhaps, eternally!!

Anthony D. Luck

Black Velvet Night

The night is a black velvet gown
For her Majesty the world to wear.
The moon is a silver ornament
To be fastened in her hair.
And all the stars together
Form a glittering ring.
For her majesty the world and beauty
Are to be married again this spring.

Frances B. Montgomery

From Me To You

Love is...sweet
Love is...mysterious
Love is...you
Love is...me

Love is...our children
Love is...our home
Love is...you
Love is...me

Love is...happiness
Love is...sadness
Love is...you
Love is...me

Love is...fear
Love is...tears
Love is...you
Love is...me

Love is...us
  Forever together.

Janet Gendron

"Unkissed"

I made the grocery list
On it I marked
When was I last
Kissed.

Was it a task not noted
Ingredient omitted
Unfinished
Label?

There were those days
We lay in bed
Our needs were
Sated.

But, oh, I cry
The years we wasted
Wine left open
Untasted.

Mark me not missed.
Mark me not on the list
Mark me
Unkissed.

Patricia M. Harrison

"Wedding Of Sorrow"

A tear fell at your wedding,
  un-noticed 'mid the throng;
A heart did softly murmur,
  "Love of life, so-long."

To think, I had to see the day,
  that you would wed another;
And leave me standing in the aisle,
  just one, amid the others.

To know that in our loving,
  your heart was never mine;
To see you take another's ring,
  Ah! Your eyes did shine.

To see the many flowers,
  spread in sweet array;
I cried a million tears, lost love,
  on that, your wedding day.

Laurence E. Smith Sr.

"The Soul"

My cruel life a burning "Hell"

The burning souls,
That's how I fell

I hate everyone,
in life I see no fun

My soul,
I've lost control

Please join me in this burning hole

Give me your soul
this is your toll

"Hell" is the soul of all
Kristy M. Burdick

"Prayer"

Prayer is the highway to heaven
Faith will open the door
The Bible will guide and lead you
On the pathway all the way through

Love and patience gives understanding
The Holy spirit is every place
Salvation is free to every one
Surely will need grace.

Satan is working every where
So prayer is needed all the way
Strength, courage and wisdom
Is needed through every day

Soon the journey is over
Jesus is waiting at the door
Oh what a wonderful welcome
When Jesus says come home
My children come home.
Nona Moore

South Carolina

Remembrances
of fishing in that rickety boat
with bamboo rods and wriggling crickets
that catch random sizes and shapes
of slimy, but soon, delectable fish.
Practically two acres
of flourishing vegetables and fruits
with lime green vines that tangle
and twist to wet dirty roots.
Tomatoes, peppers, watermelons,
cucumbers, cherries, and cabbage
grow with the statuesque pine trees.
then...
death...
and...
grey trunks replace the lively trees
as brown weeds replace the agriculture.
the boat is gone, the green is gone-
the life is gone.

I miss you, Granddad.
Sam Prince

Nature's Sounds

The wind glides through the trees
on an invisible ray of light.
The stars shine through the clouds
to light the darkness of the night.
All the sounds of nature
are in perfect harmony,
The sounds of help for the wild
go back through the trees;
where they are distributed to each of
nature's ears.
Nature is the symbol
of man's wealth and this world,
and is not to be abused.
So take care of nature's contents
and they will take care of you.
Pam Barbour

My Love

My love, my life,
  You're all I think of,
I've loved you since we met,
  And it will never end
  (That I know)

But the problem is,
  That I can't tell you,
For I scare you'll
  Break my heart,
You didn't even know
  I wrote this poem.

It's all true,
  From the bottom of my heart
I'll always love you,
  You'll always be my friend,
No matter what happens,
  Because we have a friendship,
  That is unending.
Its all true,
  That I love you...
Patrick White

Journey Of Life

From child to woman
in the blink of an eye
I watched you grow

Now you start up the hill
into the battle beyond
through wins and losses
we've all known

The wind blows strong
the wind blows cold
but in the calm of the storm
we reach into our hearts
and find the inner strength
to go on

But when you stumble and fall
turn around
and I will be there
to lift you up off the ground.
Ricky L. Shaw

I Need A Friend

All by myself I can grow a flower
  But I need a friend to give it to.

All by myself I can throw a ball
  But I need a friend to catch it.

All by myself I can tell a joke
  But I need a friend to laugh.

All by myself I can draw a picture
  But I need a friend to give it to.

All by myself I can know a secret
  But I need a friend to share it with

All by myself I can write a poem
  But I need a friend to read it.
Aubrey Latham

Daddy's' Pain

He watched his son
take his first steps.
Say his first words.
Go on his first date.
Then he put his first
baby boy in a grave
He always thought he
would die before his son

He will always remember
when he had to go
and identify his son's
body. He was so cold.
Poor daddy. All he has
now is memories, pain,
and anger. Daddy's pain
He thinks it's his
fault, but it's not. It's
the murder's fault.
Daddy's pain.
Laura Negrete

Cry To My Distant Kin

Normally, vampires do not share
And I am alone in my chair
At the wall I do stare
Seemingly, without a care.

Do not be deceived
For I have become quite peeved
At the way that humans seethe
And their hearts forever bleed!

Do the creatures not understand
It is all according to the plan
That the master of the band
Is playing out the final hand?

Smile loved ones, we are peers
The end is forever near
Through which a new world can appear
And we may all live without fear.
Jessica Leigh Black

The City

A man
sits on a curb
outside of a church
he has no where else to go.
Brian Falkenberg

Appreciation: Health Care Givers

God Love and Bless the C.N.A.'s, who
   daily make the bed.
Take residents to the dining room
   and see that all are fed
Wheel patients to the shower room
   and give a real good bath
Handle Foley-bags with caution
   connected to the cath
God Love and Bless all C.N.A.'s
   who do assignments well
Who never leave a resident without
   a signal bell.
And so it is with Faith and Prayer
   In the Golden years of Medicare.

Clara M. Collyer, R.N., B.S.N.

For New Parents On Valentine's Day

One, and the world is empty.
Two, and life begins.
Three, and the world is full again
And they wonder what happened to two.

Three, of course, is tiny
And asks ever more of two,
And two, they have forgotten
The life that was better than one.

And then comes a day to remind them
Of when one and one become two
And all of the glory that followed
The love between me and you.

Randy Ouellette

Just Open Your Eyes And See

When you open your eyes
There's a lot of surprise!

I see bees at school.
I see a frog in the pool!

I see money in the street.
I see a fly on the meat!

I see an "A" on my test.
I see my brother who's a pest!

I see Dad playing pool.
I see Mom with a gardening tool!

I see books on my shelf.
I'm reading them all by myself!

Bryan Pang

"The Ole House"

The house by the side of the road
was filled with laughter and tears.
The children played and jumped
and never dreamed of years.

I drove by the other day,
doors are gone, windows closed.
The porch was torn away.
I only saw a glimpse of yesterday.

I stood and looked with tears in eyes.
The house that used to be.
So why should I cry and mourn
when memories still are there for me.

Lowrie Brady

Condolences

On meeting with the one we know
whose one unknown to us has died
we may find conscience goading courage
to generate consoling words
born of custom's finer modes.

Then in a flash of vertigo
as awkward words fall from our lips
we hear our own cacophony,
the bounce of mocking phantom gourds
on mausoleum marble floors,
hyena howls and bovine bells
and capering hooves on hardened clay,
and we retrench to start again
but choke to silence and delay.

The one we know expresses thanks
and in an all-consoling flash
we recognize he understands
none can assuage the grief he feels
for one he knew unknown to us.

David Hyde

Let God's Will

History books have their pages;
Widows and orphans their tears
They've related to us through the ages
How on its people war wears.

Peace and good will now is spreading.
The winds of contention too blow.
Do we dare air out our bedding?
Will strife never cease here to flow?

Let God's will be here as in Heaven.
God, grant us here life eternal.
Let God's law add to us its leaven.
God, grant us here homes supernal.

Let us have peace everlasting,
The Prince of Peace reigning o'er all,
The Devil cast out—and the casting
Only the devil appals.

Katherine W. Shelton

Prayer Of The Lost

Oh dear heaven... grant me peace...
Let my heart and troubles cease,
Lay me down to rest so deep
In that blissful... eternal sleep.
Grant I not have to fight my way...
Through one more seeming endless day...
If not: At least; reach me down,
A hand to help me stand my ground!

B. J. McKee

A Grandmother's Touch

With wisdom beyond her years,
She has the power to wash away tears,
And to make a child's fears, melt away.

Her words give inspiration,
Her eyes always shine with love.
She truly is a special gift,
From Heaven up above.

For one such as I, she is a blessing,
She has shaped my life so much.
I am lucky to have known her,
And the love of a grandmother's touch.

Donna Jones

The Little Things In Life

Too often we don't realize
what we have until it's gone.
Too often we wait too late to say
"I'm sorry, I was wrong."
Sometimes it seems we hurt the ones
we hold dearest to our hearts
and we allow stupid things
to tear our lives apart.
Far too many times we let
unimportant things get in our mind
and by then it's usually too late
to see what made us blind.
So be sure you let people know
how much they mean to you.
Take the time to say the words
before your time is through.
Be sure that you appreciate
everything you've got,
and be thankful for the little things
in life that mean a lot.

Starla Staples

Untitled

Circle - up
   and circle down
In and out
   and all about
round and round and round again
   saving not time nor friend
Yet going out and in again
   round about and end to end

Judith Ann Kroll

My Fancy's Finally Turned To Love

Spring, oh spring, you've finally come,
I've waited all the year.
My fancy's truly turned to love,
Now that you're finally here.

I now know my heart was right
My mind was fooling me.
I'm truly glad I held you tight.
And did not lose you foolishly,
Your flowers will this memoir tell,
Of when I held you in my arms.
And of the sweet perfume you'd smell
And of your light and lovely charms.
With buds upon each barren branch,
Your trees have much to say.
They tell me of a new found life.
And that the world will twist and sway.
But like the buds, we're holding tight,
In life by day; in dreams by night;
In future hopes that come what may,
This life will yield a wedding day.

Daniel Arthur Emery

A Meeting

Coal black curling strands
Shower light into being
Creative expressions, in wave and emotion
Artistic, true to form
Shining with the absolute beauty
Unknowingly, filling a cup
Contact making red flow
Another cup already filled
Time taken only for worth.

Kendall L. Smith

Universal Love

Love is beauty, it is sunshine
It is a fountain of life
Love is joy the fragrance
and beauty of the flowers
love is solace to the world
brings peace and heaven on earth
love is a sweet binding force
which can bind the human mind
love is the beauty of spirit
that enhances the beauty of soul
love is eternal it never dies
always revive the human life
love is pious and sublime
it is sacrifice for human kind
love is pure and divine
where God always resides

Sarojini Sharma

Strangeness

Sometimes
you cannot see
the color of the life
You cannot say
it's red it's black it's white
Sometimes the life - night - day
is just a slough:
A big mouth ready to gulp you
    ready to slush
When it happens
it does not matter how strong you are
it does not matter
if your resistance lasts an eternity
    or an instant
it does not matter
anyway the slough swallows you
during an eternity
during an instant.

Claudia Caballero

Everlasting Love

Somewhere out in empty space
Long before the human race

A vast and timeless source began
A loving light was born and then

Power filled with universe
with the cost of nothingness

Lover is life and life is love

Everlasting love!

Emelio Stucchio

Cigarette Grump

Cigarette grump, cigarette grump
Lousy, revolting, awful
that is how I feel
my body is such a dump.

Cigarette grump, cigarette grump
disgusting mess I made
of a once proud body
smoking is a real bump.

Cigarette grump, cigarette grump
oh, how I wish I could quit,
it would be such a kick,
but to do it is a tough hump.

Daniel Wolfe

Golden Wings

You have danced your way through
    the perils of life
With the poise and grace
    of an elegant swan.

You have left a trail of sparkle
    along the way
With the warmth of your heart
    glowing from within.

You have glided over the
    mountains and ridges
With the strength and the power
    of a mighty eagle.

You have touched the hearts
    of many
With the kindness and peacefulness
    of a dove.

You are as special as a
    hummingbird in my heart
Your golden wings will take
    you soaring to the top.

Diana Blandford Lambert

Flying Away!

On the wings of eternity,
    we enter this short play,
And with initial breath,
    a pendulum begins to sway.

As life inches forward,
    a clock ticks away
the seconds and the minutes
    of each person's day.

Relentless in its movement,
    our existence as its prey,
It restrains our enjoyment,
    and holds our security at bay.

What started this continuum?
    Who sent it on its way?
Why does it happen?
    And its end, where does it lay?

Logic dictates a reason,
    why time does us betray.
For in the heart lives 'forever.'
    'Er our dread of flying away!

Richard J. Sullivan

Idle Time

I use to spend hours
with Hallmark
picking out just the right cards
for you.

Once home
I added them to my pile.

Do you have an address?
I could send them to you
so when you are old
you too can remember
the many different ways
I loved you.

Ann McLish

Spring

Tree's blowing,
Flower's growing
- It's a sign of spring

Sun shining,
Babies crying
- It's a sign of spring

People mowing,
It quit snowing
- It's a sign of spring

People swimming,
Other's trimming
- It's a sign of spring

Every kid go outside,
And slide down a great big slide
- Spring is finally here

Janet Becker

Hope

Stars, reflected in people's eyes,
Fragments of a universal consciousness,
Twinkling hopes of undying souls.

Lighthouses in the vastness of
Faraway blue prairies,
Hesitating shadows, going through the
everyday motions of life.

Existing in a metaphoric illusion,
People who never really
Lived their lives but
Empowered proxy aspirations
To improve life for them.

Oxymoronic wastelands irrigated
By dry salty tears,
Bearing no fruits, generating no
Thoughts, wandering aimlessly about.

Ordinary people, looking up, hoping
That opportunity will someday come and
Calmly knock on their rotting wooden
Door, before it is too late.

Ron Cohen

Untitled

I made it through the coldest winter
Your cold air could not
take my breath away
Through your cold sleet
I remained sane
and only dropped a bit of rain
But across the blue
shined a sun that was not you
that gave me joy
and fat white powdered snow
His rays of gold wrap and hold
Me about Him
Not like your arms
Not like your love;
for it was never everlasting
as the light from up above

Stefanie Frazier

We Are A Part Of His Creation

We are a part of his creation
We are a part of his plan
We need to reach out
Take hold of his hand
He forgives, he loves, he heals us, too
The choice he gives us is up to you
He's power, he's mighty, he's also meek
He's here for the strong
He's here for the weak
When God speaks, things get done
Jesus Christ His only begotten Son
Life without Him can be real rough
Life with Him is more than enough

Judy G. Phillips

The Water's Edge

As I walked
Down by the water's edge
Where the rivers flow like air,
I dipped my hand and sole into
The perfection hidden there
But as I glimpsed my reflection
In the drops strewn about my hand
I felt sharp pains of anguish
Bite through my flesh and bone
I fell back in agony
And felt my heated skin,
Only to find, from a thousand tears,
The red which flows within.
I looked back to the water's edge,
bleeding from my very soul,
Only to see that the glistening pools
were as innocent as before.

Rose Rittenhouse

To A Dead City

Twisted underbrush of steel
Rusted, pockmarked
Ravaged by war
That most anarchical of all disease
Which men invoke and fear

Lone stumps of buildings
Preside
Eye sightlessly
The humbled heap

Water laps
Listless, lifeless
On crumbled ramps

Glassy earth returns
No annual upspringing

No one crying

But I
Why

Doris Mayer

A Remembrance

A car bomb —
terrified innocent people
screaming children,
their playtime over —
a city in Oklahoma
America's Heartland
torn apart...
Forever

Romy Malbin Hodgson

Untitled

All I see
is darkness.

The moon
lies at my feet,
fallen to the Earth.

The stars burnt out.
Their million years reign ended.

I laugh at this,
a parody of society.

Where all great people
have fallen,
no longer to exist.
No hope to shine again.

Then on the eastern horizon, I see it,
a small speck of light,
the birth of a new star.

Maybe all hope isn't lost.

Jennifer Brant

Wind Chill

Winter memories
Not easily erased
As buds announce spring.

John M. Jenkins

A Deadly Disease

AIDS...
How do we get it?
How to prevent it?
How many will die each year?

All these questions
not many answers
I'm starting to worry-
about this fear!

How do we know
when our time has come?
Will I be next
to catch the glum?

AIDS...
How do we get it?
How to prevent it?
How many will die this year?
It's just me
Starting to worry
About this horrible fear!

Tiffiany Bates

Untitled

Lights this moments,
Shadows the next.
Joy spiralling upwards,
Then gloom, deep darkness
In the labyrinth of life
This frame a trusting one
Walking through the maze
in the guidance of his gaze.
A head in the distance
a meadow of freshness,
dews of a soft morn,
tendrils of a love song.
Just a while to go...
And aye.....
    Will soon be there.

Otulana Temitope

The Fire Leap

I am the fire!
I am the light!
Together I can fight to get the
right of love.....

If you imagine...
You can fly as high as a Dove;
If you are afraid
just think of spirit, God
He will silently guide you to the
Right Way.....
If you leap deep
You can do anything.....

Drusilla Forster

Life

Seldom we feel
alone and lost
like our problems are
there forever and no one
can help
We feel sad but also
depressed and on how
life lets it carry itself
But a question we
should ask is it the way
we choose to carry it
and make it turn out for
one other not all people
know this simple answer
but a lot ask

Natalie Pepin

The Seagull

*Dedicated to my mother Yolanda Rubio,
and to my family*
To dream and fly
Touch the sky
A dream of hope;
beautiful and free
Her wings never clipped,
her heart full and feeling
the ocean breeze
She soars way up,
no one can ever stop
her flight already made
Bold, strong, unafraid
unafraid of obstacles
no matter what they
may be
This is the life I've
chosen for me!

Hilda R. Pareja

Dreams

Painting a picture of dreams,
"What does it mean?
Why am I here?"
Her questions remain unanswered.
The moment has passed,
But the dream sits inside her,
Only to fade away and disappear,
But they don't disappear,
For dreams do not fade.
They simply hide away
And reappear in quick flashes.
But the girl,
Not realizing her loss,
continues painting.

Kelly Jackson

Good Night

The great dragon
lazily
closes
his juwell eye
stretches
his giant paw
smiles
his sharptoothed grin
curls
his spiked tail
around his firefilled snout
sighs

and

sinks
into another millennia
of blooddrenched dreams

Alexandra Hasselmann

Angel's Song

They tried to kill America
As Old Glory was unfurled
A knife plunged in her heartland
A sound heard round the world

A lifeless child for all to see
What madness man unleashed on thee
As mothers tears began to flow
America's anger would grow and grow

They broke America's heart that day
But brave and valiant we must stay
To fight for right and God each day
We owe that to those they took away

A choir of Oklahoma angels sings
For all of us to hear
You have the right to shed those tears
But remember man can't live in fear

They tried to kill America
And Yes! They broke her heart
But her spirit remains strong
Listen, you'll hear our angel's song

Thomas H. Oberle

Winooski Salmon

Below the bridge of metal, wood,
Salmon leaping
Hurl themselves up
On ledges, hurling again,
Hurling again, flesh stained
With their essence, scarred
Against rock and river
Men have destroyed,
Onion River, Winooski, other words for
Other waters, where
Natives and patriots have
Poured their own blood, we pour
Garbage, not dealing
With our size now
As beings who have outgrown
A child's body and still walk
The flower beds.

McGillicuddy

Untitled

Trickling through the icy veins
peaceful as the winter sleeps
time suspended, life sustains
the river stands in tranquility
silently, waiting.

Secrets of the ages past
shielded by the sparkling water
boulders standing ever steadfast
rolling stones, gently dancing
silently, waiting.

Spring will soon begin to push
the swell in certain fury
the roaring, surging, crashing rush
but for now, the lazy river keeps
silently, waiting.

Debra H. Williams

My Day-Off

I'm in no hurry,
   today's my day-off,
      everything takes me longer:
My waking-up,
   my bathroom-stop,
   my brushing my teeth,
   my shower-time,
   my casual reading,
   my TV watching,
   my constant munching.

And the daily loading
   of the gun.
And the nightly attempt
   at pulling the trigger,
before I sleep.

Ammar Abdulhamid

Untitled

Spring in the East,
in this country house;
leaves bursting in verdancy,
azaleas brushing color
against the windows -
this country house, to me,
forever wintry.
The still silence singing
dolefully, chilling me,
leaving me stark.
Not even a dog barks.
All the demons here roost,
like the crows
which caw their strident wrath
on overgrown grass.
The pall of this serenity
stifles me with gloom;
all this space, these trees,
this infernal rusticity.

Sandra Tollman

"He Came Into Her Room"

Death came into her room last night.
And stood beside her bed
He pulled the cover over her feet
And kissed her softly on the head

She felt his lips touch her skin
And fear struck through her bones
Death left her room last night
But he didn't leave alone

Monica Exley

Untitled

From far away
the chimes of bells
roll over hills and fields
to me
the doves fly a small circle
back to security
the sheep feed slowly
not really moving
and I sit here
still in me
filled with the beauty
of it all

Bettina Brown

My Secret Place

My secret place is in my head,
Nobody can bother me there.
And when I am inside my head,
I can go anywhere.

I can be an astronaut,
flying to the farthest stars
or I can be a millionaire,
who owns 500 cars.

I could be a basketball player,
swishing all my shots,
or I could be some clear water,
boiling in a pot.

I could be Martin Luther King Jr.
bringing together the human race.
That all happens inside my head,
and that is my secret place.

Sean Dufford

Memories

The years had built
A lengthy time behind,
Impeding us to unfold
The pages of our lives.
And working against us
Memories of our own,
As we had none
To lean upon.
But, suddenly one day,
Our paths were crossed
On the other side
Of each other's age;
And melting with joy
As well as sour notes
Your mysteries and mine
Resolved themselves.
Today, we both realized
When walking holding hands,
That finally we owned
Our memories at last!

Dunnia M. Cumpston

Memories Last

Our lives are like a painting
A piece of art we know,
These memories last forever
And never letting go.

These memories hanging proudly
Like art in our museums,
For memories are like
That art piece
We treasure and look at so.

Bobbie Payne

The Direction Of Leaves

On a bench in the sun
Sat an aging man
Leaning gently forward.
In the nearby stream
A trout looked puzzled
By the round stones.
In the air, a plane
Zipped across the sky
Filled with prisoners.
On a concrete step
A bored little girl
Danced without music.
The wind blows hard
And takes the leaves
Swirling with it.

Tom Sgrizzi

Untitled

Two bodies
Two minds
Two hearts,
Now one.
One dream unfolds another.
It's time to stroll along together,
to begin what began
before it had begun.
Time to run..
to run in time,
an island of pleasure I've found
in you,
I am the ocean at your side,
forever caressing...
forever true.
It's time to love...
to love the times,
One dream...
One wish...
I wish to dream for you.

Andrea L. Cox

The Time That Was

Walking alone in the sunset,
Seeing the beauty of the sky;
Colours entwining overpower me
As I slowly let myself cry.
I know you're still with me somewhere
As I watch the whispering sea.
White foam, the soul of unicorns,
Seems to be beckoning to me.

Tender tears trickle gently down.
Please comfort me here whilst I sleep.
All I have left now of you are
The treasured memories I keep.
Darkness around me draws me in
As I wonder where you could be.
I love you so much, it hurts still.
My sweet little one, watch over me.

Rachel Wagstaff

Christmas

Christmas is white
It sounds like bells clinging together
It tastes like candy canes
It smells like cookies baking
It looks like a big family celebration
It makes you feel like playing with
all your toys!

Stacey Schwartz

Dreams

Dreams are not real.
What's the big deal?
They are so sweet.
They don't stink like feet.
Dreams are too nice!
Now roll the dice...
Six is all you roll.
You have control.
Now let us talk real,
Let me tell you the big deal,
They sometimes never come true.
Give you a clue...
They suck because they are so fake!
Wake up for God's sake!
REALITY is here.
Don't feel the fear!
Reality can be nice.
Just don't roll the dice!
You may get a one...
And dealing with it won't be fun.

Susan Hernandez

Touchless

Not even the orange-red
flaming screams of children
could touch you

And I've seen you pass
over pools of blood
steaming shattered bodies
blown hollow, empty
in the concrete streets
of cities

Even in phonebooths
you smile and crack
splintering grim visage
with angry teeth
gleeful in your own
    destruction

Debra L. Richardson

"Unloved"

To die unloved,
like a snow white dove.
Reaching out a trembling hand,
Not a friend in this lonely land.

Eyes drenched with sadness,
a nightmare of madness.
Slipping away like morning mist,
poisonous as a viper's hiss.

Lips that cry no joy,
meaning of life we toy.
Overwhelming sense of pain,
as death makes more gain.

To die is punishment of sin,
no mortal could ever win.
To die unloved is shameful sorrow,
as death takes away tomorrow.

Wayne O'Quinn

Flower

It sits all alone
On the mantle so high
In a vase full of water
And the tears that I've cried
The petals blood red
A stem that's sea green
Sharp prickers that cut me
Un-noticed, Un-seen
Because it is picked
From the world that it knows
It starts to go limp
And no longer grows
Yet I leave it to die
Petals wasting away
Hoping it will bloom
On some other day.

Frederick E. Whitlock

Lonely Angel

Are you my sweet mommie
your face is so very sweet
I need to find my sweet mommie
To cuddle me warm my cold feet
To sing to me a lullaby
I'm just a lost, tired angel
Whose halo isn't very bright
The dark is getting creepy
A noisy - cold shadowy night
Please be my sweet mommie
I don't like being so lonely
Or having an empty tummy
I'm so lost tired cold sleepy
But my wings won't unfold
Wish I could find my mommie
For in her arms she would me hold
Your face is so loving
I'm so weary
Need some one to love me
To dry these eyes, so teary!!

Frances Rulli

My Abyss Of Darkness

Oh why do I have to
Go down and look in it.

When all I have to do
Is have a thought and be in it.

Why do I want to go down into
That bottomless pit,
Where it's dark with evil
Thoughts, evil spirit.

Abyss. You call. I come.
I look. I run.

You're a hole in my soul
My darkest fear.

You call. I come. I don't run.

John T. Shepherd

Life

For us all
   life brings
      smiles and tears;
and increased
   memories
      all thru the years.

Betty Daniel Pack

Bitter Pill

The moonlight shines
through on opening in the
curtains and rests upon a
brass chair, she is outlined
in the shadows.

A tear forms in the corner of
her saddened eyes, loneliness, she
holds in the palm of her hand.
She sits and waits for sleeps,
as she bends her head and
asks for forgiveness.

Then at last, it finds her,
she lays herself a permanent
sleep. And on the night stand
next to her lifeless body, an
open bottle of her best friend,
a bitter pill. Her life's end.

Margaret Cobb

"Grandma"

Grandma's aren't forever
    they are only here for awhile
So treasure the moments
    remember her smile

I remember mine in her purple dress
    the same one she wore
When we put her to rest

Tears never came, but they flow inside
    the memory never leaves
The pin only subsides

Grandma's aren't forever,
    for mine has died...

Cindy Nicolelli

Kick Start

You sounded down so very much
I thought I'd drop a line
It's not what's happened
That counts so much
But what you do about it.
Things always happen for a reason
Whether our mistake or no,
So now's the time to pull ahead
And straighten out the mess.
Pick yourself up and carry on
With head held high and shoulders back
You know you did your best,
Turn fate around and meet the rest
Of life's challenges head on
Cause things are always happening
To try and drain our strength
Just don't forget to keep your faith
And all will be corrected.

Margaret Westworth

If Ever An Angel

If ever an angel fell from the sky,
That wonderful angel was you.

If ever an angel had beautiful eyes,
That wonderful angel was you.

And if ever an angel was loved by me,
That wonderful angel was you.

Ashlee Hollaway

Stolen Time

'Twas a moment in time
he was taken away,
Unable to kiss him
on the fateful day.

How I cried and cried
as that night grew cold,
"He'll be back in three years"
was what I'd been told.

One juror took a nap
while the others looked on,
compromising the verdict
their decision was wrong.

One day they'll be judged
for the decision they made,
then will they know
all the pain that they gave.

Justice for all
will I no longer believe,
beware of the system
that took him from me.

Peggy Sullivan-Dooling

My Guy

When he looks at me,
I smile inside.
When he looks at another,
I wish that she would hide.
The way his hair,
Shines a sunny gold,
He looks as it,
He could never grow old.
His brilliant blue eyes.
Shine in the day.
They seem to twinkle,
When he looks my way.
He's very athletic,
And looks great in a wet tee.
I wonder if he knows how much,
I think of him and me.
I hope by day,
And I pray by night.
That my fine sweet Austin,
Will never leave my sight.

Rachel White

Granddaughter

I look into your eyes
And see a window to my past,
A mirror of my youth,
Too many years gone by too fast.

I hold you in my arms
And feel your mother's warm embrace,
The silky touch of Mommy's hair,
The trusting, loving little face.

I feel so free to love you -
No duties in the way -
No scoldings, speeches, lessons,
No warnings I must say.

It's almost like a second chance
To do the things I tried
To do so many years ago
Amid life's crushing tide.

Life's most precious moments
Are embodied in you, lass,
My ever joyful, ever darling
Mirror to the past.

Barbara J. Sanko

The Night Feed

Rocking slowly
    Late at night,

Baby gently drinking.

Rocking slowly
    Late at night,

Eyes are slowly blinking.

Rocking slowly
    Late at night,

She almost sleeping.

Rocking slowly
    Late at night,

Dawn is quietly creeping.
Rocking slowly
    Late at night,

A mother's sleeping bliss.

Rocking slowly
    Late at night,

She lays her with a kiss.

Lisa Law

Thinking

As the long day ends,
under the bridge nearby,
It attracts the conscience,
and people that like to lie.

Every so often
I visit this place,
because it's a secret
I leave no trace.

I come here to think,
and to clear my head,
I can block out the thoughts,
of what others have said.

It's not my fault I act how I do,
I come here to think
and so should you.

Boris Lehtman

A Queen No More

Sipping my tea in a dark room
Front door unlocked, now you are home
With abated breath I sat quietly
On my cheek, lips touch solemnly
Savouring memories of years past
When I was the queen in your heart
When hungry you stretched out a hand
Always I was ready with a bun
A cool drink to quench your thirst
Hugs and kisses to dry your tears
When the wind was cold and gusty
My embrace was warm and cozy
Those cherished moments of sweetness
Were a queen's treasure in loneliness
Sipping my tea, mute and alone
Happy you've found a new queen
To warm your heart and hold your hand
When I'll be gone beyond, my son.

Pacita Labayen Aliermo

Dream

Flame of untamed love
burning away at my heart
bringing only endless sorrow

Running through a field of dreams
watching words of love pass by
tears of pain from not only today
but tomorrow

The burning sensation
I know love has departed
nothing can heal it except that
gentle kiss

The fulfillment that only
dreams may bring
now is gone
it ceased to exist

Ashley Etchberger

Jesus Wonder Of Wonders

When sad and lonely,
My eyes blinded by tears
In sorrow bleeding my heart,
I feel near you, my Lord.

When all roads are closed
And I walk in darkness
Crushed by my sorrow,
You are my guide, O Lord.

And when I feel running away
On the border of despair,
With my crying heart
O Jesus, I embrace your Cross.

Emmy de Gaspar

Newfound Love

Thank you for my newfound love
A love I thought was lost.
Renewed so deeply do I feel
It must be from above
You'd showered us with many
Blessings, I'm so glad you have
It makes our days so very full,
With many surprises to add.
It makes our nights so loving
We missed so many times.
You move so gentle within
our lives and
Guiding our very stride,
We've so thankful, for you're
Loving hand.
We promise never to hide
Our newfound love we have

Janice Clare Forget

He Is Our Rock

He was there when we needed him,
Our lives were never dim,
Our hearts he did win,
Because of him.

He was also our friend,
He always had a hand to lend,
Our hearts may never mend,
Our love for him will never end.

Now he is wearing a halo,
Fishing off his own dock,
By our side he will always walk,
Because he is our Rock.

Nancy Conley

Untitled

The salt in my tears burn my eyes
    sometimes,
Flowing so deep and rapid like
    the river to my soul,
leading to the ocean in
    my heart.
Pounding and pulsing so
    hard the waves so tall,
the power, is a focus that would
    put anyone in awe,
    hypnotized
by the waves crashing.
The salt foaming creating an illusion
of its strength as it roars to
    the shore.
Proving that it will never stop.

Jennifer Bennett

Be True To Yourself...

Why be ashamed of what
you feel
Open your heart let
it be real
Don't worry about
people and what they
will say just smile
Nod and walk away.

Appreciate there comments but
don't be scared tell them
the truth "How You Feel"

Listen to your gut, follow
the way that's laid
Before you each and
everyday.
The path of feelings
Is the path to friends

So follow the path and
It'll never end

Jennifer N. Corey

Everyone Screams

I live in a world
Where words cut
More deeply than knives
Where the loneliest times
Are when I'm not even alone
And solitude
Is a memory...
Where togetherness is
A fairy tale
Told by little children
Too young to know the truth
Where tears are invisible
And screams
Inaudible...
And I know
Deep down inside
Everyone lives
In a world like that —
Behind their walls
Everyone screams...

Stephanie Chalk

Modern Life

Stop eating!
We have to *go!*

Phillip Ruben Serrato

Waterfall Dreams

Silvery water trickles,
Splashing against a rocky face,
weathered by time, smoothed with age.
Water splashes, gently trickling.
down a weathered face,
that has been aged by the years,
wrinkled by time and,
smiles of days gone by.
Ferns adorn all around,
Arranged and scattered
Darkest colours
Deepest greens
A rainforest dream.

Sparkling drops of water
Adorn graying locks
Dripping icicles
Cold and clear
Fresh new smells
An aged ones dream.

Cherie Shields

Untitled

Man tries to curb the elements
And aim for stars above
When all the time we've been endowed
With things that bring us love.

There's summer, fall and winter
And the springtime too
That send forth massive beauty
Beneath the skies of blue.

One need only look around
At this our fair domain
And study God's great gift to man
A place that's not inane.

There's wonderment and elegance
In forests, streams and trees
In every living creature
On land and in the seas.

So let us realize all this
Before it is too late
Before we change this world of ours
To a place of ill begotten fate.

Gordon A. Lawrence

Little Star, Guide Me

Little star up in the sky,
Twinkle as the night goes by.
Guide me 'til the morning sun,
Lets thy work of night be done.

Little star up in the sky,
Watch o'er me 'til morning's light.
Bless my rest and keep my soul,
'Til the morning I behold.

Little star up in the sky,
Watch o'er me, your loving child,
For I know that you're God's son,
Watching o'er this little one.

Little star up in the sky,
Lead me safely thru this life.
If my path be straight and clean,
Take me home to be with THEE.

Shirley Woodlock

A Feeling For You

I lie here by your side
listening to your heart beat
the rhythm soothes my thoughts
my lips press against your skin
I kiss you

My fingers glide over you
I feel your warmth
I am warm

Lying here so alone
my ears ringing the sound of loneliness
my lips have no place to rest
my fingers reach out but
find no smooth body to caress
I am cold

Trina Stockill

If

You turned your back.
The barrier it made
was hard and cold and stoney.
I waited inside
a frozen bubble of icy air
while you walked away.
The bubble shattered,
it fragments tinkling, falling
through the lifeless atmosphere.
Its shining shards
showered my feet
and spattered me with pain.
If had thought
that you would hate me,
I would have closed my heart
and never let you in.

Rita Summers

A Miracle

On a long ago cold morn,
A baby was born,
   And they called His name Jesus.

The angels all sang,
And three wise men came,
   With gifts for the little boy Jesus.

"'Tis a miracle," they said,
And Mary bowed her head,
   To gaze at her son, the baby Jesus.

Now today we all celebrate,
This miracle so great,
   The birth of the one we call Jesus.

Mildred S. Salisbury

Glorious War

Bombs dropping
ears popping
hearts stopping
screaming, crying
shrapnel flying
people dead
and people dying
children wonder through the street
of broken dreams with bloody feet
This is the truth we cannot ignore
what do you think of glorious war

Simon K. Browning

I Became An Inuit

I became an Inuit I.N.W.T.
To see the sights
And northern lights
In all their majesty.

The Great Slave Lake just sits there
With Yellowknife, her friend
With long full hours of sunshine
And days that never end.

MacKenzie Mountains standing there
So silent, strong and grand
We're flying to Inuvik
Cross this great and barren land.

Among the sights to see up here
Is Nahanni National Park
And just due east, Fort Simpson
Has a warm and welcome heart.

Steve Henshall

To The Sea

Roving, restless, angry sea
That's for-ever dashing
Against the rocky, sandy shore.
What makes thee have such moods?
The continual clashing
Of your foamy, foreign tongues.

With all this careless talk,
I do not implore
Thou restless minds to demand
Your boisterous waters to be calm
For-ever more,
And lay quiet, longing for dizzy life.

Cut the ropes from the rushing waves,
Let them be gone.
Wake up all the old mad sea devils.
All this turmoil makes thee beautiful.
So keep on
Slinging thy tumult spume to the winds.

Ruth Brown

A Believer's Prayer

Open our eyes Lord
   Help us to always see
The hand of someone reaching out
   So we can fill their need

Open our ears Lord
   To hear their desperate call
You will always be there
   Each time we fail or fall

Open our minds Lord
   Seeking to know of You
Striving to show faithfulness
   In everything we do

Open our hearts Lord
   Showing others that we care
Their burdens and sorrows
   We are willing to share

Open our lives Lord
   Help us do all we can
And be a willing servant
   Wherever You may send.

Janet Lee

School's Out, Summer's In

Say goodbye to your friends
   School's out, Summer's in
Make sure you give your teacher
   a farewell grin
School's out, Summer's in
Make your enemies your friends
   School's out, Summer's in
Tie all untied ends
   School's out, Summer's in

Things become easier all of a sudden
School's out, Summer's in
Can't cause trouble anymore
   School's out, Summer's in
More things in store
   School's out, Summer's in
Do whatever you want and more
   School's out, Summer's in
Having fun til you're tired
   All because
School's out, Summer's in!

Inyang Ekong

The Graveyard

The nights creeps forward,
Reaching out, o'er the yard,
Darkly hiding the stones,
With its shadowy guard.

Only sleeping bones,
The living souls are gone,
Away on a journey,
Approaching a new dawn.

The morning wind sweeps,
And rouses all the trees,
While the living leaves stir,
And rustle in the breeze.

Wind passes over,
Leaving its hope behind,
A much-valued treasure,
For the young and the lined.

Each stone names a life,
A long-ago glory,
A plot in the graveyard,
What is their life story?

Maureen C. M. C. Meyer

I Love You More

I Love you more, was her reply
and I couldn't help but smile.
   For tho circumstance keeps us apart
   I know our love grows all the while.

But a question troubles me
as the thought she did profess.
   Makes me wonder if she loves me more
   does that mean I love her less?

Still, I simply can't imagine
any way to rightly measure
   The loving way she fills my soul
   of that I truly do treasure

No number may convey the scope
nor may a mirror show fair reflection
   Of how much she means to me
   and the depth of my affection

Perhaps someday I'll find the words
that will make her understand
   How much I long to shower her
   with all the love at my command

Richard Gallison

She Is...

She Is...

A strong beautiful woman
A real person
A wonderful role model
A great grandmother, mother and wife

Caring

A person to talk to
A shoulder to cry on
A friend who can share laughter
A provider to everyone dear

Amazing

A roommate when times are tough
A ride to school when running late
A fan at softball games
A teacher in life!

Loving
Jennifer LeJeune

In The Beginning

Nothing
    Less than that
Nothingness

No dawn
    No sunrise
        No first bird

No sound
    No song
        No light

    Into the brooding darkness
Came
    The power of the word
        "Let there be..."

And the word gave birth
    To joy and misery
Twins
    Bound as one

    For all eternity...
Edyth V. Harris

Outside

            one
        drop of
        rain   is
    dangling from
    a   branch
    of   the
    old   oak
    i   know
    how   it
    feels   to
    be   suspended
    in   midair
    just   waiting
        for   the
            fall
Melody L. Schoenfeld

Did You Forget To Enjoy Yesterday?

Now, please consider this today —
Can you remember yesterday?
Was it cold or warm,
Was it sunny or grey,
Were you happy or sad?
Did you take time to pray?

Did you pause to breathe deeply,
To smile as you worked,
To say "hi" to a stranger
Behind whose eyes lurked
A longing for friendship,
A kind hand to shake?

Did you take time to marvel
At the gifts you've been given?
If you did, then you know
That they all are from heaven.
God's joys are around us,
They're for us to take.

So, don't waste today
For tomorrow's sake!
Margaret S. Herp

At Venus Pool Table

He shoots a good stick
pivots the azure tip
on the moon ball balanced
on a fringe of universe.

Eyes in a prism
he seeks out the right planet
and strokes his wrist
to the suffering delight
that rolls to his belly

Like sex
sinking down
spinning always,
Vesper is always
making cosmic business.
Real St. Pierre

Who Begun

Under the threat of war
Our hearts are filled with doubt
What are we fighting for
Why can't we work things out

Our pride and dignity
Still is the highest goal
But for our victory
Willing to risk all

No one knows who begun
Nor how this thing may end
But no one will have won
Some scars will never mend
Edgar Vos

Arthur

I look at my life and wonder
what have I done
did I do everything I wanted
Accomplished everything
I dreamed.
Then I look at you, my Son,
My dream of all dreams
And I say, yes
I've accomplished the one thing
in life most important you!
Kathleen Boos

For G. I Love You

For a sweet gentle man who
made love to me during a
long winter's night
The brush and distant man
whom I dared to kiss

He... who longed for passion
a hopeful little boy who longs
to be held and comforted in
the safety of loving arms

A man who stormed and captured
so many citadels which in his
boyhood and youth must have
seemed as fantastical and
unobtainable as Ali Baba's cave

A man of many lives
Rhonda Jaminson

The Sand-Dwellers

The sand-dwellers are now gone,
Just another disappearing tribe,
The sand dunes are all undone,
The gladiators are on the drive.

The table of arid earth,
Constantly swept by desert wind,
Turns into a defenseless fortress,
The ragged vales become unkind.

The sand is always a battleground,
Which absorbs spilt blood swiftly,
Now lizards and scorpions abound,
With rams and camels for company.

The sand-dwellers are now afar,
Their empire turned into tombs,
As the ever-consuming ancient war,
Can't be ended by words and bombs.
Elmer R. G. Valdez

Kathleen

Dedicated to the Memory of Kathleen Ferrier
Emotions redefined.
I listen, enthralled,
Enraptured, captured
In aural bliss.
My soul is shattered,
Battered then mended
As the words your voice
Sings become distilled
To something beyond
Reason, beyond experience.
Chromatic richness that
I can sometimes
Barely endure.
You sing of He who
Is despised and I feel
The guilt of those who were there.
You ask 'What is life' and
I share in Orfeo's despair.
Sing now eternally,
Where all shall come to hear.
Barry D. Johnson

Too Little Too Late

I think of snappy come backs, long after a debate.
I know just what I should have done a day or two too late.
I go to bed and try to sleep, all I can do is think.
But then sit up and realize, my mind is out of ink.

I can always pick a winner after the game is played.
My mind will always function, but the action is delayed.
Our minds are just for thinking, now tell me what you think.
What would this world be like if there wasn't any ink.

You couldn't write to relatives across the ocean blue,
And they wouldn't have no ink to write a letter back to you.
So I leave you with one thought in mind for you to stop and think.
Just what this world would be like if we hadn't any ink

Margaret Van Der Wal

Untitled

Black pearls from the sea
That's what your eyes were when they held me
Suspended in time
You let me see into your soul
And now my heart just won't let go.

When I felt your love so soft, yet strong
I knew it would not be long
But now six months have past
And the love I thought would last
Has never made it to my door
He ran away, as did I
And now I sit and wonder why.

Suellen Fagan

The Resurrection

My own two personal Hitlers are remembered
and respected well.
Through this battle I've become quite the
strong soldier.

Will I ever be my father's daughter again?
It's obvious that the answers aren't coming.

The second aggressor — the fancy named Prince
in sheep's clothing; how could I have ever let
it go so far?

Now, the various beatings are over. The one-sided
love story has finally ended happily ever after.
I am free to love, laugh, and rejoice.

The tattoo's no longer relevant and neither is
my love for him.
Both Hitlers banished and all is not lost.

Love lives on in those who are strong.

Kimberly A. Tracy

Fairyland

Baby-blue tinted
crystal mosquito wings twitch in the enchanting
tune humming wind....
A majestically sparkling glow surround
each fairy...
Tiger eyes gaze with satisfactory
along a veined courtyard wall.
Some glowing a peaceful pink-
others a moral green-
and one a crystal clear set of cluttered fairy dust wings
flies away with mischief looking for a juicy fly.
Gleefully crouching on a daffodil's stamen -
Lovingly munching on iris petal....
Awaiting a rain sprinkle to wet their wings
and give them a playful bath -
to sing or dance
or coast into an evening soar.

Sarah Fournier

Book Of Life

This is the story of the busy man, who never found time to pray.
No matter it seems how hard he tried,
   he could not find time in his day.

So busy he was gathering things, things he was sure he would need
that all of his time though he couldn't see it,
   soon was consumed by greed.

Gathering this gathering that his wants his needs soon confused
he never found time for anything,
   and most of his things went unused.

Still he kept going gathering things, loosing more time in his day
all of his time with each precious minute,
   he just couldn't find time to pray.

But time it's said waits for no man, soon his time had come
and there he stood before Jesus in heaven,
   to review the things he'd done.

Jesus stood looking down at the man, then looking back at the book
what a sad moment it must have been,
   as Jesus said with a saddened look.

I am sorry my son in my book of life your name I can not find
I meant to write it down, I just couldn't find the time.

Randy Kidwell

Robbed Of My Youth

Suspicion of lost sanity blows in the air. Deeper and darker becomes
   the night.
No longer standing this time that we've shared. It's crumbled to the
   ground.
Subdued, no conclusion but the end is coming near.
A dark new beginning, I'm lost in a stare.
Climbing or falling, illusions of hills. Night falls over day
And clouds fill the skies. Moment upon moment I've gone away.
I no longer exist, I've lost all self. Pieces on the marble floor,
   I have no eyes to see
Carried away by my heart, my greatest enemy.
Death patterns flock near corners of life, to rid me of my soul.
Time slips slowly away from my side, leaving me to face the cold.
Sunsets and sunrises have shattered on the ground
I'm no longer Daddy's little princess, when you stole my heart you
   stole my crown.

Rebecca Canuso

Affirmation

He awakens me with a painted sky of early dawn and
walks with me in the cool morning sand.
He greets me with a gentle breeze and
takes my hand in the warmth of His sun.

He shows me strength in the powerful sea and
hope in each newly-formed wave.
His promise of each new day shows his faith in me;
and from each gentle wave he whispers: "I Am!"

S. L. Smith

Love

Love is not a game to play.
Love is sweet, and then one day
Some guy thinks he has you "won."
And that's when you find he's not the one.
Love is strong.
Love is like steel.
Love goes right when you're both on an even keel.
Love is not a game to play.
Love is sweet, and then one day
one wants to choose a different road.
Just think of it as not having to worry
about that extra heavy load!

Amber Prine

Mother

So many years have long since passed by I remember your leaving
I did not cry. My heart was heavy, I tried to be brave
I had lost my best friend and the love you gave.
I remember too how you looked after us boys, your work
and planning.. keep us fed buy us toys. No mean feat without
a daddy to take a hand for you to look for a helping hand.
Mum! You did things that couldn't possibly be, giving happiness and
love to my brothers and me and if indeed there be such a person called
Christ please, take care of my mum, she was so nice.

When I think back on life with you there, oh! So much fun
we hadn't a care and that day I got hurt I remember it well.
The blood flowed freely I wanted to yell, but mother, you came to me.
Gave me a kiss and a cuddle I knew then I was not in trouble

So much I want to say about you, dearest mother, your smile, sympathy
and caring, when we were sad and shed a tear, the comfort of your arms
when bed time drew near. Silly things that may have seemed kind of
small yet to us kids they weren't really small at all Unselfish love
right from your heart, sadly to remain only as a memory now that
God has willed us apart.

Norman St. Paul

Illegal

I cannot even wrench a poem from this pain:
There are no words for being this alone.
Behind the window is the world I watch.
I cannot find its key.
I cannot find the deeds
to make you stop ignoring me.
I do not understand the sins
for which I must atone.

You see
you only give the option
of not to be
not of whom to be
of not to do
not of what to do

(And I can write, oh,
about love and learning
and laughter, maybe laughter)

But not about not being:
Death is too complete...

Maaike Ellen Onkenhout

Mother

For your loyal support in everything I do
For decisions that always are right and true
For cheering me up when I feel blue
 I Love You Mother

For truly believing that I will succeed
For supplying me with whatever I need
For making each thing you do a good deed
 I Love You Mother

For leading me in the right direction
For showering me with love and affection
For sheltering me with your protection
 I Love You Mother

For making me strive to reach my dreams
For mending my heart when it tears at the seams
For polishing my soul until it gleams
 I Love You Mother

For the constant sacrifices made
For your continuous help and aid
For your steadfast love that will never fade
 I Love You Mother

Meagan Rundell

The Gifts Of The Father

I know the sun doesn't shine everyday,
but at least I can wear a smile on my face.
The blessings I receive from above,
are sent to me as a token of my father's love.

He makes the flowers grow so bright,
to remind me of his heavenly light.
Each night as I lay down my head,
I thank him for all the things he has said,
I know one day I will see his face,
up in heaven, what a wonderful place.

Dear friend I pray each and every day,
you will join me and others to say.
Earth has been great even with all its snares
but the home we have in heaven can't compare.

So I hope to see you in that place on high,
up above the clouds one day we will fly.
To live with out father for evermore
on that peaceful, golden, shore.

Kim Evett

Ode to Sean

Your presence never leaves my mind
And your thought has never gone, and I can't keep lying
To myself that nothing can heal this pain inside
Of you dying

It seemed so long ago
That you were alive
Ever since my heart has been filled with sorrow
And I count the days until I can again see your eyes

I wish you could be here
To see the changes that have become
If you were alive and in your teenage years
Doing what teens do: have fun

A lot can be said
About you dying
Through the papers people have read
Your story left many crying

You would now be around fifteen
Your siblings are a lot older
Your parents often wonder what might have been
If you hadn't dropped your bag and folder.

Ryan Mason

A Mother's Love

Waves of pain crashing through me
that have no beginning, no end
Suddenly over, and I am awestruck
that through suffering came this gift of deliverance
in the most beautiful wrapping I have ever seen

Small and slightly wrinkled frailness
first tinged a delicate blue
Through a haze of exhaustion, exhilaration
I marvel at the perfection of his form
and listen as his feeble wail fills the air with life

Tiny fingers wrap around my thumb
the fragile pressure is exquisite
Large luminous eyes gazing up at me, into me
the depth of trust I see there is overwhelming
pure innocence claiming me as his own

Nuzzling warmth presses in close
seeking comfort and security
Breathless wonderment washes over me
I am transformed in the completeness of this moment
as I begin to know the staggering fierceness of a Mother's love

Susan E. White

Christmas Far From Home

Christmas comes but once a year,
When all you love are gathered near.
Your table full,except one chair,
In your dinner I will not share.
But it is my wish I could be there.

Christmas is a joyous day.
If you could hear me, I would say:
"Let the time be full of glee,
As big and bright as your Christmas tree;
Please don't be sad because of me."

On this day, don't be blue;
You should be happy through and through;
For at your table I will eat,
In my spirit, head to feet.

And so, dear sisters, brothers, Mom and Dad,
On this day you should be glad.
I'd feel worse if you were sad;
For in my mind it is my wish
That you will spend a Merry Christmas!

Bill Kjergaard

A Testimony Of God's Love

My whole life has been a testimony of God's love—
    I must witness to it.

Through a lost childhood, he sustained me.
Through a loveless marriage, he supported me.
Through tragedies of sudden death, he comforted me.
Through poverty and hunger, he nourished me.
Through sordid circumstances, he uplifted me.
Through births of three children, he blessed me.
Through an enquiring mind, he enriched me.
Through a near-fatal stroke, he made me well.

A witness? Yes, with praise and prayer

Behind each of the above, there is a story—
    that someday I must tell.

Estelle Lowe Kaczenas

"The Walk To A New Life"

The road I walked that day
I had walked many times before
I had no idea, what God had in store
I saw a woman, with a sadness, a broken heart
I felt compelled to hold her, and tell her
of a day, when Jesus would come, and
Take our pain away
God, had for us a plan,
that neither of us knew
And that was to love each other and
start our life anew.

Gary W. Huffer

He's Gone

He stepped out of my life as quickly as he entered
Too young
Too inexperienced with life
Not knowing what togetherness was all about
Start over they say
Meet another
Live again
It's easy for them to say
But still, he's gone.

Diana L. Parsons

A Little Mixed Up

Just a line to say I'm living,
That I'm not among the dead
Tho' I'm getting more forgetful
And more mixed up in my head.

For some times I can't remember,
When I stand at the foot of the stairs
If I'm going up for something,
Or if I just come down from there.

And there are times when it is dark outside
With my night cap on my head
I don't know if I'm retiring,
Or just getting out of bed.

So if it is my turn to write to you,
There is no need of getting sore
I may think I have written,
And do not want to be a bore.

Please remember I Love You, and wish that you were here
But now it is nearly mail time so I must say, "Good-bye", my dear.

As I stood by the mail box my face so very red,
Instead of mailing you my letter I opened it instead.

Edward J. Matlock

Gods of Ruined Temples

Where do the Gods of ruined temples go
Whose altars are broken,
Where no voice is heard to cry the lament save that of
    the winds which murmur low among the vines, and
        timid birds hiding from the hands of men speak a single note.
The temple light is darkened;
The temple light has died, the shattered winds cry.

Where do the Gods of ruined temples go
Waiting to remember a quiet midnight melody or distant chant,
The dark requiem of limpid waters.

Strange sea sounds swell from afar.
The souls of old men weep their plaint nightly through
    spectral colonnades, or wandering down vast
    corridors, lattice etched in purple shadow,
    whisper the lament in praise of dust.
Touched by silence, moonladen, listening for the swish
    of garments, the half-familiar words, the arching
    echoes ringing on stone.

George Bouthilet

Dreaming

To see the green grass, the flowers in bloom
the sunset and the morning dew a smile that says so very much
and a pretty face - filled with hard lines of grace
What if, I should someday get up and see none of this

To hear the cars swishing by honking horns and rushing no where
to hear the patter of rainfall
the giggles of children in the playground
to hear the sobs and hurt of a child who get left behind
What if, I should someday get up and hear none of this

To feel the prick of a rose bush
to feel the softness of a kitten or pup
to feel the heat of the sun's ray
or the cold sleet of a winter's day
The gentleness of a touch and embrace of someone I love very much
What if, I should someday get up and feel none of this

When I see none of the above
nor hear any sound nor feel any tender touches
I hope I wake up and remember I've only been dreaming of losing all
of these cause if you can not feel, nor hear, nor care to see, then,
there's nothing left - Wake me - Wake me... I'm dreaming.....

Mary R. Gibson

My Healing Begins

My healing begins when I can forgive myself for not living up to
expectations, and when I can forgive those who hurt me, no matter
how badly.

My healing begin when I can look forward and not backwards,
and when I can learn from my mistakes and not repeat them.

My healing begins when I can look in the mirror and say "I love you,
flaws and all," and mean it, and when I learn to think first of
others' feelings.

My healing begins when I can learn to appreciate others' individual
gifts and not concentrate on their weakness, and when I realize
that I am not perfect, never will be perfect, and that we all
have fallen short of God's glory.

My healing begins when I can turn weakness into strength,
and when I can find a way to make peace, not war.

My healing begins when I can give freely and love without boundaries.
My healing begins when I accept that I am healed and made whole.

My healing begins when I can truly feel the pain and suffering
endured by Christ and others, and when I can take my pain and
suffering to help and comfort others.

My healing began when I asked Christ into my life!
My healing begins with me!

Carol McBride

Tainted Badges Of The B.C. Sheriffs Services

As a youth my dream was to become a Canadian cop,
I became a deputy sheriff in 1981 in British Columbia,
Not soon afterwards, my personal choices took their toll.

I befriended a man I looked up to, a black supervisor who,
in the eyes of many white racist deputies, I became their target
I endured criminal acts, discrimination, and a muddied name
Now, 14 years later my evidence will show them great shame,
that they unwarrantably slipped evil into my file.

Men should be respected for what's in their heart,
for those reasons we should be able to tell them apart,
What I endured all these painful years,
has reminded me of the countless tears,
A good man's reputation was blacklisted from his police avocation
despite overwhelming odds he tried to win his aspiration,
the lies behind the badge are tainted by these acts.
In the absence of discipline there are insanities,
their clandestine acts of libel and cover-ups are profanities.
With a government investigation, courage and indisputable truth,
we hope to restore my name, dreams and justice with the proof.
The best years of my life were stolen by the black hearts of men.

Kerwin N. Maude, B.A.

A Little Part Of You

From the moment of conception, you watch your children grow.
You nurture and protect them, because you love them so.
It's not an occupation or a job that will be through.
Just eternity unfolding, from a little part of you.

Life's path is not so easy - they stumble and they fall.
First with tiny baby steps as they toddle down the hall.
A gentle hand behind they're back teaches them to stand.
And after that you're always there to catch them as they land.

You search your heart so many times, to teach them what is true.
The values of a lifetime, that your mother taught to you.
You watch each stage of growing, each set of life's demands.
Through right or wrong decisions a Mother understand.
Then comes the time, God grants you grace.
Your time on earth is through.
The legacy you leave behind is that little
part of you.

Linda Lemieux

What Price Freedom

The mighty Fraser River, rushing to the sea
Passing through lush valleys, pressing to be free.
Silent swirling under-tows, broad hustling bustling shores
Travelling from craggy narrows at her distant northern source.

Fishers, loggers, miners too, heard her roar; to thyself be true!
No respect for friend or foe, slip or loose grip, a perilous blow
She commands attention. She's unforgiving, cruel and mean,
In restless wait of a future fate, her true nature unforeseen.

She reached her height of anger in the flood of forty-eight.
All hell broke loose that summer, when she raced to break the gate.
Armies of reserves, in convoys, left Vancouver
With search and rescue and sandbag crews on a serious maneuver.

She seldom shows good manners and refuses discipline.
Great losses her flood causes can never be regained.
Her anger shows from time to time and wakens up our fears.
Has she planned another climb? It's been almost fifty years!

With power and determination, on her dedicated course,
A restless, shifting giant, with a strong unyielding force
Pushing tireless and anxious, boldly rushing to the sea.
The mighty Fraser River pressing to be free.

Florence Marion Tungehaug

Reflections From A Park Bench

She hobbles very carefully a parcel under arm,
Clutching cane and purse as though someone might cause her arm.
A group of boys begin to taunt and circle her for fun,
I can see the fear etched on her face as she feebly tries to run.

An old dog warily works his way, down the trampled path,
Looking left and right of him in case of an attack.
A park official spies the dog and then the chase is on,
It quickly bolts away in fear and then the both are gone.

A jogger is approaching, a whistle round her neck,
She looks a bit more confident than the others had and yet
I sense her fear and uncertainly as she quickly speeds the pace,
Once she's past I see a more relaxed look on her face.

A small boy wanders over, climbs up and starts to talk,
He flashes me a trusting smile, says he's on a walk.
We chat awhile until his mother grabs the boy away,
I hear him say "But he's my friend, please can't I stay and play?"

It saddens me that through the years the world has bread this fear,
Mistrust has spread, like a bad disease, to all that it comes near.
This bench was once the place I came to enjoy a summer's night,
Now I just sit and watch the world hurry by in needless fright.

Nancy Aultman

Forlorn Visitor

His feet were weary and his hands were old,
until the Adirondacks' Cambrian song
of trees and starry lakes hung in those long
resplendent distances from winter's cold.

When he was cheerless and deserted, bold
Mount Marcy and the Whiteface mountain's strong
appeal, convinced him that wretched was wrong
as he was part of all the Earth may hold.

Lake Champlain, faced serenely, like a smile
then seemed to smooth over his turbulent mind
where ice had made his thoughts rigid and raw.

Camping in the forests for a while
could make him feel that all nature was kind.
Even the Sarana began to thaw.

P. Mihalik

Blessings Of Life

How Great can the purpose of Life be?
When I have the wisdom and the eyes to see,
All the Glory and beauty I enjoy each day,
Such as the little things of Nature growing into Great things along my way.

When I am Blessed with the ears to hear,
And understand any danger or approaching fear.

When I have the voice to speak a loud,
My Love for God above any Faithless crowd.

What a Joy to have the sense of feel,
When my hands are busy at the wheel.

The sense to feel a kiss of love and appreciation upon my cheek,
And the feel of the warm tears that creep when times are bleak.

When I have my sense of smell so clear,
That I can know the wild honeysuckle trail is near

When I have good feet carrying and bringing me to and fro,
All is well with my God and this I know,

That You Lord for the strong hands I use to row,
The Boat at Life that takes me where I wish to go.

Beatrice Matthews Daniel

Untitled

One day as I was walking, an old man approached
He said he'd been waiting and to listen when he spoke
The face was wrinkled and his eyes were kind
He had lived a long life and all his wisdom shined
I knew what he was about to say was going to be true
And I should listen intently and then think everything through
He said, you dream of tomorrow, that's a waste of time
Today is the day to make all your dreams come true
Don't worry about what happens tomorrow
Cause tomorrow sure don't worry about you
And some of life's problems are just part of the big plan
So live life daily and just do the best that you can.
Your time here on earth is short so make it sweet
Don't take it for granted, and don't admit defeat
Have a free spirit, go dance in the rain
Who said life can't be fun, who said that life had to be sane
Go ahead, take a deep breath, and let life begin
'Cause having fun, laughing and being kind is not a sin
He said stop, look and listen and in my heart the answers I'll find
suddenly my soul softened and all my wisdom began to shine.

Deborah L. Reis

"The King Of Kings"

The King of Kings rules up above
And spotless sinners share His love,
The kingdom which he so wisely rules
sparks with Heaven's Saintly Jewels,
Lambs of God's white snowy fleece
They have found the joys of peace,
worthy servants to Him on high
rewarded richly with lasting joy,

Before each dawn the darkness lies
and Heavens stars light up the skies,
The moon that shines above our head
stays on watch while we're in bed.

When daylight breaks the shades of night,
the sun comes out and shows its light,
and as the hands of time resolve
brand new problems we must solve.

Despite how some may try and sway
let all that's Holy in us pray,
and shame the thought of foolish pride
that keeps the saviour from our side.

Gerald J. Tobin

Untitled

A conspiracy of merciless and villainous evil is amassing
in the shadows. This faction of malicious individuals is
trying to exploit the hidden and buried animosity in
everyone. They wish to employ this rage
to enslave and control the populace. Through brutality,
lies and deceit they will use humanity's bitterness and
hatred against itself. The final product will be a deranged
and perverse world of suffering.

So, you see, not much will change.
We will continue to live our lives except we will
begin fear the government,
instead of just hating them.

Christine Torrance

Subtle Cries

How I could I have known?
A thousand subtle cries flash through a mind that can't believe the
depth of your despair or the shock that your sudden leaving has
registered

Guilt cuts through uncertainty
Was I too cold? Could not hear the desperation in your voice?
Have I not the sensitivity to perceive something so tragically obvious

How could I have helped?
With one of a thousand subtle ways that flash through a mind that has
now turned to mutely question your blunt and final departure

Disappointment fills so many arms that will not have yours to hold
them and frustrated I share the burden of your course with so many
who loved you but were blind to your reality

How could you have stopped?
The thousands subtle beckoning's that led you down this thorn filled
path into the mind that had both the courage and the cowardice to
see it end

And the tears that run like angry, bitter revolutionaries through a
street dark and empty have no where to fall and be heard
there will be no understanding no question answered, only a heaviness that,
although lifted from your existence, has been shifted to other
shoulders, weak and confused
shoulders of those who could perhaps have helped but did not
recognize subtle cries

Darlene King

"Winter Wonderland"

Looking up, I see the sky washed clean from the freezing rain.
The air feels fresh and crisp, the wind has swept the dirt and dust from it.
All the trees along the way are made out of glass,
their branches hanging down like crystal chandeliers.
The fields are covered with a glittering, gleaming blanket of ice.
And the weeds and grass left from a summer past are formed into
shining ornaments.
Spanned from one telephone pole to the next are silver strings, and
even the wire fences look pretty as they sparkle brightly, studded
with diamonds.
The golden rays of the sun transformed Nature into a shining Beauty,
I am walking in a Winter Wonderland!
And as I walk, I think of you,
So far away now, but you loved it so much too!

Elsa Kirschenhofer

"The Pond"

You are so beautiful as I want to be
but, no I am not, look at me.
Your shaded banks are my shaded past.
Your center is the door at long last.
Your ripples are all my hurting in my life.
Your clam peacefulness is what I strive.
Your color so shiny and bright is like the light.
It's in my mind reminding me of him.
I'm scared now like the darkness in
your waters bottom.
When winter comes and you are cold.
Your ice is like his heart, piercing me inside.
I am afraid, I want to run and hide
your overall body reminds me of myself.
helplessly there I sit on a shelf.
You are always there on the land.
But, no one can hold your hand.

Stephanie Hager

The Old Oak Tree

Grandpa, I miss you more than words can say,
    and just right now, you seem so far away.

I see the empty bench beneath the old oak tree,
    where you used to sit and spend the afternoon with me.

I fondly remember the stories you would share
    of your childhood and youth when you hadn't a care.

Some of the things that I really miss
    are the hugs and even the occasional kiss,
    the grin and winks when grandma wasn't looking,
    to the teasing comments about her awful cooking,
    the detailed instructions on how to mow the lawn,
    and admonishments to be home long before dawn,
    the pat on my belly asking when the baby was due,
I should have known I would have never fooled you.

Thinking of these things makes me realize with a start,
    you are with me right in my heart,

So next time that I am feeling blue,
    all I really need to do,

Is think of you beneath that old oak tree,
    sitting there right beside me.

Gail A. Vavruska

Evenings By The Seaside

Did you ever feel the ocean mist
Spray upon your face,
Or see stars streak the heavens
Landing somewhere out in space.

Have you ever seen the milky way
After midnight in the sky,
Or hear the rolling waves come in
As nature shifts the tides.

Then there's blue skies filled with stars at night
And moonbeams on the sea,
While twinkling lights from ships upon
The horizon do I see.

They pass each other silently
In the shadows of the night,
Signaling a brief hello
While each ship sails out of sight.

Louise E. Fogell

Fifty-Four

When I was but a mere eighteen,
I wrote a poem about my youth.
But now I'm fifty-four,
I've seen it all. Or have I?
I could have gone to war,
But no war came to me.
At twenty-one I studied hard, and got a card
That said that I was qualified to do a job.
I did my job, and paid my dues,
I got some praise. I saw divorce.
I have a child, not yet eighteen;
She surfs the Net; it's awesome.
I heard a song done by a man
Who said he'd done it his way,
He'd seen a lot, much more than I.
He told me how it was, when he was thirty-five;
How wise I thought, when I was twenty-three.
So now I'm fifty-four;
Does anybody give a hoot,
Is anybody listening?

Ted Traill

Why?

Innocence suffers
The destruction of all hope
Why do they do this?

Annihilation
There are dead bodies galore
Why do they do this?

Guns, rockets and tanks
A soldier says a farewell
Why do they do this?

In lonely countries
The young men fought well and died
Why do they do this?

In the soldier's mind
He was seeking his courage
Why do they do this?

The loved ones missed him
But he will never return
Why do they do this?

That war is over but it will happen again
Why do they do this?

Ian Patrick Clements

Song Of Submission

If I should ever be so vain
to want only blessing, refuse to see pain
if my only hope becomes to gain
remind me that thy will be done.

And if my mind can't understand
what reason guides your mighty hand
than help me bear with your command
and help me be a stronger one.

And when I grope the empty air
in hope to find some answer there
don't let me dangle in despair
assure me that I'll see the sun.

Jeannie Tiemessen

Political Life

<u>left</u>   <u>right</u>
                                                                    Timed drum
                                                        on brokered beliefs
                                            Walked gum
                                    of lyrics lost
                        Curtained hue
                of mounted view
        Misery's dew
on mast seas
        Gentle breeze
                season of promise
                    Quiet tease
                        to still waters
                                Hopes bloom
                                        as rains subside
                                                Make room
        and   seE   tHE   LITE
                    timed   drum
of lyrics lost
        m. dhaemers

Roberta Rae

Although the distance and miles are far away
I hope our friendship hasn't gone astray
Has my postman mistakenly sent your letter away
The letter from a dear old friend - "Roberta Rae"

Oh, how will I find thee
So, sincere, beautiful and full of glee
Where will I go, who shall I see
With this postcard, I hope she'll find me
So that I may gladly say "wee"

It's been almost two months of anguish and pain
Not knowing where you may be, it's beginning to drive me insane
So, I hope this letter will not be in vain
For I shall sail the seven seas, or brave a ride on an amtrak train
Just to see you, my true friend of fame.

        Reynold Kung

From My Window

From my window...I can see the ivy, clinging to the weathered frame,
its surface blistered by the blazing suns of humid summers,
thick with the heavy scent of honeysuckle,
climbing toward thundering skies that boil and burst with summer rains,
and shimmering beads of crystal - to quench the thirst of ivy parched
    by August heat.

Now, longing for relief from rains
that beat against my windowpane,
and wail, at thoughts of pending gales
of gusty, swirling wintry winds,
aging the blooming ivy to a brittle, scraping frailness,

As it clings to hold its own against the ever changing seasons
of the world
I can see...from my window.

        Joyce A. Outzen

Love

Love is not a quantity, nor a tangible amount
It's not a thing that one can see, nor that one can count
It's never, ever measured, It's felt within one's heart
Its strength and size can vary, you'll know it from the start
It deepens as it ages, and warms us when we're cold
Its value lies within, it can't be bought or sold
A gift that can be given, or accepted with one's trust
To be cherished by another, only when it's right and just

        Lewis S. Dunkel

Till The End

I sit and think of who you are
What our friendship stands for
Reflecting on moments good and bad
Times when we were happy, depressed, sad

We listen to each other as we torture ourselves and rack our brain
How special it is that we understand the other's pain
To know, feel and help each other mend
This we have in common and why you are a very dear friend

At this time, I wish to thank you
For helping me to grow and look at life anew
For friendship, love, care and advice
You offered all this and more without thinking twice

Nearing the end of this work, do not frown
I pray and know in my heart deep down
That wherever our lives, fate may send
We'll be there for each other till the end

        Douglas Stromer

Arkansas Summer

Magnolias, mint juleps, Southern Belles
Good ole boys in white hats and string ties
Azaleas — white, pink, blazing reds
Adorning stately white washed mansions —
Fried chicken, catfish, hush puppies
Onions, corn-on-the cob, barbecues —
Gallons of ice tea, buckets of homemade ice cream

Half naked boys swinging on vines
Over the ole water hole
Revelling in the coldness of springs
Shouting with youthful vigor —
Girls sunning in swim suits
Baking and turning under ole Sun
A baby eating her first ice cream cone
Mothers hanging out the "wash"
And Fathers working on ole jalopies
Little boys playing cars in the dirt
Lovers hugging, kissing under moon's glow

These are the sights, sounds, smells
And tastes of summer down home.

        Joyce Rossi

My Mind

Looking out across my shadowed mind
Wondering about my undeniable angel
Where I am cannot change, my mind
I'm on the inside, stuck in the clutter
All these lost thoughts, working my brain
On the threshold of an answer, close to victory
But then now, as the last time something else
Something new to plague my soul, what now
For this insecurity, concentration is always lost
Bothered by these mere insignificances, so pointlessly
Every day and all day long my mind ponders
The possible explanations, but where I stand
It's always too simple to accept a reality
For my never ending dreams, nevertheless
I find rejection in my understanding, I often
Think if I was on the outside looking in at
My discontent posture, I could easily sort
Out every ill humor and thought, my mind
I could discover what was wrong and what was right,
But as I know, where I am cannot change, my mind

        Joshua Ansline

"Forbidden"

Thou are like forbidden fruit to me.
Is it wrong for me to want thee?
A burden on my heart too heavy to hold.
Only I know the desires and secrets untold.
No one knows the despairing torment that binds me.
My soul just aching to be free.
How can I love one, yet have feelings for another?
Thoughts of you curiously wondering, what would you be like
as a lover?
I've only known but one man in my life, and as fate would
have it he's made me his wife.
My conscience has been bothering me since I first looked
into your eyes; and my heart tells me to forget about you
which I know has to be wise.
You are a temptation, a test for me; a test of my love and fidelity.
I pray that this is a phase that I am going through.
If it isn't, I don't know what I'm going to do.
Why is this guilt so persistent and strong?
When I know in my heart I've done nothing wrong.
Forbidden.

Tanya C. Weber

Room Revisited

Cool and big, the white walls stretch before me
Where I was long ago, but still linger,
As if each breath I take is a memory wafting by.

And the floor echoes with my determination,
Seats remaining with the tell-tale marks of my past.
And this corner contains a mystery:
A place where pink on pink stood out
And a dark boy sat pondering the same thoughts as I do now.

How could it be so simple, when before it was crushing?
Blows that penetrated my heart, wounds that never healed.
But this battlefield is surreal and washed over, newly painted room.
Like a grassy knoll that drank the blood of hundreds,
Fertilizer, clean and perfect, like spring on December 1st.

What a dressing does for a room revisited.

Karen E. Lippold

Untitled

I am the voice of the island. I speak to you moment by moment each day.
You will hear me in the guttural bark of a seal, in the scream of an eagle,
in the spine-tingling bugling of a majestic bull elk. At other times my
voice can be heard in the constant scree and gabbe of myriad gulls.
At first daybreak I beckon you in the pleasant melodies of songbirds.
I even talk to you in the grating and unending caw of the crow.

Walk leisurely beside any of the numerous natural streams that
surround you. What you will hear in the noisy flow of the
crystal-clear water is my voice. I am everywhere...

You can hear me in the soft, soothing slap of gentle waves washing a sandy
beach; again you will hear me in the thunderous roar of storm-tossed water
pounding powerfully and relentlessly against a rocky headland.

I speak to you as well in the total silence of a midnight hour under the
magnificent, star-studded sky. Shhh, listen - yes...you can hear me even now!!!

It is my voice that you hear in the plaintive, bittersweet call of a loon;
in the far-distant "follow me" trumpet call of travelling Canada Geese.

When you are aware of the soft, yet persistent patter of raindrops on a roof,
you are actually listening to another of my efforts to attract your attention.

I am always urging you to slow down, to release yourself from human
pressures and to learn of me. I am the voice of the voice of the
island, the wisdom of Nature, the guidance of God!!! I have been
since the beginning, I shall be unto the end. I am here. Learn to
listen for me. Your life will be enhanced by so doing....

Allan Boyd

Love You Hon

The love we have for you.
Will be in our hearts forever
It has been four years that God,
Took you in his loving arms.

We miss you and await.
The time we will be together again.
Memories of you forever touch our lives.
And send whispers of unforgotten love.

Some people come into our lives and quickly go.
While others stay for awhile.
And leave footprints on our hearts.

And we are never again the same.
You have a place in my heart.
That not one can fill.
I love you. I miss you. I always wilt.

Thinking of you on this day.
And in our minds you will stay.
Happy Birthday dear friend.
Today, tomorrow and always.

Evelyn Tallman

Draw The Line

Life is like a journey, as we follow our own dreams
    struggling and surviving, we all know what it means.
As we start out as a child and grow into an adult
    all the things that happen, it's really no one's fault.
It's living and it's learning from all mistakes we make
    we try to do it better and do the best it takes.
The loved ones in our lives who help us all the time
    should stop, look and listen and really draw that line.
As we care for our own children and our parents job is done
    in times of troubled moments, is when we join as one.
It's time now that we grew up and did this on our own,
    but the greatest thing to remember is that you'll never be alone.
You'll always have your family through good times and bad,
    sometimes being happy and even being sad.
We pull through all the heartaches as we suffer with the pain.
    constantly reminded there's always a lot to gain.
So as each day that passes and facing a new way,
    you're the best person possible as you sit alone and pray.
And yes it may be a long road and may even take some time,
    the only one to change it, is you and your own mind.

Christine Charlton

Golden Wings

We're on this earth for a reason,
To love, to learn, and to teach.
With visions of a better place,
We have dreams and goals to reach.

When someone comes into your life
And brings you all these things,
Then you have met a special friend
Their gift is of golden wings.

They bring with them encouragement,
Understanding, compassion and more.
The lessons they will teach you,
Is their wisdom to help you soar.

If you could give them something,
A token to remember and keep.
Then give them the freedom they've offered.
To fly, be free and just be.

Your purpose has brought you together,
And distance won't keep you apart.
Your souls have touched for a reason.
You are sisters of the heart.

Roberta Venedam

The Girl On A Swing

There once was a little girl on a swing,
who soared through the air like a bird on the wing.
Up on a hill with an oak for a friend,
swinging with glee o'er a meadow without end.
Long blonde hair flowing, she dared touch the sky,
flying higher and higher, ne'er to ask why.
Her giggles and laughter filled the pure country air,
her joy was unbounded, she hadn't a care.
Hers was a spirit you just couldn't tame,
"My swing's the highest!" she oft would exclaim.

Swinging through life, with its ups and its downs,
she became a young woman with life that abounds.
And when my life's path, she passed one day,
"Come fly with me," I'd hoped she would say.
For if laughter and joy were what she's about,
I knew I'd be happier, without any doubt.
Then my life changed, and my hope turned to glee
for with these incredible words, she beckoned to me:
"I'll lift you to heights, you've never dreamt of,
for my swing's the highest, come join me, my love."

John E. Montesano

Summer You're Growing Old

Now you summer must grow old, for the autumn
winds are blowing cold. Summer you're growing old.
How many secrets do you hold, now your leaves
have turned to gold, summer you're growing old.
Soon these winds will break your hold, and your
vanish into season fold, summer you're growing old.
Many stories will be told, about your warming
centerfold, oh summer don't grow old, oh let
me find your pot of gold, which in your fragrance
do you hold, oh summer you're growing old.
I can feel your hands their so cold, oh
summer you've grown so old, but to your hands
I will hold, while these autumn winds blow
us cold, I will remember our days of gold,
which in my heart will never grow cold,
oh my summer summer old, always gold.

Kingsley Hill

Spending The Rest Of My Life With You

The good Lord must have sent you to me at a distant but yet so near.
Looking in your eyes so bright and clear, they were telling me
something I really needed to hear.

As you approached the bar and returned to your seat, I said to myself
that's the guy I really want to meet. That one night made a
change in my life and the way I felt it had to be from Jesus Christ.

The voice so soft, smile so wide, touch so gentle as I stood at your
side. Asking me to dance was a honor you see, then I knew this
man was really meant for me.

The hours days and even months went by and all I could say was my,
my, my. We shared our sweet times, up and downs, our sickness and
our death do you part and you knew that you had won my heart.

Then one day you left me alone, I started to give up but I was
strong, to my father I turned with all my pain and do you know
nothing was ever the same. He said daughter if its the man you want,
pick up the telephone, open your door for your man to come in,
that's the only way you can really be happy again.

Juanita Pennington

Tricia

Your voice is lovely music as you whisper my name,
A wife so special is far better than fortune or fame,
Your scent draws me close as you walk by my side,
Being lovers and best friends we have nothing to hide.

I look deeply in your eyes in the soft moonlight,
Your warm my body and soul as you hold me tight.
Your lips are soft as velvet as they part to meet mine,
I savor your sweetness and the taste of red wine.

Your touch is light as a feather in the breeze,
Your warm breath tickles my neck with a tease,
My hands run through your golden blonde hair,
I never dreamed I'd be with a woman so fair.

Andrew R. Rowan

The Garden

I wanted to possess your soul
I led your mind astray
I saw the passion slowly die in me
While you were father away
I walked out to the garden
Within its possible beauty I prayed
Of the day I could free you from the dream
Along with the fantasy that I made
You came with me then to the garden
Your tears watered the flowers
They bloomed brighter than ever
Its radiant loveliness gave us power
I caused that tear to fall
Or was it the rain in your eyes
I'll kiss your breath away
To wipe your tears forever dry.

Robin McGauley

Chemistry

Chemistry.
Dissolving into a positive solution.
Body and intellect performing in harmony.
Neutralizing temporal confinements.
Crystal clarity of sight, sound, and feeling
Revealed.
Odorless, tasteless and colorless.
The camel galloping through the needle's eye —
Mystifying the Learned,
Edifying the Interned.

Ursula Buehler

The Depression

Long lines and sunken faces
is evident on every hand,
with traces of little hope
throughout the width and breath of the land.

Threadbare, kitchens bare, privies there,
obligations and only despair
and everything else we see
seems in need of repair.
The skinny, the beggar, the cup
may be a fleeting thing we see,
but the God of Ages hence,
holds the secret of what they longed to be.

We look to faith and hope,
as a hand is put to the plow,
and cleave to those that love
and pray that things will improve somehow,
why? Oh why does it take so long
For man to begin to comprehend,
That God does not forsake those
Who pin their faith and hope of Him?

Emory M. Brooks

Dad

I rarely tell my terrific dad, how much He means to me,
Yet every time I need some help, it's Him that I go see.
There never was a wiser man, today or times gone past,
That could measure up in knowledge or size, to the shadow that He cast.
He stood proud and tall for years, and would never hang his head,
No matter what hard blows were dealt, or what other people said.
He been an inspiration, to everyone He knows,
Because He's felt the hardest blows, and yet He goes and goes
He's never been a quitter, He never will concede,
To the awful pain He suffers, none of us could ever believe.
So as I finish writing, and tell Him "I Love You!"
This man, my dad, lives on in me, in everything I do!!!

Janita Hofen

A Salute To Minnie Pearl

With your great sense of humor,
We loved you for that,
Especially when you wore,
Your one dollar and ninety eight cent hat.

When you said, "Howdee,"
We answered back in kind,
Because that word Howdee and you,
Stayed always in our minds.

When you knock on St. Peter's door,
And he inquires, whose there?
You reply and say, Minnie Pearl,
With her homespun stories so rare.

Yes, we loved you Minnie Pearl,
Through all these wonderful years,
There will be great sorrow at your passing,
And I know quite a few tears.

But your going home to glory,
In a far better place then here,
You'll have God's hand to lead you,
And never more have anything to fear.

Edith Craley

The Shakespeare Rose

Beside the Avon River in an English garden grows,
A flower which has been the liege of poetry and prose,
Its fragrance fills the morning mist with a scent so sweet and fair,
This rose, so perfect in its form, is quiet beyond compare.

Like a play upon an open stage, it has the starring role,
The florets gyre with every breeze to give its body soul,
The twigs and branches intertwine much like a sonnet's rhyme,
As they go through all the motions of a clever pantomime.

Its crimson nuance stands apart from petals of its peers,
The dew which clings to verdant leaves drips down like sterling tears
And when it slowly ages, blossoms turn from red to plum,
A variegated gift from those whom it descended from.

Like words upon a scripted page which have a purpose to be served,
With compact inflorescence it transcends the spoken word,
As if immortalized in thought, upon the rosettes lay,
The blessings of a namesake who has long since passed away.

And if the bard is watching from his playhouse in the sky,
A smile has surely found his lips, and make the angels sigh,
Though known by any other name its sweetened smell still grows,
But only one, this work of art, can be the Shakespeare rose.

Gregory A. Smith

"Dreams"

The beauty of love shines in your eyes
As the sunrise is paled by your face.
Your heart piercing smile has entered my dreams
Gently seizing a permanent place.

The heavens could erupt and stars could fall
And the earth would survive the act.
But a heart once pierced by the essence of you
Will never survive in tact.

So join me forever within my dreams
Banish guilt to another land.
Our world is filled with fantasy
Reality was destroyed by man.

And as our dreams transports our minds
To a safe and heavenly state.
Our soul are joined in thoughts we share
Within the bitter sweet clutches of fate.

Gary Ramsey

"The Nectar Of Mortals"

This beverage is known by many a name,
And cherished by some to a great extent.
Few achieve notoriety and fame,
Yet all share the same process of ferment.
Some are very smooth, while others are stout,
So you can't judge the swill by the label.
To Yanks it's a round, to Aussies a shout,
When mugs and pitchers cover the table.
Be they bottles or cans, barrels or kegs,
That cold, amber liquid refreshes you.
The last in line for the tap gets the dregs.
There's nothing better than a sip of brew.
A tribute, with the words I've written here,
To the nectar of mortals we call beer.

Yudi Wong

My Morning Prayer

When I awake in the morn
I take the sleep from my eyes
Go to my window
And look outside
At puppy white clouds
And the sky of blue
Also a wonderful fresh morning dew
The sounds of the leaves as they play in the trees
All the birds and the deer.
I see all around me, the things I hold so near.
But never have I really gave thanks
To the master above
For the privilege of having His precious love.
So thanks I give to thee,
My loving master above!
Amen.

Heather Vince

My Soul

Everyone should have a goal.
Mine is to keep my soul whole.
Being that I can read, write, and think,
Then form the responsibility for my soul, I should not shrink.
It is the value I place upon myself,
Whether my soul be with God, or on the devils shelf.
I am the commandant of my ship, the task master of my soul.
The Lord is my compass and will steer me past the devils shoal.
My soul should rest assured with the Lord aboard ship,
That my life will not be for naught as I make
This earthly trip.

Joseph W. Chadwick

The New Belfast

October 20, 1994

Is éire me,
The land of hibernia in two.
A common people with conflicting views.
They do not see the unity.

For centuries grudges held,
Deceived by a land opposite the Irish sea,
Gladly setting brother on another.
They were unable to see the unity.

Still, all is Sunday school to the "troubles"
For six and twenty years bloodshed of my peoples.
All for allegiance to Rome or lack of it.
They refuse to see the unity.

Now the streets are silenced,
Arms traded for slow sensitive negotiations.
I pray for mo paistí in a neutral church
That they will finally agree to unity.

Inné tá sé fuar eagcurbáistí.
Tomorrow will foggy.

Joseph James Fitzgerald

This Deep

In this deep
My heart.... My Death
A dragon lies within my soul
N' the Angel's touch ignites the flame
The passion burns deep
  Forever brandin' my heart
Deep... hidden pain
The Angel flies to heaven
  Asking forgiveness for her sins
In this deep... So cold.... So gray
May I grow wings
Will I ever know my angel's love again
My heart... My death
A dragon lies within my soul
My heart... My death
The Angel rose to heaven's hold
In heart... The death
I wish for angel's love
But I'm in this deep
  Where the dragon lies within a gray soul!

Matthew Paul Emerson

Victims

You took most of my friends
And now you want to take me
Tell me why I have to be a victim of the street
The rules you live by encompass no mercy
Each day you survive you count as a burden
Why do you take your anger out on me?
Why do I have to be a victim of the street?
You think you're mistreated
Or misunderstood
It would take just a minute
For them to respect you for good
How can you expect to be treated how you like
When you hurt and kill
People all your life
And now you've reached me
I'm the end of the line
Will you stop taking lives if I let you take mine?
Will it then be just me
The last victim of the street?

Susan Edmunds

The Kiss Of Nirvana

Life is a strange adventure,
A little joy, sorrow galore,
I get what I have to endure
And what I should be thankful for.

My mind produces many thoughts,
They take wings and fly,
Until they are permeated
With the spirit of the very high.

How much wider is my sight
On present, past and future hence,
Generations are coming, going,
A spectacle that never ends.

Nothing is stable, yet all remains the same,
All is diffused, yet the universe is one,
The creature is mortal, the creation eternal,
The show continues on and on.

Nirvana kissed me in my forehead,
I am not afraid at all,
I am doing what I will must do here,
I am ready for its call.

George G. Strem

A Spring Walk

The early morning dew sparkles like your smile,
As we walk arm in arm for awhile.
The sun's rays warm my hidden heart.
And thoughts of you can't help but start.
Birds fly by like time with you.
When we're apart the sky is deep blue.
Calm breezes wash over us
As a bird with chicks makes a fuss.
Each flower is a happy thought;
Each blade of grass a battle fought.
The winning is an April shower,
Giving us more growing power.
Like a caterpillar we grow wings;
And smile as the Angels sing.
We're going to make it - you and I.
Our hopes and dreams - we'll reach the sky!

Leila DesLauriers

Pulse Of Love

When all is quiet, your presence speaks louder
Than the booming thunder of a summer storm.
The love we feel crackles, pierces my soul
Like the lightening bolt that spears the clouds
After the thunder subsides.
You overwhelm my thoughts, tighten your grasp
On my heart with each passing minute of every day.
I beat in time with the rhythm of your heart...
Even when we are apart, I feel the pulse of your love,
As surely as blood courses through our veins.
We mesh, entwining our lives, until we flow smoothly as one,
Like the easy current of a river.
Your warmth permeates every pore of my being...
Like the grains of sand on a beach that absorb the sizzling touch of
the sun; sometimes I fear my heart will melt with the heat of our
Growing, never-ending passion.
I want you forever a part of my days on earth,
And even beyond this life...
Eternity will find us wrapped in each other's love;
One heart, one mind, one soul.

Karen Davies Laughlin

I'm So Lucky To Have Someone Like You!

You give me life that I live today
Always understanding the things I say

Never too busy to have a special talk
Love from you to me is always in stock

You've helped me through my times of tears
And cared so much all these years

We share so much and have a special bond
When I said I love you, you were there to respond

You do so much in every way
From ordinary jobs to the things you say

You've taught me the qualities of life and all right things
How I've learned so much from you

I love you so much you don't even know
That love will continue and always grow

A thousand thanks you's for all you've done.
I want you to know you're so special to me.

You and your love hold a special place in my heart
Always will and have from the very start.

Jessica Lemmon

Sometimes

Sometimes I pause to watch
The world around me I desire to touch.
The burning sun... The gleaming moon...
The silent stars that fade too soon.

Sometimes as I glance around
to find myself uncertainty-bound.
who I am, what they say I should be,
Longing...yearning to just be me.

Sometimes I wake to my dismay
to taste a fear for the coming day,
Like a butterfly with her limited age
I must find my place before I fade.

Sometimes as I dance I hear
Beyond the music a newborn's tear
who longs to be held, yearns for a touch,
wanting his Mom to care so much.

Sometimes I sit and wonder whether
I am all these things rolled together;
A burning, deaf, weeping heart,
Innocent, lonely, torn apart.

Laura Ebersole

"An Angel Came"

To each of us he gave so much,
his brightest smile, his kindest touch...

His generous heart, his gracious way,
the helping hand, he gave each day...

To all of us who loved him so,
I write these words, so we will know...

That through the dark, there came a light,
"An Angel Came" to him that night...

She held him tight and wiped his tears,
she took away his greatest fears...

Now, when it comes my turn to see,
He'll send an angel back for me...

Lynne Marie Chase

She-Devil!

Wooing her I did try
I felt my heart die.

I saw her in the altogether
She seemed to prefer I did anything with her
However I could not touch her.

We fraternized well
She urged me to leave before the gospel.

She was a Mystery
With her Sugar Daddy
Naughty!

From dusk till dawn
She used to call me a clown.

The lady-like Grim Reaper
Stepped in with her
My dear Lady Ginger.

Together they cut me down
My remains lying all around.

Hugo Hambursin

Magic Mirror

If I were a magic mirror, for a while, hanging on your wall.
I would get to see your smile, I wouldn't mind at all.
When you look at me to fix your hair, I would get to simply stare.
Into your eyes, and at your face, every time you passed that place.
Where I hung so patiently, waiting for you to smile at me.
I'd wait for you to come home, and stare when you were on the phone.
I'd wait for you to glance in my direction, so I could capture your reflection.
Remember, I would have magic power so your image I would keep forever.
I'd recall your image on the other side, the reflected room where I'd hide.
Then we could be together for a while, me , and your image, with a smile.
I don't think that it would be so great, if you didn't come home or
were very late.

If that happened, I swear, it's true,
I'd become a human and wait for you.

Michael Hamel-Smith

Morning

Feeling the morning smell marks
the beginning of new day.
The cold air bites and wakes me up
when I open the door.
Everything is fresh
with the special power of morning.

Walking to the office at eight o'clock
is my time to bask in morning.
As I walk on the grass
which is heavy with morning dew,
The green smell expands around me
with each step.

My hair absorbs the morning air
by the time to get the office
And I feel the morning
while I am working.

Morning always fades out before I'm aware,
then another day passes again.

Mihoko Ueda

Precious Moments

Children have a way of taking each and everyday,
they turn it into something special, when all they do is play.

Some children can take a simple swim,
and turn their legs into magic fins.
While others can climb an Apple Tree
and find a Treasure with a key.

One thing that children have in
common is they're pure and simple
hearts. If only we could all grow up
and keep that special part.

Sometimes Children need some help to get them
out of trouble, that's what Mom and Dad are for,
'cause they love and help you double.

Who's the one that can sense the carefree hands
of a child? Cause, even when his tail is pulled
he loves them all the while.

Children, come and gather close, and listen
to what I say, "don't ever let growing-up,
take your Childhood Dreams away."

Gail Nadasi

"Memories Of Boxcars and Baggage"

"Boxcars and baggage," she smiled at the thought
As we heard the whistle of a faraway train.
"What happy times I recall for such a poor family of six."

"See my Dad worked the railroad so our tickets were free,
But we rode that train just as proud as if we had paid full fare."

Closing her eyes, she recalled the familiar sounds and smells—
The chug, chug of a hot coal engine, freshly polished seats,
And the smell of honeysuckle growing thickly along the tracks.

"Four little girls squeezed into one row,
Each wanting the window seat
As the conductor bellowed, "All a - b - o - a - r - d!"
Oh, 'twas a jolly time back then."

"No matter if the ride was hot and soot covered our clothes.
We shared our meager lunch, then huddled together for a nap
Awaking just as the sun set and fireflies sneaked through the
still open windows."

"Yes, those were the good old days," she sighed as her eyes closed
And the nod of her head told me once again she had drifted off to sleep
Leaving me with another treasured gift —
Her memories of boxcars and baggage.

Susan L. Saylor

Comrades

Trench warfare.
A lull.

Screams radiate the darkness,
Like an electrical storm.
My tongue, veteran sergeant, surveys its losses,
Gingerly;
A melancholy tally of empty, pink, fleshy foxholes;
First, upper palate, dabbing;
One... now two... there, another, three;
Next, lower palate, poking, probing;
One... thank God, only one.
Then tending the wounded, throbbing, hot, swollen,
Nursing with soothing salve,
Twisting in gentle embrace,
Faltering,
Wanting to do more, but tasting irreparable death,
Recoiling,
Banging into one of those painless, stoic, polished replace-
ments.
Finally, extolling the precious living,
Then quickly behind the lines.

Paul Rama

The Bus Driver

She stands tall
Over everything and all.
The leader, the ruler,
The master of the big, yellow bus.

They taunt and torment her,
driving her nuts
On the floor leaving gum, garbage,
and some cigarette butts.

No matter how hard they try,
She comes out strong.
No matter what they say,
She's never wrong.
They attempt to see how far she can bend.
She always wins the fight in the end.

She chuckles at each attempt they try
to twist her and drive her mad,
But strikes them down with each
fast and intelligent command.

In the end they are beat by her.
O Hail Almighty Bus Driver!

Susan Moore

To My Only Valentine A Passage From The Heart

As I walked across the moonlit sand.
And gazed toward the ocean's tide
An image of beauty took my hand
Her warmth felt closely by my side.

We strolled along the waters edge
And stared into each others eyes
Like two roses on a window ledge
I knew our love was no discize.

I stopped and whispered into her ear.
The love I'm feeling cannot escape
Put your arms around me hold me near
Tonight is our night I shall not wait.

I love you more than you will ever know.
My heart grows fonder each day in time.
And this to you I will forever show
So tonight my love be my Valentine.

John C. Bunn

Not Yet

Pulling into the driveway,
our trip finally ended,
stretch our legs, limping up the walk
we happily greet Mom.

I look up to the doorway,
shadow of a man, older, wizened,
closer, reveals, more than wanted,
hair almost gone, wrinkles too many.

We hug and talk, share our stories
play music, laugh, and lunch together.
His mind is sharp, and clear as ever
belies the image set before us

We talk of the past, present and future
knowing our thoughts, he speaks openly,
we listen to hear something, anything,
we may have missed

Reluctantly we have to leave
his grip is firm, kisses sweet,
I pray for him, them, us
for time remaining.

Wendy Seberras

Does Friendship Lead To Happiness Or
Does Happiness Lead To Friendship

In my opinion friendship leads to happiness
Just what is friendship?
Friendship is when one can bring happiness into one's life.
Friendship begins to develop when two individuals have trust,
honesty, and compassion.
They begin to share and care about one another, and communicate
honestly with one another.
When in time yourown and blue, a friend knows exactly what to do.
She'll call you on the phone and say:
"Hey, let's go out today."
She'll say, "It's not too much trouble. I have time indeed. I am
right here in the time of need."
She has no trouble using clout. "Let's hurry and get out and about!"
A friend is there at your door. What more could you ask for? If you
have a sadness, a burial or such.
A friend is there to touch... touch.
A friendship is to value.
It's and everlasting treasure, for sure.
Friends are always here to endure,
and bring happiness with have and much, much, more.

Marlene Woodring

Reflections Of A Mother

What is the meaning of life I often query,
On those long lonely days
That go on endlessly,
With habits, rituals, and routines
That never vary.

But there in my children I find the answer.
In their baby blue eyes,
I see innocence and purity.
In their minds I find wonder,
Of the world that surrounds them.
In their hearts I find love,
A love that's unforsaken.

I dream of their future.
I wish for them happiness.
I've known not a love so deep.
Until I had children to cherish.

I live for my children,
To protect, nurture, and guide,
For a mother is my meaning,
Until the day that I die.

Debbie Sewell

For You

Though the days seem to shorten, the
    years blur from day to night
There remains one constant, so
    steadily guiding my life
It is there in the form of your comforting voice,
    the softness of your touch
It comes in the joy and laughter we share,
    the memories that mean so much
It grows and binds never ending,
    no matter the season, the hour, the day
It is together that we are one,
    forever to be that way.

Kevin Donohue

Why The Sky Is Purple

One star hovers over the horizon,
Coal black sky,
Heat rises, black becomes navy.
Navy evaporates into dark blue,
Becoming a baby boy's room.
The water color source glides,
Across the canvass.
White and gray drifts by unfinished,
As the brush drops from the painting.

Blue becomes blushing red. Layers,
Forming streaks,
Across the chapel ceiling.
Orange falling into red falling,
Into blue. Makes a purple center.
White turns into lavender,
Then drifts on by. Royal blue ink leaks,
Over the picture,
While one white dark pokes through.

Gregor Southard

A Brand New Beginning

The wonders of the world no longer mean much to me
Abuse, violence, pain is all I can see
It threatens my being, my soul, and my mind
Sends ice tingling chills up my spine
My eyes, they are weary - they look very old
I try very hard to be strong, to be bold
Tears well up and roll down my face
As I realize how much I hate this place
Sometimes as I lie awake in bed
I have feelings of hope enter my head
Abuse violence pain can come to an end
If we pull together to start a new trend
Giving life a new meaning
A brand new beginning

Hope Lawrence

Everlasting Father

Rising from Spirit's Infinity
To stand in His Holy Mountain

He opens His Eyes and universes are
He closes His Eyes and universes end

Sketching with universes, Painting with galaxies
With all of Life and Motion from His Heart and Breath

And yet He builds with grains of sand
And flutters with the hummingbird's wing
And laughs with a baby's smile
And sees a mother's toil

And before all this
He saw and chose His children
For His Own through all time

And there, there at the place
    where they said there is no God
There, There, You will be called Sons of the Living God

Alpha and Omega, Mighty Power
King of Kings, Lord of Lords
Everlasting Father
Forever!!

L. E. Cooper

When I Think Of You

When I think of you,
my heart has wings.
It soars to high places,
and explores new things.
Flying into the clouds, spirit and soul,
to find your love, pure and whole.
When I think of you,
my feelings run deep.
My mind races, and my body leaps.
Your being seems to carry me,
higher and higher.
Making my body burn with your fire.
When I think of your passion,
your touch, your kiss,
my heart cries out for it's you that I miss.
I need you so badly, every night and day,
endless...
will my love to you pay.
When I think of you, my spirit rejoices,
feeling the colors of all heavens voices.

Diana Robinson

"Essence Questing Notoriety"

Just this once, I won't summon my heavenly Muse.
For I know what I have to say, and exactly which words to use.
What utter joy it brings to read the language of a heart.
This language which sets the true and the false so far apart.
In the beginning, devoted passion pushed the ink-tipped feather;
Lilting artists so inspired by the leaves of a tree and the marvels of weather.
Today there is passion, but not quite the same.
Keys are so often pressed by the desire to build a name.
But although I'd like to think it, perhaps I truly am not alone.
For why then would I write this, if I didn't wish to be known?

Frank R. McGill

Tiny Foot Prints

Tiny footprints in the snow
Where are they going? I do not know.
"I wonder" what can it be that makes
these footprints, go around the tree,
Around and around the tree they go,
What they are looking for, I want to know.
Aha, I see them I'm lost for words.
For I know these footprints are made
by birds. They search and search for something
to eat. Until a kind friend, gives them
a treat. The birds have made a path in
the snow, "believe me" it was quiet a show.
Their tummies are full now and then
fly away. Only to return another day.

Eileen A. Ethier

"A Purpose"

With a blast of His nostrils, our lives were sprung
Our breath set in motion, our lives begun
A driving force ever changing....progressing onward until...
   progressing downward
Touching others' lives as we journey through this way
Just as the glory and splendor of spring, we quickly fade away
What is our life? but a vapor or a spray?
A sweet, sweet aroma that vanishes away
So Touch, Birth, Inspire, and Create!
Breath life into another before it's too late
And happy you will your Creator make.

Erica Rocker

A Beautiful Place To Me....

A beautiful place to me consists of me and a lovely wife,
Someone who I would have and hold and cherish the rest of my life.
A beautiful place to me would have a sun a moon and some stars,
Therefore it will have a day and a night and, no, it isn't Mars.
A beautiful place to me will have music and music galore.
Of course I'll need a CD player one that plays a hundred and four.
A beautiful place to me would have the park up Saint Louis Heights,
A place where I can study and learn while sitting and seeing the sights.
A beautiful place to me, what I deserve I will get.
This place is truly a beautiful place there is no worries and no regrets.
A beautiful place to me there is no money, everything's free.
Every single person is honest and trustworthy.
A beautiful place to me will have to have a place to feast.
I think this place is imaginary because I saw it on Beauty and the Beast.
I don't know if such a place exists, I'll have to wait and see.
But for now let's work and study hard because knowledge is the key.

Garrett Jaimes

Our Yard Fountain

We have a fountain in our yard,
Rebecca is her name.
If she were to run away,
It would be an awful shame.

She stands among the plants and flowers,
'Tis such a pretty site.
We can watch her for hours and hours,
And well into the night.

The moon above so big and bright,
Shines down on her smiling face.
It even makes the water sparkle,
As it flows from her lovely vase.

The sound of the water splashing,
Is music to our ears.
Our yard is a bit of heaven,
As it's been for years and years.

William R. Gillam Sr.

The Years Were Gray

Turbulence was the order of the day;
The sun always seemed to be hidden away.

Each day became a challenge to live through.
Instinct kept me asking, "Lord, what shall I do?"

"Fear not, I am with you," was the message brung,
But the clouds refused sunshine and heaviness hung.

Only briefly were glimpses of a fresh, new start.
And I grasped them and treasured them close to my heart.

The answers came slowly and were savored and remembered.
Their impact was strong and had to be tempered.

Only scarred hearts can heal and help our brothers,
That are struggling from bondage to themselves or others.

Christ offers forgiveness and a clean heart for believing;
A new look at yourself and a life with some meaning.

It's free to all, just for the asking...
The greatest gift of all - Life everlasting!

Ruth D. Kline

May The Puddle Hide Me

We allowed the chicken to cross the river
leaving the crocodile far, far behind
to the annoyance of mankind.
May the puddle hide me till another season to nourish.

We allowed the stranger to cross the river
leaving the crocodile far, far behind
to the annoyance of mankind.
May the Puddle hide me till another reason to nourish.

The stranger came back and claimed the river
and named her Victoria, but Victoria fell.
And still Victoria falls to nourish the path.

The path or the river, which is the elder?
The path crossed the river
and the river nourished the path.
And so I'll come back,
I'll come back to continue this service.
I'll come back to continue this love.
May the puddle hide me till another season to nourish.

T. Ebow Ansah

Together We Can

Why are we so blind to see, that I'm not better than you, and
you aren't better than me.
Discrimination has been around way to long, and if this hatred
continues, it will be twice as strong.
Whether it be a white, black, red, or yellow face, no color,
culture, religion, or appearance will ever win the race, to reign
above all the rest.
Stop being belligerent, and don't be ignorant, learn more about
yourself, and others, after all we are all sisters, and brothers.
Learn and understand more about different cultures, faiths,
and races, and you will see no more hate on any color faces.
If you take the time to think about how you feel, you will soon
realize that the bad things you thought were there are not there at all.
If we take these steps together, we can make the world a whole
lot better.
And maybe in the end we can all be friends.

Delia Smutny

Expression

I cannot express how much I love you.
Though everyday I let you know,
I don't feel as though it's enough!
I wish you could reach into my heart,
So you'd be able to feel it too.
This feeling grows stronger and stronger
Each day.
When I look into your eyes,
I know you feel the same.
But do you also feel the magic? The sparks?
Your eyes are filled with much happiness,
I can only hope that you're always this happy.
There will be tough times ahead,
And neither one of us will want to give in.
But if we both just stop for a few seconds,
And realize that our love is stronger than our dispute,
We can back down together.
Each day is a stepping stone,
And I want to take each new step with you.
I just want you to know how much I love you!!

Gina Poetsch

My Life

Grew up with drugs and guns and gangs,
People were hard core.
Never got mixed with drugs or guns,
Cause I was just too poor.

People asked me left and right,
"You wanna take a hit?"
So I figured what the hell,
And tried a little bit.

Was taking pills and drinking,
And smoking off some weed.
That was all that I could want,
All I could have, it was everything I'd need.

Got taken to the hospital,
Everyone was examining me.
Who'd of thought that I would die
Because I just O.Ded?

Now I'm dead, my life is gone,
I'll never breathe again.
My life story I o.deed
At the age of 10.

Karin McLaughlin

I'm Sleepless 'Cause Of You

Under the covers, I turn left to right,
    this one thing I need, somehow I fight;
I close my eyes, surely I'm hoping,
    the sleep that I need, yet my eyes reopen.

My eyes are heavy, burn, as if they're baking,
    my thoughts are clear, again I'm awaken;
You feel so near, yet we're worlds apart,
    somehow your arrow, shot through my heart.

I asked, was it her or is it cupid,
    well that's obvious, I know I'm not stupid,
Because her voice is alive in my mind,
    keeping me up, around the clock, even through nighttime.

Up and alone, losing my mind from lack of sleep,
    I write these rhymes, that make her weep;
I can't function, my body weakens,
    these words I write, is my heart speaking.

I'm told minds fail with inadequate rest,
    yet at this time, my rhymes seem at their best;
Sorry I'm ending this, so I'll leave you this clue,
    I know it wasn't cupid, I'm sleepless 'cause of you.

Stephen Collins

Untitled, With Luv

I looked down, it was dark, it was cold.
Tears of sorrow ringing in my ears, invading my brain
Looking frantically side to side,
Needing only somewhere to hide.
Dark, black figures, holding Kleenex to their eyes,
Were staring carefully at me.
I wanted to run, away from this empty place.
The figures sobbed, their sobs were deep,
I looked back at the man, forever asleep.
My whole body quivered, I cried painfully,
Looking at the cold man, lying beside me.
Don't bury him now, don't dig so deep,
I don't want to believe, please wake him from his sleep
Rain falling hard, like the tears from are eyes,
Rain falling fast, like the memories escaping our past.
Help us hold on,
To hope and keep
Until we too enter
That peaceful sleep.

Krista Siefried

Christmas Is Forgiveness

Potpourri everywhere!
Even some in my hair!
Itchy, scratchy, sticky things,
"You jerk!", is all that I can scream.

I guess I shouldn't have ticked my brother off;
Because he did more than sit there and scoff.
He took the liberty of pulling my hair;
And throwing potpourri everywhere!

I guess I shouldn't have called him a jerk;
Just 'cause inside me I have so much perk.
I'm sorry that I called him a jerk;
He's sorry he told me I have too much perk.

After awhile he got kind of crabby;
Then I told him he's acting very sappy.
What happened next did not make me happy;
Out came my hair...and up went potpourri!

Boy will be boys and since
    Christmas Is Forgiveness,
I think I'll do just that.
    Cori Elizabeth Racine

The Reality And The Remembrance

It's aged so much.
Been neglected too long
The atmosphere is still there though.
The doors are long gone.
Poor little house.
The tree centuries old has finally fallen.
Nevertheless.
It's still very pleasant and peaceful.
The way it used to be.
Fond memories of laughter with friends.
Settled in front of the cozy and warm log fire.
The proud tall tree towering over the perfect home.
Remembering how happy you were.
But look around at reality.
A house that could be made into that happy home again.
All it heeds is a little care.
All it needs.
Fond memories
To make them real just once more.
    Jan Leszczynski

Eighty One

I never thought the day would come when I was eighty one,
Till suddenly the days went rushing by and now have come and gone.
So I no longer think about when I'll be eighty two,
Because each day of joy or sadness simply means life starts anew.
I used to rush around with great determination and haste
in order not a precious moment of life and time to waste.
For now I think life never ends, but flows forever on
in generation after generation, the bloodlines always strong.
So I no longer worry about the passage of the time,
since it goes on and on forever and hears not the funeral chime.
Nor are days gone by forever lost, but are recorded
somewhere in the mind, and they can be re-ordered
from the marvelous memory storeroom treasure
and re-lived in fantasy, joy and pleasure.
    Jason P. Moore

"Let It Flow"

Everyday goes by,
the sun comes up, and the sun
goes down, and all around the
starlit universe.
The clouds pass by like moments
lost in a precious life.
Stuck in a room alone is not the way.
Get up, get to it, live for today, stuck
on sad memories does not mend,
Get up, get to it, break rules that
you should not bend.
Be free and choose, let your heart sore....
you can't lose
You never know what page will be turned.
Just don't be hurt by anyone,
this is something much to be learned.
    Theresa Bullock

Hold Still, Little One

Hold still, little one, and let me cuddle your soft body in my arms,
Let me kiss your dimpled cheek and soak up all your childhood charms.
How fast the stage has changed from a baby of yesterday,
To a little child who walks and talks with me today.
Will I be able to cope with all the changes in which you're about to engage —
From total dependence to being independent,
And then to "mother knows nothing" stage?
Hold still, little one, and let me grasp the beauty of your sweet innocent face,
Let me dream of you always in ribbons and bows, and dresses made of lace.
Wait for me, time...I've got to cling to each beautiful moment,
For there will never be another quite as precious, nor so well spent.
Why does God let little ones grow up so fast?
Why can't this feeling of being needed forever last?
Hold still, my little one.
    Norma Parsons

Endeavorous Journeys

There seems to be a silence
That awakens in a dream
A melted figure
A transparent seed
Even the weakest of minds
Can't escape this portal of time
Power of suggestion turns into a game
Full of remarkable and unbelievable things
Daring you to fall asleep
Taunting your every restless move
Trying to grab hold of your heart
Reading your deepest thoughts
Struggling to awaken
They turn into reality
Slipping back into the dream
Afraid you will never survive
Leading to an unknown destiny
Abruptly the journey ends
You enter a new day
Leaving behind the night
    Shannon Morningstar

Symphonic Muse

Would that the believers, ever faithful,
join in prayer. And in their differences,
like the differences in these instruments,
All contribute to the composers score.

Would that the doubters
(some even in eloquent tacit)
Offer up the counterpoint and dissonance
Necessary to the progression of the theme,
Then would there be a harmony
This universe has never heard
A Song of Peace.
    William J. Malchik

Handyman

I have a handyman called Tony, he's big and strong
He makes me tired to watch him as he moves along
Wielding his pick and spade that's kept so sharp
His antique rake, so heavy, his pride and joy to use,
He found in old Estate.
He's here at eight to start. "This won't take long", he says,
"Then I'll do other jobs", the clock to race.

See him move the gravel, and the weeds
Reluctant to unravel they claim the rock-hard place, this soil
Will soon capitulate before his toil.
I had to provide, gladly, lots of cups of tea. He likes his tea!
Here's two metal star posts in his way. Set so deep
Lots would say "you'll have to mow 'round that",
But Tony brings sledgehammer in to play with awesome whacks
Until you smell the metal hot, and when he's done he breaks them off
And with a wrench, a heave or two, he lifts. They're out! He's won.

If all Australia worked with Tony's energy and zeal
Our country would be really great. I mean it really would, I feel.

Shirley Humphrey

How Long The Night

How long the night when lights in the town are dim;
And crickets fiddle their endless prelude.
A heavy sky squeezes its moisture, making soft
rhythmical drops from the eaves.
Through the mist, a bright light searches a long
track, blurting eerie warnings not to violate its motion.
The stars are lost in a shroud.
Curtains hang limp with dew from the night air
looking drawn and pathetic.
A light steady snore from another room confirms
an aloneness to the wakeful.
How long the night!

Virginia K. Hazard

I Once Admired A Rose

I once admired a rose above my head,
With yellow petals in a fragile cup,
Which, as I stroked, it almost seemed to shed
A glow upon the hand that I reached up.
Anticipating fresh and sweet perfume
I bent it gently down, near to my nose
And saw, my cheek against the tender bloom,
Japanese beetles swarm is putrid folds.
Transfixed I watch, it seems to me an hour;
Their copper armor glints with brassy pride
As if to mock the golden colored flower
Or kindle smold'ring black decay inside.
Now, when I see a bud, my mind in part
Must fear that beetles hide within its heart.

Amanda Thomas Buck

"The Sea"

Marvelous, mighty the waves come and go
The sea foam is the color of soft white snow
The soaring sea gulls high above the sea
While the bright seashells dance toward me

The sun shines bright on my face
While I watch the red crabs race.
I love to look far away
To see the grey dolphins play.

The smooth wet sand under my feet
Hides my small toes from the heat
The wild wide sea swallows the sun
And all of my day's fun is done.

Paula Baba

Enveloped

Every night covered me with your soft skin
I was dirt and jaded edges, innocent and believing in nothing
You changed everything, turned me up and down, made me feel
holding me in your warm embrace, you pushed me into ecstasy
I formed my present state
but no longer were our souls and bodies careening together
You would slowly envelope me, sooth what you had smoothed
and I thought I knew what love was.
One night I longed for you and your warmth stopped short of me
You might reach out to me again, even pull me back a little
talk to me as if nothing was lost
a drop or two would splash onto me
You were still so close, but mostly now,
I memorized your features by pale stars
and you told me you loved me
as you receded forever into the gray of early morning
Every night I saw you and dreamt of touching your moonlight skin
I want be inside you, one last time, forever
but when I finally felt the palm of a hand
and the force of a throw
I crumbled into dust and blew far from your waves

Scott Berkley

Serenity

The sky blushes
As the sun kisses the water.
The golden ball
Is engulfed by brilliant colors.

The melancholy cries of the sea gull
The melodious swish of the waves.
The tranquil song
Echoes throughout the beach.

Hills of shimmering sand
The sweet fragrance of salt.
The water recedes
Carrying nature's wonders into its depths.

A gentle breeze
Caresses a young woman's ivory skin.
She closes here eyes
And lays down on the soft carpet.

Her flesh melts
Into the sand.
A spot in her soul is touched
And she embraces the serenity.

Krista Reale

Brother Against Brother

Flesh and blood by same mother and father
'Tis was the war between brother and brother
To claim thy heart of thee willing fair maiden
Both trying to prove a love of innocence

This duel, thus competition seeking the best
One shall die, thus winner gets thy rest
'Tis quarrel which shattered thus bond of thy family
To bitter and senseless, ruthless enemies

She lust for one thou loved truly the other
Hurting inside, thee tried leading jealousy to one another
Hoping to destroy this kinship of thus brothers
Knowing in the end would be no sincere winners

The victor, thy older, stronger brother
Thus underdog, thy one who was thee true lover
Thou realizing thus her loss was forever
Her mistake, thee would always dishonour

Thee maiden, a dagger in her hands she clenched
She pierced her heart, guilty blood on her chest
Sinking to the ground in the depths of death
Conceding thus heaven would never be her receiving bed of rest

Christine Anne Therien

Cancelled Today Only

We have a scrumptious affair
A fine selection of daily wares
To buy or sell or exchange.
Beautiful, exciting, never plain.
Red vases, two knickknacks,
Spears on display...but stay.
Here's a special travel pack,
Some fine powders, here only today!
A steady stream of baying sheep,
A baby wren, how cute-a peep,
A darling blue carpet,
Satin burgundy sheets,
Here today, it will be gone next week.
But don't despair, money still speaks.
All the beautiful hidden charms
And antiques found at the Bazaar
Down by the old abandoned farm.
Just down the street, it's not far,
It's the one with the sign that creaks
Cancelled - today only. It's been hanging all week.

Myrialynn Krause

Backyard Buddies

Prairie Chickens and a large Jack Rabbit,
Do at times our yard inhabit,
Could it be they're showing disdain,
For a countryside domain?

We wouldn't think of complaining,
Our rural runaways are entertaining,
Really making most interesting neighbours,
While performing at their labours.

The Prairie Chickens a mid-morning vigil keeping,
Give themselves away with constant peeping,
Never really minding their toil,
Scratching away in our garden soil.

A large Jack Rabbit with leaps and bounds,
Is paying a visit to our grounds,
Munching on our landscaped greenery,
He likes changing our well - planned scenery!

Though some might find nature's neighbours annoying,
We find ourselves their antics enjoying,
So we have chosen with them to abide,
And live in peace side by side.

Lynne H. Kroeker

Life Goes On

Do I live in years gone by
do I sit alone and cry?
Do I dread each new day
because you have died
and gone away?

Do I dread to make a new start
because of the empty void
you left in my heart?
Oh no I'll go on to be
the best I can be
Because you would want
nothing less for me.

There will be times I will shed some tears
There will be times I will have to
face my fears.
But with God's Help
I know I can cope
because with each new day
comes a brand new hope.

Janet Rone

Old Woman In Park

Her bare feet tread the ground.
Grasses, aromas, moisture
surreptitiously pervert her whole being
in rebellion against
her waterfalls sequestered in the past.

Incomplete gestures pulsate
for just an instant.
Only her stares attain concretion
and incriminate the fleeting light,
strive for immutability
and sunrises bathed by primeval waters.

Her spirit undulates
as if riding on edges
in an obscene dynamics disconnected
from the events of her body.
It stops at the lifeless thresholds.

Her thirsty soles will not forsake verdure.

Lillian Marta Viotti

A Lifetime In A Minute

Hurry up and wait, it takes forever, then, it is over in a second.
  Did I miss it?
Anticipate the ending, stretch for the finish, the final note sounds.
  Is it over, already?
Grueling hours spent preparing, practicing and waiting for the chance
  of a lifetime.
Do I get another chance?

I've waited a lifetime,
  for the moment when I could sit back, survey all I had done.
I've waited a lifetime,
  to see the sun come up on my face and no where to run.
I've waited a lifetime,
  and now, I no longer have the chance for any of it.

In one single minute, that's all it took,
  all I had lived for and dreamed about was gone.
Only a minute, sixty small seconds.
  Was how long I had my dreams left.
One minute, no time at all.
  Separated me from all that I believed in .

If I had known, I would have tried to put the rest of my lifetime in
  that last minute.
Before I knew it, the minute was gone, and so was my lifetime.

Barbara Markley Darrah

The Pottery Woman

Her spiritual smile wakes the dawn,
Its sweet swinging rhythm,
Brings a pretty blue peaceful and artful sky.
The morning footprints of the young lady's steps,
Masterpieces the wet clayed sands with devine courage.
The musical shores are engraved with her elegant signature.

Her shoulders, high with strength,
A reflection of the erection of bronzed jubilee.
Of a magical melody.
Her loving eyes cry a religion of freedom,
With her, the naked are given warmth,
The church-less given a redeeming soft sermon.
Thank God for this woman.

Her slender hands hold water to feed those in drought,
Those with no way out.
Those with now way,
A better way.

Her pearly white dress sweeps the dusty, cutting crosswalks,
Her head held upright, her devoted angel held tight.
Thank God for this woman, for she is a river.

Jawn P. Solomon

Mother Dearest

Sometimes I look up at the stars in heaven and I know,
that you are somewhere among them.
I have so many wonderful memories of you
and can still hear the sound of your voice,
and your words of comfort.

Years has gone by,
since I last saw you,
and there have been numerous changes,
but you will be in my heart forever.

So many secrets I would have liked to share
and whenever I think of one true friend,
I think of you.
Wishes do not always come true,
and to hope encourages me to face a brighter tomorrow.

Often I wonder, if you see me one day,
Will you remember me?
Would you know my name?
If I had the chance to see you one more time,
I would let you know just how much I miss you.
Mother I Love You.

Marcel Winter

Untitled

War is not black and white.
It's gray.
No rights.
No wrongs.
Maybes.
That is life.
Look around, view the many values.
Understand them all.
Learn.
Grow.
Then you will see.
Then and only then can you judge.
There is no judgement to black and white.
Only a narrow path
And in Nam it was not safe to walk along the paths.

Karen D. Boeddeker

Energized Emma

Just like a pep rally
Bringing good spirits to a crowd,
Emma is always there
Determined and proud.

She came to work at Wilson
Not knowing what she would find.
She brought joy and happiness
To all of us inside.

Whenever you are feeling frustrated
And at the bottom of your stairs
Emma comes and picks you up
She puts you in her prayers.
She says give your problems to a higher power.
He will lead the way.
You will wake up tomorrow
To a better, brighter day!!

Emma is extraordinary
She knows just what to say.
Coming to work with Emma is a pleasure
Each and every day!!

Karen L. Foote

Victorian Home

The house stood like a sentinel, its turret reaching high,
Guarding precious memories of times gone by.

Steadfast in structure, Victorian lines,
Foreboding special moments of joys so sublime.

Windows reflected sunlight, the doors were open wide,
Warm welcome was exuded, and music played inside.

Light filtered down the staircase, and drew one's gaze above,
To lofty heights and cherished thoughts that spoke of family love.

Spaciousness invited private thoughts, to while the time away,
Some nook and cranny could be found to house the mind at play.

Incidents sad and unrepressed joy were part of the old home's history,
Embracing strength of a presence there invited deep felt mystery.

Out on he porch were rocking chairs, and the swing looked so inviting,
Peace could be claimed; or if one wished, talk could be exciting.

Wisteria hung from the old windmill, magnolias bloomed in profusion,
And exotic scent filled the air, to create a sweet illusion.

Reluctantly, the old home relinquished anything from its hallowed walls,
Especially all the people, who graced its stately halls.

Satisfied it had served them well, it knew that they would yearn,
To relive their past contentment, and in their hearts return.

Helen B. Yarborough

Soul-Senses

Kinsman. Friend. Neighbor. Soul-senses to eternity. Body to infinity.
Called to manage heavenly rangelands in hooves-a'flying accident.

Soul-eyes see with perfect vision the most-loved vista —
Flint Hills. Dusk. Ebbing sun. Painted sky. Sculpted clouds.
Shadowed limestone. Placid cattle. Vigilant horse. Etched on
wind-rustled folds of golden grass.

Soul-ears hear perfectly Nature's silent soil-symphony.
Muted rangeland concert. Subtle. More beautiful than imagined.
Perfect soul-insight solves unfathomable puzzles among grasses,
forbs, weeds, light, soil, wind, rain, temperature, fire, time,
insect, wildlife, cattle and man. He becomes them. Truth revealed.

Bemused soul-humor marvels at the simplicity of nature's complexities;
Unveils every mystifying secret hidden within Earth's life-sustaining crust.
Mother cow licking calf. Quiet dappled fawn. Quail covey flush.
Prairie chicken boom. Coyote yodel. Instincts unwrapped.

We — with memory-eyes, memory-ears, memory-senses, and not-yet-
activated souls — still puzzle over life and inexplicable death.
We remain. Remembering. Contemplating extinguished life.
Gone for now! Until reunion — a speck of eternity beyond today —
soul-senses patiently monitor our fragile track to Earth-trail's end
... and reunion!

Thayne Cozart

Dawn's Solitude

In the sun-kissed hues of brilliant dawn and
coloured blooms iridescent in morning dew,
I drink in nature's myriadic scents as the
windows of my soul embrace tender memories of you.

Nature's music unfolds before me like rhythmic
symphonies blowing in the wind, and the strings of
my heart orchestrate the melody of my reality and
I feel as alive as the brightening sky.

I embrace life with a new serenity, peppered with
love and hope, and relish those old memories as bright
as the golden sun.

Jo Mills

Moonlight Sign

Silvery moon,
  rising high.
Glowing softly in
  the sky.

Howling dogs,
  worship your path.
You're a shining symbol
  of midnight's wrath.

For all the world,
  you light the sky.
And make the superstitious,
  cheat and lie.

To me you are,
  a beautiful sign.
While you create the waters, glistening,
  upon the mighty Rhine.
    Wendy Welles

Shattered Dreams

She will never be as beautiful
as she'd like to be
A cracked mirror holds her prisoner
and won't seem to let her free
From her shaking palm drips crimson red
Adding colour to the sheets of her unturned bed
The music unleashes her hate and desire
the words linger and set her heart on fire
Through a broken window she lets out a scream
Waking up in the morning to realize it was all a dream
She sits alone in her place
Hiding the pain of her
tear stained face
if I could help her
I would try
But I'm just a pillow
when she needs to cry
    Brandy Weir

The Christmas Tree

I never knew how much people loved their trees
until I cut one down and decorated it as I pleased.

I thought it was the most beautiful and correctly dressed of trees,
but then I watched as others did the same things as me.

Oh, they couldn't have as deep a feelings as I have when doing mine
so I watched them very closely to see what I could find.

Most were very patient when checking their strings of lights
they hung their ornaments with reverence and positioned them just right.

They strung their garland and hung their tinsel, just like God had put it there
and you should have seen their manger scene made out of angel hair.

Now as they hoist their angel to the top it's finally clear to me.
These people, just like me, they love their Christmas Tree.
    Dana Hill

"Financial Status"

No closets, no halls, no house with four walls
No couch, no chairs, no family to share
I live on the streets with calloused hands, calloused feet
No job, no cash, I dig for food in the trash
No designer clothes, no designer shoes
Just a voice to sing my blues
The working class complains of troubles on the job and at home
I would love to have the troubles you own
It's hard living on the streets alone
    Rochelle M. Tate

"A Child"

"A child" is precious in so many ways
give them your love throughout the days,
they're like a gem that sets in your heart
the magic of love will never depart.

The smile they give the laughter they show
will always be with them wherever they go,
when they are sad and start to cry
show them you care - tell them why.

"A child" needs lifting give them your hand
let them know you understand,
"a child" needs to know you can be reached
and let them learn from what you teached.

"A child" needs happiness, loving and prayer
let them know the Love is there,
"a child" is sensitive and very aware
of feelings and love.
"Handle with care!"
    Dennis D. Disbrow

White Heat

I have felt the sting of the serpent
his words like hot fire fell upon my tongue
believe and with me you will be one

I will meet you in the market place
it is I whom you will choose to follow
and in my temple you will dwell

Do you question my blasphemy
if he who honors his false Gods would turn to see my prophecy
then he would know to worship me

I will make love to the dragon
and all of you men will be left at the Tower of Babel
speaking in tongues that you don't understand

It doesn't matter what you feel
say my name and believe because it is only he who cries out to
me that with my touch I can heal

At my command the mountain will rise to meet the sky
piercing the clouds that burn with the desire to be free of the
burden inside
and nourish the land below

Come with me, feel me, give me your hand
    Michele Kuester

My Hands

I gazed upon my hands today,
And wondered what these hands would say.
If they would tell you what they could,
About their journey along life's road.

They've helped in the tragedies of life,
And aided many in times of strife.
They've soothed the ill and held the hands.
Of those in pain they could not stand.

They have cooked, and washed, and made the beds.
Washed little faces and shampooed heads.
They've spanked little britches and handed out love.
With a lot of help from up above.

These hands could tell you a whole lot more.
But my readers I do not want to bore.
Because today I am alone.
And it matters not what I have done.
    Phyllis I. McKee

Watching Clouds

Through the eyes of a child
see the clouds?

Lie down.
Look up.
Feel the magic.
The clouds go drifting by.

Over there!
That cloud looks like a bear.
The eyes, the nose, the ears,
the body shape.

It's changing, getting longer,
Stretching out
until it takes
a dragon shape,
twisting its way across
the sea of blue.

Another one!
A sailing ship!
As it sails by you wish you could get on,
and float among the other mystic shapes.

Elleen Van Ness

The Coffee Shop

The door swings open
on its large metal hinges
and the cold air rushes in.
Heads turn and smiles form
on the faces behind the counter.
The aroma of mint and sweet chocolate
fills the nose and is inhaled into the lungs
Then it is time for choosing
a place to sit, in the corner, by the window.
I see him reading while he drinks
the hot liquid from his cup
savouring every last drop.
His brow wrinkles with disgust
as he reads the headlines.
Two girls in the corner
read horoscopes and laugh.
Cold air rushes in
and on its large metal hinges
the door swings shut.

Denise M. Moore

Death Of A Dreamer

Look into the eyes of a dreamer
    And see the birthplace of affliction
    Hear the wretched sounds of a pretender
        Then put on a happy face

Savour the taste of falsified integrity
    And relish the bitter zest of regret
    Inhale the stench of dissolute jealousy
        Then put on a happy face

Though deception lies in the path of this dreamer
    And faith is an expression that can't be reached
    Laugh in the naive face of this believer
        Then put on a happy face

Shake the hand of a conquered paper soldier
    And touch the fair skin of denial
    Smell the scent of a defeated warrior
        Then bow your head in disgrace!!!

Irena Ciucianu

Untitled

The sport I love is a part of life
Not something you do with your kids or wife
You round up your buddies (no more than two)
Never forgetting to pack the brew
The peanuts, poles, worms, and sling shots
They all have their own special spots
Once you're finally ready to roll
You set out for your secret hole
There has to be fog and a little frost
That's when you seem to get yourself lost
But you suddenly stumble upon a creek
And without haste you take a peek
You have scored it's packed with trout
But your stupid friend Al lets go a shout
And off the fish go, up the strip
Now that's where it ends, the great fishing trip

Ron Davis

The Old Shoe

Sometimes new shoes are so uncomfortable you can hardly stand.

But the old shoe continues to give as much comfort as it can.
When your feet hurt you feel miserable right from the start.
You just can't seem to function and take an active part.
Many times you have a mind to throw those old shoes away.
But your better judgement tells you, you might need those shoes someday.
Although they have been battered and a little kicked around...
If you save them, when you need them, you'll be happy when they're found.
Old shoes don't always look so very good to you
However, when they're polished up...they almost look like new.
Then you can surely say "Thank God, my feet don't hurt...
Now I can be in comfort, as I do my work
My whole body seems to feel so much better too
Aren't you glad that you held on to that wonderful old shoe?

Willablanch Wilson

Don't Turn Away

Don't runaway and try to hide
Don't resist what you feel inside
Don't turn away when I want you to stay
'Cause baby I think of you day after day
My heart bleeds when you're not here
Living without you is what I fear
The days are so long when you're not around
Lost without you is what I've found
Baby I know that you feel it too
'Cause I know how much I meant to you
So let's get together and make a brand new start
Show me your true feelings that are within your heart

Steven Parak

I Am

I am a strong girl who is not afraid
I wonder if I will ever get straight A's
I hear negative things
I see nothing but violence
I want world peace
I am a strong girl who is not afraid
I pretend to be happy when I'm really mad
I feel happy when I succeed
I worry that my friends are drifting away from me
I cry when bad things happen
I am a strong girl who is not afraid
I understand life is not good all the time
I say thing's that get me in trouble
I dream of every thing that should be but is not
I hope I will fulfill my dreams
I am a strong girl who's not afraid.

Kim Reid

Soul Mates - Tekawatha Woods

They glided silently through the woods.
Two females, skin and fur, woman and dog.
They listened, sniffed, scratched, examined.

The woods inhabitants sensed their own.
Butterflies perched on leaves.
Nuthatches babbled happily.
Deer gazed silently at them.

Sunlight and shadow. Moss and rocks.
Thistles and flowers. Step by step,
souls restored.

The dog guided them out of the woods.
The woman drove them home.

Sandra Lee Peterson

Be

Perspective views opinions convictions
one, the same our end of the looking glass
I speak for no one everyone, me and he
logic of course there is none yet all is logic
God is who's to say he's not
only he only he didn't so God is
what reason do I have?
A single blades of grass a bird song
a mountain, a mole hill all are he is
we are only if we choose for ourselves to be
why should it be that we can choose? Can we?
He is, said we could, so we can
some of us do, some of us are
some of us don't, some of is aren't
If we don't, if we won't then we aren't

If we do, then we are, we have all
If you do not choose then you cannot be
because He is said he can
Be

Jeremy Saul

The Phone Call

Could a life depend on a mundane ring?
The quality of a heartbeat
Of thoughts that sing.
Sing and dance to the beat
Of one being?

Should a life depend on the sound
Of a voice so square but round
Empty yet full of reassurance but bound
To give away all but nothing?

Should the essence of a being
Be enmeshed in the non-essence of another
The immaturity of one being
Clash against the maturity of the other?

Could this moonstruck heart
Be cured of this malaise
This melting heart
Saved from the burning hearth?

Yes...pain.

Ngozi Joannis

Tears

Tears on my pillow,
Tears in my heart.
Tears are within me, since we've been apart.
Tears of sorrow, tears of pain.
Tears are within me,
For in God, I laid the blame.
Tears of regret,
Tears of my shame.
Tears I now shed,
Lord, let me try over again.
Tears of happiness,
Tears on my face.
Tears are within me,
Because of your amazing grace.
I know I'm forgiven,
My Father, Redeemer and also my friend.
You are always with me, your loving hands, you do lend.
I look forward to the future,
And all it can hold for me.
I now give you my life, and we'll meet in... Eternity!

Sharon Kaulback

"The Stars That Left The Sky Shining"

What's it like,
to be way up in the clouds?
To be at ease and peace, without the loud
what's the sky up there where birds fly high
what's light up there
when the stars left the sky
If I was a bird, where would I go?
If I was a star how long would I show?

The sky that I see, I wonder if it
leaves me a mystery
The stars that have fallen
I wonder if my wish has been called
Light be the light without no sun
The beauty of a rainbow the beauty of one
my life I am living, my soul that I keep
my long journey home

I walk with my feet
And I look right up, without no
whining, for the stars that left the sky.
The sky is still shining.

Renee Davis

DENY NOT YOUR GIFT

I am a child of THE DIVINE FORCE,
Of THE DIVINE POWER,
By which I am GIFTED with LIFE, as Thou art.
We are obligated in our Life's Journey to
AMPLIFY THE DIVINE FORCE, TO
MAGNIFY THE DIVINE POWER!
Let our Life's Journey be of errant purpose
And we shall be consumed by that errancy.
Seek Unflaggingly THE DIVINE FORCE,
Nourish Unrelenting THE DIVINE POWER,
And by so-doing,
We will be sought, and found, by THE DIVINE FORCE,
We will be Nourished by THE DIVINE POWER,
From whence we came, and of which WE ARE!

John Christy

What Is Life

Life is mopping floors, shopping stores, wiping fingerprints off doors,
Fixing breakfasts, suppers, lunches, following hunches, dodging punches,
Washing mugs, vacuuming rugs, spraying bugs,
Dusting sills, sponging spills and paying bills!

Life is making beds, aching heads, buying gifts when someone weds,
Throwing out the unread papers, airing vapors, cutting capers,
Dreaming dreams that don't come true, catching flu, liking You,
Mowing lawns, stifling yawns and waking up before day dawns!

Life is full of little woes, snagging hose, ironing clothes,
Missing busses, noon-hour rushes, fender crushes;
One encounters surly types, cloggy pipes, petty gripes,
Unfair bosses, stock losses and curves a loving husband tosses!

Life is waiting for publisher's checks, stacking decks of their rejects,
Hammering thumbs instead of nails, attending sales when all else fails;
It's a wonder, the way I blunder, I haven't gone completely under,
Yet despite occasional pain, and frequent times I'm caught in rain,
And doubting that I'm really sane, given a chance I'd try again!

June L. Willumsen

Forgive

Someone has hurt me, someone quite dear,
Hurt me so badly, I feel quite near -
Hate.
"Oh, but," God says, "To hate is as to kill.
You must forget and because it's My will -
Forgive."
"But how can that be?" my old self cries out
"I'm haunted by hurt and I will never, no doubt -
Forgive."
"Oh, but my child; hate just cannot be;
For there's never any found in Me -
Forgive."
Again I'd argue 'til once more I see,
My saviour suffering to set me free, -
Forgiven
Then my heart cries out from deep within
"Forgive me, Lord, for that awful sin -
Hate"
"And, God, bless that one who has hurt me so badly
Help me forget, as I know now I can gladly - Forgive"

Harriet Jenereaux

Shield Of Passion

   I feel deeper than a wound
Understand - it's not the surface of the skin
But the depth of the tear
   As we intertwine
I feel the suppression of my heartache
and with passion seeping through the pores of our bodies
leading to a trickle of sweat
that gets tossed within the turmoil of our ecstasy
I feel content
   Your embrace that surrounds me is like
a great wall
I feel your power
your shield
most of all I feel from all doubt
therefore may the pieces heal to an indefinite
path of existence!

Maria Tangredi

True Love

True love is giving, caring, sharing,
It's a love that comes from the soul.
It can only come from the depth of ones being,
It's the light that makes us whole.

It's the most beautiful scariest feeling,
Because with true love comes pain.
The pain that lies within our past,
So we run from it again and again.

It's not hurting each other as most of us do,
It's feeling the other ones pain.
When it comes to us and it's really real,
It will make the tears fall like rain.

Until we find it within ourselves,
We cannot give it away.
So you see when it comes from deep within us,
You know it real and it's there to stay.

Sandra C. St. Onge

To Your Health

I'm plum confused 'bout what to eat,
Some say fruit, some say meat,
Some say Veggies are good for us
But you may wind up with colitis!
You need your Vitamins and Proteins
You need your fish and you need your beans.
Eat your celery and carrots too,
But dairy products are bad for you.
Don't eat foods that have been preserved
But you can't feed millions if it's not reserved.
Count those calories, avoid that fat!
Sometimes I wonder just where I'm at.
Health reports bring fear and sorrow,
But what's bad today will be good tomorrow.
The way to solve this situation
Is to eat what you want in moderation.
Let's eat whatever tastes good to us
Then just Kick-Back and avoid the fuss.
Regardless if you're fat or thin,
It's a wonderful world that we live in!

Max D. Warren

Untitled

I hate this place, I've never liked it here
I feel used, violated and more unwanted then ever
I want to leave and go far, far away
Never to give it another thought

I want to go where someone cares
Where someone will actually listen to what I have to say
I want to escape, not to escape from fear, but for love
I need to go where I am loved and wanted
And stay there 'till they want me no longer
Then I still leave again and again 'till I'm wanted
'Till I can find someone who can hold me
Who can make me feel loved and cherished
And wanted for all of my life

This may take most of my life, to feel like I'm in heaven
And it probably will
I think I will never feel this way
But yet.....this is what I want

Wendy L. Kreutzer

House Cleaning Time

It's time to clean this house of mine
to make it glitter, gleam, and shine.
I need to wash away the dirt
and pray for someone I have hurt.
The grudges I have held so long
I need to trade them for a song.
I need forgiveness in my heart
and try to make a brand new start.

I want to try not to condemn and judge others,
but to mend a broken heart that's just like mine,
that doesn't glitter, gleam, and shine.
The things that others have done to me,
I should forgive them for eternity.

Help me to wash away all hate
and leave it at the golden gate
where it will be turned into love
cleansed by the blood of the Lord above.
Help me Lord to be more like You.
Forgive, forget, and love as You.

Phyllis Eads

Who Is Really A Friend

A friend is someone who really cares,
They don't just like you because of your looks,
But because of who you are inside.
A friend is someone you can trust,
You can tell them your deepest, darkest secret,
and they will not tell a single person what you said
A friend is someone you love and care for,
That is what a real friend is.

Sarah Huls

Dull, Matted Day

Since the Toaster lost its shine the rug's been matted and grey.
Rolling the thing doesn't help at all.
It is matted clean through.
I think you spilled cherry limeade there by the
Chili Dog Stain.
The Rug smells get all mixed together
and remind me of you.
The silver reflection of the toaster
is lost.

Maria Nicole Hadley

A Message From The Battlefield

The combat has ceased-the armament is cooling
The living are settling beneath the tent wings
The heroes from Battle - the brave victors!
On this night fruitful was death.

In the cold night the breeze is gathering,
carrying to Heaven - the moan of the dying.
A quiet whisper, a cry: "Brother, friend,
your wounds are lighter, home you will be going.

We are good compatriots - you know all of mine,
send my love to my wife, tell her death has arrived
a bullet has gone by my heart,
tell her I'm bleeding, and my days are few.

Kiss my small son tenderly for me.
My little angel will not really understand
where I have gone - why his father is not there,
that I will no longer call him by name."

The glow of bonfires sheds light upon fields,
a grave has sprouted, a hero less...
A small star on the horizon
glowed bright - and down to Earth it fell.

Theodor Zikic

A True Friend

Dear God, I have come to talk with you today,
My heart is sad and heavy, and I feel the need to pray.

My life is in such a turmoil, and the road seems so unsure,
Please guide me through the bad times, so that I may feel secure.

Joy and laughter once filled the air,
My home was warm and happy, with hardly a worry or care.

I have always tried to be a good friend, mother and wife,
However, time moves on, each person has their own life.

The children leave the nest and the house grows cold,
The husband seeks outside interests, in the fear of growing old.

So, I come to you God, and ask that you be my friend,
Please keep your warm and loving arms around me, till I
reach life's end.

Keitha Irene Allen

"Reverie"

Life is such a puzzling thing
Sometimes we laugh
Sometimes we sing
Alive with laughter
Attune with love,
With hardly a thought for God above.

Then all of a sudden, our happy days cease
Sorrow and strife
and sadness increase
While sickness and worry
and troubles ahead
Remind us of prayers, too oft left unsaid.

We long for a haven of peace and trust,
Unruffled by envy,
greed or lust,
Where patience, love,
and kindness grow
And all the deeds of friendship sow!

Would I could live this life of mine
As Thou would wish, - Lord give me time.

G. Isobel Guilboard

Spirit Brother

We used to walk in fear, yet still respecting each other.
    But as my world progressed the fear and respect
became less and less
    Now my greatest fear is that my spirit brothers
will not be around to show their beauty and grace
in this ever growing concrete world.
    Forgive me, my spirit brother for we know
not what we do we do to you and the rest
of our spirit brothers
    By stealing your hunting grounds, we have
caused your slow demise and brought you
very close to extinction in this world we both share
    Your home lands are slowly becoming lands
for our habitation
    We kill your family, your children and your
very essence for our greed of money and power,
    I pray that when we meet in the great hunting
lands of our afterlife that you will find
it in your heart to forgive me and mine

Clayton Guinn

A Tribute To My Son

Time goes so fast and it's sad you died a young man
God does these things and it's hard to understand
I regret the things I said to you, I regret the things
I didn't do for you
I always loved you, and I promise I always will
I wish this was a dream, but I know your death is real
I cannot change things or turn back the time
But even in your death, you will always be living in my
heart and mind

I pray for you every night my son and if it's only one
person in heaven, I pray that your the one

I'll try to forget the hard times we had, but I'll never
forget you or you calling me "Dad"

Jerry Sweeney

Sunrise

How shall I greet a Summer's rosy dawn?
Aurora's lovely faring and rising in the East?
Like an eagle or a coy fawn?
Like a purple Roman wine or the swelling of the yeast?
How royal is a Summer's fresh and golden morn,
The roving clouds of pure air and golden light,
A ceremony of a sparkling sun and growing corn,
That outpour of divinity and its greatest might.
Lets see now how I fare and vainly stammer,
No man has for such greatness the really proper word.
No man bears the mighty force of Vulcan's hammer
Or the gleaming power of an ancient hero's sword.
And as the clouds grow and in their dimensions tower,
The sun bathes now in purest gold the blessed land
And as I with fascination see and humbly cower,
I feel the Godhead's strong but ever gentle hand.
What do I think and what do I trembling feel?
I am silent now while I understand and finally kneel.

Werner Reinhard Schubert

The Freedom Way

I'm not in love with any girl, it's not natural
I'm in love with a country, it's not cultural
The country that I love is called the USA
I wish to visit it in the spring precisely in May
I really want to see the Democracy
But between it and me there's a sea
I want to go where I belong
But the way is so much long
AMERICA, AMERICA you're so far
To see you I'll need more than a car
Yes all that I need is a dream and some hope
And in my heart I have faith more than the Pope
I'm telling you "In God I trust"
And to AMERICA I have to go, I must,
My motto is: "Justice and FREEDOM for all".
And to all the world I'll bring that call
PLEASE Lord show me the way I want to be
A citizen in the Holy land of thee

Joseph E. Yared

Forever Young

When the deep shadows of your eyes dancing by
the fire of glad grace with the beauty
souls with loves false from true racing
across the fields of gazing grain hasted
forever toward eternity.

Minh Ha

Beauty In A Book

As you go into a book store, quickly
glancing at all the books, you noticed
the plain one.
The book is used, the title is
silly and you look inside, so many
misspelled words.
The book makes no sense to you,
amused, putting it back, thinking
what a waste of good reading, it's
not worth your time.
The book you did purchase was
new; well written, made sense. After
reading the book you found it satisfactory
but you were discontent.
The following week you go
into the book store, to your surprise
you see the used book is now on the
best seller list. As you go to purchase
the used book you notice a sign
"Rare addition, sold out."

Nilsa Lugo

Just Another Day

Echoes of a child's prayer in a world so far away.
Huddled beneath the shelter, pleading with God for just another day.

Human carnage, evidence of destruction in her life,
apparent that she constantly veering to avoid disappointment and strife.

Hunger, and the child, they are not strangers,
they've been aquatinted for far too long.
Her silent prayers with God, her faith in tomorrow's sun,
keep's the diminishing hope within her saunter on.

"Just another day"
A well rehearsed cry, yet from her tiny blistered lips it's never
questioned why.
A master plan by a higher being, calling the people back with him.
And for the villains weighing upon their shoulders,
guilt, an unforgivable sin.

Grateful for each breath she takes,
a life to her, there's no other way.
Fighting for existence to see...
"Just another day"

Jolanda L. Morrison

"When We Began"

When we began, the road seemed endless,
But you taught me to pace myself and remember to rest.

When we began, I feared the unknown,
But you stood beside me whispering you're not alone.

When we began, the world seemed so big,
But you just laughed and said it's all in how you live.

When we began, I was faced with so many things,
But you just smiled saying these things are what rainbows bring.

When we began, it was just you and me against the world,
But you taught me to reach out and now we walk with two beautiful girls.

When we began, I put my heart in your hands,
But you wanted to protect it, so you sealed it with a wedding band.

For now it seems like an eternity has past since our wedding day plans,
But so does the love we share grow more than, when we began.

Bruce P. McElroy

Enchanted Illusions

In the silent sphere of yesterday, I feel the feathery light present
of irresistible phantoms weave there cherubic chants to the
Mentor of my mind.
Silently I listen to fascinating enchanted voices
Flowing elusively through the melancholic night air with
melodious sounds, like the whisper of the wind.
Their solemn lyrics and poetic Odes spinning their mystic net with
sweet and everlasting Sonnets of Love to the metaphor of my Soul.
Dried rose petals mixed with the ancient smell of sweet aroma
and the masculine scent of musk linger in the Now.
The stillness of the night surrounds me, embracing, communicating
their Love, once reality, now Eras ago... the Love still lives beyond
the boundaries of time, even Death can not erase conquered love,
existing through Eons of time.
Tranquility encases my wearied saddest heart. I still see your face,
feel your touch, my Soul relinquishes in your nearness.
Don't weep my heart tarries... I always be near you,
Until we meet again, my Love is with you Now.

Gisela Wright

A Shadow Of Grief

I stand alone on the edge of a great emptiness.
Everyday I walk between the darkness and the light.
A shadow without a body in infinite space.
Waiting for the fog to lift from my eyes
so I can see the shining light illuminating my body.

Linda Goss

Within Me

I have all the secrets of the universe - within me.
I have all the brain power to remove a curse - within me.
I have all the knowledge I need to know - within me.
I have all extra inches when I need to grow - within me.
I have strength to overcome the worst of all - within me.
I have extra energy to stand up when I fall - within me.
I have plenty of faith to believe in true love - within me.
I have an extra eye to see from above - within me.
I have dreams that'll give me power to strive - within me.
I have peace that makes me happy to be alive - within me.
I have will power to become my very best - within me.
I have the biggest heart to share with the rest - within me.
I have all the enthusiasm to learn and explore - within me.
I have all the abilities I could ever wish for - within me.
I have a little sense of doubt to keep it all hidden - within me.

Jaime'G Jaramillo

Fall

Warm days turn colder
The grey and white appears
The leaves begin to turn color
The leaves begin to fall
The grey and white bird appears again
It is a lone bird.
Fierce at heart
It stares at me, proud, strong, dominating
It flies atop the clubhouse roof
There it sits on top of the world looking down upon me
He's up to the challenge
The leaves fall off
The fruit of the trees and bushes appear
The row of trees is the birds domain
It protects the fall harvest
It fights off the flocks of birds come to take its food
With a heart as strong as I have ever seen
it fights with courage and its last drops of strength
Until the flocks of birds overcome it

Kevin Wright

I'm Sorry And I Love You

Everyday I wonder, wonder if I
hadn't been so mad, would you
still be here and would I still be bad?

Some nights I cannot sleep
remembering the times we had when
I wasn't mad. But know I weep for you.

I ask myself, how could I be so stupid
to have been mad enough to have said
those things which I would never mean?

Now I can never say I'm sorry and I
hope you know. I still will never let you go.

Why did you have to die? Couldn't you
have made me see in a different way?
Well, now I have to pay.

I'm sorry my friend, and I love you.

Michelle Harrigan

We're All Outsiders

Anger burns my eyes red,
I cannot understand.
All the sadness deep inside me
Just cannot be expressed.

Strange mysteries in this world
Will be solved soon in time,
But the heart breaking sorrow in our hearts
Seems to be growing all the time.

The blank stares from those around me,
Those trying to hide their thoughts,
Feel that no one should know their anger;
The anger held for others.

The pain all must suffer
Seems to have no end.
All seem to hate each other;
There is no "helping hand"

Differences don't really matter
And if they were set aside,
All the pain and suffering in this world
Would then surely pass us by.

Anna Joshi

Memories

White waters flow down hill,
I'm told to let things be as they will,
As the hill levels the waters slow,
As the waters calm and things are told,
Of one's life and time in this pond,
As one lingers and grows fond,
They find that they must go on,
They then continue to flow beyond,
And mix with other waters,
They become parts of one another,
They will always be in my memory,
No less then when first parted of freed,
but only intermingled with greater memories,
Until we become all that we can be.

Edward A. Hester

A Summary Of A Day

The sun strikes earth early in the morning
People reluctantly meet the new day,
Suddenly, events pass without warning
Trying to avoid trouble in all way.

The day sees the busy people going
Walking like ants to different places,
All of these people forever roaming
So many people, so many faces.

Night has fallen, all of earth is now dark,
Moon has shone up, above living and dead
Weak and weary bodies, now left to park
Rush hour has seized, all people are in bed.

Alas, but a whole day has come and gone.
Hence! More days are coming forever on.

Elizabeth Viloria

That Dear Lady

She's a symbol of what the pilgrims prayed for,
    the day they landed on plymouth shore,
praying that God would let them live here in peace
    and that This Lady would hold her torch evermore.

It seems she's saying, it's the ultimate honor
    I'll hold this torch in honor of the sons who died-
I'll wear my crown with dignity and pride for all to see,
    and to pay tribute to all the Moms and Dads who cried."

I think I hear her softly singing "God Bless America-
    The price of freedom is never an easy price to pay
For those who paid the ultimate price-let their spirits arise-
    Let us visit their graves-get on our knees and pray."

Dear Lady, your presence will bless us 'til the end of time,
    lighting our way north to south, east to west with steadfast hand
Let's all respect her as she lifts her torch and wears her crown
    proclaiming freedom for everyone in this great land.

William H. Moore

Untitled

An Angel is on my shoulder, whispering "this way"
I question "where does it lead, this way?"
Softly reassuring, the whisper comes again "this way"
I peer into darkness. "Is that a point of light, this way?"
I feel a soft touch, a tender push.
"You will not fall or fail, this way."
"It doesn't look like a path. Are you sure it's this way?"
But, I follow the soft nudge, the touch, the whisper "this way."
I now look back and see how narrow the path of "this way"
How easy, but how sad to not have gone "this way"
Angels whisper very softly. Listen.

Doris Kauffman

The Swing

At the cottage there was a swing about eight feet
Homemade with rope and a chunk of 2x4 for a seat
I was only a child then
When I would swing for hours and hours on end
On a nice summer morning just after breakfast
I would start to get bored of dishes and Grandma being a pest
To relax myself from her
I would go outside and swing as high as a bird
I thought of school and friends
Sailing through the air I never wanted it to end
Flying high in the tree, I would challenge myself to something petty
Like trying to touch the highest branch when I was ready
I loved the feeling it gave in my stomach so high
Back and forth I felt butterflies
Well that was then and this is now I find
For the swing is gone forever, but not from my mind

Trina McInnes

Rain

It pedals down from up above,
it hits my house with a soft thud.
It fills the lakes so ducks can swim,
it grows the grass that we play in.
It washes the birds,
and clears the streets,
it gives parents a reason to get angry....
when their kids stamp in puddles of it with their feet!

It gives flowers the strength to bloom,
it eases peoples fear of a drought,
but it doesn't rain forever....
the sun will come out again without a doubt!

Stephanie Amanda Spino

School

On the first day of school I had a friend. He pushed me around and
I knew trouble would begin.
He threw a chair. It hit me in the head, but that didn't bother me.
He treated me like dirt. It didn't hurt.
Then he told all my secrets. I got mad but there was nothing to do
but laugh. I knew it was revenge time.
On the next day of school it was a blast. I sat in my chair thinking fast.
How can I trick him? What should I do?
First I will tell him, "Your breath smells like rotten egg", or
"You have a nappy head."
But first I have to hide my thoughts away.
In line I saw his spine. I put a sign on it. It would be a kick!
At lunch I had a bunch of ideas. I sneezed on his candy dots,
it was filled with snot.
On his return I'd have my revenge! When he came back he ate
his snotty dots.
He spit them out and without a doubt he caught me crying out!
I had my revenge. Then I stopped. Here comes more troubled again.
He told on me. We went to the Big Man. We spilled our guts.
He just smile and said "Be friends again.
It's better than detention in the end."

Bronn J. James

My Love

My sweat dearest one of all,
I must admit you have it all.

Your gentle touch, upon my face,
Your sweet and humble embrace.

While lying awake in my bed,
I remember all the words we've said.

I feel so wanted when you hold me in your arms,
You seem to have all the special charms.

When you touch me, I melt inside,
From you, I've nothing to hide.

I love your strong arms and tender kiss,
That brushes so softly against my lips.

I like to think of you because,
I know the feeling is true.

Because when you sit next to me,
I feel the love we share.

You give me happiness,
You give me laughter.

Along with your sweet love,
that's what I'm after.

Gidget Bates

As A Nurse

As I watch you fade away into nothing I remember all the times you smiled at me, all the punches you threw. The times when I almost lost you. Then I see your family yelling at me for something that could not be controlled. I know that is because of guilt. They feel guilty because they put you here. Now you are about to pass through the pearly gates and they fight to pull you back. They don't want to let you go, yet they visited you only once last year. By the time they accepted where you were in life you had already packed your bags and headed down that road to a better place. I argue with your doctor to find a an answer to your guest for a painless journey. I see you everyday I watch you hang on every last piece of life, I hear your pleas for mercy and I hold you tight. I know you are scared as I watch you pass on. I must carry on with my day until it is through. I see you as a friend and I know I will miss you. The work never ends. Now it's someone else's family, my staff or my boss, non stop until I leave to go home. I stop at the door and try to leave your memory there as not to bring it home with me. I drive home hoping to have peace for the quietest part of my day was spent you.

My kids are fighting, my husband wants to discuss the bills. I walk past it all for one final moment to reflect on the chance I had to know you. I fix dinner, go to bed and get up to face another day and another family member. To get punched, bit or scratched, slapped or spit on. To be asked questions that I don't have the answers to. Try to heal the pain of somebody new as for I made a promise to serve you.

Susan K. Armstrong

Dreams

In everyday life, we all have dreams and aspirations we try to obtain.
We all have goals and accomplishments yet to be attained.
From our dreams we get a glimpse of what we hope to become.
In life, love, and family.

Dreams are nothing more than a mirror in which a part of our life
    is reflected.
A doorway, that if we choose to step through, would open our eyes
    to marvels and wonders of the world.
In our dreams are our hopes and fears which can only be conquered
    by our will and determination

For without our dreams, we can never strive or reach for the stars.
Which are our goals and aspirations.
Without dreams you can never know the full potential of the person within.
The soul, the spirit, the heart, and love of a person.
For without dreams, we would fall short of many endeavors in life,
    and to give up on life is to give up one's self and no one
        wants to be alone in the world.

Dreams are just another extension of you, a way of expressing your thoughts.
To dream is to want, to want is to get, to get is to give back,
    share with others.
Because if it weren't for dreams - where would you be today?

Remember that dreams are meant to be lived out to their fullest
    and not slept away.
For you are your own destiny and only you can fulfill your dreams.

Jeffery A. Robertson

These I Love The Most

I love purple lilacs, red roses and yellow honey suckle vines,
living beside still waters and watching the morning sun as it rises through the pines.

I love to hear the lonesome whine of a train as it passes through
the night. The trill of the mockingbird and the turtle doves coo
in the early morning light.

I love to hear little children reciting special verse, and the
church choir singing praises to the heavenly host.

I love my parents, I hold their values close. I love God, family
and friends, these I love the Most.

Juanita Jones Lunsford

To Each The Other

Life is so fragile,
there are limits we are not aware of
It is a fragility of crystalline depths,
Easily opaque, equally translucent,
brittle of heart, reflective of soul.

Facets a plenty, all parts of the whole,
each of one make, all of them different
The whirlings of time and each of fates steps,
discovered anew each has its own view of
fragile life is so.

So fragile is life
fully connected each to the other.
Purination of one; with each splintered shared,
and great empires crumble, visions spent.
Fall even the mighty, many short of goal.

They have tasted of beauty its purity of soul,
unity in harmony through strengths inherent
Each ray crisply pure and simply no guard
all focused in fire, so sings clear the bard.
Is life so fragile?

Christopher W. W. Harris

"Time Was"

One day I walked an unknown path, far from
    the tedious road
Whose length and breadth had held me fast
    from a dream I longed to know
At first I thought I walked alone, but then
    you took my hand
For just a little while we shared
    a haven far from home
Few grains we took from the sands of time
    softly they shone in the dusk
To await a time we both would know
    return again we must
And so it was my chosen fate changed not
    but now embraced a tender loving
    memory not to be replaced.
From the moment it took to know you,
    I knew I could easily say
The time it would be I'd forget you
    when forever becomes today.

Ruth Henderson

A Dog's World

The world...according to canines
No ordinary canines are we,
But Bichon Frises!
Our Matriarch is Molly; our Patriarch - Cocoanut.
As for us — better known as the "Three Musketeers"
Named MacDonald, Barnaby, and Jasper.
Perhaps we'll be splendid show dogs,
Elegantly groomed...
Or fine pets; at present, we are enjoying the life
of rambunctious puppies,
Especially when people continually fuss over us
as we grow and develop.
Ah! Canine life is not too tough after all,
Although we remain small.

Audrey S. Mercer

Love And Hate

If love is a sunset them let me see it,
If love is a star then let me be one,
If love is a moon then let me have one,
If love is me then let me be myself.
If hate is a sunrise then don't make me watch
If hate is a meteor then don't make me be one.
If hate is a sun don't let me take one.
If hate is me then let me be an actress.

Ashleigh Robertson

The Voyage Home

It seems to me somewhere along the line
    humanity took a wrong turn
We toil away day after day and turn never heed
    the lessons we learn

We look to the sky and give out a cry
    "God, let me be the one"
Yet we seldom ever try, or even ask why
    or realize that damage we've done

It's so hard to love, we all look to the above
    and judge everyone's sacred space
We hold in all the pain, only looking to face
    with your divine destiny

A journey into self, there will be no one else
    the illustrious voyage home
Treat yourself so kind, keep an open mind,
    and find you never, really are alone

Christopher Laurence Souders

"Choices"

Life has a way of turning
In unexpected ways,
You never really know the road
You'll be going down each day.

When you are young
You never think and never plan your day,
You just enjoy each passing day with
friends who like to play.

When you're a teen
Life can bring some problems in your way,
You have to stop to think about the choices
of each day.

As you grow older in your life,
You reflect on roads you've took,
Some were smooth and some were rough,
But those were the paths you took.

There's never any guarantee's in life,
Each day brings something new.
Each choice we make - each road we take,
We're dealt the hands we chose.

Bonnie Sheble

When

When will He come I do not know,
but some day it will be sure to show.

I will walk with Him day and night
up in the heavens where the stars shine bright.

When will I see Him for the first time?
I think it's when the sunbeams shine.

He is kind, loving, and sweet,
and that's Someone I can't wait to meet.

When will I serve Him in the heavens?
I don't know, but it will be my pleasure.

McKenzie Fulford

A Summer Garden

I walk along a new-mown path
That borders beds of beauty and delight;
There are marigolds and pansies,
Flaming cosmos and dazzling daisies bright.
    This little garden planted here
    Invites the tiny songbirds —
    Beckons to the dainty butterflies,
    And casts a mood of hushed tranquility.
I pause a moment to enjoy
This calm and soothing scene
And revel in its peaceful spell.
    My garden of memories much richer will be
    As I take away with me
    This priceless jewel of serenity
    And add it to my growing store
    Of happy things I've known and seen.
To the recalled again
In moments of quiet reverie.

Effie Barlow

Insecurity

There's no denying when I look in your eyes
When you look back at me, I completely melt.
Of which this is a wonderful feeling
The greatest of all feelings I have ever felt.

I am very self-conscious
About the things that I do.
And when you're around me
I can't even talk to you.

I'm afraid that I'll say
Or do something wrong.
So I look off into space
And soon you are gone.

It's not that I'm trying
To ignore you at all.
But if I mess up in front of you
My heart will stop, and I will fall.

Jessica Maree Horvath

Blind

Because I could not see your rainbow
You unkindly laughed at me,
Even though I tried my hardest
To see what I could see.

There must be something wrong with her
You say to your friends
Because I can't find where your rainbow starts
Or even where it ends.

I'm sure that the colors
Make a lovely sight
In a brilliant perfect arc
The flows from left to right.

Stunning reds and vibrant blues
That splash a cloudy sky,
But I just cannot see it
No matter how hard I try.

I am so very jealous
Of this sight that you see
And I wonder If you're right;
If there's something wrong with me

Kara Ukolowicz

The Great Mystery

There are many kinds of mysteries,
good and bad.
There are many kinds of mysteries,
happy and sad.
But the greatest mystery of all
lies within ourselves,
for the greatest mystery of all is life.
Life is something that was a gift
given to us by God.
Life is something that can be taken
for granted, as quick as it can be
taken. Life is something that puzzles
us all. Something that will be...
the greatest mystery.

John Rohr

Untitled

Uncanny thing to be free
The diamond collarbone feeling heavy as a leash
The torched arrows pointing high and low
So that traffic may evenly flow

I was once told...
An automobile swerved off the happy road
Diverting off the graveled floor
Debris splattering here and fro
Just hearing the engine roar

Driving purposely along the dwindling stretch
Waiving diligently to passers-by
Their eyes huge, gasping for breath

Soon the Imperial Valley sun set
Its radiant splendor later dazzled in the west
The coronas hand propelling mother natures quest

The unknown driver
Tracking through a cacti spread
Cut convention's horns from its head

Jacqueline Lopez

Untitled

We walked together,
His fingers laced through mine.
Arthritis knobs pressed my wedding band,
Worn thin from years of touch and time.
The noonday sun warmed the breeze
Salty from the incoming tide
As it whipped my wispy gray curls
Around my face like a cloud halo.
With bared feet
Our toes scrunched in the wet sand.

Screeching sea gulls overhead
And spindly legged sandpipers
Cheered us to victory
As we played our games of hopscotch and
Tic tac toe
On driftwood-drawn lines in the sand,
And again as we played hide-and-seek in the dunes
Shielded by sea oats
Waving in the wind.

Edna G. Banov

Supernova

The soft light of morning falls on "Starry, Starry Night"
Hanging on the kitchen wall above the table.
A vase of Spring promise, daffodils, bring new hope to her mind;
She is leaving soon, not without some regret.

It hasn't worked here, not for a long time; the family, the house she grew up in
Changed over time. But she did, more than they.
In the foyer, two paintings: One by Aunt Grace, "Ruins Through the Persimmon Trees."
No persimmons here, only ruins.
The other, from the Ramayana entitled "The Happy Ending."
How ironic.

The grasscloth covered walls of the dining room hold a brass rubbing given by her mother
Alongside Chinese characters wishing good health, wealth, luck and happiness.
She has crafted a heart-shaped basket with loving hands, three strips of red border it.
The inside is empty, like her heart.

Why is it all gone? Why am I so tired? She asks herself as she packs,
Part of me is here and part cannot bear to be.
Will they put up new pictures when I am gone?
Already a replica Harley sits next to the Lladros.

Four bronze musicians from Siam and all the temple bells are silent.
I will hear their song again, she promises herself without conviction.

Carole Hasson

Remembering Pa

When I was young we were best friends
I thought you'd be there till the end.
But I am here and you are gone
Memories of you are fading on.

When you left it was a beautiful day
The sun was shining, the birds were at play.
In a way I was mad, you left me alone.
Did I do something bad? Did I do something wrong?

I was real disappointed, you never said "Bye".
The only question I had was why? Oh why?
But after all these years I've figured it out
You moved to a better place, no doubt.

Now that I'm grown, I understand -
God took you to the Promised Land.
Where the sun always shines and the birds always play
And where we will meet again some day.

Angela Alejo

"Decisions"

Thinking about what is the best to do,
How many ways in thoughts your mind does carry you?
Looking at things from all sorts of views.
Trying to decide for you, what is the best thing to do?

This decision must be one that is precise.
There can be no betting or rolling of the dice.
Before the time came that you had to make this decision your day was nice.
In coming to the right decision, what direction will you take and go?
You find that the truth is, you really don't know.
You hope you'll take the right steps and because of your
  decision be left with no regrets.
Before you had to make this decision about everything
  else you've had good wisdom and sense.
But now, you're puzzled and tensed, and feeling dense.
You decide it's time for you to take a break.
Tomorrow this decision may not be so hard for you to make.
Why not have a drink and sleep on it tonight?
Tomorrow is a new day and then you'll make the decision that is right.

Sheila C. Dozier

Jane

I depended on her.

The way a Flower depends on rain
at the end of a warm summer day.
Looking for its comfort.
A cool drink, something to help tie over the harsh, dry days.
The Cloud came sporadically,
only enough to help the Flower get by.
When it came the Flower would stand taller
confidence risen, waiting in anticipation
to hear the pitter-patter,
pitter-patter.
This last time, the Cloud was black.
Bringing poison to the little Flower.
Suffocating her in its turbulent courant.
Now, the little Flower, uprooted,
lying in a puddle,
drying on the black pavement,
swirling in circles,
hypnotized by the currents constant motion.

The car drove on, unconcerned.

Christy Barnoski

Chocolate Marshmallows

I dreamed last night and the night before of a bunch of kids
playing on the floor...one was white and one was brown and
one could smile upside down by standing on his head with his
feet off the ground...which made all the kids shout "Quit
Clownin' Around!"......while the snow white girl with the long
blonde hair planted a kiss on the big brown eye of the kid
with the coal black hair and he started to cry when the red-
haired kid with the freckles galore laughed so hard he wet
the floor...but it didn't matter 'cause the cute little twins,
one white and one brown, danced and sang "I Love You" songs
to the rainbow kids and I'm trying to sleep so I can dream some
more about the bunch of kids playing on the floor.

Christi Clarke

Au Revoir

Pictures and memories are all I have left
    Of the happy home we once knew,
You brightened my days with your innocent ways
    Now, what am I going to do?

You barked and you jumped,
    we walked and we played
Fifteen happy years through,
    You were my Buddy
My pal and my Friend
    Loyal, devoted and true.

Old age came along with its troubles galore
    Deepening my love for you even more.
You slowed down bit by bit until you finally quit
    Content to just lie down or sit.

Then come that sad day
    when you went away
Leaving my heart bleeding
    broken and sore.

My precious Jolly, Live on!

Lucille E. Ricks

Lonely Tree

As I sit here looking at the old oak tree
I can see how much it resembles me
Its trunk so old and barely alive
While the others laugh by her side
Her branches quickly falling down
She has to be the ugliest tree in town

When that tree was actually young
Her trunk was so ripe, beautiful branches hung
She looked as though she was always smiling
Nobody knew that she was really dying
She was not dying of old age
It became obvious, it was all her rage
Barely standing, she tried to be brave
And not let others drive her to the grave

But now she cannot stand so tall
Because she knows that she will fall
When she does, she'll fall deep into the ground
No one will miss her, she'll be nowhere to be found
It will be as though she was never there
Because nobody did love or care

Diana Miller

Visions Of Love

This afternoon,
    while a child was being conceived,
Your image appeared before me.
And in the time it takes
    for death to conquer,
You were gone again;
    Simply a shimmer off hot asphalt,
    a mirage, an oasis.
I believe you are, in fact, a tangible wish.
If one wants you or needs you badly enough,
    she can wish you into existence.

My mind becomes a moth
    dancing round your flame.
But the flame is lit only when called for.
So your spirit appears only when beckoned
    by this flickering soul,
    or her infinite joy.
It makes no difference,
    just so you are here for me to love.

Shannon Field

Listen Closely to the Wind

If you listen closely, you may hear the wind
Whispering its secrets as it blows across the land
If you listen closely, it will tell you where it's been
And some of its encounters will chill your soft, warm skin
And if you listen closely, it will tell you what it's seen
All the wondrous beauties, and all the horrid things

If only human souls, would act more like the wind
Never straying from its given path, and never giving in
No matter what the obstacles it must endure along the way
Never trying to go back, it just moves forward everyday

So listen closely to the wind, listen carefully to each turn
For each one of its stories, provides a lesson you can learn

Travis Inselman

Glen, Our Son And Brother

There was a time my son,
When we would talk and laugh and run,
A time for caring, a time for wishing,
We even had the time for fishing.

The joy and laughter,
Your smiles and tears,
The way you shared your hopes and fears,
In this way we spent our years.

And then while I was away,
The Lord called - you could not stay,
We miss you so and try to understand,
That you had to go - but was it planned?

We miss you - oh so very much,
Your laughter, dreams and your touch,
The way you made our lives a treasure,
Will fill our days with full measure.

As the years go rolling by,
Our memories of you will never die,
The love you left will always last,
Until tomorrow becomes the past.

Gerald G. Martin

Untitled

Look in the mirror and you will find
someone looking back who is one of a kind.
Turn around and look you'll see the same face,
Nobody else could take your place.

Phyllis M. Caternolo

We Used To Be

We used to be like two roads that intersected
On a busy highway
Leading eastward traffic westward
And southward traffic to bay.

But our hands have been reconstructed
And traffic make a detour
East doesn't on West
and North doesn't go South anymore.

I guess what I'm trying to say
Is pain enough to see
But I'm glad that you've found happiness
Even though it's not with me.

Andrea Coley

The End Of The Affair

Winter whispers with its silvery breath
And tells a haunting tale of snowy dreams
With feathery filtering shapes and shadowy schemes,
And soft gleaned whiteness of a silent death.

The snow falls lightly on the traveled paths
And covers up the footprints made in haste,
To give a grace to walkways strewn with stones,
And soften all the harshness of the past.

The trees take on new life outlined in frost,
And all the myriad branches are defined
With gossamer and lacy breath entwined:
And summer's passion seems a gentler loss.

Lorna Hamilton

Words

Restrained by circumstances, I am mute;
Forever sire of words unsaid to her.

Words that spring sourceless from deep
And innocent longings of boyhood;

Words coined crisp and clean and honest
By desires of a guileless heart.

Well up, words, sweet and uncontrived.
Let me fill my darling's ear

With whispers of ardor overflowing,
Untutored by arts and devices of romance.

Let me speak phrases pristine and fresh
As waters that flow sparkling from springs

Hidden in shades of woodland tranquility,
Away from furtive eyes and tongues plotted

With deceits and assassinations of love.
And when my beloved answers,

May enchanted words free my captive voice,
And soothe my yearning dreams.

Robert D. Richardson

Mourning Light

For the tree in winter stands, bare and naked in her hand
Stripped and bare for all to see, nothing left to rival thee.

No one knows the fruit she'll bear, Or the love and tender care.
No one see's beauty's rest, as she holds it to her breast.

Still...she is so quiet now, knowing not the why or how.

Crying from her wounded side, came the sap to her eyes.
Bitter is the winter's cold, in dying breath took her hold.

Nothing but a hole to see, where once stood a big oak tree.
It was gone it felt like death, the hole so deep within her chest.

"I am the tree of life" he said "I am not done, I am not death.
I am in your soul, I am at your breast.

Oh little tree don't you see, you have the biggest part of me.
Buried deep inside your chest, a bleeding heart is one that's blessed.

Mourning in the winters cold, Is hard to bare but free's the soul.
Winter comes to hold the soul, from what one does to what one knows.

All the time that we once shared, engraved in you with tender care.
Listen to me now and than, I'll bring you up to where I've been.

The seasons all come and go, and life goes on as you well know.
My love for you is in your hand, feel your heart and there I am.

The heart is called to newer things, that it may bring forth in you
The Spring.

Elizabeth Ann Morin

Stella Maris

Stella Maris
Home for old sea dogs.

Back from childish dreams of vaporous heat

Small dank back rooms
with tattooed nicknamed women

Sulfurous visions of Conrad and London
and sheeted ships of close-packed men

I take my memories in bulk container ships
biding in gage roads and gantry swinging docks.

L. I. Zivkovic

Today Be Happy, Don't Shed A Tear

If you must cry, don't cry too long,
I've only gone away to my heavenly home;
There is love, peace and happiness here,
My friends don't cry, don't shed a tear.

I can see Jesus, that was always my goal,
I'm now resting in his bosom, his arms unfold;
Think of all I've done on the earth below,
But when Jesus said come, I was ready to go.

No matter what I did or what I said,
Think about how many souls I've fed;
Think about how I've helped somebody along the way,
Don't cry be happy, don't shed a tear today.

I thank the Lord for letting me walk the earth for a little while,
He blessed me with one lovely child;
My loved one, I know, is in heaven above,
Heaven, indeed is the place he love.

Today, just think about me and the heavenly host,
Heaven is the place I love the most;
I've gone away to a better place, I had nothing to fear,
Today just be happy, don't shed a tear.

Georgia B. Malone

Life Being A Clown

Since I am famous clown
I'm very good at making people laugh.
I have a big red rose along with big baggy pants
and giant brown shoes to help me dance.
My face is painted white and my shirt is tucked in tight
and when people see me they laugh and say that I'm a funny sight.
I do tricks with the animals and give balloons to girls and boys
and when the circus is over, I give smaller children stuffed toys.
I like my job and I hope you like clowns too,
and maybe someday at the circus I will meet you.

Sara Stover

A Mass Of Clay

Day by day, I slowly watched her
Turn into a mass of clay.
Hardened by the angry rays of the sun,
"Oh Lord!" I asked myself,
"What has she become?"

She longs for a rainfall to moisten all the layers
All the years of pain and torment.
But she is trapped - buried alive,
In what was an avalanche of mud
Which slowly hardened into a mass of clay.

She screams for water
"There is more, the well is dry!" He angrily shouts
She shivers, huddled in a corner and begs:
"But is it not you who holds the abundant supply of water?
Embodied in your heart, your eyes, your sexual release."

"The well is dry, leave you mass of clay!"
Thus, she must leave in search of water, if only a sprinkle.
With time the layers will soften, turn into mud again,
And only then will she be cleansed and no longer be a mass of clay.
She will be free to live - oh to live again!

Lynn Bacso

Home

This world God created can be a wonderful place
But all to often, and to our disgrace
It's filled with hatred, anger, sorrow, and greed
They give no thought what they'll reap from this seed
With all the turmoil, anxiety, and stress
Home is where I go for rest.

Here I find a soft word spoken
Much love, encouragement, and bonds that aren't broken
My faith in God, forgiveness, and direction
Loyalty, honesty, guidance, and correction
Peace of heart and peace of mind
Comfort and compassion here are mine.

When out in the world and among the rat race
I think of home and set a new pace
To be a well person this knowledge I must keep
Whatever I sow - that shall I reap
Lessons are taught and examples are given
But it's up to me how I use this wisdom.

Tiffany Richardson

Inspiration

A smile displaying infinite care
The gentle caress of an age worn hand
Rather at its peak in silence than a gallant stand
Lies the honored gem seeming unattainable there

Rather in a snowflake than sparkling quilt of white
Rather in a whisper than a timeless speech
That which to the wisest can seem so out of reach
Rather in a single star than in the night

In the breath of a sleeping child not the words of man
In a letter untouched for years
In the honesty of tears
Live that which the wise may never understand
In a simple rose lies its infiltration
Seeming still inaccessible is inspiration

Rebekah Zimmerman

The Empty Cross

The cross stands empty now,
There's silence on the hill of Calvary.
What had taken place raised many a brow,
For it was really something to see.
The people had nailed an innocent man to the cross,
They jeered and taunted Him for many an hour.
But do not despair for there was no loss,
For you see, for the Christian, the victory is at that empty cross
They condemned this man, not believing;
They called Him a liar and refused any grieving.
For how could they see who He really was?
How could they ever know His identity?
They were blinked so they would not know He was our Saviour, Jesus
They were blinded to His being The Deity.
Do not weep or pine, do not feel any loss,
For christ has been the victor all the time.
He is The Royal Blood Line.
Because of the cross, He paid for our sins,
Because of His love, we the Christians win.

Rose Wegener

The Encounter

The city is glass, concrete and white for miles.
My feet are in this synthetic world. I wait and watch.
I see you coming. Full blooded Comanche, your face intent,
     magnificent.
Was ever so little learned from another?
I have been on the trains, killing your buffalo, taking
     away your livelihood.
I have been the government slowly destroying you with
     broken promises.
I have been the missionary squelching your beliefs in the
     name of Christ.
I have not honored your humanity.
In spite of this, I am woman and know the taste of hunger,
     deceit, homelessness and injury.
My white flesh is a man in me and I have become his
     stranger.
My white heritage is overcome.

Virginia Hanslien

The Turning....

As the trees are dancing naked, They hold a secret oh-so-sacred.
Sensing this, the breeze joins in; Around & thru the trunks it spins,
Twirling past the mighty Spruce, Dancing freely, intent: to seduce.
Arous'd, the green leaves rustle, free! Their quiet voices hold the key.

All around, a Shadow lurks, In the darkness, something works.
It wants to see, it wants to know, What secret tale the forest holds.
The wind has now pick'd up its pace; No more play, now it's a race.
It moves around like a sleuth, Asking questions: Why? and who?

The branches and leaves are closely-knit; They keep safe their own,
dammit! Not about to spill, are they, What knowledge haunts them
night and day. Moving on to taunt & tempt, The wind leaves trails of
leaves unkempt. It starts to play the "good old friend" And offers
rewards to no end, If only the Treasure they would share, But they
refuse — their souls — to bare.

No sooner does a sapling break, Than something stirs, at last awake.
The dark sky fills with bright white light, As all the trees shrivel, in fright.
The Secret's out, and nothing's safe —
From the nearing Doom there's no escape.
Screams are heard, last rights are read,
And then, darkness & silence — all is dead.

Dorothy Liang

Everything Precious

And you, sweet child lying tender in my arms,
Are a re-creation of life, of all that is fresh and new,
And a brand new start.
And as I rock you in dreams,
And hold you close to my beating heart,
I want only the best for you, and will always be there,
No matter what.
And even though I will sometimes get emotional,
I will never be too busy to care,
For you are everything that is precious and real,
And you mean the world to me!
So sleep, wrapped in tender dreams,
And grow in the Love of God!
And may He forever give His Angels charge of you,
To watch over you,
When I cannot.

Elaine Dinnall-Stewart

A Child For The Beating

I was only a child when I took my first beating
I wondered why this kept repeating

I worked very hard at hard at trying to be good
But it didn't matter if I did what I should

The beatings I took were so severe
I could not think about them without shaking with fear

I lived in fear most of my life
Because the looks he gave me cut like a knife

I tried to run and disappear
But he always found me after drinking his beer

I used the drinking to explain his behavior
But I truly knew I was just doing him a favor

The beatings were bad even when he was sober
I cried out and prayed for them to be over

I laid awake, many a night, trying to figure out
How to kill him, to end the fright

Rodney Timms

Human Nature

Birth is the celebration of an awakening.
Passages of life are enclosed with this gift.
Days go by, with an integrated experience,
As the appetite for survival lingers.
Watching the mind branching out into lost places.
Hearing earth's existence and feeling her beauty
With moves of body.
Destiny awaits through the maze of consciousness.
Although a physical world exists,
Someday, mind will surpass matter.
Collected temptations point to discovery,
While mystery stands in its shadow.
Seek and fulfill alerted views,
Achieve and control under creation.

Cindy Mijin Park

My Old Friend

He looked at me, and very gently said 'I have AIDS you know.'
I said 'Yes' - 'I'd heard' 'you old so and so.'
I looked at him - straight in the eye - then gave him a hug -
Embarrassment over - he looked down at me and said - 'you old love.'

Our friendship went back to his student years.
So we chatted away - told me his hopes and his fears.
We talked of the people we knew years ago.
Updating each other about friend and about foe.

He took me to dinner, said he had a white car;
I sat in his Rolls - he said 'Restaurants' not far
I said, 'I'm impressed' - I knew he was proud -
Then he looked at me and giggled then laughed out loud.

He told of the bad days - when he first knew -
Of the friends he has lost - what can you do?
He makes the most of every minute he's here.
He lives with a friend - whom he holds very dear.

He visits the places he's wanted to see
The Alps and the Islands and Egypt - and he
Knows that he lives on borrowed time
How I admire the courage of this old friend of mine.

Pamela Jean Duley

True Lies Of You

Love is at all nothing but sorrow,
Leaving empty memories of tomorrow
Giving my strength to only weakness below,
The truth beneath you, so hard to show.
Disbelieving the truth I shed a tear,
Wanting that warmth when you were hear.
It was all the softness in your touch,
The way you let it mean so much.
Now to have it ripped apart,
With questions unanswered and a broken heart
You once lifted me so high,
For when I was low you showed me the sky
You showed me the beauty in the stars above,
You once promised me the given in your love
You showed me I can be strong inside,
You told me I was beautiful, then I cried
The end was so sudden so still,
How much you cared I'll never know, I never will.

Maria Pangas

The Call

I hear a gentle calling
Like distant music in my ear
It brings an awesome feeling
And shade each thought with sense of fear
There the past before me runs
As a storm upon the mind
And sudden in a dreadful calm
I saw deeds the stained this life of mine

Who art thou that seek me
Where dost thou abide
What is this awesome prodigy
That impels the soul to hide

I hear the voice still calling
Like a stream my being flow
I feel the heart's deep yearning
The agony, the woe
There burns an inner emptiness
Taunted and wretched I am
Life seems to have some deeper meaning
I do not understand

John Adams

Villanelle

I can see as far as tomorrow
Doubts knitted in the furrow
The soulful strains of someone else's sorrow

Petals in a row
They will always be new
I can see as far as tomorrow

Tingling tonsils
How could they be so
The soulful strains of someone else's sorrow

Footprints on the road
Much that will always be in turmoil
I can see as far as tomorrow

Simmering cloves
Hand me the twirling smokes
The soulful strains of someone else's sorrow

A swiveling world
Even a poet can be normal
I can see far as tomorrow
The soulful strains of someone else's sorrow

Yuzhi Yang

Secret World

Look beyond these horizons and the glimmer of the stars
taste the sounds of
hope and tranquility, witness and touch
the vibrance of life's beauty, emotions and dreams
Travel within this secret place and feel
the warm thoughts, friendly banter and closeness
that so much belongs...
What comprises our words and thoughts, questions and doubts.
Why do we speak as if seeing, act as if hearing and do as if believing
that life centers around our needs and dreams...
Our river flows into stream and eddies with pockets of sky,
whispering the thunder of emotions
raining the sunshine of importance of need.
Why do narcissistic egos weaken our true feelings,
turn on our questions and doubt cycles
and hurt those for which we care...
Behold but the sprinkling rain as it moistens to soothe
the saddened thoughts and colder
heart that occurs beyond this secret world.

Robert William Lee

Reverie

A hole in the forest where a split tree once stood
And a small patch of sky was my place in the wood,

Where I went every day to be all alone
Just to think what I'd be when I was full grown.

I sat on a stump where half the three was cut down.
It made a grand seat; just the right height from the ground.

For a long time I thought I was hidden from view
And for awhile I suppose that might have been true.

But what was more important, in solitude there
I learned to write poetry, to dream, and to care.

Learned to listen to life all around in the air
And to make it my music, my song, and my prayer.

Today I am older; I look back with a sigh
To the thoughts that I had but let wither and die.

The poems I could have written, the stories tell
The songs in my heart that could weave a spell.

Maybe I need to find a new place in the wild
Renew acquaintance with faith I had as a child.

Then maybe the music and stories inside
Could be written and sung; told fluently with pride!

Jerri Hamilton

I Need Someone To Be My Friend

When I look at the empty landscape of our lives
Without someone it's like barren ground and dark skies
Then I acknowledge that something to each applies
I need someone to be my friend, I realize

When I see mad violence that sweeps the nations
Men, women and little ones facing starvation
Hatred, ethic cleansing, bombs and devastation
The wail for a friend is not a revelation

How many migrating boat people are lost at sea
Miles walked in the dead of night as a refugee
All looking and needing something more than their poverty
To neighbor nations, be a friend is a useless plea

Large forests have come from just a handful of seed
On the smallest sea creatures the largest ones feed
To get friends you want, the key is simple indeed
"Do to others as you'd have done to you" just heed

Shirley Sally

Feel The Fear...Do It Anyway...That's How We Heal

Two years and more have flown by since that fateful day
When you asked me to become your wife.
I'd never been so afraid in all my life,
but soon after, I received the most important
advice from a stranger, who must have been an angel.
He asked me, "Do you love him?" Of course I said, "Yes!"
So, he said, feel the fear, do it anyway, that's how we heal.
I thanked Him so sharing; I never saw Him again.
We've been through so much already, in such a short time:
life and death situations we've been able to handle one day at a time.
Just when it seemed we couldn't take anymore,
He sent more angels with his messages right to our door;
Remember, they all began with feel the fear, do it anyway, that's how we heal.
I married my best friend. He still loves me unconditionally,
even when I can't seem to love myself.
Because recently, it seems once again,
I'm consumed with fear that seems to be choking me;
but in a moment of stillness I was able to hear
another angel whisper loud and clear, just let go!
Let go of the fear! Feel the fear, do it anyway! That's how we heal.

Dorothy Marie Francis-Ball

Just An Old Shoe

In the back of the closet, far out of sight
There's a pair of old shoes, a left and a right
Now worn and scuffed, run down at the heel
Some of the leather had began to peel.
Oh, the memories are many, if they could but say
Of parties and games, of work and of play.
They had danced all night, had walked in the rain.
This old pair of shoes, never caused any pain.
Tho they had walked miles over varied terrain
It always felt good to have them on again.
Now they're stored, hidden away
The owner remembers in their better days
They had carried him faithful, as he went his way
Now he began to wonder, as time passed by
And thought aloud. With a deep long sigh
What will be done to a scuffed old man
Wrinkled and tired, shaky of hand
Is there space in a closet waiting for me
Or will I be cast out, with other debris?

Loyd D. Sallee

You Are My Mother

You are my mother
My pride and joy
I'm giving you a poem
Instead of buying you a toy,
I wrote this poem
to show you I care
And to say "I love you"
and I'll always be there
I may not say I love you enough
But I do think about it
and plenty of other stuff
The other stuff is
The things that you do
That makes me happy
And doesn't keep me happy I do appreciate
Everything you do I may not say it
But you know it is true
You are my mother and my mother you'll stay
and I love you very much
No matter what I might say.

Jennifer K. Boonstra

Beyond The Field

Beyond the field it is dark and damp,
Should I venture there?... no I can't.
It calls to me with such powerful force,
I can not follow the normal course.
I will go... no I shan't, explore there, where it is dark and damp.
Beyond the field many things hide, I will not go, I must abide.
 I miss the field where uncovered things still lay.
But I must not go that way.
 Beyond the fields is not so bad,
Although the atmosphere is gloomy and sad.
 Maybe I will go to the place where many things hide,
No, I will not abide.
As courageous as a lion I march, into darkness blocked out from sun by
an invisible arch. I enter this awkward place, and think behind me,
is there another face?
Yes there is I can tell, I hear the footsteps as a loud as a bell.
Now I hear heavy breathing, I am overcome with a frightened feeling.
Shall I spin around to see, who is following me?
What was that, it is their voice, saying "Anne we're having dinner,
to come is your choice!"

Ana Callahan

The Drunk Driver

As you stare into the night,
 You will see a terrible sight.
 As you look both far and near,
 A horrible crash you shall hear.
 There smashed upon a tree,
 Lay the lifeless body of old Gibbons McGee.
Oh, and then the very next day,
 The tabloids have swept the terror away.
 And turned it into some strange thing.
 Then and there you hear the telephone ring.
 The police begin speaking to you,
 Like the man you saw die last night was a fool.
Well, as it turns out to be,
 Old Gibbons McGee was a fool you see.
 For he chose to drink and drive,
 And God chose to take his life.

Audrey LaFave

The Symphony

Close your eyes for a moment and hear the music
Surrounding our wild souls.
Let your mind drift into a world of melodies.
Allow yourself to lose control.

Do you feel the rhythm of our hearts beating?
Can you sense the symphonic spirit
And grasp the distinct power of the unforgettable tune?
You must stop to hear it.

Each note rises and falls like our emotions.
Every vision orchestrates.
We are writing a symphony meant to be heard
Through the joy our love creates.

Smoothly combined are the harmonic tones,
Flowing at our pace.
If you let the music touch your heart,
It will be yours to embrace.

Tami S. Robb

Villanelle

They dream most restlessly who soon must wake,
they wake most fretfully who soon must sleep;
and all go lonely for the long day's sake.

To those who seek to ease the ancient ache,
maimed and forgotten children come to weep;
they dream most restlessly who soon must wake.

There are no shattered ramparts to retake,
and heroes amble stupidly like sheep,
and all go lonely for the long day's sake.

They search most uselessly who seek escape
in rest; sleep is shallow, resignation deep;
they dream most restlessly who soon must wake.

There is no broken promise to remake
there is no novel covenant to keep,
and all go lonely for the long day's sake.

Even if heroes rouse and stir and wake,
or sad dream children all begin to leap,
they dream most restlessly who soon must wake,
and all go lonely for the long day's sake.

    Daniel J. Welty

Different Road

Today I travel a different road, not knowing where it may lead me,
not caring, hoping to find peace. Searching my soul, trying to
find the answer to my thoughts.

The road I travel has been used many times over the years;
the grass has grown up, the big trees with their beauty, and the
flowers that bloom as the sun comes through the trees, make a
beautiful sight, as I walk this road.

Searching for peace or something that I may never find.
As I walk this road of no return, I have seen many things unfold,
not understanding them or why.

As I keep walking this road, and wondering will I find the
answers or will I have time.

Sometimes I am tired of walking this road.
Maybe I will give up and forget my soul.
Will it make a difference, as I travel this road,
Hoping somewhere the answer will unfold?
When I have come to the road's end, what will be
waiting for me? The answer I have been searching for
or have I came to the road's end?

    Ray South

The Dance

Sailing from wing to wing
They dance and glide across the floor
This way and that....sailing smoothly over the ice
They proceed from end to end and back again
Not a free moment, only a slowed pace
Never a shortage of partners
Pass after pass with ease and grace
Diverted from player to player
The play never falters
Round and round they go
A spin here, a side step here
Then they part....
With one swift motion it takes flight
Slipping....sliding....spinning....
Faster and faster
Then the dance comes to a jolting stop
The goal has been scored
Safe and sound, it rests for a time
Only to start once more....
The dance of player and puck

    Trish Juers

The Day America Lost Its Image

The day November 22, the year 1963
An altered Presidential motorcade route in Dallas
Was the origin of the dark and deep mystery
When our leader was slain in malice

Our Nation's course was directed by the trajectory of lead
That unforgettable and fateful day
The question still remains, why is he dead?
Does crime really pay?

Almost 33 years ago he was brutally killed
Some hated him, but many loved him
His hopes and dreams never completely fulfilled
To this day, we still do not know why he was a victim

The wall did eventually fall, detente was reached in time
Ending the Vietnam war was a long tragic stall
Had he lived, perhaps all would have been achieved during his prime

Still a mystery almost 33 years later!
Government of the people, by the people, for the people, dark shadows
    are still cast
Thou shall not kill proclaims our creators
Our future is dependent on the truths of our past

    Larry R. Fifield

On Watching Horseshoe Crabs

Each year they come
Propelled by an instinct older than man.
As the moon rises full in June, they come
To perpetuate the species.

I go down to the Middle Bridge and watch.
As the tide rises high, so do they
And engage in the age old match
Of male and female intertwined.

I stand there is awe.
Newcomer biped on the scene,
Knowing that what I just saw,
The dinosaurs watched as they
Danced in the full of the moon.

    John Elder Dick

The Wonder Of You!

It was a stroke of luck for me, our meeting the way I met you.
The meeting of two loving hearts, so honest and so true.
That we are joined together now and forever in such a way,
is a miracle and a wonder that I marvel at each day.

All the precious moments, that the two of us share,
always make me feel warm inside loved and full of care.
It's when we are together and I hold you in my arms,
that I feel the most alive, and in awe of all your charms.

In those times when I have felt afraid, as all of us sometimes do,
Those feelings were easily erased by you simply walking into the room.
How can I repay you, for all that you have given me?
I will do my best with understanding, compassion, love and by my deeds.
Now whenever I see you with a tear in your lovely eyes,
I pray it will be the joy of our love, that has made you cry.

So here we are at the doorstep of the rest of our lives,
wondering what lies ahead and ready together to give it a try.
I hope this little rhyme, has helped you to understand and see,
all the joy's and happiness you have brought to me.

As I have sworn you this oath my love, that all of this is true,
it still pales by comparison, to the Wonder of You!

    Carl Jon Poss

Imagine

People are human
they have this in common
They were all born with skin
from Brazil to Laplomin.

Black or white
Short of tall
Is this how we should choose
who is allowed in the mall.

Together we stand
Divided we fall
How can we survive
If all we do is brawl?

Life has so much meaning
If we learn some lessons
Be civil to others
And if unsure ask some questions.

Different customs and beliefs can be confusing I am told
But if it were not for these differences
Would life be so bold?

John E. Brown

Reflection

Harbouring thoughts, memories fragmented,
branches like tentacles reach out
to grasp particles suspended in time.
Stillness envelopes terror, opposites collide,
healing likened to the action of waves.
Molecules crash relentlessly
against the bombardment of hard facts,
the combined strength of each memory.
Grains of sand against glass,
the persistence of reality breaks
exposing the pounding of the psyche.
Dark as the memories that hid for so long,
secrets long past evolvement speak,
continuous as the churning
which surfaces from within.

Sharon Turner

"Faith"

True faith the living spirit of all time
Upon its rock the face of God shall shine
Spirit of light, shine on your mighty sea,
Where faith shall sail your mighty ship through thee.

Your sea of justice flowing from the deep,
Your living water bless the breath of peace.
The shadow of your peaceful wings in flight,
To guard the earth until the end of time.

Faith rolls the waves unto eternal tide,
To sail the world upon a sea of light.
With truth and life, faith reach the rainbows end,
To seal with love the unity of men.

Yolande A. Seibert

The Strengthening

   As I cry here alone in my prison cell I wonder;
will I ever make it home,
or does death awaken with the dawn?
   For hatred I pray from the Gods of my fathers...
for their hatred helps me carry on.

Rosendo Martinez III

Sister

A sister by chance that I never had,
a 2nd daughter for my mom and dad.

A sister joined by love so visibly shown,
a daughter bringing happiness into our home.

A sister to share a sad movie tear,
another daughter to ensure the table is clear.

A sister who savours a long shopping spree,
a daughter to help trim the Christmas tree.

A sister with whom my thoughts I can confide,
a daughter, forever to be at my brother's side.

A sister I can help when she's down and blue,
as a daughter, mom's wisdom you will cherish too.

A sister who will become my very best chum,
a daughter, delightfully welcomed by dad and mom.

Mary Anne White

All The Silent Streams

For three months only, do no rain fall. Soon my flighty droplets find
A bride faraway to rejoice and leave me lonely for a season.
Blessed is my land, am yet so distressed so another lover you find.
But where will you go and not find all those silent streams singing
songs of my quiet dreams, in susurrant vitality just to redeem desert
land a thousand mile spread. Though parched without, those limbs,
your tree can blossom by morn' or eventide, just hold a picture within, let
the silent streams break forth from the seams of your brimming heart.
A horizon the wandering stream surely sees, they share your dream every
time when refreshed you are, scooping a handful from unknown fountain.

You can break free to a waterfall tomorrow, then invigorate a thousand
bare trees, who yesterday lost all her magic to those hungry wind,
charm lost to empty strife. In fields of paradise, fruits quietly
paint my trees everyday, someday you'll see. When you search for a
hold, come to a place you are told where love runs and grows.
A stream is silent alone to find a new road.

Uwakwe Victor

Too Late To Bow

(Villanelle)
Each broken corpse looked the same
Lying warm at Gettysburg and Shiloh,
Too late to bow to bastard fame.

No one quite remembered what became
Of Sara Ann's engraved memento -
Each broken corpse looked the same:

Bradleys, Hunters, Websters and McClains,
Pickets lying faceless in stiffening rows,
Too late to bow to bastard fame.

Each foul ditch held all the shame
That brothers lying within could know;
Each broken corpse looked the same.

None remembered Lee's immortal name,
If he were gray or blue or black as crow.
Too late to bow to bastard fame,

But better sleep than limbless, or the maimed
Defeat of shoulders cracked and low.
Each broken corpse looked the same;
Too late to bow to bastard fame.

Judy Dunn

I Hate Those Words

The clouds in the sky are thick;
Sun shines obscurely, just as those words,
Brooks dry up, but the rain was bursting,
Just as those words—disconcert and are confusing.

People going to and fro; motivates all what they do,
Not like those words; indistinct; undefined yet exist,
Life is from above, later passes away as vapor,
Those words out from man's heart, puzzling.

Better is the ocean, deep yet fathomed;
Not like those words, shallow but penetrating,
The eagles in the air could not soar the ends of the distance;

Just as uttering those words, certain but disputable.

O heart, heart, man, why can you say it?
And you don't care even it seems dubious;
You could appear as persuading me
But you cannot because I hate those words.

O heart, heart, man why have you said it?
Better is the ocean, deep yet fathomed,
You could seem as alluring me,
But you cannot, because I hate those words!

Christian Joemyr Torres

Roy (My Daddy)

He was a man whose education spanned far beyond the years he spent
in school. He was a man who taught his children and others the joy of
living by the Golden Rule.

Her raised and trained Walker Hounds to hunt the Raccoon, and as a
hunter and trainer his fame spread very soon. Young and old, black
and white, they came to share with him the fun, the thrill of the
hunt and to train their dogs, the Coon to run.

When not working or on a hunt, he was teaching girls and boys the
ball to bunt. For baseball was his king of sports and he loved also,
to participate. So he headed up a group, the Decherd Little League,
to instigate.

A farmer, he was, who loved the land, but came to time for his
horizon to span. Tho politics was not his life's aim. He felt the
call of neighbors and friends to try this game. The first campaign
for Sheriff, he was not selected. Three terms, consecutively, after
this he was elected.

Roy William Smith was a man who believed in integrity, honesty,
hard work and also hard play. He loved dearly his God and Family
and he proclaimed these love proudly everyday. We miss you Daddy, and
though are gone, your spirit and love lives on. We are proud and honored
by the heritage you have provided your children and grandchildren.

Dorothy S. Swann

To Many Mother's On Their Day

Can you think back to when you were young?
If one was playing by a bush — did you get stung?
Who did you turn to, perhaps your Mom!!!
The thought of Mother with calm and peace,
gave a joy, and with her care, the pain would cease.
To be a strong fort in a child's life, when things
look obscure, (with maybe) a touch of strife:
Mom would be there — as a sort of rock, to make the
situation straight: at home or around the block!!!
Also she might call you for dinner — as one observes the clock!!
Take a kind word to a Mother on this day, for it by far,
is the right play!
Tell her thanks for all she has done;
If possible, under the vast sky and sun.
And tell her "Happy Mother's Day." Yes!!!

Robert Capistrand

The Flight

My father and I, were as close as could be,
We never dreamed that someday-
One of us would have to leave,
To leave one behind, is just not right,
For the other doesn't know.
When they can make that flight,
God will carry us on our way
Making sure that we meet again.
On a glorious day.

Carol A. Marsh

Ancient Limbs

As pages turn from days like these
Shades of many colors remain on trees
Virgin paths
A canvas of greens
Transit to clean to touch what's unseen
Our nature has always been here
Please walk not near
For the ancient growths have had reason to fear
Fire and destruction
Without thinking to care
Trees lay dying
Not a thought to repair

Joshua A. Paine

The Breath Of Spring

The breath of spring breaks forth
from my heart and calls to thee.
My spirit races past the miles
to tug at yours and set you free.

A daisy dance I would dance with you,
soft grasses and warm scents in your hair
Our fingers entwined, exploring,
moving softly together with care.

In fantasies of warmth we would wander,
lost each in the others embrace.
Winter wishes would come true,
let loose from some secret place.

Flowers would rise up to kiss the sun,
and bees and bugs would buzz and play
Together we would chase the butterflies,
letting our cold blue feelings slip away.

If I could be there right now,
I'd make this dream come true.
And if I had all the seasons of the year,
I would give Spring and Summer to you.

Peter A. Wetherall

My Land

The land is green
The sky is blue.
And everywhere I look
There is not a soul to be found.
This is the land I live in.
This is my land
A land of my fantasies and dreams
None can come true because
most of my world is reality.
I have so few friends.
I have so few realistic hopes and dreams.
But for now I will sit in my land and
dream up a better tomorrow.

Candice Blanchet

Walking Wounded

I hear sentences, clipping through my head,
"Do you have any regrets?"
Hitting like a bullet, I am stunned.
This question lodges itself in my soul.
A silent struggle.
I carry it forth.

Defenses down.
Alone, at last,
I sit high a top the frozen unnatural world.
Staring down, reflecting glass, bright lights,
and a questionable thing called civilization.
Above all, in contrast, rounded shaded clouds,
with hues of velvet, amble by.
How I do wish.
And I carry on and on.

And I question: Isn't doing the same thing,
but expecting something different true insanity?
Wounded I sit,
bitting the bullet,
a sour metallic taste, and still I carry forth.

Cynthia M. Baird

Turn Off That Great Big Moon

Now that you said good bye,
  "I", with a tear filled eye,
Have no desire to spoon,
    Turn off that great big moon.

No I'll never smile,
  You're gone, it's not worthwhile.
No more, to me you'll croon.
    Turn off that great big moon.

The nights we use to spend,
  Did you remember then?
Our plans couldn't come too soon.
    Turn off that great big moon.

I guess I'll have to admit,
  I'm just about to quit,
I don't want to hum a tune.
    Turn off that great big moon.

There'll be no wedding bells,
  I want nobody else.
For you, I'm nutty as a loon.
    Turn off that great big moon.

Louise Page

"My Special Place"

I know a forest still, with a carpet made of leaves,
Reaching upward toward the sky are tall proud trees,
White cotton clouds float in a sky of blue,
In the morning, the grass has diamonds of dew,
By night, the sky is velvet black,
Millions of twinkling stars always come back,
It's home to me, such an "ordinary" place,
This spaceship earth, traveling through time and space.
I have a very special place to go,
When life's problems are too heavy, and I'm feeling low,
'Tis just a quiet, lonely spot beside a gurgling stream,
A place to hide and while away the moments,
A place to think...a place to dream,
Everyone needs a place to go, to lay their burdens down,
When too heavy they may seem,
A quiet place, a private place, a place, to think...to dream.

Marie Mayo

Anatomy Of A Patient

So we fill your halls and stand in your lines
Hold our heads and our children's hands
Ask inane questions at inopportune times
While smiling red exit signs beckon, asking us to leave.

Long, beige tiled walls empty into indignity
Rubbing alcohol disturbs the air and assaults the memory
Paper gowns tear after just one arm
We're ashamed of nothing and everything all the same.

Do you try us in high court and prosecute our injuries?
Are we broken arms, blocked arteries, an untreatable social disease?
Or just the faceless, nameless, work to complete
Matching the forms that later prove we were here.

We are patients at your mercy
Our only defense is ignorance
Powerless to your knowledge, your technology, your choices
your sparkling, white uniform exactness in action
My we take up a few minutes of your everyday?
Pass through the thick walls of your sterile fortress?

We are people at your mercy
Only you can remind us we're more than simply what is wrong with us.

John A. Wehner

A Christmas List

Christmas is a load, Christmas is like a beer, slug one more down and
maybe it will all disappear. So you think I'm a Grinch, you think I'm
a Scrooge; if you had to buy all these presents you'd be one too. The
malls are all packed, the stores are all filled. I am tearing my hair
out, ahhh! I guess I'll skip Uncle Bill. I find myself in the car
again beeping and moving between lanes, trying Deliver these
Christmas cards. "To the post office!" My wife exclaims. Tis the
season of giving and boy is this true; again my wife banters about
"Twenty more things to do!" Don't get me wrong, I love my wife Sue.
I said "Just give me two more years dear, and I will have all this done
for you." Well they are done and I am whipped...what the hell is this
dear, another list?!?! Without a word we points up at the attic.
Here I go again, for some lights, a manger and a backache. So
everything is done and boy am I ready for that beer. But wait she
stammers "One more thing dear!" Now the carolers are on our door
steppen up a storm. I am not in the mood for this so I graciously
slam the door. My wife put the children to bed and I desperately
want to go too. But she turns, smile and says to me "One last thing
to do." Now I'm all for Christmas you all know tis true, but I am not
going to do one more damn thing, that's what I an going to do! And
so the mistletoe is hung - the last thing on our list to do. She comes
over to me and says "How's about a little kiss, for you know who?"
As I ponder over the things we had to do it is all a part of Christmas
- the cards, the boxes and the mistletoe too. So remember during this
this Christmas season for which all the things you had to do. Don't
forget your wife on this Christmas list, she loves you too.
Merry Christmas.

Stephen C. Bosley

Friendship

We take friends for granted while time passes by
We never appreciate them until in loneliness we cry
We don't value people until our heart beats alone
We seem not to notice others until forever they have gone

We always say too late, the things that should be said
They have already left our lives when the thoughts come to our head
The joy, the laughter, the kind words we like to share,
are wasted on the cold blank walls when there's no one else to hear

Our today and tomorrows have slowly slipped away
gone forever are our moments of play
Our days for giving and loving have ended
A slash in our lives that can never be mended

Lawrence D. Hayes

Untitled

Somehow it came
It came from the stars
From time
It came when you needed it most,
  wanted it most.
It came sliding into you by fate
  flying and flowing to you
  assisting your broken bones and emotions
It held you up, and it pushed you ahead
It taught you who you were, and what
  you needed to do, where you needed to go
It filled you with a craving to give
It filled you with desire and greed
  But just enough
It gave you meaning
It made you whole.

Deborah M. Corrigan

A Father And Daughters Love

It's not every day, a daughter can say
How her father is loved, in a very special way.
And even though its said once a year,
Her father to her, will always be dear.
For she remembers how she sat on his lap
For a hug and a kiss, before taking a nap,
Then soon he has noticed she's starting to grow
For off to school, he watches her go.
To grade school, to high school, then her first date
Giving her orders about coming in late
Soon she tells him she's falling in love
And asks for his blessings and all his love.
And then comes the day he gives her away
Wishing her happiness in his own special way.
With a lump in his throat, there's nothing he can say
But hope for their happiness, in each coming day.
But he'll always remember how she sat on his lap
For a hug and a kiss before taking a nap.

Barbara Buhl

The World

The World goes steadily forward
From whence it came, no one knows
It just keeps travelling ahead, onward, onward
No one knows where it has been, or where it goes

We tag along on the journey for a ride
Some for a time that is long, or for some is short
Many take life's steps with dignity and pride
Others waste it with spoils, and many abort

What is our purpose for tagging along?
Is it only to love and procreate?
Some see the World as a place for dance and song
While there are those who more seriously postulate

Not all are given in God to believe
They who say only in myself is there God
For those only to themselves deceive
Above this Universe, God holds this World like a pea in a pod

So to all who take this journey my friend
Take it from their infancy to their end
The length of which is short or long
Combine it all, you'll find it is to God we belong.

Bill Ruzenski

Shadowed Lives

The sun sets slowly on a distant horizon.
People walk amongst the dark streets
And stare blankly out at each other.

The coldness has captured their heats and souls
And they only live to see the light again.

The life has left their eyes
And the warmth has left their souls.

They live eternally in the shadows
Searching for a single ray of light
To penetrate the coldness.

The only hope that lives in the cold
Is the thought of feeling the warmth again.

The darkness takes hold
Of the life of all its creatures
To keep them in the gloom
And freeze their souls.

They try to escape the nightmare
But are held back by their fear
They will stay in the darkness forever
Until the grasp of the coldness is broken.

Jonna Elaine Reagan

Dawn

The sun was rising above the trees,
Casting shadows on the lake,
Birds were chirping their morning songs,
Bidding the world to awake.

He viewed the scene with pleasure,
From his look-out by the bay,
As dawn stretched out a welcoming hand.
Ushering in a bright sunny day.

He savored these quiet moments,
The gift of each new dawn,
Too soon this peaceful scene would change,
And the magic would be gone.

He then retraced his footsteps,
Heading back from his little bay,
His face revealed the inner calm,
That dawn had sent his way.

But he'd return tomorrow,
To his look-out by the bay,
Where dawn again would greet him,
At the start of another new day.

Bill Ott

The Altar

In the Holy sanctuary,
Come to the altar.
Close your eyes,
Fold your hands,
Kneel down and pray.
Reverence and Humility.

In your body, which belongs to God,
Standing, sitting, walking, riding, driving,
Come to the altar of your heart,
Kneel down in your mind and soul.
Close the eyes of your environment,
Fold your thoughts inward, and pray.
Reverence and Humility

Marjorie Faulkner

Wounded Wings

I found a bird with a wounded wing and nursed it back to health again.
I healed its wounds and gave it strength, and then too soon away it went
So I guess it seems to show, with wounded wings they're bound to go
And I guess it means it's safe to say, heal wounded wings they'll fly away

A wounded wing on a crying bird, unable to sing but trying to be heard
Is a wounded wing on a baby dove, just trying to sing its song of love
And to heal its wounds is my disease, as the Doctor of this aviary
I'll perform my knack of surgery, then nurse them back so caringly

And sometimes I'll hear the distant sound, that these birds are still around
Sailing in along a searing breeze, they sing their songs of being freed
But none stopped in to sing hello, just spread their wings and off they go
But I remember what I did, and how they got all I could give

But I guess it seems it goes to show, with wounded wings they're bound to go
And I guess it means it's safe to say, heal wounded wings...they'll fly away

Nick Robinson

Tears

We all must cry from time to time, maybe several times per year,
To release the pain of tragedy, to morn the loss of someone dear.

Or tears of joy, extremely rare, with a value that of gold,
Or tears from spineless whimpering, very worthless to behold.

Misty eyes, from a picture show, is poetic expression indeed,
And tears of your baby's crying, is an innocent call of need.

The cry of pain when wounded, is commonly understood,
But bawling from some tiny scratch, that isn't very good.

So cry if you must, I understand; we all must cry, that's fine,
That's the way we were created, just a part of our design.

Yet if tears be used to manipulate, or flow from too much introspect,
Then all your crying is in vain, it gains no comfort or respect!

Cry my friend, but know the why, if tears fall from your head,
For my dear, I warn you now, they often turn the eyes to red!

Fredrick A. Ball

Nightmare

Alone in the dark, my head buried under the blankets I hear her
cries from afar.
I struggle not to hear, desperately trying to quell the fear,
the anger, the sadness, the loneliness.
My mind wanders to a place I can only dream about,
a place that I imagine is safe.
But suddenly, as always, I am jolted back to my reality by the
sound of his hand across her frail body, his voice chiding her,
her horrific scream to stop, "Please Stop!"
But it doesn't stop, it never stops.
Finally sleep envelopes me and I dream - it is a soothing dream, a
comforting dream of that place where I long to be. It is my safe place.
There I see friendly faces, people who smile, adults who are free
of the burden of hate. There is no hitting, no chiding, no fear.
My safe place protects me from those screams in the night, the
screams of my night mere.
My safe place is a place I will find someday, a place where I will
comfort and protect those children who, like me, must endure the
sounds of their frightened night meres.

Jacqueline Scholes Eldridge

The Lee Tree (A Weeping Willow)

I'm so happy I've found a lovely new home;
No more do fear that I still have to roam.

I'll not ask much of you, My Dear Friend, Lee;
Just some water and knowing you're growing with me.

Let's pretend I'm eleven - just like you;
My limbs will be growing along with you too.

I'll shade you in summer from the blistering sun!
In winter you can climb my strong branches..
    we'll have so much fun.

When you're happy burst around me and dance with glee;
And when you're sad, you can always lean on me.

I'm your friend forever, though you'll move away;
I'll not "weep" big tears... you'll be back to visit
    me one fine day.

By then my roots will be deep... my branches strong;
I'll bless my young life, for you helped me along.

The birds will build nests and sing sweet lullabies;
On this continuous voyage through the heavenly sky.

We'll both touch the stars high in the sky;
And remember times shared, Lee, just you and I.

Donna Decker Harcourt

Somewhere In Time....

We met one night long ago, we danced the last dance of the show
He held me close, safe and secure
This man I didn't even know
We met again...became more than friends
We learned of each other, our families, our friends
We shared, we cared, we cried and we lied
Some we forgot and some we tried
We hurt - but we loved the best we could
Through thick and thin - there we stood
I hurt and I cry - now all alone
And remember these times of long ago, of love and hurt and openness
These things I know I surely miss
With my heart still broken and a love that goes on
He's not here to hold me I must carry on
To a future I'm walking with only a prayer
And God only knows if I'll meet him there
If I could go back - oh you know that I would
I'd go to the place I first understood
To a couple who danced close if only in mind
And had a dream to share...somewhere in time?

Joy Delong

Paradigm Shift

If of the conviction
Attempt not be considered
Is in itself failure

If at least not attempted change will not occur
let alone the outcome be successful

A paradigm shift has historically been seen
to bring about change

Hence a step closer to Harmony
Oh what a paragon dream
So far from reality it seems

Science Religion a Reciprocate team
Orthodox thinking is truly
Obscene

Slag the Beatnick

386

My Cup Of Joy

No label I could trace you to,
Not an import or as a reserve,
My cup of joy,
You are unique.

Your love is a liquid that flows through me,
Continuous without ending,
A quench unsatisfied,
Always fresh and changing.

Never demanding only welcoming,
A warmth that lingers on,
My cup of joy,
You can do me no wrong.

With you my cup is always full,
Regardless of your strength and size,
It is the constant joy you bring to me,
Even words fail to describe.

Svetlana Konstantinov

Heaven's Gate

She came to me on a cloud one day
Dancing lightly on the way
Her winsome smile upon her face
Her hands now old — still full of grace

Eyes still bright and full of guile
She softly said — I'll be there in a while
She reached for my hand across the sky
Looked down at the world and said good-bye

Tenderly she touched my face
Her wispy hair — a vision of lace
My arms stretched out to hold her near
Now old and grey and still so dear

She sang a song to me that night
And kissed me in the morning light
No longer do I have to wait
To greet my love at Heaven's Gate

Edith Brereton

Grungy Shirt

Grungy, grungy, grungy shirt,
Did you know how those words would hurt?
Spewing insults about what I wear
Thinking them funny, that I couldn't care!

Grungy, grungy, grungy shirt,
Not for me now the 'mini' skirt
Years of primping and off pain,
High heeled shoes designed to maim.

Grungny, grungy, grungy shirt,
My shape no longer slim and pert.
After all these years of 'we'
Don't you see the real me?

Grungy, grungy, grungy shirt,
Warm and soft, colour of dirt.
Brings me comfort at days end,
Making light the chores to tend.

Grungy, grungy, grungy shirt,
Forever! together, like Ernie and Bert.
Grungy shirt now my banner of protest,
For comfort and loving to me are what's best.

Janet Horwood

Out Of Sight, Out Of Mind

People say, "Out of sight, out of mind."
That's not true.
I've never seen my love;
he's always on my mind.
I've never seen my father;
he's often on my mind.
A lot of times things around me
I cannot see, I cannot hear,
because the things out of sight
are on my mind.

Amy Richardson

Our Song of Praise

The dawn heralds a new day:
New things to do, new things to see,
Hours filled with work and play,
New blessings for you and me.

As years pass and we older grow,
We welcome each new dawn.
Our days are limited well we know.
There are so many since we were born.

Each day's treasures we shall grasp:
The stranger well met along the way,
A dear friend's warm hand clasp,
The loving smile that makes our day.

When the evening tide of life we reach,
And count the blessings of our days
May we each join in to teach
Our song of joy, our hymn of praise.

Anna Murchison

Untitled

Our paths intertwined for a brief moment in time.
As we walked together, I thought it would be forever.
Along our journey we were able to share;
Love, Life, Friendship, Laughter, Tears and Prayer.
When the time did come that our paths continued their separate ways,
I found myself devastated for I did not anticipate the days,
That I would awake to find
I had lost those sweet, dear friends of mine.
As the paths that we take continue to curve, swerve, and wind,
I anxiously await your paths again intersecting mine.
If ever again we do embrace
I know it will bring a warm smile to my face.
My heart is heavy and my eyes are sad
Missing the friendship we all did have.
Thank you for walking awhile with me,
There is a place in my heart
That you will always be.

Teri S. Bahnfleth

You

You give me the strength to carry on,
You give me the power to succeed,
To follow my dreams, to go after my goals
to try, to hope, to believe!

In your heart there is no place for hatred,
In your thoughts cruelty would not be alive,
Your soul only carries compassion
and love, only goodness will survive.

You realize that love may not be visible,
Yet if you look deep enough you shall see,
It's there somewhere within your soul
It's there for you and me.

Vesna Michelle Jovanic

Untitled

As she walks around the room,
across the street, and to her work, he watches,
they meet but the love
was filled in only one heart,
two is needed, one is mad,
his anger and love grows when they
should have ceased, he enters, unwanted,
she throws her hands up
as desperation sets in
the fight is over,
the victory is his but
the aftermath is hers,
As the young grows
the memories are all of evil but
the wondrous dreams are of a hero,
he grows, wonders, and asks,
the answers are nothing but a web of circles

Terry Williamson

Two Matches

When the first match was lit,
Blind in the eyes if the bewildered seekers.
Something was born-living, breathing, controlling,
   exhilarating...beautiful,
As the flame progressed on with the burning
   desire of love and attraction feeding it.
The flame growing into the touch where
   elements of the spark became the
   foundation of the blinding glow that not
   so long ago was a dim twinkle in the blind
   eyes of the beholders.
To this day those two sparks have united
   to form and unimaginably wonderful
   formed love.
The love known by two matches in a book!

Jennie Erickson

A Look To The Future

A message of Altruism,
A message of Truism,
A message of Brotherhood
A message of Innate Good.

A message of Futurism,
A message to outlaw cataclysm
Of hate and prejudice
Of its evil that exists.

A message of futurism
Of love embedded in a prism
Of colors that beguile
Soul of adult and child.

A message of calm,
Of hymns and psalms,
Of peace and balm
Untouched by harm.

My message, thus,
So broad in scope
May it ever embrace
Every neck and cranny of earth and its space!

Doris Jacobs

Bipolar Depression

Standing at the back of the moving train,
Watching the past fade away in the distance
Through a dirty window set in a locked door.

Wondering of things that might have been,
And of things that had been all too real,
Not really thinking about a future,
A promise that might yet be,
But would probably not live up to the
Enticement and temptation of its lies.

The past was a bit more than sad, not quite to bitterness.
More a waste of plans gone wrong,
Plans that didn't quite work out,
Expectations of others base on a slightly different reality.

Sometimes it's just waiting for the clock to run out,
To move on to the next existence — whatever it may be —
with a forlorn hope of maybe
Some slight wisp of an improvement.

Into the mists and the fog of the snow covered fields,
Filtered by the rain-streaked dust on the glass,
The past, like the tracks, slowly fades away.

Michael A. McConnell

One's Thoughts

Words, are but a tool we use as an instrument to sculpture are
expressions of life and feelings. Compassion, humility, forgiveness
and love are but a gift we are given to share. Are we not born of and
into flesh and bone, and from birth we are given life and death.
Through living, choices are bestowed upon us. Is are direction in
life from the path we choose, a correlation by our actions or not
actions. Thus our course in life if chosen.
If a pebble is thrown into a stream of water, could you not see the
ripples of your actions. If a mighty boulder is thrown into the sea
with the strength of many, would it sink with quickness or would the
wave it caused, be felt with the unity it took.
Does the life we live have a purpose to our existence or is our being
to know the knowledge of life and its circle, from which fate seems
to play a role. Then, are we not born of and into spirit.
When opening one's mind and heart, only then are you inviting life's
wonders and beauty as it was meant to be felt and heard.

Deborah A. Westcott

Dad

The face before me seems strange in a way
I remember seeing it day after day
But now it is weathered and weary to wake
And I worry sometimes about its fate.

The voice is demanding much like before
But when it sounds I rush to the door
He wants to go home but he is already here
And he believes it is snowing when it is sunny and clear.

The man before me is that last single bond
That ties us forever from here to beyond
He helped give me life and the tools to survive
And I have grown and developed only to thrive.

The face and the voice belong to the man
Who lays in the bed unable to stand
His name is father, pops or dad
And for his God given life I am eternally glad.

Beverley Marson

Endless Flight

Life is love from the heavens above
Play with the fishes, playing with the doves
Never neglecting always apprehending
A physical being
How beautiful it seems
When the two join together and create a team
By all means unconditional mental and physical
I'll stand with you through known and mystical
Can you feel the essence
From past to present
On how life was from the beginning
Nature's flowing plus distinguished moments
With no more room, no more enrollments
Permanent bonding with natural involvement
With the sensuous Earth constantly revolving
Through space and matter
With pleasure and laughter
Legacies of creativity to compete the trilogy
With total harmony and total serenity
My sweet come to me tonight on an endless flight.

Michael D. Key

There's Something I Must Say

There's someone I appreciate that has made my world new.
She is very special and, Mother, it's you. I'm proud
that you are my mother. You make me feel alive. These
are my true feelings that I express from deep inside.
You have given me many things. Things only you can give.

They are very special feelings that help my will to live.
I feel that I'm becoming a man. I say this with pride and
joy; but, I know within my heart, I'm still your baby boy.

I know I let you down in many ways. We both know this is true.
But, now I've planned a worthy future and this
I'll show you soon.

Yes, I know I hurt you many times and I know I caused
you pain, but, even though that's in the past, I'll
remember that with shame.

I have these special feelings that come from deep inside.
It's knowing that you are my Mother and it's filling me with pride.
These things that I have said, please believe they are true.

I would like you to remember and believe that I love you.

Shawn

Untitled

Like a prince, rescuing a princess
 you came into my life
Freeing my soul, from loneliness.

Like the sun, on a warm summer's day
 you warm my heart
Making me feel, again.

Like a lock, securing a door
 you make me feel safe
Willing me, to let my defenses down.

Like a heart, beating fast
 you get my blood pumping
Making me curious about life, again.

Like the falling, of rain
 you speak rhythmically
Soothing my emotional fears.

Like a dream, coming true
 you help me to see
That love is possible, despite all the odds.

Kelly Lyn Schofield

Ideal

We're looking forward to getting away,
Whether for a long time or just a day.
We're driving out to a campsite,
With supplies, we hope are right.
Starting in the morn, or afternoon.
Looking forward to the campfire soon.
Everyone chattering with the smell of smoke.
Someone's gone for a branch that's broke.
Smells of supper that's started to sizzle,
No matter if the weather decides to drizzle.
Hunger satisfied and the peace we feel.
Just sitting, watching the fire wheel,
Tossing a log, and stoking the fire,
'Til sleep takes over, it's time to retire.

Eileen Strobl

Hazel Eyes

You won't shed a tear knowing that I am here
my dear.
When I stare at your eyes, I have a feeling I'm in the sky
When I look in the light you take me by surprise
Hazel eyes.
I don't know who you are, but by the sound of your voice I
feel you're the perfect choice
Your Hazel eyes took me by surprise
You gave me delight and so in heaven I arrived
Hazel eyes.

Jorge Ortiz

Green

The beginning of time had a color.
The color of spring is the same.
This color helps flowers grow taller.
This color has only one name.
This color represents the Earth.
This color is also the afternoon.
This color also means rebirth,
and the color of summer in June.
My favorite color is this one.
This color is always happy never mean.
With this color you can have lots of fun.
Of course I'm talking about Green.

Sylvia Diane Macias

My First Love

She was such a beautiful thing,
and there were no such things as strings or rings
She took me for rides, and stayed by my side,
she was such a beautiful thing.
And when I was sick, she put me to bed,
and layed night down by my side.
And when I was bad, boy she got mad,
but she was still a beautiful thing.
And as I sit here and wonder why,
"God" took her away, before I could say —
 MOM you were a beautiful thing

Archie Viney

Untitled

Yellow and green checkered colors govern your thoughts
stare at them, let your mind...but wait
don't forget—did you leave the Stove on?
What about Algebra Homework? Is that the Phone?
Distractions....push, push them out. Let your mind....
free this time, to roam and break free. Yes finally!
Swirling, twisting, churning, maneuvering. You hear music?
You should—it's good. If not, no matter
just like alice, it's hookah for the pipe
just colors but is it just that?
who says it can't be a way to escape?
unfold into yourself, feel the waves of individuality
pull your under into a riptide!
you hear a Familiar Voice out in the distance
the Lifeguard of Reality calling you back in
"Don't Stray Too Far. You'll drown".
But maybe drowning is the way. Who's afraid? Not you
but they are, with their sharp voices commanding; then there is
Acquiescence you sigh—another time. Calmly with assurance and
poise
the green and yellow checkered cardboard box waits for you to return

Betsy Housten

Infibulation

Oh Mother, what have I done
Why didn't you just kill me, should I have been a son
Doesn't anybody want me if I don't look like this
What is it they really want
Bloody kisses from bloody,
Bloody lips?

It is me, is it all in my brain
Don't you see me, don't you see my pain
Was I born without freedom, the only way his
How can anybody want
Bloody kisses from bloody,
Bloody lips?

He says he loves me, when I twist and turn
Because I'm only his, he must make me burn
Shall I fill his life with my apologies
Give him all my pain and
Bloody kisses from bloody,
Bloody lips?

Martin Hassel

Advise To A Brawn Hartling

As the fourscore wright, the brawn;
And the brighting thrown, the crown;
Giving the red gown some proper respect;
And the torpid gutimates with triple prospect.

Since the brown gownlock termed immense;
And the brawns are shining, with no pretense;
Hopeless are the souls in balding area;
Except the proud braughtons in the bare viscera.

But now the virgules are roundly prompted;
And the bings are moved to the bright side, instead;
So the mirates suggests the sadly vicious;
Empty to the full, a large glass of dogmarus!

What remains is to fend the paratelmic thirst;
And to earn the price of cumidum based burst;
Take advice from a friend, who knows the braggo;
Say no Hurrah to the urge — if nowhere to go!

Thomas Szirtes

The Apple - Raped

A seed
Small in size
Matures
Round
Smooth
Delicate
Firm
Sweet aroma
Juicy, wet, desired
Pierced... the knife
Uninvited, requested not
Violated... harsh...pain
Numbness
Exposed, taken (eaten)
Disguarded
Bruised, gnawed and agitated
Violated!

Carol Cowan

Dirty Ol' Dog

Dirty ol' dog
Get down and beg.
Dirty ol' dog's
Got his tail between his legs.

Dirty ol' dog's
Been scratchin' for some...
Dirty ol' dog's
Been itchin' for some love.

Some people try and push
This dirty ol' dog to the side.
But if they're not careful
This dirty ol' dog'll bite.

Dirty ol' dog
Wants to get in your kitchen.
Dirty ol' dog
Won't be around to listen
To anymore of your b*tch*n'.

Ronald Seelogy

Blood Lovers

Our mortal lives are just a mask,
For us is promised a bigger task,
Our time alive grows ever short,
Awaits our days in the devil's court.

In the inky black of night,
Clear and crisp in vampire sight,
Our time will come to join the fleet,
The dark children will our secret keep.

And never more the sun we'll see,
Entombed in death beds we shall be,
Until our hunger stirs our mind,
And blood we'll drink of every kind.

Mortal fear and death no more,
Just morbid romance lies in store,
We'll walk the streets in the dead of night,
And in human blood we will delight.

Deadly killers you and I,
Forever will hunt under moonlit sky,
Vampire lovers we shall be,
From now until eternity.

Leigh Frazer

More Than Words

To just say that I love you,
doesn't nearly say enough;
because I love not only your smile,
but also your smooth and gentle touch.
I love your soft, curly hair,
and the way it feels on my fingertips;
I love your hot, wet tongue,
and the way it glides about my lips.
I love your beady, brown eyes,
they seem to put me in a trance;
I love your tight, firm butt,
It looks so good when in your pants.
But most of all I love your chest,
from within I feel the beating of your heart;
and with each beat I love you even more,
and I hope to love you till death do us part.

N. C. Patterson

We All Fall Down

Revolting devil children
dance around my head.
I lie here waiting
for the time to strike.
The blade gleams
as I shine it nice.
Things have to look good when you die.
Perfectionist prays
for better days to come forth.
She cries cold tears to wash away hate.
Now she is ready for
the horrible fate she has set.
To stab and curse in
continuous thrusts, in pain.
Life leads the stabbing.
She lies in a pool, her own blood.
Now regretting, now ashamed. She murders her.
She is her, left on cold linoleum.
Left to fend for herself.
Left to die. To smile one last time...

Nami Matsuo

Out Of Hell A Human Meeting

Saint Paul is the predicted Antichrist testifying calamity
We Mother Church by Christ testacy should not be soul raped
    and hung on a line
I saw eagles yak yak around with their prey
Yak ambo: Man is the head divinity in a one dimensional amen,
Insidiously gaping Eagles fief goal hierarchy,
To feast on automalist homosexual soul thirst in still cell,
To chasten psychic slavery slaughter in rivers sways,
To adapt Minotaur like Teilhard de Chardin primate hazel
Yak: "We love anything 'comfort,' 'dog,' 'wife,' 'candy.'"
There are theologians paganists high jinks feazing hill,
Where feeble unconscious blindfold victims obey,
Overwhelmed by faith to height spittle sikh, jail
God forsaken Shylock sexist occult madicity,
From Genesis to Saul lynch laws to kill charter rights.
Women priest may be: To betray themselves! Sold as element of sin,
Where there is not soul triune to reach their transcendent sight.
To pertain wed sacerdotal obeying couple in God triune sing-song mystery,
In the transfiguring desire to love Orb inborn weld
To amend country slumber to vote man-woman charter rights.

Lorraine Martin

Amphitrite's Victim

She cleanses him.
He enters her feeling impudent,
wet, sure.
He can see through her,
yet accepts the seduction,
anticipating release.
She feels surprisingly warm.
Slowly, deliberately, forging deeper,
he is consumed.

He pauses,
envisioning betrayal in the eyes of his beloved.
How could he?
Why?
The inevitable pain...
He cannot stop!
This desire has waited too long.

His eyes are now wet
and he tastes the salt.
Waves of certainty comfort him.
She is gentle, she knows.

D. M. Taliento

Closin' Off And Lovin' The Groove

Sweet, man, oh so sweet; I feel it,
Callin' me down to the well.
Cleanse your soul, baby, just
Wash away the pain of emotion
And let that ol' f***er run dry.
Bleed out all your hope and let it
Run through the grass, to be lost
Down the gutters backlogged already
with half the world's rejected dreams.
chill with it, honey, when there's
no more reason to sing than a
bird has, who's barred in a cage.
or an innocent man, sentenced for a lesson.
Cry it out, doll, but save your tears,
Wasting time to give in that much.
there are no perfect stories, you writhe, toss, turn,
sleep, dream, wake, cry, rage, burn, scream, work, sweat,
bleed, curse, stumble, fall, climb, pray.
Then maybe you can smile, once, to yourself,
before it's all over...

Jan Williamson

I Take You...

I take you like a whirlwind
and set your soul on fire
Fill you with my driving love
and my urgent desire.

I captivate you with a kiss
and make your eyes light up the night
I make you feel so good inside
How could this not be right?

Still, in your heart you keep me
regardless of where you go
And I keep you with me, too
just in case you didn't know.

W. Scott Phoenix

The Road Of Life

Everybody wants their life to be
sunny skies and rainbows.
But they fail to realize were the
sun always shines there is no water below.
And they need a little rain to get the rainbow.
So as you travel on the road of life remember this.
There will be times that it's rough and
times that it's smooth, and sometimes you win,
sometimes you lose.
Everybody wants their life to be a bed of roses.
But they don't realize the roses come with thorns.
And they don't realize sometimes in
life they have to grab the bull by the horns.
Everybody wants to live on easy street,
but they don't realize it takes a lot
of work to build that street.
So as you travel on the road of life remember this.
There will be times that it's rough and
times that it's smooth and sometimes
you win sometimes you lose.

Homer Harris

A Love That Lost Its Way

Our love was always filled with happiness and fun
It was guided by the bright and shining rays of the sun
Our feelings for each other were always touched with kindness and
tenderness
The warmth from our hearts were bonded with our sincere togetherness
For now our love is deeply shattered and broken.
But it could be mended if only the true words of love were spoken
In our younger years, we met, fell in love, married and were very
happy
In our middle years we became closer and deeper in love and raised a
family
In our later years our love became lost and couldn't find away to stay
In reality, it became just another love that lost its way
Our love has gone astray
But I believe it's not far away
It will come back someday

Richard D'Amato

Little Lambs

Little lambs. You enormous bears with sharp teeth,
raging wolves, do not bite.
Bees and hornets, do not sting.
Come not near our Ma, do right.
An angel with a soft, little voice,
Listen to our soft emotions.
Emo, emo, emotions, emo, emo, emotions.

Never yell, nor scream, nor put on a spell.
Be near my sweet charmer be shone.
Relax, listen to our soft emotions.
Little Lambs. Trouble some tigers, don't come by us.
Stay away you black-striped creatures, stay away,
Horses brown, soothe us with your neigh.
Nor mouse or rat don't come near to play.
An angel with a soft little voice.
Listen to our soft emotions.
Emo, emo, emotions, emo, emo, emotions.

Never yell, nor scream, or put on a spell
Be near my sweet charmer, be shone.
Relax, listen to our soft emotions.

Tara Herron

Here

Here in my body I feel the anger,
Here in my mind I see no danger.

Here in my heart I feel the pain,
Here in my eyes I see the rain.

Here in my hand I hold you tight,
Here in these memories everything's all right.

Here in my cries I need you here,
Here in my life I need no fears.

Here in this hour I'll cry for you,
Here in this day I'll pray for us too!

Cande Emanuel

Red Flashing Lights

An ambulance, fire truck and school bus
beneath a fretful sky
compete for space in a one-way street
before three passersby.
Hope it's not one of the kids
hell you never know any more
I hear they're totin' guns and knives these days.
Young necks are craned
red flashing lights pull in the curious
two cops talking with the bus driver, ashen but still furious
he says he thought it was a goddamn firecracker
There goes the stretcher now.

Cecil O. Humphrey

Forever Until The Morning

Crystal star and darkest night,
Bring together one true light.
That for myself I always seek,
To find the one, to save the meek,
Of mind and heart and soul am I
A fledgling with no wings to fly?
I try to write down how I feel,
But words do but make myth seem real,
So I lay me fears aside,
And speak the words I tried to hide:
Field blue and sky of green,
Eyes thru love-felt blinders seen,
Coins of dust and refuse gold,
Ice is warm and fire cold.
Take my hand, and take my heart,
A frozen finish to a blazen start,
So as we part, I say farewell,
To love, to life.... and damned to hell.
And when, if e'er you need to cry,
I will be there.. far past we die.

Cyrus Malkin

The Rose

May your love blossom and grow
as a beautiful rose; growing into a
unique and perfect flower..and may
your love last, like a precious rose
Preserved to be remembered, to last
a lifetime. For a rose, like a marriage
has many thorns that prick and hurt
at times, but if handled with tender
loving care, the beauty and sweet
aroma will always overcome the pain.

Rachel Hart

Rain

O my God! How it rains again
The sweet pains of the heavens
Food for the plants, Fuel for my sorrows
a perfect patch for my broken heart

It rains even harder now
I think how much I miss her
Her every touch was a joy to me
Her very existence brought me bliss

The rain is a torrential downpour now
Her last goodbye was a sword to my heart
Our last embrace was a turning of that sword
Oh God! Make The Pain Stop, Kill Me Here, Stop My Pain

The rain is now lightering, a phone rings
It is her...she says she wants me back
She is coming over to talk
Will she twist the sword in my heart, or pull if out and make me whole

The rain is over, the world refreshed
She loves me, I am healed
My heart swims in love for her
I never want it to rain again

Jeffrey R. Werth

Run, Run, Run

Run, run, run, horsemen of the night;
Black steed on flames, sword amidst the blood;
Cry of power, laughter of valour,
Swing your blade, spring on the chase,
Arrows fly, spears pierce, cries, tears, tragedy,
Swordsmen on the field, blood, tears,
Run, run, run, horsemen of the night;
Swing your blade,
Screams, wails, crying virgins,
Bleeding ground, blood, guts, and fear.
Army of light is in retreat,
Run, run, run, horsemen of the night;
Save the powers of light, free the world of twilight;
A blade of gold, black and bold, grip of steel, strong behold;
Demons, banshees and astral nastiest,
Turn, scream and face in fear the knight of light,
A horseman in the night
Flee, flee, flee, be banished, let us be
Free, free, free,
A horseman of the night.

Mamdouh Al-Daye

Changes

Changes. Bad ones.
I have a friend.
He used to be the greatest guy I knew.
He was nice and caring with good grades.
He was in all sports and always
talked about making Varsity football.
He has changed. All he talks about now
is earings and tattoos.
His hair is long and dirty.
He has started experimenting with drugs.
He is changing for the worse.
I want to help him. But how?

Naomi Deatherage

"This Old Body"

This old body was once young and strong.
Now everything seems to go wrong
My legs bring me pain,
My brain is out in the rain,
There's plastic in the body, steel in the head,
and it's getting harder and harder to climb the stairs up to bed.
Sometimes I [think] I'd be better off dead
but I know God has better plans for me instead.

Edward Folk

Tootsie My Dog...

Born August 5th, 1994,
She played and played when she was small,
A born fur coat she bore and she never did grow tall.

A white line of fur on her breast,
Tootsie loves it here on the farm
And to lie in a box and rest, to walk around in the barn.

At any air lane she would bark,
The cat, tootsie would chase,
In the soft ground footprints would mark
She stayed away from a cat, a certain pace.

After Mrs. Cat, she would run,
The cat ran up-the ladder,
While I was having fun, that made tootsie even madder.

And when we moved away,
In the morning tootsie wouldn't come with us,
For tootsie it t'was a sad day,
of her, Mrs. Maclaughlin always made a lot of fuss.

Yvonne M. Park

These Are The Words That I Often Say

"I love you"
    These are the words that I often say.
    I whisper these words in your ear.
    I say these words for everyone to hear.
    I say these words for they are sincere.
    These are the words that I often say.

"I miss you"
    These are the words that I often say.
    When we are lying alone.
    When we are on the phone.
    I say these words to you and you alone.
    These are the words that I often say.

How, when, why,
    did these words fill my heart and mind?
I will never know and hope that you never push them aside.

But ever since my love for you has grown
    Grown into something that, to me, was unknown.
So at night I sit, sit and wait to hear your voice to heal my aches

I love you, with all my heart and hope our worlds and hearts will
never part these are the words that I often say.

Alexis Allen

Summer

Summer smells of blossoming flowers,
Summer appears as an untamed jungle coming to life,
Summer feels hot like a fiery oven on a warm starry evening,
Summer sounds of birds chirping and aged falls leaves blowing in
The peaceful breeze,
Summer tastes of tangy hot barbecue and frosty cold lemonade.

Stacy E. Forrest

Golden Years

Paul and Anna five children had
Altogether Paulette, Gwendolyn, Paul Jr., Elvira, and Ramona
Under this group bore twelve grandchildren
Lively and vivacious were Mom and Dad.

All fifty years resided in Key West
No other place did they want to rest
Down life's road did God truly test.

Asking of Hi, for guidance and strength
No man did quite know what they meant
Now on this 50th anniversary April 27, 1992, is a fact
Anna and Paul, our parents, we do love and respect.

Ramona Richardson

The Runner

Standing down by the canal on an overcast day.
Lost in my own thoughts, my own world.
Worrying about whatever there is to worry about.
I see you coming toward me.
Headphones on.
Running into the wind.
Into my world. Into me.
If I latch on, will you take me with you,
wherever you're going?
I wonder if you're running toward something,
or away.
Lost in your own thoughts. Your own world.
Why won't you look at me?
You are fast approaching.
I open my mouth to speak to you,
but you've already sped by.
I turn around to see if you will look back.
But you don't.
You're already in a different place.
I'm still standing still.

Amy Mallett

Give Me Back My Heart

I have never really felt any love quite like this,
    It has swept me away from the taste of its first kiss.
We have gone separate ways for regardless what reason,
    But to explore another lover would surely seem total treason.

Confusion sets in again and my mind wanders away,
    Concentration ebbs as I labour through each day.
Please give my heart back if you still remember me,
    And God please show me mercy so that I may see.

I would have died and still would to really hold this ground,
    My own body saturates me-does this mean I have found?
The tear that washed me away to become lost in mornings dew,
    And my dreams of all tomorrows and a lifetime with you?

The lost essence of your spirit still tortures my mind,
    Sleep comes only when this demon of love is kind.
I once believed that every soul was true,
    Substance of lost truth should have been my cue.

Man kinds power to reason and his passions of the heart,
    Open the doors of a mind's infinity, and thus his odyssey to start.
Innocence transcends all along the corridor of broken dreams,
    And it is the quest to its return that really makes love all it seems.

...Give me back my heart.

Gary Brothers

"Mommy, Daddy And Me"

So small and so precious,
What a wonder you are,
Sent from above from the
Love of two hearts.
It will be so exciting watching you grow,
We will love you and guide you and
Teach you, you know.
You are so amazing, we still can't
Believe its true, that God has blessed
Us with a perfect little you.
You are our sunshine and our breath of fresh air,
You will never have to worry because mommy
And daddy will always be there.
We will protect you and hold you ever so tight,
From things you may say, go bump in the night.
You are so tiny now, not knowing what is to be
But soon you will realize when you are one, two or three.
That we are as one, a sweet family,
Mommy, Daddy and Me.

Susan Soring

Life

We all are sent both ups and downs from day to shining day,
but He never makes our lives seem rough;
we're the ones who choose the way.
We can accept our lives with love and help as it is needed;
we can lift a fallen brother and treat as we'd be treated,
or we can bemoan our lot in life and blame the other guy,
completely overlooking our own inability to fly.
But no matter how we choose to think
God gave each of us the choice,
we can be a cowering little mouse
or from the wilderness a voice.
A voice that makes a fallen soul rise up and try again
or comfort bring to those whose lives
have almost reached the end.
So use your voice, your touch, your love to great your fellow man
and back comes love a thousand fold
to give to you a hand.

Vivian Cole Ingersoll

Angels

We all know there are angels,
Angles are so pure and white,
They are as a bird, so graceful in flight.

The beautiful birds have wings we're told,
Angels are said to have wings of gold.

The birds perch on branches of a tree,
I know angels, they're so wild and free,
We know birds jump around on the ground,
We know the angels will always be around.

Some birds can be sweet as honey,
A little touch by an angel is better than money.
Some birds can be mean as bears,
One thing we'll always know, is that, the angel always cares.

You know some birds are bright as the sun,
How about angels, I don't know, have you seen one?

Philip C. Hallmark

Seasons

As a cold wind blows, I know summer has come
to end and I am sad.
But my sadness soon goes for children's happy
cries of Halloween are here.
As their cries die, I know winter is coming. I feel
at peace when I stare out my window and see
snow falling, so cold, so quiet, so soft.
My feeling of peace leaves and turns to restlessness
when the birds start chirping announcing that
the long winter has passed and spring has arrived.

Debbie K. Stechschulte

Love....It's Something Very Special

It should be handled with care,
Not done on a dare

Don't mistake it for lust,
Love is something you can trust

When you take different sides don't toss it away
True love will never leave forever it will stay

If we try to throw it away it will be our loss
Because what made love so very special was when Jesus died on the cross

God sent love down from heaven above
to show us nothing can separate from his everlasting love

Don't try to make the passion real
for when you have true love it is something you can feel

As though some may think love is not a game
If you play you'll lose because it's not man made

Janet K. Gaugh

Growing Up In Hard Times

Just a kid growing up, in a grown up's world.
Trying to survive, fighting hard to say alive.

Just a kid growing up, when things are not all right.
Violence and bloodshed is everywhere — I stand to cry silently,
in sorrow, in despair.

Just a kid growing up, where the power and greed govern humanity.
Droplets of blood and pieces of shrapnel I see.
Fear and panic fill my brains; as I pray solemnly, down on bended knee.

Just a kid growing up, when gunshots fill the air.
Can't stop the images, I'm freaking out, but I'll fight to the end.
I won't rest until the cries of society are heard and said.

Just a kid growing up, looking through a stain glass window.
They try to hide the real world, the pains, the misery.
Knowing any time this window will open. I can still see.

Just a kid growing up, with my pen as my weapon.
I will let it be known, the wall that separated us from peace
I will take down the wall; block by block, piece by piece.

Andrew Wong

The Hollow Side Of The Moon

The forecomings of the day are forgotten
as I fall in cascades onto my bed.
The warmth of the covers comforts me
as I realize the cold outside.
Every part of me relaxes
as my head further deepens
in the cradle my pillow has created for it.
The clock no longer shows time as
I enter the threshold of dreams.
I think only now of angels and playgrounds,
laughter and innocence.
I feel the sun's rays, though being in the night,
and as my eyes slowly close,
no longer am I in my room,
but sleeping on the hollow side of the moon.

Lyndsey Anderson

It Called "My Love"

My love there is only you that fits in my heart
No lips but yours with that cute smile
That shine like the star.
Please believe when I say you are my love forever
Also the body that rocks and melts my heart away.

Susan Zelin

Clouds Of Life Parade

Clouds float by in a parade, year by year, constantly changing.
Clouds like life, are continuously transforming and rearranging.

Carefree cloud wisps, like Baby's Breath, tumble in a blue sky.
And cotton candy-pink clouds, embrace the sun as they dash by.

Lacy, pearly white clouds, dance like a bride on her wedding day.
Then tiny angle - white cloud tuffs, float in the azure sky of May.

Clouds of trial sometime overshadow life, its music I cannot hear.
Clouds, floating, dashing, dancing, tumbling, year after year.

Black clouds, clashing, lashing, smashing, stealing life's light.
Rainbow clouds, like hope rise and flash with beauty so bright.

Dark depressive, crashing, storm clouds of doubt, bring fear.
Rain clouds lashing, raindrops splashing, dash down like tears.

While watching the parade pass by, wondering if happiness can be found,
Maturing, waning fog clouds, like wisps of gray hair, fall to the ground.

Life, constantly changing, clashing, crashing, flashing, falling,
   winding,
Splashing, lashing, smashing, wondering on the wild, wings of the wind.

Patricia Stone Guynn

Night Sights.....

I love the night and the stars that I admire from afar,
The full moon is a real sight, but sometimes it gives
me fright. The crescent moon is not so bright but it
gives me great delight, makes me see things in a new
light. In my strolls about I have found a very swell
lady, we hit it off good and now we go steady. We both
love the sun and spend our evenings and days off having
fun in the sun. We love the shade, we like the night it
always seems to make thing right. We enjoy the same
things, we go out and shout to the world; how happy we
are just enjoying the sun, the moon and the stars.
Love is grand, it's great to be alive and happy with
nature, it makes one know there is a God.

Joseph A. Schwan

Ode For The Children

So many things are going on today that need our attention bad;
If we don't do something really soon, we're going to wish we had.
Our children are lost and crying out for directions we can't give;
It's all because we've closed our eyes to the filth in which we live.
Every movie that comes on T.V. now is full of sex and sin;
As if regular T.V. isn't bad enough we have some more junk cabled in.
Most movies today made "Just for kids" are filled with sex and lies;
Set forth to present themselves in a fairy tale or fable guise.
Take for instance the new Disney movies with their tempting, sexy
sirens; Is this the message we should give our young girls "Get the
man by any means?
Use powder and perfume; expose yourself; put your breasts up in his face:
Heaving and humping lie flat out on your back; for that's your proper place."
Our models are but little girls dressed up to entice grown men;
Wearing too much make-up and perfume and looking "waif-like":
Gaunt and thin. The young men too have got it bad, look at their role
model cavalcades: Athletes, politicians and singers who womanize,
do drugs, and live with or die of AIDS.
We've come so far but, lost so much. It makes me so angry, so
frustrated, so sad. Again I say, we'd better do something really
soon or we're going to wish we had.

Imogene Menzies

"Suicides Insanity"

My life drifts continuously from my will with the passing of each day. My uncontrollable thoughts grow stronger, keeping me in fear from realization that someday my sanity might not be found. Life's frustrations seem to apply pressure to the soul of my very being. My will, though a strong one, weakens from the stress of my feelings, and a sane mind looks to insanity for comfort.

How is one to live when everything worth living for is ripped away from that of a higher power. A higher power, a God, well not the "God" but god to me, for my happiness is held in its claws. Its excuse is that my mind is too weak to know the limits pertaining to my well being. The fools! Some god; rehabilitating me into a contentious monster. A monster of darkness, whose greatest loves, everything held dear to my heart, torn away like that of a baby from its mother's arms. Leaving me in bitter loneliness, withering in denial, in the cold; dark, isolation, at the bottom of a pit of misery.

Emptiness fills my heart, leaving a void big enough to kill an ordinary man, but not me - not yet. This torture inflicted from the inside out, slowly executes any hope of life in the pit, thus making a madman madder! The fear of being incapable to feel frightens me, but yet still grows to its adulthood, leaving me no choice but to kill the monster before it's too late.

The only debate for this choice is the thought that the void will be filled and happiness regained, once I climb to the top of the pit. But does the pit have a top and if so am I strong enough to make the climb? Am I truly twisted, or just a sane mind trying to make sense out of an insane world? Sometimes, I think I'll never know.

Bejamin Seymour

A Day In The Future

Yes, Love, there was a war when I was young. A war where young men died before learning that life <u>was good</u>! A war that meant that life for liberty was still in the hearts of our own! Some say, there was a mighty and worth-while cause, while others remember their grown-up soldiers as only little ones, who were called to give their youthful life for a reason no one could really understand! They went willingly off to this war and within their young minds were thoughts of home and life left behind, and to the emptiness and fruitlessness of future days of battle! Yet still in their hearts, they knew that they, and only they, could win for their homeland the freedom and liberty sought by their forefathers to make our land what it was this day. That freedom must and would be sheltered and protected at whatever cost need be. Yes, Love, he would go to war and fight as he had never before for his new arising and undying belief in what this fighting was all about. Yes, Love, Daddy was a good soldier and always remember, He died to assure that you and I were to live forever in peace and freedom, and HE DID NOT DIE IN VAIN!

Sandra M. Barthlein

A Soldier's Night

Sitting here in the middle of the night
nothing much to do; try as I might
I sit down here to type out this rhyme
listening to the tanks firing time after time
Their big guns are loud and flaring
with bright flashes of light that keeps me staring
I will be glad when this night is through
because I'm getting bored with so little to do
My Sarge is sitting here reading, rocking and half asleep
probably instead of reading; he is counting sheep
My comrades are all snoozing in their beds
while these mortars are flying over their heads
Their minds are far away dreaming of their dames
but in reality we are still here playing these war games
Soon it will be morning and everyone will be getting up
watching and waiting for the chow truck
I will quit for now; my stomach is growling and starting to moan
but I will be back again around the twilight zone

André Scott

Secrets

I've often wondered as I
stood on the shore alone just me, what
tremendous secrets the waves could
share. What do they know that I don't
know? What have they seen that no eye
has seen? What have they heard that
no ear has heard, if only the waves had
lips so they could speak of the tales of
adventure, struggle and mystery they
could tell.

If I could sail upon the
waves will I ever learn all the secrets
the waves have seen and heard, even
those who probe beneath the waves will
never uncover all the hidden mysteries
they being. If I had one wish that
would be to ride the waves into the sea.

Michael Ellick Jr.

A Garden In July

Picturesque
A garden in July.
Golden summer sun shines
Like a blessing with a smile,
Delicate flowers bloom in beauty
Coloring with fragrant scents,
The robin red breast sings
With joy to be fully spent.
Amongst the flowers and the trees
Romance grows to love abiding,
And the monarch moves in delicate grace
Beauty in freedom from its abandoned case.
The poet and the painter
Create a scene in nature's glory,
Clouds of white
In heavens of blue
Is a part of nature's story.
Summer breeze
So gentle to please
In a garden in July.

Vanessa Pinto

Untitled

I finally fall asleep
I float above the clouds
I contemplate my life
It just keeps spinning round and round.

I see you in the mirror
Your face so filled with life
Why does this void keep reflecting in my eyes.

It took my life to see
my dreams cloud come true
why you left me standing
with no wings to fly away with you.

I know that I can go through life
having no more fear
you'll always rest here
on my shoulder
and guide me year to year.

The told me time would heal my pain
I guess these words were true,
I finally found serenity
I owe it all to you.

Lorelee Johnson

"Steady The Steps We Climb"

Cleansing the earth, fell the snow.
Doth thee have a meaning? Do we know?
Take we, shall we go,
Into the never traveled. Then do we grow?

Close the mind, running slow.
Enter the light, of once a shadow.
Answers are here, in the cool air, low.
Inhale deep the breath of all our foe.

It is then, that we shall know,
What is there, and where we go.
Still falleth, steady snow.
Then in triumph, we shall grow.
Paul Finnegan

"Night Walk"

When it's dark and late at night
and the moon is shining and still,
I look up and see the stars shining bright
and listen to the call of the whippoorwill.

I walk silently on the path in the woods
straining to hear any noises around me,
listening, and shivering as I pull down my hood,
the wind is whispering around peacefully.

I hear the owl call me far-away
and know it's time to go home.
Starting on my way,
I stop and remember I'm alone.

Up head I see the well-lit house,
I shout for joy and begin to run,
calling greetings to my cat, Mouse,
glad that my night walk is done.

As I lay snuggled in bed,
looking at the moon shining bright,
I pull the covers over my head
and whisper to the world, "good night."
Camille Mendez Williams

Untitled

In the graveyard something stirs,
something strange has occurred.
With glowing eyes a scary orange,
opening its coffin with a screeching door hinge.
Its bone hand popped out of the dirt
then ribs in a tattered shirt.
One by one the bones come out,
and they start dancing about.
A werewolf howls, bats fly by
higher and higher they reach the sky.
Graves scatter and tell the deaths.
In the trees are vultures nests.
Ghosts around moaning and wailing,
werewolves find victims and start trailing.
Things come out from under the bed
to drive them away - hit them in the head.
Zombies come out and eat anyone around,
they roam and roam all over town.
Monsters... Ghouls... Ghosts... The dead... Pumpkins, tame and
mean, that's because it's Halloween!!!
Matt D. Colyer

One Day I'll Walk

When I was younger my brothers,
Sisters, and me
Used to go by the pond and go fishing,
But now those days are gone. Now
I have memories of all the good
Times we had when one of us
Would get in trouble and the rest of
us would laugh. Our Mamma would say
"I'll give you something to laugh about."
And we were all silent. I said to
myself that one day I would walk
in my Mamma's footsteps when I will
act just like her. To my kids I will
act as if I were my mother. They
might act as my brothers, sisters, and me
But I will know better. I said I will walk
one day in the footsteps of my ancestors.
I might walk one day like Martin Luther King Jr.
did, lead my people to a better future, like
he did. But I know that one day I'll walk.
Marjorie Springer

On Memories

With feelings mixed I often do recall
Events which like the tides would rise and fall.
And times in which were felt anger and pain
And others which provided worthwhile gain.
Tough times there were that brought with them distress.
And in their wake came loss and mental stress.

Rich memories there are of friendships true:
Familial love, concern and caring too
That helped dissolve vicissitudes of life
Thereby succeeding to dispel its strife.

Precious were friendships made and kept those days
Marked with goodwill displayed in copious ways.
Happy delightful times I still recall
Times when it seemed life mostly was a ball.
Eustace H. Reis

Preludes

When the hands of God rest between shadow and flesh,
and dead men learn to fly from their bodies,
all of the devils fall quietly away,
and every hour awaits a miracle.

When the wind grows tired of caressing the earth,
and the moon begins to drift to wonderful sleep,
the simple clouds freeze dreamily
in anticipation of a still sky.

Yet my blood begins to chase wild horses forever
and the strange fur of skin goes all afire,
the tongue of death seems never stranger
while the voice of my
human heart
can only
stutter,
knowing it's you.
Vlad Bar

Seasons Of You

Winter mornings with glowing drips of sunlight
cannot compete with your loving smile.
Morning doves with shades of amber
that fly across the milky white sky
could not be compared to your sparkling pure eyes.
The waves of autumn that splash against my legs
with heated passions of summers gone by
could not touch the warmth of your gentle caresses.
The fresh new breeze of young free flowers
that bask in the shades of spring
cannot compete with your sweet fragrance
That continues to linger on in my everlasting memories - of you.

Tangerine

Father

I love you, Dad, I love you so,
And my love for you will continually grow.
Your passing away is really hard for me to take,
But I know for sure that this was no mistake.
I remember all the things you did,
The love you had was never hid.
You are someone I'll always miss,
I wish I could give you just one more kiss.
I wish I could reach out and hold your hand,
Or go to beach and play in the sand.
We'll all miss you so very much;
What we need right now is your loving touch.
The memories of you will live forever;
They are much too special to ever sever.
So, as you look down from heaven with your loving eyes,
I want you to know my love for you will never die.

Jonathan Troyer

A Picture

A still portrait of yesterday — frozen in time.
smudged with fingertips inside a dusty album —
forever smiling — forever happy.
Eyes gleaming, glowing without a breath or sound.
Only scant images and memories,
sweet memories of yesterday.

Bringing sadness today.
Sadness..and tears
Regrets of lost time — lost smiles, lost love.
Now...wanting so deeply
that feeling
that day
those moments...again
knowing they're gone forever.

That instant and countless others — lost.
and now — just a faded dream.
Teaching the hardest lesson of all...
To relish the past
To embrace the present
and to love every moment before it is gone.

Troy Schwiegerath

"Rocket"

Rocket launch...rocket explode
rocket launch...rocket explode
rocket launch...rocket explode
a burning flash
rocket launch....that ingrains blindness
splinter of rocket disperse
rocket explode...metal stabbing my heart
rocket explode...time stops

Gregg Hewitt

Reflection

I remember the laughter and the games we would play
I remember my birthday parties being my own special day
I remember the egg hunts and the hidden chocolate rabbits
I remember the traditions, that now are my habits
I remember learning to skate and ride my bike
I remember the camping trips and the long mountain hikes
I remember the car rides, we took to nowhere
I remember the first time I had cut my hair
I remember walking side by side
I would look up at you and keep in stride
I remember the funny faces and jokes dad would tell
I remember the lessons, you've both taught me so well
I remember visits with family and friends
I remember hoping childhood never ends
Together you taught me what I would need
to go off on my own and someday succeed
When I wake up in the morning, I look in the mirror and see
a reflection of you both looking back at me.
I smile and think, how lucky I could be
for the parents that were chosen especially for me.

Roxeanne Schaefer

Vagabond

I stare at passerbys walking by my bench, their eyes full of caring
Arms intertwined, laughing at the simplicity of the world, memories sharing. No one feels this way for me anymore, I'm alone and inside
I feel like I'm slowly dying, This hollowness has made a void in my soul from an excessive amount of crying.

To strangers' eyes, I'm a outcast vagabond, lingering in the street,
Once a successful entrepreneur, left my dreams behind, finally admitted defeat. To avoid reminiscing about what once use to be, I find solace in drinking, Sometimes I surprise myself by realizing that a sad song I am singing.

Once I had it all, a wife, a home, beautiful children, Now I find the jaws of life closing in on me, an inevitable burden. Where did it all vanish to, my drive, my ambition, my inspiration, the support that i thought I had, it was all a figment of my imagination.

I thought that my wife who knew of my pain, would have always been there for me, Never for a second believed that she would take our children and abandon me. If anyone asks me to explain this heartbreaking shock with some clarity, I have no words, no emotion, no heart, slowly I feel that I am losing my sanity.

Looking down at my dirty attire, I think of the man that I have let myself become, I must find the strength within and this fear of starting over, try to overcome. Once upon a time, I did indeed have it all, I have nothing more to lose, some confidence in myself I must now install.

Angela Agourias

Silent Reproach

When the sky is leaden and the snow so deep
My heart has but one sigh of woe,
Like the willow tree that never ceases to weep
So do my tears never cease in their flow.
For how could this heart discard such sadness and pain
That which your hand did so consciously render?
Forever it will hold your soul in disdain
May you never know the joy of life's glory and splendor.
To forget your offense, my mind will comply
For surely your life will soon tatter and fray,
Of sorrow and regret your heart will cry
And forever be reproached by the winds of yesterday.
  For in our lives, we must lead our own way,
  So must we live with the guilt of going astray.

Melissa E. Coulombe

Thoughts Of A Bulrush

Long ago our roots would lay in pristine waters, where-ever
Water-life existed. Waterfowl were discreet, in weaving
their nests at our feet. Geese and Mallards would stay
and bear their young, for we the bulrush would shelter
them from the winds, rain and sun.

Frogs would spawn, from which tadpoles would wriggle, with
young minnows darting here and there, and turtles basking
in the sun. Occasionally, a horse-drawn jaunting cart
would pass by, leaving the water-life undisturbed.
Now high-powered vehicles fly by, leaving deadly
gases which we absorb, and will eventually die.

Now stunted in growth we carry on, but very soon we will
be gone, then only on canvas will we be seen, by human
beings yet un-born. Human beings must re-think, before
they with everything else become extinct.

Ecological preservation must be derived,
if our planet is to survive.

Albert Hale

A Gypsy Sales Girl

Oh! gypsy girl with swirling skirt,
With hawk black eyes and watchful glance.
Your tablecloths flung o'er your arm
And wicker bag with many more.
You spread your wares along a hedge,
And watch for eyes that might appear
To want to buy "mantels" today.
"These are the best, lookee, just see."
A little bit of English learned
It helps to sell to wary folk,
Who aren't quite sure if they should buy,
Or bargain first and wait awhile.
"It is nice lace, and pattern too!
"How much?" you say. "How wide is it?"
"It's your senora for dos mille."
A sale is made; the gypsy smiles
And tucks the note inside her breast.
Now she can sit and rest a spell.
Manana is another day.

Dorothy Thornton

Toll Of A Cloud

Across the sun-lit sky there strayed
A lonely ragged little cloud;
Whose tattered suit was worn so thin
That pieces floated with the wind,
Through trackless footless halls of blue.
The sun looked down and flashed a smile,
At such a challenge from a cloud.
The world turned on its side to see
This fancy floating fantasy;
That dared to raise its standard high.
And flaunt its banners in the sky;
That dared to place its flimsy veil
Across the highway of the sun,
And take a toll from out its rays.

Glen H. Byers

I Love J. T. T!

From Home Improvement to Man of the House,
he's the best one I've come across.
From Man of the House to
Tom and Huck, I love him more
and most of all.

That's J. T. T.

Pam Bushey

Teardrops In The Snow

I stood by her grave
    a young girl I never knew and cried

I bent to scrape the ice from her name
    the cold reality struck again

The scene of a year ago flashes in my mind
    her skidding car meets mine wrong place wrong time

I placed there my tangible thoughts
    a single rose a handwritten note things I brought

With eyes closed hot tears streaming
    on a winter cold face I prayed

For the joy her short time gave
    to her special love ones now missing her

For the hope her dying gift gave
    to strangers once ill whose hearts beat anew

For peace understanding and strength
    for me for all who struggle

I walked away from her grave
    leaving flowers prayers and teardrops in the snow

Joyce Elliott

"From Darkness Into Light"

I was born into the world without sight,
Then at six months of age I saw the light.
At age three I got glasses so that my vision would not be so fuzzy,
I did see things better, but they were a nuisance and a burden to me.
My Elementary School days were spent in a sight conversation class,
    which helped me with my education,
But reading regular print in High School and College gave me great
    deal of frustration.
Then I tired those hard contact lenses, which caused me much pain,
However while dating without glasses I endured the strain.
I had a cataract operation - fell out of bed and my elbow was dislocated.
My fingers had constant pain, so that for me, contact lenses could not
    be manipulated.
I was operated on my other eye — still contact lenses I would not dare,
Thus I walked in a constant haze, if my glasses I did not want to wear.
On February 24, Dr. Spencer Sherman gave me lenses that could stay,
In my eyes up until three months and that was truly a red letter day.
For the first time in my life, I wake up every morning with perfect
    sight, and see the world in focus from morning until late at night.
There are no words that can express, adequately my great indebtedness,
To Dr. Spencer Sherman for all that he has done for me,
The greatest doctor in the field of ophthalmology.

Esther Feinberg

Rights of Beast

Yes, I believe in the Rights of Man
And in a society that says "Yes, I can!"
    But overwhelming forces conspire to create
    A society doomed to desiccate
A failure to love
    An inability to understand—
Conspires to doom the Rights of Man.

The Rights of Man in the face of War
Continues to mangle, hurt, and gore.
    The continuation of this policy throws me into a fit-
    "We had to destroy this village in order to save it."
A failure to love, an inability to understand—
The Rights are reduced to the Lore of Man.

Do you believe in the Rights of Man?
Can you unconditionally love and Understand?
    Or will the extinction of hate rob you of your power?
    Reign in all your policies, prevent Your "Finest Hour"
If this is the case—
    Love and understanding will cease
and the "Rights of Man" becomes The Rights Of Beasts

Francis Jens Erickson

'Longing'

We part, a kiss for you farewell.
My lips kept moist by thoughts of you, lie melting, linger.
Time passes
a remembrance, a twinge, a smile, a sigh.
Love made in the minds of lovers longing,
for warm embrace at fires light.
Timberline in December's wake, once carried my perfume
through September.
How time can oxidize such precious memory,
my every moment, my every care, my every hope,
my every dream.
Come dance with me sailor, on wing tipped shoes.
In darkness parted by candles hue.
The wine is sweet, sultry, the dress speaks desire.
Supple, round, soft, pert, hungry, stammering.
But desires desire calls on deaf ear.
Sitting, waiting, longing again.

Kathi Lee Dobbins

Tyler's Song

You're my baby, don't you know?
You're my baby, I watch you grow.
You're my baby, baby boy.

I love you, yes I do.
I love you thru and thru.
I love you, I love you, I love you.

What can I say? What can I do?
I've always loved you!
You're my little boy, you're my little man.
Let me take you by the hand
And show you, and tell you,
All that you need to, become a man,
My little, little friend.
I love you, I love you, I LOVE YOU!

Timothy J. Weber

Live To Give

Is it wrong, to believe that I have something to give?
Is it wrong, to be willing to give what I believe I can?
Is it wrong, to try to make a contribution? Is it wrong?
Is it wrong, to feel that I should give? Is it wrong?

What happens to the youth, who believes that he or she has
nothing to give?
What happens to the youth, who has heard these things so long?
What happens to the youth, who has chosen this way to live?

So o.k. Life begins, the belief sinks in
I have nothing to give. So I can't give.
What then is made my alternative?
Getting is the only thing left.
To get, is the purpose for which I live.

So the young sister, she gets this, she gets that. She gets money.
She also gets an unwanted protruding tummy.
The young brother, he gets money. He gets a gun. He gets shirts.
He gets a pair of pants. He gets hot lead through his head,
or a life sentence.
Please, give youths the belief that they have, and could live to give!

Keith V. Joseph

Tender beauty
shining from your face,
a smile brighter than the sun,
mesmerizing eyes attracting my glance.
You — an enchanting belle of endless wondering
trapping my defenseless heart into
the web of lonely yearning . . .

Ben Forshay

Through The Artist-Hand

Light is ever new,
Pouring over the various moments of being.

Colors and sounds
Burst from their prison
Of pretense and preconception,
Come rushing through the artist-hand.

Fredrick Pritchard

Inherited Cross

As I wander down this path of life
Amongst the pain, toil and strife
I wonder, was this meant to be
Why is there so much misery

There was a time, not long ago
When everyone would say, hello
But now we just go on our way
And often times, forget to pray

Our youth are plagued with poverty
A future bright they cannot see
Asking Him to take their hand
Could rekindle hope throughout the land

As children, we did laugh and play
We went to church, on the Sabbath Day
Our family then, was closely knit
Have we lost respect for it.

This world He gave us still is good
But have we managed it, the way we should
I'll leave you now, but not in despair
There's help for the asking, your cross to bear

Nora J. Baird

The Lighthouse

The rain was hammering at the windows,
The waves were clapping against the rocks,
The wind was a clatter of sounds,
and the beacon was as bright as the stars in the sky.

A ship's horn blew signaling its arrival.
Suddenly the beacon blew out.
The Lighthouse was completely dark
and the ship was still coming.

I tried so hard to get it to light up
but nothing would work.
Suddenly on my last try the light went on.
The beacon was shining brighter than before.

But it was too late,
for the ship had hit the rock.
I looked out the Lighthouse window;
without a clear view I saw the ship sink to
the bottom of the roaring ocean.

Ashley Golden

A Silver Grey Haired Lady

One day while I was walking, I came across an old lady
Her hands aged with time and her hair a silver grey
She spoke with such tenderness my ears could not believe
The way the lady smiled and spoke about her dreams.

She smiled as she told me how she used to live
The elegant jewels and charms that she would proudly give
As she sat and told the story how I listened with intrigue
To this silver grey haired lady who told me of her deeds.

As I watched her tell the story, tears fell upon her face
Although she cherished all her memories that life could not erase
She showed me all her treasures not so long ago
I felt her mixed emotions as they would come and go.

Upon her story ending, I thanked her for her time
And offered her a token but she wouldn't accept a dime
As I slowly walked away, I turned to see her face
This silver grey haired lady had lonely tears upon her face.

Kim Hardy

Judge Us Not

Spare me the shame you feel, whenever you look
At yourself critically, we are one and the same.

Our blood is the same there
Is no need for you to feel
Ashamed, be proud of who you are and I'll do the same.

Don't criticize what we are
Our race is proud, no longer savage, so don't deny your
Heritage and be proud of who you are.

You hide behind your rejection of us and laugh at us, we do
Nothing, it is not up to us, it's
You who cannot believe enough in yourself to be one of us.

You live in the white man's world
Where Indians once ruled and roamed
Free like the wayward breeze, and
Lived in peace and Harmony, while the White man stole our world.

There will come a time my friend, when your rejection of native things
Will no longer matter, that my friend
Is the time that you will dread, so
Judge us not I beg for you will be judged
And then my friend that will be the end.

Norma Longard

My Special Tree

There was a lane, not traveled much
That lay beneath a shaded wood,
Where as a child I often walked
When grown-ups seldom understood.

And at the end of this lonely path,
There stood a great oak tree,
Its graceful branches met the earth
To offer refuge just for me.

There was a pond a few feet deep
Where "peepers" came from fields afar,
And there I'd wade on summer days
To capture tadpoles in a jar.

'Twas there I shared my deepest thoughts
With God and this old tree;
Though not a word it had to say,
How quickly answers came to me.

Now sometimes in my wildest dreams,
Once more, a child I yearn to be,
With spirits free and soaring high
Beneath the shade of my special tree.

Mary Boone Dickens

"Counting The Years"

Until thinking of you, I'd never the thought
For the count of our ages and how it is wrought.
For I can number a house or a wagon tis true,
But there isn't a number that sets beside you.

When I've needed a friend,
To hold my hand through the fears,
I'm cradled in love as there you appear.
All of the love, joy, and sorrow,
We've shared in our tears.
These times I remember,
Who's counting the years.

We'll take all your years and put each in a book.
Then we'll place them in orders in your own little nook.
Then from now on,
There won't be age and year columns.
If they want to know your age,
They'll have to read it in volumes.

James N. Marshall

Thank You

Thank you for being there whether the road is smooth or rough,
Thank you for being there whether the times are easy or tough.

Thank you for your warm and sincere friendship always there,
Serving as a comforting reminder that you really, truly care.

Thank you for the time you take to listen and suggest,
The advice you often give helps me withstand the tests.

Thank you for being a constant supporter whose patience never ends,
You've made a difference in my life by being a devoted friend

Thank you for being there, I think the world of you,
And I pray your life is blessed day by day for caring the way you do.

Annie B. Pegram

Listening To The Wind

Listening to the wind.
Wondering about everything, seeping through its invisible,
soulless, and unwanted heart.
Listening to all the conversations it passes through, passing
them to the next victims.
Slipping into the hair of unwanted children, sobbing in the fields.
Blowing through the trees, to keep them going and living.
Drifting through the music and gently passing it to the next unbelievers.
Sacredly brushing the faces of the ground, bringing up the
undesirable souls.
Floating its lifeless and effortless body back through the eyes of
the unforgiven, warning the life ahead, of the coming unborn.
Dreaming by us and barely saying a word.
Brushing against the backs of creativity, leaving it unstirred.
Pushing the fear back into the original.
Blowing gently into the back of minds, listening and remembering
all the dreams of sweet thoughts.
Drifting back and forth through feelings but thankless it rolls away
and dies, appreciation disappearing gracefully, full with ideas,
dreams, and decisions. But letting them all go, undeserved.

Andrea Gianfrancesco

Untitled

Manifesting in force behind these eyes, life comes as no surprise.
Escaping the prison of fear within thought races, dreams become
hidden behind those faces.
Trappings of the mind have no place to stay, when love works in
the most marvelous way.
Seeking expression entangled in a maze, love works in the most
spectacular way.
Guiding you, protecting you, with the onset of each new day,
love works in the most mysterious way.

Helena Mahrle

Our Flag

50 stars, a state for each
And every state of star.
Where friendly hands will always reach
The boundaries near and far.

The stars and stripes that Old Glory flies
Tells the story of great inspiration.
of love and courage and sacrifice
To make ours the greatest nation.

Our flag has proudly been unfurled
Through peace and war, on land and sea,
And our colors known to all the world
As a symbol of America Liberty.

Virginia L. Bass

Echo

The echo of life, the sound of creation,
The howl of winds in canyons of faith
Depend on greatness beyond human hands.

From the inches of rain to the floods of pain
Grow on the branch of life that emerges from
Endless seeds of hate for love of all desires
In a chest of a human over these times.

Endless tears and grief on aging of times,
Hopes die as the sun rises on the flat land
Waving and smiling with dead sense of fear
As it descends down the deep sea of fiction
The aging man changes to a ghost of dust.

Huge snow balls race west to melt and to rest. Small mounts,
narrow seas, and shadows of blue; shades of gray, waves of green
with purple tips, thin masses of tented white, and holes of
black appear like a distinctive mix of a sphere, floating deep
throughout the vast space. It bursts and wipes it all; lands
and waters. We're then spirits; the old material shatters.
Where we reside, to me it sure matters.

Ryan Alchakaki

"Junior"

You came into my life
I hardly knew you at all
But once you were in
Everything else seemed to fall

You were my light, when all was dark
I was the wick, and you, the spark.
Then, one night so sudden it came
Your guardian Angel, to extinguish the flame

Someone above, knew the time wasn't right
Descended below, to put out your light.
Although the moment itself, quickly passed
You left a memory, that will forever last

I loved you once and now I know
That one of these days, your flame will grow.

Angela C. Algar

The Dead Clown Song

As I walk home from school, from learning right from wrong...
...There it is, I hear it!! The dead clown song.
You'd think ice cream truck songs are jolly and all,
but no, not this one, with its eerie call.
We think he might be trying to call spirits from the dead,
or simply just trying to scare little kids in their beds,
but whatever he does or wants to do...
be careful, I say, he might be out to get you!

Jill Marie Bolkcom

Strangers

You don't know me, I don't know you.
You think it's weird, but it's true.
Remember all the years we've spent together?
And times we talked about the weather?
All those times we laughed and joked?
Or cried until our clothes were soaked?
We shared secrets and faced some dangers
Never knowing that we were strangers.
When I realized we were so far apart,
I reached deep down into my heart.
I finally decided what to do
So, mom, I'd like to get to know you.

Graca McKenney

"The Winds Of Life"

If I only could paint the wondrous scenes of natures glorious
colors. No one may capture the feelings, for only the heart may hold
this peaceful moment, all others would not feel as I. The leaves
swirling around failing to natures ground some never wanting to let
go of mother tree for fear of losing a place with mother nature.

Some fall gracefully soaring first for a last tumble with the wind.
Some are to concerned of where they may land sweeping the earth
for a final taste of sweetness for they are greedy of their own selves.
Some so green fall to early believing the air is more free near the
water only to be swept away with the waves as life takes one's heart.
And then there are those who are old and brown to be noticed by the
hurried crowd only hoping to find a peaceful resting place for eternity.

If only I could write the words to express the heartfelt love of
natures simple change of every year to a new dress of color. My
words are of simple nature and may not be compared to a poets
pen, but in our hearts the words are all the same....

Joyce Woodard

Untitled

The bud sits all alone now nestled deep within the thorns:
yes, the flowering has gone, yet still the bud waits for the dawn.
What color lies deep inside? What fragrance does it hide?

Who pulls the strings for this young rose?
Why was he made to wait?
All the others have come and gone yet he has never shown
what color lies deep inside: what fragrance he does hide.

Can it be that the sun will never look upon his glorious petals?
Will he hold it all inside, until the sun no longer shines?
What color does lie deep inside? What fragrance does he hide?

God, don't let this tragedy happen.
Don't let your work be lost.
Release those strings and let the sun flow down
so we may see inside; the fragrance do not hide

Charles J. Rutenberg

Gone Has The Rebel

Gone a way has the Rebel
The Rebel left with a faint good by
The adolescent try so hard to catch him
But the Rebel is truly gone now
And we can not create the new without burying the old
No
No for we the young the Rebel is dead

Claiborn Phillips

"Stop Killing My Brother"

Stop killing my brother, please Mister Cocaine
They 're sniffing up their nose and shooting it in their veins
You've taken so many, so very few are left.
They have turned to beating, killing and theft.
They will do anything now just for a hit.
Taking a life to them - it don't mean slick
I pray that you stop while a few of them remain
Stop killing my brother please Mister Cocaine

Stop killing my brother please brother of mine
It's gotten so bad you're killing your own kind
Killing, stealing, and downing your brother - that's out
That's not what brotherhood is all about.
I pray that you stop now and draw the line
Stop killing my brothers, please brothers of mine

Stop killing my brothers please Mister Brutality
Stop beating on my brothers, and just let them be
They can't even walk the streets without looking suspicious
You can't even talk to them without being malicious
I pray that you stop with the amount of fatalities
Stop killing my brothers please Mister Brutality

Zina M. Manning

"Mom"

When I was a little girl of "three"
Our Daddy left my sisters and me!
I'm sure our Mom's heart did break
When another woman he did partake!
And through it all she had a "smile,"
Today for "one" I'd walk the mile!

We three sisters had a wonderful "mom",
We grew under her guidance and her thumb!
She was always there, no matter what,
Even for "Teddy" our loveable mutt!
She never complained if we brought friends home,
Perhaps for this reason we did not roam!

She lived her life through her daughters eyes,
Taught us to spread our wings and fly!
We, three sisters, wed the men of our choice
And gave her twelve grandchildren to rejoice!
The years did pass and God took her away,
And yet, you know, she's still here to stay!

Phyllis Berry

No Dogs Allowed

I walk the dogs along the levee
Stretched out between them
My face to the river
The setting sun a glowing red ball
Like a snippet of film
From Apocalypse Now.
Riverfront Park is around the bend.
When I was small, my father
Used to keep me home from school
On a Monday (if I were very good)
And take me to the union hall
A coke for me, the possibility of work for him
And then to the park
To watch the barges.
He always said the park would not last
That the land was much too valuable to keep a park.
He is gone now.
Riverfront Park will soon be cleared
To be landing for a gambling casino.
I'm sure no dogs will be allowed.

Grace M. Strange

Yesterday's Reflections

As I walk aimlessly
Thinking of you,
Feeling empty inside,
So lonely, so blue,
Wondering what went wrong,
With a love so right,
Without harsh words,
Without a fight,
We were so close,
We seemed like one,
We shared so much,
Laughter, fears, sadness, fun
All these emotions rolled in one,
But I want you to know,
That within my heart and soul
I will never forget your smile, your touch
All the little things between us,
That meant so much,
May just be memories to you,
But they will always remain as blessings to me.

Valerie Richter

Art

Art is my escape from the real world,
into brilliant colors of my imagination.
I feel the soft pastel shades
warming the cold surface of the paper.
Using my pencil to draw places I would rather be
than sitting in a crowded stuffy classroom,
I realize that the paper has become
a window to my soul.
I have my ruler to draw the lines in perspective
to make my hideaway world as large as I want.
Suddenly the bell rings—
I am jerked back to my classroom
and my arm spills my dirty paint water across the page.
My world is once more smudged and splattered
with reality.

Laura Greenough

The Carousel Horse

As the Carousel Horse am I, trapped within the structure of my being.
My feet are immobile, my body frozen; Yet, my soul lives on.
My soul longs to be free; set me free.

The world turns around me and I around it.
Up and down and all around I ride; discontentment rages within me.
I dream the dreams of those before me, and of those who are sure to follow.

The melodious chant rings in my ears over and over again;
They have attempted to break my spirit with rhythm and routine.
Yet, each day I concentrate to destroy my boundaries, and disturb
   the never-ending cycle.

The bold blues, greens, reds, and yellows have becomes worn and frail.
Others, their tails swoon, their heads droop, and the beautiful
   eyes that were once filled with life no longer luster.
These, these have been broken.

I will never be broken! My spirit resists against the rhythm
and routine, my body becomes rigid at the sound of the tunes.

Although my colors no longer remain true, and my eyes begin
   to betray me, my spirit lives on.
My soul longs to be free; Set Me Free!

Christina Dayl

Memphis Midnight

In the quiescent for the satin night
an indiscernible breeze passes o'er.
It espouses the soul as the touch of a lover
and arouses life's stolid burden.
The rush of the wind purges the mind
like the rime of the premature dawn.

The innocence of the moon reflects its virginity
and surrounds it like a righteous crown.
Beams of light isolate the blackness
and leave the pathway unbroken.
Stars scintillating thrusts of energy
echo reflections against the shadowy sky.
The calm explores Creation's inner thoughts
and confesses the emotion out loud.
It pierces the heart and compels the moment
to whisper its most secreted trust.

Karen B. Hindman

Why

Kurt Donald Cobain,
Why did you put your life to an end?
That is the question in my head.
Why?
Why did you pull the trigger?
Why?
You left your wife, Courtney,
Your daughter, Frances,
Your band, Dave and Krist,
And your fans.
We will remember you,
by your voice,
by your music.
And we all have the same question in our heads
Why?

Jennie Nowakowski

Peanut Butter

He scurries along the floorboards
On feet as light as air
The little lord of the pantry
Has emerged from out of his lair

He feasts on cereal and crackers
On raisins and dried fruits
For the contents of the pantry
He has claimed as his personal loot

But all that glitters is not gold
The old folks used to mutter
But how many old folks can resist
The taste of peanut butter

The trap is set, the bait is too
His brain is all a clutter
He moves in close, driven to find
The tantalizing peanut butter

He grabs the morsel with his teeth but doesn't hear the click
His spine has been snapped right in two, his death at least was quick

No more scampering little feet amid the pantry clutter,
For death is close for any mouse that dines on peanut butter

Randal King

They Have Feelings Too

Could someone tell me why
some people act the way they do?
Why there is cruelty to animals?
I haven't got a clue.
Some use them and abuse them.
Some hunt then just for fun.
If they just think about what they're doing,
it could help a ton.
Don't they realize
that animals have feelings too?
They can feel the pain,
just like me and you.

Kylie Streck

A Father's Carving (Viking Head)...

What thoughts and far-off reaching speculation
Gave finer definition to each silence-hewn and care-extracted chip
in this creation?
Rebuilding from this little stump of wood
Anew the tree of knowledge, good and evil, now in retrospective
rumination.

To bear in muted lines of this and that expression
Fruits of life's great loves and labors, this and that digression
Sending branches into many winds of this and that direction
And thoughts, he had along the vales of his and their transgression.

What sadness carved the long and furrowed line?
What dashing, leaping thrust of hope in borrowed time
A shorter notch, and deeper, often made?
Just so in life, when on our longer brow, the woes, to wit, recline.

What stillness-breaking laughter rustled in the fallen leaves
As joyous mem'ry conquered one that grieves?
As days, and bits of wood, from life were torn,
And fell, these whited leaves, to leave, the naked tree, a naked head,
a life, in looking back, one sees.

Earl A. Kendall M.D. (aka Erling Koppedal)

"The Rainbow"

OH! How magnificent as it appears
Your eyes will be full of tears
The colors so bright will make your heart delight.
Red, orange, and yellow how sweet and mellow
Green and blue will sing a tune.
Purple and white what a lovely sight!
The name of the tune is in key G,
"God Almighty", whom you can clearly see
Behold the rainbow!
It is a picture of pleasure which reveals beauty
All the colors total seven,
And you will find your soul in heaven
The angels are now singing there shall be eleven.
The song is familiar it was your well being!

Gilbert F. Heiney

The Beauty of Love

There is a beginning in Love,
Casting soft warm glows of precious
sweetness which lighten a woman's world.
If it is truly a soul mate premonition,
You will be touched forever.
Many times it will come from your love to the
love that was meant to be.
It has happened to me and when the sweetness
of my man's touch alights, I feel aligned,
united, whole; never again being bruised by the
devious, rough, calloused grip of false intentions.
Go and be still and grasp your love.
Surround yourself with the beauty that was meant
only for you, forevermore.

Nancy P. Thompson

Lost

A love one lost is not really lost
if you only know where to find them.

For your lost loved one is in your heart
It is from here they will never ever part.

Remember a laugh, remember a smile
Remember for always not only for a while.

Time is something that there's not enough of
But there's always time for a little love.

For each star in the sky is a loved one lost
For everyone you cry is for a loved one lost

For each prayer you pray is for a loved one lost.
For all thoughts you may have of your loved one lost.

So feel the pain, the anger, feel the sorrow even after tomorrow.

Remember your loved one lost is without pain,
Without grief, without worry but never without love.

So keep that lost love one in your heart.
Always and forever, forever and the day
Until you see your loved one lost again someday.

Always remember that you can find your loved one lost in your heart.
It's only here were your healing can start.

Shari Strawbridge

The Beauty Of Pain

There is beauty in pain which cannot be had exultation.
Exultation pampers man but pain instructs, exultation
opens to excesses but cries for reforms.
   Man in times of exultation often forgets that his
sojourn on earth is only temporary, or such he thinks of
nothing but the enjoyment of himself regardless where he
will lead to. Only pain can awaken him from his total indifference.
   Pain is constant reminder to man, whenever he
gives way to his ferocity, pain takes hold of his ears and

pinches them. When he has to gone to far astray, pain
tortures him physically and mentally with his conscience,
if he has any, makes him mend his ways.
   Take pain away and this world would become a
world of wolves and not of men. Pain is shame a
torture a suffering for a mischief, a crime or a sin committed
willfully or unwillfully, consciously or unconsciously.
   It is a silent or nonvocal punishment for disregarding
natures laws or laws made by men.
   Man needs pain whether he likes or not. It is only through
pain that men can feel the reality of life.

Rosalina Espinosa

A Fella

At 10 a fella is a just a little fella.
At 20 a fella thinks he knows more than all the older fellas.
At 30 a fella wishes he knew what the older fellas know and rolls
   his eyes at the 20 year old fella.
At 40 a fella knows what he knows and talks about it.
At 50 a fella says "just live".
At 60 a fella knows what he knows, talks about it, and tells the
   40 year old fella to "shut up and just live."
At 70 a fella won't shut up about how it was.
At 80 a fella remembers half of how it was and fills in the rest with
   how it should have been.
At 90 a fella knows two or three things about when he was 20, and
   won't talk about anything else.
At 100 a fella says "just live".
At 110...if there is a fella, he's the one who knows more than the
   other fellas.

Michael Brainard

Ode To Nature

Rain drops glistening on window pane
bring memories back again
Thoughts of times long since gone
Thoughts so precious to my heart alone.

Winds of march with strength did blow
Bringing rain and sometimes snow
but always bringing hope you know,
that Spring time follows winds that blow.

The days of summer then appear. Causing
each in his heart to yearn for trips to
the mountain and the sea. Life's cares and
worries soon to flee.

Following Summer comes the Fall with
leaves of gold and red and green. The
seasons come and go, each one with Blessings
to bestow. The thought occurs, each one is
best that each season exceeds the rest.

Take the seasons as they appear, enjoy
each one with hearts of cheer, knowing
that as they come and go, God has a new one to bestow.

George W. Shannon

Safe At Home

Rain
I am with my people
Free from all the dangers of the world

In the morning I see the sun shine in my eyes
In the evening I see the moon and the stars
Gleaming and twinkling ever so beautifully

When it is cold I turn pure white
When it is warm I turn back to my original form
Colorless
Shapeless

But I know that I will not be safe
Anymore
Very soon
I will have to leave my people
My home
My heaven
To a world full of dangers
But I know I will find my way home
Once again

Dawne Liu

Put Him First

"Do your best to let everyone see,
Only Jesus in you, constantly —
No matter what people might say,
Trust in The Lord along life's way.

"Glorify His name with ceaseless praise,
In all you do, put Him first, always —
Victory will come, pray and wait,
Even though, the cost may be great.

"Under His wings," there is sweet release —
Place your faith in God, you will have peace.

Vicki Thompson

The Attempt

Words die and blow away
In ashes
In a crumbling tower of display
We all fall down
With our pockets full of posies
Aching for the words to mean something again
Begging for a phrase to be sensible
To be left in a silence
In a silence to be left
We lose the words
And we all fall down
In ashes
To be sensible in a phrase
With our pockets full of silence
We are blown away
Aching to mean something to the words
And we display our posies
In ashes, ashes we all fall down

James Rossillo

March Is A Wench

March is a wench who has kicked off her traces
And flung them high over winter's mill
And stolen bright April's gown and her graces
And gossamer charm that becomes her ill.
For her hair is snarled hemp done in loutish fashion
Her hands are still grimy with barnyard tasks
She walks with a lurch and the uncertain passion
Of one who has swilled and exhausted ale casks.

She flings up her arms to embrace a church steeple
A clatter of bricks pelts her head to her toes
And with nary a care for good church-going people
She flings from her bosom last winter's snows.
Now maudlin, now tearful, no longer so cheerful.
But spent and despairing and full of remorse
Now cowering in panic of consequence fearful
She falls asleep on a clump of gorse.

Betty Krantz

My Girl

She has eyes and hair of brown
She knows how to turn my frown around

She is my confidant and best friend
She doesn't keep up with fashions or trends

She doesn't ask for much, just a lot of love
A walk through the park to see the doves

She lives in a place of comfort and ease
She is one who is very easy to please

She and I are inseparable, you see
We are the best of pals in the highest degree

With a low, sad moan and a gentle nudge
This is her way of saying without a grudge

She is all furry and warm, not thin and lacey
She is my special girl, her name is K.C.

Sharon Campbell

Sounds

As I sit on top of a warm beautiful mountain looking around and
seeing the sand that holds the mountain in from falling over and
making a crashing noise like a bell. I can smell the fresh air
that's blowing against my toes that's covered in sand. I can
taste the sweet peach that I eat.

Amber Coberley

Love Stands With Us

(For Jill)

I see my friend as she struggles to regain her sanity
Trying to untangle the web and break free
Grace has been given to her from on high
For without it her attempts would be in vain

Like a warrior she unravels her pain
Bringing hope and encouragement with each victory
She rests awhile to regain her strength
Then moves out timidly to fight again

Hers is a spirit of passion
Deep sorrow has fought its fight
Now rising up from its pit
She reaches out for help

For someone to guide her to still waters
To help her lay in green meadows
I hear her call and stand at her side
But we are not alone...love stands with us

Janet Nicholson Swann

My Mother

My Mother for whom I care,
Has no memory, has no fear.
She taught me how to live each day;
Wearing a smile each step of the way.
This is indeed her final legacy to me.

Manners, she said, through the world will take you.
Speak gentle, it will turn away wrath.
Be honest, it's the best policy you'll learn.
Be thorough in your dealings, it's the best card.
Be truthful, you'll never be embarrassed.

Take time out, she said, for family fun;
You'll have lots of time for things to come.
Remember to pray whenever you feel
An important task lies ahead.
God, she says, will make a way.

Take on the world, there is a place for you.
Be alert, you shall not miss anything.
To me, this was her legacy to inherit.
She was absolutely right.
For with her legacy I've found that place today.

Harry Morrison

Grief

Gray skies are leaden as is my heart.
The chill pierces the soul.
   Loneliness is an aching void,
   And a sigh escapes pinched lips.

Flowers bloom but I don't see them.
Birds sing, but I cannot hear.
   Only sights and sounds that accompany sorrow
   Are bidden to come near.

You have gone from my life,
And I recoil from feeling.
   But pain is a garment
   I unwittingly wrap around me.

Then dormant hope begins to stir
And faith strains to rise.
   As a tiny plant struggling toward the sun,
   A promise of new life is born.

Lois J. Woodruff

Housework

I never did like housework, am I the only one?
Who doesn't like to clean and dust, it seems it's never done.
I'd rather paint a picture or else be out of doors
taking care of flowers instead of washing floors
'cause outside troubles vanish, bills to pay and such
And my pretty flowers I love oh so much
But I must face the facts no one else will do it
So I'd better stay inside, I may as well get to it.

Christina Cook

The Garden

We meet every day in the small room with a black piano.
This has become our own special place.
We share ourselves together,
Her heart flowing through her fingers onto the piano
And my own soul poured out in ink upon paper.

There, in that room we are most deeply ourselves
And that together.
We love, we hate, we laugh, we mourn, we dance, and we dirge,
We make love and we seek vengeance, feel compassion and sigh with true justice.

Together we feel these things,
Her on white magic keys and I, on paper.

Here we are like this
As we are with no one else.
Here, our spirits roam free
And we meet by the stream side among the lilies to
Share intimate moments.
Words exchanged only by a glance
And feelings shared only by a caress.

This moment is a hidden garden of love to us
But I know there will never be us again as we are right now.

Chad D. Wayne

Use It Or Lose It

Just because some people try to tell me what to do
it doesn't mean I'll always do the things they want me to.

No one can ever own my soul, or be my boss you see,
'cause I was born to live my life and do what pleases me.

I have a mind that is my own, and I intend to use it;
'cause if I don't, as the saying goes, I'm surely bound
to lose it.

Linda Mascetta

Posthumous

i am dead.
i died when the wind and sky
sang to the autumn moon on such a perfect day.

i died on the train to freedom
as if my soul could find a way to pay the fare.

i died, when the world looked at me with magical curiosity
a lost lover on the road to nowhere from whence i came.

The churning sea i am, causing the white foam to rise
and greet the new day, a power so great
as to be only seen in its entirety by God.
It is me reaching for the blue that has no memory
to envelop and protect what sense of sense i possessed
and now i lay in my coffin of blue
trying to remember how it was that i became so
and to be released.

But i am dead and there is no more.

Brian Cramer

The Whippoorwill

The whippoorwill came home today,
to his oak behind the shed.
He came to fill the nights with song,
till the eastern sky turns red.
He'll be there till the trees turn gold,
and the grain is in the bin.
Then one night he'll just be gone,
Back to the south again.
I know that he came home today,
although I did not hear.
Because it is the 12th of May
he comes this day each year.
And even though I'm far away,
with different woods to roam.
It makes me very glad to know,
The whippoorwill is home

Carrie E. Rogers

Gone?

Gone? Never, my love.
  I am with you every minute. I live with your spirit,
    your laughter your love for me.

Gone? Never, my love.

  I see you in the faces and actions of our children,
    our greatest blessing, our greatest accomplishment.

Gone? Never, my love.

  There were glad days and sad days but all good days
    because we were together.

Gone? Never, never, my love.
  It cannot be. You are a part of me.

Ida Mae Marx

Untitled

  I sit alone... for I am a great deal
different from those who sit across the room.
Why is it like this? Weird though, they say they
are my friends. They laugh and I get hurt,
my brain scrambles, and I strive to be strong,
to have a voice and to stand and fight
back — just like daddy taught me; I need
to make him proud. Disruption in my
mind, hatred in my heart, but there is
love in my face. Why can't I have
peace in this world...

Lauren Doffont

Love To My Sister

When mom passed away three years ago,
we all look it differently as you know.
The years have been long, and I know you cared.
How many countless tear's
have you and I shared?
The pain was too much for our family to bear
but you got the job done you were always there.
You've been there through times both good and bad.
I'll always be thankful for what you and I have.
The whole family has gone through a lot of turmoil
But maybe in time we can all turn back the soil.
Rose, now your job is finally all done.
And we all know, why you were the chosen one.
You've carried mom's wishes out indeed.
Because of you, I've learned to set her free.
Now, mom can finally rest in peace, it's true.
I'm proud to say were sisters and I love you!!!!!

Mary Perez

Man Enough To Cry

A man standing alone and proud.
An invisible armor, surrounding him.
A man sadly alone, even in a crowd.
Peering into a future that is dim.

His honesty is for all, except himself.
Life has been all but kind.
His heart? He keeps it on a shelf.
To his emotions he is blind.

He has all too few friends.
Love? It has always been cold and dry.
His pride never waivers or bends.
Tears? You never see one in his eye.

Too many seasons have come and gone.
He feels himself growing old.
His pride? It yet lingers on.
His heart remains lonely, covered with mold.

Still he sees himself as a man so proud.
He stands tall and unafraid to die.
Quietly his heart whispers aloud.
"How sad, you were never man enough to cry!"

Gary H. Long

Untitled

The Silver Man upon my breast
speaks to me in tongues

There's a violent cough inside my chest
a wheezing in my lungs

Everything is darker now
my vision's closing in

There's no reason to ask how
the hand of death is going to
win....

Danielle Vilella

I Just Can't Love You

It's hard for me to love you,
After you've beaten my body and soul
With your angry fists of rage
Since a time I was at such a young age,
I just can't love you.

It's hard for me to love you,
Because of the words you shouted
That were so cruel and unkind
And because they still echo inside my mind,
I just can't love you.

It's hard for me to love you,
And it's hard for me to see
A child with a loving dad
For it makes me think of what I never had,
I just can't love you.

It's hard for me to love you,
Because for all the important things in my life
You just didn't give a damn,
Now that those things are part of who I am,
I just can't love you.

Cassie Frank

The Dance

The tall, superior, dark brown rough master
keeps the irregular shaped colorful forms
from drifting free.

Their friend, the wind, tries to make the
multi-armed master let go, so the
colorful production will begin.

At the closing of fall,
he is old and quite weak.

When he is aged,
The wind can loosen his grasp and the
dance of ruby, gold, scarlet, copper and rust
may begin.

After the finale, the ground is covered with
dying dancers of the wind.

Mary Sue Bergin

God Only Knows

Only God Knows
Do you know? Or does it appear that I
know? When I really don't.
Only God Knows
Why birth was granted for me as well
as you, he never said it was gonna be
easy, please be patient with me, and
the pleasure you enjoy in each birthday
will grow. If that's to difficult to
handle and I don't have your guidance
it'll be my ashes you'll blow. But remember!
Only God Knows

If ever I feel he's not present in my
life when times get hard and I don't
get fed, I'll tell him mama said "You'll
always know just what to do," and that
I should put my trust in you." And then
mama said "When she's out of answers
she talks to you," so that's what I'm gonna do.
Happy Birthday Mama

Shevon R. Lopez

The Eyes Of The Wolf

Gaze into the spellbinding eyes of the wolf,
And he will meet your gaze.
Look into his glowing eyes,
And he will tell you his story.
From him you can keep no lies.
He will search deep in you
Looking for strengths and weaknesses,
For fear or courage,
For aggression or passiveness,
But above all for truthfulness.

Return his gaze and you will see
He is ready to befriend,
But prepared to defend.
He is the leader of the pack,
The wise ruler of wolves.
The majestic king of the Yukon,
His territory goes on and on.
The brave captain against aggressors,
Like a knight in battle.
He is the strongest and most skillful of them all.

Heather Danda

Positive Thoughts On Aging

Aging comes to the fortunate;
those who are blessed with time.....
Time to pursue those pleasures
that bring joy and happiness.
Time to spend with friends and loved ones
and not have to notice the clock.
Time to enhance ones knowledge or
polish existing skills.
Time to meditate or think or pray
for others as well as ourselves.
Time to focus on personal goals
and celebrate the fruits of our labor.
Aging is a rite of passage.....
and the journey is truly a gift.

Brenda S. Davidson

This World We Are Living In

This world we are living in
Is a world of fears
Is a world of tears
It is something that worries me
If you feel like I feel
If you see what I see
You would know all I mean
This world we are living in
Is a world without love and peace
Walking out on every streets
Looking on every faces I see
In the eyes of all the people that pass me by
I can see the reflection of pain and sorrow
Has taken the place of smile and joy
Hopelessly we are waiting what tomorrow might bring
We are victims of our own guilt
It is all because our viciousness cruelty and selfishness
Every night before I can close my eyes I think about
This world we are living in.

Claude L. Barbe

Circles And Spirals

If there is a reason for this indiscretion
Tell it to me slow so I can understand it
You know the answer?
Break it down for children's ears

Push them in a hole so we can pull them out, now
Tell ourselves we're loyal to a higher cause, how?
Throw out the paper
Break it down to flesh and blood

Make your introductions while your hand is in my pocket
Squeeze from your slush fund the dollars to back your mouth
All the while children are learning to beg

Can we show them that there is a place
For their young hearts to grow here
I fear we are losing a child a day
Throw away your arguments
Get your new boots wet

We can talk and talk and talk and talk in circles
Only those who walk the walk can understand this
Open the flood gates
Wash away our children's fears

Donna L. Gober

My Day Begins

As the float plane takes off, every morning at eight
It's my time to rise or I know I'll be late
It makes such a noise, it could wake the dead.
I slowly roll over and crawl out of bed.

My day begins bright and early
If I'm a minute late the customers go squirrely

It's not an interesting job, mostly just talk
Most of the day, I watch the clock.

I work at a meat store, what more can I tell you.
But I'm sure to bet, I've got something to sell you.

Beef, chicken, lamb or pork
I've got everything here to put on your fork.

My day ends at six, by that time I'm beat
The last thing I want to do, is look at meat

When dinner is finished and the kitchen is tidy
I retire upstairs and get into my nighty.

The moon is our only light here at night
The ferry blows its horn for boats not in sight.

Well it's almost that time, time for bed
That place I rest my body and rest my tired head.

Brenda Koroscil

No One I Know

I wonder what you're thinking. I wonder where you have been as you
kiss me goodnight, and try to tuck me in. I am not anyone you love
I'm not who you need. Just another hungry mouth in all of this
house of lies and deceit. I do not ask for anything you supply
what I need. A good place to rest. A conversation that bleeds.
A wish for the weary, a trap for the soul. My journey ahead will
bring a great toll. I watch as I dream all the things that could happen to
me. I don't write it down for these things are precious to me.
You ask a lot of questions in search of the true me. I reply with
honest answers, but you cannot see. The questions will
cease. Because you will forget this dream. You will want to
change it and that's fine with me. Because, I'm like no one you
know or will ever again meet. Just be glad we have met. I will
think of it as a treat. Don't ask where I will go or who I will
see. We had our time together if only in a dream.

Rachael Collins

Summer Vacation Memories

First there was lightning and then came rain
the glory of it all I cannot explain.
The crash of thunder and the falling limb
And then there was silence, dark and dim.

It brought back memories, of the cottage on Michigan shores
Where I spent my youth in summer lake chores.
The old pump-organ which accompanied our singing
filled the night with vibrate ringing.

The fun-filled days, sailing and kayaking
Shopping at Johnson's, frolicking and yakking.
Then came July 4th, with rockets soaring
And e pluribus dingbat, interrupting his snoring.

Searching the dunes for ripe blueberries
And eating with relish Jinny's hot gerries.
The sand scorched our feet, as we ran down the hill
But the water was quick to bring on a chill.

Hot dogs and marshmallows toasted over a fire,
Tickled the palate and satisfied desire.
This may not seem like much of a theme,
I guess you had to be there, to appreciate the dream.

Herbert A. Hudson

"Plush Raccoons"

You were there for me when I failed an important test.
You were there for me when I ripped my sister's new gown.
You were there for me when I didn't get whatever I wanted.
You were there for me when I was beaten up and pushed down.
You were there for me when I was made fun of.
You were there for me when I didn't make the team.
You were there for me when I was greatly misunderstood.
You were there for me when I wanted to kick and scream.
You were there for me when I felt alone and misguided.
You were there for me when I needed a good friend
You were there for me when I ran away — and then ran back.
You were there for me when I needed you,
    and you will be there until the end.
I love you, my plush raccoons.

David Autin

Untitled

Our worlds crossed each other by chance.
Time, that ever-winged creature, unleashed a
hurricane of emotions, unearthing all in its path.

Bound by a force greater than ourselves,
Escape is but a dream.
For this force is the fountainhead
of all that is primal, all that is untamed, all that is dark,
and all that is sensual in us.

We are caught in this whirlwind of passion
like two falcons caught in a net,
whose struggles for freedom ensnare them tighter.

Let us ride this whirlwind 'til it blows itself into a calm,
and we plummet to Earth fragmented.
Or let us clasp one another tighter
and be thrown into the net of madness...

To wish our worlds never collided with such force.
To fly away free as from an awakening nightmare.
It would be simpler to tear ourselves free
from a shroud of thorns.

Let our cupid, chance tear us apart.

Palmina D'Alelio

Unconditional Love

As we go through life today,
It's hard to know just what to say.

To those we meet in daily life,
Who may be feeling hate or strife.

It's with these many thoughts in mind,
That we should greet them and be kind.

For they may be in need of love,
Not just from us, but up above.

If they ignore or pass you by,
They may be down, forlorn, or sky.

So go just one more extra mile,
And pass on to them your friendly smile.

A small gesture it might be,
But remember this, a smile is free.

Love one another, God's great command,
It still can work across this land.

It doesn't take great things to do,
Just a simple I love you.

In this poem I've one thing to say,
Love's a meaningless word, until given away.

Josh Robinson

While

While I'm sitting here, safely, in my room,
Oklahoma is shaking,
While I'm sitting here, safely, in my room,
the federal building is falling
While I'm sitting here, safely, in my room,
many people are crying,
While I'm sitting here, safely, in my room,
innocent people are dying,
While I'm sitting here, safely, in my room,
people are becoming heroes,
While I'm sitting here, safely, in my room,
the sirens are flying,
While I'm sitting here, safely, in my room,
the doctors are trying,
While I'm sitting here, safely, in my room,
Oklahoma is growing dark.
While I'm sitting here, safely, in my room,
man is, once again, getting away with murder.

Kelly K. Howard

The Distance

It had to be something,
To keep me away from you
Now, wanting to be with you
Is more than a desire
It has become a need
I would climb mountains
Just to be with you
Is that what you really want?
I could live my life without you
....But only with regrets
I cherish the opportunity to love again,
That you have sublet
I could be the one to fill the void
The distance is making me want
To be closer to you
If you can only see the joy
It might bring
....We would share the best
Of everything

Lance M. Daniels

Walk Of The Priestess

The jungle sleeps as I walk
An ambage keeping my feet in line
Stepping slowly, silent
Deliberate, I take my time.

Pale shimmering stars fade toward day
Destiny calls as black becomes gray.

The jungle is waking my eyes can now see
The steps of the pyramid waiting for me

I begin to climb
Step
    by
        step
My heart beats faster,
Shadows lengthen behind

I quicken my pace I dare not be late
Up,
    Upward climbing toward fate

Until I can climb no higher, I have come
To face the fire
    Of the morning sun.

Verna Warren Starr

"My Friend"

My friend, I guess I can call you
a friend we have been together
through all kinds of weather.

My friend, I guess I can call you a
friend, you have been there in the
bad times but don't forget the good times.

My friend, I guess I can call you
a friend, cause when I called you
came, when I knocked you let me in.

My friend, I guess, I can call
you a friend, you've never let
me down and when I need you
you're always around.

My friend I guess I can call you
a friend because that's what you
have been "my friend."

Essie M. Kinsey

Peace!

A world shared with happiness and love
A dream sent from Heaven above
Is shattered when we awake
And feel the earth tremor and shake!

The sound of tears, grief and pain
Only add, to a world gone insane.
The agony of those we love and lose
There has to be a better way to choose!

All people, great and small
Ban together and work to stand tall
Join hands across the seas and fight
For what we know is right!

Work for peace-for our country, our land
Walk together hand-in-hand
And the joy we share from peace
As wars and turmoils finally cease!

Linda C. Knight

Found Near The Summit Of Mount Columbia

At last the height is reached!!
And here I am! Like a fool.

The wind wrenches my jacket
And with a whine howls steeply down.
Twisting demons within the arabesques of snow,
They plunge toward the valley.
Shining in the summit sun, how do they mock the darkness?

Resisting the rush, I lean into the squeaky summit
And watch the vanguard of the scorned storm
Boil over base camp...far below, and tower into the west.

Fear finally in my belly, I turn like a spinnaker in the wind
And stare into the storm of mountains, a set piece almost,
Against an impossible blue sky carved raggedly 'round me.

Islands of light; the peaks dazzle above the roiling ocean,
Breaking with bow waves through the atmosphere
They await that must inevitably come.

In this rarefied position I wait...idly wondering
What other granite souls stand lost above these islands.

Friends and lovers; we hail one other across the doomed air,
And contemplate our similar, separate and foolish fates.

Trevor J. Williams

My Friend Cora

She'd come every night dressed in white,
Up and down the halls she'd go.
Her friendly smile, her gentle touch,
All the residents know she loved them so much.

If there was a problem, if someone needed a care,
Cora always would be there.
She made our job so easy, because we always knew,
The nights that she worked, everything was done —
Even an extra job or two.

We miss her more than words can tell,
That wonderful lady we knew so well.
And now She's at rest in Heaven above.
God's giving her the love and care she's so deserving of.

I'm so proud to have known such a wonderful friend,
Who was there for so many to the very end.
As I walk through the halls during the night,
I can picture her pretty smile shining bright.

I know that She will always be,
Silently going down the hall with me.

A Co-worker and Friend
Sharon M. Parcel

The Sparkle In Her Eyes

For Anna Larsson

How can one so low as I know her who is so high
the sparkle in her eyes

A sight of her so high my spirit flies
for only her I would willingly die
the sparkle in her eyes

Like an angel her voice sings
what heavenly joy she brings
the sparkle in her eyes

Eyes a perfect blue hair a flow of gold
in her presence all is new
away from her all grows cold
the sparkle in her eyes

A goddess clothed in splendid light
oh, how she makes a gray day bright
the sparkle in her eyes

Her gait so full of elegance and grace
worthy of her, there is no such place
the sparkle in her eyes

How can one so low as I know her who is so high
captivated by her eyes

John T. Cunningham

The Dandelion Dancer

I am not a fish
And I am not a bird
I left my wish with the stars
But like light, it takes longer for words
Incognito and invisible
Like the wind I go
It's all reasonable you know
I touch everyone like the wind
I can be anyone
Lend me the answer
I'll provide the question
Who was the dandelion dancer?
It must have been someone
Someone with the answer

Richard A. York

"In The Park"

I met an old man and he asked me my name
I sat on the park bench and asked him the same
He told me some stories of life in his day
The old man was dreaming, he gave it away

Do you remember the warm summer haze
Do you remember snow on every Christmas day...in the park

He spoke of religion, his family and life
And how a car crash had taken his wife
His words were not bitter, his tears did refrain
His weary old eyes told the story again

Do you remember the warm summer haze
Do you remember snow on every Christmas day...in the park

A young man's an island with fears to disguise
But old men stop running when they realize
That the wisdom and virtues in life never last
The old man had told me his life passed too fast

Do you remember the warm summer haze
Do you remember snow on every Christmas day
And do you remember that old men fade away...in the park

Joel Gaudet

She Crouched...

She crouched
under her tree
    her favorite tree
    her sanctuary
    her second mother.

The tender
    loving
      dagger tree.

Its billion arms
    hiding her
protecting her from the world.

No one saw her
    could see her
shoving fistfuls of grass
fistfuls twice as large as her mouth — down her throat

No one saw her
    could see her madly
shoveling grass.
groundmouthgroundmouthgroundmouth.

How do you deal with your horrible days?

Carolyn Pellecchia

"Waiting"

I await with curiosity
I'm curious about what he'll be like,
I'm curious about what he'll look like,
I'm as curious as he'll probably be when he is two.

I await with excitement
The excitement of him being here,
The excitement of helping him progress,
The excitement of watching him blossom like a flower.

I await with patient hope
With the hope of being a good mommy
With the hope of doing all the right things,
Hoping he'll love me as much as I already love him.

I await frightened
Frightened of being so young,
Frightened of not knowing what to do,
Frightened, like a child, myself, who is lost in the dark.

Nakea Koontz

My Grandfather

My grandfather used to dive into the dictionary
and swim amongst the words,
and, then...

   Emerge,

Phrases dripping from his mouth,
to strut across the hot Caribbean sands.
The beaming sun reflecting on his proud, glistening back,
he'd waltz to the speech competition
and shower his witty words on the parched ears of the thirsty crowd.
"You blubbering, blustering balooga", he'd say..

And those avaricious ears with their unquenchable thirsts would cry,
"More! More!"
As his ever flowing fountain of phrases continuously drenched
their gluttonous minds.
And when those fattened brains plopped down on the sand,
drowsily basking in the rays of sunlight that reflected off his
onyx skin, a slow smile would slide across his moist, gleaming face.
My grandfather's face.
My grandfather!
Timotheus Mathias Nero.

Jenelle Nero

"The Song"

Deep within my heart and into the depths of my soul
A beautiful melody can be felt and heard.

The lyrics and its sweet sound I do not recognize.
Yet, often I feel the song and I know it is for me.

The timbre has been given by my soul for my heart to sing.
It is a joyous and thankful song known only to my spirit.

I am so happy and blessed for the occasion was given to me
That allowed the wonder of this mortal life to continue.

I am grateful, humbled and amazed for I received a second
   chance at life.
I have no special traits or talents that entitled me to this event.

But, one night many years ago I became a member of a Royal Family.
Belonging to this family carries certain rights and privileges.

The joy of life that I feel in my heart and in my soul
Helps lessen and ease any physical discomfort I may have.

To be able to feel and sense emotions can only mean one thing —
I am alive! For this song I am eternally thankful.

Linda D. Hensley

"My Dark Haired Beauty"

With lights so dim and hopes set high,
My dark haired beauty brings a sigh.

Her brown eyes set my soul on free.
They burn through me like a funeral pyre.

While in the mirror I watch her primp,
She touches me my limbs go limp.

My fantasy though it my seem,
Is she for real or just a dream.

I hold her body close to mine,
I caress her hair so soft, so fine.

Her heart beats fast as she draws near,
Her nightgown glistens so silky sheer.

Her sense of humor conquers me,
My heart keeps beating endlessly.

People tell me you're never moody.
I turn and say, "My darkhaired beauty."

Alan J. Miccio

From The Hostel

These folk who once were you and I
Now shuffle past with a sorrowful eye
Searching and seeking for something past
While moving along with their eyes downcast

With unkempt hair and floppy shoes
And going nowhere that they care to choose
Each with a story from other years
Of good times, bad times, happiness, tears

Into the maw of the uncaring beast
Shuffle these souls of the street
Coming from nowhere and going nowhere
These folk we decline to greet

Down the road, when it's time to go
When the master will pick and choose
Won't it be strange, on that heavenly range
If God wears floppy shoes

Don Pierson

Untitled

Embrace life
before it leaves you for good
for worse
come with me
embrace me
join your cold hands in mine
and I'll never let go
I won't lose you in this night
I can see in this dark
with senses different than that I was born with
close your eyes
you too can see
free fall through this time on earth with me
let go
spiral wildly
laugh
smile
life is what you make it
follow your heart to a different dream

Sherry-Lynn Hill

Child Of War

  So innocent and young are you, like a delicate flower in the
field of life. Yet why do you suffer the heartache from man's
cruel greed? Why must hunger touch your soul filling you with
uncertainty and fear, as you quench your thirst with the tears
of your sadness? "How does your innocent eyes see the world
your nurtured home?" Where do you gain the strength to carry
on, when your life seems so meaningless?

  Yet no matter your sadness and pain there always seems to be a
vision of hope in your eyes, as if somehow you see hidden beauty
in the hearts of those who should help, not destroy you with fear.

  Child of war is it that deep within you know you are free? Not
from pain and sadness, which war and man's selfish hands have
burdened your tender heart. As from your eyes of love you see
your home and family destroyed by the most dangerous weapons
that sound the music of hate that captures the innocence of your life.

  Innocent one are you free to dream, to touch the beauty of
your reality. To have faith and strength as you cover yourself
with your veil of peace, in hope that one day your veil can
somehow cover the world...

Carol Bernadette Joseph

Fairies

Fairies, nymphs, water sprites and petites,
so dainty and small,
quiet and sweet, they don't let us see them,
they are afraid.

Maybe they have colonies in our lawns,
near our streams, they live so peacefully.
They make their clothes of leaves and flowers
play all day and frolic in the grass, so green.

Dainty features, tiny noses, glittery eyes
porcelain-doll hands, wire-thin bodies
braided hair, so dark and curly
swinging in the branches, they play.

We think that we hear the frogs,
peeping loudly at night,
but what we really hear is the fairies,
singing their tribute to the moon.

Sharon Ostfeld-Johns

Killing Her Softly

Pain consumes the little girl,
Who is trying to make them understand,
That the vacant look in her eyes,
Is created by a dishonest man.

She sits in a dark corner,
Trying to hide from her shame,
He inflicted it by his touches,
By playing "his" little games.

He grasps hold of her trust,
Throwing it all away, he fills her head with thoughts,
Of the betrayals of yesterday.

The confidence she has in herself,
Flickers and slowly dies, a three-year-old girl,
Is left with a life built on lies.

She smiles on the outside,
While she cries within, for she has nothing left to give,
But a confession of his sins.

The little girl lies quietly in the dark,
Trembling with sudden fright.
For he has decided once again, to molest her in the night.

Renee Miller

Sonnet

Praxiteles, the sculptor, sought in stone
To recreate for all the flush of youth:
A statue shining bright with livid truth
For all the world to see, not he alone.
Petrarch, the crafted spinner of the sonnet,
Endeavored to shout out his love for Laura:
In burning words acclaim his passion for her
To all the listening world and creatures on it.

— I, too, search out a sounding-board to voice
A somewhat alternative ego choice:
A passive object for my gripes and groans,
Recipient most patient of my moans.
She'll diligently scrutinize this verse
And probably concede it could be worse!

Dana Dumas

Mothers Are Funny That Way

Mothers say they love you,
But when you rebel and want to go your way
They throw a fit, they yell and they fuss
And know just what to say
Mothers are funny that way.

They want you home, and they want you gone,
But when the time comes
They cry a lot and think of things to fear,
"But what if this or that," you hear this everyday.
Yes Mothers are funny that way.

"I know how you are," she'll say
"You live in a dream world, what do you care,
You'll never make it out there."
Yes Mothers are funny that way.

So she'll smile and she'll cry, she won't say goodbye.
"You'll be back" she still says.
But in her heart is a prayer,
"There she goes Lord, You take care"
Yes Mothers are funny that way.

Sadie Marjerison

Gold Or Soul

Some would prefer silver and gold
For they idolize things they can hold.

God said you'd be saved only by his word.
His word, some have never heard.

"I am the way, truth, and the light,"
to the world he must persuade.
To us, his only son he gave.

God loves the world,
Every man, woman, boy, and girl.

Still some prefer silver and gold,
But I prefer the One that can save
   my Soul.

Eboni Williams

Winter Wind

The rain pours down and winter blows in
A dream foretold for where to begin

It seems like loneliness never ends
I wish I knew what became of my friends

I set here alone and ponder a thought
I paid the price but what have I bought

There's nothing left of my worldly domain
I look to the future and have nothing to gain

My mind takes me to a place far away
With flowing streams and tall grass where I lay

The sunlight trickles through the leaves in the trees
I hear the birds sing a sweet tune on the breeze

Spring is gone and summer slowly turns to fall
I listen to the wind and I hear a voice call

The skies darken and clouds form overhead
Nothing last forever soon all will be dead

Peace and contentment and happiness abound
But the world rushes in and destroys all that I found

I scream as I feel my soul crushed under it all
With the weight of the world my kingdom will fall

Greg Matthews

What Am I Feeling?

If only I could describe what I am feeling,
It makes me happy,
And fills my heart with joy.
Many call this love,
But how will I know?
I sit and I wonder;
Can it be?
How could I deserve one such as you?
You are kind and gentle, sweet and tender,
And so very much more.
How do I make you mine?
It scares me to think of life
Without you.
If only we were together.
If only I could hold you close,
And never let you go.
For you have captured my heart,
And it is you, I will always treasure.

Katie Corradino

Pure White Flakes

So still the night all softly quiet and sleepy.
The pure white flakes begin to fall.
Slowly at a snail's pace not hurrying to my call
all pure and untouched.

Till the ground below breaks their silence
onto the hard earth so cold below.
Their glory not to last only is theirs for a short time
then to transform into drops like pearls upon mother earth.

The pure white flakes are now many
hundreds and thousands who knows
These precious flakes of untouched snow.
With their arms outstretched
begging to the cold wind to let them go.
These pure white flakes not touched by any mortal thing.

It's a knowing life is near an end as not for them eternal.
With their purity turning them into glimmering streams
and rivers that flow on for ever.

Those pure white soft and oh so quite untouched flakes
that came from Heaven today
to fall upon the cold earth below was theirs for a short time.

S. E. Bessant

Why Are We Traveling

I'm so proud of you
That my heart always cherishes a hope,
The hope we'll keep sharing together.
While the stars, they're shooting through
In the space light years away out of scope,
The scope of eternity: They gather.

Why are we traveling through the time
Is it for living?
Wish you'd never go away
With a sword that's about to be drawn now...

Whose eyes so tenderly
Watching over me from somewhere high?
No dream will soothe my pain.
Whose arms now cover me
From the wind that's coldly sly?
Hold me tight, so I'll live again.

Why are we sometimes blind to see
What we believe in?
The words you would say
I'm hearing deep inside of me now, love...

David S. Himeno

Mist On The Mirror

The faded misty image-
in the steamed up bath room mirror
does the image look like a dreamer who
never took a chance,
who never stuck his neck out for an
honorable advance -
He looks but doesn't do, he hides behind
that misty hue, the steamed up
bath room mirror.
Is a man, truly a man, when he tries to change
something wrong to something right?
Is a man truly a man when he tries to change
something bad to something good?
The faded misty image on the steamed up bathroom mirror.
Now quickly rub off the steam, smile and say to
the new image -
thanks, you're a good teacher, the faded misty
image, in the steamed up bathroom mirror.

William Smooty

Sleep

Sleep such sweet prosperity
The enchantment of night
A lifetime of dreams
Satisfaction to most and torment to others
The tradition of generations from past to future
A gift yet a curse
Only a peaceful moment in life
A time to forget and a time to remember
One of life's mysteries and wonders
Where the mind is free and the body is at rest
A world unknown yet explored by the mind
In a child a kingdom of fantasy untouched by reality
The conqueror of man and life
A journey where time is of no concern
Where boundaries are merely brushed away
The place created by each living thing
A place where the soul can be free and enlightened
Tis a necessity of life and a product of the mind
Experience of other places and times
The serenity of sleep

Amy Compton

The Crail

The Crail is a creature who tends to be lazy,
It lays in the meadow—its thoughts are so hazy.
Idling in the meadow every day and every night
It never gets up at the first ray of light.

Each has a servant—a nightingale
To clean its home and fetch its mail.
The nightingale becomes a subservient bird,
It must obey the Crail's every word.
And if it doesn't, a feather will be taken,
Its feet will be tied and its head will be shaken.

The Crail won't volunteer to help a good cause
No matter how grave, it always withdraws.
It refuses to act when someone's in danger
Whether it's family or just a stranger.
The Crail never lends a helping hand
It would rather stick its head in the sand.

The selfish Crail will do no one a favor
If one were to ask, the Crail would quaver.
Not many care about the death of the Crails
But a celebration would be held by the nightingales.

Jeremy Kinnard

The Atonement

Christ suffered and died to redeem mankind,
to restore man's spirit, heart, soul, and mind.
The power of the Holy Spirit imparts God's will,
and teaches us to listen and be still.

His death enabled us to be reconciled,
to be one with Him, as a little child.
The presence of the Holy Spirit makes us aware,
that Jesus Christ is truly there.

Comprehension of the Atonement comes from above,
when we abandon self, and receive His love.
It's then that we begin to spiritually mature,
to grow in grace, and to be sure.

While we were yet sinners, Christ died for us.
We must now renew our trust.
We thank Him for His redeeming love,
and for Jesus, who was sent from above.

Joseph B. Tribble

Skipping Stones

Two boys stand by the edge of a pond
Skipping stones, making ripples in the undisturbed surface
Hundreds of circles, patterns of waves
Touching, changing, interacting

Two boys laughing, unsuspecting
Go and leave the ripples fading
Circles flowing slowly outward
'Till the last one disappears
From the surface of the peaceful pond

Pond — still and undisturbed
No sign of who has come and gone
And all the smooth round skipping stones
Lie unnoticed at the bottom of the pond

Naomi A. Solomon

The Blood Collection

"Signatures"
When I'm pricked
my blood gushes against
my innermost skin,
anticipating that keen tickle of freedom.

      It wants no part of me.

In escape formation
it becomes a liquid herd of stampeding bloodlets.

Each one speeding DNA seeds
thru the cracks of deep, scarlet scabs.

Each one swelling, bottom-heavy like breasts,
until it snaps.

Each one   escaping me.
Until exhaustion owns the herd.

    And I'm left with permanent signatures
    in my aborted white flesh.

Mark D. Hennigar

Knowing

A beautiful swan, falls from the sky,
  Its broken wings spread, trying to fly.
Down it falls, into the lake,
  Its slender neck, the impact does break.
Down, down into the lake it sinks,
  It fears, it know, it feels, it thinks.
Silent tears the swan does cry,
  For now it knows, it's time to die.

Tasha Greiner

Little Things

When one is sad and sick at heart
One has many blue and bitter thoughts
Things well up out of the forgotten past
Things add up to break your heart.

One tries so hard to hide the hurts
Laughing a lot so no one knows
And yet within the heart still beats
Amazing thing - as we wither inside.

Somehow we know that this is life
And endless joy is a lie
Somehow we know that this will end
And joy will return again!

And remember well that God ordains
That life on earth is both joy and pain!

Mario Rangel-Bron

THINK ABOUT IT

I cannot stop the raging sea from waving,
But I could wave back to the sea.
I cannot halt gale-force winds from blowing,
But I can prevent the wind from blowing my hair.
I cannot erase dark clouds from hovering overhead,
But I can look at dark clouds and smile,
And wait for the sun to shine through.
It makes no sense to dwell on things
I cannot change from the past,
But I can enjoy the present,
Look to the future,
Correct some of my past,
To improve some of my tomorrows.
I can't stop from growing older,
But I can change from feeling old.
Lo and behold as we dwell on time;
We can't slow down the essence of time,
But we can slow down from rushing around,
And stop the time of any wasteful living.

Eddie Timak

Moments

I deposited my melancholy
in a secret place of my heart...
I brought to the surface a merry mood,
and out I stepped (with this far armour)
to acquire what spring would offer me.
I tasted its cheer for a few moments.
By its violence I was carried away
to unlikely sunny days
-for several moments,
I still had the merry mood-
but I was not misled into dreams
by its violence and joy.
Even before I could return
I had lost the false armour
and was thinking of the wilderness of men.

Jason Velisaratos

To My Father On His 92nd Birthday

You're here, you're gone, you're back again.
These are my memories of you as you have entered my life,
    then left me for a while, only to return.
Much as a spirit shadow falls upon the snow.

There is much you have missed of me and, I of you.
Sadly, time is growing too short to fill the void.
So, as we two continue our march to the inevitable,
Let us enjoy the music that each of us is playing
And listen intently to the tune.

Elinor Horton

Someone Loves You

Whenever clouds are gathering
and the skies are full of rain,
always remember that, somewhere,
the sun is shining
and someone is playing a love song.

Whenever you awaken to the dark of night,
without a ray of sunshine in your room,
always remember that, somewhere,
it is morning
and chroruses of birds are singing.

Whenever you are crying tears
and your heart is drowned in sadness,
always remember that, somewhere,
someone loves you...
and, that someone, is me.

Valerie A. Hardy

The Tyranny Of My Soul

Oh! To be misunderstood is an everlasting sad affair;
My poor heart is bombarded with a tyranny unfair.
Deep in the veins of the fibers of my soul
Buried are the secrets forlorn and untold.

To speak my mind, oft' jeered and mocked;
So afraid to unwind, to another is locked.
Fear of someone out there knows your gait,
Sometimes it may hurt you - or just wait.

What does one do with a dilemma so gaunt?
Trying to free the shackles haunt,
When the heart too has its roll call to attend,
And you feel you're just - maybe on the mend.

But you feel tormented and frail,
Like you were kneeling in front of a grail.
So wrapped up in your tears of fright,
But you must stand upright - for your right.

For life's a gift to one and all,
But the tyranny of it is the injustice of it all.

Marguerite E. J. Rolley

Yearning

Oh! This longing I feel deep inside
That robs me of my shame and pride
I want you, how to get from here to there?
I fear I don't really have a prayer.

And then, Oh then, our eyes do meet!
I feel your strength, your need, your heat
And in your arms I find release
Your love has brought my lasting peace!

Luella Ann Springham

Vision Of Peace

Silently looking at the peaceful beauty
of God's Northern Country; I see close
at hand a quilted blanket of silver clouds
covering the lake with a beauty only the
heart and mind can touch.

Below the soft white clouds and the deep
blue shield; white tipped waves from the
water reflect the unseen stars above.

In the background the tall green trees
stretch a staggered line, trying to fill the
space, where the breath of clean air escapes
through the puffed clouds to the unknown.

Delina L. Cabral

The Bus

Amongst shaded mountains lie haunting pasts
as the bus rumbled through faint steel masts.

I lingered in my sleepless daze,
when torch light ripped the chocolate haze.

The rumble clicked, then stopped. Then died.
Voices clattered, someone cried.

The stranger's boots stomped and crushed,
and each face froze as he scanned the bus.

The only farang in his sight,
I sunk beneath his sulphur light.

He glanced at me, his pistol primed,
then speared the dreams of the girl behind.

The cicadas drummed their rhythmic song.
There was no question. No right; no wrong.

The bus sleepily lumbered past the range,
and no one dared to think it strange;

Soldiers weave their webs for flies,
and no one blinks when a stranger dies.

Caroline Sag

Untitled

I could write my most melancholic verses tonight,
still the fresh scent of your skin in my mind
brings back to me only sorrow, sadness and fear
that I day after day try so dogged to disappear.

No time, no distances can tear off these thoughts,
there is no other loves that can digress yours;
the phantom you left when you went away
seems will last forever in me until the end.

I could write my most depressive stanzas tonight;
furious rain-drops against my windows fight
while I try to understand and excuse your lies;
nothing can calm this unmended broken heart.

Looking up at the sky in this moonless night
a brassy breeze wipes my tears while I close my eyes;
my lips can kiss other lips, my hand can hold another hand
but trust me, my heart will never love another one.

Marco A. Sosa

A Smile A Day

A smile is one of life's little things,
that should come each day naturally,
so when your day passes and no smile to be seen,
here is my advice to you.

Drift into the past and remember the times,
when your laughter was joyous and deep,
then carry the memory to the present with you,
and smile in spite of yourself.

Look beside you and see the faces,
of the people who give you hope,
then feel that warmth fill your heart,
and smile in spite of yourself.

Look to the future, believe in your dreams,
and share your life with the ones you love,
then embrace the sweetness of knowing your life,
can make you smile in spite of yourself.

Adria Curich

Life

Once, I had direction in my life.
I knew where I was going and what to do.
Then I met him and my world entered strife.
All I had aimed for became a dim view.
I gave my heart and soul to become his wife.
Instead, he walked away, bidding me adieu,
Leaving wounds far worse than a knife.
Since then everything has been askew....
Direction, feelings and love all stripped from my life.
I move in a numbness so very blue.
Now, you want to take away my strife.
Give me direction, feelings and love brand new...
Take my heart and soul and make me your wife.
You can't break my wall with a construction crew.
You have to carve away a little at a time with a knife.
Take the time to mend my broken heart with loving glue.
Only then can we move on with our life.

Kelly M. Bond

Where The Sea Meets The Sky

What if I was a ship setting sail on the sea
And the land that I left was a mother to me,
and the wind in my sails was a gleam in your eye?
I'd sail to a place where the sea meets the sky.

What if I was goldminer, scarring the Earth
And the ground that I dug was the land of my birth,
And my shovel and pick were your laughter and tears?
I'd dig as the sound of gold rang in my ears.

If I was a beggar, who's blind, deaf and dumb,
If I was a tortoise, a sloth or a snail,
If I was drunkard, drinking my rum,
If I was a puppy, chasing my tail,
And if you were a thought, just a blink of my eye,
I'd dream of a place where the sea meets the sky.

Hans Christian Connor

Tumbleweed

Appearing suddenly on hill's crest
momentarily poised in silhouette
they begin their deliberate advance
down the slope
wave upon wave
in disciplined array
battalions relentlessly descending
heedless on the bards of the wire fence
dying and dead
yet, in the seeds that burst from broken pods.
Immortal.

Eillen Munro

He Walks With Me

He walks with me by day
He walks with me by night
He walks with me when I sleep
He walks, He walks with me

He's by my side when I'm sad
He's by my side when I'm mad
He's by my side when I laugh
He's by my side.

He walks with me when I'm feeling down
He walks with me when I feel I've lost all hope
He walks with me to give me strength, faith and patience
He walks, He walks with me

Derek Charles Carter

417

Hurting

Tears are falling gently like the raindrops
Trickling quietly down her face.
Don't make a sound, just let them fall now,
To make a noise would be so out of place.

It's not allowed for crying to be noisy
Only she can't help the surge of fears.
Yet all this time she weeps so very softly
To make a sound a quivering of her fears.

To be questioned on her need for sadness,
To have to answer for her grief,
She only knows this is what God intended
These crystal tears bring her sweet relief.

They tell her time alone will surely heal her
To be patient, that this too will pass.
But as the joy of crying is upon her
Her heart is breaking, like a piece of fragile glass.

Only she can know the pain of hurting
She also feels the grief and strife.
But God will always guide and shield her
During these traumatic moments in her life.

Ann E. Ward

Lost

In a room of quiet intensity
Lost in a world that doesn't exist to me
Not knowing when I'd go home
Not even finding a telephone
Praying that someday I'd get to go home
For all I do in this room is roam
Roaming through junk and trash in heaps
Trying to find something I could keep
Something to help me stay together
So I can live forever and ever.

Elizabeth Diltz

A Mother's Cry

Have you watched a mother suffer
for a child she has in pain.
Wondering why the good Lord
can't make her well again.

A mother cries a tub of tears
and prays to God above.
To ease the pain she suffers
and give her all His love.

But nothing slows down the pain
the smiles are gone now too.
What she wants is God to answer
and for all the suffering to be through.

A mother cries each day and night,
and prays to God for strength.
She only wants her to be well again,
and asks God to help her go the length.

Ruth Shelton

My Mom

The morning sits outside, afraid until my
mother draws the shade;
Then it bursts in like a ball
Splashing sun all over the wall.

The evening is not night
Until she tucked me in just right
And kissed me and turned out the light.
Oh, if my mother went away,
Who would start my night and day?

Beth L. Buckley

The Last To Know

Some day soon she will wake up
And realize what she's done
She'll see that to be popular
Is not always much fun.

It hurts me so to see her change
The drinks, the drugs, and more
Always trying to be "a show"
Performing with what she wore, (her attitude, not clothes)

The late night parties, the too close calls
Praying never to be caught
Could end in a disaster
Though never to be sought

Maybe at the moment now
It hasn't been to much
But if the future takes a toll
This friend will be out of touch

So someday soon she will awake
And realize all that's past
She'll see that being popular
Is something that doesn't last

Dana C. Bonanne

Remembering

Remember, the days when we first met?
Our lives were so different, in our own ways set.
And as time went by, how we did change;
To resemble each other, on the country range.

Remember, how the family grew?
Each day would bring a promise new;
How we taught them to love, and to trust the Lord.
And no matter how hard, but to follow His word.

Remember, how the time did fly?
And each one of them would say their good-bye.
To spread their wings, and oh, the pain;
But we saw our teachings were not in vain.

And now that we're tired, and old and gray,
And look back upon our life's highway;
We thank the Lord for His gracious love;
That he sent to us from Heaven above.

Agnes Jarmuske

Bela Lugosi The Man Behind The Cape

Terror strikes within the screen
For the King of terror will make you scream.
But there was much more to the man behind the cape
A man who suffered a terrible fate.
Drug addiction was the subject
While he worked at studios of the low budget
Sadness stood within the eyes
Of this faithful man of pride.
A talented actor gone down to waste
A man who originally earned his place
Long before Karloff, Price or even Christopher Lee
It was just a terrible thing to see.
When you mention the kings of terror
The one for me is the proud Hungarian king
The one who makes me shiver
The one whom others treated like liver
Remember it was not poor Bela who is to blame
The pressures of life are just insane
poor Lugosi was practically almost driven insane
But he is not to blame, for he is the man of Dracula fame.

Christopher R. Gauthier

Dawn

Up in the dark sky, the first glimmer of dawn streaked across the
    sleeping earth.
Bright oranges and yellows spilled down like a waterfall crashing down
    on the soil.
Mother earth was flooded with the blinding light.
The chill of the night was fought back by the magnificence of the sun.

Savage creatures that dwell in the night retreat at the resilience of the day.
Happiness fills the void of the withdrawing darkness.
A tear forms in the eye of a man at the beauty of the picture.
Hatred is a coward cringing with fear at the love irradiated by the
    fiery disk.

Beauty and beasts alike dance in the brilliance of the plummeting warmth.
Know it well that this day is unable to be imprisoned by any
    photograph.
No painter can catch the colors on any canvas.
The beauty of the day is beheld by the eye of those who witness this event.

Snakes that wind along hidden valleys bask in the warmth freed by the
    daybreak.
Birds sing sweetly to themselves as if in a dream swaying in a gentle breeze.
The baby blue sky was like a pathway that led to glory and the bright
star was a fiery chariot racing across the path throwing riches to
all who saw.

Heather Williams

Today I'll Know Everything And Tomorrow I'll Know More

so you walked so you wandered so you thought so you pondered and
so close you came to what smacked you in the face that turned you
away to lead you astray in the right direction the fire burned on
because you didn't know how to use the water so you stood there
soaking in the river and caught a fish but couldn't grip it and flew
away to a higher plain and simple and everything nice but nice burns
to burns so hot that didn't stop forget me not and slip and fall and
have an upward perspective on the world below all understanding but
you don't know your mind does things behind your face that you
don't know you do what it says with the threats and the fears
even though you know better than to do everything everyone tells you
to but don't take my word for it is because eventually...

The day goes on sunny full of everything you've always known as
being what is and everything else seems to want ketchup with it
and while the day is still young

...but eventually your minds knows all and then that forgotten fire
has burned so much of what it was burning it couldn't be smoothed
out with a steamroller but try as you might or not know all but
all comes back like a click of a switch of the snapper of your brain
which has now been clicked as you reached for that last piece of
everything that drags you away and up and up and up and up and even
though it told you to, your mind has missed the flight.

Martin J. Chalk

Thinking Of You

I write to you, my mother dear,
    In memory of your fifty odd years.
You've worked and slaved for Him up above
    And for all of us, you gave your love.

No word can tell or tongue relate,
    For God alone decides our fate.
He gave me my mother and only you
    Has decided the right that I should do.

When only a babe you held in your arms,
    I loved you so and all your dear charms
My beautiful mother with lovely hair,
    With truth and honor that God places there.

He gave me you - so pure and true,
    I love you mother and honest I do.
Although I am a few miles away,
    I am thinking of you on your birthday.

Bonnie L. McClure

Lascaux (9.20.95)

Let's go Lois, like soldiers arm-in arm.
To a place where unseen rivers meet;
An underground cathedral sculpted for man to paint
Over 15,000 years ago.

As we move, it moves; layered for change.
The ceilings and walls undulate to a life giving rhythm
So much stronger than me;
Where cows are sensitive to touch,
And eyes are etched to speak of love.

Then the powerful swirl of it all in one Place
With the Bulls in your face so enormous and kind
While inside of a bull is a cow giving birth

At this moment in time where I too should have horns
Since I'm part of this dream
Without breath, without words, and as frozen as they.

Jonathan Nash Glynn

To Eat Or Not To Eat?

You should see me diet
It really is a riot,
You just would not believe, friends, what I do:
I sit down at the table,
Knowing I'm not able
to eat the things I'm really dying to;
I have to watch my calories,
But they're watching from the galleries
(Or so it seems to me while I am eating),
For all the other gals,
Together with their pals,
are on a diet too and so competing.
But some day by and by
When they see that I
show up sporting my remodeled figure,
Then they will have to say,
"Well, look at you today
The last time we saw you, you were much bigger!"

Marion W. Ahlborn

I Love Old People

I love old people and old books,
Twinkling eyes and wrinkled looks,
Real quality you can engage,
Experience written on each page.
I think that older folks are great!
They'll list their pains while you wait!
But never mind, they also know
What life's about, and tell you so.
So, for my part, "for goodness sake,"
That rocking chair and book, I'll take,
Give someone else the other kind...
The TV fool with shriveled mind!

©Judith Chadwell

My Paper, My Pen And Me!

I write my poems, and hope and pray
That some poor soul will read them one day
And get as much out, as I've put in
Me, my soul, my paper and pen
With each of these verses that I beget
I can't help but feeling some regret
These lines that once were part of my soul
These kindly words I sought to bestow
Will fall on deaf ears, and fade you see!
Like my paper, my pen, and like me!

Lonnal Davenport

The Pain Of Piano Practice

Do, sol, la, sol, do, fa, do,
Up and down again they go.
What the cause, I'll never know
That all pianists practice so.

Surely, a cat's tread on the keys
Would create tones more noble than these.
The flustering rout of a fat man's sneeze
is hymnal compared to those shivering 'C's.

Bach's etudes would be well forgotten I know
Were it found that he started the arpeggio.
Bravura, cadenza, cabaletto and rondo,
All but disguises of this do, fa, la, do.

That practice makes perfect, we all understand;
Perfection in music is not be panned;
The versatile artist is worthy our hand;
But practice, I grant you, should justly be damned.

George H. Crosby

The Ocean

As I sit and listen
The roaring of its waves lure me.

It takes me away from myself
Away from the thoughts that occupy my mind.

All I see is the beauty of it.
All I hear is the thunder of its powerful waves.
All I feel is a warm breeze
filtering through my hair.

I close my eyes
I can still see it
I can still hear it
I can still feel it.

It has become a part of me and I apart of it.

I cannot leave it now
It has too much to tell me.

I will be silent, I will be patient.
I will wait. I will listen.

I will sit here with this magnificent
wonder of the world - the ocean.

I will sit here and listen.

Evelyn Slinkard

Handicapped

Did you ever see a falling star
as it streaked across the sky?
Have you ever seen a sailboat
as it goes sailing by?
Did you ever see a sparrow
as it flies from tree to tree?
Have you ever see the white caps
upon the deep blue see?
Have you ever seen the sunset
at the closing of the day?
Or watched the little children
when they came out to play?
Have you ever seen the trees in color
on a beautiful October day.?
Have you ever heard your mother's prayers
when she kneels down to pray.
Oh! Yes I've seen and heard these things,
But only in my mind,
Because my friend I'm handicapped.
I am deaf and also blind.

Ramona Lynn Jones

Lamb In A Field Of Grass

The Aroma of fresh cut grass
awakens the silent baby lamb
from his peaceful slumber.
he sniffs the air
full of beautiful smells
of different flowers
and stands up looking for his mother.
The lamb falls down
full of confusion.
he tries to get up
but his legs are not steady.
His mother swiftly
moves through the grass field
to help her new born child.
After many unsuccessful tries to get up,
the lamb is up off the dew covered
grass once again.
Once he moves one or two steps
the lamb is back on the ground
right where he started out from.

Megan O'Mealia

Just Love Me

Others have come before,
   longing to hold this body

I long to be held,
   but not arms stretched around

Can't it be seen,
   this heart aches-withers,
      starved for emotions-
         feelings would fill

With you I see a beginning
   the end hides in a painful fog

For now I will walk in a crowded absence

Mark Curley

The Trio

At night she halos tenderly my head.
My white feline, so rabbit soft in fur.
My Molly, stalking balls with sleuth in bed
She pigeons coos and welcomes friends with purrs.

The rotund beauty black, sits sunning nigh
The window; yawning, stretching, feigning play
Chez spreads her belly bulge to sight and sigh,
She shows her trust, her sedentary way.

The clown is Lambert, devilish, spry cat.
His agile, acrobatic antics set
A circus mood, a noisy voice at chat.
He leaps, he jumps, this aerialist pet.

These cats, these wondrous, warm, wee ones delight,
With purrs and loving rubs make safe the night.

Barbara Wiese

How Did I Get To Be This Old

A moment ago I was but a lad on my parent's farm, and was my mother's boy. I was full of hopes and dreams, totally unaware that with the passage of time, loneliness would all but swallow me up. What is time, but a door we must pass through from birth to death and what we did in that brief moment in time is merely nothing more than a test God puts us through, and then we go home. The angels weep when we are born and rejoice when we die, so it has been said. My feeble being musters up all its strength to face yet another day, and I ask myself, "How did I get to be this old?"

Marilyn Craig

Squirt

When the clear cylinder gets that little
cloud of red, you get so dizzy you almost lose
your head. You know the danger, when you pull
back the plunger. See the tint of red, then
press down on the plunger. Hear the train
whistle blow in your head as loud as thunder.
For this ride, you beg, borrow, steal, or plunder
You keep on and keep on till you're six feet under.
All of this just makes a sane man just sit and
wonder why you do something so
extreme as to kill every single dream
you would ever dream.
    But to the soon-to-be junky, it seems
to be a little shame, a lot more fun
than just to stay clean. Although every junky
that lies dead in the dirt; if given the chance,
would slap the child's face and say forget about it,
"Squirt!"
    Lemuel Lee Verner

Love

Love is as red as as a ripe cherry
        on a lovely summer day

It sounds like the crinkling of paper
        on an unopened gift.

It tastes like freshly opened chocolates
        on Valentine's Day.

It smells like ground cinnamon and sugar
        on hot buttered toast.

And Love feels like the beating wings of a butterfly
        freeing itself from a chrysalis
        Marren Bailey

Tapestry Of Life

Upon this road I tread
Is not unlike a thread

Interwoven to make a pattern
Even life's small things matter

Unbeknownst to us they see
What fabric makes up you and me

Times of stress some say
Will cause the fabric to fray

The wonderment of life bedazzles
Upon this tapestry that slowly unravels

What lies around the corner from me
Is as a child peeking from the blanket to see

The warmth that feels my heart I say
Is like a blanket on a cold winter day

From beneath the cotton and lace
There is a purpose for me in this place

That I maybe a comforter to all
And not have only a place on this wall

What good is a man that has no plan
It is like cloth in no one's hand

    Arturo Venecia II

Weather The Storm

I hate frivolous flowers so weak and fragile,
bright and bold with lots of frills.
I prefer the sturdy useful oak,
thick and strong with limbs that poke
the fluffy cotton clouds above
that suddenly turn dark and the sky is black and lacking love.
Rolls of fearsome thunder shake the laboring ground
and blinding spears of light come crashing down.
And within the hour, heaven has shown such mighty power
that torn and twisted lies the oak
with no more limbs with which to poke
the once again calm puffs of cotton.
And yet, beyond the battered boughs
a little flower my attention does arouse.
Wind-whipped, battered, but still upright,
I changed my opinion about flowers tonight.
    Audrey Sherman

Different Kind Of Lady

A different kind of lady, from all the rest
God send me here—I'll do my best.
He made me "Special", is what I'm told,
A priceless treasure—much more than gold.

A different kind of lady, from all the rest,
I will not fall—I'll pass his test.
My life is cherish—I'll live it right,
I'm in his care—I'm in his sight.

A different kind of lady, from all the rest,
I'm very "particular", when I choose my guest.
There's something about, the way I carry myself,
Something very "rare"—given to no one else.

For I am me—that's all I'll be,
A different kind of lady, is what you see.
So please respect me, with all your heart,
God made me this way, right from the start.
    Charline A. Jenkins

Untitled

Twilight retreats bowing; knowing his place.
Left in the wake lies a bleeding child, chilled and muted by silent
    screams.
At first demons are banished and tears dried by golden hand.
Slowly she ascends...
as fingertips reach out further in desperate embrace
Slowly she ascends...
on angel's wing, rising to meet the oceans
Slowly she ascends...
until none could question her ardor
All the while, the child lies content in motherly arms, warm and
    devoted.
Finding salvation...
    with the coming of dawn..
For Martha
    Ernest Rivera

Beyond

Soaring through the dark blue sea,
Seeing all creatures big or tiny,
There is coral on the waters wall,
With schools of fish dashing down the hall.
Boats gliding on the top of the clear blue sea,
Orange and yellow sun shining brightly on me,
Beautiful at day but creepy at night.
The sea is amazing when you're in flight.
    Vanessa Lengies

Untitled

If you need someone to talk to,
  I will always be there.
If you need a shoulder to cry on,
  Let me be the one to wipe your tears.

If you have a problem,
  We can solve it together.
No matter what we face,
  We can waive the stormy weather.

We'll have our highs and lows,
  And some days in between.
That just goes to show
  I only say what I mean.

You are always in my heart
  You are always on my mind.
From the night we met,
  Until the end of time.

  Lisa A. Thomas

Reflections On Age

I have reached my eightieth birthday
  And I know I'm growing old.
But age is just a number.
  And as my birthday comes again,
I view with few regrets the years
  And worry not about "What might have been."

"Time Marches On" they say,
  And we know that this is so,
Some days pass on eagle's wings,
  And other days go slow.

I'm told "The Clock of Life" is wound but once,
  And the minutes pass by swiftly:
So qualities such as love, hope, faith and trust,
  Must all be conquered quickly.

For life on earth is measured.
  By the good that we have done,
And when our journey's ended,
  May we hear the words "Well Done."

  Ruth Hemp

My Poet Of The Heavenlies

Have you ever stopped amongst your very busy day,
To stand and see each grandeur God has made in his own way?
It's not just earth, it's not just sky, it's so much more than these,
So intricately designed by him, the Poet of the heavenlies!

Oh! My poet of the heavenlies draws out his pen and sheet
With one quick sweep across the page lays out his plan complete.
He leaves to us a heritage, a beauty to behold
A land that's filled with everything, a treasure chest of gold.

God's words are written in the skies, as every raindrops falls,
His clouds are wells of heartfelt love, as nature's parched land calls.
Graciously his blessings stand, as majestic statued trees,
Courageously constructed to withstand the land's unease.
His plants breathe life to fill our lungs, his water quenches thirst,
His soil brings forth our richest dreams, which one do we pick first?

His evidence is left for us to hear in nature's sounds,
Revealed in our suspension in a space we see abounds.
Yes! My poet of the heavenlies constructs a puree clean,
A marble in the spanse of love, a glimpse of wisdom seen.

  Dawn M. Thomas

Not Yet A Butterfly

I built a small cocoon in which to hide.
With gentle hands you laid those silken threads aside
(missing line it was cut)
But as I turned around and looked about,
I saw myself, it made me realize
That I was still a worm among the butterflies.

I slipped back to my cocoon again.
Re-built the wall that sheltered me from pain.
It is a lonely place but here I'll stay
Nor will I let another tear those threads away.
In my cocoon I'll hide from prying eyes,
Since I'm a worm, I will not try to dwell among the
  butterflies.

If I stay long enough in my soft bed
Perhaps again you'll lay aside each silken thread.
Into the sunshine you will lead me out.
There by your side, I'll turn and look about.
Because you love me, I will preen my wings and rise
And joyously I'll soar toward the skies.
For on that day the lowly worm will die
And, through your love, I will emerge a butterfly.

  LaVey Adams Alexander

All Alone

There I was all alone
No sound expelling from the phone.
No headlights beaming down the drive
Just me, alone, barely alive.

He said this, he said that
Mostly lies from a spineless rat.
At his tales I had wondered
As his victim, my head just thundered.

Where and who and how and why
Are questions I'll ask until I die.
There are no answers to be found
As my mind twirls round and round.

Emotions flood this heart of mine
As I pray for some kind of sign.
That, yes, a better love lies ahead
And soon no more tears I will shed.

Out there, somewhere, please be a love
That will be sent from heaven above.
And to this dream I will cling
Until our hearts meet and together sing!

  Mary Ann Tuomi

Mermaid

The wind tendrils of my hair into my face,
While the bluster of the sand envelopes me in its wrath.
Distorting my view as I try to walk
Away from you.

Into the ocean I ventured.
The bitter cold was your animosity toward me.
The salt, the bitterness you left in me.
The wave, your hand as it slapped my face.

I continued on with a stolid face.
I knew what awaited me further on.
I kept moving into the deepest parts of the water
I left you forever.

I now swim in my sapphire paradise.
While you and your world
Drag on, no purpose
Endlessly.

You did not love me.
I am gone.
My serenity is where I belong.
So strong, so long.

  Laura Margavitch

Why Are We Eating Purple Produce?

When I recall my life as the summer club of death
  I am deliriously in lust with TV
    a repulsive apparatus frantically
      incubating a sweet shadowy symphony

I have the urge to scream
  A bitter winter storm is all I need

Please worship the sordid goddess
  an elaborate vision of beauty
    her languid language manipulating dreams

A thousand beats through music
  but iron moments trudge by

Cool diamond lights sleeping in the moon
    staring madly together over flooded waters
      yet whispering mists cry

If I ask you
  will you swim about them
    through petals and wind?
      C. S. K. DeVinney

Untitled

Silk touches, warm caresses, the essence of purity and intimacy.
To sit and to hold.
Drugs can not surpass or approach.
Feeling your skin through mine as I slowly roam your body is a
great joy in and of itself
Then to receive a sigh of pleasure is extreme ecstasy.
To hold in my arms the subject of all my love is the climax of a lifetime.
I hope time will stop. For Life is gray without this passion.
My heart has stopped till your tender touch again revives it.
I pray I again live in a color filled world where through touch
I am able to both give and receive pleasures.

    Piero Sutti

All Joking Aside...

No where to run,
no where to hide,
I can only cry.
This world is coming down,
piece by piece,
no allies, no friends,
not even me.
You can't walk away,
it will find you one day,
we can only hope the kids of tomorrow won't have to pay.

    Cliff Manion

Body and Soul

The heat rises from within
Blazes red across cheeks
Ignites my soul.

A heart of glass once molten
Still defined by a memory.
Does she carry a torch for me?

One look from her cold, blue eyes
Tells me the fire's gone from her belly.

A vision for the future once seared into my mind
now scattered in the ashes of the past.

    Carrie Campbell

Repentance

Up from my desk felling so blue,
Wondering if a single verse I can do.
Down to my chair I quickly flew
To pen my thoughts - quite a few!

Some I may have to discard later,
For I don't want to suggest a hater.
Sometimes we need to throw away
What might send others deep in clay.

You know, each of you is my friend;
And I can't do without you in the end.
Some of you I may greatly offend;
And some of you may say, "That's a sin!"

My intentions are meant to right
All wrongs to have caused the fight.
Repentance is a great rod of peace
That cause all ruffed feelings to cease.

My friend, come to my house today;
And we shall have food to give away.
I like to cook when my pantry is full;
And I want you to know - scat sull!

    Lillian M. Donahoe

"The Child"

  I am a child with a world of a smile. I am a child who knows not
hate, merely love and an unfortunate sorrow. I am a child who
must fly high like snow white doves. I am a child who cheerfully
smiles, laughs even in the storm of pain.
  I am a child larger than life as the mightiest of oceans. I am a
child of beauty with loving eyes that pierce through souls.
  I am a child who knows only how to give in innocence. I am a
child who longs to wrap humanity in a legacy of love, beauty
and laughter.
  I am a child of many faults, too generous to a fault. So when you
see a joyous child running across a scented, green, rolling meadow,
stop and gaze at that innocence of life flying freely as he or she
leaps to a see of blue sky. To grasp clouds of colorful, fleeting
balloons. Listen for that child's rolling chuckles of laughter.
And allow the whispers of time gone by bring you back to
a once long ago unblemished joy and freedom.
  "I am merely a child and so is a part of you!"

    Luanda Machado

Beneath The Bridge

Beneath the bridge of the Hairy Troll,
Secrets - Long hidden - begin to unroll.
I peek down from high on the ridge.
Peeking at the Hairy Scary Troll, who dwells,

Forever,
Beneath the Bridge.
I can cover him over—with years and drugs.
But, he'll still peek out his terrifying, horrible mug.

  Quick!!
  Push him back!
   He'll squeeze through the crack!
  He'll attack!!

He's loathsome. He's awful.
He's full of glee...

He'll posses my life.
He wants only.......me
    Sharon Fultz

Life

Innocent and young, no worries at all
Growing up, learning to walk from a crawl
Many problems come along your way
With the passing of each new day
Thinking in your mind and feelings worse
Which one do you think, comes first?
When you dream at night, what do you see?
Do you wake up, to face reality?
How many feelings do you feel after each day?
And who or what made you feel that way?
What to do? Do you want to learn?
Or is it something else? What do you yearn?
How are your days? Who do you meet?
Are they exciting or do they repeat?
What are you really looking for?
And when you find it, do you look for more?
How do we act towards others?
Do we hurt or do we help one another?
Oh, and there's one other thing I need to mention,
Why are there so many unanswered questions.

Kevin Tram

Earth Day

Earth Day brings to all aware,
    A question. Do the people care?
It's clean, so nice, we'd like to think.
    But there's litter of cans, and graffiti ink.

Along the path of this green land,
    Trash is lying, thrown by man.
Wrappers from the gum we chew,
    A plastic bag, an old brown shoe.

Earth today is piling up
    With trash and garbage, messy stuff.
Plastic wrap and tin foil balls,
    Scribblings on the bathroom walls.

The toss of a can we say won't hurt.
    Bits of glass lying in the dirt.
It all adds up and in a while,
    Our treasured ground has lost its smile.

I myself have caused a mess,
    Of waste I've tossed in carelessness.
But if we all will lend a hand,
    We'll clean and shine this wonderful land.

Leah Jo Blaha

My Song

When will my song be born
Which season will it adorn
This melody of sweet caress
With lyrics that ring of gentleness

I've been searching for the longest time
For that indescribable perfect rhyme
One day, not a minute too soon
I'm sure to find this unique tune

This song will definitely carry
A beauty so extraordinary
Sensitive and full of tenderness
A rare gift of timelessness

Where do I continue to look
For that song from a fairy tale book
That can surely brighten everything
And gladly make my heart sing

Once finally found
My heart will be forever bound
By the mysterious hands of fate
To this magnificent soul mate

Vittoria Aspro

The Survivor Of His Own Island?

When one has reached the sight of expectancy,
He will travel his journey,
But he will never return,
Never return,
For he has gone beyond,
Gone beyond to start the footsteps
And to create the path of human dignity
He lives the "survivor of his own island."

Diane Blanche Marie Joanisse

The Clown

Last night I had a nice dream:
I was a funny clown
my house became the tent of a circus
so bright in a little town.

My father played a crazy flute
my mother stepped to the drum
my brothers were tickling the Sun.

"Nobody can sleep in this noisy place!"
cried the old man not believing
how a little monkey was making a cake
and two elephants were dancing and weaving.

What a beautiful team!
What a nice dream!
"Get up, boy," my mother said.
Oh, my, my circus was over
as I stumbled out of bed.

Carmen D. Coronado

Out Of My Head

I will not let you break my heart again,
another tear for you I will not shed.
I have to be comfortable being your friend,
but those old emotions keep popping up, I dread.
Why can I not get you out of my head?

I thought we might again be close,
that a future together might lie ahead,
but that subject never arose,
and my heart is left feeling like it is full of lead.
Why can I not get you out of my head?

When we talk, I try not to hope,
that, maybe in your love, I will tread,
so that I do not feel like a dope,
when I see the signs I misread.
Why can I not get you out of my head?

If my heart gets broken again,
and my tears are being shed,
it is not because I cannot be your friend,
it is because you are still in my heart
    and in my head.

Robin Ramsey

God's Love

He loved us all and he gave us life.
He gave us children, plus a man and a wife.
He gave us love in the best that he can,
but we turn away with nothing to say,
and we call ourselves a man.
There are some things that we know at the time we fall,
but the thing that gets to me
is he loved us all.
And I'm asking if you would, love if you could,
everyone like you should.
Cause I don't want an end,
to the love that he sends,
to all of us in Amen.

Jeff Thielen

Appeal To Scientists

I
lay
dull in
my bed, like
a dumped human
figure. I dummied
around my lazy weight;
my body too heavy to carry;
weak to the marrow and bones.
My bedroom, though, dun and dark,
did not appease me. Those lights like
lonely orphan-candle lights reflected into
my dull and sleepy eyes. My hands groped about
for a bed-switch that never was. I feared my
neck at sleep, electric cord not to tangle. My
restless mind was drawn to the light-switches
on the wall; my thoughts narrowed into dreams;
And there I lay, fear beside me. Scientists, please
invent light-switch remote controls for the world.

Obiora E-lk Ofoedu

To My Friend

The time has come to go our separate ways,
To say good-bye to yesterdays.
You've meant so much to me through all the years,
You stood beside me through laughter and tears.
You knew my every move and you felt my every fear,
You always knew how to make me laugh, when I would shed a tear.
You were always slow to criticize and never quick to judge,
You gave me the strength and courage that I needed to go on.
The support and encouragement you've shown me through all these years,
Will help me through a lifetime of hopes and fears.
To give you back everything you've given to me would take
    more than an eternity.
So with these words we must part,
But you'll always hold a special place in my heart.
Just remember that our friendship will never end,
And you will always remain my dear, dear friend.

Sarah Lynn Wallace

His Love

Even in our darkest hour, His love comes shining through.
There's never been a greater love and He's given it all to you.
Especially during the lonely times, when all we feel is despair;
His love will then surround us and we feel His spirit there.
It sometimes take life's hardest hits to make us really see;
His blessings are abundant and He's there for you and me.
When things look grim and all you feel is sorrow in your heart,
Look up in prayer and to His word; His wisdom will impart.
So go to Him with all your cares, anytime or anyplace.
An altar or your living room; look full into His face.
God loves His children for He's given us His greatest gift;
His only son for all our sins; our burdens He will lift.
Therefore, always turn to Him with problems, big or small.
His love forever lights our way, the sweetest love of all.

Carol N. Lawson

The Message

Every morning, at the break of day,
they start up their engines and drive on their way.
Thoroughly trained and without a fuss,
goes the operator of a wheelchair bus.
People who think that life is unfair
should view the perplexities from a child's wheelchair.
And those others constantly complaining of ills,
should see those children learning basic life skills.
Driving a school bus, you can bet,
is a real life experience you will never forget.

Gordon Johnston

I Wish I Had A Million Dollars

I wish I had a million dollars
    You would hear such a holler
The neighbors would call 911
    Thinking I was having to much fun
I'd jump up and down and run around
    Like a fool or a hyper clown
I'd look my sister square in the eye
    And say "lay a finger on my loot you die"
I'd buy my mom a brand new mop
    So her knees would heal and she could flop
My dad would get a lawnmower of course
    So he wouldn't to go to Circle K every 2 days for a thirst buster
Of course I would only buy a few simple things
    Legos, Sega, and a diamond ring
Then I would save the rest for a rainy day

    Oh no it's raining!

Sean Coleman

"Rocking Chair"

The ole' porch needs a coat of paint
    The steps are not as sturdy as
    they once were.
Many years have gone by.
Still, I can remember my granny
    Rocking and singing in her
    special rocking chair.
Holding us little ones in her lap
    Snuggling us close when we
    needed a hug.
How safe it felt — close to Granny!
    I can still hear her laughter
    and see her smile.
We always knew she loved us.
    How I liked to say, "Granny, I love you."
The rocker's been gone a long, long time
    For now I am a grown-up man.
"Oh Granny, if you were here...I'd buy
    a new rocking chair
    and I would rock and sing to you"

Sophia Simmons Borger

Mom

I wish I knew the girl before the woman
    The girl who clumsily crawled across a wooden floor
    The girl who tentatively walked across that same wooden floor

I wish I knew the girl who went to her senior prom in a beautiful
    red dress
    The girl who used to race bikes with all the boys in the
    neighborhood
    The girl who sadly said good-bye to her parents as she left for
    University

I wish I knew the brave girl who stood with thousands that
    protested "the war"

Now...

I know the woman who nursed me
    The woman who shuttled me to school day after day after day
    The woman who sang me a lullaby when I couldn't sleep.

I know the woman who yells at me when I come home late
    The woman who cleans the house too much.
    The woman who talks too much about her children going to
    University.

Sometimes I wonder what she thinks.
    I wonder what stars she sees.

Desmond Webster

City U.S.A. Today

Graffiti, fires, taxes go higher,
Morals fade, contumacy grows,
The stores are guarded, schools retarded,
While teacher strike and statesmen haggle,
Talk is redundant, crime abundant,
The aged fear and the young hold malice,
Some blame, some lie and the blameless die,
Protestors block a street or a door, against or for,
As the city declines constantly faster,
Lost, another city from greatness to pity,
No longer a big wheel, just a hub,
The people who wanted to stay,
Saw the destruction and ran away.

It was once a city with a sky clean and blue,
Few chose to sue, complain, or crave for fame,
Happy children played in an empty lot,
The Mayor's smile was bright, the law accepted,
The Flag respected, and the city was safe at night.

Then progress came - what a shame
  Instead of joy - it brought pain.

Alice Lehner

Hope

As I look up, into the sky
And see all the shining stars gaze back
I know that, someone up there
Is looking after me from above.

Where there is no hope, there is no path.
Where there is no path, there is no light.
Where there is no light, there is no life.
Where there is no life, there is no hope!

For how can there be a life
If we do no believe in one.
And how can we believe if,
We do not hope in it.

Hope! You are the sun that penetrates,
my heart, after a heavy Winter spell.
Giving me assurance that spring is yet to come.
As the light beams on my aching heart.

I am overwhelmed by the joy you give
For the spirit of hope within me,
demands that, I live my life in abundance.
Hope! My stability, my joy, my violin.

Victoria Chipoka

A Walk In Heaven

Eternal life is wonderful,
What else can I say,
For I am with Jesus,
And it is beautiful everyday.

As I walk the streets of heaven,
There are so many people that I see,
There is Saint Matthew and Saint Mark,
And they are happy to see me.

As I walk a little further,
I come to the river of life,
I am so glad,
I gave my life to Jesus Christ.

Finally, I ask Jesus, what about my family,
He says, They are sad because you are gone,
But not long in the near future,
I will bring them home.

Shawn Wells

Reunions

Reunions are planned to celebrate,
To recall the past and bring us up-to-date.

Some times we gather at the shore,
In pretty white cottages with rooms galore.

We swim a lot, walk and play on the beach, and wish-
The sandfleas we gather will help us catch fish.

We'll show our old movies, and how we will laugh
To see ourselves as we looked in the past.

There will be special T-shirts, we'll continue to wear
As a reminder of when we were there.

Along with the fun, the food's always good.
We really eat much more than we should.

The reunion is over, we all say goodbye,
Some will embrace, others will cry.

New friends have been made, relationships renewed,
And we plan to meet again in a year or two.

May God bless us and keep us close in His care,
As we await another reunion to share.

Ruby C. Henderson

The Lovers

Out of nowhere
A rush came over them
Their eyes met then their lips
To her it was beautiful and welcome, yet frightening
To him it was needed and new, yet confusing
As the moment enveloped them
Each fulfilled the others needs.
Would he ever know what he had done for her?
Would she never know how much he needed her?
Amongst their friends they wondered
Would their secret be revealed
Alone, together, they entered another world
Together they became one for the first time
His gentle touch created electricity in her body
Melting away the horrors of her past
His touch slowly crumbled the wall around her soul
Their needs satisfied,

They are friends once again.

Eileen Herron

Directions Of Life...

I looked to the north and what did I see
  the tallest trees that could ever be
They reach with their branches to the sky
  more visions ahead...now I know why.

To the south of that site - the flip of the coin
  the majestic mountains on the horizon it joins
So vivid the colors and capped with snow
  the beauty of creation and all that it shows.

I pondered that vision for a short while
  then pointed due east - I could see for miles.
The breeze travelled my direction - brought feelings serene.
  My mind takes a picture of this vast scene.

Whether north or south - east or west
  no one vision I would choose over the rest.
For no matter the direction or the choice you make
  is the one time in life it can't be a mistake.

Cat Sweetsir

The New Machine

Not like machines of yesteryear
With buttons to push on its top
Here in the garage the painted machine sits.

A mighty machine with detergent, whose motor
Is the stored energy, and its name —
Maytag. From its flip-top lid
welcoming soiled garments; their gateway
To cleanliness.

It is a machine that a company made and sold.

"Purge ancient dirt, your various stains!"
cries it,
With churning water. "Give me your pajamas,
your underwear,
Your mismatched socks yearning to be deodorized,
The wretched refuse of your work shirts,
Send these, the filthy, the smelly to me,
I lift my lid to your clothes!"

   Megan L. Severance

A Day In The Life Of A Homeless Man

He awakens and rises just before dawn,
He gathers belongings and trudges along,
He feels people stare at his dingy attire,
His hair and his skin both tainted with mire.

They whisper and laugh at him; he hears from behind,
Even though he's embarrassed, he pays them no mind.
He stops to thrust in front of him an old rusted tin,
As few people stop to drop a coin in.

When noon becomes visible, he still remains here,
But is suddenly gone by the time night appears.
Although harsh winds seep trough his old tattered clothes,
Through withered shoes and on to his calloused, icy toes.

He wanders through alleys and dimly lit streets,
Treading through garbage for any scraps to eat.
Despite his empty stomach that is grumbling for food,
He walks away, finding nothing, in a frustrated mood.

He settles for the night at a lonely, dark curb.
With no one to talk to or exchange friendly words.
So he lies on the dirty, cold, hard, frozen ground
Ignoring his pain as he tries to sleep sound.

   Leslie Jones

After The Storm

The storm has ceased its never ending torment,
The sky is placid and the clouds have gone.
Fragrance of rain arises from the garden,
Floats up unnoticed to invoke the sun.

At last, the golden star in all its splendor,
Magnificent appears in the sky
Wrapping the Earth in loving, warm embraces.
Kissed by the breeze, sweet flowers bow and sigh.

Small drops of rain dance softly leaf to leaf
Like crystal beads so delicate and clear.
Intensely they attract the sun's warm rays
And tiny rainbows charmingly appear.

The perfumed mist breathes life in every corner
While Nature smiles wisely, filled with love.
In the celestial vault azure and bright,
Like a white pearl, so pure, flies a dove.

   Cristina Necula

Untitled

My heart is like a vacant house
The fear in it, runs like a mouse
From room to room in hopes to feed
Upon my hopes, my dreams, my needs

The windows are gone, and upon the porch
A black crow sits, and with cruel retorts
Reminds it of the one who left
That it's all alone to defend itself

The wind blows in and sings a song
Of untrue love, and hateful wrong
The rain comes through the sagging doors
And drips like tears upon the floors

The flower beds are choked with weeds
They are so ugly, like hate and greed
To the casual observer, there seems no hope
But its foundation is made of solid oak

It's seen the seasons come and go
And can stand rejection, for it does know
The time will come, when someone true
Will want to repair it and make it new

   Kaye Cauley

The Nemesis Of Man

I hear the screams
I feel the pain
crashing, destroying, and annihilating whatever heart that's left
in this world.
Confusion taking over the fragile mind
Greed tearing apart so many lives
Pain amongst pain, pangs of guilt tearing apart the human heart
Can it be true?

The heavens are crying, shedding tears of sorrow
Watching us penetrate anguish into our own souls
Is it all a nightmare - a creation of our self conscious?
A quiet, ticking voice - controlling our every moment
Too invisible for the human eyes - to see, to feel, or to comprehend

We see "them" working their evil -
taken over by greed, animosity and hate
Man's worst enemy is man himself
As the sands of time continue to fall -
will civilization perish or stand tall?

   Rumana Ahmed

This Land

This land's a wondrous place for me to be.
No other do I really want to see.
To travel from each ocean side
And roam wherever country wide,
This land's the one that's really meant for me.

Where "batter up" is heard on every nine
Or where each team is urged to charge that line;
Where you can dream of rocks and rills
And shout "There's gold in them thar hills,"
I'm proud to tell you of this land of mine.

If you should ever want my recipe:
Take Liberty's ingredients, A to Z,
Add all my love and stir it well
And soon you'll have the world to tell:
This land's the place where you and I are free.

   Louis C. Renaud

The Road

Why am I here, on this road?
This road, where only the lost leave their footprints in the sand.
There are no exist, no sign posts.
I am tired and I long for rest, but there is no oasis, no end.
Faces of the unlost pass by, and I silently make my plea for understanding,
But, the faces are blank and unreadable, except for the fear, alive in their eyes.
I can smell the fear, it fills the empty space around me, it clings to my shrinking flesh, and brings tears to my burning eyes.
I cannot escape my own fear.
It stalks me, like a beast waiting to pounce.
Don't shun me, is my silent plea, to those who pass me by.
I don't belong here, for I am not a vagabond.
I did not choose this road of despair,
This road chose me, and ...
Beware!
This road may choose you.
This road has a name.
This road is called AIDS.

Daphne Patterson

Time Passing

We should seize the day, enjoy it for
all that it has to offer. Use it to try
and move one step closer to our dreams.

If we don't, there are always other
tomorrows, but they become todays
and all to quickly pass into yesterdays.

We try to be strong and regain the time
that passes, stressing and rushing through
another today; trying to make up for what
we lost, and not being able to enjoy what
it has to offer.

Slow down, grab on to today and make
it worthwhile, even if it only means a
passing smile for someone.

All too soon the today, tomorrow and
yesterday will turn into chances that
have past, instead of a lifetime of memories.

Cabrina Carlo

Twins Togetherness

My dearest twin sister,
  Why did you leave me alone?
I have always been with you.
  All the closeness we have known.

Sometimes I feel anger,
  I know not at who,
Not at God, I'm sure
  And certainly not at you

To his heavenly home, without me,
  I do not know why he took you.
I feel so much hurt,
  So much loneliness, too

You seem so very near, your spirit I am sure,
I know you are not here, you are on your heavenly tour

We were conceived together, lived, played, worked, loved.
Learned to believe in God, forever, and that He is from above

Together we gave birth to sons, they seemed to be entwined.
They were not the only ones, all your children seem like mine

It is hard to live without you, but is the thing I have to do.
I have to say goodbye - it's time, dearest sister of mine.

Jean M. Goodman

Until Your Swords

At last, I fled the safeties
And braved a midnight leap,
While dreams waged war to shred the ropes
That snatch me back from deep.

A violent dawn returned me,
Revealing steel strewn dead.
The rope-infested summit
Again reclaimed my head.

Come solve these wars that waste me.
Watch takeoffs choked by ropes.
Until your slashes spring me,
No flight can reach your hopes.

Leonardo Valle

One Nation

Beneath festering sleeves of anger and pain,
an adequate nation lay in wait.
Will we be one and whole again, and raise
the flag up high?
To this end we'll be satisfied or could it be
an empty desire, because for far too long this
country has been so stratified.
Bring the sick, the hungry, the jobless and the homeless
and pray to the end of a trifling nation plagued by
the unequal distribution of wealth and power.

Rhonda Jackson

American Ideals

Picture the high flying colors of red, white, blue.
When it calls for your service
will you be true?
The time will come when it must be defended,
but would you sacrifice?
It helps those who befriend it,
but makes those who don't fools.
Believing in its meaning is real freedom.
Flaming hearts from oppression it cools.
It asks God to bless America
for allowing it to strive.
Almost like in a Shangri-La
the Eagle of Liberty lives on.

Michael A. De Cicco

The Pebble Of Life

A stone washed up on the ocean beach,
If it could talk, what tales it might teach.
The wonder, the mysteries, of all the days.
I ponder what role in history it plays.

Could this be the stone that David did slay
Goliath the giant, thus history was made?
Could this be the stone that all cave men once knew?
If so, then the days of stone age were true.

A thousand phrases, 'Rollin' stone gathers no moss.'
A thousand seas, did this little stone cross.
How many years to cross just one sea;
A million or more, just how could that be?

A stone washed up on the ocean beach,
If it could talk, what tales it could teach.
The wonders, the mysteries, all these I do lack
So I picked it up and tossed it back.

Robert C. Toyne

I Want To Be Free

I want to be free,
And see what I hope to be.
I want to be free,
I wanna work like a bee,
I want to be free,
And staying in a room with a door, but no key.
I want to be free,
And never lie on my knee.
I want to be free,
And to be me.
I want to be free,
I wanna look around and see.
I want to be free,
Not to say I but say we.
I want to be free,
And to learn it all from A to Zee.

Bardes Ahmed Gamal

Incarceration

I felt suffocated but the breeze embraced me
I felt dark and depressed but the moon lit up my face
Diana herself had done proud
But I did not feel any appreciation
The passing of the day the coming of the twilight
Saddened me to an extent unfathomable
The loss of the sun, the gaining of the moon
Gaining of quixotic dreams, loss of hardened realities
At this I vociferously voice these opinions to myself
A tranquil and almost hypnotic silence inevitably follows
With the day hard-faced situations
With the night comforting images but unavoidable loneliness
A balance would hearten me so
But I fear it will never be possible

Chloa Cromwell Mardis

Poetic Justice

The verse that bursts with the fervor of cause,
The strophe that to virtue cajoles,
The villanelle that transgresses God's laws,
These are the rhymes that try men's souls.

Jerry Dorbin

"Letter"

I am not sending you a frown,
or even a couple of tears,
not an "I'm sorry",
or "but I've loved you all these years!"
I'm sending you a smile,
for everything we had,
don't think I didn't love you,
or that I'm not sad,
It's just I knew it had to end,
and so, instead,
this I send,
A smile.
A smile for all the times we shared,
the times we loved,
the times we cared.
For all the great times we had,
all those times when we weren't sad.
I end this letter with a sigh,
and with that,
I say goodbye.

Mary Duguid

Many A Day

Many a day we get up to wonder what pleasures this day will bring us today

Or trials and fears and things to happen to us we do not want this day to hear that may still happen this day

For each new day is a beginning of life a life we may live this day in any way

Our thoughts and actions we are masters of what may we have that we may with others share today

Better to share and learn life's lessons each and every day to treat others with kindness that they may treat us that very same way

Let not a day go by that in sorrow we may be for lessons of life not learned for that day for us there may not be a day tomorrow

So let us not miss the opportunity we may do for others a kindness that they may do for us

Then when we get up we again may wonder what this day may bring but remember we may that yesterday we were kind to another and may be today another may be kind to us this beautiful day

Edward David

It's For The Best

They took my baby from me
Did they know what they were doing?
I think they don't understand how it feels.
Imagine a hand reaching in and
    tearing your heart from your chest

The pain.

If only they had let me decide and say
I might have given my baby to them.
I'll never known, that part is over

The pain isn't.

Linda L. Martin

Epitaphs On Aborted Embryos

Your hateful mother hid you from light
You'd now have been my life's bright.

Your father didn't trust me
And he denies responsibility.

She wouldn't let you interrupt her studies
And you'd anyhow disrupt her liberties.

Your father didn't care for me,
How alone I'd I maintain thee?

It's because I told your mother whore
I didn't think you were mine for sure.

Your mother realized I didn't love her
And she wanted to be free for another.

The times I'd met your mother were few
So she feared I wouldn't own you.

"He gives me nothing," said she
"I won't bring you into poverty."

Gerald M. M. Matovu

Just A Bowl Of Cherries

If I were in charge of the world,
The day would start at noon.
So everyone could get their sleep,
Instead of waking with the moon.

The poverty stricken people
Who struggle day by day,
Would burrow out of their financial hole
And into a sunny world of pay.

World peace, so far on the horizon,
Would proceed closer by leaps and bounds.
The guns stocked with ammunition
Would refuse to shoot their rounds.

The people living in sad darkness
Would advance into a happy light.
For all the distressed people
Would achieve their goals without a fight.

If I were in charge of the world,
Nothing would go on the fritz.
This would be a bowl of cherries life,
Without these troublesome pits.

Megan McElwee

Old Yeller Unique

Furry, bold, and cunning, sad eyes.
Yellow and white.
Fast hind legs that propel him and
pointed ears.
Runs through the field like a bullet.
Despised and loved by the people who
house him, he still tries hard to be
part of the family.
Dashing and brave as he helps his neighbors.
Soft, yellow fur, warm and as cozy as a blanket.
I wish I could have a dog like him.
Similar to and different from the late Bell.
Dirty doggy dances dandily to save Arliss.
Fights off bears, chases raccoons, and helps with hunting.
He is golden with an aroma of different odors,
He is like a piece of sun that turned into a dog.
Flips cows with the greatest of ease.
Like part of the family —
Old Yeller

Burton Durand

My Love For You

We sit on the hillside late at night,
our hands closed together, the stars shining bright.
The sound of silence fills the air,
I look at your face and can't help if I stare.
Your love, your beauty, your presence so dear,
I feel your warmth as you are near.
The trees all around us sing a joyful hymn,
To this place called love. Won't you come in?
Oh, how the flowers have such a beautiful smell,
It has to be love, I can already tell.
Each minute goes by, the time I spend with you,
I will always cherish, for my love is so true.
From the depth of the ocean, to the mountain tops,
My love flows like a river that never ceases to stop.
So, as this night of all nights comes to a close,
The love in my heart for you, still grows.

Daniel Martinez

Happy Valentine's Day

"Happiness is", the less serious have said,
 "A roll in the hay"; to some, "A warm bed."

The ardent pursuer of golf in the sun,
 Says, "Happiness is a neat Hole In One."

The tennis buff staring match-point in the face,
 Says, "Please, dear Lord, just give me an Ace."

The secret of happiness time proven by sages,
 Is loving and laughing with your spouse through the ages.

The joy that you feel with your spouse by your side,
 Is one of the treasures this world can abide.

We who've had years of such marital sharing,
 Wish others had tried a bit harder at caring.

The fun is in living each year, come what may,
 So wit love we can say, "Happy Valentine's Day!"

Nell Menn

Oneness

Penetrate air and see instant color

Continuum...no break...
 Each touch...some blend...
 even flow...All one...

Add depth and definition -
 does unity and oneness collapse?

After categorize, individualize,
 divide and separate

No - Endures the name...
 pastever, forever, futurever...
Remains the "isness"...
 brotherhood of easiness

Which sound high...which side left?
 smell of rose or bala

Beholder plans...but doesn't know

It hot...then cold...then hot...then...

It round...then square...then...

Each part counts....each is the whole
 Each makes the whole...
 Infused one — change is your heartbeat...

Lynne A. Riedy

"Night"

(In Memory of Cliff Powell)
Sitting alone in the dark.
A barking dog.
The drone of a far off engine.
A siren in the distance draws close, then fades away.
Night silence suffocates just long enough to bring
a twinge of fear and loneliness, but I know in
My heart, the world is still alive.
Time leaves me behind.
Thoughts pass through my mind, like a brook
over rocks on a summer day.
I long to reach back to the time that the night
was my friend.
Two cats fighting.
A door slams.
Oh, let the light come soon and save me from
my own thoughts.

Valerie Graham

To My Woman!

To my woman I give my fries,
the gold in their color
spell the riches of a kiss
as they sooth her hungry mouth.

To my woman I give my Coke,
it sweats though
it cools me in the burn of summer,
as I sweat to cool her desire.

To my woman I give my Big Mac,
tempting with its secret sauce
so she may know all my 1,000
islands in my dressing and all
the 1,000 kisses from my heart.

To my woman
I give all of this so she can have the
extra value meal (super size) of my love.

Dylan P. McGowan

We

Like vapours floating in the night,
   or soft sounds drifting by
As fragrant scents upon the breeze
   and colors in fading skies,
Or fragile flowers come to bloom
   as time creeps slowly by.

The vapours fade and sounds slip by
The breeze has caused the scents to sigh,
While flowers, like the fading sky
   will soon have passed through time.

A. Wayne Mckay

Death's Passion

Setting out from Edinburgh on an evening tide,
He and his crew would be condemned to die.
By a tempest of relentless fury the Devil's bends,
While searching for his love to make amends.

To the mercy of the sea sinking in a ghostly mist,
The human cries faded to the last fatal hiss.
Slowly gurgling down to the quiet devouring deep,
In the sympathy of reeds sheltered consuming keep.

As seen but not spoken of the cataclysmic roar,
An undisturbed obsession lay forever more.
Until the cold winds blow to the heart shivering,
Up to the moon caressed by stars glimmering.

The unresting soul of love shall be awakened,
With a resolution too strong to be forsaken.
From his quiet cool rest of a watery grave,
He will search eternally forever a slave.

Charlene McNaughton

Love Is.....

Love is something that does not have a frown.
Love is something that helps a person when they are down.
Love is something you can not take.
Love is something you should not hate.
Love is sometimes hard to find.
Love is sometimes very kind.
Love is sometimes very rare.
Love will come to you.....If you know how to care.

Michelle Lynn Couvillon

"Gifts"

Many give gifts at special times;
most enjoy receiving them too.
But, there are many kinds of gifts
athletic and mental prowess, to name just two.

Some are gifted in the music field,
others in public speaking or art.
Individuals throughout the world contributed
to humankind since our cave-dwelling start!

A few are gifted with inventive genius,
advancing society for the good of all.
Others develop the gift of making money,
although it can be a blessing, or cause a fall.

There is one gift this planet's people
will never, never have enough of —
for everyone needs it, and that is
the gift of giving and receiving love!

Wayne Franke

That Night

Oh, what a night it must have been,
Don't you wish you'd lived back then?
To feel the difference in the air that night,
As the world paused waiting for the Light.
To see the stars brighter glistening.
To stand with the shepherds listening,
For that special sound,
To come from the stables in the town.
To hear that first soft cry from the Babe,
As in the manger he was laid.
To hear the night then burst alive,
Surrounding the shepherds on that hillside.
As the heavenly host announced His birth,
God's Love, come down to men on earth.
Oh, what a night it must have been,
Don't you wish you'd lived back then?

Patsy Cavender Ward

come to me, i'll go

the sun kisses the moon on evening's approach,
its bright adieu gently resting upon the horizon
beholds night's lunar, tender embrace,
you come to me like heavenly clockwork,

ticking away my heart, willingly, breathtakingly,
i go, as you wish, to dance on moon light beams
reflecting far beyond time as we know it,
such as stars enchant life's creative pulse, forever

a place within mirrors thy universe without,
your depth is my beauty, your beauty my depth,
rapture delights this ticking heart,
beating it into elation,

i go, arriving at your space in the heavens,
departing earthly limits, letting go of my life,
to die blissfully back again on a cloud
as your heaven embraces my earth

come to me, i'll go,
as when the sun dances around the moon, ceaselessly,
venturing always to be one,
destined, passionately, as two

Carleen Diane Mejza

Whirly Wind

It feels like heat, it feels like sweat,
Grab the family, Grab the pet.

Head to the cellar, head to the hall,
It will rip up the base and tear off the wall.

It's Big and grey and scary at sight,
That big guy will put up a fight.

It will rip out the window and blow out the door,
Wake up the children, it's no time to snore.

It might rip out the garden and pull out the trees,
There goes a potato and one, two, three peas.

There goes breakfast, there goes lunch,
Guess what dear, I've got a hunch.

Our roof is gone and so's that thing.
Listen to that sound-hear the birds sing.

Timothy Karl Kuhn II

For Granny's Sake

I feel so sad, for someone took my Granny away, but the memories of
  her still lingers with me today.
We used to sit down in the middle of her living room rug, and there
  she would laugh and play cards and games with me, and then she
  would give me a great big hug.
After we would get through with our games and such, she would sit me
  in her lap and I just loved her gentle touch.
I dream of her almost every night and wish I could hug her with all
  my might.
She was the sweetest person on this earth, for I have always loved her since birth.
She was not only my Granny, but my best friend, for I could always, on
  her, depend.
I miss her so, that I feel that my heart is breaking, upon each and
  every day when awakening.
She was my special star and guiding light, for the memory of her will
  always shine bright.
And I don't know what a difference, in this world, that I can make,
  but I'm going to try to make it a better place for my Granny's sake.

Alicia Kathleen Horner

Commencement

And so it goes: Walking up that aisle is just like hearing my boots
scrape gravel against asphalt in the dark crisp night, hearing nothing but the street,
the street responding, echoing under the presence of some miracle celestial orb,
comet, I think, but really nothing more than a strange stain on the sky.
In fact, it is the only thing that's indistinct,
unamplified, and somehow a blur:
all else is examined under a high powered microscope,
or so it would appear.

My father dreams of white trousers, like Prufrock,
on the streets of Rio de Janeiro during the Carnival,
and while I look at my classmate's wisps of hair, like melodrama,
I think perhaps my sweetest days will be spent eating peaches,
and not dreaming of peaches past.

Still, the tassels on our caps would be streams of tears
so we look like so many miracle weeping Madonnas
walking down the aisles.
And God! Here I am crying rivers down to my boots
so caked with the earth of some seven states
and the gravel of the other night and cracked practically in half
I can feel the ground in my soles.

Evelina Zarkh

Tomorrow

Tomorrow, I'll wake up early
And smell the flowers, oh! So sweet
I'll listen to the raindrops
And laugh, as I wipe them from my cheek

Tomorrow is another day
And I will have the time to say
All the things I forgot to say
Today, and yesterday

Life is so short
Where does it go?
Tomorrow, maybe I will find the answer
Surely, someone must know

Meanwhile, I'll travel down life's highway
Leave riches behind with the sorrow
But wait, this is my, life I'm dreaming on
And I must start living - tomorrow

Josephine C. Morio

An Ode To The Beach

Sometimes I want to be at the beach,
But it seems it is out of reach.

I really like to cruise in my car,
And always drive right by the bar.

The water is always crystal clear,
And that is one thing I love to hear.

The waves crashing on the shore,
But I wish I was in the water a little more.

Every time I see the surf,
It seems to bring me back to earth.

The sounds of the shore under the moon,
driving in my car with the big boom.

It has always been a dream come true,
And it is everything I want to do.

I wish I could go there now,
But I think that I've forgotten how.

Michael S. Mucha

The Weeping Rose

In this glass I'm left to stay
  All alone, to live each day.

Yes I was one of the first blooms in Spring
  And sprouted myself above everything.

I worked myself up and shouted out with a cry
  I'm so beautiful, I'll never die.

But now I'm alone; the others drifted apart.
  I know my time is short; I too shall depart.

My petals have loosened and it's quite a strain
  To hold them together and sustain.

I live for each moment in a day
  As all things living must pass away.

Beverly L. Raab

The Uncivil War

Blue and grey
Not just the uniforms, but the day.
Gunfire and cannon blasts
It went on as long as the day would last.
Many a good man dies,
And on that bloody field his body lies,
Broken and battered and covered with bruises,
It doesn't really matter which side wins or loses.
Friend was foe, foe was friend
Every day they fought that damn war over again.
Soldiers lost eyes and legs and arms
They killed each other and burned down southern farms,
Men fought for honor, men fought for slaves
But in the end no soldier's life was saved
They fought like men and were slaughtered like cattle
But not one man feared that day's battle.
After the battle Johnny Reb and Billy Yank
Sat around fires and their camps and ate and played and drank.
To all the men who fought in the heat and blood and grime,
I say to you, you have earned your place with the greatest soldiers
    of all time.

James K. Dean

In Memory Of My Beloved Cal

I lost my beloved 15 long years ago,
and through these many years I still love him so.
To me he was the stars, the moon and the sun;
my whole life through, he was the only one.
His tired heart could no longer beat.
His short life was now complete.
God wanted him to come home to stay.
I had to understand his wishes to take him away.
It was the hardest thing in my life to do;
I had to start my lonely life anew.
We were married for twenty nine years,
and we lived through both happiness and tears.
Our three children grew up to be,
the best of Cal and the best of me.
All three of our children are loving and kind;
all good people you would stand behind.
There also are a daughter in-law and son in-law he never knew,
and our six wonderful grandchildren too.
I have great sorrow they will never know his love,
but he is watching over us all from heaven above.

Ruth Loomis

So There Lies A Mother

With her new born baby on her arm,
She makes a vow never to let it feel any harm.
Reality soon shows harm is in the air,
But never will Mother not care.
As her baby grows,
It gets much harder - she knows.

Now dear Baby is on her own,
but never will she forget her true home.
Visits are always wonderful,
With not a moment dull.
But now rarely do they stop and see
How it used to be.
Time slips away,
No notice of today.
But now it's too late.
I suppose it's just fate.
So there lies a mother,
Her "baby" now above her.

Jennifer Acee

A Poets Words

These words come to me,
Like the millions of rain drops,
That fall from the sky,
They are a mix of emotions,
Sometimes happy, sometimes a mournful cry,
They pour out from my soul,
Wanting desperately to be heard,
A gift from God, A Poets Words,

When I look to others,
Who's talents I do not possess,
Their creativity eludes me,
Even when I try my best,
And when I'm feeling truly talentless,
I sit and do what I do best,
I let the words fall from me,
All jumbled and in a mess,
And from these words I will create my work,
Hoping desperately to be heard,
A gift from God, A Poets Words.

Susan Mapes Lankford

My Haunting

Hovering over every inch of my soul,
The Haunting has crept within me.
It's existed before my memory's birth,
But the Haunting I never see.

When I was child, the Haunting lingered,
Yet somehow I didn't notice.
I was happy, content with life
But this life was out of focus.

Now reality has set in,
The Haunting becomes apparent
It stays with me throughout the day,
But the Haunting is not transparent.

For I am the Haunting's captive.
Will I ever break free?
Desperately alone in this struggle,
Eternally, searching for the key.

I do not hate the Haunting,
Although, it brings me misery.
I cannot hate the Haunting,
My Haunting is a part of me.

Mary-Geraldine McNamara

Together

His body advances towards mine.
My heart beats faster and faster.
Questions running through my head
like little children in a playground.
Does he love me?
Our bodies and souls meet
and we become one figure in both.
As the sweat glistens off our bodies,
I wonder was this right, should I have done this?
He sucks the sweetness from my body
and I the same to him.
Our bodies screaming for one another.
He wipes the tears from my cheek
and holds my in his arms.
He makes me feel cared about.
He softly presses his lips to mine
and in one long sigh says:
I love you with all my heart.

Barbara McKasty

What Is Purple?

Purple is the violets and irises of spring,
And purple markers and ink are the thing.
Many look great in purple clothing.
What do you think about purple clothing?

Purple tastes like fat, juicy plums and grapes.
Purple is the chilling, delicious black cherry ice cream,
And also a grape jelly pool in your dream.
Eggplants are purple, but don't forget purple candy too!

Purple smells like spring flowers in morning.
Such as asters or morning glory.
Purple smells like the fresh breeze off the ocean coast.
Or a scary, old ghost.

Purple sounds like waves crashing in the ocean.
Or even flowers singing in the sun.
Purple is the migrating birds coming from South.
And little children on the beach having fun.

Purple feels soft and gentle like a baby's skin,
Which never makes a sin.
Purple is a rabbit's fur, or medicine to make a cure.
Purple is amazing if you think about it,
So use your imagination and sit.

Teresa Albert

I Need Someone To Be My Friend

When I look at the empty landscape of our lives
Without someone it's like barren ground and dark skies
Then I acknowledge that something to each applies
I need someone to be my friend, I realize

When I see mad violence that sweeps the nations
Men, women and little ones facing starvation
Hatred, ethic cleansing, bombs and devastation
The wail for a friend is not a revelation

How many migrating boat people are lost at sea
Miles walked in the dead of night as a refugee
All looking and needing something more than their poverty
To neighbor nations, be a friend is a useless plea

Large forests have come from just a handful of seed
On the smallest sea creatures the largest ones feed
To get friends you want, the key is simple indeed
"Do to others as you'd have done to you" just heed

Shirley Sally

Texas Blue Norther

It's cold -
The kind of cold you feel with your ears.
Sleet hitting the window
in the back bedroom of a farm house.

Whistling Wind crossing the fields and
stealing through the window cracks and floor boards.
The creaking and moaning of the great Oak limb as
it tempts the roof and dips to the ground weighted with ice.

The "Norther" has arrived.
You can hear it's cold.

Tucked warmly amongst comforters and pillows
surrounded by three bed dogs in red and white knit sweaters -
You are safe.

This is the way to experience cold - with your ears -
Soon you will pull yourself from the bed
and greet the wind full force.

It will cut across your face as you rush to the barn
and howl in your ears as you struggle with the barn door.
And you will curse the cold.

De Springer

Love, Be Not Mild

Love, be not mild
Take me as I am, engulf me in thy robust waves
And thy entangling web.
Conceive thy sentiment into thy womb
Bestow freely thy heart.

Memorize me, console thy vital spirit and take
heed to thy enchanting ways.
Let thyself be lured into my eccentric affections.
Befall to thee willingly.

Entice me with thy timeless words and inexhaustible
feelings.
Shadow thy moves, touch thy pulsating soul.
Be fruitful to thee and stay with thee forever.

Sharon E. Gibbs

America...

America, I acquiesce, in a humble way;
For I know not how to dress on your auspicious days.
Should I wear star-spangled clothes and wave your banners high,
Or would the black of mourner's clothes be more appropriate to try?

I've seen the recent winds of change blow across your land
Falling many precedents your blood was spilt to stand.
Scholars of your history, technicians of your past
Are wary of your destiny; has attrition moved too fast?

Oh, come back, come back, America! To simpler, slower days;
Reach out and help your neighbors mend their zealous ways.
Oh, come back, come back, America! To where you left your pride;
then slowly move on forward with honor at your side.

And if we pull together, we can wave your banners high,
Oh, look up, look up, America! Toward the bluing of your skies.

Norm Hansen

Juxtaposition

A strange and beautiful face, I saw
In vacuum as I opened my eyes.
She picked me, her soft touch of love
Always took me to the height of skies.

Constantly her watching eyes and stern stare
On me, did not let any catastrophe to fall.
Always beside me. She held my hand tight, took me
Through the rugged terrain, saved me from being pall.

My mother's heart is vast, with limitless horizon
Deep and soothing like ocean waters.
Taught me caring for others, love thy neighbor
Deeply rooted in me, blooming million flowers.

Now I am in the care of a foster mother
Whose lap is larger, vaster and warmer enough.
Accepted many like me, assured all, but
Could not walk with me, wherever the ground was rough.

Her exposure to multitudes is a kind of visit
To a garden, lush green, lustrous and luxurious.
Marveling at her kindness, prestige and sagacity
My heart prays for both; to prosper and forever to be virtuous.

Sushma Malhotra

The Gift Of Blood

If a few minutes of your time
Could save some dying person's life,
If several strikings of the chime
Could stay the probing surgeon's knife.
Would you give them?

If this power pulsed through your arms,
Would you share it with your brothers?
If finding there's no personal harm,
Would you share it with some others?
Would you share it?

If a mother's child lay dying
On some far away battlefield,
If on you they were relying
Praying softly as they appealed.
Could you refuse?

All have this power of which I speak.
I implore you without time's loss.
Please give this pint of blood this week
To the American Red Cross.
Go give it now.

Theodore L. De Marco

"Those That Knew"

They stood in the dark, dense forest.
Black hoods pulled over their heads.
There was nothing more than the silence
As they waited for the call of the dead.

The fire shone bright on their faces.
Each felt a cold, growing dread.
A chant rose up with the fire smoke,
Yet still no call from the dead.

The wind swept up like a gale force,
And threw back the hoods from their heads.
They grew strong and clasped hands in the fire light.
From the earth rose the call of the dead.

The evil was evident around them.
On their souls it seemed to have fed.
They writhed on the ground in the fire light.
Their life force food for the dead.

The sun rose high in the morning,
Over bodies lying still on the ground.
They had played with a magic o'erpowering.
What they sought they never had found.

Kelly Beckwith

In Silence I Love

In the darkness that is the depth of my soul,
  there is a light that is yearning to shine.
In the trembling that is the beat of my heart,
  there is a love that is waiting to be found.
In the ache that is the wanting of my arms,
  there is a longing to be entwined.
In the turmoil that is the focus of my mind,
  there is the sweetly tantalizing essence of you.

With every inhale and exhale I release and receive
  the pain of being without you.
My heart and soul cry out but they are stopped
  by what cannot be.

  I am numbed with grief. I am mute.
I cannot allow myself to speak. I must endure
this intolerable suffering alone and encased in myself.
I can only wait for the time, when lips can touch lips
and soul can reach out to soul.
  Hoping and praying in silence.

In silence I wait. In silence I weep.
In silence I mourn. In silence, I Love.

Celina H. McElvaine

My Grandfather's Garden

Each day in their seasons, he tends them for hours:
Vegetables, fruit trees, grape vines and flowers.
Of a garden more gorgeous you cannot have read,
Yet the squirrels say that Grampa is strange in the head.

He noticed the squirrels would steal, if you please,
Or at least badly damage the fruit in his trees,
So he took some old fox furs, in tatters and curls,
And slung them from branches to scare away squirrels.

That the furs aren't alive, the squirrels can well see,
And they've sure never heard of a fox in a tree!
So, fox or foxes, they'll nibble a pear,
But you won't see a squirrel if my grandfather's there!

He lavishes love upon feather and fern;
Young gardeners flock to him, eager to learn;
He's charming, intelligent, cheerful and gentle,
But all of the squirrels are convinced that he's mental!

John Cameron Stirling

A Brother's Bond

My brother has gone and moved away
In my house now he will never stay
I was there to say good-bye
It wasn't easy I'll tell you why
You see he was my big brother
I looked to him as my second father
He partly made me what I am today
And I thank him in every way,
I love my brother, whose name is Jon
And we will never lose a thing they call
A Bother's Bond!

Gregory M. Grudecki

Untitled

Tell them that you love them while they are near,
  For when they are gone, they can not hear.
Kiss their dear lips while they are warm and nice,
  For when they are gone, they are and cold as ice.
Please bite your tongue before you ever say,
  A mean word that will hurt, the rest of the day.
Put your arms around their body and hold them tight,
  And cuddle up close in bed each night.
Just take the time to say,
  "You look very special to me today."
Yes, never wait until they are gone,
  for your days and nights will be lonely and long.
Take time to thank God every day,
  For sending that "special" love your way.

Louise E. Reynolds

On My Own

I'm on my own, no place to go.
I thought I was right but didn't know.
Why did I yell and scream that night?
Why did I run out after the fight?
I left with some money and my winter coat,
I didn't say good-bye or leave a note.
Now I'm here on a lonely street,
begging for charity from anyone I meet.
I can't go home, it's been so long.
And my parents will remember the night I was wrong.

Alexa Korzenewski

"A Year In Time"

Howling winds on the barren plains
No waving grains of wheat!
No stalk of corn so green and tall
Just dry grass and blazing heat!

Dust devils dance with careless glee -
Springing up from out of nowhere.
And off in the distance a filmy haze
No clouds - just the sun's hot glare!

Where is the rain? The life-saving rain?
So many people pray.
No smiles on their faces - beseeching eyes
Pleading for rain on this day.

And then - far off in the distance
A faint rumble - can it be thunder?
Behind the haze there arise some clouds
With lightening streaks running asunder!

The wind blows cool - how good it feels!
Raindrops are pelting the ground!
The drought is broken - thirsts are quenched
Hearts are grateful - there is "joy" all around!

Agnes M. Dobias

Nursing Home Blessings

Blessed are they who knock at my door
With a smile on their face as their feet hit the floor.

Blessed are they who seem to understand
How weak my knees and trembly my hands.

Blessed are they who seem to know
My hearing's impaired and my thinking is slow.

Blessed are they who don't seem to mind
To dress and groom me, with hands always so kind.

Blessed are they who help me to the table,
Prepare my meal, realizing I'm not able.

Blessed are they with a cheery smile,
Who stop for a hug or just to chat awhile.

Blessed are they who never (ever) say,
"You've told that same story twice today."

Blessed are they who check me at night
To see that I'm breathing and sleeping all right.

Blessed are they who make it known
I'm respected, loved and never alone.

Blessed are they who ease my day
While at a Nursing Home I stay.

Faye Redding

Pray

"Hem your day in prayer, it'll be less likely to unravel";
Your day will be less ragged, when all through it you travel.
Look for God's blessings, each moment you live,
And you will realize just how much he loves to give.

Thank God for everything, every time that you pray.
Fellowship with him throughout all the day.
He will listen intently to everything you say,
And He will lead you correctly in each and every way.

Always be obedient to all of God's directions;
You'll make less mistakes, there'll be less corrections.
In your book of life, each day is a page.
Live your gathered wisdom each day that you age.

Life is a journey, written as we travel through.
My journey is different from the journey for you.
If we each weave in the guidance from our
   Author up above,
Our lives will be bound together with its
   Maker's peace and love.

Anita Cathey Ryan

London, Ont., After Forty Years

Why do my people have nothing to say to me?
Their closed minds shut the doors of curiosity.
They scapegoat me.
I did the exploring, I fell over the cliffs,
While they snuggled on warm armchairs in R25, (or higher), houses.

Tell me what you want to know. Ask me questions.
If you are not interested in my discoveries,
Did I live my life outside history?
I thought I was special. They told me I was special.
Did they not know how to facet me?

My possessions, a gross of containers,
Could be thrown on some dumpster,
Helter skelter into a landfill,
Hazardous waste for literate bag ladies.
But nothing to nourish marauding racoons.

Time is my organizer. Do something today. Plan for tomorrow.
Prioritize.
Bottom - up requires no thinking;
But, top - down...
I'm in need of beginning.

Barbara Wallace-Albu

"One In Loving Spirit"

Many messages
   We continue to receive;
To draw us near;
   And in God and Jesus believe!

They desire
   Our willing, humble return;
To make us Theirs;
   For us They toil, and yearn!

To be as one,
   Free of ways that make us grieve;
Glorify our God;
   Give honor and praise for all we receive.

Their spirit,
   Within us, helps us to learn;
Of Life's true ways,
   Which we must cease to spurn!

We sing songs;
   Of glory and honor, in a hymn;
Expressing desires,
   To be one, united with Them!

Janet M. Knodel

Renewal

Under irritating beams of light
I would like to cast off
the troubled adds and ends of my body
and stand in the light beyond
and wait for the burning sun
to warm me up again.

In vain, death with its moldy face, grinning,
lurks upon me from its lurid window,
the ardor of spring will burn it up,
the fire of summer will consume it.

Come, ray of sun, closer and closer,
all the way to my bed
come like a lover,
come kiss me
and I will kiss you back
to burn with you forever.

Agnes V. Furst

"July Jubilees" — Acrostic Sonnet

Dedication Poem — To Elfriede and Donald

Enchantingly decrees portray magnificence enamoring magnetic
   tranquil royal lures —
Luxuriantly illustrating altruistic chivalries innately
philanthropic
   loyal pures —
Fascinations interchanging loneliness alliance comfort genuinely
   virtuously cures —
Regal splendored evenings congenial idyllic visions linking special
   moments flown —
Imparting grateful tenderness nobilities prophetic winds sublimely
   generously blown —
Ecstasies fulfilling years while nurturing entwining hearts prove
   beautifully grown —
Devotedly where trusting vows rhyme balancing connecting floating
   permeating middles —
Elevated breezes lilting elegant perfuming fragrance marveling
   nocturnal epic riddles.

Declarations eloquently manifesting covenants proclaiming cherished
   valued health —
Odysseys proceeding routes contributing prolific ardent sanctuaried
   chosen wealth —
Nestling souls safeguarding troves resplendently enchant perfection
   magics learned —
Authentical dramatic lives profoundly sharing venerative grandeured
   haloes yearned —
Lustering auroras glowing picturesquely rapturing divinely charming
   blissful bonnet —
Destinies symmetrical aligning special lullabies transcending chimed
   acrostic sonnet.

    Gilbert Belmont Withers

Life Changes Things

As life goes on, people and things they change
Ever since I left for college, nothing's stayed the same

I didn't know what to expect when I first arrived at school
Initially, I felt like I was an ignorant fool

I knew only two people in this whole new world of mine
(Of course I'd meet many more in just a little time)

These first days reminded me of a time thirteen years before
That was when I first embarked upon kindergarten's door

It may seem odd, but it is really quite true
That the amount of people I knew then also happened to be two

So as I went through my first year away from the place that I knew best
I realized some things and pondered them in my chest

While I was out meeting new people and playing new games
The place that I knew best had still remained the same

At first I thought different, I thought home was a new place
But then I discovered, no, it's me who has a different face

I am not the same person that I was just a year ago
Although my body's here, my heart is not, I wonder if it shows

    Máya Camiá Sullivan

Life

   Life is like a wolf turning his back to the cold rain, he'll
Never know what is going to happen, or if he'll be safe again.
   Life can tear your family apart, just as the wolf lost his
to the storm, and all he can do is feel the pain.
   If the rain clears up, the wolf will go on with his life,
just as I'll go on with mine. But for the wolf and me, there
will always be something missing, in our heart, and I guess we'll
have to just keep wishing, that someday the rain will pass by.

    Billie Ann Bradley

"Love Is"

Love is strong - because it
   stands up to any situation.
This is the time you really see
   your love's evaluation.

Love is soft - because it whispers
   soft tones to your heart strings.
To say, "I love you" means a lot,
   when you know the happiness it brings.

Love is tender - because it shows
   compassion for one another.
What God hath joined together
   let not man put asunder.

Love is kind - like a rose.
   that spreads her fragrance in a gentle breeze.
A little calm in the midst of a storm,
   will set your heart at ease.

Love is sharing - and shows you care,
   when things go wrong.
It mends the broken places
   and puts within your heart, a new song.

    Jeanne E. Helm

Mother Of God

The mother of God was great with child;
While she carried our Saviour so meek and mild;
A woman of virtue never knew a man;
Until after giving birth by Jehovah's plan;

Conceived by the Holy Spirit in the seed of a woman;
Jesus was both God and man as he trod the land;
Son of a carpenter, prophet, priest and King of kings;
Because Jesus is God who created everything;

In the book of life Mary's name is written down;
And she, like us, will one day wear a crown;
Redeemed up in heaven so bright and fair;
Saints, the righteous people will meet up there;

It will be one great family, the nations of the earth;
Who accepted Christ's righteousness, the new birth;
Given freely to all who on the Saviour call;
Our mediator and advocate now in the judgment hall;

He loves you very much;
Will you please get in touch;
He is waiting up there;
To hear a sinner's prayer.

    Bernice Hooks

Time

A showdown of sorrow over powers thy soul.
   No longer tormented by fear, of you've grown
so used to it.
   You walk the streets alone, but only in your heart.
   You cry out for help, but you're the only
one who hears the scream.
   You feels as if you've returned to the past
you long to forget.
They say they understand but do they
   really hear you?
You stare and wonder why you can't be needed.
Is that it or is it just that nobody wants you.
Maybe both, or none?
   You blink away the tears and try to hide,
sadly it only grows stronger with time.
As your soul grows weaker.

    Michelle Smith

"Springtime Flowers"

Ah, the springtime flowers
Come to life with April showers
Dreams of tulips and daffodils
As I slowly climb the hill
Through the garden gate
Where the flowers wait
I come to see them in April and May
They glimmer in the sun's rays
Oh, what a beautiful sight
The flowers and the bees unite
Through the garden I wonder
From the sky comes the thunder
The rain begins to fall
The birds stop their call
Through the rain I make my way
Back down the hill towards the bay
I know I'll return some other day

Arthur Blank

Remembering

I was the only one
She recognized.
Old and frail,
She lay there,
Unaware of her surroundings.
Her tiny wrinkled hand reaching
Out to grab anything.
Reaching out to grab
A heart, a soul, a hand.
Alzheimer's had taken over her life.
It had taken over everyone's life.
Especially the twelve year old
Granddaughter.
I was that granddaughter,
"The baby,"
The one who
Endured the most,
For I was the only one
She recognized.
The only one.

Meredith Hillyer

The Temple

A beautiful edifice stands serene
Our temple can be seen,
As one enters the sanctuary
   there is a sight to behold
Stained glass windows standing
   tall and bold.
At sun up one can see the light
   come pouring in
And lo! one knows that God is
   within
But on Saturday morning it is
   sad to say
Very few people arrive to bless
   this Sabbath day
And to thank the dear Lord for
   all He's done.
So — forget all your grievances
Let all gripes cease,
Come to the temple and pray for peace.

Viola Campli

A Beautiful Land

When I left my country
it was not yesterday
but long ago when I decided
to start my journey far away.

Across the sea I travelled
I followed a dear person always
to find a new promised land
and I decided to stay.

This land became my country
and I'll never move away
a beautiful friendly place
to live in a peaceful way.

Assunta Mary Gava

In Trust

I've learned to trust.
In family and friends.

I've learned to trust.
My heart and soul.

Through faith with hope;
I've learned the best of all,

Has to come to trust;
The spirit of truth, through one and all

GH

Phenomena

I thrill at phenomenal life;
   I'm nature's most curious child,
But, it's not man's industrial strife
   That rouses my imagery wild.

The science of being to me
   Defies emulation by man;
The tiniest twig on a tree
   Drops genius to just "also-ran".

Louis F. Conca Jr.

The Cleft Of The Rock...Ex.33:22

Forgive me Lord, when my courage fails
And at times You seem far away;
The fault is mine, and only mine,
Because I have gone astray.

So I thank You Lord, my steadfast Rock
So eternal and so true,
For the cleft You make to shelter me
From fears that within me brew.
I thank You Lord, my steadfast Rock
Standing eternally,
For Your loving hand that holds me fast
In that cleft You have made for me.

Margaret Plenk

Snow Of Roses

Snow falls softly on the mountain
Bringing forth a gleaming fountain
The mountain echoes forth a great quiet
A hermit lives there on a herbal diet
He has his sweet dreams for friends
So lovely he hopes night never ends
He writes his rosy poetry that rhymes
He lives there out of step with his times

Michael Murphy

Another

Memories only of the time we spent
Together, apart, everywhere we went
Sadness, happiness and tears of joy

Another wind's stronger it must be
it's able to take you away from me
You feel happiness and no pain.

While I wait here for you today
Longer hours pass with each day
A few more months pass me by

All the love was in our hearts
Too many things kept us apart
You found another to take my place

Another to be close and true
Will it be the same for me and you
Times the healer of my heart

Theresa Harris

Untitled

Mastermind at ignorance
Couldn't see it coming
Faster find a moon dance
Wouldn't stop the drumming
Beating faster found the find
Feigning fast finding found
Feating master ground to mind
Reigning past minding bound
Fateful patience all but mine
Past the interest at the sign
Brown to black blast the line
Starched and stiffened fates align.

Cynthia J. Boucher

To My Wife
On Our 50th Wedding Anniversary

Finding a perfect Wife
was my greatest wish
Knew it came true
When we had our first kiss.

We were wed on a cold and windy day.
It would last forever I did pray.
You gave me three girls and a boy
They gave us a few gray hairs,
but were always a joy!

The grandchildren they gave us
were a bakers dozen
now everywhere you look
you see kissing cousins.

These 50 years have been perfect
which no one can deny
and I shall Love you, Sug
until the day I die.

Robert Bomson

To D...

When you kiss
me

It is like you
are kissing
my heart-

- It stops beating.

Hrafn A. Hardarson

Pillars Of Nature

So sensei I said
"The waves come and go
    The ocean remains"

And so leaves and buds
    once in bloom
        wither away
            The tree remains

Moonlights glow
    and the sun is born
        over and over again
            The sky remains

And my love
    as the ocean
        the tree
            the sky
    My love remains
        Yours forever

Marie-Paule Thorn

The Survivor

Why it was the way it was...
I'll never know more than 'twas.
My only guess it was because!
His madness made him stop and pause.

Somehow I found just the strength...
To endure the years full length,
The madness of his abuse...
And the horrors of his use.

From brutal beatings of the past...
Are the scars that will forever last.
From the horrors of all the use...
To never be the same is not an excuse.

Just a chance was all I asked...
For my freedom just to bask.
Stepping out from behind the mask...
A new me I did dare cast.

Not only did I break the chains...
I also removed all the pain.
I over came and even changed...
Now me and mine will not hang!

Sheila Johnson

Untitled

We are friends forever
in a fashion of a matter.
Together we can do what
ever we want to.

Friends forever
in every little snitch and snatch.
And we can pull through
little fights and stuff.

We love to dance and sing.
We can do about anything.
We'll be together till the end of time,
but that won't stop us from singing
this rhyme.

Emily Sargo

Deep End

'Tis True!...
    I'll admit.
        Awareness, is bliss!

        —oh yeah...

The price of this,
    To Understand Love's passion
        and Her intimate demands!
For, failure to grasp
    up the size a the task —
        Marks evolution,
            towar' devolution!

A kiss O' the abyss,
    Bring depth to surface.
Still...if to miss,
    will Sing Death's curses, until...

Even better though,
    Is the Soulful Watching Eye.
    So full,
        And endless as the sky!

Shawn Hoffman

How I Feel

Your hair is life long strands of gold,
glistening in the sun.
Your voice is like the sparrow's song,
a soft and tender one.
Your eyes are like the mighty ocean,
deep and bright as day.
But around you I just turn to stone,
and hopelessly crumble away.
The prettiest sunset seen on earth,
is nothing next to you.
Angels sometimes visit us,
you must be of these few.
And if you ever leave my life,
I know I'd surely die.
The reason that I feel this way,
Is love, yes that is why.

Chris Howey

Sold

Idols demand their due,
blind in turn we wander through.
Silent sadness the look directed,
hidden means seldom detected.
Wanting each of life's reward,
helpless, harmless moving forward.
Guilty, sentenced, prison term;
have yet to find a ground that's firm.
Gods to fashion, gods to fail,
torn and tattered along the trail.
Eyes sorely bend.
A truth.
Focus pain of what we are;
Idols demand their due.

Mark R. Dunson

Never

Never will I feel the way you do.
Never will I see your light.
Never will I be who you want me to be.
Never will it end.
The Journey will end and then begin.
I will never learn to love another.
Never will my head stop hurting
Never will I sleep again.

John Perry IV

And Time Will Run Back

And time will run back
To fetch the age of gold,
The good times, the bad times,
The memories we hold

And the memories we'll treasure
In all the years to come,
We don't know where we're going
But we know where we're from.

Jacalyn Burns

Red Rose

Once I saw a red, red rose.
I could smell the fragrance in my nose.
It was as beautiful as could be.
As I stared at it, I could not see.
It was so very bright,
It was like the morning's light.
And now in the grass it remains,
It will always stay the same.

Jennifer E. Trent

"Woody"

Woodrow's dead and the cat is gone
And I'm in Arkansas all alone
In some hotel off interstate
Nothing here to do but wait

Suddenly I'm very cold
One more tale of life's been told
My mind's so full, my heart so sad
I'm a little touched, nee a little mad

Woody, you just left too soon
A little man who danced in tune
In your little town you lived and died
A little man with a heart so wide

In that big house where you were born
And your children after you would come
Without complaint, you suffered so
Exchanging blood that would not flow

Borrowed time was all you had
I wanted to sit once more, so bad
And chat with you about all my kin
But here I am, alone again.

Glenda Stone

Hope For The Future

War is now upon us
The time has come once again
When will it stop?
When will it end?

The endless killing of innocence
The destruction of the earth
A horrendous look at war
Again the inevitable re-birth

The guns, tanks, and bombs
The coldness in the air
The blackness filling the earth
Why doesn't anybody care?

I hope one day we'll see
Again the clear, bright blue sky
But until that day
We may all just foolishly die

Brenda Hemmerich

"She's Gone"

Never to hear her voice
Never to see her face
Never to see her smile
Why? She's gone.

Never to feel her touch
Never to fee her good
Night kiss. Why? She's gone.

She's not next door,
Or gone to the store.
Why? She's gone.

She is gone home to be
With the Lord, yes she
is gone, she is not alone.

Venus Roberson

The Rivers Bank

I walk by the rivers bank
Throw a pebble into the water
See the splash-and like a flash
It's gone

I walk by the rivers bank
Take a look into the water
I can see how much I've changed
Time is gone

I walk by the rivers bank
Tears drop into the soft water
I can hardly recognize myself
I'm gone

I walk by the rivers bank
To see if I can still remember
All I've done in my life
Before it's gone

Ted Ebersole

Canada's Treasures

Laying in the summer breeze
Among the flowers and the trees
Rocking in Mother Nature's hand
In this beautiful Manitoba land

Watching the squirrels as they play
Listening to the birds sing all day
Thinking of every wonderful thing
This great land has to bring

Spring, Summer, Winter, Fall
These are the season, I love them all
Flowers, snowflakes, leaves and sun
These are things I find fun

Prairies, Mountains, Arctic and Sea
These are some places her you'll see
Buffalo, goat, wolf and seal
Beautiful animals that appeal

Manitoba, Ontario, The Yukon and B.C.
Wondrous places in Canada you'll see
Quebec, Alberta and the Maritimes
Happy memories for all times.

Barbara Marzoff

A Secret Place

There's a place I sometimes go
A secret place which no one knows
There I drift without a care
A state of mind beyond compare.

Scents of Jasmine in the air
Visions of colors soft and rare
The breeze is gentle like your touch
I like this place so very much.

In this world so full of despair
A shallow world, where no one cares
Where voices shout of things unfair
If love is found it's very rare.

The smells of toxic air we breathe
The colors drab and very bleak
This place where people always rush
No chance for love to ever touch.

This place for me is way too much
If I don't leave, I'll soon be crushed
I'll close my eyes and soon I'm there
A secret place which no one knows.

Margo S. Burgois

"Help!"

We climb a tree and scrape our
knee the blood will give us signs.
It will show us not to fear of
death but to know that we are dying.
We walk around being selfish
thinking of only money and gold.
We'll do anything to get it even
chop down a tree that's old.
I hear a cry of "help" when I
think of all this stuff.
Like people cutting trees down, then
think that they are tough.
But it only shows a weakness
about how they care about the
earth, when I hear this cry of
"Help" I think of what this world is worth!

Jessica Swanzy

The River

As I sat and watched the river,
flow down into the sea;
it bumped into the stones,
the fish jumped with glee.

A peaceful kind of solitude,
in this place, I was alone,
as I watched the speckled ones
playing by the stones.

A tin can came down a-bobbing,
clicking on the rocks.
On the side was a message,
please, forget me not.

As I picked it from the water
and shook the water out,
I headed straight for Grandma,
to tell of what the river brought.

Her eyes shone with laughter,
as she turned around the can,
for, now I knew the message
was written, by her hand.

Marjorie Peters (McIntosh)

Dreams

As I lay in my bed looking at
the wall,
Slowly my eyelids droop and
then close.
Clang! Goes the cymbals, loud
and clear.
Sweet dreams fight the bad
and lo!
Sweet dreams win, chasing
away the bad.
Suddenly I'm walking in the
clouds,
So high, so soft, so lovely.
Oh no, thererowing paler!
Brr! Goes the alarm clock!
Pop! Go my eyes!
Shatter! Go the dreams,
and here come the daydreams.

Sarah E. Mellen

Girls In White Dresses

God covered his eyes
Pretending not to see
The exposed back seat,
The mixture of sweat
And black leather upholstery

Innocence was destroyed
Before fingers had a chance
To part and take a peek,
Unaware of her treasure,
As cramped legs press

Against a steam-streaked window
Something sacred to protect,
Casually tossed out the window
Like a crushed cigarette butt
As church bells clang in her head:

An incessant reminder
That punishment is severe
As are the cries in the still of night
When all girls in white dresses
Stare at the silent, grinning moon

Sarah Furtek

Temptations

My thoughts wander nomadically
grasping for bits of truth
Visions force my mind a malady
as time robs me of my youth

Inhibitions forsake me today
abandoning me to vulnerability
covetousness intrudes upon me
replacing my spirituality

I succumb to visions of fantasy
excluding from consciousness my fears
I crave the sensations of ecstasy
while abiding in the midst of tears

I search for an answer to heal
that which is broken and odd
only a receptive heart can feel
the emanating love of God

Debbie E. Henry

Our Great Country

Hello out there America
The land I love so well
I'm proud to be a part of you
And on your soil, to dwell.

I love your hills and valleys,
Your sparkling waters too
Your fresh air, and your sunshine,
And your sky of azure blue.

Some try to mar your beauty,
While others your beauty admire.
You offer us many great wonders,
Anything a heart might desire.

I've often wondered how
Betsy Ross felt
As she made our red, white, and blue.
I'll bet her heart was just
Bursting with pride
For she knew it would represent you.

Ethel Hand Perry

Difference

Difference what does it mean?
   Why must we judge it?
   Why must we make it pain?
   Why must we keep it inside?
   Why must we take it in vain?
   Why must we make up names?
   Why can't we look beyond it?
   Why can't we look inside?
   Why can't we be proud of it?
   Why can't we take it for pride?
Difference what does it mean?

Anne Crocker

My Time

Do the things you want to do,
Spend your time this way.
Walk the paths you've wanted to,
It's up to you to say;
My life is mine
And precious few
The hours I have known,
That I had under my control,
No wonder I have grown,
To jealously regard my time
As moments all my own.

Dorothy Hale

Dreams And Wishes

Lie on backs in open air,
Count the satellites, away up there.
Summers night, star-lit skies,
Dreams, and wishes in our eyes.

Falling stars magnificence,
Crickets, frogs song in the distance.
Hearts awake, beat so alive,
Dreams, and wishes, in our eyes.

Bodies snuggled, deep in bags
After hide-n-seek, and tag...
Play, and laughter, voices high,
Now dreams and wishes, in our eyes.

Brother, sister, cousins then,
Under starry starry heav'n...
Before the dawn, with wonders sigh,
Dreams and wishes, behind closed eyes.

Jerrie L. Hall

Untitled

Birds sing at dawn,
the north winds blow.

The rain brings forth fine flowers,
in the dawn's sweet morning hue.

I lean forth and find a breath,
of fine fresh air.

Then my mind wonders back to you.
You are my breath,
my soul is with you.

I can try as I may,
to find the words to say,
I love you both with every fine
breath this dawn brings.

Then I realize as you sleep,
snug and warm in your beds,
just how rich I am to share
in your lives and to have
been given you.

Love,
Mother

Paula M. Jackson

Facile Enmity

Her heart, her mind, her very soul
regrets her torrent frenzy.
At times she wishes she would not be
to spill that worthless agony
on those she causes pain.
She cries, she prays repentingly,
but it is all in vain.
Deep down she knows that she herself
is her own true enemy.
If only she could control
her unwanted, facile enmity,
for it has made her pay a toll
forever and incessantly.
Her soul sinks slowly down the hole
always more irretrievably.
Oh yes! She has surely paid the price
for her noxious orifice.
She could only now be proud
when she is wrapped within her shroud.

Katherine Tessier

A Time To Rest

Across the sky I will fly
Above white clouds so very high
Upon lightning he will soar
Over the never ending moor
From a darkened valley I will strike
Down the hill into the night
Into his heart my sword will fly
Under the moon he shall die
Before his death I hear him cry
Begging, begging while he lie
In weak breath I hear him say
As he cry in loathsome display
"I am the last come take my soul"
In a tone so weak and so very droll
By his tears my eyes turn red
For all of those so long dead
Across his throat my blade then lay
Not to be used another day
A time to rest for all adrift
In vengeance they say anger is a gift

Joseph Chapman

Thank You

Thank You sounded my heart,
A little word expressing my soul.
Wonderful utterance giving joy and
Gladness to blessed One.

Tik...Tak...Tik...Tak... time goes by,
The beauty of life that never saw.
Enjoying the creation which everything
Made possible for life.

Forgetting a person,
Who blooms my very heart.
Someday, somehow I might
Thank Him.

Time is still here
Not the end of a period to change
A tune of melody came out,
Saying "Thank You my God, Thank You."

Marlynne Lourdes B. Mallari

Life

Life moves faster each day
if only we knew how short
Life really is maybe we
world stop and smell
the flowers more often.

Before we realize it the
person we cared so much
about is gone. All
we really have left is memories.

All that time we took it
for granted not realizing
what we had was so
important 'til we lose it.

We really should have
cherished each moment,
for no one knows when
life is gone, we can
never bring it back we
can only cherish it in
our hearts and souls for eternity.

Colleen M. Koceja

Forever Friends

Friends are forever we always
seem to care.
When we come together we always
like to share.
Friends share their good times,
problems, feelings, and fears,
and they're always there for us
when we break out in tears.
We're all one big family.
We call each other names,
but everyone knows that we're just
playing games.
Since we are the five of best friends.
you'll be able to see.
we'll always be able to find the
magic key.
We come hand in hand for
whatever we need,
all we need is for our friends to
make our life succeed.

Stephanie Erieg

Don't Know What To Do?

The Crying,
The Dying,
The Lying,
not to know which is true.
Always wondering what to do?
Ask the Questions,
get no answers,
And still don't know what to do.
I do it right,
plus do it wrong.
Trying new things,
learning right from wrong.
The past shows me to the future.
Leading the way,
See the guiding light,
but turn the other way.
It feels right, then wrong.
I guess that's why I'm confused
and I don't know what to do.

Brandy Marie Serin

Purple

Purple is a royal color
bright and jolly the color of
grapes, the color of the ink
in my purple pen flowers
on trees and places I've
been Purple popsicles
grape juice stains, the
color of the grocery store
lanes, the purple in the
night sky and the
tropical birds flying high.

Kimberly Martinez

"Un Known"

Who makes us laugh?
Who makes us cry?
I don't know why.
But when I think of fame,
I hear he calls my name,
He doesn't talk,
He doesn't show up,
I just listen to his laugh,
And when I go to sleep,
I see him in my dream.
I looked around the world,
I still didn't find him,
When I look deep inside my heart,
I notice his handsome face,
And there he is locked up with my lace.
He gets sentimental,
If I don't talk to him,
Who makes us laugh?
Who makes us cry?
I don't know why.

Anwara Khatun

What Is Me Without You?

What is a match without a light?
What is a voice without a song?
What are eyes without a sight?
What can be right without wrong?
What can be joy without some pain?
What can be loss without some gain?
What is me without you?

Lauren Hammett

Expansion - Explosion

I see them creeping, every town
and village, flowing, spreading.
Up hill and down.

They once were joined by country road
and held apart, distinct -
but now they crowd.

Obese and bursting, grossly full,
town holds out hand to town
and muscles pull.

Acquisitive for more and more
houses, shops and schools,
hotel and store.

Now country lanes forever shrink
as town holds hand with town
without a link.

Muriel Reed

Mother

My girl, don't lie
Why did you leave last night
Is it because of my temper
Is it because of that terrible fight

You left without a sound
Gone without a peep
Without you by my side
It's hard for me to sleep

You left me for my friend
You left me for my brother
Our children are so sad
They ask, "Where is our mother?"

Now you're gone, don't return
Don't try to mend their pain
You will just hurt them again
Have fun with your cocaine

Ross Mooney

Only The Truth

True science never has limits,
True passion has no bounds;
Only truth, has no gimmicks,
Only silence, has no sounds.
True nature never has killers,
True lies just can't be heard;
Only wars, have only losers,
Only opinion defines a word.
True beauty, cannot be drawn,
True effort, need no retakes;
Only dead, is just too far gone,
Only Gods, make no mistakes.
True friendship is truly forever,
True kindness cannot be made;
Only the truth can fail us never,
Only true love, can never fade.

Ron J. Dalueg

Lateral Drift

A poet is lost within a troubled mind
And those for whom roses are red
Know all they were told
And wish to tell it to you
But do not listen with vision
Just memorize
That violets are blue
Poetic erosion has begun

Joseph A. Phelan

Heaven

Your up there, I'm down here
I miss the smell of your clothes,
the touch of your hand, the glare
of your eyes, and most of all the love
of your smile.

Every time I bend my knees,
I pray to the Lord you can see,
something that reminds you of me.

I lie in bed and weep at night,
hoping you haven't gone into the
light, but deep inside, I know,
you've become the light.

Cherrie O'Dell

Aftermath

Today the streets of my heart
  Are the empty streets of a town
Where the singers of songs are stilled
  And the last lights flickers down

For the carnival night is past.
  And the dawn is breaking gray.
Now the mummers, stumbling home
  Have tossed their masks away

Lonely I wander the streets
  Under a weeping sky
For my King of Hearts forever sleeps
  And nobody's Queen am I!

Clara D. Ward

Two Of Us

The sky is gray
The sun can't get through
My mind is busy
Thinking of you

How are you doing?
In your busy way
Always on the run
Racing through the day

On the road
On the phone
Is your way of life
Spending time alone

I would like to be your companion
As you journey on your way
Being your friend and lover
Making it happen, everyday

We have so much common
It would be a shame
For us not to be together
Thinking and doing, one and the same

Derald Stone

Summer

Birds nest
The eggs hatch
Birds fly
Summer

Bradley Maw

Life

My life is a destiny,
A path of reality.
I walk in the fire
That burns within my soul.
When the flame goes out
And the smoke casts
Shadows on my past,
I will look back,
And realize that I was only
Living in death.

Stephanie Thanase

My Monster

He's horrible, yucky,
  Mean and green.
He's the ugliest thing
That you've ever seen.
He's gross, disgusting,
  Crude and rude.
The sound that he makes
  Is moo, moo, moo.
He's weird and sweaty
And covered with fur.
I'm not too proud of it —
But he's my brother.

Jessica Hermann

Clever Breath

Along the fervent beaches of
deft dialect,
Walk pens and toes combing
shimmering sands,

Some drink the day
Others nestle the night

We spend our warmth to
garner glory,
We sweep her floors for
reaping riches,

Some delve the depths
Others scour the surface

Quest to the end to sail
sinuous skies
Master the minds of teal
turbulent tides
Tie the loose laces of frail
forlorn faces

And with this new face
Sense the beautiful places

Andrew Hoffman

I Tried

My life was meant to be doomed
  so when will it happen?
All I ever do is F. (mess) up
  I wish I could say goodbye
I do wanna be somebody
  but all I do is lie
Where is this screwed up life going?
  Am I going to die?
I will see the future soon
  and will probably cry
For all I want to do is sleep...
And never have to say.

Paula P. Manard

Poverty's Special Touch

Only they who feel it, know it:
The lean world in a grain of sand,
The cancerous hate, the angry touch
Of poverty's intimate hand.

Only they who see it, know it:
The sad state of a face that cries,
The tortured hopes, the lifeless look
Of poverty's intimate eyes.

Only they who get it, know it:
The sometimes desperate lonesome quest,
The mocking laugh, the burning pain
Of poverty's intimate breast.

Only they who think it, know it:
The cruel world of war, so blind;
The passionless dreams and shadows
Of poverty's intimate mind.

Only they who know it, feel it:
The rich world in a grain of sand;
The peace and love and beauty
Of poverty's intimate hand.

Al Harris

An Embarrassing Moment

The audience was all seated
The orchestra's in the pit
It's curtain time, the show must start,
I'm about to have a fit.

The MC announced my number
As on the stage I glide
I opened my mouth to start my song,
And my drawers began to slide.

With both my hands I grabbed my waist
And started in to dance,
I didn't want the audience
See me lose my pants.

Well, they were none the wiser
As I finished up my dance,
And glided off into the wings
To hope for another chance.

Pauline E. Franklin

Condemned

I can't sleep tonight
Big rings under my eyes
The slight dripping of the tap
Sounds like the slight dripping
Of my sanity
Worries overwhelm my throbbing head
Everything seams too complex
I rake my hair with the filthy sering's
Why I'm I trapped
In a hell which I've created?
Chapped lips
Week old stubble
It all reeks
Reeks of disappointment
Mother is convinced that
I'm a failure
May be I am...
Though, I live in my own world now
Where, no one can come in
And, I can't get out

Jennefer Jenei

Thoughts Dreams

Fond thoughts are these,
Yet heard but once only;
To fill this heart
Once tired, left out, so lonely.

The warmth of your voice,
Unknown, yet gently spoken;
Lends solace, a comfort
To this soul, a love's token.

Now thoughts become dreams,
And in them I feel oft'ly;
A touch, an embrace,
A kiss given softly.

Oh dream never end,
Nor from sleep awaken;
Til my Soul and Spirit,
Into your arms are taken.

Mark Agnew

Good Intentions

Spread yourself
dandelion
yellow my lawn
Butter color butter flower
shower yourself
flower my lawn

Neighbors abhor
your galore
Children
gather in rays
my lawn of youthful bouquets
rape my lawn

Overnight wither
fold up close up
ugly my lawn
Thistle sprout no doubt
fledgling windy flight
seed my lawn

My lawn—gone.

Joy Flugge

The Evening Prayer

The old man knelt and bowed his head,
As he said his evening prayer,
His thoughts were of his departed wife,
And the years of love they'd shared.

Visions of the past appeared,
Floating across his mind,
Conjuring up happy memories,
But little comfort could he find.

He longed to feel her gentle touch,
At the closing of the day,
A last embrace, a tender kiss,
Had always been their way.

A tear flowed from his misty eyes,
And trickled down his cheek,
He brushed it aside, crawled into bed,
To seek solace in his sleep.

William C. Ott

Rage

Your darkness infested me;
My pale light was cluttered with hate,
A hate for all.
A hate of rage and vengeance,
Sparing no race or color.
Your blood on my hands,
On my sword,
Gives me a temporary sanity,
My now distorted mind feels focused.
Your death is my life,
My sanity and escape.
A happiness otherwise not achieved.
You were so precious.

William Ryan Cooper

"Self"

Laughter and tears are life's lessons.
Experience is gained from such.
One cannot receive it from another
nor can it be given away.
Each soul has a learning path
totally personal in its plight.
There is no right or wrong way,
the only teacher is one's self.
One cannot blame another
for choices made that have gone wrong.
The "wrong" was "right" for learning
the "thou shalt not" lessons in life.
No matter what faith one follows
to seek the "truth" in life,
There is no greater truth to follow
than the one's God cast in stone.
The path one chooses to follow
is a choice that comes from within.
No other "truth" can ever be trusted,
Like the one's we find in "Self."

Louise E. Bjorn

This Silent Silence

Sitting, Silently,
   inside my Silent room
More Silence is yet to come
   it will be here soon
Greeting me in Silence
   has been your best defeat
I tell you this in Silence
   Upon these Silent sheets
Silence steals the time
   that words are meant to take
Swallows promises
   that are made
But later found to break
   Now silence will continue
As Silence always will
   Believing all that is silent
In this Silent state of still...

Stacey Fowler

Whispers

Tickle through your ears
telling things you like to hear.
Whispers
are as soft as skin
letting little words curl in.
Whispers
come so they can blow
secrets others never know.

Candace Leigh Linyard

The Information By-Way

Passing time with restless mind
You type upon the 'board.
Click and read, find and feed
Sites across the world.

Hours are spent, reality bent
Scouring for the truth.
Find the blue, click it too
Your aims remain aloof.

It's all the rage, create a page
Bookmarks for your dreams.
Read the mind, put it on line
For others, through their screen.

Check the clock, and get a shock
Your time limit has waned.
Exit's a snap, the screen goes black
But what did you obtain?

Luke Frohling

"The Question"

If I were to be
from me
philosophically
to turn Animal,
would I grow to be
or reduce from me
to be
Animal?

Joshua Liberty Sundance Steele

Untitled

Woke up from my dreams
   Not with laughter but screams
My past went fast, my
   Future too slow, I'm happy now
But want to be laid low
   My heart begs and pleads but
No one has been there feels
   Like no one ever cares. My heart
And soul has been broken and
   Laid wide, all I want is someone
To be by my side, as my journey
   Continues for love and devotion
All I can offer is sweet emotion.

Randy Hermreck

Untitled

Twenty lines
Squeezed from the sea of words
—The strange dialects
Laughter, tears,
Screams of fear
Filled my soul,
Leaped to the sun,
Fell like rain
Through all the earth
My always joy
In knowing to say:
"Thank you, I love you,
Bless you."

John L. Speckner

Untitled

We come as strangers
   to this land
And God was guiding us
   with his hand
The winters were harsh
   and the cupboards bare
But in times of greatly stress
   the Indians were there.

And so we have travelled
   through depressions and wars
Raising our families
   Doing the chores.
But now things are moving
   With 'cyberspace' here
Will we get to hold on
   to the things we hold dear?

Irvin Grossmän

Cardinal

You are the cardinal
among the blues jays
You stand out, quietly
though boldly

Oh, they bring attention
to themselves
cackling in groups
fighting for their stand
proud to belong

You, you're different
the harder you try to fit in
the more awkward you appear
untrue to the real you
but when You let your difference shine
and take flight, your personal journey
you too shall be noticed
for you

You are the cardinal
be proud of You

Mary Oster Pollier

In Retrospect

A deserted beach.
Sun-warm sand firm beneath my feet
as I bent to reach
out a hesitant hand to meet
one cold wave before its retreat.

A wind-beaten lake.
Standing on smooth rock as the thought
of you made me break
into a smile I could not
then have known would not be forgot.

A memory now.
If possible I would suspend
those hours somehow
and as a gift to you would send
one final day to never end.

A difficult choice.
Should I now return to that place
would I hear your voice?
And could a smile still cross my face
though your footsteps I cannot trace?

Elaine Jauniaux

Sharing And Caring

Many thanks go out for your empathy,
By putting yourselves in our place,
People will help, but must be asked,
We do not expect sympathy.
Special people instinctively know,
The needs of us in distress,
Pity breeds negative thinking,
Positive thoughts are best.
We need support of family and friends,
For someday you may be as I,
So share and care as best you can,
If you cannot we understand,
you've touched my life with tenderness,
God sent you, so thee I bless.
While walking down life's pathway,
Do as the volunteers do,
Give a little time,
A small piece of you.

Audrey Major

Cameron's Creed

Listening..., not talking.
Helping ...., not harming.
Showing a stranger the way.

Giving..., not getting.
Loving..., not hating.
What am I trying to say?

Kindness and caring,
Respect and sharing,
Will help you along the way.

Cameron and Sandra Newbigging

Someone On Wanted Love

Pressures are too much
Pressure are to fear
When God brings a blessing
of life unto this earth.
Pressures are not fear.
Just grip the hand of hope
Then the pressure that you fear,
Will never hurt you as long
as you have someone that cares.

Knowing the pressure you feel.
Wanting to love the life inside.
Waiting for the time to
touch the joys in life.

Knowing that the pressure and
the fear will hurt you.
Trying to see pass that.
Finding there is someone
that wanted to be loved inside.

Kimberly A. Wallace

Storm

Torrents tear with craven grasp
my trembling outstretched arm
from the comfort of tender flesh
drifting into dreams of eyes,
and locks and quiet breaths
icy drops to batter my broken panes
stranger, passing through your nights
I stand defiant in the gale,
mute, upward gaze to drink
you in, bravest of girls,
and escape with a frozen smile.

Chris Gordon

It's Me

Look in the mirror
What do you see
Not a super star
Or a beauty queen
Just you or me
If you don't like it then leave
Cause I like what I see
It's me
There's no way I can change that
Who cares if I'm a little fat
I see it's me
No one has to tell me what I look like
I see my self alright
It's me
So I wouldn't want to change a thing
It's me...

Bridget Maria Greenwald

Forever

Forever it seemed
The light gone from his eyes
The warmth from his lips
Anxiously she awaited the answer
That lied on the lap of the Gods
And then she felt it
At first a light caress
Then escalating into a full
Thunderous blow
And she was swept away

Jena Hencin

Untitled

Living once a little girl
Given always plenty of distance
Unshared self alone and private
Lunching never with others

Seeing clear her life
Yearning still for a truth
Realized too as beyond in time
Solicitous tear through blue eyes dying

Dodging screams with clenching fists
Creeping safe through pale confines
Lonely grace from jealous darkness
Resting sodden by the mouth

Nearly over idle journey
Retarded movement from the source
Mourning past in secret sorrow
Little girl, my mother
Little girl, myself

Stacey Arthur

She Comes At Night

She comes at night when I'm sleep
And looks at me, just looks at me.
In wild delight I try to keep
Her there with me, in bed with me.

But then I wake and she is gone
I stay awake until the dawn.
Then pass the day impatiently
Awaiting night and sleep so she
can come again to look at me
My blinding, longing tears to see

She'll come one night just as before
But I'll not waken anymore.
Then I know she'll stay with me.
Then my love will stay with me.

Harry A. Sachaklian

Anza-Borrego Night

Beneath a full, April moon
Our shadows glide before us
Dark people of the earth
Made jagged by the ocotillo.
We breathe the fragrance of
A solitary red cactus bloom
As desert shapes rise up
Mysterious as a dream.
DANGER. HUSH.
MOUNTAIN LION TERRITORY.

Now across the purple bowl of night
Stars splash and toss about
The silent, rising moon...milk-white
As golden Venus of the western sky
Reflects.
Arms entwined, we freeze
Like hammered silver statues
And listen to the desert.
DANGER. HUSH.
MOUNTAIN LION TERRITORY.

Laura M. Audino

Rain

Rain
Falling from the sky
Rain
Water from heaven
Rain
Sharp, poking, needles
Rain
Natural cleanser
Rain
Drowning the world
Rain
Peaceful
Rain
Running inside
Rain
Wet, dreary
Rain
Dripping off my window
Rain

Jenny Crescuillo

A Smile

On this day, this sunny day
a challenge comes to mind,
for every frowning face I see
a smile I shall find.

So many people rarely think
what a simple smile can do
not only does it brighten ones day,
but it warms a heart all through.

No excuses needed
a frown just will not do
not only is a smile easy
but it's healthy for you too!

So walk by me and if a frown I see
I'll take it upon my self
to take that from right off your face
and put it high upon a shelf.

Vickie L. Dennis

For Joan, On Secretary's Day

I wish I could be more like you
You've got such a lovely soul
You would never harm a living thing
Not a tree not a mouse not a troll

Like a Norman Rockwell painting
Of a sophisticated lady
You carry yourself with dignity
Never pompous or mean or shady

An eccentric lass, some say of you
But that, I'll never say
You're just a little different
In a very special way

You're always there to talk to
When I need some good advice
Or to just provide a smile
From someone who's true and nice

I wish I could be more like you
Good deeds you do each day
You're the sweetest person I know
The sweetest in every way
        Francis Tate

The Scarecrow Walks At Midnight

The witch on her broomstick
     flying past the field.

The scarecrow on the stick
     watching the night grow dark.

The wolf on the hill
     howling at the moon,

The scarecrow will walk at midnight.

They'll all party until dawn and
     dance and sing; "This is Halloween,
     this is Halloween!!"
        Adam T. Hosteny

Just One Glass Of Wine

I never have to taste you
Or with you friendly be,
The misery you cause some folk
Is plain enough to see.

Your neon sign is tempting
Your path is often trod,
You know it is contrary
To the precious word of God.

Your ads are all misleading
While T.V. is warming up,
You try your very best to help
Some lad to fill his cup.

Look not upon the wine when red
Strange thoughts we all do think,
Each drink leads to another
One step closer to hell's brink.

If God can take and shake us
Before we get too much,
We will step upon the devil's toes
For Jesus has that touch.
        Emma Wagner

Flowers For February

Pieces left of a fence made long ago
I found,
And as I walked along
I thought
This aged old fence should not
Be lost.

Along came the Artist
With his book,
A sketch was made,
And then it took
A time to paint the colors rare.
Gold of daffodils to spare.
Old wood in gray
Lining knots of resin in decay.
Behind the stems and twigs
Of last years weeds
Was all it took to show
The beauty of a whim
That goes into a colored song.
        Lorene Foster

"Si jeunesse savait, si vieillesse pouvait!"

Awaiting now the distant call
I sit beside a shadowed Spring
the Summer-long but knowing well
that love so snugly set in new
environs will have no time for thoughts
of me. What childish levity
harasses old men's minds with hopes
of youth and age replenishing
the fallow land! And yet my mind
caught up in fancy falls into
a Winter's dream where constancy
the rule of law for fools becomes
the force that charts the course of mad
adventure. Like the architect
I draft the print with dreadful care
that love might keep remain in tact
and bloom again full-force in Fall.
        Bill McMinn

Mother's Day Prayer

Life is...
caring,
sharing,
working,
hurting,
tiring,
mothering,
helping,
and yelping everyday for...
caring,
sharing,
working,
hurting,
tiring,
mothering,
and yelping,
and there is only one
person I know that can
do all of this...you.
Happy Mother's Day.
        Katie Green

Untitled

My grandpa was like the northern light
Because he used to shimmer and shine
Exactly like the fair banks line.
But now that he has passed away
I think about him every day.
I remember him well with all my heart,
He always made me feel so smart.
Then one day his lights faded out.
And then I learned what death's about
        Elizabeth Mary McNicol

No More

No more fighting
No more pain
No more tears
No more shame

No more bruises
No more breaks
No more crying
No more hate

No more fists
No more kicks
No more slaps
No more hits

No more alcohol
No more beer
No more hitting
No more fear
        Melissa Napholc

Where Evil Lies

When night time shed its darkened cloak
Where evil lies and dreams are broke
Where loneliness you're soon to find
Where nightmares beat against the mind
This is my life, my favorite hell
Where all the demons know me well
I welcome you with open arms
Into a world that's never calm
A forgiving world I have not seen
Just pallid moons to ignore our screams
There is no sun, come see my night
Where there are dragons you must fight
No castles set upon the clouds
Only pits the darkness shrouds
No gallant knights in shiny coats
But rancid air to dry your throat
No more music shall you hear
Just the echoes of your fear
Come wrap yourself into my cloak
Where evil lies and dreams are broke
        Stac-E Hendon

100% Bull

The things that Bull's 91 does,
Are excusa-bull just because.
    To the reff he gave a hard butt,
He was of two hundred-thou cut.
    Rodman tells us his great excuse,
He's do better with more tattoos.
    He always leaves me in a daze,
When his hair's flared up in a blaze.
    His 'do is unpredicta-bull,
But really irresista-bull,
    And also contradicta-bull.
He's like-a-bull and always was,
    So does it matter what he does?
        Carla Urzua

Chronic And Addictive

A tear begins to fall,
Your dreams soon diminish,
All the misconceptions;
Will soon learn to finish.

Self-depreciation now magnified,
Lost in your Chronic thoughts.
Vulnerable and abandoned,
This episode is fought.

Your addiction is a killer,
And Chronic as it seems;
Try and begin to recognize —
These aren't your life-long dreams.

Worthlessness, anorexia,
Clinically depressed
Bulimia, Hallucinations,
Don't be so oppressed

Fight this longing episode;
Fight your pain and sorrow;
Fight the self-depreciation —
You'll feel renewed tomorrow.

K. J. Burger

She's Just A Ghost

She is the unkissable figure hiding
in a labyrinth of fate,
often too ironic.

Her eyes meet mine
across crowded trains and coffee shops.

"Forever may be a pretty long time,
thought I could wait that long.
I lose faith, enraged."

As time drips slowly,
my listless body weakens.

Her shadow dances in pantomimes
within my viscera
turns them inside out...

Turns me inside out, too -

Like books or
improvised plays,
they never end the way I want.

Shiu-Yeung Hui

A Young Child Cries

Deep inside a young child cries
Lost in a sea of emotion
Wave after wave rolls over her
Of emotions alien to such a young child
After each wave
She looks around to see
What the wave left her
Page after page of the adult life
She has to live again and again
Looking for a reason
For the nightmare to go on
She is but a memory
Of a child I once was
Before everything when wrong
Innocence now lost
Lost in a sea of emotion
Deep inside of me
A young child cries.

Kim Snyder

A Look At War

Why do we get crazy for war,
When he throws us on misery's shore?.
Why do we place war before peace,
When war bears great anarchy's keys?
Why, to war do we pay homage,
When war brightens no - one's image?

We see great wars across the earth,
Spreading all round untimely death;
We see warriors who know no fears
Spreading to people, bitter tears;
We see scholars, who know so well
Making bombs to make earth a hell.

What at all do we get from war?.
Nothing else but sore, gore and more;
From war, what great goods do we get?
Nothing, but mass graves and regret.
Let's see war as he truly is,
And give him the contempt that's his.

Akpenyo Kwao Agbosu

By Her Example

(Legacy of Martha Halcomb Janser)
Do the best you can
That's always what she did
By her example,
She taught us how to live

Be good to one another
Don't lie or cheat or fool
By her example,
She lived the golden rule

Work your hardest every day
Never forget how to pray
By her example,
She showed us the way

For us she was always there
No matter when or where
By her example,
We knew how much she cared

The dark day came too soon
When we had to say goodbye
But, her example will remain
With us until we die

Susan Janser Treiber

Never Having A Chance To Say Good-Bye

When I look up to the blue,
cloud filled sky above
and take a deep breath of air,
I know you can no longer do the same.

Next year when school starts again,
you won't be there to share
my excitement when I pass
that test I've studied all week for.

With each passing day the pain
I feel without you will lessen.
The memories we've
shared will be with me forever.

You were never the type
to be quiet and reserved,
you were always
your best when on the mission
of a practical joke.

And when I laugh out loud again,
I will think of you...
and all the times you made me laugh.

Jessica Kennedy

And Time Stood Still

The day we met I'll never
forget, we were so happy then.
So time went on things began
to change and I am no longer
with him. As the season's
changed we also changed and
things will never be the same
again. We thought our love
would last, but that was in
the past, and I'll probably never
see him again. His kisses
were sweet, his love was unique
in a funny yet special kind of
way, I have memories of him
and dreams of what might have
been, but that was then and
those moments have past away.
But for a few moments in time
our love was sublime, and time
stood still for me and him.

Tina Harper

The Return

I've lived on earth for 13 years
I've cried and cried lots of tears
Because I did not get my way
Or because my life was going Astray.

Sometimes I felt I was not loved
But then I thought who was above
The Lord thy God who cares for me
even in my time of need.

I think sometimes life will soon end.
Then Christ will soon come again
He will not come with pity of joy.
He will come only to destroy.

He will come and get the good
And send the Bad to satan's Hood.
And the good shall go to heaven
But the Bad will forever Burn!

Shannon Brion Chambers

Cold Love Presence

Leave me naked
like the moon
but shining like the sun
wrapped
in a blanket of stars
dreaming
of your mirror eyes
perfect flowers
vanilla glass
enamel dreams
look at the reflection
which unannounced you draw
in the shadow of your timeless scream
enclose me in the echo
of your mute blossom
wrap me in the smoke
of your blue angels
wrap me
Shelter me
in voluptuous death

Fausto Alzati

Privilege

The Lord selects a chosen few.
The art of healing his task to do.

Grants wisdom, compassion
with tender hands of infinite skill.

So, worthy physician,
hold high thy torch,
use wisely thy tools.

On a distant day
the Lord will say.

"Thy mission's accomplished
Thy assignment well done.

Oh, son of Hippocrates enter here."
Eileen A. Briley

Spring Is Here

Spring is here, come see the flowers
starting to come out of the ground,
hear the birds with song and chirping,
Oh, what pleasing, lovely sound.

Gone is ice and snow, and winter,
lovely spring is here to stay,
music sounds on streets and meadows,
and my heart sings light and gay.

Sing now songs of joy and praises,
think of nothing but good time,
Spring is here, with summer waiting
to surprise us,—anytime.

Lovely sunshine, oh so pleasant,
how I love and wait for you,
how you touch, and pat, and warm us,
even healing, you can do!

Yes, I love you, lovely sunshine,
give us more and more delight,
so when winter will arrive here,
we are full of warmth inside.
Ilse Sante

"Ode To Steve"

He met me at my door
with flowers in his hand
This very special man - it
seems that God had planned
That we should meet.

He hunts rattlesnakes and such,
of which I have great fear.
I like the theatre and all the fun,
but he is such a dear.

We're very different you can see
but there's something in his voice
That's really drawn me to him
it seems I have no choice

We both have loved before and lost
But that is in the past
We're living in the present now
Believing love can last.
Jessie B. Snider

Someone Once Said...

Someone once said
That the beauty
Of a truly great writer
Was marked
By the way
One sculptured
The words.
The bits that were chipped away
Were more important
Than what remained.

Someone once gave
That sculpture to me,
A jigsaw puzzle
Of feelings, rhythms, and warmth.
I showed that master-piece
To friends
But they saw nothing.

What keeps the soul alive
Is invisible to the eye
Someone once said...
Hannah Sklar

"The Darkness"

Darkened clouds and misty haze,
My heart filled with demonic rage.
In the dark I reach for a friend,
The only one I find is the end.
Mindless, fate in other's hands,
As I travel across these evil lands,
To carry out the devil's plans.
Sealing my fate with my soul,
The blood in my veins runs cold.
Today a thousand slain,
But in my heart is no pain.
Immune to smiles I have known,
To all the love I once was shown.
Beyond the point of turning back,
My soul has turned an evil black.
Inside all feeling is gone,
Yet through the darkness, I press on.
Tina Parish

Saying Goodbye

There once was a lady named Chris,
who all of us do miss.
She's only been gone a short while,
but how can we ever forget that smile.

I've been on her list a few times,
but off again just in time.
I appreciate the things that she did,
she showed me a way to forgive.
I will miss her with all my heart,
she will always be apart,
of the memories of the heart.
Maxine Lumicisi

Common Misfortune

Helpless amongst the guilt of fire
Burning within life's own desires
Struggling times of wants and needs
Causing uncertainty for hearts to bleed
Eager to taste a little success
To acquire more, but to receive less
To problems requiring instant attention
Are simply left - Not to mention
The unhappiness of unreachable goals
Of human flesh and mortal souls...
Keith Coleman

Veterans

Masses of nails epoxied together
Thrown in every which way
Years ago shown in splendor
Now rusting with age

Barnacles cling in grotesque fashion
Nails bent out of shape
Time wraps its shadows tightly
Stealing the chance of escape

A gnarled hand rests down
Giving glimpse to a similar fate
Fingers twist slowly around erosions
Knuckles lay limp where they fall

Veins protrude, skin hangs free
Its life caressing the cold
Aged flesh and broken metal
As winter awaits spring thaw
Denice M. Casteel

Nine Bells

Nine bells!
    This first of July.
The piloting
    They say I should try.
There's not a breeze
    Or choppy wave.
The sun shines out
    My way to pave.
There's not a bird
    Or beast.
There's not a sail
    Or sandy beach.
There's not a beak
    Or fin.
The sea's
    Like molten tin.
Ten bells!
    I spy a colored sail.
Look back.
    Our wake's a serpent's trail.
Erville Allen

Silent Virtue

The man is a beauty
Like a gem to behold
More precious than diamonds
More charming than gold
Loyal faithful
and true to the end
From him I receive
Nothing more than a friend

Should his affection turn
from her unto me
Then the gem he'd become
would a tarnished one be
So I suffer my wants
and desires alone
And pray many thanks
for this man I've not known
Linda Charlton

Rat

The rat sits,
A sniper on a cold wet night.
It peers out of the dark.
And spies a scrap of food.
It darts out and is gone.
Jaimie Lund

Love

Love is a funny word
That means so many things.
Like giving and taking and sharing
Of hearts and flowers and rings.

It can turn a house into a home -
Turn night time into day -
Go with you where "ere" you roam -
Make you happy where "ere" you stay.

It binds together with tender hands
That must be loose but strong.
It's there in gentle loving hands
When every thing else goes wrong.

Yes, love is a funny word.
But one we can't do without!
It takes the blame for all those things
That make us want to cry and shout!

So take the word and thought we share,
Sent to you on your special day.
May the gift of love so very fair
Be ever with you along your way.

H. Maxine Peters

Life

Yesterday —
    old
        warm
            everlasting.

Tomorrow —
    new
        exciting
            unexplored.

Today —
    the fabric from which
        tomorrows
            are made into
                yesterdays.

Eleanor G. Syler

The Meaning Of Life

The meaning of life will be told
at the end of this world
or when you die at ages old

The meaning of justice
of truth and of fact
what may be the universal pact
will then be known
as a matter of fact

The meaning of power
of love and of lust
can then be learned
if you know who to trust

Matt Corrales

Untitled

Little Lady dancing in the wind
Are you, you
Or, are you a part of me
That I don't know
The shamrock in my eyes
Let me smile
Let me weep
Let me see things that can't be seen
Yet the fairies must stay in the mist
And the truth be as pure as the green

Joseph Lanahan

Per Chance

If we had met
Another time
Would you be a friend of mine?
Or would you be someone whom
I'd often see across a room

I'd tell you tales
You'd tell me yours
We'd talk a while
And sometimes smile

Remembering when the times were good
The days when we just wished we could
Sometimes we'd say what's on our mind
With no response of any kind
Because if we did
We knew inside
That there'd be nothing left to hide.

Karen Aimola

Germinating Winter

To the winter that turned green
And the lullaby that turned blue
When winter came
The day turned new
Apples fell from the trees
And the words were the same
Today was washed
With the things that went away
Tuesday moved the mountain
And Monday turned to day
Winds in the orchard
Children went away
Mouths that talked of trouble
Children talked of wine
Changing the meadow slightly
Today I think of rhyme
When the truth fulfills a dream
And tomorrow words are hard
The moment turns to everything
And the meanings by the yard

Tarmo Kaard

Little Sheree

There was a littler girl Sheree
Who had a baby doll.
She kept the treasure close to her
And would not let it fall.

She loved the dolly very much
And watched it carefully,
So not to let it stain or soil,
Its dress fixed prettily.

One day the rain came falling down,
No warming, they were caught.
Her doll was splashed by maud and dirt.
She cleaned it with a cloth.

She told her doll its ok,
Sometimes, thins happen fast.
She said, "I love you very much.
We'll find another dress."

Nancy L. Brown

Birth

Blades of grass glisten listening,
To the sound of morning dew.
Dripping onto moist, once arid soil.
Droplets of vapor transform to cloud,
Yearning to return to Mother Earth.

Jerome A. Meyer

My Peace

Walking through the fields alone,
As the sun sets in the west.
Breathing in the evening air,
It seems all the world's at rest.

Stroll in silence undisturbed,
Look into the star filled sky.
The moon is so huge and bright,
I can touch it if I try.

The crickets now begin to sing.
The breeze is gentle on my face.
Looking closely I see it now,
And hasten to my special place.

An alcove across the creek,
With a carpet of moss and leaves.
Listen, to the whispering wind,
Laughing, dancing through the trees.

Here in the darkness I sit and think,
And sort my feelings out.
Here in my private world it seems,
I know what life is all about.

Patty Kauffeldt

Untitled

If I could take away your sorrow
I would.
If your pain would only
become mine.
If I had all the answers
to the questions you would ask.
This would be much better.
If time stopped
when you needed it to.
If heartaches would just disappear.
I am here for you
like I've always been.
Like I will always be.

Angel Rovinski

Carnival

It was just
The kind of day
To fit a child's best dream;
The children laughed
With glee upon the Pony ride.
But my heart
Was stabbed with pain as
I saw the curly headed girl
With crutches by her side.

She sensed my pain
Heard my unasked, "Why?"
She smiles, "Oh yes it would
Be fun to ride and laugh
To give a friendly shove;
But God has given me
Happiness in a better way
He has taught me how
To listen and to love."

Patricia Kelly

To My Children

If I am as you say,
Then you are also,
For you, are of me.

Patricia Jochum

Untitled

Falling into the
Unknown of mystere, angry
Might of mother ours.

The abyss opens,
It hungry mouth readily
Does flash the silver tooth.

Overpowering,
Thundering whisper does light
And shoot the cannon.

The sky is lit - one
Moment, then darkness gulps the
Rising sun. Tis done,

This over, mother
Silences her servants.   Their
Job is almost done.

Now all must sleep to
Yet again awaken for
Mother's fury more.

Kamil E. Kerstenetsky

Lands End

Here I am at land's end,
the open sea ahead.
Another day with you in mind,
a lonely one I'll dread.

I've pictured you a thousand times
beside you, you would stand,
as we gaze at God's creation,
while standing hand in hand.

No words are ever spoken,
no thoughts left unexpressed,
for in your arms I find myself
within your warm caress.

Now here I am at land's end,
the setting sun in view.
Now my eyes are filled with tears,
for again, I'm missing you!

Ronald A. Reyes

Dream

It's easy to just say
what to do and what's been done
Initiative... no easy task
Especially when you're the one

'Scuse the slow
Cause they're not the same
The same as who?
What is standard?

Unwritten laws...unwritten rules..
who's to say..what's to do.
just passing by
   no impressions made.

If you don't influence me,
Don't discourage me
Don't shatter my hopes
I won't set my goals too close,
   nor too far away.

Close enough to be reached
far enough to still be called
   a dream.

Sebastian Hernandez

Tear Drop

As I fall deeply into your eyes
and I think that if I were to die

The form I choose to reappear
would be that in the shape of a tear

Live my life in your eyes
until the time comes to cry

Upon which, I would gather my strength
to travel not a great length

Hugging the contours of your face
leaving behind a small wet trace

To end my life in a single trip
to end my life upon your lip.

Bruce Latham

The Holocaust

If I had lived through the Holocaust,
what could I have done?
Could I have stopped
the pain and hunger
or the malicious "making fun?"

Would I have watched
the brutal killings
or the way people were starved?
Or would I have held my head high
and watched them get their scars?

If I had lived through the Holocaust,
what could I have done?
There was no place to hide
and there was no place to run.

Monica Hardee

Untitled

Break the bread my ever sweet,
In this time we shall meet.
One day you shall see,
One love in the distance stream,
on a mountain ever high.
In the sky ever wide,
on land to see so far,
one hope.
One prayer.
Hold so tight,
don't let go with all your might.
As time passes hold your hope.
For I will come my ever sweet,
Than we shall love,
And we will meet.

Kathy Crawford

Love Bugs

Flying recklessly through the air,
It floats as if it does not care.
It gives the birds a wonderful feast,
But it's nothing but a brainless beast.
Splattered all over my car,
It looks a lot like tar.
The thing I hate the most in life,
The love bug gives me too much strife.

Jeffrey D. Perez

Things Change

When worry rips wounds across our
foreheads, in the pain of a troubled
life, we remember how
all things change.
But when the wounds heal and the pain
subsides, we always seem to forget how
all things change then, too

Ian J. Ball

The Redemption

Unspoken beauty
One seldom forgets
For not words can touch the soul.

Timeless in essence
The heart that projects
True love in which to grow.

The solace of heaven
Atoning the earth,
Redeems the Lord with man.

For light yields the hallows
That darkness entrails,
Warming the heart to understand.

Forget not the comfort
Of love set above,
To cradle our hearts as we pray.

For faith conquers sorrow
With wisdom and peace,
Granting truth to guide the way.

Angelina Archibald

To Savour A Moment...

To savour a moment
To have time stand still,
To find peace of mind
This is our will.

But do we find these moments?
Are they precious enough?
Do we remember their significance
When times are tough?

Will time ever stand still
as the days go by?
We hear ticking, we feel rushed,
Life...becomes but a sigh.

The serenity we long for
seems further away
Where is this peace?
Yes, we must pray.

We must pray for patience
For wisdom and strength,
But mostly for courage
to have faith at length.

Sandra Tuzzolino

Let

Let the days pass one by one
With gladness underneath the sun.
Let me hold my head up high,
Let me feel the summer sky.
Let me wake to happy things,
Now and forever let me sing.
Let me feel and see all of life,
Free from hate, and free from strife.

Marilyn B. Rutter

The Breath Of The Dragon

In the shadows of the night
When all is dark and all is bright
When tales of lore
Are brought ashore
And bathed in the light of the moon
The talisman sings
On the oceans mighty wings
The breath of the dragon's abode
There shall no be a sigh
From the earth sunken tie
Nor the voices of those who shall hear
For in the whisper of the dark
Without a trace, without a mark
I commend to the depths of the sea

Laureen M. Heisler

Dreams Of Love

I came to know her
by osmosis
I looted the love
    of her petulant youth
like a bee gathers honey
    from the cherished flower
I drank the exquisite perfume
    of her delicate body
in moments of eternity
I deciphered her deepest inner feelings
from the pupil of her romantic eyes
the utopia of my past dream
suspended
in the time of our
    everlasting togetherness.

Denis Brazeau

Have You?

Have you ever paused to listen
To a small child say its prayer,
How the heavenly Father's presence
Seemed to hover very near?

Have you ever closed your eyelids
And prayed in whispers low,
That He would bless and keep you
No matter where you go?

Have you ever watched the splendor
Of the change from spring to fall,
And felt the presence of the one
That watches over all?

Just steal away with Jesus
And leave your burdens there,
When you are tired and lonely
Go to the Lord in prayer.

For He is ever near you
He'll hear your faintest call,
He is a friend to everyone
And watches over all.

Pansy B. Shrader

"Tsunami"

The waves crash
solid and tight,
descending over the sand
like a Father's hand over his daughter,
Slaps down,
Again rising and falling
He is a monstrous shadow
and then the pain.

Dana Woodring

Glass Percussion

Crystal lyrics
Wreathe in me
Subtly flow
Complexly grow
Gorgeous opalescency.
And harmonic tricks.

Sharper edges
Make tintamars
Cut melancholy
Scald me —
Bright avatars
Crowd ledges.

Flames of sound
Brassy incandescence
Diamond fugues
Orchestra's huge;
Distills an essence
And I resound.

Edward St. Boniface

Mother's Day

Grandpas bark at children
    Grandmas like to scold.
Parents do the telling
    Children do what they're told.

Sons can get in trouble
    Fathers work too hard.
Daughters lose their temper
    Uncles are a card.

Brothers always rival
    Cousins make much noise
Aunts can be a bother
    Infants break up toys.

But when everyone's in trouble
    You know who they will call.
It won't be their attorney
    Cause Mother's best of all.

Robert A. Rothman

"Rainbows Of A Lifetime"

The rainbows of a lifetime
are few and far between,
Few of us can count them the rainbows
that we've seen.
It's hard to reproduce the colors no
matter how we try.
Of the masterpiece before us - the
rainbow in the sky.
When I see a rainbow I consider
it a gift,
The magnificence of color should give
our soul a lift.
God sends us gifts so very rare we
don't even realize.
It's all right here before us if we
open up our eyes.
Next time you see a rainbow take
note of it - please do,
For the rainbows of a lifetime when
we think of it are few.

JoAnne Moore

"Family Lives"

Family lives are one to treasure
The memories that come along,
For today was always a yesterday
The love must carry on.

Sometimes life can be difficult
    and hard to understand,
But we must stick together
    and lend a helping hand.

And when that touch does reach you
    the warmth will never let go,
So squeeze a little harder
    ...its love - I really know.

Holley R. Mado

Untitled

I cannot breathe
Without your breath
I cannot live my life
When it is death
The appetite is lost
Without a partner to dine
The heart will not beat for nothing
Not even the heart itself
My thoughts keep going back to the past
The mind won't let me forget
The body cannot let me live
When nothing brings it to life

Tonia D. Jack

I'll Make It

The road is long and dreary,
But I will make it there,
For at the end, there is waiting
One, I know who cares.

The load is heave that I carry
But I will get it there.
For as my shoulders begin to stop
Someone, my load will share.

My heart is heavy and full of pain
But when I ask for help.
Upon my shoulders, a hand is laid,
And some ones presence felt.

The road is made much shorter
The load is made more light.
The pain is lifted from my heart
And my day again is bright.

Harriet Floren

"If Only They Could See"

If only they could see
inside of you and me
They'd see the love we share
how much we really care
If only they could see
inside us from the start
They'd see the kind of love
that's truly from the heart
If I only had one wish in life
I know what it would be
That everyone could feel the love
I feel inside of me
"If only they could see"

Charles "Chip" Carney

Bound In Love

There are times when I find comfort
in a glimpse of way back when.
So I keep some photos in my mind
to flip through now and then.

It's my photo album of memories,
and it's bulging at the seams.
So many cherished moments
that I now see in my dreams.

Today this albums opens
to a page that I hold dear,
where I've cut, pasted and labelled
hugs and smiles of the years.

They're placed on golden pages,
family snapshots that I prize,
and as I close my book again
love oozes from the sides.

I think I'll keep my album close,
for tougher days like this
to remind me of those treasured times,
that I so often miss.

Jewel Birdsall

A Dream

A dream
woke me.

I was crying,
my pillow was soaked.

Images flash
and crash.

I tried to recall
what and who.

Only your name
came to my mind.

I reached
to touch you.

I forgot you
had never been there.

Jennifer Noble

From Where We Go

Electrical cities
High in the sky
From where lightning falls
With thunder for its cry
Mountains of clouds
Colored as amber coals
There march the soldiers
Which build dreams
In the melting sun
As the ocean swallows
The moon — the lime sphere
Dissipates without warning
Nature's new child has just
Been giving birth
It is day
The face of night.

Benjamin Eshinski

Hearts Of Gold

Going back amongst the years,
We find a valley filled with tears.

But in a heart shaped locket,
All our dreams are kept.

Sunken in a whirled round,
So that we may take our crown.

We weep no more because we feel,
In this life of drowning sea.

We see a light and forever,
To never wake again.

Sadness leaves,
Happiness goes round.

Loving always because we know,
In our hearts a sea of gold.

Heather Wood

The Gift Of Mind

Lord, I awoke so early
In the sunlit dawn
I heard a lonely bird
Sing from our lawn.

His song had power and joy
It brought me so near
To your holy presence;
In ended all fear.

And now when I awake
I hear that song,
And in Your gift of mind
That song lives on.

Katherine Benion

Nobility

Galloping
Freely over the plains
This mighty beast begins to roam.

As he approaches the hills
His muscles tighten.
He ascends,
   Up...
      Up he glides...
As this noble animal reaches the top
Steam rising from his heated body.
His thick black mane
Rippling in the wind.
His crystal eyes
Reflecting the setting sun.

Standing so proud
He sees before him...
The great...vast world which he exists.
For this is his world,
And his alone...
For no one can step in.

Catherine MacMillan-St. Germain

Spring Time

Sun is warm in the spring,
Pretty grass grows green.
Rabbits run all around,
I'm happy in the spring.
Nothing's ugly in the spring,
Grow colorful flowers in the spring.

Jessica Madau

On Possum Pike

We see her in
those old photos
leaning on the bumper
of the new Buick

She is dressed
like the city
her skirt hiked to
expose
those legs

The dirt road
in the foreground
defines, for us, the
real picture

The girl, once at home
in the country, is
now merely a visitor
in these parts.

Linda Hill

Long Distance Love

As I gaze out the window
I think of you
out a yonder
where the sky is blue

Why must our love drift apart
when our love should grow
deeper than thoughts

You are the one for me
I am the one for you
let us share with one another
all the love that is true

Lisa Clancy

My Heart

Hears my heart for you to love
A gift of God from above.

It is pure and it is kind.
My treasure of love so easy to find

As our heart's will be the key
It will be forever, you will see.

Like Heaven's angel's, all in flight
your love is my guiding light

Hear's my heart for you to love
A gift of God from above.

Wayne S. James

A Promise

If you didn't aim to keep it —
You shouldn't ever make it —
If you didn't want to share it —
Don't promise it, then break it.

I know we shouldn't judge each other,
But by a principal, we should live.
If we say we will do a thing —
No excuses can we give.

Our thoughts are put into many words,
And in so many ways,
But as long as we are living
Others judge us by what we say.

Examples of what God is like —
We should always be.
As others look to us,
Our integrity they will see.

Dorothy Carter

What Is Love?

Love is beautiful
Love is pain
Love is hatred
Love is game
To love is to be kind
To love is to be brave
To love is to be different
To love is to be strong
  For one must love from the heart
  For one must love to learn a lesson
  For one must love to tell the truth
  For one must love to take a chance
Love is to go through living life
Love is to face your biggest failures
Love is to gain a certain life
Love is to raise a precious thing.
  Love is understanding
  Love is trusting
  Love is powerful
But most of all, Love is life

Lesley Napier

What Is It Lord

What is it, Lord, you ask of me?
What is it that I fail to see?
  I've baked and sewed
  And scrubbed and hoed
And tried to do it all for thee.

What is it, Lord? What's that you say?
Have I not lived the whole long day
  To tidy my own life,
  To being just a wife?
Nor cared who fell along the way?

Oh, God. Oh God, don't let it be
That I am thinking just of me.
  Help me lift up
  And hold a cup
To those who weep and cannot see.

Blanche P. Zimmerman

Spring At Last

At last the winter snows have melted,
Leaving a blanket of green.
Streams flowing down the mountain
It's all signs of spring.
Buds bursting out all over
With a lovely fuzzy hue;
Fluffy clouds floating along
In a sky of azure blue
Everything is coming alive
Birds singing their sweet refrain
Tulips and jonquils are blooming
At last, at last it is spring!

Ruth Woods

I Love You Forever

Loving you is eating me
The love you give I cannot see
I share my pains, to give you pleasure
I shed my tears to fall like feathers-
I give you love from all my heart
And pray to God we never part
To tell you how I love you so
And on with life we shall go
But now we've gone our separate ways
And still apart I count the days
I wait the day we'll be back together
I want you to know I love you forever.

John Pierce

What I Know About God

God is merciful,
and almighty.
God is full of strength,
and he keeps the earth tidy.

God created the heaven and the earth,
the soil which is dirt.
The planets and the stars,
including Mars.

God loves all sinners,
even shoplifters.
God is full of love,
and is as swift as a dove.

I worship and cherish,
God the creator of my life.
I love him so dearly,
with all of my might.

To conclude this rhyme,
that has twenty lines.
I would like to say,
For life, to God I must pay.

Ivan Learmont

Heal The Children

Heal the children
That are entrusted to our care.
Protect the children,
Help them face their fear.

Honor the children,
There's so much that they know.
Cherish the children,
Through their love we grow.

Look into the children's eyes
And you will see
The glorious beings
These children can be.

They are our teachers,
Innocent and wise,
Teaching us to love,
Seeing through our disguise.

Inspire the children
To be all that they can be,
For the children are our link
With Eternity.

Beverly Nadler

Memories of Gabriel

The time will come tomorrow
When I know we both must part
But remember little grandson
I'll always hold you in my heart.

A face that's so angelic
and a voice so crystal clear
The times that I did hold you
To chase away your fear.

The early-morning clowning
And the mid-day escapades
Will stay with me forever
When all else starts to fade

Many miles now I must travel
To return home safe and sound
But with me I will take, that day
New riches that I've found

Judith A. Brown

Untitled

To shop in a mall
To try everything on
To look for it all
And use coupons

Roots is too expensive
Then Bi-Way is too cheap
Go ahead and spend it
Just hope the bill is not too steep

Shopping really ain't bad
If you have money you should be glad
The clothing is really quite cool
But in the end money rules!!!

Shira Lifschitz

Flowers

Flowers are very pretty
and they come up every year.
You grow them in you garden
and you always have some near.
The flowers are always scented
like a lovely smelling cake
which has green and yellow icing
that you're putting in to bake.
You should pick some for your mother
and put them in a vase.
When you give them to your mom
you'll put a smile upon her face.
So please, take my advice.
run on home, my little friend.
Pick your mom some pretty flowers,
'cause now we're at the end.

Erika Littles

A Playground For Children

There's a playground for children
There's a place for them somewhere
There's a playground for children
God made so fair
Even the ones in far away lands
Know there's a place for them to stand.

Lottie Brinson Lockey

On The Verge

On the verge of something wonderful
The far and wide unknown
On the threshold of eternity
With so much to be shown

Standing here and looking
At the never ending sky
Hoping for so many things
Your soul begins to die

The sky shows your emotion
As darkness starts to fade
Tears give way to peaceful dreams
As night evolves to day

Standing at the edge of nothing
As your life begins
Each day becomes a miracle
As you search within

Looking back at nothing
As you start anew
Learning so much more of others
By first understanding you

Rachelle E. Scheel

"Me"

When I walk into a room
  all eyes turn to me
The whispers and questions
  "who could she be?"

The women they stare
  and wish they had what I do
The men come with the line
  "can I get to know you?"

I have a beautiful spirit
  that shines through my eyes
I have a strut in my walk
  that makes men watch my thighs.

I am Isis, Neferetiri, Cleopatra
  all wrapped in one
Malcolm, Martin and Medgar
  were all my sons

I am mother earth, the sky,
  mountains and sea
A beautiful black woman
  - yeah, that's me.
  Dinah Gourdet

Untitled

Memories of Hell
Come in soft colors
To those who might forgive
The terror of love.

Worthless possessions,
They die for the chance
To own the things
That will destroy them.

Unseen by the eyes
Of a believer
In the empty promises and lies
Of the God of the Blind.

Already dammed
By the mind-washed living-dead,
I walk by the light
Of a candle burning low.

Listen to my words,
See through my eyes
To understand my thoughts;
We're saved when we die.
  Katie Rose Bozic

Good-Bye

You said you loved me and you'd
always be there.
You said you'd call and you'd
always care.
So where are you?
You have my number.
I cried over you.
I was stupid to think it would work,
wasn't I.
I got to close to you.
You had my heart in your hand.
You threw it on the floor and
crushed it into a million pieces.
You lied!
I can't take it anymore
you don't love me,
you never did, you never will.
So now I'll say goodbye.
  Janice Stamm

A Harp Is Wanted

Glitter for ever, o magic light
revealing the beauty to the world.
Chase the dragons out of sight,
a harp is wanted not a sword.

A harpweaver is a dreamer
like a dancer and a dance.
They always radiate and shine,
they are like fire and wine.

When I hear the harpist playing
cascades and waves are hugging me,
I feel as touched by a starry-sky
music like river is a lullaby.

Happy and alone by the river
I am listening to the harpweaver,
enchanted, I whisper to the world:
A harp is wanted not a sword.
  Nina Novak

All It Needs Is Water

When roses were red
And violets were blue
Oceans were clean
And race was not an issue
In the all perfect world
Lift the shades
And see the horizon of hope
Hope of a better place
To walk the streets
Without getting hit
To go to school
And not worry about being called names
It has come down
That even children
Innocent children are affected
And as long as that rose
That once was red
And all other flowers remain wilted
So will be relations
Between you and me.
  Stephen Berger

"Little April Fool"

Just around the corner
Lurks my old friend
Death

Laughing up his sleeve
at me

The little April fool
Who always made a joke
of life

To get through the gates of Hell

To the other side
Life

Can I survive the lies?
the snares

Get through the maze
the tricks?

Or will next

Up jump
the Devil?
  Maria Schuyler Kirsh

Untitled

Disturbing distilled darkness
Slips in the window
Haunting sibilant sounds
Silent reveries drift down
Sneaking pages of life from
Between the cracks in the
Paper - walls containing
Imprisoning thoughts - vision
Slips through and breaks
On new shores of being
Washing of caressing
Rocky shores or sandy
Beaches of continuity
And continuations of long
Past conflicts and molting
Feathers of hubris breaking
Up on cloudy days and
Rushing along fast moving
Rivers of time
  Karen LaRue Mooney

Shooting Stars

I've known so many people
they come searing through my life
like fiery shooting stars
then quickly drop out of sight
but not out of mind
a fading trail of disintegration
remains behind to remind me
they were in the air...
but like faint fragrances
now they're in the wind
blending as they bend
to their selfish wills
blinded by self-erected walls
of total indifference
doomed to partial existence
  partial extinction
  impartial ISOLATION
never fully being
never being full
never.
  Tim Currier

Some Time Ago

Some time ago,
But not long ago;
I dreamt of being in heaven,
seeing the angels that once was,
and seeing daisies growing.

Then I see him...
The one true God.
I'd ask him if
It's my time to go,
He'll say no.
Then I wake up to a bright,
new day.
  Kimberly Beem

To Chris

My soul flies,
My heart stirs,
For it is you
Whom I yearn.
  Wendall Carnes

Memories

A child ran down the street
He didn't see me look;
He tripped and skinned his tender knees
And dropped his story book.

Then he gathered up his things
And brushed his dusty knees,
He was up again and off with zest
His journey full of ease.

He ran with scurried steps
That hurried to his goal-
Determined to be where he wished
With adventures to unfold.

The park was just a block away,
With trees and fields of grass!
To start a grand adventure
In daydreams that forever last.

I followed him with just my eyes,
He took me back long years;
To all the memories a boy collects
In which he knows no fears.

Leo Green

One

One candle melts to smoke,
One more cigarette is stubbed while
One wonders about you, or,
One sits in wonder of you.
One is the same as the other.
One time there was surety,
One did not question,
One just was.
One is such an easy number.
One way or another now,
One needs strength, for
One ton of restraint balances
One ounce of desire as
One dreams of two blue eyes,
One silverine smile,
One sweet,
One deep,
One lingering kiss that would at
One time both soothe and fire
One troubled soul.

Ron McConaughy

Sister

Sister
To the birds that sings so well.
Sister
To the music that have you in a spell.
Sister
To the children run and play.
Sister
Our friendship is here to stay.
Sister
To the whisper that's in your ear.
Sister
My love for you is always here.

Ellis Marshall III

Winter Sleet and Snow

Winter sleet and snow
Brush against my windowpane
Sparkling in the sun.

Sarah Beth Vogt

Untitled

Today is a day
    of autumn beauty,
October winds rustling,
    up multi-colored
    leaves thru the air.

Fall will not last.
Winter steps in sprinkling,
    snow flurries upon
    the ground.

'Til spring flowers arrive,
    summer seeds bloom
Fall will come again and again.

Josephine Mele Koumas

The Judgement Within

I must be deep,
beyond all depths.
I must be dark,
far too dark for any light.
I must be angry,
over and above the color of passion.

The night winds crack my lips.
The sandpaper cuts to the bone.

My falseness must be.
Why that is all.

My mind cannot exceed yours,
it is lower than Luther's playpen.
Don't disgrace my passion.

Elizabeth Marie Rich

Hospital Bed

Why did you leave me here,
Lying in this bed?
How could you put me here
In this hospital bed?

Walking along the road I was,
When you came around the bend,
Drunk and driven insane,
Then leave me here to die in pain.

I cannot move,
Nor eat or drink,
Not even blink,
But you don't even care.
You just kept on driving,
Then leave me here lying
In this hospital bed.

You didn't stop,
Not even think,
Just keep on driving
Drunk and driven insane,
Then leave me here to die in pain.

Katie Ferreira

His Name

The name we pick for our new boy,
We'll pick with lots of love and joy,
It maybe Samuel, Jake, or Terry.
Maybe even Pete or Gary,
If we pick from Jean or Ted,
David, Matthew, Jim, or Fred,
We'll pick a name that suits him fine,
Our little Boy both yours and mine.

Theresa Weybrecht

Love From Afar

All these feelings I have
for you are hidden
For feelings like this
are forbidden
All the emotions I have
buried beneath
Just in case someone
Might suspect or see
Wish we could be together
But I know that will
never be
Because you belong to
another and not to me

Myo Hyang Lee

From This Day Forward

This is the day I dreamed of
The day we say I do
This is the day I dreamed of
The day I start my life with you.

From this day forward
I'll do it all for you
From this day forward
I'll keep on loving you.

This is the day I've waited for
The day we're joined as one
This is the day I've waited for
The day two become one.

From this day forward
I'll do it all for you
From this day forward
I'll keep on loving you.

Corine Mellor

Beyond The Bend

Take a look beyond the bend,
And tell me what you see
of darkened halls
And cold stone walls
or ships upon the sea.

Take a look beyond the bend
your misty past recalled
of former lives
And mystical ties
To ancient souls revealed.

Take a look beyond the bend
Into tomorrow's face
of things to come
And tasks undone
Into the hidden place.

Marc Rosenfeld

If I Could

If I could reach out and touch someone
And change anything at all
I might touch the wrong person
And cause them to fall.
If I could help someone
And ease their pain
I might hinder their lesson
And the knowledge they must gain.
Maybe I should just
Walk beside someone
And help them carry their load
And always be a friend
Along life's many roads.

Peggy S. Nelson

Fall

I watch the leaves so madly chase
Around the yard they wildly race
The dance of fall in her cool embrace

I see clouds as they skittle by
In pale sun of the winter sky
All blue gray and laden they fly

I glimpse the golden russet whirl
As brown grass catches up a squirrel
Gathering mutts with tail afurl

I gaze upon the brown trunk of a tree
Knobby limbs blown so free
Turning toward heaven to say look at me

Grace Ellen Wallis

Unplanned

Laying covered in the street
Without life's beat.
One minute alive
The next second survive.
People driving by
Asking why?
No one knows how much time is left.
Each day the last or one more yet?
A gamble of emotion — time.
How to, when to, what to — time.
Go here, go there, go everywhere.
Fast, slow, without despair.
Have to care — have to share.
Need to love — need to live.
Want to live — want to give.
Can't stop now — wasn't planned.
The end.

Alan Nasits

Fairy Tale

Cinderella found her prince,
Sleeping Beauty discovered too,
Open up your eyes,
Realize I've finally found you.

I want you to be my destiny,
I want to live in a fairy tale,
Just you and me,
I want to sore high above the clouds,
And venture into the sea,
I want you to be my destiny.

I'm not wearing a crown,
And I don't see a crown on you,
But if we lived in my fairy tale
We could wear whatever we desired to.

The Little Mermaid got her wish,
And, I want my wish to,
If you'd just step into my fairy tale,
All my wishes would come true,
Then you would know,
That I love you.

Kelly Nowicki

Untitled

I was dead
covered in silk and shadows
My head surrounded by roses
She kissed me on the forehead
And I left for heaven...

Rich Schilling

Shells

Neat little shell
Shape like bells

I like to watch you brighten
When the day lightens

Nice little shells you look like hair
When the day turns pail

I like to watch you in the bay
In the black seas make me stay

Neat little shells
Shaped like bells

I like to see you play
When the bay turns gay

Nice little shells you look like water
When the day turns later

I like to watch you in the sand
In your very big band

Neat little shells
Shaped like bells

Rachel Rincon

Riverview Terrace

Riverview Terrace at Sutton Square —
I sit here again and wonder where
My much loved friend is sitting now,
Of what he thinks and feels and how
He'll manage what seems an awesome feat
To put himself finally on my street.

I need him badly and can't wait long,
Tears are more frequent than any song.
The years go by and much time is lost.
My sadness grows and at great cost
For my well-being does depend
On seeing this most beloved friend.

Patricia Schwarz

A Young Marine

Left a boy, came back a man, a
young Marine has made a stand.
Left his home to a foreign land,
shedding blood in the sand. A young
Marine has made a stand.
Mixed feelings about the war, not
knowing what might be in store.
A young man doing what he can,
a young Marine has made a stand.
Left a boy, came back a man,
A young Marine has made a stand.
This young Marine who left a boy,
has filled my life with love and joy.
The man who returned, of which I'm
glad, is now called my dad.
Left a boy, came back a man,
A young Marine has made a stand.

Tatum Mahoney

Last Night

If I should die tomorrow,
If dusk would come without me,
Let me make a note
For those who gather 'bout me.

If life embraces just one moment
Of brief transcendent light,
Rest easier in knowing
I danced with God last night.

Ward Nay

The Giving Of Tears

She begged my eyes to look upon
the tears that fell from hers
bleeding hearts becoming one
after all these years

My fingers danced across her face
where pain once ran like wine
replaced within a moment
by a tear of mine

I let it rest so stagnant
my heart left in a drop
beating twice as hard
for my lovers heart that stopped.

Paxton Tyler Bowman

Love Eternal

Looking back over several years
That special day once again nears
That is the day two became one
Our life together had just begun

The visions and dreams we could see
Many plans for you and me
Some roads were rough-some hills steep
Some nights lacking needed sleep

Feeling each others concern and care
The wink and smile that's always there
I sure do have that special smile
We'll talk about it after while

Life with you has been so very good
I dare not change it if I could
I'm so in love I'm sure you see
On this day-our anniversary

Jodi Hill and Andy Anderson

Tell Me

When can love be enjoyed
Without hurt without pain
Can two people love
And still be free
You tell me, for I don't know

Do the stars shine at night
The sun each day
Will you have me always
Is our love meant to be
You tell me, for I don't know.

Arthur Osborne

Composed Upon A Platform

I
Behold it's winter.
Morning.
  Am
Jolted from a reverie
Three women gathered on a platform
Two were white,
The other, well...
  Coloured
A yellow-eyed monster
came snaking in
vomited an undigested meal
and hungrily grabbed the three
Two went to the back
The other in front.
In this chain of friendship
am I
a link?

Robert M. Marankey

Paradox

The first sign of spring
is the gift of the past
to man's wondering mind

Without transiency
no harvest
no abundance of flowers
no game of love

What once was
presupposes eternity
and what is today
shall tomorrow be hidden
from my sight

Charles Racine Bergesen

The Invisible Candle

I am like the candle
burning by his bed.
Beautiful, alluring and mysterious.
Yet dangerous to touch.
He ignores me,
While I burn low,
Each drop of wax
falls from the flame,
like tears from human eyes.
Yet he doesn't notice
that he despaired me.
When he threw me away
because I no longer suit his need
and he replaced me
with a new, young candle.
Only she won't have anyone
to warn her of what will happen...
later.
Like no one warned me.

Judy-Lyn Ogilvie

The Leprechaun

One fine day while fast asleep
In my dreams I chanced to meet
A funny wee man who hopped along
Calling himself a Leprechaun.

This funny wee man with coat so red
And strange black hat upon his head
In his hands he did hold
A copper pot so full of gold.

He placed it beneath a Shamrock plant
Then began to sing and chant
"Oh fiddle dee Oh fiddle dit"
"My gold is yours if you find it"

I looked upon that Shamrock green
The pot of gold was plainly seen
But when I went to make it mine
The funny wee man began to whine.

Then I awoke with open eyes
And found to my sudden surprise
My dream had burst, all was gone
The pot, the gold and the Leprechaun.

Robert C. Dennett

A Plain

A beautiful plain
shines below the mountain side,
grass blows in the breeze.

Courtney Figg

The Brotherhood Of Man

All peoples of the earth,
Were born to brothers be,
To live in peace and love,
From sea to shining sea.

All peoples of the earth,
Love not as brothers should:
Some hate and watch and fight,
While others strive for good.

All peoples of the earth,
Could be as brothers now,
If they would follow God,
And truth and freedom vow.

Some peoples of the earth,
One day will brothers be,
While living up on high,
In love and ecstasy.

Some peoples of the earth,
One day will brothers be,
While living down on earth,
In love and ecstasy.

Helen S. Penney

On Answering The 'Phone

I love it when my kid says "Ma?"
To answer and to hear a voice -
so welcome, young and dear to me,
How sweet it is!

I love it when I think the ring
is just another routine call
and find my child is on the 'phone
How great it is!

I love it when the news is good
he's got a job - she met a man!
What joy I feel, my day's complete
How thankful, God, I am.

The days are full
My life is good
I thank my God above,
For every time my kid says "Ma?"
My heart just bursts with love.

Theresa Lang

'I Touched Him'

I touched Him,
I touched Jesus.
I touched Him,
When He came by.

I touched Him,
I touched Jesus.
I touched Him,
As I cried.

I touched Him,
I touched Jesus
I touched Him,
For all the world
To see.

He saved my soul,
He made me whole.

That's why I touched Him,
I touched Him just for me.

Dorothy J. Taylor

I Wonder

Thoughts is where
I live, I think, I stare.
I see the unseeable air.

With heartbeats of joy.
I gladly share,
the treasures, I wonder.
For those who care.

Thoughts of wonder
young and old.
The greatest stories
ever told.

What would our
world be.
If no man ever,
wondered to be free.

Thoughts is where
I wonder best.
I will meet my maker.
My wonder thoughts
and I shall rest.

Arthur Vines

Bedouin Market

In the market
on thursdays
you sit,
eyes veiled
legs crossed.
Bare feet
sandals
english oxfords
yankee macys
all pass,
you sell dreams
and grass.

Flora McIntosh

Lost

All the force of fighting is gone
All the words look not enough
I gave my heart, the spirit sore
Dust, blown in some part.

All the force of fighting is gone
Having nothing, in this life, a ghost.
I called, yelled, tried and cried
But, I lost what I loved most.

All the force slowly vanished,
No reason and no explain
In my fate, with sweet memories
Shrivelled, dumbed, iced,
With no more joy and pain.

Emil Asdurian

Beaches

My feet sink into the hot sand
as a strong breeze whispers in
my ear. Shells surface and
waves let out their furry.
The sun's rays come down and
hug me and I feel their heat
and see their happiness as they
bless the beach with their
never-ending love.

Ariel Wallingsford

My Savior

I stood upon the edge of life
Beside an open door
I heard a voice from heaven say
That time would be no more
Again I looked beyond the door
The judge was on his throne
My knees began to tremble
And I felt so all alone.

For a moment there was silence
There was nothing I could say
It was too late to run and hide
Too late for, me to pray
So as I stood there trembling
The gate began to close
There is a debt for everyone
But that's when Jesus rose
He gently raised his nail scarred hand
This soul has been set free
'Twas then I knew the Son of God
Had paid the debt for me.

Gordon R. Hall

My Teacher

The hour when I am in your room
Is short and never any gloom
My teacher is so kind and neat
She always treats me very sweet
I never like to come to class
Without my work, which is my pass
I never like to hear the bell
Because it seems to say farewell.

Clara Harper Urlicks

Dogs

Dogs are brown
Dogs are black
They liked to be patted
On the back

If you tickle them
They won't laugh
But if you train them
They might learn math

They like to be played with
They like to fool around
If you play around with them
They'll hide and won't be found.

I have a puppy dog myself
She loves to play around
It is true that if she hides
She truly can't be found.

Kerri Swail

Paradigms

See...
    to feel without hearing.
Feel...
    to hear but not touch.
Hear...
    to touch without seeing.
Touch...
    to see but not be.
See...
    to be.

Karen Novak

untitled

as we road along
the blue ridge parkway
redwood highway
going-to-the-sun-road
or sat breathing fumes
in yosemite, yellowstone
staring at a winnebago wall
plastered with stickers
honk for jesus
she would turn to me
with satisfied looks
sighing a smile at the glass
i scowled at the drive-thru scenery
thinking of this perfect trail
paved

Susan King

This Time

I know you don't understand
And we both know
Things aren't going right
So now it's time to say good-bye
And put our love aside

Maybe for only a short time
But now we must go on
As friends
But not as one

Although this time
Our love is gone
We have the strength
To move on
And keep our friendship
Safe from harm

Sharon Schwar

Hanging Out To Dry

Swinging in the mid-day sun
I've played the games,
I've had my fun.
Gazed in awe at the summer sky
Left out to drain,
Left out to dry.
In all this wonder I fall in love
The Earth below,
The sky above.
No-one here to make a sound
I sense my world go around and round.

Lee S. O'flaherty

Christmas

Carols are being sung.
Happy people all over the earth.
Reindeer are flying.
Is the time of year, when...
Surprises are everywhere.
Toys are being made by elves.
Merry Christmas say everyone
Angels are all around.
Saint Nicholas is laughing like a
Bowl full of jelly.

Charles Kenkel

Love

Love is Beauty,
Love is Grand,
It is a duty,
That many have had.
It brings thy happiness,
It brings thy joy,
Thy love for someone,
I always show.
Thy love I cannot hide,
But thy shyness may be the foe.
However, thy still young,
And have a lot more to love.

Voula Viglis

Not So Lonely

Have you ever taken a walk while
it's raining,
Or watched the moon in its nightly
waning?
Have you ever waited around for some-
one
to meet,
Or found a tree with the perfect
seat?
I often think of how it would be,
If everyone wanted to climb that
tree.
I will admit, sometimes it's lonely,
Still sometimes you think you're the
only.
No one else watches the sky when it
gets clouded,
But then I think, at least it's not
crowded.

Steve Allen Moore

"No Longer"....

This will be my last poem to you.
This will be my "good-bye."
No longer can I feel the joy.
No longer can I cry.

No longer can I sing to you.
No longer can I write.
No longer can I live the hope.
No longer can I fight.

I wrote my poems to someone there,
Someone in fantasy.
Someone I needed once to have,
To hold, to hear, and see.

And now the dream has gone for good,
And took you far away.
No longer can I be with you.
No longer can I stay.

This will be my last song to you.
My melodies will die.
Until I live the dream again,
This will be my "good-bye."

Ghazi Asaad, M.D.

The Falling Star

The night is dark,
but still is light.
The world is day,
but still is night.

There is no love,
but there is no hate.
When you are early,
You are most surely late.

The fire is down,
but still is a blare.
You might be cruel,
but still you care.

The answer is right,
but you cannot be sure.
You have enough
but still you want more.

The star is falling,
in the dark night.
Things may look wrong,
But still they are right.

Pouneh Aravand

Aging

Time decays
It bumps and bangs
Along the way.

Needless to say
Same can endure
Some pass away
And others stay the course.

Thus to delay, to estimate
Events, achieve and proceed
Or initiate new ones
Like a fickle wind teases leaves
And branches sway
To leave a layer of color
Along the path
Or color half the town like
A blanket, red, yellow or brown.

Zelia Jane French

Love

Love is a river that flows through
a man's soul to the very depths of
his being

Flowing over the rivers and
valleys of his mind

Rushing warmly through his
heart, and raging wildly through
his life

Twisting and turning until he is
completely covered in its beauty.

Becky Elkins

See The Sunrise

Death before life on a dreary day,
Absent sunrise after sunset,
The blackness of a barren world,
Where dreams will not become their own.
'Cause dreams awake the morning light,
Allowing everyone to see,
That day is now and night is never.
Forever will the sun shine bright,
Life to only those who see,
The rest are dead in darkness.

Amber Barkey

To Spring

Spring with its backaches,
Spring with its flu,
Spring with its sniffles,
Spring with ka-choo!
Spring with its ague,
Spring with its gout
Spring with my grass seed
Refusing to sprout,
Spring with tornadoes,
Spring with its flood,
Spring with spring cleaning,
Spring with its mud,
Sprint's out of favor,
Spring's for a lout,
Spring's what I wish
It were....out!

Clyde E. Borman

My Mother

As I gaze upon you, I
see a woman
with a soul that can see
the true me.
Some have a soul as blind
as can be,
but not you, you can see
what I'm going
to do without a second
thought.
You of all people who can
see and understand me
almost better than I can
are,
my mother.

Amy Fortunato

FLORIDA:
SUN AND FUN UNLIMITED

Proud feelings well inside of me,
So this I must proclaim
About the state I love so well,
And FLORIDA is its name.

And as you travel here and there
Among its utmost reaches,
You'll surely see, without a doubt,
The world's most famous beaches.

Now if you're strolling leisurely
Or really on the run,
You'll never fear the smog or soot;
We've only fun and sun.

Come here as a necessity,
Or merely come by chance,
But you will find no better place,
A setting for romance.

So if you favor big, bright lights
Or dimly lighted corridor,
The place that's next to Paradise?
Exotic, stately FLORIDA!

Delia M. Long

The Vanquished

To see their dull shrunken eyes
Skin drawn taut across
Those trusting hungry faces
Beneath the hot blue skies.

Distended bellies and their poor, thin
Emaciated sick brown bodies
Sends a pain as sharp as any knife
Deep, deep into my skin.

While man ignores and wines and dines
Carefree, with liquor on his breath
The vanquished, too weak and tired
Lie down, and patiently wait for death.

Patricia Paterson

For The Sake Of The Children

Let the blossoms bloom
On the chestnut tree.
The rosebuds in the valley,
Let them be.
And the birds in the tree,
They belong to you and me.
May they fly across
The fields and mountains,
And soar along
A deep and endless see.

Let our children live,
They should laugh and play.
For life's a wonder to them,
Let them be.
As the birds in the tree,
They belong to you and me.
May they linger
Watching crimson sunsets,
And fleetingly
Glimpse at eternity.

Gisela Seifert

Life Is Good

Life is good
Life is fun,
Life is never done.

I am good
I am fun,
I am never done.

I must be life!

Rachael Hernandez

It Passes

So soon it passes,
  like a bird on the wing.
Morning dews and rising suns
  are brushed aside and spat upon
  as things that must be borne
To reach the morning coffee
  and the office,
Where the world is far away
  and the noon-hours turn up empty
  and the sun arcs down unseen.
So soon it's gone the way of
  other days and other suns

John McKinley

Just Wondering
(Post Mortem Questions)

We never got to know you, Mom,
The way we wanted to.

'Tho you gave us all your writings
(A partial record of your life),
We look at the table of contents
And wonder about that empty span
From when you married daddy
'Til your life in Coram began.

Was there a special reason that
No secrets of yours were revealed?
We remember your saying one time
That those were the years about which
We'd have our own stories to tell.

Mom, what really happened?
Did you ever break out of your shell?

We're leaving for home tomorrow,
We'll be wondering all of the way
What capers and gambols
You hid from our sight
So as not to shock or dismay.

M. Jane Popolizio

Realization

We sat
In the sweet summer grass
Searching
For four leaf clovers
The bees — pollen-ladened —
Hummed and buzzed
Overhead..
We vowed
That the one
We might find
Would be a token
Of our love..
We finally found - one
With the fourth leaf
Dead..

Rollie C. Dowdle

Old Folks

Hello, how are you today
Are your eyes growing dim
Can you still go out and play
And do you have a double chin

Are you legs growing weak
And your tummy getting fat
Do you wander down the street
And don't know where you're at

Do you go from room to room
And can't filled with gloom
That's the way we old folks fly

Now, my body needs ironing
And some grey in my hair
But my heart is still singing
So - I really don't care

Margaret Deer

A Memory Of Us Together

I have a memory of our first
glance into each others eyes.
I have a memory of our first kiss,
your lips were so soft and tender.
I have a memory of the first
embrace into your arms.
They held me so tight and I
felt so safe and secure.
I have a memory of our courtship.
Each and every day it seemed
to become more of a dream.
I have a memory of the first time
you took my hand into yours.
Hands that were strong and held
onto me so I wouldn't fall.
I have a memory of your words
saying you would love me forever.
These are all memories to me
now that you are gone.
Memories are all I have left of us.

Denise Marie Trieglaff

"That Fat Buddha Man
Ate My Religion"

Wise sage
crazy fat faced little man
sez to me
"God Barbara
praying is for fools
and this is the last of the poundcake"
I wrote it down.
As he stuffed his face with yellow
sponge that
would last for ages
lingering
on my mind as he looked up
squeezing his eyes
to include me in a crazy whacked out
ethereal vision
munching away on dumb symbolic
poundcake
that would invade my brain for weeks.

Jennifer Keel

The Tree Of Life

If I could be the tree of life
How strong would my roots be?
If I could be the tree of life
Could you depend on me?
If I could be the tree of life
Would it be with your time
To look upon this tree of life
And venture forth to climb?
If I could be the tree of life
Would I have limbs of strength
To hold you with security
As you explore their length?
Would I have limbs that flourished with
A brilliant coloured leaf
Or would the bareness of my tree
Just cause you pain and grief?
If I could be the tree of life
And this would be my prayer
That if you need a tree of life
Always would I be there.

Mark Durfor

The End

Off in the distance
The sound of drums
Hooves beating on ground.
It's coming.

Clouds gather
Harbingers of storms.
The rumble mimics the horse.
It grows closer.

Lighting flashes
Power yet untold
Near to being unleashed.
He is nearly upon us.

We have not yet heard the thunder
Seen the lightning
Understood the end.
He has come.

"And I saw a pale horse,
Upon it a pale rider
The horse's name was Pestilence
The rider's name was Death."

Revelation.

Jason Tauber

Home

They say home
Is where the heart is.

But I disagree.

Home is where
The spirit rests.

When it's finally set free.

Following the brightest
Light

That you have ever seen.

Flying thru a sea of clouds
your feelings are serene

You're floating in a mist
When suddenly the
Bright light's gone

And there in a blanket
of darkness
You hear the faintest song.

Molly Newkirk

Untitled

The digger digs a tender trough
and down I lie amongst the stones
in damp dark earth.
Its walls are wet, and crumble
beside my skin with roots and shells.
My eyes catch dust.
I am not buried yet, I see the sky
and hear the birds or angels sing.
Very sweet yet quiet here.
Blue sea sky and yellow sun
find a spot to glimmer down
upon my face and give me once
a little warmth.

Andrea Anderson

Captured Memories

Two hearts a fire,
    captured by a past
        that cannot be forgotten.
Separate lives by choice,
Stolen moments with love,
Soulmates by heart.
    Rekindled promises
        of yesterday.
Tomorrows future held
    gently upon our sleeves.
Cherishing each today,
    as if it were our last.

Millie Reich-Peek

My Family And I Lost

A loved one
To God she went
for all time
I wondered so
Why did she have to go
but my Mom and Dad
reassured me
God is there forever and ever
he called her because He loved her too
I was told not to be greedy or selfish
So later that night
I made a wish to God
to please tell my loved one
I loved her so.

Lisa Truwe

Stitha-Pragna

A great surge of land
enclosed a fluid muse.

Transient powers held
by a sheath of black.

I looked, dazed at
that lustrous calm.

A flood of memories
of the same still life.

Happy, painful, solvent
all water washed.

Sucking at my past,
my present, my future.

Not yet ready to give-
I simply stood there.

In a trance. In siege of
the velvet conqueror.

I then left - my secret safe
beyond the rising hill.

Pallavi Nagesha

As I Remember

When I button my blouse
in front of the mirror
and see my hands
they remind me of my aging mother
then I was so very tolerant of her
it bothered me not at all as I remember
now I shiver a little
my mother's generation
was the last wave off the shore
before me

Lisa Steckler

The Sum Total Of All My Parts

I am a mind.
A personality.
I'm cold hands
And curly hair.

I'm a loud laugh
And obsessive worrying.
I'm walking in the snow
And swimming at two a.m.

I'm the romance of Bronte
And the melodrama of a Harlequin.
I'm bright yellow roses
And a pretty lousy game of pool.

I'm Mom's Christmas gift from '76.

I don't have a double D-sized chest.
But I do have double D-sized dreams.
I don't have really big hair.
Instead I have a really big heart.

I don't have a flat personality.
And I don't have a flat mind.
I don't even think my stomach is flat.

Dana Yates

Mourners Of The Silent Sunday

They crowded around and
watched, speaking not a word,
looking on as the sky
cried.

Silence fell, like the leaves
of the Fall, and the shadow
crept farther over the dark
unmoving

Wilted and dried, the petals
fell, and were buried under
the dirt of the earth for
eternity

Loud wails sporadically
came and joined the sobs
of the high and mighty
above.

Lasting darkness and
ever wondering fear lurked
unveiling, and the sky continued
to cry.

Amy Straub

The Journey Within

As in "miles to go before I sleep"
Which road to leave, which road to keep
I fear to choose, that I might weep.
And never find myself.

The journey often long and tiring
Always dreaming and aspiring
To higher ground before retiring
Perhaps to never find myself.

Looking inward, looking out
Realization belying doubt
My destination is life throughout
And I will always find myself.

Anita Weeks

The Things I Love

I love the way you dance with me
    To music sweet and clear,
The way you hold me in your arms
    And whisper in my ear.

I love the way you talk to me
    When we are all alone,
The way you kiss my lips, my dear,
    And know they are your own.

I love the very thought of you
    That's with me everyday,
I even love the love the loneliness
    I feel when you're away.

The things I love are countless
    As are the stars above you,
But what I love the most, dear one,
    Is the way you say, "I Love You."

Evelyn Masek

Peas

I don't know about you
but this is a fact.
When you have peas for dinner,
watch them attack.

It starts with one
rolling off the plate
you hear "there they go"
replies your mate.

And when you clean up
they are on the floor,
one needs to sweep
them out the door.

The answer to this
the next time you eat,
is to fix green beans,
they can't be beat.

Susanna G. Taubenberger

"Fear"

Hate
hate
loss of control
unseen forces, blacken your soul

Fate
fate
lack of power
despair strikes, begins to devour

Nod
nod
nod to commands
it's not your mind guiding your hands

God
God
tyrant master
Lord of plagues, Lord of disaster

Death
death
end of it all?
Only fear can keep our life small

Matt Thrift

Untitled

When we first met,
I'd never have thought,
If you didn't love me,
I'd fall apart.

I never believed you.
When you said you loved me,
I always wondered,
how could that be?

The feeling of love,
is strange and new,
And when you hold me in your arms.
We know the love is true.

I finally realized,
That we really had love,
It was sent to us,
By our Lord from above.

Nicola Hamby

Night Frights

I lay upon
My bed at night,
Waiting for a signal,
A sign of light.
I look out my window
And I shall see,
Many frightening,
Haunting trees.
Many sights
May give me fright,
But as I turn
My head at night,
I see a room
full of light.
My mother then comes,
And tucks me in.
Then all my troubles
Drift away in the end!

Shana Shawver

Winter Eden

An encompassing hush falls
while I sleepily dance,
barefoot and sleep-dazed,
on cold concrete that bites
my toes, as I
listen to the lack of the sound
of snow falling.
The silence is deafening.
It holds me in an obedient trance,
captivated.
Transformed by angels —
the flight of the Canadian Geese
enveloped my entire being.
Their migration in the sky,
poetry.
The brush of snow,
whisper of wings,
icy lace draped delicately
on the limb of a weeping willow.
Signs of life.

Heather Thayer

Untitled

Children are the innocent,
  The joy and love of life.
They look at you in wonder,
  In happiness and delight.
They're busy little bodies just
  jumping all around.
With energy and enthusiasm
  sure to abound.
One minute they are angels,
  so sweet you love them so.
Then next they're way too rowdy,
  you'd like for them to go.
No matter if you're Mom or Dad,
  Grandma or Grandpa . . .
They're still your little angels,
  you love and want them all.

Lynda Gable

Expectations

Love may be explained
  in many different ways
It can bring you pleasure
  it can also cause you pain.

In love there must be trust
  and with this you can expect
There should be a little patience
  and a whole lot of respect.

Be a little sympathetic
  and have an opened mind
Or otherwise for you
  Love will be very hard to find.

Just watch what you might say
  and be careful what you do
For if you can wait patiently
  true love will come to you.

Angela Culp

Untitled

You don't even know me
  I don't even have a name,
But we have something in common
  That is very much the same.
In each of our own lives
  They play a different role.
They care about us all
  Deep within their soul.
I cannot say exactly when
  We'll meet face to face.
I guarantee the time will come
  And only with His grace.
I hope you will be proud of me
  Just for who I am.
Because I am a part of you
  and That is who I am.
See you soon,
  Baby Redmon

Yvonne R. Redmon

Only Man

I love my only man.
I love his tender touch
So when I am around him
I need not every much.

Melanie Pelot

Where There Is

Where there is laughter,
there is a smile.
Where there is fashion,
there is style.

Where there is smoke,
there is pollution.
Where there is a problem,
there is a solution.

Where there is a beginning,
there is a end.
Where there is a companion,
there is a friend!

Jodi Fechtelkotter

"Just A Picture"

There's a picture in my heart,
holds a thousand memories, and
each day that passes by, it keeps
looking back at me, each heartbeat
of my heart, paints that picture
bright and clear, it makes me
feel like living although I know
that she not here, just a heartbeat
and a picture is all she left for me,
but that heart beat and that picture
means all the world to me,
you could give me all the money,
that this old world can hold, but
it will never buy that heartbeat.
or that picture that I hold,
Just a heartbeat and a picture
is all she left for me,
I will cherish them forever
until "Eternity"

Benjamin A. Jeremiah Sr.

Let's Talk

Let's talk all through the
night, hold me tight with
all your might. Without
any pain that will gain
my heart. Hearing you
say "that it's better
apart". My sun won't shine
again, unless you cure all
the pain, by saying "you'll
stay" and never be ashamed
because I will always
remember your name, and
will always love you the same.

Edna Morales

"Nature's Way"

So many nights have come
and gone... restless nights
so alone...
    Then there are nights you
are there... visions of you
in which we shared....
    As I see you in nature
way... how beautiful you
are as I see you this way...
    The beauty of you fills
my heart as I remember you
in the dark...
    To this day I see you
in nature's way...

Billy Angevine

Dream Wishes

Two ladies by a river stray
While walking down the lane,
Lady Anne the wild one
The dreamer Lady Jane.

The dreamer sighed then said
"I wish my life were as a stream
So peaceful and so still,
Kind of like a dream."

"I would be a little drop
In the greatest rolling fall;
I'd never choose the gentle lake
For it wouldn't please me at all!"

It was lady Anne who spoke
Those words to lady Jane,
As they continued on their walk
Down the peaceful lane.

So if you carry out your dreams
Be full of smiles or of tears,
As God has planned well
Should help bear the years.

Miranda B. Squires

Geese

Raindrops fall softly,
  on my brow,
and the ice cold wind, rips
  through me, like the
  slice of a blade.

The geese move slowly,
  inspecting, each morsel
  of earth,
  for what might be their
  feast.

Lovingly they group together,
  as to protect their
  massive clan.

The winter cometh,
  Where will I go?
The geese have their
  destination,
  and soon will depart from me.
  I'll miss them.

Deborah Simpson

Chance

  Take a chance worth taken,
it could be a love worth making.
  When most would say no, only
I say yes.
  After everyone has walked away,
there's only one right here that
will always stay standing by the
one only I could, and will truly love.
  Total dedication can be given
to you, when most are left only
wishing.
  So take that chance and you
to, may stop wishing and start
truly living.
  Someday soon you to will
understand that this chance is
waiting for only one, to take it,
but that one, happens to be you,
so please don't be left only wishing.
  Take this chance worth taken.

Tammy D. Mann

"The Man I'll Never Know"

As I sat there thinking
'Bout days gone by,
I couldn't help
But remember,

Would he ever be
That man that stole my heart,
Would he ever be
That man I'd see again,

His rope sang a tune,
As it danced through the air,
He was the guy of my dreams,
But I would never have,

So I sit here crying,
Remembering the past,
And the man I love,
He is a star I'll never touch

Cortney Bramwell

Names, Tags, And Labels

The pinkerton says a thief.
Mother says my favorite son.

The priest says a lost sheep.
Father says a trif'lin boy.

The educator says potential.
Sister says a lunatic.

The judge says an addict.
Brother says a lazy punk.

The tudor says a poet.
Uncle says a worthless youth.

The parole officer says confused.
Janey says he's mine.

The first Sergeant says a brave one.
Send him to the land of the Sun.

The coroner says another one.
Where's his tags, what's his name,
He's already been labeled.

Ronald Phillip Bowles

Untitled

Run with me,
  down to the river....
To collect my spirit for your
  memory book.
I want to be sure that
  you remember
Me
  In the right way.
For who I am, not
  who I seem to be.
For what I believe, not
  what everyone says I should believe.
For the way I jump from rock
  to rock
With the smile on that you
Cannot understand.

Jessa N. Goldstein

Ode To A River

Oh, river, so strong, so fast;
You run by without a care.
I listen as you go past,
And wonder if you know I'm there.

The water's cold to my feet,
And you seem to know I'm there.
You dance around my cold feet
To say "your burdens I'll share."

I find a great place to sit,
Warmed in the afternoon sun.
How good to relax a bit,
And learn from you a lesson.

Why can't I gain strength, be slow
And let life run on by me?
For then is when strength I show;
Life is the river in me.

Joy E. Krumdiack

"A Photograph"

Black and white
Left and right
Style and smile
Click and clack
Step forward step back
Light I need
Shutter speed
Focus thoughts
Emotions caught
Zoom lens dark room
Squint and print
Oh how I love to
Capture the rhythm
of life on film

William C. Papke

Baby Blue Eyes

Oh child of mine
So young and fair
With baby blue eyes
And long blonde hair
Pretty as a picture
And quick as a whip
Make your life count
For the goodness in your soul
And the love in your heart
So your spirit can soar
To places unknown
To those with no eyes
And a heart that is stone.

You are the love of my life
And the soul of my being
With those baby blue eyes
And your spirit of freedom.

Candice Cossitt-Bennett

If My Finger Nails Were Candy

If my fingernails were candy,
I would bite them all day.
If my finger nails were candy,
I'd say hip-hip hooray.
If my finger nails were candy,
I would bite them all the time.
If my finger nails were candy,
They'd be peach, lemon, and lime.

Rebecca Suriano

Friendship

Friendship is a gift.
It cannot be bought or sold
With silver or gold,
but lives within our hearts.

Friendship shares the times
when sorrow comes our way.
To have a friend who really cares
lightens the burdens we must carry.

Friendship brings back long
forgotten memories of the past
as we bring them out to share
with that very special friend.

Margaret Roy

"Ode To A Root Cellar"

There are many kinds of roots
As our ancestors often told
But the only ones worth climbing
Are those in Jack's root cellar
And believe me they are bold
Roots-roots-roots
Climbing up and down again
Proud to get the best of men
They catch us on the stairs
And they grab us any where
Quite often you don't dare
To risk it down the stairs
To Jack's root cellar.

John F. Whitaker

Origins

An isle as beautiful as they say,
such as the shore by Galway Bay.

Tis but a piece of darkened turf,
pushed up from mother earth.

A place washed gently by the sea,
made for the likes of you and me.

And now I understand as if been told,
just who I am and from what mold.

This is not done for which I've come,
until my soul and yours are one.

Thomas F. Gillen

Run Away

I wish I could run away into your arms
And leave the world behind
To walk along the breezy beach
And watch the sun rise

I wish I could tell you all my fears
And cry them all away
And melt within your tender kiss
Until the break of day

But my heart has been shattered
And my love has gone away
Like a fire drowned out by water
What is there left to say?

Uncorked champagne will go flat
And, I guess, so have I
But I did before I was put on the shelf
And now, alone, I must cry

Erica Dorfler

Unmet

At first she is a person,
Who you have feelings for.
The feelings don't fade or worsen,
They grow more and more.

You yearn just to hold her,
To have her by your side,
Your arm on her shoulder,
Fills your heart with pride.

She's a lady you're thinking of,
While she is Lord knows where.
She's a woman you can love,
A good friend who does care.

When troubles have you pressed,
She can make you laugh!
The key to your success,
She's your other half.

Worth more than any treasure,
Keep her safe from harm.
An asset beyond measure,
She is your Lucky Charm!

Ronald Wood

Time

Our paths have crossed
Our lives have touched
I'll never be the same.
For someplace deep within my heart
You're more than just a name.

Jason Lefebvre-Spence

Best Friends

You're my friend forever
as long as that might be.
You've stood by me through days of bad,
and shared my joys with me.
I've known you for a very long time;
and each day has been the best.
Stay as you are forever
and our friendship will forever last.
But in the times that follow
be yourself the whole time through,
and stand by me as I stand by you.
The way Best Friends do.

Jimi Ann Ayers

The Dawn After Death

Serene
in the still silent solitude
of death.

Liberated
from a life
none of us
completely comprehend.

Released
from a body
that has filled
its final purpose.

Free
Forever
in some invisible paradise
where wisdom
is the wings of wholeness
and peace and love
a Heaven of Now.

Therese M. Turner

The Unborn

A glimpse of life did I share,
Beautiful and glorious do not despair,
Life of ninety did I know,
Days were all I had to grow.

Never to know what was my name,
Never to reach fortune and fame,
Not to feel happy or sad,
Never to be good or bad.

Innocence was my way,
Why on earth could I not stay,
Boy nor man will I be,
What could have been I'll never see.

I am well being here,
Having not life nor death to fear,
So do not cry and do not mourn,
I am simply the unborn.

Luis M. Elizalde

A Dream

A dream is something special.
A dream might amazingly come true.
A dream is something secret.
Your dream is only for you.

You might have many dreams.
You know what they could be.
One dream might be to go swimming,
The other to climb a tree.

Everyone in the world has a dream.
You certainly have your own.
If you have a dream,
You'll never be alone.

Nancy Marsden

Communication

Stimuli of minds
Balm for souls
Release of emotion
 Speech!

Comfort of closeness
Contact of compassion
Proof of caring -
 Touch!

Relief of tension
Outpouring of hurts
Rivers of loving
 Tears!

Sharing of joy
Lighting of eyes
Conveying empathy
 Smiles!

Torrents of inspiration
Feelings demanding expression
Thoughts communicated
 Poetry!

Honoria A. Groves

Love

Love is wind, rain, fire, burning sun
Love there's only one
Love is a heart set on fire
Love is passion, romance and desire
Love is cool
Love is nice
Love is fire, rain, sun and ice

Katrina Steigerwald   Age 12

The Grief Of War

Shattered earth
upon the realm of reality.
In strangeness shapes
the wailers wailing
as only they know how.
Colour in the darkness
covering all that was
but are not now.
The wailers trained to be the soul
as all and one but not today,
they are themselves.
Not one or many more could be,
in unison they cry as only
they know how.
No poetry or rhyming grief,
today they cry
at what they see,
reality.

Dennis Sean

Someone Something Special

Something special grows in me
more and more each day.
It feels like it wants to burst,
to share,
or to give to another.

Maybe one day someone
will come into my life
and love me for me
and not judge me
by what they hear
or the way I look.

This someone would stop
the nightmares,
the loneliness,
and the pain, that I have in me

This someone won't break
my heart or play with my mind.
But when I find someone
this something will love them
the way they have love me.

Paul M. D. Patterson

Choices

Visions of motion,
Forever in change.
Shades of night.
Days in the dark.
Shadows of light
While day turns to night.
Forever in change,
Light and dark.
Time to look,
Feelings, left so far behind,
And a darkness to shine.
One to choose the light of day.
Choices made so long ago.
End of tomorrow,
Forever in sight.
Look through the window,
And events to pass.
Balance in motion
Visions through time.

William Hall

To Be With Jesus

Momma and Daddy are in heaven
Where the angels sing
Holding the hand of Jesus
Their eternal king.

He takes them to the Throne
Where they'll praise his name
He says, welcome to your new home
I'm your eternal king.

They walk the promised land
To the Golden Shore
To their mansions so bright
Where they'll live for ever more.

Their children below are waiting
For their turn on High
To be with Jesus in the sweet by and by.

Marlyn Johnson

Remembering The Years Gone By

For many years I climbed,
For many years I fell
For many years I lived
Enclosed in an empty shell
And then one day....
I found the rose,
That very day I lost my soul...
For when I plucked it
From where it lay,
It dried in my arms,
And withered away.

I feel too old, to start anew
But this I say to those of you
Whose lusty ambitions
Rule your lives...
"Search not for roses,
Search not for strife,
For love can be the cruelest knife."

Ramona M. Soto

Love

Quiet stirrings from within
creep forth on silent feet,
like morning fog
that veils and shrouds
the tell-tale light of dawn,
wending thoughts
and clouding minds
till hearts are strong
and intertwined.

But as the day
wears thin the veil,
realities unfold.
Dewdrops wither
in the sun,
and young hearts
oft grow old.

Lew Hofmann

STEVENSON

There he is
    Might as well capitalize
He needs a stone formation
To match his glorified ego
God help his invisibility
Lest his heel be once exposed
And grounds
    His sole life purpose.

Sugar Boese

Desert, Sand, and Sea

Dry bushes, hot sand, and a
    shining blue sea.
On occasion there is shade
    near a twisted smoke tree.
Seagulls are finding their way
    to the shore.
Looking for whatever sea gulls
    like to explore.
Continuous hills in the distance
    Oh what a great sight!
Their colors ever changing throughout
    the day into night
Creosote leaves, lacy in their
    silhouettes against the sky
So peaceful, so quiet with exception
    to a cotes cry
This desert is home and
    forever there'll be
Dry bushes, hot sand, and
    a shining blue sea.

Vivian F. Wilkeson

My Heart...

My heart is were I will
always keep your love in mind,
My heart will love you till
the end of time,
My heart will keep you
safe and warm,
My heart will keep you
safe from harm,
My heart is were I'll
keep my love for you,
I hope your heart's there
for me too

Trenna Scott

Brink

The brink of death
Can happen so fast
Jaws of life
Are opened wide
Ready to swallow
It's next victim
Down to its shallow grave
Bones turn to dust
Wandering out through the eaves
Blowing far and away
Above the earth and out
Some more and more and more
Finding things never seen
And floating beyond anything
Chasing after stardust
In an atmosphere full of fear
Things shall never ever seize
Cause everything is free
Wandering in a place full of wonder

Pamela Ryan

Friends

Together we came
Even though apart
Hearts without aim
Formed like art
Valued is friendship
Born is trust
Together we're its
Most precious must!

Friends

Ricky J. Brown

Light Of Hope

Light in the night
Beaming bright
Beacon of hope
Words unspoken
Through the darkness you shine
Your soul reaching mine
Is it frustration,
Inspiration,
That keeps you glowing?
Or a way of knowing,
Knowing you care
You're always there
You help me carry on
When hope seems gone
When desperation takes its toll
You are the light of my soul

Lynne Ford

"To Shed A Tear"

On a cold winter's night
his father left town;
left a small little boy,
with his face to the ground;
I said to the little boy,
have no fear,
he smiles and looked up;
and shed a single tear,
as time passes by;
he gets stronger each day,
for I am his mother;
I'll mend his heart
in every way.

K. Merritt

Child Abuse

I can see them
everywhere
Little children
of despair
Trapped inside a world
that's old
Void of feelings
dark and cold
Ghostly shadows
dance about
Making the children
scream and shout
Trying to hide
to no avail
Ghosts still find them
alone and frail
With bodies so fragile
they fall apart
And inside their bodies
a broken heart

Ellen Kelly

Untitled

I'm drowning
in the air
of this
empty room

Michiel Arts

Unclaimed Ruby

Sunlight penetrates
Deep turquoise waters.
A ruby bounces gently
To the rhythm of the ocean.
Entangled by seaweed,
It remains prisoner to the ocean floor.
A ray of sunlight touches deep into
Its heart,
A blood red screens its surroundings.
Unclaimed;
Waiting to be discovered.

Anna Marie Capasso, M.D.

Rose Of Life

The pedals of a rosebud,
    soft as a baby's hand,
Eager to open and reach the sun,
    and spread beauty to all the land.

Those soft hands of a baby,
    so eager like the rose,
To reach out to another
    and bring joy as new life grows.

Who could dare to sever the rose,
    before it blooms in Spring,
Before it shows its beauty rare,
    to every living thing.

And who could dare to sever the life,
    of a helpless unborn child,
Before he has a chance to love,
    before he's ever smiled.

Verlina Gutierrez

The Emigrant

Thought we were special,
I have my doubts.
Thought to be Canadian,
I have my doubts.
When we left our home;and
To start a new life and
Feuds and bitterness forgot.
You are now Canadian,
Stand straight and tall
To make this the best land of all.

Grace Stoddart

Thank You Lord

Thank you Lord,
for blue skies above
For robins, and turtle doves,
For green, green grass,
on yonder hill,
For the mournful cry
of a whipper-poor-will,
For snow mountains,
that reach the sky,
For the majestic eagle,
that sours on highly.
For all Gods creations,
great and small,
For your love of people,
the most of all.

Iman C. Wintz

Revolving

Sitting in circle
Indian style
Thinking about what you're thinking
What are you thinking about?

Is it me? Do you know who I am?
How could you when even
I can't decipher

Fact from Fiction
Opinion oriented answers
staring at me like Russian roulette.

Who am I in the huge void
traveling down roads
that lean into the horizon?

How do you know me
when even I don't know me?
Who are you?
Why are you here
    knowing me - going me
    reaping and sowing me
in his huge void of Russian roulette?

Katharine L. Maguire

Like An Angel

Like an angel he can fly
Like an angel in the sky

Like an angel he can sing
Like an angel with its wings

Like an angel he can dance
Like an angel and its prance

Christina Grbesa

Sister

Saw your face in the
mirror today.
Eyes full of life.
Face with lines of wisdom
and a life well lived.
You smiled at me and your
face radiated love and kindness.
You eyes laughed with mischief.
I started to touch
your face and realized I
Saw your face in the mirror today.

Crystal L. Ambrose

Eight Days Of Seven

Sun peaks through
Yet, you speak of rain.
Who could resist ice cream
You think of gain.
Bubble baths are fun
You say "it's time."

Your steps are wide, rush to keep-up.
Making eight days of seven,
you try, you try.

Amidst smiles and warm hugs.
You make broccoli taste good
    and learning a game.
"It's time" - again, before I'm snug.
Quietly down the steps to your bath
    I'll add some bubbles,
    today...

Manny Franqui

It's Dinner Time Again

It's dinner time again, I catch the smell,
Of fresh-baked bread upon the evening dwell,
Buttered corn, T-bone steak, done well,
Hot coffee's taste, a golden bit of jell.

It's dinner time again, a baked potato steams,
With sour cream a-melting, in it in seams,
Blueberry muffins bursting at the reams,
My waiting appetite in hunger screams!

It's dinner time again, hot gravy strains,
Across mixed vegetables, its luscious stains
rich dark brown where baking meat has lain,
A green salad where chopped tomatoes, reigned.

It's dinner time again, I taste the sweet,
Of cinnamon apple pie, and greet,
The mellowness of my first luscious treat,
For this wondrous dinner, and repeat!

Lucille M. Kroner

Beau

Please love me? I am beautiful.
I need your love, I can be dutiful.
I am not a Poodle dog,
I am a Portuguese Water dog,
No one sees me, but I am not a log.

We met under the table, your belly near the floor,
Your legs almost vanished through the door,
You took my heart when I said, come,
So scared, and yet it was your floor,
You clung to me as if for ever more.

Finding care, and friendship you became quite a comic,
Your days so full loosing your panic,
My beautiful Beau I loved you so.
How could some one hurt you more,
I'd promised to shield you ever more.

For such a short time we had fun,
Your life a joy to see, and run
Neighbors did not see your love
Once more hate under your sun
Rat Poison on chicken, I lost you forever my precious one.

Ruth Dyson Hadfield

The Fall

Afraid of this life, willing to die
    The hope for the future has just passed by.
Dry tears I'm crying, no emotion at all
    Just one of the many discounts of the fall.

An adventure that ended, and started again
    For the one's who survived November's rain.
The wall crumbled down by a victim's hallow eyes
    Because of believing a beast's truthful lies.

The world keeps on fighting for nothing at all
    Just one of the many discounts of the fall
We make our future, the wrong path we chose
    Just look at the tombstones standing in rows

A hand reaches out for nothing to hold, and
The child's body shivers from the force of the cold.
    A picture is shattered by the touch of a hand.
    A woman is running from the fear of this land.

We watch our children grow into men
    Knowing they'll never be young again.
The bell of God's children rings to tell all
    Just one of the many discounts of the fall.

Cassie Altheim

Bahama Mama

Hey, Bahama Mama, some island here!

Seized by the smooth-silken sand between
    my toes. Carrying the footprints of its prey.
Water so clear I can see my feet.

Mama, some island here!

Native Mamas bagging big bags of bright-colorful
    beads.
Enticing tourists as they plead: "Cornrows, cornrows,
    $2.00 a braid".

Mama, some island here!

Bahamian brothers hanging 'round, down
    by the smooth seaside.
Shouting, "Boat ride, boat ride".

Sailboats boasting brilliant colors.
Striped in yellow, orange and blue.

Little boys begin to holler, "T-shirts, T-shirts,
    only a few dollars".

"Cornrows, boating, T-shirts"
"Cornrows, boating, T-shirts"

Hey, Bahama Mama, some island here.

Jacquelyn Bryant

Untitled

Once upon a time
when misery haunted my mind
I was falling...

Down the dawn of the drab gray skies
where the treetops trail the tides
It was you and I as I looked in your eyes
as you whispered a thousand whispers
and I sighed a thousand sighs

So the autumn breeze breathed sweet brilliance into my body,
and you, my chariot, carried me through chilling rains
Yet...I just stood there getting wet

Then you, my valiant Poseidon
you penetrated my palace with no regret
and as the dawn came dashing down
The stars then silently seized my soul
That being so, you danced like a billow in blithe stance
When you then touched fantasy at my request

Racheal Thomas

The Picture

With his finger he slowly traces
Her smooth, delicate cheekbones
The soft, puffy lips
And looks deep into eyes as blue as the sky

He hears her joyous laughter
And catches a sorrowful tear
He leads her through the nights
With his gentle caress

Long walks on the beach, hand in hand
The kisses stolen in the moonlight
As the waves crash against the sand
And the breeze gently blowing through her hair

He fights back the tears starting to form
As every memory of her floods through him
These emotions are now frozen in time
In the picture

Camille Johnson

"Blessed Are The Merciful"

Their dog was old, paralyzed and in pain.
The vet said,
"I can give him a needle,
To put him to sleep,
For he could live six months like that,"
The dog's eyes
Were soft with mute appeal,
So they said,
"Go ahead"
  And the world well knew, they loved their dog.

Their mother was old, paralyzed and in pain.
The doctor said,
"I can give her needles
To prolong her life,
So she may live six months like this."
The mother's eyes
Were frantic with mute appeal,
But they said,
"Go ahead"
  So the world would know, they loved their mother.

   Jean Crook

What's Your Age?

To be "young" is to know the joy
Of sharing and loving and caring,
To look for new horizons to conquer
And to view life's challenges with daring

It's nothing to do with numbers or dates
And it matters not if your hair is turning.
It's how you feel inside that counts
That's what keeps life's fires burning.

If some dusty stranger should save you
From flood or quake or the fires that rage
Would you turn to him and say
"Thanks friend, I'm so grateful - but what's your age?"

Some day a great discovery will turn our world around-
The "old" will younger grow and take centre stage.
And when that time comes (as it surely will)
It won't matter what your age!

When such a miracle is found (and it will surely be)
Will mankind turn a brand new page
Or will he still be tradition bound
And say "I wonder - what's your age?"

   Kathy Arsenault-Cameron

My Buddy

He sits beside me day and night.
His eyes sparkle with a loving light.
His love is pure and sweet,
All he wants is food and a warm place to sleep.
His loyalty is honest and true.
My love for him is nothing new.

Tho hugs and kisses we do not share
Our closeness has nothing to compare.
He is my friend it's true to say
And by my side he'll always stay.
One day he'll be gone, this I know
But my pet, my buddy in my mind, will never go.

   C. King

Black And Gold

The curling fingers slowly closed the galaxy.
The cloudy breath of stars have passed their apogee.
The whirling worlds, receding, soon will turn to black
The final pages of its space-time history.

Ten billion years, or more, this darkness will remain.
No spark will light a dream in this deep-sleep domain.
Since all created must traverse this rounded universe,
The galaxies will reunited again.

Such speed occurs when two huge galaxies collide,
That atoms loosen leaving naked their inside!
In passing through each other leaves an endless cloud of fire
That parts in half as they reluctantly divide.

Electrons golden threads with patterns soon appear
For suns and satellites that follow in their sphere.
The final fabric is the curving diamond veil
That hides the secrets that the magic may prevail!

   Leland Embert Andrews

Memories

I have an Uncle, and his name is Don.
With which I have, a special bond.
He's one of a kind, and is like a second Dad to me.
And it's something that, I never let him see.
Now I think it's time, that everyone should know.
And it's something that I should have told him, many, many, years ago.
Growing up as a kid, we all had so much fun.
And the memories he's left me, add up to be ton.
I just wish that we were, as close knit as before.
And what I have to tell you, we all can't ignore.
Grandma and Grandpa, had only one wish.
That when they departed, we would all surely miss.
This wish that they had, was that things wouldn't change.
That we would just stay, as the family we became.
But families just grow, where we get wrapped up in our own.
And no one knows why, it will always be unknown.
I'm not really saying, that anyone is to blame.
We all eventually new, things wouldn't stay the same.
I wish we can go back, and reminisce the past.
But I know that this surely, will just not last.
But I just want to say, for old times sake.
That what life has dealt us, we all have to take.

   Laurie Oddo

Cosmic Voyager

Holding on to twilight's hand
my soul ascends above the land,
and so the voyage begins.
Travelling past the milky light
a billion stars absorb the night,
then through the veil I gaze.
Finding refuge outside the maze
I journey far to what will be,
unlocking the riddle that is me.
Wondering just how long I'll stay,
if only a moment to hide away
and dream awhile with you.
Remembering when the world was new
I begin to see the clearest picture,
the story of my past and future.
Touching eternity for that split second,
the ground beneath my feet will beckon
for me to come home.
Knowing that I'm never alone,
a part of you remains to hold
as another day starts to unfold,
and so the voyage ends.

   Frank Ciofalo

Silent Screams

Silent screams of a broken heart
  Twilight at my door
I play the moon as the stars cry out
  Dance with us once more
The darkness cloaks me within its folds
  Where you once held me near
I reach for the night to accept me as one
  But I'm alone, now it's clear
As the stars serenade the ocean
  You once called my name
Now you caress another
  While the poison slowly fills my veins
My heat ebbs away
  Now cold and wet with fear
All I leave for you my love
  Is
    Just
      One
        More
          Tear
    T. Rene Kittle

"You And I"

I've realized now that I have to let go
Though you were never mine
Your love was just a fantasy in the corner of my mind
All at once I fell for a dream
I hoped and prayed each day
That my visions of "you and I" would come true
and you would be here to stay
Then just as quick as those visions came
they began to fade away
My dreams turned to stone, my visions were gone
and I was alone
I was too blind to see that the love held in your heart
Wasn't meant for me
Now I've come back to reality but I know for sure
My love for you will always be there
even though "you and I" never were.
    Devon Davis

The Cross

Jesus died on the cross, I will never forget his pain and his loss.
  He hung there in fear, he hung there in fright, but he
never once gave up that fight.

  He will always be alive in our hearts, when we think of
him we are never apart.

Now we sit every Sunday in his house, to give our thanks and
our prayers. It is time to come stop being delayers.

  His heart was full, his hands were out. He wanted to help,
He wanted to save, but the people broke out into a big out rage.

  To give our thanks we should pray, at least once or twice a day.
    Jessica Page

A Storm.....

A Storm is upon my life, its ominous that it's tearing me apart.
The lightning has struck me leaving excruciating pain to fill my heart.
The wind is blowing frantic, powerful and free
that it's pushing and hurling every feeling from me.
The rain is falling so hard that it's blinding my way,
I'm in total darkness each step of the way.
I've fallen so many times Lord looking for extra strength and
love, but only to get up hurting, shivering and wondering if
you'll hear my prayer above?
I know that somewhere in this clouded life of mine there has
to be some light from a sun that shines, but until I find that
path that I should go and that light to let me know.....
I guess things will remain pretty much the same.....
.....A Storm.....
    Amy Mole

I Promise

In sickness and in health,
I promise to be there.
Richer or poorer,
I promise to be around.
If your world crumbles or falls,
I promise to put it together again.
If your dreams should come true,
I promise to be there, to help you through.
If anything was to happen to you,
I promise to carry on your name.
If you should find someone new,
I promise never to forget you.
    Tabitha Streetman

Path In Heaven

As I stare deep into the starry sky,
  A world of enchantment is all I see.
I am no longer left wondering why;
  Finally love is true, for you and me.

Our path's lighted with a radiant glare;
  where we are headed, I really don't know.
Down the long road of happiness we stare;
  with each step taken, the closer we grow.

As we progress, not a problem we meet,
  For the answers we have always seem right.
We look ahead and enjoy our defeat,
  For winning your heart was my only fight.

Then when this world isn't a distant gleam,
I wake to sadness because it's a dream.
    Roy Mejia

Lost Alien

The other day I took a trip
In a earthing spaceship
I left Jupiter at half past three
Soaring over a valley of trees
The planet Earth was my first stop
Then onto Antarctica with a plop
I was surprised when I opened the door
Earth didn't look anything like the brochure
I took pictures of this odd sight
Then I became filled with delight
Suddenly, I heard a knock
I opened a door, what a shock
I saw an alien named Lars
He was from the planet Mars
His spaceship sunk in the sea
He asked if he could travel with me
I said yes and we became friends
I knew our fun would never end.
    Stephanie Young

Valor

Deep in the jungles of the dark far east,
Large battles rage at a terrific cost.
Forgetting the pressure for worldwide peace,
Unwilling boys defend their freedom lost.
A soldier thins the thickness of the dawn.
A witness to some wounded comrade's strife.
An instinct of compassion pressing on,
Brings about changes from a death to life.
To risk his life so others can survive
Shows how our duty to each other.
With selfless love, hope for peace is alive
Throughout the world, brother loving brother.
Where soldiers are still men and hearts still feel,
The threat of war gives way for pain to heal.
    James Murphy

Sometimes I Wonder Why

When I am lonely
Or when I cry
No one is there
And I wonder why.
When I am hurting
And need a friend
Nobody tells me
That it's not the end.
I'm all alone I feel despised
If someone showed they cared
I'd probably be surprised.
Sometimes I do things
That I always regret
Maybe that's why no one cares and yet...
Everyone does things that they regret
So I'm no different
Yet they have friends
People to be there for them until the end.
So sometimes when I'm lonely scared and I start to cry.
I realize no one's there, and I wonder why.

Kristin Szebenyi

Dark Sibling

His life,
an unending cycle of destruction
like the Black Plague,
sweeping through humanity causing pain, misery,
drowning in a quagmire of his own making
sucking those close into the vortex that is his nightmare,
sapping strength, sympathy, love
while simultaneously repelling them,
he careens wildly round,
wrecklessly, dangerously,
he knows, but does not care, of the havoc he wreaks,
tempting death
while others cling tenaciously to life,
taunting death at every turn
because he is already decaying in the
malignancy that is his life,
the cycle is unbreakable,
unavoidable,
like the Black Plague
he must run his course.

M. A. Champion

The Promise Land

A place where I can dwell in peace,
it is a search worldwide,
the fighting never seems to cease
for it goes way back in time.

A place where I can call my own,
and have no thought of fears,
how far back does this saying,
go where I can smile and have no tears.

What started all this distress
for once it was only land,
was the world crowded, or not;
did someone have a plan?

Why can't I say my prayers;
is it wrong or right?
Does it matter, that the skin is not white;
it's said at one time, there was no light.

The promise land I have not found;
Is it because we haven't met on a common ground?

Rita R. Jamialkowski

A Song To Ruth — Words Are Tied To The Heart

Whenever we utter a sound,
It need not be so profound,
Make certain that it helps to lift
The soul and spirit, causing no rift
In a mind so young and pure.
For negative words grow as one matures
Into the heart, taken as true
Then, with growth and maturity, it's hard to undo.

Hearts are broken and hard to mend
Because criticism or judgment went out to send
Illusions of a cruel ego world and mind
To an innocent child who could not find
Her own truth for many, many years
Her worthlessness was heartfelt, dissolved in tears,
Until she found that we are all one,
Loved by Him, blessed by Him, excluding none.

Now her spirit shines brightly each of her days
From morning till evening as she prays,
She uses only those words that impart
Words tied with a golden ribbon straight to her heart.

Dorothy Gemino

Buffalo Lake Is Dry

I am looking at a sea of shimmering grass.
The visions that appear are ghosts of the past.
A baby swims to its mother's breast.
A skier flashes by, then glides to shore for
a much needed rest.
A fisherman yells, "I got one, I got one."
"Oh damn, he got away!"
There's the smoke of burning oak as hotdogs
roast at the end of the day.
The Sunset in all its splendor fades beyond
the Canyon walls.
Children sleep, and grown ups talk quietly as
darkness falls.
Then from the feedlots flow the poisons and the
fishes die.
Across the streams the damns were placed and
the lake went dry.
Yes, Buffalo Lake is dry; and all that remains on this
hot Summer's day is a lonely silence, a bird, and a blowfly.
Sadly I watch as the bird flies away.

Charlie A. Miller

Winter at the
Chautauqua Institute

This mystical, spiritual retreat, nestled by the water,
Sleeps in silence like Snow White awaiting the kiss of her lover.
Chautauqua fills my soul with peaceful contentment.
I close my eyes, breathe deeply, and sense the unseen energy
Of creative minds that preceded me here.

Strolling through now quiet pathways,
I see quaint Victorian cottages,
The outdoor lecture hall, the amphitheater, and
The old stately library.

Chautauqua looks as if some magnificent baker
Frosted it heavily with glistening diamonds.
A gentle wind dances with the evergreen trees and
Playfully scatters sparkling snowflakes as it swirls about.

Motionless, the lake has become an enormous sheet cake,
Where hungry fishermen scoop away layers of icy crystals,
Seeking the hidden treasures below.
Gifts of the earth; gifts of the spirit; gifts of God abound here.

Mary Nasits

Over Seven Bodies Found - Mutilated

Found at the innocent age of fifteen. Thrown upon our steps on a
breezy afternoon as effortlessly as the paperboy tosses out the evening post.
Eyes empty and dark, full of nothing, as he sat cringing from the
world, all alone in a room full of strange people.
Unfamiliar faces talked of 'doses', and theories.
Windows barred, nailed and painted shut.
The smell of urine consumed every corner of this seemingly sterile
place. The boys crime?....Brilliance...

Born with superior intelligence exceeding normal magnitude.
His parents however, could not begin to grasp this child's gift.
Instead, they preferred to grasp their needle, their pipe, their solitude.
And sadly, this impecunious child sat in a locked closet, days on
end, emptied and alone.
Alone, as his mind reeled and clanked, thought after uncontrollable thought.
Needing to be nourished with endless books, literature and theories.
Instead, fueled with horrid torture, neglect and unimaginable torment.
Starving, in all senses, with no guidance, no knowledge, no love.
Knowing only resentment, tribulation and hatred.
Demonstrous screams filled his ringing ears, instead of symphonies
as this prodigy sat alone...in soiled pants...afraid to blink, afraid
to cry. Labelled as a runaway at nine. Arsonist at ten...and now?
After being taught all the wonders of life, he decided to give a
little something back to his community just to say thanks.

Dawna Schwiegerath

Heritage

In my slumber as I sleep, there are visions running deep,
And in my mind, they're haunting me about a past I'll never see.
I dream of souls of long ago who started a heritage I now know,
And who produced a family that somehow is a part of me.

There are ancestors of the past who lived their lives that were to last
And become the beginning of a family tree that resulted in the birth of me.
I remember my grandparents, loving and dear, who go back no further than yesteryear,
But no one ever described my family line to take me further back in time.

There were no records or pictures taken that in my mind could help awaken
Memories of a family, generations ago, that I shall never be able to know.
All I can do is continue to dream of visions that passed but will
    never be seen;
Yet I know that these people who lived long ago, will always live on
    in the depths of my soul.

Jack A. Feldman

"The Derelict"

Alone is he who sits and broods
A broken man with purpose naught,
We look askance and pass him by
Not caring what his needs or trend of thought.
If we but knew, he longs for her
Once more to feel the touch divine
Of better days when they were young
Of soft dim candlelight and wine
How, on their wedding night he'd swept her 'cross the polished floor
And she had laugher and whispered "Darling, swing me just once more,"
He had, with bursting heart complied, and pressed her oh so close,
His newfound bride.
Then she had gone. Oh God! the pain. The thought of never holding her again
Had swept him into solitude, so dark, profound,
Oft time he'd vent his wrath to God, upon the new formed mound.
Bewhiskered, red of eye, he sprawls and dreams,
For with him there is she, of so it seems.

Patricia Watson

The Homeless

He froze to death in the cold.
Distracts bureaucrats from empires old.

But prodded by scribes
Each political tribe
Happily prescribes
its diatribe.

Solutions they demand
Make budgets to spend,
'Fore fiscal year end
Why not just give 'em a grand?

Civil servants now spring into action
To affirm their important position
With a carefully crafted proposition,
Ignoring fundamental supposition.

Guess this could have all been foretold
When we put his options on hold.
But when plans are unrolled
Guess what — spring will unfold!

The martyr vindicated — or at least syndicated —
His blood our machinations lubricated.

Robert Innes

My Best Friend

It started out as love at first sight
I picked him from the litter because
it just seemed right

No I'm not talking about a boy or guy
I'm talking about a puppy as black
as the night sky.

As time went on he became the best
he had won my heart, it was no contest.

I shared my secrets I shared my dreams and
through all tough times we worked as a team.

After one long weekend I returned home to
find that the dog I loved who was gentle
and kind had to leave this world with no good-bye

He left in the spring not in the fall but
I know he died proud and tall.

And still to this day it makes me cry
to think of that wonderful dog in heaven's sky.

Amanda Jones

Chances Are

Chances are, you never could love me.
chances are, it would never be true.
But if the Chances were in our favor,
I'd take a chance and be with you.

Chances are, I'll never feel
Your tender arms around my chest.
But if the Chances were to be ignored,
I'd take a chance and be their guest.

Chances are, the kiss you hold,
Will never be my valentine.
But if the Chances were to be forgotten,
I'd take a chance and give you mine.

Chances are, if we felt the same,
And I loved you and you loved me,
If Chances said our love would fail,
I'd take a chance and set you free.

Bridget Burke

The Mirage

All Summer trails tell tales to remember.
Fiery sunsets on mountains of splendor.
Meadows spilling a rich golden yield,
Colours constantly changing from furrow to field.

Valleys that dip to the centre of earth.
The road runs down steeply to find its own birth,
Over bridges and culverts and creeks filled with mirth,
And a spirit of gladness marks our country's worth.

There is mirage on the Number One Highway.
A huge tree appears on the centre right-of-way,
Hanging down on the road, like a sheltering palm.
It seems to be there to save us from harm.

As we travel along, the tree moves to the right,
Now towers beside us, majestic and bright.
The mirage moves away with the fading of light.
Now to Portage and the 'Peg, a most welcoming sight.

Now back to the West as we turn to go home,
Grateful and glad we had highways to roam.
On the newest horizon, the place we remember,
And the feelings of home and a lovely September.

Alice Potier

My Children My Lifeline

My children are my lifeline. I depend upon them most,
for now that I am older, they have become my host.

I try to be independent, my scooter helps with chores,
but, sometimes it's impossible to weave my way round stores.

I have come to a happy medium, when the weather isn't "grand,"
from this lifeline of my children I accept a helping hand.

I know that they are willing, their kindness is more blessed,
because they work so hard, they also need a little rest.

I say "God bless," my children. My grandchildren too.
My lifeline of the future, your strength will see you through.

So trust in God and always pray, for when he lends an ear,
to all your joys and sadness, respond with love not fear.

I know that I must say, "so long," as I journey on today,
but loud and strong, I sing my song, I did it all...my way.

Nan Mathews

Outside My Window

Outside my window I see... clouds billowing into a mushroom sky.
Birds are pecking, picking, swooping and dashing through the chilly
air. I see flowers smiling, waving and swaying in the autumn sun.
I see leaves scraping, dancing and crashing down the old dirt road.
I see frost sparkling in the cold chilly breeze.
Next to an old oak tree curving like a snake is a fence that is
dented like old cars that had an accident. I can feel the
grass tickling my toes. I imagine a river gently gliding through
a dark tunnel. That's what I see outside my window.

Kellye Leonard (Age 9)

heartwood

i walk in forests so dense
no universal light trickles in
no prophetic truths hang over the head of humanity
like a religion of clouds armed with javelins of lightening
poised and aimed at towers of heartwood
ah, if but our hearts would be so pure
and our deeds as gentle as pine needles against bare soles

Margaret Milroy

Understanding Is The Meaning Of Life

The search for happiness is not so much fulfilled,
In being loved as it is in being understood.
To not so much understand another,
but for ourselves to be fully understood.
Understanding,
It is the reason we love, that in giving our heart,
Another will look inside at our very soul,
And in looking they will know our pain, fears, and dreams.
It is also the reason we hate, that in giving our heart,
Another was allowed to look inside and failed to see,
We were revealed yet, not understood in the least.
To not be judged by the world's standards,
But with loving, kind, eyes to be revealed completely;
That is, to be understood for who we really are.
I believe this is the greatest struggle of life,
To find one who knows us more intimately than we know ourselves,
It is not enough to merely be loved,
We are complete only when we are understood for who we are.
To be naked, unashamed and unafraid,
To know for certain we are understood is the greatest joy.

Debra C. Hurd

Never

The coldest part of never, is never far away
It seeps into your spirit, and keeps your strength at bay
It whispers words of envy, of other pastures green
Then leads your soul to peril, with thoughts all filled with dreams.

The world has many faces, hid behind the sculptured masks,
Of most important people, and most important tasks
Of those so filled with wisdom, and some that aren't too bright
Of them that praise the sunshine, and those that roam the night.

Of little spaces, that belong to each of us
that ward off armed intruders, that try to make a fuss
That dare to change our thinking, and turn it to their way
Demanding we take action before the light of day.

To them that just hear silence, when the clock has struck high noon
When storm clouds sail forever, and shadows shade the moon
Of fields that crack with dryness, and rivers void of fish
The coldest part of never stays gentle in the mist.

Awake, rejoice, seek comfort, your grasses may be green
Thoughts you keep so secret, so quiet and serene
Are also hid by others, that to you have made impressed
Your most forgotten treasure, is your search for happiness.

Eliza R. Campbell

An Object Of Art

A fistful of brushes
A rainbow of colours
A sheet of rag paper
A skillful hand
Which can translate thoughts and visions
Into colour language.

A splash of cerulean blue and payne's gray washed aside
To build a menacing thunder cloud
Yellow ochre streaked across the paper
Lets the feet feel the hard, cold sand
A medley of prussian and antwerp blue
Sparsely applied
Give rise to the white-crested sea
A thin line of new gamboge
Wedged between sand and cloud
Gives the setting sun a radiant evening glow
Two shadows, hand in hand, disappearing in the distance.

Adelheid Jacob

Angel's Song

Out of the dreary depths of night,
touched by kindness and goodness' light.
You lifted me without knowing,
and helped me down the path I'm going.

Raven hair and winning smile.
Fair face and heart, no hint of guile.
Your aura sparkles for all to see,
and you chose to shine your light on me.

You gave me purpose when I found none,
helping me up life's cold dark mountain.
Taught me how to love myself,
All this, and oh, so much else.

Never asking, always giving,
into this dreary shell of my living.
If it were all to end tomorrow,
I would feel both joy and sorrow.

Sorrow that you would be gone,
and I'd be left so all alone.
But joy, although it was not long,
I once did hear your angel's song.

Richard E. Spencer

Accidental Happiness

See me stand
and watch my eyes.
Can you see what it's all about,
the pain and sorrow
of how yesterday was
and every other day
before the day
that I fell in love with you?
The sun shines on the coldest day,
and the moon glows for nights never ending.
My face hurts
from the laughter you cause,
the happiness you bring me,
and the accidental attraction
has completely evolved into eternal love,
joy never experienced before,
and I hope will never end.
For I want every day, every moment,
to be as beautiful
as today is with you.

Jennifer D. Stuckey

Make Yourself A Note To Meet Me Halfway

Your words are ambiguous,
    and so are your ways.

Didn't you know that,
    that was the problem from the very first day.

Stubborn and set in your ways;
    here we are, once again.

I'm receiving messages, while you are in silence.
Yet I'm trying to let you know that,
    that is not what the time is.

Cause I feel we need to speak, but;
    you must let yourself be, distinctly.
        Cause I am not in favor of obscurity.

For if not then; in a moment,
    I'll say good-bye, one day.

So make yourself a note, to meet me halfway!

Nancy Brown

Trapped In Insanity

Insanity... not a choice... a trap.
Insanity... not in your mind, free in your soul.
Insanity... not a medical problem, yet another pressure in everyday life.

Insanity is being in life and wanting to die.
It doesn't need padded rooms or heavy drugs, It's not a disease!
It doesn't need therapy or jokes.
Insanity needs love and understanding.
Insanity is me... I'm trapped... I'm confused...
I know insanity though I don't know me.
No one person can understand until they have lived it.
It is an emotion as is fear and loneliness,
Not... like happiness and love.
I'm insanity... I'm trapped... I'm confused...
Insanity is the questioning of the mind and soul.
Insanity ain't fists, it's tears, it's not what you see on t.v. or
pulling out hair,
it's not murdering innocent people.
Insanity can fool you... Watch out it fooled me!

Nicole Marie Rozgonyi

Differences

Our differences make us special, it is no
more black and white. It's all colors of the
rainbow that make the world so right. It's
the blending of the races that continue
day by day and it is God who made all people
in this very special way. So who are we to
judge another for the color of their skin.
For it is God who made all people the one
who's always been. So when you have a
hatred and that goes for black and white,
because of one's complexion then we doubt
God's work and might. He made all the
angels, the sun, the moon, the stars. He also
made the animals look how different they
all are. Respect and love each other and
open up your mind to all the world around
you and let your heart be kind. For when
you die and go to heaven he just may not
let you in. It will be because of all your
hatred and not the color of your skin.

Dolores DiMarco Cinema II

Dreams Come And Go

Dreams fade away
Striving for goals that are hard to obtain
People make their dreams stay
Minds form ideas and ideas form dreams.

Striving for goals that are hard to obtain
Most falling short
Minds form ideas and ideas form dreams
Those that remain hold tight.

Most falling short
Images and intentions all turn to myths
Those that remain hold tight
Because everyone needs dreams.

Images and intentions all turn to myths
Dreams fade away
Because everyone needs dreams
People make their dreams stay.

Josh Garvey

A Faraway Friend

I know him on a different level.
He's not for me to have.
He's never been there for me to see,
Never for me to touch.
His voice I've never heard, but he's touched me so.
A relationship, not based on appearance.
A relationship, not based on perception.
A relationship, based solely on words.
I know, if I could look upon him, my love would not be shattered.
To look upon his eyes only once, I'd remember them forever.
To hear him say I Love You, the words would last a lifetime.
To kiss those lips just once, the memory would never die.
On paper I could always trust my non-judgmental friend.
My lover of sorts, his words will never leave me.
I thank you for the gentle words, and for your patience.
I'll love you forever.

Kelly Shannon

Prejudice

I had a dream...

White called me black;
Black called me white;
So I called out in my dream,
"What color am I?"
"You're human my friend," a voice replied,
"But 'human' is not a color," said I,
"Neither is 'black' nor 'white,'" it cried,
"Be not afraid, there is nothing to hide,
In who you are, not what you are, take pride!"

But the dream was real.

Hilary De Cambra

Why Don't You Take A Weekend

I couldn't tell my husband anything, concerning our son,
Raising him lately, has not been fun.
"Oh, he's just three and a half, he seems good to me,
And I love having Don - for my company."

"Why don't you take a weekend. Go and visit your Mom.
I'll hold the fort, while you are gone."
So I packed and left early on a Friday night,
With my intuition warning - things would not go right.

On returning Sunday evening and opening and front door,
In a cycloned front room, my tired spouse was lying on the floor.
From the kitchen doorway I saw our ketchup-splattered kid,
Standing on a floured floor amid rice, beans, pot and lid.

A cheerful "Hi Mommy!" Just a I closed my eyes,
"Am I glad that you're back." My husband's voice caused no surprise.
"Now I'll tell you one thing," he added sheepishly,
"That little monster did not inherit this from me."

Verna Wantnuk

So-o-o Small

Blood rushing through my fingers
Blood thumping in my heart
I guess this is the end of what had seemed the start.

As I watched siblings ripen
I stand alone so small
Thinking back...
The years weren't very good at all,
Now all the life is gone from me.

They've drained it all away
So here I sit alone
Passing by the day

Tara Brian

In So Many Ways Love Is Portrayed...

Love cultivated as such simplicity
arts of words and feelings so delicately composed
A recollection of nature's beauty and creativity
One's intuition so interesting reposed
Love is constituted in those who believe
Confluent in nature's idealistic trend of patchworks
Infinite not only to conceive but as well to receive
And even pacified through a hurting extent of the heart
Love is nurtured through its maturities
From captivity into a duration of departure
Love is so unmeasurably endured
and simplified from its insecurities
Love is expected for its longevity
and nature's essence so highly exposed
In so many ways love is portrayed
A four letter word defined so implicitly
so vividly fulfilled I suppose...

Pamela Denise Singletary

Orbits

Like a comet approaching the sun with its spin
    Caressed and shaped by the solar wind,
Its tail ever pressed and directed away,
    While its heart is drawn closer by gravity's play.
So, two souls interact, their forms gently molding.
    Pushing some there, while here lightly holding.
Perihelion closeness warms hearts and emotions.
    Periodic opening helps cool seething notions.
Yet the system is filled with an energy field,
    Whose strength is increased as the souls are revealed.
And orbits may close to tightly concentric,
    Or be loose, double focused and very eccentric.
The form flows freely from the soul's constellations,
    And takes natural shape from the interrelations.
Let's flow with the ether through space unconstrained.
    And love nature's methods and music refrain.
No time for the future, the past, or their load,
    It's the present we're walking on life's open road.

John Fitzgerald

Reading Can Be Hazardous To Your Mental Health

I shudder to think that this is realistic, checks issued after retirement, according to statistics. Only twenty checks they expect to pay. This is currently the average as of today. So it is written and so it must be? Shortly after retirement, deep six me? I have never been average, ordinary, or run of the mill, and when I retire, I'll leave big shoes to fill. Heads up big company, you will see, my pension you'll be paying me. For years and years I will collect, all I deserve and expect. There are so many plans that I have made, not a hammock in the shade. I will cruise the Caribbean real slow, then dance the night away in Acapulco. I will go to Europe, Africa, and Asia too, and there is so much more I want to do. Just too many things for me to mention, while I collect my well deserved pension. The condo on a golf course, for those golden years, and I will have forgotten all my fears about the thing I read today, to hell with statistics anyway...

Inez M. Seminerio

To My Artist

My artist is a genius, the best you'll ever find,
For her can paint a rainbow and sunbeams in my mind;
I close my eyes and see his work, every shadow, every leaf,
Every ripple in a tranquil pond, or crashing wave against a reef.
I watch him with his brushes, a masterpiece his goal,
Shimmering on canvas, the reflections of his soul;
If I traveled to a gallery, with the finest works of art,
None could surpass the rapture, that he paints within my heart.

Jean C. Bafia

Appreciation

Thanks a lot for addressing my concerns,
You've earned my respect in return.
I have no doubt you'll treat me right,
So I'll continue on and start to type,
Some more poems from my insight.

The poem cards were wonderful,
I slowly read them as I pulled up a stool.
They were exactly what I had in mind,
The job you did was really fine.
I am delighted to give them to my friends,
It gives me a sense of satisfaction within.

Sandra K. Wilson

Six Months

I look down at my Dayton
so comfy in my arms
and I'm amazed at this miracle
so full of love and charm.

In this life, so hurried and so busy,
with those big blue eyes and hair a little frizzy.
He looks up - he - smiles - his eyes begin to close,
I realized all at once what every mommy knows.

With all the bills and money owing,
With all the errands and a van for towing;
I look down at him, my heart goes pitter-pitter
He's so beautiful, so peaceful, nothing else could matter.
As his tiny fingers tickle my lips
I realized how precious he is, right from the toe to tip.
I want to keep him so safe and protected
there is nothing like a baby to put life in perspective.

The love I feel for him is so wonderful and great,
words can't begin to show this lucky stroke of fate.
Being a mommy is so fulfilling and so fun
It's the best job in the world, Oh I love you little one!

Twyla Senchuk

Farewell My Friend

I never thought that I would give up
On someone or anything,
It just seems too hard to let go
Of something that used to be so close.
But today I held on to all that I had
And realized I had nothing.
To leave empty handed with scars on not the hand
But the heart
For it is the one that bleeds.
And to shed a tear for the last time brings pain
To the face that was once filled with happiness and joy.
Pain is forever
And the memory will never die.
It grows inside the broken heart not to mend
But to remind me of countless times of sorrow.
It is so hard to say good-bye
To someone I have just said hello to,
Or someone who would not give me a chance.

Karyn S. Forsyth

His Magical Touch

As the suns rays dance upon the oceans shimmering blanket....
The water arching up to meet the warmth of your touch,
Your never changing facets.....
Beauteous!

Teanne L. Steinetz

A Desert Life Scene

A lone flower - lovely and serene,
blooming alone in a desolate scene.
The harshness of nature takes its toll
and the flower that was loses its soul.
As time goes on, the earth's surface
is dry and does crack, a little at
a time the flowers life comes back.
The dormancy time that the flower
did take, gave food for the soul
and a strong life did make.
As we look hard at nature in all its wonder, we can
follow the example and not stay down under.
We can bloom and we can fade on our
journey thru life, recover our joy and let go of strife.
The lesson is there for all to embrace, showing directions
for how to keep pace. Remembering the flower,
when the rains come and wash out our path,
we will gather our forces and put aside our wrath.
Following the pattern there for all to see, helping us to know
what will be will be!

Sally A. Seth

Transcendental Meditation

blue speckled blue/green
southern sky
redi-whip grey/white
cotton clouds
tippin' past egg yolk sun
beamin' like hot shower warmth

bronzed octogenarian sittin' on porch
rockin' question mark bent
dronin' "What a friend we have in Jesus"

"good mornin'" cuttin' back my harlem jive tone
"respectin' the right - us her eyes hear slow trackin'
brown face/hairs silver
thrustin' she zero on's the inner you
her voices speak sing song baptist ringin'
"mornin' son"

i pass yet remain
Momma Dawson
lips smilin'
ridin' her time capsule brain scramblin' spirits
transcendental meditat...ion...

len fraser

Education

Those that learn only from books and papers,
Know not the world's passions.

Those that learn only from the world,
Know not the world's academics.

Those that fear the world,
Know only their home.

Those that love only their travels,
Know not a love for one's rightful place.

Neither has their intelligence as a result of education.
For what is the knowledge of books and papers
without a world to apply it.
And for what is the knowledge of the world
without the facts and figures it has produced.

Education comes only when one has known both
And applied it in both books and on the streets.

Tara Simms

Reverie

I saw her turn around as if to see
Once more, her school, her teachers, and I thought,
Why are we loathe to leave what used to be,
So much ahead for youth - surely they ought
To hasten forward - reach with outstretched hands
For life - no need in youth for fettering bands.

I could not see her face as I stood there,
Only her figure poised to take its flight;
I thought of all that I should say to her
To tell her life is love, and truth is right,
And as I moved to wake her from her reverie
I saw the girl I was, look back at me!

Doreen Christie

Today's Reality

As I view the World of this Age
Everyone seems to be full of rage.
What are we supposed to do?
Crush the hate, don't sit and stew.

We need to change the world of today.
Make it safer for our children to play.
Come together to join as one
To right the wrongs that are done.

I want the world to be a better place
For all to unite as one human Race.
Only at this one given time
Will we then do away with crime.

Hopefully in the near future everyone will see
That we need to open our eyes to Today's Reality.

Terry Wirtel

Blanket Blue

She's gone and he lives there only
Lying still in a coffin of the lonely
The bed posts where she once draped her gown
Her spirit has flown
He lies in bed alone
Fascinated by the visions of her
Fluttering through the blades of the ceiling fan.
He still tastes her tears on his hand
An ally in a foreign land
Walking while he wraps himself in a
Comforter of pain and delight
Matrimonial memories
He smells her hair on the pillow
He cannot release her—the poor fellow
Restless sleep
Not to dream but to weep.

Jeffrey D. Wyrick

Beautiful You

Everything that's beautiful you are.
Stars and the moon that glisten in the sky,
Flowers that grow Oh! So high,
Shells and pearls from the ocean deep,
The sunset that shows us now we must sleep,
The snow that has fallen,
So white and so bright,
With icicles forming a winter's delight,
The rain that is falling,
From the heavens above,
Each drop telling you,
How much you are loved,
Everything that's beautiful you are.

Angela Dimare

Time Goes By So Quickly

I'm sure you remember the day I was born,
I was so tiny and so warm,
you never let me out of your sight,
you knew I needed to be held tight.

You made things easier when you were around,
like when I stumbled and fell to the ground.
You picked me up and took care of me,
you were the best mommy that could ever be.

Sticking out in my memory are all the things
that you taught me.
I hope your kind and loving ways will stay with
me through all my days.

All the wisdom you gave to me takes me places
I dreamed to be.
You never let me down or made me frown.
You will always be so dear to me,
the mommy I hope some day I will be.

Janel Stewart

A Young Blind Man Weeping In A Subway Train

In sorrow, himself he endures to brace;
Tears tear his dams and flood his faded face.
The trampling torrents roll and will not cease;
He prays in his life-lasting darkness, "Please!"

Six sportive students stampede through the door;
They thump and bump, and burst out laughing more.
Then all at once they see the weeping blind;
They pause their actions with their young hearts kind.

He locks his lips and holds his forehead high;
He turtles to the door and will not sigh.
"Saint George's next stop!" a boy awakes to shout;
The blind man cane-detects his dark way out.

The small boy prays, "Hope God will be your guide;
"He'll journey life with you, right by your side."
"Then you will see with sparkling eyes your own
"The splendid heaven you have never known".

Martin Yam-tin Wong

I Often Wondered Why

There were so many times I often wondered
why, when I was little and a wee bit shy, I
saw things in others that I couldn't see in I.
I felt I couldn't do much of anything I didn't
really try, I often wonder I often wondered
why, My mother often told me that everyone
has a hidden talent, I didn't realize
what mine was so who was I to challenge.
And then one day a voice spoke to me and
said you're what you ought to be. And I discovered
that poetry was bestowed upon me, I took one good
look at myself and realized poetry is all that
is left. And now I sometimes wonder why I
still don't use my talent, with my gift of
poetry there's many yet to challenge.

Brenda L. Edwards

Human And Animal

Sitting here pondering life's little pleasures,
caught in a dream world plucking my feathers.
Take off these chains so I'm able to fly,
soaring up high and touching the sky.
Where is it that all of your anger stems?
Why must I have to be always condemned?
This is really my life I do fear
and this dream world is actually realities tear.

Leanne Parisien

Old Yeller

Long nose, soft eyes
stingy yellow and light browm
tail, short and stubby
love, like a wild flower garden in a heart
many people love others, but don't put their life on the line
for them like he always did
fearless and unselfishly, he gives up his life
dress him up in gold for saving Arliss's life
wishing he could be the hero of the day
dog above all other dogs
dingy, dirty dog was he
Arliss showed love for the yellow dog
dirty odor from outside adventures
gentle as a new summer breeze
coming into the family by stealing
a male's best friend, Old Yeller

Valerie Courville

Rainbows In My Medicine Cabinet

A portrait of dismal emotions
Running stalwartly through my head
A subtle feeling of contentment
As I purposely wet my bed

Approaching my medicine cabinet
I hear a child-like voice summoning me
I unconsciously unfold a new world —
Rainbows are all that I see

Red stands for the innocence of my blood
Orange is for the fruit of my womb
Yellow is for the non-shining sun
Green is for the mold growing in my once vacant tomb

Blue is for my lifeless lips
Indigo stands for my non-functioning veins
Violet is for my decaying tongue
That awkwardly licks my brain

The rainbows flow through the depths of my stomach
But never again will they run stalwartly through my head
The rainbows are now the cushion in my make believe coffin
Absorbing the dampness as I once again wet my bed

Destenie Vital

Life Without Love

Live without love is like
A flower that doesn't open to greet the day
It is dead.

Life without love is like
A war without casualties or death
It isn't real.

Life without love is like
A hawk without feathers
It isn't free.

Life without love is like
A wolf without a pack
It is alone.

Life without love is like
An adventure without risks
It is boring.

Life without love is like
A baby that isn't born
It isn't a life.

Michael Groves

Broken Wing

You're lying there, in front of me
I'm looking down to You.
Your eyes are open, yet You can't see
My love for you was true.

Like a bird with a broken wing I feel,
I cannot set off for a flight.
And my wound will never heal,
Now, that You have died.

I'm saying: I'm sorry, I'm sorry, and how,
For all the things I've done!
I've made a mistake, I've noticed by now,
But not it's too late, 'coz You're gone.

There You are lying lifelessly.
You cannot hear a word,
Can't hear that You meant the world to me,
Like its wing means the world to a bird.

You could fill a lake, even a sea
With the many tears I shed.
Yet, still You're lying in front of me
And still, still You are dead.

Annika Weyhersmueller

Dare To Fear

I met a man his eyes talked to me.
He was a man of wisdom, which few could understand.
He told me things I thought
I could never learn.
God sent this man to me.
I met a man his journey was about to end.
He told me of a place where life will begin.
He dare fear this place where men
have gone before him.
God bless this man who dare to fear.
I met a man his eyes touched my soul.
I asked this man if heaven or hell existed,
he told me of this place
where stories will never be told.
God bless this man who dare to fear.

Sheila Smith

Eyes Of Remembrance

I see things I never thought I'd see.
People crying.
People dying.

Friends and family so pale and so thin.
I just want to take them in my arms.
I want to say it's OK...
But it's not!

Tomorrow is another day.
When people are killed for what they say,
For who they are.

My eyes are shut.
It is dark and yet,
I see a light.
A light that takes me away.
I hope.....

Rebecca Wolf

Have You Ever Wondered

Have you ever wondered....
Where the sun goes at night
Or the stars in the new light of day
Is it the sun that puts the stars on the run...
And chases the moon away
Or is it the moon that chases the sun
Until it falls out of sight
Telling the stars the coast is all clear
So they'll come out and play through the night

Loretta Hibner

Majesty Of Our God

Splendor fills the morning sky.
Songbirds serenade on the wing raising high.
Day and night rings forth powerful speech:
Wisdom of creation beyond our reach.

There is no speech; not a word spoken,
Yet the voices reverberate; the silence is broken.
Creation itself sings a delightful song
Of our mighty reverential Creator; to Him laudation belong.

The heavenly expanse makes a tent for the sun.
The earth travels its course and benefits from the run.
As the sun pours forth its life-giving rays
It nourishes its ward from the light it relays.

The wisdom of God sets the boundary line.
The law of nature opens instruction; line upon line.
So every creation great and small
Unfolds its life story on this, Earth's ball.

There is life, and there is death.
There is good and evil; we endure the test.
But the test is revealing the majesty of our God,
Echoing through the ages—through the corridors we trod.

Wanda L. Holcombe

One Day At A Time

Behind a dead bolt and chain
High above a sparkling city
A rain soaked coat
Strikes a senseless floor

Darkness observes indifferently
Tears drop incessantly
Hot stinging darts, like acid rain
On floral garden bed sheets

The poisoned linen
Snakes through silent corridors
Rustles across blistered hardwood floors
Oblivious to the splinter-needled stairwell

Then gentle cycle begins
Hot milky water seeps into the garden
Trapped in a cavity of metal and glass
It wilts, then drowns

I close the lid and wait
As I did yesterday
As I will do tomorrow
Until the water runs clear

Daphne Tsang

Let It Wave

The flag hung proudly over
   the land.
The people there have taken
   a stand.
From the big White House of the USA,
   the decision, it was made today.
Stop! Halt! Was the demand.
   Whoever heard of such a man?
Trying to take from people
   so near.
The hurting and crying, it rings
   in the ear.
Strength is ours from God's quiet command.
   Justice will be yours again.
On across seas, and many a mile,
   under storm clouds or skies of blue,
   it waves, and from the front porch
   of me and you!
Let it wave!

Bonnie Meredith

The Message

Upon a wing of a Mighty One,
   A messenger from heaven will come,
But, will all listen to where it's from?
   Oh yes, there will be some.

What will this message be?
   Will the people hear and see?
And will it set us free?
   Yes, and there will certainly be a key.

How will this message appear?
   How else, but through someone very dear,
I know, everyone's heart will be seared,
   And all will truly fear.

Now, this word has come to light,
   The Lord is grieving deeply, as in His sight,
He see's that His people do not seek, all they do is fight,
   Even the meek, who are all uptight.

Soon the Lord will come,
   Soon all healing will be done,
All people must become His one,
   Soon, soon, soon, the victory of God will be won.

Anne M. Leslie

"Daddy"

She wanted him to come to her from the peaceful world above,
She wanted comfort and advice from the one she could never love.
Her first breath was for him and he was gone from the start,
He left her with a puzzle and a missing piece in her heart.
She never cried or even thought,
what he could have done for her or what he could have taught.
He always made her wonder how things would be,
If he hadn't taken a sip or left without a key.
Her mother told her how good he was and what he would've done,
If he could've taken her out just once to have a little fun.
She wondered why her mother told her all these things,
Why was she always so careful to pretend it didn't sting.
She wanted an answer to the world of mystery,
She needed to know why he left her without some history.
What was to become of her? She needed someone new,
To tell her how to get things right and always what to do.
She'll never get him back, all the damage is done.
Her image of him and his say in all matters is still
   never and none.

Stephanie Oakley

"We Three"

Nothing outdoors, can replace the shade of a tree
Especially if one lives in very sunny country
Tho the moon, shining bright at night - up above
Is a favorite setting for couples in love.

Nothing is as beguiling as a loved ones smile
It lights your whole being; all the while
Knowing he loves you, and you love him too.

Birds on the wing, for "you" they sing.
The blue skies above - can't encompass your love.
Your heart begins to dance - it's an avalanche!
Yesterday is gone - today you wear a crown!

Then one day, when he holds his own precious babe
Nothing gives a proud father more reason to rave!
Those little fingers and toes and little button nose,
Take hold of a big man's heart, even in repose.

No one has ever had a babe like this!
His dear, dear wifie - deserves a big kiss!
Papa's heart begins to dance, his limbs want to prance
The heavens have opened wide - and blessed is his wife.

Lorena Barrett

Dilemma Of A Heart

I had made myself open, someone came and roped me in
I had given love and trust to the one that I had lust
Love and contentment had made me blind
I never saw the blade from behind
I felt an extreme pain in my chest
Since that time my heart has had no rest
I feel moats being made, I feel mines being laid
I fell walls being built, for this I feel guilt
I do not want to be this way, but my heart sees no other way
When a heart has been stepped on
The inclination to expose it is gone
However if it is hidden
The chance of of feeling is ridden
Should I be open, should I make myself vulnerable
Should I trust, should I love
I want to let someone close
But my heart can not take another painful dose
Love, joy, pain, and sorrow, do I take part
For this is the dilemma of my heart

Jason Baumohl

My Children Will Never Be Gone

My children are playing outside in the yard.
I hear their laughter, feel their joy.
I want to join in but there is no time.
Their laughter fills me, beckons me...I am drawn outside.
What will I do when they are gone?
I miss them already, no hand to hold, no song to sing.
What will I do when they are gone?
This depth of emotions amazes me, this kind of love is so strong.
My heart is heavy as my mind leaps ahead
to the day they say good-bye. I can feel the
regret I will have for all those times I said, "I have no time";
I realize as my children yell,
"Mama, mama come play." That as long as I
listen to my heart there will always "be time" and
that my children will never leave me because the
bond between our hearts will keep us together forever.
My children will never be gone.

Debora Muilenburg

Untitled

I loved you more than anything.
We flew so high,
Like birds on the wing.

When you said goodbye,
I tried so hard —
But I did cry.

We went together,
Just like
A bird and a feather.

Forever's what I thought we'd always be,
But now,
We are both free.

Katie White

Time Yet To Go

To have already failed
And have time yet to go
That is a beautiful thing in life.
To have not surrendered, many times after losing,
To find oneself as unvanquished as the enemy,
To feel the blood still coursing
In torrents through the bodily accoutrements,
To sense again the willingness to fight
And the incomparable preference for love,
That is the glory of life.

W. Stuart McCloy Jr.

Chocolate Chip

The first day I saw him,
I knew he was mine.
The waiting I did was a matter of time.
He was eight weeks old, when he came to our house,
No doubt about it, not as big as a mouse.
He was no bother, and learned real fast,
That his outside habits will always last.
We bought him some toys, well worth the money,
He knows them by name, even the bunny.
He eats when we do morning and night,
And if there's a goodie he gives us a fight.
His sparkling bright eyes are like his gold collar,
His black button nose, shows he's scholar.
My scooter basket, he really does like,
And begs me to take him wherever I might.
He has two blankets which he knows are his own,
And loves to drag them all over our home.

Cleo C. Gould

The White Fence

Scraping and painting the white fence,
we talked about death and those we loved
who had gone.
We talked about the mechanics of it all;
the family in attendance, the ending ceremony,
and the facts; brain and lung tumors, that she had smoked
or hadn't, that she loved herself or not.

We avoided the other stuff
that creeps among us in light or darkness
lurking behind a familiar smell, word, or song.
It comes unannounced and uninvited
pushing aside those carefully erected barriers
to our emotions forcing us to peer into the deep
dark cave of our emptiness remembering those other times
like the brilliance of fall ended by winter's grays.
It is this we avoid in our wordplay talking about the end
always fearful of losing it all
right here,
painting a white fence.

David Fowler

"Love's Treasure Chest"

Irreplaceable moments,
and the splendors of yesterday,
silly little love taps,
all can never be taken away,
Yet love shared by two,
should never be taken for granted
Consume yourself in each others love,
take complete advantage,

Treasure the love you've found,
Ponder it to its highest elevation,
Make it as innovative as it is profound,
Enjoy love's revelation,
of experiencing the pirate's quest,
the long awaited finding of love's treasure chest,

Treasure the melodic memories,
playing over and over in your head,
like the rhythms of no rhythms,
the visionary moments,
of where your heart's been lead,
Treasure the love you've found

Shelley S. Madkins

Come, My Friend

Come have a cigarette, my friend. Let's sit and talk a while.
Let's talk of what our world is like and "face it all in style."

Come have a beer or two, my friend. Let's drown our fears in wine.
Let's let our brains decay with age, pretend that it's all fine.

Come have an acid trip, my friend. Let's fly until we fall.
Let's see some things we know aren't there. Then we would "have it all"

Come take a drag of pot, my friend. Let's smoke until we're through.
Let's laugh at everything we see...and then what could we do?

Come look at what we've done, my friend. Let's see what we've become.
We've wasted everything we had and now our minds are numb.

Come try to fix your past, my friend. Let's take a look around.
Let's see the big mistake we made with all the drugs we found.

Come see the lessons learned, my friend. Let's see what fools we've been.
Let's show the people that we've found we can't begin again.

Come teach the children now, my friend. Let's tell them what we know.
Let's tell them that a high's not high...it's nothing short of low.

Rebecca Lynne Hesselman

The Disastrous Mistake

I sat there one late night
The sky was dark, and the moon shone brightly while
I watched a teenage boy get drunk.

I sat there one late night while
He went for a drive, and as he turned the corner,
Going as fast as a bullet, crashed into a car.

Crashed.

I sat there one late night while
The family from the car went through the hard windshield
And impacted the cold hard ground.
Death is the outcome for a family.

Death.

I sat there one late night while
The driver sat there paralyzed in his car for he could not move.
One mistake drastically changed his life forever.
He will never walk again.

Never.

As I think of this every time I am tempted by that cold killer
I get a chill that runs up my spine. I vow never to make his mistake.

Ever.

Theresa Forrester

Weathervanes

The steaming mug of early morning coffee warms my hands
As I sit quietly by the kitchen table.
The pain of the restless night slowly drifts away.

My eyes see again the handstitched sampler hanging on the wall,
Its weathervane figures poised forever in mid-turn,
Their colors faded gently by time.

The rust colored eagle perches atop its westward pointing arrow,
While the black horse and turquoise rooster face east.
No breath of air will ever move them.

Please let me not live to see myself never changing,
Sewn forever in place by threads of pain and despair,
Unwilling to move in a new direction.

"The wind does change and the creek will rise"
The words sewn long ago in jest now become the morning's prayer.
Thank you Father, for the wind and the creek

Karen Bruggemann

A Winter's Snow

In wind blown mounds and curling drifts
    Our life is filled with winters gifts
It comes to tell us, this winter day
    That nature's show has come our way

That life is similar to the flakes
    That fills the sky with magic shapes
That we are formed from magic parts
    And fashioned by a loving heart

In curling mounds and blowing drifts
    Silently and soft, who brings these gifts
Gifts that press upon our hearts
    And say to us, you are a part

In song and laughter, grief and tears
    Blown by winds of fleeting years
We gather like the magic flakes
    To form the imperfect human race

Good will to all, love and respect
    Will guide our thoughts
As we retreat to contemplate
    The curling mounds of drifting flakes

Walter E. Teague

Tall Abe Lincoln

A better man has never lived
    Than tall Abe Lincoln, the Kentucky kid
With hands so big, and feet so long,
    The boy who never did anyone wrong.
He always thought all men were equal
    And got along with all sorts of people.
Who freed the negroes from slavery
    In the Civil War, fought with great bravery.
    Against the Confederacy in the south
Until freedom for all was brought about.

Abe Lincoln studied day by day
    And borrowed books from miles away.
For all his neighbors and his friends
    Gladly to him their books would lend.
Everyone trusted Abe, so tall.
    A man who was loved by one and all.
A better man has never lived
    Than tall Abe Lincoln, the Kentucky kid.

Vivian L. Merrill

"Winter's Night"

The moon, snow, and barren trees
    all seem mysterious to me
The moon with his beams
    of shimmering silver
    piercing through the velvet of night
The snow turns the dark to a world of beauty
Trees take their barren branches
    and reach into the sky
The majestic world of a winter's night
    stars ray through sky's blackness
    as shining diamonds
    moon enlightens all
    to deadly paleness
    snow, a soft blanket
    covering the world as a whole
    trees which grab into the sky with their
skeleton's
    claws
    reaching
    and grasping
For you or I

Golden Delismon

Will You Answer

You have chosen the way of life
you're walking the path with me
I'm your light shining through you.
Take my love with you into the world
Tell everyone what I've done for you
And I'll do the same for all who
Will come to me and believe.
That I am the way to life
Then people can start living the life
I had for them long ago
I'm calling you, will you answer the call?

Gregorio Garcia

When Will He Love Me?

When will he love me?
Will he love me when I'm 133 or when I'm 123?
When will he love me?
Will he love me when I'm finally working?
Will he love me when I'm singing his song?
When will he love me, and for long?
Will he love me for a second, an hour, a day or for years?
Or, will I have to find more things to master to impress
   him before I receive this most precious gift?
When will he love me?
Will we ever be together, married and living happily near
   beautiful green trees?
Will he love me if I have his child?
Will he love me for just my smile?
Will I ever live up to his expectations?
I wish he loved me now, for me, right now
But apparently I'm not worthy of his love.

Denise L. Rene

Treasured Memories

The value of love, faith, and hope goes beyond measure.
Memories of Mom, and Grandma, are among my greatest treasures.
They gave those gifts, upon which to base my life, so that I might
face daily trouble, and strife.
I could always take my problems to mom, her way of handling things
was soothing, and calm.
Mother thought God gave parents, the greatest of tools, if they'd
teach their children the Golden Rule. If, you'd dare take your
responsibilities light, you washed those dishes over till they were
done right. I have so many memories of yesterday, doesn't, feel like
20 long years, since moms passed away.
She was careful of others feelings, with judgement so wise, with God
she surely found much favor, for, she, was a "Soul Winner", for her Savior.
Mother believed everyone had a purpose, you see, our main life's
goal should be making "Heaven our Destiny".

Sandra Morton

Street Song

I been turning around everyday of my life
to an empty and endless surround,
I go on my way, nothing to say
to the nobody I ever found.
The street is my home, my visitors few,
a sometime smile shared with someone passing thru
on their way to their place where the warmth lightens blue.

I travel alone, rubbing right hand with left hand,
perhaps artificial, but warmth nonetheless-
A drink from a running brook soothes my throat on demand
I offer to passers a sip, and I guess,
from their uncertain eyes that they don't understand
as they try to disguise a sigh of relief that
"Thank God it's not me or the ones that I love" for
life is too sweet, as they all have discovered,
and I smile too, I get by in the street.

Ken Wolpert

Vintage Era

On the brink of winter love,
sophisticated women primped
in crimson velvet gowns
weave through the elaborate ballroom,
displaying delicate collars and lace gloves,
elegant pearls soft on fair necks.
The mesmerizing hope of romance
holds the entire audience captive
under its tempting spell.
Deep golden shadows
elicit mysteries in each lady's eyes.
The gentlemen, polite and handsome,
stand back to admire the scene.
All people poised and excited
as long, plush skirts glide by still.
And in the most bashful countenance,
a humorous grin radiates.
How fancy to dance
through such a charmed era.

Janelle Hoopes Weber

For The Love Of...

The unobtrusive things of life...
passed by
the common look, the quick glance
small, insignificant seeming...
but...deep in the meaning of all life...
natures domain
parts of us all
evolving, temporal, mystic...
why? Do we miss this
why? Passing by
why? Not seeing
   nor hearing
   nor feeling
it's...all of us

Jessica Chatles

Thoughts, Faces And Places

Hi, and how are you today?
Do you need some help?
Have a nice day!

Hi, how's it going?
(I see you, I see your face, I see
your hands, you look tired, I see you.)
Anything else? Thank you, enjoy your day!

Hi, and how's your day going?
You look tired, long day I ask.
Well, now you can kick up your heels
and relax, make the best of it.

(I would love to chat, I'm sorry...
The line is building up!
I'm on the clock, and so are you!)
Thank you, and enjoy your night!

Next please - and how are you this evening?

Reina Santana Dominguez

Joy In The Morning!

I've got cancer and God didn't give it to me,
He gave me a challenge to help me with, you see,
Most of us have the tools of the greatest
importance, a Bible, and a positive
approach to pain, to be sure.
Just learn to adapt to the physical
changes it takes to ensure,
That all go ahead and live,
With all you've got to give.

Julianne Scarbrough

"Come - Oh Spirit"

Come, oh spirit and fill my heart,
Let my weakness be given over to strength,
Assist me in my trials
Enlighten me in my doubt.

Help spirit in all my needs
Protect and console me in affliction
Give strength to fulfill my duties
Gracefully hear me -

Pour your light into my mind and being,
Protect my soul in all my endeavor,
There are souls to care for.
Wounds to heal, and hope to give.

As the Lord is our Saviour
We must atone for our sins,
Give heart to the weary,
Food to the hungry.

Give clothing to the poor
Inspire hope to the hopeless
Wisdom to the needy
Love and good-tidings to all.

Johanna Wolfe Dubensky

Breathing In The Night

Tis my heart that beats the still nights breath,
tasting its enviousness of the futuristic day.
The death of the night now supersedes what was kept,
alive and vibrant, yet only in the light may it stay.

Oh time is forsaken and wakes not the eye,
left in dreary, sleepful dreams of moon covered sky.
The sleepy tears of clouds tremble like fall leaves,
a sample of our thoughts, dreams not to be.

For when you said goodbye, and bid your adieu,
my heart broke in instance, found pieces, few.
So here we stand in darkness, awaiting the day,
when loving and living, again comes our way.

Kimberly Kristenson

The Gift

Chubby fingers, nudging, tugging,
earth releasing on command.
Clinging as a friendship soil
remains on little hand.
A breeze skips sprightly
through a furl of golden untamed hair...
Sunlight slipping like a ribbon
honey color everywhere.
Faded dress parading rosebuds
Pockets filled with secrets rare
a different rock, green colored glass and
brittle locust shell.
Dancing blue pools of innocence,
feelings stir the heart
as smiles embrace each other
echoes of a thought.

Crystal holds great beauty,
gold is worthy, too.
Flower fragrance of perfume
will linger all day through.
But the treasure of my memory,
one that I desire
is the stately, golden dandelion
given by a child.

Edna Collins

"I Wonder"

I wonder why the sky is blue.
I think it is because people store
all their happy thoughts in it.
If all the happy thoughts go away
then the sky will turn all gray
and no one will run and play.
That is why I like the sky so blue and high.
I like the sky because it brings us
many happy bye and byes.

I wonder why I wonder,
I wonder why I always do.
I would just let it be,
but then I wouldn't know why I am me.

Megan Lindley

I Would Miss You

As I lay awake in my bed last night thinking,
A strange and frightening thought came into my mind.

If you should suddenly leave, and pass on before me,
And with out any warning, I should wake to find,

Just how much I love you, and need my precious wife,
And how tightly our love does surely bind,

As I lay there awake and thinking, 'twas then I realized
How our savior loved each one of us, and how in love he died.

Of all the things God gave to me, my precious wife I prized.
For her love, was real love, and not in any way disguised.

So if I should stay to face the world, and you should pass away
If you should leave this wicked world, and I should have to stay.

No one else could ever take your place, is all that I can say.
But I know that will never happen, for to my God, I pray, each day.

But, if I should loose my sweet wife, as time goes marching on,
I'd simply live in our past life until this life is gone.

The sun would rise again someday, for with Jesus comes the dawn,
And life in His great kingdom will go forever on and on.

So as I lay awake just thinking, of our sweet life and love,
My mind turned then to heaven, and Christ's kingdom up above,

Harry D. Palmer

My Dream

My dream is rather simple.
I want to see often a smile's dimple.
I want to make others worry-free.
I want to see them full of glee.
I haven't yet an idea or even a clue
But somehow I will make a difference in this world -
bring a smile, share a hurt, fulfill a dream.
I know it will not be as easy as whipping cream
But still I must try
Or many souls may cry.
You see, whether I am teacher or a writer does not matter
For my dream must not shatter.
Yes, I have a dream of what I want to be and do,
But will I be happy not sharing anything with you?

No, I must seek more.
I must not lock the door.
My dream is rather plain.
It is about easing other's pain.
I want to live in peace forever
And my dream will cease never.

Cheryl Mrazik

My Memory Of Pee Wee

Here it is another day,
And Pee Wee is still away.
Pacing up the street each day
Pee Wee? Has he gone to stay?
Always asking, looking to see
Pee Wee! Where can that child be?
Needing help to carry things big and small
Still Pee Wee has not come back at all.
Where is that child? To send to the store,
As I continue to look out my door.
I suddenly sit with a thud
As tear fall heavenly to my rug
I'm old and have forgotten the way
Pee Wee was murdered the other day

Pee Wee
Murdered April 25, 1996
He now rests
Forest Lawn
Buffalo, NY
Rest My Child

Sheliah A. Carrier

A Summer's Work

Whose bull this is, I think I know
He's from the pasture down below.
A hole in the fence I think I see,
and fence posts flat, all in a row.

I may ask the powers that be,
to look around for help for me!
Preferably a man with a good horse,
this would probably be the key.

A man to set him on his course,
over the hills, without much force.
Then the fence we'll have to mend
summer's work brings much remorse.

I hope this doesn't establish a trend
of fixing fence for days on end.
My back begins to throb and ache
from thoughts of all the fence he'll rend.

I wish his owner would come and take,
him to a sale barn for my sake
or at least to take him home,
come on bull give me a break.

Jeanne Uhl

Summer

On a long hot summer's day
heat was smoldering on the
fresh cut hay.
Not a breeze was blowing, just the
thick summer heat,
ripening the crops on the farm
for winter's keep.
As time and season had their own cycles
to go through,
after planting the ripening did prevail
of the vegetables and berries coming on the vine,
all waiting their harvest from off the farm.
From the roof in the corner of the porch,
wisteria was hanging down,
like clusters of purple grapes and
fragrance filled the air.
Whippoorwills and Bob whites were
calling and saying, "It's harvest time, it's harvest time,"
from everywhere.

Mary Elizabeth Green

"Love"

Love is a game
Which each of us will choose to play

Love is a bitter medicine
That each of us will swallow someday

Love is a dream
Which will soon be forgotten

Love is a memorable lesson
That each of us will learn often

Love is a blind devotion
Which may block us from reaching our true destination

Love is a beautiful rose
But its thorns can be very painful

Love is an aching experience
That can lead to tearful moments

Take the advice from this experienced soul:
"Please be patient with love 'cause love is cruel."

Van Huynh

"Magical Dreams 0f Forever"

Invincible thoughts of you is what
brings my courage of love to your heart,
with the remains of time, to show
this love without prejudice
To look in the background for
promise of a sincere devotion for
infatuation of two souls too
correspond as one

To form life, love and happiness
on the response of hate
With the fruits of harmony which
pulsates through our bodies, from
an overflow of hibernating thoughts
Which you can feel through ones
touch of passion
To let the demons of sorrow, regret
And sin pass us by
As long as the elaboration of our
hearts last for the lifetime of infinity

Javier Echevarria

Summoning The Hermit

A stroke of lightning, lovingly aimed,
Can split 'yes' and 'no' into Maybe.
The laughter of children, digging in sand,
Can charm a whale and tickle the sea.

But you, my friend, though you mean us no harm,
Have forgotten yourself and hardened your mind.
Obsessed with perfection and perfectly wrong,
Your silence breeds fury as you wane sublime.

So come down from your mountain, your breath is too cold.
And there's much more to learn before you grow old.
With your taste for the truth, you've been swallowing stones.
Spit them back out and add sand to our beach.
Come skip with chance and dance out of reach.
But, first, could you please pick the ice from your teeth!

David Lawrence McPhail

The Crush

Lying here all alone in the dark
Wishing you were here to comfort my heart.
My friends all say you like me
I've opened my eyes and tried to see,
if there are hints that you like me.
Your hints are so few,
But I don't give any hints, that I like you
They say you look, and sometimes stare
I'm usually hiding behind a book or I'm not even there
You are my inspiration and I like you so much
I can imagine what it would be
like to have your loving touch
I will always feel your kindness in my heart
It won't matter a bit how far we are apart
You have fulfilled my standards for a
kind, caring, and loving guy
I'm happy when you say hi, to me, but
sad when you say bye
I have had a crush on you, and I wonder if you knew
how much I liked you, and how much I still do.

Kelly Schulz

A Mother's Warm Love

As I doze off and close my eyes
A new world shows as the old one dies

Pictures of families full of love and joy
The older ones laughing and having fun
While the little one is content in its new toy

Far off in the distance I see a familiar face
Of a young girl fallen from grace

Her face - a blur nothing is clear
Is it my face, no it can't be, it's not fair

I look at the face no life do I see
As I look in deeper I know it's me

I quickly jerk up as I am awakened by a gentle shove
I am comforted by a mother's warm love.

Becki Beardsworth

Succession

A single tear, an abolished cry.
A single tear must drip, from your drab, dismal eye.
You look down at the uncovered grave,
neither heaven nor hell will he not become a slave.
Cemeteries so big, but still have to expand.
Soon the domain of the dead will own the mournful land.

It starts with a tear, the succession of pain,
just like a storm as it starts to rain.
So many stages still left to endure.
A problem with pain is you know there's no cure.
There's no way to fix the unforgiving past,
someday, a single tear will be y doleful last.

Drip after drip, tears roll down your cheek;
every drop of pain makes you more and more weak.
Living in a world that lives off despair,
all the pain the same, yet unable to share.
A grassy envelope of earth puts the casket in disguise;
and a final tear must drip, from your drab dismal eyes.

Tony Foster

The Invisible Ladder

You tremble and shake as you look about - and wearily think-
There's no escape, no ... all hope's gone-nothing but fear
As you dash about in a maze of confusion and doubt-
Knowing not where- or - whom to turn in that dark, lonesome haze.
Homeless, you say — do not despair —look up
'Tis a ladder of infinite hope and mercy there, to be found
Within its grasp lies the key that will, your life turn around!

Not a thing, nor anyone with it can compare-God's ladder -
Indeed, God's ladder of mercy and love you'll find there
For, He, alone, knows when you're in utter despair!
You're cast in a perilous abyss of fear, hopelessness and gloom,
You're tossed about in a sea of turmoil storms and utter doom
Grasp on, hold tight - as you come into the "light"-The Holy Book!

Your body shakes, ill and numb- you wonder- "Is this the end?"
So severe the pain, you cannot tell a foe from a friend;
Then, from error and darkness to truth and the "Light" you're led
The "light" of His wisdom, only, there can be found
He'll stand by your side, and your life, He'll turn around
No longer, forsaken, lost or bound, will your life be-
For, by His word, He'll lead you to Victory!

Marguerite Rocco Orsomarso

Awakenings

She sleeps soft like the golden ray pushing through the clouds,
I catch myself falling yet I fall further.
I can't explain the way I feel or why I feel,
But I know my heart is pounding like the waterfall on the rocks below.
To look at her is to catch my breath, as she paralyzes me,
    thoughts only,
Never before have I known the depths of my heart, yet now I
    visit frequently.
I Love her so much, it hurts, for I know that given all eternity,
    I could never have enough time to explain how much.
Her eyes open quietly as rose petals beginning to bloom.
A smile.

I melt as the warmth from her heart pours onto me.
Is it possible that she loves more deeply than I?
Our hearts are open to each other like the empty book awaiting
    a chapter, a verse.
I choose to write...
    Until you, I never knew. Until you, I never lived.
    Until you, I never loved. You, my life
It is on this day, at this moment, that I awaken.
If I give of myself for the rest of our love, I will give you forever.

Thomas A. Domino

Fun On A Rainy Day

Dark clouds are looming about in the sky
Seems the raindrops will be falling bye and bye
A dismal day outdoors means there's time on hand
To bake, cook, sew or create something grand
Perhaps cut out scraps for a patchwork quilt
If not a seamstress, then a cake can be built
With two tiers and a layer of filling supreme
Iced with whipped topping it looks like a dream
When there are children it certainly is a shame
Don't spend the day moping, get out the Monopoly game
Maybe chinese checkers, dominoes or you might even pick
That 3D puzzle you think can be worked real quick
Those interested in stamps will fill hours with delight
Licking hinges and placing them onto pages and might
Learn about people, places and animals one never dreamed
Existed in our universe, very educational it seemed
Whether we accomplished anything or just had some fun
Made no difference to us when the day was done
Tomorrow would hold more surprises and then
Decisions on what to do would be made all over again

Lucretia A. Gorham

Eternal Spouse

Heed this warning, handsome Pirate
Should your eyes meet with mine,
lest the spell that we created would surely catch you quick time
Beware your capture, loving Pirate
When my beauty draws you near,
for the time will be at hand and fate shall reappear
The vow fulfilled doth bring us peace
until our death once more when parted
Anguished and lost, forced to continue
though we've been beaten and broken hearted
Remember well, my dearest Pirate
On our souls we vainly swore
no other could we marry through this life and evermore
then with our hearts we sealed the bargain
Thus forever it keeps us searching
Each time on Earth, each time in Heaven
Still you wait, my lonely Pirate
O'er the years and many lives
Pray it not be an eternity to make me yours, Your loving wife.

Yvonne R. Auxier

An Aging Musician

Sometimes I wish I could go back, to the old Cajun Bandstand
Where I danced with and romanced the young girls
But never asked one for her hand
For years I used and abused them, I always looked for a ten
Now I could sure use, just one or two
Of the ones that I turned down back then

It started with Phyllis and Charlotte, then Cindy, Missy and Sue
Joanne, Diane and so many more
I know I've forgotten a few
One by one they left me, until I had no-one to hold
I thought they'd found somebody new
The truth is I was just growing old

The years have gone by too quickly, my lines just don't work and more
Girls who once thought, I was clever and cute
Now just think I'm a bore
Young girls still come and smile at me, some of them laugh right out
  loud
They think I'm a fool with an old bass guitar
Just another old man in the crowd

Jackie J. Gantt

The Ink On The Page

With our first-drawn breath, we receive our book.
This book? The Book of Life; daily entries recorded upon pages of
Parchment...White.
With our first murmur the Quill stands ready, recording steadily,
ink flowing 'till the end of day.
Upon sunset and still of night, Rest silent the Quill aside its page
of Parchment bright.

People change, as seasons do, daily entries not so pure. The
Parchment...grey.
Moon and stars shine softly, a gift, God's heavenly love; the soul rest.
Silently turns a page.

Morning light breaks over the sleep, reprieve; a new page in life.
The Quill quivers as it's raised...the question comes with its task,
"Can this day bring the change of our sullen, discontented past?"

With each new dawn, we decide; Heart and Soul distinguishes what is
wrong or right, What should be recorded upon Parchment White.
There are no erasures to our Book of Life, each day brings forward a
new page with choices for
Parchment White.

Choose carefully my dear, what's recorded each day...for you alone...
are the ink on the page.

Estelle M. Stanton

Heavenly Homage

Galaxy of countless stars
Twinkle down from afar.
Darkened visions fill my head
Of legendary warriors dead.
Dwellers deep within your midst
Shower meteoric gifts.
Hues of yellow, red and green...
Jewels fit for King and Queen.
Radiant adornment in ebony hair;
Positioned with the utmost care.

Collage of wishes and unfulfilled dreams,
Echoing vacuum of soundless screams.
Keeper of secrets too great to be known
Imprison the life forms of the curious and bold.

Patricia L. Shjeflo

He's There

As I sensed the first flutters of life inside me
  I thought, He's there?
As I left you on the first day of school,
  I thought, He's there?
As I watched you lead the team to victory,
  I thought, He's there!
As I placed you on the bus for military training,
  I thought, He's there!
As I saw your face when you became a father.
  I thought, He's there!
As I looked at you and your Medal of Merit with glee,
  I thought, He's there!
As I listened to the Taps and held the flag in my arms,
  I thought, He's there?
As I gazed at the beautiful, wooden structure with you inside,
  I thought, He's there?
As I heard the crusty earth fall upon your final womb,
  I thought, He's there?
As I stared toward heaven at the rainbow arched to earth,
  I thought, Hallelujah! He is there! He's there!

A. V. Rogers-Younger

It Is A Matter Of Trust

It is a matter of trust.
To reach beyond the past into the present.
To see the future with love and hope in your heart.
It is a matter of trust.
To give your heart to another.
To reveal goals and dreams.
It is a matter of trust.
To grow from where you are.
To be challenged and happy instead of being impatient and sad.
To look at what you are going to receive instead of what you had.
It is a matter of trust.
To hold fast to truth, in the midst of lies.
To release the tears in the night.
To embrace the joy that comes in the morning.
To know that you have a future and a hope.
Even though you are not sure what it holds.
To expect the impossible...is a matter of trust.
Remember to trust God.

Charlotte Dyson

Have You Ever?

Have you ever seen the sunset,
On a warm summer day?
Have you ever felt the ocean's wind,
And heard what it has to say?

Have you ever looked at a flower,
As a bee was tasting its pollen?
Have you ever paused to listen to,
The crickets so tenderly calling?

Have you ever noticed the snow,
As it falls upon the mountains?
Have you ever stopped to laugh in the park,
At a child trying to drink from the fountain?

Have you ever noticed the creatures,
That walk beneath your feet?
Have you ever seen a honeysuckle,
And tasted the honey so sweet?

Have you ever thanked the Lord above,
For all that you can see?
Have you ever took the time to stop,
And wonder how they came to be?

Leslie Power

The Man I Love

Tonight before I say "good night,"
I'll say "I love you!" and hold him tight.
For he is the one I have always cared,
and he is the one I have never dared.
He is the one I will always love,
and he is the one I will never put above.

We laugh and we cry.
But if I ever sigh,
he'll look at me with his loving look,
the kind of love expressed in no book.
A kind of love so special and sweet,
it keeps out all the cold and holds all the heat.

This is a bond my mom never had,
this is a bond between me and my dad.

My daddy's the one I'll love for all time,
for which is why I wrote him this rhyme.

Candy Breyer

When Lovers Dream

Oh, to go for a walk on a winter night
When the stars hang big and bright
And the moon hangs low in the sky above
And the night seems filled with light.

'Tis on nights like this that lovers walk
And plan of days to come
When two shall become one and dreams come true
And love shall overcome.

When lovers grow old and dream no more
Still there's magic in the night
When the moon hangs low in the midnight sky
And the stars are big and bright.

Audrey Morrow

Together

I stood upon the tallest peak, to view the world below.
I walked in lush green valley fields and heard the cattle low.
I laid upon the clean white beach, to watch the waves roll in.
I dreamt that you were there with me to see the New Year in.

But after all the years rolled by with all those wasted tides,
I searched for you in every place, to keep you by my side.
And when my heart was sure at last that you were gone forever,
I saw your smile on every face that we begat together.

For on each youthful face I saw, a carbon of my love.
No other ever could replace on land or sky above.
We walked together hand in hand and cried for what we'd lost,
And always on this very spot we meet at any cost.

When life is gone from this old soul, my spirit left to soar,
We'll meet once more beside the sea and walk along the shore.
I'll know my search has reached an end, with ebbing of a tide.
Eternal love will be our song... with thee we shall abide.

Jo Vissotzky

Inspiration

At times the inspiration seems to flow,
  And needs no bridge to make it go.
    But then again it slips away,
      And dies as if to always stay.
It gives to wonder why it's so,
  Unless it too needs rest to grow.
    And can't be stirred up everyday,
      But must come back to its own way.
Then, too, it makes one want to know,
  If we're inspired down here below,
    By some mysterious outer ray,
      From out beyond the human play;
For inspiration has a glow,
  And burns the mind as if to show,
    The inner conscious, if we may,
      The picture in its full array.

Annie J. Carlisle

Was Love Not Meant To Be?

Your love has overcome,
shattered all boundaries,
endured all pain.
To hear you whisper my name... Desiree!
stops the beating of my heart.
My love,
never shown, barely spoken,
yet always existing, never fading.
Now our love has combined, embracing one another's hearts.
Needing and wanting each other.
For what we thought was meant to be...
To only find out that our love wasn't meant...
For you or me!

Deidra Desiree Dodd

Forsaken Echoes

Who is to say who is to die...Are you not innocent like a new born lamb, vibrant and ready for life?

Yet you are led to slaughter...

Severed from the very closeness that brings you life
Ripped raw from the rhythmic echoes that soothe and lull.

Gone is the echo that mellows the soul
Gone are the arms that will never caress nor hold
So tender the heart now lies gaping and holed.

Half naked and split... still willing to live...
Looking for life...clinging to life!

Lee Lewis

My Teddy Bear

Peace has captured my heart today
All worries and pressures have drifted away
For though I stand by myself in the cold
I've allowed your warmth to enter my soul

Thoughts of you put my mind at ease
Dreaming with you sets my spirit free
Holding you close, my dreams are fulfilled
Held tight in my arms, all's good in the world

You stalwartly stand, in your own special way
Casting out fear with your love, every day
Eyes and ears open; lips sealed tight
Keeping me safe 'til dawn's early light

My fuzzy-faced dream
Confidant, love, and friend
I'll carry you close
For as long as I can.

Christine E. Somerville

My Mother

A lady,
Kind at heart,
Gentle thoughts in her care-free mind,
And never looking down on anyone with a frown.

Giving a helping hand-
Turning defeat into victory,
With moments of happiness,
Understanding the sorrow.

Always doing her best,
Turning hope into success,
A teacher of all teachers;
This is my Mother.

Matthew L. Schedlosky

The Guardian Angel

She's with you in all of your troubles,
She comforts you when you are sad.
She always has time to forgive you,
When you have done something that's bad.

She's with you in sickness and sorrow,
She tries to bring you up right.
She watches you all through the daytime,
She's always near you at night.

I guess you might call her an angel,
This wonderful person we know.
She has her own heartbreaks and sorrows,
But she fights to get us to our goal.

You must know of whom I am speaking,
There never could be any other.
An angel who'll always stand by you
That one and only is Mother.

Evelyn Roberts

World

Quietly I watched my horse die,
then all the flowers started to cry.
all the leaves fell off the trees,
as I watched my horse die with ease.
the skies turned gloomy and grey, as
mother nature washed my world away.
Then I sat by my horse once again,
and prayed "Dear God don't wash my world
away again."

Breanne Hrin

Preceding The Dawn

Beauty precedes the dawn,
You precede it too.
Your words equivocal of psalms.
Your sentiments hold true.
You taunt me with your riddles - I answer them in time.
You speak of all your troubles - I remember your lies and lines.
But what you seek is Beauty; I yearn to help you find.
Your happiness my duty-without me peace of mind.
You hold back all the flowers.
I try to hide the sun.
And as we stared for hours,
I realized the battle was won.
There lies a solitary mountain,
Brown, tattered and very weathered.
Near a once flowing fountain,
Objects that saw my structure severed.

Our beauty precedes the dawn.
Our bodies feel weak and numb. Left longing, deaf and dumb.
On the grass so very calm. Your words are equivocal of psalms.
Now my beauty precedes it too.

Mona Morsy

Answers

I am focusing on the small patch of road
That rises up from the blackness, in the
Arc of headlights, shortened by a wall of water
Which encloses our car in a womb-like space.
My young son is lost in thought.

His earnest face, dimly lit by the dashboard light,
Brow furrowed with intensity, turns to me.
"Is there really a God?" he asks from the
Bottom of his soul. My hearts stops.
In the moment of silence I feel God hesitate,

Halt momentarily, His lonely surging force.
Ah — a real question — how to answer?
Shockingly the car is filled with lightning,
Revealing the world in stark detail. Then
Darkness descends. I guess that's your answer.

My son does not remember. He was too young.
But within his being he has an awareness
Of the meaning of unconditional love. He does not
Call it God. There is just a sure and steady
Knowing, that he is love and loved.

Maureen Moore

Reminiscent Love

Love is the thing that brings us together.
We all feel it and cherish its lore.
Whether Love comes from your friends or mother,
We can all say that we always want more.

When someone says "I will always Love you,"
Do you think they mean what they are saying?
Stop to ponder if this feeling is true.
Or you might find yourself without feeling!

We all take emotion for granted.
Step back, look deep into the empty souls,
To embrace the bleakness that lies behind.
Ask within, "Do I want these burnt out coals?"

You can ignite the embedded ember.
Choose to let Love live, as you remember.

Composed By: Derek Berrisford

The Prisoner

The prisoner walks within the walls of the prison
He does not walk alone; God walks along beside of him
There is not a moment that he does not feel God's presence
It is a sense of comfort to him
Even though he is where he is, he knows
God will protect him from harm wherever he goes
He is a messenger, a messenger of God
Inside his heart he is a good man
Helping whenever he can
one of the guards became his friend
The guard had a heart attack and fell to the floor
The prisoner fell down to his knees
and, to everyone's shock and amazement, and prayed for him
with tears streaming down his face
The guard was in critical condition
until the next day, a miracle no one could explain
The doctors could not understand what happened or why;
a complete turn around, can't you see?
God heard the prayers from a prisoner

Alma Jean Epps

Pension

Some folks get old hoping money to spend;
   Some folks spend a lot of time getting old;
Other folks take time to spin their webs
   And make all the other people get very old.

Youth is a state of mind as the story has been told;
   Aging is a state of grace to endure as years unfold;
Living brings the present state as time claims the past;
   Hope drives hard towards the future with endurance, the
      proof to last.

We all lay claim to ability,
   To withstand daily trials at hand;
Maintaining the path of resistance and faith,
   To gain as the years expand.

We plain with a king's ransom,
   The future treasure yet to build;
And rest and live on measure,
   But our pension holds dreams unfulfilled.

Beatrice B. Mackin

"A SPECIAL PLACE"

There is a very special place
For the loves I mourn and can't replace
They live inside my heart and mind
Their unmatched grace I will not find

Cherished moments I recall so well
Flash through so often, clear as a bell.
Special warmth enfolds me and holds me tight
I dream their love throughout each day and night

Ecclesiastes stated "For Everything a Season . . . "
My soul-mates' sacred visits really need no reason
Treasured memories take me back in time
When life was easy and peace sublime

My loved ones spoke no evil, each a special soul
Unselfish wisdom and kindness ever was their goal.
Is there then any wonder that I do not erase
The beauty of such pure and everlasting grace?

Be good to each other, I would caution you
Time moves much too quickly to undo.
Show care, give care and pleasure throughout their lives
Take care deep regrets do not survive when tragic loss arrives!

Lucille D. Lucks

A Store Trapped In Time

Upon walking down the sidewalk, thinking my deep thoughts,
I happened quietly to walk inside a store of which I'd sought.

Gingerly and with utmost care, a prize I'd hope to find,
But something sparked a memory, hidden deep within my mind.

The stairs, rails and ceiling fans, were still within their place,
The dimness of the glowing lights, reflected in my face.

Back in time my mind did go, to wander far away,
Taking me back to the place, the place I'd love to stay.

The store was old and the floors did creak with such a rusty sound,
Things were so much simpler then, with so much that could be found.

The time was quaint and people spoke, while shopping for their lot,
Greetings, smiles and a happy air, something not soon forgot.

The smells were there and were just the same as many years ago,
Those special, precious innocent times, the ones that we all know.

Deftly my mind brought me back, to where I stood in deepest awe,
A spark of memory in distant time, and what I thought I saw.

The time and timbre of the moment put a smile into my mind,
Of memories, fondness and moments of a store trapped in time.

Cheryl Walker

Computers

Each man today evolved from single cells;
Vague knowledge where and how we came to be,
Or did we just appear (the good book tells).
Life's current charges forth on land and sea
Unleashing change: mutating DNA
That links such cells to form some fish or flesh,
Immune so it survives - it's never prey.
Of elements like ours, it is so fresh:
Now mimics humans - the computer's born!

Oh true; they'll talk, and see, and walk, and think:
Fact is, they'll never love, shed tears nor mourn!

Man may connect his mind and feel in sync,
Although he'll never share his soul or heart.
No life! They'll play an artificial part.

Bartondox

Intangibles

My dreams I can share,
my love I can give,
but try to take it and you have nothing.
You can have my trust and my respect,
but they are mine, take care,
if broken,
they cannot be replaced.
You can never own me, nor I you,
we can only own ourselves,
our feelings, our thoughts,
our souls.
We don't own the stars, the sun or the moon,
the wind, the rain,
or the colours of the rainbow,
but we can share them,
just like dreams.

Gillian G. Kadiri

My Spirit Lives

My spirit lives, - it soars with the eagle,
Riding unbounded in the open skies.
I am the wind that blows the golden prairie grain;
The winter stillness of my northern home.
My soul is lifted to the mountain peaks.
I catch the diamond sparkle of new-fallen know.
I glide in peace across the shining lake,
Where sunshine dapples water, - crystal clear;
And salmon flashes silver from the deep.
I am content that I have helped my fellow man,
And shared my happiness with friends, and those I love....
I've met the daily challenges of life;
I've won, - I've lost, but most of all, I tried!
I did not die, - my spirit lives.

Edna F. Neely

By Love Empowered

Love strengthens the soul, the mind, the heart,
It mellows the surging heart to restrain the evil of confusion.
It allays bitterness, and forces understanding in the midst of chaos.
It burrows into the deepest spaces of the mind, and soul.

Love needs to be remembered and must be constantly practiced.
It needs to be regenerated and energized with kindness and concern.
It must be dispersed liberally and with compassion;
And it must be accepted whole-heartedly and unconditionally.

Love changes the face of all emotions.
It blocks out the torture of jealousy and despair.
It gives us the satiated calm after desire; fulfillment; life.
It joyously allows us the freedom of dancing and song.
Love can he everywhere and nowhere.

Mina B. Clappison

I Am

I am a young woman struggling to find herself
I wonder if there really is a God
I hear voices crying our for justice
I see blood-stained countries
I want to enfold the world in my arms
I am a young woman struggling to find herself

I pretend to be someone I am not
I feel as if there is nothing I can do
I touch those who I can
I worry about what will happen to us all
I cry when I am moved
I am a young woman struggling to find herself

I understand that it takes a lot to survive in this world
I say our world needs some major repairs
I dream of a good world
I try to do my best
I hope to make a difference
I am a young woman struggling to find herself

Trinity Peacock-Broyles

Depressed And Alone

It's cold and bitter outside, like me inside I guess,
No room in my life for pride, my mind a state of undress.
Depressed and unhappy, but never knowing why.
I could laugh it's so scatty, instead I sit alone and cry
Afraid of what I am not in control of, the future just empty dreams,
A life shattered and hollow, and inside I can't silence the screams.
Everyone around me, content and happy, I guess I envy everyone.
Their lives warm and fulfilling, mine empty over and done.
I need to be attended, loved, secure, safe and well.
But I know that's not going to happen, my life a hollowgram of hell.

Elizabeth A. Hobbs

Waters

I looked into the mirrored waters....and what did I see,
The image of Jesus....looking at me

I heard a voice say go forth my son....do not hesitate,
Live your life in forgiveness...before it's too late.

Make those around you enlightened... and smile,
Your past is behind you.....yes it is on file.

You have done many a thing....in which I disagree,
You shall forever be forgiven....if you put your trust in me.

All you have to do is ask....and I shall be there,
For whatever you have heard my son....I really do care.

I have shone down upon you....with all of my love,
You have seen my angel....come down from above.

I love you my son...

The waters started to ripple....the image disappeared,
I shall never be alone....for this I had feared.

I set off on my journey....the task to uphold,
The meaning is so precious....more precious than gold.

I am quite thankful....for that day in the park,
The light continues to shine....way after dark.

Randy Garrett

Serenity

In Summertime
The fields of green
Beckon to me.
And inside of myself unseen
Grows a desire to be free.

To be free and tread
Upon the velvet grass,
No fear, no dread;
And as I pass
A mystery surrounds me.

The mystery of life, behold,
Unfolding energy
With strength untold
Consumes my senses, thoughts and dreams,
And carries me aloft.

And life rises up to meet my step,
To thrill and excite and enthrall.
The joys of this beauty must be kept
To savour for one and all.
And this shall be my home.

J. Perry Grandel

One Last Show

Gossip has it, rumors abound
Elvis Presley's back in town
Fans line up to catch a peek
To hear him sing, or just lip sync
To see the King in all his glory
To tell the tale and sell the story
To snatch a button or lock of hair
To auction at the county fair
And tell their friends and Uncle Jack
They'd always said that he'd be back
To sing a song for one and all
In Hackensack or else St. Paul
So get your pass from the man called Pete
Demand is high for a worthy seat
Yes, hurry now and don't be late
'Cause they're selling fast at the Pearly Gate

Deanne Mazur

"Breaking The Chain, Finding Love Again"

There is a priority I must address!
For thousands of people who live in unrest.
From generation to generation, I pray its not to late!
One wonders how we can allow so much garbage on our plate.
Its humiliating, its deceitful, and the fear of it can make you lie.
But the most devastating of all, is when we see it through our children's eyes.
There are many different kinds of it, found in every walk of life.
But no matter what kind it is, it still cuts like a knife.
Go ahead and ignore it, but it won't go away.
Its putting down roots and its planning to stay.
So many will suffer through another's hands.
That is why its imperative, we must take a stand.
Because abuse is so powerful when it takes on human shape
So many different kinds of what we call rape.
It makes ordinary people kill and go wild.
Unforgiveable when its done to an innocent child.
Children are our legacy so we must make them understand
That the future of our nations in the palm of their hand
So once again God I'm depending on your power as my friend
Help us start the healing process, so all abuse can finally end!

Marcella Leasak

Looking Back

Looking back over the years of my life
Much happiness, some sorrow, a wee bit of strife
  Parents who gave me a really good home
  From which I never wanted to roam
A desire to help others - hurting, in pain
Led me to nursing school, my RN to gain
  If you really want joy your life to fill
  Try helping someone is really ill
Life goes on - I had a date
With the man who would become my mate
  And then as it happens in the course of time
  Came two little girls - his and mine
Now dad's gone on to eternal rest
But he'd be so happy if he could just
  See his little girls grown and away
  Busy with their careers and families every day
So when Gram's alone and feeling sad
In pop the grandchildren who make her glad
  And while she dreams of days long gone
  She finds in her heart there is a song

Helen Erickson

Rose Of Gold/Rose Of Love

R isen from the land in awesome beauty,
O ut of the soil like the sun almighty,
S even petals of sun-lit glory,
E den's flower I pluck for thee.

O mega can not touch this gift,
F or ageless and endless it shall live.

G olden fire sweeps its graceful form,
O nly you behold it every morn.
L ike my love for you was born,
D eath alone will cease my mortal norm.

R oses of stone, gold, and nature combined,
O nly with these three elements will thee find,
S uspended within my heart a love so fine,
E ternal death himself shall not confine.

O h my love, these three gifts I offer thee,
F orever will you be the only love for me.

L ong lost love, like long lost brothers,
O nly is found when both ends bother,
V ainly we may love in lives another,
E ternally united by the grace of our Father.

Sean Hsu

In Just One Minute

In just one minute,
That we take for granted,
A whole life is lived,
All around our planet.

Young ones falling in love, weddings being performed,
Loved ones passing on, babies being born.

Wars taking place with turbulent noise,
Little children playing with their favorite toys.

All around the world,
In just one minute,
A life is being lived,
Bonding us all in it.

Tears of joy, for those who are meeting,
Tears of sorrow, for those who are weeping.

People taking and people giving,
People asking and people receiving.

In just one minute,
That we all shared,
A whole life was lived,
Shouldn't we have cared?

Patricia Lalonde

The Season's Bride

Watch the lady in her slumber.
Soon to awake surrounded by beauty
and splendour

Watch the lady as her body lies still,
Soon she shall move
She shall move at free will.

A petal has fallen to the ground
within thy shadow the rose makes no sound.

Watch the lady stretch abroad
her eyes now in opening peer out to the light,
And she is charmed by the sun so bright.

Her face utterly florid
drawn to visions of flowers, with sweet shade
Watch the empty grass
with her pattern she once made.

Melinda Kay Jacobs

A Time To Break

At first we're dazed and then we cry and then we bow to reason
Go silently through our days
As winter follows autumn's haze and love is a past season

We read poetry and we repeat: Was it ever less than a treason
To part, to follow strange new ways
To cry, still dazed, yet yield with grace and then begin to reason

That life continues and there is a time for every season
That winter solstice heralds May
When winter follows autumn's day and love is a past season

We work, we dream and travel abroad, but find it sill a treason
To wake up as one where two once lay
To walk dazed again through a whole day and bow again to reason

When in our heads the voices cry: Treason, treason, treason
And urge us on to seize the day
For winter may end autumn's play and love is a past season

And then we feel that we must face the last and greatest treason
And not go on, but pause and gaze
And cry, awake, not in a daze, and break this cage of reason
And rage that death ends our days and love is a past season

B. B. Harsanyi

God Rides The Wings... And More

I was flying high above earth's ground one dark and dreary night
With lonely Sunday feelings abound and nary a smile in sight
I thought of God and wondered just where he was right now
Out ridin' the wing came a whimsey thought, a hangin' on somehow

He seemed to pop up more and more this Christmas time of year
A prayin' n' singin' n' workin' hard to spread his year long cheer

He is alive thought I, a smilin' in every young child's heart
In every candle's flame so high, in every prayer we start
So raise your spirits silly boy, my tearful mind did cry
And search for God's beauty, as in His air you fly

For beyond the dark of rain and this dreary lonely night
Spring clouds of joyful hope and days of lasting light.

Ronald J. Unterreiner

The Performance

Practice makes perfect, I often hear people say,
Week after week, day after day.
Over and over parents and teachers stalk,
Never letting you get away, not even to talk!

Rehearsing together, the performance grows near!
Hurry, oh hurry! Production's not ready, I fear.
The weeks fly by with a wink,
Minutes seem to be just tiny measures of ink.

Time is running short, I do believe,
Soon our goal of musical beauty we'll achieve.
Finally the big day rolls around,
One last get-together, then the final count-down.

Black and white, everyone is dressed up nice,
Almost like perfectly groomed little mice.
Gleaming instruments in shiny hues of brown,
The orchestra is seated, members from all over town.

Silence creeps forward as we wait to begin,
Mrs. Conductor steps up and we warm our violins.
Starting the concert, awe charms the great music hall,
Applause fills the room as the music is stalled.

I guess it really isn't that bad, being in this classical band.

Ann Pearson

A Salute...

If I could write a poem of love, its title would be you
And though no words could quite contain the recognition due,
Its message I'm sure would suffice, its meaning clear and true,
Would be a phrase of just three words, and they are I love you.

If I could bend a rainbow, a ribbon "way on high",
For you I'd wrap the gift of love, a tribute in the sky.
This unique dedication is intended to express,
Soft autumn colored ecstasy, tranquility at best.

If I could write a poem of love with rainbow colored flair,
For you upon the heavens, a tribute beyond compare....
To you this dedication with poetic verse of true.
Gift wrapped in autumn beauty is this ribbon just for you.

Robert Hellom

Untitled

A loud bang, the dull thud of a body.
Skittering of feet, a growing pool of crimson blood.
As life ebbs and nears death,
Events in that life appear before a pair of deadening eyes.
Sirens are heard, the heart slows down, and vision blurs.
Police rush about,
Paramedics look at the body and shake their heads.
Darkness envelops the body, a heart stops,
And another life is lost to violence.

Brian Vasquez

Makes Me Think Maybe God's A Woman Too...

I've had a dream of my own, it is mine and mine alone.
I've had it since I was just a girl,
    And when I think about it, it puts
My head in a whirl.
    It makes me think maybe God's a woman too..

I used to walk my head held high,
    Until the day came and you said goodbye.
And I wonder how God thought to make someone
    like you,
And it makes me think maybe God's a woman too..

I see you in the spotlight,
    But I always wake up to the cold, dark night.
I try and go back to dreaming, like I know I
    should not do.
    But it makes me think maybe God's a woman too...

I close my eyes and whisper your name,
    Only to cause myself more grief and more shame.
And if God would only make this dream come true,
    It would make me think maybe God's a woman too.
Yeah, it makes me think maybe God's a woman too..

Jacquelyn Sturdivant

Mothers

Mothers are the storytellers of all children
The lawyers of life
The educators of man kind
The nourishment of young souls

Mothers are the total existence of our nation
The stepping stones of success and the comforts of failures

Mothers are the powers to control poverty or riches
The difference between good and evil
The back bone of man

Mothers are the silent strength of our nation
For without Mothers, man will not be man
Mothers: The power and glory of all nations within man

Veronica Bean

The Peace Tower

I've head nightingales sing in England,
I've heard Opera sung in Rome,
But the sweetest of songs to an airman,
Are sung by engines that carry him home.

So I'm flying back to my loved one,
To the girl who is waiting for me,
Tho' I've seem half the world in my Service,
It's the Peace Tower I'm longing to see.

My home-town in Canada calls me,
I've left England's cities so grand,
The engines are singing of Maples,
My girl will be there when we land.

We will sail on the Ottawa River,
We will ski in the Gatineau Hills.
We will sit on the grass by the Peace Tower
And listen to carillon bells.

Harold T. Kay

My Star

Shadows echo as their whispers dance in this fading light
I wait for stars, yet stars are only seen when my
    world lies in darkness
I am afraid to touch this glitter of hope, for I am
    told that stars are merely lights in the sky which
        show the brilliance of what must ever remain far away
For if we capture our star, its radiance dims, for
    who can contain the passion of its fiery burn

Douglas James Getgood

491

Alzheimer's

(To Mary Ruth Oldt French, M.D.)
No more with the landscape of the cell
And the caverns of flesh and bone
Reveal to her searching eye
The enemies that ravage body and mind.

No more will the light of science
Beam from her caring heart
To brighten her way in the healing art
In a calling loved and duty bound.

Now shadows fill this once bright mind
And a stark repose has stilled a lively face.
Yet a generous smile breaks through the mask,
Glowing from a heart that nurtured family and friends.

What triumph is there for this treachery
Of robbing the memory of its treasured past,
And of taking away the happy hours
Of days so bright and playful?

Those she touched still feel the glow
Of a fulfilling past so presently felt.
No darkness can fall upon that life,
And that is where the triumph lies.

H. Nelson Fitton

Ode To A Mechanics Life

Grease on our clothing, oil in our hair,
Trans oil and lubricants are everywhere.

We stay up real late, lying in puddles on the ground
There are stains on our furniture, it's all around

Our clothes are all stained and our carpets are too.
We track in the crap on the bottom of our shoes.

Our children are filthy. They just can't stay clean.
'Round here clean kids, will never be seen.

Parts stores and suppliers sell all sorts of cleaners
But it seems like the harder you scrub, the stains just get meaner.

We sleep not a wink before it's running just right
But the son-of-a-b____ will be back the next night.

Our feet are soar and our backs feel like they're broken.
All of this for only a small percent of the token.

Use extra caution when you are checking their air.
The problem, no matter, it started from there.

You messed up my carb when you checked my tire
The guy knows, full well, he's a gosh darned liar.

They cry, "It's all your fault, we will not pay."
In a Mechanic's life, it's just another day.

Julie A. Johnson

In Loving Memory

Like a bird let out of its cage,
You flew away at an early age;
you suffered so much while on this earth
But God knew your destiny even at birth.
God stopped your pain and took you home,
He always knew you were one of His own.
You are in a much better place
God did not make a mistake.
Of course, we'll miss you
as the days go by.
And in loving memory, sometimes we'll cry
As the angels sing with you and rejoice,
we find comfort in knowing you made the right choice.
We'll see you again at heavens door,
Smiling and more beautiful than ever before.

Kathy D. Calhoun

The Flame

Sitting in the candle light, thinking of you, constantly.
The candle flickers, reminding me of how life is and can be.
Life had its ups and downs.
The flame is blue, peach, orange, and yellow.
Blue, sadness, I miss you, I wish you were here.
Peach, cheeriness, you and me together.
Orange, the sunset dream I wish would come true.
Yellow, the flame lighting up our room.
The heat of the candle, lying in each others arms, bare.
I hope our flame of our candle will burn forever.
But if it doesn't, I hope we remain friends.
I hate candles most when they go out,
The room goes black, you feel alone.
Smoke fills the room from the extinguished flame.
Something like a relationship.
Your heart breaks, and you feel alone.
The missing flame, doesn't leave smoke, it leaves tears.
Now there's no candlelight, no flame, love, I am now alone.
Alone again, afraid of what the future holds,
For myself, my candle, and my flame.

Shayna Dawn Booth

Angels

We hear Angel songs a ringing in the ears;
Angel voices releasing all from fears.

A guiding presence likened to a bond of love;
A blessed power sent down from Heaven above.

Who are these Angels hovering on the air?
Do they have wings and softly flowing hair?

Are they called when sadness holds full sway?
Or perhaps they're present any night or day.

Are they perched upon a pink cloud in the sky?
Or on a shoulder to calm an urgent cry?

Maybe they are neighbors, friends at hand,
Or dear folks strewn across the land.

No matter where they may be all the while —
We hold in awe the magic of their style.

We know a sense of Peace in a world of daring,
As they fold us in their arms, gently caring.

Evelyne Day

Eleven-Three

How far have we fallen
since the days of eternal bliss
uncomplicated days
and endless nights?
What was it that had gotten into us?
What happened to the feelings that ruled those priceless
autumn hours?
I suspect I will never learn the truth
about what happened to you
and what happened to me
as the days grew longer
and our time grew shorter
and eventually dwindled to nil
but I'll forever memorize the love and laughter
that possessed us shortly before and not too long after
eleven-three...11/3/93

Joseph R. Songco

Chief Joseph '94

Lo! The great spirit chief,
Whose eyes have forever seen and protected,
The inheritance of the Indian,
Whom gave them the vast plains and waters and sky,
And the Buffalo and the Deer and the Antelope,
Whom ordained the earth a Chief of living flesh on the creation,
To give all manner of guidance and spiritual,
To his Braves and his Squaws and their children,
To live in harmony as the beast and nature itself.

Now! The great spirit chief,
His eyes have seen and his heart is in sorrow,
For alone stands Chief Joseph,
There with his back against his foes,
Tired to agony of his living soul he alone cries.

"I shall fight no more..for the sake of my people.
To hot barren reservations we shall live on,
And our generations of children shall pray for peace,
That the Great White Father shall be spiritually awakened,
When our great spirit chief will war his judgment,
And our foes awaken plagued on the greatest reservation of death."

Roy Hernandez Sr.

Of Deals Most Haunting

On a dark and windy, stormy night,
The thunder claps and leaves take flight,
My thoughts turn black, as black as can be,
For tonight is the night you come for me,
The deal I made, lo, those years ago,
Is a deal I repay, with my very soul,
You came to me in my deepest despair,
I was so young then, little did I care,
Your soul, he said, and I cringed at the thought,
For the life you dream, but forget me not,
For I will return to collect what is mine,
You'll surrender to me, at the appointed time,
I could not refuse him, my life was so bleak,
So the deal was then struck, a deal I must keep,
Now lightning does strike, and my heart grows cold,
For now here you are, purest evil, I behold.

Kim Catherwood

An Enchanted Moment

Standing, staring in wind driven skies,
like life forgotten...she appeared there
standing, staring at me.
And so it was, through awe struck eyes
she looked like heaven,
and I unknowing, looked back.
Was it the time of angels, or sinners.
Was it transparent like me.
To wish and pray...to hold time as it was.
To hear a heartbeat echo within all of me...whispering her name.
Then it was broken just as it began...unknowing...
I believe in enchanted moments
and the sorrow they bring when they end.
And so it was
I was left standing, staring...
like life forgotten...she was no longer there.
I can feel myself dying when I think of her,
her heartbeat absent in my arms.
And so it was...

Ryan Lee Gardner

But For A Word

There are those moments, few in life,
when, resting from the daily strife,
I can recall the joy we'd seen
and wonder, now, what might have been.

Would love have bloomed if had been heard
the sound of just one spoken word?
In utter quite, love wilts to die,
we pass aside with silent sigh.

You did not speak what's in your heart
and now we drift so slow apart.
As ships drift on the ebbing tide,
from here to there, so slowly glide.

But for a word you might have spoke.
My soul's in tears. My heart's now broke.
But for a word kept in your heart,
we go our ways... on paths apart.

David M. Simms

Day Dreaming

These funny little thoughts
That run through my funny little head,
Keeps turning somersaults
Making strong juices, from which my brain is fed.
Now this sounds very funny
to most of you I know,
But how else could my little brain grow?
An enema won't help,
What's wrong with me.
That will only tend to help,
Set the lower half free!
But that's not the subject,
That my mind is dwelling on.
The checks have just arrived
And I'm gone! Goodby.

Grace Hearn

To My Mother

When I think of all the things you've done for me
The times you've held my hand,
I look at you and think I see
God's loving gift to me.

Because you are my Mother,
And your being has graced my soul;
No other woman will ever make me feel as whole.

As life for me began with you,
Your breath of courage does see me thru.
So, Mom, I write this to you
In celebration of the most special love I know.

Barbara Donner

Spring Creek

Downward the flood waters rush,
Brown with the silt of the land.
The roaring, tumbling, powerful flow
Make the banks of the stream expand.

The will of the water rips at the fields
Gouging out thicket and shrub.
Over the acres so tenderly tilled,
Wild water now laden with scrub.

Tomorrow this torrent reverts once again
To the trickling creek in the glen,
So pretty and harmless it glides
And murmurs like words of a friend

Kathryn I. Strauch

Solitude

I saw a pretty sight today,
It was the ocean with its gentle wave.
Far beyond the ocean line;
There were great colors all combined,
It was the golden sunset there;
That spread its golden light
As I saw the water come onto the shore;
It made it's path like an opening door.
The birds were gone, there was no sound;
    only the ocean roar.
As I sat there in my solitude;
Along came the night.
Then the sky opened its eyes,
And they all shined oh, so bright.

Yvette Yslas

An Old Man

Forgotten and neglected
Dirty
Hungry.
Oh the frustrations of being old!
Alone - an old man fears falling,
Children dying before he does.

He hopes though -
Another birthday, Christmas — perhaps another Spring.

But mostly he dreams of youth.
School days, falling in love.
His first son,
Oh yes, he dreams.

Lucille S. Barry

April Sunshine

Chippen when I'm slippen
Don't preach me to me, reach to me
Smoken, Pretty soon you're on the floor choken
Use to play the yo yo
Now we play slow mo
Dreaming the dream, April Sunshine
Lying in my arms
Standing in my charms
We all breath the same air
Cut me I bleed, April Sunshine
Cook the corn, feed the kids
Scrub the floor
Got time for more
Two flowers in a row
Needs water to grow
Heart to Heart
Dreaming of a dream, April Sunshine
April Sunshine in my mind

Gregory G. Haats/Toyota

Visualize

When the whole world seems to be, coming down around you,
and old memories want to make you blue,
close your eyes and visualize, my arms wrapped tightly around you.

When you feel that you are all alone and full of despair,
close your eyes and visualize, and I will be there.

When your body aches all over and you have a need of love,
close your eyes and visualize,
that we're together and our bodies are just one.

When work is long and your day seems dank and dreary,
close your eyes and visualize,
our kisses and how they're made with such great fury.

Tim Discher

Oxbow Lakes

The piercing carelessness of the children's laughter
seducing us. Should we now abandon our
well-worn lenses for the screening gauze?

The stylites descend to solutes for the
bazaar-vat of thronging mindlessness?

(For the oxbows exiled veering sharply
from the headlong torrents blindly surging
in still aloofness gaze cyclops-eyed at
a nuded sky, eyes now saline
with dredged up secrets of the earth)

And siblings of Galileo that we are
dare spell 'pope' with a puny P, with
hilarious tears pun to The Vulgar the vulgate

But then fragile clingers, torque-cursed,
immured in the monolith of a shattered
cosmos; fleeting loungers for the childhood
haziness and the headlong plunge-
    Eden of the unplucked apple

    And still, from the street, the gay
    laughter of children in play

Rotimi Opeyemi Babatunde

Eyes Of A Little Girl

As I look through the eyes of a little girl, I see a wonderful
man holding her hand. Sometimes staying quiet and out of the
way, at other times, eager to jump in to help and learn more. She
watched as he worked endless nights to achieve his goals and that
checked flag. Every time those glorious moments came, she vowed
to be a little more like him. Never did he keep the glory to
himself, his joy was to share it with everyone. She was so proud
of him — he was the best. She would take him into school for
"show and tell" — she would stand tall and proud saying, "my
dad's a race car driver".

Twenty years later, she still watches him working endless nights
through love to pass the moment of glory down to his little
girl. Every time that checkered flag falls for her, in her
heart, she is still aware of who makes it possible — that man
who held her hand so many years ago. As I look to the future, I
have many goals, the greatest of which is to be more like you.

I love you dad.

Kelly Sutton

Songs

Some station is playing old songs tonight
With a mixture of static and crackle,
But they come to me with a fond delight
Through my worn-out radio.

These old tunes set the mood I'm in
That makes me think of you,
For I want so much your love to win
And keep it ever true.

I've tried in different ways to say
How much you mean to me;
Like the songs, it was only yesterday
When you touched me tenderly.

You pieced together a shattered year
That I could hardly bear,
And you erased a grievous tear
When nobody else would care.

There is a song only I can sing,
Some day I'll let it flow;
'Till then, accept this love I bring
For it's the finest gift I know.

Gordon Dean Schlundt

Changes

What makes my arm go up and down,
What causes my lips to part.
Is it the work of my brain alone,
Or also the beat of my heart.

The strength in the grip of the hand,
That keeps me from losing my place.
The pleasure I feel when that same strong hand,
Reaches out and caresses my face.

The lull of the river as it flows over the rocks,
Brings peace to my soul, while I fish in its pool.
Now churns ever so swiftly, as it comes to the falls,
And the roar becomes frightening and cruel.

As the bright blue sky lures me outside,
To enjoy the long summer days.
Soon I search for a tree in the shade to hide,
From the heat of the suns sweltering rays.

The breeze softly flutters the papers at rest.
And brings the scent of the lilacs across my face.
Suddenly the wind quickens and rustles the leaves.
Sending whirl winds that make a chaotic place.

Nancy Thomas

The Cure

Feeling pressed to do it all,
I call upon the wisdom of the past.
Gestures of reconciliation, so simple then.
A hen... token of apology,
becomes a part of our anthology.
Offenses were forgiven, forgotten and done.

"That was then, this is now!"
How sad we always work at hurting,
flirting with disaster.
Speaking words that cannot be recalled,
we fall, into a time of great distress.
Why can't offenses be forgiven, forgotten and done?

Sisters,
each one vying for the top.
I stop, and realize,
no one else can close the gap.
The strap... maybe it wasn't all that strange.

A little pain might help,
offenses to be forgiven, forgotten and done!

Lori Hoose

Forever And A Day

I want you with me always
If you'll only stay
Here by my side, as my guide
Forever and a day

Never will I seek
New grounds on which to play
Cause it pleases me to be with you
Forever and a day

I long to hear those three sweet words
Whom only you know how to say
Cause they sound so sweet, as you repeat
Forever and a day

I hope my words don't seem
To real cause in any way
I'll love you, hope you'll love me
Forever and a day

Linda J. Robinson

Mother's Day

Dear Mom,

You make my life a wondrous dream
Your love is like a light's strong beam

You care for me, you love me
For my future you hold the key

You may think I don't really care
But to say I don't would be unfair

You supply all of my needs
And try to answer all of my pleas

You give me all the love I can use
Your love is like an eternal fuse

I really do love you
A love this is straight and true

You seem to do all I ask
If you don't like it you seem to use a mask

Just so you won't hurt my feelings
If I'm ill your touch is healing

For all of these reasons in the beginning of May
We celebrate a wonderful day!

Happy Mother's Day!
Kelly E. Crawford

For An Aging Poodle

I look into your face and see the time is coming when
I'll have to learn to do without my constant, loyal friend.
The large, soft eyes are clouded now, they don't see quite as well,
Your handsome head hangs lower, you don't always hear the bell.

You run to chase your ball, the way that you have always done
Your legs are weak, they can't fulfill your need to have some fun.
You bravely make the effort as you answer to our call,
But more and more it seems, these days, you stumble and you fall.

We lift you gently to your feet, you seem to be confused
You cannot understand defeat, you've never been abused.
You follow in my footsteps, even up and down the stair
But now you move more slowly, taking every step with care.

Fourteen years of love have gone into your every act
Your time with us ending and it's hard to face that fact.
God bless you, Max, my loving friend, I'll serve you faithfully
And be with you until the end, as you would be with me.

Irene Kane

Equinox

The year's wavering
Between these fogs and silences
That on the fields call forth the hours
Of steady council and iron hands.
So darkening to its utter day
When bracken bends to one thin line
And gray vapors trade again
This dim half dream of cold for miles of heath from the hills.

The fire that burns to winter's end
Spreads its fogs from frozen brakes
And rivers of ice steam into mist
From stars wild out of the north
And nights lie dead in the early time
White knighted by the glittering reeds.
Crested by some tall lord to a fire
Where silver goes stale against a moon.
Aft of any point to a newer green
Burning from Arcturus to the sands
Seas going south take up this wind
Weedy with fathoms falling to land.

Mary Kellerman

I Arrived In Paradise

Anticipated for a long time
Afraid of the unknown
Finally I arrived in Paradise

Blinded by the lights
Deafened by the hums
Cooled by the gentle breeze

I was standing on the clouds
Suspended by air
There was nowhere to fall

The light cleared
The hums faded
The gentle breeze stopped

I expected to see multitudes of humanity
I thought there would be friends and neighbors
People of status and rank

But in this great vast of nothingness
All I saw was you
Solomon Poll

Your Stepping On Me

I'm trapped in the mind of me,
I'm being bothered and I'm bothering.
Everything I've done and do aren't me,
It's something new.
I'm going through changes
Greatly disapproved,
But I can't help me for
I'm not sure what to do.
Everything I'm doing now I do only for me,
I care about no one else!
Nobody I see.
I'm asking
But not out loud.
If you'd please lend me a hand.
For I say I can make it on my own.
But really,
As you can see
I'm as helpless as a snail.
And it's like you're
Stepping on me.
Connie Morrison

The Flower

What a beautiful sprout
poking up through the ground.

It looks like it holds so much promise.
If it lives, I know
that it will make a fine flower.

I can supply the rain,
but not the warmth of the sun.
That is your job.

Together, we can help it grow
into something wonderful, and more
beautiful that it had ever hoped to grow alone.

Separately, it will die.
The sprout will shrivel up,
and go back under the ground to hide,
until it's warmer outside.

Tell me,
what's the weather like
where you are?
Suzanne Chaney

Black Owl's Night Of Love

The darkness surrounds the world with a certain aspiration
to give time a rest. Peace is what it wants, wandering
around, around and around. It falls when it is expected,
but then sometimes not. The black owl covers the golden
coin in the sky, and what proceeds is darkness.

There is so much darkness it surrenders us to its depths.
We are lonely for the black easy way out, through our
hopes and dreams. Without a doubt it controls our
very sanity in which we live. For if we did not have
darkness, we would surely strive for insanity.

When it calls we beckon to its one wish, do not watch
it sleep. You become weak, and you will power will
not hold up, you do its bidding. It may surround you
with warmth, but then turns and a cold mist comes
your way. Though in any city, century of country it will always
be called the black owl's night of love.
Kyle A. Hein

Fall From Innocence

A mysterious kid the neighbourhood,
at the oak tree is where all stood,
staring at the figure in the dusk-end sun,
in this struggle for life, death had won.

Gazing upon a darker sky,
wondering why he chose to die,
hanging above with head bowed down,
silence wearing an expressionless frown.

Thirteen and hanging before his day,
to a down-wind the body sways,
twilight sweeps the burning ash of day,
swallows the autumn leaves away.

Celestial voices sing for those who die,
angels claim his soul, onward they fly,
the sun breaks, a new day born,
as night passes and brings on dawn.

Months on end the memory haunts me,
returning from the grave forever to taunt me,
a kid from school, one more face in the hall,
no one was there to catch our innocence in the fall.
Kenny Hawkless

The Day Of Eternity

The day of eternity has finally arrived,
And bringing with it in its deathly rage,
Is a torment known worse than the plague.

As a menacing haze it slowly emerged,
And billowed on up through the sky,
Its searing glow was a sight to behold,
Even though I knew we would die.

The earth became covered in a blanket of dust,
As it moved closer and closer,
In its bloodthirsty lust.

Cities and people began to melt,
And turn rancid to the core.

For this was the beginning,
And end.
To a nuclear activated,
Man-made war.
Richard S. Jowett

A Father And Mother Tribute

My Father and Mother were very special to me,
They were the best parents, that can ever be.

The affection, love devotion they shared,
They were always there, no matter what they cared.

Thanks to the good Lord for His blessings above,
And my Father and Mother's eternal love.

The humour, laughter, excitement they brought to my life,
They were a good team, husband and wife.

The tolerance and patience they both endured,
Bringing up seven children, had to be a difficult chore.

Remembering the wisdom, dedication, respect and good advice,
The everlasting impact, they had on my life.

You see my Father and Mother meant the world to me,
Nobody else can take their place, no matter what it maybe.

Dianne Richardson

What Is Love?

A fragile piece of glass
A cool breeze on a summer's day
A rose gleaming with light and radiating through the garden
A smile so warm it seems as if it were always there
A ray of sun that enters your body
A feeling of uneasiness at the mere thought
Like a butterfly flying blind
Like a kitten's eyes, so innocent yet so fragile
Like a songbird laced with a bow
Or like the rain on a sunday afternoon, peaceful and sweet
So What Is Love?
A feeling so cherished, so hard to find
A feeling so fragile almost like a falling teardrop
A feeling of warmth, of peace
A cleansing tingle that runs up and down your spine
Love is natural and beautiful, something to discover
and always cherish

Marie Palmer

Limits

Walking down this deserted gravel road
I remind myself of how it used to be:
Sitting in a meadow
With the aroma of flowers you would pick me.
Cold, damp sand on the beach,
Water splashing at my feet.
Swallowing the air,
The taste of sweet nothing.
Gliding down my throat.
Listening to the lonely cries of the birds,
Just moaning maybe some laughing.
Bright blue sky above me,
The world had no limits.
I guess I was wrong
Look at me now.

Michelle Demchuk

Life

The rusty summer light,
Leaves purple petals into the night.
Lying weak in the desert, the spring,
fades away like an ancient king.
But bare thy love to thy day,
and let the sun spread light on fields of hay.
The orchards of apples we have to eat,
would fall to the ground,
and under our feet.
The spring starts in every May,
and then the next year on that same day.
All is well until,
life fades away like life in a hunter's kill.

Leeann Schmalzel

The Bridge

Ellis is my name and I touch the sky
Whether bleak or crystal blue
I soar with my feathered friends,
Tho I cannot follow their distant ventures
They caw their tales of far away places seen
They are my only companions.

I am two countries, with no one loved more
I cater to all those with no bias everyday,
Every person is embraced in my presence,
If just for a short while.
I've seen millions embark my grace with,
Joy, fear, excitement, hesitation and awe.

I stand proud and strong with a view remarkable
For miles, unlike any other, only majestic
Mountains compare to my sight and sights.
Far below is my reason for being,
Beautiful yet deceiving it licks and taunts me.
Without it I fear I would not have been

Her name is Erie

Cindy Madden Gevaert

All Little Things We Lose

I have been sitting on the bathroom floor for a long time now, staring out the window and my legs are numb from the knees down. A small silhouetted figure hangs in the window; a dead leaf left over from winter, or maybe some small child's long lost mitten, perhaps even my own. The mitten hangs from a five-toed claw, at first between me and the setting sun, now between me and the tasteless, blue-grey of twilight. Not only can I not feel my feet, but I can no longer see them. I have been sitting absolutely still for an hour and forty five minutes, but my vigil is finally rewarded as the mitten begins to move. A twitching, it smells that now it is night; a stretch and it grows legs, not a thumb, and wings like arms with which it makes its sticky, wet-looking way across the screen. In the three seasons for which it has left and come back again, this is the first time that I have ever seen it move with my own two eyes. But somehow I know that after tonight it will not return again next summer because to see it move and spread its wings is the closest I will ever come to understanding how all little things we lose turn into bats and fly away to Mexico.

Dean Mosher

The Boardwalk

Along the faded boardwalk, I travel quietly.
 With each step, a memory unfolds to my dreary eyes;
A recollection long since packed away, creeps into my mind.
 How long has it been since I've seen your smile?

A tear slowly runs down my cheek, a pain I can't hold back.
 Across the outlying bay, a bird soars in the cool breeze.
The memory of that cold November night haunts my soul,
 The mystery is still locked within this boardwalk.

As I recall, you were so young and beautiful;
 Your long golden hair danced around your soft face,
Your emerald green eyes shone deeper than the sea.
 Oh! Why did you leave me that night on the boardwalk?

Because it was here on this boardwalk that I fell in love;
 To the most amazing person who ever existed,
It was right here where I had lost a piece of myself,
 When death came to claim my best friend.

I still wander along this boardwalk and think of you;
 I try to keep good thoughts and reminisce about happier times,
But it's difficult to stay strong, when you are not here with me,
 Here; standing empty, cold and so alone upon the boardwalk.

Kymberly Kennedy

My Children

Oh dear God, protect my children,
 To me they mean so much,
They are together but apart from me,
 And I cannot feel their touch.

'Tis a lonesome feeling that builds in me,
 And so impossible to control,
But the love I have for those two kids,
 Fill my entire heart and soul.

Please show them God, the love of man,
 And what they are to do,
That the love they have for someone else,
 Is the love they have for you.

I love them Lord, more than life itself,
 So guide them with your hand,
Because when you're four and six years old,
 Life is so hard to understand.

 Douglas Wayne Pedersen

Caesar's Generosity

Crossing the country by wagon train surely was a hardship
And the adventure, more arduous than the one that I endured
The valley then was only a stop along the way
The rainbow's end was another state away
Only decades ago, it is often told
That dreams once came true here with the dice or the shoe
It is dusk now as I walk along this road
Only Caesar could have helped me with my one-way ticket home
The glowing city lights reach out to the mountains on each side
As I wave my thumb as some sort of good-bye
I find peace as I look to the west
For God's sunset has silhouetted the mountain crests
But soon the mountains will disappear into darkness
And the jubilant city lights will dim all but the brightest of stars

 Anthony Essy

Two (As In You And I)

Why is it when you are not around,
I am so profound...
It appears I have lost our past, but his doesn't last,
The moment we meet again,
I know I will always love you,
Time will pass, our love will last,
As our love will forever be,
In our hearts and soul,
We have planted our seeds,
And they will forever grow,
For love is all we know,
Till death due us part,
In our own hearts.

 Patricia Ann Baines

Love Poem

My feelings for you is a perpetual fire
It fills my heart with love and desire
You are more to me than a mate or a wife
Each day is worth living, for you are my life
Without you I'd find my existence a bore
Instead I end up loving you more
You fill all my dreams, my hopes and my wants
You are my best friend, a true confidant
Although there's been trials and sadness it's true
We've faced life together and always come through
The bond that we have is solid and strong
Our life will continue to be happy and long

 R. D. Winterbottom

Memories Of A Friend

It was a cold night in December
A night I'll always remember,
Your sister phoned me that you had attempted suicide
But she didn't know if you had died,
I hurried to visit you in your hospital bed
But you weren't there, you were dead,
Feeling empty, sick, and shattered inside
Part of me went with you, when you had died,
I guess the life road that you were trudging was a bit too rough
Or maybe the love and compassion of your friends just wasn't enough,
I wish that you would have shared your pain and sufferings with me
So that I could have tried to stop a death that didn't have to be,
But no, you took a loaded gun instead
And shot yourself in your head,
When I went to your funeral, I had tears in my eyes
Realizing I was the only one present which was quite a surprise,
I guess in a sense you were always alone
That's one reason your body laid in your coffin cold and dead as stone
Now I understand the heartaches that you were going through,
And I want you to know that this world was never meant for
someone as sensitive and as wonderful as you.

 Sheryl Amato

If

If I were a bird,
Singing for you in front of your window every night,
Would you recognize my voice?

If I were a candle,
Burning for you, giving my life for you,
Would you see my tears in the dim light?

If I were a star,
Shining eternally in your sky, in your dream,
Would you understand my solitude and pain?

If I were the wind,
Following you everywhere all my life,
Would you sense me at your side?

If, in anguish, the bird were dying in her melancholy song,
If, in silence, the candle were shedding her last drop of tear,
If, in darkness, the star were falling with her broken dream,
If, in despair, the wind were languishing with her withering heart,
Would you wake up
From your dream?

 Zhang Dan

Mixture Of Joy And Ambiguities

Without a warning, a flood of joyous mirth
Envelopes the soul like a drifting wave;
And like a surfer, waiting for
The perfect colossal ride, body, mind, and soul
Commit themselves to this, ecstatic joy.

Then suddenly, like an avalanche,
The flood of joyous mirth came cascading
Into a pillar of darkness
Over body, mind, and soul.

But this is life!
It offers a hand in friendship sometimes,
Then suddenly withdraw that friendly
And not so friendly hand
If as though, a thought of recollection
In its euphoric gestures, simply evaporated;
Leaving body, mind, and soul
In a knocked out, dragged out, discarded rubble,
All because, life gives no guarantees
Of total joy, without some form of ambiguity.

 Joan E. Gettry

Look To The Future

As you journey down life's golden path...
It can be filled with joy and lots of laughs...
At times it may be filled with pain and sorrow...
Never give up... there's a brighter tomorrow...
Keep alive your hopes and your dreams...
Never give up your pride and self esteem..

Reach for the stars and beyond...
Never lose sight of your golden pond...
Keep your spirit alive and your heart free of love...
For peace in life is as free as a dove...

Keep alive your dreams and your heart free from sorrow...
For your future is bright with each new tomorrow...

And when you grow older and your hair has turned gray...
Keep your memories alive and in your heart each day...
Never forget the pat you chose along the way...

Carlene June Rose

Rebirth

Yesterday, my fingers touched eternity, as the eternal soul
surrounded and enveloped me.
The night slowly lifted from my eyes, in the hazy mist, I
beheld an aura of surprise, as if some strange infinity
had descended upon the finite me.

Shadows seemed to disappear, my troubled mind was somehow
clear. The turmoil locked within my heart I seemed to
touch, it stood apart. This compassionate soul of mine
had somehow touched the ultimate divine!

"O God!" I cried, "Why is it me you have chosen to touch eternity?"
Yet, I knew, I was among the precious few, that whose soul
could not identify the body in which to occupy.

Somehow my life had purpose still, my soul was washed and saved
from hell. With fresh new eyes I saw the world, the world
that which was hurled at me, so rapidly, I could not see the
laughter from a child's heart, the daffodils, a work of art!
These things were but blind to me, until my fingers touched eternity.

Virginia Kulhanjian-Freeland

Untitled

Where does fantasy end, reality begin
Once there was only a dream...

A peasant girl, sweet and dainty
Destined to one day reign
Placed upon a throne, scepter in hand
Hair and eyes of mother earth
A nymph from days of old

A heroine then and now
Vanquishing the eternal darkness
So that mine eyes could behold
Beauty to make a goddess green
A passion to out brilliance the sun

A queen of light so pure
A vision of etherealness
She cleansed my soul and claimed my heart,
A kingdom of love for two

So joyous a reunion, when fantasy became flesh
Then gone again...A whisper of smoke through a field of dreams

Though time was short my heart still yearned, mind recall
A vision of fantasy and the fleshy surety of what reality could be

Jeff Stephens

The Old House

The old house sits by the side of the road.
　Inside, the rooms are empty and still.
The woman and little dog who once lived there,
　were taken away against their will.
The light still shines bright hanging there
　on the side of the house.
One wonders why it's left to shine,
　with nothing to benefit but rats and mice
　　and the passage of time.
Many feet have passed through the old door.
　some were happy and swift, some slow and sad.
It makes you wonder why things change and turn out to be so bad.
It's true, we all have to grow old.
　our steps grow slow and our mind gets dull,
But who should decide our fate,
　and why should others say from your home you must go.
If the old cuckoo clock hanging on the wall could turn back time.
The rooms would once again come alive.
The old lady and little dog would come home again,
and would once more there abide.

Betty Kopf

Two Hearts

The love that was within my heart, will hurt again they say.
The sadness I feel inside, remains in my heart to stay.
The fire which was hot and ablaze, has turned to smoke and embers.
The coals are hot, but the fire is gone only pictures to remember.
What happened along the way, only you and I will know.
So it's time to choose our paths, and watch our children grow.
To hurt each other more would mean, heartache and despair.
Our love we have is not enough, but we will always somehow care,
Memories will forever linger, in the cobwebs of our past.
Our dreams which seemed so real. Though faded oh so fast.
Our hurts will be mended, because time heals most pain,
Although we must continue on, inside the scars remain,
So we must follow our rainbows, and continue to chase our dreams.
Two hearts that became one, are two again it seems.

Thoralee Schneider

A Coastal Sunrise

Out beyond the horizon,
Gleaming heartily in the breeze,
Is the semi-circle sun,
As it rises with such ease.

Brighter than the brightest light,
More glorious than a rose,
Is the breathtaking sun,
That forever and ever glows.

Waves crash onto the shoreline,
Dragging seaweed to the sand,
Then they pull back out to sea,
Mopping the golden beach clean again.

The sun has risen higher now,
Looking brighter than before,
For it must take its place up there,
Where the gulls and songbirds soar.

The blue sky lights up
Behind the puffy, cotton clouds,
It surely is a beautiful day, you think,
As out rush the happy crowds.

Bethany Green

Mother, Teacher

My mother is a teacher, she works hard
I hear stories of long days with difficult kids
I see her toil many hours over papers of unappreciative youth
She comes home tired, exhausted, weary and worn
She wakes early, goes to bed late.
I watch as she spends her time, money, and effort
To further the education of her students.
She gives of her life for the kids that are not her own
And they don't know...but I do.

Nathan Powers

If I Die

If I die
Will you give it a second thought?
Am I worth that?
Would you go to see me—**dead.**
Would you cry? Would you ache?
Or would you try to save face?
Would you care?
What-would-you-wear?
Would two hours of your so precious time
Be two too many to spare—
To see a kid that you barely even knew
That you never got to know and never will know again?
Or would you rather go run and jump and play
In the cold, cold snow?
What am I worth warm or cold?
Am I worth more young?
Or worth more old?
Do you feel a pain in your chest?
Or laugh and blow it off as another kid like the
Rest.

Gregory M. Albert

Untitled

Mr. Pall Mall went to dine with Mr. Philip Morris,
and they roomed at the Chrsterfield Hotel, pretty
soon they got a tip from Mr. Filter that
Sir Walter Raleigh was in town. So they
took some money, mounted a Camel and rode.
While riding along they say how Lucky can
you get. I hope we reach L&M by ten;
if not Viceroy's got it at both ends. Smile.

Rosellar Barber

The Naturalist

Wildflower jewel in field encrusted with emerald blades
just outside the tread of the path's dirty feet
the wildflower, a ruby starburst of petal tongues
high upon rocket trail of glass green stem
spinning missile
pollen is the falling glowing ash snowing on a honeybee back

Back to the hive

Buzzing back by my ear
and spiraling down a drain against a placid sky

Sweet clover honey is like the yellow sun's warm light
is like the breeze carrying another bar of the bird's
sweet chorus by my ear
from high.
In the tree he sits, the bird mocking
my crutched legs and digits
sore is my neck from craning it to see the music
the winged cherubs sings, trapped in the halo of my binoculars.

Robert Price

I See

I see the sun, that reminds me of smiles and pods and melting
ice-cream. I see houses, that remind me of sleep and TV and
family. I see the parks, that remind me of bikes and skateboards
and a game of chase. I see trees, that remind me of beauty
and peace, and drinking lemonade in the shade.
I see the rain that reminds me of catching bull frogs
and turtles, and swimming in the ditch,
and watching water valleys. I see the world, that reminds
me of friends and penpals and the first to blast to the moon.
I see a rainbow that hugs the world and reminds me
of brightness, beauty, peace, friends, and harmony.
I see these things because God chose for
me to see them. So take a long, hard look
at these things . . . aren't they
Beautiful?!

Sydney V. LeBlanc

Walking Walls

Monumental walls tombstones that can walk
are fashioned from materials not of common stock,
are made of many colors in every shape and size
with visible foundations hollowed out by pride.
Prepared illusions
facades perceived as clean,
hatred poured as mortar
supporting shallow beams,
with the catalyst of ignorance
forging bitterness for seams.
The parapets are raised
without a leveled line
by the uneven setting of bigotry's design.
Prejudice the architect
from the tower waves, lending misdirection to
walls which have no sight;
for all the walls of mention
have been constructed in the night!

Peter F. Serra

The Poet-Aster

I saw a child running through
a golden field of wheat ready for harvest.
The light of a full moon
glanced off his fair head.
He was so beautiful I cried.

A mischievous towhead
out in the middle of the field
after dark, but the moon was bright.
He touched the wheat's kernel;
I saw him pull it from its spike.

I saw a towhead child taste the grains
which thresh free of the chaff.
Then the light of full moon brought the child home.
He picked up a book to read.

The light of the full moon was brighter than the old lamp,
glowing behind his shoulder.
I could see what the child read;
he had tasted a golden harvest,
but was reading graffiti.
For the Poet-Aster I cried.

Lynne S. Chaplin

Dear Holy Spirit Take Control

Dear Holy Spirit take control
It's you Lord, only you Lord that can fill me and make me
be whole again.

Dear Holy Spirit take control
There's a valley in my life today and things don't seem to be
going right.
But in my mind Lord I know there's a blessing in it.
There's no valley to low or problem too hard for God to solve.

There's a valley in my life but there's a blessing in it I know
For Gods gonna make it be right

Dear holy spirit take control, its you Lord only you Lord

that brings peace to a valley or a mountain top.

And when my valleys come in my mind, Lord I know
There's a blessing in it.

In my heart soul and spirit Lord I know, there's a blessing in it.
This valley of mine Lord I know you've got plans
for a blessing in it.

Dear Holy spirit, take control for this heart,
mind and soul of mine is longing for.
All the love Lord, happiness, peace, and joy
that only you Lord can bring
   Ruby Noel

The Gathering Of Angels

Dawn approaching with the brilliancy of the sunrise shimmering with
the early dew in the morning light. Birds singing softly, a calm
breeze flowing

Another day showing its glorious beauty in sight
Early morning embraces a mother's smile, a pat of encouragement and family blessings.
A kiss, a hug and away

Innocence walking their familiar paths, together hand in hand,
reminiscing of a yesterday yet so vivid today.
A child's faith and wonderment blindly walking to eternity..

Only to walk once again cheering to one another with great
excitement the beauty they see.
With outstretched arms the path so great shining before them,
leading them on to whatever might be.

Forgetting forever the pain... the fright
Happy once again and eagerly awaiting their new found home of eternal
happiness. A home with so much love and kindness and visions in sight.

There's so much "Greatness" before them and so dear. Bless our
children, our dear sweet angels, you will always be so very near.

This poem is dedicated to the pre-school children who were taken so
swiftly in the Oklahoma City bombing along with their dear parents
and families who have felt and still are feeling this great loss.
   Cloie Caudill Dale

Resurrection

He took the brittle seed and flung it from him.
The man's search for beauty continued to haunt him.
Never knowing, never even suspecting,
Beauty lay in the seed, waiting resurrection.

A more peaceful place to dwell he tried to find,
In nomadic discontent he spent his time.
Never knowing, never even suspecting.
Peace lay within the man waiting resurrection
   Clarise Dover

Embark

The rain and the solitude embark
   upon the happiness

The Passion and the firefly explicit
   on the verge of eternal orgasms

The countless creatures with light wings, conscience
   and dire rationalities

What next on the wagers
   of human life and companionship.
   Varun Budhiraja

"Your Name"

We bleed every month
For your name.
Just so yours can continue.
Our cramped bellies and
Flooded organs far reach
Any pain you could suffer
For any "brother" or "war."

For we suffer justly
Without complaint or
Particularly want.
Our hormonally off-set minds
Feel only the love
For you or for life, and
Thus will endure our bodies.
For this we do not suffer
For our name, but only
For your name.
So we can continue your name.
   Shannon Baker

The Fossil

The beetle wandered wayward
Over the weary weathered stone.
The fossil figured faintly,
Is it looking for its own?
I've had one trapped for eons out,
But time's changed my furrowed brow.
Winds wash will and water runs by
Will the beetle find out how?
I've worked and slaved and fought and sung
To ease my heavy heart
Of one whose form was first among
The species, grains apart.
   Joan B. Shannon

To Live Is To Love

   Life is worth living when there's someone to love,
To be loved by someone that's sweet as a dove;
   Loving that someone comes because of caring,
Being loved by someone is the cause of sharing;
   Learning to live is to bring someone close,
Sharing life with someone you love most;
   To love someone is the right key of living,
For that special someone love is for the giving;
   Loving that someone feels so right,
Life feels real good and soars high like a kite;
   To love someone feels good in life,
I'll love that special someone wit all my heart and night;
   In this life my love is to be claimed,
My undying love will always rename to same.
   Paul Dorsey

Joy And Love

Suddenly the hole in my heart has been filled.
When your love entered me I was thrilled.
I will have no more longing and no more tears,
But joy and love throughout the years.

Your patience more than a Virtue.
Your love that says "I'll never hurt you."
Your joy in times of pain.
Your voice that will call my name.

The love I will always need
comes from you and will always heed.

Tracey Virtue

Two

When summoned upon to articulate,
By a handsome gentleman who queries,
Precisely how he shall unlock the gate
Of my passion, in practice or theory...

Butterflies in my uterus panic.
Perspiration beads between my fingers.
Potential requests of him race manic.
The mystery, unanswered still lingers.

Plainly, I fear that which makes me feel good.
I'm not certain why 'tis; I fear not him.
I do know why.... he'd leave me if he could.
Countless others all wooed and left by whim.

Perhaps my bedside manner be latent.
Should he stay, I must beg of him, "be patient."

Holly K. Gibson

Precious Moment

We may never live to see tomorrow
and the past cannot be undone
life is not always what we wish it to be
but I will continue loving you.

We may never live to talk about yesterday
remembering that day when I first saw you
hoping someday you would be my shining star.
You showed me how much you really care
and I cherish every moment being with you.

We are together today, and I take this opportunity
to tell you
my wife, my lover, my friend
you have made my life complete
and I Love You.

Marcel Winter

Untitled

There are motes of dust
on my window panes -
That are visible when you take
the time to see.
It is time for water again,
to shine them up and gaze out,
with an unimpeded view.
Everything looks a lot dusty now,
another summer is almost over.
Soon - fall will be here,
and the winds will blow,
and the leaves will turn,
Into a lovely show
of yellow and red and finally
a dusty hue.
Even dust, can't impede
my view.

Dorothy Diana Petrie

Past And Gone

The Ice Wagon pulled by horses coming down the street.
Children running out to get a chip, it was their special treat.
The butcher with a side of beef upon a wagon bed of ice,
covered with a new white sheet your purchase he would slice.
School lunch in a shining pail of tin with fried chicken,
mother had killed a hen.
Washing on a wash board and drying them in the sun.
It all sounds so miserable, but was really lots of fun.

Memories are a blessing when you are growing old.
Pray for a lasting mind. It is more valuable than gold.
I have enjoyed the things of old and lived to enjoy the new.
God has blessed me with good health; on June 2nd, I turned 92.

Writing poetry is like a tonic, it keeps you alert.
Even if you have a pain, it doesn't seem to hurt.
The Conventions are so special; meeting friends we hold so dear.
I am already looking forward to seeing you again next year.

Mamie Hodge

Bereavement

I was lead up the aisle to you, by my father,
And you lead me down the aisle and out
Into a world as partners, lovers, spouses,
Homemakers, facing every kind of strife.

Now they bear you aloft, down the aisle,
In your bed of flowers, satin pillow and lace,
In the grey suit you wore at our first-born's wedding, not long ago.
I follow meekly out and into the world,
Alone, though crowded by friends and relations.

After years of taking each other for granted,
"My clothes, my food, my papers in order,"
you demanded. My bills unpaid, I'd make louder claims.
Alone, now, I face each area of life's frictions.
"Trust God," I'm told.
"Don't question sudden death," they say.
My rights now merge into responsibilities,
Despite God's presence, I am afraid.

Iris Devadason

Galaxy

In spite of the heat seeping from the stars
In spite of the sun burning all my scars
My life goes at an amazing speed towards the dark

Look at the farthest spot in the sky
Look at the darkest side of my life
Look, but forget what you pry

When the dice of life is thrown
Truth already lies in your hand
Forget for a while what is inside
Weep and enjoy the tremors in your eyes
Crush the fake desire
Hide your feelings and burn 'em in a fire

Jump to the nearest galaxy
Feel all the energy engulfing your body
You're dashing through space
Intense heat carry you in waves
Asteroid belts and meteorites
Time crushes to a halt
Well where's the feeling inside...
It's all gone.

Naushad Dulymamode

My Life

My life is sand through the hourglass.
My friend is a rock.
My life is shattered.

Kim Martin

Here And Now

Here and Now,
Where the infinite lies,
Here and now,
Where the stars shine bright,
Here and now,
Where truth is discovered,
Here and now,
Where life is not bothered.
Alon Sitzer

The Call

The geese call me to follow
Where mist hangs over lakes and forests

The Loon calls
Come to mirrored lakes where
Peace and Quiet reigns.

The giant pine sighs as the wind whispers
Come to green meadows
Here the sun warms the earth and
The land bursts forth in flower.

Come to majestic snowcapped mountains
Where the deer and sheep play
in sheltered valleys.

Come where God's good earth sings
And steams laugh as they tumble
over creek beds to the sea.

Come - come with me.
J. M. Monahan

Russel

Straying eyes on nothing specific, missing words he's never heard.
Conversations with laughter,
in uncomprehensible emotion he wallows,
silent ... like a profound thinker.

What wonderful inventions in a mind so quiet, what wonderful intentions?
Deathly silence betrayed only by reaction.
Awkward.
Cannot stare into his eyes.

On my level his music is the same but why can't ask him?
It's all so unfair.

Languish in words, feel pleasure in them,
sweet as they ooze over your tongue, he's never has that ...

Scorned ... shunned ... outcast of his own people.
Misunderstood by us, he stands alone a world he rules,
hidden from harsh words and deceitful words
and most of all caring, soothing, loving words.

I want to tell him the of the world,
but this eyes, brown and unmoving stare at the wall as we speak.
He'll never know.
Simon Du Plooy

"YOU WILL ALWAYS BE THERE"

You fell down when you were one; your first steps so unsteady.
I picked you up and kissed your cheek; to walk, you weren't ready.
You tripped and fell another time, and skinned your tiny knee.
I picked you up and held you tight, your pain was felt by me.
Years went by, you fell again; First love had broken your heart.
I was there to pick you up, to mend the broken parts.
The last time came, you fell once more; too soon it was for good.
I tried so hard to pick you up; there was no way I could.
I fell down, my loss so great; I wanted to stay down.
The memory of you picked me up, and willed me to go on.
I now feel stronger in many ways; my newfound strength from you.
You've picked me up and made me see, I have to live for you.
Connie Kay Zaffino

Life

Life is not a bubble of air,
That blows up like a balloon;
Nor a weakling that totters
And falls on a wind-swept dune.

Life is not a wayward plaything,
We can break in our iron hand,
And re-create, joining the pieces
With the mixture of blood and sand.

Life is not flesh and bone,
Nor the five senses that decry,
Nor the heart that feels, nor the mind
That thinks, of the breath that will die.

Life is a recycled birth, wrought
To mingle with his image, his thought.
Nooroon Dossal

An End

Painless I hope it be.
For my world is painful.

I'm happy for others sake.
But me all I know is pain.

I love happy colors, yet,
It seems black is always on my mind.

Past and Present there have been happy times,
But the pain inside seems to conquer all.

I feel my insides sagging,
Lower into the pit of blackness they go.

I still hold some joy,
But it's only a temporary release,

From the pain so deeply run,
That I'll never recover.

No, medical help will do.
Only a painless end will cure all.
Misti Jo Degner

Listen

Listen to everything,
    what we hear
    and what we can't.
And when we can't hear anything,
    listen with your eyes, body, and soul.
    There is still so much to be heard
    without any noise at all.
Look into a pair of eyes and
    tell me what you see!
Look at the way one moves
    and it can tell you what you need.
Listening is not only what we hear,
    But what our heart and soul tell us.
And we our thus guided into helping
    by listening to ourselves.
Sandy Barry

May I Have This Dance

I stroll across the dance floor.
Our eyes lock.
The music begins playing in our hearts.
We begin to dance.
I lead only a short while,
then turn the responsibility over to her.
She leaps and glides
through the air
like a ballerina jets across a stage.
The dance ends.
I regain control
of my horse
as we leave
the jumping arena.
Terry Williams

Untitled

This day I will marry my best Friend,
the one who shares
my Laughter and Joys,
my Sorrow and Tears,
the one who Supports and Comforts me,
the one who brings
Meaning and Happiness to my life,
the one who I share
my Life and Dreams with.
This day I will marry
the one I Love.

Becky Dinesen

The Coming

Brightness shrouds my face
I beam like a light tower
Between heaven and earth I rest
As if possessed by mystic powers
None alive can break my faith
For I foresee many great tomorrows
But it's my keen belief of today
Which could make any man stand and say
"Thank you"
There is heaven on this earth
For those who live life good.

Mesha Polk

Outer Spring

Spring has sprung, the flowers
Bloom; within me black as night,
In sorrow both are my heart and soul.
Although my outer spring is green
As grass; for what you see is just
A mask.
It covers my true feelings of pain
For thee; for the man I love I know
Loves me, but lacks a bit of
Maturity.
For he not realizes that whatever
Outer spring I still posses, is
Merely a cover-up like the leaves
Of a tree or green of the grass.
My Lord help my love see past my
Outer spring, so that in time he
May gain and see this outer spring of
Life is not a game that he might lose.

Noemi Espinoza

The Sting

Alas!
The Sting of Death is triumph over
The Breath of Life
I Cry
I scream
Is the only path to immortality
Death?
Why?
This path the living daily tread
Why?
When the foot steps cease
Why?
Must they too, be dead

There is no other path to follow
There is no place to hide
The Sting will triumph
The Breath will Die
And I shall
Cry

Cora Freeland

Yesterday And Tomorrow

Beauty will change as time goes by...
To somewhat regarding our lives.
Our feeling of yesterday
Is different to now-a-days.
For the world is round and wide,
To riches or poverty one shall glide.
So don't get snobbish with what we're now.
Our lives shall become,
Or what we'll have done.

Hok-Swie Liem

Brooke Ashley

I can't believe she's only three, her mind is so mature.
She reasons like an older child, her actions are so sure.
She'll formulate a dance as the music stirs her soul.
The melody will make her spin, around and around she'll twirl.

Her deep brown eyes shine bright with joy, her smile brings mine too.
Her dark brown hair with lustrous gleam is so silky smooth.
The softness of her olive skin curves round her dimpled cheeks.
Behind a pair of rosy lips are beautiful tiny teeth.

Her thoughtfulness and caring amaze all of those who hold her.
How old? they ask, she can't be three, she really must be older.
She's so wise for her size, they say with pleasant wonder.
How is it that she understands things that should be beyond her?

Yet only three is what she be and there are times she shows it.
Like, when she's tired and sleep's required a fit she'll get and throw it.
Tears will flow, why? She don't know, but love is all about.
Hugs and kisses soothe her spirit and calm her need to shout.

Her faults are lost amid my love for I am her Poppy.
A name she gave that, when she speaks it, makes my heart feel lofty.
A gift of love from above, she makes my life so sweet.
Expectantly, I'll watch her grow beyond the age of three.

Richard N. Valentine

"A Girl That Normally Look Okay, But Tonight Looks...."

The dress was a green, sequined web, in which
everyone in the room was instantly entwined.
The web would strike you blind as you stared,
Relentlessly.
Your feet were numb, your ears were numb
But your mind and heart were left alone
to sprint away.

And so the girl that normally looks Okay
but tonight.... wears a green dress
and brings to the room her hidden
lethal outline.

Matthew Seilus

Standing On My Own

Who am I?
Nobody knows, sometimes...not even I.
What do I want to do with my life?
Everybody knows...
That's perplexing to me.
Whose principles, guidelines and standards do I live by?
Only God knows but it's really up to me.
What do I really want?
Interestingly...no one understands this but me:
To be accepted for whomever I am, for whatever I choose
To do and not to be judged for choosing to live by
My standards...standing on my own!!!

Tonya Revonne Truesdale

Time Erases

Time Erases life of the past
In doing, brings the future
We are works of art
Created by heaven and earth
We are the Universe's display
For Universal eyes look upon us

Time erases sudden hurt
Brings the love that is sought
But in doing so, soon will let go
We mold our life as planned
But in time the eyes of the universe.
Will take a few away for Universal eyes look upon us.

Time erases the things we must not see
We are a world that's on stage
We are stars, we do our part
In work and in play we come and we go
Whenever it is time for time erase us all
But every man, woman and child will live in a kingdom
Where time does not erase the factors and the hurt
But remembers as life goes on.

Rick Bull

Love's Lament

A brawling dove coos from his
lonely perch receiving no reply,
How barren, how dry seems the
restless sky,
And everyone around alive and hearty,
Has muffled out woman's inner cries,
And she reaps the lamentation of a new
beginning.

Such a bitter mystery this thing called love,
It rules our prudent years and dries our tears,
But lover to lover we awake under sleeping
stars and a warm embrace.

Underneath a brilliant moon a coo is heard,
thru a Westward wind,
Flowing so gently across the water,
Awakening my hopes and fears,
And under the full moon the white foam of the
dim lit sea breaks on the shore under
wandering stars.

Cotton Essex

Untitled

We want you to know on this special day
there's several ways we'd just like to say
    we love you,
we could give you hugs and all our kisses
flowers, and dinner, even help with dishes
cut the grass, vacuum the floors
do the laundry, and stop slamming doors

Wipe the mud, and grease off our feet
and try not to spill our drink in the seat
pick up our things and take out the trash
clean up our room and not charge you cash

All of these things we'll be happy to do
cause this is your day, the one just for you
we hope you feel special, and to us there's no doubt
your the one in a million we can't do with out

So when tomorrow comes, and we're missed just a few
or most of those things we we're gonna do
we hope it reminds you, and this is so true,
without you, we don't know what we would do.

Daniel Hudson

Stale OM In The Hollowing Grotto

The light of his smile couldn't touch the sun-
The sun which set at her breast.
Cracked lips a reminder that he hadn't won,
Salt- water tasting of the meat eating test.

Will the priestly mourning pray for that smile-
While frantically searching for his cap and bells
The cutting cruel laughter echoes all the while
His childlike beads tell of heavens and hells.

Paradise is a moment, she mutters with grace;
Her words taste like weapons, and he struggles to meet
The smile of deceit on her twisted face,
Yet winged words will touch but those feet.

Is he a jacobin now, under a monk-like hood,
With pale face on fire, not surprisingly jaded-
Touch grown unknown, laughter misunderstood,
Wailing: 'Pour water on my head before the light has faded.'

Pitie, pitie, Il a ete pris par son truc.
Call forth the bells-let's mark with a parade
The self eating snake and the cackling rook.
Leave cracked bones to dust, preparations are made.

John James Bernard Ford

Untitled

Out under the night sky
dark descending,
I am comforted by your presence,
with no thought given to the raven above our heads,
or its shadows underneath.
We lie content and laughing,
at ourselves, each other, and the wonder of this life.
The choice is ours to make,
we know,
so,
we dream while waking,
delighting in each moment,
each beating of our fragile hearts,
wrapped in the strongest resolve to gaze,
not at the night,
but at the stars in the sky,
falling down,
cascading all around us,
certain to find refuge,
in your eyes.

Melanie Adele Davis

Unchained

If I could I would-
no earthly boundaries impeding me,
save those of the greatest good
    setting me free.
As I am I said I am human in every way;
filled with doubting emotions,
sinful day to day I am,
dreaming beyond this turning orb.

Kept to my place by pride,
I am humbled by a book.
Filled with myself inside,
guilt shames my very core.
Sleeping on the highway
my nightmare wrecked this life.

To be unchained, on bended knees I look up
with a heavy soul.
Tears falling down and sadness in my heart,
light filters into darkness
Folded arms in meditation, the unchained mind soars
beyond this turning orb.

Hicks E. Maples Jr.

The Funeral Home

Scared, so scared, as scared as can be.
Our first date, to his Funeral Home, the Undertaker took me.
It wasn't the movie, the mall, or to bed,
In his Funeral Home hair stood up on my head.

Trying hard to be brave
With things erie from the grave.
Things that go Boo and bump in the dark,
I'd rather be anywhere, even in a dark park.

Chains didn't rattle, my skin didn't crawl.
There were no footsteps down the long hall.
Embalming tables I saw and caskets of white.
We stayed in that place and had a good night.

Suddenly, the Funeral Home became a place so dear.
The scary and creepy I wanted to be near.
From my heart I rejoiced, from the depths of my heart.
From this place I never want to ever depart.

Our first kiss, hug, even love under the tree
Lots of good memories in this Funeral Home for me.
First time we made love, second time too,
No longer afraid of the dead saying Boo!!!

Veronica G. Taylor

What A Gas

I came to the oil and gas capital of Canada,
A lobotomized bearded Schizophrenic,
With the threadbare threads on my back,
A one-way Grayhound bus ticket
And two measly bucks in my pocket
Along with a huge battered suitcase
Crammed with a lifetime's excellent poetry.
I ended up in a commune, now razed,
Sleeping on the funky library floor
Where the incongruous judgmental creep
In oxfords, carrying a furled umbrella,
Had to step over me to reach the door
When he went to his work cage
Punctually at 7 a.m., He made is known
To everyone but me that he considered me
An undesirable damned renegade intruder
And that if he were king of the universe
Which he was in all but name and fact,
I would be the very first to get gassed.

James E. Cooper

Ode To My Mother

No masterpiece you painted
    One ceiling high in Rome,
But both your girls and son remember
    You lived one in your home.
You panned no epic poem
    That critics might call art,
But with a grander vision,
    You wrote one in you heart.
You craved no Parian marble
    In sculptured greek design,
But with you God Blessed loving fingers,
    You shaped this life of mine.
You built no white cathedral
    By echoed footsteps trod,
But in simple faith you made
    Our home a house of God.
Not the hand of Raphael,
    Or Michelangelo,
Could paint my Mother as she is -
    Only her children know.

Mary V. Prisock

Along.....

The grains of sand beneath your feet
may sometimes cause you pain
yet sometimes they may give you strength
to walk into the rain

This path was chosen for you friend
walk gently as you go
you have so many gifts to give
it's time for letting go

So much has passed and caused you harm
today you should feel strong
you've gotten past the obstacles
and overcome the wrongs

With all the love inside your heart
be whatever you can be
and peace will come to you my friend
you will finally be set free...

Dee O'Neill

Biographies
of
Poets

ABED, SANY R.
[pen.] Sonny Abed; [b.] May 26, 1968, Beirut, Lebanon; [p.] George and Salwa; [ed.] Business Management Diploma - Douglas College New Westminster B.C.; [occ.] Public Relations and Hospitality Industries; [memb.] Young Entrepreneurs; [pers.] If more people could recognize the simplicity of life, there would be a unity on earth that would make us all equal and eternally peaceful; [a.] Coquitlam, British Columbia, Canada

ACOCELLA, MIKE
[b.] June 29, 1975, Edison, NY; [p.] John B. Acocella and Linda J. Acocella; [ed.] Montgomery H.S. Class of 94' full time student Santa Rosa Junior College; [occ.] Student; [hon.] Outstanding Offensive Player Award for Baseball Team in 92' for Montgomery H.S.; [oth. writ.] Poems and Short stories but they have not been published.; [pers.] I write to display my thoughts in a colorful and detailer manner without stating the obvious. I try to leave everything open ended so that anyone else who reads my poems or stories can assign their own personal meaning.; [a.] Santa Rosa, CA

ADAMCZAK, ANNETTE I.
[b.] November 27, 1967, Virginia Beach, VA; [p.] Rosemary and Daniel Zmuda; [m.] Dwayne D. Adamczak, August 13, 1988; [ch.] Jessie Rae, David John, Emily Rose, and another child due in September.; [ed.] Graduated from Alden Central High School in 1986; [occ.] Chiropractic Assistant; [oth. writ.] I have compiled a collection of poems, but none have been published to date. These poems date back to the early 1980's; [pers.] "Jonathan's Promise" was written for a very close friend whose life was cut short in a car accident. It is at times like this, in the darkest and saddest of all places, when it is the easiest for me to compose my work.; [a.] Akron, NY

ADAMS, KRISTEN
[b.] September 14, 1982, Laguna Beach, CA; [ed.] Currently a freshmen at Santa Margarita Catholic High School, Accepted into 4 Honors/AP Courses (out of 7 course) including English; [occ.] High School Student; [hon.] Top 10% in Math, Scat Test-UCI College, Outstanding Achievement in the CA Mathematics League, 2 yrs. in the UCI talent search, Participant in the Knowledge Master Open, Participated in the Imagination Celebration of Orange County for Art.; [oth. writ.] Participated with Distinction, Mater Dei H.S. English Department Essay contest 1996, won a Sapphire Jem Stone in a Mother's Day Poetry contest (2nd place, 1996); [pers.] Go for it!; [a.] Laguna Beach, CA

ADAMS, PATRICIA J.
[pen.] Patricia J. Adams; [b.] January 3, 1952, Anguilla; [m.] Calvin B. Adams, August 12, 1972; [ch.] Patvin, Dwayne, Amanda, Candis, Jared; [ed.] College of Further Edjucation, St. Kitts. B.W.I.; [occ.] (Trained) Teacher; [oth. writ.] Anthology of Poems 1995 entitled "A Jewel Made Of Sand" folk songs, children's stories, poems in local magazine/newspaper.; [pers.] Strive to promote Anguilla, its culture and other aesthetic beauty through poetry. Inspired by West Indian writers.

ADAMS, RENEE
[pen.] Renee Adams; [b.] March 16, 1950, Nashville; [p.] Ruby and Otis Morris; [m.] Kenneth Adams, August 5, 1968; [ch.] Aleathea, Kenneth, Michael; [occ.] Self - AAA Lock and Key; [oth. writ.] Other poems

ADAMSON, GLORIA
[b.] Kansas City; [p.] Marie and Harold Adamson; [ch.] Three; [ed.] Boulder, Colorado, University of Colorado, BA in Studio Arts, an MA in Art, Education, and a Teaching Certification in the

same K-12 (1995); [occ.] Teacher; [memb.] Past Director on The Board for the Village, Arts Coalition and the Boulder Artists Gallery. Past Boulder of Delta Theta Chi National Women's Sorority and Boulder and Boulder International Folk Dancers. Volunteer for the Talented and Gifted Program and the Boulder Public Library Children's section. Past dance performer with Tapestry Ethnic Music and Dance Ensemble, Postoley Folk Dance Performing Grope and the BOulder Scandinavian Dancers. Present dance performer with Hoofin' High Country Cloggers and Skandia Dance, L.T.D. (Love to Dance).; [oth. writ.] Kosmos - 20th Century Icons, House of Hours, Mathematical and Historical Poetry, Philosophical Poetry for both adults and children, A Renaissance of the Modular Interdisciplinary View of Intelligence and Learning Capabilities, Humorous Etiological Poetry, Tales from A Winters Night, Beyond the Issue of Assessment in the Visual Arts, Creativity - Processing Self-Discovery, Creatively Teaching your child at Home to Learn, House of Hours myth for above mentioned work of art; [pers.] Strives to be reflective on life's experiences and observations and to research and educate others to learn how to learn and remember through personal example, poetry and writings.; [a.] Boulder, CO

AFROZE, ZEENAT
[b.] January 1, 1957, Bangladesh; [p.] Kazi Z. Rahman, Zahura Begum; [m.] A.F.M. Billah Khan, October 3, 1976; [ch.] Almansur, Nadia, Lamia; [ed.] Master in Social Science and Diploma in Computer Programming; [occ.] Secretarial Job in Sales; [oth. writ.] Published in College and University Magazines.; [a.] Scarborough, Ontario, Canada

AGEE, ERIC MATAIEU
[pen.] Eric Mataieu Agee; [b.] November 23, 1957, Staten Island, NY; [p.] Cecil and Irene Agee; [m.] Susan Costales Agee, June 7, 1994; [ed.] AA at Monterey Peninsula College, B.S. James Madison University Harrisonburg, V.A.; [occ.] Ortaotic Retailer and Pedortaist; [memb.] Shoreline Community Church Pacific Grove CA Peportate Footwalk Ass., Nature Susaine Inc.; [pers.] That is my view on those seeking a lifelong husband or wife. "It be honours a man, or a woman to marry one of conviction, charity, character, and wit. If not, they marry their Myta, destined to be its foot stool.; [a.] Pacific Grove, CA

AGNEW, MARK
[b.] March 29, 1951, Odessa, TX; [p.] James and Eva Agnew; [ed.] Crane High, Univ of Central Oklahoma, Calif. state Univ of Sacramento; [memb.] Canterbury Choral Society, Canterbury Chamber Choir, Red Lion Pipe Band; [hon.] National Honor Society for Century 21 Accounting, Best Vocalist '88, '90 at Regency Talent nationalist, Best Pop Vocalist '89 at Discovery Television Nationals; [pers.] If you follow your heart, your dreams and wishes will come true, and if you don't know how to unlock your dreams, wait, someone else in your life may have the key.; [a.] Oklahoma City, OK

AGUILAR, CASSIE
[b.] January 1, 1969, Tilden, NE; [p.] Dwight Detlefsen and Lila Bliss; [m.] Thomas T. Aguilar, July 18, 1992; [ch.] Jesse Emmanuel Aguilar; [ed.] Apache Jct. High School and Apollo College Medical; [occ.] Mother and Housewife otherwise a medical assistant; [memb.] Childrens book clubs; [pers.] Dedicated to my son Jesse for giving me all your precious love and memories the first year of life. I love you.; [a.] Superior, AZ

AHMED, RUMANA S.
[b.] July 8, 1983, Queens, NY; [p.] Bayezid Ahmed and Rabia Ahmed; [ed.] Rachel Carson Intermedi-

ate School (8th grade); [occ.] Student; [hon.] Honored as a young author by Queens College/Ford Fdn., National Ged, Literary contest winner (daily news, NYC), won Dep of NYC poetry contest, was interviewed by Bangladesh t.v. and voice of America.; [oth. writ.] Poem titled "A Changing World" published in Unicef, poem, "A Cold Reality" published in "I Danced all the Way Home", several other poems were published in newspapers in NYC and Abroad.; [pers.] Living in harmony in our world doesn't mean that we exactly have to be the same, for we could be like a bowl of fruits-different yet united.; [a.] New York City, NY

AHMED, SULTANA RAZIA
[b.] October 22, 1980, Dhaka, Bangladesh; [p.] Bayezid and Rabia Ahmed; [ed.] I attend Francis Lewis High School in Queens, New York. I will be in the Eleventh Grade in September 1996; [occ.] Student; and also I dedicate sometime volunteering at the New York Hospital Medical Center in Queens, N.Y.; [pers.] "Surely, time's passing and so are our days. All those sweet memories are long gone... So let's all make the best of our lives, which are beautiful - but short".; [a.] Flushing, NY

AIVAZ, DAVID
[b.] 1925, Bronx, NY; [ed.] A.B., A.M., Ph.D., Harvard University; [occ.] During most of my working years, was a teacher.; [oth. writ.] As a graduate student, published a few poems in "Little" magazines. In regent months, Pieces in Mystery Time (Decatur, Illinois), The Ultimate Writer (Metairie, Lousianna), and (accepted, not yet in print) Ellery Queen Mystery Magazine.; [pers.] At age seventy, I have resumed writing verse after a 45-year lapse.; [a.] Bronx, NY

AJIGBOTAFE, WEMI
[b.] August 11, 1975, Chicago, IL; [p.] Christopher and Eunice Ajigbotafe; [ed.] Rosary High, La Sierra University; [occ.] Full time student; [memb.] United Negro Collge Fund; [hon.] Elementary/Jr. Track team, Honorable Lawyer for Rosary Mock Trial Team, Co-director of High School Production.; [oth. writ.] Entered a short story into The Jessamyn West Young Writers Conference in 1989, have collection of unpublished poetry.; [pers.] I am greatly moved by the romantism coursing through the lives of those around me. I feel a kinship with their passion and their pain. Therefore I strive to reflect that rainbow of emotion into my poetry.; [a.] Yorba Linda, CA

AKANDE, AZZIZA OLUWAKEMI
[b.] June 27, 1973, Ibadan, Nigeria; [p.] Mr. and Mrs. A. B. Akande; [ed.] Ramses College for Girls, Cairo. St. Catherine of Sienna School, NY. New Era Girls' Secondary School, Lagos. University of Ibadan, Ibadan, Oyo.; [occ.] Medical Student University of Ibadan, Nigeria; [oth. writ.] Other poems - all unpublished; [pers.] In all that I do I make God the centre of it. That way I know I can't go wrong.; [a.] Ibadan, Oyo, Nigeria

AL-ZAID, BASMA
[b.] April 19, 1980, Kuwait; [p.] Mr. and Mrs. Al-Zaid; [ed.] Currently in high school (Islamic, Saudi Academy in Alexandria, VA); [pers.] I was born and raised in Kuwait. In the year 1992, I was forced out of my beloved country due to the war. From there I went to England to start a new life. There I learned to read and write in English. In England I became a fluent English speaker, and soon the English language became like my first. Now I have been living in the U.S. for almost 2 years due to my father's occupation as the Bureau Chief of the Kuwait News Agency. I have been writing poetry as a hobby, but many people thought of it as being a talent. I have one important philosophy that I would like to share with you: "Confidence is the

first step, then the next steps will flow like water." The reason why I write these words on paper is because of my past experiences as a child in a foreign country and I think that, without my confidence, I would have never made it this far.

ALBERT, GREGORY M.
[b.] March 10, 1979, Harrisburg, PA; [p.] Kendrick and Mary Ann Albert; [ed.] Central Dauphin High School; [occ.] Student; [memb.] Christ Lutheran Youth Group, National Honor Society; [oth. writ.] Commentary published in school paper.; [a.] Harrisburg, PA

ALGAR, ANGELA C.
[pen.] Angela C. Algar; [b.] May 19, 1973, Belleville, Ontario, Canada; [ed.] Quinte Secondary School; [occ.] Radio - Broadcasting, Student at Loyalist College; [pers.] I am aiming for a successful career in Broadcasting, so I can use the media to the benefit of animals and senior citizens. Follow your intuitions and work hard for your dreams, remembering that everything is possible.; [a.] Corbyville, Ontario, Canada

ALIERMO, PACITA LABAYEN
[pen.] Pacita Labayen Aliermo; [b.] January 25, 1924, Philippines; [p.] Sebastian and Angela Labayen (Deceased); [m.] Eduardo A. Aliermo (Deceased), June 20, 1948; [ch.] Rodolfo, Reynaldo, Ma. Cecilia, Rolando, Ramiro, Rogelio; [ed.] Courses in secretarial, Journalism Social Sciences, Real Estate Management, Development, Appraisal and Brokerage; [occ.] Visual Artist; [memb.] Past Member Quezon City Board of Realtors, PAREB, Philippines, Distinguished member, ISP, 1996; [hon.] ISP Editor's Choice Award; [oth. writ.] Inspirational poem for hospitals and homes to comfort and inspire, "Eternal Wisdom"; [pers.] Humility is the key to peace of mind and a happy disposition.; [a.] Thornhill, Ontario, Canada

ALLEN, ERVILLE
[b.] February 3, 1919, Lucknow, India; [p.] Floyd and Florene Smith; [m.] George Allen, June 16, 1941; [ch.] William White and Robert Irving; [ed.] Los Angeles Academy, White Memorial School of Nursing, Pacific Union College (Nursing), U.C. San Francisco (Maternal Child Nursing); [occ.] Retired after 50 years of nursing and teaching nursing in the U.S., Nigeria, and Kenya; [oth. writ.] Published — article on hydrotherapy, a story article about Flickers (birds); In process — children's and parents' stories and articles; [pers.] God has made a beautiful world. We can cooperate in making it better.; [a.] Saint Helens, OR

ALLEN, LAURA ELLEN REED
[pen.] Lera; [b.] October 18, 1959, Indianapolis, IN; [p.] Jack P. Reed, Anna Reed Gallert Kirkpatrick; [m.] Carl W. Allen (Deceased), January 18, 1994; [ch.] Scott Reinhart; [a.] Fontana, CA

ALPHONSO, MS. PRIYA
[b.] July 18, 1972, Hodeidah, Yemen; [p.] Mr. Augustine Victor Alphonso, Mrs. Carmelina Alphonso; [ed.] Nichols College, Dudley, MA, Bachelor of Science in Business Administration Magna Cum Laude, double major: Accounting and Finance, Minor: English and Humanities, Dean's List/Dean's High Honors; [occ.] Experienced Business Assurance Associate at Coopers and Lybrand, Boston, MA; [memb.] Zeta Alpha Phi Delta Mu Delta, Omicron Delta Kappa - "Eldridge Boyden Society"; [hon.] Who's Who Among Students in American Colleges and Universities, Robert Henry Eaton Dean Emiritus Trophy for Dedication, service and commitment to Perfection - Awarded by Nichols College.; [oth. writ.] Several poems published in Windfall - Nichols College's Literary Magazine.; [pers.] Poetry has always fascinated me and it allows me to express my views of this world

in my own style. I find nature very inspiring and I enjoy poems that are rich in irony along with those that are woven with timeless truths.; [a.] Chelsea, MA

ALTHEIM, CASSIE
[b.] February 7, 1984, Edmonton, Alberta, Canada; [p.] Ray and Catherine; [ed.] Grade 8; [occ.] Student; [pers.] I like poetry, arts. I play the organ and guitar, and I like to sing. Have had some poems put in school and community papers.; [a.] Spruce Grove, Alberta, Canada

AMATO, SHERYL
[b.] Brooklyn, NY; [p.] Doris Majoros; [m.] Joseph Amato, August 27, 1966; [ch.] Dante Amato; [ed.] Baruch College, Queens College, St. John's University; [occ.] Real Estate Investor; [hon.] Dean's List; [oth. writ.] Several articles published in "Show Business Magazine."; [pers.] I am very much persuaded by authenticity, honesty, and sincerity not only in others but also in myself.; [a.] Kew Gardens Hills, NY

AMPRINO, MARCEL
[b.] December 21, 1927, Modane, France; [p.] Luigia Barone and Giuseppe Amprino; [m.] Margareta Zec, October 4, 1975; [ch.] Step Daughter; [ed.] Technical School, Isalesian Mother House Torino, Italy; [occ.] Retired; [a.] Edmonton, Alberta, Canada

ANAKAER, BRITT
[pen.] Britt; [b.] January 10, 1983, Calgary, Alberta, Canada; [p.] Nicola and Gary Anakaer; [ed.] Grade 7 student, Dr. George Ferguson School, Regina, Sask, Canada; [occ.] Student; [oth. writ.] Working on it!; [pers.] I love reading all sorts of poetry and when I'm older I hope I can be a well known author.; [a.] Regina, Saskatchewan, Canada

ANDERSON, ANDREA
[pen.] Andrea Anderson; [b.] September 1, 1962, Guilford, England; [p.] John Anderson, Nicolete Anderson; [m.] Albert Sgambati, November 9, 1992; [ed.] West Surrey College of Art and Design, England Bath Academy of Art, England Cooper Union for Advancement of Science and Art NY, NY; [occ.] Painter, Tattoo Artist; [hon.] Pollock Krasner Foundation Grant for Painting; [oth. writ.] Poems, Short Stories; [a.] New York, NY

ANDERSON, DESMOND
[b.] December 23, 1977, Africa; [p.] Samuel and Fredricka Anderson; [ed.] New Brunswick High, Middlesex County College; [occ.] Cashier, Edwards Super Food Stores, Somerset, NJ; [memb.] United Methodist Church at New Brunswick; [hon.] Highest Average in Accounting 1994-95, member of the "Vocational Education High Achiever's List" for New Brunswick public schools, winner of the Frank Reen Memorial Award 1994-95; [oth. writ.] "The Real Me", "The Tree", and "The Truth Like the Sun"; [pers.] Interdependent is and will always be greater than independence, but like a star, you can still be independent and shine brighter.; [a.] Somerset, NJ

ANDERSON, JOHN C.
[pen.] Jonah; [b.] July 13, 1923, Springfield, NJ; [p.] Augustus and Lyra Anderson; [m.] Ann Thacher Anderson, June 24, 1961; [ch.] John Thacher, Lucy Reeves; [ed.] A.B. Kent State Univ. 1951, S.T.B Gen'l Theological Seminary 1958; [occ.] Retired Priest (Episc) Poet, Artist, Spiritual Director; [memb.] Third Order Society of St. Francis; [hon.] Shows at Finkelstein Library, Spring Valley, NY (2) and 1 at Grace Church Nyack, NY; [oth. writ.] Little poems and little pictures w. Betsydo Giger, Aspen Colorado n.d. "The Hunting" poem Chelsea Review 1957 General Seminary; [a.] Grand View, NY

ANGER, VICTORIA
[b.] October 16, 1943, Warspite, Alberta; [p.] Teodor and Anne Ewaskow; [ed.] Grant MacEwan Community College: Special Needs Teaching Assistant, Life Management Skills Coach, N.L.P. Practitioner Certified; [occ.] Special Needs Teachings Assistant, Life Skills Coach; [memb.] Advisory Council, G.M.C.C. IA Faculty; [oth. writ.] Poetry, articles, short stories written for workshops and teachings programs; [pers.] It is my desire of coming to know myself as a woman and my search for what that means to me in my daily life.; [a.] Edmonton, Alberta, Canada

ANGEVINE, BILLY L.
[pen.] Bill Angevine; [b.] March 31, 1937, Binghamton, NY; [p.] Harold and Vivian Angevine; [m.] Barbara; [ch.] Trisha Lynn, Cynthia, Kim and Michael Angevine; [ed.] Chenango Forks Central NY, Syracuse Univ. B.A., UCLA Masters B. Admin.; [occ.] Laundry and Dry Cleaning Consultant; [memb.] American Quarter - Horse Assoc., BASS Masters Assoc., National 4H Assoc.; [hon.] Awards: Public Speaking, Leadership and Teaching, Scholarships: Baseball, Football; [oth. writ.] 148 poems and other writings, my first for publication. I'm in pursuit of writing and publishing a book of poems.; [pers.] I'm a romantic at heart. I'm inspired by my surroundings feelings, people. At times I awake at night and write a poem with a pattern of words which seem to materialize from my sleep.; [a.] Phoenix, AZ

ANGULO, GERARDO L.
[b.] June 26, 1972, Nogales, Sonora; [p.] Alejandro A. Angulo and Bertha M. Angulo; [ed.] Bachelor of Arts Degree in Human Services; [memb.] Member of Phi Theta Kappa International Honor Society (1993); [pers.] I wrote the poem a dying rose in honor and memory of my beloved mother, Mrs. Bertha Maxie Angulo. My mother will always be my greatest inspiration.; [a.] Nogales, AZ

ANSAH, TUMI ELBOW
[pen.] Santrofi Ansah; [b.] July 18, 1939, Winneba, Ghana; [p.] Joe E. Ansah and Efua Tanoa Ansah; [m.] Ka Waano Paado; [ch.] Ojo, Paintsil-Paa Gyesi, Nana Nketsia - Efus, Tanao, Boss; [ed.] Putney College, London Film School, London Academy of Music and Dramatic Arts, Jinley Theatre, Royal Court Theatre, London; [occ.] Ethno-Musicologist, Folklorist, Research, Scholar; [memb.] British Equity-Actors Union, Performing Rights Society, Songwriters Guild, American Guitar Society, L.A. City Harmony.; [hon.] 1st Prize - Song for Peace Award, London, '86. Best Original World Music Award for "Stage the Raft" production, London,'86.; [oth. writ.] Film Music for "Farewell to Dope" and "His Majesty's Sergeant". Articles on "African Ethnic Cultural Diversity" for Smithsonian Institute in Washington, DC. Other short stories and poems published in local magazines.; [pers.] Denkyemireku, Funtumireku a twin-headed crocodile with one stomach. The only time they fight is when they are eating, which signifies "Unity in Diversity". I have heard it and I have Kept it.; [a.] Los Angeles, CA

ARAUJO, JOHN F.
[b.] December 27, 1963, Parnaiba, PI; [p.] Raimundo Jose Araujo and Maria Cleide Araujo; [m.] Marise R. Freitas, April 6, 1989; [ed.] MD UFPI, Teresina PI, 1991, Certificate in Chronobiology, USP, 1991, MS in Psychology, Sao Paulo University, 1994, PhD in Neurosciences, Sao Paulo University, since 1995; [occ.] Assistant Professor of Physiology, UFRN, Natal, RN; [memb.] International Society of Chronobiology SBNec, SBPC; [oth. writ.] Several poems published in local newspaper, Poetas Brasileiros de Hoje 1985, Escritores Brasileiros.; [pers.] My writings have reflected my

personal vision the condiction of mankind and their social relation. I have been being influenced by dialectical materialism.; [a.] San Paulo, SD

ARMSTRONG, HELEN M.
[b.] January 2, 1932, Almonte, Ontario, Canada; [p.] Harold and Esther (nee Morrison) Laidlaw; [m.] John Edwin Armstrong, April 21, 1962; [ed.] Carleton Place High School, Ottawa Teachers College; [occ.] Retired Teacher Ottawa Board of Education Ottawa, Ont, Elementary School Grades 1-5, Librarian, Teacher of Learning Disabled; [memb.] Canadian Diabetes Association, Various Genealogical Associations (15) including Ontario Genealogical Society, British Isles Family History, Society of Greater Ottawa; [oth. writ.] Poems and stories, family history for personal and family enjoyment only.; [pers.] We must understand and appreciate people and the past if we are to understand ourselves and the future.; [a.] Aylmer, Province of Quebec, Canada

ARMSTRONG-MOSELY, GLORIA
[b.] Condem County, GA; [p.] Mrs. W. E. Armstrong; [m.] Kenneth E. Misely - Deceased 1990, May 10, 1957; [ch.] Adrienne, Kevin, Kenneth II; [ed.] Washington Irving, H.S. N.Y.C. NY. Fort Valley State College, Ft. Valley GA. (B.S. degree), Calif State Univ. at Dominguez Hills, Carson, CA (M.A. Biological Science); [occ.] Retired Educator, Volunteer; [memb.] Phi Beta Kappa, Delta Sigma Theta Sorority, Phi Delta Kappa Sorority, Nat'l Asso. of Science Teachers, Calif State Univ Dominques Hills Alumni Asso., Northwest Baptist Church, Alpha Mu; [hon.] Calif Teacher Instructional Improvement Program (CTIIP), Calif. Education Asso. Distinguished Service Award, NASA Special Award, other Distinguished Service Awards: Compton H.S., Willowbrook Jr. H.S., Phi Delta Kappa Sorority, Judson Baptist Church: 1991 and 1992 second place ribbons, Univ. of Florida Cooperative Extension Services Arts/Crafts Festival; [oth. writ.] Poems published in the Atlanta Constitution, poems and articles published in the peachile (Ft. Valley State) College.; [pers.] I believe that everyone can learn something from someone, some event, some situation.; [a.] Cocoa, FL

ARSENAULT-CAMERON, KATHY
[pen.] Kathy Cameron; [b.] Tidnish, NS; [p.] Deceased; [m.] James Richard Cameron, December 23, 1989; [ed.] High School and 2 yrs. of University; [occ.] Still writing but retired.; [memb.] Sunday School, Canadian Girls in Training, Was Home Cave Worker in Halifax for sometime as I loved "helping people.", Member RCAF (W.D.) During W.W> II 1942-1944; [hon.] I don't think anyone does anything just for the "awards". The "awards" sort of help to make up for the awards I never knew existed!; [oth. writ.] Scrapbook of articles in Moncton Times/Transcript. Also wrote a book a number of years ago that is still waiting publication. It is titled "A Storekeeper's Touch" and contains mush humor.; [pers.] Sooner or later everyone becomes recognized!

ASARE-WILLIAMS, KELVIN
[b.] 9 November 1973, Tema; [p.] Ms. Florence Gaveh; [ed.] Accra High Secondary, University of Ghana; [occ.] Student; [memb.] Legon Tourist Club, Association for the Study of Classical African Civilization. (ASCAC); [hon.] Best Literature Student - Zion College; [oth. writ.] Several unpublished poems, plays. Published articles in newspaper and magazines.; [pers.] Most often I laugh, giggle, smile at the truth of mankind. Most often I cry, moan, wail and pity. But there was and will always be sadness and happiness. In the character of the human nature within a complex universe and it's beyond. I observe these and I write.; [a.] Accra, Ghana

ASDURIAN, EMIL
[b.] November 15, 1958, Tirana-Albania; [p.] Pavllo and Zoica Asdurian; [m.] Teuta A. Asdurian; [ch.] Pat and Anig Asdurian; [ed.] Gymnasium Musami Frasheri, Albania Medical Faculty - University of Tirana Albania (M.D.) - Neurosurgeon specialization - Alabania; [occ.] Neurosurgeon - University of Tirana - Albania; [memb.] Congress of Neurological Surgeons - USA member of European Committee of Brain Trauma and rehabilitation.; [oth. writ.] Scientific Safer for neurosurgery in Europe (France and Albania); [pers.] I want to express the human feelings so undiscovered, so changeable, so cleansing in sorrow and joys.; [a.] New York, NY

ASEOCHE, ANNA LIZA
[b.] January 8, 1983, Monterey Park, CA; [p.] Reynaldo and Alma Aseoche; [ed.] Attends Olde Middle School in the Bellevue District; [occ.] 8th grade student in Olde Middle; [memb.] Member of the School's Orchestra; [hon.] Received many "Student of the Month" awards, and honored 4th place in Grade School spelling Bee. Was promoted twice in Grade school.; [pers.] I not only make poems to inspire the reader, but to inspire myself. The words that I use I can sometimes relate to myself and others. I make a decision before I write a poem that it will not only attract the reader physically, but also mentally and emotionally.; [a.] Kirkland, WA

AUSTIN, DOUGLAS S.
[b.] August 2, 1946, Port Jervis, NY; [m.] Carol A. Austin, May 12, 1973; [ch.] Bryan D. Austin; [ed.] B.A. SUNY Geneseo, MA Montclair State; [occ.] English teacher, director of drama and communications Saffern Senior High; [memb.] NEA, NYS Council of English Teachers; [hon.] Outstanding Teacher (NYS Council of English Teachers, 1995), Who's Who Among Americas Teachers (1996), Suffern High School Yearbook Dedication (1975, 1993), Poetry Winner NYS Department of Education Contest (1987); [a.] Tuxedo, NY

AUTREY, LEON
[b.] December 22, 1941, Mountainair, NM; [p.] Alfred and Marie Autrey; [m.] Darla Autrey, June 17, 1961; [ch.] Two sons; [ed.] High School Four years Military Service Fort Collins Colo, Vet School; [occ.] Cowboy and Cattle Rancher; [memb.] New Mexico Cattle Growers Assoc. Americal Farm Bureau National Cattlemans Assoc. Torrance County Farm and Livestock Bureau Beef Master Breeders United to name a few; [hon.] Award of Merit for Outstanding Accomplishments in Resource Conservation Presented by Goodyear NACD Salt of the Earth Award Presented by N. Mex Cattle Growers Ass. and Outstanding Rancher, Presented by - Claunch Soil and Water Conservation District; [oth. writ.] Book entitled I dreamed last night I seen daddy - cowboy poetry; [pers.] I write about life, people horses and cattle and about the land, things I've seen! I believe we should leave this world better than we found it we've just borrowing from the next generation.; [a.] Mountainair, NM

AUXIER, YVONNE RENEE
[pen.] Yvonne Renee Auxier-Young; [b.] May 9, 1968, Seattle, WA; [p.] Gene E. Auxier I, Trudy Auxier; [occ.] Small Business Entrepreneur/Fiction Writer; [pers.] Beauty and the Beast in the Poet's heart. Thank you, sweet Beast. I send you a kiss...; [a.] Cortland Manor, NY

BABB, SHERON
[b.] August 25, 1951, South Carolina; [p.] LeRoy T. and Dena Hucks; [ch.] One son, Chris; [ed.] Attended Shorter College, Rome, GA, University of S.C. Columbia, SC, Tarrant County Junior College, Texas; [memb.] ASPCA, American Humane Assn., National Wildlife Assn., The Humane Society of the United States

BACKMAN, INGRID
[b.] April 19, 1947, Vancouver, BC; [p.] Gustav F. Backman, Edith Amanda Backman; [occ.] Wildlife Artist; [memb.] Coquitlam Art Club and Art Focus Port Coquitlam; [pers.] I endeavor in my waiting and drawing to capture the joy and strength of spirit nature gives me. Writing and drawing are a part of me as much as breathing.; [a.] Coquitlam, British Columbia, Canada

BAEZ, SANDRA L. G.
[b.] November 18, 1966, Brooklyn, NY; [p.] Lucy Gonzalez, Enrique Gonzalez; [m.] Joshua D. Baez, November 18, 1989; [ch.] Sophia Joy, Naomi Emilia, Amanda Celeste; [ed.] Queens Vocational HS, New York City Technical College; [occ.] Home maker - by day, telemarketing, evening; [pers.] Writing is an awesome way of expressing your feelings without saying a word. Once feelings fill an empty page, it provides a wonderful sense of release...then peace. For readers, a sense of familiar grounds and realization that what we have in common is our bond.; [a.] Ridgewood, NY

BAFIA, JEAN C.
[pen.] The Poet; [occ.] Entrepreneur; [hon.] To have my talent recognized and published, by the National Library of Poetry.; [oth. writ.] The Artist And The Poet, published in Morning Song.; [pers.] Believe, in the magic of your dreams.; [a.] Mesa, AZ

BAGAGLIA-WOOD, CYNTHIA E.
[b.] April 17, 1961, Warren, OH; [p.] Frank R. Bagaglia Jr. (Deceased), Linda M. Colecchi-Bagaglia; [m.] Harry R. Wood, March 20, 1982; [ch.] Nicole Marcella, Ashley Marie and Shante Danielle; [ed.] Warren G. Harding High School, (1979), Warren, OH, USA Training Academy (1988), Colombus, OH and Jackson Community College, Jackson, Michigan Associate Degree in Business Management; [occ.] Documentation Department, Tecumseh Products Company - International Division, Tecumseh, MI; [memb.] Bethany Assembly of God Church, Adrian, MI; [hon.] Honors Program, Business Secretary, Graduated with Honors from Jackson Community College; [oth. writ.] "Dear Dad" will be published in the anthology "Portraits of Life", Fall 1996 and various others poems written. Some have been published in my home-town newspaper.; [pers.] This poem is in honor of my Mom, Linda M. Colecchi-Bagaglia, who has always been there for all six of us, Anna Maria, Frank, Ron, Mike, Marina and myself. I love you Mom. Thank you for all you've done.; [a.] Tecumseh, MI

BAHNFLETH, TERI
[b.] July 24, 1965. Peoria, IL; [p.] William Bahnfleth and Barbara Baum; [ch.] Ricky, Lynse, Brittney; [ed.] E. Peoria High, Illinois Central College, Carl Sandburg College, Community College of the Air Force, PTI U of I Champaign; [occ.] Police Officer; [pers.] Life gives me feelings I want to write down and share with others.; [a.] Morton, IL

BAILEY, MRS. ALMA
[b.] November 12, 1927, Washington County; [p.] Mr. Byrd Lacy, Mrs. Elizabeth Lacy; [m.] Rev. James Bailey, December 10, 1994; [ed.] 11th grade; [occ.] Retired; [memb.] Mainst Baptist Church Friends Club; [hon.] Radio, Coffee Mater Grandparent Trophy Mission II Lincoln District certificate of Recognition; [a.] Lyons, TX

BAILEY, WILLIAM
[b.] May 7, 1980, Somers Point, NJ; [p.] Richard and Blanca Bailey; [ed.] Ocean City High; [occ.] Full time student, tenth grade; [pers.] For me

writing has always been enjoyable. I love writing because it allows me to express myself in all kinds of ways. I also strive to someday become a novelist.; [a.] Seaville, NJ

BAIMEL, JOSHUA DAVID
[b.] November 12, 1976, Huntington, NY; [p.] Jerry and Rosalynd Baimel; [ed.] Hollywood Hills High, currently attending University of Florida; [occ.] Student pursuing degrees in Civil/Environmental Engineering; [memb.] Sigma Tan Sigma, Florida Engineering Society, American Society of Civil Engineers, B'hai B'rith Hillel Foundation; [hon.] Phi Eta Sigma, Dean's List, Chi Epsilon; [pers.] Writing has a relaxing effect on me, yet it is so powerful. Express yourself openly, don't keep the feelings bottled up, and never deny your inspiration.; [a.] Gainesville, FL

BAIN, JULIEN L.
[pen.] Jules; [b.] July 25, 1967, Port of Spain, Trinidad; [p.] Lucia M. Bain; [ed.] Humber College: Arts and Sciences, Seneca College: Marketing Admin.; [memb.] International Society of Poets, World Vision Canada, American Marketing Asso.; [hon.] Editor's Choice Award - 1996 Re: The National Library of Poetry; [oth. writ.] National Library of Poetry: "Seasons", "Remember", "Heavenly Creatures"; [pers.] "I believe in love! That, the impact of its power will one day sprinkle throughout all eternity...enter the souls of all people...spread throughout all this land, embracing all thoughts toward the unity of living."; [a.] Toronto, Ontario, Canada

BAIRD, CYNTHIA M
[pers.] God's gift to the poet, words, insight and feelings.; [a.] Danville, CA

BAKER, ELIZABETH DUDLEY
[b.] September 16, 1906; [p.] George and Grace Dudley; [m.] Harold Munroe Baker (Deceased), 1st marriage to Frederick Radcliffe, March 10, 1933; [ch.] Seven children, 12 great granchildren; [ed.] One year of college (Boston University); [occ.] Retired postmistress, 20 years as a newspaper reporter, 7 years at Biddeford Daily Journal, 5 years on the Homestead Daily Messenger, also worked for Fairchild Publications; [memb.] St George's Golf Club, Several poems published in journal member in 1951 of League of American Penwomen; [oth. writ.] Poem in the NY Times, One selected in magazine as best in mag. Several in Three Village Herald where song for autumn was published on November 4, 1966; [pers.] Just try to live by the Golden Rule; [a.] Setauket, NY

BALASUBRAMANIAN, ASOKAN
[pen.] Ashok; [b.] May 2, 1964, Madras, India; [p.] Balasubramanian and Vasantha; [m.] Manimekalai Asokan, August 28, 1996; [ed.] M. Sc., Post Graduation in Computer Application, Dip in German; [occ.] Software Engineer; [a.] Rogers, AR

BALLANTYNE, SARAH I.
[b.] October 25, 1917, North Sydney, NS; [p.] Cavanaugh Daniel, Emma Jane (Bonnar); [m.] Emery Roland Ballantyne, June 30, 1941; [ch.] Emery III, Evelyn, Brenda; [ed.] St. Joseph's Convent School finished high grade 12 - typing computer - photography course (night school) cooking - sewing, still learning (Charles Givens "How to Succeed"); [occ.] Retired (from) Finance Dept. Federal Government Securities - Bonds Heart Institute; [memb.] In Canada - Ottawa Civic Hospital Heart Insititute, all - Aleonquin life long Learning College, Roman Catholic Church Sodality of the children Blessed Virgin Mary - in America US Smithonion recently International Society of poets 1995-96 distinguished member.; [hon.] Editor's Choice Award 1995 by the National

Library of poetry (Outstanding Achievement in Poetry). The International Poet of Merit Award plaque 1996. A bronze medallion also.; [oth. writ.] The National Library of Poetry poem in Anthology book 1995 (Shadow) Sparkles In The Sand, first attempt published and career writing continuation. Kanata Courier newspaper, second poem being published also the Lonely Heart.; [pers.] Positive realistic - live by the "Golden Rule." Love Thy Neighbor. Do all I can to make someone happy in any way possible within reasons. The world is one family. I see my self in every face. And feel the joy pain sorrow they experience a common bond humanity.; [a.] Kanata, Ontario, Canada

BALLOY, MAGDALENE PATRICIA
[b.] November 6, 1932, Grenada, B.W.I.; [m.] Arthur J. Balloy, November 23, 1955; [ch.] Michael, Dennis, and Noelle Rose; [occ.] Cosmetic Sales; [oth. writ.] A book in progress, Beyond The Darkness, an autobiography. "God Is Seeded In Man's soul". "Heaven Is". "A Life Worthwhile" "Hasten Darkness In It's Flight". "This Is My Desire" "The Answer Is Love" "His Light Will Shine". "My Awakening" "Magdalene's Prayer". And many more.; [pers.] my poetic writing began in 1963, after Jesus appeared to me, through a death like occurrence. That phenomenal event, drastically transformed my life, by awakening me to the "Presence of God" within myself. Since that moment in time, I have been pushed and shoved, by a hungering desire, to share my life experiences through poetry.; [a.] Palm Desert, CA

BARBA, CARLOS M.
[b.] July 31, 1930, Havana, Cuba; [p.] Osvaldo Barba, Ana Garcia; [m.] Esther Palacios Barba, December 28, 1957; [ch.] Lourdes B. Ridyard, Charlie Barba; [ed.] Dr. in law (Havana Univ. 1955), Revalidation (University of Fla) 1975, (Cuban-American Lawyers Program); [occ.] Assistant controller, University: Florida Technology (F.I.T.); [memb.] Last Secretary (1960): Rotary Club of Havana, Rotary Club of Indialantic, Fla, Knights of Columbus, Fla-Columbia Partners), Spanish American Club of Brevard, Fla, "Our Lady of Lourdes, Church"; [hon.] Valedictorian Class 1950 high school: Escolapios Habana, Eucharist Minister and Lecturer at "Our Lady of Lourdes Catholic Church", Melb., "25 years service at "Florida Institute of Technology", Melbourne, Fla (F.I.T); [oth. writ.] Editor: First Spanish publication (1971) in Brevard County, Melbourne, Fla, several articles (cultural, political) in local newspaper.; [pers.] In my poems and writings I try to send a message of human values, love for country and love of family and of God.; [a.] Melbourne, FL

BARBE, MR. CLAUDE L.
[b.] March 6, 1961, Victoria; [p.] Mother only; [ch.] 'A Girl'; [ed.] 'Form III Secondary School', To Junior Secondary F. III; [occ.] Asst. Coordinator; [oth. writ.] (Lyrics songs), (Lyricist); [pers.] "Common everybody get together, try to love one another right now. And give peace a chance.; [a.] Victoria, Seychelles

BARBER, ROSELLAR
[b.] July 4, 1910, Windsor, NC; [p.] Lillie Whitehurst; [m.] Albert Barber, May 1935; [ch.] Eight; [ed.] 7th Grade; [occ.] Retired; [memb.] Green Memorial Church. Williamstons, NC, article member of Senior choir 301 Years.; [pers.] Is it possible to have my photograph on the back.; [a.] Williamston, NC

BARRY, LUCILLE S.
[b.] June 25, 1923, Uledi, PA; [p.] William and Viola Smith; [m.] Wester B. Barry, September 14, 1985; [ed.] East Huntingdon Township High, PA, KEK School of Practical Nursing, Essex County

Community College, Associate Degree in Music - with honors; [occ.] Housewife; [oth. writ.] Children short stories, musical composition for piano and flute; [pers.] Greatly influenced by the Truth of God contained in the Bible as my guide in life; [a.] East Orange, NJ

BARTHLEIN, SANDRA M.
[pen.] Sandra Francine Murden; [b.] October 25, 1946, Norfolk, VA; [p.] George William and Mary Frances Murden; [m.] Jimmy Dan Barthlein, October 14, 1978; [ed.] Princess Anne High School, Virginia Beach, Virginia top ten (10) of my graduation class!; [occ.] Retired Exc. Secretary for the Federal Government; [memb.] Distinguished member IPS, National Piano Guild, American Diabetes Asn. Norfolk Savoyarads, Ltd. Hospital Volunteer Committee Sweet Adalines, Int'l. Health Spa, Norfolk Theater Productions, National Modeling Academy, Nat'l Wildlife Federation!; [hon.] Beta Sigma Phi, VA. Volunteers Awards Committee, over 2,000 hours, Editor's Choice Awards, NLP, Plank Owner, U.S.S. Mississippi.; [oth. writ.] Publications for NLP. Poetry and short stories featured in various newspapers, periodicals and magazines. Reporter for local Govt. and civilian newspapers, inspirational work for local church. Past editor for hospital newsletter.; [pers.] My works are strongly influenced by my love of life, my observation of my surroundings and people and nature in general, as I was first inspired thirty plus years ago, when I was in my low twenties (20's)!; [a.] Norfolk, VA

BARTLESON, MARY ANN
[b.] September 15, 1980, Bridgeton, NJ; [p.] William Bartleson Sr., Mary Bartleson; [ed.] Maurice River School, American School; [pers.] You never really understand the greatest gift that mankind can ever have until you experience the joy that each small package brings.; [a.] Port Elizabeth, NJ

BARTOLO, ELIZA CAMPBELL
[pen.] Eliza R. Campbell; [b.] May 3, 1950, Scotland; [p.] John and Margaret Campbell; [m.] James D. Bartolo, March 15, 1969; [ch.] Three sons; [ed.] College Grad.; [occ.] Registered Nurse; [memb.] Ontario Nurses Association; [oth. writ.] Personal non-published short stories and poems.; [pers.] I believe to look behind slows movement towards the future but can also steady the steps.; [a.] Mississauga, Ontario, Canada

BASTIAN, WALTER
[m.] Carolyn S.; [ed.] B.A. (Summa) American University, M.A. Yale, Graduate Senior Foreign Service Seminar, U.S. Dept. of State; [occ.] Retired Foreign Service Officer; [memb.] Omicron Delta Kappa (hon.) Alpha Sigma Chi, American Foreign Service Assoc., Visiting Professor, National University of El Salvador Cultural Attache - Cuba, Ecuador. Argentina, Turkey, Public Affairs Officer/Counselor of Embassy - Colombia, Venezuela; [a.] Chevy Chase, MD

BATES, TIFFIANY
[b.] July 23, 1980, LaPorte, IN; [p.] David Bates, Constance Bates; [ed.] Grade 11 at Washington Township High School, preparing for college; [memb.] American Heart Association, CPR Certified; [oth. writ.] "A Deadly Disease" is my first published poem, but I have a complete book of my own.; [pers.] This poem came from the bottom of my heart, and if I could have one wish, it would be to find a cure for this terrible disease.; [a.] Valparaiso, IN

BATMAN, KELLY A.
[b.] November 17, 1964, Reading, PA; [p.] Earl and Claire Batman; [ed.] Sahuarita High School, Pina Community College; [occ.] New Restaurant Opening Training Specialist; [memb.] The Body of the

Lord Jesus Christ, His Bride; [hon.] Employee of the Quarter on two occasions, voted most courteous employee by customer vote. I'm honored to teach Sunday school at living word Tabernads in Gastonia, NC ages 3-10 years old.; [oth. writ.] Sahuarita High School News, youth related newspapers; [pers.] I strive toward the mark of the high calling which is Christ Jesus. The birth of this poem came, when I was a brand new Christian, I give the glory to the Lord of whom the inspiration was given. I ask one question of you - you probably know much about my Lord, but have you met him personally?; [a.] Gastonia, NC

BATTLE, SPENCER O.
[pen.] John E. Battle; [b.] April 11, 1967, Warwick, GA; [p.] Sallie Waters, Frank Waters; [m.] Mary E. Battle, July 26, 1995; [ch.] LaKeisha Evans, Frederick Evans, Lagunda Battle; [ed.] Worth Co. Comprehensive High School; [occ.] Laborer; [pers.] I write and strive to my best ability, in the phases of life, that we go through every day of our precious life.; [a.] Albany, GA

BAUER, CHRISTINA D.
[b.] September 4, 1977, Hamilton, OH; [ed.] Hamilton High School - graduated in 1995; [occ.] Customer Service Rep. - Viking Office Products; [a.] Hamilton, OH

BAYCAR, POET
[pen.] Robert Baycar; [b.] June 3, 1929, Slovakia; [m.] Dr. Irene Bajcar, 1952; [ch.] Two; [ed.] M.Sc. (Physics), Ph.D. (Physics); [occ.] President of Company; [a.] Bramalea, Ontario, Canada

BAZEWICZ, JOAN A.
[b.] December 10, 1938, Mt. Vernon, NY; [p.] Fredrick Spicer, Marietta Spicer; [m.] Anthony J. Bazewicz, December 24, 1964; [ch.] Darryl Raymond, Steven Anthony, Kimberly Rose, Sean Joseph; [ed.] Edison High School; [occ.] Retired - Foster parent and Day Care Professional; [hon.] Foster Care Association of CT. for outstanding service for over 25 years. Child Care Association of CT. for excellence in service.; [oth. writ.] Articles and poems relating to children in need. Awareness articles to correct misconception and create awareness of numerous ways to enhance extended family potential.; [pers.] I strive in my writing to reach out to others to create a better understanding of children in need. Wether thru adoption or foster placement. To show the values of extended family life in todays changing world.; [a.] Honesdale, PA

BEAN, HELEN E.
[b.] October 19, 1921, Mercer Co., PA; [p.] Gilbert and Jessie Dick; [m.] Robert "Ike" Bean, October 30, 1943; [ch.] Kenneth R., Cheryl L., Sandra L., Larry H., Robert I. Jr. Deceased at age 16; [ed.] Graduate of Rocky Grove High School; [occ.] Retired Bookkeeper; [memb.] Worden Chapel U.M. Church, U.M. Women; [hon.] From World of Poetry: Merit Awards - 2 for 1983, 1984, 1985, 1986, 1987, 1988, 2 for 1990, 1991, Golden Poet Awards - 1985, 1986, 1988, 1990, 1991, Who's Who in Poetry 1990, Editor's Choice Award 1994.; [oth. writ.] Poem published in Book "Clover Collection of Verse", Church papers, Children's School papers, My biography in "Who's Who in Poetry"; [pers.] Altho my poems cover many subjects, in most of them, I try to make people more aware of God. He is Alive and Will Return!; [a.] Franklin, PA

BEAN, VERONICA
[b.] April 9, 1950, Saint Louis, MO; [p.] Gertrude and George Matlock; [m.] Divorced; [ch.] Donnell Bean; [ed.] B.S. from Columbia University, Beaumont High School in Saint Louis, MO; [occ.] 13

yrs. U.S. Army; [pers.] I wrote this poem to reflect the importance of Motherhood.; [a.] Westland, MI

BEARD, TIMOTHY G.
[pen.] Timly Grae; [b.] December 20, 1968, Pittsfield, IL; [p.] Dean Beard, Carolyn Beard; [ed.] Seneca High, Freed-Hardeman U., University of Louisville; [occ.] Operations Clerk; [pers.] Poetry is the voice of the soul.; [a.] Louisville, KY

BEARDSWORTH, BECKI
[b.] June 3, 1972, Attleboro, MA; [p.] Betsy Balduf and Clyde Perry; [m.] Sean Beardsworth, June 6, 1992; [ch.] Kayleigh and Alexandra; [ed.] Foxboro High School; [occ.] Jewelry Manager at Wal-Mart #2158; [hon.] Golden poet (for a Mother's Warm Love); [oth. writ.] Not yet, planning to submit some other writings in the future.; [pers.] For my mother and grumpy, for whom nothing would be possible. Thank you, my dearest friend.; [a.] Foxboro, MA

BEARE, PAUL
[b.] July 22, 1961, Albuquerque; [p.] H. W. and Rita Beare; [m.] Carol Beare, December 24, 1986; [ch.] John, Matthew, Tamara; [ed.] West Mesa High School - 1979; [occ.] Phillips Semi Conductors; [oth. writ.] "From My Pen To The Paper", this is my personal notebook with all my poems from February 23, 1981. I have currently 234 poems in my notebook.; [pers.] I like to write poetry free style. A thought or words come to mind, and from there I write out the poem.; [a.] Albuquerque, NM

BEAUDET, DANIELLE
[b.] January 8, 1946, Arthabaska, Canada; [p.] Odina Garneau, Marie-Anne Langlois; [m.] Andre Beaudet, August 25, 1973; [ch.] Michelle and Catherine; [ed.] Nursing, Laval University Music, CND Montreal Hospital Admin, Montreal University Enterprise Sc. Org., Montreal; [occ.] Writer, Musician, military wife, mother.; [memb.] Laval Univ. grad. Association.; [hon.] Music Festival Bursary Recipient, Semi-Finalist 1980-1981 'Prix Robert Cliche' 1981; [oth. writ.] Songs, short stories for children, two novels in french.; [pers.] I strongly believe that beauty reality is in the eyes of the beholder.; [a.] Ottawa, Ontario, Canada

BEEM, KIMBERLY
[pen.] Tweety; [b.] May 13, 1982, Aurora; [p.] James Beem and Mata Harders; [ed.] 8th Grade; [occ.] Babysitting; [hon.] Poem published 3 times, at Waters Edge and another book.; [oth. writ.] When I Look In His Eyes; [pers.] Reading and writing are my favorite subjects, when ever I feel bad or happy. I write.; [a.] Pittsfield, IL

BELLS, SHARON
[b.] January 5, 1961, Toronto, Ontario, Canada; [p.] Allen and Donlyn Workman; [m.] Jeffrey Bells, September 9, 1983; [ch.] Wesley Jeffrey; [ed.] Richmond Hill High School, Visual Arts and Instructor training at Seneca College in King City (High Honours List) School of Interior Design in Montreal, Quebec; [occ.] Home Based Learning Pilot Treeographer - Oil Painter; [memb.] Greenpeace, McMichael Art Gallery, Ontario Fibromyalgia Association; [pers.] I explore my world with the eyes of a child, so to see beyond the subject matter. I feel life is a continuing education with no place for boredom. I strive to achieve calmness, enlightenment and courage through my writing, to expose who I am and then to be her, in the most caring and creative way possible.; [a.] Aurora, Ontario, Canada

BEMBURY, ARTHUR A.
[pen.] Keetie and Henare; [b.] October 21, Boston, MA; [p.] Elva L. Bembury and Wm. A. Bembury; [ch.] Diego, J'mal, Shannel Henare of Hollywood, Ca.; [ed.] W.L.A. College...Immaculate Heart

College of Hollywood, Ca.; [occ.] Musician/Composer; [memb.] International Guitar Registry, San Fernando Valley Bd of Realtors Inc. C-21 Careertrak; [hon.] Salesman of the Mth. C-21, San Fernando Valley-Central Valley Ca. Real Estate License; [oth. writ.] Song Catalog of over 50 subjects and several poems. Currently composing for new Catalog.; [pers.] I attempt to write based on life's experiences and believe that there's a song in each of us and a voice nearby to sing it. My influences are taken from the likes and stylings of Vocalist Nancy Wilson, Regina Bell, Anita Baker. My hero is songwriter Sammy Cahn.; [a.] Boston, MA

BENION, KATHERINE D.
[b.] August 15, 1919, Sunbury; [p.] Paul and Elfrieda Dietterle; [m.] Harold H. Benion; [ch.] 4; [ed.] B.A. Susquehanna University M.A. Bucknell University; [occ.] Writer; [hon.] Class Poet - High School, Scholarship to Susquehanna University, Won "best one-act play contest" written by a student during college.; [oth. writ.] Many article and poems for Grit Newspaper throughout the years, articles for the Sunday Patriot News and many other news articles, articles for the Lutheran, Guideposts, Seventeen and many others.; [pers.] I believe that my talent in writing is a gift from God and that I want to use that gift for the rest of my life to glorify God in every possible way.; [a.] Milton, PA

BENJAMIN, VINAY
[b.] 16 February 1958, Vrindavan, India; [p.] Late Emmanuel E. Binapani Benjamin; [m.] Avis Lovelina, 28 December 1981; [ch.] Neha Sarah, Samuel Neville; [ed.] Saint Xavier's School, Maharaja's College (University of Rajasthan); [occ.] Manager - Graphic Arts Xerox - Bahrain; [memb.] Indian Fine Arts Society, Voluntary Blood Bank Associations (Jaipur, Oman, Saudi Arabia, Bahrain), Distinguished Member - ISP; [hon.] 3 Editor's Choice Awards from National Library of Poetry, "Poet of Merit award" 1996, International Society of Poets, Xerox Commendations; [oth. writ.] 6 unpublished anthologies of poems including one in Hindilang. 5 poems selected for 5 NLP anthologies 2 poems released on "Sound of Poetry" and 2 being reviewed for "The Poet's Corner."; [pers.] "Tragedy is an unavoidable consequence but joy is a personal creation."; [a.] Manama, Bahrain

BERGESEN, CHARLES RACINE
[b.] April 1922, Stavanger, Norway; [ed.] Educated a market gardener.; [occ.] Until the end of the 1980-ies he was the Chairman, of the Board of same. President of Norwegian Shipowners Association, Oslo, for two years (1976-78). Consul of France for 12 years and for more than thirty years Consul, later Consul General, for Sweden in Stavanger.; [oth. writ.] He wrote four books of poems: "Min tid" published in 1986 (under pseudonym B.H. Grau), "Underveis" in 1990, "Sommerblomster of Tistler" in 1992, "Irrganger" in 1994. He also translated into Norwegian some of P.B. Shelley's poems, among those the beautiful "The Sensitive Plant". This book was published fall 1993. Later he translated some of his poems into English. This selection called "That I may Live", all from the books mentioned above, was released this autumn in London. In 1993 the composer R. Ronnes wrote music for piano, bassoon and recitation to twelve of his poems. The concert was first presented at Bjergsted Music Centre in Stavanger December same year. This performance was also repeated at Haugesund. Translated into Russian the concert was performed in Moscow during a Scandinavian Music Week in March 1995. He took park in the annual literature week in Stavanger for several years. He was asked

to read his poems at many arrangements in the district.

BERLIN, ROBERT S.
[pen.] Bob; [b.] August 7, 1938, Bronx; [p.] Bernard and Beatrice Berlin; [m.] Joan, July 26, 1969; [ch.] Laura Charlotte - Anne Louise; [ed.] CCNY College; [occ.] Stockbroker, Paine Webber Senior Vice President Investments; [memb.] Frances Tavern Museum Advisory Board; [pers.] I strive to challenge myself and beat my own records.; [a.] Scarsdale, NY

BERRISFORD, DEREK S.
[pen.] Saxon; [b.] January 25, 1978; [p.] Hal and Nora; [m.] Sara R. MacDonald (love and inspiration); [ed.] Orchard Park Secondary School; [occ.] Business Entrepreneur; [hon.] Regional winner of the 1996 Marion Drysdale awards for my poem the united colours of all; [pers.] Imagery is a wonderful thing. Creativity is your tool. Use it to your full extent, and you will discover a jewel.; [a.] Stoney Creek, ON

BESHIR, BETTY O.
[b.] December 26, 1953, Grand Rapids, MI; [p.] Donald and Wilma Overbeek; [m.] Aladin Beshir, January 8, 1984; [ch.] Christopher, Alexander, Amy; [ed.] B.S. in Nursing from University of Alabama in Huntsville (UAH), Advanced Training in Psychiatric/Mental Health Nursing through US Army; [occ.] RN Working in Psychiactric Home Health Care; [pers.] I believe we all are dependent on each other for our well being. Therefore we should praise others for their achievements and support them during rough times. Eventually we will need them to do the same for us.; [a.] Stone Mountain, GA

BESSANT, SANDIA ELIZABETH
[b.] 24 September 1944, Shoreham-by-Sea, Sussex, UK; [p.] Sionega Rosetta Backhurst; [m.] Maurice Santo Bessant, 21 September 1968; [ch.] Cara Elissa; [ed.] Grammar school; [occ.] House duties; [oth. writ.] A booklet of mixed poems and proses titled Innermost Thoughts

BIRDSALL, JEWEL
[pen.] Jewel Mae Thiessen; [b.] May 8, 1961, Kerrobert, SK, Canada; [p.] Menno and Eileen Thiessen; [m.] Edward Zerr, July 15, 1978 and Ronald Birdsall, July 2, 1988; [ch.] Barry, Bradley, Brent; [ed.] James Charteris Composite School; [occ.] Aerobic Instructor, School Supervisor, Model; [oth. writ.] Memorials; [pers.] Positive thoughts bring achieved goals.; [a.] Kerrobert, Saskatchewan, Canada

BLANCHARD, NICKY
[pen.] Nicky Blanchard; [b.] December 18, 1980, Singapore; [p.] Guy and Kathy Blanchard; [ed.] James Fowler High School; [occ.] Student; [memb.] Victory Cornerstone Church; [pers.] All my poems are from my heart, a part of who I am.; [a.] Calgary, Alberta, Canada

BLANCHET, CANDICE
[b.] March 5, 1982, Pawtucket, RI; [p.] Normand and Sandra Blanchet; [ed.] Smithfield High School, Gallagher Jr. High School, Anna M. McCabe Elementary School; [occ.] Student; [memb.] Girl Scouts of Rhode Island; [hon.] High Honors (School), 2nd Place in School Science Fair; [pers.] Remember joking about someone can really hurt. It doesn't make you anymore popular by doing this.; [a.] Smithfield, RI

BLASY, YVONNE
[b.] November 29, 1948, Michigan; [p.] Ruth and R. Keene Evans; [m.] George Blasy, January 20, 1979; [ch.] Joy Ruth Blasy; [occ.] Surgical Technologist, sidelines, Yvonne Blasy Fine Arts studio,

also singing for weddings, Special Occassions, Etc.; [pers.] It's important for us all to be encouraged in life. I want my work to provide some of that. I'm inspired by the mystic, Meister Eckhart, who said "It is in the darkness that one finds the light, so when we are in sorrow, then this light is nearest of all to us. "This is one of those paradoxes of life which needs to be seen in this way".; [a.] Stevensville, MI

BLOOD, BILL
[pen.] Culpeppervon Rattus Rattus; [b.] October 28, 1968, Michigan City, IN; [ed.] BA - Anderson Univ. Fine Art/ Psychology; [occ.] Social Service Instructor; [oth. writ.] I am currently working on several projects; [pers.] I try to make relevant commentary on the human condition, but an often only abole to make a joke about the absurdity of life.; [a.] Indianapolis, IN

BLUDAU, DEBORAH LEE
[b.] May 7, 1955, Toronto; [m.] Roland Bludau, October 9, 1993; [ch.] Tasha, Elizabeth; [ed.] Incomplete Psychology Masters at U.W.O. Canada; [occ.] Health Care Worker and Assistant Program Co-ordinator; [memb.] Black Parent Association, West Park Baptist Choir, Red Cross Volunteer Program; [hon.] Christopher Leadership Program; [oth. writ.] "Publishers Choice" selected poems, 1989 and 1990 American poetry anthologies and one article in the Edmonton Community Newspaper; [pers.] As we reflect in growing, we come to realize that life is simply sharing the best of ourselves that we can in as many ways that we can; [a.] London, Ontario, Canada

BLUE, MRS. MARY MARVA
[b.] New Road, LA; [p.] Mr. Raleigh Ford, Florence J. Ford D.; [m.] Rev. Edward Blue Sr.; [ch.] Yolanda, Jimmy, Edwina, and Edward Jr.; [ed.] Attended Washington High School. A Graduate of the University of Michigan-Flint. Located in Flint, Michigan.; [occ.] Retired-Teacher; [memb.] Old Emmanuel Baptist Church, Reverend M.C. Guillery, Pastor, Member of Deaconess Board and mass choirs. Interdenominational Ministers wives fellowship - vice President.; [hon.] Have been given to Mary Marva Blue from the National, State, Local level, and her church, for her Accomplishment in the work of the Lord.; [oth. writ.] Five songs published, 45 songs ready for publishing and 3 books ready to be published.; [pers.] My aim is to please God in all that I do and say. My goal for each day that I live, is to do unto others, as I would have them do unto me. And we do that by putting God first, others second and self last. I was influenced by my mother, the late Mrs. Florence Jackson Ford and my father, Mr. Raleigh Ford.; [a.] Lake Charles, LA

BLUE, ROSALIND D.
[pen.] Rocky or Daphne Blue; [b.] February 2, 1944, Birmingham, AL; [p.] Robert E. and Ada Lewis Jones; [ch.] Danielle Patrice and Donald R., Darius R.; [ed.] Immaculate Heart of Mary, Rosedale High, Birmingham Al. Southern University, Baton Rouge Louisiana; [occ.] Teacher of Youngsters of Emotionally Handicapped; [memb.] Delta Sigma Theta, Sorroity, New Testament Baptist Church, Council of Exceptional Children; [oth. writ.] Short Stories and poems, unpublished; [pers.] I am challenged to reflect the joys found in the smallest measures of life and to raise the social consciousness of people.; [a.] Syracuse, NY

BOALS, GRETCHEN
[pen.] Gretchen Boals; [b.] July 5, 1966, Charleston, SC; [p.] Herbert Zeller, Carol Zeller; [m.] Randall Boals, September 17, 1987; [ch.] Dominique, Adrienne; [ed.] Columbia River High, University of Phoenix, Southern Illinois University; [occ.] Electrician, United States Navy; [oth. writ.] Various poems not published.; [pers.] When the

mood strikes me. I am compelled to write. My poems are an expression of whatever emotion I am trying to capture.; [a.] Great Lakes, IL

BOLKCOM, JILL MARIE
[b.] October 25, 1983, Idaho Falls; [p.] Ken and Kris Bolkcom; [ed.] Thomas Jefferson Jr. High (UT) 7th grade; [occ.] Student; [hon.] Hope of America Award (6 grade), 3rd place for "Me" (poem) 1st grade; [oth. writ.] "Me" (poem) published by "Anthology of Poetry by Young Americans"; [pers.] Enjoy every wonderful day, because it will never come again. Be glad after a bad day, because that too will not come again. Because every single day is different.; [a.] Kearns, UT

BONHAM, ELIZABETH A.
[b.] October 27, 1973, Belleville, Ont.; [p.] Elizabeth A. and William B. Burgess; [m.] Matthew A. Bonham, August 6, 1994; [ed.] O.A.C. Diploma (Quintie Secondary School - Belleville, Ontario) and two year Accounting diploma received from Loyalist College, Belleville, Ontario; [pers.] I enjoy the peace and tranquility of losing myself in writing. One of my long range goals is to be an accomplished writer.; [a.] Dartmouth, Nova Scotia, Canada

BONNIER, NANCY
[pen.] Maria Perez; [b.] February 24, 1965, New York; [p.] Rosemarie Bonnier, Joaquin Perez; [ed.] Graduated top ten percent American Senior High. Seeking to continue education this winter; [occ.] Community Services Coordinator in AIDS related field; [memb.] Active member of St. Lawrence Parish Hospice Volunteer Sponsor to New Church Members; [hon.] National Honor Society Who's Who High School 82-83 National Recognition Young Business Women of America 1986 Outstanding Service, HIV Aids Planning Florida rep in National Haiku Contest; [oth. writ.] Poetry the voice of imagination (collection of poetry, songs, inspirations); [pers.] My overall goal in life is to have made a difference in as many lives as possible. Through the tears come inspiration, through despair, hope...I am the Phoenix; [a.] North Miami Beach, FL

BOOTHBY, ANDREA
[b.] June 3, 1971, Oakville, Ontario, Canada; [p.] Anita and Michael Boothby; [ed.] Gordon E Perdue High School, University of Toronto, Canada, University of Wollongong, NSW, Australia; [occ.] Student; [memb.] Student Council; [hon.] Ontario Scholar, O.S.S.T.F. Award Recipient, Perdue Teacher's Award, Dr. Bruce Tovee Memorial Award, B.A. (4 yr.) from U of T Majorina in English and Anthropology, Diploma of Education from University of Wollongong, Australia; [oth. writ.] I have been published in local newspaper in addition to writing children's stories I use in the classroom when teaching.; [pers.] This poem is dedicated to all of those who could not find their way back from the bitter edge of loneliness.; [a.] Oakville, Ontario, Canada

BORGER, GERALDINE
[b.] September 2, 1942, Clarence, PA; [p.] Mr. and Mrs. Frank Waxmunsky Sr.; [m.] Stanley W. Borger, September 19, 1964; [ch.] Vonda, Beth Ann, LeAnn, Doyle; [ed.] Graduated from Bald Eagle High School, attended classes at Centre County Vo. Tech. School and Penn State Univ.; [occ.] Housewife; [memb.] Snow Shoe Ambulance Club, Mountaintop Alliance CMA Church; [hon.] Cub Scout Den Mother Award, School Newspaper Staff Editor Award, School Library Staff Award; [oth. writ.] Several editorials and articles published in local newspaper, poems and writings in local Church newspaper and bulletins.; [pers.] A great deal of my poetry expresses the love of God and His

creative handiwork. I see His touch in all of nature, as well as, mankind. My parents instilled within me the love of nature and good Christian values.; [a.] Snow Shoe, PA

BORMAN, CLYDE E.
[pen.] Clyde Kalaila Borman; [m.] Rosaia M. Borman, January 21, 1967; [ch.] Six children; [ed.] A.B. Degree, McKendree College in Lebanon, Illinois. Graduate School of Banking Univ. of Wisconsin.; [occ.] Former Banker, now retired; [memb.] American Legion, S. Pauls' Church, Honalo, Hawaii. Member-Gudacama Veterans', Rotary Club; [hon.] Silver Beaver, Boy Scouts of America; [oth. writ.] Trusts and Estates Magazine Burrough's Clearing House, American Banker Magazine, Mid-West Banker Magazine Honolulu Magazine; [pers.] Other writings, cont. — Aloha Magazine, Hawaii Magazine, Other writings are serious, I write poetry for fun.; [a.] Kailua-Kona, HI

BOSLAUGH, EDGAR P.
[b.] May 7, 1912, Frankport, SD; [m.] Emma Clayton, September 7, 1939; [ch.] Paula, Douglas, Vicki; [ed.] H.S. Grad. and just over one year of college; [occ.] Retired; [memb.] Model A (Ford) Club of America, 3rd Degree Masonic Lodge, Good Sam chapter; [hon.] A scad of bowling Trophies and some ribbons in 2nd World War; [oth. writ.] Contributor of letters to the editor and a lot of poems in a loose leaf binder.; [pers.] Ve git too soon old and too late schmart!!; [a.] Everett, WA

BOTELHO, ROXIE
[b.] January 9, 1939, Laurel, MS; [p.] Lillian and Houston Richard; [m.] William, October 9, 1960; [ch.] Traci and Michael; [ed.] High School Hattiesburg, MS; [occ.] Housewife/Widow; [memb.] None published; [pers.] I have written many poems for other people, mostly on the lighter side, but some were serious. I have been called the "Erma Bombeck" of the neighborhood.; [a.] San Jose, CA

BOURGEAU, MARK JAMES
[b.] December 15, 1948, Detroit, MI; [p.] David C. Bourgeau Sr., Phyllis Louise Bourgeau; [m.] Tamara Lynn, October 23, 1982; [ch.] Mark, James, Oliver, Marthins, Benjamin, Robert, Adam Alexander, Lauren K. Louise, Christopher Coates; [ed.] Pontiac Central High, Ferris State Univ., B.S. Bus Admin. Central Michigan Univ.; [occ.] Seeking Employment; [memb.] Nat'l. Kidery Foundation, American H. Assc.; [hon.] Dean's List; [oth. writ.] Several poems published in College; [pers.] To observe reflect and then to touch the hearts of others.; [a.] West Bloomfield, MI

BOUTHILET, GEORGE
[b.] November 1, 1924, St. Paul, MN; [ed.] M.Ed., St. Thomas Univ., St. Paul, Minnesota; [occ.] Retired teacher; [memb.] Phi Alpha Theta, Historical Honorary

BOWLBY, JULIA
[pen.] Juliana Blawyn; [b.] February 7, 1945, Modesto, CA; [p.] W. J. and Rosemary Culver both Deceased; [m.] Elmo Bowlby, August 4, 1963; [ch.] Sonja Bowlby; [ed.] High School; [occ.] Self; [hon.] Won contest - Charcoal Art - Stanthorpe, Queensland Australia (now in gallery); [oth. writ.] The Chakra Workout pub. Llewellyns 1993 (co-author and illustrator).; [pers.] My study of eastern philosophies and quantum and metaphysics inspired me to write the poem, "Contrasts".; [a.] Petersburg, AK

BOYSE, IONA
[pen.] "Iney"; [b.] September 23, 1917, Mosherville, MI; [p.] Chloe and Montie Bater; [m.] Charles, June 18, 1937; [ch.] Dale, Douglas, and Dorothy; [hon.] Many church awards - first Methodist Church, Life member of American

Motherhood Club; [oth. writ.] My mother wrote poems to her children. I put my poems together in a book and dedicated into my husband and our children in 1982.

BRADFIELD IV, JAMES R.
[pen.] Cabbage; [b.] September 26, 1971, Baltimore, MD; [p.] James R. Bradfield, Theresa Bradfield; [ed.] Cardinal Gibbons, C.C. College; [occ.] Professional Skateboarder, play music; [pers.] The more you give, the more you get. "Helen Steiner Rice" that is the philosophy I believe in. Less gets more.; [a.] Baltimore, MD

BRAZEAU, DENIS
[b.] May 7, 1944, Ottawa, Hull; [ed.] B.A., B.L.S. Ottawa University and St. Paul University; [occ.] Retired; [pers.] I am very much attached to lyricism. Poetry is for me a way of expressing my emotion, the very essence of my soul and the soul of humanity and I see it.; [a.] Vanier, Ontario, Canada

BREAZEALE III, BURCH O.
[pen.] Buck Breazeale; [b.] September 11, 1979, Henderson, NE; [p.] Burch and Carolynn Breazeale Jr.; [ed.] Elementary, Jr. High and High School at McCool Jct., Public High School; [occ.] Student; [memb.] National Honor Society, Hoby Alumni, National Cufflink Society; [hon.] National Honor Society, Hoby Alumni, Honor Roll and McCool Public High School; [pers.] Do not accept mediocrity.; [a.] McCool Junction, NE

BRENART, RACHEL A.
[pen.] Alexandria Francis; [b.] February 28, 1975, Elmhurst; [p.] Dr. Robert and Margo Brenart; [ed.] National Honor Society Yorkville H.S. High Honors 4 years CNA; [occ.] CNA and full time student; [pers.] I am inspired by natures beauty and tranquility.; [a.] Yorkville, IL

BRERETON, EDITH
[b.] October 17, 1924, Toronto, Ontario, Canada; [p.] John Hamilton, Edith Hamilton; [m.] Leonard Brereton (Deceased), October 27, 1951; [ch.] John Richard, Julie Kathleen; [occ.] Retired; [oth. writ.] Several poems (I have never attempted to have them published or entered a poetry contest before).; [pers.] It is never too late to accomplish your dreams. I belief all things are a gift from God. - Many of my poems reflect this.; [a.] Scarborough, Ontario, Canada

BRILEY, COLLIN
[pen.] Collin; [b.] August 4, 1984, Monterey, CA; [p.] Barbara and Patrick Briley; [ed.] Prunedale Elementary, Gambetta Middle School; [occ.] Student, water meter reader; [hon.] Honor roll, Principal's List of Academic Excellence; [pers.] "Take control of your life"; [a.] Prunedale, CA

BROOKS, GARY
[pen.] Bucket, Sweething; [b.] August 5, 1960, Lonoke, AR; [p.] Wardell Brooks and Mildred Brooks; [m.] Pamale Talley, August 16, 1996; [ch.] Jermaina; [ed.] Wabbaseka Tucker High, South Central Career; [occ.] Self Employed; [memb.] WH Thomas Lodge, Tomeblin Baptist Church; [hon.] Arts Band Music Certificates; [oth. writ.] Band Reporter; [pers.] I strive for the better of this world and mankind in my writing. I have been greatly influenced by the romantic poets in my life; [a.] Tucker, AR

BROTHERS, GARY
[b.] August 30, 1950, Toronto; [p.] Wilford Brothers Marion and Nadine Brothers; [m.] Irene Aworak, August 18, 1973; [ch.] Brandi Theresa Marion, Darryl Roy Vincent; [ed.] Alderwood Collegiate Inst. Toronto; [occ.] Car Sales Larry Hudson, Pontiac, Buick, GMC, Listower Ont.; [memb.]

Mankind; [hon.] Life itself and many trivial others; [oth. writ.] Several hundred poems printed locally - songs in process of recording; [pers.] When the essence of love gets lost in the cluster and every magnitude of itself - it is time to take back your heart.; [a.] Palmerston, Ontario, Canada

BROWN, A. J. DANRE
[pen.] Butter Pecan; [b.] January 17, 1979, Galveston, TX; [p.] Jorenda Bolden and Geoffery Wayne Foughnor; [ch.] Sadeja M. Tucker (2 years old); [ed.] Crystal Elementary and Middle School, Sullivan Middle School, Ida B. Wells High School, San Francisco State College; [occ.] Student; [memb.] Celebration of Life, Church of God in Christ, Judah Christian Fellowship, N.A.A.C.P., Step II College/ascend program; [hon.] African American Honor Roll award, Dean List (honor roll) award; [oth. writ.] Young Nubian Princess, The Fingersmith, peace and sweet and soft: Several other poems published in school newspaper and high school yearbook.; [pers.] My writing is a reflection of my everyday life. I write about things that are close to my heart and in my presence. I have been greatly influenced by my daughter because through her I see better days.; [a.] San Francisco, CA

BROWN, PETER LANCE
[pen.] Lama; [b.] March 23, 1959, Brooklyn NY; [p.] Sarah Brown Satterwhite, Fred Satterwhite; [ch.] Jamel, Navasha, Rachel; [ed.] St. George Auxiliary High, New York Interpreters for the Deaf; [occ.] Interpreter for deaf and merchandising agent; [oth. writ.] Many but not yet published.; [pers.] Do not fault people because their beliefs are unacceptable to you. It may be the only means for their survival.; [a.] Phoenix, AR

BROWN, RICKY J.
[pen.] Rick Brown; [b.] April 9, 1951, Greensboro, NC; [p.] Joe and Stella Brown; [m.] Claudia Leigh, June 11, 1986; [ed.] B.S. Business Management University of Maryland; [occ.] Personnel Management Specialist; [memb.] U.S. Air Force Sergeants Association; [hon.] Decorated Military Veteran; [pers.] Inspired by I.E. Cummings

BROWN, VELMA
[b.] April 13, Truro, NS, Canada; [p.] Elsie and Gordon Purdy (Deceased); [m.] Fredrick Brown, August 17, 1940; [ch.] Carolee; [ed.] High school; [occ.] Retired; [memb.] Canadian Vice-President of V.A.P.A. - United Amateur Poetry Association, U.S.A. in the late '70's, Scotian Pen Guild, Dartmouth, N.S., Canada, member - Clover International Poetry Association, 1973; [hon.] Best Poet, 1973, AWJ Amateur Writer's Journal, Poet Laureate, 1972, United Amateur Press, U.S.A.; [oth. writ.] Poem: The Matriarch - Pub. in "Clover Collection of Verse - 1973 several articles for "The Atlantic Charismatic" (recent); [pers.] 81 in age, but young in spirit. Still writing.; [a.] Halifax, Nova Scotia, Canada

BROWNING, SIMON K.
[pen.] Tethodii; [b.] March 2, 1971, Southampton, England; [p.] Keith and Yvonne Browning; [ed.] Insufficient; [oth. writ.] 1. "Magic Man" published in anthology `Gentlemen of Television' GB 1993, 2. "Untitled published in `The Space Between' 1994 (Editors choice award), 3. "The Mountain Top of Stability" published in `Best Poems of 1995", 4. "I Hate (Pc 1) published in `Best Poems of 1996' (Editors choice award), 5. "Judgmental" published in GB Collection `Footprints in Time 1996; [pers.] Always listen but don't always do what people tell you to do! I dedicate this poem "Glorious War" to all the war makers in the world especially those behind the scenes with hidden agendas that usually concern financial gain.

BRUEGMAN, CHARLES E.
[pen.] Charle Bruegman; [b.] January 5, 1955, Cincinnati, OH; [p.] Mildred Baudendistle; [m.] Renee Bruegman; [ed.] Cincinnati Technical College; [occ.] Airline Employee; [oth. writ.] Published in Morning Star by the National Library of Poetry. The poem was titled "Alone". A poem book will be published in 1997.; [pers.] Reach for the truth in all things you seek. Set your goals without hurting other's smile.

BRUNELLI, JEANNE M.
[b.] January 19, 1959, Waterbury, CT; [p.] Eugene Ozerhoski Helen Ozerhoski; [m.] Anthony L. Brunelli, July 3, 1993; [ch.] Thomas Charles; [ed.] 1977 Graduate Thomaston High School Thomaston, CT, 1978 Graduate Torrington Beauty Academy Torrington, CT; [occ.] Hairdresser/Cosmetologist Daves Family Hair styling Center Thomaston, CT; [hon.] Had my picture published in an international hair styling book called inspire volume sixteen page 36; [pers.] My poem was written in memory of my grandparents. They had a tremendous influences on me through out my life. I love them both dearly and am waiting til the day I can see them again; [a.] Plymouth, CT

BRYAN, LOUIS
[b.] 1944, Atlantic City, NJ; [p.] Helen Manning Bryan, Louis E. Bryan Sr.; [ed.] Clinton H.S., Clinton, MA, Unity College, Unity, ME; [occ.] Poet, Fiction writer, Writing consultant, Medicaid health care provider; [hon.] Dean's List; [oth. writ.] Poetry and fiction published in various literary and commercial publications: New Mexico Humanities Rev., Pacific Rev., Hayden's Ferry Rev., Seattle Post Intelligence, The Crisis, etc.; [pers.] In poetry, as in fiction, I try to explore, unflinchingly, and with compassion, the African American experience, and the universal human condition.; [a.] Bellingham, WA

BRYANT, JACQUELYN
[b.] Newark, NJ; [p.] Joseph H. Howard, Jessie M. Howard; [ed.] Certified Medical Staff Professional, Professional Licenses: New Jersey Real Estate and New Jersey Life Insurance; [occ.] Manager, Medical Staff Office, University Hospital Newark, NJ; [memb.] National Assoc. Medical Staff Services, NAMMS North Jersey Chapter, Faith Fellowship Ministries World Outreach Center Intercessory Prayer Minister, National Association of Realtors, New Jersey Association of Realtors, Greater Eastern Union County Board of Realtors; [oth. writ.] Author of "The Power Tower", a powerful book of prayer. Published by End Time Wave Publications.; [pers.] As a prayer advocate and intercessor, my purpose is to deliver people from bondage to spiritual freedom through Jesus Christ. The Book that has influenced me the most has been the Holy Bible.; [a.] Linden, NJ

BUCKLEY, BETH LORRAINE
[b.] March 2, 1956, Peterborough, Ontario, Canada; [p.] Fay E. White, Elias White; [m.] Glen, May 7, 1977; [ch.] Jason William, Benjamin Clayton; [ed.] Millbrook High School, Sir Sandford Fleming College; [occ.] Not employed now but I am a medical Secretary; [oth. writ.] "Cherish Your Tokens" in "The Millbrook Times", poems written for a bereavement group.; [pers.] This poem is dedicated to my mother, in her honor and my great loss. It was written by my heart and hands in grade 1 or kindergarten.; [a.] Peterborough, Ontario, Canada

BUEHLER, URSULA
[b.] July 4, 1932, Winnipeg, Manitoba; [ch.] Two daughters; [ed.] BA degree - Algoma University College; [occ.] Semi-retired Correctional Officer; [oth. writ.] Unpublished poetry 1 lyric poem set to music L. Tobin unpublished.; [pers.] Presently working on short stories.; [a.] Sault Ste Marie, Ontario, Canada

BULL, RICKY
[pen.] Rick Bull; [b.] December 23, 1953, Elrose, SK, Canada; [p.] Richard and Verna Bull; [ed.] Sweft Current Saskatchewan, Swift Current Comp. High School; [occ.] Lakeside Packers, Brooks Alberta Canada; [oth. writ.] Have many writings like to have a book published one day.; [pers.] I started writing prayers for the church and end up writing poems as well.; [a.] Brooks, Alberta, Canada

BUNN, JOHN CHARLES
[b.] May 19, 1964, Brampton, Ontario; [p.] Lorne and Shirley Bunn; [m.] Leslie Ann Bunn (Ne-Young), October 13, 1990; [ch.] Lauren Ashley, Jackson Garnet; [ed.] Stayner Collegiate Institute Georgian College of Applied Arts and Technology (Barrie, Ontario), Monhawk College (Hamilton, Ontario); [occ.] Electrician; [memb.] Stayner Lions Club, Member of Ontario Championship Senior "A" Hockey, and Baseball Teams; [pers.] My father always told me that there is no such things as "I can't".; [a.] Stayner, Ontario, Canada

BURGER, JUANITA VAUGHN
[b.] October 19, 1937, Chatsworth, GA; [p.] Winfred and Bertha Vaughn; [m.] Single "Grand Mother"; [ch.] Barry Witherow, Marlon, Kenny and Jacqueline Burger; [ed.] Herron School of Business, School of Cosmetology, and C.A.S.A Training also Foster Parenting Training Master - Life Leadership; [occ.] Care-giver for handicapped and Foster Parent of two young girls.; [memb.] Creative Arts Guild (Previously) Baptist Convention of Chatsworth, GA and Canton, GA, Senior Citizen, M.A.P.P. (Organization for care of children); [hon.] I can't think of any.; [oth. writ.] Poems, short stories for children enjoyment. "A Mother Thoughts" published in local newspapers. "Po' lil' ole' houn' dog', published in Creative Arts Guild Publication.; [pers.] I had the advantage of being reared in a small town with 6 sisters and 1 brother, a loving gentle father and firm but patience mother, and hundreds of aunts, uncles, cousins, nieces and nephews - All close to each other.; [a.] Chatsworth, GA

BURGOS, YDALIZA M.
[pen.] My lady; [b.] October 10, 1979, New York City; [p.] Arlette Avillan; [ed.] I am presently in my senior year in high school; [occ.] I babysit and work at Loeman's Clothing Factory; [memb.] I am part of the creative writing workshop at my school and have been published in the school poetry book; [hon.] I've won awards for my participation in the school poetry magazine and for excellent achievement in English and creative writing; [oth. writ.] I've been published in Lehman College's Newspaper and my school poetry magazine. I am presently working on novels and short stories which I hope to publish.; [pers.] I write because its the only way I understand myself, reflect what's in my heart. I owe everything I've ever accomplished to my ever supportive mom. Arlette Avillan; [a.] Bronx, NY

BURNS, JACALYN
[b.] September 10, 1956, Spokane, WA; [p.] John Strope and Charlotte Strope; [m.] Kenneth Burns, January 1, 1995; [ch.] Peter Fitch, Michelle Strope; step-children: Michael Burns, Nicholas Burns; [ed.] Shadle Park High, Spokane Community College A.A.S. Mechanical Engineering Technology; [occ.] Housewife and Mother; [hon.] Graduated from S.C.C. with honors (Dean's List); [pers.] This contest has brought a great feeling of achievement to my life. Thank you.; [a.] Loon Lake, WA

BURREL, FREDA
[b.] April 4, 1956, St. Louis, MO; [p.] Felix and Christine Fullerton; [m.] Ralph L. Burrel, February 27; [ch.] Michael David; [ed.] North Montgomery High School; [occ.] Rehab Tech. — Continental Rehabilitation Hospital of Terre Haute, IN; [oth. writ.] I have written several poems. For one of them, I received an honorable mention.; [a.] Farmersburg, IN

BUZZUTTO, PENELOPE
[b.] February 15, 1943, S. Windham, ME; [p.] Clyde and Barbara Wiggin Sr.; [m.] Michael Buzzutto, September 30, 1988; [ch.] Edmund Ebert III and Christopher Ebert; [ed.] High School Graduate Gorham, Maine; [occ.] Chambermaid; [oth. writ.] Many poems, I printed in a church bulletin, words to a song plus some reflections. None have been published until now.; [pers.] I am born again believer in Jesus as my Savior. He has been my help and my hope in many times of trials and sorrows. I thank God for the talent he has given me.; [a.] West Buxton, MN

BYRD, JESSICA LAUREN
[pen.] Jessica Lauren Byrd; [b.] August 10, 1983, Oklahoma City, OK; [p.] Reside with grandparents - James and Suzanne Jesse; [ed.] 8th Grade Student - Marlington Middle School; [memb.] Marlington High School Marching Band, Suzuki Association of Canton, Ohio (Violin); [hon.] Power of the Pen-State Competition Finalist, Aguest Violin Soloist for the Canton, Ohio Symphony Orchestra (May 1996) "Vivaldi's Spring; [oth. writ.] The Cat Who Dreamed of Far Away Places a children's book currently submitted for publication; [pers.] I plan to attend The Ohio State University to study literature and music.; [a.] Atwater, OH

CABALLERO, CLAUDIA
[b.] July 19, 1963, Mexico City; [ed.] Spanish Language and Literature in Universidad Automa de Mexico (UNAM); [oth. writ.] I was published in the anthology El Libro de Lo Insolito by Emiliano Gonzalez of Beatriz Alvarez Klein, 2nd edition, editorial FCE, Mexico City 1994, (13 poems). Also published in Plural Magazine in Dec. 1993; [pers.] "A wet bird never flies at night." W.C. Fields; [a.] Fairfax, VA

CALLAHAN, ANA
[pen.] Colleen Ham; [b.] September 21, 1984, Valley Stream, NY; [p.] Michael Callahan, Irma Callahan; [ed.] East Northport Middle School; [occ.] Acting, Violin; [memb.] National Wildlife Association; [hon.] Principal's List, 95 or above average, Citizenship award, honor roll; [oth. writ.] Poems, short stories, essays, nominational letters; [pers.] There is no failure in trying, except for not trying at all. Most people spend more time, and energy going around problems than trying to solve them.; [a.] East Northport, NY

CAMARENA, IGNASCIO G.
[b.] September 19, 1946, San Jose, CA; [p.] Francisco and Valentina Camarena; [m.] Anita Hope Camarena, April 14, 1969; [ch.] Ignascio, Kristine, Michel; [oth. writ.] Several articles have been published in the local newspaper. I am in the process of writing my first book.; [pers.] "Teach your children to love their children. For that is the essenes of life." My thinking has been molded by the beauty of the souls, of the people that have crossed the road that is my life.; [a.] San Jose, CA

CAMPBELL, CARRIE J.
[b.] August 21, 1967, Westwood, NJ; [p.] Richard Campbell, Carol Campbell; [ed.] B.A. Susquehanna University; [occ.] Health Promotion; [memb.] NJ Society of Public Health Education, National Wellness Association, Transplant Recipients International Org.; [hon.] Sigma Tau Delta, Pi Delta Phi; [a.] Mountain Lakes, NJ

CAMPBELL, MD. ROBERT ALLEN
[b.] December 21, 1924, Toledo, OH; [p.] Glenn and Harriet Campbell; [m.] Mary Christine Campbell, September 21, 1949; [ch.] Robert Perry, Mary Ellen and Catherine Anne; [ed.] Columbia U., Univ. Calif. SF, Oregon Health Science University, BA, MD, Post-Doctoral Fellowship (USPHS).; [occ.] Physician, Professor Emeritus, Active Oregon Health Sci. Univ. Nephrology Research; [memb.] Numerous basic Science and clinical organizations, emphasis on kidney specialties.; [hon.] Phi Beta Kappa, Alpha Omega Alpha (Medical), Wyatt fellowship, and others. WW II Pacific theater combat medals.; [oth. writ.] Seventy six book chapters and original articles and one hundred and twenty and scientific abstract. Wrote one lay poem published years ago. 120 pg. $10.00 for it and decided I'd better be a doctor. We were hungry.; [pers.] Take time to fiddle, diddle, whittle, or what have you.; [a.] Portland, OR

CAMPBELL, PHILIP N.
[pen.] Philip Campbell; [b.] April 1, 1977, Las Cruces, NM; [p.] Wanda and Billy; [ed.] College Student - Life Student; [occ.] Struggling Author, Waiter, Life Traveler; [hon.] War; [oth. writ.] Numerous poems and short stories in personal portfolio.; [pers.] No one appreciates my insanity.; [a.] Las Cruces, NM

CAMPBELL, R. WALLACE
[b.] December 31, 1916, Pelly, Saskatchewan, Canada; [p.] Milton Neil Campbell and Hazel May Campbell; [m.] Alberta Jane Campbell, August 23, 1953; [ch.] Elaine Lois Campbell and Barbara Anderson; [ed.] Graduate of Queen's University, (Kingston, Ontario) and the University of Toronto; [occ.] Retired-Elementary School Principal and High School teacher of English during work years; [memb.] Golden (Senior) Kiwanis Club, Superannuated Teachers of Ontario, Member Collier Street United Church (Akin to Presbyterian and Methodist) Golf Club; [oth. writ.] Regular writing and broadcasting of own radio, short stories. Editor of local church magazine and Kiwanis Club bulletin. Milton Neil Campbell - A political and governmental Biography (by my Brother and me); [pers.] Having spent 14 years in parts of Northern Canada, I have learned to appreciate the vastness and variety of my country and the many aspect of the cultures of our native peoples.; [a.] Barrie, Ontario, Canada

CAMPOS, EVE O.
[b.] March 13, 1979, Riverside, CA; [p.] Miguel and Dolores Campos; [ed.] Currently senior in high school and sophomore in College (through running start); [pers.] My poetry reflects my faith in my religion and my relationship with my Lord Jesus Christ. Without him my poetry is worth nothing! Thanx mom, dad, Max and Sofia for everything!; [a.] Grandview, WA

CANUEL, M. J.
[pen.] M. J. Canuel; [b.] February 28, 1951, Halifax, Nova Scotia; [p.] Gabriel and Philomene Canuel; [m.] Donna Aziz Canuel, June 30, 1973; [ch.] Maryssa, Phillip; [ed.] - Universite De Montreal, Summa Cum Laude/B.A. Literature, Loyola/B.A. Economics, Concordia University; [occ.] Director of Manufacturing Operations - Okaply Industries, President - Mont Belliard Impex; [oth. writ.] Poem: Stainless Steel Reflections - Published in Reading for the Write Reasons - Prentice Hall (Canada) 1996. I hope to have a poetry volume published early in 1997.; [pers.] I am a poet by nature, a teacher by vocation and a businessman by livelihood.; [a.] Lorraine, Province of Quebec, Canada

CANUSO, REBECCA
[pen.] Rebecca Canuso; [b.] July 9, 1979, Abington; [p.] Mary Spencer and Craig Spencer and Francis Canuso; [ed.] I am entering my Sr. year at Abington High School; [occ.] Student and P/T Adm. Asst.; [memb.] Roslyn Softball Club; [oth. writ.] I have written many other poems, although I have never sent any others for publication.; [pers.] My poems are my tears, my laughs, my passion and my pain, I am thrilled to be able to share them with others. I hope other teenage girls will relate to my poem.; [a.] Abington, PA

CAPISTRAND, ROBERT J.
[b.] July 24, 1960, Toronto, Ontario, Canada; [p.] Robert and Helen Capistrand; [ed.] Secondary Education, Dr. Norman Bethune C.I.; [occ.] Clerk Toronto - Dominion Bank.; [memb.] World Wide Church of God.; [hon.] Nominated for Award of Excellence (Internal Service) with the Toronto Dominion Bank.; [pers.] Philosophy of life. Truthfulness, kindness, and doing things with care.; [a.] Thornhill, Ontario, Canada

CARLISLE, ANNIE J.
[b.] June 1, 1942, Cleveland, OH; [p.] Sam and Johnetta Lentini; [ch.] Michael, Cindy, Marie and Erik; [ed.] Phoenix College Arizona State University Jane Addams School of Nursing; [occ.] Nursing - Specializing in ventilator dependent children and adults.; [memb.] Arizona State Board of Nursing Ohio State Board of Nursing; [hon.] High School Valedictorian National Honor Society; [oth. writ.] Children's book "Stinky"; [pers.] I wish to dedicate "inspiration" to my beloved parents, my brothers and sister, and all of my children, grandchildren, neices and nephews.; [a.] Queen Creek, AZ

CAROLINE, MARY
[b.] October 5, 1946, Seattle, WA; [p.] Mary Effie Wetherington and Kinney Leonard; [ch.] Rebecca Skye; [ed.] The Pincipia, Alaska Pacific University, Boston University, M.Ed, PHR; [occ.] HR, OD Consultant; [oth. writ.] Personal, philosophical, and political pieces in Gay and Lesbian Press; [pers.] I believe using metaphor to explore our pain and despair elevates and shifts our experience so the light of understanding can begin to ease our struggle.; [a.] Seattle, WA

CARLSON, JANE TAMAE
[pen.] Tamae Matsuo; [b.] Wahiawa, Kauai; [p.] Ichiji and Suzu Matsuo; [m.] Sigfred Robert Carlson (Deceased), December 9, 1943; [ch.] Sighe, Sigfred Jr., Sydney and Sylvia; [ed.] Kahuku Hi-Oahu Adult Ed. - (Pt. T) Shoreline C.C., Settle, WA - (Pt. T) U. of Hawaii, Kauai Campus; [occ.] Japanese Speaking Gardener; [memb.] Kapaa Hongwahji Mission - Temple, Kauai, HI, Greenpeace; [oth. writ.] "Over The Fence", a segment from Veggic - Life, published my "Skating Along" tip in the garden, which I submitted in the January 1996 issue.; [pers.] I believe, a single person can make a difference in this world.; [a.] Wailua Homestead, Kauai, HI

CARMICHAEL, LILIAN S.
[b.] July 4, 1956, Scotland; [m.] Douglas W. Carmichael, December 31, 1993; [ch.] Lindsay Stirrat Carmichael (Deceased); [occ.] Air Canada, Customer Service Co-urd-cargo Toronto Ontario Canada; [hon.] Royal conservatory of music piano - grades 1-6; [oth. writ.] 30 plus poems in memory of death of baby girl.; [pers.] This poem was written to honour the loving memory of our beautiful precious angel, Lindsay Stirrat Carmichael. She was burn on October 9, 1995 with congenital heart disease, and sadly passed away on January 28, 1996. After heart surgery. My poems reflect how much she was loved and how sadly she is missed.

CARPENTER, LINDA
[pen.] Linda; [b.] December 7, 1962, Patterson, NJ; [p.] Ted and Nancy Mills; [m.] Stephen Carpenter, September 23, 1995; [ch.] Billy, Brandon, Kurtis; [ed.] Mountain View High School, Kingsley PA; [occ.] Waitress; [oth. writ.] Not published "My Father", "My Love, My Life", "Alone"; [pers.] My writing's always involve. Situations that are going on in my life, all my writing are of real emotions from the heart.; [a.] Uniondale, PA

CARRIER, SHELIAH A.
[pen.] Ricki; [b.] August 7, 1949, Lake Charles, LA; [p.] The Late Joseph and Fretty Carrier; [m.] Divorced; [ch.] Doral and Charles; [ed.] Graduated Bennett High, "68" Buffalo School of Practical Nursing; [occ.] Retired Psychiatric Nurse; [oth. writ.] Only short stories in High School for English Assignment just for fun. Teacher read to class. Stated the story was an a for the assignment only I got; [pers.] I love my young black Afro-American please, don't destroy our youth's of young lawyer, Dr's judges Scientist's poet's stop the violence; [a.] Buffalo, NY

CARTER, DEREK CHARLES
[b.] October 11, 1969, Corner Brook, Newfoundland, Canada; [p.] Eric Carter, Elizabeth Carter; [ed.] Queen Elizabeth High School, Southern Alberta Institute of Technology, Mount Royal College; [occ.] Canadian Armed Forces; [oth. writ.] Several letters published in the Alberta Teachers Association Magazine; [pers.] Never give up on your dreams because the very instant you give up, the reality of your dream coming true lies just around the corner.; [a.] Calgary, Alberta, Canada

CARTRIGHT, MICHAEL
[b.] October 23, 1964, Joplin, MO; [oth. writ.] "Vision West" a triptych broadside Co-authored with David Ashmore published 1986 by Vision West Press/Stone in Shoe Press. "Broadsheet" Broadside published 1987 by Sunburnt West Press. "Newsreel" published 1991 by other sources. Dan Dryden, and Fireproof Press.; [pers.] The history of my voice originates from four points: The sound of Lew Welch, Stuart Z. Perkoff, John Macker, and American Vernacular.; [a.] Carthage, MO

CARVALIS, HARRY
[b.] November 25, 1952, Pensacola, FL; [p.] Violet Lucille Hayworth, Harry Carvalis Sr.; [ch.] Kenneth Warren, Michelle Lee; [ed.] St. Petersburg High School, St. Petersburg Junior College, University of South Florida; [occ.] Letter Carrier, St. Petersburg, FL.; [memb.] Mensa Society, National Assoc. of Letter Carriers, American Poolplayers Association; [hon.] Honorable Discharge, U.S. Army; Several work-related awards; Regional and National Pool Competitions; [oth. writ.] None published; [a.] Saint Petersburg, FL

CASEY, TAWNYA
[b.] May 27, 1983, Grants; [p.] Jean and Alan Casey; [ed.] Marzano Vista Middle School; [occ.] Baby sitter, Poet; [memb.] Youth Drama, First Baptist Church Bosque Farms; [hon.] Math, Social Studies; [oth. writ.] Several Poems that were kept private; [pers.] In my writing I like to show that no matter what you do life always, goes according to a plan just the plan changes.; [a.] Bosque Farms, NM

CASKEY, DONNA R.
[b.] May 19, 1958, Racine, WI; [p.] Lester Werlein, Jo Ann Werlein; [m.] Gleen G. Caskey Jr., July 4, 1995; [ch.] Cory Robert Lamp, Christa Rae Lamp; [ed.] Burlington High School; [pers.] I want my poem to show there is hope. Family, good friends and God, will always stand with you.; [a.] Burlington, WI

CASSIDY, PATRICIA
[b.] England; [pers.] I wrote this poem to give people a better understanding of persons suffering from schizophrenice and other serous gentle illnesses. I hope to create awareness and erase stigma attached to this terrible disease.

CASTRO, OMAR DAVID
[pen.] Om's; [b.] June 20, 1979, Andrews AFB, Prince George's City, VA; [p.] Edgar N. Castro, Yvette M. Daniel; [ed.] High School Student; [occ.] Student; [hon.] 2 Art Awards, one in Miami, Fla., in pre-school and the other in the Washington D.C. Arch-Diosan (D.C., VA, and MD) Art Contest, I came in 2nd Place for 2nd Grade; [oth. writ.] I keep a journal - I have several now.; [pers.] I was 12 when I started writing. I am inspired by the music I listen to, incidents that happen in the world, people and feelings or thoughts that I have. I write songs, not poems really, I write the lyrics and my friends in my band play the music to them. I want to be a lyricist - a song writer.; [a.] Scottsdale, AZ

CATER, BERNICE E. J.
[b.] November 14, 1979; [p.] Noel and Julie Cater; [oth. writ.] Published in Dance on the Horizon and Best Poems of 1996; [pers.] They say the only thing that stands between you and perfection is fear. What you should really be afraid of is what you'll miss if you don't try.; [a.] LaRiviere, Manitoba, Canada

CATHERWOOD, KIM
[b.] November 13, 1965, Brantford, Ontario, Canada; [p.] Graham Harris, Eve Harris; [m.] James Catherwood, July 8, 1988; [ch.] Darrell James, Jacob Tyler; [ed.] Pauline Johnson Collegiate and Vocational School; [pers.] I am an avid daydreamer who see's a poem or a story in everything around me. I am currently at work on a novel that I hope to get published someday, but poetry will always be my first love.; [a.] Brantford, Ontario, Canada

CELESNIK JR., SYLVESTER P.
[pen.] Joe; [b.] August 14, 1948, Greensburg, PA; [p.] Sylvester P. Celesnik Sr. and Frances Perne Celesnik; [m.] Sharon Schall Celesnik, June 7, 1969; [ed.] Hempfield High School, Military: United States Air Force, Vietnam Veteran; [occ.] Home Improvement Contractor in Northern Virginia; [pers.] I began writing poetry after the tragic death of my beloved youngest brother in March 1996.; [a.] Vienna, VA

CEREZO, REUBEN A.
[pen.] Rey Cerezo; [b.] September 13, 1965, Philippines; [p.] Ben Cerezo, Rose Cerezo; [m.] Mae P. Cerezo, February 14, 1996; [ch.] Jonathan Marcus, Angela Noelle; [ed.] Bishop England High The Citadel; [occ.] Auditor, U.S. Dept of Commerce/Inspector General; [memb.] Association of Government Accountants, Shao-Lin Do Association; [hon.] Bronze Medal Award, Certified Government Financial Manager, Third Degree Black Belt; [oth. writ.] My Secret Adoration, Escape, My Lover...My Best Friend, The Rose, Dreams, Lessons; [pers.] I thank God for blessing me with my devoted parents, beautiful wife and loving children.; [a.] Loganville, GA

CHACON JR., FELIPE
[pen.] Flip; [b.] September 23, 1951, Fabens, TX; [p.] Felipe Chacon, Rita Sigala; [m.] Sandra Quintana, June 30, 1979; [ch.] Randy, April, Rodney; [ed.] St. Louis H.S. (Honolulu, HI) University of Texas at El Paso; [occ.] Driver for furniture company; [oth. writ.] Several other poems, including, "You", "When Engels Cry". For first book of poetry titled, "The Voice from Within."; [pers.] The most beautiful song in the world, is the smile of a child.; [a.] El Paso, TX

CHADWICK, JOSEPH W.
[b.] August 5, 1920, Muskegon, MI; [p.] Joseph and Della Eddy Chadwick; [m.] Juliette I. LeBoux Chadwick, June 14, 1951; [ch.] Lavientia Joette Chadwick, Julianne Marie Chadwick; [ed.] Graduate Muskegon High School completed course at Hope College completed course Oklahoma Baptist University, graduate of Army Air Force Engineering School; [occ.] Retired; [memb.] Boy Scouts of America Lake Herbon Grange United States 5th Army Air Force. Local 1015 Union of Papermakers, Hope College Alumni; [hon.] Distinguished myself by running a record amount of paper on 3 different machines on 3 consecutive days. No one had ever done this before. I was awarded a letter of commendation. I am a 13th generation American; [oth. writ.] I have written several thousands poems. I was a papermaker tending a large machine for 8-12 hours a day. Setting, watching, waiting, poems would flash through my mind. 20 years at this.; [pers.] Reflections of my mind. I try to find some good in most things. God created the world. We create our thoughts let us be Christians. Let us have patience and understanding; [a.] Muskegon, MI

CHAKRAVORTY, ANUPA
[b.] August 4, 1967, Yamunanagar, India; [p.] M. L. Banerjee, Nihar Banerjee; [m.] Soumya Chakravorty, March 6, 1991; [ed.] Doctorate (Ph.D) in American Literature from Kurukshetra University, India; [occ.] Currently homemaker (in USA) previously Lecturer in English (in India); [memb.] American Studies research Centre, India; [pers.] Preserve nature - the one true inspiration for poetic thought. I have ben greatly influenced by wordsworth's poetry.; [a.] Santa Clara, CA

CHALK, MARTIN JOHN
[b.] March 17, 1977, Barnstaple, England; [p.] Stephen and Daphne Chalk; [ed.] Advanced High school diploma from New Sarepta Community High School; [occ.] Farm hand at Telawsky Holsteins; [a.] New Sarepta, Alberta, Canada

CHAMP, THOMAS
[b.] May 20, 1957, Princeton, WV; [p.] Betty and Ed; [m.] Katerina Alexandra; [ed.] B.S.E.E.; [occ.] Supervisory Engineer for U.S. Dept of Veterans Affairs; [memb.] Captain in the U.S. Air Force Reserves; [hon.] Eagle Award in Boy Scouts; [oth. writ.] "Patience", "Love State To Make", "Your Love", "Kate", "Miss You", "My Love", "The Proposal", "Someone To Hold", "Vilnius and a Love Rendezuous".; [pers.] From my heart to Katerina the lady of my dreams. May our life's together always be filled with love and happiness.

CHANDRA, SHIVANI
[b.] April 5, 1983, Carboneer, Newfoundland, Canada; [p.] Dr. Lokesh Chandra and Mrs. Vandra Chandra; [occ.] Student; [memb.] Active Basketball, Volleyball and Band School Member; [hon.] Academic and French Excellence; [oth. writ.] Many poems for school and other writing competitions, especially for my own interests.; [pers.] I'd like to dedicate this poem to my brother Samarth Chandra and to you in Whitby. "Remember love is like water, it holds many mysteries."; [a.] Burr Ridge, IL

CHARLTON, LINDA L.
[pen.] Linda Dearden; [b.] August 6, 1961, Endicott, NY; [p.] Z. Thomas and Roberta L. Dearden; [m.] Keith S. Charlton, March 8, 1991; [ch.] Levi and Noel; [ed.] Osbourn High, Northern Virginia College; [occ.] Full time parent and entrepreneur as Courier for Red Riding Hood Delivery; [memb.] Manassas Church of Christ; [hon.] Awards for jams, jellies, and plants; [a.] Manassas, VA

CHAVEZ, NOEMI ESPINOZA
[b.] October 15, 1968, Los Angeles, CA; [p.] Juan and Hermelinda Espinoza; [m.] Cuauhtemoc Chavez Cerros, August 14, 1996; [ed.] Finished up to 3 years of college at the University of Oklahoma, John Marshall High.; [occ.] Bilingual Teacher Asst. at Edgemere Elementary, Oklahoma City, OK; [pers.] I'm inspired to write practically only when I've been heart broken or sad. This poem was influenced by my first boyfriend Salvador Sauceda.; [a.] Oklahoma City, OK

CHAVIS, ROCHELLE
[pen.] Rochelle Chavis; [b.] February 17, 1981, Riverside, CA; [p.] Guy and Cindy Chavis; [ed.] Sultana High School; [occ.] Student; [memb.] Air Force Junior Reserves Officers Training Corps. Kawanis Key Club; [hon.] Principal's Honor Roll, Vice Principal's Honor Roll, Outstanding Achievements in several school subjects.; [pers.] I write what I feel. This is the way I express my mind through my hands and my heart... my words.; [a.] Hesperia, CA

CHESANEK, BEVERLY A.
[pen.] Anya Chesanek; [b.] October 23, 1944, Norwich, CT; [p.] Francis Chesanek, Ida Sherwood; [m.] Divorced 1995; [ch.] Catherine Monique; [ed.] Norwich Free Academy; [occ.] Medical Transcriptionist OB/Gyn Services, P.C.; [memb.] American Assoc. for Medical Transcription, National Museum of the American Indian (Smithsonian), Volunteer for Native American Awareness Program, Am. Indian Movement Support Group, and Native American Community and Cultural Development Agency; [hon.] Head Librarian, Board of Directors; [oth. writ.] Wrote several articles and a column for a newsletter entitled "On The Wing" in 1994 for War Chief Moonface Bear of the Golden Hill Paugeesukq tribe.; [pers.] I was once advised to write what I feel and this is what I strive to do, especially when presenting native issues to a non-native society. I have been greatly influenced by the work of John Trudell, A/M activist, poet and actor.; [a.] Norwich, CT

CHIN, KATHERINE
[ed.] Father Michael McGivney, Catholic High School; [hon.] Patricia Zoskey Award for Creative Writing; [a.] Markham, Ontario, Canada

CHIPOKA, VICTORIA
[b.] April 23, 1976, Zimbabwe; [p.] Shingairai and Jephais Chipoka; [ed.] Sophomore at College (Valley City State); [occ.] Student; [oth. writ.] Responding to newspaper articles. And live a book on its way.; [pers.] A poet at heart I am and wish to share the beauty of words to all who appreciate. Perfection should be the goal to every artist. To improve on our inabilities and always live room for improvement.; [a.] Valley City, ND

CHUKWUEKE, EMMANUEL U. N.
[b.] August 26, 1965, Ovim, Nigeria; [p.] Emmanuel and Catherine Chukwueke; [m.] Loveth Chukwueke, October 28, 1994; [ed.] Ugwunchara Pry. School Umuahia, Govt. College Umuahia, Institute of Management and Techn., Enugu, University of Portharcourt, Nigeria; [occ.] Former Immigration Officer in Nigeria, Store-Keeper, Phila Aviation Country Club, Blue Bell, PA; [hon.] Of Excellence and Distinction, Nigeria Immigration Training School, Kano (Aug. '88); [oth. writ.] Several incisive articles on African Socio-political problems published in Nigeria's local newspapers.; [pers.] Like the Biblical Solomon, I believe that world's socio-economic and political puzzles can be solved by fearing God and having mutual respect for one another.; [a.] Woodlynne, NJ

CIRKSENA-BAUMGARTNER, STACY
[b.] October 8, 1972, Manchester, IA; [p.] Russell and Patricia Cirksena; [m.] Daryl Baumgartner, March 26, 1994; [ed.] American Institute of Commerce, Hotel/Restaurant Degree; [occ.] Manager of The East Inn Motel; [oth. writ.] "My Daddy's Hands", "Baby Sister", "Silent Love", "Just Dreamin'"; [pers.] My inspiration is my family. They've given me this gift of writing poetry. Thank you I write as a hobby, but one day would like to write a book!; [a.] Manchester, IA

CLAPPISON, MINA
[pen.] Mina Smith; [occ.] Water colour Amateur Artist; [hon.] Bachelor of Arts, Deg. Trent. University (1982); [oth. writ.] Unpublished book of poems all original from never been submitted for print.; [a.] Cobourg, Ontario, Canada

CLARDY, SHERRY WRIGHT
[pen.] Sherry Wright Clardy; [b.] December 8, 1956, York County; [p.] Mr. and Mrs. William D. Wright Sr.; [m.] Michael Dean Clardy, January 6, 1979; [ch.] Michael 17, Bryan 13; [ed.] Completed High School Attended Technical School (Horry Georgetown); [occ.] Director of Child Care at First Presbyterian Church; [oth. writ.] My Paw Paw, The Man with the Sticks, Dreams, Clouds, and more!; [pers.] Upon the death of my Maw Maw I was inspired to write this poem, feeling that I had only answered her poems in which she had written to me earlier in my life, (asking God to take her to live with him up there (in Heaven) when she died down here (On earth)). I usually am inspired to write by something or someone that I love and my Maw Maw was very dear to my heart.; [a.] Myrtle Beach, SC

CLARK, JOAN E.
[pen.] Evelyn Sefton; [b.] 21 August 1924, Liverpool, England; [p.] Frank and Olive Leeson (Deceased); [m.] Widow; [ch.] David, Lucinda, Paul, Joanne; [ed.] Convent - Grammar State Registered Nurse - Midwife Health Visitor; [occ.] Retired - Writer; [memb.] I.S.P.; [oth. writ.] 'The Brooch' (Evelyn Sefton) a dozen poems published in authologies and local publications.; [pers.] I was very honoured to be made a life member of the International Society of Poets, last year. The beautiful countryside of Wales in which I now live, inspires my poetry and my forever busy life provides memories to recall in my novels.; [a.] Llanabystud, Wales, UK

CLARK, MADELINE
[pen.] Madeline Deniellcia Brown; [b.] September 28, 1973, Kansas City; [p.] Elliott J. Clark and Madeline Romero; [ed.] Central Classical Greek / Computers Unlimited Magnet High, American Institute of Business; [occ.] Bead Builder, Bridgestone-Firestone; [memb.] Business Management Association, American Heart Association, Who's Who Among American High School Students 1988-90; [oth. writ.] Just leisurely, but will be writing a book of poetry.; [pers.] As long as the Good Lord lets me live I will not let any type of negativity enter my life or stop me from succeeding.; [a.] Des Moines, IA

CLARK, W. DRURY
[pen.] Drury (DRU); [b.] August 10, 1913, Owensboro, KY; [p.] John and Annbell Clark; [m.] Katherin Meehan (Deceased), June 8, 1940; [ch.] Two; [ed.] Four Years of College Gmt. Teacher of Math night School Anderson, IN (War years); [occ.] Retired; [memb.] Elks; [hon.] GM Safety Director (Award) Guide Lamp Div Emc Pres. Gamm Mu Tau, GM School Pres, Senior Class 1940 GM Tech at Flint, MI; [oth. writ.] Letters to personal friends with a always a theme regarding a happening or a thanks for what they had given me "love, understanding" and help; [pers.] All men or

women create their own destinies, "They made me do it", applies to a greater authority (parents government, war); [a.] Kalamazoo, MI

CLARKE, MRS. KATE
[b.] 8 December 1940, Hinckley In., Leicestershire; [p.] George and Muriel Wormleighton (Deceased); [m.] David Anthony Clarke, 29 October 1960; [ch.] Sally and Nathan; [ed.] Secondary Modern Girls School, Vice Head Girl in final year; [occ.] Medical Secretary for 3 G.P. Practice for 15 yrs.; [oth. writ.] Several poems - none published; [pers.] I like to write about the emotions I feel and the funny side of human nature; [a.] Billericay, Essex, UK

CLENDENIN, JANET E.
[b.] June 7, 1931, Charleston, WV; [p.] Wilburt and Maudie Cavender; [m.] Kermit M. Clendenin, October 29, 1955; [ch.] Richard Wayne Clendenin; [ed.] High School and some College; [occ.] Retired Kindergarten Aide - Woodlawn/Sugar CK and Chandler Elem.; [memb.] Charleston Mountain Mission; [pers.] Sweet Sixteen was written for a very special (great nephew, Justin Underwood, for his sixteenth birthday.; [a.] Charleston, WV

CLICK, VIRGINIA
[b.] September 5, 1950, Kentucky; [m.] James Click Jr.; [ch.] 2 children, 2 step-children; [ed.] Clinton Central High School; [occ.] Business Office Manager, Sisters of St. Joseph, Tipton, IN; [memb.] Forest United Meth. Church; [pers.] Until now I have only written for family and friends, for birthdays, weddings, and other special occasions. My dream would be to write a song and have it recorded.; [a.] Forest, IN

CLINTON, SUZANNE
[b.] November 17, 1982, New Haven; [p.] DaLoyd and Anson Clinton; [ed.] Entering 8th grade September 1996 at Sacred Heart in Groton; [occ.] Student; [memb.] Christ The King Singers, National Honor Society, Student Council; [hon.] Principal's Award, student of the month; [pers.] I wrote this poem in honor of my brother's memory, Anson B. Clinton Jr. He was murdered 3/10/94. I strongly believe in the Kingdom of God.; [a.] Old Lyme, CT

CLISU, CONSTANTIN
[pen.] Constantin Clisu; [b.] October 14, 1931, Birlad, Romania; [p.] Iordache and Aneta Clisu; [m.] Ecaterina, January 20, 1951; [ch.] Corina and Nausicaa; [ed.] University of Bucharest - Romania; [occ.] Retired; [hon.] Prizes for poetry in Romania (1979, 1990), Italy (1965), Greece (1986); [oth. writ.] 8 volumes of prose and poetry published in Romania; [pers.] Based on the saying that "A poet is a world within one person", I try through my poetry, to make my fellow travelers better and wiser, and more sensitive. I strive to help them believe in truth and justice and friendship, in the sunrise, in the birds' song, in the green of the forest, in gentle rains that bring forth bountiful crops. I want them to feel, at each day's end, one step further along on their inner journey.; [a.] Edmonton, Alberta, Canada

COETZEE, MARTHA M.
[b.] April 8, 1953, Pretoria, South Africa; [p.] Willem J. Q. Ras, Susanna M. Ras; [m.] Felix Strumwasser, August 16, 1996; [ch.] Susanna Maria, Suzaraii Johanna; [ed.] Pretoria Gardens High, University of Pretoria (Medical School), College of Medicine of South Africa (Psychiatry); [occ.] Psychiatrist; [memb.] SAS Biological Psychiatrists, SA Pharmacological Society; [hon.] 1993 Travel Award in Neuro-Science (SA); [oth. writ.] Several poems in annuals, novel and self-help guide in preparation; [pers.] I strive to serve and love God and mankind.; [a.] Cape Cod, MA

COHEN, JENNIFER KRISTEN
[b.] December 31, 1984, Carmel, NY; [p.] Jill and Larry Cohen; [ed.] James Mastricola Elementary School; [occ.] Student; [memb.] Girl Scouts of America; [hon.] Citizenship Award James Mastricola Elementary School 1996; [pers.] I am eleven and one half years old, so I'd like to say you're never too young to write.

COHEN, RON
[pen.] Yanur Mulash; [b.] September 16, 1947, Cairo, Egypt; [p.] Nissim and Esther Cohen; [ch.] Yaron Cohen; [ed.] Fairfax High, A.A. Los Angeles City College, A.A. West Los Angeles College. B.A., M.A., U.C.L.A; [occ.] Judaic Studies Teacher L.A. Unified, Kadima Academy; [memb.] United Teacher's, Los Angeles; [hon.] Alpha Mu Gamma, Tau Alpha Epsilo, Benel Zion Gold Medal Award, Bible Champion of L.A. 1971, Dean's Honor List (5 times) graduated U.C.L.A. with Honors; [oth. writ.] Several poems published in local newspapers. I wrote the Couse Outline for L.A. Unified School District the teaching of Hebrew for Adult Education. Soon to be published Book "Beginner's Israel Hebrew for Adults"; [a.] Los Angeles, CA

COLBERT, DAMON RX
[pen.] Dx Holmez; [b.] May 10, 1976, San Diego, CA; [p.] Vemla Smittick and Titus N. Colbert; [occ.] Security Guard, AACE Security; [memb.] Nation Of Islam Muhammad Mosque #8 And FOI.; [oth. writ.] Had a poem published in the book full of poets called the Path Not Taken and another called poems of the 90's.; [a.] San Diego, CA

COLE, LAURENCE
[pen.] Laurence Cole; [b.] 16 January 1972, St. Albans, England; [p.] Mr. and Mrs. H. F. Cole; [ed.] Beechwood Park School, Aldengham School (both Hartfordshire, England) English BA Honours degree at University of York, England; [occ.] Rights Assistant, British Broadcasting Corporation (BBC); [oth. writ.] Nothing as yet published - one novel, about fifty poems.; [pers.] I enjoy using the beauty of nature to reflect emotions. Greatly influenced by early 20th century English poets, especially Rupert Brooke.; [a.] Milton Keynes, UK

COLEMAN, KEITH
[pen.] Kewe Benton; [b.] December 21, 1963, Texarkana, USA; [p.] Lester Coleman and Dorothy Traylor; [ch.] Keyon (5), Darion (2), Stormie (9); [ed.] Greenville High School, Metrocrest Med Services (E.M.T.); [occ.] (E.M.T.) Emergency Med Tech, Lab Aide, Med. Courier; [hon.] Military Vet (US) Interlochen Arts Academy Acceptee (1981); [oth. writ.] Quill books Harlingen, TX; [pers.] If we were ever in love before, there is nothing more than being with the person that shows so much love towards you. Love cannot be expressed in many words of lovers but it will be reminisce in your heart and mind for eternity.; [a.] Garland, TX

COLLETT, JULIA DIXON
[b.] September 3, 1923, St. Louis, MO; [p.] Irene Rives and Forney Dixon; [m.] Leslie, July 17, 1944; [ch.] Juleta, Stephen, Douglas, Melissa and Rosanne; [ed.] Normandy High Grad. 1941, Wash. U. Psychology Courses; [occ.] Retired Executive Sec.; [memb.] Assembly of God, International Society of Poets, St. Louis Genealogical Society; [hon.] National Library of Poetry Editor's Choice Award 1995. Famous Poet 1996- Famous Poets Society Hollywood, CA; [oth. writ.] Eulogy on Groundhog Day, Julia's Country Kitchen, Hershey Hugs, Co-dependency Release, Country Typewriter, Ozark Cookin, Orchid Blankey, True Co-dependent, Valentine Thoughts, My Valentine, in this Anthology; [pers.] Just completed manuscript for 300 page book: 'Co-dependency in verse and my way out.'; [a.] Saint Ann, MO

COLLIER JR., ULYSSES
[pen.] Cesar; [b.] January 15, 1959, Nashville, TN; [p.] Raymond and Joyce Jamar; [m.] Angela Jenee Collier, August 18, 1996; [ch.] Darius Atwaurn Baker; [ed.] J.O. Johnson High School; [occ.] Machine Operator at AUEX Electronics; [hon.] Wrestling; [oth. writ.] Stop the violence published in Famous poets Society Book; [pers.] My writings are about the worlds, everyday life.; [a.] Huntsville, AL

COLLINS, STEPHEN
[pen.] Heavenly Father, COL; [b.] May 14, 1965, Yeadon, PA; [p.] John and JoAnne Collins; [m.] Jesus Christ (My Confirmation), April 7, 1975; [ed.] Highland High (Auto Mechanics) presently Educating Myself, on a wide variety of subjects of interest, particularly - Religion.; [occ.] Carpenter, also posses other trades, not a jack of all trades-yet.; [memb.] Philadelphia Church of God; [hon.] Various Swimming honors and Awards, from age 6 to 18.; [oth. writ.] May other poems of various topics, long and short. Numerous lyrics for songs, especially "Makin Money" a rap song, that I believe will be a "Smash Hit" like no other, once released. Also, writing a Modern Day Bible, to unravel it's text.; [pers.] I live for the end, when righteousness rules Eternity, and oppression on mankind, through breed and power is destroyed forever, whereas peace, love and happiness, will be the way life.; [a.] Port Saint Lucie, FL

COLVIN, ANN C.
[b.] 7 June 1951, London; [ch.] Madeleine J., Jennifer L., James R.; [ed.] Meols Cop High School, Local Comprehensive, Southport Technical College Merseyside, England; [occ.] Self-employed cleaner/mothers help; [oth. writ.] Several poems written but nothing as yet submitted for possible publication.; [pers.] In wanting to relate my thoughts of a personal nature, I have learnt to express my emotional feelings in writing mainly romantic poetry, inspired by my fiance, Dave.; [a.] Southport, Merseyside, UK

CONANT, PHYLLIS
[pen.] Queen Angel of Philadelphia; [b.] March 26, 1920, Rives Junction, MI; [p.] Frank and Murle Brodock; [m.] Clarence "Pete" Conant, January 28, 1945; [ch.] Kim Rene Conant; [ed.] Graduated Concord High School in Concord, Michigan in 1938; [occ.] Retired from the Aero quip Corp. in Jackson, Michigan; [oth. writ.] "I Am That I Am" which is my first book and that is not yet published was dictated to me, The Angel of Philadelphia by the Holy Spirit. I have also written various works of poetry; [pers.] God numbered and predestined that I was to be the barren woman in Isaiah 54, The Queen in Matthew 12:42 and The Angel of Philadelphia in Revelation 3:7-13. Now I say to you: Peace is my star shining so bright. It comes from my soul where God is the light.; [a.] Horton, MI

CONCA JR., LOUIS F.
[pen.] Francis Sylvan; [b.] March 26, 1921, Providence, RI; [p.] Louis F. Sr. and Rose Marie (Both Deceased); [m.] Marguerite M. (Devitt) Conca, October 18, 1947; [ch.] Nancy Jean, Mary Lou, Stephen, Michael, James, Elizabeth and Thomas; [ed.] High School and Army Civil Service Schools, Active Air Force Military Schools (1942-1945), Oxford University Honorary Attendee (1945), Ministry Study (3 Yrs.), Army Air Force Communications Schools in New York, Wisconsin and California; [occ.] Retired from New England Division Corps of Engineers (33 yrs. Tenure), Administrative Officer.; [memb.] Leisure Learning Group, Knights of Columbus (former), Eucharistic Minister and Treasurer of Senior Citizens Group.; [hon.] Numerous outstanding performance awards from New England Division Corps of Engineers during 33 years tenure, Army Civilian Service Meritori-

ous Award (2nd Highest given by the Army to Civilians) and Editor's Choice Award for Poetry, 1996, awarded by The National Library of Poetry.; [oth. writ.] Numerous poems written and assembled in one volume (as yet, unpublished) also, am writing a novel (150 pages, unpublished); [pers.] Until submitting a number of poems to The National Library of Poetry, I've always written for my own pleasure. I have been greatly influenced in my writing by the master poets, namely, Shakespeare, Shelley, both browning Riley, Sandberg, etc; [a.] Providence, RI

CONLEY, JOAN
[b.] September 22, 1941, Melita, Manitoba, Canada; [p.] Jim Conley, Zetta Conley; [m.] Wayne Conley, March 5, 1960; [ch.] James Stanley Wayne (Deceased), Jeffrey Todd; [ed.] Jasper Place High School, Edmonton, Alberta, Canada - Senior Matriculation Degree; [memb.] Kamloops Family Historical Society, Aberdeen Hills Gulf Course; [oth. writ.] Poems published in The Compassionate Friends Newsletter, (for Bereaved Parents), poem published in Kamloops Daily News; [pers.] Seven years after the sudden death of my oldest son, Jim, I began writing poems. These written words have helped me express feelings I had suppressed for all those years.; [a.] Kamloops, British Columbia, Canada

CONLEY, NANCY L.
[b.] September 21, 1951, Silver City, NM; [p.] David and Betty Miller; [m.] Michael Conley, August 12, 1971; [ch.] Tracy Conley; [pers.] Upon the death of my father, we made a discovery of amethyst rocks at his grave sight. I took a piece and had a necklace made for my mother. I wrote "He Is Our Rock" so my mother had thoughts of the necklace other than a rock from my father's grave.; [a.] Tampa, FL

COOPER, JAMES E.
[b.] June 27, 1935, Hamilton, ON, Canada; [ed.] Journalism degree from Ryerson University, Toronto, graduate working communication at Michigan State University, East Lansing, MI; [occ.] Retired (Between stays in mental hospitals, have worked in journalism public relations, college teaching, wrecking buildings, washing dishes, etc. in Toronto, Montreal, Halifax, Thunder Bay etc.; [hon.] Maclean Hunter Gold Watch for excellence in journalism, Cliff Peters Memorial Award as best editorial writer; [oth. writ.] Autobiographical novel Far From Feeling Sorry published in Montreal, many poems published in Canada and U.S. including Dalhousie Review and Antigonish Review, manifesto published in Iconomatrix; [pers.] Dedicated to writing to combat the stigma attached to schizophrenia.; [a.] Calgary, Alberta, Canada

COOPWOOD, KEN
[pen.] Ken Blulicious; [b.] December 29, 1964, Gary, IN; [p.] Theodore and Emily Coopwood; [ed.] B.S. Business Administration M.P.A. Public Administration, Phd Candidate for Education Administration; [occ.] Asst. Director of African American Cultural Center Ind. State Univ.; [memb.] Phi Beta Sigma Frat, Inc. Pi Sigma Alpha Nat'l Honor Society Alpha Kappa Psi Prof Business Frat Ind. Coalition of Blacks in Higher Education; [hon.] Big Brothers Big sister Volunteer of the year project mentor volunteer of the year. President of ICBNE - ISU Chapter; [oth. writ.] Song - down for your love poem - what happens when I think; [pers.] In a nation where speculations of money, health, poverty and policy rank supreme in the conscience of the public and mind, the most tragic and destructive display of human judgement is still that which conceals the absolute truth of a people.; [a.] Terre Haute, IN

CORCORAN, JOE
[b.] May 17, 1957, Wilmington, DE; [p.] Frank and Patricia Corcoran; [m.] Carla Corcoran, May 28, 1987; [ch.] Jennifer Erin, Kevin Connor; [ed.] Master of Arts in Public Communication, CSU Chico; [occ.] Communication Instructor, Santa Rosa Junior College; [oth. writ.] Walden Three, Colors of The Wasteland, An Introduction to Nonpolicy Debate; [pers.] The only muse worth invoking is the Holy Spirit of God. As my title for my unpublished book of poetry might indicate, T.S. Eliot is my inspiration.; [a.] Windsor, CA

CORONADO, CARMEN D.
[b.] Dominican Republic; [p.] Altagracia Suriel and Domingo Coronado; [m.] Justo Soriano; [ch.] Lourdes Karenina and Hansel; [ed.] Bachelors in School Counseling and School Psychology, Master's Degrees in Adult Education and School Counseling; [occ.] Guidance Counselor, PS 156, The Bronx, New York City; [memb.] His panic Educator's Association American Counselor's Association; [oth. writ.] Adventure Roads (Poetry) Enchanting Stories Forest Land (Stories) Color Land (Stories) Human Relations (Essay) Interiors (Poetry); [pers.] I pursue to foster happiness and love to Nature and family in my writing. I have been influenced by Juan Ramon Jimenez, Gabriela Mistral, Pablo, Neruda and Salome Urena.; [a.] Yonkers, NY

COSSITT-BENNETT, CANDICE
[pen.] Candice Cossitt-Bennett; [b.] November 9, 1947, Oakville, Ontario; [p.] Gerald and Audrey Cossitt; [m.] William L. C. Bennett, March 10, 1979; [ch.] Zara Bennett - 22, Cam (Deceased); [ed.] Grade 10 - Thomas A. Blakelock, Oakville, Ont. (1963) Legal Administrative Assistant Toronto School of Business (1994/95); [occ.] Writer; [memb.] Anglican Church; [hon.] Student-of-the-Year, Legal Secretary 1994/95; [oth. writ.] Poetry, short stories for children (Aspiring); [pers.] Life is a learning experience and as long as we keep learning and growing we feel alive. I like to share my experience through writing.; [a.] Toronto, Ontario, Canada

COZART, H. THAYNE
[b.] January 30, 1943, Kansas City, MO; [p.] Harry and Ida Cozart; [m.] Sharon A. Cozart, August 16, 1964; [ch.] Amy and Shanna; [ed.] B.S. Agricultural Journalism, Kansas State University, 1964, M.S. Journalism Management, Oklahoma State University, 1967; [occ.] Director of Marketing and Communications Agri-One-The Internet Ag Marketing Co.; [memb.] National Organization for Raw Materials; [hon.] American Soybean Associations Communicator of the Year, Association of Ag Communicators in Education Communicator of the Year, Honorary American Former from the Future Farmers of America; [oth. writ.] Poem's title "Soul Senses". Here written a syndicated rural humor column, weekly, titled "Viewing The Field by Milo Yield" also a column titled "Laugh Tracks in the Dust"; [pers.] I am personally moved by the beauty of rural landscapes and by the dignity and character of farmers, ranchers, and the citizens of small rural communities. Our highly urbanized citizens need constant reminding of their connection to the land for food and fibers.; [a.] Madrid, IA

CRABTREE, JENNIFER
[pen.] Jennifer C.; [b.] June 15, 1965, Meridian, MS; [p.] Bidwell Land, Mary Carney; [m.] Thomas J. Crabtree, October 1, 1992; [ch.] Michael Conley, Kevin Conley; [occ.] Wal-Mart Garden Center Mgr.; [oth. writ.] This is my first published work.; [pers.] The mind carries us away, the heart brings us the joy, the passion makes it worthwhile, and the soul makes it all eternal.; [a.] Melbourne, FL

CRAIG, RUTH R.
[b.] March 13, 1920, Dallas, TX; [m.] Wesley P. Craig, July 11, 1943; [ch.] Claudia Baughman, Lynnea Dunn, Diane Herrera; [ed.] B.A. Univ. of California, Berkeley; [occ.] Artist; [memb.] Nat. Assoc. Pen Women, AAUW, Artists Round Table, DAR, TROA Silver Singers; [hon.] Second in only other contest I have entered; [pers.] Since my poetry has arisen from deep emotional feelings and need, I have rarely shown it to anyone until now, as it has revealed too much about my life, but as it is now past and I can view it with critical equanimity.

CRANDDENT, YANDHI T.
[pen.] Yandhi T. Cranddent; [b.] November 20, 1964, Copenhagen, Denmark; [ed.] Vishal Arts/ Commercial and Business Management (1986) studied at "Algonquin College", Ottawa, Ont. Canada; [occ.] Full time clerk in retail business; [memb.] H.F.C.W/Canada Local 175, United Food Commercial Workers Union of Canada, P.R.O. Canada - Socan; [hon.] High school honor diploma, "Editor's Choice Award" from National Library of Poetry in '94-'95-'96; [oth. writ.] Wrote songs, available through PRO/Canada for copies of lead sheets, wrote many poems, published by "National Library of Poetry" "Sparkles in the Sand", "Beneath The Harvest Moon", "The Ebbing Tide", "Day - Break On The Land"; [pers.] Road to success always under construction! Always believe in your dream, hard work, determination, set you goal, don't pretend to be someone you're not. Always have a lot of love to share!; [a.] Ottawa, Ontario, Canada

CRAVEN, RUE ANN W.
[pen.] Rue Ann W. Craven; [b.] January 17, 1932, Cushing, OK; [p.] Rulon W. and Minnie Schick Winter; [m.] C. Richard Craven (Dick), February 11, 1954, (Div. September 12, 1995 - He went the way of the world); [ch.] Debbie, Rick, Janie; [ed.] American Fork High Brigham Young University; [occ.] Elem. School Teacher, (26 yrs.) 3 yrs. 2nd grade, until opening in Kindergarten. Major: Elem. Ed and Minor in art. Kindergarten Proficiency also.; [occ.] I retired from school last June 1994. I am still busy writing for people, poems, tributes, stories, special celebration poems, anniversaries, poems, tributes, stories, special celebration poems, anniversaries, working on my home, which really needed some upgrading, working in my yard, which I dearly love, tending my darling grandchildren, family get-together's made. Church jobs, and charity work for my L.D.S. Church, helping families with yards, and homes, and in general busier now that I was for my 24 hours a day when teaching. But...better busy than bored, which I have never had the privilege of being. I love life, and enjoy helping others to do so.; [memb.] Delta Kappa Gamma, NEA, UEA, AEA. American Heart Assoc.; [hon.] Sang in Double Trio for many years, in school and out, and won many honors throughout our county. Honored by school, along with five principals I worked under for my School Pep song, I wrote the music and words for. "Westmore Wildcats". I received a plaque and Honorable mention certificate for my poem, "Smile" from the National Library of Poetry in 1994. I have since them made it into a book mark, which has sold extensively in bookstores.; [oth. writ.] I have been writing poetry all my life, and dedications, retirement poems, tributes, and really do enjoy the challenge. I intend to one day, put all my poems etc, into a book for each of my children and grandchildren; [pers.] I love life, and love doing for others. I always try to look for the best in everyone and everything. My mother always taught me to seek beauty in all things. I have tried to do the same with my children. Life is what you make of it. I enjoy trying to help my fellowman.; [a.] Provo, UT

CRISP, WILLIE MAE
[b.] November 6, 1935, Reidsville, NC; [p.] Mr. and Mrs. William McGee; [ch.] John and Joseph Crisp; [ed.] High School and Some College; [occ.] Private Cleaning Service an Holiday Inn Salad Tech; [memb.] American Red Cross; [hon.] Awards for Church Leadership and participation.; [oth. writ.] I have written poems and some plays for church I tried to write a small book also.; [pers.] Some of my inner thoughts can best be spoken in writing.; [a.] Reidsville, NC

CROMWELL, RUDI
[b.] March 26, 1973, Collingwood, Ontario, Canada; [p.] Pat Cromwell and Jr. Cromwell; [ed.] Grade 12 graduate, currently in 2nd year of a three year Graphic Design Course at George Brown College; [memb.] Humane Society, Foster Parents Plan, Canadian Geographical Society; [pers.] The only way to really live life is to experience everything possible and then some. I try to do this and convey my experiences through my writing.; [a.] Collingwood, Ontario, Canada

CRONK, JAMES D.
[pen.] Free Lee; [b.] September 13, 1963, Winnipeg, MB, Canada; [p.] Mary Hellen Cronk, adopted mother Florence Hunt; [ed.] Grade 12 Tec-Voc High School; [occ.] Self Employed (Shielded Butterfly Ent); [memb.] A distinguished member (The International Society of Poets); [hon.] A distinguished member of the International Society of Poets, Editor's Choice Award 1995 from National Library of Poetry; [oth. writ.] People are People (The Path not Taken), Dawn the Break of Day (The Ebbing Tide), The Past (Day Break on the Land); [pers.] Four year from the beginning of the new century! Peace among all people soon to be here! We must all P; [a.] Winnipeg, Manitoba, Canada

CROUSE, MICHAEL SHAWN
[pen.] Mr. Brownstone; [b.] June 22, 1973, Richlands, VA; [p.] Arbutus and John Henry Crouse; [ed.] Grundy Senior High, Southwest Virginia Community College, North American School of Gun Repair; [occ.] Musician; [memb.] National Rifle Association, North American Hunting Club, Dismal River Hunt Club; [oth. writ.] Small pieces for local papers; [pers.] Poems, music and art in general are the highest forms of emotion. For the most part I am a dark, moody person, and I suppose my work reflects this.; [a.] Grundy, VA

CUTLER, R. B.
[b.] November 8, 1913, Dover, MA; [ed.] Noble and Greenough School, '31, Harvard AB '35, M Arch. '39; [occ.] Assassinologist; [memb.] The Conspiracy Museum, Director; [oth. writ.] Grassy Knoll Gazette, alias Oswald, Explo 007, The Umbrella Man, Evidence of Conspiracy, Goodnight, Mr. Callabash; [pers.] The Conspiracy's Coup d'Etat in Dallas has run its course, Ahimsa.; [a.] Beverly Farms, MA

D'ANTONO, LEA
[b.] July 25, 1975, Montreal, Province of Quebec; [p.] Leo and Cira D'Antono; [ed.] DEC Commerce Danson College Concordia University- Economics Certificate of Excellence -Picai Diploma of the Italian language and culture -P.I.C.A.I.; [occ.] Administrative assistant; [hon.] Public speaking track and field; [pers.] I like to words to describe situations we all have to face.; [a.] Montreal, Province of Quebec, Canada

D'SOUZA, GLEN
[b.] May 23, 1972, Kuwait, Middle East; [p.] Joachim and Philomena D'Souza; [ed.] Don Bosco Secondary, York University; [occ.] Student; [oth. writ.] Fantasy or Reality (song) and other short poems.; [pers.] This poem is dedicated to S.B. you will always be in my heart.; [a.] Toronto, Ontario, Canada

DAHL-AUDZISS, PATRICIA
[b.] July 2, 1955, Vancouver, BC; [occ.] Retired; [oth. writ.] Previous poems published in a newsletter as well as "The National Library Of Poetry". Future prospects await with publication of my own books of poetry.; [pers.] There is no greater purpose to life then to fulfill ones dreams and share the wisdom gained deep within our souls. To be remembered for what we gave for those yet to follow. Stay connected to your inner self. God Bless.; [a.] Coquitlam, British Columbia, Canada

DALE, CLOIE CAUDILL
[b.] November 11, 1924, Lothair, KY; [p.] Anna Morgan Caudill and Ervin Caudill (Deceased); [m.] Homer Dale Jr., April 6, 1946; [ch.] Sherryl Anne Shelton and Teresa Elaine Degelmann, Six Grandchildren Cloie is from a large family of eight and one of six girls; [ed.] Marion High School - Marion, Indiana Chicago School of Interior Decoration; [occ.] Retired to Venice, Fl. in 1993; [hon.] We were Mr. and Mrs. Bicentinial in 1976 in Anderson, Indiana and celebrating our 50th Anniversary this year in Venice, Florida-1996; [oth. writ.] Have written many short poems and writings over the years, but never tried to published any.; [pers.] I started writing poems after my daughter were born - such miracles- I hold them dear to my heart also have written two memorials-have written songs to my grandchildren; [a.] Venice, FL

DALTON, EVE
[b.] February 10, 1958, Dayton, OH; [p.] Elmer Madden, Ruth S. Madden; [m.] Roy C. Dalton, July 31, 1978; [ch.] Valerie Elizabeth, Monica Faye; [ed.] Carlisle High, Kettering College of Medical Arts; [hon.] National Honor Society; [pers.] I dedicate my poem, "Do You Know Me?" To my late father, Elmer Madden, who shaped my life in many positive ways.; [a.] Franklin, OH

DALUEG, RON J.
[b.] December 24, 1964, Edmonton, Alberta, Canada; [p.] Don and Merna Dalueg; [ed.] Queen Elizabeth High, University of Alberta (B. Sc.); [occ.] Scientific Researcher, Construction Assistant; [oth. writ.] "Poetry in Motion", some personal birthday and greeting cards.; [pers.] I try to write with my heart and soul while using my words to spark a little honest thought.; [a.] Edmonton, Alberta, Canada

DANIEL, BEATRICE M.
[b.] October 8, 1914, Dinwiddie, VA; [p.] Rufus Lafayette and Florence Clark Matthews; [m.] Rufus Carlton Daniel Sr., December 25, 1935; [ch.] Ellen, Peggy, Ruth, Nell, Susan, Rufus Jr.; [ed.] Dabney High School 1932; [occ.] Retired Clothing Buyer for Belks Department Stores; [memb.] Carey Baptist Church; [hon.] Salutatorian 1932 Class; [pers.] I appreciate God's blessings in my life and I love everyone.; [a.] Henderson, NC

DANSBY-GLES, GLORIA F.
[ed.] B.A., M.A., Ed.D., Licensed Professional Counselor, National Certified Counselor, National Certified School Counselor, National Certified Career Counselor; [occ.] College Professor; [memb.] American Counseling Assn., American School Counselor Assn., American Mental Health Counselor Assn., Mississippi Counseling Assn., President - Mississippi School Counselor Assn.; [hon.] 1993 - Teacher of the Year - Jackson State Univ. School of Education; [oth. writ.] This is my first poem submitted for publication. I have primarily written for professional counseling publications.; [pers.] I am interested in assisting in the growth and development of each individual.; [a.] Jackson, MS

DANT, MICHAEL J.
[pen.] Mike Dant; [b.] May 19, 1970, Louisvile, KY; [p.] Raymond and Beverly Dant; [ed.] St. Xavier High School, University of Louisville, College of Business and Public Administration Finance Degree; [occ.] Personal Trust Assistant/ Business Owner (3 Businesses); [memb.] New York Institute of Photography, International Freelance Photographers Organization; [pers.] I strive to live life to the fullest extent, and believing in one's dream is all that is needed to be successful. Never give up in the face of adversity.; [a.] Louisville, KY

DAVENPORT, LONNAL
[pen.] Leonnie Davenport, The Poet Prophet; [b.] October 6, 1949, McMinnville, TN; [p.] James and Florence Davenport; [ch.] Crystal Dawn Davenport; [ed.] Public Education, GED and Masters degree (from my Lord and Master Jesus Christ) from the school of the streets; [occ.] Prisoner, revolutionary and prophet (inspired poet); [memb.] In the family of man; [hon.] Gold and Silver Poet Awards from world of poetry and publication in poetry contest in South Bond (Indiana) Tribune Newspaper; [oth. writ.] Collection of 177 poems in unpublished back entitled "The Mystery of Life Unraveled" copy right number TXU708-152 Library of Congress; [pers.] Lonnal is a street poet and used to travel the tourist circuit meeting people from every corner of the nation and sharing his poems of peace and love with them. In New Orleans, LA. he was known by the artist community and street people as the poet of the French Quarters.; [a.] Michigan City, IN

DAVIDOWICZ, JOYCE
[b.] April 22, 1959, Baltimore, MD; [p.] Mildred and Henry Davidowicz; [occ.] Aspiring poet; [hon.] Poet of the Year, 1988; [oth. writ.] Several poems published in several anthologies.; [pers.] May we breath clean air always.; [a.] Crisfield, MD

DAVIDSON, DALE
[b.] April 11, 1943, Melfort, Saskatchewan, Canada; [p.] Herb and Mary Davidson; [m.] Barbara Ann Davidson, April 30, 1971; [ch.] Sandra and Shawn; [ed.] Grade 11; [occ.] Chef, Retired; [oth. writ.] Short stories, unpublished.; [pers.] "People helping people".; [a.] Surrey, British Columbia, Canada

DAVIS, MELANIE ADELE
[b.] November 30, 1958, Charlotte, NC; [p.] Pat and Lee Kennedy; [ed.] B.A. Political Science, East Carolina University, M.A Social and Emotional, Disturbances - University of Northern Colorado; [occ.] Recently retired Special Ed. Teacher, Advocate for persons with disabilities; [hon.] 1996 Olympic Community Hero Torchbearer, Greeley, Co.; [oth. writ.] "From Where I Sit", regular column for center on disability and deafness newsletter, various poems, including "In Memory Of Diet Rich Bonhoeffer".; [pers.] I have always viewed my writing ability as a gift from Jesus Christ for myself and for others. I hope my writing bears witness to the love I've been given and to the love I hope to give.; [a.] Greeley, CO

DAVIS, NICOLE ANTOINETTE
[pen.] Nikki D.; [b.] October 31, 1976, Long Branch, NJ; [p.] Yvonne Davis and Carrie Ritchie; [ed.] Mount Carmel Holy Rosary School in New York (Elementary School) also Calvin Coolidge Senior High School in D.C.; [occ.] Babysitter at home; [memb.] Teachers Profession Program Step Club (TPP) and The Writers Workshop; [oth. writ.] Poems written for School and honored for my writings and a poem in the papers.; [pers.] I want people to know my thoughts and to get a since of other people writings.; [a.] Washington, DC

DAVIS, RENEE
[b.] November 26, 1980, Saint Louis Park, MN; [p.] Marge Davis, Willie Davis; [ch.] Ryane Davis, Eric Minea, Charles Minea; [ed.] Roosevelt High School 9th grader; [occ.] Babysit; [oth. writ.] My poem about a friend I lost, was put on a plaque and was on showcase at my middle school, also had one poem published in school yearbook.; [pers.] When I write poems, I don't write about what I see, I write about what I know. Poets, like Iangston Hughes, Maya Angolou, influenced me to do something I am best at and that is poetry.; [a.] Minneapolis, MN

DAVIS, RON
[b.] January 12, 1979, Bremerton, WA; [p.] Mark and Karen Davis; [ed.] High School; [occ.] Construction - (Weekends and summers); [memb.] High School Football and, Baseball teams, Natural helpers program; [hon.] Baseball all star team seven years.; [oth. writ.] Poems published in School newspapers, and many songs for my band.; [pers.] Whenever you get the chance to do something - no matter what it is do it!.... You'll always regret it if you don't.; [a.] Bremerton, WA

DAVIS, SEIJA
[b.] April 24, 1966, Heinola, Finland; [p.] Aini M. Taberman - Marvin W. Davis Jr.; [occ.] Computer Technician at Level Computers, Fullerton, CA; [oth. writ.] "Firestorm 1993" published in "Straight Streams" volume 90 (magazine for L.A. Country F.D.) I have 3 books full of poetry since 1984, and currently I am working on a 4th.; [pers.] I am inspired by tragedy with the intent to search out the positive. I believe all negative has a positive message which in turn creates a positive result.; [a.] Garden Grove, CA

DAY, STEPHEN
[pen.] Philip Mundane; [b.] June 6, 1939, France; [p.] Archibald Day, Alice Mondain; [m.] Margaret Cooper, June 6, 1964; [ch.] Marion, Allan; [ed.] B.A., M.A. (Canada) Doctorate France, Teaching Certificates in Canada and France, Queen's, Toronto, Dijon.; [occ.] Associate Professor, French Studies, Translator, TV Educational Programs in English and French.; [oth. writ.] Poems and short stories, children's stories, in progress: "A Book Of Beasties", "More Beasties", "Beasties Galore" (inspired by my daughter in the poem "Negotiations"). Academic books and articles, mostly on French language and literature.; [pers.] Enjoying giving and receiving wonderment in all forms of thought and language; [a.] Kingston, Ontario, Canada

DE ANGELIS, ANN
[b.] July 26, 1930, Pittsburgh, PA; [m.] May 8, 1952; [ch.] Mark, David and Paul; [ed.] St. John the Baptist H.S., Cheerleader, some college courses at CCAC; [occ.] Nurses Aide, taking care of sick elderly for 25 yrs.; [memb.] Franciscan Associate since 1992. St. Joan of Arc Member; [oth. writ.] Five short stories.; [pers.] I was inspired from within a feeling of inner peace and happiness.; [a.] Finleyville, PA

DE CAMBRA, HILARY
[b.] June 2, 1935, New Amsterdam Berbice, British Guiana; [m.] Maureen Ann De Cambra, July 2, 1994; [ed.] St. Stanislaus College, Georgetown, British Guiana, West Indies; [occ.] Desktop Publisher; [memb.] St. Anne De Beaupre; [oth. writ.] "Random Thoughts About Intangible Things" (Unpublished); [pers.] My credo. I believe in: - The equality of man, - The sanctity of human life and the immortality of the soul without this, I am nothing with it, I am immune to harm.; [a.] Brampton, Ontario, Canada

DE GASPAR, EMMY NIELSEN REYES
[b.] La Paz, Bolivia; [p.] Friedrich Nielsen, Sara Reyes Nielsen; [m.] Dr. Victor Gaspar, January 15, 1949; [ed.] Deutsche Realschule, La Paz, Lette Verein Institute and Staats Kunstakademie, Berlin. Continuous studies in various Europian countries, also Literature and Philosophy.; [occ.] Painter, Fine and Decorative Art. I decorated residences in Paris and New York; [oth. writ.] Poems and essays. Two books Moral Beauty and a biography in Spanish Federico Nielsen Reyes, Intellectual great patriot, diplomat. Subtitle: "Memories Of His Sister".; [pers.] I consider a priority in our lives the necessity of developing our faculties - the power of the mind and the sensitivity of the heart - to attain, in despite our frailties, the dignity that demands to be human beings created by God.; [a.] New York, NY

DE LACERDA, EDUARDO G.
[b.] November 27, 1929, Azores, Port.; [p.] Jose and Maria; [m.] Fernanda, November 12, 1960; [ch.] Edward; [ed.] Elementary - Portugal; [occ.] Retired from Pan Am Airways; [memb.] Poetry Vortex Wilmington, DE National Geographic Society Washington; [hon.] A grant from the government of the Azores to publish my book "Ecosdasaudade" 1994; [oth. writ.] Publish 30 poems in the Portuguese Times New Bedford, Mass. continued to write.; [pers.] A veteran of the US Army - 1951-1953, Nato Democrat; [a.] Wilmington, DE

DE LAND, CHARLES A.
[b.] July 22, 1926, Livingston Co., MI; [p.] Orlo E. and Ethel E. De Land; [m.] Louanna M. (Seavolt) De Land, May 31, 1947; [ch.] Charlene McKenna, Theda O. (Deceased); [ed.] Sunfield High School, General Motors Institute; [occ.] Retired Gen. Mot.; [memb.] Oldsmobile Exc. Club, Charlotte Assembly of God, Adult Bible Class Supt.; [oth. writ.] Several poems in local newspapers and newsletters - 1 book entitled "To God Be The Glory" containing 53 poems.; [pers.] Started writing poetry in second or third grade, then got away from it after marriage until in Oct. 1981 I accepted Jesus Christ as my Lord and Saviour and He immediately renewed my love for poetry, since then God reestablished my talent for His Glory.; [a.] Sunfield, MI

DE MARCO, THEODORE L.
[pen.] Theodore L. De Marco; [b.] June 4, 1923, Philadelphia, PA; [p.] Alberico and Irene De Marco; [m.] Gloria De Marco, June 1, 1946; [ch.] Theodore, Ronald, Dennis; [ed.] Graduated Ben Franklin Vet, H.S. Charles Morris Price School of Adv. and Journalism (Life Insurance School 2 years), (General Motor Sales 2 years), Customer Service Rep for Post Office School), Bethesda MD for 4 years; [occ.] Retired from US Post Office; [memb.] Over brook IAD Club hole in one club. National Post Service Union Branch 35. Marlyn golf Club. Phila. Boxers Association; [hon.] President of Special Delivery Messengers Union of the A.P.W.U. Secretary of the welfare fund U.S. Post Office Recipient of Variety Club Award and Darby, PA. Lans Doune Rotary Club Award. US Postal Service Special Achievement Associate Editor of American Postal Worker Union Paper. (Phila. PA); [oth. writ.] Five stories that have not been submitted for publication and about 100 other poems.; [pers.] When I wrote the gift of blood I watched a blood mobile of the red cross taking blood. I felt very badly because I ad contracted malaria and was unable to give, so I wrote the poem.; [a.] Philadelphia, PA

DEER, MARGARET C.
[b.] April 2, 1921, Harrisburg, PA; [p.] Peter and Annie Christmas; [m.] Widow; [ch.] Daughter: Mardeen Olmstead, grandchildren Jeff 20, Ann 18; [ed.] William Penn High School; [occ.] Retired;

[memb.] Poetry Society of OK; [hon.] HOnorable Mention in Poetry Society of OK, "My Grand-daughter."; [oth. writ.] Now You Are 21, "Dreamer's Journey" Poetry Society of OK, Honorable Mention in OK Society of Poets "Last Love", The Rainbows End; [a.] Tulsa, OK

DELANEY, ELAINE PATRICIA
[b.] 11 September 1945, Pambula, NSW, Australia; [p.] Ruby Ellen Roberts; [m.] Michael Delaney, 17 April 1965; [ch.] Three; [ed.] High School Certificate Business Course Certificate (Shorthand/typing, administration); [occ.] Home duties, casual receptionist/typist; [memb.] Faw (ACT) - fellowship of Australian Writers (ACT), NBPA (National Bush Poets Association) Wildcare Queanbeyan Inc. Cultural Centre Queanbeyan (CCQ); [oth. writ.] Numerous poems published regularly in local newspapers, Radio broadcasts a poem published in National Poetry book - 'Road to Reality' 1995. Articles in newspapers, faw (ACT) magazine ABPA Magazine, Canberra writers centre letter.; [pers.] My heart 'home' belongs to the Australian Bush and empathy with the land, its people and all her inhabitants. My writings spring from inspiration and emotion's stirred by things seen and felt, rather than a knowledge gained by intellect of even education.; [a.] Queanbeyan, New South Wales, Australia

DELANEY, ROBERT
[b.] August 7, 1961, New Orleans, LA; [p.] Margaret Delaney; [ed.] Educating myself; [occ.] Striving poet; [oth. writ.] Poems published in 4 poetry anthologies and local newspapers.; [pers.] I am highly influenced by my lovable deceased mother, whom spirit lives within me daily.

DENNIS, ERLINE
[b.] May 8, 1953, Bridgeport, CT; [p.] Adgie and Bertha Dennis; [ch.] Shanté R. Randall; [ed.] Warren Harding High School, Bridgeport, CT; University of Bridgeport, Bachelor's Degree - Business and Humanities; [occ.] Single Mom - work a full-time job; [memb.] Member of Messiah Baptist Church - Bridgeport, CT; [oth. writ.] Wrote my very first poem 11/23/95 - "A Message to My Sister from Heart to Heart" - have written about 30 poems since that date; [pers.] I thank God Almighty for allowing me to write. If my poetry can touch someone's heart or soul then I know I have done my job. And thanks to my dear friend who has been a great inspiration for me.; [a.] Bridgeport, CT

DERYNCK, TRACY
[b.] April 5, 1978, Calgary, Alberta; [p.] Bea Derynck, Paul Derynck; [ed.] Queen Elizabeth High (Advanced Diploma with Excellence), entering the University of Calgary; [occ.] Student at the University of Calgary; [hon.] Alexander Rutherford Scholarship, various awards for achievement in art, band and several academic subjects; [oth. writ.] Two letters and one essay published in "The Calgary Herald". Working on several novels.; [pers.] I use my writing to explore an individual's experience with darkness and personal demons. It is my belief that one must understand and compromise with the darkness within before one can mature.; [a.] Calgary, Alberta, Canada

DHAEMERS, MARK NEAL
[pen.] M. Dhaemers; [b.] September 5, 1972, Davenport, IA; [p.] Mark R. Dhaemers, Laura Lee Irwin; [ed.] Graduate of Lost Nation Comm. School, Current Freshman at Leeward Comm. College; [occ.] Student; [oth. writ.] Currently working on a collection of poems to be "hopefully" published as a book entitled, poetry 2 Appease The Minds; [pers.] The beauty of "home" is always close to hand as well as heart.; [a.] Pearl City, HI

DICK, JOHN ELDER
[b.] June 4, 1939, Providence, RI; [p.] Bowman and Sarah; [ed.] Ed.B. Ma, LCT; [occ.] Retired English Teacher; [memb.] Narrow River Preservation Hospice; [oth. writ.] Short stories, local historical sketches, poetry, history pamphlets, churches; [pers.] Nature lover, live on unique estvarine sanctuary, (Pettaquamscuit River) awed by nature and man's fleeting moment devort and go-eatholic; [a.] Wakefield, RI

DICKENS, MARY B.
[b.] April 25, 1942, Bascom, FL; [p.] C. E. and Inez T. Boone; [m.] Jimmie Dickens, June 17, 1966; [ch.] Kenny, Gina; [ed.] Malone High, Chipola Jr. College; [occ.] Accountant; [oth. writ.] I have written poems for several years only as a hobby; [pers.] I have been influenced by childhood experiences and poets of the Romantic and Victorian Periods; [a.] Bascom, FL

DICKENSON, MARIA
[b.] October 16, 1974; [p.] Raffaele Pane, Lucie Coiefyr; [m.] Widow, July 19, 1947; [ch.] One boy; [ed.] M. Superior in Stage and Classic Course of Celtousbell I'm on war 13 died, married in Wis. lived in the wildness, five years.; [occ.] Exformer wife; [hon.] I wrote composition in stug has published in local paper in Sheldon Wis. in NY. I been writing song in foreign language, some in English.; [oth. writ.] I published my self a book in 1992, title Mipote Oli fuencesco Souchi's Nitti. I translated myself in English, "The nephew of Franci's and his love; [pers.] I write at Columbia University 6 months, grammar and composition. I did because I love to express myself and communicate. T'is has been the old man of my life.; [a.] New York, NY

DIEL, MARGUERITE
[b.] January 18, 1927, Buena Vista, TN; [occ.] Homemaker and Baby setter; [hon.] I was Salutatorian of 8th Grade Class. I am a member of "Good Hope Baptist Church"; [oth. writ.] My book is published entitled "Poetry That Tells Of God's Love For The World"; [a.] Paducah, KY

DILL, EDNA
[pen.] Swan; [b.] January 13, 1946, Greenville, GA; [p.] Levon and Roena Skinner; [m.] Dwain Miller, October 12, 1995; [ch.] Britt Shuman; [ed.] Richmond Hill High, Augusta College, Savannah Univ. of Cometology; [occ.] Retired; [memb.] Beta Club; [oth. writ.] The Adventures of Puppy Jo, many songs, poems and short stories; [pers.] With pen in hand I travel to the reach of my imagination and hopefully touch a heart.; [a.] Ludowici, GA

DILTZ, ELIZABETH C.
[pen.] Elizabeth; [b.] December 27, 1984, Frankfurt, Frg; [p.] Michael and Ellen Diltz; [ed.] 6th grade; [occ.] Student, Terrell Intermediate School; [memb.] A.I.M., D.A.R.E., Yearbook staff honor choir, Band, UIL, Awana S.; [hon.] A honor roll, 4th place UIL; [oth. writ.] Poetry, stories, musical lyrics - "The ghost in the barn", "Purple", "Helen", "Love", "My Angel", "Ring of Endless Night", "Your Home", "Blue", "Chocdate, Chocolate, Chocolate", "Everything will be alright" etc.; [pers.] When I write, I let my imagination run free. I have loved to write, since I was a small child, and find it very peaceful and relaxing.; [a.] Terrell, TX

DINESEN, BECKY L.
[pen.] Becky Dinesen; [b.] August 16, 1969, Vancouver, BC, Canada; [p.] Mr. and Mrs. Frank and Lorraine Dinesen; [m.] Jeffrey John Wick, June 15, 1996; [ed.] Diploma of Biotechnology, BSC. Biology from U.B.C. (University of British Columbia); [pers.] Below the gold embossed roses, on our wedding invitations, is the poems I wrote to my fiance to express my love and understanding of our relationship.

DINH, ANDREW A.
[b.] June 2, 1972, South Vietnam; [p.] Dr. and Mrs. Anthony Dinh; [ed.] B.S. Wake Forest University; [occ.] Student, Ski Instructor, Tennis instructor; [hon.] Presidential Leadership Conference, Wake Forest University 1993; [pers.] Life is full of interruption. Focus!; [a.] Beckley, WV

DINNALL-STEWART, ELAINE
[pen.] "Epiphany"; [b.] Jamaica, WI; [p.] Charles Dinnall and Leah Adams; [ed.] Dunrobin High, Kingston, Jamaica, Nursing Diploma from University College Hospital Kingston, Jamaica; [occ.] Peri Natal Nurse. San Bernardino Medical Centre. RN 22 years in various ares including medical/surgical, psychiatry, pediatrics and ophthalmology; [hon.] Diamond Homer Trophy - 1996 from Famo Poets Soceity for "Place of Grace" my first submitted piece.; [oth. writ.] I write daily to date over three hundred title poems plus two children gift books several poems being submitted on currently and awaiting acceptance one submitted children's book; [pers.] I look for love, life and passion in each new moment and want to give back only the positive parts of my self. I strive for expanded awareness of the sacred and write from my heart.; [a.] Mentone, CA

DOBBINS, KATHI L.
[pen.] Kathi Lee Dobbins; [b.] May 24, 1966, Astoria, OR; [p.] David and Colleen Thompson; [m.] Steve Dobbins, September 5, 1992; [ch.] Kevin 12, Jason 9, Kamille 3, Craig 1; [ed.] High School grad. (Astoria High School) College 3 yrs. (Clatsop Comm. College); [occ.] Registered Nurse/Stay-at-home-mom.; [memb.] Who's Who among American High School Students, National Thespian Society; [hon.] Best Supporting Actress 1985-85, Clatsop Community College performance of 'Grease'; [oth. writ.] (Short Story) 'The Neighborhood' (unpublished), (Poem) 'Restored' (unpublished); [pers.] I'm a hopeless romantic and love to read poetry that causes me to think. I write from matters of my heart, in hopes that someone might relate. My favorite poets: Emily Dickinson, Robert Frost.; [a.] Ridgefield, WA

DOMINGUEZ, REINA ESTHER SANTANA
[b.] June 3, 1948, Jayuya, Puerto Rico; [p.] Georgina Fernandez Klute, Francisco Dominguez; [ch.] Eric M. Schubert; [ed.] Austin High School - Chicago Illinois, Watterson College, Pasadena, California; [occ.] Cashier - Walgreens Data Entry - Sears National Bank; [memb.] Boy Scouts of America Den mother Room Mothers Association; [hon.] Certificate of Merit - for Art, displayed at Wiebolt's department store. Several Certificates of Achievement and appreciation awards with various organizations; [oth. writ.] Farewell Address - Elementary-Manley School; [pers.] Embrace each day with an open mind and thank God for your achievements as well as your shortcomings. Always have a song in your heart.; [a.] Tempe, AZ

DONNELLY, STACY
[b.] September 24, 1961, Philadelphia, PA; [pers.] I can only pray that mankind will learn that it is alright for people to disgrace and be different. Disagreeing is better than Death.; [a.] Bensalem, PA

DORBIN, JERRY
[pers.] Jerry Dorbin ("Poetic Justice," Pg.429) is a jogger and autodidact. He lives in Santa Fe, and is currently working on a volume of light verse.

DOVER, CLARISE
[pen.] Clarise Turner, Polston; [b.] May 26, 1912, Cord; [p.] Mr. and Mrs. Kin Reaves; [m.] Herman Dover, February 17, 1986; [ch.] Four - boys; [ed.] One and half years of College; [occ.] Housewife; [memb.] ME. Church Order of Eastern Star Home Demonstration Club; [oth. writ.] Gift of Prayer,

River, Big Foot, Afraid, God Is There, Ice Storm, Baby Growing, Shadows Just Tomorrow Away, Rain Almost Fall; [pers.] I am 84 yrs. old, I have been married 4 times. They all past away except the last one - He is in a nursing home. Do the best you can all time. Trust God in everything. Live each day as if it were your last.; [a.] Cord, AR

DOWD, LINDA L.
[b.] July 30, 1949, Niagara Falls, Ontario, Canada; [p.] Gerald E. and Patricia M. (nee Pattison) Herries; [m.] Gerald F. Dowd, August 23, 1969; [ch.] Shannon Lyn, Erin Marie and grandson Michael Patrick Dowd; [ed.] Graduated from the Mack School of Nursing in 1970, Saint Catharines, Ontario, Canada. Have since taken numerous credit courses in a wide variety of subject matter.; [occ.] Artist (Pioneer Studios). My watercolour paintings have also been reproduced in limited edition prints. Registered Nurse (Psychiatry, Public Health); [memb.] Meadowvale Art Group (Founder, Past President), College of Nurses of Ontario, Mississauga Arts Council, Civic Centre Art Gallery, Visual Arts Mississauga, Lady of the Knights (Blue Knights (Ontario VII), Bruce Trail Assoc.; [hon.] Editor's Choice Award (NLP 1993 - The Mighty Oak), Editor's Choice Award (NLP 1994 - The Night Shift), Editor's Choice Award (1995 - The Twilight Hour), Editor's Choice Award (NLP 1996 - Two Thousand And One), 1996 - Inducted into the International Society of Poets as a lifetime distinguished member.; [oth. writ.] Poetry published by NLP in the following anthologies: A Question Of Balance 1992, Distinguished Poets Of America 1993, Dance On The Horizon 1994, Echoes Of Yesterday 1994, Best Poems Of 1995, Best Poems Of 1996, Best Poems Of The '90's - publishing date 1996, Daybreak On The Land - publishing date 1996, my poems have been well receive at public poetry readings. I have also written over fifty songs and instrumental pieces for the guitar - many of which I have performed professionally.; [pers.] It is important for each of us to periodically take an overview of our life. By carefully looking at our past and present experiences, we acquire valuable insight into ourselves and the world around us. The knowledge we gain will hopefully light the way to a happier and more successful future.; [a.] Mississauga, Ontario, Canada

DOWLE, MARILYN J.
[b.] June 5, 1949, Chicago, IL; [p.] Edward and Darlene Meier; [m.] Richard William, April 17, 1976; [ch.] Brian Richard; [ed.] Oak Lawn Community High School, B.A. St. Xavier College, M.S. North Central College (all located in Illinois); [occ.] Antiques Dealer; [hon.] Illinois State Scholar, National Honor Society, President's List; [oth. writ.] Many other poems, book in progress; [pers.] My goal in writings is to uplift, inspire, and bring hope and meaning to the lives of others through an infusion of spirit and love.; [a.] Scottsdale, AZ

DREW, LENORA R.
[b.] June 30, 1968, Philadelphia, PA; [p.] Stanley and Mary Drew; [m.] (Fiance) Darnell A. Johnson, October 12, 1996; [ed.] Pemberton Twp. High School, Hampton University, Lincoln Technical Institute, Manna Bible College; [occ.] Legal Secretary; [memb.] Second Baptist Church; [hon.] Dean's List; [oth. writ.] Several poems not yet published, including christian poetry; [pers.] Jesus Christ died for your sins, accept him today.; [a.] Pemberton, NJ

DRIESBACH, MARK SHANNON
[pen.] "Sir Markus"; [b.] September 12, 1973, Palmerton, PA; [p.] George (Deceased) and Ellen Driesbach; [ed.] L.B. Morris Elementary, Jim Thorpe Junior High and 2 years, Jim Thorpe Senior High, Then GED and The School of Life; [occ.]

Fast Food Worker and part-time Songwriter; [hon.] Various NLP Editor's Choice Awards; [oth. writ.] 5 poems in local paper, 3 in High School paper and 1 in another company anthology and many in NLP Anthology!; [pers.] Without support life falls apart. Amie, Rachel, Greg, Walter, Danielle, Tim, Mom and Dad, Tim, Natalie, Mrs. Pfingstler, Mrs. Burke, Lois, Aunt Patti, David and Shannon, thank you for keeping My life together and going in new directions! You all mean a lot to me!; [a.] Jim Thorpe, PA

DRISCOLL, MIKE
[pen.] Guardian Angel; [b.] August 23, 1950, Ottawa, Canada; [p.] Dominic Driscoll, Connie Driscoll; [m.] Lucia Castelli-Driscoll, February 14; [ch.] Michael Jr. and Matthew Driscoll; [ed.] High Schools of St. Pats in Ottawa Gloucester H.S. in Ottawa and North Grenville in Kemptville Ontario. Two year course in Counselling, Policing courses of Breathalyzer search and Rescue, Police College Training in Toronto and Aylmer Ontario; [occ.] Formerly a Police and Enforce Officer for over 20 years. At present I am a Cancer patient with a terminal Brain cancer.; [memb.] I have actively been involved with issues that harm Cancer patients. Many years of fund raisings within minor hockey as well as other communities to out north for needy service clubs.; [oth. writ.] Poems, editorial to local newspapers on occasion.; [pers.] All my life I have always believed in a Special One who lives in a place called Heaven. He is known by many as Our Spiritual Father. He has been sought by many of these times. People ask our Hearts. I can honestly assure our people of the world He lives in all. His conversations come to us in poetry of all kinds. We are His children whether we are poets or not. He loves us all!; [a.] Lansdowne, Ontario, Canada

DUBENSKY, MRS. JOHANNA WOLFE
[pen.] Johanna Wolfe Dubensky; [b.] Alamogordo, NM; [p.] H. Joseph Wolfe and Clara C.; [m.] George Dubensky (Deceased); [ch.] Two sons and four grandchildren; [ed.] Three years College and Continued Education for Permanent, Catholic Deacons and Spouse Since 1976. Several Schools Fed. Gov. Civil Service (Military Personnel Mgn.) Kelly AFB.Hq. Randolph MP Ctr Brooks AFB, DMA Hq. IAGS Ft. Sam Houston, TX; [memb.] Ministry, 104, Pastoral Counseling, (Seminar) Training Program Hospital Ministry, Local Hosp. (1991) Outstanding Service and Courtesy Artist Oil Paintings Display, Local Library; [hon.] Eucharistic Minister since 1979, Facilitator Church Renew Program 3 yrs., Poetry published in two poetry books, poetry broadcast, 1946, "The Exposition Press, N.Y.; [oth. writ.] Two Songs - No Hits," (Note Hq. Headquarters.) Military Bases San Antonio, TX; [pers.] To brings "A Little Sunlight" in to the hearts of all Gods Children, with cheer and hope for the future.; [a.] San Antonio, TX

DUDLEY, MARGERY M. L.
[b.] July 7, 1918, Washington, DC; [p.] Margery Mitchell, William A. Mitchell; [m.] Military Eng - Historian and Teacher, June 1937 and August 1980; [ch.] 3 Minister, Lawyer, Social Worker; [ed.] After high school, attended Columbia - NY, George Washington, DC Cornell - Summer courses; [occ.] Twice Widowed, am going back to writing poetry; [memb.] Episcopal Church Daughters of the US Army; [oth. writ.] Never for publication. Letters in times of crisis. Which I save with hope that they may be of help to heal the wounds of crises for my family. My writings simple reflect the world.; [pers.] The world as I see it - its beauty and its mystery.

DUFRESNE, EDNA BOUDREAU
[b.] March 14, Bellingham, MA; [p.] Jack and Rose

Boudreau (Deceased); [m.] Wilfrid B. Dufresne, January 7; [ch.] Billie Diane, Jackie Wilfrid - Grandchildren - Nelson Cook, Jackie and Jessica Dufresne; [ed.] Boston University Liberal Arts, Boston University Masters of Education (Reading) Retired Reading Co-ordinator; [occ.] Co-Owner Sunburst Show Gardens Hybridizev of gladiolus, dahlias and lilies; [memb.] American Dahlia Society, No. American Gladiolus Council, Chairman of Speaker Program 1996, No Am. Gladiolus Convention - Tucson 1996. Federation of Garden Clubs, Judges Council - Orlando - R.I - Winter Haven; [hon.] Seedling Awards - Top Floral Design Ribbons in Table Artistry Award, Winter Haven, FL, 1996. Photography exhibited at Ridge Art, Association - Winter Haven FL.; [oth. writ.] Gladiolus - Commercial Growers Associate Editor; [pers.] Life is an adventure to be shared. My dream is to be a poet. I have been writing for myself.; [a.] Lake Wales, FL

DUKES, DONNA L.
[pen.] Lady D.; [b.] February 23, 1971, Sumter, SC; [p.] Ada Dukes and Harry Dukes; [ed.] Sumter High School Central Carolina Tech. College American Institute of Banking; [occ.] Customer Service/ Sales Rep., Wachovia Bank of S.C.; [hon.] K-Mart, Chairman's Award, S.C. Career Center, Most Creative Student, American Institute of Banking, High Grade Award (Honor Student); [pers.] To me, poetry is a form of self-expression. Like the eyes, poetry is the key to one's soul, and you can enter a whole new world through the eyes of ones poetry.; [a.] Sumter, SC

DUKES, JENNY
[pen.] Jenny Dukes; [b.] 13 June 1944, Luton, England; [p.] George Rowe, Vera Rowe; [m.] Alan Dukes, 2 December 1966; [ch.] Roger, Michael and Susan; [ed.] Luton Girls High School, Barnfield and Dunstable Colleges; [occ.] Housewife and student; [memb.] Stopsley Baptist Church; [oth. writ.] "Thoughts In A Spring Garden" published in an anthology in England; [pers.] My Christian faith gives me a greater insight into the beauty of God's creation and inspires my poetry. For 2 years (94-96) I lived in Troy Michigan; [a.] Luton, Beds, UK

DUNCAN, DEBBIE
[b.] March 16, 1963, Vancouver, BC, Canada; [ed.] High School Graduate, Parksville British Columbia; [hon.] Tap Dancer, Baton Twirlist in my early years. For 12 years I won many awards and certificates.; [oth. writ.] Many other poems written to family and friends.; [pers.] Thank you to everyone involved for this publication. This is the 1st.; [a.] Parksville, British Columbia, Canada

DUPONT, DEBRA ANN
[pen.] Catherine Bridge; [b.] April 29, 1975, Toronto, Ont.; [p.] Donald Dupont, Gloria Dupont; [ed.] St. Roberts Catholic High School, York University 2nd yr. creative writing/History Honours Major; [occ.] Full-time student; [memb.] The League of Canadian Poets, Epilepsy Association; [oth. writ.] Several poems published in University and local newspapers, as well as for the Epilepsy Association's newsletter.; [pers.] I wish merely to pass on a great truth that my dear friend, Robert, once blessed me with in a letter: "To be passionate about life and what you do is crucial to ones existence." I believe it.; [a.] North York, Ontario, Canada

DUQUETTE, DR. GEORGES
[b.] February 18, 1947, Thunder Bay, Ontario, Canada; [ed.] Ph.D. - State Univ. of New York, Buffalo, B.Ed., M.Ed. - University of Ottawa, B.A. - Laurentian University (Philosophy and English); [occ.] Professor of Education; [oth. writ.] Duquette, G. (1995). The Undiscovered Country, (revised

Edition). Lewiston, N.Y.: Edwin Mellen Press. Duquette, G. (1995). Second Language Practice. Clevedon, England: Multilingual Matters D. G. (1992). Methods et strategies pour l'enseignement an secondaire. Welland: Soleil Publications. Malave, L. and Duquette, G. (1991). Language, Culture and Cognition. Clevedon, England: Multilingual matters. Duquette, G. (1982). A Voice In The Wilderness, Ottawa: Heritage Press.; [pers.] Each person has inner dreams which can come to life, flourish, and become reality. All one has to do is be true to oneself and let one's light shine through. I have been influenced by the romantic poets, especially Keats and Woodsworth.; [a.] Sudbury, Ontario, Canada

DURE, REMY
[b.] February 2, 1955, Haiti; [p.] Fernand Dure, Elizabeth Dure; [m.] Carolle Dure, August 22, 1981; [ch.] Robert, Rachel, David and Dominique Dure; [occ.] Supervisor North General Hospital (New York); [a.] Brooklyn, NY

DURFOR, MARK ANTHONY NEALL
[pen.] Skeeziks; [b.] May 28, 1975; [ed.] Senior at Seattle Pacific University; [occ.] Security Officer at SPU; [pers.] I was surprised when God blessed me with the words of this poem. Normally writing in the style of my favorite poet Dr. Seuss, I found myself blessed and challenged to write this. I hope others feel that from reading it.; [a.] Seattle, WA

ECHEVARRIA, JAVIER
[b.] December 12, 1970, Bronx; [p.] Armando, Carmen Echevarria; [m.] Noemi Cotto Echevarria, January 18, 1988; [ch.] Jovan, Adrian Echevarria; [ed.] Passaic High School, Edison Job Corps; [occ.] Truck Driver, Painter; [pers.] I would like to dedicate this poem to my wife. Noemi, I love you.; [a.] Passaic, NJ

EDGCOMB, CHERYL B.
[b.] August 22, 1954, Marion, OH; [p.] Helen Cizek Wagner and William C. Bowman Jr.; [m.] Brian W. Edgcomb, June 15, 1974; [ch.] Shannon M. and James R.; [ed.] High School - Cowanesque Valley Jr./Sr. High, Westfield, PA, Currently enrolled at Liberty University, Lynchburg, VA, for a Bachelors Degree in Christian Counseling; [occ.] Postmaster Knoxville PA; [memb.] National Association of Postmaster of the United States (NAPUS) Board for Congregational Life - Jemison Valley Brethren In Christ Church, American Philatelic Society; [hon.] Exceptional Individual (1995) Performance Award for US Postal Service, 1995 Ernest A. Kehr Award for philately, Dale Carnegie Special Achievement Award; [oth. writ.] Special feature articles for philatelic publications such as "The American Philatelist" and "The Philatelic Observer" and local newspapers.; [pers.] I try to live my life as such, that which God's help, one person can make a difference!; [a.] Knoxville, PA

EDGERSON, MORSSIE L.
[b.] April 10, 1947, Swan Lake; [p.] Dorothy and Rubin Guein; [m.] Raymond B. Edgerson, December 31, 1970; [ch.] Brandon and Adrienne; [ed.] Bachelor of Science - Lincoln University in Jefferson City, Missouri and Masters of Art - University of Missouri - Kansas City; [occ.] English Teacher; [memb.] Ebenezer AME Church, Delta Sigma Theta Sorority, Inc.; [hon.] Outstanding American Educator; [a.] Raytown, MO

EDMUNDS, SUSAN
[b.] March 18, 1983, Auckland, New Zealand; [p.] Christine and David Edmunds; [ed.] Westlake Girls High School (still attending) Takapuna Normal Intermediate School Willow Park Primary School; [occ.] School student; [oth. writ.] Short stories in local magazines - all sorts and write on.; [a.] Auckland, New Zealand

EDWARDS, BRENDA LEE
[b.] July 10, 1961, Marion County; [p.] Johnny Havvard and Mary Brown; [m.] Robert E. Edwards, October 18, 1984; [ch.] Six, 3 boys and 3 girls; [ed.] Broad Ripple High School, 6 months of college in the medical field (Dental asst); [occ.] I'm an inspector of Sculptors; [hon.] As a child I was not so popular but did manage to receive a few awards for talents I didn't realize I had.; [oth. writ.] I have many poems that I have written in which I keep in a book, all of my poems are of different topics.; [pers.] I've always written poems as a child and still as an adult. I pretty much do it as a hobby. But everyone tells me I have a wonderful gift and talent. If given the chance I'll pursue it.; [a.] Indianapolis, IN

EDWARDS, SHIRLEY DICKENS
[b.] April 24, 1954, Reidsville, NC; [p.] Martha Grubbs Cromer; [ch.] Robert Cromer, Angela Cromer, Guy Edwards Jr.; [ed.] Happy Home School, Ruffin NC, Guildford Tec. Com. College GED; [occ.] Painter, South Eastern Ind Painting Eden NC; [hon.] Served in U.S. Navy and U.S. Army; [oth. writ.] I had a dream published in Shadows and Light. Have numerous poems on all topics, been writing since second grade.; [pers.] I dedicate my appreciation for poetry to Mrs. Coey Underwood my second grade teacher. She was more than a teacher, she was my inspiration my friend, the one person who made me believe in myself. A special thank you. I love you Mrs. Underwood.; [a.] Reidsville, NC

EKONG, INYANG
[b.] August 17, 1983, Dallas, TX; [p.] Patrick Ekong, Affie Ekong; [ed.] Richardson West Junior High School; [hon.] Beta Club, "A" Honor Roll, Most Valuable Player Award in Track; [a.] Richardson, TX

ELKIN, FRANK JACKSON
[b.] November 10, 1923, Toronto, ON; [p.] Frederica Lovell - George Elkin; [m.] Doris Ellen, August 2, 1946; [ch.] Frank Jr., Carol, Suzanne; [ed.] Elementary, High School, Sir George William College; [occ.] Retired (Ex Toolmaker and Tool Designer); [memb.] Royal Canadian Legion; [hon.] Canadian Voluntary Service Medal and Clasp, '39-'45 War Medal, Defence of Britain Medal; [oth. writ.] I have composed a number of songs and written many others poems. Some copyrights. Nothing published.; [pers.] Sometimes it is better to keep your mouth shut and let people think you are. A fool than open your mouth and confirm it.; [a.] Lachine, Province of Quebec, Canada

ELLEN, PATRICK
[b.] 19 November 1959, Freetown, Sierra Leone, West Africa; [p.] Major J. H. Ellen Obe Lpm; [ch.] Shana-Tamsin (9), Timothy (6); [ed.] Various Schools and Colleges; [occ.] Offshore Engineer; [hon.] My children love me; [oth. writ.] Nothing published (haven't really tried); [pers.] Celebrate each new day, and remember what peace there may be in the beauty of your own mind.; [a.] Nr Cambridge, UK

ELLICK JR., MICHAEL
[b.] January 18, 1975, Cook County; [p.] Michael B. Ellick, Carolyn R. Ellick; [ed.] South Shore High School, Columbia College Chicago; [occ.] Doormen Hyde Park; [pers.] I maintain writing poetry from what my feelings and knowledge of recognizing, the talent when I'm alone from, the goodness of accomplishing of understanding myself.; [a.] Chicago, IL

ELLIOTT, JOYCE
[b.] June 15, 1958, St. Charles, IL; [p.] David, Dorothy Lindahl; [m.] Craig S. Elliott, September 27, 1980; [ch.] Jennie, David, Linnea; [ed.] Geneva

Community High School Geneva, IL. B.A. Augustana College Rock Island, IL; [memb.] Geneva Evangelical Lutheran Church, Mother's Club of Geneva, Girl Scouts, P.T.O.; [pers.] Being able to express my emotions in the words of this poem helped in my grief over a tragic can accident. Perhaps these words can help another through a similar tragedy. The poem is dedicated to the memory of Krissy Terada.; [a.] LaFox, IL

EMERSON, MATTHEW
[b.] April 3, 1974, Minot, ND; [p.] William J. Emerson and Sandra Kellogg; [m.] Kristie I. Emerson, June 15, 1996; [oth. writ.] Thorns, Shadow On The Hillside, Sweat Promising Kiss So Soft N' Special, Little Emotion, A Magical Whisper, Money For The Moon, Scare Crow, Every Nothin' (all unpublished); [pers.] All is all not, A puppet in life, Cut the strings with your knife; [a.] Bismark, ND

EMERY, DANIEL ARTHUR
[pen.] "Dae"; [b.] June 5, 1948, Burlington, VT; [p.] Charles E. Emery and Myrtle "Stanhope" Emery; [m.] Laurie E. "Thomson" Emery, February 13, 1982; [ch.] Daniel Jr. (Deceased, 1970), Todd, Heather, Terr, Tammy and Tanya; [occ.] Self-employed; [memb.] American Legion Post #59, President — I.D.D.C.O.A. (International Dedicated Dumpers Club of America); [oth. writ.] "Remember", "The Winner".; [pers.] "Think, don't dwell, try to find a plus in all happenings, for one is only on earth a blink, compared to the universe!"; [a.] Waterbury, VT

ENGLUND, BARBARA ANNE
[b.] October 7, 1966, Menominee; [occ.] I'm a cook at a restaurant. Becca's Diner'n Dairy Trent; [pers.] I write with the idea of making a difference in people's lives. Influenced by life experiences.; [a.] Menominee, MI

ENLOW, W. H.
[b.] April 26, 1903, Glen Rose; [p.] Albe - Florence Enlow; [m.] Georgia Enlow, March 3, 1931; [ed.] 9th Gr. Railroad Employee from February 1942, January 1945 Tinker Air Force Base January 42; [occ.] Retired to July 31, July 31, 1970; [memb.] Union R.R. Machinists Union T.A.F.B.; [hon.] Tinker Air Force Base Outstanding Performance Rating Dept. of Tinker A.F.B. Superior performance. Air Force Logistic's Command Bronze - Zero Defects Awards Dept. of the Air Force - Superior performance Dept. of the Air force - Certificate of service - July 31, 1970 Retired; [pers.] Worked for Rock Island (Shawnee) OR. Union Pacific (Omatta NE) Riogrande (Denver) Co. Georgia Enlovy (Wife) Died April 9, 1993.; [a.] Shawnee, OK

ENRIQUEZ, RICARDO C.
[b.] November 30, 1973, Cd Juarez, Chihuahua; [p.] Ricardo B. Enriquez, Enedina Enriquez; [ch.] Amanda N. Enriquez, Ricardo Enriquez III; [ed.] GED, Associates Degree (Auto-Technician); [memb.] Low-Rider Car Club Advocate; [pers.] Dreams, nothingness, contact with thy deteriorated dejavu, leads thy to the pungent, decomposed breath of a canister embedded on the poles.; [a.] El Paso, TX

ERICKSON, ARLENE
[pen.] Pat Erickson; [b.] May 30, 1931, Minneapolis, MN; [p.] Lois Hurst and Emil Roepke; [m.] Gerald (Jerry) Erickson, July 5, 1957; [ch.] Sherrie, Daniel, James, Jodie; [ed.] 9th grade got G.E.D. in 1983; [occ.] Bar Ownen - Tender; [oth. writ.] More poetry.; [a.] Owatonna, MN

ERICKSON, FRANCIS JENS
[b.] October 28, 1962; [p.] Joseph and Mary Erickson; [m.] Tracey Kaye Hoyle, November 4,

1985; [ch.] Son: Paul Jens, daughter: Kayci Marie; [ed.] B.A. of Ed., Arizona State University; [occ.] High School History Teacher; [memb.] Alpha Phi Omega, Phi Theta Kappa; [pers.] To know and understand history is to comprehend the world, leaving one with the challenge to master himself.; [a.] Mesa, AZ

ERICKSON, HELEN
[b.] June 27, 1921, Camden, NJ; [p.] John Mylet, Helen Mylet; [m.] John Erickson (Deceased), July 21, 1948; [ch.] Kathleen, Janice; [ed.] Collingswood High School, Philadelphia Bible College Cooper Hospital School of Nursing; [occ.] Retired School Nurse Deptford NJ Public Schools; [memb.] First Baptist Church Woodbury NJ, National Education Assn. Ret N.J. Education Assn. Ret Gloucester County Education Assn Ret; [hon.] Medical Nursing Award Cooper Hospital Class of 1948; [oth. writ.] Various poems for friends. Church functions etc.; [pers.] Reading poetry has always been a favorite pastime of mine. I enjoy writing poems fro and about friends who seem to enjoy them. I guess you could call it a hobby.; [a.] Mantua, NJ

ERICKSON, JENNIE ANNE
[pen.] Jenn; [b.] June 23, 1978, Rockford, IL; [p.] Kent and Terry Erickson; [ed.] Going to be a Senior in High School Hononegah High, CNA (through the High School); [occ.] CNA at Swedish American Hospital (Family Birth Center), Played High School Tennis for 4 years.; [memb.] Tech Prep (program I was selected to be in, gives hands on experience with my CNA and we receive scholarship) been on "Who's Who Who Among American Teens for 2 yrs. received Academic Award at School; [oth. writ.] None published write to please my mood. Never entered anything else; [a.] Roscoe, IL

ERIEG, STEPHANIE
[b.] July 31, 1983, Memorial Hospital, Delaware Country; [p.] Raymond and Mary Ann Erieg; [ed.] Ridley Middle School 8th grade; [a.] Ridley Park, PA

ESPERSCHIED, IDA MAE
[b.] March 25, 1918, Fremont, NE; [p.] Mary Elizabeth and Otto Ibsen; [m.] Deceased, June 10, 1941; [ch.] Sally, Sue, Cindy, 1 son deceased Wesley; [ed.] 8th grade; [occ.] Retired House Keeper; [memb.] Jesus Christ of Latter Day Saints; [hon.] Being a parent and grandparent - 7 grandchildren, great grandchildren - 5; [oth. writ.] Many poems from age 13; [pers.] Raised on a Dairy Farm one of 11 children. Love writing poetry but due to Parkinsons - writing is difficult.; [a.] Fremont, NE

ESPINOSA, ROSALINA
[pen.] Lyn; [b.] October 10, 1923, Philippines; [p.] Deceased; [m.] Jose Vidal Espinosa Sr. (Deceased), January 2, 1943; [ch.] Jesse Manuel, Vincsan, U-XH, Merarie, Charmie, Dan, Judy and Joel; [ed.] High School Grad; [hon.] Hon. Mentioned by the: Golden Poet World of poetry (1990); [oth. writ.] The Ugliness of Ease; [pers.] If at first you don't succeed try and try and try again until you succeed.; [a.] Greer, SC

ESSELEN, AURET
[pen.] Auret; [b.] October 24, 1986, Johannesburg; [p.] Sue and Dr. Michael Esselen; [ed.] Grade 4; [occ.] Student; [oth. writ.] To My Sister Liat; [a.] Richmond, British Columbia, Canada

ESSEX, IRIS DARLENE
[pen.] Cotton Essex; [b.] March 4, 1954, New York City; [p.] Charles Lee Metz and Betty Iris Helms-Metz; [ch.] Charles Robert Atlee Essex; [ed.] Fairmont State College West Virginia University; [occ.] Artist; [memb.] Smithsonian Institute National Teacher's Association WV-AMI Affiliate of the National Alliance for the mentally Ill Alpha Phi Omega; [hon.] Whet Stone bi-yearly

publication graphic design. World of Poetry poetry award.; [oth. writ.] Fairmont State College bi-yearly publication, whetstone. West Virginia University Literary publication, Calliope. World of Poetry; [pers.] As a universal being I'm influenced by the positive and negative energy of humanity and nature. By writing, I wish to help someone on their journey here, as well as my own.; [a.] Fairmont, WV

ETIM, ESSIE KINSEY
[pen.] Essie M. Kinsey; [b.] April 14, 1957, Los Angeles; [p.] Mary E. Washington; [m.] Mr. Ime O. Etim, June 6, 1991; [ch.] Janelle Miranda, Udokah and Shaka Etim; [ed.] High school; [occ.] Songwriter; [memb.] Member of Top Records Songwriters Association in Nashville; [hon.] Won award from NCA Recording Co. in Nashville, for excellence in lyric composition in 1976; [oth. writ.] I have written over 60 songs; [pers.] I have a song entitled, I Wish coming out on an album by Earl "Wildcat" Ellis.; [a.] Los Angeles, CA

EVANS III, WILLIAM ROBERT
[pen.] William Robert Evans; [b.] May 13, 1940, Camden, NJ; [p.] Mr. and Mrs. William R. Evans Jr. (Bernice); [m.] Elaine-Parker (Deceased), May 5, 1967 (Widowed); [ch.] Sean William Evans; [ed.] BA in Anthropology 1969 (with honors) (University of South Florida - Tampa, FL), Berklee College of Music 1964 (Boston, MA), Rollins College (Winter Park, FL); [occ.] Musician (Arranger, composer, woodwinds), grad. student.; [memb.] American Fed. of Musicians, Amer. Society of Composers, Authors and Publishers (ASCAP), Florida Anthropological Society.; [hon.] Downbeat Magazines Scholarship Award (1964), (Berklee College of Music - Boston, MA) Dean's List of scholars (U.S.F. - 1969), B.A. Degree with Honors (U.S.F. - 1969); [oth. writ.] Two poems ("A Tree In Sawgrass Park" and "Beach Walk") published in Russian-American Anthology - 1994 English Poetry Edition by the Open Poetry Society of St. Petersburg, Florida.; [a.] Palm Harbor, FL

EXLEY, MONICA
[pen.] Monica Exley; [b.] September 26, 1981, Savannah, GA; [p.] Angela, Ricky Exley; [ed.] I am currently in the 9th grade; [occ.] Student; [memb.] Effingham County Band; [pers.] I enjoy expressing my feeling and thoughts through poetry.; [a.] Guyton, GA

FABRIZIO, LAUREN
[b.] March 11, 1983, Bethpage, NY; [p.] Linda and William Fabrizio; [ed.] Sunquam Elementary Schook (K-2), Signal Hill Elementary School (3-5), West Hollow Middle School; [occ.] Student; [hon.] National Junior Honor Society; [pers.] I enjoy playing soccer, reading poetry, writing poetry, and listening to music. I think kids should be treated equally because many time we have the same ability as adults. I hate ignorance and prejudice.; [a.] Melville, NY

FAGIANI, PATTY
[pen.] A. J. Tamara; [b.] September 24, 1971, Montreal; [p.] Maria Noce, Guglielmo Fagiani; [ed.] Lester B. Pearson High School, Dawson College; [occ.] Graphic Designer/Receptionist; [hon.] Reading Award, Honor Roll List; [oth. writ.] Personal Collections, distributed several Copies of Poetry Requested.; [pers.] Poetry is really a true expression of oneself, once it is written on paper one's reflection appears.; [a.] Montreal, Province of Quebec, Canada

FAJDICH, LAURA M.
[pen.] "Bagora"; [b.] July 2, 1966, Chicago, IL; [p.] Beatrice Fajdich, The late Michael "Big Mike" Fajdich; [ed.] George Washington High - South

Suburban College; [occ.] Pre-K teacher; [memb.] C.F.U. Tamburitzan music and Kdo group. Chicago Special Olympic Asst. Coach and Volunteer; [oth. writ.] I have had a few poems published. Where as others are framed and hung in special friends homes. An honor in itself!; [pers.] This poem was written with warm memories of my father and friends who are forever loved and remembered! Even a small star shines bright in the darkness!; [a.] Chicago, IL

FARLOW, JOHN KING
[b.] July 9, 1932, London, UK; [p.] Dengs King Farlow, M.B.E. Gaggenheim; [m.] Elizabeth Ann King Farlow, R.N., May 16 1992; [ed.] Westminster School, London and Christ Church, Oxford U., Duke U. (A.M.) Stanford U. (Phi. D.) - Post Doctoral Fellowship at U. of Pittsburgh, U. of California, U. of Liverpool U.K.; [occ.] Professor of Philosophy, University of Alberta; [memb.] Fellow, Royal Society of Canada, Past President, Canadian, Philosophical Association, founding Editor, Canadian Journal of Philosophy, Member, the Athenaem, London, U.K., Past Director, the Stroll of Poets; [hon.] See 'Memberships' above, Commissioned Service, Royal Pair Forces Distinguished Member, International Society of Poets, Co-Chairman of (World) International Congress of Philosophy of Montreal; [oth. writ.] 10 Philosophy books, The Dead Ship (Advent Books London), poems in magazines and anthologies of five countries including, Commentary, poetry London New York, Oxford Magazine, Isis, Gulles Jail Review, New Laurel Review, Best Poems of 1996 etc.; [pers.] Joys of my life have included, my wife, Liz Faith, friendships, poetry, philosophy travel.; [a.] Edmonton, Alberta, Canada

FAROOQUIE, KHURRAM A.
[b.] July 2, 1974, Karachi, Pakistan; [p.] Mr. Ajaz and Mrs. Rana Farooquie; [ed.] Bachelors in Aviation Computer Science from Embry - Riddle Aeronautical University; [occ.] Student, Computer Programmer; [memb.] President of Pakistan students and Scholars Association.; [oth. writ.] My compilations.; [pers.] A lifetime can pass by in seconds and sometimes a second seems like a lifetime. It is in this lifetime, that I'll write my poems, which come from inspirations that only take a second.; [a.] Daytona Beach, FL

FARRAR, CATHY
[b.] September 27, 1974, Rolla, MO; [p.] Jack and Sonja Farrar; [ed.] Salem High School, Southwest Baptist University - Salem, MO; [occ.] On-air Personality, KSMO Radio, Salem, MO; [a.] Salem, MO

FAULKNER, MARJORIE
[pen.] Marjorie Faulkner; [b.] April 1, 1937, New Jersey; [m.] James Faulkner, June 27, 1987; [ed.] Orange High and Montclair University; [occ.] Teacher, Eng., Orange Middle School; [memb.] N.T.E.A., N.E.A., Shiloh Baptist Church, Manna-Feed the Hungry; [hon.] Governor's Recognition Teacher of the Year Award, 1991; [oth. writ.] Plays and others poems written and used for special occasions. "No Matter What," performed at Monclair State, and Symphony Hall, Nwk., NJ; [pers.] Poems and plays must give a central theme touching on sincere attitudes and beliefs that pierce the soul.

FEASTER, WILLIAM
[b.] March 7, 1981, Chester, SC; [p.] William Feaster, Olivette Feaster; [ed.] Greenbrier High School; [oth. writ.] Several poems published and short stories published also.; [pers.] I hope to be come well known at pro sports to give the future generations of my family a sense of pride not to "succeed" but to be.; [a.] Evans, GA

FEINBERG, MS. ESTHER
[b.] May 4, 1919, Brooklyn, NY; [p.] Sarah and Samuel Feinberg; [ed.] BA degree Brooklyn College MA degree New York University; [occ.] Travel Agent; [memb.] Board of Directors Day Care Council, President Thomas Toback Chapter AMC Cancer Research, Board of Directors Combined Health Services. Member of IATA.; [hon.] Woman of Distinction AMC Cancer Research.; [a.] New York, NY

FELDMAN, JACK ALLISON
[pen.] Jack A. Feldman; [b.] December 19, 1923, Amsterdam NY; [p.] Leon Feldman and Anna Esther Olender Feldman; [m.] Margaret Waldman Feldman (Deceased), July 19, 1946; [ch.] Robert Louis and Diane Lynn; [ed.] High School and Valedictorian of Electronics, Naval Air Apprentice School 1948-1952 (7588 hours), also taught math in school of study; [occ.] Retired from 35 1/2 years with Naval Air Station: Electrical Engineering Tech., set-up Electronic Standards (World-Wide); [memb.] "Senior Engineering Technician" with "Institute for Certification of Engineering Technicians" by "National Society of Professional Engineers" Member of "Jewish War Veterans of America", Medic in World War II, Platoon 7, Battalion D; [hon.] World War II: Two Battle Stars, Asiatic Pacific Ribbon, American Area Ribbon, Philippine Liberation Ribbon, "Honorable Discharge" (Navy), While working in Electronic Standards Laboratory, I won several money awards for inventions in calibrating electronic standards in Electronics all over the world as well as The United States.; [oth. writ.] As a Senior in Wilbur H. Lynch High School, Amsterdam, New York, I won first prize in the city, and honorable mention for state of New York, and a certification for an essay titled, How the Spanish American War helped to Influence Our Present Latin American Policy.; [pers.] I was inspired in poetry by Robert Frost, Bliss Carmen, Henry Wadsworth longfellow, William Shakespeare, Virgil and Homer (Greek Poetry). Inspired by my deceased wife, Margaret Alice Waldman Feldman, by my present wife, Shirley, and her friends as well as my friends.; [a.] Norfolk, VA

FERNANDEZ, FAUSTO ALZATI
[b.] 27 September 1979, Mexico City; [p.] Marie del Consuelo and Fausto A. Alzati; [occ.] Guitar teacher, student other unstable jobs; [pers.] See beauty in rage and pain, just like in love and bliss.; [a.] Mexico City,, Mexico

FERNANDEZ, JOE
[b.] April 11, 1976; [a.] Walnut Creek, CA

FERNANDEZ, VERONICA
[b.] November 23, 1942, New York; [p.] Jean Schutt and Henry Schutt; [m.] Jorge (George) Fernandez, March 5, 1991; [ch.] Five grown Adult Children; [ed.] High School plus I enjoy playing Tennis, play the Piano, and Card games to relax, I love to read inspirational books, and lots of humor in life.; [occ.] Writer, Songs, Poetry, also Manager of own Business Maint, repair and Cleaning Services; [hon.] Silver Poet Award from World of Poetry California; [oth. writ.] Songs, Just A Woman My Son, after 40, choices, I Am Me, New Beginning, many more.; [pers.] In life look back don't stare, only to learn from ones past choices, no pain, no gain always go forward at your own pace, be proud of your accomplishments, life is not a contest, we are all special in our own unique way, we learn from each other.

FERRARI, JOHN
[pen.] Shadow; [b.] December 31, 1971, Philadelphia, PA; [p.] Phylllis and John (Deceased); [ed.] St John Newmann High, Temple College, Slicher

Kratz Real Estate; [occ.] Counselor/writer; [memb.] Disabled Veterans Asso. Mr. Solution (Private Writers Column National Inquirer and Local Schools) acting Vice President; [hon.] Local Counselor of the year foreign language honors I (Spanish); [oth. writ.] I am the proud owner of 417 poems and writings waiting to be discovered I was elected to write eulogy's for family and friends; [pers.] To be a poet or writer you have to reach somewhere inside yourself that no one else can. That is why I respect the work of Jim Morrison. He reached deeper than himself.; [a.] Philadelpia, PA

FINDLEY, TRACI D.
[b.] June 14, 1971, Frankfurt, Germany; [p.] Linda and Patrick Schmidt; [m.] Richard A. Findley Jr., November 6, 1993; [ed.] Raytown High School, Longview Community College, and Central Missouri State University; [occ.] College Student; [pers.] Poetry is but only one way to express oneself. I find it healing and therapeutic to put my thoughts into a written form.; [a.] Lee's Summit, MO

FINK, SANDY
[b.] August 9, 1935, Chicago, IL; [p.] Jeanette Walker Deike, Harry Walker; [m.] John Fink, October 15, 1987; [ch.] Perry Hornkohl; [ed.] Major in Philosophy and English, Minor in Psychology; [occ.] Retired; [memb.] Life membership in Florida Freelance Writers' Association and International Society of Poets, annual membership in Rockford Writers' Guild.; [hon.] Numerous competitive poetry awards including first, second, third and honorable mention in Oregon, Florida and other states; [oth. writ.] I've written and been published in newspapers, magazines, newsletters, brochures and television (t.v. commercials). Key images, a book of poetry (with illustrations and in my calligraphy) was released by Distinctive Publications January, 1992; [pers.] I'm at my best in distillations of any kind, especially when I can apply humorous twists to material. I enjoy paradox caught within a person's life, and the individual way it plays out. I'm hooked on the written word and go through life trying to make as much of it mine as possible.; [a.] Chiefland, FL

FIRTH, ROBERT AARON
[b.] March 28, 1967, Winnipeg; [p.] Anna and Robert John; [ed.] High School graduate, University graduate from the University of Winnipeg, Bachelor of Arts Degree in environment studies; [occ.] Employed at Manitoba Liquor Control Commission; [oth. writ.] Have had two other poems published by the National Library of poetry I should have been a doctor and the Hitchhiker's Query.; [pers.] Each of us has the right to journey to those unknown places where dreams are told and realities unfold, the trick is in discovering who and what we are along the way.; [a.] Winnipeg, Manitoba, Canada

FISHER, FRED E.
[b.] January 2, 1925, Indianapolis, IN; [p.] Edward E. Fisher, Verna L. Fisher; [ed.] Mich. State University, University of Indianapolis, Purdue University, Indiana University, Ivy Tech; [occ.] Retired Engineer for GM 1950-981; [memb.] American Radio Relay League (call sign AA9OP), Indianapolis Scottish Rite Orchestra, Viola; [hon.] Phi Theta Kappa Society; [oth. writ.] 1949-50 new articles as a reporter for Portland (Indiana) daily sun, letters and poems to and for my friends.; [pers.] After serving as a radio operator in the army signal corps in world war II, I pursue my three main interests....music, writing and engineering all were fulfilling. Mostly, I enjoy life on this wondrous planet.; [a.] Indianapolis, IN

FITZGERALD, JOSEPH J.
[pen.] Deidre J. FitzGerald; [b.] March 21, 1976,

Pueblo, CO; [p.] Joseph N. FitzGerald Lorraine FitzGerald; [ed.] Pueblo South High, University of Northern Colorado; [occ.] Student; [memb.] Irish - American Cultural Institute, U.N.C. Track Team, Co PIRG, Irish National Caucus, Pol, Science Club.; [hon.] 1993-'96 Academic Dean's List, '95-'96 Academic Athlete, 95-96 Departmental Scholar Political Science; [oth. writ.] No other nationally published creative writings. I am currently finishing work on a novel and a collection of on a novel and a collection of short stories dealing with Ireland and Irish - America.; [pers.] I have been an Irish Historian for ten writing deals with the struggles, dilemmas, and history of the Irish peoples.; [a.] Greeley, CO

FLAUTT, AGNES OSBORN
[m.] James R. Flautt, MD, March 21, 1987; first husband - John E. Osborn, M.D. (1944-1957); [ch.] Four: 2 sons in medicine, 2 daughters married to physicians - Michael J., Stephen J., Julianne Osborn Rooke, Mary Osborn Sciallis; 15 grandchildren; [ed.] College Graduate BBS Major Systems and Procedures, Worked as Editorial Coordinator and Copy Editor - 2 Medical Journals and 4 medical textbooks; [occ.] Retired; [memb.] Doctors Mayo Society, International Society of Poets, Heritage Society, Spring Hill College Medical Auxiliary; [pers.] As a widow raising 4 children, one just born and oldest 12 at time of husband's death, I have tried to incorporate in my poetry my observations of small children and children in general. I am in the process of writing a book expressing my experiences with young people; [a.] Rochester, MN

FLAVIN, EDWARD M.
[pen.] E. M. Flavin; [b.] June 21, 1952, Los Angeles; [ed.] B.A. Anthropology; [a.] Sun Valley, ID

FOGEL, BARBARA
[b.] February 11, 1954, Hillsdale, MI; [p.] Eleanor and Cecil Clevenger; [m.] Michael Fogel, June 19, 1976; [ch.] Victoria, Roxanne; [ed.] Camden-Frontier High School, Hillsdale College, Siena Heights College; [occ.] Middle School English Teacher; [memb.] American Morgan Horse Association, Rainbow Morgan Horse Association, The Lippitt Club, Ohio Education Association, Camden Missionary Church; [oth. writ.] Several articles for The Morgan Horse Magazine, Classic Morgan Admirers, High Percentage, The Western Horseman; [pers.] I believe in the power of the pen. As a teacher, I encourage my students to write everyday. Good things can happen if you do!; [a.] Edon, OH

FOLK, EDWARD
[pen.] Easy Eddie; [b.] July 6, 1937, Brooklyn, NY; [p.] Frank Mary; [m.] Kittee; [ch.] Two Twin Boys, Girl; [ed.] Maybe 9th Garade; [occ.] Tukee it nice and easy; [memb.] A-A National Wild Life; [hon.] Born July 6, 1937 - Still here August 1, 1996 Thank God; [oth. writ.] Short story's; [a.] Atlantic Beach, NC

FORD, JOHN JAMES BERNARD
[b.] May 30, 1972, Kindersley, Sask.; [p.] Alfred and Mary Ford; [ed.] BA (Honours) in English from The Royal Military College of Canada; [occ.] Writer; [memb.] Kingston Panthers Rugby Club; [hon.] The Judge's Award - RMC Rugby; [oth. writ.] Several essays on literary theory and comparative literature. I am currently working on my first novel.; [pers.] I hope to take my MFA in creative writing at the University of British Columbia.; [a.] Nepean, Ontario, Canada

FORREST, STACY E.
[pen.] Stacy; [b.] December 3, 1983, Indianapolis, IN; [p.] Ted and April Forrest; [ed.] Student entering 7th Grade fall 96; [occ.] Student; [memb.] Fall Creek Baptist Church, Belter Middle School Choir;

[hon.] Honor Student - 6th Grade, Issma Solo Competition - 1st Place, Issma Group Competition 1st Place, Math Pentathalon - 2 Gold Medals; [pers.] I am inspired by the early poets. I strive to bring beauty to my poems because I have always loved nature.; [a.] Indianapolis, IN

FORRESTER, THERESA
[b.] August 28, 1981, Rockford, IL; [p.] Howard and Linda Forrester; [ed.] Sophomore at Boylan Catholic High School; [occ.] Student at Boylan Catholic High School; [memb.] Spanish Club, Studies classical ballet and pointe, and jazz dance for 8 years.; [hon.] Honor student; [pers.] I feel my writings reflect the realities on issues that the younger society of today tend to deem acceptable.; [a.] Rockford, IL

FORSHAY, BEN
[b.] September 28, 1979, Peru; [p.] Rick and Liz Forshay; [ed.] New Hampton School; [occ.] Student; [oth. writ.] Some other poems. Nothing published.; [pers.] For the Beautiful girl you've lost all courage to talk to.; [a.] Exeter, NH

FORSTER, DRUSILLA
[b.] March 19, 1983, Tampa; [p.] Dr. George, Regina Forster; [m.] April 3, 1981; [ed.] Calvert Private School Tampa 8th Grade; [occ.] Performing Arts Student; [memb.] Vinoy Club, YMCA Unity Church, Art Club, Sea Ray Club; [oth. writ.] Take a stand Tampa Tribune 3rd place "Dangers of Smoking", poetry collection.; [pers.] "What goes around, comes around.".; [a.] Tampa, FL

FORSYTH, NANCY
[pen.] Nancy Forsyth; [b.] April 10, 1950, Toronto, Ontario, Canada; [p.] Cecelia Elias; [m.] Barry William Forsyth, May 15, 1976; [ch.] Mark William; [ed.] Eastdale High School, Shaw's Business School; [occ.] Secretary, G.E. Multilin Markham, Ontario, Canada; [oth. writ.] National Library of Poetry Published in The Path not taken poem. (Days Gone By). Also published in the Relay Times Multilin Magazine; [pers.] There us beauty in everything if you can find it. I can find it. It is expressed in each of my writings; [a.] Markham, Ontario, Canada

FORTUNATO, AMY ELIZABETH
[b.] April 6, 1984, Tague, South Korea; [p.] Frank Wayne and Debbra Ann; [ed.] Notre Dame Catholic, Elementary School in Santa Barbara, California; [occ.] Student; [memb.] Girl Scouts: Cadette Notre Dame Student Council: Commissioner of Public Relations; [hon.] 14 "A" Honor Roll, 5 Superior Citizenship, Citizenship pin, 4 Effort Awards, 1 Standard of Excellence, 1 Academic Studies, 2 Catholic Daughters Award's, Dare Gold Essay Plaque, Science Fair Ribbons, and winner of several school sponsored writing contests; [oth. writ.] Several short stories, award winning essays, a poem book, and poem written with different techniques such as haiku; [pers.]I hope that one day I can inspire young girls everywhere.; [a.] Carpinteria, CA

FOSTER, LORENE
[b.] June 5, 1916, Shelby Co., TX; [m.] Woodrow Foster, September 9, 1936; [ch.] Sara Beth Foster Hancock; [ed.] Center High School; [occ.] Songbird Carvings (Wood) Paintings and Housewife; [memb.] Center Art League; [hon.] Awards for Carvings and Paintings; [oth. writ.] My poems are writings I have done over the years I have kept in notebooks.; [pers.] Beauty found in the simple things of nature is the greatest gift for me. Radio Poetry (Between the Book ends) had a great impression on my youth. Read by Howard Ely and Ted Malone.; [a.] Center, TX

FOWLER, STACEY MARIE
[b.] December 24, 1977, Boaz, AL; [p.] Wesley and Belinda Fowler; [ed.] Crossville High, Snead State Community College; [occ.] The Video Store in Albertville, AL; [hon.] First and Second place in honors in school papers (Poems and short stories).; [oth. writ.] The Bible (one true Friend) published in famous poem of today by the famous poets society.; [pers.] Sometimes we find ourselves very alone and scared. But it's in these times of silence we often find the strength to pick up the pieces and go on.; [a.] Crossville, AL

FRANCIS, KELLEY MARIE
[b.] November 21, 1976, Phila., PA; [p.] William and Sheryl Cooper; [m.] Fiance Gary D. Luckey; [ch.] Christopher, Michael and Vachon; [ed.] Darnell Phila. High School for Girls, National Education Center; [occ.] Physical Therapy Aide; [oth. writ.] A few poems have been published in high school literary magazine.; [pers.] I am truly thankful for the love and words of encouragement from my fiance and children. Also I wish to thank Ms. Colleen for entering my poem.; [a.] Philadelphia, PA

FRANCIS-BALL, DOROTHY M.
[pen.] Dorothy M. Francis-Ball; [b.] September 7, 1965, Lansdale, PA; [p.] Joan and John Francis; [m.] Joseph Ball, April 30, 1994; [ch.] Angel Marie Ball, Lee Andrew Francis; [ed.] North Penn High School, Lansdale, PA, Class of 1983 Bradford School of Business, Philadelphia, PA, Class of 1984; [occ.] Legal Secretary, wife, mother; [memb.] Tri-County Crossroads Friends of Bill; [pers.] One day at a time; [a.] Lansdale, PA

FRANK, GERALD B.
[pen.] Forthright; [b.] September 22, 1928, New York, NY; [p.] Blanche Baumann Frank, Morris Henry Frank; [ch.] Daniel B. Frank, Jonathan W. Frank, Louise B. Frank; [ed.] B.A. Colby College Waterville, Maine, Class of 1950; [occ.] Retired; [memb.] The Cliff Dwellers of Chicago; [hon.] My three children, the wives of two of them and the sons of one of them!; [oth. writ.] Lotsa advertising copy over the years...mostly in "Plain Talk"; [a.] Chicago, IL

FRANKE, WAYNE
[pen.] T. H. Hunter; [b.] September 26, 1935, Beaumont, TX; [p.] Deceased; [m.] Divorced; [ch.] Aurel Wayne Franke III; [ed.] B.A. Hardin Simmons University Abilene, TX 1958; [occ.] Retired Military; [memb.] VFW; [oth. writ.] "101 Treasure Poems" (to be published treasure stories in prose) poems published in: "Th'ers Express" quarterly journals, "The American Dawson" quarterly digest.; [pers.] Have author 300 treasure stories in prose.; [a.] Abilene, TX

FRANKLIN, KAREN A.
[b.] October 11, 1948, Washington, DC; [p.] Mary E. Libby, Richard L. Libby; [m.] Dennis E. Franklin, February 12, 1972; [ch.] Jeanne, Anthony, Matthew; [ed.] B.A. Nazareth College of Rochester, NY, M.A.T. State University of New York at Binghamton; [occ.] Instructor (part time) at Broome Community College (Binghamton, NY); [memb.] AAUW, Cousteau Society, Girl Scouts, Congress of Parents and Teachers (PTA), John Libby Family Assoc.; [hon.] B.A. Magna Cum Laude, Kappa Gamma Pi, Thanks Badge, Girl Scouts of U.S.A., Life Membership in PTA; [oth. writ.] Article for the Teaching Professor.; [pers.] I believe there is a divine light illuminating the universe and it shines brightest when a human being cares for other people and conserves natural resources; [a.] Endicott, NY

FRANKLIN, PAULINE E.
[b.] October 12, 1923, Penn Yan, NY; [p.] Leland

and Grace Gray; [m.] Paul Franklin, August 25, 1968; [ch.] Paul, Elaine, Alan, Neil; [occ.] Retired housewife; [hon.] Won many blue ribbons on my oil and pastel paintings.; [oth. writ.] This was the first time I have ever had my poems reviewed.; [pers.] I really enjoy putting my thoughts and to make people happy.; [a.] La Luz, NM

FRANQUI, MR. MANNY
[b.] February 8, 1960, NY; [m.] Mig Franqui, August 7, 1982; [ed.] Current Student - "College of Life"; [oth. writ.] Often wrote poems and letters to my then, steady girl - now wife Mig. during my old school days.; [pers.] "Hope for more days of smiles than tears and never surrender."

FRASER, LEONARD
[pen.] Len Fraser; [b.] June 23, 1932, Harlem; [m.] Shirley; [ch.] Ruwanda and Zinga; [ed.] B.S. LIU, Fredrick Douglas Creative Arts Center; [occ.] Retired Teacher; [memb.] PSI CHI Psychology Honor Soc.; [hon.] "Excellence in Teaching" (1993) N.Y.C. Bd and Ed.; [oth. writ.] Poems/Articles/Short Stories Amsterdam News, Afro/American Classical Music-Jazz News, Garvey's Voice, Nommo Black Scholar; [pers.] Special thanks, Quincy Troupe, Jayne Cortez, Abba, Martin Simmons, Lloyd and Joyce, Greenidge, Ruwanda, Zinga, Shirley Fraser, "Blues Songs, Black Words - The Universe"; [a.] Brooklyn, NY

FRAZER, MS. LEIGH MACKAY
[b.] 29 September 1978, Redruth, UK; [p.] Brenda and Stewart Frazer; [ed.] Pool School and Cornwall College; [occ.] Engineering; [hon.] Award from the Royal Association of British Architecture for Prose and Verse; [oth. writ.] A fiction story printed in a schools magazine. Poems written for personal use.; [pers.] I have always had a love for the mysterious and beautiful. I hope to convey that through my poems.; [a.] Portreath, Cornwall, UK

FRECHEN, ROBERTA MARIE
[b.] July 23, 1964, Honesdale, PA; [p.] Henry Frechen (Deceased), Jeanne Dirr Williams; [ed.] Blue Mtn. Academy, Andrews University (B.A., English, 1996), also beginning work on a M.A. in History; [occ.] Student, part-time employee, adult foster care home; [memb.] Sigma Tau Delta, Phi Alpha Theta; [hon.] All-American Scholar (1994), Who's Who Among students in American Universities and Colleges (1995), Dean's List; [pers.] Two things motivate my writing: personal experiences, and experiences of those around me. Whether I write poetry or short stories, I strive to always be realistic and descriptive in my writing. I credit my enjoyment of reading and writing to my father - who early instilled in me a love for the written word.; [a.] Berrien Springs, MI

FREELAND, CORA M.
[b.] February 26, 1932, Chelsea, MI; [p.] Clare/Mammie Futtle; [m.] Howard Freeland, November 4, 1950; [ch.] Susan, John, Lela, Harold; [ed.] B.S. in Social work; [occ.] Retired; [pers.] The common denominator of dealing with death is the silver molter falling from the eyes after the volcanic eruption go a broken heart.; [a.] Ann Arbor, MI

FREY, BRADY
[pen.] Brady, Eris, B.J. Smith, Brady Frey; [b.] January 21, 1981, Great Lakes, IL; [p.] Mr. Richard Frey, Ms. Marsha Frey; [ed.] Currently attending Zion - Benton High School, Presently Sophomore; [occ.] Student, part-time job; [hon.] High Honors in academies and physical fitness. Several achievements towards drawing and painting; [oth. writ.] Several poems published in school newspaper.; [pers.] I yearn to reveal the simple loveliness and bitter darkness blinded in creative silence that survives in poetry.; [a.] Zion, IL

FRIESE, DORIS M.
[b.] December 17, 1942, Somerset, CA; [p.] J. Harold and Luha M. Fisher; [m.] Cecil E. Friese, October 1, 1972; [ch.] Cecil and Friese Jr.; [occ.] House wife; [oth. writ.] Never had any of my poems printed before - as I played around with words - in my early teens; [pers.] I enjoy, put words together. In expressing the love and kindness I see in others.

FRISCHMUTH, KIM
[pen.] Kim Frischmuth; [b.] 15 January 1971, Footscray Victoria; [p.] Fred and Heike Frischmuth; [m.] Jason Brown (Defacto); [ed.] Wheelers Hill High School (Victorian Certificate of Education) year 12; [occ.] Accounts Co-ordinator at 7/11 stories head office/Musician; [hon.] Certificate of Creative Writing from Holmesglen College; [oth. writ.] Numerous poems previously unpublished and short horror stories one published in a local magazine. I've also written songs performed and recorded by myself and my back bones.; [pers.] My inspiration for writing poetry is life experiences and my goal is to have a book of all my poems published; [a.] Melbourne, Victoria, Australia

FRY, MELISSA
[pen.] Tweetey; [b.] September 5, 1981, Belvidere, IL; [p.] Steve Fry, Bertha Fry; [ed.] Parview Jr., Sr., High School; [oth. writ.] Several poems not published.; [a.] Orfordville, WI

FURST, AGNES V.
[b.] December 24, 1946, Hungary, Budapest; [p.] Eugen Woltzinger, Rosalia Meszaros; [m.] John Furst, May 1, 1992; [ch.] Dora Hiba, Zsuzsanna Hiba, Demeter Konstantinides; [ed.] Trade School for Food Sales, Gyorgy Dozsa High School, Word Processing Courses, Typist, Shorthand School; [occ.] Medical billing student; [MEMB.] ASA Institute of Business and Computer Technology; [hon.] I won second place in the typing and shorthand contest in 1980 in Hungary's capital of Budapest in 1980; [oth. writ.] I won second place in the "Modern World" International Poetry Contest in the Hungarian Language. My poem was published in Canada by the poetry club in the book entitled "Metamorphosis". Several poems were published in the newspaper "American Hungarian Peoples Voice."; [pers.] "Money is not everything" The goodness and mankind are more valuable than a cold money bag.; [a.] Brooklyn, NY

GABLE, J. LYNDA
[b.] December 1, 1941, Delaware Co, IN; [p.] Lawrence C. and Leona J. Hammer; [ch.] Kimberly Brown; [ed.] Attended some College-Ball, State University - Muncie Indiana; [occ.] Manufactures Rep. - Gift Industry; [hon.] Sales awards; [oth. writ.] (Insurance related training manuals - only published writings). I've always put my thoughts on paper, but never submitted any writings before.; [pers.] I want to express my love for life, children and nature, thru words. I really want to touch others and leave something to my grandchildren.; [a.] Muncie, IN

GACK, KIMBERLY A.
[pen.] Learmouth; [b.] September 6, 1971, PA; [ed.] Lutheran Private School, W.B. Saul H.S. of Agricultural Sciences, Art Institute of Philadelphia; [memb.] St. Michael's Lutheran Church, Workout For Hope, Future Farmers of America; [hon.] Three years perfect attendance award, Senior Prom Queen; [pers.] My love for my boyfriend James, gave more inspiration to write than I have ever had before. Such a great opportunity as this has caused me to chose this poem over all my others. I am extremely proud to have "A poem for James" published in such a fine anthology. Thank you.; [a.] Philadelphia, PA

GAKERE, ANN M.
[b.] June 24, 1974, Nairobi, Kenya; [p.] Keziah N. Gakere, Jamleck N. Gakere; [ed.] St. Ursula Primary Sch. (Kenya), Maryhill High Sch. (Kenya), West Los Angeles College (CA); [occ.] Student; [memb.] Writers' Association of Kenya; [hon.] British Council and Ministry of Education (Kenya), National Poetry Award, Dean's List (West L.A.); [oth. writ.] Different poems published in Kenya magazines, the 'Jambo Unlaut' (Goethe Institute), 'Writer's Forum', and in a poetry book by the Kenya Institute of Education.; [pers.] This poem is dedicated to my late father, J. N. Gakere. We miss you Dad, and we love you!; [a.] Los Angeles, CA

GALASSO, JEANNA MARIE
[b.] November 30, 1984, New York City; [p.] Norma Galasso and John Galasso; [pers.] Even though I am still young, I intend to continue writing because I enjoy it so much.

GALLARDO, DONNA J. WAKIYAN CHANTE
[pen.] Celine Santiago Talbot; [b.] April 23, 1954, Hawthorne, NV; [p.] Donald L. Gallardo, Amalia Gomez; [m.] Dennis 'Spotted Eagle' Dews, December 26, 1992; [ch.] Travis Adrian Duncan; [ed.] Hawthorne High, Wooster High University of Nevada and Reno (UNR) Life; [occ.] Finance and Accounting, Chinook Winds Casino; [oth. writ.] Several poems published in local newspapers.; [pers.] For open eyes, and my heart to see - I think creator and his magnificent creations.; [a.] Lincoln City, OR

GANTT SR., JACKIE
[pen.] John Henry Scott; [b.] November 28, 1943, Concord, NE; [p.] Jack Gordon Gantt, Bertha T.; [m.] Gina Clark (Fiance); [ch.] Jackie Gantt Jr., Alene Gantt; [occ.] Clown, Actor, Magician, DJ; [memb.] International Brotherhood of Magicians screen Actors Guild, AFTRA, past president Cajun French Music Association; [hon.] DJ Hall of Fame, Cajun Bass player of the year, Best performance by an actor, 86-87 New Orleans, Magician of the year 1969, NC; [oth. writ.] Donse Donse (song) Masked mayhem (Play-produced Oct. '94), the Cajun Fiddler (poem); [pers.] Life is so fleeting, if it's not fun, why bother.; [a.] Wilmington, NC

GARFIELD, LOTTIE
[m.] Bertram; [ch.] Ellen and Louise; [ed.] High School Graduate, Continuing Education Program University of Toronto Studied Art Central Technical School Art Department; [occ.] Retired from work at a treatment centre for emotionally troubled youth; [memb.] Board Member and past Vice President, Thyroid Foundation of Canada, past Vice-President Family and Child, Service of Metropolitan Toronto; [oth. writ.] Published in Periodical of a National Organization; [pers.] Keenly interested in poetry while in High School, particularly the classics and wrote poetry. This has resurfaced in my later years. I write spontaneously and often in response to events that interest me or happenings in my personal life. One of my favorite poets is Elizabeth Barrett Browning, but in contrast, I also appreciate the poetry of Ogden Nash and have been told there is some similarity to my own work.; [a.] Toronto, Downsview, Ontario, Canada

GARIFO, LAWRENCE
[b.] February 22, 1920, Philadelphia, PA; [p.] George and Jennie Garifo; [m.] Jeannine Rita Garifo, October 31, 1953; [ch.] Jacquelyn, Lawrence and Sallyann; [ed.] High School, Stenotype Institute - Phila.; [occ.] Court Reporter, Reporting Agency - Owner; [memb.] American Legion, Knights of Columbus, Man of Malvern - Malvern Pennsylvania; [hon.] Certificate of Merit — World War II - European Theater of Operations —

General Dwight D. Eisenhower, Commander in Chief; [pers.] Have written countless poems in my lifetime. Never bothered to save a copy.; [a.] Cherry Hill, NJ

GATLIN, JANIS
[pen.] Passion or CC; [b.] November 18, 1960, Pittsburgh, PA; [p.] Clarence Jackson, Eliza Jackson; [ch.] Eric, Jason, Mashawntla, and Marquita; [ed.] Farragut High Sch, Malcolm X College; [occ.] Bus driver of U 46 School District, Elgin Illinois; [memb.] Philadelphia Baptist Church mem of the church committee, member of the YMCA; [hon.] Dean's List in College many times; [oth. writ.] I have several other poems that reflect. What is, or what I expect to happen in my or my childrens future and present; [pers.] My philosophy is that life is what you make of it. If you use the ability that was given, then you will more than likely succeed in your endeavors; [a.] Elgin, IL

GATTO, GIUSEPPE
[b.] June 14, 1976, East York, ON, Canada; [p.] Leonard and Margaret Gatto; [ed.] Jean Vanier Catholic Secondary School, The University of Toronto; [occ.] Student and part-time worker at Garden Centre and Supermarket; [memb.] Leader - Boy Scouts of Canada.; [oth. writ.] A vast array of poems that have never else been revealed.; [pers.] My poetry reflects my on going journey through life, within my soul and in the world around me. It also reveals the inquisitiveness I have for everything that exists and doesn't exist.; [a.] Scarborough, Ontario, Canada

GAUGH, JANET K.
[b.] April 22, 1981, Jackson, TN; [p.] Neil B. and Lori K. Gaugh; [ed.] Chester County High School; [occ.] Student; [a.] Henderson, TN

GAUTHIER, CHRISTOPHER ROBERT
[b.] February 22, 1983, Montreal; [p.] Robert Gauthier, Lillian Comeau (Deceased); [ed.] Grade 7 Student; [occ.] Student; [hon.] Represented St. Gabriel's School for "Story Telling", Festival 2 times.; [oth. writ.] Assortment of Poems.; [pers.] I hope someday to be successful. I was greatly influenced by three people: My mother, sister, and Bela Lugosi, also my twin brother.; [a.] Montreal, Province of Quebec, Canada

GAYLORD, STANTON RAY
[occ.] Editor, Christian Faith Advocate Magazine; [oth. writ.] Miscellaneous publications, poem book - "Butterlings and Other Things"; [a.] Fort White, FL

GAYSEK, KARIN
[b.] May 12, 1941, Germany; [p.] Theresa and Herbert Luck; [m.] Stan Gaysek, April 21, 1961; [ch.] Carl and Linda; [ed.] Grade 12; [occ.] Health Care Aid - Dijl.; [memb.] Concordia Club, Concordia Bowling Ligue St Peter's Lutheran Church a Kitchener; [hon.] Royal Canadian Mounted Police Chalelain Magazine; [oth. writ.] "The Grapevine" - Peter Island - Conrdia News, Writing Awards, "Canadian Living" Recipe entering Contests.; [pers.] Striving for harmony and peaceful Co-existence within families, multinational races and all countries of our Earth.; [a.] Kitchener, Ontario, Canada

GEBRAN, NICOLAS NICOLAS
[pen.] Gebran; [b.] August 5, 1934, Bouweida, Lebanon; [p.] Nicolas Gebran, Ramzia Salum; [m.] Joumana Adib Rubeiz, September 28, 1974; [ch.] Nicole, Carla, Dalia; [ed.] B.Sc. Chemistry, 1958 (American University of Beirut, Lebanon; [occ.] Retired from proctor and gamble as of 5/96, after 34 years of managerial responsibilities; [memb.] 1) President of the Syndicate of Chemists in Lebanon, 2) Responsible Director of the Journal "World of Chemistry"; [hon.] Several service pins and awards;

[oth. writ.] 1) Several poems in Arabic and English (Most of them not published), 2) Write ups on industry and technology in local press, 3) A book in preparation entitled "Multinational companies in the Middle East and North Africa".; [pers.] "Strive to deliver to mankind with generosity"; [a.] Beirut, Lebanon

GENDRON, PIERRETTE
[b.] April 24, 1944, Northern Ontario, Canada; [p.] Yvette Poulin, Balthazar Proulx; [m.] John; [ch.] Renee, Tracey (Step daughter); [ed.] B.A. Laurentian University, B. Ed. Nipissing University, Specialist, Ottawa University; [occ.] School Teacher; [memb.] Professional Associations; [hon.] Stratcona Trust Committee Bursary from Teacher's College, Assistant Graduate, Dale Carnegie Course Several Recognitions for Artwork, Oil Pointing, Displays; [oth. writ.] Short stories, poems, in progress; [pers.] I often depict real life situations. When writing fiction, I contribute positively to society.; [a.] Osgoode, Ontario, Canada

GEORGE, BRIANT
[b.] September 18, 1962, New York City; [p.] Joan George and Elmo Johnson; [ed.] Marist College; [occ.] Corcraft Industry, "Machine Operator"; [memb.] Full Gospel Business, Men Fellowship Treasure (Chapter #1570); [hon.] School of Commercial Arts, Creative Writing Awards, Magazine Writing awards, Newspaper Writing awards, and Advertising Design and Layout awards.; [oth. writ.] Poems published in "Black Family" Magazine, C.O.P.E. Magazine and "Words of Faith" publication; [pers.] God is the source of my strength, the light of my life, and the joy in my heart! And I give all glory and honor to him... I greatly admire and love the poetry of Helen Steiner Rice...; [a.] Brooklyn, NY

GEORGE, STEPHEN
[b.] March 24, 1948, Brooklyn, NY; [p.] Mary and Joseph George; [m.] Marilu, May 8, 1971; [ch.] Christopher and Geraldine; [ed.] New York Institute of Credit; [occ.] Sales; [oth. writ.] Short Stories "Our Love Story," "The Book"; [pers.] Live each day as though you would live for a thousand years with haste to perfect the remaining years.; [a.] Old Tappan, NJ

GERVIN, LORI
[b.] October 16, 1965, Deloraine, Manitoba, Canada; [p.] Bill and Shirley McKinney; [m.] Alton Gervin, October 6, 1990; [ch.] Kara Faye-Ann Gervin; [ed.] B of S in Agriculture from North Dakota State University (1990) B.A. in Elementary Education from Moorhead State University (1989); [occ.] Grade 5 and 6 Teacher at Waskada School; [oth. writ.] Several poems related to my faith, family and or feelings.; [pers.] Several weeks after I became engaged I was inspired to write the poem, Side By Side. My writings are influenced by the two most important relationships in my life. My relationship with the Lord Jesus and my family.; [a.] Waskada, Manitoba, Canada

GETTIG, TIMOTHY A.
[pen.] TG; [b.] October 27, 1959, Panama City, FL; [p.] Ronald E. Gettig, JoAnne Green; [m.] Janice M. Gettig, March 9, 1979; [ed.] Graduated from Perrysburg High School, 1978, in Perrysburg, Ohio. Graduated from Michael J. Owens Technical College, January, 1984, in Perrysburg, Ohio, with an Associate Degree in Applied Business in Computer Programming, with a Major in Computer Programming; [occ.] I run my own Computer Consulting and Programming business. I engineer networks and program many practical business applications. I, also, sell advertising, as an Internet Consultant, to businesses wanting to advertise in

the iMALL on the Internet; [memb.] I've been awarded, "Distinguished Membership", by the International Society of Poets; [hon.] My poem, Thoughts Of A Seed..., appeared on the nationally syndicated radio show, Poetry Today, with Florence Henderson, on January 14, 1996, heard throughout the U.S., Canada, and the Caribbean. I've, also, received, Editor's Choice Award for, Thoughts Of A Seed..., from The National Library of Poetry's 1995 North American Open Poetry Contest. Nominated, one of the Best Poets of the Year for 1996, by the International Society of Poets, and visited their 1996 symposium and convention in Washington, D.C. the first week in August, 1996. Asked by the National Library of Poetry to include another poem of mine, in their upcoming anthology, Best Poems of the '90's, due Winter, 1996. I am proud to have my poem, Just Me!?, published in this special edition. Only 2% of the individuals whose poetry were examined were selected to be a part of this distinguished group of outstanding poets.; [oth. writ.] My poem, Thoughts Of A Seed..., was published mid-year, 1996, by the NLP, in their anthology, The Voice Within. My poem, Just Me!?, is scheduled for publication Winter, 1996, by the NLP in an anthology entitled, Best Poems of the '90's. My poem, You're My Butterfly, is scheduled for publication, Winter, 1996, by the NLP in an anthology named, Morning Star. My poem, Lil' Birdy, is scheduled for publication, Winter, 1997, by the NLP in an anthology entitled, The Colors Of Thought.; [pers.] As I make my way along life's path, searching for what it is I want, many times, usually more than not, I come across another of God's wonders. Surprised I am not, awed by your miracles, I Am.; [a.] Margate, FL

GETTRY, JOAN E.
[b.] Jamaica, West Indies; [p.] Deceased; [m.] Martin D. (Deceased); [ch.] An adorable 9 yr. old English Springer Spaniel Dog; [ed.] An Associates Degree, La Guardia Community College. Future Goals - Hunter College; [occ.] Homemaker; [memb.] Women's Auxiliary, N.Y., Medical Center. International Society of Poets.; [hon.] Dean's List; [pers.] Life, is not only beating of the heart and workings of other organs, but a life-force that teachers the in's and out's of conflicts and strife which an only be unravelled by careful reflectivity.; [a.] Beechhurst, NY

GEVAERT, CINDY
[pen.] C. J. Madden; [b.] January 23, 1962, Montreal, Quebec; [p.] Neil and Shirley Madden; [ch.] Christopher, Camile, Amy, Shirley; [ed.] Howard S. Billings H.S.; [pers.] My poems are a definite part of me. I write to go places that cannot and I hope to take others along. Nature rules me.

GIAIMO, FAY
[pen.] Renee; [b.] November 14, 1943, Cleveland, OH; [p.] Franklin and Arline Eldred; [ch.] Joseph and Anthony Hlavinka; [ed.] Parma Senior High, Cuyahoga Community College; [occ.] Customer Service Representative; [memb.] Florida Motion Picture and Television Assoc., Wyoming Antelope Club; [oth. writ.] Poem published in poetry anthology; [pers.] Through my poetry I hope to inspire those who may be suffering mentally, emotionally, or physically by bringing forth a reflection of the love that the spirit has to offer to them.; [a.] Largo, FL

GIBBONS, COURTNEY REISS
[pen.] Andrea Frumples; [b.] April 13, 1982, New Haven, CT; [p.] Thomas W. and Gail Reiss Gibbons; [ed.] Amity High School; [occ.] Stablehand, Student; [memb.] Sleeping Giant Pony Club, Student Council, Drama Club, Life; [hon.] Honoured by my school for artistic and creative ability. I've

been honoured by my family for caring and by caring unconditionally.; [oth. writ.] I write to bring joy to others. This is the first I've had published. I hope it isn't my last!; [pers.] To all that have suffered or are suffering, the only way to be healed is to learn to heal others. Use what you have and let your heart become your brain! I have found happiness this way.; [a.] Woodbridge, CT

GIBBS, JESSICA
[b.] February 27, 1980, Sault Ste. Marie, Ontario, Canada; [p.] Heather Gibbs, Bob Gibbs; [ed.] Currently a grade 11 student at Bawating Collegiate High School; [hon.] Writers and Sports Awards for grade 8 graduation; [oth. writ.] More poetry and short stories.; [pers.] My poetry comes from my feelings that I don't usually express and the pain and hurt going on all over the world.; [a.] Sault Ste. Marie, Ontario, Canada

GIBBS, SHARON E.
[pen.] Seg, L.A.S.S.I.; [b.] January 14, 1971, Lewis Delaware; [p.] Nathaniel and Christine Gibbs; [ed.] Dover High School, Delaware State University Majoring in Hotel Restaurant Management; [occ.] Room Service Supervisor with four season luxury Hotel in Autumn, TX; [memb.] Zeta Phi Beta Sorority, Christian Hope Cogic; [hon.] Deans List Attended School of service and hospitality for wine. Seminars, President of YWCC; [oth. writ.] Several poems published in the eye magazine other poems such as silent rage, my shepherd dream a dream within a dream, questions, a vow, life's a privaledge, just a hug, I love you Matthew; [pers.] "To live your life your own way, to reach for the goals you have set to yourself, to be the you that you want to be, that is success". Don't ever let anyone dictate your life but you. Life is about being truly happy; [a.] Justin, TX

GILLIS, CHRISTINE
[b.] August 24, 1970, Brooklyn; [p.] Pam Ferolano; [ed.] Tottenville High School, College of Staten Island; [memb.] National Asthma Association, American Cancer Society, V.A. Red Cross Search and Rescue, C.C.E.; [hon.] Track team, Spelling bee champ, Cert of accomplishment from P.H.P., Award of merit in poetic art, Awards of honor from Y.P.D.C., Honor Student; [oth. writ.] Many other poems published in Anthologies, writing in magazines, essays of life stories.; [pers.] This specific poem is dedicated and written especially for my mother, who had battled all my problems with me so patiently and loving. I reflect all my feeling and life stories through my poetry and writings.; [a.] Staten Island, NY

GISCLAIR, ERICA LYN N.
[b.] September 18, 1981; [p.] Yenton and Debra Gisclair; [pers.] I feel like when I write about Mark and his death in a sense it keeps his spirit alive with me.; [a.] Cut Off, LA

GODWIN, LORI CAMILLE
[pen.] Cami Godwin; [b.] July 8, 1975, Washington, DC; [p.] John B. Stewart II and Fran Williams; [m.] Bobby A. Godwin, April 25, 1994; [ch.] Samantha Godwin; [ed.] Junior at UNC-W (currently) majoring in Psychology UNC-W - University of North Carolina at Wilmington; [occ.] Student; [memb.] UNC-W Track Team; [hon.] Dean's List 3 Times; [oth. writ.] This will be my first publication.; [pers.] As I lay across my bed, with my dog Poddie, I spotted the evil red fuzz ball. The dark warrior Poddie abruptly ate the fuzz ball and we won the battle! This poem holds the key to my childhood.; [a.] Wilmington, NC

GOLDBERG, YVONNA
[pen.] Iwona Opoczynska; [b.] October 24, 1955, Poland, Wraclaw; [p.] Jakub Opoczynska, Edwarda

Opoczynska; [m.] Norman Goldberg, November 29, 1988; [ch.] Paul, Adam; [ed.] Wroclaw University, Poland Teachers College, Columbia University, New York; [occ.] Computer Teacher, St Mary Star of the Sea School, Bayonne, NJ; [oth. writ.] Reports, articles, reviews and short stories published in Polish regional newspapers and national periodicals (1968-88).; [pers.] I believe in immortality of words.; [a.] Iselin, NJ

GOODMAN, JEAN M.
[b.] November 26, 1931, Rhineland, MD; [p.] Fred H. and Florence E. Saak; [m.] Hugh W. Goodman, April 16, 1988; [ch.] Stanley R. Shaw and Nickie J. Shaw; [ed.] Rhineland Elementary School, Eureka High School, National School of Dress Design; [occ.] Retired; [memb.] Bethal United Church of Christ, The Twin Foundation; [hon.] It was an honor to be a twin (identical). It was the greatest honor I ever had.; [pers.] I wrote this poem after my twin sister died. We were very close. We had our first sons about two hours apart. I lost my father two months before my sister. I still have my mothers, two sisters and a brother.; [a.] Florissant, MO

GOPINATH, KALYANI
[b.] 24 January 1971, Kerala, India; [p.] K. Gopinath, Girija Gopinath; [ed.] Bachelor of Arts (English Literature); [occ.] Freelance Journalist; [hon.] First Ranker in the University. Awarded a scholarship under The National Scholarship Scheme of the Government of India; [oth. writ.] Written stories and articles pertaining to children, while working for a children's magazine, a weekly supplement of the Khaleej times, the leading English daily in the UAE.; [pers.] I feel strongly for the children of the world. I wrote 'Down the Ages' during the height of the Bosnian struggle. I wish it would all end. I have been a great admirer of T.S. Eliot.; [a.] Dubai, United Arab Emirates

GORDON, INA
[b.] September 19, 1911, Schuler, Alberta, Canada; [p.] William Peterson, Mary Hingsburger; [m.] Second Marriage, Harold Gordon (Deceased) October 14, 1973; [ch.] One (Deceased); [ed.] Grade 12; [occ.] Retired; [hon.] Honors, old time fiddler contest; [oth. writ.] Over 300 selection of Poetry.; [pers.] Natural Musical talent, and Humanitarian Nature. Two languages able to speak.; [a.] Edmonton, Alberta, Canada

GOSS, EVELYN
[pen.] Evelyn Goss; [b.] June 3, 1917, Canton, OH; [p.] Sadie and Adelbert Danner; [m.] Pete Maurer of 46 yrs. now deceased, 2nd George Goss, August 31, 1986; [ch.] Tim and Bob Maurer; [ed.] High school graduate from McKinley in 1935. Now attend Malone College as Auditing each year.; [occ.] Retired; [memb.] Belonged to Leaders Club in high school, and Christian endeavor at church of God, now belong to Unity Church of Truth; [hon.] Won quite a few gold medals while performing in senior olympics when I was in my sixties, biking, bowling, tennis, long jump, running horseshoes, golf, and table tennis; [oth. writ.] Story of my skydiving at age of 79 to the Reader's Digest (not as yet printed or returned). Special article to the Canton Repository; [pers.] Thank God for my life and hope to keep on being alive while living.; [a.] Canton, OH

GOSS, LINDA D.
[b.] July 9, 1959, Muncie, IN; [p.] Ruby and Jerry Smith; [m.] Robert C. Goss Jr., September 4, 1982; [ed.] University Southern Colorado; [occ.] Registered Nurse; [pers.] This poem was inspired by nature and is in memory to my husband who lost his physical bonds to mother Earth in January 1996.; [a.] Rifle, CO

GOSS, YVONNE BROWN
[b.] March 19, 1947, Hodge, LA; [p.] James V. Brown, Caryol Holtzclaw; [m.] Divorced; [ed.] Jonesboro Hodge High Quachita Votec School - (Nursing); [occ.] Licensed Practical Nurse; [oth. writ.] Have had two poems published in local newspaper. Have written one for wedding.; [pers.] I write simple poems but everyday happenings. Poems ordinary people can read and understand. They're usually the ones living the everyday things I write about. I like writing science fiction poems the most, however. I guess I'm very much a dreamer about the future but I don't forget the realities of life.; [a.] Jonesboro, LA

GOSSE, PABLO
[pen.] P. W. Gosse; [b.] October 1, 1974, Grand Falls, NF; [p.] Walter Gosse and Maria Gosse; [ed.] Graduated from Botwood Collegiate in June, 1992. Graduated from Memorial University of NF in April 1996, with B.A. in English and Philosophy; [occ.] Student at Lawrence College, St. John's, NF. (Journalism); [pers.] Write not to please others, but to satisfy one's inner-soul.; [a.] Botwood, Newfoundland, Canada

GOULD, CLEO C.
[pen.] CCG; [b.] March 4, 1927, Regina, Saskatchewan; [p.] Connie and Harry Taylor (Terzakis); [m.] James Robert Gould, May 28, 1972; [ed.] Wellsley High School - Toronto, Ont. Canada Shaw's Business College - Toronto, Ont. Canada (Secretarial Course); [occ.] Housewife; [memb.] "Golden Gators of Gainesville, FL", American Kennel Dog Club, Was Secretary of the Chihuahua Club of Florida. (1960's) Dragon Keep - Personal Computer Communication Freenet/ Internet Communication Programs; [hon.] Many trophies/ribbons Awards for showing in AKC Dog Shows; [oth. writ.] None, but have several started in my computer.; [pers.] I have strived to be a good citizen, always willing to listen to other people's troubles and to help when possible. Most of all enjoy being with my Spouse and our little "Chocolate Chip," a 3 pound Chihuahua which I take with me on my electric scooter wherever allowed.

GRAHAM, PETER J.
[b.] July 31, 1971, Calgary, Alberta; [p.] Sharon and Elgin Graham; [ed.] Lorne Jenkin High School, currently attending Mount Royal College, Faculty of Education; [occ.] Past jobs include everything from Beekeeping to sales to construction to tutoring English; [memb.] National Qi Gong Association; [hon.] Honors in English and Economics; [oth. writ.] I have no previously published poetry, this is the first time I have sent something in.; [pers.] I believe poetry unlocks the gate to our soul and connects us with a deeper world consciousness. I try to and reflect the world as it feels.; [a.] Calgary, Alberta, Canada

GRANDSTAFF, NIKKI
[b.] December 4, 1962, Oklahoma; [p.] Patricia A. Melton; [ed.] Midwest City High, currently taking college courses; [occ.] Interactive Coordinator; [pers.] I gratefully acknowledge my mother's influence on my life, her heart and her love. I also hope that somehow my writings can positively affect others.; [a.] Irving, TX

GRAY, ERIC JAMES
[pen.] Eric James Gray; [b.] January 27, 1957, Cincinnati, OH; [p.] William Gray, Mary Gray; [m.] Susan Jean Gray, August 7, 1979; [ch.] Stephen, Peter-Joseph, Emma-Christa, Jonathan; [ed.] Aiken Senior High, University of Cincinnati; [occ.] Math Teacher, Hughes Center, Cincinnati, OH; [pers.] I try to express sound good with good sound, personal feeling with public beauty, and Yeats has been my own works springing ground.; [a.] Cincinnati, OH

GREEN, GWENDOLYN NORRINGTON
[b.] October 11, 1952, Newton County, GA; [m.] Charles Green Jr., October 24, 1971; [ch.] Shely, Coretta, Charles III, Mathew; [ed.] R.L. Cousin High School Dekalb Technical Institute; [occ.] Housewife; [memb.] Graves Chapel A.M.E. Church; [pers.] I write of feeling that move the soul, mind and heart that tell the truth about life. I write about serious feeling.; [a.] Oxford, GA

GREEN, SHANNON
[b.] November 18, 1976, Kenora, ON; [p.] Glen and Cathie Green; [ed.] Beaver Brae Secondary School; [memb.] Keewatin Ringette Association, Kenora Rowing Club; [hon.] Graduated from High School with honours with assd.; [oth. writ.] Several other poems, none of which are published.; [pers.] My poetry is sacred to me. It comes from my hopes, my fears, my dreams and most importantly it comes from my heart. I am a poet and an artist as well as many other things.; [a.] Keewatin, Ontario, Canada

GREEN, STAN
[pen.] A.K.A. Norman St. Paul; [b.] April 19, 1918, Horizon, London; [p.] Clara Grace and Bertram James; [m.] Patricia A., February 4, 1950; [ch.] Paul Michael; [ed.] Degreed Civil Eng.; [occ.] Retired, Writer - Artist; [memb.] London Society of Art, ISP Hit Soc. Poets, British Legionnaire; [hon.] Mention in dispatches WW II, British Sports Car Champion; [oth. writ.] The Shame in Spain, There Ain't No Justice, We'll Meet Again, Go To Hell!; [pers.] Prolific writer in many genes industry Poetry. Offending me the opportunity to express concern of a sad world which appears to be lost and struggling for survival.; [a.] Coquitlam, British Columbia, Canada

GREENWALD, MS. BRIDGET MARIA
[b.] June 29, 1983, Detroit, MI; [p.] Amelia and Henry Greenwald; [ed.] Omni Elementary Middle School Boca Raton, FL, in the 8th grade; [pers.] My sister Annette Juanita put the positive outlook in me. Yes I wore glasses and was a bit chunky so when I looked in the mirror I was happy looking at me!; [a.] Boca Raton, FL

GREGORY, MARK ALLEN
[b.] October 12, 1957, Indianapolis, IN; [p.] H. W. Gregory, Katherine Gregory; [ch.] Nichole D. Gregory; [ed.] Perry Meridian High University of Indianapolis; [occ.] Quality Control Manager; [memb.] South Port Baptist Church Tri-Country Counselling Committee, Alpha XI Delta; [oth. writ.] Several poems published in local newspapers.; [pers.] I believe that by sharing of life we can be happy. I believe that life should be lived each day to it fullest degree that I can live it. In finding and losing love - we grow.; [a.] Indianapolis, IN

GREINER, TASHA
[b.] July 6, 1981, Winston Salem, NC; [p.] Steve Greiner, Teresa Deadmon; [ed.] 9th grade; [occ.] Student; [pers.] Hobbies and interests: play clarinet, guitar, some piano. Write often. Plant to study in Archeology, loves the ocean.; [a.] Wilmington, NC

GRETCHEN, DENISE
[b.] North Arlington, NJ; [p.] Carolyn R. Gretchen (m), Dennis A. Gretchen (p); [ed.] M.A., Ed.M - Teachers College, Columbia University, B.A. (Cumlaude), University of Delaware. Pursuing a PhD. Counseling Psychology; [occ.] Research Assistant, Institute for Urban and Minority Education Information Specialist - Eric Clearing House on Urban Education; [memb.] Phi Beta Kappa, Golden Key National Honor Society, American Psychological Association, American Counseling Association.; [hon.] University of Delaware De-

partment of Communication Faculty Award - Outstanding Senior Communication Major, 1994. Several awards for creative writing - from primary and secondary (high school) grades.; [oth. writ.] Professional Publications - Study on Magnet Schools, Study on the process of out placement counseling, study on teacher's views of violence in the schools. Editor of student journal of counseling psychology.; [pers.] To me, writing poetry is quite therapeutic. Through the years, it has given me an outlet to express raw emotions, reflective thoughts, and the very essence of my experience.; [a.] Brooklyn, NY

GRIFFITHS, EDWARD
[pen.] Edward St. Boniface, The Bromechanoid; [b.] April 16, 1967, Winnipeg, Canada; [p.] Unit 97, CyberGene Experimental Labs Inc.; [m.] Estella The Xylopede, Shortly after her metamorphosis; [ch.] Various Grubs, Chrysalides and Pupae; [ed.] Scattery; [occ.] Elastic; [memb.] I hope one day to join the human race; [hon.] Life (by who/whatever); [oth. writ.] A novel of the far future and numerous paranoid - supernatural stories, all requiring a publisher-some E-Zine publication in columns and a rag-tag collection of reviews, verse and minuscule 'psychopace' preces.; [pers.] Never Trust: Rust Lepers or, Stargenies or, Alrens or, Blondes or, Bromechanoids.; [a.] Cosmopolis, Cosmic of Fear

GRIFFITHS, MILDRED P.
[pen.] Pearl; [p.] Mildred Gray Griffiths; [oth. writ.] My mother from Old Furge, Pa., has written and pub. 22 poems: My Pet Lacry, Memories of Childhood, Flying by Wire, Who Shall I Vote E or Etc. Artist Paint, Picturer, Coal Brakers-pets for humane Dr. Blomawe Society, Purchased two paintings I am also writing a story about our town. Spike Island and the Coalmones. From creative arts and science and world of poetry this poem I have written about the "Gray House" my mother lived and was born in, and her maiden name was Gray also. Poem A Minors Life Cast, a poem about rocky glem park mystery name of Spike Island poems about Christmas past, Where do we go from here, It's Ninty Six, A Thanksgiving poem. Mother, Mildred Gray Griffiths, published twenty two poems, One about John Glenn's space flight received letter from John Glenn and wife and Nacsao sent an appreciative letter for poem Flying by Wire by my mother.

GROVES, HONORIA A.
[b.] April 26, 1923, England; [p.] Lloyd and Jessie Norman; [m.] Ernie Groves (Deceased), September 10, 1955; [occ.] Retired; [memb.] Church of the Nazarene; [oth. writ.] Five Booklets of Inspirational poetry self published as a ministry to hurting people.; [pers.] I believe emotional and spiritual needs can be met through a relationship with Jesus Christ.; [a.] Oakville, Ontario, Canada

GRUVER, KELLY
[b.] October 8, 1977, Chambersburg, PA; [p.] Jim and Barb Gruver; [ed.] Shippensburg High School, Shippensburg University; [occ.] Student; [pers.] I pray for inspiration and use the gift of God has given me to write the best poetry I am able to.; [a.] Shippensburg, PA

GUARDADO, MARTHA
[b.] August 16, 1945, El Salvador; [p.] Andres Leonor and Leonor Merino; [m.] Luis Guardado, October 24, 1970; [ch.] Katherine; [ed.] 11 years; [occ.] Office Clerk; [oth. writ.] Poems; [pers.] Every raindrop has the possibility to create a rainbow.; [a.] San Francisco, CA

GUERRA JR., GUADALUPE J.
[b.] February 25, 1956, Laredo, TX; [p.] Guadalupe and Irene Guerra Sr.; [m.] Carol A. Guerra. Decem-

ber 10, 1992; [ed.] J.W. Nixon High, U.S. Navy 6 years; [occ.] Disabled; [a.] Austin, TX

GUNTON, SUSAN ANN
[pen.] Mother - Dorcus Bell / Kemp, Dorcus Bell; [b.] 15/02/49, Norwich, England; [p.] Regonald and Dorcus Kemp; [m.] Malcolm Gunton, 2/10/71; [ed.] Secondary Modern; [occ.] Royal Mail NCH(First Aid); [hon.] First Aid / Cup first; [oth. writ.] Several stories of life in Norfolk. Other poems of feeling on how I feel. Stories as my mother told of how life was for many folk in Norfolk.; [pers.] I have listened and read stories of life in Norfolk of life hopes and dreams and so often letdowns loneliness; also of hope and love, which is life.; [a.] Norwich, Norfolk, England

HAACHIZO, PIOUS
[b.] December 7, 1969, Chirundu, Zambia; [p.] Peter Haachizo and Edina Muleya; [ed.] University of Zambia; [occ.] Student (BSC Bio/Chem); [memb.] Martin Luther King Jr. Memorial Library, British Council Library, A Childhood Memory: The Staid Flow of River Zambezi; [hon.] Second Best Student award - Grade Eleven 1986, Canisius Secondary School (Zambia); [oth. writ.] A few poems (unpublished), a novel in prose (unpublished); [pers.] Up the narrow staircase, to entirety of absence, of hate, haste, greed, they make their tread. They are the poets.; [a.] Lusaka, Zambia

HAAS, BRENT
[m.] Mary Jo, January 1, 1990; [ch.] Kristine, Christopher; [ed.] BA - Holy Cross Seminary, BA - University of Wis/Whitewater, MS - Governors State University; [occ.] Teacher/Coach - Naperville, North High School - Naperville, IL; [oth. writ.] Numerous poems published in poetry magazines; [pers.] Aging is not an option but it is an opportunity.; [a.] Aurora, IL

HAATS, GREGORY G.
[pen.] Toyota; [b.] August 6, 1961, Vancouver, WA; [p.] Shirley Ann Arionus; [ed.] G.E.D. 1992, Fbks. Ak., Hutcheson Career Center; [oth. writ.] (Little Book of Poems and Paint) Dedicated to, Ms. Shirley Arionus, Dedicate (Video), 100% proceeds goes to United Way Foundation and Dorbecers Children Hospitals.; [pers.] Again I'm just one person trying to do the right thing and or say the right thing...; [a.] Vancouver, WA

HAGBERG, ANNETTE
[b.] May 3, 1961, Uppsala; [p.] Mona and Thorsten Borgehammar; [m.] Lars-Ake Hagberg, November 19, 1983; [ch.] Emma, Mattias, Lucas; [ed.] Undergraduate at the University of Uppsala (currently). Main subjects - English and German.; [occ.] Student; [hon.] I was awarded the prize for English at Observatory East School, and St. Angela's Ursuline Convent (both schools in Johannesburg, South Africa, where I lived for six years).; [oth. writ.] One poem (Swedish) published in a Swedish anthology; [pers.] I'm a lover of literature. During my English studies I wrote two large essays within the subject of American literature (authors: Faulkner and Kate Chopin). (Exam projects); [a.] Uppsala, Sweden

HAGER, STEPHANIE RENEE
[b.] May 26, 1968, Bloomfield, IA; [p.] Jerry and Patricia Hyde; [m.] Douglas E. Hager, July 30, 1993; [ch.] Evan Joseph and Dillon James; [ed.] Albia Community High School; [oth. writ.] One other poem published in Rainbows end titled "Broken Heart Former"; [pers.] I write personal feelings in my poetry and strive for awareness of my talents. Hoping to reach out to others.; [a.] Ogden, IA

HAHN, DAE SOO
[b.] March 12, 1948, Pusan, Korea; [m.] Oxana - Mongolian princess; [occ.] Poet-Songwriter-Pho-

tographer; [hon.] 1. Best Ten - 1st Korean Pop Song Festival - for songwriting, 2. Awarded "Kook-Jun" Korea's prestigious art exhibition - for photography; [oth. writ.] 1. Photographed and edited "History of Korean Costumes" - Suk Joo Sun, 2. Photographic prints for "Manhattan Lightscapes" - N. Lieberman, 3. Released 7 albums and CD's of own composition - Seoul; [pers.] "We must fight against our malicious nature to find beauty and spread the seed of kindness"; [a.] New York, NY

HAIDER, SYED IFTIKHAR
[pen.] Iftikhar Haider; [b.] November 14, 1929, Pakistan; [p.] Syed and Khurshid Haider; [m.] Mahmuda Haider, April 1961; [ch.] Sadia and Faiza; [ed.] Various Technical Diplomas; [occ.] Retired; [memb.] Member Writer's Guild; [hon.] Gold Medal (Literature) 1996, Philips International Light Design Award.; [oth. writ.] Author of 4 books.; [pers.] Truth remains truth even if nobody accepts it.; [a.] Toronto, Ontario, Canada

HAIRSTON, DEACON JOHN W.
[b.] December 24, 1951, Ararat, VA; [p.] Agnes V. Hairston; [m.] Leatha Hairston, November 30, 1996; [ch.] Kerion; [ed.] 12th grade GED; [memb.] Miracle Temple Fellowship Church; [hon.] Certificate of Appreciation Sheraton - Harrisburg Inn one year, loyal and conscientious service 1980, Gospel Echoes team, certificate of completion of 8 series courses Home Bible study in 1994; [pers.] I thank God for being God, is my prayer. I truly love poetry as the one's in proverbs.; [a.] Lancaster, TX

HALE, ALBERT VEARDY
[b.] December 3, 1921, Wales, UK; [m.] Mary Margaret, October 22, 1946; [ch.] Two - Brian and Michael; [ed.] Electrical Engineering - Technical Institute and Colleges South Wales, UK; [occ.] Retired; [memb.] Member of DACETT, Certified Engineering Technician Ontario; [oth. writ.] I have written several poems over the years.; [pers.] I try to provide a message in my poetry to mankind.; [a.] Aurora, Ontario, Canada

HALE, DOROTHY
[pen.] Dorothy Hale; [b.] Peterborough; [p.] Wm. Rose, Elizabeth Rose; [m.] Leslie R. Hale (Deceased); [ch.] Three sons: Jackie, Kim, Alan; [ed.] St. Peter's High School, St. Mary's Convent all in Peterborough; [occ.] Retired for three years, owned and operated bridal salon; [memb.] Peterborough Branch Canadian Opera Guild Peterborough Horticulture Society; [hon.] My highest honour has been going blessed with three wonderful sons. Nothing could possibly top that.; [oth. writ.] Various subjects private collection never published.; [pers.] Inspired by William Blake and Robert Browning. I write for my own enjoyment and relaxation and interested in spiritual themes.; [a.] Peterborough, Ontario, Canada

HALEY, BARBARA
[b.] May 4, 1945, Plainview, TX; [p.] Woodrow and Ruby Surratt; [m.] Jerry Haley, November 30, 1963; [ch.] Stacey Dawn; [ed.] Muleshoe High School, Clovis Community College; [oth. writ.] Recently had a poem and short story published in an anthology at the college I attend.; [pers.] I have always enjoyed reading and writing poetry. My writing has always been influenced by my surroundings and the events of my life.; [a.] Muleshoe, TX

HALL, ALISON
[b.] June 30, 1965, Berkshire, England; [p.] Thomas and Pauline Hall; [ed.] Rosary High School, California State University at Fullerton, Rancho Santiago College; [occ.] Child Care Director, Univ. of Calif., Irvine; [memb.] National Association for the Education of Young Children, California Elementary Education Association; [hon.] Dean's List - Calif State Univ., Fullerton

HALL, ELVIE D.
[pen.] "S"; [b.] May 5, 1966, Aurora, IL; [p.] L. V. Hall, Carla Brown; [ed.] Oswego High; [occ.] Motorcycle Mechanic, Aurora Cycle; [memb.] Klingon Armada; [pers.] Life is short, so make the most of it. When looking back. Remember the good times, have no regrets, and be happy.; [a.] Aurora, IL

HALL, JERRIE LYNN
[pen.] J. L. H.; [b.] April 25, 1951, Everett, WA; [p.] Arnold R. Meyer (Deceased) and Alta M. Ross; [m.] Thomas A. Hall, December 11, 1971; [ch.] Jonathan A. Hall, Jennifer C. Mafli, Heather M. Hall, and David B. Hall; [ed.] Forks H.S., Northwest College, A.A.; [occ.] Valet, Sis of Providence St. Peters Hospital, Olympia, WA; [memb.] Sponsor, WA. St. Law Enf. Assc., Sponsor, WA. St. Council of Fire Fighters, Past Mem. and Renewing Mem. with Williamette Writers, Portland, OR; [hon.] Best Actress and Most Insp. Player, H.S. Play "The Lark". Best Actress, All District Drama Festival and Competition, Grays Harbor College, (The Lark), H.S.; [pers.] I express, and seek to convey the wonder, and intricacies of creation, both through the eyes of and hidden within the heart, of one...; [a.] Lacey, WA

HALL, LISA R.
[b.] July 26, 1964, Leoti, KS; [ch.] Cameron; [ed.] B.S. Medical Technology; [occ.] Medical Technologist

HALL JR., JAMES
[b.] February 9, 1971, Okinawa, Japan; [p.] James Hall Sr. and Anise E. Ritchie; [m.] Tai Said-Hall, June 2, 1995; [ed.] High School Diploma; [occ.] Office Clerk; [oth. writ.] In the works, God Willing; [pers.] To the next generation, Jesus Christ was my only way home. Satan almost deceived me/ my soul, but thanks to God's amazing grace...He saved us!; [a.] Portland, OR

HALLMARK, PHILIP
[b.] July 23, 1979, Florence, AL; [p.] Harlon Hallmark, Brenda Hallmark; [ed.] Currently a senior in high school; [occ.] Bagger at Food World; [a.] Russellville, AL

HALPERN, KATE ALLISON
[b.] June 16, 1980, New York City; [p.] Ronnye and Richard Halpern; [ed.] Currently attending Brooklyn Technical High School (Major: Environmental Science); [memb.] Student Government, Leadership Training, and Raices Literary Magazine; [hon.] Certificate of Excellence for Freshman and Sophomore English, 2nd place in DC-37 art contest, acceptance to the Manice High School Leadership Training Program and, Who's Who Among American High School Students; [oth. writ.] Several unpublished poems and short stories as well as a novel in the works.; [pers.] Words I live by: If you want something, get it yourself. Luck is when preparation meets opportunity and life is a writer's best inspiration and smile.; [a.] Roosevelt Island, NY

HAMBLETON, JEN
[pen.] Epona; [b.] October 16, 1980, Wilmington, DE; [p.] Rebecca Hambleton; [ed.] I am a sophomore at Concord High School in Wilmington, DE; [occ.] Student; [pers.] In my poetry I reflect the symbolism of the earth and of mankind. I have been influenced by Edgar Allen Poe.; [a.] Wilmington, DE

HAMILTON, ALEX
[pen.] Alex Bennett; [b.] May 31, 1984, Carmichael, CA; [p.] Hugh Hamilton, Susan Bennett and Wesley Bennett (Stepfather); [ed.] Currently in 7th grade; [occ.] Student; [memb.] Student Council; [hon.] Academic Achievement awards in Math, Writing and Reading. Citizenship awards. Student Council award.; [oth. writ.] The Storm,

The Mad Cat, The Leprechaun, Trees My Summer, Fall, Changes, Seasons, Winter, Favorites.; [pers.] It's an honor to have my poem published in this book, and I hope to have more done in the future.; [a.] Orangeville, CA

HAMILTON, ELLEN GERALDINE
[pen.] Jerri Hamilton; [b.] February 5, 1922, Green County, IN; [p.] Robert W. and Eva Geraldine Chipman; [m.] Floyd P. Hamilton, October 29, 1939; [ch.] Elizabeth, Larry, Ronald, Sandra Myron, Ted; [ed.] High School, grade school writing course; [occ.] Retired; [memb.] Russiaville United Church, First Niters Home Ec, Lay Speaker for Church, Member of Lay Witness Missions Group; [hon.] Two poems, special recognition in County Homemakers, one poem published in American Poetry; [oth. writ.] Poems, articles, children stories, newspapers (Kokomo, in Tribune) and (Evening World - Bloomield, IN); [pers.] My church work and personal relationship with God and Christ is my inspiration to write. I love to write about animals children and my faith. My poetry and writing reflect this. I love the outdoors and have written poems about this.; [a.] Russiaville, IN

HANEY, ERIN
[b.] February 8, 1986, Pittsburgh, PA; [p.] Dan Haney and Vicky Haney; [ed.] Graduated from 4th grade at Heritage Elementary School, Murrysville, PA; [occ.] Student; [memb.] Girl Scout Troop #104, Ballet and Jazz at Christine's School of Dance; [pers.] I think poetry should be fun. I get most of my ideas from the world around me.; [a.] Export, PA

HANSEN, ROBERT L.
[b.] September 1, 1947, Toledo, OH; [p.] Leonard C. Hansen, Virginia I. Hansen; [m.] Divorced, married for 20 yrs; [ch.] John Charles, Kristen Lynn; [ed.] Gallup High School, New Mexico State University; [occ.] Sr. Maintenance Planner for Saudi Aramco Oil Company; [memb.] Dhahran Chap, S.A.M.E., MILO 938 AF and AM, BPOE #1747.; [oth. writ.] I have written many other poems I hope to soon have published.; [pers.] My poetry reflects my personal walk through divorce. And all the emotions that accompanied it. Presently working and residing in Saudi Arabia.

HARCOURT, DONNA DECKER
[pen.] Dona Decker Harcourt; [b.] December 7, 1933, Long Beach, CA; [p.] Elmer L. Decker, Alma R. Decker; [m.] Divorced, August 31, 1957; [ch.] Two; [ed.] Graduated from Marymount College in Los Angeles with a B.A. Degree 1954; [occ.] Rancher, Farmer raise Quarter Horses; [memb.] A.Q.H.A., A.P.H.A.; [hon.] Long Beach, CA. Sports Boosters Hall of Fame, World American Stock Seat Medal Competition. (A.H.S.A.) in 1949, Queen of the Long Beach Float for Rose Parade in Los Angeles, CA., Equestrian Award (1949) for Best Western JA. Rider Judged by the So. California Equestrian Paradesmen's Assn. (Committee of 6).; [oth. writ.] Personal; [pers.] Life itself is poetry. It offers a myriad of opportunities... Unimaginable. The "Lee Tree" is just a simple reminder. I offer this poem to my grandson, Lee.; [a.] Paso Robles, CA

HARDEE, MONICA NICOLE
[pen.] Monica; [b.] December 28, 1981, Myrtle Beach, SC; [p.] Benjy and Lynda Hardee; [ed.] North Myrtle Beach High School; [memb.] Young Life Youth Group, NMB J.V. Cheerleaders, Hap Ki Do Karate Team; [hon.] National Beta Club, 8th Grade Creative Writing Award, Horsemanship Awards; [pers.] In my writings I express the torture and pain that took place in the Holocaust. The inspiration to write was given to me by the famous Ann Frank.; [a.] Little River, SC

HARDING, KRISTEN MICHELLE
[b.] February 28, 1979, Guelph, Ontario, Canada; [p.] James and Kathleen Harding; [ed.] Brookville Public School and Milton District High School; [occ.] Ontario Ranger (Summer '96); [memb.] Girl Guides of Canada; [hon.] Honor (Public School - gr. II) Girl Guide: All Round Cord and Canada Cord; [oth. writ.] Several articles and a poem in my school yearbooks.; [pers.] Life doesn't take you where it wants to go, you take life where you want to go. In other words, only you can lead your life, so make it the best one possible.; [a.] Campbellville, Ontario, Canada

HARDY, BRENDA
[b.] October 21, 1957, Alexandria, LA; [p.] Lee and Lucille Johnson; [m.] Ronnie Hardy, February 14, 1984; [ch.] Sonia Cheree, Tarence Logan; [ed.] Manual High School, Aurora Community College; [occ.] Special Needs Scheduler for Aurora Public School Transportation Dept.; [memb.] Bone Marrow Donor, National Kidney Transplant, Victorious Youth of America, Red Cross Instruction/ AIDS Gethsemane Program Director; [hon.] Colorado Dept. of Education Central High Ace Award, Aurora Leadership Institute (1990), How to Lead a Team; [oth. writ.] Several poems have appeared in my church bulletin.; [pers.] My walk with God enables me to seek and find the best in everyone.; [a.] Denver, CO

HARDY, KIM
[pen.] Nikki Nightingale; [b.] November 20, 1962, Edmonton, Alberta, Canada; [p.] Ettie Hardy; [ch.] Tarah Janine (February 18, 1994); [occ.] Computer Operator; [pers.] "The only thing in life that is consistent is change. Don't fear happiness that success can bring, the excitement and challenges of your life long dreams."; [a.] Calgary, Alberta, Canada

HARKINS, TAMIE
[b.] December 29, 1976, Goshen, IN; [p.] Weston Fields, Beverly Fields; [m.] Timber Harkins, May 28, 1995; [ed.] Warsaw High, Currently Freshman at Trinity College of Florida; [occ.] Student; [hon.] Dean's List; [pers.] In all things, I try to be original, looking at the world from a perspective no one has ever looked at it from something I learned from 2 teachers in high school.; [a.] Ekalaka, MT

HAROUTUNIAN, JULIE
[b.] May 28, 1976, Toronto, Ontario, Canada; [p.] Susie and George Haroutunian; [ed.] Second year University student studying English Literature at Carleton University; [pers.] The willow trees are talking, and spectrums light the sky, the triangle girl is born again, and the moon reflects its shadow light.; [a.] North York, Ontario, Canada

HARRIGAN, MICHELLE
[b.] September 2, 1982, Meriden; [p.] Brian and Bea Harrigan; [ed.] Freshmen; [occ.] Student; [pers.] I wrote this poem because I had a friend that I got in a fight with. I said some really mean things. She committed suicide which made me realize I still loved her.; [a.] Plantsville, CT

HARRIS, AL
[pen.] Al; [b.] Saint Kitts, WI; [m.] Dr. Ratna Dan; [ed.] Trained Family Therapist, and Theologian (Registered pastor); [occ.] Psychotherapist; [memb.] Canadian registry of Professional Counsellors and Psychotherapist, Association for Education and Evangelism; [hon.] Numerous awards for arts and poetry; [oth. writ.] Memories and Projections (Book of poetry) Novel - I-Man: A West Indian Dilemma, a West Indian Hope.; [pers.] I believe that a positive state of mind allows one to feel the blissfulness and joyfulness of life. That means experiencing the Kingdom of God within.

HARRIS, HOMER
[b.] June 8, 1938, Tulsa, OK; [p.] Ulice Harris and Ruby Harris; [m.] Divorced; [ch.] Glen, Gary, Michelle; [ed.] Graduated Tulsa Central High School, Tulsa Okla 1957; [occ.] Construction worker; [memb.] AARP; [hon.] I never missed a day in high school and was never late; [a.] Fort Worth, TX

HARRISON, FRANCES
[b.] February 10, 1950, Winnipeg, Manitoba, Canada; [p.] Leo and Kathleen Fierce; [m.] Paul Harrison, April 2, 1977; [ch.] Kathleen Claire, Jesse William; [ed.] Sisler High, Pacific Vocational Institute, Kwanten College; [occ.] Co-Founder/Director of a non-profit Society to help sexually abused teens.; [memb.] Hermenic Order of the Golden Dawn International; [hon.] Soroptimist Award, 1987, Dean's List, 1986, '87, '88; [oth. writ.] Much other unpublished material; [pers.] I am inspired to write by the light of love, shining as an eternal halo, an angel with healing in its wings.; [a.] Surrey, British Columbia, Canada

HARRISON, PATRICIA M.
[pen.] Rain; [b.] October 26, 1937, Fairview, Alberta; [p.] Kenneth and Nellie Paul (Both Deceased); [m.] Divorced; [ch.] Carmen Patterson and Robert Harrison (Zuzanah) and Grandson Luke Harrison; [ed.] Graduate of Fairview High School, Fairview, Alberta; [occ.] Artist, Lyricist, Writer; [oth. writ.] Published "Winter Heart" in "Path Not Taken", National Library of Poetry, Spring 1996; [pers.] Recognition and validation is a great jump start for creative arts.; [a.] North Vancouver, British Columbia, Canada

HARRISON JR., RICHARD S.
[b.] May 12, 1971, Vallejo, CA; [p.] Deloris Harrison, Richard Harrison Sr.; [ed.] Vintage High School; [occ.] Produce Clerk; [oth. writ.] "Unspent Love" published in the Rippling Waters by The National Library of Poetry.; [pers.] She is the most beautiful woman in the world and although I have never had the courage to tell her she is my love and inspiration. My poetry is my voice to express my love for her. Her name is Denise; [a.] Vallejo, CA

HARRISS, JULIE L.
[b.] January 14, 1961, Chicago, IL; [m.] Mark Harriss; [ed.] Maury H.S. Norfolk, VA, South FL, Community College; [occ.] Citrus and Cattle Farmer; [pers.] I wrote this poem for my husband when I was suffering from depression due to a thyroid condition. I'd like to dedicate it to my best friend, Vinnie.; [a.] Arcadia, FL

HARSANYI, BARBARA B.
[b.] November 23, 1933, Budapest, Hungary; [p.] Dr. L. Budinszky and Margaret Budinszky; [m.] Rodney E. Vaughan, December 1985; [ch.] Daina M. Kulnys; [ed.] BA, DDS Universidad Nactional de Colombia, 1960. MS Oral Pathology U. of Ore., Portland, Ore., 1968 DDS Dalhousie Univ., Halifax, NS., Canada. 1977, FRCD(C) in Oral Path., Toronto, 1977; [occ.] Semi-retired, Adjunct prof. Oral Pathology, Dalhousie U., Halifax, N.S., Canada.; [memb.] Canadian Academy of Oral Pathol., Universalist Unitarian Church of Hlfx., Canadian Physicians for Global Survival; [hon.] Honorable mention N.S. Writer's Federation Poetry Contest 1978., N.I.H. Fellowship in Oral Path. 965-1968. Past President Canad. Academy of Oral Path.; [oth. writ.] Scientific papers in Oral Surg. Oral Pathol. Oral Radiol and Journal of Dental Research.; [pers.] I write because I must. Poems and songs from several languages inhabit my mind, sometimes I recognize a particular influence. Mostly I just have a sense of some other, larger voice speaking through my writing.; [a.] Mahone Bay, Nova Scotia, Canada

HART, JOHN
[b.] May 9, 1954, Edmonton, Alberta; [p.] Richard and Grace Hart; [ed.] Matriculated from Fort Saskatchewan High, B.A. in English from the University of Alberta; [occ.] Courier; [pers.] I try to write poems that have lyric intensity. Some of the stronger influences on my poetry have been: Emily Dickinson, Thomas Hardy, A. E. Housman and Leonard Cohen.; [a.] Edmonton, Alberta, Canada

HARTLEY, SALLY
[pen.] Sall (Tyndale) Hartley; [b.] December 26, 1921, Lansing, MI; [p.] (Long Deceased) Howard and Pearl Tyndale; [m.] Bill Hartley (Deceased) 1982, February 7, 1991; [ch.] Richard Hartley - teacher, Mary Anne - Private Sec.; [ed.] High School and some College and short courses in creative writing and history; [occ.] I sold real estate for over 20 years and also did assist teaching. I am now retired; [memb.] Church "yesterday's youngsters" a group of senior citizen who do video tapes. "National Assoc. of Romance Writers; [hon.] I am a mother grand mothers and great grand mother 2 children and son and daughter 5 grand children 3 great grandchildren and one on the way. All of my children and grandchildren are college educated. God has blessed me; [oth. writ.] Children stories and other short stories and prose I am now writing a novel of the Civil War called "O Why Should the Spirit a of Mortals be so Proud" title prose written by Abraham Lincoln; [pers.] I hope to published my novel this year - it is a love story of a girl of Miched Blood and the civil war and I slovery and the meaning of freedom (P.S. I am white and English); [a.] East Lansing, MI

HARVEY, ELISABETH NICOLE
[b.] November 1, 1979, Iowa City, IA; [p.] Richard and Shirley Harvey; [ed.] Mid-Prairie Senior High School. I will be a junior for the '96-'97 years.; [occ.] Waitress and Babysitter and Student; [hon.] Honor roll 7th 10th grades, certificates stating I went to the Young Writer's Conference 4 years in my school career.; [oth. writ.] I am in the process of writing a short story that I am very proud of. It's called "Obsessed." I have many other short stories also.; [pers.] You can't be a truly good writer unless you read. It's helped me a great deal. I love poetry. It gives me a sense of stability in a world full of chaos.; [a.] Wellman, IA

HASANI, TANGERINE
[b.] April 29, 1972, Vancouver, B.C.; [p.] Lisa; [ch.] Aziza; [ed.] Bradford District High School; [occ.] Poet and Psychic and Full-Time Mother; [hon.] Acting awards throughout schools; Actress since the age of two years; [oth. writ.] I have been published in the local newspaper and was on a local T.V. programme to read my own poetry.; [pers.] I believe children are our future, so never lose the child in yourself! [a.] Hawkesbury, Ont., Canada

HASSON, CAROLE LOUISE
[b.] April 9, 1947, Georgetown Univ. Hospital, Washington, DC; [p.] Gloria Carole Ryan, James William Ryan (Deceased); [ch.] Catherine Carole and Daniel Joseph Hasson; [ed.] 1995 AA Degree - Bucks County Community College, Newtown, PA, also attended Temple University and Wharton School of Business (U. of P.), 1965 Grad Neshaminy High, Langhorne, PA; [occ.] Full time Liberal Arts Student, Clemson University, SC, former Insurance Underwriter and Real Estate Agt; [memb.] Phi Theta Kappa Internat'l Honor Society, Calhoyn College Honor Society, Mortar Board Honor Society, Nahnemann University Breast Cancer Survivors Support Group; [hon.] BCCC AAJCU All Academic Team Nominee, President's Cup Nominee, Dean's List 1993, 94, 95, 96, Secretary, then V.P. Tyler Literary Magazine at

BCCC, BCCC Women's Intercollegiate Tennis Team; [pers.] Poem written in response to my father's death from cancer and my own diagnosis the same year, which provided the strength to reject an unhealthy relationship and to begin in a period of personal growth. I hope to inspire others to meet such challenges in a positive way.; [a.] Clemson, Tiger Town, SC

HASTINGS, STEPHANIE MICHELLE
[pen.] Michelle; [b.] February 9, 1980, Danville, VA; [p.] Steve and Vickie Hastings; [ed.] Junior at Chatham High School in Chatham, VA and dual - enrolled at Danville Com. College in Governor's School for the Gifted and Talented; [occ.] Student; [memb.] BETA Club, FBLA, Junior Volunteer at Danville Regional Medical Center, Spanish Club, Volleyball Team, FHA, FTA; [hon.] Spanish Excellence Award, Honor Student Award, Presidential Academic Fitness Award; [oth. writ.] Poems for Church newsletter and school student booklets; [a.] Dry Fork, VA

HAWKINS, LYNN MARIE
[b.] February 18, 1984, Burbank, CA; [p.] Lori and Steve Hawkins; [ed.] Graduated from 6th grade at Lincoln Elementary; [occ.] Student; [memb.] American Girls Club/Historical Society; [hon.] Honor Roll, Principals Award, Student of the Month for creative writing; [oth. writ.] Young Authors Fair books 6 years in a row; [a.] Lancaster, CA

HAWKLESS, KENNY
[b.] 19 September 1973, Katoomba, NSW; [p.] Neville Hawkless, Judith Hawkless; [ed.] Berkeley High School, Australian College of Journalism; [occ.] Hospitality; [memb.] Australian Writers Guild; [hon.] Diploma in Journalism and currently studying for diploma in Script writing; [a.] Berkeley, New South Wales, Australia

HAYES, ELAINE
[pers.] Through her intuitive writings, Rev. Elaine expresses the mysticism of religion, mind, and science. Her goals are to awaken mankind to his true nature of being—— the All, knowing of Spirit, All that Is is the Essence of God, Love, Energy!

HAZARD, VIRGINIA
[b.] April 29, 1930, Springfield, MA; [p.] Stuart and Stella Kibbe; [m.] Rev. Gerald Hazard, June 1955; [ch.] Ronald Hazard, and Brenda Hazard; [ed.] Agawam High School Adiron Dack Community College (AA) Univ. of Hartford, Ct. Univ. of Ct.; [occ.] Homemaker, life long Church Voluntier; [memb.] Bethlehem Art Assoc. Presbyterian Church; [hon.] Various Awards for Watercolors; [oth. writ.] Children's Stories (nothing published); [pers.] I'm inspired through my faith in God to be helpful in my writing especially to the disadvantage and also reflect the goodness and greatness of God.; [a.] Delmar, NY

HEIN, KYLE
[pen.] Blake Black; [b.] September 5, 1971, Winnipeg, Manitoba; [p.] George Hein, Beverely; [ed.] Graduated from Ernest Manning High School in 90' and also went to Mount Royal College - both are School in Calgary, Alberta.; [occ.] Actor/Screenplay Writer; [oth. writ.] "Chesire Cats! - Screewplay and also "Stalkers" - Screenplay.; [pers.] A mask in the deepest form of the subconscious dwells inside a man which brings these thoughts to life. This person is myself, I think of the world as a playground that has not been touched yet by man in the endless tunnels of his mind.; [a.] Calgary, Alberta, Canada

HEINEY, GILBERT
[b.] June 25, 1932, Northampton, PA; [ed.] Northampton High, Northampton, PA '50, Kutztown University (25 credits) (BS), United

Wesleyan College (39 credits) (BS) '76; [occ.] Telemarketer (P.T.), Home Improvements; [hon.] Honorable Discharge, A/1C (U.S.A.F.) '56, (United Nations), (Korean Campaign), (Good Conduct); [pers.] Interpretations: (11 Angels), 7 Colors of Rainbow, 2 God and Yourself, (Angels, 2 Past and Future), Well Being (Admiration of Rainbow), William Shakespeare (Favorite Poets), and Robert Frost. I'd like to write more for humanity about the awareness of beauty.; [a.] Allentown, PA

HEISLER, LAUREEN M.
[b.] November 4, 1956, Calgary, Alberta, Canada; [p.] Philip and Catherine Heisler; [m.] Norman Barnett; [pers.] I strive to live in truth, however gentle or brutal it may be. I believe the greatest gift I can offer my spirit, my fellow man, our animal friends and mother earth herself, is to live by the untainted truth of who we "Really" are. It is from this depth that my poetry springs.; [a.] Saanichton, British Columbia, Canada

HELLOM JR., ROBERT
[b.] January 7, 1960, Toledo, OH; [p.] Kathryn Olive; [ch.] Kevin Myesha, Jamie; [memb.] Public Service; [a.] Toledo, OH

HENDRIE, MRS. JEAN
[pen.] Jean Hendrie; [b.] 7 February 1929, Dundee, Scotland; [p.] Mr. William and Jean Simpson; [m.] Mr. John Hendrie (Deceased) 5 September 1990, 2 October 1948; [ch.] Sheila, Ian; [ed.] Butterburn Primary School, Rockwell Secondary School, Rockwell Sec. School night classes, Stobswell Night Classes, short hand, typing, book-keeping; [occ.] War widow (retired secretary); [memb.] 'Solitaire' Pen-friend Club, St Pius Pensioner's Club, Anchor's Aweigh Poetry Club, 'Saga' Magazine Club; [hon.] 46 poems published in poetry books, 11 published in papers, 2 poems in solitaire magazine, 2 Editor's choice certificates (Int. Soc. Poets. G.B.), 1 poem on tape - (Nat.l Poets, USA), 1 poem on tape - (Int. Poets GB), 4 poems on tape - talking tapes for blind, Tayside, Dundee; [oth. writ.] I have another 24 poems sent in to various poetry clubs for assessment, and I am awaiting the results.; [pers.] Since the death of my husband John, and my only daughter Sheila, I find writing poetry, has been good therapy for me, to overcome my grief. I intend to write a book of poems, "My life and thoughts in verse" to leave with my family tree book.; [tn.] Dundee; [a.] Tayside, Scotland

HENDRIX, MARGARET G.
[pen.] Goldie Xavier; [b.] June 6, 1953, Talledega, AL; [p.] Marguerite and Leoba Garrett Sr; [m.] Howard Hendrix, August 31, 1985; [ch.] Anthony, Stevie, Levinia Garrett; [ed.] Massey Business College Atl. Ga. Tongue Pt., Job Corp. Ctr., Astoria, Oregon Associate Degree, Massey Institute; [occ.] Independent distributor; [memb.] Bally's Total Fitness Captain - Senior Choir, Mt. Ephraim Bpt. Church; [hon.] Outstanding Achievement, Dean's List, Hall Leader, Employee of the Year Award - Rich's Dept. Store, Honor Roll; [pers.] I express my inner feelings in my writing. I have been influenced by the great Poet Maya Angelou.; [a.] Smyrna, GA

HENNING, ANNE
[b.] May 6, 1982, Huntington, NY; [p.] Michael Henning, Catherine Henning; [ed.] Entering 9th grade at Huntington High School September 96; [occ.] Student; [hon.] Honorable mention for poem in Junior High; [oth. writ.] Poem published in literary magazine.; [pers.] My work reflects my inner thoughts. All I see I filter thru my heart; [a.] Huntington, NY

HENSHALL, STEVE
[b.] England; [p.] Bert and Margaret Henshall; [ed.] Completed grade 12 in Britain University of

Manchester Teacher Cert in Education 1975, BC Teaching Cert 1990; [occ.] Industrial Education Teacher (Woodworking-Cabinet Making); [memb.] Robin Hood Society BC College of Teachers; [hon.] City and Guilds of London Institute final and Advanced Cert in Cabinet Making, U of Manchester Teacher's Cert in Education, English Speaking Board, Cert: How to teach adults, British Columbia Cert in Benchwork Joiner (Red Seal), British Columbia Teaching Certified; [oth. writ.] Besides poetry writing that I find very fulfilling and rewarding I also design educational curriculums and course outlines. Have had one poem Published in the mackenzie Times in Northern BC; [pers.] A proud Canadian, a lover of Canada and the North Country. I live here by choice, we have the greatest county in the world. Canada is a wonderful, colorful Mosaic of Geography and people.; [a.] Agassiz, British Columbia, Canada

HENSLEY, LINDA D.
[pen.] Linda D. Hensley; [b.] March 15, 1952, Galax, Grayson County, VA; [p.] James C. (Deceased) and Helen L. Donithan; [ch.] Chad Steven Hensley, Luciana Adele Hensley; [ed.] Bachelor of Science in Nursing, Gardner - Webb University Boiling Springs, NC; [occ.] Registered Nurse; [memb.] American Red Cross, Cliffview Church of God, Galax, VA, Virginia Nurses Association, Acoustic Neuroma Association; [hon.] Phi Theta Kappa 1985-'86, Who's Who/American Junior Colleges 1986, Graduated Cum Laude, WCC (Wytheville Community College) 1986; [oth. writ.] Books entitled - The Summer of My Forty - Second Year and I Will Always Remember You (unpublished at present time), poems published in church magazine; [pers.] I love and enjoy life. Basically I find much goodness in mankind and I strive to help and improve life for others. My feelings and thoughts regarding life have been greatly influenced by Robert Frost.; [a.] Mount Airy, NC

HEPBURN, LEONA ENNS
[occ.] Music Teacher; [oth. writ.] Have had an Easter and a Christmas card published by a renowned card company, and signed papers for another Christmas card to be published. I have written nearly ninety poems, most of them are about nature.; [pers.] A lot of my poetry expresses the pain of nature, and the conflict in my soul, how to help.; [a.] Colorado Springs, CO

HERMRECK, RANDY
[b.] April 10, 1975, Garnet, KS; [p.] Louis Hermreck, Velma Hermreck; [ed.] Garnett High School; [occ.] Carpenter; [pers.] I strive to encourage people to write what they feel in their hearts.; [a.] Garnett, KS

HERNANDEZ, JOHN GUADALUPE
[pen.] John G. Hernandez; [b.] July 8, 1949, Los Angeles, CA; [p.] John P. Hernandez, Amparo O. Hernandez; [m.] Divorce but friends, Lorraine M. Avilla Hernandez, re-married, 1971, 1974; [ch.] Joseph John Hernandez 23 yrs. serving and getting Ed. U.S. Air Force; [ed.] Grad. 1968 Woodrow Wilson H.S., drafted February, 1969 by April I was serving in Viet-Nam; [occ.] Construction, labor and foreman 23 yrs. labor member, Union #1082; [memb.] E.L.A. Tennis Club, Captain and Instructor, Viet-Nam Veteran Outreach Program, E.L.A. Vet-Center; [hon.] As a Viet-Nam Veteran I was honor and awarded the purple heart and the bronze star, Rank Sp4 U.S. Army; [oth. writ.] None, never been published, began writing one yr. ago.; [pers.] I wish to someday visit our Nation's Capital and the Viet-Nam memorial and to be inspire. Inspiration will live on forever as long as humane minds, and human hearts our inspire with-in it will never die. My father was a great man, now decease, heart attack world war II Veteran and much more. U.S. Navy, my mother still active a 70 yrs. a great

woman in her own right a story in it self.; [a.] Diamond Bar, CA

HERNANDEZ, SUSAN
[b.] January 30, 1976, Dimmitt, TX; [p.] Virginia and Ignacio "Chief" Hernandez; [ed.] Caprock graduate of 1994 A few semesters at Amarillo College, looking forward to going back.; [occ.] Restaurant Management, pursuing a career in writing of nutrition.; [hon.] Poem of the month, National Vocational Technical Honor Society Scholarship, Home Economics Cooperative Education Scholarship, Francis C. McLoughlin Scholarship J. Fred and Estelle Balderston scholarship; [oth. writ.] I am a young beginner who will earn my success in the future.; [pers.] You have a voice, to use it, its your choice.; [a.] Amarillo, TX

HEVI, MARY
[b.] December 20, 1975, Cairo, Egypt; [p.] Vincent and Bintou Hevi; [ed.] Anglican International School in Jerusalem, Israel; [occ.] Student; [hon.] Bradnack memorial Award for placing high values on dedication, commitment and integrity in every area of school life! 1 or 4 class valedictorians.; [oth. writ.] Poetry influenced mainly by what I see around me.; [pers.] I'm a perfectionist. I always try to do the very best that I can.; [a.] Jerusalem, Israel

HEYLIGER, WILHELMINA
[pen.] Willie; [b.] Digby Co., NS, Canada; [p.] Nelson and Lena; [m.] Andre Cromwell; [ch.] Nelson, Taylor; [ed.] Weymouth Consolidated High School, Mount Saint Vincent University; [occ.] Accounts Clerk; [oth. writ.] Poetry published in the Toronto Sun, writes short stories, articles reflecting on everyday family life.

HILL, DANA R.
[pen.] Drew Mitchel; [b.] April 1, 1955, Pickford, MI; [ed.] Ferris State University; [occ.] Manager 1st Optometry Woodhaven MI; [oth. writ.] Optician Moving On, My Daughter, I Have A Friend I Have A Lover, Love And Will Flowers; [pers.] I strive to find and point out the love in our daily lives.; [a.] Southgate, MI

HILL, JOELLA PALMER
[pen.] Joella Palmer; [b.] September 4, 1941, Trinidad, CO; [p.] Mr. and Mrs. Billie Palmer; [m.] Bob Hill, June 28, 1959; [ch.] 3 sons; [ed.] High school grad. - HOEHNE, Co., Bette Bonn Modeling school grade., (Des Moines, Iowa) (finishing school); [occ.] Rancher, Model, Charm, and Horsemanship, Teacher for Rodeo Queens; [hon.] Recognized for my teaching Rodeo cow girls how to be Rodeo Queens - also Judged Rodeo Queens in 5 state.; [pers.] I have to be moved to write poems - sad or happy you are the first to get a poems - I did not think it was any good.; [a.] Model, CO

HILL, LINDA A.
[b.] February 21, 1951, Washington, DC; [p.] Doris and Orville Mill; [m.] Gary Hill, July 22, 1990; [ed.] B.A. English, Northern AZ Univ - 1974; [occ.] Information Management Administrator; [memb.] SAFE, AAUW, ASN; [oth. writ.] 60 poems published to date including: "Oh Souls", "Posing the Question", "The Lingering Instance", "Contemplation After the Bath".; [pers.] Nature is my favorite theme. I express my feelings in both poetry and photography. My creative energy has returned after 20 years.; [a.] Alexandria, VA

HILL, SHERRY-LYNN
[b.] November 19, 1966, Brantford, Ontario; [p.] Beth Hill and The Late Carl Hill; [m.] Ralph (Bunny) Hill, April 30, 1992; [ed.] Currently taking a photography course.; [occ.] Cashier; [memb.] WWF (World Wildlife Fund) PETA (People for the Ethical Treatment of Animals); [oth. writ.] Never been published!; [pers.] I'm

greatly inspired by nature and the weather and the seasons!; [a.] Ohsweken, Ontario, Canada

HILLYER, MEREDITH
[b.] November 14, 1982, Sylacauga, AL; [p.] Billy Hillyer, Linda Hillyer; [ed.] Edgewood Elementary K-5, Homewood Middle School 6-8; [memb.] Dawson Concord Choir, Dawson Concord Handbells, Homewood Middle School Chorus, Cahaba Girl Scouts; [hon.] National Junior Beta Club, Young Actors Conference; [oth. writ.] Editor of All Star Kids (Class Newspaper), Cupid - published in Anthology of Poems by Young Americans; [pers.] I feel very strongly about my work, in that most of my poems are reflections of my personal experiences. I have had a large support group of friends, family, and teachers to help me along the way.; [a.] Birmingham, AL

HILMAN, DARREL
[b.] November 22, 1954, Rimbey, Alberta, Canada; [p.] Ray and Irene Hilman; [m.] Janet Hilman, February 21, 1975; [ch.] Erin, Brianna, Meghan, Aubrey; [ed.] Goldendale High School, BEd - University of Alberta, Mech. Trades Jrny - S.A.I.T.; [occ.] Project Coordinator, Southern Alberta Institute of Technology, Calgary, AB; [memb.] Alberta SCC; [pers.] From the crucible of such moments as God allows us, those in which we see who and how we truly are, come the surest steps of our journey.; [a.] Calgary, Alberta, Canada

HOEY, KATHLEEN M.
[b.] September 22, 1906, Canada; [p.] Peter and Mary Hoey; [ed.] Academy of Holy Names (High School), Valleyfield, Quebec, Canada; University of Montreal (French); University of Detroit - B.A.; [occ.] Retired; [memb.] Hudson Ridge Tenant Association, Senior Citizen Volunteer Association; [hon.] Award for excellence in teaching - Montreal, Quebec, Canada; [pers.] "Love God and go your way."; [a.] Rochester, NY

HOFEN, JANITA
[b.] May 19, 1958, Alva, OK; [p.] Everett W. Hofen Jr., Jeanene Hofen; [ed.] Alva High School; [occ.] Postal Clerk; [memb.] Hopeton Wesleyan Church, American Postal Workers Union; [a.] Enid, OK

HOFFMAN, CAROL BALDWIN
[pen.] Carol Baldwin Hoffman; [b.] July 23, 1947, East Liverpool, OH; [p.] Allen and Rachel Baldwin; [m.] Divorced, June 5, 1965; [ch.] David and John Hoffman; [ed.] Wellsville High School, Kent State University, Mahoning Vocational College; [occ.] Disabled - Notary Public; [memb.] Trinity Presbyterian Church, Eastern Star Chapter 18 - Demolay Mothers Past President of Columbiana County Health Board, Col., County and State Arthritis Board - North Eastern Ohio Arthritis Advisory Board - Wellsville Alumni Ass.; [oth. writ.] Poems and articles in local newspapers. Poem in 30th Alumni Book.; [pers.] "I believe life should always be a continuing education. I approach it with the guidance of God, a sense of humor, and by being true to myself."; [a.] Wellsville, OH

HOLCOMBE, WANDA L.
[pen.] Wanda L. Holcombe; [b.] December 14, 1944, Cobb Co; [p.] Fairrie Mac and Orth Stanley; [m.] Joseph Wayne Holcombe, May 31, 1968; [ch.] 3 boys Brian, David, Brandon; [ed.] High school, Diploma 1964, The Institute of Children's Literature diploma 1-4-90; [occ.] Housewife, mother and amateur writer; [memb.] Walnut Baptist Church; [oth. writ.] Written many poem, articles and writing a book, none published; [pers.] The Lord is my helper and I desire that He receive any honor that comes my way.; [a.] Hoschton, GA

HOLLENBACK, MARYANN MARIE
[b.] July 25, 1948, Perth Amboy, NJ; [p.] Steve and Isabelle Bodnar; [m.] William Adam Hollenback, September 7, 1974; [ed.] High School Graduate, Woodbridge High School, Woodbridge, NJ (1966); [occ.] Housewife; [a.] Edison, NJ

HOLLOMAN, QUINTON
[b.] June 11, 1965, Newport News, VA; [p.] Richard Williams Sr., Alice M. Williams; [m.] Yolanda E. Holloman, January 25, 1991; [ch.] Eboni A. L. and Reygan E. Holloman; [occ.] Customer Service Technician, U.S. Air Force; [hon.] Air Force commendation Medal Air Force Achievement Medal, PTA appreciation certificate for volunteer service; [pers.] To create and a spiritual legacy for generations to come and to manifest God's spirit in my life and writings. Influenced by langston hughes.; [a.] Grand Prairie, TX

HOOFE, MARGARET G.
[b.] October 16, 1929, South Jersey Seashore; [m.] William J. Hoofe, February 14, 1957; [ch.] One daughter, 3 sons and 4 grandchildren; [oth. writ.] Hobbies: Writing children's books and illustrations; [pers.] I take great pleasure from writing and illustrating new stories for my grandchildren.; [a.] Newport Beach, CA

HORNER, ALICIA K.
[b.] December 15, 1984, Columbia, TN; [p.] James Earl and Marilyn Horner; [ed.] Hickman County Middle School - 6th Grade; [occ.] Student; [memb.] 4 - H Club, Pep Club, A Club, Band, Book Club, D. A. R. E. Club.; [hon.] President's Award for Outstanding Academic Achievement, Academic Award - An Average, Citizenship award, first place in Women's Club Poetry Contest.; [oth. writ.] "Life Before The Mystery" "Granny's Front Yard", "The Creek" and "Mr. Gilbert" (other poems); [pers.] I wanted to dedicate this poem to my Granny, who has been missing since her house burned in Jan. of 1994. (Her case is still under investigation.); [a.] Centerville, TN

HORWOOD, JANET
[b.] September 2, 1951, Leicester, United Kingdom; [p.] Thomas Davies, Dorothy Peet; [m.] Terence Horwood; [ch.] Jason, Kristian, Jessica; [ed.] Mary Linwood Girls School, Southfields College, U.K., E.C. Drury High School, Milton Ont.; [occ.] Catering and Food Consultant - Chef; [oth. writ.] Art Critic Articles in Local Newspapers; [pers.] I returned to school in my forties and discovered a talent to write. This proves we are never too old to learn. Go for it!; [a.] Georgetown, Ontario, Canada

HOSTENY, ADAM T.
[b.] May 15, 1989, Hoffman Estates, IL; [p.] Jerry and Marlene Hosteny; [oth. writ.] This is Adam's first poem written.; [pers.] Adam has a delightful imagination and is very creative. Adam does very well in school and enjoys playing with his younger brother, Kyle.; [a.] Huntley, IL

HOTTE, NGAIO
[b.] April 14, 1982; [p.] Paul and Vicki Hotte; [ed.] In June 1996, I completed the grade 8 gifted program at King City Public School.; [occ.] Student; [hon.] 1. York Region Environmental Leadership (1995), 2. Certificate of Distinction for Canadian Math Competition (1996), 3. Consumers Gas Certificate of Environmental Achievement (1996); [oth. writ.] "To Walk In The Trees" published by Consumers Gas in Earth Day 1996 Environmental Story Challenge.; [a.] Kettleby, Ontario, Canada

HOWARD, CLEVIA
[pen.] Sis. Howard; [b.] January 20, 1933, Trezevant, TN; [p.] Mr. and Mrs. Charlie and Cealma Howard; [ed.] Attended Douglas High School; [occ.] Pastor Baptize Believers Fullgospel Church; [memb.] United Christian Fellowship; [oth. writ.] Several unpublished poems, spiritual writings and many Gospel songs; [pers.] I strive to achieve the goodness of God in my life, and relate that goodness to mankind through my writings and songs; [a.] Oklahoma City, OK

HOWARD, KELLY K.
[b.] October 4, 1980, Moskegon, MI; [p.] Ike and Dee Middleramp; [ed.] Oakridge Sr. High School, will be a junior in the fall of 1996; [memb.] Oakridge Sr. High Band; [hon.] Baton, gymnastics, jazz dancing, also school awards in band (playing the flute) and perfect attendance; [oth. writ.] I have created a personal book of original poems I wrote. Also, I have wrote a few short stories.; [pers.] Special thank to Sheryl Swainston for her learning experience and my mam for all her support.; [a.] Muskegon, MI

HUBBARD, EUGENE
[b.] August 4, 1912, Michigan; [pers.] One year at Cal Tech was ended by the stock market crash of 1929. I was a navigator in the merchant marine. I then turned to overseas construction work. I have had cosmic experiences: In Alaska North of Fairbanks, a vast aurora boreal is cast pastel colors on the snow. I was at one with every living thing! When I discovered that $eitt+1=0$, I was overwhelmed in a blinding flash of unblinding light! That is the most poetic statement in all of pure mathematics! Evil is generated by a lack of cosmic evolution. Eternity is not a number: It is a concept. Life and death are unified in the Eternal Now!

HUDSON, DANIEL K.
[pen.] Daniel Hudson; [b.] June 1, 1962, Tuscaloosa, AL; [p.] Robert Hudson, Ann Spann; [m.] Sheila M. Ray; [ch.] Shanna Ray, Alicia Ray; [ed.] 8th Grade, Priceville Jr. High, Decator, Ala; [occ.] Auto Body and fender; [pers.] It's the poet that brings out what's in other peoples heart's, and give's us all an easier way to express ourself.; [a.] Columbus, MS

HUDSON, HERBERT A.
[pen.] Herbert Hudson, Alex Hudson; [b.] June 5, 1924, Galesburg, IL; [p.] Later Charles Hudson and Late Adelaide Hudson; [m.] Chloie D. Hudson, February 7, 1948; [ch.] Charles, Pamela, Lawrence and Danial; [ed.] BS Foreign Service, 1952 Georgetown University, MA Far Eastern Studies, University of Michigan 1955; [occ.] Retired; [memb.] Washington Metropolitan Golf Association Director, Executive Committee, Georgetown Alumni Ass. U. of Michigan Alumni Assc. Charter Member Assc. Former Intell. Off.; [hon.] Combat Stars with U.S. Marines in World War II, King of Beaux Arts ball, TOKY 1957 Key to City of New Orleans 1957, CIA Service Medallion 1970, Distinguished Member, International Society of Poets, Poet of Merit 1996, Awarded Medallion of Convention Washington, D.C. August 1996; [oth. writ.] "Nagasaki Revisited", 1st Prize Regional contest Hilton Head Island. Short story. National Legacies Contest Pending; [pers.] My poetry and short stories are all based on personal experience; [a.] Silver Spring, MD

HUGHES, AARON
[b.] August 25, 1976, Renton, WA; [p.] Duane and Carolyn Hughes; [ed.] High School Diploma; [occ.] Chemical Operation Specialist — US Army; [hon.] Eagle Scout, climbed Mt. Rainier twice; [ot. writ.] I have written about 50 poems about Bosnia. None were published or sent in except "Emptiness."; [pers.] I was first turned on by poetry when I heard "The Cremation of Sam McGee." Hearing that while I was camping up in Alaska was unbeatable.; [a.] Kent, WA

HUGHES, NANCY GAY CASE
[b.] June 30, 1898, LaGrange Co, IN; [p.] Riley C. Case, Mary Elizabeth Eshelman; [m.] Wayne Philo Hughes, December 26, 1926; [ch.] One Son Wayne P. Hughes Jr.; [ed.] B.S. Purdue University, 1921; [occ.] Paying Guest (by invitation) Betty Thomas; [memb.] College Pi Beta Phi, Delta Chapter. Indiana. Daughters of American Revolution (8 years Secretary) Recebeca Dewey; [hon.] Published "Up the Trail", Feb. 1960 American Heritage chap. won a 500 dollar scholarship for student at St Andrew U. Scotland granddaughter giving Scots Lineage; [pers.] Ruskin's quote: "To get peace if you want it make for your selves nests of pleasant thoughts. I call mine Pockets of Pleasant thoughts. When I read Franklin's Autobiography I did what he suggested. Wrote all things I wished to be concentrated them. Later was surprised how Robert Louis Stevenson summed his: Courage, Gaiety and The Quiet Mind. Hold eternal Truths and Everlasting ideas.

HUGHES, PAUL
[pen.] "Pablo"; [b.] September 7, 1946, Winthrop, MA; [p.] Russell Hughes, Ana Sirtowtis; [ed.] Cathedral High, Boston MA., Oblate College. B.A. Theology, Washington D.C.; [occ.] Roman Catholic Priest Parish Ministry in San Juan, Puerto Rico; [memb.] Member religious congregation, Missionary Oblates of Mary Immaculate (OMI); [hon.] Poem entitled Tale Of Two Universities on record with the National Commission of Parks and Momunments (Ireland); [oth. writ.] Booklets of verse: "From Dublin Fair City", "From Desert Well", "I Dig Animals, Do You?"; [pers.] "Good poetry is good Theology, it participates in some small but significant way in the divine paradox...."; [a.] San Juan, PR

HUMPHREY, SHIRLEY
[b.] 3 June 1928, Dulwich Hill, Australia; [p.] Harry and Bess Moyle; [m.] William Fergus Humphrey; [ch.] Wendy Elizabeth; [ed.] Gosford High School N.S.W. Australia; [occ.] Writer/Artist/Pianist; [memb.] Fellowship of Australian Writers A.C.T. (F.A.W.); [hon.] As in "Best poems of 1996" The National Library of Poetry. Very proud to be made honored international member of the Society of Poets by N.L. of P. Played the grand piano at the albert Hall for the A.C.T careers' Luncheon 1994.; [oth. writ.] Autobiography/on-going artist's journal/poetry/short stories.; [pers.] Poetry is emotion made visible. Electric enthusiasm turns me on, where, ever I find it.; [a.] Chisholm, Australian Central Territory, Australia

HUNT, CAROL A. JACKSON
[pen.] Carol A. Jackson Hunt; [b.] September 14, 1957, Bracebridge, Ont.; [p.] Marvin and Lillian Jackson; [m.] Thomas F. Hunt, October 25, 1985; [ch.] Jason, Vicky, Johnathan, Lenny; [ed.] High School, University College; [occ.] Greenhouse owner, artist, writer; [oth. writ.] Chatelaine Feature Item; [pers.] "Grass doesn't grow on a busy street."; [a.] Calgary, Alberta, Canada

HUNT, KATHERINE M.
[pen.] Amanda O. Lin; [b.] October 14, 1959, Cincinnati, OH; [p.] John E. Meyer Sr. and Donna R. Lewis; [m.] James M. Hunt (P. J. Bottoms), November 15, 1991; [ch.] Julia M. Wixom, Kevins, Cox; [ed.] High School Graduate; [occ.] Housewife; [oth. writ.] Hitting Post, (Tomorrow's Dream), Signed: Love Mom (Recollections of Yesterday) both National Library of Poetry Anthologies.; [pers.] I write about other people's lives, what affects me in my life and situations in the world around me.; [a.] Cincinnati, OH

HURD, DEBRA C.
[b.] August 18, 1972, Tampa, FL; [p.] Dwight and Colleen Wray; [m.] Philip W. Hurd, May 1, 1993;

[ed.] Plant City High, Cochise College; [occ.] Information Systems Specialist, SEABHS; [memb.] Phi Beta Lambda; [hon.] Meritorious service metal, good conduct metal; [pers.] I wish to express the feelings of life through my poetry. I want to touch lives and make a difference.; [a.] Sierra Vista, AZ

HURD, J. MARTIN
[pen.] J. Martin Hurd; [b.] November 8, 1929, Mpls., MN; [m.] Dr. Richard N. Hurd, December 22, 1950; [ch.] Melanie E. Suzanne; [ed.] A.A. Maryland College Women B.A. Univ., of Minnesota and Bus. degree American Institute of Wash. D.C. and graduate courses; [occ.] Poet and Home manager; [memb.] Girl scouts of American (Officer, Wabrush Valley, Indiana) Phi Omega Sorority, The Presbyterian Church Post for and Music for special days also 1st pres. (Much in Mass and Austin, TX, Michigan Share Club, Wilmette, Ill.; [hon.] Nationalist: World of poetry Las Vegas - 1989: Featured: Pennyland" A and E network, the Sutby Dews, Austin, Texas PBS, featured spoken garden club of America and Texas gardens, pres. Univ. of Minn. Alumni of Central Texas - also, Boston, Mass.; [oth. writ.] Poems published in newspapers from: Mpls. Minn- St. Paul, Minn College Musical Program St. Louis Post, Austin (Tx) statesman.; [pers.] My life - expressed in poetry - minors of experiences.; [a.] Evanston, IL

HURWITZ, LEIALOHA
[b.] February 15, 1985, Kailua-Kona, HI; [p.] Steve and Deena Hurwitz; [ed.] Hawaii Preparatory Academy; [oth. writ.] Several others that are unpublished.; [pers.] I try to put all my heart and soul into my writings. I was greatly influenced by my fifth grade teacher Ms. Lolly Davis.; [a.] Kamuela, HI

HUSSER, MICHELLE R.
[b.] December 10, 1981, San Jose, CA; [p.] Robert and Barbara Husser; [ed.] Freshman, attending Leigh High School; [occ.] Student; [hon.] 8th Grade, "Spanish student of the Year Award, Honor Roll all through Middle School, Young Author's Award for Children's Literature, (Young Author's Faire).; [oth. writ.] I write short stories and many poems but none of my writings published, (yet); [pers.] Through my writing, I hope to influence many people to reach their goals. Follow the path of your heart and there you will truly be satisfied for life. I learned success is failure, turned inside out.; [a.] San Jose, CA

HUTCHINSON, MARLENE
[pen.] Rae Morier; [b.] January 18, 1943, Glasgow, Scotland; [p.] John Beaver, Elizabeth Beaver; [m.] William Hutchinson, February 29, 1964; [ch.] Grant William, Bill Scott Fraser, Paul Thomas, 1 grandson Kyle William; [ed.] Wellshot High School Scotland; [occ.] Buyer (Hospital); [oth. writ.] Songs inspirational writings; [pers.] I endeavor to glorify God in all that I do. I am a descendant of the author, James Justinian Morier, world classic "The adventure of Hajji Baba of Ispahan".; [a.] Burlington, Ontario, Canada

HUTCHISON, LESLIE JAMES
[pen.] Les Hutchison; [b.] October 16, 1902, Leeds County, Ontario, Canada; [p.] Joseph and Pattie Hutchison; [m.] Jean Joffry Cooper, May 29, 1992; [ch.] Dr. Patricia A. Hutchison by 1st marriage; [ed.] University of Saskatchewan, Saskatoon, Sask., B.S.A. 1927; [occ.] Retired 1967, now 93 years old; [memb.] Life Member, Saskatchewan Agricultural College Graduate Association Institute of Canada, Ontario Institute of Agrologists, U of S. Athletics Wall of Fame.; [hon.] Chiefly in athletics tracks: pole Vault, broad, jump and high jump, Thirteen Medals. Polevault Record for 2 yrs.; [oth. writ.] "The South Saskatchewan - River Dam.", The Dream's I've Had" Les Hutchison

Joins the club, A Nostalgic Return, "When Baseball was the king of sports and feathers were in fashion."; [pers.] Dealing mostly with humorous situations, praise-worthy events of sentimental happenings.; [a.] Ottawa, Ontario, Canada

HUYNH, VAN
[b.] May 10, 1977, Vietnam; [p.] En Huynh, Dung Doan; [ed.] Joseph H. Brensinger School, Dickinson High School; [occ.] Full time student, candy striper at Jersey City Medical Center; [memb.] Who's who among American, High school students, Quill and scroll society, Asian club, School's newspaper and High school science magnet prog.; [hon.] Honor and merit rolls, salutatorian of Joseph H. Brensinger School (PS #17); [oth. writ.] Several sport articles published in school newspaper, short story published in school magazine (Aries).; [pers.] Dealing with beauty, misery, conflict, peace, hate, and love through writing help me overcome stress, fear, and depression. Writing is the most articulate expression of oneself. Expressive writing is my path toward improvement.; [a.] Jersey City, NJ

HYNCIK, AMY J.
[b.] May 3, 1943, Newark, NJ; [p.] Mary Landow, J. Leonard Landow; [m.] Joseph W. Hyncik, November 8, 1980; [ed.] Hillside High School, BA and MA from Newark State College, now Kean College in Union, NJ; [occ.] 3rd grade Teacher, Wayside Elementary School, Ocean Township, NJ; [memb.] NJEA, Ocean Fitness Club, President - Condo Association; [a.] Belmar, NJ

IAUKEA, LIANE
[b.] February 7, 1943, Christchurch, New Zealand; [ch.] Sydney (26 years), Lesley (25 years); [ed.] Now Practising Registered Nurse. A college student at this time; [occ.] College Student/Sales/First Aid Attendant; [memb.] Canoe Club, The Gym; [hon.] First place Mother/Daughter Pageant Hawaii 1991. Outrigger Canoe/and IOK Running awards, Third Place Honolulu Marathon Mother/ Daughter Division 1995; [oth. writ.] None first poem I've ever written. I've ever written. My eldest daughter Sydney, formed a kindergarten in the interior on the edge of the Rainforest in Costa Rica. She is in the Peace Corps. I wrote the poem for the experiences she was going through at the time.; [pers.] I believe patience, love, education and participation in sports is what helps children to evolve into caring adults.; [a.] Honolulu, HI

IGHEDOSA, STEPHANY UDI
[b.] December 13, 1952; [p.] Mr and Mrs Ighedosa; [ed.] M.B.B.S. (1976), Ph.D (Glasgow, 1983), BFHI Master Trainer (UNICEF, 1995), Advanced Modelling Course (KCMO, 1996); [occ.] Public Health Physician with focus on: Int. Breastfeeding Advocacy; [memb.] Academy of Breastfeeding Medicine (US, 1996), FWACP (1985), NMA (1976); [hon.] 1. ABM (1996), 2. FWACP (1985), 3. National Certificate of honor (1979), 4. Best Student's Award (1976), 5. University Certificate of honor (1974), various scholarship awards; [oth. writ.] Ph.D Thesis (Glasgow, 1983), "Weanling Diarrhea", Poems, Guest Lectures, Int. Conference Reports, Several Community Development Reports, and Philosophical statements.; [pers.] Confidence derives from being in the conscious presence of success.; [a.] Kansas City, MO

INGRAM, CARLENE
[b.] June 14, 1950, Detroit, MI; [m.] Lee R. Ingram; [ch.] Sharena NaCole, Roummel Jerome, Shanai Moniece; [ed.] Southern High, University of Detroit, Wayne State University, Business Administration; [occ.] Self-employed, Oak Park, MI; [memb.] Dayton-Hudson's Contract Authors List; [oth. writ.] Author of a newly designed memorial book titled "The First Step", published in 1993; [pers.] I endeavor to inject the impor-

tance of love and unity within the family in my writing. A characteristic that motivates me from the early teachings and memories of my father.; [a.] Oak Park, MI

ISON, KATHERINE J.
[b.] January 12, 1953, Isonville, KY; [p.] Mary and Everett Elliott; [m.] Willis J. Ison, August 7, 1970; [ch.] Willis David and Williams Arlis; [ed.] High School; [occ.] Housewife; [memb.] Sumter Baptist Temple Church, Life Member Weight Watchers, Distinguished Member ISP; [oth. writ.] Several poems published in other anthologies and on cassette tape. Others still unpublished.; [pers.] I strive to encourage through my work. Helen Steiner Rice and Pannie Crosby have been a great inspiration to me.; [a.] Wedgefield, SC

IVIE, KAROLYN
[pen.] Karolyn Ivie; [b.] December 31, 1939, Delta, UT; [p.] Marion Davis, Orda Allen Davis; [m.] Divorced; [ch.] Karry, Alan, Tracy, Mindy, Larry and Danny; [ed.] Delta High, Utah Tech College, Utah Community College, Red Cross; [occ.] Home Health Nursing; [memb.] Red Cross; [hon.] Interim Award of dedication and Professionalism; [oth. writ.] Several stories in women's magazines, several biographies in process of writing several books and children's stories. Wrote and put on two plays while on High School.; [pers.] Take life's experiences, write about them to educate and fill others life with hope for tomorrow.; [a.] Trenton, NJ

JACKSON, BARBARA BENICE MILES
[pen.] B. Miles Jackson; [b.] June 24, 1948, Fort Worth, TX; [p.] C. B. Miles and Maybelle Dugan Miles; [m.] Divorced; [ch.] Tracy D. Jackson; [ed.] I. M. Terrell Class of 1966; [occ.] Hear start - Day Care Association of Ft. Worth and Tarrant County.; [memb.] Carter Metropolitan, CME Church; [hon.] State Employee of the year 1990, Usher of the Year for Carter Metropolitan Church; [oth. writ.] Poetry - Atmospheric Condition Renewal, Go Your Way, Ancient of Days, Silent Voice, A Sign, Void of Times, Be Sure, Answer, Keep, Times Changing Times, House on Southcrest, Listen See, Verses, Death Comes at God's Will; [pers.] In great times of sorrow and sadness - look up and know; [a.] Fort Worth, TX

JACKSON, PAULA
[pen.] Paula Jackson; [b.] October 9, 1957, Springfield, IL; [p.] Edna Jean Morse (Deceased); [m.] Divorced; [ch.] Daughter: Sarah Lynnee Jackson, son: Courtney Myles Jackson; [occ.] Home Educator - Homemaker, Adoptive Mother and Breeder of Long Hair Chihuahuas; [memb.] First Baptist Church of Lockesburg, Or.; [hon.] I am honored to have been given two wonderful, bright, intelligent children through adoption.; [oth. writ.] Poems and children's book(s) not submitted for publication at this time.; [pers.] I strive to give children Christian insight into life. As well as to give thanks to those thankless people that do good deeds and feel forgotten and may God bless you.; [a.] Lockesburg, AR

JACKSON, RICHARD C.
[pen.] Vincent J. Michaels; [b.] September 2, 1951, Saginaw, MI; [p.] Mr. and Mrs. Albert Curtindale; [ed.] Associate in Arts, Delta College, Bachelor of Arts, Central Michigan University, now attending Graduate School, University of Hawaii; [occ.] Supply Clerk, U.S. Government; [memb.] 1) Amnesty International, 2) Christian Reformed Church, 3) Air Force NCO Club, 4) ACLU, 5) Sons of the American Legion; [hon.] 1) Journalism Award, Douglas MacArthur High School, 2) Journalism Award, Delta College, 3) Rehabilitant of the Year, Metro Section, State of Hawaii; [oth. writ.] News writing, daily newspaper 1967-1975, including a music column, I had a folk song released nationally

and I am half finished with a novel.; [pers.] I am offended by what illegal drugs are doing to our young people, because God is a God of love and not a God of hate, my faith is strong.; [a.] Honolulu, HI

JACOB, ADELHEID
[b.] March 6, 1939; [p.] Peter and Anna Jost; [m.] Karl H. Jacob, February 16, 1963; [ch.] Christine, Marlene; [ed.] B.A. Wilfrid Laurier University, Canada M.A. University of Waterloo Canada; [oth. writ.] Poem "Sharing Love, Sharing Life", in reflections by moonlight, Poetry Institute of Canada; [pers.] It is my goal to: Paint a picture, create a mood, translate feelings into words.; [a.] Whitby, Ontario, Canada

JACOBS, DR. TIMOTHY A.
[b.] November 5, 1944, St. Petersburg, FL; [p.] Bill and Virginia Jacobs; [m.] Carolyn M. Jacobs, November 4, 1972; [ch.] Jenny Thuy Ha Jacobs; [ed.] BSN (70) Univ. of Fla., MS (76) Univ. Utah, PhD (79) Greenwich Univ., MPH (91) Yale Univ., CTM (82) Liverpool Sch. Tropical Med.; [occ.] Infectious Disease Epidemiologist, Capt., US Army, Ret.; [memb.] Amer. Public Health Assn., Royal Society Trop. Med. and Hygiene (London, Eng.), Assn. of Military Surgeons of US, Fla. Public Health Assn., Doctorate Assn., NY Educators; [hon.] Sigma Theta Tau, Sigma Xi, Phi Kappa Phi, Fellow, Royal Society Trop. Med. and Hygiene, Fellow, Amer. Biographical Assn.; [oth. writ.] Poems: 1) "What's Race-Walking: A Collection of Humorous Poems", poem "A Broken Caduceus", poem "The Corps at 89", poem "Images from the Past: An Army Nurse in Vietnam"; [pers.] I have traveled extensively in S.E. Asia, especially Vietnam, since the war. And my poetry attempts to reflect the work, valor, and sacrifice of those who cared for the injured in Vietnam.; [a.] Tampa, FL

JACOBSON, SANDY
[pen.] Sandy Schimdt, Sandy Jacobson; [b.] September 6, 1958, Los Angeles; [p.] Art and Ruth Schmidt; [m.] John Jacobson, June 27, 1981; [ch.] Jeanne Marie Jacobson; [ed.] B.A. Elementary Education From Calif. Lutheran University Westchester High School; [occ.] Desk Manager for Westside Academy of Dance in Santa Monica, CA; [memb.] Westside Ballet Co. Guild; [hon.] Student Gov't.-High School Honor Society - High School Head Cheereader - High School Cheereading - College Co-President Westside Ballet Co. Guild; [oth. writ.] "In Memory of Mom", "Goodbye, Again"; [pers.] At age 19, I lost my mother cancer in a matte of months. I forged ahead with college, because I knew my mother would have wanted me to. Without my mother to talk to, I turned to writing letters, poems, and stories. My mother loved the ocean, and I spent my formative years at the beach. "Goodbye to Summer" is a Philosophical and Symbolic reflection on the loss of my mother - and changes that occur in life from season to season, and year to year.; [a.] Los Angeles, CA

JAMES, BRONN JARRELL
[b.] January 7, 1986, Nurnberg, Germany; [p.] Freddie L. and Shelly J. James; [occ.] Student, Newsome Park Elementary School; [memb.] Pack 358, Patrol "Bad Badgers" Cub Scouts, Warwick League Basketball; [hon.] AB honor roll, Computer Club, CHROME Club, Presidential Physical Fitness Award, Young Authors Award; [oth. writ.] Short stories for special school projects.; [a.] Newport News, VA

JAMIALKOWSKI, RITA R.
[b.] November 17, 1929, New Haven, CT; [p.] Alvos and Anna Sarno Garcia; [m.] Frank T. Jamialkowski, May 4, 1949; [ch.] Lisa Ann Jamialkowski King; [ed.] Hamilton Elementary, Fair Hillhouse High School (NM) Folt and Tarvond Compt. School; [occ.] Retired; [hon.] Essays in

Grammar School, Graduated with honors from Elementary, The National Library of Poetry, Famous Poets Society, a poem accepted by country Music; [pers.] Writing was a field I had hoped to inspire to; I thank God for the gift and foresight to pursue it. By accepting my poem, the National Library of Poetry realized this ambition. My favorite expression is I am major of all trades and master of none.; [a.] Spokane, WA

JARRELL, SHEILA ROSE JOHNSON
[pen.] ,S. J.; [b.] July 26, 1949, Pontiac, MI; [p.] Betty Lou McDermit, Edward Leroy Johnson; [m.] Douglas Kevin Jarrell, October 17, 1987; [ch.] Connie Lorrane, Martha Rose, Albert Edward, Joseph Nathaniel, Joshua Michael, Crystal Corette; [ed.] 2 yrs. Cambridge Business School, 2 yrs. Petosky Beauty Academy, 2 yrs. North Cen. MI. Comm. College - Bus. Management, 1 year Central MI, University, - Bus. Management, also special studies in law and phychology; [occ.] Business Management; [memb.] Women's Bowling Association; [hon.] Received award and Honor from Jerry Lewis for telethon work and fun raising NCMC and JTPA for opening the college doors for women to attend college without a diploma but with enough work and life exp., misc. education, Personal Merits and efforts in that area; [pers.] To overcome any trial or challenger in life, be it most inhumane, unexpected or ecstatic, one has to only keep the inner strength and desire to raise above it and seek only inner peace with one's self, not anyone else. You can never make anyone else happy. They have to do that themselves. It is everything life itself entails that gives me the inspiration whether positive or negative, also the need to let go of emotions and the desire to share them with others in a non confrontational way that enables me to express anything in the challenging and fun form of poetry.

JASOL, FATEH SINGH
[b.] 15 January 1940, Jodhpur; [p.] Rawal Amarsinghji, Rani Basant Kanwar; [m.] Sita Ranawat, 24 June 1974; [ch.] Manu Vikram, D'Anuradha; [ed.] B.A. (Eng. Lit., Delhi - 1963), M.A. (Eng. Lit., Jodhpur - 1965), MPA (Harvard - 1983); [occ.] Public Administration; [memb.] Life Member, WWF-India, Wild Life Conservation Society, Bhavnagar, Bombay Natural Hist. Soc., Administrative Staff College of India, Hydrabad; [hon.] Best alround student Gold Medal, St. Xavier High Jaipur 1959, D.S. Bhandawat Gold Medal, Jodhpur Univ. 1963, Director's Medal, National Academy of Administration, Mussoorie 1966, President of India's Medal for Meritorious Serive, 1973, Second prize, Vineet Gupta Memorial All India Poetry competition, 1989.; [oth. writ.] Several Professional Papers, Poetry, Prose, Short Stories, Articles, Radio Talks, TV Interviews, Two Bird Books currently with Publishers.; [pers.] I have deeply loved life and living and the beauty of all created things and try to reflect this in all my writings.; [a.] Gandhinagar, Gujarat, India

JEAN, TODD L.
[b.] October 16, 1968; [memb.] Veteran Administration; [hon.] The Army Achievement Medal, to the security and safeguarding of several thousands soldiers against possible enemy activities. United States of America War Office. Anti tank weapon, expert Rifle, sharpshooter Grenade launcher, marksman Machine gun, sharpshooter Law, expert Basic training, diploma Basic training cord National defense ribbon Overseas ribbons Combat patch Combat badge, German infantry cord Certificate of Recognition, helped break Warsaw pact which broke the iron curtain and Berlin wall, helped German unification and the extension of freedom to eastern Europe Certificate of Achievement, exceptionally meritorious service 45 caliber pis-

tol, sharpshooter; [oth. writ.] Unpublished works Here, There Planet Earth, For Us, Future books: Here, There Planet Earth II, For Us, Un-Market-able Soviet Inventions, At the Pentagon, Bond to the President; [pers.] Everyday I dream of that special woman who will love me at first sight, for the rest of my life. I guess good things come to those who wait. To all my readers, I wish you all peace, love and prosperity. Remember, I love all of you, the same.; [a.] Bellmore, NY

JEFFRIES, ANN
[b.] November 12, 1937, Joplin, MO; [p.] Wayne and Audrey Jeffries; [ch.] Rebecca Naylor, Cynthia Sweeney Paul Jones, David Jones; [ed.] Stuttgart High Arkansas, BA Ottawa U. Ottawa KS Masters of Divinity Saint Paul School of Theology Kemo; [occ.] Chaplain/Pastor; [memb.] World Ministry Fellowship, Women's Project - Arkansas AARP; [hon.] Alpha Chi (Academic); [pers.] We are unique earth lings, created by God who love us, calls us, and sustains us, as we respond to God, God emblem us to become our very best.; [a.] Kansas City, KS

JEFFS, HENRY
[b.] July 23, 1955, Jersey City, NJ; [p.] Henry Jeffs, Catherine Supple; [m.] Tina Marie Bellavance Jeffs, November 19, 1994; [ch.] Henry, Shawn, Rebecca, Tabitha; [ed.] Plainfield High School, Plainfield, CT; [occ.] Electrician; [pers.] I write of things that Inspire me, I don't worry about specifics, the Rhyming comes naturally.; [a.] Brooklyn, CT

JELSO, CLARA
[b.] May 5, 1928, Tacoma, WA; [p.] Peter and Sina Petersen; [m.] Samuel Jelso (Deceased); [ch.] Toni, Dominic, Sandra, Stephen; [ed.] Stadium High School - Tacoma, studied anthropology and archaeology - U.N.M.; [occ.] Retired; [hon.] Senior Olympics Medalist; [pers.] I have traveled throughout the world and am always amazed at the natural beauty that surround us; [a.] Albuquerque, NM

JENEI, JENNEFER
[b.] September 11, 1979, Royal Victoria Hospital, Montreal; [p.] Mrs. Helen Jenei and Ernest; [ed.] Dawson College Student Creative Arts Program!; [occ.] Actress/Model; [memb.] Member of Leave Out Violence, Photojournalism project; [oth. writ.] Other Poetry and Children Stories; [pers.] I think of my poetry as intense feeling which has been formulated in a particular, obscene order of thought.; [a.] Chambly, Quebec, Canada

JENEREAUX, HARRIET
[b.] December 21, 1941, West Point, PE, Canada; [p.] Edison and Helen Smith; [m.] Keith, May 19, 1962; [ch.] 4 - Sheryl, Angela, Susan and Keith Scott; [ed.] Teacher's Certificate Prince of Wales College Normal School; [occ.] Operates a Christian Seniors Boarding Home; [memb.] Member of different Baptist Churches for forty years, member of the International Christian Mission, International Society of Poets; [hon.] My greatest honor is to be a wife of 35 years and a grandmother of eleven beautiful grandchildren given me as an award by my three lovely daughters. I also feel honored to have such a son as I have. The international past of Merit Award 1996.; [oth. writ.] "Fit for the Master's Use" in Sparkles in the Sand, several in newspapers and private Christian works. I also write Christian fiction and non-fiction.; [pers.] I serve the Lord Christ and I write to honor Him.; [a.] Kingston, Nova Scotia, Canada

JENKINS, ANN SHANNON
[b.] August 19, 1951, San Antonio, TX; [p.] Dr. and Mrs. George Shannon; [m.] Len Jenkins; [ch.] Grey Davis; [ed.] Master's in Education (media degree); [occ.] School Library Media Specialist;

[pers.] This poem is based on childhood memories I have of a large oak tree in my backyard in my hometown of Laurinburg, NC.; [a.] Wilmington, NC

JENNINGS, VANCE S.
[b.] August 10, 1925, Oklahoma City, OK; [p.] Reedy V. and Bess Cudd Jennings; [m.] Chris Boyd Jennings, November 26, 1969; [ch.] Terri and Sherri; [ed.] B.M. Eastman School of Music of the Univ. of Rochester (NY) (1950) M. Ed. Univ of Mississippi 1952 Doc. Mus. Ed. Univ. of Oklahoma - 1972; [occ.] Retired Professor, Active Professional Musician; [memb.] TTKA, OAK, KATT, OMA, TTKA, Scabbard and Blade York Rite, Masonic Bodies, Florida Bandmasters Assoc. Nat'l Assoc. of Wind and Percussion Instr.; [hon.] Performer's Certificate, E. S. M., Who's Who in South and Southwest, Who's Who in American Music; International Who's Who in Music. Professor Emeritus from Univ. of South Florida, Tampa, FL; [oth. writ.] Numerous Prof. Articles in professional periodicals such as The International Musician, The Instrumentalist Music Educators Journal, dissertation of 20th Cent. Clarinet Music; [a.] Tampa, FL

JENSEN, ALLAN L.
[b.] November 17, 1942, Salt Lake City, UT; [p.] Norman Curt Jensen, Doris Walker Peirson; [ch.] Karen Gagnier, Alexis Lane Jensen; [ed.] San Francisco State University California State University, Hayward; [occ.] University Administrator, University of California at Berkeley; [memb.] National and Western Associations of Student Employment Administrators (NASEA and WASEA), Marina Bay Yacht Club; [hon.] Margene Orzalli Award for Leadership in Student Employment; [oth. writ.] Self-Published "Marblehead Remembers" a small anthology of romantic poetry. One prior issue of The National Library of Poetry, numerous postings to Internet World Wide Web poetry sites. Personal WWWeb site is: Http://members. Tripod. Com/ Gramps/index. html; [pers.] The most powerful impact on my writing is Stanley Burnshaw's "The Seamless Web". I hope I am not among the last of the romantic style poets. I believe poetry is one of the finest legacies that one generation can leave to future generations.; [a.] Marina Bay at Richmond, CA

JOANNIS, NGOZI
[b.] May 13, 1964, Jengre, Jos, Nigeria; [p.] Prof. and Mrs. Oluikee; [ch.] Theodora Onyinyechi Joannis; [ed.] Mus. Ed (diploma), B.A - Music, LPN (Licensed Practical Nurse); [occ.] Nurse; [hon.] Best All-Round Performer (1990), University of Nigeria, Nsukka; [oth. writ.] Unpublished poems written from the age of nine to seventeen; [pers.] Keeping a healthy stride with the bitter and sweet, adds up to living life to its Fullest.

JOCHUM, PATRICIA
[b.] August 11, 1930, Dubuque, IA; [p.] Anton Pearl Baumhover; [m.] Charles G. Jochum, February 3, 1951; [ch.] Mary Kay, Tonette, Robert; [ed.] High School, Creative Writing Course, Sinipee Novel Course; [occ.] Retired; [memb.] National Writers Association, John Tigges School of the Novel, V.F.W. Auxiliary; [hon.] First place Award Sinipee Writers Workshop, Poetry contest.; [oth. writ.] Three short stories published; [pers.] Most of my writings are dawn from the love of my family.; [a.] Dubuque, IA

JOCHUM, VALERIE
[b.] February 14, 1955, Sayre, PA; [ch.] Three Sons; [ed.] High School; [occ.] Fashion Consultant; [memb.] Washin - Ryu Karate; [oth. writ.] "The Strongest Little Hands in the World." "Love is not alternative." "Dreamship" "The Dawning" - many more...; [pers.] I have no need for honors,

awards or credentials. My gifts are given freely from my heart, directly to the readers. My greatest honor is when my listeners want more.; [a.] Warren Center, PA

JOHNSON, BARRY DAVID
[b.] 25 June 1947, Hastings, UK; [m.] Sandie Johnson, 9 October 1982; [ch.] Samuel; [occ.] Medical Laboratory Scientist

JOHNSON, JASON C.
[pen.] Jordan, Jason C. Johnson; [b.] September 11, 1980, Hammond, IN; [p.] Carl Johnson and Terri Ellis; [ed.] Enrolled in Greenbrier High; [occ.] Student; [memb.] FFA, Beta Club; [hon.] Straight A's, A's and B's, entered a poetry contest in middle, and published in a state wide school book; [oth. writ.] A few poems have been looked at, one has been published besides this one.; [pers.] I strive to reflect my feelings in most of my poems. I have been influenced by my feelings, imaginations, and thoughts.; [a.] Greenbrier, AR

JOHNSON, LORELEE
[b.] September 7, 1969, Edson, Alberta, Canada; [p.] Ed and Ursula Brandle; [m.] Calvin Johnson, June 10, 1995; [ed.] Grade 12 Diploma, Grand MacEwan College for 1 year, Office Automation Diploma; [occ.] Secretary, Office Clerk; [a.] Edmonton, Alberta, Canada

JOHNSON, LORELEI
[b.] September 5, 1949, Norwalk; [p.] Mary and Gordon Tingets; [ch.] Kristin Lorelei De Rosia, David Keith De Rosia; [ed.] Norwalk High School, National Academy, U. Conn, Post College, Paier College of Art, C.P.I.; [occ.] Self Employed/US Government; [memb.] Past and present volunteer for American Heart Assoc., Cancerfund, Arthritis Foundation, Special Olympics, Leukemia Assoc., Diabetes Assoc., Bristol Civil Theater, SFX Choir, Dance Workshop; [hon.] Numerous awards for academics, Art, Literature and volunteer work; [oth. writ.] Poems published in local newspapers and school journals; [pers.] My poems and writings have been influenced by my life, family friends and artists I have admired; [a.] Waterbury, CT

JOHNSTON, JEFFREY L.
[b.] May 18, 1982, Jena, LA; [p.] Debbie Johnston, Gene Johnston; [ed.] Kindergarten through 8th grade at Quitman Public Schools in Quitman, AR; [occ.] Student - 9th grade; [memb.] Gifted tallented, FFA, Chess Club, School band, basketball team, Ozark teenage rodeo Association; [hon.] Band awards (3), 3 belt buckles for bull riding in O.T.R.A., 3 recognitions for short stories.; [pers.] I write exactly what I feel about the people in my Life, that have encouraged me to do well and strive to accomplish mu goals in the road of life. I owe everything to my mother - Debbie, father-Gene, sister-Amy, and brother-Brent. I also owe a great of gratitude to my 4th grade teacher - Mrs. Hankins.; [a.] Quitman, AR

JONES, ROGER P.
[b.] April 24, 1944, Mize, MS; [p.] Mr. and Mrs. C. M. Jones; [m.] Lois, September 29, 1966; [ch.] Christy and Amber; [ed.] B.S., M.S, Ph.D.- Mississippi State University; [occ.] Chairman of Agriculture Dept. Hinds Community College, Raymond, MS.; [memb.] American Vocational Assoc., American Neat Science Assoc., American Association of Neat Processors; [hon.] Outstanding Vocational Teacher Award - 1989, 3-E Award - 1995; [pers.] I wrote this poem as away to cope with the death of my granddaughter to Sids.; [a.] Raymond, MS

JONES, ROWLANDA
[b.] January 16, 1942, Hongkong; [pers.] Rowlanda was born in a concentration camp in Hongkong,

during Japanese occupation of the island. A heightened awareness of the abuses of power, have guided and shaped her life.; [a.] Mississauga, Ontario, Canada

JONES, WILLIAM H.
[pen.] William Henry Jones, W.H. Jones, Captain J. Bill Jones; [b.] April 1, 1924, Black Diamond, WA; [p.] Helenor Jones - Father Deceased; [m.] Barbara A. Jones, May 17, 1960; [ch.] Robert Jeffery Jones, Denise Lynn Williams; [ed.] B.A. San Diego State Naval School of Hospital Administration; [occ.] Captain, U.S. Navy (Red); [memb.] (1) Federal Health Care Executives, (2) Fleet Reserve Association, (3) Distinguished Member International Society of Poets; [hon.] Legion of Merit (Navy), numerous service medals and awards, graduated with honors 5 military schools, advanced from Apprentice Seaman to Captain during Naval career. Editor's Choice Award 1995 (1), Editor's Choice Award 1996 (7); [oth. writ.] Sparrowgrass Poetry Forum: Endless Thought, Am I Worthy, In His Wisdom We Must Trust, Garden Workshop, Sequins on the Floor, Symphony of the Night, Charlie, Lady of My Dreams, Dearest Mom, A Humble Apology, Customary Places and Faces, To Hell with Diamonds, Man's Best Friend, Dreams I've Had, The Window of His Soul, The Looking Blass, Believer or Deceiver, Chiqui is Her Name, Sweet Pixie, Tears of Joy. The National Library of Poetry: Songs Unsung, Catacombs of the Night, Stop and Smell the Roses, Home Alone, Devil's Wind, Ascent from Hell, No Perfect World, Please Another Chance, Poems Unpublished, Embers, Lonely is the Poet, The Hand that Stroked My Brow, Embers Lonely is the Poet, You were a Good Man Billy Jones. Mercury Register: The Infamous Still in Oroville. News Reporter: Father's Day is Everyday; [pers.] I believe in personal achievement, inspiring others to fulfill their dreams, at peace with self and others, all with a sense of humor, dedication and perspective.; [a.] Lake San Marcos, CA

JORDAN, SANDRA
[b.] April 6, 1961, Dayton, OH; [p.] Risteen Jordan, Opal Jordan; [ch.] Godson Matthew Tackett; [ed.] West Carrollton Senior High; [memb.] Buckeye State Sherriff Association; [pers.] I can't write about anything that I don't have a passion for.; [a.] West Carrollton, OH

JORDAN, SARAH ASHLEY
[b.] October 1, 1985, Charleston, SC; [p.] James B. and Bonnie F. Jordan; [ed.] Entering 6th grade - I'm in advanced Math; [occ.] Student; [memb.] Jr. Atlanta Faloon Cheerleader and Girl Scouts; [oth. writ.] "Koalas" and The Day That Easter Almost Didn't Come; [pers.] I like to write the stuff that would make people smile. Unlike Lights in the Attic. Lights in the Attic talks mainly about scary and disgusting stuff, while I talk about the beautiful facts of the Earth.; [a.] Marietta, GA

JOSEPH, CAROL BERNADETTE
[b.] January 10, 1964, Trinidad; [p.] Jamil and Sarah Joseph; [oth. writ.] "Find Four Dreams Within Your Heart", book of poetry published (1985), Lyric to Songs, verses for greeting cards, articles and commercial in newspaper.; [pers.] When a smile touches your lips and kindness is spoken, when you can feel caring in your heart and learn to share it. It is the greatest gift to the world. If only we can understand, respect and accept it.

JOSEPH, KEITH VINCENT
[pen.] Gambie; [b.] October 6, 1958, Saint Vincent; [p.] Eileen and Arthur Joseph; [occ.] Building Contractor; [oth. writ.] A Jewel Heart; [pers.] Live unselfishly.; [a.] Lansing, MI

JOSHI, ANNA
[pen.] "Jannat"; [b.] August 26, 1979, Sydney, NS; [p.] Mr. and Mrs. P. Joshi; [ed.] Grade XII High School Student, Riverview Rural High School; [memb.] Literary magazine Club, Peer Education, Environment group and School Band; [hon.] Chiropractic Award in Science Competition, achieved Honors distinction status throughout Junior High/ High School, chosen for National Youth Leadership Forum in Boston.; [oth. writ.] Several unpublished poems such as "Mysteries" etc.; [pers.] My life is based around two concepts: Lewis Grizzard, yesterday is history, tomorrow is a mystery, today is a gift, and that's why we call it the present. Life is like a dog sled team. If you aren't the lead dog, the scenery never changes.; [a.] Sydney, Nova Scotia, Canada

JOU, MARGARET
[b.] October 29, 1975, Toronto, ON, Canada; [p.] Paul S. M. Jou, Julian Jou; [ed.] University of Toronto, St. George Campus; [occ.] Math, Biology Student; [pers.] This poem is written to give spirit to those conditioned to misfortune, category or disability. Unfortunately, society has many closed minds who force people to be trapped within a rotting world with no escape. Thanks to all who give me life, love and respect.; [a.] West Hill, Ontario, Canada

JOVANIC, VESNA MICHELLE
[b.] 11 October 1979, Sydney, Australia; [ed.] Third year high school student; [oth. writ.] Poems: "Forgive Me For Loving You", "All I Ever Wanted Was You", "Sweet Dreams", "Thank You", "Hello", "Believe", "You Make Me Feel", "Sorry", "Why", "Choice", "Stop! Don't Look", "Rose", "Not Alone, "It's You I Miss", "Our Loved Ones", "My Victory", "Passionate Sorrow", "Midnight", "Disappointment", "Monami"; [pers.] Many poems are dedicated to someone special who will be in my thoughts and cause fiery passion to burn inside of me. Otherwise, as H. Keller said: "The best and most beautiful things can not be seen, nor touched - only felt in the heart. "I'll continue" listening to my heart" for, that is where my inspiration lies.; [a.] Belgrade, Serbia-Yu, Australia

KAARD, MR. TARMO
[pen.] Tarmo Koarel; [b.] June 19, 1955, Penrith; [p.] Margrette, Arno; [ed.] Leaving Certificate, School Certificate; [occ.] Medical Officers Assistant; [memb.] Schizophenia fellowship, Powerhouse Museum Society

KADIRI, GILLIAN GAIL
[b.] January 19, 1950, Liverpool, England; [p.] Stanley and Iris Williams; [ch.] Kia Louise and Craig Michael; [ed.] University of Liverpool, Camoun College and University of Victoria; [occ.] Student/Sales; [memb.] International Society of Poets; [hon.] Several Community Service Award; [oth. writ.] Published in other anthologies, some newspapers.; [pers.] Being able to enjoy life, sharing it with the unconditional love of family and friends - whom I am fortunate to have.; [a.] Sooke, British Columbia, Canada

KALMAN, JEFFREY
[pen.] Joe Frye; [b.] May 15, 1974, Detroit, MN; [p.] Joan and Ernie Kalman; [ed.] Bucknell University, New York University; [occ.] Student; [pers.] Night withdraws our sight and gives us inner eyes to view the visions of the soul.; [a.] Bedford, NY

KANE, IRENE
[pers.] Irene Kane is a graduate of Adelphi University with a Bachelor of Arts in English Literature. She has had many poems published in local newspapers and magazines.

KANEGAE, RUBY ANN
[pen.] Ruby Moreno; [b.] October 23, 1965, Las Cruces, NM; [p.] Beatrice Moreno; [m.] Blake Kanegae, May 16, 1987; [ch.] Angela Marie, Akemi June; [ed.] Willow Glen High, Mission College; [occ.] Digital Imaging Hitech Publications, Beaverton, OR; [oth. writ.] Children's stories, and other poems unpublished.; [pers.] My work is dedicated to all English teachers who encourage their students writing abilities. Teaching them patience, creativity and self-confidence; [a.] Aloha, OR

KARIDES, TOULA P.
[b.] March 24, 1926, Milwaukee, WI; [p.] Strat and Doris Petropoulos; [m.] Peter George Karides, October 24, 1948; [ch.] Marlene, George and Steven; [ed.] Two years college; [occ.] Real Estate, Investments; [pers.] Wish I knew yesterday what I know today!!; [a.] Caledonia, WI

KASUN, ALISON D.
[pen.] Ali K.; [b.] September 9, 1982, Indiana, PA; [p.] David and Diana Kasun; [occ.] 9th grade student; [hon.] Basketball, softball, and rolleyball awards, distinguished honor student; [pers.] This is dedicated to all of my family and friends.; [a.] Indiana, PA

KAWAKAMI, BARBARA F.
[b.] August 24, 1921, Kumamoto Japan; [p.] Torashku Oyama (Mother), Matsu Oyama (Father); [m.] Douglas Y. Kawakami, February 1, 1944; [ch.] Three Children; [ed.] MA in Asian Studies, BS in Fashion Design and MDSE. Bilingual English/Japanese; [occ.] Historian, Consultant on Japanese Immigrant History and Clothing, Lecturer, Story telling on Japanese Immigrant, Experience and "Picture Brides"; [memb.] Toast Master Int'l., District 49, Mililani Toast Masters, #5244. (ATM), Bishop Museum of Hawaii, Japanese Cultural Center of Honolulu, Japanese American Nat'l Museum, Hawaii Buddhist Womens Ass. Hawaii's Plantation Village Part and Museum; [hon.] University of Hawaii. B.S. in Fashion Design/University of Hawaii. MDSE Dean's List, 1979, Myrle Clark Creative Writing Award (1986), (UH), Golden Poet Award. Immigrant Child's First Day in School", named in Who's Who Among Students in American Junior Colleges, 1976, Association for Asian American Studies 1994 outstanding book award in history for "Japanese Immigrant Clothings in Hawaii, 1885-1941 (UH Press at Ann Arbor, Michigan, second award for book: KA Palapala Do'Okela, Excellence in Reference Books Award, "Japanese Immigrant Clothing in Hawaii, 1885-9141" 1996. Na Hulu Makua (An honor society for adults returning to education 1996. Silver gavel award: Toastmasters Int'l, Hawaii, District 49, 1993; [oth. writ.] "A Christmas story", published in Hawaii Herald 1983. Hawaii's Japanese American Journal: Japanese Immigrant Clothing in Hawaii, 1885-1941 (University of Hawaii Press), 1993, Kasuri to Palaka: Journey through clothing: from Japanese Villages to Hawaiian Plantations, 1885-1941. In Issei Pioneers: Hawaii and the mainland, 1885-1924. Japanese American Nat'l Museum, 1992. (Poem) Immigrant's Child, First Day In Scool, Hawaii Herald, 1982. Hawaii's Japanese American Journal.; [pers.] Education is a life long process. Although I had a late start in formal education (started as a freshman at age 53), my life has become richer and more meaningful. I find joy in sharing my life experiences with others through my writings, lectures and story telling. I learn as much from the many people I meet in all walks of life and diverse ethnic groups of people.; [a.] Mililani, HI

KEATON, PERRY
[pen.] PK; [b.] March 15, 1960, Welch, WV; [p.] Robert and Addie Keaton; [m.] Imogene Keaton; [ch.] Amber and Anthony; [ed.] Iaeger High School; [occ.] Power Line Construction; [a.] Glen Easton, WV

KEISER, RICHARD
[b.] May 13, 1941, Cambridge, OH; [p.] George and Agness Keiser; [m.] Laura, April 23, 1966; [ch.] Brian, Bill, Tony; [ed.] H.S.; [occ.] Machine operator; [pers.] Poems must come from the heart not from the head in order to have lasting value.; [a.] Sherrodsville, OH

KELLER, ROBERT
[pen.] Edgar Max; [b.] January 14, 1952, Baltimore; [p.] Edgar and Anna Keller; [ch.] Erika Brumett, Robert Keller; [ed.] Overlea Senior High School; [occ.] Fire Protection Engineering, Technician/Part-Time Cab Driver; [memb.] National Institute for Certification in Engineering Technologies; [oth. writ.] 'Curtain Call' published in 'Frost at Midnight', several other unpublished poems, currently working on musical arrangements for song lyrics, and fictional short story.; [pers.] Answer the voice that calls from deep inside, without love, there is nothing. We love because he loved us first.; [a.] Baltimore, MD

KENDALL, EARL ALLEN
[b.] July 16, 1933, Madison, WI; [p.] Einar and Henrietta (Fischer) Kloppedal; [m.] Ann Marie (Hovre) Kendall, June 6, 1964; [ch.] Michael Lee (30) and Karen Sue (29); [ed.] Concordia H.S. and Jr. College, Milwaukee, Wis. Pre-med. and Medical School, Univ. of Wisconsin, Madison, Wis. BA and MD degrees Radiology residency, VA Hosp., Minneapolis Minnesota; [occ.] Physician - Staff Radiologist at Morton Plant Hospital, Clearwater, Fl. for 20 years.; [memb.] National, State and Local Medical and Radiological Societies; [hon.] Summo Cum, Concordia College; [oth. writ.] 30 poems, none before submitted for publication. 4 articles in medical and radiologic literature.; [pers.] I write poems when "mad, sad, or glad", and for occasion, birthdays, etc. Usually philosophical or humorous to encapsulate feelings about issues of current or lasting interest.; [a.] Clearwater, FL

KENKEL, CHARLES WILLIAM
[b.] October 10, 1985, Saint Louis, MO; [p.] William and Deborah Kenkel; [ed.] Finished 4th grade in June 1996 - Joe T. Robinson Elementary in Little Rock, AR; [occ.] Student; [memb.] Boy Scouts of America; [hon.] "A" Honor Roll, "Superstar" Award at school, various scouting awards; [oth. writ.] "Love" - Robinson Reporter - March 1996.; [pers.] I would like to dedicate my poem to my grandfather and namesake, Charles Kenkel (1919-1995). Also to my family and friends.; [a.] Roland, AR

KENNEDY, JEANNE
[b.] October 17, 1911, Huntsville, Ontario, Canada; [p.] Henry and Elsa Forde; [m.] Nicholas Kennedy, July 2, 1936; [ch.] 2 sons; [ed.] Business College; [occ.] Retired; [hon.] Literature Awards High School

KENNEDY, KYMBERLY ANN
[b.] January 12, 1971, Guelph, Ontario; [ch.] Jossyca-Lynn, Jacob-Andrew; [ed.] High School grade 13 and correspondence courses; [occ.] Mother, School Bus Driver, Writer; [memb.] Brampton Writer's Workshop; [hon.] Journalism award for school newspaper. Several articles and poems published in the Royals Reporter, Centre Duffrin District High School Newspaper.; [oth. writ.] 1st Volume of "The Soul Within" copyrighted 1994, several short stories and a manuscript called "Penny Fields"; [pers.] Being a strong believer in world peace, I pray I live to see the day when our world will sign away negative power and

hug for peace and freedom.; [a.] Brampton, Ontario, Canada

KENYON, KATIE I.
[b.] October 31, 1982, Portland, OR; [p.] David and Leah Kenyon; [ed.] I will be attending the 8th grade at J.B. Thomas Jr. High in Hillsboro, Oregon; [occ.] Student; [hon.] I've earned a silver award for physical fitness, and a gold award for music; [pers.] I'm a very happy person. I wish to achieve a lot of success in my life. My grandpa influence me to play the piano, and I look to my parents for guidance and values.; [a.] Hillsboro, OR

KERSHAW, ELAINE M.
[b.] May 17, 1944, Kimberley, British Columbia, Canada; [p.] Gilbert and Dorothy Kershaw; [m.] Divorced; [ch.] Daniel, Milton, Laura, Martin; [ed.] Graduate of St. Joseph's School of Nursing, Victoria, BC; [occ.] R.N.; [a.] New Westminster, British Columbia, Canada

KERSTENETSKY, KAMIL E.
[b.] October 13, 1979; [p.] Julie and Manuel Kerstenetsky; [ed.] Senior in high school; [hon.] High Honor Roll Silver Medal, Maxima Cum Laude, in National Latin Exam, Honorable Mention (4th place) in CT Latin Exam, International Awareness Award; [oth. writ.] Numerous poems, short stories, columns, and articles, published in local newspapers, literary magazine, and yearbook. One-act play locally produced, directed, and performed; [pers.] "One can have no smaller or greater mastery than mastery of oneself" - Leonardo da Vinci; [a.] Norwalk, CT

KESSLER, JEREMY
[b.] July 30, 1984, New York City; [p.] Robert E. Kessler, Dr. Margaret L. King; [ed.] Kew-Forest School; [occ.] Student; [hon.] Accepted to Hunter College High School, 1996, Participant, Center for Talented Youth 1995-1996, Johns Hopkins University; [a.] Douglaston, NY

KEY, MICHAEL D.
[pen.] Harmony and Prettyboy; [b.] January 24, 1973, Manhattan; [p.] Albert Key, Celeste Key; [ed.] Pacific H.S., H.S. Diploma Wallace Community College Selma, Alabama 1 1/2 year experience; [occ.] Songwriter, and a Lifeguard; [memb.] Independent; [hon.] 1st place in a rap contest. 1st place in a spelling B contest. 1st place in a science fair contest, 4 gold medals for swimming. Trophy for a basketball tournament.; [oth. writ.] Life as a student, lover's paradise, ups and downs, spreading my wings, the harmony syndrome, and creative thoughts.; [pers.] I am deeply honored to be a semifinalist. I surely hope everyone takes pleasure in my talent. Working hard to achieve, has payed off for me in the long run in life.; [a.] Brooklyn, NY

KHAN, A. F. M. BILLAH
[b.] January 1, 1948, Bangladesh; [p.] Mustafiz B. Khan, Jahanara; [m.] Zeenat Afroze, October 3, 1976; [ch.] Almansur, Nadia, Lamia; [ed.] Bachelor of Engineering (Mechanical); [occ.] Engg. Service, Scarborough Public Utilities Commission; [memb.] IEEE, P. Eng. (Ontario) in progress; [oth. writ.] Published in Bengali Papers in Bangladesh; [pers.] Human feeling has no time or place boundaries. We must believe either in love or in God.; [a.] Scarborough, Toronto, Canada

KHATUN, MRS. ANWARA
[pen.] Saika Chowdhury; [b.] February 9, 1946, Dhaka Bangladesh; [p.] Mr. Ainuddin Ahmed and Amina Khatun; [m.] Mr. Shafkat Hossain, January 15, 1960; [ch.] Four sons and four daughters; [ed.] Secondary School; [occ.] House wife; [oth. writ.] Short stories, poems, songs, novels published in different publications and news papers in the native country

KING, CARMEN
[b.] March 24, 1947, Toronto, Ont.; [p.] Evelyn and Delmar Dillon; [ch.] Erik and Karen Persson and Brittany Dahl; [ed.] Graduate of Loyalist College Belleville Ont.; [occ.] Mental Retardation Counsellor now call Residential Life Counsellor; [memb.] March of Dimes South Marysburgh, Ann Farwell Library Board, Prince Edward Animal Welfare Society; [oth. writ.] Poems and articles published in local papers. Short story written for children; [pers.] I like to write poems and stories expressing my feelings and to attempt to teach my children and others the morals in life.; [a.] Milford, Ontario, Canada

KING, DARLENE
[b.] May 8, 1959, Nanaimo, BC; [p.] Eileen Murray and Bert Hill; [m.] Tim King, June 30, 1986; [ch.] Boy-Taylor (9), Twin Girls Kennedy, Sheridan (7); [ed.] Graduated with honors from Nanaimo Senior High, Royal Jubilee Hospital School for Registered Nursing graduated 1981, 1 yr. obstetrics specialty; [occ.] Head Coach and Owner of Kings National Baton Club - National Champions 1986 - present; [memb.] Registered Nurses Association of Ontario, Canadian Baton Twirling Association.; [hon.] Nursing and District Scholarships for outstanding grades. Numerous National and International and world championship titles in Are of performance sports.; [oth. writ.] For provincial and National performance sport news papers and magazines. This is 1st poetry ever submitted for publication.; [pers.] Through poetry I enjoy the exploration of occurances in our lives that elicit emotional responses - These responses being our most powerful fuel for enlightenment.; [a.] Georgetown, Ontario, Canada

KING, RANDAL
[pen.] Randal King; [b.] February 15, 1956, Toronto, Ontario; [p.] Colin and Elspeth King; [m.] Patricia Ann King, January 23, 1993; [ed.] Mohawk College Hamilton, 3rd year Television Broadcasting Student; [occ.] Student; [oth. writ.] Various other poems published in local and city (Toronto Sun) newspaper.; [pers.] Poetry is a side dish for the soul.; [a.] Brantford, Ontario, Canada

KINNEY-GORDON, KATHLEEN
[pen.] Kathleen K. Gordon; [b.] August 15, 1969, Verdon, Quebec, Canada; [p.] Bernard Kinney, Irene Kinney; [m.] Bruce Gordon, August 24, 1991; [ed.] Villa Maria High School Vamer College; [occ.] Technical Writer, Graphic Designer; [oth. writ.] Currently completing Sci-Fi Novel and Rock Opera Project.; [pers.] I do not wish to be the servant who was thrown out for burying his talent in the ground. (Matthew 25:30); [a.] Chanteauguay, Province of Quebec, Canada

KIRKNESS, DONNA A.
[pen.] Herb and Mary Gunsch; [b.] April 1, 1961, Billings, MT; [m.] R.D. Kirkness, May 5, 1984; [ch.] Brandelyn (12), Britney (10), BreAnna (7), Jayde (4); [occ.] Business Owner/Self-Employed; [hon.] The gift and honor of my 4 children, during this the awards are plentiful!; [oth. writ.] Many; [pers.] God has directed me and has given me the talents to write poetry. I wrote this poem for my children that they acknowledge God daily and all he has done for us as a family.; [a.] Billings, MT

KITTLE, T. RENE
[b.] December 1, 1963, Missoula, MT; [p.] Lyle and Delores McLaughlin and Frank Lee; [m.] M. Jess Kittle, August 21, 1993; [ch.] Brandon Joseph and Spencer Jordan; [ed.] 14 years; [occ.] Legal Assistant and child care provider; [oth. writ.] Recently finished first novel titled "From The Ashes Of Deceit"; [pers.] I believe out children are our future and the children deserve our love and a gentle guidance.; [a.] Polson, MT

KLEIN, WADE
[b.] January 24, 1977, Calgary, Alberta; [p.] Brian Klein, Mary Klein; [ed.] Grade 12 Diploma, Forest Lawn High; [occ.] Continuing Education; [oth. writ.] Three books of poems and stories and an unfinished screen play, all writings are still not published.; [pers.] I am but one voice whose decidedly dark views on the world are not to be forced upon any one. On the highway of love and life I'm no different than anybody else surviving if they can. My strongest poetic influence has been Leonard Cohen.; [a.] Calgary, Canada

KLIMITZ, MRS. BETTY
[pen.] Bette Elly; [b.] August 30, 1949, Toronto; [p.] Diane and Sam Sniderman; [m.] Stanley Klimitz, July 10, 1973; [ch.] Jordan and Jesse; [ed.] Honours B.A. York University, Bachelor of Education Degree, University of Toronto; [occ.] Founder and Owner of Private School Called "Speaker Skills" also teaches High School English and Theatre Arts, part time through the North York Board of Education.; [hon.] Honours B.A. York University - 1975 Honour Graduate from University of Toronto - 1976; [oth. writ.] Writes fiction, short stories and plays; [pers.] "Where there is a will there is a way." If you work hard and believe in yourself you can accomplish your goals and dreams.; [a.] Toronto, Ontario, Canada

KLOPPENBURG, MICHELLE
[b.] October 24, 1960, Joliet, IL; [p.] Roberta, Robert Knapp; [m.] Louis S. Kloppenburg, November 19, 1988; [ch.] Malinda, William, Alycia; [ed.] High School Grad.; [occ.] Homemaker; [oth. writ.] Your Smile, Your Eyes, Who Would Have Thought, It Will Get Better, and more. Nothing published yet.; [pers.] I always write about feelings. If I can't say it I write it. My greatest influences are family, friends. My work to me is a great work of heart!; [a.] Lowell, MA

KNIGHT, AMANDA REGINA
[b.] June 24, 1985, Kingston, PA; [p.] James Knight, Dianajo Trevethon; [occ.] School Student; [memb.] Y.M.C.A.; [a.] Nanticoke, PA

KNIGHT, LINDA C.
[b.] January 21, 1948, Tampa, FL; [p.] W. R. and Rosa Ve Clark; [m.] Divorced; [ch.] Michael Darren, Wendy Diane; [ed.] Hillsborough High Tampa FL; [occ.] Secretary; [pers.] I enjoy writing on any subject matter. My faith, family and country are very important in my personal life and are reflected in my writings.; [a.] Crystal River, FL

KNOLL, PHYLLIS
[b.] September 17, 1922, Toronto, ON, Canada; [p.] George Lehman, Katie Lehman; [m.] John E. Knoll, August 21, 1948; [ch.] Esther, Ruth, Robert And Sylvia; [ed.] Bolton Ave., and Withrow Ave., grade schools, Danforth Technical Bible College Kitchener ON; [occ.] Retired Pastor's wife; [pers.] I've been writing poems for many years on request, for special occasions. Since feeding the birds, their very human characteristics have been a delight to watch. I prefer to capture these with pen for total viewing.; [a.] Caistor Centre, Ontario, Canada

KNOWLES, RICHARD N.
[b.] August 8, 1935, Wilmington, DE; [p.] Dorothy and Frank Knowles; [m.] Claire E. F. Knowles, December 31, 1988; [ch.] 3 daughters, 1 stepdaughter, 1 Grandson, 3 granddaughters; [ed.] BA Oberlin College, Ph.D U. of Rochester in Organic Chemistry; [occ.] Director of Emergency Response and Community Awareness - DuPont Co.; [memb.] Board-Berkana Institute, Board-National Institute of Chemical Studies, Audubon Soc., American Chemical Soc., Westminster Presbyterian Church; [hon.] Who's Who in the World 1993 - Present, Who's Who in the US, 1997, American

Men and Women of Science, Crystal Award - Championing Human Potential DuPont Co., Chemical Emergency and Preparedness Partnership Award - Region III, U.S.E.P.A.; [oth. writ.] 40 U.S. Patents, Journal for Quality and Participation, 6-1995 Expanding Self-Organizing Systems, 1-1996 Measurement of Self-Organizing Systems; [pers.] I deeply believe we need to shift our paradigm from the world as a machine to the world as a living system so we can find ourselves and our spirits again.; [a.] Niagara Falls, NY

KOCH, LEIGH-CHANTELLE
[pen.] Charlotte Rain; [b.] 4 December 1979, Perth, Western Australia; [p.] William Koch, Gwen Koch; [ed.] Bovo International Primary School (PNG), Dubbo West Primary School (Australia), Rochedale State School (Australia), Redeemer Lutheran College (Australia); [memb.] Singer in a band, Inc (Music info.); [hon.] A few community service awards, goalie (for hockey) award; [oth. writ.] Song lyrics that I sing with a band, other poems, a few short stories and I am starting to plan a Soapie for television.; [pers.] It is best to always have an open mind about everything in life. And you must always believe in your dreams - it doesn't matter whether anyone else thinks you will achieve or not as long as you believe in yourself you dreams with be fulfilled.; [a.] Rochedale, Queensland, Australia

KOCHER, NATASHA
[b.] November 4, 1983, Walkerton; [p.] David Kocher, Dianne Kocher; [ed.] Mother Teresa Elementary School; [hon.] Remembrance Day Literary Contest (2nd place); [pers.] I look deep into people's souls, reaching beyond what truly exists, bringing to surface the unbelievable. Hopefully enhancing people's awareness of each others unique qualities.; [a.] Walkerton, Ontario, Canada

KOLENSKI, NANCY A.
[b.] December 31, 1963, Hamilton, ON; [p.] Marjorie and Edward Kolenski; [occ.] Computer Operator; [oth. writ.] Novel chapter, accepted for "Inter Novel", California.; [pers.] I write for my own pleasure, but if I move one person with the words I pen, I have achieved a far greater goal than self-satisfaction. I feel I have been paid a compliment so great, I am speechless.

KOLLIAS, PANAGIOTIS
[b.] November 12, 1928, Athens; [p.] Spiros Kollias, Kaliopi Kollias; [m.] Olympia Iatridou, September 15, 1963; [ch.] Spiros Kollias, Vassilios Kollias; [ed.] Dr., Civil-Sanitary Engineer; [occ.] Research in Sanitary Engineering and Environmental Sciences; [memb.] Technical Chamber of Greece, Association des Hygienistes et Techniciens Municipeaux, France, I.S.W.A, I.A.C.T.; [oth. writ.] Mainly poems, some narrations and a novel. Also more than 50 papers presented to Seminars, Congresses, Magazines, etc. and three technical books; [pers.] I love the nature, the work of God. I strive for the protection of the Environment and the improvement of life quality standards; [a.] Athens, Greece

KONSTANTINOV, SVETLANA
[b.] November 25, 1968, Montreal, Province of Quebec, Canada; [p.] Victor and Halina Konstantinov; [ed.] Rosemount High School, Dawson College, Concordia University - took some literature courses; [occ.] Records Assistant, Office of the Registrar, Concordia University; [hon.] Editor's Choice Award 1996 - The National Library of Poetry.; [oth. writ.] "A Blood Red Rose". Published in A Moment In Time, as well, "A Shining Star". Published in Best Poems of 1996. By the National Library of Poetry.; [pers.] Poet's thoughts that are into words come directly

from his or her soul.; [a.] Montreal, Province of Quebec, Canada

KOPF, BETTY
[b.] June 10, 1939, New Albany, MS; [p.] Cleve and Clemmie Garrison; [m.] Aubrey W. Kopf, June 20, 1959; [ch.] Alicia, Sheila; [ed.] H.S.- Dublin, MS 1 yr College - Northwest MS Comm. College Licensed Practical Nurse; [occ.] Licensed Practical Nurse; [oth. writ.] "Hauntings at the Brown Cabin" (unpublished book); [pers.] I write about true events that have affected my life.; [a.] Pearl, MS

KOSENA, DONNA M.
[b.] February 13, 1948, Seattle, WA; [p.] Dean Hess, Eva Hess; [m.] Bruce A. Kosena, December 14, 1985; [ch.] Donna S. Chandler, Rebecca Kosena; [oth. writ.] Several, but none in print; [pers.] I feel a kinship for the "Twilight Mystery", philosophers of life, and an awe, when their hand moves my pen.; [a.] Kalispell, MT

KOTO, DORINA
[pen.] Donna Koto; [b.] November 18, 1955, Alexandria, Romania; [p.] Ion Radu, Maria Radu; [m.] Kin-ichi Koto, December 1979; [ch.] Junko-Lorena Koto; [ed.] Public School of 12 years; [occ.] Housewife; [oth. writ.] I have written an intense, absolutely original and romantic novel, my first roman I wrote, the title is "Sashimi". This work was accepted and right now is on the way for publishing by Vantage Press Inc., New York.; [pers.] I believe the loneliness was an ideal impulse which drove my hand and inspired me with fervor. To be honest, it is very first time when I have tried to write a poem. That was the sway of the destiny which inspired me in a moment of depression, and it happened to me in the right time. Many times the disappointment or despair is the most brainstorm muse. Makes you create.; [a.] Minoo, Osaka, Japan

KRAMER, ROSE
[b.] January 29, 1919, Roselle, NJ; [p.] Tamara (Deceased) and Louis Hoffman; [m.] Irving Kramer, October 15, 1946; [ch.] Jonathan - 48, Jacquilin - 45, Greg - 43; [ed.] B.S. - Magna Cum Laude, Phi Beta Kappa New York University 1968 - graduate fellow special education, Univ. 7 Southern California; [occ.] Retired and writing when able; [hon.] QBK, graduate Fellow U.S.C. Ascal, etc. Honorary Glum Society Honorary English Society, Ellectic NYV - etc; [oth. writ.] Too many to list. I wish lyrics and poetry and prose since I was three or five.; [pers.] I feel very ambivalent, not having head of your organization and hoping it is not a "Vanity" firm as poets, even poets Laurei, aurarely given recognition and/or money. But I want to get my "juice" running and this may just be the tickets needed.; [a.] Santa Rosa, CA

KRISTENSON, KIMBERLEY
[b.] July 24, 1975, Lehighton, PA; [p.] Arlon and Anna Kristenson; [ed.] Custer County High School, 2 years at Miles Community College - both in Miles City, MT. Currently enrolled at Montana State University Northern in Havre, MT, 3rd year; [occ.] Counselor working in habilitating persons with Developmental Disabilities. Also a full time student - enrolled in Elementary Education; [oth. writ.] This is first published poem, yet I have been writing poetry consistently since age 13.; [pers.] Believe in yourself and others, the truth will guide you through the many obstacles we face. I find I enjoy writing about people most, and the courage and strength that can be found in every living thing.; [a.] Havre, MT

KRONEN, ARI
[b.] September 28, 1984, New York City; [p.] Jerilyn and Ken Kronen; [ed.] Ramaz School, New York City - 6th grade student; [pers.] I have always

had many questions about God, So I decided to express it in a logical creative way, which was inspired by the teaching of poetry by Ms. Victoria Ginsburg, my fifth grade teacher, at Ramaz School.; [a.] New York, NY

KRUMDIACK, JOY E.
[b.] August 3, 1952, Spokane, WA; [p.] William and Eleanor Hughes; [m.] Bryan, December 21, 1974; [ch.] Kristen Ann, Karolyn Amy; [ed.] Spokane Falls Community College, Eastern Washington University; [occ.] Medical Transcriptionist/medical Assistant; [memb.] Whatcom County Chapter Medical Assistant, Sophomore Women's Honorary (SELEAH) in College (President); [oth. writ.] A collection of poetry/Prose titled song of joy, yet to be publishes.; [pers.] I attempt to express my feelings in my writing so that others may be able to identify with them as well.; [a.] Bellingham, WA

KUNTZ, LARRY L.
[pen.] "The Big L", "Lucky Larry"; [b.] January 22, 1918, Brooklyn, NY; [p.] Otto and Anna; [m.] Belle, December 6, 1950; [ch.] Four; [ed.] Thomas Jefferson H.S., Brooklyn College; [occ.] Retired from New York Times, Originating poetry items; [hon.] Poetry and Sports, items in various Newspapers and Magazines; [oth. writ.] New York Times, New York Post, Daily News; [pers.] In all course of human events these five things observe with care, "Of Whom You Speak, To whom You Speak, How, When and Where!!!"; [a.] Brooklyn, NY

KURUP, SANDRA
[pen.] Sandra Kurup; [b.] February 12, 1984, Houston, TX; [p.] Rajendra and Nirmala Kurup; [ed.] Going into 7th grade; [hon.] Harmony Middle School, Blue Valley Principal's Honor Roll Award, Participation in U.S. Academic Triathlon, Straight A award, and Promotion in Piano class.; [oth. writ.] Stories: Mary's Vision, The Day My Enrichment Sister Came Poems: My Dearest Grandfather, Star of Love, Imagination, Mother Earth, Fond Memories, My Child is Growing Up! etc.; [pers.] My writing skills has improved over the years due to the encouragement I got from my family members and teachers.; [a.] Overland Park, KS

LABUCKAS, HOLLY
[b.] January 14, 1980, Hamilton; [p.] Rick, Judy Labuckas; [ed.] Battlefield Elementary, Princess Margret Puble, Stamford Collegiate; [occ.] I just filled and application for work; [hon.] Graduation Award; [oth. writ.] My guardian angel, one good man, beware, you are my every thing, thank you, pay backs, here with you.; [pers.] I feel a great need to let my feelings out on paper. Therefore I can look at the world in a more positive way.; [a.] Niagara Falls, Ontario, Canada

LAKE, BRENDA
[pen.] Brenda Heron-Lake; [b.] November 8, 1949, Toronto, Canada; [p.] June Coulson - Mother and Best Friend; [m.] Alan Lake - Police Detective and Car Buff; [ed.] Huron Heights Secondary School, Newmarket, Ontario; [occ.] Office Supervisor, Drew Chemical Limited, Div. of Ashland Inc.; [oth. writ.] The sudden death of my youngest brother, Bob, in 1982 inspired me to compose memoriams. Since then I have written poems for family and friends.; [pers.] I am an avid antiques enthusiasts, enjoy gardening, reading, car shows, and spending quiet moments with my 3 cats. I dedicate "Bobby's Gift" in loving memory of Robert James Heron whose sparkling personality and keen sense of adventure will never be forgotten.; [a.] Mt. Albert, Ontario, Canada

LAKIN, BOBBI OMORI
[b.] January 29, 1988, Enid, OK; [p.] Sid and Linda Lakin; [ed.] Presently enrolled in 3rd grade at Hillsdale Christian School, Hillsdale, OK

LALIBERTE, LISA
[b.] February 19, 1974, Soo, Ontario; [p.] Roland and Maureen; [m.] Jon Burns; [ch.] Hailey Patricia Burns; [ed.] Bawating Collegiate graduate; [oth. writ.] "First Family Christmas" published in "Fields of Gold" 1996; [pers.] Poem written as a gift to Jack and Shirley Smith for their 50th wedding anniversary, with love.; [a.] Sault Ste Marie, Ontario, Canada

LAMBERT, DIANA BLANDFORD
[pen.] Diana Blandford Lambert; [b.] September 20, 1950, Portsmouth, VA; [p.] Samuel James Blandford and Dolores Newlands Blandford; [m.] Fergason Warren Lambert, November 25, 1985; [ch.] Jeffrey Markus Collins, Kevin Ian Collins; [ed.] Nathan Bedford Forrest High School Jacksonville, Florida; [occ.] Student Programs Coordinator, Eastern Virginia Medical School; [memb.] American Business Women's Association; [hon.] Eastern Virginia Medical School, Staff Recognition Award, 1991, 1992, 1993, 1994, 1995, 1996; [oth. writ.] "Tribute to Nana"; [pers.] "Life's real treasures come from the heart".; [a.] Virginia Beach, VA

LAMBERT, WILLIAM J.
[pen.] William J. Lambert; [b.] December 24, 1919, Camden East; [p.] The late Winnifred and John S. Lambert; [m.] Evelyn, September 21, 1977; [ch.] Three; [ed.] Very little - grade 8; [occ.] Propane Operator, Gardener, Soldier Farmer, Construction Foreman and Poet I have been successful in all walks of this life; [memb.] Var Amps of Canada, Distinguished member of The National Poetry; [hon.] Poetry elite - 1985 Public Recognition 1939/45 Canadian Forces of Canada - Editors Choice Awards 1993/95/96 National Library of Poetry; [oth. writ.] The poets corner in local paper 2 yrs, I have 3 books of poetry on the market "Treasured Thoughts" Vol. I, II and III; [pers.] My inspirations as swift as the waters nature is my educator, the best teacher of man I am a lover of binds, flowers and all nature around now retired look back on my childhood years and put life time thoughts into poems.; [a.] Village Morton, Ontario, Canada

LANCASTER, TIMOTHY DAVID
[b.] March 10, 1971, Jackson, TN; [p.] James Lancaster, Sarah Lancaster; [ed.] Various public schools, Jackson State Community College, Lambuth University; [occ.] College student at Lambuth University, hospital volunteer; [hon.] 7th grade i received award for Best Short Story; [oth. writ.] In 1992, I privately published a collection of poems and drawings under the title "Bitter Streams". My poem "Sleeper" originally appeared in this collection.; [pers.] I seem to understand the infinite realms of the human imagination and have been influenced by Shelley, Byron, Baudelaire, and Hemingway.; [a.] Jackson, TN

LANDRY, TIMOTHY
[b.] November 17, 1982, New Iberia, LA; [p.] Tim Landry and Cathy Landry; [ed.] St. Edwards Elementary, Catholic High School; [hon.] In a school contest I received 1st in nonfiction and in a DAR essay I received 4th; [pers.] I want to thank my teachers, especially Mrs. Karen Foret, who introduced me to poetry.; [a.] New Imberia, LA

LANDY, ALVIN
[b.] January 21, 1920, Savannah, GA; [p.] Deceased; [m.] Deceased; [ch.] Hilary Joyce and Anne R. Landy; [ed.] AB Univ. Calif. Berkeley 1994 English, MA Ohio Univ. (Athens) 1951 English MSW Simmon Sch. of Social Work, Ph.D. Higher

Ed. emphasis Soc. Wk.; [occ.] Retired February '96 Counselor with terminally ill pts and families, earlier: college teacher, therapist; [memb.] National Associations of Social Workers, when working full time, belonged to other prof. organizations; [oth. writ.] Write poetry, but never published.; [pers.] I have been influenced by W. H. Anden, E. Bishop, James Merrill, among others: Whitman, D. H. Lawrence.; [a.] Wilmington, NC

LANG, JENNIFER M.
[b.] March 17, 1969, San Anselmo, CA; [p.] Joan Aufricht; [m.] Robert Lang, September 4, 1994; [ed.] University of California; [occ.] Multinational Specialists; [memb.] Kappa Delta Sorority; [pers.] I believe that in every story there is a lesson to be learned. My hope is that children everywhere can learn from mine.; [a.] Simi Valley, CA

LAPHAM, TREVA
[pen.] Treva Lapham; [b.] February 20, 1921, Lima, OH; [p.] William and Cora Reed (Both Deceased); [m.] (Divorced) Leland Lapham, November 14, 1937; [ch.] Anita J. Janice S, Shirley S. Treval, Melvin A., Marolyn A-deceased); [ed.] Nine Grades of Education Church Old German Baptist; [occ.] Retired L.P.N. of 25 years caring for the elderly; [memb.] Member of the old German Baptist Church; [hon.] Just friends telling me I should let others enjoy my poems. It was a great "honor" for you to select my poem. I feel great about it.; [oth. writ.] I write about all topics for poems. Have written several shortstories. Had 2 poems books published but never done anything with them. Gave some away for gifts. I really needed to take this step forward.; [pers.] My poems are for lonely and hurting hearts with help from Jesus.; [a.] Elida, OH

LAPOINTE, BRENDA L.
[b.] September 22, 1942, Tampa, FL; [p.] Leon H. McLain and Jacquelyn Clark McLain; [m.] Charles E. LaPointe, December 27, 1972; [ch.] Debra Lee, Jacquelyn Leon, Geri Elaine and Linda Sue; [ed.] Gulf High School; [occ.] Administrator, First American Title Insurance Co.

LARSON, TASHA
[pen.] Tel; [b.] July 31, 1980; [p.] Lori and Don Larson; [ed.] Still in School, High School; [pers.] This is the first time I've entered a poem contest. And I hope that when someone else reads my poem (s) they see what I see and feel what I feel.; [a.] Palmer, NE

LATHAM, BRUCE EDWARD
[b.] September 20, 1972, Trenton, Ontario, Canada; [p.] John Norman and Audrey; [ed.] 2nd Year of Information Systems at Loyalist College in Bellovile, Ontario; [a.] Trenton, Ontario, Canada

LATTANZIO, TONY
[b.] October 11, 1942, Italy; [p.] Tolmino and Fenisia; [ed.] Up to High in Italy then L.I.F.E. Bible College, Los Angeles (Not graduated); [occ.] Product Manager (Television Commercial Area); [memb.] Travelled too much to stay put and hold any.; [hon.] Never looked or strived of any - looks like I was very successful in this.; [oth. writ.] Mostly humorous stories all with me and never shown - most of them in Italian (of course); [pers.] Life is beautiful even at his lowest point. In my stories I can't seem to be serious, in my poetry (limited, indeed) I can't seem to get funny.; [a.] Rome, Italy

LAUTERBACH, ROLF FRITZ
[b.] July 17, 1949, Saxony Germany; [p.] Hilde Gramatke; [m.] Divorced; [ch.] Karl, Clinton, Brennar; [ed.] 12 plus College Courses in Writing and Literature; [occ.] Disabled; [oth. writ.] In process of writing some more poetry starting 2

books and various thesis and articles to come porth soon; [pers.] I am a student of all history and a quester for truth in all writings or music I read 3 to 400 books a year and I'm an inpoholic on current events; [a.] Ucluelet, British Columbia, Canada

LAUZIER, GENEVIEVE
[b.] July 2, 1965, Verdun, Quebec; [p.] Francoise Pelletier, Gerard Lauzier; [m.] Andre Joly, July 16, 1994; [ch.] Alexandre, Xavier; [ed.] L.C.C.H.S., Vanier Cegep; [a.] LaSalle, Province of Quebec, Canada

LAVALLE, CONNIE
[b.] August 25, 1948, Perry, FL; [p.] David and Genevieve Gamble; [m.] William M. LaValle, November 26, 1976; [ch.] Eric - 18, Heath 16, Benji 13, Joseph 11; [ed.] Taylor County High School 12th Gr.; [occ.] Cartographer - Computer Mapping; [memb.] Spring Warrior Church of Christ; [oth. writ.] This is my first. I've never attempted to have any of my work published, but have always had a secret desire to do so.; [pers.] Writing has always been a part of my life, but I've always held back, thinking I wasn't good enough. My advice is go for it.; [a.] Perry, FL

LAW, LISA
[b.] December 11, 1960, Springfield, OH; [p.] Ron and Ann Delfans; [m.] Scott, July 31, 1982; [ch.] Jennifer, 9 months; [ed.] Grade 12; [occ.] Office Mgr.; [a.] Bragg Creek, Alberta, Canada

LAWRENCE, CAROLE E.
[b.] 1 March 1945, Abergavenny, South Wales; [p.] J. R. Barlow (Deceased), N. M. Barlow; [m.] Charles Bernard Lawrence, 18 February 1967; [ch.] Michelle Louise Lawrence; [ed.] Margaret Glenn-Bott Secondary School - Nottingham Clarendon College - City of Nottingham; [occ.] Artist; [memb.] Weyford Arts Centre Enniscorthy Golf Club; [hon.] Maths Hons - English Literature Hons., Business/Secretarial Hons., Swimming Award, Domestic Science Award, Golf World Magazine Award for Most Improved Player 1982 Golf Prizes; [pers.] Through my poetry I try to express my thoughts and feelings of the natural beauty of this world that touches us all.; [a.] Enniscorthy, Eire, Ireland

LEASAK, MARCELLA MARIE
[b.] December 2, 1952, North Battle Ford, Saskatchewan; [p.] George and Eva Frehlich; [m.] James Aurtor Leasak, November 10, 1988; [ch.] Robin, Denis, Jessica Evan Marie - Kasie Jean Leasak; [ed.] Gr 1 to 9 Meota School Sask. Gr 10 COGJ North Battle ford Sask Canada; [occ.] Wife, mother of three children helping to run our farm in Edam; [memb.] Rural Area PETA, Protection, Education Towards Animals, Humane Society of Canada, Distinguished Member, International Society of Poets 1995; [hon.] Editors Choice Award for Outstanding Achievement in Poetry for 1995 given for poem, called "Gods gift of love to me", put on tap and sounds of poetry 1995, Pub in sparkles in the sand" National Library of Poetry; [oth. writ.] Where love grows, courage follows, the visitation, pub. in "The Ebbing Tide", Mothers Take a Stand" pub, in "Best poem of the 90's," Tears for Jimmy pub. in portraits of life, "Abuse-Breaking The Chain, Finding Love Again," pub. National Library of Poetry 1996 day break of the land; [pers.] God has given me a chance to make a difference in the world, to take a stand and help give back faith in human nature, I am trying to do this through the messages in my poetry. I pray people will gain hope by reading it.; [a.] Edam, Saskatchewan, Canada

LEE, DEBEVON
[b.] October 6, 1953, Los Angeles, CA; [p.] Finis

and Rosalie Duncan; [m.] James Gordon Lee (Lt. Col. - U.S.A.F.), August 15, 1980; [ch.] Shaun Duncan Lee; [ed.] South Hills High, have attended various colleges and universities - have moved eight times in past fifteen years - e.g., no B.A./B.S. Degree Earned yet; [occ.] Administration of Justice, Homemaker, Student, Second Counselor in Relief Society - Church of Jesus Christ of Latter - Day Saints; [memb.] Rainbow Girls - Harlaxton Society, Morgan Horse Club - Ridge Riders, Clan Donnachaidh Society, PTA Secretary in Virginia and Australia; [hon.] 500 hour service pin for hospital volunteer work, 1971 Award from Citrus Valley Optimist Club; [oth. writ.] Poems printed in High School "Laurel" book; [pers.] I want to thank my heavenly Father for the talent I've been given, and thank my parents, husband, son, and friends for their support and encouragement.; [a.] Vandenberg Air Force Base, CA

LEE, JENNIFER
[b.] August 12, 1976, Vancouver, British Columbia, Canada; [ed.] Eric Hamber Secondary and the University of British Columbia, entering third year of an English Major; [occ.] Student; [hon.] Dean's list, finalist in the 1994, Stephen Leacock International Poetry Contest.; [oth. writ.] I have had poetry and short fiction published in several student publications local to the Vancouver area, including the Claremont Review.; [pers.] I am in love with the idea of being an artist, and although that doesn't necessarily bring home enormous pay cheques, it certainly supplies some pretty fulfilling daydreams and sometimes some amazing realities.; [a.] Vancouver, British Columbia, Canada

LEE, PETER B.
[b.] May 10, 1971, Baltimore, MD; [p.] Thomas J. and Susan E. Lee; [ed.] McDonough High School (Owings Mills, MD) Mary Washington College, B.S. Business Admin.. United States Sports Academy, M.S.S. Sports management; [occ.] Assistant Men's Basketball Coach/Part-time Instructor-Faulikwer State Community College; [pers.] Imagination and creativity are the keys to everything we have. They are our faith. They are our science. They allow us to explore a world where anything is possible. Most importantly they provide us with the ability to hope and love.; [a.] Daphne, AL

LEE, THOMAS E.
[pen.] Suppz; [b.] December 2, 1954, Burlington, IA; [p.] Delbert Lee and Norma Lee; [m.] Hyon Lee, March 22, 1980; [ch.] Thomas Jr.; [ed.] Trevor Browne High, Univ Kentucky, Univ Maryland Glendale CC. Grand Canyon Univ; [occ.] U.S.P.S.; [pers.] To give more than I take, and leave something behind for others.; [a.] Glendale, AZ

LEE, YUK WOR
[b.] June 1, 1924, Burma; [p.] Ping Cheung and Liu Che Lee; [m.] Shui-Ming Lee, August 28, 1957; [ch.] Wendy Lee; [ed.] Northcole college of Education, Dip., Hwakui College of Commerce and Engineering H.K., B.A., Biology Teacher's Course, University of H.K., Cert., The use of Visual and Audio Aids. Wandsworth Tech. College London and Cert. Institute of Ed. U. of London, Institute of Education, University of London, Associaship; [occ.] Retired; [hon.] Hong Kong Government Civil Servants Scholarships (1960), Commonwealth Education Fellowship (1973); [oth. writ.] Reports on field trips with special reference to the plants of Hong Kong in the capacity as former Hon. Sec, of H. K. Natural Hist. Soc. Produce, and 8 mm Film on "Hong Kong in Blossom" (Running time 60 mins, seasonal plants, 100 local species 43 fam.) "Hong Kong In Blossom" Flowers of the Four Seasons in H. K. incl. some rare species all with photos to be published "In the Land of the Mid-Night Sun-Iceland" to be published.; [pers.] 30

poems of The Tang Dynasty (618-906) in English (translation).; [a.] San Francisco, CA

LEFEBVRE-SPENCE, JASON
[pen.] Colten Lafaue, Jason Lefebvre; [b.] January 21, 1972, Sudbury, Ontario, Canada; [p.] Robert and Wanda Lindsay; [m.] Douglas O. Spence, May 16, 1992; [memb.] Member of GLOW (Gay and Lesbian Organisation of Waterloo); [oth. writ.] Your Birthday, Marriage Is..., Who Am I to You?, Hate, Gone, True Love, Love vs. Importance, If God Went on Strike, and the Harvey Saunders Poem.; [pers.] Never judge a person's chosen path in life until you judged your own, because that person might be following you. Comments: All my writings are influenced by Love and Relationships. All my work is copyrighted by: Jason W. Lefebvre-Lefave Interprize.

LEMIEUX, LINDA JEAN
[b.] July 10, 1951, Eau Claire, WI; [p.] Donna and William Morissette; [m.] Charles Lemieux; [ch.] Michelle, Shannon, Ryan, Cara; [ed.] Memorial High School - Eau Claire, WI; [occ.] Asst. Supervisor Food and Nutrition Luther Hospital; [memb.] Samaritan Club - Luther Hospital; [pers.] My poems are a reflection of my love for my family.; [a.] Eau Claire, WI

LEPAGE, MELISSA
[b.] March 16, 1984, Saskatoon, Saskatchewan, Canada; [p.] Gerald and Judy LePage; [ed.] Melfort and Unit Comprehensive Collegiate Grade 7; [oth. writ.] I have written 15 other poems besides alone. I keep my poems in a little book that I hope to publish in the future. Favorite poem, "Confusion"; [pers.] I live with my parents and older brother Mikal. I have one dog, Brandy. I have juts recently started writing poetry and am very proud of my accomplishments so far.; [a.] Melfort, Saskatchewan, Canada

LESLIE, ANN M.
[b.] April 22, 1996, Toronto; [p.] James and Marjorie Mutch; [m.] Clifford Leslie, October 15, 1988; [ch.] Marjorie-Anne, Lorne, Laura and Ralph; [ed.] Grade 12 and Business College, Real Estate; [occ.] Homemaker; [memb.] St. John's Lutheran Church; [oth. writ.] "The Promise" being published in the Field of Gold through The National Library of Poetry.; [pers.] My heart is in tune with the wonders of creation that surrounds us all with all its mysteries which can bring us hope, peace and joy and I try to reflect this within the poems I have written.; [a.] Waterloo, Ontario, Canada

LESSER, ROSE
[pen.] Sobi-An; [b.] March 24, 1908, Berlin, Germany; [p.] Julius Lesser, Sylvia Kahle; [m.] Kenji Takahashi (died December 28, 1948), May 1933; [ch.] Elizabeth, September 28, 1940; [ed.] 6 years Primary School, 3 years to work for a living. Had to quit school when a 3 penny roll casted DM 87.000.000.000. In the worst postwar time went to Tubingen, working 4 years as a micro analyst in 1929 I left and went to Japan.; [occ.] Author, Educator, Language Teacher, Youth Adviser (Jugendberater); [memb.] ASJ: (Asiatic Soc. of Japan) East Asiatic Soc. FTAJ: Foreign Teachers' Ass. of Japan/Self Realization Fellowship, California; [hon.] For 3 times, used reduced size copies from Mayor of Tokyo for good deeds, from Mayor F Kawasaki for daily every morning while running, picking up litter for donating books to the Library; [oth. writ.] Jap. Volksmund (Proverbs) Other writings Jap/Philosophy and Poetry 1942 Japan die Fremde - Japan de Heimat: 1970 Taifun und. 1981/ Typhoon and... 1982 Hyoko, Winterhabitat of Wild Swans at Suibara (Int. Wildlife Research Bereau. England 1990: Anthology and Biography

and others; [pers.] Definition of Joy: Everything that gives nourishment to the upward thoughts, that adds to our strength and causes us to love life, our neighbor and the world better, is Joy.; [a.] Kawasaki, Tokyo

LESZCZYNSKI, JAN
[pen.] Nathan Alex Prey; [b.] September 9, 1962, London, England; [p.] Mary and Richard Leszczynski; [ed.] Bishophalt Grammar School, Hillingdon, England; [hon.] Black Belt, Tang Soo Do (1st dan); [oth. writ.] Several poems in fanzines, Magazines in Europe

LEVINSON, SAM
[b.] March 28, 1985, London; [p.] Barry Levinson, Diana Levinson; [ed.] K-5; [occ.] Student; [oth. writ.] A Forgotten Cry, A Fallen Angel, A Remembered Image, Common Difference, School Playground, Shadow land, The Dark Side of Happiness, The Men In The White Suits, Bared, The Eye Of Your Mind, etc; [a.] Ross, CA

LEWIS, ABIGAIL
[pen.] Twiggy; [b.] July 7, 1978, Milwaukee, WI; [p.] Stephanie Sperry, Bennie Lewis; [ed.] Nicolet High School, Glendale, WI, Alverno College, Milwaukee, WI; [hon.] National Honor Society, Dean's List, Merit Award; [pers.] I wrote this poem specifically for males, I believe strongly in this poem and hope others will too, also in God.; [a.] Milwaukee, WI

LEWIS, CAROLYN
[b.] June 28, 1949; [p.] Mattie L. Donaldson; [m.] Eugene Lewis, September 11, 1982; [ch.] Twins; [ed.] Franklin High School, Rochester, NY; [occ.] Machine Operator at my Company were I work; [memb.] End Time Miracle Ministry Church; [oth. writ.] I've loved to write poems all my life. It's a gift from God.

LEWIS, JOAN
[b.] May 20, 1948, Cincinnati, OH; [m.] Marshall Lewis, April 26, 1968; [ch.] Tanya and April, grandchildren Tyana and Kayla; [ed.] Hughes H.S. (Cincinnati, Ohio), Monroe Community College (Rochester, NY); [occ.] ITT Automotive, receiving coordinator; [memb.] National Writer's Union (Rochester, NY Local), Writers and Books (Rochester, NY), Toastmasters International, International Society of Poets; [hon.] 1. Editor's Choice award 1996, 2. Semi-finalist - International Society of Poets Convention '96, Top 2%, 3. Best poems of the '90's; [oth. writ.] Essay on Poets - published September '96 Democrat and Chronicle (Rochester, NY) Mar '96, Poem - Gates/Chili news (Rochester, NY) May '96, Poem - Rochester shorts (Rochester, NY) magazine, Contributed articles published for Black History Month 1994, Democrat and Chronicle (Rochester, NY) essay on my mother 1989, Democrat and Chronicle (Rochester, NY) self-published Poetry on the Patio '95; [pers.] It is my opinion that we are all poets during one time or another... simply by the words we speak, the actions we display or the thoughts we write.; [a.] Rochester, NY

LIANG, DOROTHY
[pen.] Requiem; [b.] October 26, 1981, Ottawa, Ontario, Canada; [p.] Dr. David Liang, Dr. Hwa Cheng Liang; [ed.] Bell High School; [occ.] Facepainter, High School Student, X-Phile; [memb.] EP, Xangst Anonymous, GANTA, GAGA, SYX, WXFC, XPRA, Ratboy Brigade, ONLFC; [oth. writ.] Numerous pieces of X-Files Fanfiction; [a.] Kanata, Ontario, Canada

LIEM, HOK-SWIE
[pen.] Hok-Swie Liem; [b.] November 21, 1934, S'baya, Indonesia; [p.] Liem Sing-Lian and Tan Tjoen-Nio; [ed.] After graduating from Lian-Hua High School, I furthered my education in Gameliel Univ. in Jakarta, majoring in English Literature and dropped out in 1956; [occ.] Word Perfect and Proofreading; [oth. writ.] My Adorable Girl, Be on the Alert, Spiritual Life, The Wonderful Couple of Lian Chung, Easter Day; [pers.] I hate to be spurned by those who flaunt off their wealth, I would rather humble myself in the sight of God and be a law-abiding citizen of the United States of America the greatest country in the world and forever.; [a.] Woodhaven, NY

LILIENTHAL, JASON HAWORTH
[b.] March 4, 1974, Santa Fe, NM; [p.] James and Jeanette Lilienthal; [pers.] Your mind is the most powerful thing you have, so use it.; [a.] Albuquerque, NM

LINK, HANNAH
[b.] August 10, 1980, Topoka, KS; [p.] Mary Jane and Tony Link; [ed.] Brookstone Lower, Middle, and High Schools; [occ.] Jr. year of high school; [memb.] International Society of Poets; [oth. writ.] Several other poems published by N.L.P. short stories in progress; [a.] Midland, GA

LIPE, ROGER A.
[b.] February 22, 1948, Hillsboro, IL; [p.] Charles and Bonnie Cozart Lipe; [ed.] Hillsboro High School, AA, BS Scouthern Illinois University, Carbondale, IL - University Honors; [occ.] Director - Mercury Software Systems Inc., Data Processing Consultant; [memb.] Vietnam Veterans of America Deadhead, Military: Served with USAF 1967-70 in Vietnam and Thailand; [hon.] University Honors; [oth. writ.] Roger has a large body of over 300 poems written from 1970 to the present.; [pers.] "Day Break On The Land" are words from a grateful Dead song. This poem is dedicated to Jerry Garcia and the Grateful Dead. They helped to instill compassion, love, tolerance and the joy of being in my heart and soul. The fact that the moment is it, as are each one of us. Be in the moment.; [a.] Schram City, IL

LIPMAN, DANIELLE A.
[b.] October 30, 1987, Wilmington, DE; [p.] Mark and Karolin Lipman; [ed.] Mt. Pleasant Elementary Burnett Elementary; [occ.] Student; [memb.] Junior Girl Scouts Troop 1413; [hon.] 1st Latin Contest in Gifted Program; [oth. writ.] Day and Night; [pers.] This poem is dedicated in memory of my cousin Adam Spizz. He died out age 18, which is the same age that I am now. Although I never knew him his memory lives on in my heart.; [a.] Wilmington, DE

LIPPICK, AMBER
[pen.] Amber Keryn; [b.] June 11, 1985, Philadelphia, PA; [p.] Edward and Charlotte Lippick; [ed.] Homeschooled; [memb.] Girl Scouts of USA; [hon.] Volunteers time and talents to N.J. Cat shelter (makes kitty toys for homeless cats); [pers] I enjoy writing poetry about things I like.; [a.] Philadelphia, PA

LIPPICK, CHARLOTTE
[pen.] Charlotte Virginia; [b.] August 20, 1952, Philadelphia, PA; [p.] Gustan and Dorothy Anton; [m.] Edward Lippick (Lipczynski), November 11, 1978; [ch.] Kimberly Anne, Amber Keryn; [ed.] Kensington High Sch. for girls (grad. 1970); [occ.] Homemaker and Homeschooling Parent; [memb.] Girl Scouts of USA, Member of St. Michael's Lutheran Church of Phila., Penn. Home Education Network (Penn. Hen); [hon.] Library Volunteer; [pers.] I keep in mind, everyone has some intimate thoughts they would like to share.; [a.] Philadelphia, PA

LIPPOLD, KAREN E.
[b.] January 30, 1972, Walnut Creek, CA; [p.] Eve H. Lippold, Joseph C. Lippold; [ed.] University of California, Los Angeles; [pers.] Behold the serenity of my family. Thank you Toby.; [a.] Los Angeles, CA

LITTLES JR., ALTON L.
[pen.] The Music Maker-Turk Littles; [b.] May 27, 1942, Florida; [p.] Adopted Mom - Bessie Mae Sutton; [ed.] High School/many private lessons plus USAF 1960-1968 "Trumpeter"; [occ.] President/Owner T-Top records of Arizona (TTR); [memb.] BMI; [hon.] The first musician to qualify for the USAF band and drum and Bugle Corp the same day; [oth. writ.] 300 (non-published) poems, 1,300 completed song catalogue (both music and lyrics) 3 screen plays, 4 commercials.; [pers.] Writing is my life and ambition. The gift is one of my most honored possessions. Self discipline and dedication introduced me to a love for writing at an early age and writing gives me a daily dose of probity and proclivity which sustains me daily.; [a.] Chandler, AR

LIVERMORE, LORRI ANN
[b.] December 15, 1965, Toronto, Ontario, Canada; [p.] Ken Livermore, Elke Jockschus; [ed.] Pickering High School (gr. 12) George Brown College, Centenial College, English, (Graphic Design 2 yr. Diploma); [occ.] Illustrator, lyricist; [memb.] Greenpeace; [hon.] I survived a fatal horseback riding accident in 1979 - was in coma 6 weeks from head injury. I appeared on the Camilla Scott Show (Program Titled: Against All Odds 1996) and spoke for a radio interview for "The Ability File"; [oth. writ.] Worked with various songwriters, I wrote the lyrics, currently working on an autobiography.; [pers.] Make the most of the life you have now, because it can be taken away from you in a heartbeat. My live experience is my poetic inspiration.; [a.] Pickering, Ontario, Canada

LLOYD, TINA LOUISE
[b.] February 9, 1972, Terre Haute, IN; [p.] Roger Rayhel and Sheila Monk; [m.] Greg Lloyd, May 23, 1992; [ed.] Marshall High School, Indiana State University, Indiana Business College; [occ.] Secretary, LLoyd Excavating, Inc.; [memb.] North Terre Haute Christian Church, Big Brothers and Big Sisters of Vigo County; [hon.] City of Marshall Scholarship; [oth. writ.] Poem published in local newspaper; [pers.] I thank God for my talent and Mrs. Bennet, my high school English teacher, for encouraging me to continue writing poetry.; [a.] Terre Haute, IN

LOCKAMY, MARY F.
[b.] January 8, 1958, Fay, NC; [p.] Wilma and Bruce Files; [m.] Divorced; [ch.] George F. Lockamy Jr.; [ed.] High school graduate; [occ.] Spinner - for a textile company. As you can see, I'm not a very interesting person. I work 1st shift in a textile plant. When I was on 3rd shift, the Lord literally gave me the words to the poem. I give God the glory and honor for "mama, will you pray?" If the poem can touch someone's heart or win a soul to Christ, then that's worth more than any amount of money.; [pers.] I feel that it's a precious treasure, to have a praying mama. I thank God for my Christian mama. It's my wish that everyone could experience a mama that prays with and for them.

LOCKHART, DRAPER
[b.] October 25, 1910, Whitewood, VA; [p.] Jennie Draper and Frank Hand; [m.] Walter, Deceased, 1994, August 20, 1994; [ch.] Howard; [occ.] Retired; [memb.] Raven Pentacostal Holiness Church; [pers.] I always have and always will love poetry! I was greatly inspired by my late brother, Ed Hand and his works of art! Since day one of Sandy Barthlein's published poetry, I think her poetry is so beautifully written and deserved to be published!; [a.] Cedar Bluff, VA

LOEWEN, ANGELIKA
[b.] May 31, 1950, Hamburg, Germany; [p.] Fritz Erding, Hilde Erding; [m.] Dr. Dale Loewen (MD); [ch.] Kim Erding, Molly Loewen, Joshua Loewen; [ed.] High School, (Post-Ed) Cosmetology; [occ.] Distributor, "Sweet Shalom" Therapeutic Skin Care and Vitamin Therapy at "Total Health Centre"; [oth. writ.] "Quiltwork of Poetry," several articles in local news papers: "Tribune," also "Poetry"; [pers.] From an early age I have enjoyed writing! Since 1976 I have been a "Born Again Christian," and it is my prayer and to goal to let "Shine Through The Prince of Peace, Jesus" and His love and wisdom.; [a.] British Columbia, Canada

LOHMAN, DONNA
[b.] October 18, 1955, Saint Louis, MO; [p.] Mary Lou Austin nee Heumann; [m.] Matthew W. Lohman; [ch.] Christina, Jennifer, Matthew, Tayler; [occ.] The hardest job I ever loved: Mom; [pers.] Thank you God! Thanks for the inspiration. This poem is for our homeless. May we all love one another more.; [a.] Brentwood, MO

LOMAX, JOHN A.
[ed.] Radio Eng. PWTI, AA degree Psy, DCCC; [occ.] Writer: Creative; [hon.] Dean's List and President's List: DCCC

LONG, DELIA MARIE
[pen.] Mardelo Glow; [b.] September 27, 1939, Lamont, FL; [p.] James and Savannah Williams; [m.] Henry A. Long Sr., June 8, 1979; [ch.] Darryl, Tommy, Kathy, Bernard Henrietta, Henry Jr., Van; [ed.] BS/Business Education, Med/English; [occ.] Retired English Teacher; [memb.] Fort Clarke Baptist Church; [hon.] Williston High School, Teacher of year 1994; [pers.] I enjoy imparting knowledge to others. I am fulfilled by helping others in need.; [a.] Gainesville, FL

LONGARD, NORMA
[b.] February 21, 1967, Fort Vermilion; [p.] Cecil and Therese Mitchell; [ch.] Victoria, Lee, Therese, Tyrell and Alex; [ed.] Grade 12, Spirit River Secondary; [occ.] Green House (Marg's) Employee; [oth. writ.] A Collection of poems; [pers.] I want people to feel the emotion in my poetry when they read them.; [a.] Fort Vermilion, Alberta, Canada

LOOMIS, RUTH
[pen.] Ruth Loomis; [b.] January 24, 1929, Chicago, IL; [p.] Mr. and Mrs. J. P. Klaus; [m.] Calvin J. Loomis (Deceased) April 5, 1952; [ch.] Curt James, Susan Jane, Fantus and Jeffrey Roy; [ed.] High School Education; [occ.] I am currently on disability leave from my job.; [oth. writ.] This is the 1st poem I've ever written.; [pers.] I leave this poem as a legacy to my children. Their father meant the world to us all.

LOPER, JANET LYNAS
[b.] Windsor, Ontario; [p.] Bob and Joyce Lynas; [m.] Dr. David Loper D. C., October 2; [ch.] Alex, Ashlyn; [ed.] B.A.- Dance, B.S. Education, A.A. Early Childhood Education, Stephens College for Women; [occ.] Owner Artistic Director Ennis School of Ballet and Dance; [memb.] Ennis Chamber of Commerce, First Presbyterian Church, Stephens College Alumni Ass.; [pers.] I look for depth of life and inspiration in all things.; [a.] Ennis, TX

LORT, MARGARET A.
[b.] July 3, 1939, Denver, CO; [p.] Charles and Clara Armstrong; [m.] Art Lort, July 24, 1959; [ch.] Becky Campbell, Matt Lort; [ed.] 3 years at University of Northern Colorado (formerly Colorado State College); [occ.] Administrative Assistant at Denver Seminary; [oth. writ.] Poem and one article published in Local Point Magazine, Three poems published by the National Library of

Poetry.; [pers.] Grandchildren are a marvelous creation of God. My two have inspired me to reach depths of feelings, through my poetry, that I've never tapped before.; [a.] Denver, CO

LUCAS, MARY CHRISTINE
[b.] January 18, 1958, Kirkwood, MO; [p.] Frank and Patsy Lucas, step parents Donna Lucas and Gary Bustraan; [ed.] Quit school freshman year; [occ.] Disabled; [memb.] Belong to The Rose of Sharon Pentecostal Church of DeSoto, MO; [hon.] Two Editor's Choice Award's from this National Library of Poetry; [oth. writ.] Many other writings one published in newspaper seven by the National Library of Poetry; [pers.] I've been given a gift of love from God and love does over come everything; [a.] DeSoto, MO

LUCK, ANTHONY D.
[b.] October 11, 1953, Pittsburgh; [p.] Marcellus and Elsie Luck; [m.] Shirley Anne Luck, December 15, 1972; [ch.] Stacey, Peter, Stephen, Nicholas; [ed.] Central Catholic High School, Assoc. Degree in Bus. Mgt.; [occ.] Self-Employed; [memb.] Chamber of Commerce, N.A.S.E.; [hon.] Dean's List, Honors for Highest G.P.A. in Math and Spanish, listed in "Who's Who among American High School students; [oth. writ.] Two books - "Don't Tell Stephen!", "I Miss You Daddy!"; [pers.] Believe in yourself, and you can accomplish anything!; [a.] Penn Hills, PA

LUDWIG, JENNIFER
[b.] November 21, 1979, Wilmington, DE; [p.] Mr. and Mrs. Gail Robert Ludwig; [ed.] High School: Junior year: (That's the current extent of my education); [occ.] Student (high school) at Newton High School; [oth. writ.] I've never written into (any other poetry contest) anything else, but I have other poems: Truth In Love, World Volts and Thunder Bolts and Crimson Terror (please remember that these are not published); [pers.] When I write I think about whether or not I would be proud to share it with someone. I hope that my poetry reflects my convictions and defies the stereotype of the youth poetry of my generation.; [a.] Newton, NJ

LUMLEY, BOBBI LYNN
[b.] July 22, 1962, Petrolia, Ontario, Canada; [p.] Ross and Eleanor Parr; [m.] Phil Marsh; [ed.] St. Phillips School, L.C.C.V.I., Petrolia, Ontario; [memb.] Bitch Wednesday Club; [oth. writ.] Stored away in the anal's of my memory box.; [pers.] In memory of my stepbrother David Ross Parr, (August 8, 1995) and 'our' Dad, Ross Cameron Parr, (May 27, 1996). I'm sure they're both smiling like skunks eating bumblebees. Isn't this a Gene Autry! Love you both.; [a.] Sarnia, Ontario, Canada

LUPER, BETTY MILLS
[b.] May 17, 1949, Durham, NC; [p.] Walter Richardson, Mary Tew Briley; [m.] Jimmy A. Luper, May 14, 1991; [ch.] Kenneth Wayne and Daniel Lee Mills; [ed.] Balboa High, Panama Canal Zone Edgecombe Community College; [occ.] Homemaker; [hon.] Cub Scout Den Leader Coach, CNA; [oth. writ.] Short story published in Colorado City High, Texas newspaper; [pers.] I thank my Mother for teaching me strong moral values and self respect. Her love has always inspired me.; [a.] Wilmington, NC

LUSK, STEVEN WAYNE
[pen.] Steven Lusk; [b.] July 7, 1955, Bluefield, W. Virginia; [p.] Edith Juanita Lusk, Bobby Joe Lusk; [ch.] Steven Wayne Lusk II; [ed.] Southwestern High School, Flint, Michigan; [occ.] Artist, Poet

LYNCH, EBONY
[b.] May 16, 1981, Honolulu, HI; [p.] Mary C. Lynch and Willie Lynch; [ed.] Mathews High School Graduation in future (1999); [memb.] Pep

Club, Bible Club, Future Business Leaders of America, Zion Baptist Church Choir; [hon.] Merit Award; [oth. writ.] "Father Father oh Dear" "Rainbow Day" "Angels" "My First Love" "School (Daze)"; [pers.] I would like to dedicate this poem to my mother for encouraging me to do my best at whatever I do.; [a.] Cardinal, VA

MACEACHERN, RHONDA
[b.] August 13, 1971, Schefferville, Quebec; [p.] Kathleen and Loyal MacEachern; [ed.] Tumbler Ridge Secondary, Grant MacEwan Community College, College of New Caledonia; [occ.] Early Childhood Educator, Prince George, Selody Centre (Pre-School Teacher); [hon.] First Prize Remembrance Day Poetry Contest, Tumbler Ridge, British Columbia, Canada; [pers.] With each poem I write, I try to convey strong emotions that the reader can relate to. Family plays an important part in my life and I try to focus much of my writing around this.; [a.] Tumbler Ridge, British Columbia, Canada

MACHADO, LUANDA
[b.] April 9, 1964; [p.] Jose-Maria Machado; [ch.] Shaun; [ed.] High School; [occ.] Model, Writer and Poet; [hon.] Outstanding Poetry; [oth. writ.] 25 poems - 50 short stories and 915 page novel - "A Rose Is Weeping" a small percentage of my work has been published.; [pers.] I believe I was given a grave gift of expressing the pure passions of emotions. I have always had a faithful love of man and all life. My greatest wish is to instill beauty of life.; [a.] Londonderry, NH

MACK, ADRIANNA T.
[b.] October 30, 1977, Seattle, WA; [p.] George and Beatrice Mack; [ed.] The World I now live in, life's lessons and it's teachers, there's too many to name.; [occ.] None aspiring clothes designer.; [hon.] The gift of grace is an honor, bestowed upon me through my nine years of ballet dancing: age 6 to 15 years.; [pers.] My poetry spills from a chalice that occasionally fills too full.; [a.] Edmonds, WA

MACK, WALTRAUD I.
[pen.] Ingeborg Von Finsterwalde; [b.] September 18, 1938, Germany; [p.] Alfred and Frieda Mueller; [m.] Alfred Mack, May 4, 1959; [ch.] Son: Dennis Mack; [ed.] In Germany; [occ.] Homemaker P.T Collectible Dealer; [oth. writ.] Several poems published by The National Library of Poetry"; [pers.] Through the poem in this Anthology I was able to express my deep and profound love for this great country. The greatest country in the world. The scenic beauty, the kind and gentle people I have meet. A heritage we should never take for granted.; [a.] Poughkeepsie, NY

MACKEY, JAMES D.
[pen.] "Jim Me" on the internet; [b.] October 30, 1947, Vancouver, BC; [p.] Thomas and Anna Mackey; [ch.] Kelly, April, Thomas and Tabi; [ed.] Forty eight years of life and eleven of school; [occ.] Purchaser and inventory clerk for Parks Canada/Yoho Nat'l Park; [memb.] Human Race - lifetime member; [hon.] Honored to have the love and caring of my friends and fellow writers; [oth. writ.] Stopped counting when the pile got about three inches thick. Writing is a pleasure and a joy that calms and quiets the mental ogres.; [pers.] Words can be a pleasure or a pain. I consider words to be like an aboriginal weapon. Whether good or bad, they always come back on you.; [a.] Lake Louise, Alberta, Canada

MACPHAIL, HAZEL F.
[pen.] Hazel MacPhail; [b.] August 10, 1943, Surrey, England; [p.] Frances A. Bernhardt and Leslie M. Bernhardt; [m.] Frank MacPhail, August 19, 1967; [ch.] Karen, Christine and Andrea; [ed.]

Worthing County Girls School, W. Sussex, England and W. Sussex College of Art; [occ.] Office Manager, Sun Life of Canada, Scarborough Branch; [oth. writ.] Short stories esp. humor - published in local newspaper/poetry in school magazines; [pers.] All my life I have loved poetry, I cannot imagine my life without the work of Nash, Noyes, Shelley, Yeats or Milton - Music for my soul; [a.] Bon Mills, Ontario, Canada

MACPHERSON, JOY ELIZABETH
[pen.] Beth MacPherson/Cathrina Slozn; [b.] April 26, 1954, Saint John, New Brunswick, Canada; [p.] Newton Halley MacPherson, Christine Mae Patterson; [ch.] Pascha and Liza; [ed.] Special interest in Psychology, Literacy early childhood education, student of Jazz guitar, songwriter; [occ.] Administrator, Communications Consultant in my own company (Continuum); [memb.] Honorary member of College of Family Physicians of Canada; [oth. writ.] "The Resplendent Heart", "The Secret of Simone"; [pers.] Special devotion to the pursuit of Divinity and how it is reflected in our lives day to day. The historical oppression man has inflicted upon man is use a major source of scrutiny in my work.; [a.] Tuntulon, Halifax Co, Nova Scotia, Canada

MADDOCK, K. A.
[ed.] Honours Bachelor of Science Degree (Micbrobiology), Diploma (Medical Laboratory Technology); [pers.] In the tradition of some of the great masters, I like my writings to achieve epic proportions. I feel that this best pays homage to the unlimited potential that we, as a species, aspire to. I have hope that grand deeds and grand words may finally propel us down a pathway to an enlightened age in human evolution.; [a.] Shakespeare, Ontario, Canada

MADRID, TIFFANY RENE
[b.] May 4, 1983, Farmington, NM; [p.] Kathy and David Madrid; [ed.] Simpsom Middle School; [occ.] 8th Grade at Simpson Middle School; [memb.] 7 and 8th Grade Chorus, 8th Grade band, National Junior Honor Society, Student Council; [hon.] Numerous Awards for Academic Achievements and activities from School.; [oth. writ.] Numerous short stories and poems that I hope one day will be published.; [pers.] I've learned that no matter how young or how old you are, you can always do whatever you want, example, I'm only 13; [a.] Phoenix, AZ

MAHONEY, MARIE
[b.] April 2, 1916, Aurora, IL; [p.] George Hoffman, Antionette Hoffman; [m.] Leo L. Mahoney, August 1, 1934; [ch.] Frederick; [ed.] High Fresno St. Jc. Polamar J. C. San Marcos Ca. Creative Writings Class Four Years.; [occ.] Retired Housewife; [memb.] Charter Member Women's, V.F.W., St. Marks Women's Guild; [hon.] None so far; [oth. writ.] I've written many essays one publication on Bryce Canyon also many poems; [pers.] I had a very good education from the Nuns in High School where they stressed Literature; [a.] San Marcos, CA

MAHONEY, TATUM A.
[pen.] Tatum Mahoney; [b.] June 17, 1983, San Jose, CA; [p.] Michael P. Mahoney; [ed.] 8th grade student; [occ.] Student - Canfield Middle School, Coeur d'Alene Idaho; [memb.] Select Chorus, Canfield Middle School, Ed Parkers American Kenpo Assoc., Green Peace (save The Whales); [hon.] Honor Student 5th thru 8th grades.; [pers.] I hope to progress in my writings as I continue my education Thru High School and College.; [a.] Coeur D'Alene, ID

MALANDRA, MARIA LOUISA
[pen.] Ann Tony; [b.] April 2, 1950, Montreal,

Canada; [p.] Frank and Adeline; [m.] Jim; [ch.] Cynthia Jayne, Frank James; [ed.] Malcolm Campbell High School Night Studies: McGill University, Universite de Montreal; [occ.] Mother and Housewife former: Personnel consultant; [hon.] Some poetry published in Local Colleges; [oth. writ.] Some poetry published in Local Colleges: Numerous poetry writings published in Church bulletins: One poem published in Newfoundland Telegram (newspaper); [pers.] Writing poetry is putting a piece of my soul on paper. It is exhilarating to share it with others.; [a.] Saint Lazare, Province of Quebec, Canada

MALANOT, CAROLE
[b.] March 8, 1947, Jersey City, NJ; [p.] Raymond and Evelyn Chmielewski; [m.] William J. Malanot, April 25, 1996; [ch.] Michelle, Michael, Mark, William, Megan; [ed.] St. Michael's High School - Union City, NJ; [occ.] U.S. Postal Service Clerk; [pers.] To all who have found their "Place in the Sun," a special dedication to Timmy Burke; [a.] Sebring, FL

MALCHIK, WILLIAM
[b.] January 26, 1911, NYC; [p.] Deceased; [m.] Deceased; [ed.] 1929-31 (2 years) CCNY, NY, 1932-33 (1 year) Cooper Union Art, 1934 Delahanty Police Academy; [occ.] Final Retirement from Police - Artist Draftsman - Musician - Sculptor; [memb.] Honor Legion - NYC, PD West Orange (FL) Arts 8C Historical Assoc. 1970 - 1st Violin Fla. Symphony 1984; [hon.] 1929 St Gaudens Medal for Fine Draftsmanship (NYC) 1942 Legion of Honor Medal - NYPD 1979-80-81-82 Blue Ribbon Awards for Metal Sculpture (Reposse) local shows - Fla 1982 hon mention - W. Orange Poets Corner; [pers.] (Quotation of Oliver W. Holms to Louis Brandies upon viewing the Feminine Pulchritude on Campus) (Oh - to be 65 Again!) me too!; [a.] Winter Garden, FL

MALHOTRA, SUSHMA
[b.] June 26, 1956, Phillaur, India; [p.] Late Mr. R. L. Puri, Nirmala Puri; [m.] Dr. Ved V. Malhotra, June 16, 1978; [ch.] Gaurav Malhotra, Saurabh Malhotra; [ed.] Guru Nanak Dev Univ., India (M.A.) City University, New York (M.S.); [occ.] ESL Teacher, CS102, Bronx, New York; [memb.] American Federation of Teachers, United Federation of Teachers; [oth. writ.] Poems published in local newspaper and magazines in Punjab, India; [pers.] I try to express my feelings through various aspects and forms of nature. My love for nature made me like the work of great romantic poets, from William Wordsworth to John Keats. I try to face the realities positively in my writing.; [a.] Flushing, NY

MALIK, TARIQ H.
[b.] July 10, 1964, Khushab, Pak; [p.] Mohammad Amir Malik and B. L. Malik; [ed.] B.A. Eco. and DMS, M.A. Economics (Pb), MBA, MBS and Wales (UK), Ph.D. Conducting Research; [occ.] Lecturer, Management Studies, Greenwich College; [memb.] MIPM, AIBFS, ACIB, IAPA, Pilots; [oth. writ.] Book - "Norms in the Arcane", book "Travelling Stranger", autobiography; [pers.] Supported by many, win and have societal space, though egoistic neither reach, nor have solace.

MALKIN, CYRUS
[b.] February 17, 1980, New Denver, British Columbia, Canada; [p.] Paul Malkin, Wendy Malkin; [ed.] Honours Student Since Grade School; [occ.] High School Student Grade 11 and F. H. Collins High School, Whitehorse, Yukon.; [memb.] Active member of his church youth group, Ft. Collins concert band; [hon.] "Student of the Year" 94/95 (In Jr High, Gr. 9), numerous academic achievement awards.; [oth. writ.] Poems entered and

accepted into the young author's conference "The Gates of Eden" 4/96.; [a.] Whitehorse, Yukon Territory, Canada

MALLETT, DEANNE R.
[b.] September 26, 1985, Bellflower, CA; [p.] Richard and Debra Mallett; [ed.] 5th grade, Carpenter, Elementary School and South Middle School, Downey CA; [occ.] Student; [memb.] Girl Scouts; [hon.] 3rd grace, 1st pl, safety poster, 4th grade, student council poetry contest 1s place, 5th, 1st pl "Reflection" literature contest/PTA, 3rd pl Mathfield Day, Presidents National Academic Excellence Award; [a.] Downey, CA

MANATT, ABBY RENEE
[b.] September 22, 1981, Leon, IA; [p.] Cheryl R. Kelly, Robert A. Manatt (Deceased); [occ.] High School Student; [pers.] I've struggled all my life with depression and found comfort and sometimes joy in writing poetry. I've found writing to be a great release of inner pain. I am happy to have my depression under control, and to still find writing fun.; [a.] Kansas City, MO

MANCINI, ANNE
[pen.] Sam; [occ.] Teacher; [pers.] To be remembered as someone who tried to touch all people with love...; [a.] Fort Lauderdale, FL

MANNING, ZINA M.
[b.] December 17, 1962, Roberson, CO; [p.] Samuel Lee and Thelma McPhaul; [m.] John David Manning, January 24, 1987; [ch.] Kieona Manning and Twalla McPhaul; [ed.] Rowland High - Rowland N.C. Received GED Roberson Tec in Lumberto N.C.; [occ.] Dillon County Sheriff Dept. I am a Correctional Officer; [oth. writ.] I do have other poems that I now save. I have never sent any of my poems off anywhere. But my husband would often tell me that I need to send it off to see what would happen. I also have other relative to tell me that. (My sister); [pers.] I think that by trying to put God first in your life anything can happen. I also believe if you a spouse to help push you along and to back you, you can do more than you think life is hard and nothing comes easy with out a hard price to pay. Except salvation its already been paid for.; [a.] Hamer, SC

MAPLES JR., HICKS E.
[pen.] Gene Maples; [b.] April 7, 1956, Hemet, CA; [p.] Hicks E. and Ruth E. Maples; [m.] Deborah J. Maples, February 8, 1986; [ch.] Matthew A. Maples; [ed.] Two Years of College; [occ.] Medical Supply Technician; [memb.] Currently None; [hon.] Alpha Gamma Sigma twice, award for work with spinal injuries in a therapy environment I created.; [oth. writ.] Various poems in School currently working on a book titled "Dorian"; [pers.] I would like to complete and publish the book I am working on. Also, I would like the wherewithal to give to those that have given to me in my time of need.; [a.] Redlands, CA

MARBUT, CHAD A.
[pers.] Apply Romans 12

MARCOTTE, GLENN
[b.] July 20, 1972, Montreal; [ed.] Currently enrolled at Concordia University; [occ.] Bank Teller with the T.D. Bank; [pers.] If not at the insistance of my girlfriend, Gina De Luca, I'd never would have submitted one of my poems. All my thanks, and all of my love goes to her.; [a.] Montreal, Province of Quebec, Canada

MARCUS, MS. PEARL
[b.] 4 October 1910, London, England; [p.] Deceased; [m.] Deceased, married in London; [ch.] 1 daughter in London; [ed.] I was a secretary, I went

to special school for 2 years; [occ.] Work in office secretary; [memb.] I belong to Wayman Center I do make Cosmetic Knitted Bays.

MARKELL, RANDY G.
[b.] February 19, 1965, Ottawa, Ontario, Canada; [p.] Harold Markell, Donna Markell; [ed.] Sir Wilfrid Laurier High, Carleton University; [occ.] Records Classifier, Human Resources and Development Canada; [memb.] Rite of Christian Initiation for Adults Assumption Parish, Canadian Bible Society, International Society of Poets, Luis Tae Kwon-Do; [hon.] Secondary School Honours Graduation Diploma, English Award Carleton Univ.; [oth. writ.] Several books of personal poems, two previous publications in N.L.P. Anthologies, Lyrics to many fun song, A Few Children's poems; [pers.] I am inspired by each and every person around me and I strive to reflect the joy I feel, with my poetry. My words always speak kindly (but truthfully). With the help of the Lord Jesus, I long to spread smiles all over (I have been called "The Smile Maker"); [a.] Ottawa, Ontario, Canada

MARLATT, ORLO
[pen.] Orle Orlo; [b.] March 15, 1922, Isabella, OK; [p.] Mr. and Mrs. C. H. Marlatt; [m.] Bernice Bochmon Marlatt, June 18, 1946; [ch.] Two daughters; [ed.] 17 years of schooling, Plus 1942-1946 in the US! Coast Guard, during World War two; [occ.] Traveling, author, writer, poet, and doing volunteer work, who needs help; [memb.] B.M.I. Membership; [hon.] 12 songs out of Nashville, Tenn., 5 songs out of Hollywood Calif., 2 songs out of Mass., 1 song out of Enid, Okla.; [oth. writ.] Two Novels - We Cry Aloud and Someone Lives There. 200 songs and poems Vantage Press, Out of New York, want to make 160 pages book out of my songs and poems.; [pers.] I write from the heart and soul. And all my songs and poems are true, because I live there, go with truth and with God help and He will see you through.; [a.] Waukomis, OK

MARQUARDT, MICHAEL
[b.] October 6, 1951, Elgin, IL; [ed.] Fox River Grove Grade School Barrington High School; [pers.] I think poetry is an excellent vehicle for expressing thoughts and feelings.; [a.] Woodstock, IL

MARR, DAVID
[b.] June 5, 1979, Spokane, WA; [pers.] In passion or in hate, do not be blinded by the smoke from the fire in your eyes.

MARRIN, ROBIN COX
[b.] April 19, 1959, Fort Myers, FL; [p.] Robert and Mildred Cox; [m.] Alfred Marrin, October 1, 1980; [ch.] Kate Briana; [ed.] Fort Myers High School, Edison Community College, University of Florida; [occ.] Computer Analyst at Univ. of Florida; [memb.] Aircraft Owners and Pilots Association; [oth. writ.] One historical fiction novel of 12th Century Ireland; [a.] Archer, FL

MARSHALL, MRS. PATRICIA NANCY
[b.] Richmond Hill, Ontario, Canada; [p.] Jeremiah Smith and Effie Smith; [m.] Brian Marshall, July 21, 1961; [occ.] Honourable Wife and Homemaker, Writer and Poet.; [memb.] Distinguished Member of the International Society of Poets in 1996; [hon.] Having attended art classes I excelled in oil painting and one of my paintings hangs on the wall of a Nursing and Retirement home; [oth. writ.] "My New Song", "Miracles Of Spring", "The Earth Is The Lord's", "We Are All God's Children"; [pers.] I am reminded of my mind's marvellous activity-directing my memory and my thinking to heights of joy and success, and causes me to carry a song and a poem in my heart and a prayer on my lips, thus enabling me to express thoughts through poetry to be appreciated.; [a.] Wyevale, Ontario, Canada

MARTIN, LORRAINE
[pen.] Lorraine Martin; [b.] April 6, 1918, Franklin, Quebec; [p.] Joseph Martin, Angeline Gregoire; [m.] Ernest Tremblay, August 16, 1941; [ch.] Colette, Louise; [ed.] Autodidact; [occ.] Multidisciplinary Artist; [pers.] My life commitment has been as a multidisciplinary artist and as a universal researcher in sciences of humanities (psychology, theology, philosophy, sociology), aiming at the liberation of man and woman soul from all feudal laws, as well as the request of man-woman charter of rights. My knowledge comes from "The Four Gospels in one" by the four Evangelists, to recognize Jesus as the founder of the eternal soul liberation where the man and woman represent individually a part of the three-dimensional divinity.

MARTIN, MICHAEL L. J.
[b.] June 22, 1950, Ottawa, Ontario, Canada; [ed.] Camosun College, Victoria, British Columbia, Public Administration graduate; [pers.] Dedicated, Christmas 1995, to my precious daughter, Rebecca Mae Martin, who will always hold a special place in my heart.; [a.] Victoria, British Columbia, Canada

MARTINEZ, BOB G.
[b.] June 7, 1949, New Mexico; [p.] Mrs. Mary Jane Martinez; [m.] Annette (Poopsie), February 10, 1973, (Valentine); [ch.] Lita (19 yrs.: in College); [ed.] High School graduate from Denver North High in '68; [occ.] Security Guard at the Denver Merchandise Mart; [memb.] Distinguished Member of ISP-NLP - Mile High Chapter Society - and Columbine Poets of Colorado; [hon.] Several Editor's Choice Award and over 20 anthology publications in past one and one half years (Feb '95 to July '96); [oth. writ.] My personal compilation of poems: "Sidetracks" and personal journal of my life (1949-1994) in single unbroken poem...(over 300 pgs.); [pers.] Some words cast shadows while others shoot beams. Some are demanding...some offer a hand. Some unfold the truth while others hide schemes. They all usher in daybreak on the land.; [a.] Denver, CO

MARTINEZ, DANIEL
[b.] March 10, 1979, Corona, CA; [p.] Linda and Juan Martinez; [m.] Girlfriend: Jennifer Pruett; [ed.] Centennial High; [occ.] McDonald's; [memb.] New Beginnings Community Church; [pers.] "I think poetry is a way to look and write about life and scenes around, and feelings." My favortie poet is Edgar Allan Poet and I also love Romantic poets.

MARTINEZ III, ROSENDO
[pen.] Rosendo Martinez III; [b.] February 19, 1973, Corpus Christi; [p.] Rosendo and Maria Martinez; [ed.] High School Equivelency; [occ.] Writer/Poet (novice); [pers.] My poems are personal views of: Life, nature's mysteries, the doings of man, and the current state of mankind's existence. Attempt to use the viewpoint of: A prisoner away from home, an orphan, or a veteran (in reading).; [a.] Iowa Park, TX

MARTINSON, HANNA
[b.] July 10, 1983, Danville, PA; [p.] Mark and Beth Martinson; [ed.] Danville Middle School; [occ.] 8th grade student at Danville Middle School; [memb.] AYSO Soccer, Catherine Treon School of Dance; [hon.] Honor Roll, Chorus Award; [pers.] In my free time I enjoy reading, swimming, dancing, and playing soccer and my flute. I would like to thank my seventh grade English teacher, Mary Ann Swisher for inspiring me to write.; [a.] Danville, PA

MASEK, EVELYN
[b.] May 9, 1929, Columbus, OH; [m.] Lawrence Masek, May 7, 1949; [ch.] Guidetti Sherryl, Masek Joseph, Guidry Carolyn, grandchildren Jaime,

Guidry, Casey Masek, Tracy Guidetti, Paul Masek; [occ.] Retired Bookkeeper; [memb.] Reorganized Church of Jesus Christ of Latter Day Saints, also a member of the Czechoslovak Society of America.; [oth. writ.] A variety of material, including poems, short stories, responsive readings, essays, have been published in Fraternal journals, Church Devotional Handbooks, etc. my poem, "Happy Birthday, Jesus" written for our grandchildren and published in Beneath the Harvest Moon was selected for Editor's Choice Award, and my pome, "Tribute to Breanna" is scheduled to be printed in Best Poems of the `90's; [pers.] I take great pleasure in writing for those who are an inspiration to me my family, church and friends. This poem, "The Things I Love" was written for my husband of 46 years.; [a.] Kirtland, OH

MASON, MARK
[b.] June 10, 1976, Edmonton, Alberta, Canada; [ed.] Sir Winston Churchill High School, Mount Royal College; [occ.] Student; [pers.] You must unlock the part within to be at peace. Explore every emotion for without sadness, happiness cannot exist. You must accept the ugliness and evil in mankind to appreciate the beauty and goodness. Always keep it real.; [a.] Calgary, Alberta, Canada

MASON, RYAN
[b.] April 8, 1982, Bay City, MI; [p.] Doug and Jan Mason; [ed.] Sophomore at Dow High School, Midland, Mich.; [occ.] Student; [memb.] Jefferson School Newspaper, Boy Scouts of America; [hon.] Outstanding Journalist, All A Honor Roll many times; [oth. writ.] Many unpublished stories; [a.] Midland, MI

MASON, STAN
[b.] June 19, 1934, London, England; [p.] Doris and Joseph; [m.] Angela, January 11, 1986; [ch.] Sarah; [ed.] Davenant Foundation Grammar School, London, England; [occ.] Writer; [memb.] FRSA, FCIB, FI MGT, ACIS, DIPM, M. INST, M. INST. AM, MIBC, ET ALL.; [oth. writ.] Numerous films, books, TV, theatre plays, radio, poetry, short stories. (Latest book "The 21st Century Crusaders" published June 1996); [pers.] Writing is the most thrilling activity in life. A writer creates characters, plots and stories and can manipulate them at will. Excitement in writing has no end. It is infinite!

MASON-MCLEMORE, G. D.
[b.] October 17, 1963, Saint Louis, MO; [p.] Hardin and Vivian Peterson; [ch.] Dominic C. R. Mason; [ed.] Southwest H. S., St. Louis/Columbia Coll. Columbia, MO; [occ.] Budget Analyst at Defense Language Institute, Foreign Language Center Presidio of Monterey, CA; [pers.] This poem was writen as a tribute to my grandmother, the late Maggie Williams, who died February 14, 1996, whose love had no limits.

MASSIMILLA, STEPHEN
[b.] May 31, 1964, New York; [p.] David Massimilla, Arlene Massimilla; [ed.] Roslyn High School, Williams College and Columbia University; [occ.] Adjunct writing professor, Barnard College and S.V.A. (School of Visual Arts), also art dealer New York, NY; [hon.] Phi Beta Kappa, Kauffman prize, Academy of American poets prize; [oth. writ.] Poems published in literary journals, such as Tampa review, Re: Arts and Letters, poem, descant, the distillery, atom mind, black Buzzard review, pointed circle and local newspapers.; [pers.] I am interested in the irreducible enigma of the human condition. My favorite American poets are Emily Dickinson and T.S. Eliot; [a.] Sea Cliff, NY

MATSON, SANDRA K.
[b.] April 11, 1945, Minnesota; [hon.] My awards

in life were being my kids mother.; [oth. writ.] I have wrote several short stories I also wrote a novel, I have not published.; [pers.] The mind speaks through the heart and the heart speaks through the hand, that's how I think when I write.; [a.] Brooklyn Park, MN

MATSUO, NAMI
[b.] April 6, 1981; [occ.] High School Student; [pers.] To my parents, my circle of friends, and to Steve.; [a.] Tenafly, NJ

MATTHEWS, GREGORY CARLTON
[b.] April 25, 1965, Dallas, TX; [p.] Luther H. and Virginia B. Matthews; [oth. writ.] Many unpublished poems reflecting my lifes journey from the darkness to the light; [pers.] I spent my youth searching for the meaning of life only to find that I knew it all along.; [a.] Dallas, TX

MATTIA, PHILIP S.
[b.] November 16, 1984, Livingstone, NJ; [p.] Philip F. and Elaine C. Mattia; [occ.] Student; [oth. writ.] Mystic Dreams, A Changing Future, The Both Taken, Dreamer's Wish, Soaring Wind; [pers.] When I was a small child (in second grade to be exact) my teacher, always encouraged me as well as the rest of the class to be creative - you can do anything if you put your mind to it. And I believe this encouragement helped me broaden my horizons and look at life, not as something to do and get over with but as something to enjoy all the aspects of and get as far as possible in doing so.; [a.] Caldwell, NJ

MAW, BRADLEY
[b.] June 25, 1989, Newmarket, Ontario, Canada; [p.] Wendy and James Maw; siblings: Crystal Ashley and Jason James; [pers.] At age 6, Bradley is currently a student at the Newmarket Montessori School and studies under the direction of Mrs. Donna Hilsenteger. An avid naturalist, Bradley spends his spare time studying fish, frogs and insects. His motto is "All things deserve to live."; [a.] Newmarket, Ontario, Canada

MAYO, MARIE LUNSFORD
[b.] August 9, 1937, Richland, GA; [p.] Alexander and Elva Mills Lunsford; [m.] Benjamin William Mayo, November 28, 1954; [ch.] Ben (Deceased), Anna Laura, Thomas, Julia; [ed.] Mercer University, Shorter College, Wesleyan College, graduated Columbus College 1980, Bachelor Music Education; [occ.] Retired Elemen. Teacher, Church Organist, Writer, Performing pianist; [memb.] Daughters American Revolution, Stewart County Historical Association, First Baptist Church Richland; [hon.] Valedictorian High School Class, Dean's List Wesleyan College, Columbus College, Volunteer of Year "Westville" 1990, Winner in poetry contest of Evangel Temple (Columbus, GA), poems and short stories published in book called "Hearts Over America"; [oth. writ.] Collection of poems entitled "Words for Reflection" contains "Emerald Lake," "The World Comes Rushing In," "Lifescapes," "Love Song," also essays and short stories, much of my work has been published in the local newspaper, Stewart-Webster Journal; [pers.] Living in a rural area gives me much opportunity to write about nature. I use my poetry to express my feelings. Being a descendant of pioneer families, I am knowledgeable about the past. Much of my writing reflects this. It's an expression I enjoy.; [a.] Richland, GA

MAYVILLE, KELI
[b.] October 29, 1981, Georgetown, TX; [p.] Randy and MaryAnn Mayville; [ed.] Tabernacle Christian Academy Sr. '99; [occ.] Student/Singer/Construction Helper; [memb.] B.M.I./Youth Choir; [hon.] Woodsmen of the World Historical Award,

"A" Honor Roll Student; [oth. writ.] "Counter-clockwise," "Memory", poems published in local newspaper; [a.] Burton, MI

MBREY, OBIORA OHIA
[pen.] Rey Ohia Jacobs Jnr; [b.] January 31, 1961, Nigeria, West Africa; [p.] Jacob Mbrey, Christy Mbrey; [m.] Gloria Vanderbilt Mbrey, June 10, 1994; [ed.] Government Secondary School, Power Training Institute Kainji, City and Guilds Polytechnic London; [occ.] Quality Assurance Inspector Utilise Laser Weld Inc., Detroit, MI; [memb.] Institute of Training and Development (Britain) - Institute of Energy Engineers, American institute of Training and Development, National Safety Council; [hon.] Standards and Safety Code Award, Employee Outstanding Award; [oth. writ.] Several writings published in other or foreign newspapers. Also acknowledgements from "Readers Digest" and "Newsweek".; [pers.] I relate to the faith that "No man is an island - every man is a piece of the continent. Any man's pain diminishes me, because I am involved in mankind". I am inspired by the faith that God still fulfills himself in Sunday ways lest one good wisdom corrupt the world.; [a.] Detroit, MI

MCANDREW, SHAWN P.
[b.] June 17, 1975, Columbus, OH; [p.] John P. McAndrew, Sharon L. McAndrew; [ed.] Grove City High School/Columbus State Community College (not completed yet); [occ.] Computer Repair Tech. and Cook; [hon.] Governors Gold key Award (for Computer Graphics) several merit awards for Drawing and Photography; [oth. writ.] Several (not others ever published); [pers.] Life is like a melting ice cube, each day passing with a single drop of water.; [a.] Grove City, OH

MCBRAYER, GLORIA JULIANN
[b.] June 29, 1953, Fort Morgan, CO; [p.] George Edward and Marjory Cook; [m.] Robert Donald McBrayer, January 10, 1980; [ch.] Norma Renay, Leesa Kay, Tommy Alken, Donna Marie; [ed.] Weldona Valley High School, South Plains College, Methodist, Hospital School of Nursing; [occ.] Registered Nurse, disabled; [memb.] Friendly Roller Club, Secretary/Treasurer; [hon.] Phi Theta Kappa, Dean's List, Friendly Roller Club's M.V.P.; [pers.] If you have more to gain, than to loose, then go for it.; [a.] Clint, TX

MCCARTHY, DEVON
[b.] 6 November 1962, Saint Andrew, Jamaica; [p.] Pearl Beadle and Eustace McCarthy; [m.] Audrey McCarthy, 15 February 1987; [ch.] One; [ed.] University of Technology, Jamaica College High; [occ.] Accountant; [memb.] Hope Seventh Day Adventist Church, Youth Leader; [hon.] Won prize in a national poetry competition by a local radio station.; [oth. writ.] One or two short stories and a couple poems unpublished; [pers.] I write whenever I feel inspired or I am faced with a situation that lends itself to poetic expression.; [a.] Kingston, Jamaica, West Indies

MCCARTNEY, ENRIQUE ALEJANDRO
[pen.] Alejandro and Enrique McCartney; [b.] February 9, 1972, Puerto Rico, USA; [p.] Henry and Norma McCartney; [m.] Sophia Nyoka (future spouse); [ed.] B.S. Florida Memorial College; [occ.] Seminary Student Codrington College Barbados, WI; [memb.] Alpha Phi Alpha Fraternity Incorporated; [oth. writ.] I have published only one other poem in a Bahamain Newspaper. I have an unpublished collection of over 400 poems.; [pers.] As a young afro-carribean male I am cognizant of the need to be a positive influence. I let my poetry speak so that obstinate ears may listen.; [a.] Nassau, Bahamas

MCCOLLUM, ELOIS L.
[pen.] Elo; [b.] June 21, 1961, New Haven, CT; [p.] Allen and Bernice McCollum; [ch.] (One daughter) Rashanda McCollum; [ed.] James Hill House High School, Albertus Magnus College; [occ.] Lead Customer Service Representative; [memb.] Walk of Faith Church of Christ Disciple of Christ, Crusade for Life Ministry (AIDS Patients), Youth Ministry, Sandwich Ministry (Feed both Physically and Spiritually the Homeless); [hon.] Honored at the City of West Haven, Conn's Black Heritage Celebration; [oth. writ.] An excerpt of a poem published in our local newspaper, poetry writing for local Elementary School, writing and reciting for church affairs, expressive writing for a Black Heritage Celebration.; [pers.] My strength comes from the Lord. Through God there is love, and because he lives in me, I also love. God has given me the talent of poetry writing to reach and teach others. I pray that through my writing someone is inspired.; [a.] Hamden, CT

MCCOMB, MICHAEL LUCIEN
[b.] October 27, 1946, Portsmouth, NH; [p.] Lucien and Ayned McComb; [m.] Ute (Beck) McComb, December 1, 1978; [ed.] High School Graduate, Various Business and Trade Schools in Civilian and Military Sectors, Fine Machanics Graduate; [memb.] FLAAG, Royal Canadian Legion, E.V. (Assoc. member); [hon.] Editor's Choice Award, National Library of Poetry, 1996; [oth. writ.] Published Songwriter, with two works published/sub-published in 1991, on Bella-Musica Label (Germany), Have written hundreds of songs as collaborator, and as "Ghost Writer", Two poems published in Anthologies with National Library of Poetry in 1992, and 1996; [pers.] When the going gets rough, don't give up, just keep pushing, even if the whole world seems to be against you! The most beautiful works of creativity come about due to those desperate hours and times which you have lived through. Share those feelings, no matter how long it may take!; [a.] Ettenheim, Germany

MCCONAUGHY, RON
[b.] March 23, 1952, Montebello, CA; [p.] Howard and Dorothy; [pers.] To Beverly, The words were always there. It just took you to set them free.; [a.] Redondo Beach, CA

MCCONNELL, MICHAEL A.
[pen.] I-Gor; [b.] May 30, 1948, Honolulu, HI; [p.] Yes, one each sex (in spite of rumors); [m.] Taking Applications, Pending (See Spouse); [ch.] D. 21 y.o.; [ed.] 48 schools world wide, to the Postgraduate Level, extensive course work in "School of Hard Knocks"; [occ.] Living the Adventures of Life, and Writing; [memb.] Human Race (On Alt. Rainy Thursdays), others: Depends on size of the Bribe they are willing to pay; [hon.] A few paperweights, and "Stuph" to hide the holes in the walls made by doorknobs.; [oth. writ.] Tech Writing, Historical Fx, Science Fiction and Fantasy, Children's Short Stories, Occasional Irate Letter to whoever; [pers.] There's too much anger and violence. We must relearn to laugh at ourselves and with others, the universe is too precious to waste.; [a.] Albuquerque, NM

MCCULLOUGH JR., WILLIAM D.
[pen.] Davey; [b.] August 15, 1972, Tallahassee, FL; [p.] William and Nelle McCullough; [ed.] Graduated from Tampa Preparatory in 1990, currently a second year Senior at Guilford College. Majoring in Management; [occ.] Student; [memb.] FCA, Intervarsity, Apartment Association, Co-Captain Varsity V-Ball Team; [hon.] Tampa Bay All-Conference, AAU ALL Star, Designed High-School Logo; [pers.] Shining brightly, a star's prisms are made by those who have contributed to the light.; [a.] Greensboro, NC

MCDANNELL, AMANDA MARIE
[b.] May 12, 1984, Upper Sandusky; [p.] Roger and Linda McDannell; [ed.] I graduated from St. Peter's Elementary School; [memb.] Girl Scouts, 4-H, Kendall's School of Baton, Upper Sandusky Jr. High Band and Choir, Secretary - Treasurer of Older Girl Scouts Youth Advisory Committee; [hon.] Young Author 1995, Numerous State Fair level awards in Creative writing and other Arts for Girl Scouts 2nd place in Wyandot County for 4-H Creative writing plus many other 4-Hand girl scout Awards. Numerous award at both local and State levels for Baton twirling. Many titles and awards for local beauty's Awards.; [oth. writ.] Club news articles for both Girl scouts and 4-H. Numerous short stories, mysteries, folk tales, fairy tales and poems of all kinds such as free verse, rhyming, Haikus and Cinquains. I've also written six young authors books.; [pers.] I have enjoyed learning from great poets and writers and it has always been exciting to express my feelings and creative thoughts through my writing. I hope to further my writing techniques in the future because there are always so many wonderful ideas to share; [a.] Upper Sandusky, OH

MCDONALD, MARY B.
[pen.] Mary McDonald; [b.] April 6, 1944, Simpsonville, SC; [p.] Jack and Annie Brown; [m.] Billy McDonald, May 29, 1965; [ch.] Larry and Bobby McDonald; [ed.] Hillcrest High School, La Salle Extension University; [occ.] Bookkeeper - Mauldin Methodist Church Owner - Professional Tax and Bookkeeping Service; [memb.] Liberty Baptist Church, American Institute of Professional Bookkeepers; [pers.] The Lord gave me the words to this poem one Sunday afternoon as I thought about my mother and mother-in-law just before Mother's Day. The last verse was in honor of a lady of my church.; [a.] Simpsonville, SC

MCELROY, BRUCE
[b.] August 30, 1959, Mineola, NY; [p.] Richard McElroy, Margaret McElroy; [m.] Renee McElroy, August 17, 1983; [ch.] Kristian Elizabeth, Jessica Yvonne; [ed.] Prince Georges Community College, Univ. of Maryland, Univ College; [occ.] Accountant; [pers.] I have always been encouraged by my mother and my wife to write. My inspiration comes from: That which crosses my mind and touches my heart.; [a.] Columbia, MD

MCGILL, FRANK R.
[b.] May 16, 1977, Brooklyn, NY; [p.] Richard and Catherine McGill; [ed.] Monsignor Farrel H.S., St. John's University; [occ.] Full time student at St. John's University.; [memb.] Amnesty International, Speech and Debate Team, St. John's University Newspaper.; [hon.] National Honor Society, Dean's List, Winner of various writing contests.; [oth. writ.] Several poems published in local and school newspapers. In the process of creating on a personal anthology.; [pers.] In my writing I strive to extol the unappreciated facets of our everyday existence. I have been influenced by the early romantic poets. My works are solely dedicated to the three most important women in my life. My ever-present grandmother, Victoria, loving mother Cathy, and my love, Sharon.; [a.] Staten Island, NY

MCGOWAN, DYLAN
[b.] 8/2/79, La Paz, Bolivia; [p.] Maricruz McGowan; [ed.] High School Senior, The Lab School of Washington; [occ.] Student

MCINNIS, LINDA
[pen.] Terry Shaw; [b.] March 27, 1947, Edmonton, Alberta, Canada; [p.] Finley and Ellen Shaw; [m.] Mike McInnis, October 5, 1969; [ch.] Paul and Dan McInnis; [ed.] Grade 12 diploma RPN courses.; [occ.] RPN; [pers.] Being greatly influenced by my late mother's talents poetry being one, I feel the warmth of her presence in my verse.; [a.] Leamington, Ontario, Canada

MCINTOSH, MARJORIE PETERS
[pen.] Maggie Peters; [b.] Farewell, Ont., Canada; [p.] Harry and Linda McIntosh; [ch.] Laurie, Ivan, Lois; [ed.] Graduate - Stratford Career Inst., Toronto, Ont. Canada - awarded highest honours, Int. Correspondence Schools - Montreal, Que, Canada - awarded highest Honours. Owner/Operator Sarnia Bus Depot and Airbas Transportation Bus liners 1967-1989; [occ.] Retired Business Woman, Disabled.; [memb.] CDN Corp. Br 10, Sarnia, Ont., Canada Eagles Club. Sarnia. Ont; [hon.] Album by - Composition Writer will gentry lyrics writer M. Peters McInstosh, titled album - Walk Out Backwards which was the name of my song.; [oth. writ.] Memoriams and poems local papers only. Lyrics: Ole Time Gang, Walk Out Backwards, and Renting Out of my Limousines, Give me A Chance, all recorded Nashville/Tenn.; [pers.] Poetry is a memory in tune with a heartbeat.; [a.] Sarnia, Ontario, Canada

MCINTYRE, GLEN V.
[b.] August 15, 1947, Edmond, OK; [p.] Dr. and Mrs. Ray V. McIntyre; [ed.] B.A. and M.A. in History-University of Oklahoma, Masters of Liberal Studies with Museum Emphasis-also at university of Oklahoma; [occ.] Assistant Curator, Museum of the Cherokee Strip, Enid, Okla.; [memb.] Oklahoma Historical Society, Oriental Institute of Chicago, Society for Roman Studies, Federated Church - Kingfisher, Oklahoma; [hon.] Scholarship for Masters of Liberal Studies Degree, When I was Curator of Chisholm Trail Museum that Museum won Tourism Dept. award in 1984 and 1989; [oth. writ.] Articles in: Chronicles of Oklahoma, Saturday Evening Post, American West, Westview and KMT magazine. Poetry in Crosstimbers and Westview Magazines.; [pers.] My poetry uses images of the outside world to reflect inner feelings.; [a.] Kingfisher, OK

MCKINLEY, JOHN
[b.] May 31, 1921, Wheatland, IN; [p.] Lester and Emma McKinley; [m.] Maxine Shake McKinley, January 17, 1944; [ch.] Lee, Nancy, Allen; [ed.] B.S. Indiana State U., M.A. Indiana Univ., Ed. D. Indiana Univ.; [occ.] Retired Professor of Adult Education, Indiana Univ.; [memb.] AARP, Indiana Adult Ed. Assoc., Trinity Episcopal Church; [hon.] 1975 Distinguished Service Award, Indiana Adult Ed. Assoc.; [oth. writ.] 5 books on adult education; [a.] Bloomington, IN

MCKINNON, CAROL MARIE
[b.] October 26, 1964, Calgary, Alberta, Canada; [a.] Calgary, Alberta, Canada

MCLOY, ANITA RHUE
[pen.] Nita Rhue; [b.] October 31, 1960, Johnston, CO; [p.] Tessie and Alexander Rhue; [m.] Divorced; [ch.] Farah and Donald Rhue and Lenora McLoy; [ed.] Ged Johnston Tech Col. 2 years incomplete Atlantic Christian; [occ.] Certified Nursing Asst. and Team Leader; [memb.] United Full Gospel Overseers Committee; [hon.] Certificates - Team building nursing asst, employee of the month (Brittmens and Smithfield) others; [oth. writ.] Two editorials published in the news paper for Smithfield Heralds. Other poems waiting to be published in the future. Book in the making.; [pers.] The poems are for inner healing and a reflection of one self in the mirror. Only God can receive the glory honor and praise of the writings for they come from him.; [a.] Smithfield, NC

MCNABB, HOPE
[b.] March 26, 1936, Renown, Saskatchewan; [p.] F. G. and Annie Patrick; [m.] Gordon McNabb, November 24, 1953; [ch.] Cynthia-Ann Rocky Gordon, Todd Daiton - Grandchildren: Lasha, David, Amberlee, Brittany - Hunter.; [occ.] Small Business Owner; [memb.] Poets Corner International Society of Poets; [hon.] Several Time's In Newspaper, three times in National Library of Poetry. Once in Canada institute of Poetry.; [oth. writ.] Birthday Card's, Wedding Invitation; [pers.] To inspire is to be inspired.; [a.] Nanaimo, British Columbia, Canada

MCNAMARA, JESSICA
[pen.] Jessica McNamara; [b.] August 29, 1977, West Branch, MI; [p.] Larry and Sue McNamara; [ed.] I am entering my junior year at Florida Southern College; [occ.] Student; [memb.] I am a member of the Florida Souther Women's Basketball Team; [hon.] I was the valedictorian of my 1995 high school graduating class; [pers.] A good person is a well-rounded person. The Renaissance Man of the Renaissance needs to expand into the present in order to bring our society back to a level of peace and intelligence.; [a.] Englewood, FL

MCPHAIL, DAVID LAWRENCE
[pen.] Dave McPhail, Radsickle; [b.] February 16, 1972, Toronto, Canada; [p.] Larry McPhail, Peggy McPhail; [ed.] Ernest C. Drury High School, Trent University; [occ.] Shipper/Receiver of Applied Wiring Assemblies; [memb.] I'm a member of the Milton Players Theatre Troupe and The National Trivia Network's Players Plus."; [oth. writ.] High school yearbook and English Class Publications. "Detour" Trent, student-run, monthly poetry publication.; [pers.] This poem was written for and about an annoyingly stubborn person in my life, who reads too much and enjoys to little....; [a.] Milton, Ontario, Canada

MCQUADE, ELIZABETH A.
[b.] March 24, 1930, Dundolk, MD; [p.] John Blackhurst, Annie Blackhurst; [m.] Monroe M. McQuade, March 24, 1948; [ch.] John and Michael McQuade; [ed.] High school; [occ.] Retired from - Church Home Hospital, Balto. MD 21231; [hon.] Only those from N.L.O.P.; [oth. writ.] "Swift As The Wind", "Missing You", a book ("It's A Bunnie World") in rhyme (not published) (1990) a long poem "If I Were A Rose".; [pers.] I have a dream of doing something really good. Because writing is fun and is a great joy in my life. It helps make friends from strangers.; [a.] Baltimore, MD

MEJZA, CARLEEN DIANE
[pen.] Carly M.; [b.] February 12, 1956, Bermuda; [p.] Helen and Conrad Mejza; [ed.] B.A. Psychology MSW Social Work; [occ.] Psychotherapist, CSW; [memb.] NASW, NYSEPH; [oth. writ.] "Good night Sweet Prince" tribute and metaphor of the death of my father.; [pers.] In every souls, under the sun, a seed of life is planted deeply; [a.] New York, NY

MELLEN, SARAH E.
[b.] April 25, 1985, West Germany; [p.] Joseph and Patricia Mellen; [ed.] Kindergarten, 5th Grade Homeschooled, 6th Grade Jesus is Lord Academy; [occ.] Student; [hon.] 1st Place Science Fair 1996, 1st Place Fine Arts Day 1996, poems published in local newspaper.; [oth. writ.] Numerous poems and creative writings reflecting humor and intricate settings and characterization.; [pers.] I desire to honor the Lord Jesus Christ in all that I do.; [a.] Gettysburg, PA

MENZIES, IMOGENE
[pen.] Imogene Jackson/I. M. Luv; [b.] July 9, 1951, Sunflower County, MS; [p.] Thomas Jackson - Johnnie M. Jackson; [m.] Bobby J. Menzies, April 25, 1971; [ch.] Joy Angelique; [ed.] Vashon

High, Forest Park Community College; [occ.] Community Health Worker; [memb.] M.A.S.W, Rowell, Comm. Health Adv. Team, N.S.T.M. Youth Activity Board; [hon.] Forest Park Community College - Dean's List '87 and '92.; [oth. writ.] Non - published; [pers.] The health (mental, physical, sociological, and spiritual) of our race (human) is at stake. Our children are our only hope of ever becoming a safe, sane people. We need to rally behind our children for the betterment of us all.; [a.] Saint Louis, MO

MERRILL, VIVIAN L.
[b.] November 6, 1926, Byesville, OH; [p.] Rovert O. Mullen; [m.] Frank R. Merrill, June 28, 1947; [ch.] One son, 2 grandaughters; [ed.] High School at Clairton PA and Pgh Business College; [occ.] Retired housewife; [hon.] Ribbons as winner in China Painting and ceramics plaques for service in Hospice and Masonic Service Organization; [oth. writ.] Many poems but none published.; [pers.] I'm a craft person, seamstress, China Painter and Ceramist. Have never tried to get my poems published, so am very honored that my poem has been chosen for publication.; [a.] Summerfield, FL

MERRITT, MISS K.
[b.] April 25, 1958, Oakville, Ontario, Canada; [p.] Mr. and Mrs. William Merritt; [ch.] Sharon and David; [ed.] K-8 Elementary (Oakwood) Public. 9-12 Perdue High School Oak Ontario Canada (Hairdresser); [occ.] Operator stackpole Ltd Miss. Ont.; [memb.] Block Parent Program; [hon.] Excellent attendance Awards from stackpole Ltd, Perfect att. award from high school. G.R. Technology Certificate Award.; [pers.] I love to write poems to people I love or my children. I have a great personality due to romance poems.; [a.] Waterdown, Ontario, Canada

MICCIO, ALAN J.
[pen.] Alan J. Miccio; [b.] December 15, 1956; [p.] John and Margaret Miccio; [m.] Lisa Miccio; [ed.] Deer Park High, SUNY Farmingdale; [occ.] Electrician; [oth. writ.] Other poems, none of which have been published, but who knows!; [pers.] Poems have always been my source of serenity and inner peace.

MIDDOUGH, LISA
[b.] November 9, 1959, Santa Barbara, CA; [p.] Charles Cantello, Marilyn Cantello; [m.] Michael Middough, July 15, 1995; [ch.] Matthew, Morgan, Lindsey; [occ.] Sales Representative; [pers.] Poems I write directly reflect personal experience and true love of life.; [a.] Ojai, CA

MILES, ASHLEY
[b.] July 2, 1984, Saint Joseph; [p.] Rodney and Lana Miles; [ed.] 7th grade; [occ.] Student; [a.] Houston, TX

MILES, SAMUEL C.
[pen.] Sam, Sammie, Dedga; [b.] February 20, 1955, Galveston, TX; [p.] George L. Miles, Eddie Gayle Miles; [ed.] Thomas Jefferson High School, Crenshaw High School, Maricopa Technical community College (now gateway); [occ.] Disabled; [hon.] Editor's Choice Award, nominated by the International Society of Poets for Poet of the Year in 1994-95, nominated for Inductee as International Poet of Merit; [oth. writ.] Euphoria (Winner of Editor's Choice Award, National Library of Poetry Contest 94/95 The Answer, published in one of your anthologies.; [pers.] Friends are forever. Friendship should be cherished. Acceptance is the key, love is the most powerful force in the universe.; [a.] Phoenix, AZ

MILGRAM, ISAAC
[pen.] Isaac Milgram; [b.] March 19, 1937, City Kiev, Ukraine; [p.] Clara Vyazovskaya, Zuss

Milgram; [m.] Sophie Redko, February 15, 1983; [ch.] Ernest Milgram; [pers.] Love and beauty are my tragedy and my religion.; [a.] Toronto, Canada

MILLER, CHARLIE A.
[pen.] Charlie A. Miller; [b.] March 15, 1918, Mississippi; [p.] Lawrence and Vergia Miller; [m.] Sue Barnnett Miller, December 23, 1940; [ch.] 3 Daughters, 1 son; [ed.] Pieayune High, Pieayune, MS, Bachelor of Art - LSU, Master in Economics, LSU; [occ.] Retired Military, Retired Teacher; [memb.] Retired Officers Asso. Retired Teachers Ass. (Texas), AARP, Omicron Delta Epsilon, National Democratic Party; [hon.] Military - Bronze Star Purple Heart as my commendation Medal, National Honor Society (Economics); [oth. writ.] Term papers, Master's Thesis, other poems letter to the Editor; [pers.] I am a child of the Universe, no more nor less than the flowers and the forest, the animals of land and sea, the mountain and the moon, the sun and stars. I will endeavor to live in harmony with all elements of the universe in difference to the common creator. All living have a life cycle, when must be accepted. My life cycle is birth, then living, learning, loving, crying, and dying.; [a.] Canyon, TX

MILLER, CHARLOTTE
[b.] 1908, Piene, Germany; [p.] John and Martha Blazek; [m.] Vance Balih (Deceased), October 20, 1928; [ch.] One; [ed.] High School and Elementary Grad. 1927. Was married to Ralph Miller a few years is deceased; [occ.] Housewife and gardening, flowers; [memb.] Reliecked at one time Homemakers, and president Ladies Aid President Member of Cemerion Lutheran Church, taught S. and Bible; [hon.] Awards and pin of P.L.A.; [oth. writ.] A selection of poems, some published in newspapers, always fell, strong on patriotism people and nature; [pers.] I write poems in sympathy each, I write what I feel for the other person and angry, live and song sales for many years; [a.] Richey, MT

MILLER, HELEN
[b.] December 15, 1915, Toronto, ON, Canada; [p.] Bill, Liz-Fairbrass; [m.] Edwin James Miller, August 11, 1934; [ch.] Five Children; [ed.] Carlton School Toronto; [occ.] Army Widow; [hon.] Grandmother to 56 Grandchildren, 6-5th generations; [a.] Stayner, Ontario, Canada

MILLER, JENNYE S.
[pen.] J. Miller; [b.] June 3, 1950, Paducah, KY; [p.] Virgil and Eva Osborne; [ch.] Lorri and Angie; [ed.] Life; [occ.] Director of Convention Development, Chattanooga Convention and Visitors Bureau; [memb.] People for the Ethical Treatment of Animals Humane Society of the U.S. Center for Marine Conservation Defences of Wildlife Doris Day Animal League World Wildlife Fund; [hon.] My two daughters my granddaughter, Kali Vinny, my love; [oth. writ.] Other poems.; [pers.] My writing reflects the constant, and sometimes hopeless struggle, to survive the never ending battle between good and evil, and sanity versus insanity.; [a.] Chattanooga, TN

MILLER, RICKEY PAUL
[pen.] R. Paul Miller; [b.] May 1, 1953, Oxford, MS; [p.] H. P. (Shorty) Miller, Rose Davis; [m.] Barbara Lynn (Watts) Miller, July 17, 1980; [ed.] 20 years in Law Enforcement, 2 years different Schools, and life its self.; [occ.] E.911 Operator, La Fayette County Sheriff Dept.; [hon.] Some but who cares.; [oth. writ.] 2 poems published in A Sea of Treasure and A Travesty of Thoughts, several for friends and several for my own mind.; [pers.] I must say, if not for my wife, I do not believe I cold have made it. I've try hard to treat her right. This woman, my wife, Barbara Lynn (Watts) Miller. I love and care for you. Thanks for putting up with me.; [a.] Abeville, MS

MILLER, TEHRANIQUE
[pen.] Tehranique Khalyla Miller; [b.] September 22, 1978, Nassau, Bahamas; [p.] Terry Miller, Melvern Miller; [ed.] Kingsway Academy High School, College of St. Benedicts/St. Johns University, Bahamas Campus; [occ.] Marketing Director of Intellect Public Relations and Marketing; [memb.] CACP - Citizens Against Capital Punishment; [oth. writ.] Why?, Life, Sunrise, Love; [pers.] Art never expresses anything but itself!

MILLER SR., CHARLES G.
[b.] September 23, 1949, Leeds, AL; [p.] Catherine Miller, Frank Miller; [m.] Jacqueline R. Miller, April 8, 1981; [ch.] Charles Jr., Teaon, Jeremiah, Joshua, Ayanna, Alishia; [ed.] R.R. Moton High, Southern Business, Lawson State Jr. College, Birmingham, Metro Area Skill Center; [occ.] Building Maintenance Supervisor, North East Branch YMCA, Birmingham AL; [memb.] Board of Director's Member of Clear, Mt. Calvary Baptist Church program for affordable housing. Assistant Pastor New Hope Church of God in Christ; [pers.] I love to write about all aspects of life such as love, sorry, pain, joy, (etc). But I especially love being creative and imaginative, letting my mind sojourn to it's full potential. I have been greatly influenced by God's inspiration.; [a.] Leeds, AL

MILLS, JO
[pen.] Jo Mills; [b.] June 11, Amboy, CA; [p.] Joseph and Audrey Mills; [ch.] Three Donis Paul, Tammy Jo, Dana Marie Mills; [ed.] San Bernardino High School, Northridge University, Northridge, Calif.; [occ.] Clerical Manager Quality Staffing; [memb.] National Assn. for female executives; [hon.] American Legion Award, Jewish war veterans scholarship, honor "Connecticut Foundation" Youth Motivation task force national model program"; [oth. writ.] "Joshie's Adventures", "Russell's Earthquake Rumble", "Tides of Deception", "Stolen Moments"; [pers.] My creative endeavors and artistic talents are the windows of my soul and existence. I have been greatly influenced by poetic writings of Florence Burrill Jacobs; [a.] Indianapolis, IN

MITCHELL, ERIN
[b.] June 30, 1983, Victoria, BC; [p.] Peter and Suzanne; [ed.] I am in grade 8 at Bayside Middle School in Brentwood Bay, Victoria B.C., Canada; [occ.] Baby sitter; [hon.] 3 "Creative writing awards from Seaview Elementary school and 1 citizenship award for helping my best friend Ashleigh Dukoff; [a.] Brentwood Bay, British Columbia, Canada

MITCHELL, PATRICIA A.
[pen.] Pat; [b.] January 20, 1962, Lake Charles, LA; [p.] Albert Mitchell, Ernestine Mitchell; [ch.] Aubrey Alexander, Terrance Lee; [ed.] Sherwood High Portland C. College; [occ.] Dining Room Attendant/Cook; [oth. writ.] Several poems published in newsletter at Beaverton Lodge, where I work.; [pers.] I receive great pride in writing poems that touch ones lives. My poems reflect my inner being.; [a.] Beaverton, OR

MOBLEY, JEFF
[b.] October 18, 1974, Greenville, NC; [p.] George and Christine Mobley; [ed.] J. H. Rose High School, East Carolina University; [occ.] Full-time Student; [hon.] Alpha Epsilon Delta, Premedical Honor Society, Dean's List, Honor Roll; [pers.] I endeavor each and everyday to project the image of Jesus Christ in everything I do, for he is who my life revolves around.; [a.] Greenvile, NC

MONTANEZ, ALICE
[b.] May 8, 1950, Ayer, MA; [p.] Francisco and Gladys Zina; [m.] Divorced; [ch.] 1 son Guillermo

III, 3 daughters, Celeste, Melody and Amy; [ed.] Union School, Dunstable, Mass., Fairgrounds Jr. High, Nashua, North Groton High School, Groton, Mass., some courses at Middlesex Community College, Lowell and Bedford Mass Campuses; [occ.] Produce Dept., Market Basket Stores, Lowell, Mass.; [memb.] Amway Distributor, Vineyard Christian Worshippers; [hon.] National Honor Society - (Jr. and Sr. years) Groton High School $500.00 Scholarship while attending Middlesex Community College; [oth. writ.] Did several poems and short stories but didn't like them so I threw them out. Didn't like "You're Not Alone" either but didn't throw it out. Look what happened!; [pers.] All my tests in school pointed toward my literary talent. I didn't have enough confidence in myself to believe I could do anything with it. The first time I tried, I got published! Just try!; [a.] Lowell, MA

MONTESANO, JOHN
[b.] December 10, 1946, Chicago, IL; [p.] Rose Montesano and Nick Montesano (Deceased); [m.] Brenda Lead Montesano, January 15, 1995; [ch.] Robert, Michael and Dustin; [ed.] Weber High, De Paul University; [occ.] Waiter/Captain in Gourmet Restaurant, Interests, I am very involved in music (mostly from a listening stand point), classical, rock and blue grass mostly. I have been involved in church choir, as a singer, flutist and director.; [hon.] I have produced and directed a musical presentation of the passion of Jesus, which is the greatest achievement of my life to date; [oth. writ.] I have written several poems over the years that reflect my then current involvement and the people in my life poems about my belief, philosophy, children, parents, spouse and friends. "The Girl On A Swing" is my spouse "Brenda Leah"; [pers.] My writing usually reflects my feelings and responses to my surroundings and the people in my life. Many poems have been written about people who have touched me and reflect the spirit of that person. I believe in, live and let live, be true to yourself, the goodness of man, and kindness to all.; [a.] Aurora, IL

MOON, DANIEL JODY
[pen.] Daniel J. Moon; [b.] February 10, 1965, Flin Flon, Manitoba, Canada; [p.] Elsie and Dan Moon; [ed.] High School Graduate, 4th Class Stationery Engineer Certificate; [occ.] Stationary Engineer, Revenue Property Owner.; [hon.] High School President; [oth. writ.] Nationally published in High School. "Argyle Aware" book, published in local newspapers and aired on C.B.C. (Canadian Broadcasting Corporation); [pers.] Greatly influenced by the environment, nature and those close to him. Poem "A Man's Sonnet" inspired by his girlfriend.; [a.] Winnipeg, Manitoba, Canada

MOORE, DEBBIE
[pen.] Debbie S. Moore; [b.] December 19, 1958, Topeka, KS; [p.] John Holt and Dorothy Holt; [m.] Vernon Moore, April 16, 1987; [ch.] Trish Rainey, Megan Rainey; [ed.] Seaman High, University of Maryland, U.S. Army; [occ.] Electrical Electronic Quality Control Test Technician, Savannah, GA; [memb.] American Heart Association, Isle of Hope Volunteer Fire Dept.; [hon.] Letters of Commendations for saving a child's life (chocking) and an adult (drowning), Military Awards: Military Service Award, Army Commendation, Overseas Ribbon, and several others.; [oth. writ.] Childrens books: Penelope the Peculiar Purple Porpoise, Carlton the Crosseyed Crab.; [pers.] I love life and helping people. There is a message for peace and preserving the world in the books I write. I read, learn and grow by reading every type of poetry and this helps with my writing.; [a.] Savannah, GA

MOORE, JASON P.
[b.] January 22, 1915, Bell Co., TX; [p.] Lawrence H. and Dessie L. Moore; [m.] Virginia B. Moore, August 24, 1940; [ch.] Marjorie Shaefer, Jon L. Moore, Elizabeth Moore, Jason H. Moore; [ed.] Denton High School, TX, 2 yrs., North TX University, 5 years The University of TX, Austin, 1939, B. Arch.; [occ.] Retired Architect, Poet, Gerontologist; [memb.] American Institute of Architects, Senior Archt., Int. Soc. of Poets, Chairman, Duke City Marathon, Mem. Master Runners Unlimited, AARP, Amer. Running and Fitness Assn.; [hon.] Numerous Architectural Awards for Excellence over 50 years of professional practice, various age group awards for running since 1978, Club and State Free-Style Archery Champion 1959-70; [oth. writ.] Buildings and articles in architectural magazines over the last 50 years. Was Ass't Prof. of Arch., Texas A&M 1946-'48, poems published in Nat'l Library of Poetry and in Master Runners Unlimited; [pers.] Would like to be known as a wise man who expresses the imprint of the experiences of a long lifetime in rhythm and beauty.; [a.] Albuquerque, NM

MOORE, MAUREEN
[p.] Eric Liddell, Florence MacKenzie-Liddell; [occ.] Artist and Poets; [pers.] My paintings and poems are a vehicle for expressing my view of the world and finding out who I really am. They are also a blueprint for the new life which I am in the process of creating. Currently, I am mounting prints of a painting and a poem on laminated plaques. I have been watching for the right publisher. This is my first submission.; [a.] Ancaster, Ontario, Canada

MORANCY, TYE JASON
[b.] September 11, 1974, Jacksonville, FL; [p.] Timothy Morancy, Patricia Wilson; [ed.] Uxbridge High, Holy Cross College, Candidate for PhD in Radiology at UMASS Lowell; [occ.] Student/Teaching Assistant UMASS Lowell; [memb.] Society of Physics Students, American Assoc. for the Advancement of Science, National Honor Society, Holy Cross Brand Honor Society, Premed Society; [hon.] National Science Foundation Fellowship, Holy Cross Scholarship, Oceanstate Power Academic Scholarship; [oth. writ.] Large collection of unpublished poems covering many themes.; [pers.] I wrote toe express my thoughts and feelings. I believe poetry to be the trust expression of our inner selves and can be found in all of us.; [a.] Uxbridge, MA

MORGAN, CORY
[b.] August 5, 1982, Metairie, LA; [p.] Cathy and Terry Morgan; [ed.] Elgin High School; [occ.] Student; [memb.] Collect Precious Moments; [hon.] Won all school Spelling Bee 5 times, Presidential Physical Fitness Award 4 times, Academic Honors; [pers.] I have been influenced to write by: Other authors, my best friend; [a.] Elgin, IL

MORRISON, CONNIE J. M.
[b.] April 7, 1977, Hinton, Alberta, Canada; [ed.] Elementary School, Peers and Grande Cache Alberta Canada Junior and High Schools - Edmonton Alberta Canada; [occ.] Waitress; [oth. writ.] Numerous poems not yet published; [pers.] This poem was written when I was 15 years old and is directed towards people who suffer from Alziehmers disease and the mental anguish that both the individual and the family might go through; [a.] Honolulu, HI

MORRISON, JOLANDA L.
[b.] November 11, 1966, Red Deer, Calgary AB, Canada; [p.] Dwight and Lynn,; [m.] Tracy Behrens; [ch.] Kristyn Lorraine-Lynn, Kyle William - Mark, Melissa Rae-Joyce; [ed.] Calgary, Alberta, Canada; [occ.] Financial Services Industry; [hon.] The honor of bringing 3 healthy, beautiful and fortu-nate children into this world.; [oth. writ.] I have been using poetry as a means of self expression and growth since I was twelve years old. Personal writings total 500 +, never published.; [pers.] Although, I hold no firm political views. I can't help but cry out for the children. The real victims of our Adult ignorancy. "From my small eyes if you could only see". "The examples of human kind you instill in me."; [a.] Calgary, Alberta, Canada

MORROW, DOROTHY D.
[b.] September 21, 1952, Orillia, Ontario; [p.] Helen LaHay and Archie LaHay; [ch.] Paul (P.J.) O'Halloran; [pers.] My poems come from my feelings and from my heart. I have been greatly influenced by my family and friends, and most of all "my mother."; [a.] Owen Sound, Ontario, Canada

MORSY, MONA
[b.] October 26, 1974, Montreal; [p.] Mohammed and Anahid Morsy; [ed.] Miss Edgar's and Miss Cramp's High School, Marianopolis College, McGill University; [occ.] Student full time expecting to graduate in a B.A. this year; [hon.] Dean's List, Honor Roll, (College Level) Art History and Leadership Award at the High School Level; [oth. writ.] Article published in the Montreal Gazette entitled "Longing for Mountains or at least Hills. A girl should be happy with the body parts she has."; [pers.] I enjoy communicating through my writing. Even if each individual is different, there are similar experiences and emotions that can be translated by the written word. I have been greatly influenced by the 20th century and its break from contormity.; [a.] Montreal, Quebec, Canada

MORTON, SANDRA ROMELLE
[pen.] Sandra Griggs Morton; [b.] July 13, 1942, Putnam Co, MO; [p.] Leonard and Letha Maude Griggs; [m.] James Curtis Morton, July 16, 1960; [ch.] 3 two girls, and one boy; [ed.] High school grad; [occ.] Store Clerk R&R Market Queen City, MO; [memb.] Member Queen City First Baptist Church; [hon.] I once received a $10 gift certificate, when I was ask to write something for a IGA Christmas Party while working there.; [oth. writ.] I've mainly written memorials for friends and etc. in my hometown newspaper, and for things at church, also I've written several Gospel type songs which I usually sing myself. I make up my own tunes because I can't write notes; [pers.] I strive always to promote the gospel through my poems, and songs especially. If just one lost person is saved, I've met my goal.; [a.] Queen city, MO

MOSHER, DEAN ALAN
[b.] September 27, 1970, Arlington, VA; [ed.] Annandale High, currently attending Northern Virginia Community College; [occ.] Pipefitter's Assistant; [hon.] Inaugural class of Ameri Corps, 1995; [pers.] Humanity is incredibly beautiful, but why must we be such a pain in the ass?; [a.] Alexandria, VA

MOUNTS, JAMES T.
[pen.] Tommy; [b.] June 23, 1954, Matewan WV; [p.] Raymond and Obera; [ed.] High School Grad. from Magnolia High, Matewan, 42 yrs of daily life and still attending; [occ.] Retired; [memb.] National Rifle Association (NRA); [oth. writ.] Jim and Debra, Only the Good Times; [pers.] Sometimes I laugh, sometimes I cry, my words are my words; [a.] Wyandotte, MI

MREMOVICH, MARIJA
[pen.] Nina Novak; [b.] August 15, 1942, Croatia, Yugoslavia; [oth. writ.] To speak out in order to prevent the triumph of evil and injustice - that's what's poetry all about...

MUHLHAUSER, JANN
[pen.] Jenna Taylor Smith; [b.] January 22, 1948, Aberdeen, WA; [ed.] Certificate of Completion Office Occupations, AAS-Office Tech grays Harbor College, Aberdeen, WA; [occ.] Volunteer - Rape Crisis Center, Author; [oth. writ.] I'm working on a novel.; [pers.] I'm a romantic who was born a century late. I believe that people are inherently good, and that all they really need is a chance. I get angry at injustice and have no patience with intolerant people.; [a.] Aberdeen, WA

MUILENBURG, DEBORA
[b.] January 28, 1969, Sisseton, SD; [p.] John R. and Donna Wegleitner; [m.] Scott Muilenburg, June 3, 1989; [ch.] Jessica Renee, Nicole Lynn and Stephanie Marie; [occ.] Housewife; [pers.] I have two goals that I feel I must achieve in this lifetime. My first is to raise my children to be honest, sincere and strong. I want them to be strong enough to stand up for what they believe in. To hold fast to their convictions, no matter how wrong the world tells them they are. I do not want them to be easily led. My 2nd goal is that I, as a wife and mother always strive to do the right thing. I never want my husband or my children to feel that I let them down.

MURPHY, AMY
[b.] December 3, 1978, Seattle, WA; [p.] Margaret and Randy Murphy; [ed.] Snohomish High School; [memb.] Active in Bits N Spurs 4-h Club, 1995-96 State and National 4-h Horse bowl Team; [oth. writ.] Two other poems, "To Catch The Moon" and "Rage", published in 1995-96 Within Reach, my schools literacy magazine. Plus many other unpublished poems.; [pers.] Life is given to us for a purpose. My purpose in life is to write what flows from my heart and soul into the minds of others.; [a.] Snohomish, WA

MURPHY, CHRISTINE
[b.] February 14, 1973, Catskill, NY; [p.] James Poole and Claire Bucholtz; [m.] Todd Murphy, November 27, 1993; [ch.] Amanda Jean; [occ.] Customer Service; [pers.] This is my first published writing. I very much look forward to enlightening readers world wide with my words in the future.; [a.] Buffalo, NY

MYERS, AMBER
[b.] August 26, 1980, Mattoon, IL; [p.] Steven and Debora Myers; [ed.] Junior at Neoga High School, Neoga ILL; [occ.] Student; [memb.] Scholar Bowl, Science Club, Neoga High School Band Member; [hon.] High school honor roll; [oth. writ.] Novel "Shades of Iniquity"; [pers.] I think of myself mainly as a novelist, but occasionally philosophical musings flow through my pen, resulting in poems like "If Only". The fact that I have never intentionally written a poem confirms my suspicion that the best works of literary art are compulsive and not planned.; [a.] Neoga, IL

MYRMINGOS, DENOS
[pers.] "Your father Abraham rejoiced to see my day, and he saw it and was glad. The Jews therefore said to Him, `You are not yet 50 years old, and have you seen Abraham?' Jesus said to them, `Truly, truly, I say to you, before Abraham was born, I am.' John 8:56-58; [a.] Burr Ridge, IL

NADASI, GAIL
[b.] October 26, 1959, Encino, CA; [p.] Clyde and Elizabeth Marshall; [m.] Leslie Nadasi, December 28, 1977; [ch.] Ryan Nadasi, Brandin Nadasi, Amanda Nadasi; [occ.] Homemaker; [hon.] This is my first; [oth. writ.] Short stories, other poems. This is my first publication.; [pers.] Live by the "Golden Rule" and what goes around comes around.; [a.] Simi Valley, CA

NAGAMORI, SHINYA DAVID
[pen.] David Himeno; [b.] October 4, 1969, Tokyo; [p.] Eiji Nagamori, Yoshika Nagamori; [ed.] Waseda University (B.A. in Western History) and Aoyama Gakuin University (B.A. in English and American Literature); [occ.] Composer; [memb.] The Alien Flower; [hon.] The Alien Flower-Poetry Workshop "Guest Poet of the week".; [oth. writ.] More than 10 lyrics and translated lyrics published.; [pers.] William Blake through me into the poetical, imaginative world which, I believe, should be more realistic than the real one in a way that help us all live day by day.; [a.] Tokyo, Japan

NALIVAIKO, KATYA
[b.] February 23, 1973, Russia; [ed.] Seattle Central Community College, WA; [occ.] Student, Western Washington University; [oth. writ.] Few poems and fiction, never have been published.; [pers.] English is my second language. Writing poetry was a challenge for me, because of the language barrier. I enjoy to do it now.; [a.] Bellingham, WA

NAPHOLC, MELISSA
[pen.] Mel, Melis.; [b.] November 5, 1979, Hamilton, ON; [p.] John and Brenda Napholc; [ed.] Attending grade 12, Scott Park Secondary School, Ham. On.; [hon.] On honour roll, grade 11, 1995-1996; [oth. writ.] Another Race, Good-Bye, Faith, Father, Un Wanted, Guiding Me, Waiting Seems Forever, The Time Will Come, His Side, If You Listen..., Today.; [pers.] I have always tried to do well, and live life to the fullest. The greatest gifts that have ever happened in my life, are my niece and nephew. They are both my pride and joy.; [a.] Hamilton, Ontario, Canada

NASITS, ALAN
[b.] January 6, 1946; [p.] Julius, Sarah Nasits; [m.] Mary Nasits; [a.] El Paso, TX

NASITS, MARY
[b.] October 4, 1950; [p.] Mr. and Mrs. Wesley Keyson; [m.] Alan Nasits; [ed.] RN, BS Hotel Dieu School of Nursing, College of St. Francis; [a.] El Paso, TX

NASON, CHARLES T.
[b.] April 22, 1946, Pittsburgh, PA; [p.] Raymond W. and Helen T. Nason; [m.] Marlane, 1968; [ch.] Rebecca Anne, Jill Nicole; [ed.] B.A. Washington and Jefferson College, MBA U. of Pittsburgh, Grad of School of Business; [occ.] Chairman and CEO, The Acacia Group; [memb.] Greater Washington Board of Trade (Base Chairman 1994-95), American Council of Life Insurance (Board of Directors), Greater Washington Boys and Girls Clubs (Board of Directors); [hon.] Who's Who in America

NATANBLUT, DANIEL C.
[pen.] Danny Natanblut; [b.] December 6, 1970, Montreal; [p.] Samuel and Bruria Natanblut; [ed.] Vanier College and McGill University with a Bachelor of Social Work; [occ.] Social Worker presently working in a Golden Age Association; [memb.] Hockey player and guitar player/songwriter; [hon.] Dean's Honour List graduating year 1993. Currently completing a Master's in Education. Poem: My Eve - published in N.L. of Poetry's book "Sparkles in the Sand."; [pers.] Art is the emotional release of the creative mind - Daniel C. Natanblut, Hashem is my shepherd, I shall not lack. Quote from Tehillim #23.; [a.] Montreal, Province of Quebec, Canada

NECULA, CRISTINA
[b.] January 14, 1975, Bucharest, Romania; [p.] Nicholas Necula, Maria-Ana Necula; [ed.] Mt. Vernon High School Febbraio School of Music Suny Purchase College Private Voice and Piano Lessons; [occ.] Still a student in Final Year at Suny Purchase; [hon.] National Honor Society Scholarship in Praise of Merit (College) Dean's List (4 years) Talent prize for singing contest in New York (Miss Romania-USA Pageant); [oth. writ.] Several poems in English, Romanian and French; [pers.] I am in love with life. My singing and my writing help me to express this passion. I have been influenced by Eastern European poets and writers and by my study of Philosophy.; [a.] White Plains, NY

NEDROW, VIRGINIA VINE FAGER
[pen.] Virginia Nedrow; [b.] July 6, 1918, Akron, OH; [p.] Raymond and Clara Fager (Deceased); [m.] Richard Eugene Nedrow Sr., June 11, 1949; [ch.] Margaret Ann Zures and Rick Jr.; [ed.] A.B. Cum Laude, Beaver College, 1941, Graduate study in the Humanities Stanford University, 1946-1948, Graduate study teacher training California State University, Fullerton 1961-1962; [occ.] Retired; [memb.] Charter member Women in Military Service for America (WIMSA), California Teachers Association, AARP, National Geographic Society, Smithsonian Associates, Stanford Club of Orange County; [hon.] P. Delta Epsilon (Honorary) Dean's List, Outstanding Graduate W. W. Kimball first on scholarship, W. W. Kimball first prize, 1942-43 competition by Chicago Singing Teacher's Guild for song Lyric to Paul Koepke's music "The Ivory Tower" published by Carl Fischer, 1943; [oth. writ.] Several poems published in Poets of America 1940, several poems published in college journals, song lyrics for "The Ivory Tower" published by Carl Fischer, 1943; [pers.] As a midshipman in the very first class of Wave officers training at Smith College in 1942, I was greatly impressed by the frequent admonition, "Forget you're a woman, and remember you're a lady, "In my life and in my writing and as a teacher, I have always tried to follow the precepts of respect, honor, service, and love of God and country to be worthy of being called a lady.; [a.] Placentia, CA

NEELY, MRS. EDNA F.
[b.] May 9, 1951, Dorchester, ON, Canada; [ed.] Grad. Hamilton General Hosp. School of Nursing/ 42. (Leiut N/S, R.C.A.M.C. - W. Witt.); [occ.] Retired Registered Nurse; [memb.] IODE, Royal Canadian Legion, Westminster Historical Society, Nursing Sisters Association of Canada, Orchestra London, Untied Church Women; [hon.] Occasional prizes for posters (work themes) prizes for christmas window painting.; [oth. writ.] 1. Humorous play 'Who Me?' for church organization. 2. Christmas Hymn 'Christmas Birthday Song' (tune, Kum-Ba-Yah). Nothing published.; [pers.] "One may lose a parent, spouse, or sibling, and live to accept the loss, but to lose a child at any age there is no recovery. When my son Kerry (41) was drowned - I sat up all night and composed 'My Spirit Lives' as a memorial to publish in the local paper, instead of an obituary".; [a.] London, Ontario, Canada

NESS, RUTH A.
[pen.] Ruth Dodge; [b.] April 23, 1943, Union City, NJ; [p.] Edward and Annie Dodge; [ed.] Some College; [occ.] Disability; [memb.] Flemington Rotary, United Methodist Church; [oth. writ.] Poems for Weddings Funerals and Affairs; [pers.] In 1988 while attending a "Psalms" seminar the Lord blessed me with the instant ability to write poetry and it has not stopped yet I wish to express God's goodness in all my poetry!; [a.] Flemington, NJ

NEWMAN, ANNA LEWIS TEEMS
[pen.] Anna Newman; [b.] July 19, 1922, Atlanta, GA; [p.] Edith R. and Lewis Teems; [m.] William Franklin Newman, September 25, 1940; [ch.] Sherrolyn, Billy, Tony; [ed.] I graduated from Commercial High School in Atlanta, GA; [occ.] Retired; [memb.] Rose of Sharon Garden Club, Graybonnet Grandmother's Club, Eastside Baptist

Church; [oth. writ.] Poems Our Love, Our Roots of Life, The Light of God, This Boy, This Girl, Little Hook, story - And Away We Flew, poems - My Last, Strange but Not Alone, What Seem to Be; [pers.] I have never published any of my writings. I write poetry when inspired. I write a story when I get a strong desire as I do when I sketch a picture.; [a.] Decatur, GA

NICHOLSON, CRAIG D.
[b.] April 8, 1958, Johannesburg, South Africa; [p.] Denis and Norma-Anne Nicholson; [ed.] Jeppe Boys High (Johannesburg); [occ.] Helicopter Pilot (extended unemployment), Calgary, Alberta; [oth. writ.] Several articles and poems published in magazines, self-published a book of poetry and a booklet: "Freedom for South Africans."; [pers.] I would like to inspire the joy and power of integrity and honor within everyone. I seek to help others unfold their unique and immense but often suppressed virtues and gifts to the world.; [a.] Calgary, Alberta, Canada

NIELSEN, ERMA E.
[b.] August 14, 1929, Co. Bluffs, IA; [p.] Roy B. Pruett and Kathryn McIntosh Pruett; [m.] Harold D. Nielsen, September 21, 1946; [ch.] H. 'Don' Jr., Lois, Brenda, Mark, Myra; [ed.] Iowa Western Community College, Council Bluffs, IA, Bible Training Institute, Cleveland, TN; [occ.] Homemaker, Ret. LPN; [memb.] Church of God of Prophecy, Co. Bluffs. IA, Historical Society of Pohawattamie Council Bluffs, IA, Pohawattamie Geneological Society Co. Bluffs, IA.; [oth. writ.] 2 poems "The White Wing Messenger - Church God of Prophecy", Cleveland, TN.; [pers.] We're proud of our 5 children, and 13 grand children. I enjoy writing poetry, reading, making quilts, genealogy, traveling, also spending time with our family. I enjoy people try to encourage them to be and do the best they can to believe their goals. To enjoy life.; [a.] Treynor, IA

NIELSEN, MARY LEE
[pen.] Blondie; [b.] March 6, 1938, Salinas, CA; [p.] Mr. and Mrs. L. M. Shannon; [m.] Widowed twice, my husband, Kenneth Nielsen; [ch.] Marvin Rianda, Alan Rianda; [ed.] Finished my junior year of Hi School in SaLinas Calif. 1955; [occ.] Home maker grandmother; [hon.] Meanings I have only wrote for friends, and family they award me with their thanks and that means much to me; [oth. writ.] None only for family, and many I have wrote have been burned, as I felt they where not any good my husband always encouraged me to write my poems; [pers.] All of my poems are almost about every day, and from my heart as to how I feel about the weather, friends and family. Some are happy ,some are sad to me, depending on my mood. Some days I can write 10 good poems; [a.] Salinas, CA

NIGAM, MR. B. P.
[b.] December 3, 1917, Hamirpur, Uttar Pradesh, India; [p.] Dr. G. P. Nigam and Mrs. Krishna Kumari Nigam; [m.] Mrs. Savitri Nigam, April 25, 1937; [ch.] Two Daughters: Mrs. Ragini Narain and Mrs. Nirja Savill; [ed.] M.A. (Eng. Literature), L.Lb. (Law); [occ.] Social Work and Writing; [memb.] World Constitution and Parliament Association, English-Speaking Union of India, All India Crime Prevention Society, Indian Humanist Union, Indian Federation of U.N. Asscns., Delhi Gymkhana Club; [hon.] First Prize on the spot essay competition held in Lucknow, India; [memb.] Rukmini and other stories (a collection of short stories), Dayanand (a Philosophy Novel), Articles on current problems published in national newspaper and journals; [a.] New Delhi

NIVEN, RAYMOND GARTH
[pen.] R. Garth Niven; [b.] May 12, 1950, Nagara-

on-the-Lake, Ontario; [p.] George Raymond and Helen Eileen Niven; [m.] Carol Ann Niven; [ch.] Robert, Michelle A., C. Ashley and C. Andrew; [ed.] BS Honors, McMaster University (Magna Cum Laude), M.A. McMaster University, Ontario, Canada, MLS University of Western Ontario, Canada; [occ.] Chief Librarian Dept. of Justice, Province of Manitoba; [memb.] Manitoba Library Association, American Library Association and American Association of Law Libraries; [hon.] Governor's Scholarship, Paikin Scholarship, Jury Scholarship, Dean's Honors List; [a.] Winnipeg, Manitoba, Canada

NORMAN, NELSON
[pen.] Nelson Norman; [b.] August 30, 1966, MT. Vernon; [p.] Verlee Norman, Ernestine Scott; [ed.] Mt. Vernon High School, Graduated and moved on to the best things of my Education, poetry; [occ.] Song Writer Hip-Hop and wiser; [memb.] Apple Cap Productions, Entertainment for the youth; [hon.] Hollywood Artist Record Company Contract M.V.H.S. Diploma, Merit Award, All student listen up and more; [oth. writ.] God Bless Us Yolanda, Nelson, Ernie, Gene Pam, Michael, Debra, Dawn, Verlinda, Verlee Jr., Juanita Mom and Dad who's in heaven I love you N.N.; [pers.] To me writing is like an old antique you cherish it. For life it takes time and space that's the word. Never give end, to this society, worlds family poetry by E...everlasting; [a.] Mount Vernon, NY

O'DONNELL, CHRISTINE
[b.] September 5, 1975, Hagersville; [p.] Edward and Shelby O'Donnell; [ed.] Hagersville Secondary, Mohawk College, Honors Diploma in Police Sciences at Stratford College; [hon.] College Diploma with honors; [pers.] Remember all your memories for you cannot relive them.; [a.] Hagersville, Ontario, Canada

O'DONOGHUE, NORA
[b.] 29 March 1926, Ireland; [p.] John and Kathleen Bromell; [m.] Dan O'Donoghue, 26 June 1951; [ch.] John, Donald, Thomas; [ed.] St. Mary's Convent School, Limerick, O.L.S.H. Convent School Isle of Wight England Music Teacher Training; [occ.] Piano and Class Music Teacher, Speech and Drama teacher Amateur Director and Producer of Videos of Ireland. Arranger of Irish; [memb.] Music and Piano Acc., Associate London College of Music, European Piano Piano Music Teachers Association, Local Poetry and Drama Group; [hon.] 1st prize for a poem on National T.V. Diplomas (Music) A.L.C.M., A.R.I.A.M., F.T.S.I.M., Founder member of Tara Board of Irish Music, Honorary member Freeman of Chicago City U.S.A., Profile in Irish Post Newspaper England and by Sean Mc Carthy Poet and songwriter in the Kerrymiral Newspaper Ireland; [oth. writ.] Three Novels, Fact and Fiction A book of poems (not yet published). Most of my work is centered around real life situations. Greatly influenced by my mother's love of reading poetry to her 10 children; [pers.] My three years as a nun in a Convent gave me a great sense of love, compassion and hope, which is reflected in my writings.; [a.] Killarney, Ireland

O'RILEY, CAROLYN A.
[pen.] Carolyn A. O'Riley, Carolyn A. Van Cleave; [b.] June 23, 1946, Vicksburg, MS; [p.] Jean Davis Brown, E. Foster Van Cleave; [m.] Ronald Patrick O'Riley Jr., December 23, 1978; [ch.] Sonia Ann Millar, Lucian Christopher Millar; [ed.] Associate Degree of Fine Art, continued education and diploma in Paralegal Studies; [occ.] Office Manager; [memb.] Distinguished member International Society of Poets; [hon.] Editor's Choice Award for "The Willow Tree" in the Spirit of the Ages; [oth. writ.] Published in poetry journal, magazines and

books; [pers.] I am a writer and an artist. I've been doing both since I was a very little girl. I derive great joy from painting word pictures that reflect the Creator's love and touch the readers' hearts.; [a.] McKinney, TX

O'ROURKE, MELISSA
[pen.] Emelie Grey; [b.] March 15, 1975, Manchester, NM; [p.] Diane Belcourt, Leonard Couldrige; [m.] Patrick O'Rourke, October 26, 1996; [ed.] Memorial High, University of New Hampshire at Manchester; [occ.] Student (College); [hon.] Dean's List; [pers.] I believe humans have the ability to fly, but its individual ambition that will determine how high one will soar. I desire to soar above limits and boundaries rather than be contained within them.; [a.] Derry, NH

OAKLEY, STEPHANIE
[b.] April 8, 1982, Stanford, CA; [p.] Terri Oakley; [ed.] Will be a freshmen at San Mateo High School in Fall of '96; [occ.] Student; [pers.] When people read my poems, they are actually reading about me. My goal in my poetry is to leave the reader wondering what the real meaning is. I like to make people think and ponder.; [a.] Foster City, CA

OATES, CLARA
[b.] November 24, 1913, Keyser, WV; [p.] John and Naunie Triplett; [m.] Daniel Oates (Deceased), September 1, 1932; [ch.] Marian Elanie Oates Booth; [ed.] Graduate of Keyser High School have worked in a jewelry store for 8 years, married to Daniel Oates in 1932 - have one daughter (Marian Oates Booth); [occ.] Housewife (husband deceased); [memb.] Member of Methodist Church, Member of 4-H Club, Member of Reading Circle; [hon.] Am a High School Graduate have one daughter (married) 4 grandchildren (grown) have taken extra courses at night school; [pers.] My mother wrote poetry and I think I learned from her.; [a.] Keyser, WV

OLIVER, JOY
[b.] December 25, 1962, Stonewall, MB, Canada; [p.] Alma and Ernie Oliver; [m.] John Hearn; [ch.] Tara-Rose, Kristofer, Cody and Kirby; [occ.] Homemaker; [pers.] I try to see and enjoy the humorous side of things without humor we would lead a very dull life.; [a.] Marquette, Manitoba, Canada

ONKENHOUT, MAAIKE ELLEN
[b.] 5 July 1996, Laren, NH, The Netherlands; [ch.] Bart and Max; [ed.] B.A. International Relations Mount Holyoke College (USA), M. Phil. International Studies Oxford University (U.K.); [occ.] Disability Pension Royal Shell; [memb.] Dutch; [pers.] T.S. Elliot.... "I keep my countenance I remain self-possessed...are these ideas right or wrong?..."; [a.] Moordrecht, The Netherlands

ORLO, ORLE
[b.] March 15, 1922, Isabella, OK; [p.] Mr. and Mrs. C. H. Maslatt; [m.] Bernice Bockman Maslatt, June 18, 1946; [ch.] Two daughters; [ed.] 17 years of Schooling Plus 1942-1946 in the U.S. Coast Guard - World War Two.; [occ.] Author poet and Traveling, Writer.; [memb.] B.M.I. Membership; [hon.] I have five songs out of Hollywood, Calif, this is on tapes. (I Want Your Love) (Homeward Bound) (Widow Town) (A Christmas Love Song) and dreaming of and (Appalachian Christmas); [oth. writ.] These five songs are with Hilltop, Records and Rainbow Records. I also have written 182 other songs and poems, also two novel. I burnt one novel, because, they said at the time, that it was too hot to handle (We Cry Aloud) written in 1946 - Destroyed in 1996.; [pers.] I write from the heart, I can not write anything bad about anyone, and all my writing tells a true story.; [a.] Waukomis, OK

ORR, DALLAS
[b.] January 17, 1957, Lethbridge, Alberta, Canada; [p.] Vera Chamberland, Lorne Orr; [m.] Cindy-Lee Orr, September 15, 1979; [ch.] Dylan Gordon, Shannon Maureen; [ed.] Athabasca University, Calgary, Alberta, Canada; [occ.] Chemical Blender, Baker Performance Chemicals, Calgary, Alberta, Canada; [memb.] Odd fellows and Rebekahs, Calgary Motorcycle Club; [pers.] I write poetry to express my emotions. If these emotions reverberate through to someone else then I've done okay; [a.] Calgary, Alberta, Canada

ORSOMARSO, MARGUERITE ROCCO
[pen.] Marguerite Angelica; [b.] New York, NY; [p.] Benjamin Rocco, Gilda Rocco; [m.] Dom. Orsomarso, July 2, 1955; [ch.] Donald F. and Gail M.; [ed.] Mother Cabrini High School, Hunter College (B.A.) Hunter College (M.A.) Graduate Studies Cornell University, Graduate Post Master's Courses in Ed. (N.Y.C.); [occ.] Teacher (Elem. Jr. High Long Island) N.Y.C. Connecticut-Retired.; [memb.] Volunteer (Local Hospitals, Nursing Homes), Christian Assembly, Educators Association, Society of Professional Women; [hon.] Dean's list (4 yrs.), throughout College, Medals (High School-History, English,) (College) language (Romance) Medalist Iota Tau Alpha Honor Society, Pi Phi Alpha (College Societies) Education Honor Society, Member of "In't Society of Poets" Member of Society of "Long Island Poets".; [oth. writ.] Numerous poems published in previous anthologist, poems distributed to churches Local Papers, Nursing Homes and to individuals throughout the US. Presently, compiling book of poetry for publication!; [pers.] I endeavor to bring readers to the realization that their main concern in life should be to go to the "Source" of their strength, their needs, their goals "The Supreme God" the "Source" of all things! Establish a "Daily" relationship with God!; [a.] East Islip, NY

ORTIZ, MICHELLE
[b.] September 18, 1981, Springfield, MO; [p.] Karen and Gose Ortiz; [ed.] Home Schooling for 2 years, a much more open and desirable learning experience.; [hon.] Tested IQ of over 160. Awards of Excellence in Art, Piano and Violin; [pers.] My poetry is reflected from the darkness and pain of everyday life and inner feelings from within. Inspired and influenced by the work and personal lives of Jim Morrison, Edgar Allan Poe, Anne Rice.; [a.] Springfield, MO

OSBORN, KAITLYNN ANN
[b.] May 23, 1987, La Jolla, CA; [p.] Dr. Terry Osborn, Barbara Main; [ed.] 3rd grade; [occ.] Student; [memb.] Girl Scouts of America, U.S.S. (United States Swimming); [hon.] Kumon North American Mathematics Honor Roll Jan 8'5 thru 1996, Swimming awards for 1995-96; [a.] Dunlap, IL

OSBORNE, JENNIFER
[pen.] Janer; [b.] September 22, 1961, Buchanan; [p.] Curtis and Helen Blankenship; [m.] Steve Osborne, July 19, 1986; [ch.] Chancy and Staci Osborne; [ed.] Grundy Sr. High 12 yrs., Buchanan Co. Voc. School, (LPN Nursing), Wytheville Community College, RN Nursing.; [occ.] Register Nurse, full time mom, follower of Christ; [pers.] Dedicated to my husband Steve, who this was wrote for several years ago and is a night-n-shining to me.; [a.] Grundy, VA

OSBORNE JR., ARTHUR ANTHONY
[b.] March 9, 1946, Shelburne, Nova Scotia; [p.] Arthur and Marie Osborne; [m.] Bonnie Lynn, May 21, 1991; [ch.] Six; [pers.] To understand the people in the countries of the world around us, we must first understand ourselves and those around us.; [a.] Sutton West, Ontario, Canada

OTT, WILLIAM BILL
[pen.] Bill Ott; [b.] June 18, 1920, California; [p.] Roy and Mirle Ott; [m.] Frances Ott, 1943; [ch.] William Gary, Kathryn Mirle; [ed.] Shillingly Staff College Army School of Physical Training University of New Brunswick; [occ.] Retired; [memb.] International Society of poets; [hon.] Five 'Editors Awards from-the National Library of Poetry; [oth. writ.] Book - Poetic Musings Book - More Poetic Musings, poems in local newspapers.; [pers.] I strive to write my poems in an easy flowing cadence with a musical quality.; [a.] Ottawa, Ontario, Canada

OTTOSEN, WENDY
[pen.] Ashley Aschenbach; [b.] November 5, 1960, Lakewood, CA; [p.] H. D. Ottosen and Joyce Ottosen Miller; [ch.] Kristina Renee; [ed.] Third year psychology major at CSU Dominguez, A.A. Degree from Cerritos Community College; [memb.] PsiBeta Honor Society, PsiChi Honor Society, CSU Dominguez Psychology club, former President of Cerritos College Psychology club, former President of Cerritos College club, honors program; [hon.] Cerritos College Bronze Falcon Award, Metropolitan State Hospital outstanding volunteer award, Dean's Honor Roll; [oth. writ.] A collection of not yet submitted poems.; [pers.] Vengeance and hate keep the cycle of turmoil - Love, intelligence and empathy slow it down. Quick-fixes are needed for now, but deep-rooted solutions helps prevent future adversity at every level; [a.] Bellflower, CA

OUELLETTE, RANDY
[b.] December 5, 1964, Chatham, Ontario, Canada; [p.] Gerard and Beulah; [m.] Kim, May 7, 1994; [ch.] Rejean, Annapolis; [ed.] Grad., St. Clair College (Business); [occ.] Factory worker; [memb.] United Steelworkers

OWEN, NANCY H.
[b.] April 22, 1929, Mass., U.S.A.; [m.] February 1958; [ch.] Two; [ed.] M.A. London; [occ.] Retired; [a.] The Sea Ranch, CA

PAIXAO, CHRISTINA
[pen.] Kisstina; [b.] November 23, 1983; [p.] Pamela Paixao and Rob Cox; [ed.] Calvary Lutheran School; [occ.] Student; [hon.] $5.00 gift certificate; [oth. writ.] This was my first, "Monday's" and "eyes in the Night."; [pers.] Write what you think and feel, it doesn't have to be understood by anyone but you!; [a.] Hayward, CA

PALMER, SHERYL LEANNE
[b.] March 8, 1948, Rushville, IN; [p.] Harold (Pete) and Bessie Palmer; [ed.] Rushville High School, Career Academy of Chicago; [occ.] Medical Assistant and Pulmonary Function Tech (Certified Respiratory Therapy Tech) Pulmonary Associates of Indianapolis Rushville Church of Christ; [pers.] I have always enjoyed reading poetry, but this is my first attempt at writing a poem.; [a.] Indianapolis, IN

PANGAS, MARIA THERESA
[b.] December 3, 1980, Royal Columbian; [p.] Theresa and Nick Moudatsos; [ed.] Currently in grade 11 (My Senior Year); [occ.] Part time working at Maple Ridge McDonalds; [hon.] Honor Roll Student since grd. 8 public speaking awards since grade 8. Student of the week awards. Completed a volunteer program at Ridge Meadows Hospital; [oth. writ.] Hundreds of poems I've written, many made into personal books; [pers.] My poetry has deep meaning within its words. Through love and hate through nature and kindness.; [a.] Maple Ridge, BC

PANVELLE, TARALEEN
[b.] June 1, 1959, Thibodaux, LA; [p.] Ernest J.

Gaudet Sr. and Rosie Adams; [ch.] Trinity Knight (son); [ed.] High school graduate of Central Lafourche High School 1977; [occ.] Secretary of U.S. Financial Corporation; [pers.] This poem represents me being a victim of domestic abuse as a child and again personally as an adult. No matter what lifestyle you have, God will protect and love you, never forget it.; [a.] Thibodaux, LA

PAPATHANASIOU, CHRISTIAN
[b.] February 10, 1984, Montreal; [p.] Mary and Hippocrates; [ed.] Carlyle Elementary, 12th year Centennial Academy; [occ.] Student; [a.] Montreal, Quebec, Canada

PARSONS, NORMA LYNNE
[b.] September 19, 1936, Mayfield, KY; [p.] Wrenn Barton - Faye Barton; [m.] Bob Parsons, June 8, 1968; [ch.] Melanie Lynne, Melissa Faye, grandchildren - Alexis, Erica, Andre; [ed.] Sedalia High, Murray Univ, Memphis Univ, other courses at Univ od Las Vegas; [occ.] Substitute Teacher Elementary Schools, Las Vegas, NV; [memb.] First Baptist Church Preservation Assoc. of Clark Ctny - Las Vegas; [hon.] "Teacher of the Month", "Parent of the Month", Sunday School Teacher Awards Poetry Published; [oth. writ.] Several poems published in local newspaper, personal poetry for family members and friends, writing a book on "U.S.A. and Southern Sayings."; [pers.] My poetry is a reflection of the happy memories I've had watching my children grow and become the individuals they are today my family and friends have had the greatest influence on my writing.; [a.] Las Vegas, NV

PATE, JOAN E.
[pen.] Jeep (Initials in name); [b.] August 28, 1934, Winston-Salem, NC; [p.] Sylvester Williams Sr., Eleanor R. Williams; [m.] Tom H. Pate, October 13, 1956; [ch.] Stephanie Pate-Thomas, two grands, Aimee and Brittany Thomas; [ed.] 1948 Kimberly Park Elem Sch, 1952 Atkins High School, 1956 Winston-Salem Teachers College, Yr Graduated, all schools located in Winston-Salem, NC, Graduated Studies - Columbia NYU and Bank Street Univ College; [occ.] Retired Elem Tchr from PS 200 Man 1989 - taught 1963-1989; [memb.] Zeta Phi Beta Sorority, Leaders of American Elem, Education Convent Baptish Church, (AFT) American Federation of Tchrs, (UFT) United Federation of Tchrs; [hon.] Honors: 1983 Teacher of the Yr. UFT Retirement Certificate Awards: 1) 6th Grade Essay Contest High School - Essay - Bio on Abraham Lincoln, 2) College 1955, Scholarship from Rho Zeta Chapter, Zeta, Phi Beta Sorority, Z0B, 3) Graduation Caswell, County Alumni Whitaker Hanes Award Anna H. Hanes Award, 4) BS Degree in Educ, Numerous teaching certificates for graduate studies; [oth. writ.] Unpublished, 1) Graduation, 2) Vowels and Consonants Rhyme, 3) tribute to Arsenio Hall Rap, 4) Numerous Wake-Up Rhymes, 5) Esplanade Gardens - Lyrical a directional wonder song, 6) Keep Ike on the mike, 7) Bio Rhyme on is age Hayes, 8) 1996 NBA Championships Finals, 9) Showtime at the Apollo.; [pers.] My creative expressions are based on my reactions to the five senses of seeing, hearing, touching, feeling, tasting.; [a.] New York, NY

PATTA, YODA
[pen.] Amy Oscar; [b.] March 12, 1983, Bandung, Indonesia; [p.] Johnny Patta, Ida Ramelah; [ed.] 1996 graduate - Sampson G. Smith Intermediate School, Somerset, NJ; [occ.] 9th grader at Franklin High School, NJ; [hon.] 1996 8th grade Outstanding Science Student, Outstanding ESL Student, Outstanding Computer Student and The President's Award for Academic Excellence (Sampson G. Smith); [oth. writ.] 2 other poems, "A Light in the Dark", and "A Teenager Is..."; [pers.] Friends are

always changing overtime, as we move from time to time and from one environment to another. However, the true spirit of friendship will never change forever, even in this turbulent world.; [a.] Somerset, NJ

PAUL, TRACY
[pen.] Tracy Paul; [b.] December 19, 1980, Ont., Canada; [p.] Helen, Gerald Paul; [ed.] Grade 9, St. Mark High School; [occ.] Student; [pers.] I like to write on legends and myths and the subconscious mind.; [a.] Ontario, Canada

PAVICH, ELIZABETH
[b.] December 30, 1912, Waraine; [p.] Deceased; [m.] Deceased, December 20, 1940; [ch.] One; [ed.] Two years College Work! Work! Work...; [occ.] Housekeeper; [hon.] Always high-praise no awards, "I have my memories" someday I hope to have it published soon... I hope...; [oth. writ.] My favorite poems "Because I Love You, Mother Darling", "Those Happy Days", "The Leaves Are Turning Yellow", "Dreams Of Mine", "Soldier Great Soldier", "Othis Memoria Day."; [pers.] "Wherever I pay - that's where - thank my hat; [a.] New York, NY

PAVLOVIC, ALEKSANDRA
[b.] October 25, 1981, Dubrovnik (former Yugoslavia); [p.] Idravko and Borka Pavlovic; [occ.] Student at Gunderson High School; [a.] San Jose, CA

PAWELKA, RICHARD
[b.] September 13, 1947, Wisconsin; [pers.] Is anyone out there?; [a.] Pflugerville, TX

PAWSON, BETH L.
[b.] May 29, 1954, Onsted, MI; [p.] Ronald and Leona Pawson; [ed.] Graduated from Onsted High School; [pers.] I dedicate this poem to my brother, Bruce K. Pawson who died of AIDS. I try to promote AIDS awareness through my poetry.; [a.] Adrian, MI

PEGRAM, ANNIE B.
[b.] January 2, 1933, Charlotte, NC; [p.] Fronies and Lizzie Mae Belk; [m.] John R. Pegram; [ch.] Maria, John Jr. and Regina; [ed.] Second Ward High, North Carolina College at Durham, NC, University of North Carolina at Chapel Hill; [occ.] Retired Teacher/Public School Administrator; [hon.] North Carolina Teacher of the year 1991-92, Cum Laude, NC Central University, NC Legislative Black Caucus Leadership Award, NC Math Teacher Award; [pers.] I view poetry as a unique way to communicate. I aspire to uplift, comfort, inspire and entertain people through my writing.; [a.] Darham, NC

PELLECCHIA, CAROLYN
[b.] January 28, 1978, Columbus, OH; [p.] Cesidio and Rita Pellecchia; [ed.] The Columbus Academy, currently a freshman at Kenyon College; [occ.] Student, Kenyon College, Gambier, OH; [memb.] Holy Spirit Catholic Church; [hon.] Cum Laude at The Columbus Academy, Co-Captain of Girls' Basketball team, M.V.P., 2nd Team All-League, and Honorable Mention Central District; [oth. writ.] Poems published in my High School Literary Magazine, articles for High School Newspaper; [pers.] Thank you to mom, dad, Anna, Anthony, grandfather, Sara, Jen, Laura, Beth and Kelly. I love you. This poem is dedicated in memory of Nonna. My life hasn't been the same. I love you.; [a.] Columbus, OH

PELTER, RUTH
[b.] January 31, 1925, Detroit, MI; [p.] William and Blanette Brooker; [m.] Ben Pelter, January 11, 1947; [ch.] I have 3 children - Bill, Mark, Madeline, I have 2 grandson - Justine West, James Simonoro; [ed.] Graduated Dorsey High School - January

1943, Fred Sands - Real Estate Course; [occ.] I'm in Real Estate in Mergers and Acquisitions. Also Sell Blue Cross Health Insurance; [memb.] Beverly Hills Golf Club was President for 2 years was Den Mother for Cub Scouts active in PTA while my children were in school; [hon.] Won Piano Scholarships for 3 years thru Herald express newspaper contests which paid for my piano lessons.; [oth. writ.] This is my 1st poem that I submitted and is going to be published. I'm very excited about this. I've written other poems but this is my best one so I submitted it.; [pers.] On January 11, 1997 my husband and I will be celebrating our 50th wedding anniversary. I want to write a new poem about our wonderful life together. My motto: Smile and Enjoy Life; [a.] Sherman Oaks, CA

PEMBERTON, CAROL
[b.] February 4, 1962, Winchester, ON, Canada; [p.] Don and Janke Morrow; [m.] Chris Pemberton; [ch.] Mark Pemberton; [ed.] Dundas High School, College, (Social Work); [occ.] Home maker; [memb.] Present Parent Council Ladies Legion, and many other; [hon.] Public Speaking; [oth. writ.] Only in over local newspaper. I would really appreciate it if my personal mate could be included.; [pers.] To Mom and Dad who alway's loved me to be heard. To Chris and my son Mark who enrich my life every day. To always go through life with fear of taking chances you miss alot of opportunities.; [a.] Chesterville, Ontario, Canada

PEMBERTON, RENEE
[b.] September 25, 1956, Fort Thomas, KY; [m.] Dave Pemberton, April 14, 1984; [ch.] Tara Lynn, Taylor Anne; [ed.] Bellevue High; [occ.] Housewife and Writer; [oth. writ.] I've written poem books and other books.; [pers.] I thank God for a talent to write. I hope my writings encourage others.; [a.] Elsmere, KY

PENNEY, HELEN SILKA
[p.] Doris MacWhirter-Bazan-Radomska, John Cybulka; [m.] A. Charles Penwill-Penney; [ed.] B.A., Univ. of Windsor, Masters Courses - Univ. of Windsor, Post-grad Univ of Toronto; [occ.] Teacher; [memb.] Women Writers of Windsor, Canadian Authors Association, International Society of Poets, Royal Country Scottish Dancers, the Scottish Club, Can-Am-Friendship Centre, Windsor Home and School Council; [hon.] From Students and Parents (Toronto) Social Studies - W.D. Lowe 100% average Univ. Course, from husband law - top class marks 1986, Poet of Merit Award - (International Society of Poets); [oth. writ.] Gems of Peace (all Poetry) Devon, England, 5 plays in the past, in-progress - "Wee Bobby of Greyfriars" - short story, India Catholic Journal (Univ. of Chicago) short story, many writings (yet) to be published, (general); [pers.] I try to instill in my readers on appreciation for the aesthetic qualities found in Creation and Creatures. Also I hope that readers will learn to appreciate the necessity of all cultures to practise the "Brotherhood man" idea.; [a.] Windsor, Ontario, Canada

PENNINGTON, JUANITA H. S.
[pen.] "Weeder" or "Nita" Swanson; [b.] February 4, 1940, Knoxville, TN; [p.] Raymond Hammonds, Ola Bell J. Hammonds; [m.] Robert Harris Pennington (Deceased), February 26, 1972; [ch.] Nathaniel Jr. Tyrone, Helen, Maxwell Swanson; [ed.] Knoxville Evening High School, Coopers Business College 4 yrs. Knox State Area Vo-Tech School; [occ.] Retired from University Hospital Nursing Dept.; [memb.] Knox Country Family Resource Center, True Vine Baptist Church Choir Executive Committee and Advisory Council of K.C. Family Resource Center, Chair person for Neighborhood Walk Committee; [hon.] Phi Beta Lambda, Membership Committee, Devoted and

Invaluable Services, Positive Attitude Award, and Letter of Appreciation for Great Services from University Hospital, Distinguished Service Awards from Knox Country School System, Certificate of Merit from County School Inc.; [oth. writ.] Several poem written, ne published in "Great Poems of Our Times", in the National Library of Poetry - Honorable Mentions for poems - "I Thought I Saw Her" and "God's gift and My Life." And there are others.; [pers.] To God I give the glory, for had it not been for my Lord and savior Jesus Christ I would have no words to write these poems. Since the Lord is my leader, I pray that these words will be helpful to someone a long the way. "Let Him Lead You".; [a.] Knoxville, TN

PEREZ, MARY
[b.] February 16, 1951, Buffalo, NY; [p.] Lloyd and Bernice Weatherbee; [m.] Raul Perez, May 11, 1991; [ch.] Tony and Shawn Vrenna; [ed.] Graduated from Tonawanda Sr. High School also went to and graduated beauty Schools of America; [occ.] Beauty Salon Owner and Stylist; [memb.] St. Andrews Church in Coral Springs, FL; [hon.] Student of the Month; [pers.] This is a thank you to Sister Rose for helping me deal with Mom's death and family. I hope to write more in future.; [a.] Tamarac, FL

PERLE, ADAM
[b.] June 20, 1949, Forest Hills, NY; [p.] Miriam and Sidney Perle; [m.] Joi Perle, February 3, 1991; [ch.] Kamal Jackson - 17; [ed.] B.A. Psychology Graduate of Adelphi University (Cum Laude); [occ.] Inn Keeper/Restaurateur the 1770 House in East Hampton, NY; [memb.] I am a member of the Mysterious Enterprises of Life; [hon.] I have been awarded the gift of life and am deeply honored; [oth. writ.] Journals, essays, poems, songs published song writer and singer. Turned down major record deal in 1982 with Arista producer Clive Davis of Billy Joel, and Whitney Houston Fame for a quite, contemplative life style; [pers.] With Whitman I embrace the cosmos with emerson I rely on the self with socrates I examine my life with love I navigate within the unfathomable mystery of life which is all things, beings, and worlds.; [a.] East Hampton, NY

PERRY, JOHN
[b.] 6 September 1943, Ireland; [p.] James and Eileen; [m.] Margaret, 23 June 1978; [ch.] Celine, Sean and Seamus; [ed.] De La Salle's, St. Patricks Classical College; [occ.] Real Estate and International Finance.; [memb.] Real Estate Institute of Western Australia, Australian Institute of Management; [oth. writ.] First book coming out soon! 'Something rotten in the "State" of Ireland'. Can be purchased direct from: JPA International PO Box 750 Mamdurah 6210, Western Australia; [pers.] "Make the most out of life as best as you possibly can".; [a.] Mandurah, Western Australia, Australia

PFANNKUCHE, MRS. DENISE
[pen.] DD; [b.] October 14, 1955, Oak Lawn; [m.] Joseph Pfannkuche, July 12, 1980; [ch.] Mark (6), Matthew (14); [occ.] Housewife; [oth. writ.] This is my first time every; [a.] Chicago, IL

PHILLIPS, PLES MASON
[b.] September 11, 1926, Buffalo, OK; [p.] William and Hettie Phillips; [m.] Guadalupe Martinez De Phillips; [ch.] Rose Mary, Effie and William Lee; [ed.] Some College; [occ.] Retired from Federal Civil Service with 32 years of service; [hon.] Albert gallatin award June 1, 1987. Dept of the treasury, James Baker; [oth. writ.] One book will be ready for publication in 1997. The title like the poem "No Time For War"; [pers.] Mankind must clean up the environment, build habitable cities in the solar

system, and begin the task of growing breathable air on Mars.; [a.] Sacramento, CA

PIERCE, BRIAN
[pen.] Syk.; [b.] June 15, 1973, Korea; [p.] Eiligh Raftery and Ken Pierce; [ed.] Bridgetown Vocational College, Weyford, Ireland; [occ.] Musician; [oth. writ.] Songs and lyrics, some local Irish publications.; [pers.] My poetry and writing is my life as I saw it through my eyes, and undoubtedly felt through my heart. My feelings, thoughts and dreams.; [a.] Montauk, NY

PIETON, JONATHAN
[b.] May 11, 1987, Voghera, Italy; [p.] Richard Pieton, Elizabeth Pieton; [ed.] I will start 4th grade in September 96 in Roosevelt Elementary School, Santa Monica, CA; [pers.] I am 9 years old, I enjoy nature and music. One day I hope to travel in space.; [a.] Santa Monica, CA

PILAPIL, MICHAEL A.
[b.] August 3, 1944, Wailua, Oahu, HI; [p.] Teodoto and Raymunda Pilapil; [m.] Arlene Espina Pilapil, October 6, 1965; [ch.] Lem, Armi, Carrie, Keith and Gunder; [ed.] Immanuel Bible College - Phil.; [occ.] Pastor; [memb.] General Council of the Assemblies of God; [pers.] We can be co-workers with God each day for results that are eternal.; [a.] Kailua-Kona, HI

PINTO, VANESSA
[b.] February 19, 1979, Chicago, IL; [ed.] Grade 12 - Cardinal Carter Academy for the Arts, Ontario, Canada; [pers.] Writing to me is freedom, expression, and life. I dedicate this poem to my mother Joan, Koji Nakamachi, and Elfreda Castonguay.; [a.] Scarborough, Ontario, Canada

PITCHER, PAULINE
[b.] July 28, 1964, London, England; [p.] Yvonne Pitcher, Grandmother, Else Smith; [ed.] Dante Alighieri Academy, University of Toronto, Bachelor of Arts Degree in English; [occ.] Student, enrolled in George Brown College in a 2 year Career and Work Counselling Program. Eventually I would like to find employment in an educational setting; [memb.] Toastmasters — I am a recent member and hope that some of my fear and anxiety about public speaking will be alleviated; [oth. writ.] Currently working on a children's picture book. I would also like to break into the magazine writing industry.; [pers.] It is important for me to approach my work in a spontaneous, lighthearted manner. I have been greatly influenced by Dr. Seuss. I would like to thank my mom for fostering my love of reading and writing, and for Mrs. Carrigan, my elementary school teacher's encouragement and recognition of my writing potential.; [a.] Weston, Ontario, Canada

POLK, MESHA ARTAH
[b.] March 14, 1968, New Iberia, LA; [p.] Ralph Polk and Janie Polk; [ed.] Graduated from the University of Southwestern Louisiana in The Field of Communications; [occ.] Marketing Rep., and Freelance Writer; [memb.] I belong to the human race.; [oth. writ.] Published works found in Amherst Society, and Nat'l Library of Poetry (bls) 1995.; [pers.] Seeking comments and writings from all who respond. Write MAP, 220 Verdun St., Lafayette, La.; [a.] Lafayette, LA

POLL, SOLOMON
[b.] February 26, 1921, Austria; [p.] Erno Poll, Leah Lipschutz; [m.] Ruth Z. Poll, January 24, 1950; [ch.] Leah P., Erno C., Seema B.; [ed.] Temple University, BS 1995 University of Pennsylvania, Ma. 1957 University of Pennsylvania, Ph.D. 1960; [occ.] Professor Emeritus of Sociology, Univ. of New Hampshire; [memb.] American Sociological Association; [hon.] PI Gramma Mu;

[oth. writ.] The Hasidic community of Williasburg, free press, 1962, ancient thoughts in modern perspective, philosophical library, 1968, several papers on social linguistics, sociology of religion.; [a.] Miami Beach, FL

POLLENDER, MINDY LYNN
[b.] January 22, 1981, Simcoe, Ontario; [p.] Don Pollender, Susan and David Marquis; [ed.] Grade 10 Student; [hon.] 2nd place in Science Fair, Honorable Mention in a Public Museum, Top Student in French Camp and many awards for basketball.; [oth. writ.] Other poems I have written: Real Friends, Mothers, Special Friends, Roses, Ending A Relationship, Men, Amazing Grace, A Dear Friend, Feelings and Life.; [pers.] I feel that everyone should be loved and if everyone was loved no one would be homeless and going hungry. I think that it would make the world a better place.; [a.] Brantford, Ontario, Canada

POTIER, MRS. ALICE LILIAN
[pen.] Alice Bridge; [b.] March 19, 1914, Winnipeg, Manitoba, Canada; [p.] Alexander James Dryton-Bridge and Emily Ellen, nee Baker Bridge; [m.] Paul Edward Alcide Joseph; [ch.] Robert William Squires Potier; [ed.] Kelnin High, Honours in 13 subjects, Academics and Business, Graduated at 14 years, Father in Africa as Bugleboy. Boes War, 1st World War. Wounded, died too young I was head of family, 2 younger brothers; [occ.] Just living, loving and enjoying; [memb.] 685 Centennial Legion Calgary. Fish Creek Senior Bridge Club. Kerby Seniors, Political groups, always working toward a good life for all seniors; [hon.] Medals for Dancing, a Plate for Participation, a Park Named for my brothers, alexander James Dryton-Bridge and John Liberte Dryton-Bridge, best High School Teacher ever born; [oth. writ.] Section in book 1.E. the Winnipeg Flood, Schoolbook, "Great Canadian Disasters."; [pers.] Please plant a tree, anywhere, everywhere, one child per family! No more war. Any religion can use the Ten Commandments all will be well.; [a.] Calgary, Alberta, Canada

POWELL, BARBARA
[b.] August 13, 1963, Cape May Co., NJ; [p.] Sandra Williams and James Bogan; [m.] Reginald Powell, March 28, 1992; [ch.] Tamyra Robinson; [ed.] Wildwood High School, Wildwood NJ; [occ.] House wife; [oth. writ.] Sorrow Cry, Stand Tall; [pers.] First I want to thank God for giving me the gift to write. I also would like to thank the National Library of Poetry for giving me a chance. I'd like to dedicate my poem to my loving husband and daughter.; [a.] Portsmouth, VA

POWELL, W. F. PETE
[b.] June 12, 1908, Converse, IN; [m.] Edith Leighton, September 3, 1930; [ch.] Jane, Kimbely, Shauna Sue, Devreux Lox; [ed.] Illinois Wesleyan BA Garret Seminary - M.S.TH., E. Ill. State Univ., M. Sci. Educ.; [occ.] Social Activist Taught H.S. 20 years; [memb.] Methodist Minister CA. Teachers Union ACLU; [oth. writ.] How to teach English learn the evil of Atomic energy save the church - a new way chaff in a whirl wind (a book 1st family to drive a cross. A column out on a limb (40 years).; [pers.] There are only 2 ways to evaluate life - one is money other is people. I choose people.; [a.] El Vacon, CA

PRADON, CORI
[pen.] K. C. Dragan; [b.] November 20, 1976; [p.] John Pradon and Janice Bruby; [occ.] Opening T-shirt/Art/Literacy business - Gothic Art Ink; [oth. writ.] Works in Progress "Gargoyle Waking" a fantasy epic, and "Perilous Thoughts" a sci-fi/fantasy adventure; [pers.] Cast off your drab raiments of mortar and stone. Feel night's sweet kiss and gentle touch of wind on your skin. Spread

wide your wings and fly fast and far to your destiny.; [a.] Otsego, MI

PREDA, LUCIA
[pen.] Lusita; [b.] November 5, 1978, Romania; [p.] Mariana Preda; [ed.] Graduated High School and now I'm starting college; [pers.] Leo I love you with all my heart. Love you Lucy. Love what you have and that way you'll live forever.; [a.] Rego Park, NY

PRICE, LOYD L.
[b.] Fairbanks, AK; [pers.] Loyd Price has lived in Yosemite National Park for thirty years. Loyd began his rock climbing career the moment he stepped foot in Yosemite. In 1973 he became the first Chief Guide in the newly created Yosemite Mountaineering School. In 1980 he became the Director of the Yosemite Mountaineering School and held that position for six years. Those that have experienced a Yosemite climb will understand the emotion and sentiment of this poem.

PRICE, ROBERT
[b.] February 26, 1976, Milton, Ontario; [p.] John and Carol Price; [ed.] Student at University of Toronto, Erindale Campus; [occ.] Student; [oth. writ.] The Medium, U of T newspaper; [pers.] If I was musically inclined I would be a rock star. I am not. I was given poetry instead.; [a.] Burlington, Ontario, Canada

PRICE, WILLENE
[b.] October 5, 1942, Winnipeg, Man; [p.] George and Belle Howes; [m.] Jim, August 28, 1959; [ch.] Lori, Shelley, Verna and Danny; [ed.] John Oliver High School; [occ.] I assist people in their self empowerment; [memb.] Ladies Oriental Shrine of North America; [hon.] High Priestess in Ladies Shrine 1995/1996; [oth. writ.] On Nov. 7th 95 I fell down 14 stairs. I was critical suffering a hole in my forehead, a broken nose a fractured jaw, 2 severely broken wrists, 2 black eyes and a hemorrhage. About Jan. 96 I started; [pers.] To write poetry until then I had never written a poem. Since then I have written approx. 40. I have been asked twice and responded by reciting 2 different poems for large groups of people. I am thankful for this wonderful gift.

PRINCE, SAM
[b.] June 17, 1971, Detroit, MI; [p.] Janis Prince, Samuel Prince; [ed.] Univ. of Detroit Jesuit High, University of Michigan; [occ.] Business Manager, Voice Classified Advertising - Kalamazoo, MI; [hon.] Evans Scholarship; [oth. writ.] Blue Mountain Arts greeting cards, Michigan Daily, American Greetings; [pers.] I primarily write about what's on my mind at the time. I try not to get too complicated. Complication usually leads to misunderstanding.; [a.] Kalamazoo, MI

PRISOCK, MARY
[b.] December 6, 1943, Hot Springs, AR; [p.] Steven and Estelle Ross Vander Ziel; [m.] Stephen O. Prisock, September 21, 1991; [ch.] Steven John and Tonya Lynn; [ed.] Pearl High, University of Arkansas Hinds Junior College B.A. Nursing. Nurse during Vietnam War; [occ.] Hospice Setter and Private Duty Nurse; [memb.] Christian Nurses Assn., Hospice Setter Inc., FBLA; [hon.] Hospice Setter of the Year, Sweetheart of Sigma Chi two years in a row, Honorary Chaplain of the Vietnam Veterans, Poet of the Year at the local chapt. of poetry writers.; [oth. writ.] Had my poem published in religious publications, newspapers and church bulletins.; [pers.] I try to convey my spiritual belief and my strong love of family, country and God in everything I write since I've been greatly influenced by past passionate poets like Lord Byron, Tennyson and Milton.; [a.] Pearl, MS

PRZYBORSKI, GLORIA
[b.] November 4, 1935, Chicago, IL; [p.] Frank and Celia Menze; [m.] Edmund Przyborski, June 12, 1980; [ch.] Donna, Douglas, William, Deborah, Frank, Darlene, Dale, many grand.; [ed.] Carl Schurz High School, Business Course, Elgin Comm. College; [occ.] Housewife; [hon.] Listen in Newsletter Editor's Who's Who - Newsletter Editor for parents without partners - 5 years: Newsletter Editor for Lake Marian P.O.A. 3 yrs.; [oth. writ.] Have had several poems and writings printed in Maplewood Care Nursing Home Newsletter and Hometown Newspaper; [pers.] I enjoy writing about personal or true life stories or incidents.; [a.] Carpentersville, IL

PURDY, DAVID. J.
[pen.] David J. Purdy; [b.] March 11, 1974, Oshawa, ON, Canada; [p.] Karen Babineau, Kevin Craig; [ed.] Attended Oneill Collegiate and Vocational Institute in Oshawa; [occ.] Civil Rights Activist; [memb.] Canadian Spokesperson for the Congress of Racial Equality the Native Canadian Center; [hon.] Attended the Ontario Literary build in 1987 for short story writing.; [oth. writ.] Article on drugs used by the school board, such as Ritalin, printed in Hampton, New Brunswick. Various unpublished forms such as darkness, your skirt, and innocent times.; [pers.] The only goals that should be formulated by the human species is to stop all forms of discrimination, to stop violence, and to destroy all misused drugs before we wife ourselves into extinction. We aren't that smart, to live forever.; [a.] Toronto, Ontario, Canada

QUINN, ELIZABETH
[b.] December 3, 1914, Carrickfergus; [p.] Alice and Henry Finlay; [m.] Samuel Quinn, September 4, 1939; [ch.] Sandra; [ed.] Methodist College Belfast, Diploma in Music Trinity College London; [occ.] Retired from Teaching, Supplying my work to schools, colleges, and festivals as requested. Also plays and musicals.; [memb.] Woman Institute (Retired), Towns Woman (Retired), Clubs and Choirs. Work through various Councils for good Cross Community Relations. Belfast Musical and Drama Festival and have made my Anthology "Reflections" included in the 1997 Syllabus.; [hon.] Made an Honorary Georgian Citizen in November 1988, nominated for Poet of Year National Library 1995 (USA), in 1996 Editor's Choice Award, now have been nominated for "Making a Difference award Saville and Lisburn Borough Council. Results later this month. A number of other organizations have included my work over the past year in various Anthology publications. I have set all my poems to music.; [oth. writ.] Musicals "The Old Wishin' Chair," "The Time for Living is Today", The Joy of Living, Official Recognition, The Honest Man, A Dead Cert. Also a large selection of I act plays for women. A Step in the Right Direction (music tutor Liquid Sunshine Book of Wine Recpts. Reflections (Poetry Anthology); [pers.] If you do not get what you like, learn to like what you get. Yesterday is gone forget it. Tomorrow may never come, today is here use it. Practice Love, Peace and Understanding everyday.

RACANELLI, TERESA
[b.] June 20, 1983, Queens, NY; [p.] Luigi and Rosanne Racanelli; [ed.] John Young Elementary, Hunter's Creek Middle School; [hon.] I have gotten the Academic Excellence Award for World Geography, life Science and Applied Technology for the 7th grade.; [oth. writ.] Several poems about love, relationships and thing's going on around the world and around us.; [pers.] In this poem I show how I'm feeling in certain situations when the rain falls or when fall is coming. I am expressing how the tree feels and looks when fall comes. I have written other poems, on other subjects such as love,

and how it can be pure and true.; [a.] Orlando, FL

RACOMA-LESSNAU, LEILANI C.
[b.] October 19, 1973, Racine, WI; [p.] Fiping and Bjorg Racoma; [m.] Jason Lessnau, July 26, 1994; [ch.] Dakota Winter and Ariana Summer; [ed.] J.I. Casehigh School Palm Beach Community College; [occ.] P/T Office Manager and P/T Student; [pers.] Poetry is my expression, my reflection, and my art. I see a picture of life in my mind, and the words flow boldly from my heart onto my canvas to reflect the pictures I see. Like abstract art, the observer will comprehend what he may and my poem will image it self accordingly.; [a.] West Palm Beach, FL

RAGSDALE, ROY A.
[b.] January 16, 1942, Springfield, MO; [ed.] High School; [memb.] American Quarter Horse Association; [hon.] Its an honor to be alive and part of HIS creation and a chance to grow and fulfilled in every aspect of who I am. The awards will follow; [oth. writ.] None, been to busy working and making a living for me and family. This is my first poem and I enjoy expressing my feelings, thoughts and experiences on paper. I intend to do more and write more. Thank you very, very much this opportunity.; [pers.] Is enclosed in this envelope.; [a.] Springfield, MO

RAITT, JACOB R.
[b.] May 2, 1936, New York City; [p.] Mollie Rothwacks, David L. Rothwacks; [m.] Dana M. Raitt, May 8, 1976; [ch.] Hope Karyn, Christina Marie, Apryl Richelle, Heather Lorien, Jennifer Michelle, Jacob R. II; [ed.] Ohio State University, MS, Ph.D., Columbia Univ., B.S.; [occ.] Consultant Pharmacist, Director of Pharmacy; [memb.] Amer. Soc. Health Care Pharmacists, Amer. Pharmaceutical Assn., MD. Society of Hospital Pharmacists, Amer-Assoc. Advancement of Science, Ad Hoc Director Laurel Oratorio Society; [hon.] Rho Chi, Phi Lambda Upsilon; [oth. writ.] Multiple Scientific Publications; [pers.] Self-esteem is a virtue - egoism is not. Justice is a virtue - law is not. Reason is a virtue - blind faith is not. Reason, justice, self-esteem!!; [a.] Laurel, MD

RALEY, JESSICA ADRIANNE
[b.] January 8, 1976, Fairfax, VA; [p.] James and Brenda Raley; [ed.] Graduated from South Burlington High School, VT., One year in Burlington Tech for Performing Arts; [occ.] Government Sales Manager Comfort Inn Tysons Corner; [hon.] Several Musical and Drama Theatre Performance Awards; [oth. writ.] Just personal poem journals, this is the first one I have ever entered into a contest.; [pers.] My father is the one who urged me to enter this contest. I thank him for giving me the opportunity and support to share my thoughts and poetry with you.; [a.] Centreville, VA

RAMAMURTY, MISS VIDYA
[b.] September 13, 1968, Madras in Tamil Nadu; [p.] N. Ramamurthy (Father), K. Bhuvanalakshmi (Mother); [ed.] Master of Arts (M.A.) in English; [occ.] Assistant Editor in a publishing firm; [a.] Delhi, India

RAMAN, MS. RAMA
[b.] March 28, 1966, New Jersey; [p.] Mother - (C. S. Lakshmi); [m.] Kasturi Raman, March 14, 1994; [ed.] Master of Commerce and Management; [occ.] Seeking for job opportunities in the field of literary work; [oth. writ.] Have written around 20-25 poems till date. Two poems have been published in an anthology 'Golden Thoughts' edited by Dr. Mohammed Fauruddi, Bangalore, India. Have a talent for writing short stories, limericks and possibly not.; [pers.] By keeping the language simple and easily understood, I want to gain the

attention of a wide audience through my writing. With my subconscious ever working, I tend to write on God, and nature.; [a.] Sayreville, NJ

RAMOS, CYNTHIA A. N.
[b.] January 18, 1946, Honolulu, HI; [p.] Joseph Demicola, Eleanor Demicola (adoptive parents) Alexander Burgess Jr., Edith Burgess; [m.] Joseph P. Y. Ramos, March 12, 1962; [ch.] Jennie, Jeannette, Joseph P.Y. Ramos Jr., and Alexander Jerome; [ed.] Kaimuki High

RAMPANI, ROBERT
[pen.] Bob Eagle; [b.] July 1, 1928, St. Louis Co., MO; [p.] Mike and Etta Rampani; [m.] October 23, 1950; [ch.] Steve, Gene, Ralph, Aaron Rampani, Roberta Dame; [ed.] High School; [occ.] Retired-McDonnell-Douglas Corp.; [memb.] 45 yrs. I am Machinist Union Office-Greater St. Louis Archaeological Soc.; [hon.] Single male parent raised (5) children awards in Archaeology writing honors in news papers, journals and newsletters.; [oth. writ.] News papers, journals, magazines, poems in many anthology's. Poem excepted for largest poem for peace. Poem "God's Land" submitted to president of the U.S.A. acknowledge, by Bill Clinton.; [pers.] I write from real life in a heart felt way. Can write from dreams and vision. Relate well to our door life, with interest in saving the land and Gods creatures. Special interest in early man and Pioneer days.; [a.] Bridgeton, MO

RANDALL, SARAH ALEXANDRA
[b.] March 9, 1973, Bury, Lancashire; [p.] Dilys Randall (Mother), David Alick Randall (Father Deceased); [ed.] Completing grade 12 by correspondence because I have Chronic Fatigue Syndrome. I have dreams of becoming a doctor and author of children's books.; [memb.] Past Honoured Queen - International Order of Job's Daughters, Bench Club; [hon.] Young Canadian Authors Award, Honour Roll, Western Civilization 12 Award, Passport to Education; [oth. writ.] Contributed articles to the Spartan. (School newspaper) "The Edge" and "Recycling Newsletter" - Salvation Army publications.; [pers.] Thank you Mr. Stott, Miss Johnson and Mr. Young - teachers who encouraged me to continue writing. Thank you Mum for your love and support, you have always encouraged me to follow my dreams.; [a.] Victoria, British Columbia, Canada

RANGEL-BRON, MARIO
[b.] Camaguey, Cuba; [p.] Easther Margarita and Ricardo Rangel; [ed.] Primary School - Camaguey Jesuit American College St. George in Kingston, Jamaica; [occ.] School Teacher Elementary or High School but on Sabbatical; [memb.] University of Toronto, Catholic activities, University, Membership etc. Some semi-private charity activities etc. etc.; [hon.] Don't deserve any really - shy away from "Limelight" have been told I was "bright" even "brilliant" flattering, yes, but entirely undeserved and laughable.; [oth. writ.] Yes - but not entirely confirmed to "poetry" although poetry so succinct - is a favorite. Am interested in everything in the world history, politics, art, languages, music (classical, popular etc, etc.); [pers.] Am not in the least bit interested in wealth or "fame" (which is not possible anyway) but I do treasure minimal security, privacy, family circle - and a small and varied circle of relatives and friends. I do some charity work but it has to be backstairs and unnoticed.

REASINGER, PENNY LEE
[b.] March 10, 1954, DuBois, PA; [p.] Emery Franklin and Josephine Bell Powers; [m.] Perry L. Reasinger, December 1, 1979; [ch.] Shawn Michale and Chad Edward; [ed.] DuBois Area High School, Penn State University; [memb.] American Heart

Association, United Methodist Women, Mid-State Literacy Council; [hon.] National Honor Society; [pers.] Within the chambers of my mind, I have discovered the truth about the adage that freely chosen discipline is absolute freedom. My true self lives within the lines of my writing.; [a.] DuBois, PA

REDIFER, ILO JEAN
[pen.] Ilo Jean Hunter, Ilo Munoz, Jean Randall; [b.] June 19, 1922, Salem, OR; [p.] Leda M. and James S. Ramsey; [m.] Jesse A. Munoz, February 26, 1945, Zack T. Randall, March 17, 1969, Everett W. Redifer, November 23, 1970; [ch.] Tedde D. and Marna L. Munoz; [ed.] Excelsior High, Norwalk, Calif., Woodbury College (3 mo.), Fauerhyte Maternity Cottage, L.A., Calif. (6mo grad.), Licensed Practical Nurse, Forest Grove, Or. (1 yr grad.), Society of Arts and Crafts School, Portland, Or. (3 1/2 yr); [occ.] Freelance artist, writer, poet; [memb.] Portland Fine Arts Guild, Portland Organ Guild, Wahkeena Chapter, Amer. Bus. Women's Assn., Arleta Chap., Amer. Fed. of Garden Clubs; [hon.] Many ribbons (mostly blue) of various competitions of oil on canvas and sculpture categories. Honorable mention on "Two Faced Jardenier" at Or. Ste. Fair, 1973, 3rd Place in Or. Mothers in Art on "Reveree" a small figure sculpture - award presented by Or. Gov. Neil Goldsmith, 1985. 6 Service awards from "Friends of Vista House" of the Columbia Gorge (Or. tourist site) 1983-6, Outstanding Service Award Plaque from Portland Fine Arts Guild, 1995. Editor's Choice Award from the National Library of Poetry for "The Dance of Words Upon The Mind."; [oth. writ.] "Lily Pearl Field" a short biography about the life of a pioneer woman and niece of Eugene Field, published by Chula Vista Star News, Calif. 1962 "The Little Practical" poem published in an Or. Ned. Journal, 1965. "Prism Reflections" book of poems self published, 1993.; [pers.] I receive inspiration through nature's beauty, dreams, and outstanding personages.

REEDER, LORELEI
[b.] October 14, 1971, Gaspe', Province of Quebec, Canada; [p.] Cecil Reeder and Judith Reeder; [ed.] C.E.G.E.P. Dela Gaspesie et des Iles (D.E.C. Computer Science), Bishop's University (B.A. Classical Studies), Tesol Certificate; [pers.] In my poetry I try to evoke various feelings that awaken our senses and emotions.; [a.] Gaspe', Province of Quebec, Canada

REICH, LISELOTTE
[b.] January 12, 1920, Germany, Flensburg; [p.] Andreas and Berta Riggelsen; [m.] Deceased; [ch.] Son and daughter; [ed.] 8 years public school, 3 1/2 years Trade school in Germany; [occ.] Retired; [memb.] Distinguished Member of International Society of Poets; [hon.] Editor Choice Award for contribution to "Best poems of 1996" by the "National Library of Poetry" or few price Awards in my time; [oth. writ.] I have a great volume of poetry in English and German, also several fairy tales and other children's stories - also in both languages, - reason that I came out so late is given below.; [pers.] My regret is that I came so late in life to this country, being nearly 42 yrs. of age and unable to speak English. All by myself, totally without training I've tried to adapt, with Dictionary as my friend and helper.; [a.] Lethbridge, Albert, Canada

REICH-PEEK, MILLIE F.
[b.] June 19, 1944, Olathe, KS; [p.] Geri Tetreau; [m.] Divorced; [ch.] John (31), Phillip (30), Vincent (28) and Beverly (27); [ed.] 10th grade/H.S., 4 yr. College (for fun); [occ.] I love crafts and writing; [hon.] 4th Grade perfect attendance at Central Grade School in Olathe Kansas '54; [oth. writ.] Personal poems to friends and family. Sometimes

when I write its as if someone else is writing. I also enjoy writing short stories.; [pers.] Writing is good for the soul. Do it for yourself. Write from your heart.; [a.] Puyallup, WA

REILLY, ERNEST J.
[pen.] BMW; [b.] October 19, 1957, New Orleans, LA; [p.] Norbert and Myrtle Reilly; [m.] Tammy L. Reilly, May 5, 1979; [ch.] Chad and Jeremy Reilly; [occ.] Owner of Designer Vans, Owner of Global Internet Consulting and Marketing Services; [memb.] BSA, United Methodist Church of Picayune; [oth. writ.] Vera Jean's Star, In Honor, The Doors, All We Can't, See, my Boys, It's All in a Nutshell, Always Out There, What is It, A Son's Letter to His Father, and several other sayings and poems; [pers.] I believe in protecting love and defending good and as long as love is protected and good is defended, we will always be safe. In this I strive for, by this I live for, for you and for me.; [a.] Carriere, MS

REIS, DEBORAH VESTAL
[pen.] Sarah Elizabeth; [b.] March 18, 1953, Dallas, TX; [p.] Calvin and Louise Vestal; [m.] Michael Reis; [ch.] Michael Christopher Hayes, Bobby Brandon Kinsey; [oth. writ.] "Dance On The Horizon", "The Space Between", "The Best of 1995", "The Best of 1996" and various other publications.; [pers.] My writings come from my own continuing spiritual growth and the knowledge I receive on walks taken with the old man. I'm currently expressing myself through a novel based on a beautiful metaphysical story of love.; [a.] Miami, FL

REISINGER, BRYAN J.
[pen.] J. Bryan Keats; [b.] June 10, 1973, Naperville, IL; [p.] Brenda Marple and Donald Reisinger; [ed.] Archbishop Mitby High School, DeAnza Community College; [occ.] Technical Administrator; [hon.] Published in "Amidst the Splendor"; [oth. writ.] Several poems in a currently unpublished Anthology; [pers.] This is for Jerry and Morpheus who were my soul and strength in my darkest hour. Eres Oso, Hermano, and shall we walk out twisted path, my dark angel?

RENNOLS, VAUGHN M.
[b.] May 8, 1967, Jackson, MS; [ed.] Tottenville H.S., SI, NY; [occ.] Rennols Contracting Tile and Stone Setter; [oth. writ.] I only wright for my own satisfaction and therapy.; [pers.] This poem is dedicated to the memory of Steven Langan, 16, who was killed by a drunk driver the night of Aug. 8, 1984.; [a.] Staten Island, NY

RHANEY, ANTHONY
[pen.] Anthony Rhaney; [b.] December 31, 1955, Bronx, New York; [p.] Willie Rhaney, Orine Rhaney; [m.] Dawn L. Rhaney, August 26, 1989; [ch.] Anthony Rhaney II, Candace Simone Rhaney; [ed.] Sweetwater High School, San Diego City College, Clearfield Job Corp Center; [occ.] Prison Ministry Evangelist, Self-Employed Auto Dealer; [memb.] Christian Faith Center; [hon.] Officer of the Quater; [oth. writ.] Poems read at churches, prisons, published in newsletter; [pers.] My poetry writings are what I see, feel and experience in everyday life. I write in reality; in effect, it's poetry in motion.; [a.] Pensacola, FL

RHEA, NICHOLAS
[pen.] Nicholas; [b.] May 7, 1979, Boise, ID; [p.] Kasi L. Rhea (Mother) and fellow writer, David L. De Roest, General Contractor; [ed.] Junior in High School Football and baseball; [occ.] Life; [hon.] When I was a freshman in High School, I won $25 for writing the school motto. In addition to that, the motto is now printed on T-shirts all over the country; [oth. writ.] Other short poems such as

"Love Is, Dreams Are" and The Prayer. Wrote Baker Hs Motoe in Fresh year.; [pers.] Poetry is a way of communication, communication is a way of life. "The pride and power that we hold is found in the heart of the purple and gold (HS School colors); [a.] Baker City, OR

RHOADES, SHANNI
[pen.] Rose; [b.] July 30, 1971, Flint, MI; [p.] David and Shelia Rhoades; [ed.] Fenton High School hope College; [occ.] Missionary (Asia); [memb.] Tried Stone Church Alpha Gamma Phi Sorority; [oth. writ.] Unpublished; [pers.] I began writing poetry to soothe a broken heart but now I tend to write whatever touches that mended heart, whether grief or joy. I was influenced by Emily Dickenson and Sharon Olds.; [a.] Fenton, MI

RICE II, DAVID WAYNE
[b.] September 17, 1976, Joliet, IL; [p.] Jane Rice; [m.] Mickey Jones, July 5, 1997; [ed.] Dropped out senior year only to get G.E.D; [occ.] Cook for Applebees; [oth. writ.] Confinement Of The Damned, My Soul, Concept Of End, Heartbroken, Shallow Sorrow, Passing Freely, Dying, Reap To Sow, The G.O., Blues, Untitled and more!; [pers.] Release your aggression on paper, it's the only way one will listen.; [a.] Columbia, TN

RICH, ELIZABETH MARIE
[pen.] Elizabeth Marie Rich; [b.] January 31, 1979, New York City; [p.] William Rich III and Joanne Elizabeth Sweeney; [ed.] Current School is (High School) Convent of the Sacred Heart, (Elementary) - The Little Red School House; [occ.] Student; [memb.] Of Womyn of Proud Heritage, Poetry Club and Forensics and Womyn's Issues (these are clubs); [hon.] Honorable Mention in school poetry contest.; [oth. writ.] Personal book of poetry, short stories - mainly horror and plays.; [pers.] Insanity will always be a fascination when you never know who is truly insane.; [a.] New York City, NY

RICHARDS, LEE
[b.] March 12, 1979, Zion, IL; [p.] Evelyn Richards, Jim Nutter; [ed.] Senior at Zion-Benton Township Highschool; [occ.] Construction Worker; [memb.] 4-H, Habitet For Humanity, The Encore Players, International Thespian Society; [hon.] National merit scholarship, candidate, various 4-H livestock and electronics awards, best actor as "Lenny" in Neil simon's Rumors (at school), recognized by Teacher Council for academic and community service achievements.; [oth. writ.] "Letting Go", a short story submitted for the NCTE competition.; [pers.] I write what I feel. My style is influenced by a great number of diverse authors and poets.; [a.] Zion, IL

RICHARDSON, AMY
[b.] August 12, 1980, San Bernardino, CA; [p.] Rea Richardson (Mother); [ed.] San Bernardino High School (current); [occ.] Student in the 10th grade; [hon.] Honor roll at SBHS; [oth. writ.] This is my first published poem, but I have been writing poems and prose since the 6th grade.; [pers.] "Do your best and leave the rest, it will all come right some day or night". A quote I heard once and took to heart.; [a.] San Bernardino, CA

RICHARDSON, RAMONA
[b.] January 20, 1952, Key West; [p.] Paul and Anna Richardson Sr.; [ch.] Ramon L. Richardson; [ed.] Key West High School, Florida Southern College - Major, Elementary Education Minors, English and Spanish; [occ.] Language Arts Middle School Teacher, Horace O'Bryant Middle School, Key West, FL; [memb.] Cornish Memorial A.M.E. Zion Church, NAACP, and United Teachers of Monroe County.; [oth. writ.] I composed a poem

for the printed program in celebration of my Grandmother's 90th Birthday.; [pers.] The inspiration of family friendship, spirit, love, and cohesiveness motivates my creativity as a gift to everyone. I teach and enjoy the reading of all poetry.; [a.] Key West, FL

RICKS, LUCILLE F.
[pen.] Lucille Ricks; [b.] November 7, 1917, Spokane, WA; [p.] James W. and Rosalie W. Bailey; [m.] Deceased, Cecil C. Ricks; [ch.] Rosemary Vinson, Peggy Sterling, James Hall, Wanda Mattucci and Candy Richichi; [ed.] Some College; [occ.] Retired; [memb.] Retirees of the Chapel (R.O.C.) Greater So. Arizona Area Chapter 9th and 10th (Horse) Cavalry Assn. Chapel I, Davis-Monthan Air Force Base Humane Society of Tucsan; [hon.] Honorary member 9th and 10th Cavalry Assn. Letter of Commendation from General Colin Powell re: My book Plaque of Commendation for speaking to troops at Fort Huachuca, Arizona.; [oth. writ.] Book: "A Buffalo Soldier's Legacy" (Published) Many poems as yet unpublished.; [pers.] I am a widow of an Army officer, I try to reflect truth and the love of God for His creation, both mankind and animals, I look for goodness in man. I love animals and try to make life easier for those who are the unwanted and unloved.; [a.] Tucson, AZ

RIDDLES, ESTONTENA
[pen.] Eleanor Williams; [b.] Galey, IN; [p.] Sadie and Eston (Blindford); [ch.] Sarah Rose, Francis Riddles; [ed.] Fisk University City of Memphis School of Nursing Northwestern University Kennedy King College; [occ.] Registered Nurse; [oth. writ.] Male Malthusianism Chrishology, Civil Hiberatism, "The Oak of M.", The Glass Gross"; [pers.] I read great poets and my philosopher is Bertrand Russell; [a.] Chicago, IL

RILEY, CARLENE
[b.] August 11, 1981, Newark, NJ; [p.] Avis Riley and Lloyd Reynolds; [ed.] Will be a sophomore at Clifford J. Scott High School; [occ.] Student; [memb.] Explorers Club - Boys Scout of America, America Heart Association, Park Ave, St. Johns UMC Junior Choir; [hon.] Music and Spanish - High Honors, Maths - Honors 1995 - '96 school year.; [oth. writ.] If accepted "Mother Oh! Mother" will be my first poem published; [pers.] I wish to dedicate my poem to my mom who is the greatest person I know.; [a.] East Orange, NJ

RINCON, RACHEL ANN
[b.] December 24, 1984, San Dimas, CA; [p.] Sharon and Jose Rincon; [ed.] I go to Hawaii Preparatory Academy, grade 6; [occ.] Student; [oth. writ.] I Am, The Magical Mountain Experience; [a.] Kamuela, HI

RIPP, CAMDYN
[b.] October 21, 1970, Chadron, NE; [p.] Robert Ripp (Ed.D.), Linda Ripp; [ed.] Wray High, University of Nebraska at Kearney; [occ.] College Student; [hon.] Having my poem published is a great honor and ward; [pers.] Life is too short to hold grudges against other human beings, to be consumed with hate and hostility towards other human beings, and to throw garbage into the lives of other human beings. Cherish the simple things in life, cherish the time spent with family and friends, and cherish life itself because never is an eternity.; [a.] Grand Island, NE

RITCHEY, WANDA
[b.] March 14, 1980, Holy Spirit Hospital; [p.] Bonny Shull; [pers.] Every path, I choose, I will choose the right one. I will continuously reach for my dreams, no matter how hard the may be.; [a.] Dillsburg, PA

RITTENHOUSE, ROSE
[b.] November 3, 1980, Seoul, S. Korea; [p.] Donald and Marie Rittenhouse; [occ.] Sophomore, Virginia City High School; [pers.] I believe that exposing the dark side of life in turn discloses the light side.; [a.] Virginia City, NV

RIZZO, MARIANNA
[pen.] Marian Rosen; [b.] November 9, 1937, Philadelphia, PA; [p.] Martin P. Maguire, Marie A. (Smith) Maguire; [m.] Theodore Charles Rizzo Jr., September 9, 1956; [ch.] Donna M. Martin F., Theodore C., Tina J., David M., Daniel G., Anthony J., Steven S.; [ed.] St. Hubert High School for Girls, Community College of Philadelphia; [occ.] Personnel Manager and Executive Secretary for Bachmann Ind. Inc., Philadelphia, PA (Model Trains); [memb.] National Association of Female Executives, St. Hubert's Alumnae, Single Parents Society; [hon.] The love of my children and grandchildren; [oth. writ.] Several poems published in "The Gleaner" (a local newspaper), "The Nanny Series" (Children's books), several short stories and commemorative articles.; [pers.] My stories and poems express the joy and sorrow, peace and confusion, humor and depth, all aspects of my life experiences as single-parent/grandparent, daughter, sister, friend and lover.; [a.] Philadelphia, PA

ROBERTS, KRISTIN MICHELLE
[b.] March 17, 1982, Houston, TX; [p.] Mary Roberts, Mike Roberts; [ed.] St. Timothy Catholic Primary School, Gr 8; [occ.] Teenager Poet; [memb.] St. John Ambulance Cadet; [pers.] The blindness of the world often causes us to feel alone but always remember that God will never let that happen! This poem is dedicated to Miss Liberator, my 8th grade teacher.; [a.] Toronto, Ontario, Canada

ROBERTS, MURIEL F.
[pen.] Siams-Tha-Tala; [b.] July 6, 1944, Sardis, British Columbia, Canada; [p.] Deceased: Nellie and Francis Roberts; [m.] Companion: Vernon I. Brown, C/L 30 yrs.; [ed.] grade 12, 3 yrs University College, Alcohol and Drug Sexual Abuse Counsellor; [occ.] Regional Coordinator and Executive Director; [memb.] Hey-way-nogu' Healing and Addictions Society - International Membership for A/D, S/A Counsellor - Northwest College, Bellingham WA 98226; [hon.] Softball Honors Awards for Recreational Fastball 1987. Honored Indian Homemakers Association of B.C. August 6, 1996 for Recognition and Support; [oth. writ.] Sacred Sharing, Thoughts By The Ocean, Tribute To Alum, Grandma, Walking With A Spirit, Tree My Friend; [pers.] I have been greatly influenced by my Grandmother with whom I walked with for a short 13 years. She supplied me with the spiritual up bringing that has inspired me to always write poetry for pleasure.; [a.] Vancouver, British Columbia, Canada

ROBINSON, JACKIE
[pen.] Jackie Robinson; [b.] January 21, 1941, Salinas, CA; [p.] Al and Jackie Woggermon; [m.] Ron Robinson, 1966; [ch.] One son, Robbie; granddaughters, Nichole and Danielle; [occ.] Artist, "painter" - Landscapes in oil and acrylic; [memb.] W.B.A. Art Assoc., Local Band "Sax and Guitar"; [hon.] Several Art Awards for oil paintings, song writing awards, short story award; [oth. writ.] Poems published by National Library of Poetry etc.; short stories and articles published in local newspaper.; [pers.] I believe we must contribute to our world, to leave behind a poem, a song, a story, or a kindness done for others.; [a.] Los Banos, CA

ROBINSON, LINDA J.
[pen.] Linda J. Cousins; [b.] November 13, 1955,

Indpls; [p.] Jeanne E. Cousins; [ch.] Chiffonda Ducking, Frances D. Cousins, Arturor Casimiro III, Jametrice Robinson; [ed.] Harry E. Woods Clark College ICS Scranton Pennsylvania; [occ.] Advanced Marketing Woods Wire; [memb.] 100 Best Poems, World of Poetry Association Crusaders for Christ Pentecostal, Zion Tabernacle; [hon.] Silver and Gold Awards 93, 94, 95, 96 World of Poetry Editors Award from National Library of Poetry Silver and Gold 81, 82, 83, 85, 87 90, 91, 92, 93; [pers.] I want the world to know we and how I feel through my poetry and remember me always I give my special thanks to my sister Cheryl Flora Casimiro, ex mother In Law, Sister Leronica Martin. For encouragement; [a.] Indianapolis, IN

ROBINSON, TANISHA
[b.] June 18, 1980, Orange, NJ; [p.] Deborah Robinson; [ed.] East Orange High

ROBINSON, TAYLOR
[b.] May 13, 1988, San Antonio; [p.] Darren and Cathrine Robinson; [ed.] 3rd grad; [occ.] Student; [memb.] Brownies all Saint's Episcopal Church in Pleasontan; [hon.] Presidents patch accelerated reader field day patch all A's; [pers.] I think people should live in freedom and peace.; [a.] Pleasanton, TX

ROCKEFELLER, RUSSELL
[pen.] Zalek Medain; [b.] November 18, 1976, Welland, Ontario, Canada; [p.] Lillion Caldwell, Evan Rockefeller; [ed.] Centennial Secondary School, E.L. Crosley School for the Arts; [occ.] Writer, Artist, Musician; [memb.] The Hyborian Age, Gen Com Academy, The Canadian Tolkien Society; [hon.] Proprietor of local theatrical group, responsible for several concerts and benefit punk rock shows; [oth. writ.] Several short stories, publishings for a variety of music orientated magazines. Currently working on several full length writing projects.; [pers.] In the words of the immortal Robert E. Howard (creator of Conan) "By crom, living or dead, I will not be a slave to such dogs for long."; [a.] Welland, Ontario, Canada

ROCKER, ERICA
[b.] May 16, 1966, Waynesville, NC; [p.] James Bryant, Alpha Bryant; [m.] David Rocker, June 27, 1992; [ch.] Twins: Gavin Chamberlain and Gabrielle Chastain; [ed.] Lakeshore High School, Emory University B. S. 1988; [memb.] National Advisory Board for the Association of Emory Alumni, Womens, Fellowship Coordinator-World Changers Church International.; [oth. writ.] "There I Stood" an essay (unfinished) to be published in a book titled "Different Voices." (A collection of unfinished essays written by the Alumni of Emory regarding a unique experience while at Emory); [pers.] I like to be hold the simplistic essence of life. My writings immensely reveal my heart and my appreciation for nature, family and for the human spirit; [a.] Fairburn, GA

RODRIGUEZ, NELIDA VERNASSA
[pen.] Nelida Vernassa Rodriguez; [b.] September 7, 1960, Montevided, Oruguay; [p.] Aida Dattoli, Hector O. Vernassa; [m.] Richard Rodriguez; [ch.] Christopher Daniel Rodriguez; [ed.] Grade 13 Ontario Equivalent. Sheridan College: "Using the English Language" Chiropractic Seminars. Premed School (Faculty of Medicine Radio in Montevided - Oruguay) - Administrative studies - Radio Broadcasting; [occ.] C.H.A. Chiropractic Health Assistant; [oth. writ.] "When I think of you", "Discovery", "Perfect World", "True Love" also earlier writings in spanish published in the spanish community's newspapers in Ontario.; [pers.] Writing is an affair of the soul, where the distant point of imagination confronts our most inner perception of the world, leaving us surrender to the sublime beauty of inspiration...; [a.] Etobicoke, Ontario, Canada

ROGERS-YOUNGER, ADA V.
[pen.] Ada V. Rogers-Younger; [b.] August 1, 1947, Oklahoma; [p.] Will H. Rogers, Effie L. Rogers; [ch.] Diana L., Jerol L. II, Kasandra E., A. Michelle, LaDonna Kaye; [ed.] Vocational Instructor Woodruff Center Delta College, Stockton, CA. Dujee High, Oklahoma; [occ.] Vocational Instructor Cosmetologist (Hair Consultant); [memb.] Progressive M. B. Church - Youth Teacher Sunflower Presents - Senior Agency (Vocal) American Singers Association National Beauty Culturist League; [hon.] 100 Most Influential Business Women (Locally 1985) 1st Place styling competition.; [oth. writ.] Several poems published in job newsletters - day written and presented locally (youth); [pers.] The reflection of my writings are from the heart. I have been influenced by the great writers of positive life application.; [a.] Stockton, CA

ROJAS, JHADRAN A.
[b.] September 5, 1966, Bogota-Columbia, SA; [p.] Guillermo Rojas, Giovanna Gomez; [m.] Sarah Rojas, November 26, 1995; [ch.] Matthew, Kimberly and Keith; [pers.] If we could only see the world through the eyes of a child maybe life would not be so complicated. We forget that we're just borrowing the earth from our children.; [a.] New York, NY

ROLLEY, MS. MARGUERITE
[b.] August 18, 1953, Maui, HI; [p.] Mother side - Japanese and Hawaiian, father side - Spanish and North American Indian; [ch.] 1 Jean-Christophe Philippe Sonny; [ed.] University majored in Psychology and 5 languages/college-diploma in Early Childhood Education/lived abroad to study people's culture, languages and art/worked with people from all walks of life, also the underprivileged/worked with the airlines as a stewardess and also in the public relations dept.; [occ.] Translator; [oth. writ.] Soon to be published. Non-fiction, greeting cards, short stories, songs, poetry, inspirational, narrative reflecting the life of today, our youth, the environment; [pers.] In one of my poems I have written: "If my poems touch even one who knows it may be catchy and something's done even if to the smallest degree I'll be happy to hear and see it helped to set a soul free." Through my work I wish to bring back the lost human touch. Where has the human touch gone? Are we so far from it? After all, it doesn't take that much. My profound admiration for our greatest Poets of the World, brings out the inner feelings of the heart and soul, throws a "Beacon of Light" to the World then and now. In expressing ardent feelings of love, sorrow, compassion, sublimity, calamity, courageousness, fortitude of all human virtues, they weave a fabric of the finest tapestry taking us through almost every stage in Life (before Death). The ardour in which they expressed the profoundness takes up permanent residence in my heart. I journey through days gone by. At times, it makes me feel I've lived then and now. I share in their vividly expressed sentiments, searching to the depths of the soul, the mind playing a very big role.; [a.] Toronto, Ontario, Canada

RONDEAU, JOANNE
[b.] October 12, 1955, Dubuque, IA; [p.] Helen and Edward Rondeau; [ed.] Dubuque Senior High School, Northeast Iowa Community College; [occ.] Certified Respiratory Therapy Technician; [pers.] I'd like to wish peace and happiness to all; [a.] Freeport, IL

RONE, CONNIE
[b.] December 20, 1952, Williamsburg, VA; [p.] J. C. and Dale Yeager; [m.] Sherman Rone, November 2, 1985; [ch.] Eden Hill, Josh Henderson, Hunter Hill (grandson); [ed.] G.E.D.; [occ.] Hairdresser 27 years; [pers.] To my husband for loving me, my children for believing in me, and my friends

Rick and Terri Anderson for encouraging me to reach for the unreachable!; [a.] Newport News, VA

RONE, JANET
[b.] March 9, 1937, Baltimore, MD; [p.] Deceased; [m.] Charles Rone (Deceased), March 9, 1979; [ch.] Four; [ed.] G.E.D. - I am now attending B.C.C.C. for my A.A. Degree; [occ.] A.B.E. Teacher at The Lellie Ross Learning Center; [hon.] Outstanding Volunteer Service and Commitment Award of Excellence; [pers.] Always have a goal to strive for. Never be discouraged if it doesn't materialize immediately. With discipline, hard work, faith in God and yourself it will happen. You are what you think; you act the way you think so always think positive.; [a.] Baltimore, MD

ROOD, MARY E.
[b.] November 24, 1950, Kansas City, MO; [p.] Wilbur Owen and Rose Mary Row; [m.] Ronald S. Rood, November 17, 1978; [ch.] Janice Lori, Jonathan, Charlene and Ross; [ed.] B.S. University of Kansas M.A. Ottawa University at K.C.; [occ.] Programmer/Analyst IBM Midrange Computers; [memb.] CPU, Who's Who International; [pers.] The written word captures language at its best and communicates to others what our minds think and what our hearts feel.; [a.] Stilwell, KS

ROSE, CLIFFORD
[pen.] Clifford Rose; [b.] January 12, 1941, Florida; [p.] Navy - 20 yrs; [m.] Divorced, 1961; [ch.] Five; [ed.] Working on BA in Political Science at NYU, San Francisco Art Institute; [occ.] Paralegal for NY State Dept. of Insurance; [memb.] New York Sports Club, Immanuel Lutheran Church; [hon.] AA degree, letter for running track; [oth. writ.] Vantage Press, New Voices in American Poetry 1980, 1981, 1983, 1985, 1986; [pers.] Life, a changing process as: Death/pleasure and pain/life, is multi-emotional, in that, God reuses humans, as humans reuse trees, after Death, a tree is reused for building.

ROSS, PHILLIP A.
[b.] November 14, 1947, Denver, CO; [p.] Allan R. Ross Jr., (Step Father), Doris M. Ross (Madsen); [m.] Stephanie Taylor Ross, July 17, 1982; [ch.] Adam, Austin, Justin; [ed.] Univ. of Colorado - 1926 Pacific School of Religion, Berkeley CA - 1980; [occ.] Pastor - Putnam Congregational Church, Marietta, OH; [memb.] Conservative Congregational Christian Conference, National Association of Evangelicals; [oth. writ.] The work at zion: A reckoning, fairway press Lima, OH, 1996, 756 pgs. and other misc. unpublished poetry.; [pers.] I describe myself as a post-ordinatin, born-again, reformed Christian.; [a.] Marietta, OH

ROSSI, JOYCE
[pen.] Marie Bell; [b.] March 7, 1942, Searcy, AR; [p.] Marion and Gracie Quattlebaum; [m.] Divorced; [ch.] Tony Rossi, Eric Rossi; [ed.] Conway High, Central Baptist College; [occ.] Clerk-Typist II, Dietetics Conway Human Development Center, Conway, AR; [memb.] Antioch Baptist Church, Rebel Reelers Square Dance Club, Ozark Creative Writers; [oth. writ.] Several poems published in local newspaper - Log Cabin Democrat 1058 Front, Conway, AR 72032; [pers.] I feel my poetry is a gift from God reflecting life, emotion, and nature. With much encouragement I am pursuing developing my talents.; [a.] Conway, AR

ROSSILLO, JAMES
[b.] July 2, 1975, Covina, CA; [p.] Dominick Rossillo and Carol Rossillo; [ed.] Redland High School, Crafton Hills College, Humbolt State University; [occ.] Student, Humbolt State English/Philosophy Major; [oth. writ.] Previously unpublished. Currently finishing a collection of 400

poems, continuously growing many short stories and starting first book.; [pers.] Integrity is the highest price. With this one day I strive to be wealthy.; [a.] Redlands, CA

ROSTA, ENDRE
[b.] July 18, 1909 [p.] Sándor D. Roth, Josephine Roth; [m.] Simone Pasche, June 21, 1946; [ch.] Clara, Vera, Agnes; [ed.] Budapest Grar, LLD, 1933, Counselor-at-Law 1938, + 1919-27 Calvinist College (founded 1531), Pápa, Hungary; [occ.] Retired Chairman, Institute for International Cultural and Scientific Relations; [memb.] New York Academy of Sciences; [oth. writ.] Articles about international legal protection of softwares; [pers.] Leisure interests: Logic, Mathematics; [a.] Budapest, Hungary

ROTELIUK, MAXINE
[b.] May 28, 1960, Berwyn, Alta; [p.] Dora and Alvin Simpkins; [m.] Phillip Emile Roteliuk, October 2, 1976; [ch.] Twins - Cortney and Curtis; [ed.] Grade 7; [occ.] Housewife; [memb.] Twins and Triplets Club; [oth. writ.] Poetry - The Road To 45, that has been published with poetry guild. I also have many other poems I have written, but not published as yet.; [pers.] I like to write what means a lot to me and also what I feel in my heart. And I like to be able to share my poems with every one.; [a.] Red Deer, Alberta, Canada

ROULEAU, SANDRA
[pen.] Sandy; [b.] October 20, 1953, Lethbridge, Alberta; [p.] Mel Langager and Birdeen Newsom; [m.] Conrad F. Rouleau, June 30, 1972; [ch.] Derek James Rouleau and Kent Douglas Williams; [ed.] Graduated Victoria Composite High School, Edmonton, Alberta; [occ.] Now on permanent disability since January 1992, after 11 years as an Administrator with the Life Insurance Industry; [memb.] Huntington Society of Canada and Multiple Sclerosis Society; [hon.] Was named Ched "Good Gal" of the day through C.H.E.D. 630 AM radio station for donating a poem for their Santa's Anonymous Program in 1978. In Edmonton, Alberta and was played repeatedly each year for approximately 15 years.; [oth. writ.] Was awarded first place in a contest with a community news bulletin. In high school my English/Literature Teacher published my first poem "The Poet" in the school newspaper and convinced me to continue writing.; [pers.] "The Journey" was written as a dedication to my good friend Gloria Williams who passed away in July of '93. I have been writing poetry since 1970 and it is my wish to have a book of my poems published as a legacy to my memories and lifetime experiences.; [a.] Village of Acme, Alberta, Canada

ROY, JERRIE
[b.] August 19, 1946, Gilmer, TX; [p.] Eugene and Betty Brooks; [m.] James R. Roy Jr., November 15, 1963; [ch.] James C. Roy, Barbara Ann Roy, Cynthia Ann Roy; [ed.] Gladewater High School, Gladewater, Texas, Career Development Center, Lufkin, Texas - 6 mo. business school; [occ.] Housewife - baby sitting; [memb.] Oak Grove Baptist Church, Nacogdoches, Texas; [hon.] Second Division Rating in (Solo) Band Contest, Saxophone, Future Homemakers of America, Choir in Church and School, Junior Red Cross Council; [oth. writ.] Wrote articles for Godtel Ministries Newsletter; [pers.] I wrote articles about how God had delivered by husband and I from alcohol and other problems. I wrote about homeless people in the ministry.; [a.] Nacogdoches, TX

RUDOLPH-ABERNETHY, ROBERT A.
[b.] February 1, 1955, Cranbrook, British Columbia, Canada; [ed.] Mt. Angel College, BA, MA, Philosophy, English Literature; [occ.] Private

Business; [memb.] The Shire Fellowship, Foundation of advanced thought and creativity, (Poets, Artists, Philosophers); [hon.] Graduation, Summa Cum Laude, Dean's List Honours; [oth. writ.] Pieces published in local arts magazines, and gay publications.; [pers.] The influences upon my work, the Canadian landscape, Scottish heritage, quantum physics, wicca, racism. Influential poets/writers, E.J. Pratt, Robert Frost, Dylan Thomas, Gerard M. Hopkins, William Shakespeare, Madeleine L'Engle, W. O. Mitchell.; [a.] Calgary, Alberta, Canada

RUSSELL, BRIDGET
[b.] February 8, 1984, Manhattan; [p.] Kathleen Russell, Alexander Kovzelove; [ed.] Graduated P.S. II Elementary School, going to Baruch 104 Middle School; [pers.] I wrote the poem, "My Father", when my dad passed away. I owe this to my mother and father who taught me never to give up. and thanks to my sister, Karen who gave me the idea to enter my poem.; [a.] New York, NY

RUSSELL, SHAUN JAMES
[pen.] E. S. Russell, E. Shaun Russell; [b.] Burnaby, [p.] Paul and Kathleen Russell; [occ.] Student, Musician, Lyricist; [memb.] Covenant of Unanimous Consent; [oth. writ.] Within the past year, I have written 150 poems, including "Quaenos' Pillar," an epic in excess of 2000 words.; [a.] Langley, British Columbia, Canada

RUTHER SR., STERLIN' O'KEITH
[b.] March 4, 1969, Rochester, NY; [m.] Shlonda N. Nash-Ruther; [ch.] Sterlin' and Donavan Ruther; [occ.] CEO/President of small two big tyme productions, Inc.; [pers.] Life is a big stage and everyone has to play their role...but, only a few can be recognized as stars! Dedicated to my children of which I love so dearly.; [a.] Rochester, NY

RUZENSKI, WILLIAM G.
[pen.] Bill Ruzenski; [b.] February 21, 1927, New York, NY; [p.] Madeline and William V. (Deceased); [m.] Ivy, September 30, 1950; Four; [ed.] Bach. of Civil Engineering from Polytechnic Institute of NY; [occ.] Retired Land Surveyor, Retired Associate Professor; [memb.] ASCE, ACSM, LIALS, NYSAPLS; [hon.] Previous semifinalist in my first contest for poem entitled, "Our Mom and Dad" published in the anthology of," Recollections of Yesterday."; [oth. writ.] "Before The Flood" (Copyright) Unpublished. Negotiating Contract at Present. "A Collection of Philosophical Poems" In Process of Copyright, Also unpublished.; [pers.] Writing for only a little more than one year, is due to my father's passing away that I have been inspired to write in poetic verse.; [a.] Levittown, NY

RYAN, MARY ANITA CATHEY
[pen.] Anita Cathey Ryan; [b.] May 9, 1937, Winston Salem; [p.] Mr. and Mrs. Joe J. Cathey (Mother deceased); [m.] Kevin Ryan, July 30, 1989; [ed.] College graduate plus many more education courses, I'm certified in teaching gifted children; [occ.] None - I'm a Retired Elementary and Middle School Teacher of average and gifted children. I taught 30 years; [memb.] Locke Home Economics Club, First United Methodist Church Salisbury, NC; [oth. writ.] None that have been published. I've written about 40 some poems no one knows about and about 200 four-line verses on my little dog.; [pers.] My purpose in life is to live far and honor Jesus Christ. My hobbies include reading, cooking, working with crafts, writing poems, traveling around the world, tatting, sewing, decorating, listening to sermons and doing anything artistic.; [a.] Salisbury, NC

RYAN, PAMELA
[b.] November 17, 1981, Chicago, IL; [p.] Donna

and Jim Ryan; [ed.] Lane Technical Institute H.S.; [a.] Chicago, IL

RYANE-MILLER, MELISSA
[b.] October 1, 1961, Winnipeg, Manitoba; [p.] Beth Graham; [m.] Les Miller, May 17, 1987; [ed.] J. G. Diefenbaker High, Southern Alberta Institute of Technology, Mount Royal College.; [occ.] Certified Masseuse and Health Instructor; [memb.] CACHS - Health Instructor, CNIB- Ceramics Instructor, Volunteer Secretary/Treasurer for Mountain Sanctuary S.D.A. Church in Canmore.; [hon.] "Scrivner's Palsy" Submission, Vocal Music Awards and a Blue Ribbon for baking.; [oth. writ.] I co-published a monthly news letter, several poems published in church news letters, wrote, reported and broadcast stories on Radio, and have put poems in personalized cards.; [pers.] To accept others and ourselves fully, without judgement,..is true, Christ like love. Only this will bring peace and heaven to earth. This is the belief behind my writing.; [a.] Calgary, Alberta, Canada

RZADCA, SOPHIA
[pen.] "Morning Glory"; [b.] October 26, 1931, Warsaw, Poland; [p.] Jan and Bronislawa; [m.] Ken Vavrousek, July 22, 1963; [ch.] John Vavrousek; [ed.] Polish High School in Lubeck, Germany 2 yrs. SF City College; [occ.] Writer of Religious poetry; [memb.] I am guard an of, family of God Evangelical Assn. San Francisco, Cal.; [hon.] I also paint in oils and I got honorable mention of my painting of our Lord and Saviour Jesus Christ at Methodist Church, Palo Alto, Cal.; [oth. writ.] Many inspired writings - Psalms, on Many Different "Basis of thought" - truths.; [pers.] I hope and pray for a "new earth" where love is triumphant and righteousness peace reign for God's Glory and ours.; [a.] San Francisco, CA

SAG, CAROLINE ELIZABETH
[pen.] Caroline McCullough; [b.] November 4, 1971, Adelaide, Southern Australia, Australia; [p.] Andrew and Janice Sag; [m.] John Wayne McCullough, March 30, 1997; [ed.] Bachelor of Arts in English at Ambassador University, Texas USA, currently pursuing Master of Business in Communication at Queensland University of Technology Brisbane, Queensland, Australia; [occ.] Graphic Designer, Writer; [memb.] Australian Journalists Assoc.; [hon.] Honorary mention in 1994-95 Texas Intercollegiate press assoc. awards.; [oth. writ.] Have published articles in Youth Magazine, and self-publish writings and poetry on the Internet.; [pers.] I am influenced by my travels throughout Asia, The USA and the Middle East. Travel can help define your outlook and I like to bring those defining moments to my audience. I am greatly influenced by Elizabeth Barrett Browning's Poetry.; [a.] Brisbane, Queensland, Australia

SAINT GILLES, MANOUSKA
[b.] June 27, 1976, Haite; [p.] Jeronne Alerte and Jacques Saint Gilles; [ed.] Midwood High School, Brooklyn College; [occ.] Student; [hon.] Music Award, Midwood High School, French Honor, Midwood High School and Brooklyn College; [oth. writ.] I have written several other poems but unpublished.; [pers.] In my writing I tried to reflect the troubles of life, most importantly the troubles of being in love. The humiliations, disappointments one faces once being in love.; [a.] New York, NY

SAKANO, ISAO
[b.] June 8, 1941, Osaka, Japan; [p.] Masaharu Sakano, Shie Sakano; [m.] Eiko Sakano, November 3, 1971; [ch.] Haruh, Eimi, Issei; [ed.] Tondabayashi High School, Osaka University, Emory University, Atlanta, GA, Ph.D.; [occ.] Manager, Parke-Davis Research Laboratory, Warner-Lambert K.K.; [memb.] American Pharmaceutical Association,

Pharmaceutical Society of Japan, Japan Society for Analytical Chemistry; [oth. writ.] Several haikus, tankas and essays published in local newspapers and books.; [pers.] I strive to reflect dream, hope and will in my writing.; [a.] Machida, Tokyo, Japan

SALATA, TERRY
[b.] October 15, 1968, Lethbridge, Alberta, Canada; [p.] Wendy Dawson, John Salata; [m.] Colin Callihoo; [oth. writ.] Numerous poems, several short stories, books-in-progress; [pers.] Hardship comes into everyone's life. Some try to translate it into sense, others try instead to beautify the nonsense. I hope to be one of the beautifiers.; [a.] Lethbridge, Alberta, Canada

SANDS, MICHAEL ALEXANDER
[b.] 9 November 1958, Nassau, Bahamas; [p.] Hazel Williams, Ruben Sands; [m.] Tracey Sands, 27 December 1985; [ch.] Three; [ed.] High school; [occ.] Pest Control Operator, gardener; [memb.] Miracle Valley High-way Church; [hon.] Marriage officer; [oth. writ.] Songs "Remember The Bridge", "Mother's Pray", "Determine to Pray"; [pers.] To God be the glory; [a.] Nassau, Bahamas

SANFORD, DEBORAH L.
[pen.] Deborah Manze; [b.] May 12, 1970, Norristown, PA; [p.] Mary Ellen (Lutz) Manze; [m.] Mark A. Sanford, October 14, 1995; [occ.] Secretary, Heyser Landscaping, Norristown, PA; [memb.] All Saints' Episcopal Church, Norristown, PA; [pers.] "My Mother, Myself" was written in honor of my mother who, faced with the adversity of raising a child on her own, did so with bravery, courage, and a lot of love. I'm proud of my mother, and even prouder to be like her. I love you Mom!; [a.] Royersford, PA

SASS, THERA B. ABBOTT
[pen.] Thera B. Abbott; [b.] August 31, 1929, Joplin, MO; [p.] Addie and Charles Loomis; [m.] Robert E. Sass, April 6, 1974; [ch.] Herbert L. and Bruce C. Abbott; [ed.] Quincy College, B.A. 1969, University of Pennsylvania, MS 1972, Washington University, St Louis; [occ.] Consultant and Teacher in nursing education; [memb.] American Nurses Association, American Association of University Women, Business and Professional Women, (Sec); [hon.] Honorary: Signa Theta Tou, Scholarship 1971, Award for Graduate study, University of Pennsylvania, Philadelphia, Pa.; [oth. writ.] Monograms, in pediatric nursing, Developing new programs in nursing education, BS degree Student programs in schools of nursing.; [pers.] My writing reflects the need of the countries to share in athletic events, to establish report and better understanding of each other.; [a.] Tyler, TX

SAVOY, RONDA
[b.] June 16, 1955, Evanston, WV; [p.] H.G. Jones and Beverly Corbridge Jones; [m.] Harold M. Savoy, Jr., October 13, 1985; [ch.] H. Mitchell Savoy III; [ed.] Marion Abramson High School, New Orleans, LA; New York University Real Estate Institute; [occ.] Real Estate Broker - New York, NY; [memb.] Church of Jesus Christ of Latter Day Saints, Real Estate Board of NY; [hon.] Award Winning Salesperson; [oth. writ.] I won a poetry contest in 2nd grade and have been writing poetry since. My grandmother was also a poet and wrote of our pioneer ancestors.; [pers.] I believe that poetry is the most personal type of history.; [a.] New York City, NY

SAWATSKY, BESSIE
[b.] June 21, 1922, Belmont, Nova Scotia, Canada; [p.] Bent Roode and Ethel Roode; [m.] Henry Sawatsky (Deceased), December 24, 1943; [ch.] Charles A., Kenneth P., Beverly K. and Betty J. (Twins); [ed.] High School - Colchester Co. Acad-

emy, Truro, NS Provincial Normal College (Teacher) Truro, Nova Scotia; [occ.] Retired; [memb.] Belmont United Baptist Church, Retired Teachers Association of N.S., Royal Canadian Legion, Branch #26 (Associate Member); [hon.] Editor's Choice Award - The National Library of Poetry - 1996; [oth. writ.] 1994 - Poem "Winter Storm" published by The Canadian Chamber of Contemporary Poetry, 1995 Poems published by Sparrowgrass, Poetry Forum Inc. Spring, 1995, Poem "Autumn Splendour" published by Sparrowgrass Forum Inc. Fall, 1995, Poem "Winter Magic" published by The National Library of Poetry - 1996.; [a.] Belmont, Nova Scotia, Canada

SAYLOR, SUSAN L.
[b.] December 1, 1948, Chambersburg, PA; [p.] Preston Cook and Dorothy Cook; [m.] David M. Saylor, July 2, 1972; [ch.] William Ryan, Wade Preston; [ed.] Chambersburg Area, Senior High school - 1996; [occ.] Executive Secretary; [pers.] My writings are inspired by my love for the Lord God and for my family. Many are personal experiences that have created special memories.; [a.] Fayetteville, PA

SCARBROUGH, JULIANNE
[b.] December 29, 1931, Columbus, OH; [p.] Mr. and Mrs. Burleigh Billingsley; [m.] John Scarbrough, December 29, 1985; [ch.] Three grown; [ed.] OSU College of Ed. R of S Courses for exceptional children Xavier Bowling Green; [occ.] Retired; [memb.] O.E.S., American Legion Aux., Cancer, Heart Ass., West High, O.S.U.; [hon.] Freedoms Foundation for a booklet called Footsteps to Freedom worked on the textbook done by Columbus Teachers about Columbus out of use.; [oth. writ.] As school teacher "Foot-steps to Freedom" for the Ford Foundation, Essays as a child for national contests. I have a little ready for teaching reading.; [pers.] Love as the vines entwine in John 15.; [a.] Columbus now Waverly, OH

SCHAEFER, ROXEANNE
[pen.] H. B. Ashley; [b.] March 6, 1970, Perth Amboy, NJ; [p.] Carole I. Knapp and Andrew Schaefer; [m.] Robert M. O'Neill (Fiance); [ed.] Toms River East High School, Brookdale College, Monmouth County, NJ; [occ.] Legal Secretary; [pers.] My writing reflects experiences and special memories I have shared with my family, whom I love and admire.; [a.] Toms River, NJ

SCHEMELEY, CORRINA L.
[b.] November 5, 1966, Salem, NJ; [p.] Diana Gates, James Gates; [ch.] James Neil Schemeley; [ed.] Delsea Regional, Glouc. Co., Vo-Tech., N.J. the N.J., Warden's Association, Correction Officer Training Academy; [hon.] Academic Achievements in High School, Dean's List in Vo-Tech 2 yrs., N.J. Warden's Association Professional Development Award; [oth. writ.] Articles in local newspaper; [pers.] Being an observer and good listener are two of my main ingredients to a well-rounded writer. "She walks where angels fear to tread" is dedicated to my mother, Diane S. Gates.; [a.] Clayton, NJ

SCHILLACE, PATRICIA
[b.] August 23, 1937, Alderson, OK; [p.] James Tucker, Willie Mae Tucker; [m.] David Schillace, September 9, 1957; [ch.] Rocco Schillace; [ed.] Guymon, Oklahoma High; [pers.] I have been inspired by my husband David in the writing of my poetry. My writings are for the pleasure I receive from those I love and remember.; [a.] Pittsburg, CA

SCHILLING, RICH
[b.] November 30, 1975, Saint Louis, MO; [ed.] Vianney High School Atn. Southeast, MO State University; [occ.] Student; [oth. writ.] Have writ-

ten many other poems and also songs. I front a band called Noise Star.; [pers.] I hope someday people will read my poems not just words on paper but as words to live by. I try to be my own influence.; [a.] Saint Louis, MO

SCHLUNDT, GORDON DEAN
[pen.] Dean Gordon; [b.] May 10, 1934, Michigan City, IN; [p.] Deceased; [ch.] Cindi; [ed.] 1 1/2 yrs. Indiana Univ. 1953-54; [occ.] Retired buyer, sales clerk; [memb.] Dist. Member I.S.P., AARP, Amer Bowling Congress; [hon.] Ed. Choice Award for poem in Harvest Moon anth. "Misfortune of a Damaged Man", 1952 High School Journalism Award for school news reporting, LaPorte Herald Argus; [oth. writ.] 5 other poems, accepted to be published in upcoming anthologies N.L.P.; [pers.] A poet can look either forward or backward, or at his present state. As we advance in age, there is more territory behind us than the future holds. Nostalgia, like daydreaming, can set a certain mood, and is often pleasant, but never forget to live life to its fullest each day. Tomorrow will be yesterday's dream.; [a.] Mattoon, IL

SCHOCH, PAUL T.
[pen.] Michael Freedom; [b.] March 26, 1971, Allentown, PA; [ed.] Allentown Central Catholic H.S.; [occ.] Foreman, Keystone Automotive Bethlehem, PA; [oth. writ.] Several poems and song lyrics compiled into an unpublished book; [pers.] Life is not about what you do. It's about what you have inside and never losing sight of your dreams.; [a.] Hellertown, PA

SCHOENFELD, MELODY
[b.] October 4, 1973, New York, NY; [p.] Gloria T. Edis, Myron R. Schoenfeld; [ed.] Horace Mann High School, University of Wisconsin/Madison; [occ.] Production Assistant at Doremus Advertising, NY, NY; [hon.] Golden Key National Honor Society, Dean's List; [oth. writ.] Active Writer of songs, short stories, and poetry; [pers.] I write from the heart, as it is the part of me I listen to most.; [a.] NY

SCHOTT, SEYMOUR
[b.] October 14, 1930, Toronto, Ont.; [ed.] N.P.C. School of Horticulture, University of Guelph; [occ.] Landscaper; [hon.] Botany Award, Botany Medal; [pers.] I express thoughts as I experience them. My thoughts run the entire range of emotions!; [a.] Windsor, Ontario, Canada

SCHROEDER, SHIRLEY MAYE
[b.] March 10, 1953, Pendleton, OR; [p.] George W. Rubbert, Sarah Mae Rubbert-Onstot; [m.] Philip Gerard Schroeder, August 3, 1985; [ch.] Sarah Grace Rubbert, Michelle Christian; [ed.] Pasco High, Trend Business College, Inland Empire School of the Bible, Moody Bible Institute; [occ.] Navy Wife, Homeschool Mom, Homeworker; [memb.] Body of Christ; [oth. writ.] Several poems.; [pers.] "You must be born again".

SCHUBERT, WERNER REINHARD
[b.] November 26, 1928, Mannhein, Germany; [p.] Wilhelm and Karolina Schabert; [m.] Ilje Ingeborg Ferlcin Schabert, September 2, 1961; [ch.] Reinhard and Alexander; [ed.] Elementary School, Secondary School Studies in Philosophy, history and Arts, Professional education in Church - and work, and Illustrations; [occ.] Retired Artist, once active in Man and his world in montreal (Expo 67); [memb.] I belong to no organization but work in freelancing of creative art; [hon.] I was honored in the year of 1956 by MWM for an Analysis in cypernetical Production Technology and for the Creation of Two Sculptures; [oth. writ.] I have been writing poetry in Germany since 1947, in 1960 I began to write poetry in English as well and

I have kept to myself.; [pers.] I believe in the classical conception of Socrate's and Plato's Philosophy and in the teaching of Nicolans de Casano who enriched Medieval Germany and the Renaissance to come.; [a.] Montreal, Quebec, Canada

SCHWAN, JOSEPH A.
[b.] November 30, 1915, Saint Louis, MO; [p.] George N. Schwan (Sonoria Fochee); [m.] Marie T. Schwan, February 23, 1939; [ed.] 2 years college; [occ.] Retired; [memb.] VFW, American Legion; [hon.] Many minor awards, nothing great; [oth. writ.] Songs; [pers.] It's great to be alive in the USA.; [a.] Saint Louis, MO

SCHWARTZ, SHERYL MARCIA
[pen.] Sabrina Black; [b.] February 25, 1962, Philadelphia, PA; [m.] Ronald Tab Schwartz, September 16, 1984; [ed.] George Washington High, Temple University, John Barth Center for Performing Arts.; [memb.] Head Injury Foundation, Endometriosis Association, Computer user groups.; [hon.] Won Karaoke Contest, got to cohost with DJ; [oth. writ.] Poems, (only began writing poetry early spring 1996), short stories, radio synopsis for school production of "Harvey"; [pers.] If I can affect people in some way through my poetry, then I feel like I've accomplished something. Thank you to all those who encouraged me.; [a.] Philadelphia, PA

SCOTT, KELLY DEANNA
[pen.] KDS; [b.] April 23, 1964, New York City; [p.] Harry and Eleanor Scott; [ed.] St. Nicholas of Tolentine H.S. Bx New York, John Jay College New York, Alliance Francise Paris France; [occ.] Filmmaker, Screenplay Writer, Independent Producer; [memb.] SAG-AFTRA, BFF; [hon.] Certified Independent Filmmaker, producer, Hollywood Film Institute; [oth. writ.] Several poems published in local magazines; [pers.] It is my destiny to be the best being I can be. I strive to make a difference in at least 1 million lives. I thank the universe for my cosmic being.; [a.] New York, NY

SCRABA, BRANDICE
[pen.] Brandice Scraba; [b.] April 25, 1981; [p.] Ervin Scraba, Elaine Scraba; [ed.] Grade 10; [occ.] Student; [oth. writ.] Several poems that have not been published.; [pers.] Brandice has always enjoyed writing either stories or poems. She reads any book she picks up. Poetry seems to be a favorite little pastime for her. She'll make a poem about anything.; [a.] Andrew, Alberta, Canada

SEARCH, JOHN
[pen.] Search; [b.] February 10, 1951, Chillicothe, OH; [p.] Mary Alice Copley; [ed.] Some College, mostly life; [occ.] Van Driver for the Desert Sun Hotel; [memb.] Life is my only membership and I'm strugglin' for the dues!; [hon.] Honored with this chance for publishing and I hope awarded with $1,000!; [oth. writ.] I have written around 700 poems in less than a year and a lot more, I fear!; [pers.] Anxiety, is in existence, where, there should be resistance! Search "96"; [a.] Phoenix, AZ

SEARS, TAMLA PATRECE BOLTON
[pen.] Tamla or Tamla Sears; [b.] August 14, 1976, Denver, CO; [p.] Tyrone and Patricia Bolton; [ch.] John Tyrone Sears (J.T); [ed.] University of Colorado at Denver; [occ.] Child Care Provider (Licensed); [hon.] Dean's List; [oth. writ.] Several personal poems, (Unpublished).; [pers.] "If you think education is experience try ignorance" Derek Bok.; [a.] Westminster, CO

SEBERRAS, WENDY
[b.] September 5, 1953, Toronto, Ontario, Canada; [p.] Lois McGarvey, Howard Payne; [m.] Robert Seberras, May 5, 1979; [ch.] Rob, Melissa, Matthew and Jeff; [ed.] Mimico High, Sheridan and Conestoga College; [occ.] Dog Breeder and Kennel

and Farm Operator; [memb.] CKC Member, Rare Breed Assoc.; [oth. writ.] Mostly poetry, short stories and many ideas for future.; [pers.] To achieve in poetry, what Trish Romance does in painting. Create and recognize a special moment, in a slice of everyday life.; [a.] Belwood, Ontario, Canada

SEED, MRS. TERESA ROSE
[b.] 13 February 1962, Gt. Yarmouth, England; [p.] John and Patricia Stone; [m.] Quenton Seed, 14 December 1984; [ch.] Cassandra, Melissa and Robert Seed; [occ.] Homo Executive, Receptionist abilities and writing poetry; [hon.] Guest poet for "Crossway Publications" on Internet; [oth. writ.] Friend and The Newness of Another Day. Published by C.C.E. NSW. Australia. In a volume called 'Poets Cry Out', soon to be printed.; [pers.] I endeavour to record life and it's lessons and hope to inspire "eyes of faith" and appreciation" - in myself, my family and others. A hopeless romantic at heart, a mother and wife - I'm busy in this game called life.; [a.] St. Mary's, Tasmania, Australia

SEGAL, RUTHIE
[b.] 23 November 1944, London, England; [p.] Ann and Philip Meyers; [m.] Alexander, 24 October 1992; [ch.] Karen, Tanya, Claudia, Alixandra; [ed.] Skinner's Companies School for Girls - Open University - City University; [occ.] Health Psychologist - Practitioner of BUQI - Chinese Healing, Hypnotherapy and NLP - Neuralinguistic Programming Herbal Life Distributor; [memb.] National Council for Hypnotherapy (The Hypnotherapy Register), The Scientific and Medical Network, The Doctor-Healer Network, British Psychological Society, Vice-Chairman of the International Centre for Special Needs Education, Rescare (National Society for the Mentally Handicapped in Residential Care) Committee. Honours and awards, BA(Hons) Msc Health Psychology H.B.E., Reg. Hyp.; [hon.] Poems and articles in UK various publications - Psychology Research Studies; [oth. writ.] I love it when the poems flow and I can evoke sounds, for portraits and feelings all in one outpouring! I heal myself and others too with my writing - that's great!; [pers.] London; [a.] UK

SEILUS, MATTHEW RICHARD
[b.] February 8, 1978, Summit, NJ; [p.] Richard and Suzanne Seilus; [ed.] Bridgewater-Raritan HS, incoming freshman, U, of Vermont; [occ.] Student; [hon.] Top 10 in NJ for extemporaneous speaking 1994-5; [pers.] Poetry can get me the chicks I don't get in reality.; [a.] Bridgewater, NJ

SERIN, BRANDY MARIE
[b.] March 14, 1984, Adrian, MI; [p.] Tammy Keller, and Louis Serin; [ed.] Going into 7th Grade; [pers.] My writings reflect my present moods.; [a.] Tecumseh, MI

SERRA, PETER F.
[b.] October 31, 1946, Brooklyn, NY; [p.] Margaret Cavaliere and Peter F. Serra; [m.] Rosalie A. Mangone Serra, November 18, 1967; [ch.] Lorianne, Peter, Stephen; [occ.] Senior Stationary Engineer with New York City Police Department.; [oth. writ.] Unpublished book of poetry "Christian Visions From A Common Man."; [pers.] My writing is greatly influenced by the truth contained within the Holy Scriptures. Hopefully the poetry will add to the glory of God and lend insight to his truth.; [a.] Brooklyn, NY

SEVELLE, TAJA
[pen.] T. A. Sevelle; [b.] Minneapolis, MN; [occ.] Songwriter, Singer, Author, Songwriter for Warner/Chappel Music, c/o John Titta; [hon.] Wrote song "Love is Contagious" which hit the top ten pop charts in England.; [oth. writ.] Released two solo albums on warner Bros/Reprise/Paisley Park Records, have placed songs on various albums throughout the world, including Johnny Mathis", "All About Love" (song: "Let Me Be The One" written with Burt Bacharach and Denise Rich). Currently recording upcoming album with Nile Rodgers.; [pers.] Truth and love, as summed up in the poem, are not measured by time or perfection. Truth and love stand alone, quietly, nobly, with a sovereignty of their own.; [a.] New York, NY

SEXTON, RUPERT
[pen.] Lurch; [b.] September 20, 1971, Limerick, Ireland; [ed.] High School, part Educated Accountant; [occ.] Full time writer of Novels, Poems, Articles; [oth. writ.] Several poems and I am presently writing my first novel and looking for interested publishers; [pers.] Image is an exploration, adventure and journey restricted by stigma, low intellect, and bitterness. Treasure the gift of image and portray and share it at every opportunity.; [a.] Mississuaga, Ontario, Canada

SEYMOUR, DANIEL T.
[pen.] Daniel Frost; [b.] December 30, 1962, New Brunswick, Canada; [occ.] Sous Chef; [oth. writ.] "Togetherness" (81), "Blue Sky" (93), "To Have My Arms Around You" (89), "Clear Skies", "Jimnys Rainbow" (95), (Rainbow Eve 90) "In the Mist of My Confusion" (90), "Friendship" 89; [pers.] "To Be Wise Is To Stay Young, And Not To Grow Old Inside" (89). My inspiration comes from the special people I have met in my life. For without them I would not be able to.; [a.] Calgary, Alberta, Canada

SHABRONSKY, ERIC S.
[pen.] Eric Cess; [b.] August 21, 1967, NY; [p.] Stanley, Dorothy Shabronsky; [m.] Alison; [ed.] Master of Social Work Yeshiva University, NY; [occ.] Psychotherapist Specializing in Children and Adolescents; [memb.] AOPA, NASW; [hon.] Private Pilots License; [oth. writ.] Several poems focusing on the beauty of our natural world and universe.; [pers.] Take a moment, look, listen, touch and smell the beauty all around. An autumn leaf, a singing bird, a summer's evening, a child's giggle. Take a moment and enjoy.; [a.] Long Beach, NY

SHAFER, JOYCE E.
[b.] August 3, 1928, Wisner, LA; [p.] J. Lester and Alva Cupit Evans; [m.] Deceased; [ch.] Charles Davis Jr., JoLynn Wallace and Albert Davis; [ed.] Alexandria Business College, Alexandria, LA; [occ.] Retired; [memb.] First United Methodist Church, God's Recycled Angels, Internation Society of Poets, Co-ordinate Children's Bible Club; [hon.] Editors Choice 2 Previous publications of poems with National Library of Poetry; [oth. writ.] Poems published in school and local newspapers, Reflections of Light and Best Poems of 1996.; [pers.] Most of my poems try to reflect the joy and serenity and peace in my Christian walk. My deepest desire is to help and reach out to others and to be an encourager. I work with Seniors in Nursing Homes and children K-6th grade. I love people.; [a.] Alexandria, LA

SHANNON, GEORGE WARD
[pen.] "Ode To Nature"; [b.] September 22, 1920, Tazewell, VA; [p.] Rev. and Mrs. Beverly O. Shannon; [m.] Frances Terrell Shannon, November 4, 1946; [ch.] Sandra, Ann, Carol, Karen, George Jr.; [ed.] B.S. Davidson College 1942, MD University of VA 1945 Diplomat of America Board of Urology 1957.; [occ.] Retired; [memb.] AMA Carolina Urological Assn Rotarian, Civitan - Wrightsboro Baptist Church.; [oth. writ.] Medical publications; [pers.] I see in nature, God's Beauty and love.; [a.] Wilmington, NC

SHARMA, SAROJINI
[b.] November 2, 1938, India; [p.] Brahma Swarup, Kanta Sharma; [m.] Raja Ram Sharma, January 26, 1964; [ch.] Priti Bhardwaj, Samir Sharma; [ed.] M.A. (History) Agra University, India, B.T. Agra University, India; [occ.] History Teacher, Govt., Girls Hr. Sec. School Delhi, India; [oth. writ.] Some poems published in Indian magazines in India; [a.] Torrington, CT

SHARPE, LOUISE K.
[b.] January 15, 1929, Scotland Neck, NC; [p.] Willie L. and Carrie P. Keel; [m.] Thomas B. Sharpe, June 16, 1950; [ch.] Larry Thomas Sharpe; [ed.] High School Graduate 1948 Whitakers High School Whitakers, NC; [occ.] Retired Carolina Telephone and Telegraph Co. 1991; [memb.] South Rocky Mount Church of God Senior Adult Sunday School Teacher.

SHATZEL, GEORGE F.
[b.] July 20, 1921, Rochester, NY; [occ.] Retired - McCurdys and Co Dept Store - Clerk in men's Dept; [memb.] VFW - Post 6259 American Legion - Post 100; [hon.] World War II - 5 Battle Stars; [oth. writ.] After my 170 oil painting I decided to write a poem for each one I painted in the future; [pers.] I am primitive started painting when I was art at 60 yrs old retired as store clerk when I was 69 wrote my first poem when I was 74 present age 75, completed 188 paintings, completed 21 poems; [a.] Rochester, NY

SHAW, ROSEMARY
[pen.] Rose Shaw; [b.] March 25, 1931, Detroit, MI; [p.] Charley and Lillian Jackson; [m.] Alphonso Robert Shaw, July 7, 1951; [ch.] Leslie Cornelius, Susan Hosey, Judith Wood; [ed.] Eastern High, Wayne State University; [occ.] Retired Dance Accompanist, Kettering High School; [memb.] Former member of: Wayne University's Bonstel Theatre, Peddy Players, Detroit Civic Center Theatre, Director and Sponsor of Christian Drama Guild; [oth. writ.] Black Lady, Some Place To Be Nobody, Prayer Express, What Is, songs and short poems by "Beaver Rose" Paid in full (song), They Didn't Know A Class Is A Gas, Moma, etc.; [pers.] My writing is as diversified as my life's experiences, when the earth has claimed my body. My thoughts shall forever remain with my family and closest friends and those who would dare ponder their deeper meaning.; [a.] Detroit, MI

SHAW IV, NORMAN
[b.] March 3, 1970, Lowell, MA; [p.] Peter Delmore, Diane Delmore; [ed.] Chelmsford High School; [occ.] Concrete Finisher; [pers.] Live each day like it was your last, for it just might be! [a.] Lowell, MA

SHEBLE, BONNIE
[b.] October 7, 1943, Des Moines, IA; [p.] Albert Gail Wolfkill and Zella Wolfkill; [m.] William L. Sheble Jr., June 22, 1963; [ch.] Bill Leo III, Bruce Albert, Bradley Charles Shannon Lee, Shawn Gary; [ed.] San Bernardino High School; [occ.] Homemaker; [pers.] I write poetry for myself when an occasion moves me to put thoughts down on issues that matter to me. When I wrote "choices" it made me reflect on how our lives really rotate around the decisions we make in our lives.; [a.] San Bernardino, CA

SHEPPERD, MRS. SYLVIA
[b.] May 11, 1944, Hawthorn, NV; [p.] Mr. and Mrs. Robert J. Evans (both Deceased); [m.] Milton R. Shepperd, May 1, 1991; [oth. writ.] I've keep my songs that I have wrote. None have been published. I don't know if any are good enough, they are mostly country/Western.; [pers.] My poem friends came from finding a wonderful friend from church, so I wrote it for her since she'd the

one who aspired me to write this poem. My special and dear friend is Velda Doye from Waco, Texas.; [a.] Waco, TX

SHERMAN, VIVIAN
[b.] New York; [ch.] Kristina and Brownie; [oth. writ.] I've also written several poems and plays.; [a.] Sunshine, FL

SIEFRIED, KRISTA
[b.] January 1, 1983, Kitchener, Ontario; [p.] Joe, Sue; [ed.] I'm in the eight grade at Blessed Sacrament in Kitchener, Ontario; [hon.] Won for public speaking, honored to have an excellent family! Led my county to winning the "Thinkbowl Competition"; [oth. writ.] Many, many other unpublished poems...; [pers.] I was told by someone to make the most important thing in your life into your Philosophy. That being my family. All of them. Stick with the people who stick to you. For life.; [a.] Kitchener, Ontario, Canada

SIEMEN, PAUL
[b.] October 25, 1919, Chicago, IL; [m.] Myong-Hi Moon Siemen, September 1, 1988; [occ.] Engineer; [pers.] Poorly mated sounds make noise, not music. Similarly, poorly matched words make little sense and offer no pleasure.; [a.] Los Angeles, CA

SIEV, ISRAEL
[pen.] Izzy Siev; [b.] May 29, 1929, New York, NY; [m.] Yasuko Morita Siev, June 30, 1960; [ch.] David and Kenneth Siev; [ed.] Queens College Graduated, 1979 (Adult Collegiate Education, at age 50); [occ.] Retired Postal Clerk Edits Crucial Concepts, a newsletter Mainly as a hobby.; [memb.] Toastmasters Jewish War Veterans; [hon.] Assorted Plaques and Commendations for community work.; [oth. writ.] Poems, letters-to-editors, and smaller pieces appearing mainly in local neighborhood papers.; [pers.] I believe that over populations is the most dangerous problem confronting the human race today. Fewer children will produce a world in which there is enough for everybody. And will go a long way in producing stable and happy homes.; [a.] Ozone Park, NY

SIMON JR., MIKE
[b.] July 20, 1981, Aurora, CA; [p.] Mike Simon, Terry Simon; [ed.] Pearblossom Private School; [oth. writ.] Not published yet; [pers.] My poetry at best is an attempt at putting my feelings on paper.; [a.] Fallbrook, CA

SIMONSON, SHEILA
[b.] July 26, 1966, Winnipeg, Manitoba, Canada; [ch.] Robert Simonson; [ed.] John Rennie High, University of Manitoba; [memb.] Adult Student Association, Student Ambassador Program; [hon.] Dean's List; [oth. writ.] Several poems, short stories and articles published in local newspapers, opinions column in campus paper 'Manitoban'.; [pers.] In my writing I hope to capture the essence of the human experience and to reflect the many shades of womanhood.; [a.] Winnipeg, Manitoba, Canada

SINCLAIR, DAVE
[pen.] Raddy Daddy; [b.] September 11, 1965, Jamaica; [p.] Basil Sinclair, Lorna McKoy; [m.] Olga Walcott; [ch.] Dave Jr., Alexis, Damian, Richard, Danica, Davon, Trisha, Daquan Sinclair; [ed.] Prospect Heights High School, American Business Institute and Allen School for Nursing; [occ.] Nurse Assistance/Orderly; [hon.] A medal received from Korea: Painting of Rasta farian in water color. Recognition of hardwork and talent.; [oth. writ.] Songs lyrics, What If The Babies Stop Crying, The Bad Side, Why Some People Don't Like To See Others Survive, Forbidden Fruit, Luck Shot; In my writing and try to reflect on what's happening now. Reaching out to all mean

people of the world, it is not what you see. If you don't have any love in your heart, then how do you expect to cross?; [a.] Brooklyn, NY

SKILJ, PAM
[b.] October 16, 1980, Santa Clara, CA; [p.] Stane Skilj, Niko Skilj; [ed.] Saint Francis High School; [occ.] Student; [pers.] I play soccer year round and am going for a college scholarship. I push myself to be the best in anything I do and I settle for nothing less.; [a.] Los Altos, CA

SKILTON, JOAN COTE
[b.] July 1, 1920, London, England; [m.] July 18, 1942; [ch.] One son; [pers.] I joined the women's auxilary air force in 1940 working for air ministry London on long distance communications. I met my husband, french Canadian, and we married in 1942. I came to Canada as a war bride in 1944. His family were wonderful to me.; [a.] Dollard Des Ormeaux, Province of Quebec, Canada

SLINKARD, EVELYN
[b.] November 11, 1948, MO:; [p.] Josephine and Martin Backes; [m.] Greg Slinkard, September 22, 1990; [ch.] Michelle and Megan; [ed.] B.S. in Education Assoc. of Arts in Nursing; [occ.] RN - staff nurse at St. Mary's Health Center; [oth. writ.] Poems about my children. Poems written to husband; [pers.] I love to write about my children. Strive to do your best and look within yourself for strength and answers.; [a.] Jefferson City, MO

SMALL, DARLENE
[b.] North Carolina; [p.] Mr. and Mrs. Charles J. Mitchell; [m.] Mr. Clarence Small, July 7, 1991; [ch.] Cody; [ed.] BS in Secondary Education, Biology, Religion, Oakwood College; [occ.] Principal/Teacher; [oth. writ.] Written over a 100 poems and in search for a publisher.; [pers.] God has given us so much, yet we use so little. I write to reach people and to make a change.; [a.] Kansas City, KS

SMITH, ADAM D.
[b.] December 9, 1976, Marianna, FL; [p.] Ralph L. and Mary E. Smith; [occ.] An Employee of Russell Corporation; [memb.] First Baptist Church of Malone, FL; [oth. writ.] Several of my poems were published in the school newspaper when I was in School.; [pers.] I never focus on a certain subject to write about it just sort of comes together all at once in my mind.; [a.] Bascom, FL

SMITH, BLAIR
[pen.] Blair Smith, Blair Ruby; [b.] March 19, 1957, CA; [p.] Leon and Charlotte Smith; [ed.] California State University - Northridge; Santa Monica College - Santa Monica, CA; [occ.] Freelance Writer; [memb.] American Red Cross, United Way, Westside Neighbors; [hon.] Finalist in first two poetry contests; [oth. writ.] I submit ideas to movie production companies and local television stations; I write lyrics and publish stories.; [pers.] Be all you can be, Work for world peace, Laissez Faire, Keep your head up; [a.] Los Angeles, CA

SMITH, BRENDA
[ch.] Stephen Todd Smith; [ed.] White Co High, Kennesaw Jr. College, Medical College of Georgia Honor Graduate from H.S. and College; [occ.] Registered Nurse - St Mary's Health Care Systems - Athen's; [memb.] Sigma Theta Tall; [hon.] Honor Graduate from H.S. and College; [oth. writ.] I have written many poems, but have not pursued publication until presently.; [pers.] My heavenly father gave me the gift of poetry so he could send to us a message of hope, joy and love.; [a.] Athens, GA

SMITH, JERREL DEAN COLE
[pen.] Jerri Smith; [b.] November 15, 1946, Livingston, TX; [p.] Reverend and Mrs. J. C. Cole;

[m.] James E. Smith; [ch.] Jonathan Cole Smith; [ed.] Jacksonville Baptist College, Jacksonville, TX, Lower Columbia, Washington State; [oth. writ.] "A Dream Or Not" published 1988; [pers.] This is for you, my special friend, Carol Ann Pixley Thank You!; [a.] Livingston, TX

SMITH, KENDALL LEY
[b.] October 9, 1971, Slidell, LA; [p.] Wilbar Ley and Hilda Jones Smith; [ed.] Northshore High University of Southern Mississippi, BS in Biology; [occ.] Research Assistant; [memb.] Ducks Unlimited, U.S.M. Rugby Club; [hon.] National Deans List, Golden Key National Honors Society, Graduated with BS degree with Honors Biological National Honor Society; [pers.] Jesus Christ is my Lord and Savior our smallest actions or statements cause a direct impact on people we see everyday and ripples through their lives affecting many lives we never see we must consider what we do and say carefully.; [a.] Slidell, LA

SMITH, LAURENCE E.
[b.] May 6, 1932, Penna; [m.] M. Christine; [ch.] 9 boys; [occ.] Road-driver at Yellow Freight Systems; [memb.] Baptist Ministers Union of K.C., MO; [pers.] A gift from god that I haven't used until this attempt. Who knows what tomorrow holds?

SMITH, LISA
[b.] 1981, New Hampshire; [p.] Herb and Doris Smith; [ed.] Lawrence High; [occ.] Student; [hon.] Who's Who in American High School Students, completed circumnavigation of the world aboard 56' schooner with family.; [pers.] I enjoy writing poems that reflect on the realities of life.; [a.] Albion, ME

SMITH, MICHELLE HELENE
[b.] September 28, 1981, Denver, CO; [p.] Michael Smith, Christine Smith; [ed.] Sandia High, Cleveland Middle; [occ.] Student; [hon.] Honorary Aide to Martin Chavez Mayor of Albuquerque; [oth. writ.] Life, stolen memories rape, me alone, always, sorrow lost love, awake; [pers.] My work is a reflection in words of my emotions and thoughts, I have been inspired greatly by Edgar Allen Poe.; [a.] Tijeras, NM

SMITH, SHARRY
[b.] February 27, 1955, Three Rivers, MI; [p.] (Late) Robert L. Hackenberg and Mary Patterson; [m.] Michael P. Smith, July 5, 1992; [ch.] Heidi, Bambie, Mike Parsons; [ed.] Vicksburg High - Vicksburg, MI, Davenport College - Kalamazoo, MI; [occ.] Word Processer for Criminal Div. State Attorney's Office Clearwater, Florida; [hon.] (For Writing), (For College), Dean's List; [pers.] "Every living thing is a component of one entity, God the universal law of life."; [a.] Saint Petersburg, FL

SMITH, SHEILA
[b.] November 13, 1959, Augusta, GA; [p.] Frank and Mattie Hatcher; [m.] Walter V. Smith Jr., April 18, 1992; [ch.] Ahmid G. Kabba Jr.; [ed.] George P. Butler High 1 1/2 year. Augusta State University; [occ.] Control Clerk; [oth. writ.] Unpublished, do you know your name, flower of the morning, man hood, to be a woman, and solitary.; [pers.] Inspiration is not only gained from Human-Kind, it is also gained from the smallest wonder of nature.; [a.] Waynesboro, GA

SMITH, VONCILLE
[pen.] Veronica De Paul; [b.] September 20, 1956, Saint Petersburg, FL; [p.] Otto Woodbury and Ella Woodbury; [m.] Daniel Smith, September 14, 1991; [ch.] Joy Smith; [occ.] Metaphysician and Counselor; [memb.] National Psychic Network Corporation, Albuquerque Chamber of Commerce, National Audubon Society; [pers.] Somewhere

between Earth and the spiritual plane lies one's true identity.; [a.] Albuquerque, NM

SNEAD, DEBORAH LEE
[pen.] Deborah Myers Snead; [b.] November 27, 1951, Portsmouth, NH; [p.] Elben Thomas Myers, Myrtle Myers; [m.] Joseph Samuel Snead Jr., June 18, 1988; [ch.] James, Christie Stachura, Jennifer Folden; [ed.] High School; [occ.] Sales Associate, 8 yrs for Leggett Department Stores; [hon.] Silver Certificate Award (for Superior and Outstanding performance in customer service). Four consecutive times.; [oth. writ.] Many poems written but never published or submitted - because of recent death of nephew 6/15/96. I wrote a poem for grave side service will be published by Richmond Times Dispatch soon.; [pers.] I have found, it is not so much the level of experience or how many you witness in life. It is how one deals with that experience. "Choices", one's soul difference in the way you live your life and what you make of it.; [a.] Rice, VA

SNYDER, DOLORATA M.
[pen.] D. Catananzi Snyder; [b.] October 19, 1939, Jersey City, NJ; [p.] Carmine Catananzi and Giovanna Tamburri; [m.] John H. Snyder, February 5, 1959; [ch.] John H. Snyder II; [occ.] Executive Asst./Secretary The Richard E. Jacobs Group, Inc.; [pers.] Poetry (and the written word, in general) connect and bind all of us in their truth and reflections of our lives. Poetry makes us better people and thinkers when we experience it.; [a.] New York City, NY

SOCCI JR, ROBERT
[pen.] Rob "$tati¢", aka $¢arz; [b.] June 25, 1970; [p.] RD$R and PEB$; [ed.] EM High, Nassau Community College; [occ.] Blue Collar; [memb.] EMI - Entirely Malicious Intent, NYHC; [hon.] Awarded Permanent $¢arz from NYC Streets; [oth. writ.] Have to do with the reality and illegal ideas of the criminal world we live.; [pers.] Strive to survive. Things can always be worse. Life goes on...; [a.] E.M., NY, 11554

SOLOMON, JAWN P.
[pen.] J. P. Solomon; [b.] January 25, 1965, Bronx, NY; [p.] Laurence Solomon and Sylvia Mills; [ch.] All of God's Children; [ed.] Liberal Arts A.S., currently attending Hunter College in New York; [occ.] Bellman; [hon.] The smiles of my mother after reading my verses; [pers.] Poetry is bringing the sounds and colors of the earth and those who inhabit mother earth to a high pitch and speak the hues.; [a.] Saint Albans, NY

SOLUM, NANCY CAROL
[b.] December 29, 1953, Oakland, CA; [p.] Carolyn Solum, John Solum; [ed.] Chabot College, Ohlone College, Washington School of Art, Oakland Metropolitan Ballet Co.; [occ.] Aspiring Writer; [memb.] The Humane Society of the U.S.; [hon.] Dean's List; [oth. writ.] Recently completed over, 100 illustrated children's poems.; [pers.] "Poeta nascitur, non fit." ["A poet is born, not made."]; [a.] Castro Valley, CA

SONGCO, JOSEPH
[pen.] Joe Songco; [b.] June 9, 1969, New York City; [p.] Felice Alam, Santosa Alam; [ed.] St. John's Preparatory, St. John's University; [occ.] Litigation, Musician; [oth. writ.] Several poems published in "Culture Voice" and "Meridian", St. John's University Student-run literary publications.; [pers.] "Catch your magic moment and do it right here and now...it means everything" - VH '92; [a.] Astoria, NY

SORRELLS, LINDA K.
[b.] October 13, 1949, Fort Meade, MD; [p.] Bradford A. and Beatrice H. Keatley; [m.] John

Robert Sorrells, July 18, 1970; [ch.] Christopher John, Eric Robert; [ed.] Butler High School; [occ.] Homemaker; [memb.] St. Mark United Meth. Ch., International Society of Poetry; [hon.] NL of P. Editor's Award for "Sea" pub. in Spirit of the Age.; [oth. writ.] "Trust Is The Key" pub in The Best Poems of the 90's, N.L.O.P. A children's Christian book not yet pub. It is from a hard childhood that the wounded heart has rendered 106 poems since 1993, for it's healing and forgiveness of others.; [pers.] I think of myself not as a poet but a writer of universal thoughts. For it is by God's grace that He has made me the humble tool of the writer, for the inspired words of the author. I can do nothing on my own, only by Him who calls me. To God be all the Glory.; [a.] Martinez, GA

SORRELS SR., JAMES DAVIS
[pen.] Jamey Earl Fox; [b.] December 20, 1935, Gulfport, MS; [p.] Mr. and Mrs. Roy Wilson Sorrels; [m.] Divorced after 25 years, July 3, 1960; [ch.] Jimmye Lynne Roy, and James, Jr.; [ed.] Belzoni (MS) High School, Belzoni, MS 1954, Kemper Military College, Boonville, MO, MS Law Enforcement Officers Training Academy Jackson, MS and National Police Fire Arms Instruction School also at the Police Academy; [occ.] Retired Police Supervisor "Ole Miss," or at UMC (State) Jackson, MS, and city of Florence, MS; [memb.] Mason, (Blue Lodge at Brandon, MS) Lions Club, (Little League Baseball Coach (Formally) also at Brandon, MS, MS Law Enforcement Officers Association. (Membership #08486). Member of the American Legion Post 60 (MS); [hon.] 1952 Golden Gloves Champion (Welterweight Division: for 15 and 16 year old) in: The State of Tennessee, Held School Records: Boxing and Football at Columbia Military Academy, Columbia, TN, and Football, and College Track Records in Kansas, and Missouri, while attending Kemper Military College ('54-'55) in Bonnville, Mo. - Member "K" Club at Kemper (College) and Semi-Finalist: 1996 N.A.O.P. contest (in Maryland) held by the Nat'l Library of Poetry...; [oth. writ.] Only with the help of God I wrote: "Father's Day," "Mother's Day", "Love", "Valentines Day," "Christmas Past," "Love Child", "A Prayer Poem", plus others or etc., some were published in MS newspapers... and "Snow" (was written and published in the Belzoni Banner (MS) with the help of God, and I couldn't write anything worth reading without his help.; [pers.] "God is Love," and so, since love is the most powerful force in "Our" world, I use love, and I try to do as the Bible says, when it tells "us": "Think With Your Hearts!!!" I would like to thank The National Library of Poetry Selection Committee for selecting me to be one of their semi-finalist...God Bless.; [a.] Belzoni, MS

SOTIROPOULOU, MARGARITA
[b.] 28 October 1966, Athens, Greece; [p.] Elias Sotiropoulou, Idanna Sotiropoulou; [ed.] The American College of Greece, Georgetown University, City University; [memb.] The Cultural Society of Pendeli; [hon.] Academic Honorary Award/distinction in Sports and Languages; [oth. writ.] (English and Greek) novels, poems, short stories high - school newspaper's editor-in-chief, class representative: Literary magazine published in: Greek Newspapers, magazines and "Hoya" newspaper (of Georgetown University".; [pers.] I love to make people happy. If I don't achieve that through my writings, at least make them think....; [a.] Athens, Greece

SPARKS, JERRY L.
[pen.] Chance Matthew; [b.] January 19, 1952, Tulsa, OK; [p.] James C. and Frances Sparks; [m.] Koko, June 26, 1972; [ch.] Chance and Matthew; [ed.] B.S. University of Central candidate for Okla. - Masters of American History History working on

thesis; [occ.] Territory Manger for Interstate Supply Co.; [a.] Oklahoma City, OK

SPEAR, CONSTANCE
[pen.] White Magnetic Wizard; [b.] October 19, 1934, St. Albans, ME; [p.] M/M Reginald S. Clark; [m.] James Bennett Spear Sr., September 14, 1958; [ch.] Lori Spear Higgins Deanna Spear, and James B. Spear Jr.; [ed.] Graduate of Maine Medical Center School of Nursing Registered Certified Psychiatric Nurse Masters in Psychology from Washington College, Chestertown, MD.; [occ.] Pedratric Psychotherapist Hypnotherapist; [memb.] World Congress on Illumination, Flower of Life Sacred Geometry Alumni Joyful Child Alumni Facilitators; [hon.] A few professional awards in nursing; [oth. writ.] Short stories, and professional articles.; [pers.] I am trying to live the present moment of truth, beauty, goodness love, peace, trust, and harmony and all the rest of God's virtues. May you remember God with every breath, may you see Christ in eyes of everyone who comes before you and you and all the rest will follow.; [a.] Oxford, MD

SPEARS, PHIL
[b.] December 9, 1941, Ashland, KY; [p.] Oscar Spears and Christine Spears; [m.] Arleen Simon-Spears, December 19, 1981; [ch.] Holly-Noelle-Heather-Shan-Jason; [ed.] BA, MA Marshall University Grad. Courses - Univ. of Ky.; [occ.] Prison Warden; [memb.] American Correctional Association - Vietnam Veterans of America; [hon.] Dean's List, Bronze Star - Army Commendation Medals; [oth. writ.] Articles in Local newspapers.; [pers.] If it's going to be, it's up to me and I am the Captain of my soul.; [a.] Newburgh, NY

SPRAGUE, DEBORAH LYN
[b.] September 10, 1972, Hamilton, ON; [p.] Ron and Lyn Sprague; [m.] William Hayes; [ch.] Liam Allen Robert Hayes; [ed.] M. M. Robinson High and Sheridan College where I studied to become a Health Care Aide.; [occ.] Homemaker and mother of one son; [oth. writ.] I have written several other poems which I keep in my own collection of poetry.; [pers.] I have been influenced by several poets, personal friends and my lifes events. My poetry reflects my own personal feelings of love and life in general.; [a.] Burlington, Ontario, Canada

SPRINGER, MARJORIE
[b.] August 1, 1982, Livingston, NJ; [p.] Mr. and Mrs. Springer; [ed.] St. Mary's Elementary, Benedictine Academy; [hon.] First honors at St. Mary's School. Scholarship to Benedictine Academy; [oth. writ.] Some of my poems are being sent to various publishers.; [a.] Newark, NJ

ST. JEAN, ALMA
[pen.] AGBS; [b.] October 29, 1923, Manchester, NH; [p.] Joseph-Anna Labrie; [m.] Paul St. Jean, December 21, 1946; [ch.] Six; [ed.] High School - 4 yrs. 2yrs. Correspondence College Course; [occ.] Retired-writer of Poems-English and French; [memb.] St. Felix Golden Agers; [hon.] 1st poem - published in your book, 2 write poems and short stories in a small paper; [pers.] Writing Poems and Stories

ST. ONGE, SANDRA C.
[pen.] Sandy; [b.] December 13, 1944, England; [p.] Mr. and Mrs. J. Ratcliffe; [m.] Ex - Vernon J. St. Onge; [ch.] Three; [occ.] Teachers Aide; [oth. writ.] Touched by Angels. I unite many spiritual writings. I have had many near death experiences, not from near death but from blocking out my childhood memories. This is reflected in my writings.; [pers.] I was abused as a child. I wrote True Love because I believe we have to have this love inside to forgive. It comes from our inner child's love, which is unconditional.

ST. PIERRE, REAL
[b.] September 27, 1944, Sanford, ME; [m.] Paula, June 29, 1970; [ch.] Chelsea, Shawn, Nathan; [ed.] BA Literature UCONN - 1972; [occ.] SR Operations Analyst Fleet Bank; [oth. writ.] In Progress - Novel Sepkee Mine; [pers.] We are all one another's witness.

STAGG, TREVOR P.
[b.] April 9, 1982, Corner Brook; [p.] Debbie and Jimmy Stagg; [ed.] Going in grade 9; [occ.] Going to School to take grade 9; [oth. writ.] Poems published in local newspaper; [pers.] Trevor was 12 years old and in grade 7 when he wrote this poem. His school teacher Mrs. Griffin sent it to the local newspaper and they published it, saying they knew talent when they say it. Trevor is now 14 yrs and entering grade 9.; [a.] Petites, Newfoundland, Canada

STAKEM, MARY SUSAN
[b.] June 25, 1950, Cumberland, MD; [p.] C. A. and Joan Lancaster; [m.] William F. "Bill" Stakem, November 24, 1989; [ch.] Jamie Erin and Meghann Caroline; [ed.] Bishop Walsh High School Memorial Hospital, School of Nursing Certification in Rehabilitation Nursing; [occ.] Rehab. Nurse Consultant Memorial Rehab. Unit - Cumb, MD; [memb.] Association of Rehabilitation Nurses; [hon.] Won the Short story Award in 1967 while a Junior at Bishop Walsh School, National Honor Society; [pers.] Writing has opened a new creative world for me. I hope to honor my creator thru it.; [a.] Cumberland, MD

STAMBLECK, MARGO A.
[b.] June 6, 1956, Norfolk, VA; [p.] Ralph Allen, Marjorie Allen; [m.] David P. Stambleck, October 19, 1978; [ch.] Bayside High, Old Dominion University; [ed.] Senior Secretary; [occ.] Hace; [pers.] I am a returning student in women's studies. I have discovered a "Voice Within Me" motivating me to resume my writing.; [a.] Chesapeake, VA

STAMM, JANICE MICHELLE
[pen.] Janice Stamm; [b.] May 27, 1978, Reading, PA; [p.] Warren Stamm, Maylene Stamm; [ed.] Schulkill Valley High School; [occ.] Student; [oth. writ.] I have other poems but they have not been published or discovered yet.; [pers.] If it wasn't for men, I wouldn't have been able to write this poem. My boyfriend, Robert, gave me the courage to send it in.; [a.] Mohrsville, PA

STANLEY, REV. WILLIE FRANK
[pen.] Rev. Willie Stanley; [b.] April 27, 1944, Macon, GA; [p.] Benjamin and Leolia Stanley; [m.] Clara L. Stanley, April 14, 1984; [ch.] Andrea and Adreinne (twins), Sandra, Cheryll, Calethia, Kenneth, Michelle; [ed.] 14 yrs.; [occ.] Pastor, Receboro Ga., First Zion Bapt. Church; [memb.] IMA, Vice Mordirator of Progressive Missionary Ass.; [hon.] A tribute to Rev. Stanley my high school sweetheart.; [oth. writ.] Love Is, Halleluyah in Jesus Name, Now I can Journey On.; [pers.] I am sending this poem to you in memory of my husband. He died Feb. 1, 1996. I am so happy its game to get recognition for he was the love of my life. After 23 years, in 1984 we were reunited.; [a.] Savannah, GA

STARR, VERNA
[pen.] Starr Van Tilborg; [b.] September 19, 1940, Prescott, AZ; [p.] Mildred Warren, Vernon Warren; [ch.] Steve and Dan Starr and Kellie Whitehead; [ed.] Mayer Arizona High School, Phoenix College, Famous Writers School Crown, King Grade School; [occ.] Lyricist/Composer; [oth. writ.] Short stories and poems and religions Cohemn for Kingman daily miner newspaper (Arizona); [pers.] I try to bring the feeling of peace and heritage into the present.; [a.] Buckey, AZ

STECHSCHULTE, DEBBIE K.
[b.] October 2, 1983, St. Rita's Hospital, Lima; [p.] Mangie S. Techschulte, Arthur S. Techschulte; [ed.] Going into the 7th grade; [occ.] Student; [memb.] 4-H; [hon.] Gold Medal for reading over 200 books in 6 mo. while in the 2nd grade, 4 Blue Ribbons (over 3 yr.) in 4lt, 2 First Place (over 3 yr) in County in 4-H, 2 Second Place in County in 1996 in 4-H; [pers.] I'm 12 years old and I would like to dedicate my poem to the U.S. Women's Gymnastics Team and both of the Women and Men Swimming Teams.; [a.] Fort Jennings, OH

STEELE, JOSHUA
[b.] June 21, 1976, Mt. Lennon; [p.] Mary Ganey, Jon Steele; [m.] Anne Steele, June 15, 1996; [ch.] One on the way; [oth. writ.] Over 100 poems go for unpublished. A play written and performed in 8th grade.; [pers.] I seek to know myself and find truth in my heart. I write poetry to explore and reflect upon my own thoughts.; [a.] El Cajon, CA

STEEPLES, DARLISSA A.
[pen.] Dotti/Sis. Darlissa; [b.] December 5, 1956, Saint Louis, MO; [p.] Charles and Juanita Steeples; [ch.] DePorres, Duanita, Deana, Doron, Davina, Darlissa; [occ.] Nursing Tech; [memb.] St. Samuettemple Cogic, The concern Women of God Jesus, DePaul Hospital Nursing Staff, Lab Professionals; [pers.] This poem was written that all of mankind be reminded of the "Existence of He who is for greater than the works of science". God - Jesus; [a.] Saint Louis, MO

STEGEBY, EVA-MARIE
[b.] December 11, 1975, Sundsvall; [p.] Hakan and Inga-Lena Stegeby; [ed.] 9 years of Grammar School, 4 years of junior college (gymn.), 1 year communication/media (univ.), 1 year creative writing (univ.), 2nd year started; [occ.] Studying and management director of SWWE; [memb.] LDS, MHF-ungdom, Sundsvalls IBF; [hon.] Third price in the local contest "sundsvall-sekel-skiftets stad".; [occ.] Church paper article about BYU-dancers visit to sundsvall.; [pers.] There is so much evil in the world and I would like to make a difference - at least for some moments - and give people hope about a better world.; [a.] Sundsvall, Sweden

STEINETZ, TEANNE L.
[pen.] Marilyn Stein; [b.] November 29, 1962, Hartford, CT; [p.] Theodore Steinetz and Judith A. Steinetz; [ed.] Conard High; [occ.] President - Bunds by Teanne, Inc.; [memb.] American Cancer Society, National Geographic, Audobon Society, National Park Trust, Farmington Ave Baptist Church, North Shore Animal League, Salesian Mission; [oth. writ.] "Insatiable Passion", in Poetic Voices Of America 1989; [pers.] If our love was unchanging, our emotions would grow stugment...allow them to flourish - nourish them!; [a.] West Hartford, CT

STEPHENS, CARRIE
[b.] April 25, 1983, Ottawa; [p.] Charis and Larry Stephens; [ed.] Entering gr. 8 at Dunning Foubert Elementary School. (Last year) French Emmercian A average student. Going to Sir Wilfred Laurier high school in 2 years and plans to attend university or college to study to become a graphic designer or an actress or to study dance. Plans to study the arts.; [occ.] Student; [pers.] I have always enjoyed writing and I like to write sometimes in my spare time. After being selected for the semi finals, I think I may start thinking more seriously about writing. I would also like to thank my family and friends for all their love, help, encouragement and support. Thanks! tn.] Orleans; [a.] Ontario, Canada

STEPHENSON, KIMBERLY D.
[b.] July 25, 1976, Americus, DA; [p.] Houston Stephenson, Abbie Stephenson; [ed.] Honor graduate of Sumter County Comprehensive High, with extensive study in college prep. and Technical studies. Received diploma in Accounting at South Georgia Technical Institute; [occ.] Assistant Manager with Bargain town in Americus, Georgia; [memb.] Phi Beta Lambda, Science Club, Spanish Club; [pers.] I do my best with the hands that belong to I and the Lord. I write as often as he lets.; [a.] Americus, GA

STEPHENSON, RONALD VERNON
[pen.] Sacre Couer; [b.] April 17, 1971, Everett, WA; [p.] Rodney Vernon Stephenson; [m.] Fiance - Jennie Lynn Howe; [ed.] G.E.D. - Florida High School; [occ.] Night Stocker, Sams Club; [memb.] P.A.I.N., Pagan, Atheist, Independent, Nation; [oth. writ.] Nothing published; [pers.] Originally, my writings were more like diary entries. Eventually, I learned it was a great way to express, myself to others. Now, I need tog et others to understand the meaning.; [a.] Fort Myers, FL

STEWART, VIRGINIA E. WEST
[b.] July 6, 1964, South Charleston, WV; [p.] Thomas G. and Sally West; [m.] Ronald E. Stewart Jr., November 1, 1991; [ch.] R. Ethan Stewart; [ed.] South Charleston High School, Marshall University - for BA and MA; [occ.] Speech - Language, Pathologist Roane Co Board of Ed. Spence's, WV; [memb.] American Speech Language - Hearing Association (ASHA), West Virginia Speech-Lang.- Hearing Assoc. (WVSHA); [hon.] Gamma Beta Phi Society, Dean's List, Graduated Summa Cum Laude from Marshall U. in Speech Path., George J. Harbold Award for top Grad. student in Speech Path.; [pers.] I most enjoy my family and writing about and for family members.; [a.] Reedy, WV

STOKER, SARA
[b.] September 3, Illinois; [p.] Patrick Stoker, Ruth Stoker; [ed.] Oakton Community College, University of Illinois at Urbana-Champaign, University of Illinois at Chicago, University of Chicago, Rosary College; [occ.] Student - Head Librarian - Des Plaines Bible Church; [memb.] International Society of Poets; [hon.] Degrees - AA - Liberal Arts and Sciences (OCC), AA - Business Administration (OCC), BA English (UIUC), BA - Economics (UIC); [oth. writ.] "Alzheimer's Disease" poem in A Voyage To Remember, "My Friend, The Lord Jesus Christ" poem in best poems of the '90's.; [pers.] In everything that I do or write, to God be the glory.; [a.] Park Ridge, IL

STONE, GLENDA
[b.] March 15, 1952, Erwin, NC; [p.] Ted C. Stone, Christine Seymour; [ch.] Josie; [ed.] Brunswick Academy High School, Medical College of Virginia/Virginia Commonwealth Univ.; [occ.] Account Executive - Sterling Diagnostic Imaging; [memb.] Phi Kappa Phi, National Asso. of Female Exec., American Registry of Radiologic Technologists, American Society of Radiologic Technologists; [hon.] Who's Who of Women Executives 1989-1990; [a.] Nashville, TN

STONNINGTON, HENRY H.
[b.] February 12, 1927, Vienna, Austria; [m.] Constance Stonnington, September 19, 1953; [ch.] Six; [ed.] Physician, Specializing in Rehabilitation. Graduated in Australia in USA since 1969, Mayo Clinic, Prof and Chairman, Med. Col of Virginia and Univ Missouri-Columbia; [occ.] Medical Director Rehab Center, Memorial Med. Center Savanna; [memb.] Fellow Royal College Physicians of Edinburgh, American Academy of Physical Medicine and Rehabilitation and many other learned

Med Societies in USA and Australia; [oth. writ.] 60 some articles in Medical Journal and book chapters Editor in Chief of an International formal: "Brain Insury"; [pers.] The highest achievement in life is to pass on to your children the importance of creativity not our in art but also in everyday life and in your profession.; [a.] Savannah, GA

STORY, PAUL
[pen.] Paul Story; [b.] October 20, 1979, Burlington, VT; [p.] Anna Story, Richard Story; [ed.] Stowe Elem. School, Mater Christi Middle School, Rice Memorial High School; [occ.] Student 11th grade; [oth. writ.] Short stories published in school literary magazine. Writes songs for piano for self playing.; [pers.] I try to capture the pessimistic mood for the past-modern industrialist so that the reader can, while feeling the poems negative emotion, also acknowledge the positive side of existence.; [a.] Stowe, VT

STOVER, SARA
[b.] October 27, 1986, Payallup, WA; [p.] Lori and Scott Stover; [ed.] Sara is 9 years old and entering 4th grade in the fall; [pers.] Since she was 4 years old she has said she wished to write and illustrate books when she's older.; [a.] Bonney Lake, WA

STRANGE, GRACE
[b.] July 10, 1962, Chicago; [p.] Hoyt and Virginia McGuyer; [m.] Significant other: William David Sovern; [ed.] B.S. History issue 1995; [occ.] Wage Slave; [memb.] Founding Member Redbird, Restroom Poetry Company, Actress - Repertory People of Evansville; [hon.] This is my first Professional Award. Thank You!; [oth. writ.] Self published chapbook "Telstar On The Accordion"; [pers.] I see poetry and other forms of creative self expression as one of the last lines of defense against the total destruction of the traditional American way of life. Influences: William David Sovern, Brenda Coultas, The Beats.; [a.] Evansville, IN

STRAWBRIDGE, SHARI
[b.] December 16, 1963, Somers Point, NJ; [p.] Shirley Borosh, Allen Borosh; [m.] David J. Strawbridge Sr., October 22, 1981; [ch.] Cherie, Sarah, David, Allen; [ed.] Saugus High School, Mass. Atlantic County Vo Tech, NJ, Atlantic Community College (Present); [occ.] LPN; [memb.] LPN Association; [oth. writ.] Only personal writings; [pers.] Future plans to continue for RN then to become a Nurse Practitioner. "Let children dream for as long as they can, because the older they get the more reality gets in their way!"; [a.] Linwood, NJ

STRUDWICK, CANDI CHERENE
[b.] January 24, 1980, Marlton, NJ; [p.] Edward and Kathy Strudwick; [ed.] Junior in High School; [Occ.] Cashier; [hon.] High School Honor Roll, Softball Varsity Letter; [pers.] I like to make people have fun with my poetry.; [a.] Collingswood, NJ

STUART, DAVID
[b.] November 9, 1949, Bluefield, WV; [p.] Bob and Anna Mae Stuart; [m.] Loretta Stuart, October 25, 1992; [ch.] Julian Adam and Eva Sophia; [ed.] St. Andrews Presbyterian College, Night School Art Institute of Ft. Lauderdale; [occ.] Contractor; [pers.] I can feel the sound of harmony, the swirl of time dancing on it's feet, by walking along a sandy beach listening to the sighs of a vanishing wave.; [a.] Warwick, NY

STUCCHIO, EMELIO
[b.] May 4, 1955, New York; [p.] Neil and Nancy; [ed.] Farmingdale College, Suffolk Community College, Edison Community College, Calgary Institute Fine Art; [occ.] Restaurant Manager; [memb.] Church Committee For Art and Service, Leukemia Fund Raiser; [hon.] 1986 Mr. Suffolk County Body

Building, Dean's List Lindenhurst High School; [oth. writ.] Closest thing to heaven. Take life easier. Breeze of summer; [pers.] Dedicate my poem to Laura. For our love is everlasting!; [a.] Punta Gorda, FL

STUMBRIS, JODI
[b.] December 12, 1984, Waukesha, WI; [p.] Eileen Stumbris/Daryl Droese, Randolph Stumbris; [ed.] Going into the 6th Grade at Whitman Middle School, Wauwatosa WI; [occ.] Student at Whitman Middle School, Wauwatosa WI.; [memb.] Band, Orchestra; [hon.] Miss Jr Wisconsin 1992; [pers.] This poem is dedicated to my family whom I love very much.; [a.] Wauwatosa, WI

STURDIVANT, JACQUELYN LEIGH
[pen.] Jacquelyn Sturdivant; [b.] April 21, 1981, Baton Rouge, LA; [p.] T. G. Sturdivant Jr. and C. E. Richardson; [ed.] Just completed 9th grade - now I'm in 10th at Southpike High School in Magnolia, MS.; [occ.] Student; [memb.] National Rifle Ass., B.A.S.S. Member; [hon.] MPSEA 1st place Art Award, 1st place District Art Award, 1st place State Art Award, 2nd place Art Award yr. 1987, 1988.; [pers.] Happiness is not having what you want, but wanting what you have. Count your age by smiles - not tears.; [a.] Magnolia, MS

STUTTARD, LUCY
[b.] 16 May 1981, Dartford, England; [ed.] Dartford Grammar School for Girls; [oth. writ.] Two other poems previously published.; [pers.] I have been seriously ill with me. Over the past four years and my poetry is an expression of my feelings during this time.; [a.] Dartfort, Kent, UK

SULLIVAN, BESSIE
[pen.] Peggie; [b.] November 18, 1940, Green Coen. Hos.; [p.] Mrs. Hannah Brezeale, Father (Deceased); [m.] James R. Sullivan (Deceased); [ch.] Anthony E. Jones (he loves music); [ed.] Sterling High School: Went to one day in twelfth grade, I love attending school but, my habits didn't except school.; [occ.] My occupation is around the house and try to help my mother when I'm asked.; [memb.] It's in Columbia Video's and Cassettes. I love music. I tried to write poems and I try to see if someone would try end sing from what I have written. If not, I tried.; [pers.] Do not give out: More than I can take back. Most of times you can give and you do not know what you are giving or how much. As a matter of facts, you have to be mighty careful. As for me I have learned from hard experience, drinking.; [a.] Greenville, SC

SULLIVAN, JEANETTE Y.
[b.] October 15, 1968, White Plains, NY; [p.] Erna Sullivan and Joseph Sullivan; [ch.] Michael Sullivan, Jessica Kaylor; [ed.] New Fairfield High, CPI School Children's of Literature ICL Course. Institute of Children's Literature; [occ.] Group leader, Shepards Inc. Bethel, Ct.; [hon.] Poetry Awards Diploma ICL writing for children; [oth. writ.] Children's Stories, Poems published in other contest; [pers.] I enjoy writing poems to share my feelings with others. I also love writing for children.; [a.] Bethel, CT

SULLIVAN, MAYA C.
[b.] January 22, 1977, Minneapolis, MN; [p.] Lois Webb-Bradford and Henry Sullivan; [ed.] Received High School diploma June 1995, currently enrolled at Tennessee State University (Aug 1995-Present) classification: Sophomore; [occ.] Full-Time Student; [hon.] Dean's List, Tennessee State Univ. Presidential Scholarship recipient (1995), Pillsbury Company Scholarship recipient (1995), Voice of Democracy Speech winner (1992), various Inroads Academic Excellence Awards (1991-1995), various Basketball awards/letter (1991-1995); [oth. writ.] I have many other poems. However, none

have been published.; [pers.] I have always been inspired by things and people around me. I am grateful to God for blessing me with this special talent and my mother who has pushed me to use my ability to the fullest. Fav. poets: Maya Angelou and Sarah Johnson (my great aunt); [a.] Minneapolis, MN

SULLIVAN, RICHARD J.
[b.] July 12, 1950, Harlingen, TX; [p.] Richard and Angie Sullivan; [m.] Delia L. Sullivan, December 24, 1969; [ch.] Sandra D. Sullivan; [ed.] High School; [occ.] Self-Employed, Cleaning Service; [oth. writ.] Various poems written over the years.; [pers.] When I write poetry, it allows me to express my most inner feelings. But sometimes it helps me to ask questions about myself and about the world around me.; [a.] Salinas, CA

SULLIVAN-DOOLING, PEGGY
[pen.] BiB, Babycakes; [b.] April 26, 1954, Boston, MA; [p.] Joe and Pat Sullivan; [m.] Tom Dooling, September 8, 1975; [ch.] Patti Jean, Shanna Shirley; [ed.] Quincy High, couple of courses at Quincy College; [occ.] Mom and Care-Giver; [oth. writ.] Opinions published in local Patriot Ledger and Boston Herald newspapers.; [pers.] I try and multiply the love inside to give myself where it's needed. I give credit to Jesus my God and my parents for molding me into a caring person.; [a.] Quincy, MA

SULPIZIO, FRANCISCO
[pen.] Francisco Sulpizio; [b.] March 9, 1959, Guatemala; [p.] Ronald and Aura Sulpizio; [m.] Divorced, September 13, 1988; [ch.] One daughter: Alejandra; [ed.] B.A. in Political Science and Communications, Speak, Read and Write in English, Spanish and Portuguese.; [occ.] Full time writer. Correspondent to "Antorcha" magazine.; [memb.] The university of Pennsylvania museum.; [hon.] On Dean's List every term at Rowan College, NJ, graduate of special program for Foreign students at the University of Pennsylvania. First Prize: Inter Collegiate state tournament for public speaking. First foreigner to win such award; [oth. writ.] I am currently writing my memoirs with the hope it will save others from my mistakes, and help them, through my experiences, live a more spiritual and healthy life.; [pers.] My writings are utopical visions of how I would like the ral world to be. I have been greatly influenced by the works of Pablo Neruda and Ruben Dario.; [a.] Cherry Hill, NJ

SULTANA, BIANCA
[pen.] Bianca Sultana; [b.] June 10, 1981, Manhattan, NY; [p.] Olga Sultana; [ed.] I'm starting 10th grade in September 1996 at Hunter College High School NYC.; [occ.] Figure Skater and Student; [memb.] Member of the United States Figure Skating Association; [hon.] Won many figure skating awards in Regional and sectional championships as well as numerous educational awards; [oth. writ.] I enjoy writing children's poetry, seeing little faces light up over your creation the big greatest reward; [a.] New York City, NY

SUMMERS, HENDRIKA
[b.] 10 April 1954, Newmarket, Ontario, Canada; [p.] J. and H. Niebuur; [m.] Ian Charles Summers, 31 August 1974; [ch.] Heather Elizabeth (17 years old), John Henry (14 years old); [ed.] Holland and Marsh Christian School, Toronto Christian High School - Ontario, Canada; Queechy High School, Launceston Matriculation College, College of Advanced Education - Tasmania, Australia; [occ.] Teacher and writer; [memb.] Tasmanian Branch of Society of Women Writers (Aust.), Christian Women Communicating International (Inc.), St. Helens Neighborhood House Assoc. (Inc.), "Pieria" Writers Group, St. Helens; [hon.] 1991 - Equal first prize in Professor Louis Triebel Award for article

on Tasmanian History -1991, First Prize in Nairda Lyne Children's Short Story Award; [oth. writ.] First book of poetry published Sept., 1996 by Ye Olde Font Shoppe, Connecticut, entitled "An Unsorted Drawer", poems featured on Internet by Poetry Cafe, Live Poets Society and Crossway Publications, poems and articles published by several National Australian Magazines, (i.e. Grass Roots, Christian Woman and Hope!); [pers.] I have been writing seriously for about 10 years, but poetry only for about one year. I especially enjoy writing poetry, and feel that this is the type of writing I really want to concentrate on.; [a.] St. Helens, Tasmania, Australia

SWANZY, JESSICA
[b.] June 10, 1984, Hurst, TX; [p.] Robin and Dennis Swanzy; [ed.] Grades 1-6 Shady Oaks and Donna Park Elem., Hurst, TX; [memb.] Involvement with children that are specially challenged.; [hon.] 1st place in writing competition in first grade; [oth. writ.] 5th gr. Author of the semester (work was place in a location for public reading.); [pers.] My writing always reflects on nature and how creatures are mistreated. I love to think about nature; it always makes me happier. I hope people start to care more about the world before it disappears.; [a.] Hurst, TX

SWENSON, ROBERT
[b.] April 16, 1916, Mass; [p.] Born in Sweden and deceased; [m.] Charlotte B., September 12, 1943; [ch.] Five children; [ed.] Barrington College, R.I., The King's College, Newcastle, Del.; [occ.] Minister, Briley Chapel, Lewis, In; [memb.] Past Member of Optimists; [hon.] The only honor I have had bestowed on me is the 'Pastoral Care Award' given to the pastor of the year. I have no fame nor fortune.; [oth. writ.] Some poetry in local newspaper.; [pers.] My only philosophy is the bible. I believe it. When it comes to hobbies, I am just a big kid. I play with my electric trains.; [a.] Terre Haute, IN

TALLMAN, EVELYN
[b.] November 13, 1922, So. Westerlo, NY; [p.] Mrs. Hazel F. Mabie; [m.] Deceased, January 23, 1940; [ch.] One; [ed.] Greenville Central High School, National Baking School, Chicago, IL; [occ.] Retired and write poetry; [memb.] Social Service by Albany County, Social Security Benefits; [oth. writ.] Golden Poetry Gram - World Peace Poem to World of Poetry; [a.] Sacramento, CA

TAMIR
[b.] Jerusalem, Israel; [m.] Andrew Vidich; [ed.] MA in playwrighting, MA in Tesol (Teaching English as 2nd language), Rubin Academy of music and Dance-Israel; [occ.] Actress/voice over artist, creater and performer of 3 One Woman Shows, books and poetry, classical roles, particularly Shakespeare is my great love.; [oth. writ.] Poetry, short stories; [pers.] I write through pain, pressure and need. Miraculously the transformative power of words acts as a healing blam to my soul. Then there are the times that explode out of joy and wonder and I merely round. I love the sounds of language, the play, shape and beauty of ideas.; [a.] Riverdale, NY

TANAKA, HEATHER
[b.] October 25, 1981, High Level, Alberta, [p.] Alan and Margaret Tanaka; [ed.] Currently in High School; [occ.] Student; [memb.] Swimming Association, Wrestling Federation; [hon.] First in short story writing, numerous sports awards; [oth. writ.] All my poetry is posted on my home page on the worldwide web. hhtp://www. angel fire/pg O/ Heather/index. Ltml; [a.] High Level, Alberta, Canada

TANGONAN, PAUL
[b.] March 2, 1970, Quezon City, Philippines; [p.] Dr. Sinforiano and Edith Tangonan; [ed.] Univ. of Mo. St. Louis - Bachelors Degree in English Lit., St. Louis Community College - Associates Degree in the Arts

TAYLOR, DOROTHY
[pen.] Luta Baby; [b.] August 4, 1950, Gary IN; [p.] Wm. Jack Brown, Martha Brown; [m.] Lawrence Taylor, December 31, 1990; [ch.] La Vonya Mae, Joshua De Wayne; [ed.] Roosevelt High, Gary Career Center; [occ.] School Crossing Guard - Gary Aetna Ele. School; [memb.] American Tract Society, Abyssinian Missionary Baptist Church, Missionary Society, Vice President of the Abyssinian Choir, Sunday School Teacher; [hon.] Cert. of Appreciation The Gary Community School, Corp., Cert. of Recognition Universal Church of the Nazarene; [oth. writ.] Unpublished book - "Christ", "Sweet and Pure"; [pers.] I love to share the goodness of my Lord and Savior Jesus Christ in my poems. He has done great things in my life and I truly love him very much.; [a.] Gary, IN

TAYLOR, RITA
[b.] October 4, 1912, Victoria Harbour, ON, Canada; [p.] Jane and Ludger Gouin; [m.] Fred Taylor, September 5, 1981; [ed.] Hich and Business School Secretarial; [occ.] Retired

TAYLOR, VERONICA GRANT
[pen.] Poogie; [b.] September 22, 1949, Norfolk; [p.] Mr. Gennie Grant, Mrs. Jeanette Holley Grant; [ch.] Kada, Decaya, Elvin III, Elron Taylor, grand children: Unique Taylor, Mikia Taylor, Baby Boone and Sugar Broker; [ed.] Graduated Norfolk State University with B.S. in Accounting, Studied Theology and went to the school of hard knocks.; [occ.] Child Care, Special Friend: E. Hughes; [memb.] Member of the Church of God and Saint's of Christ, Daughters of Jerusalem and Sisters of Mercy. On the Baptizing Committee at Church, Trustee, and Member of the Financial Committee; [hon.] Was Honored twice as a team mom by coaches and recreation board.; [oth. writ.] The Saab, The Undertakers, Your Face; [pers.] To God be the glory for the things He has done. Never put your trust in man (note to females), for the hand of flesh will fail you. Trust in God and lean not to your own understanding; [a.] Portsmouth, VA

TESSIER, KATHERINE
[b.] June 6, 1957, Vancouver, British Columbia, Canada; [p.] Edmund and Valeria Glaeser; [m.] Jerome Leo Ray Tessier, November 5, 1977; [ch.] Jason and Nicole; [ed.] Community College L.P.N. Nursing Program; [occ.] I am presently a "homemaker". I used to work as an L.P.N. in Vancouver, BC and Maple Ridge, BC, Canada; [oth. writ.] I have over 20 other poems that I have written.; [pers.] I agree with the proverb: He that fears death lives not.; [a.] Maple Ridge, British Columbia, Canada

THIELEN, JEFF
[b.] March 22, 1981, Fort Myers, FL; [p.] Bill and Lynn Thielen; [ed.] Southest High; [occ.] Student; [memb.] Southeast High School Marching Band; [oth. writ.] This is my first; [pers.] Being at the age of 15, it is a real honor to have my poem published and read.; [a.] Bradenton, FL

THOMAS, CATHY DAWN
[b.] December 22, 1956; [p.] James Simmons, Jean Simmons; [m.] James Thomas, August 4, 1974; [ch.] James, Crisha, Gregory; [ed.] Harding High; [occ.] Purchasing - Buyer AMF, Inc. Richmond, Va; [hon.] Being selected to have one of my poems published in "Best poems of the '90's"; [oth. writ.] "Reflections in your eyes", "Destiny", "Serenity

of our souls", "Illumination".; [pers.] I have always enjoyed writing for personal gratification as well as the desire to be creative through the imagery of words. I love the outdoors and really draw from all that it has to offer as a source of creativity. I hope to develop my writing into new and different areas.; [a.] Mechanicsville, VA

THOMAS, DAWN MICHAL
[b.] July 31, 1961, San Mateo; [p.] Dianne Livergood, Bud Brewer; [m.] Richard Allen Thomas, March 25, 1990; [ch.] Michael, Richard, Sarah; [ed.] Leroy Andersen, Fountain Valley High, Golden west College; [occ.] Hair Designer; [memb.] Christian Coalition, National Right To Life, American Family Association.; [hon.] 8 poems in Anthologies, Poem "Auspicious Dissension" to be read by Congressman Bob Dornan at the Republican National Convention. Editors Choice Award.; [oth. writ.] Short Stories, many poems, letters to Editors "Editorials".; [pers.] Sharing the truth of God in poetry is by far the most exhilarating experience my soul has encountered! Read with your heart!; [a.] Garden Grove, CA

THOMAS, JEANNETTE EILEEN
[pen.] Jet, Net-Net; [b.] March 6, 1981, Norfolk, VA; [p.] Larry Joe and Evonne Jean Thomas; [ed.] I attended public school until seventh grade. I now attend a private school in Virginia Beach where I will graduate from.; [occ.] Student; [hon.] I have received awards for earlier writings in school, also for attendance and for citizenship.; [oth. writ.] I have written other poems, a few short stories but some have not been read.; [pers.] Once again, God receives all credit for this, along with all my other poetry success. My favorite poets are Robert Frost and Edgar Allan Poe.; [a.] Chesapeake, VA

THOMAS, LISA ANN
[b.] July 19, 1969, Saint Joseph, MI; [p.] Gerald and Beverly Hoadley; [m.] Daniel Jeffrey Thomas, June 29, 1992; [ch.] Michael, Ashley, Christopher, Daniel; [ed.] I graduated from Watervliet High School in 1987, I took some college courses at Southwestern Michigan College; [occ.] Machine Operator at Modern Plastics in Coloma; [pers.] I love to express myself through my writing. It helps me to release my feelings, my fears, and so on. I feel very satisfied and proud when I am able to write a good poem. It's a real accomplishment.; [a.] Coloma, MI

THOMPSON, JAMES
[pen.] Jamie Tomas; [b.] Philadelphia, PA; [p.] James Thompson, Lucille Meadows; [m.] Jannie Louise; [ch.] James Stephen; [occ.] Musician; [a.] Philadelphia, PA

THOMPSON, NANCY P.
[pen.] Anne Tomerlee; [b.] November 9, 1951, Monmouth, IL; [p.] Anne and Dean Pieper; [ch.] Liz and Chris Meazell; [occ.] Labor Law Clerk for the state of Georgia; [memb.] Georgia Poetry Society, National Federation of State Poetry Societies, Academy of American Poets; [hon.] My poem "One Moment In Time" published October 15, 1996 in Embers, from Armadillo Poetry Press, St. Augustine, Florida; [oth. writ.] All my current writings reflect the sincerest and most memorable qualities of what it means to be in love or to love someone to the fullest.; [pers.] I believe that love stands above most other qualities in life. It is the most important ingredient left when everything else may have fallen.; [a.] Atlanta, GA

THORN, MARIE-PAULE
[b.] July 15, 1949, Madagascar; [p.] Thorn, Marcel and Rossignol, Marthe; [m.] Bergeron, Lorenzo (Common Law); [ch.] Emilie-Childe; [ed.] Comparative English, French Literatures, University

of Montpellier, France Theatre Studies, Cardiff University College (United Kingdom); [occ.] Communications Advisor for the Canadian Government; [memb.] Former Member of Institute of Linguist (England), Yoseikan Academy of Martial Arts (Ottawa), Tadist Taichi of Ottawa (None currently); [hon.] Honors with universally degree - No awards of any kind.; [oth. writ.] All unpublished French poetry.; [pers.] Greatly influenced by English, French and Spanish poets and writers, I love working to come close to perfection in various disciplines (painting and drawing, martials arts, writing), Love to find goodness and joy in all people.; [a.] Hull, Quebec, Canada

THORNTON, CATHY LEE
[b.] February 9, 1967, Trenton, NJ; [p.] Raymond P. and Louise C. Mulrine; [m.] Keith A. Thornton, October 3, 1992; [ch.] The Late Ashley M. Thornton and Matthew A. Thornton; [ed.] Graduate; [hon.] Editors Choice Award for outstanding achievement in poetry presented by: The National Library of Poetry 1993; [oth. writ.] "Wanting To Know You" published in the edition of, "The Coming of Dawn", The National Library of Poetry.; [pers.] Don't take children for granted, for someday they may not be here. I love you Ashley and Matthew, Love Mommy!; [a.] Trenton, NJ

TIMAK, EDWARD
[pen.] Eddie Timak; [b.] Thorold South, Ontario; [p.] Aleksander (Alek) Timak and Engenia (Jennie) Bodnaruik; [m.] Divorced; [ch.] Glenn and Steve; [ed.] Grade 11 (High School Dropout); [occ.] General Motors Retiree.; [oth. writ.] Songwriting. I've written more than 40 songs in the last 3 years.; [pers.] I've decided to seriously pursue poetry and songwriting. I'm also taking singing lessons so I could sing my own songs publicly. My late father was a gifted singer even though he had no formal education I have his desire to sing.; [a.] Thorold, Ontario, Canada

TIMMS, RODNEY
[b.] September 17, 1953, Frederick, OK; [p.] Wayne Timms, Vida Timms; [m.] Shauna Timms, January 31, 1970; [ch.] April Timms; [ed.] Chattanooga High - Chattanooga, Oklahoma; [occ.] Owner of a Trucking Company; [memb.] Overdrive - Round Table; [hon.] Valedictorian - Jr High Hollister, OK; [oth. writ.] 1 - Poem published in rpm Magazine; [pers.] I try to write poetry with true feelings. I use life's events and people for my poems.; [a.] Oklahoma City, OK

TITUS, GEORGE
[b.] Quilon, India; [p.] George David, Rasalamma George; [m.] Shirley Rachel Titus, January 21, 1995; [ch.] Raeann Rozele Titus; [ed.] Master of Arts in English Literature, Bachelor of Dental Surgery; [occ.] Student; [hon.] Three time prize winner in essay contest (all India level) conducted by the "competition success Review" magazine, the most widely circulated English magazine in India; [oth. writ.] Several essays, poems, and stories published in college and church magazines.; [pers.] I firmly believe that every life on this earth has a purpose in the eyes of God. Fascinated by the American literature especially the writings of Robert Frost.; [a.] Jersey City, NJ

TOMPSETT, KAREN SYLVIA
[b.] October 19, 1973, Summit, NJ; [p.] Margaret, Michael Tompsett; [ed.] Summit H.S., Dartmouth College (1995), University of Pennsylvania School of Medicine (2000).; [occ.] Medical Student; [memb.] Kappa Kappa Gamma, Phi Beta Kappa; [hon.] Twentieth Century Endowed Scholar at University of Pennsylvania School of Medicine; [pers.] Writing is my way of participating and rejoicing in the overwhelming beauty of life's joys, sorrows and sensations. This poem is for you

Jonathan you are a beautiful person and my best friend. I love you always; [a.] Summit, NJ

TORRES, CHRISTIAN JOEMYR A.
[pen.] C.J.T., Mr. Majesty; [b.] August 31, 1978, Iligan City, Philippines; [p.] Jose O. Torres, Myrna A. Torres; [ed.] Lala National High, Mindanao State Univ., Delano High; [occ.] Student; [memb.] United Filipino Organization, Boys Scouts of The Phils., MSU Academic Scholars; [hon.] LNHS Valedictorian; [oth. writ.] Several poems and short stories unpublished; [pers.] I can't let my pen to rest in my pocket without using it during the day. My pen has much more to say than my tongue can. "My pen expresses feelings and everything more beautifully than my tongue can."; [a.] Richgrove, CA

TORRES, DEBRA LEE
[pen.] Debi Torres; [b.] September 3, 1966, Somerspoint, NJ; [p.] Mr. and Mrs. W. L. Koteles Sr.; [m.] Joaquin Torres, November 29, 1991; [ch.] Ethan L. Torres; [ed.] Bass River Elementary, NJ Pinelands Regional High School, NJ; [occ.] Employee of Lenox China; [memb.] Local 236 A and various committees in my work place; [oth. writ.] Numerous poems and song lyrics that have yet to see the public eye.; [pers.] I have been greatly encouraged by my family and friends to pursue whatever direction my poetry may go. May this lost be the beginning.; [a.] Newtonville, NJ

TORRES-GERMAN, ZAIDA
[b.] October 20, 1960, New York City; [p.] Irene and Fernando Torres; [m.] Ramon I. German, September 3, 1994; [ed.] Seward Park High School, State University of New York at Albany; [occ.] Educator of Foreign Language, Walt Whitman J.H.S; [pers.] This poem is dedicated to Lt. Harry Thompson.; [a.] New York City, NY

TRACY, MISS KIMBERLY ANNE
[pen.] Kimberly A. Tracy; [b.] June 6, 1975, Buffalo, NY; [p.] Jean and Richard Tracy; [ed.] Grade school - Southtowns Catholic, 9th 10th - Immaculata Academy, 11th and 12th - Frontier Central High

TRAILL, TED
[b.] June 4, 1942, Toronto, Canada; [p.] George Traill, Gert Cannon; [m.] October 1985; [ch.] Daughter Stacey; [ed.] BSC, Toronto; [oth. writ.] Available on request.; [pers.] Dedicated to those who did have to go to war.; [a.] Toronto, Canada

TRENT, JENNIFER
[pen.] Midnight Crystal; [b.] July 23, 1985, Saint Petersburg, FL; [p.] David and Elena Trent; [ed.] St. Petersburg Christian School/6th grade; [hon.] Honor Roll, Dean's List, Spelling Bee Awards, P.E. awards, Awards of Merit from Hollywood's Famous Poets Society, and President's Awards.; [oth. writ.] My Cat, My Family, My Family II; [pers.] When I grow up, I want to be a veterinarian. I would do that because I love animals.; [a.] Saint Petersburg, FL

TRENTHAM, PAT D.
[pen.] Pat Whaley Trentham; [b.] November 6, 1942, Sevierville, TN; [p.] Lincoln and Cora Whaley; [m.] Divorced; [ch.] Steven, Michael (Deceased); [ed.] Pi Beta Phi High School; [occ.] Specialized Equipment Operator, Electro-Voice, Inc., Sevierville, TN.; [memb.] East Tennessee Ballroom dance Club, united we stand, America, first Baptist Church, Sevierville; [hon.] Beta Club, Miss Junior, Girls State Alternate; [oth. writ.] Unpublished poetry, (this is the first one to be made public), (past) reporter for company newsletter and league of women voters; [pers.] My poems are just my personal feelings that I expressed on paper but never shared with anyone until the recent death of my son.; [a.] Sevierville, IN

TRIES, MARK A.
[b.] October 17, 1962, Salem, MA; [p.] James H. and Rita T. Tries; [ed.] B.S., M.S. University of Massachusetts at Lowell; [occ.] Health Physicist; [memb.] Sigma Xi Research Society, American Physical Society, Health Physics Society; [pers.] This poem is dedicated to my older brother, James M. Tries (U.S. Air Force pilot), who said, "The person who is HIV-positive or has AIDS will need every single bit of love, care, and support that everyone can give in order to combat the illness."; [a.] Beverly, MA

TRUESDALE, TONYA R.
[b.] March 28, 1969, Mecklenburg, CO; [p.] Noah and Ruby Truesdale; [occ.] Teacher Assoc., Dilworth Elementary Charlotte, NC Student at Southeastern College of Beauty Culture; [oth. writ.] The Black Woman, Cowards and Love and other short stories; [pers.] I'd like to think of myself as a positive individual with lots of talents and skills. My family, 4 brothers and 4 sisters, as well as my parents I could ask for all are all very influential as well as inspirational to me which exude through my writings; [a.] Charlotte, NC

TRUONG, PETER QUIOC
[b.] April 28, 1976, Vietnam; [p.] Tony Truong and Tina Ha; [ed.] Graduated from Marshall High and From J.T.T. with my AAS. Studying for my Bachelor's degree in Automated Manufacturing (Robotics); [occ.] A Test Technician at Hewlett Packard; [memb.] Christian Youth Group on 72nd and in National Honor Society in Electronics. Also a member in society of Manufacturing Engineers (SME); [hon.] Certificate in SME and AAS degree; [oth. writ.] Was offered to write poetry in Marshall, but I refuse too. I didn't think I was good enough.; [pers.] My writings is an image of feelings and thoughts on paper with the perspective of the human heart. I am greatly inspired with wisdom by all the early philosopher, and I wish I was one of them.; [a.] Portland, OR

TSANG, DAPHNE
[pen.] Daphne Lou; [b.] July 9, 1968, Scarborough, Ontario; [ed.] University of Toronto, B.A. (Hon.) English (1990), University of British Columbia, L.L.B. (1993); [occ.] Lawyer; [hon.] English Award - high school graduation, C.L. Burton Scholarship - University of Toronto, Grade X Piano Performance Diploma, Royal Conservatory of Music (Toronto); [oth. writ.] Former freelance news reporter and arts review writer for college journals and publications, Ind. The Varsity, Queen's Journal.; [pers.] I search for the essence eclipsed by the masks we create.; [a.] Vancouver, British Columbia, Canada

TSOTETSI, POET
[pen.] Kamoho Paul; [b.] July 15, 1966, Tweeling; [p.] Jors and Anna Tsotetsi; [ed.] Matric and Pastoral Diploma or Theological Diploma; [occ.] Pastor; [memb.] United Apostolic Faith Church and Industrial Mission of Botswana; [pers.] Hobbies: Reading, Church Attendant, Gospel Music, Watching T.V. and Soccer; [a.] Orange Free State, R.S.A.

TUBBS, TREANN K.
[b.] February 12, 1979, Springfield, OR; [p.] Jerome, Charlene Tubbs; [ed.] Lane Community College, McKenzie High School; [occ.] Student (Work - Baskin Robbins and Ihop); [hon.] Column in local newspaper; [oth. writ.] Reporter for local newspaper (Register Guard), personal book of poetry (about 70 poems); [pers.] After battling a severe cocaine addiction I finally went to a drug rehab center and got my life straightened out. I went on to graduate high school a year and a half early. I started volunteering at a center for abused low

income children that I where I met the little girl who inspired this poem. I am currently a theatre major at Lane Community College in Eugene.; [a.] Springfield, OR

TUNGEHAUG, FLORENCE MARION
[pen.] Florence Marion, Main Wallace; [b.] June 19, 1931, Vancouver, BC, Canada; [p.] Leonard Charles West, Marion Gertrude West; [m.] Widow, 1st April 30, 1951, 2nd April 24, 1971; [ch.] Kenneth Montgomery Keillor, Dianne Rae Nelson, Candice Rae Nelson; [ed.] Renfrew Elementary School, Vancouver Technical High, Simon Fraser University; [occ.] Wedding Wear Designer Bridal Consultant; [memb.] President, poets potpourri society Abbotsford BC, Member - Abbotsford Christian writers, Member Abbotsford homepassed business group, Member Abbotsford City fellowship, Member seven oaks alliance church; [oth. writ.] Many unpublished poems and writings; [pers.] I strive to truthfully provoke thought and inspiration in others while spreading joy, happiness and love where possible. I enjoy the poetry of Kahlil Gibran and other spiritual and religious poets.; [a.] Abbotsford, British Columbia, Canada

TURNER, SHARON ANNE CLARK
[pen.] Sharon Turner; [b.] December 6, 1950, Vancouver; [p.] Herb and Verna Clark; [m.] Divorced; [ch.] Nicole Dawn, Cari Mae, Garret Colin and Skyler Gabriel; [ed.] Bachelor of Fine Arts - Major Visual Arts - graduated with distinction May 1995 from the University of Victoria, Victoria, BC - Summer '96 diploma in Applied Arts Tech.; [occ.] Student in Sewellry, Art and Design - VCC - CC Sept. '96- May 1998; [memb.] University of Victoria Alumni Assoc. Vancouver Community College Alumni Assoc.; [hon.] (Visual Arts related - Burseries and Scholarships The Helen Pitt Award) being the most noteworthy; [oth. writ.] Various poems including "Reflection" with images on CD ROM class project Summer '96 - VCC-CC (Vancouver Community College - City Center) Vancouver, BC; [pers.] "Reflection", speaks of - childhood coping skills and survival instincts, the eruption of hidden memories, churning emotional states, the emergence of renewed hope, trust, peace, love and wisdom. "Reflection", is dedicated to Patricia Marilynne Russell.; [a.] Vancouver, British Columbia, Canada

TURNER, SHAUNA
[pen.] Mus; [b.] 1956, L.A. County, CA; [occ.] Servant; [oth. writ.] 20 years of raw personal journals documenting struggling with the something between life and death lived by most in L.A. area. I write because I live, as a means to survive barely making a living (laugh); [pers.] The spirit of mus is the power of creation resisting destruction claim her to lift your own.; [a.] Pasadena, CA

TUTTLE, YASHICA LANIQUE
[pen.] Shica; [b.] November 12, 1980, Winston-Salem, NC; [p.] Jerry W. Tuttle, Sadie C. Tuttle; [ed.] Sophomore of North Davidson High School, in Welcome, NC; [hon.] Crown Miss. Unity for Community Pageant. On the Honor Roll of North Davidson Middle School. Editor's Choice Award presented by The National Library of Poetry; [oth. writ.] A poem published in the book The Rainbows End.; [pers.] I strive to do the best that I can and to achieve all that life offers me. I feel that through writing poetry you can express your inward feelings without being shy.; [a.] Winston-Salem, NC

TUZZOLINO, SANDRA
[b.] May 16, 1970, Winnipeg, Manitoba; [p.] Saverio Tuzzolino, Carmela Tuzzolino; [ed.] Gordon Bell High (Wpg), University of Manitoba; [occ.] French teacher, W.J. Mouat Secondary, Abbotsford, BC; [memb.] Dean's list, University

of Man.; [pers.] Timing is everything in this lifetime and patience is the key to attaining the perfect timing.; [a.] Coquitlam, British Columbia, Canada

UEDA, MIHOKO
[b.] October 18, Japan; [p.] Yoshinari Ueda, Shuko Ueda; [ed.] University of Delaware; [occ.] Working at Automotive Company in Kentuckey; [pers.] I'm just writing this personal note to make my parents in Japan happy. Your daughter is doing fine here in the United State.; [a.] Frankfort, KY

URZUA, CARLA
[b.] January 7, 1981, Blue Island, IL; [p.] Salvador and Guillermina Urzula; [ed.] Freshman year at Our Lady Immaculate Academy in Oak Park, IL ('95-96); [occ.] High School Student; [pers.] I would like to thank my parents, Mr. Noppen my literature teacher, my friends especially Jill and Marcia who encouraged me to senf it. Paul Carugati who helped me rhyme, and above all God.; [a.] McHenry, IL

VALDEZ, ELMER ROMULO G.
[b.] July 11, 1953, Luna, La Union, Philippines; [p.] Patricio B. Valdez Sr., Marcela G. Valdez; [m.] Venecia M. Valdez, December 22, 1978; [ch.] Elvin, Aivee Grace, Timothy James; [ed.] B.S. Civil Engg, Saint Louis University, Grad. Stud. - Civil Engg, Univ. of the City of Manila, Grad. studies - Business Adm., M.L.Q. University; [occ.] Senior Quantity Surveyor, Armed Forces Works and Engg. Unit, Qatar; [memb.] National Geographic Society, Philippine Institute of Civil Engineers, Assn. of Government Civil Engrs. of the Phil. Iota MU; [hon.] Academic Excellence awards, Leadership award; [oth. writ.] Several poems published in Gulf weekly magazine. Compilation of poems: Flashes and Attempts, Solitary Thrusts, The Power Beyond, Rhythms of Power, and Shadows on the Sands.; [pers.] To be able to maintain my individuality amidst the mass is to live life in my own terms.; [a.] Doha, Qatar, Arabian Gulf

VALENTINE, DANIEL
[pen.] "Kimashando"; [b.] August 31, 1963, Bronx, NY; [p.] Jesus Valentine and Elba Davila; [ch.] Tito Valentine, Daniel Valentine; [ed.] New York University, New York, New York; [occ.] Professional Writer; [memb.] Pilgrims Assembly Inc.; [oth. writ.] "Women, God's Creation" and "A Touch Of A Woman", article for college newspaper, the ECCD.; [pers.] Women are the divine wound through which life and creativity come into the world. Dedicated to an influential woman, Annette Williams; [a.] North Bergen, NJ

VALENTINE, RICHARD N.
[b.] August 5, 1945, Camden, NJ; [p.] Robert Joseph and Mary Jane Valentine; [m.] Leanna Lee Valentine, January 4, 1975; [ch.] Cynthia Lee and Bryan Matthew; [ed.] Lower Care May Regional High School, Upsala College, St. Petersburg Junior College; [occ.] Retired; [memb.] Fraternal Order of Police, Lodge #10; [hon.] Famous Writers School, The Institute of Children's Literature; [oth. writ.] Children's Newsletter for Church called Joy Junction. Articles for a Local Fraternal Organization Unpublished stories.; [pers.] I try to write that which a reader will enjoy and will want to read again Brooke Ashley is my Granddaughter.; [a.] Palm Harbor, FL

VAN ECK, FRIEDGARD
[m.] Walter Van Eck; [ch.] Jonathan, Clara, Alex, Julia; [ed.] Reed College, Univ. of Puget Sound, B.A., Eastern Washington State University, M.A.; [occ.] Home Schooling Parent; [memb.] The Academy of American Poets; [hon.] Elected City Councilor 1991-94 City Council President 1993-94 in Wilsonville, Oregon.; [oth. writ.] Beginning -

collection of my poetry self published.; [pers.] In my poetry I wish to portray the beauty of life and nature, and the renewal of the human spirit.; [a.] East Haven, CT

VARA, DARRIN R.
[b.] February 17, 1967, Los Angeles, CA; [p.] John Vara, Maria Vara; [ed.] San Gorgonia High, Community College, Platt College, Summit College; [occ.] Freelance Illustration and Computer Graphic Design; [memb.] Victory Outreach Ministry Volunteer to Light House for the blind.; [hon.] No previous work ever entered.; [oth. writ.] No work ever published previous only personal hobby; [pers.] Inspiration is the key to my poetry. This piece was inspired by family dealing with the passing away of a family member, trusting and having faith in Jesus to heal our saddened hearts.; [a.] San Bernardino, CA

VARMA, BAIDYA NATH
[b.] March 10, 1921, India; [p.] Mr. Ananta Lal and Mrs. Shakuutala Devi; [m.] Savitri Devi Varma, April 30, 1942; [ch.] Ashoka Varma, Rani Varma, Ravi Varma, Sarita Varma; [ed.] BA (Distinction), Patna University, India, MA Missouri School of Journalism, Ph.D., Sociology, Columbia University; [occ.] Professor Emeritus of Sociology, The City University of New York; [memb.] Founding Member, Lincoln Center for Performing Arts, New York, President, South Asian Sociologist, U.S.A., Fellow Oxford University and T M Sombonne; [hon.] Elected to the American Film Institute, and New York Academy of Sciences, Judge, Permanent People's Tribunal on Industrial and Environmental Hazards, Trustee, United States Capitol Historical Society and Insunational Foundation for Vedic Education, USA; [oth. writ.] Articles in the Encyclopedia Americana, Books: The Sociology and Politics of Development, The New Social Sciences, New Directions in Theory and Methodology in Social Sciences, Social Sciences and Indian Society: A Civilizational Perspective.; [pers.] "Man belongs to this world, love is eternal. Let the young and old of this nervous century know the dimensions of love."; [a.] Yonkers, NY

VASQUEZ, BRIAN
[pen.] Baldomero Vasquez III; [b.] February 19, 1982, Houston; [p.] Baldomero and Leonor Vasquez; [ed.] Meadows Elementary, St. Hilary, Park View Elementary, Washington Elementary; [occ.] Incoming Freshman to Maine East High School; [memb.] Project plus, young Author's (Park View Elementary); [hon.] Finalist Young Author Society at Park View; [oth. writ.] Two books for young Authors at Park View.; [pers.] No matter who you are, how you act, we all have something in common: Stories, you could walk into a room, and look around, then you'll see what I mean. Every person you talk to or meet to or meet in life has some sort of story it tells how they got where they were's no matter how bring or exciting people of all ages, shapes, sizes, races, religions, you kind all have a story to tell.; [a.] Niles, IL

VAVRUSKA, GAIL A. CONKLIN
[b.] November 19, 1962, Lakewood, OH; [p.] John and Gail Conklin; [m.] Paul B. Vavruska, June 29, 1985; [ch.] Alexandra Nicole Vavruska; [ed.] Brunswick High School, Baldwin-Wallace College; [occ.] CPA; [memb.] New Mexico Zoological Society; [hon.] Omicron Delta Kappa Society; [pers.] One of the most important things in life is to believe in magic and dreaming.; [a.] Albuquerque, NM

VENECIA II, ARTURO
[b.] December 2, 1965, Elgin, IL; [p.] Arturo Venecia Sr. and Eula Venecia; [m.] Abigail Venecia; [ch.] Alejandro Nigel Venecia; [ed.] MBA Marketing North Park College Chicago IL BA - Finance and Economics Aurora University Aurora, IL;

[occ.] Assistant Vice President Bank of America; [memb.] American Management Association, National Society of Hispanic MBA, Hispanic Alliance for Career Enhancement; [hon.] Who's Who Among American Colleges and Universities, Recipient Aurora University Faculty Scholarship, National Beta Club; [oth. writ.] A collection of poems and quotable quotes yet to be published.; [pers.] I seek to provide words of encouragement through my writings. We live in a day and age where encouragement is scarce, like a four leaf clover.; [a.] Chicago, IL

VENEDAM, ROBERTA
[pen.] Bobby; [b.] September 24, 1958, Sudbury, Ontario, Canada; [p.] Paul and Ruth Anderson; [ch.] Wendy, Micheal, Brent; [ed.] Certificate in Environmental Horticulture; [oth. writ.] Poem published in Quill Book, several poems published in local newspapers.

VIDEON, JUNE M.
[b.] June 20, 1931, Kansas City, MO; [p.] Mr. and Mrs. John L. Arnold; [m.] December 22, 1948, Deceased, December 21, 1970; [ch.] 5 children, 18 grandchildren and 2 great grandchildren 1 stepdaughter; [ed.] I went up to 9th grade a half year, on Soc. Sec. and VA pension; [occ.] I grow plants at home and make crafts I crouched; [memb.] A Archer Nazarene church I joined the National Home Gardening club this month.; [hon.] At 17 years I received a wood plaque God is Love for memorizing the 10 commandments at Archer Nazarene church in bible school. I received a certificate award for helping in bible school, July 1983.; [oth. writ.] Other poems I write some songs not published I got a picture of Webb pierce Guitar Swimming pool with my name by if for song writing in Nashville, Tenn., in writing about my life too.; [pers.] I'd like to encourage everyone to read the bible and live their life by it. Go to church and play for others it would make the world a better place to live in.; [a.] Archer, FL

VIGLIS, VOULA
[b.] February 27, 1983, Brooklyn, NY; [p.] Hrisanti and Steven Viglis; [ed.] Dimitrios and Georgia Kaloidis Parochial School; [occ.] Student; [pers.] The world needs peace with love and we aren't giving it enough.; [a.] Brooklyn, NY

VILELLA, DANIELLE
[b.] May 11, 1981, Lansing, MI; [p.] Shawn Fuerch, Thomas Vilella; [ed.] City High School - 10th grade; [memb.] National Honor Society, PTSA; [pers.] My writing is an outlet for my anger and depression. It is a release that gives me the freedom to be happy. It is often a reflection of my environment.; [a.] Grand Rapids, MI

VILORIA, ELIZABETH AQUINO
[b.] November 29, 1981, Hayward, CA; [p.] Romeo Tolentino Viloria and Alejandro Aquino Viloria; [ed.] St. Bede Catholic Elementary School, Freshman at Moreau Catholic High School; [occ.] Student; [memb.] Private piano lessons, High School Band Member; [hon.] Runner-up in The Sister Rose Marie Hennessy Arts Scholarship, High School Honor Roll; [oth. writ.] School Class Assignments; [pers.] Not much to say about me! I'm only a 14-year old high school student.; [a.] Hayward, CA

VISION, MUTIYA SAHAR
[b.] May 24, 1969, New York, NY; [p.] Rahil Taalibat (Mother); [m.] David Vision; [ch.] Davina Emily, Corinthis Kenya and Edna Alannah; [ed.] Bachelor's Degree in Business. Audrey Cohen College. Beach Cannel High School; [occ.] Writer, Entrepreneur; [hon.] Presidential Scholarships Dean's List; [oth. writ.] Other positive, inspirational poems include Aging Beauty, Connectivity,

Child of God Rhythm, Black Essence, Favors Illusion, Union, God's Grace, Conditioning, Purpose, Vision, Success Discipline, Karma, Marriage and Life Energy.; [pers.] I am divinely inspired to fulfill my life purpose by writing positive, thought provoking poetry designed to nourish the mind and spirit. I am true believer in the concept that providing service and unconditional love are the key to abundant blessings.; [a.] Canarsie, NY

VISSOTZKY, J.
[b.] March 26, 1933, Pecos, TX; [p.] Rev. and Mrs. John W., Helen Byrd; [m.] Col. Raymond W. Vissotzky, USAF, Ret., July 20, 1953; [ch.] John, Steve, Nanette, Toni and Suzanne, and 12 grandsons; [ed.] Sanderson High, TX., Texas Tech, Lubbock, TX., Trinity University, San Antonio, TX.; [occ.] Housewife and struggling writer; [memb.] Presbyterian Church, Delta Kappa Phi, IWWLA, not all current; [oth. writ.] Several songs, poems, short stories and four novels - all unpublished.; [pers.] Even though I have never been published, I am one of those individuals who has to write to remain happy. My greatest support comes from my family and friends. I believe everyone should leave something, to show they existed, and to help others.; [a.] Big Fork, MT

VOORLAS, STEPHANIE
[pen.] Stephanie Voorlas; [b.] April 1, 1951, Racine, WI; [p.] Peter Harry and Athena Callas Voorlas; [ed.] American University of Beirut University of Utah; [occ.] Freelance writer and amateur photographer; [oth. writ.] Articles, Journalistic for Sketch international magazine, Beirut, Lebanon. Photographs published in Sun Tennis, Phoenix Arizona and Kena, Mexico City, Mexico; [pers.] Just as each photograph has endless possibilities to be unique by isolating a moment of time a poem is my way of saying - this is what a short experience means in extended languages.; [a.] Park City, UT

WADMAN, NOREEN A.
[b.] April 5, 1935, Glace Bay, Nova Scotia; [p.] Charles and Margaret; [m.] Divorced; [ch.] Paula and Peter; [ed.] Glace Bay High School; [occ.] Retired; [memb.] I do a lot of volunteer work; [pers.] I have never submitted anything for publication although I keep a file of everything I write. I write what I feel inside. I love poetry.

WAGNER, JESSICA
[pen.] Zoey, Dafney; [b.] April 19, 1982, PA; [p.] Robert Wagner, Darlene Wagner; [ed.] 8th Grade; [oth. writ.] Lots; [pers.] Stay true in all you do; [a.] Dillsburg, PA

WAGSTAFF, RACHEL
[b.] 5 February 1980, England; [ed.] St. David's College, West Wickham, Old Palace School, Croydon; [occ.] School student; [memb.] Norwich City Football Club Member; [oth. writ.] Poems published in school magazine; [pers.] This is the first poem I wrote, and since then I have developed an intense love of reading and writing poetry.; [a.] Croydon, Surrey, UK

WALKER, DALE
[pen.] T. Weed; [oth. writ.] Fool's Paradise, published by Rondom House, USA and Canada, and Bloomsbury Press, London, 1988 (short listed for the Pulitzer Prize in 1988) Natural Enemies (by T. Weed) published by Free Press Books, Box 5124, Hoboken, NJ 07030

WALL, SHARLA KAY
[b.] January 3, 1982, Odessa, TX; [p.] Clifford Wall, Rena Turner; [ed.] 8th grade and still attending; [occ.] Student; [pers.] I try to relate my poems to both real life and fantasy. When a poem comes to me, no matter what time it is, I have to write it down or I lose it. I am influenced by Edgar Allen Poe

and Robert Frost. But most of all my Mom.; [a.] Lampasas, TX

WALLACE, KIMBERLY A.
[pen.] Kim or Kimmy Leasure; [b.] September 1, 1971, New Kensington, PA; [p.] Bloom S. G. Leasure and Linda L. Murray; [ch.] Brittany Wallace and William Rautenstrauch; [ed.] Getting my G.E.D. and going to College; [occ.] Student at Highlands Family Center and Even Start Program; [memb.] Springdale Open Bible Church, the chair person on the Goal Committee also on parent activity committee; [hon.] Volunteer award at Citizen General Hospital New Kensington also award for school newspaper at Valley Middle School; [oth. writ.] I have other poems published in the Even Start Newsletter, and the Alle-Kiski Area Hope Center Newsletter.; [pers.] I try to open my mind and heart in all of my poems. I was influenced by my grandmother who is also a good writer.; [a.] Natrona Heights, PA

WALLACE, VICTOR S.
[b.] November 30, 1924, Harrisburg, IL; [p.] William F. and Verba P. Wallace; [m.] Ruby V. Wallace, February 3, 1964 2nd Marriage; [ch.] David E. Wallace and Linda L. Bishop, 1st Marriage; [ed.] High School Grad., plus Grad. as a Hydro., Electro., and Physical Therapist. Age eighteen, about eighteen months in the front lines World War II, European Theater, 27 months over seas. World War II was a full Education.; [occ.] Writer of Short Stories, Lyricist, and Songwriter, plus 140 pieces of Poetry.; [memb.] American Legion, International Society of Poets, Dial-A-Demo.; [hon.] U.S. Army, Good Conduct Medal, European Theater of Operations Ribbon, French Medal of Appreciation Africa, Italy, France, Germany, and Austria.; [oth. writ.] Publishing a Hard-Back book, 23 short stories, called, "Action Galore", Love, Surprise, Jou, Mystery, Adventure, Torture, Murder Romance, Rape, Ghosts, Sex, Hope, with Surprise Endings. Publisher, Wayne Country Press, Illinois. Over 400 pages, will be out by Oct. 1996. Also publishing a hard-back book of poetry, called "Rhyme With Reason", about 120 pages, will be out by Dec. 1996. I have two song contracts with "Big Wedge Music", Nashville, Tenn. for songs, "The Upper Hand" and "On Hold To Hold Me Darling", I have written about 35 songs. One published in Calif. called "Los Angeles", another one published in Florida, called, "Sanibel-Captivia", on a 20 minute Video Called, "A Vacation To Remember". I have poems published. "Flowers", published in hard-back book called, "Beyond The Stars", NLP, another poem, "New Year", published in "Through The Hour Glass", another poem called "Love At First Sight", published in, "The Best Poems of the 90's ". Another poem called, "March Winds", published in "Of Sunshine and Daydreams". Another poem called, "June Wedding", published in, "Daybreak on the Land", and another poem published in "Whispers At Dusk" called impersonator".; [pers.] Stay healthy, — eat correctly!; [a.] Cape Coral, FL

WARD, RUSSELL
[b.] January 23, 1964, Liberal, KS; [p.] De Wayne Ward, Dee Anne Ward; [occ.] Office Manager, Sales Jewelers, Amarillo, TX; [oth. writ.] Several poems yet to be published.; [pers.] My poems reflect what I wish life would really be like.; [a.] Amarillo, TX

WARREN, MARY ALICE
[b.] March 15, 1927, Kershaw, SC; [p.] Johnny and Della Jones; [m.] Amos Ennis Wilkins (Deceased), June 1945; [ch.] Dianna and Laura; [ed.] High school graduate Nursing Classes - did not complete Forsyth Technical Community College; [occ.] Retired; [memb.] AA and A Scottish Rite Eastern

Star, Zeta Amicae; [pers.] Faith in God and then one's self.; [a.] Winston-Salem, NC

WARTENBERG, VIVIAN
[b.] September 20, 1940, Elgin, IL; [p.] Earl Beu, Vera Beu; [m.] Glen Wartenberg, June 11, 1966; [ch.] Mary Abbott, Steve Wartenberg; [ed.] RN, BSN, Northern Ill. Univ. Dekalb, Ill. 1996; [occ.] Nursing; [memb.] Fox Valley Mixers, Square Dance Club; [pers.] I try to show admiration and affection for people in my writing.; [a.] Elgin, IL

WASHBURN, GWENDOLYN PLOTKIN
[b.] October 17, 1955, Rantoul, IL; [p.] Bobby Heard, Barbara Heard; [m.] Donald Washburn, December 21, 1994; [ch.] Diane Wills (Deceased), Tina Yvonne Cook; [ed.] Hot Springs Schools, Garland County Community College; [occ.] Attending G.C.C.C. towards a degree in Journalism and Art; [memb.] Glory Temple Church in Reno, NV; [hon.] Dean's List, Red Cross Swimming Medal; [oth. writ.] Poems published in local newspapers, Children's Book Copyright Pav 1-426-159 unpublished, collection of songs copyright Pav 1-425-530 all unpublished.; [pers.] I enjoy writing, and my life long dream is too touch the hearts of mankind with my words. I enjoy expressing my feelings on Paper and canvas.; [a.] Hot Springs, AR

WATROUS, ANNIKA LAGER
[b.] November 17, 1960, Norrkoping, Sweden; [p.] Ingemar Lager, Inger Lager; [m.] Fred S. Watrous, January 2, 1988; [ch.] Karl, Kristin; [ed.] B.S. Theology, Orebro Theological Seminary; [occ.] Studying Cognitive Science at Linkoping university Sweden; [oth. writ.] I've written poems since I was a teenager, but never tried to published any of them until now.; [pers.] Don't just read about life, live it! Some Christian believers in a quaint Romanian village in the Carpathian mountains contributed to an impression I'll never forget.; [a.] Skarblacka, Sweden

WATSON, PATRICIA V. SISSON
[pen.] Elizabeth Wilman; [b.] Ontario; [p.] Robert and Sarah Sisson; [m.] John Alexander Watson; [ch.] Four; [ed.] High School; [occ.] Housewife; [oth. writ.] Unfinished Novel. Poems.; [a.] Saint Catharines, Ontario, Canada

WATTS, NASEEMA
[pen.] Luciene Azique; [b.] 29 September 1946, India; [p.] Rabia Patel; [ch.] Marcus and Jason Simpson; [ed.] Secondary Modern; [occ.] Secretary; [memb.] World Federation of Healing; [oth. writ.] Several poems published in various anthologies. Self-published a poetry anthology, and a book titled Meditation, Mysticism and the Mystery Vol. 1. Vol. 2 to be published sometime in 1997. Also on disk, and on Internet web site,; [pers.] "Let the Light descend into our world to cleanse, heal and renew."; [a.] Leicester, UK

WAYNE, CHAD D.
[b.] August 3, 1973, Lancaster, PA; [p.] Dennis and Lynette Wayne; [occ.] Student at Columbus State University, Majoring in English; [a.] Columbus, GA

WEAVER, DAWN
[pen.] Day Break; [b.] February 21, 1962, Minneapolis, MN; [p.] Dan and Loraine Luby; [m.] David Weaver, September 12, 1981; [ch.] Derek - 13, Thad - 9; [ed.] H.S. and Bus Mgt., Computer Classes, Ins. Classes; [occ.] CSR - Commercial Ins., Wife, Mother; [memb.] B and G Club of America, ASA, AANR; [pers.] Most of my inspiration has been from my childhood but when situations arise in a daily atmosphere, it seems that if its on my mind enough, I can make the pen flow.; [a.] Murrieta, CA

WEBB, ELLEN KAYE
[pen.] Ellen Kaye Webb; [b.] March 19, 1941, Monticello, IL; [p.] Mrs. Ida Rogers; [m.] Mr. Rex "Bud" Webb, February 14, 1993; [ch.] Julie Parker, Samuel Haight; [ed.] Registered Nurse - graduated 1962; [occ.] Day Care Center Worker in Infant Room, Monticello, IL; [memb.] First Christian Church Monticello, IL, International Society of Poets 1996; [oth. writ.] "Rodney Kruse", to be published in "Whispers at Dusk", Winter 1996, "Give Your Soul To God Sam" - published 1996 Spring in "A Tapestry of Thoughts", "Thanks Be To God" to be published in "Lyrical Heritage" Winter 1996 and also in a book entitled "Famous Pomes of the 20th Century", by Famous Poets Society in California.; [pers.] My mommy is a strong person always there when I need her. My writings are mostly about family and friends and prayers to God. Helen Steiner Rice is my inspiration.; [a.] DeLand, IL

WEBSTER, DESMOND
[b.] March 23, 1978, Houston, TX; [p.] Star Webster, Lynette Webster; [ed.] The Columbus Academy High School; [memb.] Planetary Society; [hon.] National Merit Scholar; [pers.] I wanted to show my mother that I loved her. Hopefully, I did that in some small way in my work. Thanks Mom.; [a.] Columbus, OH

WEEKES, SERENA
[pen.] "Rainy"; [b.] Monteserrat, W.I.; [p.] Eleah and John Ryan; [m.] Jesse Lewkowicz, March 26, 1988; [ch.] Love "Em; [ed.] Westmount High, Montreal Canada, Vanier College Montreal Canada; [occ.] Entrepreneur; [oth. writ.] Poem published in Elementary School poetry handbook; [pers.] My writing is of many characteristics, like or unlike myself in circumstances. I look forward to the day that people will be heard through my writing.; [a.] Montreal, Province of Quebec, Canada

WEGENER, ROSE
[b.] September 18, 1952, Turner Valley, Alberta; [p.] Sophie and Ernest Wegener; [ch.] Robert - 25, Tanya - 21; [ed.] High School, Classical Guitar, Teacher's Aide; [occ.] Custodian of Empire Maintenance, Janitor of Topper Chopper Barber Shop; [memb.] Member of High Country Gospel Hillbilly Band, Canadian Red Cross, National Library of Poetry; [hon.] 11 years volunteer work with Red Cross, 3 years with Canadian Heart Fund.; [oth. writ.] Poetry and editorials for Eagleview post, poetry for bulletins at Oilfields Church in Turner Valley. Wrote songs for church functions and for coffee house.; [pers.] To write poetry so that others will learn that Jesus Christ is Lord and Savior of this world. I love the Cremation of Sam McGee poem and V. C. Andrews stories.; [a.] Black Diamond, Alberta, Canada

WEGNER, IDA-MAY
[b.] May 5, 1960, Fort Saint John, British Columbia, Canada; [p.] Isabele and Theodore Stark; [m.] Neil Robert Wegner, April 11, 1986; [ch.] (1 daughter) Alysha Katrina; [ed.] Lampman High, Saskatchewan, Canada numerous Accounting and Bookkeeping Computer courses.; [occ.] Office Manager/Accountant at Tar-Ific Dev. Red Deer, AB; [oth. writ.] Numerous poems.; [pers.] As a young girl I loved to write poems, and gave them away as gifts now that I'm older, my ultimate goal is touching hearts. I want the reader to live and feel my passion.; [a.] Red Deer, Alberta, Canada

WELCOME, KIMBERLY
[pen.] Cameron Kaine; [b.] November 21, 1982, Miami, FL; [p.] Yolanda Ebanks and Dwight Welcome; [ch.] Wendy Benedict, Becky Sprouse, Dwight Welcome; [ed.] Oak Grove Elem. Thomas Jefferson Mid.; [occ.] Student; [hon.] Florida Writes

Test (I got a five, highest score is six); [oth. writ.] Several other poems kept in a book. A play I entered in a contest, entitled "I Was Lost, But Now I'm Found."; [pers.] I write what I feel, I feel I what I write. The Passion, you see, is a reflection of me.; [a.] Miami, FL

WELLS, KATHLEEN N.
[pen.] Shots Blackwell; [b.] November 12, 1989, Greensboro, PA; [ed.] BA Eckero College 1981, Nat'l Dean's List, Tavpin Global Markets, Grubb and Ellis Real Estate Truing, Howard Shersen's Consultancy, How to make a sale; [occ.] Leader/talk Show Host and Entrepreneur and Lyricist; [memb.] Take Back New York; [oth. writ.] Passion's Bridge Home, Moving Essence, The Ascension, Teach reach to Upward Forward Fast, Sorrow's Reconciliation, The Healing Heart, Telepathy Line, Rock me to Silence, To Barney the Kiss, Rocking with the Divine...; [pers.] I am "in this world, but not of it." I enjoy being a channel for the higher power's messages. My emotional pain influences my metaphysical/Classical Work and my hope is a complete healing for the planet inhabitants.

WELSH, AMY M.
[pen.] Amy; [b.] July 25, 1975, Cambridge, MN; [p.] Dottie and Marvin Welsh; [ed.] Albert Lea Sr. High; [occ.] Entertainer; [memb.] Animal Humane Society, National Parks and Conservation Assoc.; [oth. writ.] Stories - Editorials; [pers.] The things to remember, is that life is not that bad. Poetry is what saved my life in my depression. If you are depressed, try turning your feelings into writings. Keeping a journal and writing has become my poetry.; [a.] Goldfield, NV

WEST, GAIL JENNINGS
[pen.] Gail Jennings West; [b.] November 1, 1938, Tuscaloosa, AL; [p.] Daniel Web Jennings and Adlene Jennings; [m.] Melvin Wade West, February 26, 1953; [ch.] Michael Wade West and Jeffrey Lane West; [ed.] Holt High School; [occ.] Manager Alabama Central Credit Union P.O. Box 40205 Tuscaloosa, Al. 35404; [memb.] Old Salem Baptist Church Sunday School Teacher, poems published in newspaper, church literature and other books; [hon.] First place talent trophy Shocco Springs Retreat Talladega, Alabama "Man of Galilee"; [oth. writ.] Book of Poetry "He Speaks To Me" 1982, Nest Of Baby Birds - short story, Tapes Of Music and Songs 1988-90, "Melodies To The Lord" 1988, "Songs From The Heart" 1990 writing inspired and in many cases, amplifies scriptural text.; [pers.] I had written poetry since my childhood as a hobby. I was reluctant to share them with others once written, and would pack them away in boxes and put them away. A Bible study of the parable of the talents encouraged me to share my writings with others. I now do speaking engagements for civic clubs, churches, socials and other events.; [a.] Cottondale, AL

WEYHERSMUELLER, ANNIKA
[b.] February 22, 1981; [ed.] Werner-Heisenberg High School, Weinheim, Germany; [occ.] High School student (Sophomore); [pers.] I hope that I can send a message with my writing and that people will understand that message.

WHITE, ELGA HAYMON
[b.] January 4, 1931, Flatwoods, LA; [p.] Rev. William C. Haymon, Eula P. Willis Haymon; [m.] Rev. Nedgel J. White, October 23, 1971; [ed.] Louisville High School, Louisville, Co, University of Colorado, Denner University, Denner, Co.; [occ.] Retired; [memb.] League of Women Voters, Shadow Wood Condominium Association, Board of Directors, Former member: Red River Writers Association, Louisiana, National Management

Association, Founder Rio Grande, Valley secretarial Assn. Many other Associations.; [oth. writ.] "Springtime" and "Night Fall" American Poetry Anthology - Vol IX, No. 2, 1989 Issue. Several poems that have never been submitted for publication.; [pers.] Beautiful Communication happens when beautiful words and phrases are chosen to convey your thoughts...that romantic, magical touch of your pen! Your heart and soul become entwined..imparting the intangible.; [a.] Denver, CO

WHITE, JOHN W.
[b.] April 6, 1925, Struthers, OH; [p.] John J., Victoria White; [ch.] John J., Thomas L., Diana D., Victoria M.; [ed.] Mt Union College; [occ.] Retired: Student, Hotel Manager, Miner, Insurance Office Manager, Fisherman, Hunter, Aireal Gunner Sailor, Poet.; [memb.] V.F.W. American Legion; [hon.] Fire Decorations World War II; [pers.] May God protect me from my friends, for I can fight my enemies.; [a.] Louisville, OH

WHITE, MARJORIE POWERS
[b.] January 18, 1925, NYC; [p.] Frank Powers, Mary Powers; [m.] Willard D. White Jr., May 20, 1950; [ch.] Shawn, Stephen, Catherine and Nicholas; [ed.] Ethel Walker School, Sarah Lawrence College, Arts Students League, Arts Schools in Florence Italy, Paris, France, New School of Social Research, (N.Y.C.) Poetry Society (N.Y.C.); [occ.] Artist; [memb.] Reading and writings groups.; [oth. writ.] Poem published in East Hampton Star; [a.] New York, NY

WHITE, PATRICK
[pen.] Dork; [b.] August 5, 1983, Winston-Salem, NC; [p.] Jim White and Desiree Ginanni; [ed.] Wiley Middle School, 8 grade; [occ.] Full time student!; [memb.] I am a member of Redeemer Presbyterian Church; [pers.] I'm a student striving to become an artist. My goal is to someday have my art/drawings published!!!; [a.] Winston-Salem, NC

WHITE, SUSAN E.
[b.] November 7, 1964, Timmins, ON; [p.] James and Marmion Clarke; [m.] Robert White, September 7, 1991; [ch.] Joshua Robert; [occ.] Full time mom and home maker; [pers.] In my writing, I endeavour to express those things that have influenced and changed me throughout the course of my life. My aim is to effectively communicate moments of truth and faith, of beauty and courage, and most importantly of God's tremendous transforming power and love amongst us. To Him who has given me life will be eternally thankful.; [a.] Cambridge, Ontario, Canada

WHITLOCK, FREDERICK E.
[b.] June 10, 1975, New Milford, CT; [ed.] University of Connecticut; [pers.] Each and every individual is blessed with unlimited potential. The challenge lies in discovering it, and finding the will to exercise it constructively.; [a.] New London, CT

WHITNEY, G. R.
[pen.] "Mitheldae, " which means Grey Star Shadow; [b.] May 30, 1963, Los Angeles; [p.] Bob and Lois Whitney; [ed.] Claremont College's Theater, School of Life; [occ.] Computer Support Professional; [memb.] Thespian, National Geographic; [hon.] Second Place for direction and acting of group scene — Cal Poly Pomona Shakespeare fest; [oth. writ.] Much poetry: sad, glad, and romantic; a short fable; the first half of a fantasy novel about elves, humans, and wicca; self-help article — none published; [pers.] "Remember the wings within your soul . . . and FLY!" from "Wings" by G.R. Whitney; [a.] Chicago, IL

WILKESON, VIVIAN
[b.] January 20, 1919, Santa Ana, CA; [p.] Roy Noble, Mary Noble; [m.] Samuel L. Wilkeson,

August 10, 1945; [ch.] Benton, Joycelyn, Samuel Jr.; [ed.] High school; [occ.] Homemaker; [memb.] Salton City Church of Christ, Shadow Mt Pallett Club Palm Springs Calif.; [hon.] Fine Arts, Pallett Club, Two Ribbons; [oth. writ.] Poetic Voices of America Spring, 1994, Sparrowgrass Poetry Forum Inc., 2 poems; [pers.] I really like the challenge of making words rhyme even when it takes long hours to do it. Which it does.; [a.] Salton City, CA

WILKIE, WILLIAM
[b.] December 14, 1931, Aberdeen, Scotland; [p.] William and Catherine Wilkie; [m.] Mary Jane Wilkie, March 29, 1957; [ch.] Fiona, Colin, Edna, Susan, Andrew; [ed.] Scottish Education - Frederick St. Secondary Pattern Making - Hall Russell, Aberdeen Technical Assistant, Royal Artillery, - British Army, Egypt Law and Criminal Code, - Metro Toronto Police College, Canada; [occ.] Pattern Maker, Terminal City Iron Works, Vancouver, Canada; [memb.] Aberdeen Gunners Club, Metro Toronto Police Association Worldwide Church of God.; [hon.] National Service Medal - Egypt 53-54 graduated - Spokesman Club, WWCE. Deacon - Worldwide Church of God.; [oth. writ.] Apart from the poems I have produced - unpublished, I wrote and gave many speeches. I also have written and given many sermonettes in church service.; [pers.] Whether writing for poetry, speeches or small sermon's, I have always enjoyed putting together, words, that help to draw pictures in the minds of people.; [a.] Surrey, British Columbia, Canada

WILLIAMS, CAMILLE MENDEZ
[b.] February 12, 1984, Fontana, CA; [p.] Thomas Richard Williams, Josefina Valdovinos Mendez; [ed.] K-7 Parochial School; [hon.] 2nd-6th grade Honor Roll (1991-1996), 1996 - Excellence in the Area of Reading (school); [pers.] My mom, my sister and I moved to a hilly area when I was seven years old. My mom made us exercise with her by walking through the hills in the evening. In order for me to endure our walks, I had to use my imagination to forget the pain of exercising. This poem is the outcome of one of my imaginary walks.; [a.] Yucaipa, CA

WILLIAMS, DEBRA H.
[b.] February 11, 1953, Savannah, GA; [p.] Byron and Corrie Hatcher; [m.] Bruce E. Williams, September 4, 1993; [ed.] Groves High, Savannah State College; [occ.] Student; [memb.] St. Peter's Catholic Church; [hon.] Pathways Scholarship, Dean's List, Second Place History Essay Contest.; [a.] Black Creek, GA

WILLIAMS, GAYLE VOWELS
[b.] Jonesboro, AR; [p.] Raymond and Marian Vowels; [m.] Preston Williams; [ch.] Brent, Blake, Brandon; [ed.] B.A., M.A. - Arkansas State University Ph. D. - University of Mississippi (not quite complete); [occ.] English Instructor, Arkansas State University; [a.] Jonesboro, AR

WILLIAMS, PATRICK
[b.] Elizabeth City, NC; [m.] Marilyn; [ed.] Central Texas College (European Campus) U.S. Army Engineer School; [occ.] Process Technician; [memb.] Several Martial Arts Asso. 700 Club. National Union; [hon.] Black Belt and Self Defense Instructor with a total of 14 years in the Arts.; [oth. writ.] Several unpublished novels and poems.; [pers.] My objective when writing, is to stimulate the imagination of the reader.; [a.] Pine Bluff, AR

WILLIAMS, T.
[b.] December 24, 1959, Vancouver, British Columbia, Canada; [p.] Ron and Jeannette Slate; [m.] Ethelyn Agustin, September 1, 1990; [ch.] Stephanie (1991) and Matthew (1993); [ed.] Por-

tage Collegiate Institute and Arthur Meighen High School both in Portage la Prairie, Manitoba. Portage la Prairie School of Psychiatric Nursing; [occ.] Warehouse worker, no jobs in medical field; [memb.] Registered Psychiatric Nurses Association of Manitoba, Registered Psychiatric Nurses Association of Alberta, Canadian Parks and Wilderness Society; [oth. writ.] Poetry, short stories, essays, few submitted and none published. Published a few poems in newsletters.; [pers.] Influenced by writings of Earl Birney, Prutt, Robert Service, Frost, John Muir, Thoreau, Frey Owl, and Shakespeare, Coleridge, etc. "If people don't dream, then all that's left are nightmares."; [a.] Edmonton, Alberta, Canada

WILSON, JAMES G.
[b.] April 14, 1948, Listowel, ON, Canada; [p.] Murray and Priscilla Wilson; [m.] Ann Crawford; [ed.] Business Management Studies, Conestoga College Kitchener Ont.; [occ.] Student; [hon.] Editors Choice Award for Natures Call; [oth. writ.] Several poems Natures Call published in A Path Not Taken.; [pers.] I have always written poetry for my own and family enjoyment. Lately I find that social and ecological issues are becoming major topics in what I write.; [a.] Cambridge, Ontario, Canada

WILSON, RODNEY
[b.] January 4, 1951, Battle Creek, MI; [p.] Harry and Bennie Crandell; [ch.] Scott, Michael, Wendi; [ed.] 1969 Grad Battle Creek Central High School 1990 Grad N.E.A./N.F.T. Electronics School; [occ.] Machine Operator; [memb.] 1st Baptist Church of Springfield; [oth. writ.] Bear traxs (A group of poems based on native American insights and outlooks); [pers.] I'm an avid camper and canoeist. My newest hobby is rock climbing, thanks to my very close friend, Vadwa Berg. I'm single but working on it. I have to be able to "Live" my writings even if only in my mind.; [a.] Battle Creek, MI

WINFREY, BERNARD A.
[pen.] Denard, Tamiko Turner; [b.] May 16, 1964, Indianapolis, IN; [p.] Andria L. Jenkins; [ch.] Crystal, Devin, Twyla Winfrey; [ed.] Electrical, Electronic, Mechanical; [occ.] Engineer; [oth. writ.] Many other poems, available apon request.; [pers.] I write poetry from my heart and soul, never from my head. And it is my desire to give to the world what God has given me. And it is by his spirit to whom I am influenced, as well as the reason why I seek to bless the world with his gift.; [a.] Indianapolis, IN

WINNESHIEK, RACHAEL DAVA
[b.] June 13, 1978, Chicago, IL; [p.] Dorothy Kellett, Wayne Winneshiek; [ed.] Always had A's in all my art classes in Grammer School - Stocton and Peirce School; [hon.] Won Art Scholarship at the age of "7" in 1985; [pers.] I'd like to complete my goal at becoming an Artist. Poetry is something magical to me, very touching I'd like to submit more poems in the future.; [a.] Chicago, IL

WINSHIP, ANNETTE
[b.] September 1960; [occ.] Publisher of Environmental Magazine; [oth. writ.] Has been wiritng poetry and essays since age ten; currently working on a book of poems; [pers.] "The only constant is change." [a.] Toronto, Canada

WINTER, MARCEL
[pen.] Yanz Malkovich; [b.] April 6, 1962, Saint Lucia, WI; [p.] Joseph Thomas, Esther Winter; [m.] Francine DePont, January 15, 1991; [ch.] Miguel Winter, Stephanie NaDean Maika Winter; [ed.] Vieux-fort R. C. Boys School; [memb.] Distinguished Member of the International Society of Poets; [oth. writ.] Several poems published in

Anthologies by the National Library of Poetry.; [pers.] Mother Dearest is dedicated to the late Mrs. Jeanne D'Arc Riverd Gagne' (1926-1991) mother of Mrs. Nicole Gagne' residing in Granby Quebec. And precious moment to my loving wife and friend. "The desire to love or hate depends on the different emotions we feel, emotions that could destroy our ability to learn or to experience the positive side of loving and caring, and it all depends on the heart and the way we love."; [a.] Granby, Quebec, Canada

WOJTOWICZ, RANDY J.
[b.] May 31, 1972, Grand Rapids, MI; [p.] Gerry Wojtowicz, Carolann C. Rushlow; [ed.] Randolph High School; [occ.] Temporary Work (Marketing AT&T); [hon.] Navy Achievement Award while serving in the USMC; [pers.] If love makes the world go 'round, the money makes altas hold the sphere.; [a.] Budd Lake, NJ

WOLFE, DANIEL
[b.] February 10, 1944, Bloomsburg, PA; [p.] Mr. and Mrs. Daniel Wolfe Sr.; [m.] Sharon Ann, July 1, 1967; [ch.] DeAnn, DeDra; [ed.] B.S. Secondary Education, Major - Chemistry - Bloomsburg University, M.S. Chemistry - University of Scranton; [occ.] Chemistry - Physics High School Teacher; [memb.] National Science Teachers Association, American Association of Physics Teachers; [hon.] Who's Who of American Teacher's last 2 years.; [oth. writ.] Science Scope Magazine - February 1994, "Go For An Expo."; [a.] Susquehanna, PA

WONG, YUDI
[b.] February 14, 1963; [m.] Brenda Mares, September 2, 1995; [ed.] United States Military Academy, Class of 1985; [a.] Santa Fe, NM

WOOD, KATHRYN
[b.] December 5, 1983, Markham, Ontario, Canada; [p.] W. B. Wood, Mary Wood; [ed.] James Robinson P.S.; [occ.] Student; [memb.] Markham Softball Assoc.; [pers.] I would like to thank my uncle Chic for encouraging me.; [a.] Markham, Ontario, Canada

WOOD, RONALD K.
[pen.] Ronald K. Wood; [b.] February 23, 1962, Kingston, Ontario; [p.] Arnold and Eileen Wood; [m.] Cheryl A. Wood, February 21, 1991; [ed.] Mechanical Engineer, Carleton U., Ottawa, Ont., Ordained Minister for the Church of Scientology, Ottawa; [occ.] Estimator, Road Building; [pers.] "Unmet" was written in April 1983. Since writing this poem, I met Cheryl and all longings expressed in this poem have been realized.; [a.] Wakefield, Province of Quebec, Canada

WOOD, STEPHEN COTTER
[pen.] S.C. Wood; [b.] June 15, 1977, Atlanta, GA; [p.] Bob and Mary Wood; [ed.] Sophomore in College; [occ.] Student/Musician; [hon.] I received the Quill and Scroll creative writing award from my high school.; [oth. writ.] Children's poems and short stories and a number of songs (folk).; [pers.] I hope my poetry can help people see the world as a happier place. My biggest influence is Shel Silverstein.; [a.] Greenville, SC

WOODBERRY, HILDRETH E.
[b.] August 12, 1949, Zeeland, MI; [p.] Preston and Angeline Kroll; [m.] John Woodberry (Deceased), May 23, 1981; [ch.] Kristi, Kimberly, John; [ed.] Zeeland High School, Zeeland, Mich.; [occ.] Laundry attendant; [memb.] Church of God (Penticostal); [oth. writ.] Several poems written for friends and family. One submitted before with honorary mention and set to music.; [pers.] I wrote his poem after coming out of a detox center and struggling with the drinking after my release. A man promised to stand by me but my drinking drove

us apart. I want to dedicate this poem to Billy so he may know I finally succeeded and kept my promise.; [a.] Beverly, MA

WOODLOCK, SHIRLEY
[pen.] Shirley Wollard Woodlock; [b.] August 4, 1947, Waco, TX; [p.] Alsa Wollard and Jennie Summers; [m.] James Q. Woodlock, February 23, 1964; [ch.] Randy Keith and Donna Joyce; [ed.] LaVega High School, Waco Beauty School; [occ.] Stylist-Salon Owner, Substitute teacher, free lance writer; [memb.] Northside Church of Christ, Central Texas Genealogical Society, Henry Downs NSDAR, Waco Chapter 2381 UDC; [hon.] Texas 4-H Salute to Excellence Award, City of Bellmead, TX, Golden Deeds Award; [oth. writ.] Freelance Columnist, Waco Tribune Herald, other poems, book, "They Came To Farm, Hill County, Texas."; [pers.] Kindness to all mankind, believe and trust in God.; [a.] Waco, TX

WOODS, ELLEN
[b.] February 15, 1948, New Brunswick; [p.] Marion and Roy LaSalle; [m.] Carmen Woods, May 28, 1966; [ch.] Cheryl (Woods) Graham, John Woods (deceased), Grandson Tyler, Son-in-law Jim; [ed.] High School; [occ.] Running a small farm; [memb.] Porcelain Doll and Plate Club I make porcelain dolls; [memb.] I just write poems in my spare time also do oil painting.; [a.] Colborne, Ontario, Canada

WRIGHT, GISELA
[b.] December 19, 1937, Biebrich, West Germany; [p.] Irmgardt and Anton Mehler; [m.] Jesse Franklin Wright, May 15, 1962; [ch.] Jorgen Fochler, Ramona Zeisler, Carmen Wright, Sherrie W. Mitchell; [ed.] Educated in West Germany; [occ.] Artist/Writer; [memb.] International Society of Poets, Computer - America-On-Line (Moon Raven 6); [pers.] Writing to me feels like painting pictures with words. I am the artist, words are my brush. I endeavor to lift mankind from the mundane to the ethereal beauty of life. Together we all transcend.; [a.] Glen Allen, VA

WURZELBACHER, JENNIFER PATRICIA
[b.] March 18, 1974, Toledo, OH; [p.] Colin C. and Nanette M. Gates; [m.] Samuel Joseph Wurzelbacher, August 18, 1992; [ch.] Samuel Joseph, July 18, 1995; [ed.] Grammer School, High School, Vocational School; [occ.] Proud Mother, and Writer; [oth. writ.] Currently unpublished poetry, short stories, and children's stories; [pers.] Poetry is a strong or subtle emotion spoken through words.; [a.] Toledo, OH

WYRICK, JEFFREY DOUGLAS
[pen.] Elijah Blue; [b.] March 8, 1977, Lubbock, TX; [p.] Boyce Wyrick, Julie A. Wyrick; [ed.] Coronado High School, Texas Tech University; [occ.] Student; [memb.] Disciple Student Fellowship; [hon.] Life Scout, Order of the Arrow; [oth. writ.] Short story: Donzels of the Down, Collections: Leaves on a Tree that Leans and Memoirs of Happiness, Rage, and Pain; [pers.] Poetry has given me a voice in which I can be heard and understood — a voice that cannot be produced by word of mouth alone.; [a.] Lubbock, TX

XANTHAKIS, DEBORAH
[pen.] Deborah - Sharabi; [b.] December 7, 1950, Los Angeles, CA; [p.] Ron and John Sorensen; [m.] Jawdat J. Sharabi (Fiance); [ch.] Alison and Melissa; [ed.] South High, Riverside College, Riverside Nursing Program; [occ.] Registered Nurse; [memb.] American Cancer Society Work; [hon.] Gave Graduating Speech at Nursing School Graduation, voted for by Nurse Colleagues; [oth. writ.] Magazine articles published. Orange County register short stories - starting a teen girls adventure series.; [pers.] Writing is my best friend and entertain-

ment. It is stimulating, fascinating and challenging. Combining words to create mental visions with vivid portrayals for page-turning excitement is my sweetest passion!; [a.] San Clemente, CA

YARED, JOSEPH E.
[b.] January 10, 1978, Zahleh, Lebanon; [p.] Elias Yared, Denise Kazan; [ed.] Finished High School, still studying computer science at the Lebanese University (first year); [occ.] Student; [oth. writ.] Several short poems, country music, songs, church songs, but this is my first publication.; [pers.] In my poems I talk about "the land of the free and the home of the brave", about many people's dream, to go to America; [a.] Zahleh, Lebanon

YATES, LAURA MARY
[b.] January 18, 1916, Shallow Lake, Ontario; [m.] (1st Husband) James Anderson, (2nd Husband) Ron Yates; [ch.] Doris, Patricia, Ann, 6 grandchildren; [occ.] Deceased October 6, 1993; [oth. writ.] Gentle Breezes - (a collection of her poems). Her first was printed when she was 15 by the Detroit Free Press.

YEE, TRISHA ELIZABETH
[b.] November 21, 1979, San Francisco, CA; [p.] Allen Yee, Marlene Yee; [ed.] Sacred Heart Cathedral Preparatory; [pers.] To follow your heart is to fall in true love. Special dedication...much love and thanks to my first love, Marco, who is inspired me to write "True Love."; [a.] San Francisco, CA

YORK, RICHARD ALLEN
[b.] August 30, 1978; [pers.] For all the wishes we ever made, that were never granted. From all of the mist behind our eyes, that hides there. Where those wishes wish to be pranted.; [a.] Caneencastle, IN

YOUNG, KATHERINE M.
[b.] July 15, 1914, Hill City, ID; [p.] Roy Hanford and Katherine Barns; [m.] Merlin L. Young, April 29, 1934; [ch.] Five children, 2 girls, 3 boys - Barbara, Ruth, Richand, David, Bill; [ed.] 1st yr. College - Childrens Literature Course - Compositions Courses BMCC College 1 yr.; [occ.] Retired house wife; [memb.] Bahai Faith; [hon.] Honorable Mention-World of Poetry Contest 1989 "Did you ever see my Spider"; [oth. writ.] Local newspapers page, article on "Equality of Women", to a child, the thinker (acceptedly LPS in competitions in 1996 Annual Awards) now watiki - published in Childs Way "Understanding", story on "Clumseyfunny Bear", published anthologies manchtleir; [pers.] I wish to thank ISP for the opportunity for individuals to express their innermost thoughts on verse or poetry; [a.] Pendleton, OR

YOUNG, SANDRA
[b.] August 16, 1966, St. Johns, Nfld; [p.] Fred and Phyllis White; [m.] Paul Young, July 7, 1990; [ch.] Robyn Lisa; [ed.] Holy Trinity Central High Level 3, Memorial University of Newfoundland. (3 semesters) Karen Hall, Bank Teller/Data Entry; [occ.] I was involved in an Auto accident, I had a serious head injury and can no longer work.; [hon.] Public speaking, Athlete of the year. (2 years in a row) Sportsmanship awards. (2 years in a row) most valuable basketball player, 1983-84.; [oth. writ.] I have several that has been written before the accident, but I was 25 at the time of my injury and never fallowed through on it before and now I can't well, I can not write new ones.; [pers.] Even though I have a very hard time getting my feelings out, almost impossible I still have the same feelings. I thank God for giving me the courage to send in my poem. Even though it is 10 years old.; [a.] Twillingate, Newfoundland, Canada

ZABALA, LINDA K.
[pen.] Linda K. Zabala; [b.] March 1942, Manhattan, NY; [p.] Adopted (Deceased); [m.] Jorge S.

Zabala, February 1993; [ed.] Columbia High School, June 23, 1960, Maplewood NJ, USA; [occ.] House-wife and semi-retired previously in child care (1969-1976); [memb.] Habilitation Div., U.b.H.C., New former members E. Bruns. Assembly of God, and crystal Cathedral Ministries, an excellent proofreader in 1995-96.; [oth. writ.] Daffodils (3/96) poem Jesus our "King of everything (1987)" Taffy, Woody and Kip My three dearest and special deceased friends and pets. (Stories) Brunswick, NJ (with Sue, Debby and Faith); [pers.] In 1984, a member of A.A. and Al-anon, Mrs. Zabala found hope after a lonely and difficult childhood... Several members of the clergy, and social workers and Therapists extended love under-standing and encouragement. Writings and gift from God."; [a.] New Brunswick, NJ

ZELIN, SUSAN
[b.] October 4, 1971, Brooklyn; [p.] Arthur, Myrna Zelin; [m.] Fiance Eric Nagel, March 27, 1997; [ed.] 9/87—8/90 Edward R. Marrow HS Graduate, Computers 3/91—12/93 Kingsbrough College (Fine Arts); [hon.] Vocational School Computers, Bowl-ing and Karate; [oth. writ.] None expect what I write to my finance Eric Nagel; [pers.] Write poetry to the way you feel for someone or about the world; [a.] Brooklyn, NY

ZIKIC, THEODOR
[b.] Stari Becej; [m.] Desanka; [ch.] Srdjan and Vukan; [ed.] Faculty of Civil Engineering, Belgrade, Yugoslavia; [occ.] Retired; [oth. writ.] 53 poems published in local newspapers (Yugoslavia) and recited in Church. "Philosophical Observation of Man's Character (book published) "Sparks of Spirit" - collection of 240 own proverbs (Book published); [pers.] I strive to commemorate the ultimate price what freedom fighters have to pay.; [a.] Vancouver, British Columbia, Canada

ZIKIG-KARADJORDJEVIC, LJILJANA
[B.] March 9, 1957, Krdgvjevac, Serbia; [p.] Milica Zikic-Karadjordjevic; [m.] Zoran Vuletic, Dino Galorini, April 17, 1980 and September 28, 1986; [ch.] Deni and Marko Vuletic; Dino, Mauro, Dina, Ablberto Galorini; [ed.] Academy of Stage Art, Department of Drama, School of Labor Organiza-tion; [occ.] Poet, Writer, Humanist, Ambassador of Peace; [memb.] Member of Belgrade Writer's Association, Member of the Humanitarian Orga-nization for Aid to Infants and Children of Serbia, Ambassador of Peace and Poets of Serbia; [hon.] Poetry award of the Serbian radio program "Rauna Gora" Literary, Toronto, April 1994, First Prize for Literary Prose, work My First Steps in Canada Festival of Music, Dance, Poetry; [oth. writ.] Collection of love poems, "How's It Feel," Belgrade, 1993; Collection of Children's poems "My Little Mauro," Belgrade, 1993, "Lilies" — love, children's, and patriotic poetry, Toronto, 1994; [pers.] We are all guests on this planet. Death awaits us all. Let us do battle on the playing field and compete to decide who will love the other more.; [a.] Toronto, Ontario, Canada

ZIMMERMAN, JAN
[b.] May 19, 1950, Michigan; [p.] Lee and Jane Marrison; [m.] David Zimmerman, July 20, 1984; [ch.] Steven, Teresa and Christopher, Stepchildren David, Lynn, Andrew; [ed.] Diploma - Nursing 1971; [occ.] Public Health Nurse Muskegon County Health Dept. Prenatal; [memb.] Board Member - Easter Seal Society. Eucharistic Minister, Our Lady of Grace Catholic Church; [hon.] Personal rewards, cards and letters from my clients is honor enough.; [oth. writ.] The Farmer (not published).; [pers.] Poem reflects feelings I had during a diffi-cult time in my life.; [a.] Muskegon, MI

ZIMMERMAN, LUCINDA
[pen.] Lucinda Steigerwalt; [b.] January 30, 1972, Newton, NJ; [p.] David Steigerwalt, Bonnie Begraft; [m.] Wayne Zimmerman, April 22, 1995; [ch.] Hunter Scott; [ed.] Vernon Township High School, Centenary College; [occ.] Riding Instructor, Mother; [memb.] American Riding Instructors Assoc., United States Equestrian Team; [hon.] 1989 Governor's Scholar in Creative Writing, Dean's List; [pers.] "There are poems going on inside us all of the time - and when they're ready to come out, they will - with only their fears to guide them..."; [a.] Highland Lakes, NJ

ZIMMERMAN, REBEKAH
[b.] February 13, 1978, Dennison, OH; [p.] David Zimmerman, Maxine Zimmerman; [memb.] Mem-ber of Harvest Christian Center of North Canton; [oth. writ.] Various poems such as: Truth, Rain, Winter and Release, Revelation, etc.; [pers.] I believe that Jesus Christ is the son of the living God, and is alive today, and I wish more than anything to reflect that truth in my writing and my lifestyle.; [a.] Canton, OH

ZIVKOVIC, LUKA IAN
[pen.] L. I. Zivkovic; [b.] April 10, 1958, Perth, West Australia; [ed.] University of Western Aus-tralia Major: English Literature 1st Class Honours Degree (Equiv. to U.S. Summa Cum Laude); [occ.] English Teacher in Tokyo, Japan; [hon.] B. Arts with 1st Class Honours; [a.] Tokyo, Japan

Index
of
Poets

Index

X

Y

Z